HARVARD
CONCISE
DICTIONARY
OF MUSIC

HARVARD CONCISE DICTIONARY OF MUSIC

compiled by

Don Michael Randel

THE BELKNAP PRESS
OF HARVARD UNIVERSITY PRESS
Cambridge, Massachusetts
London, England

Library of Congress Cataloging in Publication Data

Randel, Don Michael.
Harvard concise dictionary of music.

1. Music—Dictionaries. 2. Music—
Bio-bibliography. I. Title.
ML100.R28   780'.3   78-5948
ISBN 0-674-37471-1 (cloth)
ISBN 0-674-37470-3 (paper)

PREFACE

THIS BOOK is intended to serve the needs of a variety of readers, including students of music history and performance, amateur musicians, and those who simply listen to music and occasionally read about it. Its subject is principally the tradition of Western concert music. The intersections of this tradition with others, however, have been so numerous, especially in the twentieth century, that a number of entries relating to non-Western music and to Western music outside the tradition of concert or "classical" music have also been included. Current popular music, however, is not among the subjects represented.

Biographical information is given for over 2,000 composers. It is my hope that most composers likely to be encountered in the histories of music now in general use as well as on concert programs, recordings, and radio will be found here. The amount of space devoted to each does not necessarily reflect a judgment about relative importance in the history of music; rather, I have tried in each case to give just enough facts about life and works to suggest the nature of the composer's career, and this has determined the length of entries. No attempt has been made to characterize the music of any composer with a few well-chosen adjectives. In the context of extreme brevity, such adjectives are likely at best to be amusing, at worst to impede further understanding of a composer's works.

Entries on compositions, instruments, and terms are based in large measure on the *Harvard Dictionary of Music,* second edition, by Willi Apel and others (Copyright © 1944 and 1969 by the President and Fellows of Harvard College; copyright © 1972 by Willi Apel). This material is often changed in form or substance here, however, and I am responsible for any resulting faults.

Alphabetization of entries is of the separate word type; thus, "Ballad opera" appears before "Ballade." Abbreviations consisting of initial letters have been treated as a unit in alphabetizing; thus, "c.b." comes after "Cazzati" rather than after "c.a." Within entries, the asterisk (*) refers the reader to other entries that bear directly on the entry at hand. The asterisk is not used, however, in conjunction with the name of any composer, since very few composers mentioned anywhere in the book do not have separate entries. And within the entries on composers, the asterisk is almost never used except with the titles of works. The reader may simply assume that terms such as *symphony, sonata,* and *motet* included in the entries on composers have entries of their own.

Titles of works are given in the original language if this is English, French, German, Italian, or Spanish. Otherwise they are most often given in English with the original in brackets immediately following. Foreign titles appearing as entries are followed by an English translation. Well-known English titles appear in the alphabet with cross references to the original titles. The dates of works are intended to be the dates of completion and/or publication unless otherwise indicated; for operas the city and date of first performance are given. However, since many of the sources I used to compile information do not always make clear whether a particular date is the date of composition, publication, or first performance, a similar ambiguity has been inevitable here. Dates of birth and death for Russian composers are given in new style unless otherwise indicated. Complete consistency in the spelling of Russian names has not been achieved, in part owing to the widespread use of spellings such as "Tchaikovsky." This composer will be found here among the T's rather than among the C's, as consistency would have dictated. Patronymics in the names of Russian composers have been routinely included. For other composers, names not normally used are printed in boldface type within parentheses. Alternative forms, pseudonyms, and the like are printed in normal type within parentheses.

Among the many sources consulted in compiling information on composers, the following were especially useful, and readers wishing further information may wish to turn to them as well: *Baker's Biographical Dictionary of Musicians,* fifth edition with 1971 supplement; *Contemporary American Composers: A Biographical Dictionary,* compiled by E. Ruth Anderson, 1976; *Dictionary of Contemporary Music,* edited by John Vinton, 1974; *Grove's Dictionary of Music and Musicians,* fifth edition; *Die Musik in Geschichte und Gegenwart,* of which 15 volumes have appeared since 1949; *Riemann Musiklexikon,* twelfth edition with 1972 and 1975 supplements.

Numerous people have been helpful in the preparation of this book, and I am grateful to all of them. Eve Adler gathered most of the material for the entries on composers. Vito Imbasciani also contributed to this effort. Laurie Shulman and Laurel Fay typed the first draft and offered many suggestions on matters of substance along the way. Steven Stucky and Christopher Rouse read portions of the manuscript and offered much valuable advice. The illustrations appearing here for the first time were prepared by Barbara Boettcher. With one exception, supplied by Steinway and Sons, the others were executed for the *Harvard Dictionary of Music*. Revision of the first draft and preparation of the final typescript and of the magnetic tape from which the book was printed were done through the facilities of the Office of Computer Services at Cornell University. George Cameron, of that office, was helpful and generous with his time beyond all reasonable expectations. Nothing said here could appropriately express my gratitude to my wife and children, whose most immediate, though not their most profound, contribution to this book was their patience.

Don Michael Randel

Ithaca, New York

ABBREVIATIONS

abbr.	abbreviation, abbreviated	*LU*	*Liber usualis,* editions with
Arab.	Arabic		neumes, 1961; see Litur-
b.	born		gical books.
bapt.	baptized	maj.	major
c.	circa	masc.	masculine
Cat.	Catalan	min.	minor
cent.	century	movt.	movement
Cz.	Czech	no.	number
d.	died	op.	opus
D.	Dutch	orch.	orchestra, orchestral
Dan.	Danish	perf.	performance, performed
E., Eng.	English	pl.	plural
Ex.	example	Pol.	Polish
F.	French	Port.	Portuguese
fem.	feminine	prod.	produced
fl.	flourished	Prov.	Provencal
G.	German	Ps.	Psalm
Gael.	Gaelic	pt.	part
Gr.	Greek	publ.	published
Hung.	Hungarian	rev.	revised
Icel.	Icelandic	Rus.	Russian
ill.	illustration	sing.	singular
incl.	include, including	Sp.	Spanish
It.	Italian	Swed.	Swedish
Jap.	Japanese	Univ.	University
L.	Latin	vol(s).	volume(s)

Pitches are designated according to the system, described under Pitch, in which middle C is represented by c′, the C an octave lower by c, the C two octaves lower by C, and the C an octave higher by c″. Psalms are numbered according to both the King James and the Vulgate, as explained under Psalm.

HARVARD
CONCISE
DICTIONARY
OF MUSIC

A

A. (1) See Pitch names; Letter notation; Hexachord; Pitch. (2) On the title page of *partbooks of the 16th century *A* stands for *altus*. In liturgical books it stands for *antiphon. (3) *A* [It.]; *à* [F.]. To, at, with; e.g., *a piacere; a 2, a 3 voci*, etc. See *A due*.

A battuta [It.]. See *Battuta*.

A bene placito [It.]. *A piacere*.

A cappella [It.]. Designation for choral music without instrumental accompaniment. Originally the term referred to unaccompanied church music; today it is used for both sacred and secular. Historians of the 19th century believed that all music before 1600 was *a cappella*. Recent investigations, however, have clearly shown that instruments played a prominent role in the performance of much early music, at least as an *ad libitum* addition to or substitution for one voice-part or another. See also *Cappella*.

À deux [F.]. See *A due*.

A due [It.]. Direction in orchestral parts indicating that two instruments notated on one staff (e.g., Flutes 1 and 2) should play in unison (*all'unisono*) [see Unison]. However, the term is also used in the almost opposite meaning, synonymous with *divisi*. The same ambiguity exists with the French term *à deux*. For *a due corde*, see *Due corde*. *A due mani*, for two hands. *A due voci* (*cori, stromenti*, etc.), for two voices (choirs, instruments, etc.).

À la. See *Al; Alla*.

À peine entendu. See *Peine entendu, à*.

A piacere [It.]. Indication for the performer to play according to his own pleasure, particularly with regard to tempo and the use of *rubato*. See also *Ad libitum*.

A tempo [It.]. Indicates return to normal tempo after deviations such as *ritenuto, più lento, ad libitum*.

Ab [G.]. Off, with reference to a *mute or an organ *stop.

Abaco, Evaristo Felice dall' (b. Verona, 12 July 1675; d. Munich, 12 July 1742). Violinist, cellist, and composer. From 1704 to his retirement in 1740, cellist and then *Kapellmeister* at the court in Munich. Composed numerous violin sonatas, trio sonatas, and concertos.

Abandonné [F.]; **con abbandono** [It.]. Unrestrained, free.

Abbellimenti [It.]. Embellishments, ornaments. See Ornamentation.

Abbreviations. For the most important abbreviations used in musical notation, see Notation.

Abdämpfen [G.]. To mute, especially kettledrums.

Abduction from the Seraglio. See *Entführung aus dem Serail, Die*.

Abegg Variations. Schumann's Variations for piano op. 1, dedicated to his friend Meta Abegg. The first five notes of the theme are a' b♭' e'' g'' g''.

Abel, Karl Friedrich (b. Köthen, 22 Dec. 1723; d. London, 20 June 1787). Viola da gamba player and composer; pupil of J. S. Bach. Dresden court musician, 1748–58; chamber-musician to Queen Charlotte of England from 1765. Composed parts of several pasticcios (incl. *Love in a Village*, London, 1760, and *Berenice*, London, 1764); overtures and symphonies; string quartets; harpsichord sonatas.

Abendmusik [G.]. Evening musical performances, usually of a religious or contemplative nature. The term applies particularly to the famous concerts started in 1673 by Dietrich Buxtehude in the Marienkirche of Lübeck. These took place annually on the five Sundays before Christmas, following the afternoon service, and consisted of organ music and pieces of sacred music for orchestra and chorus. They continued until 1810.

Abgesang [G.]. See under *Bar* form.

Abnehmend [G.]. Diminuendo. See Crescendo, decrescendo.

Abschieds-Symphonie [G., Farewell Symphony]. Popular name for Haydn's Symphony no. 45 in F# minor, composed in 1772. It refers to the last movement, whose closing section is so designed that the players can leave one by one, the last measures being played by only two violins. This jest was meant to inform Prince Esterházy, whom Haydn served as a conductor, of the orchestra's desire to leave his summer palace in the country and return to Vienna.

Abschnitt [G.]. Section of a piece.

Absetzen [G.]. (1) To separate, either notes [*détaché;* see Bowing (b)] or phrases. (2) In 16th-century terminology, *absetzen in die Tabulatur* means to transcribe (vocal music) into *tablature.

Absil, Jean (Nicolas) (b. Bonsecours, Belgium, 23 Oct. 1893; d. Brussels, 2 Feb. 1974). Pupil of Gilson. Music director of the Académie de musique at Etterbeck, 1922–64; professor at the Royal Conservatory of Brussels, 1930–59. Composed ballets; symphonies and symphonic poems; concertos for piano, for violin, for viola; cantatas; string quartets and other chamber music.

Absolute music. Music that is free from extramusical implications. The term is used most frequently in contradistinction to *program music, which is inspired in part by pictorial or poetic ideas. It usually excludes vocal music, especially the type in which the text clearly influences the musical language and structure (e.g., a song by Schubert).

Absolute pitch. Properly, the position of a tone in reference to the whole range of pitch as determined by its rate of vibration. Usually, however, the term is used for what might more accurately be called absolute judgment of (absolute) pitch, i.e., the capacity of a person to identify a musical sound immediately by name,

without reference to any previously sounded pitch [see Relative pitch]. This faculty, also called *perfect pitch,* is a tonal memory that is sometimes innate. In some cases it can be acquired by training.

Abstossen [G.]. (1) In violin playing, same as *abgestossen,* i.e., *détaché* [see Bowing (b)]. (2) In organ playing, to take off a *stop.

Abstract music. *Absolute music.

Abstrich [G.]. Down-bow. See Bowing (a).

Abt, Franz (b. Eilenburg, near Leipzig, 22 Dec. 1819; d. Wiesbaden, 31 March 1885). Conductor at the Brunswick court, 1852–82; toured to Paris, London and Russia (1869), and America (1872). Composed operas; 7 secular cantatas; numerous songs (incl. "Wenn die Schwalben heimwärts zieh'n").

Abzug [G.]. *Scordatura. Also, older term for *appoggiatura.

Academic Festival Overture. See *Akademische Festouvertüre.*

Academy. A term used for scholarly or artistic societies and musical organizations of various types. The rediscovery, in the late 15th century, of Greek antiquity and Greek literature led to the foundation in 1470 of an Accademia di Platone at the court of Lorenzo de' Medici in Florence, in direct imitation of Plato's Academy. In the 16th century a number of academies were established in France, among them Baïf's Académie de poésie et musique (1567), which played a role in the development of the *vers mesurés. With the beginning of the 17th century, the movement spread widely in Italy; every city of some repute had its *accademia,* and larger cities had several. They were of two types: (a) learned societies founded for the promotion of science, literature, and the arts, part of whose activity was the encouragement and cultivation of music; (b) organizations of professional and amateur musicians whose sole purpose was the cultivation of music. Today there are many similar institutions, some no longer using the name "academy." The term is now also used synonymously with *school* and *conservatory*.

Accelerando, accelerato [It.; abbr. *accel.*]. Becoming faster; faster.

Accent. (1) Emphasis on one pitch or chord. An accent is *dynamic* if the pitch or chord is louder than its surroundings, *tonic* if it is higher in pitch, and *agogic* if it is of longer duration. In measured music, the first beat of each *measure is the strong or metrically accented beat. The creation of regularly recurring accents of this type depends on the manipulation of groups of pitches or chords (e.g., according to the principles of *tonality) and not solely on the placement of dynamic, tonic, or agogic accents. Thus, the strong beat in a measure need not necessarily be louder, higher, or longer than the remaining weak beats. When the regular recurrence of metrical accents is contradicted (e.g., by means of loudness, pitch, or duration), *syncopation results. See Dynamic marks; Notation.

(2) [F.]. In French music of the 17th and 18th centuries, an ornament belonging to the class of the *Nachschlag. In Bach's table of ornaments (in the *Klavierbüchlein für Wilhelm Friedemann Bach*), a long *appoggiatura.

(3) Any of the signs used in ancient Greek writing to indicate a change of pitch of the voice in recitation: *accentus acutus* (´), for a rise; *a. gravis* (`), for a lowering; *a. circumflexus* (ˆ), for an inflection (rise, followed by a lowering) of the voice. These signs are now thought to be the origin of the accent *neumes and certain other related systems of notation, called *ecphonetic notation.

(4) Any of the notational signs, *ta'amim*, used in Jewish chant [see Ecphonetic notation].

Accentuation. The proper placement of *accents, especially in music set to a text. See Declamation.

Accentus, concentus. Terms, perhaps used first by Ornithoparchus (in his *Musicae activae micrologus*, 1517), for two opposite types of *plainsong: the simple recitations, such as lesson tones, psalm tones (*accentus*); and the chants having distinctive melodic contours, such as antiphons, responsories, hymns, Mass chants (*concentus*). The terms also imply a distinction between two kinds of performer: the *accentus* is sung by the priest; the *concentus* by the trained musicians (*schola*, with soloists and choir).

Acciaccatura. Italian name for an ornament of keyboard (harpsichord) music (*c.* 1675–1725) that calls for the playing, together with the normal note, of a neighboring tone (usually the lower second), which is to be released immediately "as if the key were hot" (Geminiani). This ornament usually occurs in connection with chords, the chords often including two and occasionally even three *acciaccatura* tones. The tones are written as ordinary notes, so that the chord takes on the appearance of an extremely dissonant *tone cluster [Ex. 1].

The French counterpart is the *arpègement figuré*, in which the dissonant tone (usually only one) is indicated by a diagonal dash; as the name implies, it is performed as an *arpeggio [Ex. 2]. For an incorrect usage of the term, common in modern writings, see Appoggiatura.

Accidentals. The signs used in musical notation to indicate chromatic alterations or to cancel them. The alterations valid for the entire composition are contained in the *key signature, while the term *accidentals* refers specifically to those alterations introduced for single notes. The signs for chromatic alteration, together with their names in English, French, German, Italian, and Spanish, are given in the following table:

	♯	♭	𝄪
	sharp	flat	double sharp
E.	sharp	flat	double sharp
F.	dièse	bémol	double dièse
G.	Kreuz	Be	Doppelkreuz
It.	diesis	bemolle	doppio diesis
Sp.	sostenido	bemol	doble sostenido

𝄫		
E.	double flat	natural
F.	double bémol	bécarre
G.	Doppel-Be	Auflösungszeichen, Quadrat
It.	doppio bemolle	bequadro
Sp.	doble bemol	becuadro

The sharp raises the pitch one semitone, the flat lowers it one semitone; the double sharp and double flat raise and lower two semitones, respectively; the natural cancels any of the other signs. The use of the compound signs ♮♯, ♮♭, or ♮♮ to cancel partly or entirely a previous ✕ or ♭♭ is common but unnecessary. The simple signs ♯, ♭, and ♮ can serve this purpose. In modern practice a sign affects the note immediately following and is valid for all the notes of the same pitch (but not in different octaves) within the same measure. Some modern composers add bracketed accidentals to those demanded by this rule in order to clarify complicated passages or chords, and some specify that each accidental applies only to the note immediately following it. For the problem of accidentals in music of the 13th to 16th centuries, see *Musica ficta, musica falsa.*

Accolade [F.]. *Brace.

Accompagnato [It.]. Accompanied. See Recitative.

Accompaniment. The musical background provided for a principal part. In piano music, the left hand often plays chords that are an accompaniment for the melody played by the right hand. Similarly, a solo singer or instrumentalist may be accompanied by a pianist or an orchestra.

Accord [F.]. (1) *Chord. (2) Manner of tuning, especially of such instruments as the lute, for which various systems of tuning were in use during the 17th century. See also Scordatura.

Accordare [It.]; **accorder** [F.]. To tune.

Accordatura [It.]. *Accord (2).

Accordion. A portable musical instrument consisting of two rectangular headboards connected by a folding bellows. Inside the headboards are metal tongues that act as free-beating reeds. The instrument has pushed-out and drawn-in reeds, the former sounding when the headboards are moved outward, the latter when they are moved inward. The modern accordion has a keyboard on the right side for playing melody notes, while buttons on the left side operate bass notes and full chords. See ill. under Wind instruments. The earliest instruments of this type were made by Buschmann (1822), Buffet (1827), and Damian (1829).

A similar instrument, preferred in England, is the *concertina,* invented by Wheatstone in 1829. It is hexagonal in shape and has a number of buttons on each side. The *bandoneon* is a related square instrument invented by Band in the 1840s and still popular in Argentina.

Accordo [It.]. *Chord.

Accusé [F.]. With emphasis.

Achromatic. *Diatonic.

Achron, Joseph (b. Lozdzieje, Lithuania, 13 May 1886; d. Hollywood, Calif., 29 Apr. 1943). Violinist and composer. Pupil of Liadov. Settled in the U.S. in 1925. Composed various works on Hebrew subjects (incl. *Hebrew Melody,* for violin and orchestra, 1911); 3 violin concertos; chamber music.

Achtel, Achtelnote; Achtelpause [G.]. Eighth note; eighth rest. See Notes.

Achtfuss [G.]. Eight-foot (stop). See Foot (2).

Acis and Galatea. A dramatic cantata composed by Handel (about 1720) for the Duke of Chandos. Originally designated a *masque, *pastorale (pastoral play), or *serenata,* it was intended to be sung in costume but without action.

Acoustic. A term often used to distinguish instruments from their electric counterparts, especially guitars.

Acoustic bass (also called resultant bass). On organs, a 32-foot stop that is obtained as a differential tone of a 16-foot stop and a 10 2/3-foot stop. According to the acoustic phenomenon of the differential tones [see Combination tone], the simultaneous sounding of C (produced by the 16-foot) and of G (produced by the 10 2/3-foot) produces the tone C_1 (32-foot).

The acoustic bass is frequently used where the expense of the large 32-foot pipes is prohibitive.

Acoustics. The science that treats of sounds and therefore describes the physical basis of music. Perceived musical sounds are usually described in terms of *pitch, *timbre, *loudness, and *duration, and each of these perceived characteristics of musical sound has some basis in physically measurable acoustical phenomena. The human hearing apparatus is itself, moreover, a physical instrument with its own properties and limitations. The relationship between the perceived characteristics of musical sound and physically measurable acoustical phenomena is thus not always simple and direct, and many aspects of this relationship are still not well understood. The human perception of sound is touched on in the entries for pitch, timbre, and loudness.

Sounds are produced by vibrating systems that transmit their *vibrations* through some medium (such as air, though liquids, solids, and other gases can also serve this purpose) to the ear (or some other receiving instrument). For musical purposes, the most common vibrating systems are built upon strings or columns of air. If, for example, a string is stretched between points X and Y and its midpoint A is displaced to point B and released, it will vibrate in such a way that its midpoint repeatedly traverses the course A-B-A-C-A, as illustrated in Fig. 1, assuming for the moment the absence of friction, stiffness in the string, and the like. If one then imagines that the midpoint of the string is a point of light and that a light-sensitive paper is passed along the string at a steady speed, in a direction parallel to the length of the string, and in a plane parallel to the plane in which the string is vibrating, the vibrations of the string can be understood as represented by waves traced by the midpoint like those of Fig. 2. The distance *l* encompasses one complete wave or vibration, during which the midpoint of the string has traversed the course A-B-A-C-A, and is thus called the *wavelength*. The number of complete waves (or vibrations or cycles, as they are also called) occurring per unit of time is the *frequency* of

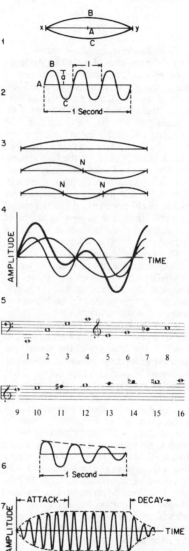

vibration and is measured in cycles per second. (A cycle per second is also called a *Hertz*, abbr. Hz., after the German physicist Heinrich R. Hertz.) The distance *a* is the *amplitude* of vibration. The frequency *f* of a string of length *L* meters, stretched at a tension of *T* newtons, and with a mass *m* kilograms per meter of length is expressed as follows:

$$f = \frac{1}{2L} \sqrt{\frac{T}{m}}$$

From this relationship it can be seen that if the tension and mass of a string remain constant, the frequency will rise as the length of the string is reduced. Similarly, if the length and mass remain constant, the frequency will rise with increases in the string's tension. In practical terms, this means that if a violinist shortens a vibrating string by stopping it at some point on the fingerboard, the frequency of vibration is increased. It is this increase in frequency that accounts for the listener's perception of higher pitch. Similarly, if the tension of an open string is increased by means of the tuning peg, an increase in frequency is produced and thus a higher pitch.

This relationship also shows that frequency is unrelated to amplitude, which depends on the amount of energy imparted to the string when it is set in motion and is thus related to the amount of energy that the string can impart to the surrounding medium. This energy, measured in watts per square meter at any point, is the *intensity* of the sound. An increase in intensity produces a sense of increased loudness, though the ear is not equally sensitive to changes in intensity over the whole range of either frequencies or intensities that it can detect. (At some extremes of frequency, intensity seems also to affect the perception of pitch.) In practical terms, if a violin string is plucked with increased force, that is if the point at which it is plucked is displaced a greater distance from the line that describes the string at rest, the amplitude of vibration is increased, and with it the intensity of the sound produced and the loudness perceived, while the pitch remains constant.

The entire length of the string described above is vibrating as a single segment and is thus producing a single frequency. This mode of vibration and the resulting frequency are given the name *fundamental*. Strings and most other vibrating systems, however, generally vibrate in several modes simultaneously. In the case of strings, these modes consist in the vibration of segments shorter than the total length of the string. Thus, strings can vibrate in halves, thirds,

fourths, and so on. Fig. 3 shows each of the first three modes of vibration of a string. In any single mode of vibration, all of the vibrating segments are of equal length and are called *loops*. The points (N) between loops, where for a given mode the string is stationary, are called *nodes*.

Because each mode of vibration results from a division of the string into some integral number of segments of equal length, it follows from the expression for frequency given above that the several modes of vibration will produce frequencies that are integral multiples of the fundamental frequency. Thus, when the string vibrates in halves, the frequency produced will be twice the fundamental, when in thirds the frequency will be three times the fundamental, and so forth. A series of frequencies consisting of a fundamental and ascending through integral multiples of it in this way is called a *harmonic series*. The fundamental is called the first *harmonic*, the frequency that is twice the fundamental is called the second harmonic, and so on. Frequencies above the fundamental in this series are also sometimes called *overtones*, the first overtone being the second harmonic, and so forth. (Many vibrating systems used in making music also produce inharmonic frequencies.)

In practice, then, a single string or other vibrating system used in music produces a series of discrete frequencies (called *partials*) simultaneously and thus a series of discrete pitches. But since the fundamental usually has much the greatest intensity, the ear, while assimilating all of the frequencies present, recognizes only the pitch of the fundamental. The presence or absence of the remaining harmonics and their relative intensities contribute to what the ear perceives as the *timbre* or *tone color* of the fundamental pitch. The vibrations producing each of these remaining harmonics can be represented as a wave of a certain length and amplitude, and the waves representing all of the frequencies present in a steadily sounding tone can be added together to produce a single complex *waveform* that describes the tone with respect to what is heard as both pitch and timbre. Fig. 4 shows the waveform resulting from the addition of the first and second harmonics where the two are of equal amplitude. Another way of representing such a tone is as a *spectrum*, each line of which represents the intensity of a particular harmonic.

It will be seen from Fig. 3 that a string can be set in motion in such a way as to emphasize one or another of the harmonics. If, for example, the string is plucked at its midpoint, the first harmonic or fundamental will be emphasized and the second deemphasized, since the midpoint is a node for the second harmonic. Similarly, plucking or bowing the string closer to the end will tend to emphasize one or more of the higher harmonics with respect to the fundamental. Differences in the point at which the string is plucked or bowed are heard as differences in timbre.

The physical characteristics of instruments, like the means by which vibrations are produced in them, affect the relative intensities of the harmonics and thus the waveform or spectrum of the tones produced. The spectrum does not, however, remain the same for pitches throughout the range of a given instrument. Instead, it appears that at least some instruments have one or more regions of frequencies in which harmonics are emphasized no matter what the frequency of the fundamental. Such regions, called *formants,* may be an important element in the production of what is perceived as timbre.

The pitches produced by the frequencies in the harmonic series form intervals with the fundamental that are said to be *natural,* or harmonically or acoustically pure. Except for the octaves thus produced (whose frequencies are related to the fundamental by powers of 2), these are not the intervals of the tempered scale used in Western tonal music [see Temperament]. Fig. 5 shows the pitches corresponding to the first 16 harmonics of the tone C. The pitches represented in black notes and thus the intervals that they form with the fundamental are distinctly out of tune with respect to the corresponding pitches of equal temperament. This suggests that there are clear limits to the extent to which the major scale, and by extension the system of Western tonality, can be derived from the harmonic or overtone series. The pitches of the harmonic series represented in white notes are those of *just intonation, and, except for the octaves, they too differ from those of equal temperament. For the sizes of the intervals occurring in the harmonic series as compared with those of other systems such as equal temperament, see Intervals, calculation of.

Vibrating columns of air can be understood to function in ways analogous to those described for vibrating strings. Here, the configuration of the pipe containing the column and the means by which the column is set in motion will determine the character of the waveforms produced. For example, a pipe stopped at one end produces only the odd-numbered harmonics. Suffice it to note, in addition, that the pitches that can be produced with a pipe of fixed length, such as a bugle or natural trumpet, are those of the harmonic series as illustrated in Fig. 5, the fundamental being determined by the length of the pipe; see Wind instruments.

The steady tones thus described might be produced on some ideal string free of the effects of stiffness and friction or on a continuously bowed string or continuously blown wind instrument. In practice, however, musical sounds have beginnings and endings of distinctive character, since the physical characteristics of instruments and the medium in which they operate make it impossible for the vibrations that characterize the steady tone to begin or end instantaneously. Plucked or struck instruments, such as the piano, in fact produce no steady tone at all. From the moment they are first produced, the sounds made by these instruments begin to die away or decrease in amplitude. This decrease in amplitude is called the *decay* of a sound and can be represented by a wave like that of Fig. 6, where the amplitude decreases with each cycle. The rate and character of decay is then illustrated by the curve connecting the peaks of successive cycles. Similarly, a curve can be drawn to illustrate the building up or *attack* of a sound from the point at which the system is first put in motion to the point at which the steady tone is reached. Taken together, the attack and decay characteristics of a given sound are called its *envelope* (Fig. 7). This feature of musical sounds differs significantly from one instrument to the next and is quite important in the ear's identification of instrumental timbres.

See also Beats; Combination tone, resultant tone; Consonance, dissonance; Intervals, calculation of; Loudness; Pitch; Resonance; Temperament.

Act tune. See Entr'acte.

Action. Any mechanism used in instruments as a means of transmitting the motion of the fingers (or feet) to the sound-producing parts. For ill. of the piano's action, see Piano.

Actus tragicus [L.]. An early cantata (no. 106) by Bach, composed in Mühlhausen (1707–8) for an occasion of mourning. The German title is *Gottes Zeit ist die allerbeste Zeit* (God's Time Is Best).

Ad libitum [L.]. An indication that gives the performer liberty to: (1) vary from strict tempo (contrast *a *battuta*); (2) include or omit the part of some voice or instrument (contrast *obbligato); (3) include a *cadenza according to his own invention.

Adagietto [It.]. (1) A tempo somewhat faster than *adagio. (2) A short composition in slow tempo.

Adagio [It.]. (1) Slow, between *andante and *largo. See Tempo marks. (2) A composition in slow tempo, especially the second (slow) movement of a sonata, symphony, etc.

Adagissimo [It.]. Extremely slow.

Adam, Adolphe-Charles (b. Paris, 24 July 1803; d. there, 3 May 1856). Pupil of Boieldieu. Composed ballets (incl. *Giselle*); 53 operas, mostly comic (incl. *Le postillon de Longjumeau*, Paris, 1836); numerous songs.

Adam de la Hale (Halle) (b. Arras, *c.* 1240; d. Naples, 1286 or 1287). In 1271, entered the service of Robert II of Artois, whom he followed to Naples in 1283. Composed numerous monophonic songs; 16 *rondeaux* for 3 voices; several motets for 3 voices; 2 dramatic works, *Le jeu de Robin et de Marion* and *Le jeu de la Feuillée*.

Adam of St. Victor (b. Brittany, 12th cent.; d. Paris, 1177 or 1192). Augustinian monk, poet, and composer. Lived in the Abbey of St. Victor in Paris and composed both text and music of numerous *prosae* [see Sequence (2)].

Added sixth. The pitch a sixth above the root when added to a *triad, or the entire chord thus obtained; e.g., c–e–g–a. Chords of this type are common in jazz and popular music, in which context they are often designated, e.g., C6. They are not to be confused with any of the chords described under Sixth chord.

Additional accompaniment. Revisions or enlargements, particularly those made in the 19th century, of earlier orchestral scores. In many instances the original intention of the composer is misunderstood or disregarded. Handel's *Messiah* has been particularly unfortunate in this regard. Mozart was among the first to make a more modern arrangement of it.

Adelaide. A song by Beethoven (op. 46), composed in 1795 or 1796 to words by F. von Matthisson.

Adélaïde Concerto. A violin concerto attributed to Mozart and edited by Marius Casadesus from a violin part dedicated to the French Princess Adélaïde. The orchestral accompaniment was added by Casadesus. Although it is known that Mozart did write such a piece for the princess, it is almost certain that this is not the work.

Adeste, Fideles [L.]. A Latin hymn usually sung today in the English translation beginning "O come, all ye faithful." The words and music are attributed to John F. Wade, and it was published in 1750 for use in the English Roman Catholic College in Lisbon; hence, the tune name "Portuguese Hymn."

Adieux, Les [F.]. Beethoven's Sonata for piano op. 81a, in E♭ major (1809), entitled (in full) *Les adieux, l'absence, et le retour* (Farewell, Absence, and Return). Also known as the Farewell Sonata, it was inspired by the Archduke Rudolf's departure from Vienna.

Adler, Samuel (b. Mannheim, 4 Mar. 1928). Pupil of Piston, Thompson, and

Hindemith. Teacher at the Eastman School of Music from 1966. Composed an opera, *The Outcasts of Poker Flat,* after Bret Harte, 1959; 5 symphonies and other orch. works; choral works (incl. the cantata *The Vision of Isaiah,* 1949); synagogue services; string quartets and other chamber music; piano pieces; songs.

Adriana Lecouvreur. Opera in four acts by F. Cilèa (libretto after E. Scribe and Legouvé), produced in Milan, 1902. Setting: Paris, 1739.

Aeolian, aeolian mode. See under Church modes.

Aeolian harp. An instrument consisting of a long narrow box with six or more gut strings stretched inside over two bridges. If the box is placed in a free current of air (preferably in an open window), the strings vibrate and produce a large variety of harmonics over the same fundamental. The sound varies considerably with the changing force of the wind. The instrument enjoyed special popularity about 1800.

Aeolopantalon. An instrument invented in 1825 by Jozé Dlugosz in Warsaw; it was a combination of a harmoniumlike instrument (*aeolomelodikon,* with brass tubes affixed to the reeds) and a piano, which could be used in alternation. It is remembered largely because the young Chopin played on it in various recitals.

Aequalstimmen [G.]. (1) The eight-foot pipes of the organ. (2) *Equal voices.

Aerophon. See Aerophor.

Aerophones. See Instruments.

Aerophor. A device invented by B. Samuel in 1912 that provides the player of a wind instrument with additional air from a small bellows operated by the foot. By means of a tube with a mouthpiece, air can be supplied to the player's mouth whenever his breath is not sufficient for long-held tones or long melodies in full legato. R. Strauss wrote passages requiring this device, as in his *Alpensinfonie* (where it is incorrectly called "aerophon").

Affabile [It.]. Gentle, pleasing.

Affannato, affannoso [It.]. Excited, hurried, agitated.

Affections, doctrine of [also doctrine of affects; G. *Affektenlehre*]. An aesthetic theory of the baroque period. With respect to music, it was treated in greatest detail by J. Mattheson (*Der vollkommene Capellmeister,* 1739), who enumerates more than 20 affections and describes how they should be expressed in music, e.g.: "Sorrow should be expressed with a slow-moving, languid and drowsy melody, broken with many sighs." A basic principle is that each composition (or, in the case of composite forms, each movement) should embody only one affection.

Affektenlehre [G.]. See Affections, doctrine of.

Affetti [It.]. The term appears in the title of various publications of the late 16th and early 17th centuries (*Dolci affetti,* 1582; S. Bonini, *Affetti spirituali* . . . *in istile di Firenze o recitativo,* 1615; B. Marini, *Affetti musicali,* op. 1, 1617; G. Stefani, *Affetti amorosi,* 1621), probably to emphasize the affective character of the music. It is also used in early violin sonatas to designate certain types of ornaments [see Ornamentation].

Affettuoso [It.]. Affectionate, tender.

Affinales [L.; sing. *affinalis*]. In medieval theory of the *church modes, the pitches a, b, and c', which occur as the finals of transposed chants.

Affrettando [It.]. Hurrying.

Africaine, L' [F., The African Woman]. Opera in five acts by Meyerbeer (libretto by E. Scribe), produced in Paris, 1865. Setting: Lisbon and Madagascar, end of the 15th century.

Afternoon of a Faun, The. See *Prélude à "L'après-midi d'un faune."*

Agazzari, Agostino (b. Siena, 2 Dec. 1578; d. there, 10 Apr. 1640). Theorist and composer. *Maestro di cappella* at the Siena Cathedral from 1630. Composed Masses, motets, and church music for voices and instruments; a pastoral drama (*Eumelio,* 1606); madrigals. His *Del sonare sopra il basso,* 1607, is one of the earliest treatises on the realization of a figured bass.

Agende [G.]. The liturgical book containing the entire ritual of the German Protestant Church.

Agevole [It.]. Easy, smooth.

Agiatamente [It.]. With ease.

Agilmente [It.]. Nimbly, with agility.

Agitato [It.]. Excited.

Agnus Dei [L., Lamb of God]. The last item (except for the *Ite, missa est*) of the Ordinary of the *Mass; therefore, the final movement in Mass compositions.

Agogic. An *accent is said to be agogic if it is effected not by dynamic stress or by higher pitch but by longer duration of the note. The German term *Agogik* (translated "agogics") is used to denote all the subtleties of performance achieved by modification of tempo, as distinct from *Dynamik* (dynamics), i.e., gradations that involve variety of loudness.

Agon [Gr., Contest]. Ballet by Stravinsky (choreography by George Balanchine), produced in New York, 1957.

Agréments [F.]. The ornaments introduced in French music of the 17th century and finally adopted into all European music; generally indicated by stenographic signs or notes in small type. See Ornamentation.

Agricola, Alexander (b. Flanders, *c.* 1446; d. Valladolid, Spain, 1506). Served the Duke of Milan, 1472–74, and Philip I ("Philip the Handsome") of Burgundy and Spain from 1500. Composed Masses, motets, and numerous chansons.

Agricola, Johann Friedrich (b. Dobitzschen, near Altenburg, 4 Jan. 1720; d. Berlin, 2 Dec. 1774). Organist, theorist, and composer. Pupil of Quantz and J. S. Bach. Court composer to Frederick the Great from 1751 and director of the royal chapel, succeeding K. H. Graun, from 1759. Composed 8 operas; church music; keyboard music; arrangements of the King's compositions.

Aguilera de Heredia, Sebastián (b. Aragon, *c.* 1565; d. Zaragoza, 1627). Organist at the Huesca Cathedral, 1585–1603,

then *maestro de música* at the Zaragoza Cathedral. Composed works for organ; polyphonic psalms and Magnificats.

Aichinger, Gregor (b. Regensburg, 1564; d. Augsburg, 21 Jan. 1628). Pupil of Lassus and G. Gabrieli. Served as *Kapellmeister* and vicar of the Augsburg Cathedral. Composed Masses and other sacred vocal works, some with instruments.

Aida. Opera in four acts by Verdi (libretto by A. Ghislanzoni), commissioned by the Khedive of Egypt for the celebration of the opening of the Suez Canal and produced in Cairo, 1871. Setting: Egypt under the Pharaohs.

Air. (1) French 17th- and 18th-century term for song in general [see Chanson]. (2) In French opera and ballet of the 17th and 18th centuries, an instrumental or vocal piece designed to accompany dancing but not cast in one of the standard dance patterns such as the minuet or gavotte. (3) In *suites written about and after 1700, a movement, found in the optional group, of a melodic rather than dancelike character. (4) See Ayre. (5) Any tune, song, or *aria.

Air de cour [F.]. A type of short strophic song, sometimes with a refrain, for one or more voices usually with lute or harpsichord accompaniment, cultivated in France in the late 16th and in the 17th centuries. The songs are in simple syllabic style, and some texts are in *vers mesuré*. See also *Vaudeville*.

Ais, aisis [G.]. A-sharp, A-double-sharp; see Pitch names.

Akademische Festouvertüre [G., Academic Festival Overture]. Orchestral composition by Brahms, op. 80, written for the University of Breslau in appreciation for the degree of doctor of philosophy conferred on him in 1879. It includes several German student songs.

Akathistos [Gr.]. A famous hymn of the Byzantine Church, in honor of the Virgin.

Akimenko, Feodor Stepanovich (b. Kharkov, 20 Feb. 1876; d. Paris, 3 Jan. 1945). Pupil of Rimsky-Korsakov, 1895–1900, at the St. Petersburg Conservatory.

Later, Stravinsky was among his own pupils there. Settled in Paris after the Russian revolution. Composed an opera; a ballet; orch. works; chamber music; piano pieces.

Akkord [G.]. Chord.

Al [It.]; **à la** [F.]. To the, at the; see, e.g., *Al fine*.

Al fine [It., to the end]. Indication to repeat a composition from the beginning (*da capo*) or from the sign 𝄋 (*dal segno*) to the place marked *fine*.

Al segno. See *Segno*.

Alalá. A type of folksong from northwest Spain (Galicia).

Alba [Prov., dawn]. In the repertory of the troubadours, a poem dealing with the lover's departure in the early morning. It is usually cast in the form of a dialogue between the lover and a watchman (*gaite de la tore*, guard of the tower), who warns him of approaching danger.

Albéniz, Isaac (b. Camprodón, Spain, 29 May 1860; d. Cambo-les-Bains, France, 18 May 1909). Pianist and composer. A child prodigy, he traveled extensively giving concerts in Spain, Puerto Rico, Cuba, and the U.S. until age 15. Thereafter, studied with Brassin and Gevaert at the Brussels Conservatory and with Jadassohn and Reinecke at the Leipzig Conservatory. Settled in Paris, 1893. Composed several operas (incl. *Pepita Jiménez*, Barcelona, 1896); numerous piano pieces (incl. **Iberia; Navarra*, completed by Sévérac) and the shorter works *Seguidillas, Córdoba*, and the *Tango in D*); orch. works (incl. *Catalonia*, with piano, 1899); an oratorio.

Albert, Eugène (Francis Charles) d' (b. Glasgow, 10 Apr. 1864; d. Riga, 3 March 1932). Pianist, conductor, and composer. Studied first under his father, Charles Louis Napolean d'Albert, a dancing master and composer of popular music; later a pupil of Pauer, Stainer, Prout, Sullivan, Richter, and Liszt. Appointed court pianist at Weimar, 1895, and director of the Berlin Hochschule (succeeding Joachim), 1907. Composed operas (incl. *Die Abreise*, Frankfurt, 1898; *Tiefland*, Prague, 1903; *Die toten Augen*, Dresden,

1916); choral works (incl. *Der Mensch und das Leben*); orch. works; concertos for piano and for cello; chamber music; piano pieces, incl. transcriptions of Bach's organ works; songs.

Albert, Heinrich (b. Lobenstein, Saxony, 8 July 1604; d. Königsberg, 6 Oct. 1651). Pupil of his cousin Schütz. Appointed organist of the Königsberg Cathedral, 1631. Composed 8 volumes of *Arien*, which incl. secular songs and chorales for one and more voices with accompaniment.

Albert Herring. Comic opera in three acts by Britten (libretto by E. Crozier after "Le rosier de Madame Husson" by De Maupassant), produced at Glyndebourne, 1947. Setting: England, late 19th century.

Alberti, Domenico (b. Venice, 1710 or 1717; d. Formio or Rome, *c*. 1740). Singer, harpsichordist, and composer, after whom the **Alberti bass is named. Pupil of Lotti. Composed 3 operas; several motets; numerous keyboard sonatas.

Alberti bass. Stereotyped figures of accompaniment for the left hand in keyboard music, consisting of broken chords [see also Murky]. They are named for Domenico Alberti (d. *c*. 1740), who used them extensively.

Albinoni, Tomaso (b. Venice, 8 June 1671; d. there, 17 Jan. 1750). Violinist and composer. Friend and admirer of Vivaldi. Composed numerous operas (incl. *Griselda*, Florence, 1703; *I veri amici*, Munich, 1722); violin sonatas and trio sonatas (from which Bach took the themes for two fugues); violin concertos and oboe concertos.

Albisiphone. See under Flute.

Alborada [Sp.]. A type of Spanish music, played on the *dulzaina* (rustic oboe) and *tamboril* (small drum), originally a morning song.

Albrechtsberger, Johann Georg (b. Klosterneuburg, near Vienna, 3 Feb. 1736; d. Vienna, 7 Mar. 1809). Theorist, teacher, and composer. Appointed organist at the Abbey of Melk, 1760; court organist at Vienna, 1772; *Kapellmeister* at St. Stephen's Cathedral in Vienna, 1792. A friend of the Haydns and of Mozart. Among his pupils were Beethoven (1794 –95), Czerny, Seyfried, Hummel, and Weigl. Published several writings on theory and composition, incl. *Gründliche Anweisung zur Composition*, 1790. Composed fugues; organ preludes; string quartets and other chamber music; Masses and other sacred works; oratorios.

Albright, William (b. Gary, Ind., 20 Oct. 1944). Organist, pianist, and composer. Pupil of Aitkin, Finney, Bassett, and Messiaen. Teacher at the Univ. of Michigan from 1970 and associated with its Electronic Music Studio. Has used elements of jazz and popular music. Has composed works for organ; piano; orchestra; chamber ensembles; multimedia, combining film, tape, and improvising ensembles (incl. *Tic,* 1967).

Albumblatt [G., album leaf]. A fanciful name used in the 19th century for short piano pieces such as might be inscribed in an autograph album.

Alceste. Opera in three acts by Gluck (Italian libretto by R. di Calzabigi, based on Euripides' tragedy), produced in Vienna, probably 1767. Revised French version produced in Paris, 1776. Setting: Thessaly, in legendary times.

Aleatory music. Music in which the composer introduces elements of chance or unpredictability with regard to either the composition or its performance. The terms *aleatoric, chance music, music of indeterminacy* have been applied to many works created since 1945 by composers who differ widely as to the concepts, methods, and rigor with which they employ procedures of random selection. In the composition process, pitches, durations, degrees of intensity, and other elements may be chosen or distributed in time by dice throwing, interpretations of abstract designs (Cage), and the like, or according to certain mathematical laws of chance (Xenakis). In performance, chance is allowed to operate by leaving the choice or order of appearance of some elements to the per-

former's discretion (Brown, Boulez, Stockhausen, Pousseur). Most of these procedures are derived from and motivated by new general concepts of music, according to which form and structure are no longer regarded as definitely fixed and final but as subject to partial or total transformations from one performance to another (*open forms, mobile forms*). The first well-known example of 20th-century aleatory composition was John Cage's *Music of Changes* for piano (1951).

Alfano, Franco (b. Posilippo, Naples, 8 Mar. 1876; d. San Remo, 26 or 27 Oct. 1954). Studied in Naples and with Jadassohn in Leipzig. Director of the Liceo musicale in Bologna, 1919–23, and of the Turin Conservatory, 1923–39; superintendent of the Teatro Massimo in Palermo, 1940–42; from 1947, director of the Rossini Conservatory in Pesaro. Composed operas (incl. *Risurrezione,* after Tolstoy, Turin, 1904; *La leggenda di Sakuntala,* Bologna, 1921; and the completion of Puccini's *Turandot*); several ballets; several symphonic works; chamber music; piano pieces.

Alfvén, Hugo (Emil) (b. Stockholm, 1 May 1872; d. Falun, 8 May 1960). Stockholm court violinist, 1891–97. Musical director at the Univ. of Uppsala, 1910–39. Composed 5 symphonies; 3 rhapsodies for orchestra (incl. *Midsommarvaka,* 1904, also produced as a ballet, *La nuit de Saint-Jean,* Paris, 1925); chamber music; piano pieces; songs.

Aliquot strings, aliquot scaling. *Sympathetic strings added by some piano makers (first by Blüthner) above the strings of the upper register in order to produce a fuller sound through *resonance.

Alkan, Charles-Henri Valentin (real surname Morhange) (b. Paris, 30 Nov. 1813; d. there, 29 Mar. 1888). Pianist and composer. Entered the Paris Conservatory at age 6, studying with Zimmermann. Later became a member of the circle of musicians and writers incl. Chopin, George Sand, Hugo, and Liszt. Composed mostly piano works: programmatic pieces (incl. *Le chemin de fer* and *L'incendie au village prochain*), etudes (incl. two sets in all the major and minor keys, op. 35 and 39), concertos, a sonata, some chamber music with piano, and transcriptions for piano.

All' ongarese [It.]. See *Ongarese.*

All' ottava [It.]. See *Ottava.*

All' unisono [It.]. See Unison.

Alla, all' [It.]; **à la, à l'** [F.]. In the manner of; e.g., *alla *turca, alla *zingarese; à l'espagnol,* in the Spanish manner.

Alla breve [It.]. A *tempo mark (equivalent to the time signature ₵) indicating quick duple time, i.e., with the half note rather than the quarter note as the beat; in other words, 2/2 instead of 4/4. Both the name and the sign are vestiges of *mensural notation and of the *proportions *(tempus imperfectum diminutum).* Originally (and properly), *alla breve* meant that the unit of musical time *(tactus)* was represented by the *brevis* (corresponding to our double whole note), not, as was usual, by the *semibrevis* (corresponding to our whole note).

Allargando [It.]. Slowing down, usually accompanied by a *crescendo.

Allegretto [It.]. (1) A tempo between *andante and *allegro; see Tempo marks. (2) A short piece in fast (allegro) tempo.

Allegri, Gregorio (b. Rome, *c.* 1582; d. there, 17 Feb. 1652). Pupil of Nanino. Singer in the papal chapel from 1629. Composed the *Miserere* for 9 voices which was performed in the Sistine Chapel during Holy Week until *c.* 1870. Its publication, though forbidden on pain of excommunication, was effected by several people, incl. Mozart, who wrote it out from memory after hearing it performed twice in 1770. Composed Masses, motets, and other sacred works.

Allegro [It.]. (1) Fast. See Tempo marks. Originally the term was employed primarily as an expression mark [It., cheerful, joyful], as appears from designations such as "allegro e presto" (M. Cazzati, *Il secondo libro delle sonate,* op. 8, 1648) or "andante allegro" (first movement, Handel's Organ Concerto no. 6, op. 4). (2) A composition in fast tempo, especially the first or last movement of a sonata or symphony.

Alleluia [L.]. An exclamation of praise to God (from the Hebrew **hallelujah,* praise ye the Lord), which occurs in some Psalms. More specifically, *Alleluia* refers to an elaborate chant sung as the third item of the Proper of the *Mass, except during Lent, when the *Tract is sung. The Alleluia of the Mass consists of the word *alleluia* followed by a brief sentence called the verse *(versus alleluiaticus,* abbr. ℣), e.g.: "Alleluia. ℣ Surrexit Dominus de sepulcro" [see *LU,* p. 790]. The music for the word *alleluia* closes with a long vocalization on the final "a," the so-called *jubilus. See also Psalmody; Sequence (2).

Allemande [F.]. A dance in moderate duple time that first appeared in the early 16th century. Like the *pavane and *passamezzo, the allemande was frequently followed by a jumping dance in triple meter (called *tripla, *Proportz)* or, in the 17th century, by the *courante. In the 17th century the allemande became a stylized dance type regularly used as the first movement of the *suite. These allemandes are in moderate 4/4 time, with a short upbeat, and frequently make use of short running figures that are passed through the various voices of a pseudo-contrapuntal fabric. In the late 18th century the name Allemande was used in South Germany as an equivalent for *deutscher Tanz,* a quick waltzlike dance in 3/4 or 3/8 time. Pieces of this type occur in Beethoven's *Bagatellen* op. 119, where he uses the phrase "à l'Allemande," and in his *Zwölf deutsche Tänze* (1795) for orchestra.

Allende Sarón, Pedro Humberto (b. Santiago, Chile, 29 June 1885; d. there, 16 Aug. 1959). Professor of composition at the National Conservatory in Santiago, 1928–45. Composed a symphony and other orch. works; concertos; choral works; chamber music; numerous piano pieces (incl. *12 tonadas de carácter popular chileno);* songs.

Allentando [It.]. Slowing down.

Alliteration. The grouping of words with the same initial letter. A characteristic feature of ancient North European poetry *(Beowulf, Edda),* it was adopted by Wagner in *Der Ring des Nibelungen.*

Alma Redemptoris Mater [L., Nourishing Mother of the Redeemer]. One of the four Marian antiphons [see Antiphon (2)].

Alman, almayne. Sixteenth-century English corruptions of *allemande.

Alpaerts, Flor (b. Antwerp, 12 Sept. 1876; d. there, 5 Oct. 1954). Pupil of Blockx. Professor at the Royal Flemish Conservatory from 1903 and its director, 1934–41. Works include an opera (*Shylock,* Antwerp, 1913); a symphony and symphonic poems (incl. *Pallieter,* 1921); the *James Ensor Suite* for orchestra, 1929; a violin concerto; incidental music for several plays.

Alpensinfonie, Eine [G., An Alpine Symphony]. A long *symphonic poem in one movement by R. Strauss, op. 64 (1911–15), describing a day of Alpine climbing.

Alphorn, alpine horn. A primitive wind instrument found in various parts of the world and used by herdsmen in the Alps for signaling over a great distance and for simple melodies [see *Ranz des vaches*]. Made of wooden staves bound with strips of birch bark, it is 3 to 10 feet long and appears in various shapes, straight or bent. See ill. under Brass instruments.

Alpine Symphony, An. See *Alpensinfonie, Eine.*

Also sprach Zarathustra [G., Thus Spake Zarathustra]. *Symphonic poem by R. Strauss, op. 30, completed in 1896. It is based on Nietzsche's work of the same name.

Alt [L.]. (1) Term for the tones of the octave above the treble staff (g″ to f‴), which are said to be "in alt." The tones of the next higher octave are called "in altissimo." (2) In German, the lower of the two female voices, i.e., the contralto [see Alto]. In connection with instruments, the term denotes the second highest member of the family (*Altklarinette,* alto clarinet; *Altsaxophon,* alto saxophone). See entries for the various instruments. *Altgeige* is the viola alta [see Violin family], rarely the ordinary viola.

Alteration. (1) See Mensural notation. (2) The raising or lowering of a note by means of a sharp or flat, also called chromatic alteration. See Accidentals; Chromaticism.

Altered chord. A chord in which one or more pitches have been chromatically altered, e.g., the Neapolitan, German, and French *sixth chords.

Alternation [L. alternatim]. A term used with reference to early liturgical compositions (12th–16th cent.), primarily to indicate the alternation of *polyphony and *plainsong. The practice of alternation is particularly important in liturgical organ music. Here not only the psalms, the *Magnificat, the *Salve Regina, and the hymns consisted of organ music alternating with plainsong, but also the various items of the Mass [see Organ Mass; Verset]. The normal scheme for the Kyrie was as follows (organ music in italics): *Kyrie* Kyrie *Kyrie* Christe *Christe* Christe *Kyrie* Kyrie *Kyrie.*

Alternativo [It.]; **alternativement** [F.]. Indication for one section to alternate with another, as in an A B A structure (ternary form; see Binary and ternary form). In the suites of Bach, an indication such as "Bourrée I, alternativement—Bourée II" calls for repetition of section A (first bourrée) after section B (second bourrée). Schumann occasionally used the term *alternativo* as a designation for an internal section.

Altgeige [G.]. See under Alt (2).

Althorn [G.]. See under Brass instruments II (f).

Altissimo [It.]. See Alt.

Alto [It., high]. (1) A female voice of low range, also called contralto. See Voices, range of. (2) Originally the alto was a high male voice that, through the use of *falsetto, nearly reached the range of the female voice (contralto). This type of voice, also known as a *countertenor, was cultivated especially in England, where the church music of the 16th and 17th centuries definitely implies its use. [For an explanation of the term, see Contratenor.] (3) The second highest part of the normal four-part chorus; L. *altus.* (4) In French and Italian, the second highest instrument of the violin family, i.e., the viola. (5) Applied to clarinet, flute, saxophone, etc., the term refers to the second or third highest member of the family.

Alto clef. See Clef.

Alto Rhapsody. See *Rhapsodie aus Goethe's "Harzreise im Winter."*

Altra volta [It.]. *Encore.

Altschlüssel [G.]. Alto *clef.

Altus [L.]. See under Alto (3).

Alzati [It.]. Indication to remove the *mutes.

Am Frosch [G.]. Bowing with that portion of the bow nearest the hand, i.e., near the *frog.

Am Griffbrett [G.]. Bowing near or above the fingerboard (*sul tasto*) of a stringed instrument. See Bowing (l).

Am Steg [G.]. Bowing near the bridge (*sul ponticello*) of a stringed instrument. See Bowing (k).

Amabile [It.]. Amiable, with love.

Amahl and the Night Visitors. Opera in one act by Gian Carlo Menotti (to his own libretto), produced in New York by N.B.C.-TV Opera Theater on Christmas Eve, 1951, the first opera commissioned specifically for television. Stage premiere, Indiana University, 1952. Setting: near Bethlehem, birth of Jesus.

Ambitus [L.]. See under Church modes.

Amboss [G.]. *Anvil.

Ambrosian chant. A repertory of liturgical chant named after St. Ambrose (340? –97), Bishop of Milan, and still in use in the cathedral of that city; therefore also called Milanese chant. One of the four or five branches of Western Christian chant [see Chant].

Ambrosian hymns. The hymns of the Roman and Milanese (Ambrosian) rites written by St. Ambrose (340?–97), or others of the same type written later. Formerly nearly all the hymns (*c*. 120) of the *antiphonarium* [see under Antiphonal] were ascribed to Ambrose, under the generic name *hymni Ambrosiani.* The number of true Ambrosian hymn texts is much smaller, hardly more than a dozen. Ambrose's authorship of four of

them is placed beyond doubt by the testimony of St. Augustine; these are *Aeterne rerum conditor, Deus creator omnium, Jam surgit hora tertia,* and *Veni Redemptor gentium.* It is not certain that any of the surviving melodies is by Ambrose. The term *Ambrosian hymn* [G. *Ambrosianischer Lobgesang*] is erroneously used for the *Te Deum.

Ambrosian modes. See under Church modes.

Âme [F.]. The *sound post of the violin.

Amen. A Hebrew word, meaning "so be it," which occurs in the Scriptures as an affirmative expression and is widely used in Christian rites. In Gregorian chant it occurs at the end of the Lesser *Doxology, and, in the Mass, at the end of the Gloria as well as of the Credo. In the polyphonic Masses and other choral works of the 17th and 18th centuries the confirming character of the Amen led to the writing of extensive closing sections in fugal style, called Amen fugue or Amen chorus, in which the word is repeated over and over. For Amen cadence, see Cadence (1).

Amener [F.]. A 17th-century dance in moderate triple time with phrases of six measures (three plus three or four plus two) as a characteristic feature. It occurs in the suites of Heinrich Biber, J. K. F. Fischer, Alessandro Poglietti, and others.

American organ. See under Harmonium.

Amfiparnaso, L'. See under Madrigal comedy.

Amor brujo, El [Sp., Love the Sorcerer]. Ballet by Manuel de Falla, produced in Madrid, 1915. The music includes numerous dance pieces inspired by folk dances, the best known being the "Ritual Fire Dance." A unique feature is the inclusion of two songs for the ballerina.

Amore, con; amorevole [It.]. With love.

Amour des trois oranges, L'. See *Love for Three Oranges.*

Amplitude. See under Acoustics.

Amram, David Werner (b. Philadelphia, 17 Nov. 1930). Pupil of Giannini. Music director of the New York Shakespeare Festival, 1956–68, and of the Lincoln Center Repertory Theater, 1963–65. Composer-in-residence at the New York Philharmonic, 1966–67. Has composed operas (incl. *The Final Ingredient*, for television, 1965; *Twelfth Night*, Lake George, N.Y., 1968); incidental music for plays; orch. works; choral works; chamber music; jazz; songs; music for films.

Amy, Gilbert (b. Paris, 29 Aug. 1936). Pupil of Milhaud, Messiaen, and Boulez. Succeeded Boulez as director of the Domaine musical in Paris, 1967. Has employed serial procedures, sometimes combined with elements of chance. Works include a piano sonata, 1960; *Cantate brève* after García Lorca, 1957; *Antiphonies* for two orchestras, 1963; *Trajectoires* for violin and orchestra, 1966.

An die ferne Geliebte [G., To the Distant Beloved]. Song cycle by Beethoven, op. 98 (1816), consisting of six songs to poems by A. Jeitteles.

Anacrusis. *Upbeat.

Analysis. The study of the relationship to one another of the elements of actual works of music. In principle it is concerned with all aspects of music, including *pitch, *rhythm, *tone color, and *dynamics, as well as matters of general *style dependent on these. In practice, aspects of the organization of pitch have received much the greatest emphasis [see Harmonic analysis]. It is an important part of musical *theory.

Anapest, anapaest. See under Poetic meter.

Anche [F.]. *Reed. *Anche battante,* beating reed; *anche double,* double reed; *anche libre,* free reed. Also *anches,* reed stops of the organ; *trio d'anches,* trio for reed instruments.

Ancia [It.]. *Reed. *Ancia battente, doppia,* etc., as under *Anche.

Ancora [It.]. Once more, repeat. *Ancora più forte,* still louder.

Andacht, mit; andächtig [G.]. With devotion.

Andamento [It.]. In 18th-century writings: (1) *Sequence. (2) A special type of fugal subject [see *Soggetto*]. (3) In more recent writings the term is used to denote a fugal episode.

Andante [It.]. Tempo mark indicating very moderate "walking" speed, between allegretto and adagio [see Tempo marks]. There is no agreement as to whether andante belongs to the quick or the slow tempi, and this makes ambiguous such terms as *più andante, meno andante, molto andante, andantino*. According to the former interpretation of the word, *più andante* and *molto andante* indicate a tempo quicker than the normal andante, while *meno andante* indicates a slower speed. In Brahms' Andante from the Piano Sonata op. 5, the closing section, marked "andante molto," is quicker than the preceding *andante espressivo*. However, other composers, perhaps the majority, use *molto andante* to mean a tempo still slower than andante. See Andantino.

Andante con moto. See *Moto.*

Andantino [It.]. Diminutive of *andante,* used mainly to characterize a short piece of andante tempo or character. If used as a tempo mark, it means a slight modification of *andante,* whose direction is, unfortunately, a matter of divergent opinion [see Andante]. Most modern musicians apparently use the term to indicate a tempo quicker than andante.

Andrea Chénier. Opera in four acts by Umberto Giordano (libretto by L. Illica), produced in Milan, 1896. Setting: Paris, French Revolution.

Andriessen, Hendrik (b. Haarlem, 17 Sept. 1892). Pupil of Zweers. Organist at the Utrecht Cathedral, 1934–42. Director of the Utrecht Conservatory, 1937–49; of the Royal Conservatory in The Hague, 1949–57. Works incl. 3 symphonies; several Masses; a cello sonata and a violin sonata; a song cycle (*Miroir de Peine,* 1923); an opera (*Philomela,* Amsterdam, 1950).

Andriessen, Jurriaan (b. Haarlem, 15 Nov. 1925). Son of Hendrik Andriessen. Studied with his father, in Paris, and with Copland. Works incl. 4 symphonies; a symphonic poem (*Berkshire Symphonies*, 1949, produced as a ballet, *Jones Beach*, with choreography by George Balanchine, New York, 1950); a piano concerto; chamber music; songs; music for radio and films.

Andriessen, Louis (b. Utrecht, 6 June 1939). Son of Hendrik Andriessen. Pupil of his father, of van Baaren, and of Berio. Works incl. the opera *Reconstructie*, with Schat and van Vlijman, 1969; works for orch.; chamber music; piano pieces; music for theater and films.

Andriessen, Willem (b. Haarlem, 25 Oct. 1887; d. Amsterdam, 29 Mar. 1964). Brother of Hendrik Andriessen. Pianist and composer. Director of the Amsterdam Conservatory from 1937. Composed mostly pieces for piano and organ; also a Mass and numerous songs.

Anerio, Felice (b. Rome, *c*. 1560; d. there, 27 Sept. 1614). Pupil of Nanino. Succeeded Palestrina as composer to the papal chapel, 1594. Collaborated with Soriano on the Medicean edition of the Roman Gradual (publ. 1614–15). Composed numerous madrigals and sacred choral works, some with instrumental accompaniment.

Anerio, Giovanni Francesco (b. Rome, *c*. 1567; d. June 1630, traveling from Poland to Italy; buried Graz, 12 June 1630). Brother of Felice Anerio. Sang with him at St. Peter's under Palestrina, 1575–79. *Maestro di cappella* at the Lateran Church in Rome and later a member of the court of King Sigismund III of Poland. Works incl. numerous Masses, motets, and other forms of sacred music; madrigals.

Anfang [G.]. Beginning; *vom Anfang,* same as **da capo.*

Anfossi, Pasquale (b. Taggia, near Naples, 25 Apr. 1727; d. Rome, Feb. 1797). Pupil of Piccinni, Durante, and Sacchini. Director of the Italian Opera in London, 1781–83. *Maestro di cappella* at the Lateran Church in Rome from 1791. Composed over 70 operas (incl. *Le gelosie fortunate,* Vienna, 1786, to which Mozart contributed an aria; *L'incognita perseguitata,* Rome, 1773); 12 oratorios; Masses and other sacred music.

Angelica [L.]; **angélique** [F.]. See under Lute.

Anglaise [F.]. A 17th- and 18th-century dance in fast duple time, obviously derived from the **country dance. It occurs in J. S. Bach's French Suite no. 3 and, under the name "balet anglois" or "air anglois," in J. K. F. Fischer's *Musicalischer Parnassus* of *c*. 1690. The name was also used for other dances of English origin or character, e.g., the (syncopated) **hornpipe and, *c*. 1800, the **country dance and the **écossaise.*

Anglebert, Jean-Henri d' (b. Paris, *c*. 1628; d. there, 23 Apr. 1691). Pupil of Chambonnières, whom he succeeded as harpsichordist to Louis XIV. He was succeeded in this position by his son Jean-Baptiste Henri d'Anglebert, 1674. Works incl. the *Pièces de clavecin,* 1689, containing suites, arrangements of passages from Lully's operas, and 22 variations on *Folies d'Espagne,* with instructions for *clavecin* (i.e., harpsichord) performance.

Anglican chant. The harmonized singing of prose psalms and **canticles, so called because it is extensively used in the Church of England. Extended four-part settings by Tallis, Byrd, and Gibbons, which had the Gregorian **psalm tone in the tenor and which were referred to as "festival psalms," were published in John Barnard's *The First Book of Selected Church Musick* (1641). They correspond to the **falsobordone settings of Josquin, Victoria, and others on the Continent. The modern abbreviated Anglican chant was first published in 1644 in the second edition of James Clifford's *The Divine Services.* The psalm tone remained in the tenor part until the 18th century, when all memory of plainsong singing had passed and melodies were shifted to the treble or soprano part. The following example is "Christ Church Tune," psalm tone I_4, as printed in William Boyce's *Cathedral Music* (1760):

O come, let us sing un-to the Lord:

This is a *single chant,* designed for use with a single verse of the psalm at a time. *Double chants* are twice as long and take two verses at a time.

Angoscioso [It.]. Sorrowful, grieved.

Angst, ängstlich [G.]. Anxiety, anxious.

Anhalt, István (b. Budapest, 12 Apr. 1919). Pupil of Kodály and N. Boulanger. Teacher at McGill University in Montreal from 1949. Active in composition and performance of electronic music. Works also incl. piano pieces; chamber music; a symphony; and works combining voices and/or instruments with magnetic tape.

Anhalten, anhaltend [G.]. To continue (e.g., sounding, as when a tone is not damped); continuing.

Anhemitonic. An anhemitonic scale (also called a tonal scale) possesses no semitones; e.g., one of the four *pentatonic scales or the whole-tone scale.

Animando, animandosi [It.]. Animating, becoming animated.

Animé [F.]. Animated.

Animo, con animo, animoso [It.]. Spirit, with spirit, spirited.

Animuccia, Giovanni (b. Florence, *c.* 1514; d. Rome, 25 Mar. 1571). Succeeded Palestrina as *maestro di cappella* at St. Peter's, 1555. Palestrina returned to the position after Animuccia's death. Worked also in the oratory of San Filippo Neri from 1570. Works incl. several Masses; Magnificats; madrigals; *laude* [see *Lauda;* Oratorio].

Anmutig [G.]. Graceful.

Années de pèlerinage [F., Years of Pilgrimage]. Collective title for three volumes of piano music by Liszt, composed over the years 1836–77. Each volume contains several pieces with descriptive titles.

Annibale Padovano (''Il Padovano'') (b. Padua, *c.* 1527; d. Graz, 15? Mar. 1575). Organist at San Marco in Venice, 1552–66, under Willaert, Rore, and Zarlino; succeeded by Merulo. *Kapellmeister* at the court in Graz from 1566. Works incl.

ricercars and toccatas for organ; madrigals; motets and Masses.

Anreissen [G.]. Forceful attack in string playing. See Attack (2).

Ansatz [G.]. (1) In singing, the proper adjustment of the vocal apparatus. (2) In playing wind instruments, proper adjustment of the lips [see Embouchure (1)]. (3) Crook or shank of brass instruments [see Wind instruments (b)]. (4) In violin playing, *attack.

Anschlag [G.]. (1) In piano playing, touch. (2) An ornament explained by K. P. E. Bach [see Appoggiatura, double].

Anschwellend [G.]. *Crescendo.*

Answer. In fugal writing, the answer is the second (or fourth) statement of the subject, usually in the dominant (occasionally in the subdominant); so called because of its relationship to the first (or third) statement, which is in the tonic. See Fugue; Tonal and real; Antecedent and consequent.

Ante-Communion. The initial portion of the Anglican Holy Communion, usually ending with the Creed or the Prayer for the Whole State of Christ's Church. It is used as a separate service, similar to the Roman Catholic Mass of the Catechumens.

Antecedent and consequent. The terms are usually applied to melodic phrases that stand in the relationship of question and answer or statement and confirmation, as in the accompanying example (Beethoven, String Quartet op. 18, no. 2, 4th movement). Here, as in other instances, the dialogue character of the melody is emphasized by its distribution between two instruments. The two phrases often have the same or similar rhythms, but have complementary pitch contours and/or tonal implications, e.g., a rising contour in the first and a falling contour in the second, or a conclusion on the dominant in the first and a conclusion on the tonic in the second. The terms are also used as synonymous with *subject* and *answer* in fugues and canons [see Answer].

Cello   Violin

Antes, John (b. Frederickstownship, Pa., 24 Mar. 1740; d. Bristol, England, 17 Dec. 1811). Moravian minister, missionary, watchmaker, inventor (devices for violin-tuning and page-turning). Composed numerous anthems to German or English texts for chorus, winds, strings, and organ; three string trios, the earliest known chamber works by an American-born composer.

Antheil, George (b. Trenton, N.J., 8 July 1900; d. New York, 12 Feb. 1959). Pupil of Bloch. Composed operas (incl. *Transatlantic,* Frankfurt, 1930); ballets; symphonies; concertos; choral works; *Ballet méchanique* for pianos, percussion, and airplane propeller, New York, 1927; string quartets; piano pieces (incl. *Airplane Sonata,* 1922; *Mechanisms*). Published articles and books on a wide variety of subjects.

Anthem. A choral composition in English, with words from the Bible or some other religious text, performed during the worship service of Protestant churches, where it holds a position similar to that of the *motet in the Roman Catholic rites. An anthem may be accompanied by the organ or orchestra or unaccompanied.

The anthem dates from the Reformation and the consequent establishment of English as the liturgical language of Great Britain. Although the anthem developed from the Latin motet, the first anthems, written by Christopher Tye (*c.* 1500–1573), Thomas Tallis (*c.* 1505–85), and Robert Whyte (*c.* 1535–74), are markedly different in style from previous and contemporary motets. They are rhythmically square, more harmonically conceived, more syllabic, and in shorter phrases, all features resulting from the greater consideration given to text and pronunciation. However, a few anthems are merely motets with texts translated into English (e.g., Tallis' "I call and cry" from *O sacrum convivium;* Byrd's "Bow thine ear" from *Civitas sancti tui*). Towards the end of the 16th century a new form, the *verse anthem,* was introduced by William Byrd and developed by Thomas Tomkins (1572–1656) and Orlando Gibbons (1583–1625). This form, in which sections for full chorus alternate with sections for one or more solo voices, was preferred throughout the 17th century, with the *full* (i.e., completely choral) *anthem* returning to prominence in the subsequent period. John Blow (1649–1708) and Henry Purcell (1659–95) introduced instrumental interludes into the anthem.

Anticipation. See Counterpoint (5); also Nachschlag.

Antienne [F.]. (1) *Antiphon. (2) *Anthem.

Antiphon. (1) A short text from the Scriptures or elsewhere, set to music in a simple syllabic style and sung before and after a psalm or canticle. The repertory of Gregorian chant includes more than 1,000 such antiphons. The melodies can be classified into about 40 groups of chants related to each other through identical beginnings and other common material.

(2) The term is also used for two types of chant that do not as a rule embrace a psalm or canticle but are independent songs of considerable length and elaboration. The first includes the processional antiphons, sung during processions on certain feasts (Palm Sunday, Purification). Comprising the second group are the four antiphons *B.M.V.* (*Beatae Mariae Virginis*) or B.V.M. (Blessed Virgin Mary): *Alma Redemptoris Mater,* *Ave Regina caelorum,* *Regina caeli laetare,* and *Salve Regina* [see *LU,* pp. 273–76]. These chants, also known as Marian antiphons, are sung at the end of Compline, one during each of the seasons of the year. In the 15th and 16th centuries they were frequently composed polyphonically, for voices or for organ.

(3) In historical studies the name is also applied to certain chants of the Mass Proper, namely, the *Introit (Introit antiphon, *antiphona ad introitum*), the *Offertory (*antiphona ad offerendum*), and the *Communion (Communion antiphon, *antiphona ad communionem*). These chants originally sprang from the same method of antiphonal psalmody that survives in a different form in the antiphons embracing a psalm or a canticle [see Psalmody III].

Antiphonal, antiphonary, antiphoner [L. *antiphonale, antiphonarium*]. A liturgical book containing all the chants for the Office, as opposed to a *gradual, which contains all the chants for the Mass. See Gradual (2); Liturgical books.

Antiphonal singing. Singing in alternating choruses. Originally and properly the term should be applied to plainsong [see Psalmody III]. The term is also used with reference to polyphonic music composed for two or more alternating groups [see Polychoral style].

Antiphonia. In Greek theory, the octave.

Antoniou, Theodore (b. Athens, 10 Feb. 1935). Conductor and composer. Pupil of Kalomiris, Papaioannou, and Bialas. Teacher at the National Conservatory in Athens, 1956–60; at Stanford Univ. from 1969, where he founded the ensemble *Alea II;* at the Philadelphia Music Academy from 1971. Has worked with serial, electronic, and aleatory procedures and with mixed media. Has composed a ballet; orch. works (incl. *Mikrographien,* 1964; *Events II,* 1969); choral works; chamber music; piano pieces; *Cassandra* for mixed media, 1969.

Antony and Cleopatra. Opera in three acts by Barber (libretto by F. Zeffirelli), produced in New York, 1966. Setting: Alexandria and Rome, 1st century B.C.

Antwort [G.]. Answer, in fugues.

Anvil. Anvils proper have sometimes been used as percussion instruments in operas, usually as stage properties (Auber, *Le Maçon,* 1825; Verdi, *Il trovatore;* Wagner, *Das Rheingold*). What is often intended by the term in works of the 20th century is a small steel bar struck with a hard wooden or metal mallet. Anvils may or may not be of definite pitch.

Anwachsend [G.]. Growing, swelling.

Aperto [It.]. Open. (1) In horn playing, the opposite of *chiuso.* See Horn. (2) An indication in 14th-century music; see *Ouvert, clos.*

Apollon Musagète [Fr., Apollo, Leader of the Muses]. Ballet, scored for string orchestra, by Stravinsky (choreography by Adolph Bolm), produced in Washington, D.C., 1928, and in Paris (with chore-ography by George Balanchine) later in the same year.

Apollonicon. See under Mechanical instruments.

Apostel, Hans Erich (b. Karlsruhe, 22 Jan. 1901; d. 30 Nov. 1972). Pupil of Schoenberg and Berg and active principally in Vienna. Composed orch. works; a piano concerto; string quartets; piano pieces.

Apothéose. See under Lament (2).

Appalachian Spring. Ballet, scored for thirteen instruments, by Copland (choreography by Martha Graham), produced in Washington, D.C., 1944. Its setting is a pioneer wedding at a Pennsylvania farmhouse. Much of the music is incorporated in a suite for full orchestra of the same name completed in 1945. It includes variations on the Shaker hymn "Simple Gifts."

Appassionata; Sonata appassionata [It., impassioned]. Name customarily given to Beethoven's Piano Sonata op. 57 in F minor (1805). The title was not his but was added by a publisher. The original title is *Grande sonate pour piano.*

Applicatur. An 18th-century German term for fingering.

Appoggiando [It.]. "Leaning," i.e., emphasized; also, full *legato.*

Appoggiatura [It.]. (1) See under Counterpoint. (2) Originally, an appoggiatura [F. *port de voix;* E. forefall, backfall, half-fall; G. *Vorschlag;* Sp. *apoyadura*] was an ornamental note, usually in the lower second, that was melodically connected with the main note that followed it (i.e., the appoggiatura was sung in the same breath or played with the same stroke of the bow or articulation of the tongue or, in the case of keyboard instruments, slurred to the following note). It was indicated by means of a small note or special sign but was also frequently introduced extemporaneously in performance. The interpretation of the appoggiatura has varied considerably since the 17th century, when it first became a conventional ornament.

In the baroque period the appoggiatura was exceedingly flexible as regards both notation and rhythmic execution. Ex. 1 shows the various ways of indicating the appoggiatura; Ex. 2 the methods of performance that were prevalent around 1700. The choice among these interpretations was left to the discretion of the performer—a "discretion," however, that was not haphazard but was governed by rules (based upon the conduct of the melody and other parts, the tempo and phrasing of the passage in question, and the expression of the accompanying text) that were formulated in textbooks (e.g., B. Bacilly, *Remarques curieuses sur l'art de bien chanter*, 1668) and taught to every student of performance. With the exception of Ex. 2a and 2b, which are exclusively French, these interpretations were taken over by musicians of all nationalities, and they are valid for the performance of music by J. S. Bach, Handel, Purcell, D. Scarlatti, and their contemporaries. See also *Appuy; Port de voix.*

After 1750 the performance of the appoggiatura was systematized by the German teachers and writers K. P. E. Bach, Leopold Mozart, F. W. Marpurg, and D. G. Türk. The ornament was then divided into two types: the long, or variable, appoggiatura (*veränderlicher Vorschlag*), and the short appoggiatura (*kurzer Vorschlag*), both to be performed upon the beat. The duration of the long appoggiatura was proportionate to that of the main note with which it was connected, according to various rules. The short appoggiatura was to be performed as a short note, regardless of the duration of the main note.

The notation of the appoggiatura in this period had no definite relationship to its performance. A few composers wrote the long appoggiatura as a small note of the exact value in which it should be performed and distinguished the short appoggiatura from it by means of a single stroke across the stem (for a 16th note) or a double stroke (for a 32nd note), but this practice was by no means consistently carried out.

The 19th century brought still further changes in the treatment of the appoggiatura. The long appoggiatura became absorbed in the ordinary notation, and the short appoggiatura was invariably indicated by a small note with a single stroke across its stem, called a grace note or (erroneously) an **acciaccatura*. The question then arises whether this grace note should be performed on the beat or in anticipation of the beat. The latter possibility had already been admitted by some late 18th-century authorities (who referred to it as a *durchgehender Vorschlag,* distinct from both the *langer* and the *kurzer Vorschlag*) for certain exceptional circumstances. After 1800 this execution became decidedly more popular. It seems to be indicated for most of the grace notes in the works of Chopin, Schumann, Brahms, *et al.,* but lack of material evidence leaves the matter open to controversy in many cases. Schumann often prescribes it by placing the grace note before the bar line. In modern music it is customary to snap the grace note sharply onto the following note, so that it slightly anticipates the beat and imparts a decided accent to the main note. See Ornamentation.

Appoggiatura, double. The term *double appoggiatura* has been applied to each of the three distinct ways two appoggiaturas can be used: two appoggiaturas performed simultaneously, at the interval of a third or sixth; two conjunct appoggiaturas approaching the main note from the interval of a third above or below it; two disjunct appoggiaturas, one being placed below the main note, the other above it.

Little need be said of the *simultaneous double appoggiatura* save that each of its components is performed as though the other were not present, as in Ex. 1 (Bach, Suite in Eb, Sarabande).

The *conjunct double appoggiatura,* or *slide,* was a common **agrément* in the 17th and 18th centuries. The 17th-century English lutenists and viol players referred to the ascending slide as an *elevation* or *whole fall* and called the descending slide a *double backfall.* The signs and execution of these ornaments

are illustrated in Ex. 2 and 3. Their German equivalent is the *Schleifer,* which is indicated in the music of the baroque period by a *direct (custos) or by two grace notes, as in Ex. 4. It should always be played on the beat.

The *punctierte Schleifer,* or dotted slide, is a complicated ornament very popular with composers between 1750 and 1780. Its performance is shown in Ex. 5 (by K. P. E. Bach). Another special form of slide, peculiar to keyboard music, is that in which the first note is held throughout. Introduced by the French clavecinists, who called it *coulé sur une tierce* or *tierce coulé,* this *agrément* is indicated and performed as shown in Ex. 6. It was adopted by Purcell and other English composers, who used the same notation but called it a *slur.* In romantic and modern music this execution of the slide is indicated with a tie, as in Ex. 7 (Schubert, *Moments musicaux* op. 94, no. 3). The performance of the slide in general has changed very little since the 18th century; it is still begun on the beat, as in Ex. 8 (Beethoven, *Bagatellen* op. 119, no. 5).

The *disjunct double appoggiatura* was written in ordinary notes until the last half of the 18th century, when K. P. E. Bach gave it the name *Anschlag* and introduced the two tiny grace notes that have since been used to represent it [Ex. 9]. The first of the two notes that make up the *Anschlag* may be at any distance from the main note, but the second is only one degree removed from it. The ornament should always begin on the beat, as in Ex. 10 (Chopin, Rondo op. 16) and Ex. 11 (Chopin, Polonaise op. 44).

Apprenti sorcier, L' [F., The Sorcerer's Apprentice]. Symphonic poem by Paul Dukas, composed 1897, based on Goethe's ballad, "Der Zauberlehrling."

Appuy [F.]. An 18th-century term for a note having the quality of an appoggiatura. It usually refers to the appoggiatura that constitutes the first note of the *tremblement* or *cadence* [see Trill].

Appuyé [F.]. Emphasized.

Après-midi d'un faune, L'. See *Prélude à "L'après-midi d'un faune."*

Aquitanian neumes. The neumatic script

from southern France (Aquitaine). See Neumes.

Arabella. Opera in three acts by R. Strauss (libretto by H. von Hofmannsthal, after his short novel *Lucidor*), produced in Dresden, 1933. Setting: Vienna, 1860.

Arabesque [F.]; **Arabeske** [G.]. An ornament characteristic of Arabic art and architecture; hence, similarly decorative or florid musical material or a composition employing such material. As a title, the term is used by Schumann (op. 18), Debussy, and others.

Aragonaise [F.]; **aragonesa** [Sp.]. See under *Jota*.

Araja, Francesco (b. Naples, 25 June 1709; d. Bologna, *c.* 1770). Music and theater director at the Russian court from 1735. Composed over 20 operas, incl. *Lo matremmonejo pe' vennetta* in Neapolitan dialect, Naples, 1729; *La forza dell'amore e dell'odio*, Milan, 1734 (the first Italian opera produced in Russia, 1736); *Cefal i Prokris*, St. Petersburg, 1755 (the first opera on a Russian-language libretto).

Arcadelt, Jacob (b. Liège?, *c.* 1505; d. Paris, after 1562). Member of the papal chapel, *c.* 1540–*c.* 1550. Court musician in Paris, *c.* 1560. Composed Masses and motets; numerous Italian madrigals and French chansons.

Arcata [It.]. See under Bowing (a); *arcato,* bowed.

Archduke Trio. Beethoven's Piano Trio in B♭ major op. 97, composed in 1811 and dedicated to the Archduke Rudolph.

Archer, Violet (b. Montreal, 24 Apr. 1913). Pianist and composer. Pupil of Donovan, Hindemith, and Bartók. Has taught at various universities in the U.S. and since 1962 at the University of Alberta, Canada. Has composed orch. works; a violin concerto; choral works, incl. settings of poems by Donne, Shakespeare, and Raleigh; chamber music.

Archet [F.]; **archetto** [It.]. Bow (of violins, etc).

Archlute [F. *archiluth;* G. *Erzlaute;* It. *arciliuto;* Sp. *archilaúd*]. A lute with two

pegboxes, one for the fingered strings, the other for the bass courses; e.g., the theorbo or the chitarrone. See Lute.

Arcicembalo, arciorgano [It.]. Microtonic instruments of the 16th century, described by N. Vicentino in his *L'antica musica* (1555) and *Descrizione dell' arciorgano* (1561). Each had 6 manuals containing 31 keys to the octave, and these gave all the tones of the diatonic, chromatic, and enharmonic genera of ancient Greek theory.

Arco [It.; pl. *archi*]. Bow (of violins, etc.). See *Col arco.*

Ardévol, José (b. Barcelona, 13 Mar. 1911). Founded the Havana Chamber Orchestra, 1934; from 1959, National Director of Music for Cuba and editor of the music journal *Revolución*. Has composed a ballet; symphonies; a concerto for 3 pianos; *concerti grossi;* cantatas (incl. *Lenin,* 1970); *Cantos de la revolución* for chorus, 1962; string quartets and other chamber music; piano pieces.

Arditamente [It.]. Boldly.

Ardore, con [It.]. With ardor.

Arel, Bülent (b. Istanbul, 23 Apr. 1918). Studied at the Ankara State Conservatory. Music director of Radio Ankara, 1951–65. Has taught composition and electronic music at Yale, Columbia, and from 1971 at the State Univ. of New York at Stony Brook. Has composed orch. works; chamber music; electronic works, incl. some with conventional instruments and some for dance.

Arensky, Anton Stepanovich (b. Novgorod, 12 July 1861; d. Terijoki, Finland, 25 Feb. 1906). Pupil of Rimsky-Korsakov and Johannsen. Teacher at the Moscow Conservatory, 1889–95; conductor of the imperial chapel in St. Petersburg, 1895–1901. Among his pupils were Rachmaninov, Scriabin, and Glière. Composed 3 operas; a ballet, *Egyptian Nights,* 1900; 2 symphonies and other orch. works; vocal works; chamber music; piano pieces.

Argento, Dominick (Joseph) (b. York, Pa., 27 Oct. 1927). Pupil of Weisgall, Nabokov, Cowell, Dallapiccola, Bernard Rogers, Hanson, and Hovhaness.

Teacher at Hampton Institute, 1952–55; at the Univ. of Minnesota from 1958. Has composed operas (incl. *Voyage of Edgar Allan Poe,* St. Paul, Minn., 1976; *A Water Bird Talk,* Brooklyn, 1977); incidental music for the Tyrone Guthrie Theater; orch. works (incl. *In Praise of Music,* 1977); choral works; songs (incl. *From the Diary of Virginia Woolf,* Pulitzer Prize, 1975).

Aria [It.]. (1) An often elaborate composition for solo voice (occasionally for two solo voices; see Duet) with instrumental accompaniment. The aria figures prominently in the cantatas and oratorios of the 17th and 18th centuries and in opera from its beginnings in the 17th century up to the end of the 19th century except for the Wagnerian type. In the context of such works, the melodic and often lyrical character of the aria stands in contrast to that of *recitative. The most important type in the period up to *c.* 1630 is the *strophic-bass aria in which successive strophes of text are sung to new melodies composed over the same bass line. The prologue to Monteverdi's *Orfeo* (1607) is an example in which the strophes are separated by statements of an instrumental *ritornello.* Shortly after 1630 a new type appeared in the *ostinato* aria, which is through-composed over a short *basso ostinato* or *ground bass. The century beginning in about 1650 sees the establishment of the *da capo* aria as the preferred form, so called because it consists of two sections followed by a repetition of the first, resulting in a tripartite structure A B A. The numerous examples from the middle of the 17th century in the works of Cavalli, Carissimi, Cesti, and others are usually brief and in triple meter. The early 18th century brings the rise of the grand *da capo,* characterized by considerably larger dimensions, virtuoso style of singing, and a more elaborate structure in which the A section includes a modulation to the dominant or some other key before closing in the tonic and in which the B section is of somewhat different (though not strongly contrasting) character and in a key related to the tonic. The A section often begins with an instrumental introduction. Widely used by such composers as

Alessandro Scarlatti, Bach, and Handel, this type became the basic ingredient of the *opera seria,* which usually consisted of some 20 such arias connected by *secco* recitatives. The strict conventions of *opera seria* (related to the doctrine of the *affections) resulted in the classification of arias according to typical situations of the plot, e.g.: *aria di bravura* (quick and virtuosic, expressing passion, vengeance, triumph, and the like); *aria di mezzo carattere* (moderate tempo, expressing gentle feelings); *aria cantabile* (slow and lyrical, expressing grief or longing); *aria parlante* (declamatory in character). After 1750 the conventionalized *da capo* aria was gradually replaced by arias written in a variety of forms and showing more individual expression. Such freer forms characterize the works of Gluck, Mozart, and many others in the late 18th century and throughout the 19th century. The principal exceptions are found in the mature works of Wagner and his followers, where the distinction between aria and recitative is largely replaced by a more continuous style throughout.

(2) In the 16th and early 17th centuries, a model melody used for singing texts of similar poetic structure (e.g., "aria di cantar sonetti," aria for singing sonnets) or strophes of a strophic poem.

(3) A short instrumental piece with a songlike character.

Ariadne auf Naxos. Opera in one act and a prologue by R. Strauss (libretto by H. von Hofmannsthal), originally produced in Stuttgart in 1912 as an entr'acte for Molière's play *Le bourgeois gentilhomme,* for which Strauss also wrote the incidental music. Setting: Vienna, 18th century, and Naxos, ancient Greece. In 1916 it was produced in Vienna as an independent work, with the addition of an introductory scene representing the stage rehearsal of the work.

Arietta [It.]; **ariette** [F.]. (1) A small aria, usually in binary form and lacking the musical elaboration of the aria; thus rather a song or a *cavatina. (2) In French operas before 1750, an aria to Italian words, usually in brilliant coloratura style. (3) In the *opéra comique* of the second half of the 18th century, a solo song (aria) in French, preceded and followed by spoken dialogue, the work being known as a *comédie mêlée d'ariettes*. See Comic opera.

Arioso [It.]. Properly, *recitativo arioso*, that is, a *recitative of a lyrical and expressive quality, not the more usual narrative and speechlike recitative. The arioso style, therefore, is midway between that of a recitative and an *aria.

Ariosti, Attilio (Malachia) (b. Bologna, 5 Nov. 1666; d. probably in Spain, *c.* 1740). Court musician at Mantua, 1696; at Berlin, 1697–1703; at Vienna, 1706–11. Lived and worked as an opera composer in London, 1723–28. Composed numerous operas; 5 oratorios; numerous cantatas; instrumental music.

Arlésienne, L' [F., The Woman of Arles]. Incidental music by Bizet to Alphonse Daudet's play *L'arlésienne*. It is usually played in the form of two orchestral suites, the first arranged by Bizet in 1872 and the second by E. Guiraud after Bizet's death.

Armonica. See Glass harmonica.

Armure [F.]. *Key signature.

Arne, Michael (b. London, 1741; d. there, 14 Jan. 1786). Son of Thomas Arne. Actor, singer, harpsichordist, and alchemist. Composed numerous theatrical works (incl. the operas *Hymen,* 1764; *Cymon,* 1767; and *The Choice of Harlequin,* 1781).

Arne, Thomas Augustine (b. London, 12 Mar. 1710; d. there, 5 Mar. 1778). Composed numerous operas, masques, and other stage works (incl. *Comus,* London, 1738; *Artaxerxes,* London, 1762; *Alfred,* containing the song "Rule Britannia," Cliveden, 1740); songs to Shakespeare's plays (incl. "Where the Bee Sucks" for *The Tempest*); 2 oratorios, *The Death of Abel,* 1744, and *Judith,* 1761; 2 Masses; cantatas; organ works; glees and catches.

Arnold, Malcolm (Henry) (b. Northampton, 21 Oct. 1921). Pupil of Jacob. Trumpeter at various times with the London Philharmonic and the B.B.C. Symphony. Has composed 2 ballets, *Homage to the Queen,* 1953, and *Solitaire,* 1956; symphonies and other orch.

works; concertos for oboe, for clarinet, for harmonica; chamber music; songs; film scores.

Arnold, Samuel (b. London, 10 Aug. 1740; d. there, 22 Oct. 1802). Pupil of Nares and his successor as composer to the Chapel Royal, 1783. Organist of Westminster Abbey, succeeding B. Cooke, from 1793. Composed several dramatic works (incl. *The Maid of the Mill,* a pasticcio, London, 1765); several oratorios (incl. *The Prodigal Son,* 1773). Published an anthology, *Cathedral Music,* 1790.

Arpa [It., Sp.]. *Harp. See also Psaltery.

Arpègement [F.]. Older term for *arpège* (arpeggio). For *arpègement figuré,* see *Acciaccatura;* Arpeggio.

Arpeggiando, arpeggiato [It.]. See Bowing (i).

Arpeggio [It.; F. *arpège;* Sp. *arpegio*]. The notes of a chord played one after another instead of simultaneously. In modern music the arpeggio is indicated by one of the signs given in Ex. 1. Its execution always starts with the lowest note, and as a rule it should begin at the moment when the chord is due (i.e., on the beat), whether indicated by sign or by tiny notes [Ex. 2, Mozart, Sonata in C major, K. 309 (K. Einstein 284b); Ex. 3, Chopin, Nocturne op. 62, no. 1]. There are cases, however, in which the melody carried by the top note of the arpeggio will not bear the delay caused by this execution, so that the last note of the arpeggio must then be made to coincide with the beat [Ex. 4, Mendelssohn, *Songs Without Words,* no. 30]. The latter performance is generally to be recommended in piano music whenever the arpeggio occurs in the left hand alone, as in Ex. 5 (Chopin, Mazurka op. 7, no. 3). A distinction should be made between an arpeggio played simultaneously with both hands [Ex. 6] and a long arpeggio in which the right hand succeeds the left [Ex. 7]. The latter is (or should be) indicated by a long arpeggio sign, joining the two staves. For the violin arpeggio, see Bowing (i).

In the 17th and 18th centuries, the execution of the arpeggio varied considerably (often at the discretion of the indi-

vidual performer) in respect to direction and number of notes. In music of the time of Bach and Handel, the word *arpeggio* is sometimes found written at the beginning of a sequence of chords. In this case, the player is at liberty to break the chords up and down several times, to extend them, and to interpolate extraneous notes, as shown in Handel's own notation of the last four bars of the Prelude to his keyboard Suite in D minor.

Arpeggione (also called guitar violoncello, *guitare d'amour*). A stringed instrument the size of a cello but with a guitarlike body and six strings tuned E A d g b e', invented in 1823 by G. Staufer. It is played with a bow. Schubert wrote a sonata for arpeggione and piano D. 821 (1824).

Arpicordo. Italian 16th-century name for a harpsichord that differed in some now unknown detail from the clavicembalo. Perhaps it is identical to the *Arpichordum* as described by M. Praetorius (*Syntagma musicum*, 1619, II, ch. 43), "a jack-action instrument or virginal on which a harplike sound is produced by means of a special stop which governs brass hooks under the strings."

Arraché [F.]. Forceful *pizzicato.

Arrangement. The adaptation of a composition for a medium different from that for which it was originally written, so made that the musical substance remains essentially unchanged. The practice is widespread at least as early as the period from the 14th through the 16th centuries, when numerous vocal works (both sacred and secular) were arranged for keyboard instruments and the lute [see Intabulation]. From the baroque era Bach provides the most celebrated examples in his arrangements of works by Vivaldi. Numerous works from the 18th and 19th centuries were arranged for piano, often, in the case of operas, orchestral works, and some chamber music, for the sake of aiding the study and dissemination of the works in question (a need not so strongly felt since the advent of the radio and the phonograph). Some such arrangements, however, notably those of Liszt, were clearly intended to have artistic merit in their own right as well as to serve as vehicles for the display of virtuosity by performers. More recently, there has been a considerable vogue for arranging Bach's keyboard works for the modern symphony orchestra and for the piano.

The terms *transcribe* and *transcription* are sometimes used interchangeably with *arrange* and *arrangement*. Often, however, the former imply greater fidelity to the original musical substance. The former terms are also used to describe the translation of works from earlier forms of musical notation into the notation now in use. See also Additional accompaniment.

Arriaga (y Balzola), Juan Crisóstomo (Jacobo Antonio de) (b. Rigoitia, near Bilbao, 27 Jan. 1806; d. Paris, 17 Jan. 1826). Studied with Fétis at the Paris Conservatory. Composed an opera, *Los esclavos felices*, Bilbao, 1819; a symphony; a Biblical scene, *Agar;* 3 string quartets and other chamber music; several piano pieces.

Ars antiqua [L., the old art]. The term *ars antiqua* (*ars veterum*) was used by writers of the early 14th century to distinguish the late 13th-century school (Franco of Cologne, c. 1260; Petrus de Cruce, c. 1290) from that of their own day, which was called *ars nova (or ars modernorum)*. Today, the two terms are usually employed in a wider sense to distinguish the music of the 12th and 13th centuries from that of the 14th century. The *ars antiqua,* then, includes the school of Notre Dame with its two masters Leonin (second half of the 12th cent.) and Perotin (*c.* 1160–*c.* 1220) as well as the period of the theoretical writings of Franco of Cologne (middle 13th cent.) and the compositions of Petrus de Cruce (late 13th cent.). The period as a whole brings striking developments in the systematization of rhythm [see Modes, rhythmic] and its notation; the emergence of composition for more than two voices; the beginnings of the motet; and the flowering of important repertories of monophonic music in France, Spain, Italy, and Germany.

See also *Cantiga; Clausula; Conductus;* Discant; *Estampie;* Hocket; *Lauda;* Mensural notation; Minnesinger; Modes, rhythmic; Monophony; Motet; Notation; Notre Dame; Organum; St. Martial; "Sumer is icumen in"; Troubadour; Trouvère.

Ars nova [L., the new art]. Generic name for the music of the 14th century, in contradistinction to the **ars antiqua,* i.e., music of the 13th century. Properly, the name should be restricted, as it originally was, to French music of the first half of the 14th century, represented by the latest compositions in the ***"Roman de Fauvel" and by the works of Philippe de Vitry (1291–1361), who employed the term *ars nova* as the title of a treatise dealing primarily with the notational innovations of the period. The most important of these innovations was the systematization of rhythmic notation in such a way as to provide equally well for duple and triple meters [see Notation]. The most celebrated French composer of the 14th century was Guillaume de Machaut (*c.* 1300–1377). Italian music of the period, to which the term is now also applied by some writers, differs strikingly with respect to notational practice, the forms cultivated, and general musical style. Important composers from midcentury here are Giovanni da Cascia and Jacopo da Bologna. The leading composer thereafter is Francesco Landini (1325–97).

See also *Ballata; Ballade* (1); *Caccia;* *Estampie;* Isorhythm; Madrigal; Notation; Prolation; *Rondeau; Virelai.*

Arsis and thesis [Gr.]. *Arsis* means "lifting" [G. *Hebung*], and *thesis* means "lowering" [G. *Senkung*]. Thus, *arsis* originally referred to the unstressed part of a poetic foot, *thesis* to the stressed part. The meanings were reversed, however, by Roman and medieval writers, and this usage persists in French and German. Modern English usage, including the application of these terms to music, coincides with the original meanings.

To 16th- and 17th-century theorists, the phrase *per arsin et thesin* meant "by contrary motion," i.e., by inversion. The same phrase was used in the 18th century to designate a fugue in which the answer is in contrary rhythm, i.e., what is on a strong beat in the subject is shifted to a weak beat in the answer.

Art ballad. See *Ballade* (2).

Art of Fugue, The [G. *Die Kunst der Fuge*]. The last work of J. S. Bach, written in the 1740s and published posthumously in 1751. It contains in its last version some 14 fugues, called *contrapuncti,* and 4 canons, all based on the same theme [see Ex.] and in which the various devices of imitative counterpoint, such as inversion, stretto, augmentation, diminution, canon, double fugue, and triple fugue are exploited. Extended controversies have arisen as to the proper order of the *contrapuncti,* the role of the last (unfinished) fugue, and the intended medium of performance.

Art song. A song of serious artistic intent written by a trained composer, as distinct from a folksong. See Song; Song cycle.

Articulation. In performance, the characteristics of attack and decay of single tones or groups of tones and the means by which these characteristics are produced. Thus, **staccato and *legato are types of articulation. In the playing of stringed instruments, this is largely a function of **bowing; in wind instruments, of *tonguing. Groups of tones may be articulated (i.e., phrased) so as to be perceived as constituting phrases [see Phrase, phrasing]. Notational symbols for articulation first occur around 1600, are not uncommon in compositions from c. 1620 to 1750, and occur with increasing attention to detail in works thereafter.

As, ases [G.]. A-flat, A-double-flat; see Pitch names.

Ashley, Robert (b. Ann Arbor, Mich., 28 Mar. 1930). Operated the Cooperative Studio for Electronic Music with G. Mumma, 1958–66; director of the ONCE Group (multimedia ensemble) from 1963; director of the Mills College Center for Contemporary Music from 1969. Has composed electronic theater works (incl. *Kittyhawk (an Antigravity Piece)*, 1964); *Untitled Mixes*, 1965; *She Was a Visitor* for speaker and chorus, 1967; other instrumental and vocal works; several film scores.

Asioli, Bonifazio (b. Correggio, 30 Aug. 1769; d. there, 18 May 1832). Theorist and composer. Served in the courts at Turin and Milan. Composed 7 operas (incl. *Cinna,* Milan, 1793); an oratorio, *Giacobbe in Galaad;* many cantatas, antiphons, motets, hymns, Masses; instrumental music.

Aspiration [F.]. See under *Nachschlag.*

Assai [It.]. Much, e.g., *allegro assai,* quite fast.

Assez [F.]. Rather, e.g., *assez vite,* rather fast.

Astorga, Emanuele Gioacchino Cesare Rincon d' (b. Augusta, Sicily, 20 Mar. 1680; d. Spain or Portugal, c. 1757). Baron and amateur of music: singer, harpsichordist, composer. Composed at least 3 operas (*La moglie nemica,* Palermo, 1698; *Dafni,* Genoa, 1709; *Amor tirannico,* Venice, 1710); numerous chamber cantatas; *Stabat Mater* for 4 voices and instruments.

Atem [G.]. Breath. *Atempause* (breathing pause), a very short rest used in instrumental performance for the sake of articulation or phrasing. It is sometimes indicated by an apostrophe.

Atonality. Literally, the absence of *tonality. The term is most often applied to music of the 20th century in which pitches are not treated in accordance with the particular principles of tonal centers, consonance and dissonance, and harmony and counterpoint that prevailed in various forms in Western music from the end of the 17th century through the 19th and into the 20th. Thus, the term generally refers to the absence of a particular kind of tonality, sometimes called tonic-dominant or triadic tonality. Many works that are "atonal" in this sense do in fact treat pitches in a hierarchical fashion in which one or a few pitches play a central role. Sometimes included in the category of atonal works are those based on the twelve-tone system (see under Serial music), in which the creation of tonal centers is often rigorously avoided. A more precise use of the term restricts it to works such as Arnold Schoenberg's op. 11 (1909) through op. 22 (1913–14), which are examples of neither triadic tonality nor the twelve-tone system.

Attacca, attacca subito [It.]. Attack suddenly; an indication at the end of a movement that the next movement should follow without a pause.

Attacco. See under *Soggetto.*

Attack. (1) The characteristics of the beginning of a sound [see under Acoustics]. (2) [F. *attaque*]. Promptness and decision in beginning a phrase, especially in forte passages. Also precision in orchestral entries. In French orchestras, the concertmaster is called *chef d'attaque.*

Atterberg, Kurt (Magnus) (b. Göteborg, Sweden, 12 Dec. 1887; d. Stockholm, 15 Feb. 1974). Pupil of Hallén. Music critic, 1919–57; Secretary of the Royal Academy of Music in Stockholm from 1940. Composed 5 operas; 3 ballets; symphonies and other orch. works (incl. *Värmlandsrhapsodi,* 1933); concertos; choral works; chamber music.

Attwood, Thomas (b. London, bapt. 23 Nov. 1765; d. there, 28 Mar. 1838). Organist and composer. Pupil of Mozart, some of whose teaching materials for him have been preserved. Very active in English musical life, he held numerous positions from chorister at the Chapel

Royal under Nares to conductor for the London Philharmonic Society (of which he was a co-founder, 1813). Composed more than 30 operas (incl. *The Prisoner*, 1792; *The Mariners*, 1793; *The Adopted Child*, 1795); church music (incl. the coronation anthem "I Was Glad"); chamber music for keyboard and strings; songs and glees.

Aubade [F.]; **alborada** [Sp.]. Morning music, as distinct from *serenade, evening music. The term has been used by various composers (e.g., Bizet, Rimsky-Korsakov) to denote a sort of idyllic overture. See *Alba*.

Auber, Daniel-François-Esprit (b. Caen, Normandy, 29 Jan. 1782; d. Paris, 12 May 1871). Pupil of Boieldieu and Cherubini. Successor of Gossec in the Academy, 1829; director of the Paris Conservatory from 1842; imperial *maître de chapelle* under Napoleon III from 1857. Composed over 40 operas (incl. *Le maçon*, Paris, 1825; *Masaniello, ou La muette de Portici*, Paris, 1828; *Fra Diavolo*, Paris, 1830); a Mass; a violin concerto; 4 cello concertos (under the name Michel Hurel de Lamare).

Aubert, Jacques (b. Paris?, 30 Sept. 1689; d. Belleville, near Paris, buried 19 May 1753). First violinist in the orchestra of the Paris Grand Opéra, 1728–52; participant in the Concert spirituel, 1729–40. Composed numerous instrumental concertos (the first by a Frenchman) for 4 violins and bass; other instrumental music; an opera; a ballet.

Aubert, Louis-François-Marie (b. Paramé, Ille-et-Vilaine, 19 Feb. 1877; d. Paris, 9 Jan. 1968). Pupil of Fauré. Composed an operatic fairy tale, *La forêt bleue*, Geneva, 1913; a symphonic poem, *Habanera*, 1919, and other orch. works; sonatas for piano and violin; choral works; ballets; songs.

Auctoralis [L.]. Authentic; see Church modes.

Audition. (1) A hearing given to a performer, often for the purpose of determining the performer's level of ability and therefore admissibility to a particular school, class, or ensemble; to perform for such a purpose. (2) The faculty of hearing.

Audran, Edmond (b. Lyon, 11 Apr. 1842; d. Tierceville, 17 Aug. 1901). Pupil of Saint-Saëns. Organist at St. Joseph's Church in Marseille from 1861. Composed over 30 operettas and comic operas (incl. *La mascotte*, Paris, 1880).

Aufforderung zum Tanz [G., Invitation to the Dance]. Piano composition by C. M. von Weber, op. 65 (1819), in the form of a waltz, preceded by an introduction (the "invitation") and concluded with an epilogue. It was arranged for orchestra by Berlioz and by Weingartner.

Aufführungspraxis [G.]. *Performance practice.

Aufgeregt [G.]. Excited.

Auflösung [G.]. (1) Resolution (of a dissonance). (2) Cancellation (of an accidental). *Auflösungszeichen*, the natural sign, ♮.

Aufsatz [G.]. Tube of an organ reed pipe. See Organ.

Aufschnitt [G.]. The mouth of an organ pipe. See Organ.

Aufstrich [G.]. Up-bow. See Bowing (a).

Auftakt [G.]. *Upbeat.

Auftritt [G.]. Scene of an opera.

Aufzug [G.]. Act of an opera.

Augenmusik [G.]. *Eye music.

Augmentation and diminution. The presentation of a subject in doubled values (augmentation) or in halved values (diminution), so that, e.g., the quarter note becomes a half note (augmentation) or an eighth note (diminution). The note values may also be augmented (or diminished) in higher ratios, such as 1:3 (triple augmentation) or 1:4 (quadruple augmentation) or in other more complex ratios. These devices provide an important element of variety in fugal writing. They are usually introduced toward the end of the fugue. Examples are: Bach, *The Well-Tempered Clavier*, I, no. 8 (augmentation), and II, no. 9 (diminution); *The Art of Fugue*, nos. 6 and 7 (simultaneous appearance of the normal form, diminution, augmentation, and double augmentation); Beethoven, Piano Sonata op. 110, last movement (similar combinations). Augmentation and diminution are also used in other types of works, e.g., the development sections of symphonies.

Augmented intervals. See Interval. For *Augmented sixth chord, augmented triad*, see Sixth chord; Triad.

Aulos. The most important wind instrument of the ancient Greeks. It is not a flute (as has frequently been stated) but an oboe with double reed and a number of holes, ranging from four in the oldest instruments to fifteen in later specimens. The numerous pictures of aulos players show that the aulos usually consisted of two pipes; probably the larger pipe provided a drone or a few tones that were missing on the other. Many pictures show the player wearing a leather band over his mouth and tied at the back of his head. This probably served to increase the resistance of the cheeks, which acted as bellows, and enabled the player to build up considerable air pressure, thus producing a sound that occasionally must have been as shrill as that of a modern bagpipe.

Auric, Georges (b. Lodève, France, 15 Feb. 1899). Pupil of d'Indy, influenced by Satie. A member of "Les *six." Director of the combined theaters of the Grand Opéra and Opéra-Comique in Paris from 1960. Has composed ballets (incl. *Les fâcheux*, 1924); film scores (incl. *À nous la liberté*, 1931, and *Moulin rouge*, 1952); *Suite symphonique*, 1960; piano pieces; other instrumental works.

Aus Italien. A symphonic fantasy composed in 1886 by R. Strauss and inspired by a trip to Italy in that year.

Ausdruck, mit; ausdrucksvoll [G.]. With expression.

Aushalten [G.]. To sustain a note.

Auslösung [G.]. The repeating mechanism (escapement) of the *piano.

Äusserst [G.]. Extremely.

Austin, Larry (b. Duncan, Okla., 12 Sept. 1930). Pupil of Milhaud. Founder of the New Music Ensemble, 1962; cofounder (1967) and editor of the journal *Source*. Has composed numerous works in "open style" (his own term), involving improvisation techniques. Has taught at the Univ. of California at Davis, 1958–70, and at the Univ. of South Florida from 1970. Works incl. *Improvisations for Orchestra and Jazz Soloists*, 1961; *Open Style for Orchestra and Piano Soloist*, 1965; *The Magicians* for mixed media, 1968; *Catharsis: Open Style for Two Improvisation Ensembles, Tapes, and Conductor*, 1967; *Agape*, electronic masque for soloists, dancers, rock band, celebrants, tapes, and projections, 1970.

Auszug [G.]. *Arrangement, usually for piano [*Klavierauszug*] of an opera, oratorio, etc.

Authentic cadence. See under Cadence.

Authentic modes. See under Church modes.

Auto [Sp.]. Spanish and Portuguese dramatic play of a religious or contemplative character, frequently with incidental music [see Liturgical drama]. Such plays were written by Juan del Encina (fl. 1500), Gil Vicente (1492–1557), Lope de Vega (1562–1635), Calderón (1600–1681), and others. These religious plays were introduced into Latin America by missionaries as early as the 16th century and soon became very popular throughout the Spanish and Portuguese colonies.

Autoharp. Trademark for an instrument of the *zither family, on which simple chords are produced by strumming the strings (with fingers, pick, or plectrum), while button-controlled damper bars damp all the strings except those required for the chord.

Auxiliary tone. See under Counterpoint.

Ave Maria [L., Hail, Mary]. (1) A prayer of the Roman Catholic Church; see text and plainsong in *LU*, p. 1861. In a shortened form it is used as an *antiphon for the Feast of the Annunciation [*LU*, p. 1416]. There are polyphonic settings, some of them based on the plainsong melody, by Ockeghem, Josquin, Willaert, Victoria, and others. (2) The same title was used for a piece by Schubert (based on a song from Sir Walter Scott's *Lady of the Lake*) and a piece by Gounod in which Bach's C-major Prelude from *The Well-Tempered Clavier* (vol. I) is used as a harmonic background for a new melody.

Ave maris stella [L., Hail, Star of the Sea]. A hymn of the Roman Catholic Church, sung to various melodies in different modes [see *LU*, pp. 1259 ff.]. There are polyphonic settings (Dufay), Masses (Josquin, Morales, Victoria), and organ compositions (Girolamo Cavazzoni, Cabezón, Titelouze) based on one or another of these melodies, most often the first melody in *LU*.

Ave Regina caelorum [L., Hail, Queen of the Heavens]. One of the four Marian antiphons; see Antiphon (2).

Avison, Charles (b. Newcastle-on-Tyne, bapt. 16 Feb. 1709; d. there, 9 May 1770). Pupil of Geminiani. Organist at St. John's and then at St. Nicholas' Church, Newcastle, from 1736. Composed numerous instrumental concertos and sonatas; several vocal works. Also published a theoretical work, *Essay on Musical Expression*, 1752.

Ayala Pérez, Daniel (b. Abalá, Yucatán, 21 July 1908). Violinist, conductor, and composer. Pupil of Chávez. Has worked with Mayan and other native Mexican material. Taught at the National Institute of Fine Arts, Mexico City, 1933–67. Has composed symphonic suites; vocal works with instruments; chamber music.

Ayre. (1) A late 16th- and early 17th-century type of English song that is derived from the French **air de cour* and, like it, was primarily a solo song accompanied by the lute (orpharion, theorbo, occasionally also virginal), often with the lowest part of the accompaniment doubled by a bass viol (viola da gamba). In many cases the composers provided for an alternative (or additional?) vocal accompaniment, printed separately on the opposite page so that the parts could be read simultaneously by three additional singers. (2) In the 17th century, a movement of a suite [see Air (3)]. (3) English writers of the 17th century use the term ayre (aire) in the sense of "key" or "mode" or to refer to the general character of a piece.

B

B. (1) See Pitch names; Letter notation; Hexachord. In German, *B* stands for B-flat. (2) In *partbooks of the 16th century, *B* stands for *bassus* (bass).

B-A-C-H. The letters forming Bach's name, each of which denotes a tone (if the German terminology is used, in which *H* is B natural while *B* is B-flat; see Pitch names). The resulting theme, B♭ A C B, has been repeatedly used in compositions, first by Bach himself in his **Art of Fugue* (in the last, unfinished fugue), and by Albrechtsberger, Schumann, Reger, Piston, Casella, and Busoni.

B-minor Mass. A great Mass by Bach, for soloists, chorus, and orchestra, composed 1733–49 to the (Latin) text of the **Mass*. The five items of the Mass are subdivided into many sections treated as choruses, arias, duets, etc. Several of these are rewritten from earlier cantatas, among them the *Crucifixus* (from Cantata no. 12, *Weinen, Klagen*).

B moll [G.]. B-flat minor.

Baaren, Kees van (b. Enschede, Netherlands, 22 Oct. 1906; d. Oegstgeest, 2 Sept. 1970). Pupil of Pijper. Director of the Utrecht Conservatory, 1953–57; of the Royal Conservatory at The Hague, 1957–70. Adopted serial techniques. Composed works for orchestra, piano, and chamber groups.

Babbitt, Milton (b. Philadelphia, 10 May 1916). Pupil of Bauer, James, and Sessions. Member of the music faculty of Princeton Univ. (where he also taught mathematics briefly) from 1950. A director of the Columbia-Princeton Electronic

Music Center from 1959. Active in the development of total serialism, its theory, and its application to electronic means. Has composed *Composition for 4 Instruments*, 1948; *Composition for 12 Instruments*, 1948; the song cycle *Du*, 1951; *All Set* for jazz ensemble, 1957; *Partitions* for piano, 1957; *Relata I* and *II* for orch., 1965 and 1968; *Composition for Synthesizer*, 1963; *Vision and Prayer*, 1961, and *Philomel*, 1964, for soprano and tape; *Ensembles for Synthesizer*, 1964; 4 string quartets, 1948, 1954, 1969–70, 1970; *Reflections* for piano and tape, 1974; *Phonemena* for soprano and tape, 1974; *Concerti* for violin, orch., and tape, 1974–76; *More Phonemena* for mixed chorus, 1977.

Baborak. A Bohemian national dance that has alternating sections in duple and in triple time.

Bacchetta [It.]. Drumstick; *b. di legno*, wooden; *b. di spugna*, spongeheaded.

Bacewicz, Grazyna (b. Lodz, Poland, 5 May 1913; d. Warsaw, 17 Jan. 1969). Violinist and composer. Pupil of Sikorski and N. Boulanger. Teacher at the Lodz Conservatory, 1934–35, 1945; at the Academy of Music in Warsaw from 1966 until her death. Composed ballets; 4 symphonies and other orch. works (incl. *Music for Strings, Trumpets, and Percussion*, 1958; *In una parte*, 1967); concertos for violin (7), for cello (2), for piano, for viola; 7 string quartets, 5 violin sonatas, and other chamber music; piano pieces.

Bach, Johann Christian (the "London" or "Milan Bach") (b. Leipzig, 5 Sept. 1735; d. London, 1 Jan. 1782). The youngest surviving son of J. S. Bach, he studied with his father, his brother Karl Philipp Emanuel, and Padre Martini in Bologna. Organist at the Milan Cathedral, 1760–62. Music master to the Queen of England from 1763; with Abel, offered a series of London concerts from 1764 to his death. Admired and instructed the young Mozart, who played in the Royal Palace in 1764. Composed 13 operas (incl. *Orione*, London, 1763; *Lucio Silla*, Mannheim, 1776); symphonies; chamber music; concertos; church music; piano pieces.

Bach, Johann Christoph (b. Arnstadt, 8 Dec. 1642; d. Eisenach, 31 Mar. 1703). Uncle of J. S. Bach. Town organist of Eisenach from 1665; court chamber musician there from 1700. Works include cantatas, motets, and other choral works; preludes, fugues, and other organ works.

Bach, Johann Christoph Friedrich (the "Bückeburg Bach") (b. Leipzig, 21 June 1732; d. Bückeburg, 26 Jan. 1795). Second-youngest son of J. S. Bach. Court chamber musician at Bückeburg from *c.* 1750. Composed sacred and secular cantatas (incl. *Die Amerikanerin*, 1776); 3 oratorios; symphonies; concertos; keyboard works; songs.

Bach, Johann Sebastian (b. Eisenach, 21 Mar. 1685; d. Leipzig, 28 July 1750). Admitted as a chorister in St. Michael's Church, Lüneburg, 1700. From 1704 to 1707, served as organist of the Arnstadt Church, with an extended visit to Buxtehude in Lübeck in 1705–6. Appointed organist of St. Blasius' Church in Mühlhausen, 1707. Court chamber musician at Weimar from 1708 and *Konzertmeister* there from 1714, while touring periodically as a virtuoso organist. Appointed *Kapellmeister* and director of chamber music to Prince Leopold of Anhalt at Köthen, 1717. In 1723, succeeded Kuhnau as cantor at the Thomasschule in Leipzig and became music director of the two main churches there, the Thomaskirche and the Nikolaikirche. Had 7 children (incl. W. Friedemann B. and Karl Philipp Emanuel B.) by his first wife, Maria Barbara Bach (1684–1720), and 13 children (incl. J. Christian B.) by his second wife, Anna Magdalena Wilcken (1701–60).

Vocal works: nearly 200 sacred cantatas (incl. *Ein' feste Burg ist unser Gott; Wachet auf, ruft uns die Stimme; Christ lag in Todesbanden*); *St. Matthew Passion*, 1727, and *St. John Passion*, 1724; **Christmas Oratorio; *B-minor Mass; Magnificat;* motets (incl. *Jesu, meine Freude*); secular cantatas (incl. the **Coffee Cantata*). Organ works: the **Orgelbüchlein* and other *organ chorales of various types; preludes and fugues; toccatas; trio sonatas. Harpsichord or clavichord works: the **Well-Tempered Clavier; *Chromatic Fantasy and Fugue;* 6 *English Suites and 6 *French Suites; 15

two- and three-part *inventions; the *Clavier-Übung, in four parts, containing (in addition to some works for organ) 6 partitas, the *Italian Concerto, and the *Goldberg Variations; the *Art of Fugue (though there has been disagreement about the intended medium of performance). Chamber music: sonatas for flute, for violin, and for viola da gamba with harpsichord or continuo; 6 suites for unaccompanied cello; 3 sonatas and 3 partitas for unaccompanied violin; *Musikalisches Opfer. Orchestral works: 6 *Brandenburg Concertos and other concertos; 4 suites.

Bach, Karl Philipp Emanuel (the "Berlin" or "Hamburg Bach") (b. Weimar, 8 Mar. 1714; d. Hamburg, 14 Dec. 1788). The second surviving son of J. S. Bach, he studied with his father; his own pupils include his brother J. Christian Bach. Court musician in Berlin to Frederick the Great from 1740; succeeded Telemann, his godfather, as musical director of the Hamburg Church, 1767. Composed numerous keyboard works, orchestral symphonies, concertos, pieces for wind instruments, and other instrumental works; numerous choral works, incl. oratorios, Passions, cantatas. Also wrote an important theoretical book, Versuch über die wahre Art das Clavier zu spielen (Essay on the true art of playing keyboard instruments), 1753–62.

Bach, Wilhelm Friedemann (the "Halle Bach") (b. Weimar, 22 Nov. 1710; d. Berlin, 1 July 1784). Eldest son of J. S. Bach. Pupil of his father and of Graun. Organist at the Sophienkirche, Dresden, 1733–46; music director of the Marienkirche, Halle, 1746–64. Composed numerous cantatas and other vocal works; organ works; keyboard works, incl. fugues, polonaises, concertos, sonatas, and fantasias; other instrumental works, incl. trio sonatas and symphonies.

Bach trumpet. See Clarino (2).

Bachiana [Port.]. Title employed by Heitor Villa-Lobos for some of his compositions that he said were the product of applying Bach's contrapuntal techniques to Brazilian folk music. He wrote nine such works, for solo piano, full orchestra, or voice and smaller ensembles, following the general plan of a suite.

Bäck, Sven-Erik (b. Stockholm, 16 Sept. 1919). Violinist and composer. Pupil of Rosenberg and Petrassi. Works incl. string quartets and other chamber music; chamber operas; orch. pieces; ballets; film scores.

Backer-Grøndahl, Agathe (Ursula) (b. Holmestrand, 1 Dec. 1847; d. Ormøen, near Oslo, 4 June 1907). Pianist and composer. Pupil of Kjerulf, von Bülow, and Liszt. Composed piano works and songs.

Backfall, forefall. English 17th-century names for two types of *appoggiatura, the former from above, the latter from below, indicated and performed as follows:

Bacon, Ernst (b. Chicago, 26 May 1898). Pianist, conductor, and composer. Pupil of Oldberg and Bloch. Teacher at Converse College, S.C., 1938–45; at Syracuse Univ., 1945–63. Works incl. settings of poems by Goethe, Whitman, Sandburg, Emily Dickinson, and others; 4 symphonies; a musical play, A Tree on the Plains, 1940, rev. 1962; an oratorio; Riolama, concerto for piano and orch., 1964; a folk opera, A Drumlin Legend, New York, 1949; other vocal and instrumental works.

Badinage, badinerie [F.]. A dancelike piece of jocose character that sometimes occurs as a movement in the optional group in 18th-century suites, e.g., in Bach's Suite for orchestra in B minor.

Badings, Henk (b. Bandung, Java, 17 Jan. 1907). Pupil of Pijper. Taught at the Rotterdam Conservatory, 1934–37; director of the Royal Conservatory at The Hague, 1941–44; teacher at the Hochschule für Musik in Stuttgart from 1962. Has employed a scale alternating whole and half steps and microtonal scales. Has composed 12 symphonies; violin sonatas and concertos; string quartets; piano sonatas; electronic music for several ballets (incl. Cain and Abel, 1956); operas; Genèse for 5 tone-generators, 1958, later produced as a ballet; other instrumental, vocal, and electronic works.

Bagatelle [F.]. A short piece, often for piano. The name was used by F. Couperin ("Les bagatelles"; see his *Pièces de clavecin*, ordre 10) and, in particular, by Beethoven (op. 33, op. 119, op. 126).

Bagpipe [F. *musette;* G. *Dudelsack, Sackpfeife;* It. *piva, zampogna;* Sp. *gaita*]. Generic name for a number of instruments having one or (usually) several reed pipes (single or double reeds) attached to a windbag that provides the air for the pipes; also, specifically, the name for the Irish and Scottish varieties of this family. [See ill. under Wind instruments.] One or two of the pipes, called *chanters* (chaunter), are provided with finger holes and are used for playing the melody, while the others, called *drones,* produce only one tone each and provide the accompaniment. In some bagpipes the wind in the bag is supplied from the mouth through an additional blowing pipe, while in others it is provided by a small pair of bellows placed under and operated by the arm. To the former type belong the *Old Irish bagpipe, Highland bagpipe* (Scotland), *biniou* (Brittany), *cornemuse* (France), *Dudelsack* or *Sackpfeife* (Germany), and *zampogna* and *piva* (Italy); to the latter, the *Northumbrian bagpipe* (England), modern *Irish bagpipe, gaita* (Galicia), and *musette* (France). A more primitive instrument was the *bladder pipe,* a single or double clarinet with a bladder used as a bag.

Baguette [F.]. Drumstick; *b. de bois,* wooden drumstick; *b. d'éponge,* sponge-headed drumstick. Also the baton of the conductor and the stick of the violin bow.

Baird, Tadeusz (b. Grodzisk, Poland, 26 July 1928). Pupil of K. Sikorski. Adopted twelve-tone procedures in the late 1950s. Works incl. the opera *Jutro* [Tomorrow], Warsaw, 1966; 3 symphonies, a *Sinfonia brevis,* and other orch. works (incl. *4 Essays,* 1958; *Psychodrama,* 1975); songs with orch. accompaniment; chamber music.

Baisser [F.]. To lower (in pitch), e.g., a string.

Bakfark, Valentin (b. Kronstadt, now Rumania, 1507; d. Padua, 13 Aug. 1576).

Hungarian lutenist and composer. Served at courts in Hungary and Poland, finally settling in Padua. Published collections of lute music in tablature.

Balada, Leonardo (b. Barcelona, 22 Sept. 1933). Studied in Barcelona and with Copland, Tansman, Persichetti, and Markevitch. Teacher at Carnegie-Mellon Univ. from 1972. Has composed orch. works (incl. *Guernica,* 1967; *Transparencias,* 1973); concertos for piano, for guitar, for bandoneon; choral works (incl. *María Sabina,* with narrator and orch., 1970); works for band; chamber music (incl. *Geometrías* for 7 instruments, 1966; *Cuatris* for 4 instruments, 1969); songs.

Balakirev, Mily Alexeievich (b. Nizhny-Novgorod, 2 Jan. 1837 [old style 21 Dec. 1836]; d. St. Petersburg, 29 May 1910). Active in collecting, arranging, and publishing Russian folksongs. With Lomakin, opened the Free Music School in St. Petersburg, 1862. Music Director of the Imperial Chapel, 1883–94. His pupils incl. Cui, Rimsky-Korsakov, Borodin, and Mussorgsky [see Five, The]. Composed numerous instrumental and vocal works, incl. *Russia,* otherwise known as *One Thousand Years* or *Second Overture on Russian Themes,* 1864, rev. 1884; *Islamey,* oriental fantasy for piano, 1869; *Tamara,* symphonic poem, 1867–82; 2 symphonies; 2 piano concertos (one unfinished); *Chopin,* orch. suite, 1910; song albums; piano arrangements of works by Berlioz, Chopin, and Glinka (incl. the latter's *The Lark*).

Balalaika. A popular Russian instrument of the guitar family, characterized by a triangular body, long fretted neck, and (usually) three gut strings tuned in fourths. It is played with a plectrum and is made in six sizes that together constitute a balalaika band. [See ill. under Guitar family.] The forerunner of the balalaika was the *domra.

Balancement [F.]. An 18th-century name for *tremolo. It is sometimes used synonymously with *Bebung.

Balbastre, Claude (Balbâtre) (b. Dijon, 22 Jan. 1727; d. Paris, 9 May 1799). Pupil of Rameau. Participant in the Concert spirituel, 1755–60. Organist (alternating with Couperin, Daquin, and Séjan) at Notre Dame Cathedral, 1760. Harpsichordist to Queen Marie-Antoinette. Composed numerous works for harpsichord or piano and for organ.

Ballabile [It.]. A name given occasionally to dancelike pieces (ballets) in 19th-century operas.

Ballad. The term derives from medieval terms such as *chanson balladée, *ballade, *ballata, all of which originally denoted dancing songs [L. *ballare,* to dance] but lost their dance connotation as early as the 14th century and became stylized forms of solo song. In England this process of change went still further, and eventually (16th century) *ballad* came to mean a simple tale told in simple verse. There may have been a transitional period during which the recitation of the poems was still accompanied by some sort of dancing. Most ballads are narrative, and many deal with fabulous, miraculous, or gruesome deeds. Ballad singers made a living by singing their newest productions in the streets and at country fairs and by selling the printed sheets (broadsides), which usually gave the instruction: "to be sung to the tune of . . . ," e.g., "Greensleeves." In its more recent (19th-century) meaning, a ballad is a popular song usually combining narrative and romantic elements, frequently with an admixture of the gruesome. These ballads are mostly written in common meter (8 6 8 6; see Poetic meter). Today the term *ballad* is loosely applied to any kind of popular song. For art ballad, see *Ballade* (2).

The word *ballad* is also used as an anglicized form of *ballade* [F.], *ballata* [It.], or *Ballade* [G.]. These terms, however, denote entirely different things.

Ballad of Baby Doe, The. Opera in two acts by D. Moore (libretto by J. Latouche), produced in Central City, Colo., 1956. Setting: Colorado and Washington, D.C., 1880–99.

Ballad opera. A popular form of 18th-century stage entertainment in England, consisting of spoken dialogue alternating with musical numbers taken from ballad tunes, folksongs, or famous melodies by earlier or contemporary composers and

including occasional satire or parody of serious opera and current events. *The *Beggar's Opera* (1728) by John Gay, with music arranged by Johann Pepusch, the first important example of this type, was also the most successful. Two ballad operas (or farces) by Charles Coffey, *The Devil To Pay* (1731) and *The Merry Cobbler* (1735), played a decisive role in the development of the German *Singspiel.*

Ballade. (1) [F.] One of the three *formes fixes* of 14th-century French poetry and music. The poem usually has three stanzas, each of seven or eight lines, the last line identical in all the stanzas, forming a *refrain. The form of the stanza is thus: *a b a b b c C* or *a b a b c c d D* (capital letters indicate the refrain), a scheme that, so far as the music is concerned, can be represented as follows: A A B (section A = the lines *a b;* section B = the remaining lines). Some *ballades* have the musical form A A B B, the music for lines 5 and 6 being repeated for lines 7 and 8. *Ballades* sometimes conclude with an *envoi.

The *ballade* played a prominent role in the work of Machaut and in the work of his successors in the late 14th century, for whom the polyphonic *ballade* became the most representative type of music. The form continued to be cultivated, though much more sparingly, during the 15th century.

Monophonic songs with the form A A B are common in the repertory of the *troubadours and even more so in that of the *trouvères, though most of these differ from the *forme fixe* in some details of versification (e.g., absence of refrain, having more than three stanzas). See also *Ballade* style; *Ballata; Bar* form; *Canzo.*

(2) [G.] A type of poem derived from the English ballads but having greater artistic elaboration and poetic refinement. These poems usually deal with medieval subjects, either historical or legendary (e.g., Goethe's "Ballade vom vertriebenen und zurückkehrenden Grafen"), or with romantic tales (e.g., Goethe's "Erlkönig"). Such *Balladen* were frequently set to music (e.g., by Schubert, Loewe, and Zumsteeg), usually as *through-composed songs of great

length. In the later 19th century, they were sometimes set for soloist and/or chorus with orchestra. Chopin, Brahms, and others have used the term for piano pieces, sometimes citing literary models.

Ballade style. A term referring to the typical texture of the 14th-century French *ballade* (Machaut), that is, in three parts, the top part vocal and the two lower parts (tenor, contratenor) instrumental. The same style was used for *rondeaux, virelais,* and occasionally for Mass compositions as well. The terms *cantilena style* and *treble-dominated style* have been suggested as substitutes for *ballade style.*

Ballata [It.]. The chief form of Italian 14th-century music, as represented in the works of Francesco Landini. Not related to the French *ballade,* it is practically identical with the **villancico* and the **virelai,* which was also called *chanson balladée.* As a poem, the *ballata* consists of a refrain (called the *ripresa*) and, normally, three stanzas that alternate with the refrain: R S_1 R S_2 R S_3 R. The stanza consists of two so-called *piedi* (feet) one or more lines long and of identical versification and a *volta* (turn) having the same structure as the *ripresa.* Music is composed only for the *ripresa* and the first *piede.* The second *piede* repeats the music of the first, and the *volta* repeats the music of the *ripresa* as follows:

	R		S₁		R	
Text	*ripresa*	*piedi*		*volta*	*ripresa* etc.	
Music	A	bb		a	A	etc.

Ballet. A theatrical performance by a dancing group, usually with costumes and scenery, to the accompaniment of music but customarily without singing or spoken words. The origins of modern ballet date from the 15th century, when dance performances were introduced at the French, Burgundian, and Italian courts for weddings, receptions of foreign sovereigns, and similar festive occasions. In their early stages these performances consisted of loose sequences of dances, based on the steps of the conventional courtly repertory but performed in sumptuous costumes and sometimes embodying the general theme of the occasion (e.g., dances of the European nations paying homage to a visiting prince, dances of the Four Continents in honor of a newborn royal baby). In the course of time, elaborate decorations were added, a story or plot provided dramatic interest and unity, and the music, originally played by small instrumental ensembles specializing in dance accompaniment, began to be performed by the full court orchestra (or even orchestras), often together with vocal soloists and ensembles.

When, in the early 16th century, the traditions of the Italian *intermedi* and *trionfi* on the one hand and the *horse ballets* (*balletti a cavallo, carrousels, danses equestres*) on the other merged with the art of ballroom dancing, the *ballet de cour* was born. The *Balet comique de la Royne,* a choreographic invention of the ballet master Baldassare de Belgioioso (de Beaujoyeulx), performed in the fall of 1581, is the earliest *ballet de cour* for which the music has been preserved. Throughout the 17th century the *ballet de cour,* which was the French counterpart of the English court **masque,* remained the undisputed favorite at the royal court and in the palaces of the French nobility.

The golden age of ballet came under Louis XIV (reigned 1643–1715), who himself liked to dance and was fond of appearing in ballets. With the ballet master C. L. Beauchamps and the musicians Jean de Cambefort (1605–61) and Jean-Baptiste Lully (1632–87), the French ballet attained great cultural importance as well as musical significance. It became the origin of a large number of new courtly dances, such as the gavotte, passepied, bourrée, and rigaudon, which were later used as optional movements of suites. Of particular importance among these was the minuet. In 1664 Lully and Molière jointly created the *comédie-ballet,* a union of stage play and ballet. Lully also introduced the ballet into French opera. His successors, Campra and Rameau, went further in this direction by establishing the *opéra ballet,* in which dramatic content was reduced to a minimum in favor of dancing.

In the second half of the 17th century, Vienna was a center of elaborate presentations, especially of equestrian ballets (*Rossballett*), and soon after 1700 the imperial court of Vienna, always in competition with Versailles, became one of the foremost centers of professional ballet in Europe. During the reigns of Charles VI and Maria Theresa, almost all the leading dancers and choreographers of the time came to Vienna, either as dancing masters at the court or as guests or permanent members of the two main theaters in the city.

From 1750 to 1850 the history of the ballet includes a galaxy of famous dancers, such as Marie Camargo (1710–70), J.-G. Noverre (1727–1810), the brothers Angiolo Maria Vestris (1730–1809) and Gaetano Apollino Vestris (1729–1808), Maria Taglioni (1804–84), and Fanny Elssler (1810–51). Unfortunately, little of the music used in their presentations has survived. Noverre, the great reformer of the ballet, found musical collaborators in Stuttgart (Florian Deller, 1729–73; Jean J. Rudolphe, 1730–1812) as well as in Vienna (Ignaz Holzbauer, 1711–83; Gluck, 1714–87; Josef Starzer, 1726–87; and Mozart, 1756–91). Gluck's *Don Juan* (1761), Mozart's *Les petits riens* (1778), and Beethoven's *Die Geschöpfe des Prometheus* (1801) are the best-known ballets from this period. After the French Revolution, the emphasis in ballet shifted from feudal elegance to patriotic fervor, drama, and frank burlesque, which in turn were followed by the advent of romanticism and the emergence of its great representatives, Maria Taglioni, Fanny Elssler, and others. Some outstanding roles in the romantic ballet, with its emphasis on idyllic or supernatural rather than heroic or tragic subjects, were created by Taglioni (*La Sylphide*), Carlotta Grisi, and Elssler (see *Cachucha*). Of the numerous ballets of this period, one has survived to the present day, *Giselle,* produced in Paris in 1841 with Grisi as *prima ballerina,* choreography by Jean Coralli, and music by Adolphe-Charles Adam.

In the second half of the 19th century, ballet was cultivated particularly in Denmark and Russia. The Russian center of greatest vitality was St. Petersburg, where Marius Petipa (1822–1910) prepared the way for the modern ballet. Tchaikovsky's *Swan Lake* (1876; perf.

1877), *The Sleeping Beauty* (1889; perf. 1890), and *The Nutcracker* (completed and perf. 1892) represent the culmination of this activity. Two other important ballets of this period are *Coppélia* (1870) and *Sylvia* (1876) with music by Delibes, both produced in Paris. Also in this period, as in preceding centuries, ballet continued to be an essential ingredient of opera in France.

The great flowering of modern ballet began in 1909 when a touring company of Russian dancers under director Sergei P. Diaghilev and dancer-choreographer Michel Fokine began to perform in Paris. Diaghilev's Ballets Russes attracted composers, artists, and writers to create music, posters and scenery, and plots for their performances. Léon Bakst and Picasso created decorative and exotic backdrops. The group's outstanding musical collaborator was Igor Stravinsky, who wrote the scores for *L'oiseau de feu* (The Firebird, 1910), *Petrushka* (1911), *Le sacre du printemps* (The Rite of Spring, 1913), and others. Ravel contributed the music for *Daphnis et Chloé* (1912), Richard Strauss for *Josephslegende* (1914), Falla for *El sombrero de tres picos* (The Three-Cornered Hat, 1919, with décor by Picasso), Milhaud for *La création du monde* (1923), and Debussy for *Jeux* (1913; choreographed by Vaslav Nijinsky, leading male dancer of the troupe). Other works of this period were Stravinsky's *Les noces* (1914–19; perf. 1923); Prokofiev's *Chout* (1915–20; perf. 1921); Satie's three ballets, *Parade* (1917), *Mercure* (1924, with décor by Picasso), and *Relâche* (1924); Poulenc's *Les biches* (1923; perf. 1924); Hindemith's *Der Dämon* (1924); and Bartók's *The Wooden Prince* (1914–16, perf. 1917 and 1922) and *The Miraculous Mandarin* (1919, perf. 1926 in an altered version).

With Diaghilev's death in 1929, the company disbanded, and the dancers and choreographers either joined other companies or formed their own. Ida Rubinstein, a choreographer with the Diaghilev Ballets Russes, had already left the company in 1925 to form her own, for which she choreographed Ravel's *Bolero* (1928) and a new version of his *La valse* (1929). In England Ninette de Valois, who had also left the Diaghilev company in 1925, founded a small company of dancers that became the Sadler's Wells Ballet, later the Royal Ballet. Notable works performed by this company were Ralph Vaughan Williams' *Job* (1931) and William Walton's *Façade* (1931) with choreography by Frederick Ashton. In France after Diaghilev's death, Serge Lifar was choreographer and ballet master of the Paris Opéra. Among well-known French composers active in this field have been Roussel, Ibert, and Auric.

Along with the continuation of some older traditions, particularly in the Soviet Union, the 20th century has seen the development of new modes of dance to which some of the classical implications of the term *ballet* do not apply. Many such developments, particularly in the United States, have their origin in the work of Isadora Duncan (1878–1927) around the turn of the century. A few among the many other important figures for the United States, where dance began especially to flourish after about 1920, have been Ruth St. Denis, Ted Shawn, George Balanchine (a Russian associate of Diaghilev who came to the United States in 1933 and thereafter choreographed numerous important musical works by Stravinsky, Webern, and others—works often not conceived as music for dance), Martha Graham (who commissioned works from Hindemith, Riegger, Cowell, Copland, Barber, and others), Doris Humphrey (works by Cowell, Riegger, Luening, and others), and Merce Cunningham (whose collaboration with John Cage has been particularly influential). The roles of electronic and aleatory music have become increasingly prominent.

Ballett. German spelling for **ballet.* Also 16th- and 17th-century English or German for **balletto* or for **ballo.*

Balletto [It.]. (1) A type of polyphonic vocal composition of *c.* 1600, dancelike in character, written in a simplified madrigal style, and frequently provided with a **fa-la refrain, which may occasionally have been danced. The first publication in this genre was by G. Gastoldi (1591). His example was imitated by T. Morley (1595) and others until *c.* 1620. (2) A dance of the 17th century, usually in 4/4 meter, bipartite form, and in a sim-

ple, nearly homophonic style (somewhat similar to the early allemande), mostly for ensembles.

Ballo [It.]. Dance.

Ballo in maschera, Un [It., A Masked Ball]. Opera in three acts by Verdi (libretto by A. Somma, based on Scribe's *Gustave III, ou Le bal masqué*), produced in Rome, 1859. The original play was based on historical fact; Gustavus III of Sweden was shot in the back at a masked ball in Stockholm in 1792. To avoid inciting violence against royalty during a period of political unrest, Verdi was forced by the authorities to change the scene of the opera from Sweden to colonial Boston. Some modern performances revert to the original Swedish setting, while others set the scene in Naples.

Bamert, Matthias (b. Ersigen, Switzerland, 5 July 1942). Pupil of Veress, Rivier, and Boulez. Principal oboe of the Mozarteum Orchestra in Salzburg, 1965–69. Assistant Conductor of the Cleveland Orchestra from 1971. Has composed orch. works (incl. *Septuaria lunaris,* 1970; *Mantrajana,* 1971); *Inkblot* for band, 1971; chamber music; *Organism* for organ, 1972.

Banchieri, Adriano ("Adriano da Bologna"; pseud. Camillo Scaliggeri della Fratta) (b. Bologna, 3 Sept. 1568; d. there, 1634). Organist, theorist, and composer. Entered the order of Olivetan Benedictines, 1587; named abbot, 1620; organist at San Michele in Bosco, Bologna, from 1608 to his death. Active in Bologna's Accademia filarmonica, where he was given the nickname "Il dissonante." Composed dramatic madrigals and other dramatic works, incl. *La pazzia senile,* 1598; Masses and other sacred vocal works; keyboard and other instrumental works. Theoretical works incl. *L'organo suonarino,* 1605, on the realization of a figured bass.

Band [It. and Sp. *banda*]. An instrumental group composed principally of woodwind, brass, and percussion instruments. In earlier periods the name was used for any group of instruments. Different types of wind band include the **brass band, military band, *symphonic band, wind ensemble, jazz or dance band.

Bandoneon [Sp.]. See under Accordion.

Bandora, pandora, pandore. A 16th-century stringed instrument of bass size [see ill. under Lute], with a characteristic scalloped body. It had seven (originally six) pairs of metal strings tuned G_1 C D G c e a and as many as 15 frets. A smaller instrument of the same type was the *orpharion.

Bandurria. A Spanish instrument of the guitar family, still widely used in Spain. In its present-day form it has six double strings tuned in fourths from g♯' to a'' and is played with a plectrum. See ill. under Guitar family.

Banjo. A stringed instrument of varying size and type with a long neck and a body in the form of a shallow, one-headed drum spanned with parchment. Usually fretted, it may have four to nine strings. Often it has five, the highest of which, called the thumb-string, is shorter than the others and is placed next to the lowest, in the following arrangement: g' c g b d'. It is plucked with either the fingers or a plectrum. It was imported to America by slaves from West Africa and has been widely used in the performance of jazz, folk music, and country and western music [see ill. under Guitar family].

Bantock, Granville (b. London, 7 Aug. 1868; d. there 16 Oct, 1946). Composer and conductor. Succeeded Elgar as professor of music at Birmingham Univ., 1907–34. Composed operas, especially on Celtic subjects (incl. *Caedmar,* London, 1893; *The Seal Woman,* Birmingham, 1924); ballets (incl. *Egypt,* 1892); 6 tone poems (incl. *Fifine at the Fair,* 1901); *Hebridean Symphony,* 1915; choral works with orch. (incl. *Omar Khayyam,* 1906–9) and unaccompanied (incl. *Atlanta in Calydon,* 1911); chamber music; piano pieces; *Songs from the Chinese Poets,* 1918–20, and numerous other songs.

Bar. (1) In English, *bar line or, more usually, *measure (included between two bar lines). (2) In German, see *Bar form.

Bar form [G.]. A term used frequently in modern studies for an old, very important musical form, schematically designated A A B. The name is derived from the medieval German term *Bar,* a poem consisting of three or more *Gesätze* (i.e., stanzas), each of which is divided into two *Stollen* (corresponding to musical section A) and an *Abgesang* (section B). The form is found in the repertory of the *troubadours and particularly of the *trouvères [see also *ballade*]. The *minnesingers and *Meistersinger, who called it a *Bar,* used it for nearly all their lyrical songs. It is equally common in the German polyphonic songs of the 15th and 16th centuries (e.g., in the Locheimer Liederbuch, the Glogauer Liederbuch, and the works of Hofhaimer, Stoltzer, and others), as well as in the Lutheran chorales and the various compositions based on them (organ chorales, chorale cantatas, etc.).

Bar line [F. *barre de mesure;* G. *Taktstrich;* It. *stanghetta;* Sp. *linea divisoria*]. A vertical line drawn through the staff to mark off *measures. The general use of the bar line is relatively recent (the 17th century). Until 1600, bar lines were used only for keyboard and lute (vihuela) music, the earliest known being from the late 14th century (Codex Faenza). The use of bar lines in 16th-century compositions frequently differs from present-day practice, since the lines served primarily as a means of orientation, without necessarily implying a regular meter.

Barati, George (b. Györ, Hungary, 3 Apr. 1913). Cellist, conductor, and composer. Pupil of Weiner, Kodály, and Sessions. First cellist in the Budapest Opera, 1935–38; founder and conductor of the Princeton Univ. Chamber Ensemble, 1939–43; conductor of the Barati Chamber Orchestra of San Francisco, 1948–52, and of the Honolulu Symphony Orchestra, 1950–68. Works: a symphony; concertos for cello, for guitar, for piano; *The Waters of Kane* for chorus and orch., 1966; other orch., choral, chamber, and stage works.

Barber, Samuel (b. West Chester, Pa., 9 Mar. 1910). Pupil of Scalero. Teacher at the Curtis Institute of Music. Was awarded the Pulitzer Prize in 1958 and

1963. Has composed operas (incl. *Vanessa; *Antony and Cleopatra*); *Essay for Orchestra*, nos. 1 and 2, 1937 and 1942; *Capricorn Concerto*, in the manner of a *concerto grosso*, 1944; *Souvenirs* for orch., 1952; a piano concerto, 1962; a cello sonata, 1932; a String Quartet in B minor, 1936 (slow movement arranged as *Adagio for Strings*); *Hermit Songs* for voice and piano, 1953.

Barber of Seville, The. See *Barbiere di Siviglia, Il.*

Barbershop harmony. Colloquial term for a type of harmony used in popular American part singing as formerly practiced in barbershops. It is typically arranged for four unaccompanied male voices, the melody being carried by the second voice from the top.

Barbiere di Siviglia, Il [It., The Barber of Seville]. (1) Opera in two acts by Rossini (libretto by C. Sterbini, originally entitled *Almaviva o sia L'inutile precauzione*, based on Beaumarchais' *Le barbier de Séville*), produced in Rome, 1816. Setting: Seville, 18th century. It is one of the last examples of the style of 18th-century Italian comic opera and, in particular, the last to use the *secco* *recitative. (2) Opera in two acts (4 parts) by G. Paisiello (libretto by G. Petrosellini, based on Beaumarchais). Produced in St. Petersburg, 1782. Setting: Seville, 18th century.

Barbieri, Francisco Asenjo (b. Madrid, 3 Aug. 1823; d. there, 17 Feb. 1894). Music historian and composer. Composed 77 *zarzuelas*, incl. *Gloria y peluca*, 1850; *Jugar con fuego*, 1851; *Pan y toros*, 1864; *El barberillo de Lavapiés*, 1874.

Barcarole [F. *barcarolle*; It. *barcarola*]. A boat song of the Venetian gondoliers [It. *barca*, boat], or an instrumental or vocal composition in imitation thereof. Well-known examples for the piano are found in Mendelssohn's *Songs Without Words* (op. 19, no. 6; op. 30, no. 6; op. 62, no. 5); others were written by Chopin (op. 60) and Fauré. Vocal barcaroles occur in various operas with Italian settings, e.g., Offenbach's *Tales of Hoffmann* (1881). Barcaroles are always in moderate 6/8 or 12/8 time and use a monotonous accompaniment suggestive of the movement of the waves and the boat.

Barce, Ramón (b. Madrid, 16 Mar. 1928). Literary historian and composer. Pupil of Gombau. Founded the Nueva música group in Madrid, 1958, and the Círculo de investigación musical, 1964. Has composed theater pieces (incl. *Abgrund, Hintergrund*, 1964); orch. works; chamber music; piano pieces.

Bard. The pre-Christian and medieval poet-musician (minstrel) of the Celts, especially the Irish and the Welsh. In the early Middle Ages bards exercised great political power, serving as historians, heralds, ambassadors, officers of the king's household, and, in brief, constituting the highest intellectual class. Their activities are documented as early as the pre-Christian era by Greek writers such as Diodorus Siculus (1st cent. B.C.), who refers to the *crwth, the traditional instrument of the bards. The bards continued to be active (though at a level far below their former high station) in Ireland until 1690 (battle of the Boyne) and in Scotland until 1748. Annual congregations of the Welsh bards, called *Eisteddfod*, were revived as a regular practice in the early 19th century after an interruption of about 150 years. These now also include choral competitions. [Also see Pennillion.]

Bargiel, Woldemar (b. Berlin, 3 Oct. 1828; d. there, 23 Feb. 1897). Pupil of Hauptmann, Moscheles, and Gade at the Leipzig Conservatory. Close associate of Robert and Clara (whose half-brother he was) Schumann, Brahms, and Joachim. Composed a symphony in C major and 3 overtures; psalms for chorus and orch.; a string octet; 4 string quartets; piano pieces; songs.

Bariolage [F.]. A special effect in violin playing, obtained by quickly shifting back and forth between two or more strings in such a way that either the lower strings are used to produce relatively higher pitches or a tremolo or rapid repetition of a single pitch is produced by alternation between a stopped string an an open string. The type of bowing required and the resulting tremolo in the latter case are called *ondeggiando* [It.] or *ondulé* [F.]. See Tremolo.

Baritone or (rarely) **barytone.** (1) The male voice between the bass and the tenor; see Voices, range of. (2) Applied to instruments (oboe, horn, saxophone), any size above the bass size. (3) Abbr. for *baritone horn;* see Brass instruments II (c).

Baritone clef. See ill. under Clef.

Baritone horn. See Brass instruments II (c).

Barlow, Wayne (b. Elyria, Ohio, 6 Sept. 1912). Pupil of Hanson, Bernard Rogers, and Schoenberg. Taught composition at the Eastman School of Music from 1937; organist and choirmaster at St. Thomas Episcopal Church, Rochester, from 1945. Works incl. *The Winter's Passed* for oboe and strings, 1938; a cantata, *Wait for the Promise of the Father,* 1968; *Missa Sancti Thomae* for chorus and organ, 1959; *Concerto* for saxophone and band, 1970; *Soundscapes* for tape and orch., 1972; *Psalm 97* for chorus, organ, and tape, 1970; organ pieces; chamber music.

Baroque. In the history of music, the term applied to the period *c.* 1600–1750. It was first applied to the visual arts of roughly the same period and in a distinctly pejorative sense now largely discarded. The *thoroughbass, by which name the period is also known, is the principal technical device common to the repertory in question. Beyond that, however, the period saw numerous significant stylistic developments, and this has led to a distinction between the early baroque (including the rise of accompanied *monody, *opera, and the *concertato style and the works of composers such as Caccini, Monteverdi, Frescobaldi, and Carissimi) and the late baroque (beginning in the late 17th century and including the full establishing of tonic-dominant or triadic *tonality, the rise of *opera seria, and the culmination in the works of Bach and Handel of international styles of vocal and instrumental music including Italian, French, and German elements). The terms *Renaissance* and *rococo* are generally applied to the periods immediately preceding and following, respectively.

Barraqué, Jean (b. Paris, 17 Jan. 1928; d. there, 17 Aug. 1973). Pupil of Langlais and Messiaen. Member of the Groupe de recherches musicales in Paris, 1951–54; developed his own system of serial composition. Works incl. *Séquence* for soprano, piano, harp, strings, and percussion, 1955; a piano sonata, 1952; *Concerto* for clarinet, vibraphone, and 6 instrumental groups, 1968; a large cycle, *La mort de Virgile* (after H. Broch's novel *Der Tod des Vergil*) for voices and instruments, containing *Le temps restitué, Au-delà du hasard, Chant après chant,* begun in 1956.

Barraud, Henry (b. Bordeaux, 23 April 1900). Pupil of L. Aubert. Music director of the French Radio and Television Network, 1944–65. Has composed the comic opera *La farce de Maître Pathelin,* Paris, 1948; *Le testament de François Villon,* cantata, 1945; *Le mystère des Saints Innocents,* oratorio, 1946; *Te Deum* for chorus and winds, 1955; symphonies; instrumental, vocal, and stage works. Has published several books.

Barré, grand-barré [F.]. In lute and guitar playing, the stopping of all strings with the forefinger at some specified fret. See also Capo, capotasto.

Barre de mesure [F.]. *Bar line.

Barrel organ. See under Mechanical instruments.

Barsanti, Francesco (b. Lucca, *c.* 1690; d. London, before 1776). Flutist and composer. Performed at the Italian Opera in London. Works incl. 6 flute solos with bass; 6 sonatas for 2 violins with bass; 6 antiphons; *concerti grossi* and other instrumental works.

Bartered Bride, The [Cz. *Prodaná Nevěsta*]. Opera in three acts by Bedřich Smetana (libretto by Karel Sabina), produced in Prague, 1866. Setting: a Bohemian village, 1850.

Bartók, Béla (b. Nagy Szent Miklós, Transylvania, 25 Mar. 1881; d. New York, 26 Sept. 1945). Pupil of Koessler. Began collecting Hungarian folk music with Kodály in 1905 and remained active in this field; appointed to the Hungarian Academy of Sciences, 1934, to prepare collected folk music materials for publication. Professor of piano at the Royal Academy of Music in Budapest from

1907; toured Europe and the U.S. several times as a pianist. After World War I, a member of the Music Directorate with Dohnányi and Kodály. Settled in the U.S. in 1940. Works: *Kossuth*, symphonic poem, 1903; ballets (incl. *The Wooden Prince*, 1914–16; *The Miraculous Mandarin*, 1919, rev. 1924, 1935); an opera, **Bluebeard's Castle; Concerto for Orchestra*, 1943; *Music for Strings, Percussion, and Celesta*, 1936; pieces for violin, incl. 2 concertos (1908, 1938), 2 rhapsodies, 4 sonatas, and a set of 44 short duos based on folk music; works for piano, incl. 3 concertos (1926, 1931, 1945), *Allegro barbaro* (1911), the sets *For Children* (1909, rev. 1945) and *Mikrokosmos* (1926–37); 6 string quartets (1908, 1917, 1927, 1928, 1934, 1939); numerous other instrumental and choral works.

Bartolozzi, Bruno (b. Florence, 8 June 1911). Violinist and composer. Close associate of Dallapiccola. Has explored expanded resources of wind instruments. Has composed works for orchestra; woodwinds, unaccompanied and in combination; unaccompanied violin; voice and instruments; chamber ensembles.

Baryton. (1) French and German spelling for **baritone* (voice, size of instruments). (2) An instrument of the **viol* family. See ill. accompanying Violin family.

Barzelletta [It.]. A type of Italian poetry of about 1500, generally in the form of the **ballata*, sometimes with only one stanza. More than half of the **frottole* are *barzellette*.

Bass. (1) The lowest of men's voices [see Voices, range of]. (2) In both German and English, **double bass*. (3) Applied to instruments, the term indicates the lowest and consequently largest type of any family, e.g., bass clarinet. (4) In musical composition, with rare exceptions, the lowest of the parts. For the origin of the bass, see Contratenor. See also Thoroughbass.

Bass-bar. In instruments of the viol and violin families, a strip of wood glued inside the belly, about 11 in. long in violins and narrowing at both ends. Its function is to support the left foot of the bridge

and to spread over the belly the vibrations of the bridge produced by those of the strings.

Bass clef. See under Clef.

Bass-course. See Course.

Bass drum. See under Percussion instruments.

Bass horn. See under Cornett. For ill. see under Brass instruments.

Bass lute [G. *Basslaute*]. The chitarrone, or the theorbo. See Lute.

Bass viol. Originally (17th century), the **viola da gamba*. See also Viol. Today, the **double bass, a descendant of the old double-bass viol.

Bassa [It.]. Low. *Ottava bassa* (abbr. *8va bassa*), the octave below the written notes. *Con 8va bassa*, doubling of the written notes by playing or singing also in the lower octave.

Bassadanza [It.]. See *Basse danse*.

Bassani, Giovanni Battista (Bassano, Bassiani) (b. Padua, *c.* 1657; d. Bergamo, 1 Oct. 1716). Organist, violinist, and composer. *Maestro di cappella* to the Duke of Mirandola from 1678; at the Accademia della Morte in Ferrara from 1684; at the Ferrara Cathedral from 1688; at the Basilica of Santa Maria Maggiore in Bergamo, 1712 to his death. Composed oratorios, Masses, motets for solo voice with instruments, and much other sacred vocal music; secular cantatas; operas (incl. *Amorosa preda di Paride*, Bologna, 1683); instrumental works.

Basse [F.]. *Basse chiffré* or *b. continue*, **thoroughbass; basse contrainte*, **ground* (*basso ostinato*); *basse profonde, chantante*, see Voices, range of; *basse fondamentale*, **fundamental bass; basse à pistons*, euphonium, and *basse d'harmonie*, ophicleide [see under Brass instruments].

Basse danse [F.]; **bassadanza** [It.]. A dance of unknown origin cultivated at the courts of western Europe during the 15th century and, in a somewhat debased form, cultivated more generally during the early 16th century. The name (*bas*, low) probably refers to the gliding or walking movements of the feet, in contrast to the livelier steps of the *pas de Brabant* (It. *saltarello*, Sp. *alta* or *altadanza*), which often followed the *basse danse* proper. In the 15th century, Italian treatises give prose descriptions of the choreographies and very little of the music; French sources record the steps of each dance in a simple tablature notation and give a monophonic tenor for each dance. The tenors included in the French sources are written almost exclusively in black breves, each note of the tenor corresponding to one step unit of the dance. Above the tenor, one or two parts of a livelier character were improvised. In the 16th century, the *basse danse* became a simpler, more stereotyped dance, its music no longer based on equal-note tenors but on discant melodies. The great majority of the *basses danses* are in slow triple meter (3/2). Sometimes the 16th-century *basse danse* is followed by a *recoupe* and a *tordion*.

Basset horn. See under Clarinet family.

Bassett, Leslie (Raymond) (b. Hanford, Calif., 22 Jan. 1923). Pupil of Finney, Honegger, N. Boulanger, Gerhard, and Davidovsky. Teacher at the Univ. of Michigan from 1952. Has composed orch. works (incl. *Variations for Orchestra*, Pulitzer Prize, 1966; *Five Movements*, 1962; *Echoes from an Invisible World*, 1976); a concerto for 2 pianos and orch., 1977; choral works; *Five Pieces*, 1957, and other works for string quartet; other chamber music; *Three Studies in Electronic Sounds*, on tape, 1965.

Bassetto, bassett, bassettl. Various 18th-century names for the *cello.

Bassflöte [G.]. (1) Bass flute. (2) An 18th-century name for the bassoon.

Bassist [G.]; **bassista** [It.]. (1) A bass singer. (2) In English, a bassist is a double-bass player.

Basso [It.]. Bass. *B. profondo, cantante, buffo*, see Voices, range of. *B. continuo*, see Thoroughbass.

Basso ostinato [It.]. See Ground; also under Ostinato.

Basso ripieno [It.]. In 18th-century orchestral works, a bass part for the tutti (*ripieno) passages only, i.e., not for the solo sections.

Basso seguente. An early type of *thoroughbass that merely duplicated (usually on the organ) whatever part of a vocal composition was the lowest at any given time.

Basson [F.]. Bassoon. See under Oboe family. *B. quinte*, a smaller bassoon, also called tenoroon. *B. russe*, Russian bassoon; see under Cornett.

Bassoon. See under Oboe family.

Bassschlüssel [G.]. Bass *clef.

Bastien und Bastienne. Opera in one act written by Mozart at the age of twelve and first performed in the garden theater of Anton Mesmer in Vienna in 1768. The libretto is based in Favart's parody of Rousseau's *Le devin du village.*

Bateson, Thomas (b. *c.* 1570; d. Dublin, Mar. 1630). Organist at Chester Cathedral and later at Dublin Cathedral. Published two sets of madrigals.

Bathyphone. See under Clarinet family.

Battaglia [It., battle]. A composition in which the fanfares, cries, drum rolls, and general commotion of a battle are imitated. This was a favorite subject of *program music from the 16th through the 18th centuries.

Battement [F.]. French 17th-century term for any ornament consisting of an alternation of two adjacent tones, e.g., *mordent, *trill, *vibrato. In modern parlance, *battements* are the acoustical *beats.

Batten, Adrian (bapt. Salisbury, 1 Mar. 1591; d. London, 1637). Organist and composer. Lay vicar at Westminster Abbey, 1614–27; vicar choral at St. Paul's Cathedral, London, 1627 to his death. Composed 15 services and 47 anthems (incl. "Out of the Deep" and "Hear My Prayer O Lord"); numerous transcriptions for organ of sacred choral works.

Batterie [F.]. (1) The percussion group of the orchestra. (2) A drum roll. (3) An 18th-century name for arpeggio, broken-chord figures, Alberti basses, etc. (4) A manner of playing the guitar by striking the strings.

Battery. Old term for *arpeggio;* see *Batterie* (3).

Battle of the Huns, The. See *Hunnenschlacht, Die.*

Battle of Victoria. See *Wellingtons Sieg.*

Battle pieces. See *Battaglia.*

Battre [F.]. To beat, e.g., *battre à deux temps,* two beats per measure.

Battuta [It.]. Beat. *A battuta* indicates a return to strict time after some deviation (*ad libitum, a piacere,* etc.). In particular, *battuta* means the strong beat at the beginning of a measure; hence, Beethoven's indication "ritmo di tre [quattro] battute" (Scherzo, Ninth Symphony) means that three (or four) measures are to be grouped together, the tempo being so fast that there is only one beat to the measure.

Baudrier, Yves (b. Paris, 11 Feb. 1906). Associate of Messiaen, Jolivet, and Daniel Lesur, who called themselves "La jeune France." Has composed much film music; orch. works; chamber music.

Bauer, Marion Eugenie (b. Walla Walla, Wash., 15 Aug. 1887; d. South Hadley, Mass., 9 Aug. 1955). Studied in Paris with Gédalge and N. Boulanger, in Berlin, and in New York with Huss. Taught at Chautauqua, New York Univ., the Juilliard Summer School, and the Institute of Musical Art. Composed orch. works (incl. *Sun Splendor,* originally for piano, 1926); choral works; chamber music; piano pieces; songs. Published several books on music.

Bauernkantate [G., Peasant Cantata]. A secular cantata by Bach, written to a text by Picander in Saxon dialect ("Mer hahn en neue Oberkeet," We Have a New Magistrate) and performed in 1742 to celebrate the installation of a new magistrate in a rural district of Saxony. The music includes several popular tunes of the day.

Bax, Arnold (Edward Trevor) (b. Streatham, England, 8 Nov. 1883; d. Cork, Ireland, 3 Oct. 1953). Pupil of Matthay and F. Corder. Succeeded Henry Walford Davies as Master of the King's Music, 1942. Composed ballets; 7 symphonies, several symphonic poems (incl. *The Garden of Fand,* 1916; *Tintagel,* 1917), and many other orch. works; chamber music; piano pieces; music for films; choral works; songs.

Bay Psalm Book. A book of psalms, *The Whole Booke of Psalms Faithfully Translated into English Metre,* published in Cambridge, Mass., in 1640 (the first book printed in North America). It had numerous subsequent editions over more than a century. In 1698 music (in two parts) was added for thirteen tunes.

Bayreuth Festival. Annual festival held in the opera house of Bayreuth (Bavaria) for the performance of Wagner's operas. It originated in 1876 with the first complete performance of the **Ring des Nibelungen.*

Bayreuth tuba. Same as Wagner tuba; see under Tuba.

Bazelon, Irwin (b. Evanston, Ill., 4 June 1922). Pupil of Milhaud and Bloch. Has composed 6 symphonies; overtures; other orch. works; string quartets and other chamber music; piano sonatas; music for films.

BB♭ bass. Double B♭ tuba. See under Tuba (2).

B.c. Abbr. for *basso continuo* [see Thoroughbass].

Be [G.]. The sign ♭.

Be-bop, rebop, bop. Terms coined about 1945 to describe jazz characterized by improvised solo performances in a dissonant idiom with complex rhythmic patterns and continuous, highly florid melodic lines. Sometimes nonsense syllables are sung, a practice from which the name is thought to have originated. It became popular after World War II under the leadership of trumpeter Dizzy Gillespie and alto saxophonist Charlie ("Bird") Parker.

Beach, Amy Marcy Cheney (known as Mrs. H. H. A. Beach) (b. Henniker, N.H., 5 Sept. 1867; d. New York, 27 Dec. 1944). Pianist and composer. Works incl. a Mass; 2 piano concertos and other piano works; *Gaelic Symphony,* 1896; cantatas; a violin sonata; numerous songs.

Beak flute. *Recorder.

Bearbeitung [G.]. *Arrangement, transcription.

Beat [F. *temps;* G. *Zählzeit, Schlag;* It. *battuta;* Sp. *tiempo*]. (1) The temporal unit of a composition, as indicated by the up-and-down movements, real or imagined, of a conductor's hand (upbeat, downbeat). In moderate tempo, the 4/4 measure includes four beats (one on each of the four quarter notes), the first and third of which are strong, the others weak, while the 3/4 measure has three beats, only the first of which is strong. In quick tempo, the 4/4 measure may be treated as having only two beats to the measure, corresponding to the first and third quarter notes, and the 3/4 measure as having only one. In very slow tempo, the beats may be subdivided into twos or threes, with the result, for example, that the 4/4 measure is treated as having eight beats (two for each of the four quarter notes). See Accent; Meter.

(2) A 17th-century English ornament that may be performed in two ways, depending on whether it is a *plain beat* (indicated by an ascending oblique line placed before or over the written note) or a *shaked beat* (indicated by a wavy line resembling the French sign for the trill). The plain beat is an *appoggiatura below the main note, performed on the beat and of flexible duration. The shaked beat consists of several rapid repetitions of such an appoggiatura and its resolution, beginning with the former, so that it resembles an inverted trill. In the 18th century the term *beat* is often applied to the ornament commonly known as a *mordent.

(3) See Beats.

Béatitudes, Les [F., The Beatitudes]. Oratorio by Franck for solo voices, chorus, and orchestra, set to the well-known text from the Scriptures (Sermon on the Mount, Matt. 5:3–12). It was completed in 1879.

Beats [F. *battements;* G. *Schwebungen;* It. *battimenti;* Sp. *batimientos*]. An acoustical phenomenon resulting from the interference of two sound waves of slightly different frequencies. It is heard as minute yet clearly audible intensifications of the sound at regular intervals. The number per second of these intensi-

fications, or beats, is equal to the difference in frequency of the two tones.

Bebung [G.; F. *balancement*]. A *vibrato effect peculiar to the clavichord, whose action allows for a repeated pressure of the finger without releasing the key, a motion causing the tangent momentarily to increase the tension of the string and thus producing slight variations in pitch. It is indicated as follows:

$$\widehat{\overset{\ldots}{p}}$$

Bec [F.]. The mouthpiece of the clarinet or recorder; see Mouthpiece (b), (d).

Bécarre [F.]. The natural sign [see Accidentals]. In the 17th century it also served to indicate the major mode, e.g., *mi bécarre,* E major.

Becerra Schmidt, Gustavo (b. Temuco, Chile, 26 Aug. 1925). Pupil of Allende and Santa Cruz. Member of the faculty of the Univ. of Chile from 1947. Has composed an opera, *La muerte de Don Rodrigo;* numerous choral works; ballets; theater and film scores; 3 symphonies; 2 guitar concertos; string quartets and other chamber music; other vocal and instrumental works, some with tape.

Beck, Conrad (b. Schaffhausen, Switzerland, 16 June 1901). Pupil of Ibert, Honegger, Roussel, and N. Boulanger. Active in collecting and arranging Swiss folksongs. Music director of Basel Radio, 1938–66. Has composed 7 symphonies; cantatas; oratorios; a piano concerto and other piano works; chamber music; choral works; songs.

Becken [G.]. Cymbals.

Becker, John J. (b. Henderson, Ky., 22 Jan. 1886; d. Wilmette, Ill., 21 Jan. 1961). Associate of Cowell, Ives, Riegger, and Ruggles. Minnesota state director for the Federal Music Project, 1935–41. Associate editor of *New Music Quarterly,* 1936–40. Composed 7 symphonies and other orch. works; choral works; stage works (incl. *A Marriage with Space,* 1935); drama and film scores; *Soundpiece,* nos. 1–8, 1935–59, for various instruments; 2 piano concertos; a violin concerto; songs.

Beckwith, John (b. Victoria, B.C., 9 Mar. 1927). Pianist and composer. Pupil of N. Boulanger. Member of the faculty of the Univ. of Toronto from 1952; its Dean from 1970. Works incl. piano pieces; a chamber opera, *Night Blooming Cereus,* Toronto, 1959; musical collages (incl. *A Message to Winnipeg* for 3 speakers and instruments, 1960); *Circle, with Tangents* for harpsichord and 13 strings, 1967.

Bedächtig [G.]. Unhurried, deliberate.

Bedford, David (b. London, 4 Aug. 1937). Pupil of Berkeley and Nono. Works incl. *Piece II* for electronic instruments, 1962; *Music for Albion Moonlight* for soprano and chamber ensemble, 1965; *A Dream of the 7 Lost Stars* for chorus and instruments, 1965; *The Tentacles of the Dark Nebula* for tenor and solo strings, 1969; *18 Bricks Left on April 21st* for 2 electric guitars, 1967; didactic works for children.

Beeson, Jack (Hamilton) (b. Muncie, Ind., 15 July 1921). Pupil of B. Phillips, Bernard Rogers, Hanson, and Bartók. Member of the faculty of Columbia Univ. from 1945; of the Juilliard School of Music, 1962–64. Has composed operas (incl. *Hello out There,* New York, 1954; *The Sweet Bye and Bye,* New York, 1957; *Lizzie Borden,* New York, 1965; *Captain Jinks of the Horse Marines,* Kansas City, Mo., 1975); a symphony, 1959; *Transformations* for orch., 1959; 5 piano sonatas; other instrumental and vocal works.

Beethoven, Ludwig van (b. Bonn, probably 16 Dec., bapt. 17 Dec. 1770; d. Vienna, 26 Mar. 1827). Pupil of his father, then of Neefe, Haydn, Schenk, Salieri, and Albrechtsberger. Assistant court organist at Bonn, 1784–92. Visited Vienna in 1787 to study with Mozart, but was recalled to Bonn by his mother's fatal illness. From 1788, played viola in the Electoral Orchestra at Bonn under Reicha. In 1792, went to Vienna to study with Haydn. Beethoven pursued his studies with Albrechtsberger after Haydn's departure for England in 1794. His hearing began to fail shortly after this; by 1820 his deafness was nearly total, forcing him to abandon his activity as a virtuoso pianist and conductor.

Instrumental works: 9 symphonies (incl. the *Eroica;* the *Pastoral;* the *Choral,* with vocal soloists and chorus); 2 romances for violin and orch.; a violin concerto; 5 piano concertos (incl. the *Emperor*); a triple concerto for piano, violin, cello, and orch.; *Choral Fantasia* for piano, chorus, and orch.; overtures (incl. *Leonore,* nos. 1–3, *Coriolan, Die *Weihe des Hauses*); incidental music to *Egmont, Die *Ruinen von Athen;* the ballet *Die *Geschöpfe des Prometheus;* an octet and a sextet for wind instruments; 3 quintets for strings; 16 string quartets and the *Grosse Fuge;* 6 piano trios; other chamber works for various ensembles; 10 sonatas and other works for piano and violin; 5 sonatas and other works for piano and cello; 32 sonatas for piano solo; several sets of variations for piano (incl. the *Diabelli Variations*); *Bagatellen* and numerous other piano pieces.

Vocal works: an opera, *Fidelio;* 2 Masses (incl. the *Missa Solemnis*); an oratorio, *Christus am Ölberge;* cantatas (incl. *Meeresstille und glückliche Fahrt*); other choral works; numerous songs with piano (incl. the cycle *An die ferne Geliebte*) or piano and string accompaniment.

Beggar's Opera, The. Ballad opera with music arranged by J. Pepusch (libretto by John Gay), produced in London, 1728. The plot is a satirical presentation of life among the lower classes in early 18th-century London, the characters being highwaymen, pickpockets, and harlots. The most successful of all *ballad operas, it has been revived several times. Weill's *Dreigroschenoper* is based on it.

Begleitung [G.]. Accompaniment.

Behaglich [G.]. Comfortably, with ease.

Behende [G.]. Nimbly, quickly.

Behrman, David (b. Salzburg, of American parents, 16 Aug. 1937). Pupil of Riegger, Piston, Stockhausen, and Pousseur. Co-founder in 1966, with Ashley, Lucier, and Mumma, of the Sonic Arts Union for the performance of electronic and mixed media pieces. Has composed works for 1 and 2 pianos; works for instruments with tape or other electronic devices (incl. *Net for Catching Big Sounds,* 1974); mixed media and collaborative works.

Beissel, Johann Conrad (b. Eberbach on the Neckar, Palatinate, Apr. 1690; d. Ephrata, Pa., 6 July 1768). Settled in America in 1720 for religious reasons and founded the religious community at Ephrata in 1735. Composed texts, melodies, and harmonizations of numerous German hymns.

Beisser [G.]. An 18th-century name for the *mordent.

Bel. A unit for measuring changes in the intensity of sound, i.e., loudness, named for Alexander Graham Bell. One bel is equal to an interval of intensity corresponding to a tenfold increase in sound energy. Because 1 bel represents a considerable change in loudness, the more commonly used unit of measure is the decibel (db), equal to one-tenth of a bel.

Bel canto [It., beautiful singing]. The Italian vocal technique of the 18th century, with its emphasis on beauty of sound and brilliance of performance rather than dramatic expression or romantic emotion. Its early development is closely bound up with that of the Italian *opera seria* (A. Scarlatti, N. A. Porpora, N. Jommelli, J. A. Hasse, N. Piccinni). More recently the term *bel canto* has been associated with a mid-17th-century development represented by L. Rossi and G. Carissimi, who cultivated a simple, melodious vocal style of songlike quality, without virtuoso coloraturas. It is also applied to the vocal style of early 19th-century Italian operas such as those of Bellini.

Belcher, Supply (b. Stoughton, Mass., 9 Apr. 1751; d. Farmington, Maine, 1836). Writer of hymns, called "the Handel of Maine." Associate of Billings.

Belebend, belebt [G.]. Brisk, animated.

Bell. (1) The bell-shaped opening of wind instruments such as the horn or trumpet.

(2) A metal percussion instrument in the shape of a hollow vessel and sounded by a clapper, usually placed inside the bell. The tone of a well-tuned bell is characterized by a great number of partials [see Acoustics], which in old bells

(chiefly those of the Continent) are slightly out of tune; owing to the efforts of English bell-founders, modern English bells have five prominent partials (including the minor, not the major, third) tuned with absolute accuracy. The frequencies of bells vary inversely with the cube roots of their weights. Thus, if a bell weighing 8,000 pounds has a frequency of x, a bell of 1,000 pounds will have a frequency of 2x (and will therefore sound an octave higher), since the cube root of 1,000 (= 10) is half the cube root of 8,000 (= 20).

There are three chief ways of sounding bells: (a) chiming, in which a rope moves the bell just enough for the clapper to strike it; (b) ringing, in which the bell is swung round full circle, thus giving a more vigorous sound; (c) clocking, in which the clapper is moved instead of the bell—a method that should not be used since it is likely to cause the bell to crack. See also Carillon; *Campana;* Change ringing.

In the modern orchestra, real bells have been replaced by "tubular bells" (*chimes; see also Bells; Percussion instruments), i.e., a number of cylindrical metal tubes of different lengths, hung in a frame and struck with a hammer.

Bell harp. A sort of *psaltery invented *c.* 1700 by John Simcock. The name comes from the bell-shaped form of its frame.

Bell lyre. See under Glockenspiel.

Bell ringing. See Change ringing.

Belle Hélène, La [F., The Beautiful Helen]. Satirical comedy in three acts by Offenbach (libretto by H. Meilhac and L. Halévy), produced in Paris, 1864. Setting: ancient Greece.

Bellini, Vincenzo (b. Catania, Sicily, 3 Nov. 1801; d. Puteaux, near Paris, 24 Sept. 1835). Pupil of Zingarelli in Naples, where he also became acquainted with Donizetti and Mercadante. Composed operas (incl. *I Capuleti e i Montecchi,* Venice, 1830; *La *sonnambula; *Norma; I *Puritani,* for Paris at Rossini's suggestion); numerous sacred and secular vocal works and several instrumental works.

Bells. Recent name for the orchestral

glockenspiel or the chimes [see Percussion instruments].

Belly. The upper plate of the resonant box of violins, lutes, etc. Also called the table.

Bémol [F.]; **bemolle** [It.]; **bemol** [Sp.]. The flat sign [see Accidentals; also Pitch names]. In the 17th century it served also to indicate the minor mode, e.g., *mi bémol*, E minor.

Ben-Haim, Paul (b. Munich, 5 July 1897). Composer and conductor. Pupil of Klose. Left Munich for Palestine in 1933. Has made use of Jewish and Arabic folk materials. Works incl. symphonies and other orch. pieces; chamber music; piano pieces; a Friday evening service.

Benda, Georg (Jiří Antonín) (b. Altbenatek, Bohemia, 30 June 1722; d. Köstritz, 6 Nov. 1795). Member of a large musical family. Chamber musician at Berlin, 1742–49; *Kapellmeister* at the Gotha court, 1750–78 (with a visit to Italy, 1764 –66). Composed several *Singspiele* (incl. *Der Dorfjahrmarkt*, Gotha, 1775; *Romeo und Juliet*, Gotha, 1776); several melodramas (incl. *Ariadne auf Naxos*, 1775; *Medea*, 1775; *Pygmalion*, 1779); symphonies; concertos and sonatas for piano and other instruments; church music; secular cantatas; songs with piano accompaniment.

Benedicamus Domino [L.]. A salutation (Let us bless the Lord) of the Roman liturgy, with the response "Deo gratias." It is used, instead of the *Ite missa est*, in Masses lacking the Gloria (e.g., during Lent; cf. *LU*, pp. 22, 28, etc., with pp. 62–63). It is also sung at the end of all Offices, for which purpose various melodies (*toni*) are provided [*LU*, p. 124]. It was often set polyphonically during the Middle Ages.

Benedicite [L.]. The *canticle of the three children, "Benedicite, omnia opera Domini, Domino" (O all ye works of the Lord, bless ye the Lord; Dan. 3:57 –88, 56 of the Vulgate), sung at Lauds in the monastic Offices, and in the Anglican Morning Prayer.

Benedict, Julius (b. Stuttgart, 27 Nov. 1804; d. London, 5 June 1885). Pupil of Weber. Conducted theater orchestras in Vienna and Naples; music director of the Opera Buffa in London from 1836 and later of Her Majesty's Theatre and the Drury Lane Theatre. Concert director for Jenny Lind on her tour of the U.S., 1850–52. Composed operas (incl. *The Lily of Killarney*, London, 1862); cantatas; 2 symphonies; 2 piano concertos; other instrumental works. Published lives of Weber and Mendelssohn.

Benedictus Dominus Deus Israel [L.]. The *canticle of Zachary (Blessed be the Lord; Luke 1:68–79), sung at Lauds, in the monastic Offices, and in the Anglican Morning Prayer. Not to be confused with "Benedictus es, Domine Deus Israel," the canticle of David (I Chronicles 29:10 –13). The term Benedictus alone nearly always refers to *"Benedictus qui venit."

Benedictus qui venit [L.]. The second part of the Sanctus of the *Mass. In polyphonic compositions it is usually treated as a separate movement.

Benevoli, Orazio (b. Rome, 19 Apr. 1605; d. there, 17 June 1672). Pupil of Ugolini. *Maestro di cappella* at several Roman churches, including St. Peter's (1646– 72), and at the Vienna court (1644–46). Composed Masses (incl. a Mass for 12 choirs in 53 parts for the consecration of the Salzburg Cathedral in 1628); psalms for 10–24 voices, motets; other sacred vocal music.

Benjamin, Arthur (b. Sydney, 18 Sept. 1893; d. London, 9 Apr. 1960). Member of the faculty of the Royal College of Music, London, where Britten was among his students; conductor of the Vancouver Symphony Orchestra, 1941– 46. Composed operas (incl. *A Tale of Two Cities*, London, 1953; *The Devil Take Her*, London, 1931); a ballet, *Orlando's Silver Wedding*, 1951; orch. works (incl. *Jamaican Rumba*, 1938); numerous other instrumental works.

Bennet, John (b. Cheshire?, *c*. 1575; d. *c*. 1614). Composed a group of *Madrigalls to Foure Voyces;* 6 songs for Ravenscroft's *Briefe Discourse;* a contribution to *The Triumphes of Oriana*, "All creatures now are merry minded"; other vocal works.

Bennett, Richard Rodney (b. Broadstairs, Kent, 29 Mar. 1936). Pupil of Berkeley, Ferguson, and Boulez. Has employed serial techniques. Has composed operas (incl. *The Mines of Sulphur,* London, 1965; *Victory,* London, 1970); cantatas (incl. *The Approaches of Sleep,* 1959); orch. works (incl. 2 symphonies; *Aubade,* 1964); a concerto for horn and one for piano; violin pieces; flute pieces; piano pieces; guitar pieces (incl. a concerto with chamber ensemble); 4 string quartets; much music for films; other vocal and instrumental works (incl. *Calendar* for chamber ensemble, 1960).

Bennett, Robert Russell (b. Kansas City, Mo., 15 June 1894). Pupil of N. Boulanger. Active in orchestration of Broadway musicals and revues (incl. *My Fair Lady* and many others). Has composed several operas (incl. *Maria Malibran,* New York, 1935); numerous orch. works (incl. *Sights and Sounds,* 1929; *Abraham Lincoln Symphony,* 1931); choral works (incl. *Stephen Collins Foster* for orch. and chorus, 1959); band pieces; chamber music; piano pieces; songs; scores for musicals, films, and television.

Bennett, William Sterndale (b. Sheffield, 13 Apr. 1816; d. London, 1 Feb. 1875). Pianist, conductor, and composer. Pupil of Potter and close associate of Schumann and Mendelssohn. Conductor of the London Philharmonic Society, 1856–66; principal of the Royal Academy of Music from 1866. Composed *The Naiads,* 1836, and other overtures; 4 piano concertos; an oratorio, *The Woman of Samaria,* 1867; a cantata, *The May Queen,* 1858; piano pieces, chamber music; songs; other vocal and instrumental works.

Benoit, Peter (b. Harlebeke, Belgium, 17 Aug. 1834; d. Antwerp, 8 Mar. 1901). Pupil of Fétis at the Brussels Conservatory. Active in the development of a Flemish national music; founder (1867) and director of the Flemish Music School (later the Royal Flemish Conservatory). Composed operas (incl. *Isa,* Brussels, 1867; *Le roi des Aulnes,* Brussels, 1859); cantatas (incl. the *Rubens Cantata,* 1877); oratorios (incl. *Lucifer,* 1866; *De Waereld in,* 1878); church music; some instrumental music. Also published numerous writings on music.

Benson, Warren (b. Detroit, 26 Jan. 1924). Timpanist and composer. Self-taught in composition. Teacher at Ithaca College, 1953–67; at the Eastman School of Music from 1967. Has composed works for band; solo wind instruments and wind ensembles of various sizes; percussion instruments; chamber ensembles; chorus.

Bentzon, Jørgen (b. Copenhagen, 14 Feb. 1897; d. Hørsholm, 9 July 1951). Pupil of Nielsen and Karg-Elert; cousin of Niels Viggo Bentzon. Composed an opera; 2 symphonies; string quartets and other chamber music.

Bentzon, Niels Viggo (b. Copenhagen, 24 Aug. 1919). Pupil of Knud Jeppesen. Member of the faculty of the Royal Danish Conservatory from 1949. Has composed 10 symphonies; 4 piano concertos; *Meet the Danes,* 1964, and other orch. works; ballets (incl. *Metafor,* 1950); an oratorio; an opera, *Faust II,* Kiel, 1964; sonatas for violin, for cello, for horn; numerous piano sonatas and other piano works; 9 string quartets; film scores.

Bequadro [It.]. The natural sign. See Accidentals.

Berceuse [F.]. Lullaby. Usually the name refers to instrumental pieces (piano, orchestra) in moderate 6/8 time and with an accompaniment reminiscent of the rocking of a cradle. A famous example is Chopin's op. 57.

Berezowsky, Nicolai (b. St. Petersburg, 17 May 1900; d. New York, 27 Aug. 1953). Emigrated to New York in 1922; pupil of R. Goldmark. Violinist in the New York Philharmonic, 1923–29; member of the Coolidge Quartet of the Library of Congress, 1935–40. Composed 4 symphonies; concertos for several instruments, incl. violin, viola, cello, harp, clarinet; *Suite hebraïque,* 1928, and other works for orch.; chamber music; a cantata, *Gilgamesh,* 1947; a children's opera, *Babar the Elephant,* New York, 1953.

Berg, Alban (b. Vienna, 9 Feb. 1885; d. there, 24 Dec. 1935). Pupil of Schoenberg and closely associated with him and with Webern. Composed the operas **Wozzeck* and **Lulu;* a violin concerto, 1935; *3 Pieces* for orch., 1914; *5 Orches-*

tral Songs on Picture Postcard Texts of Peter Altenberg, 1912; *Der Wein* for soprano and orch., after Baudelaire, 1929; a string quartet, 1910; *Lyric Suite* for string quartet, 1926, parts of which he subsequently arranged for orch., 1928; *4 Pieces* for clarinet and piano, 1913; *Chamber Concerto* for piano, violin, and 13 winds, 1925; a piano sonata, 1908; songs.

Bergamasca. (1) A generic term for dances, dance-songs, and popular poetry from the district of Bergamo in northern Italy. Many compositions—even sophisticated ones—written in the 17th, 18th, and 19th centuries bear the title because of a real or fancied relationship to Bergamo.

(2) Late in the 16th century, the term was attached to pieces composed on repetitions of a specific harmonic pattern: I–IV–V–I. In the 17th century, hundreds of compositions, largely for the guitar, were written on that pattern. Early in the 17th century, a single discant began to be associated with it and in some cases supplanted the pattern itself.

Berger, Arthur (Victor) (b. New York, 15 May 1912). Music critic and composer. Pupil of Piston, Milhaud, and N. Boulanger. Member of the music faculty of Brandeis Univ. from 1953. Has composed a ballet, *Entertainment Piece*, 1940; *Ideas of Order* for orch., 1953; *Serenade Concertante* for violin, woodwind quartet, and small orch., 1945, rev. 1951; chamber music; piano pieces; songs.

Bergerette [F.]. (1) An 18th-century type of French lyric poetry with a pastoral or amorous subject [F. *berger*, shepherd]. (2) In the 15th century, a fixed form of French poetry and music, identical in structure with the *virelai but having only one stanza. (3) In the 16th century, a title (rarely used) for instrumental dances in quick triple time, similar to the *saltarello.

Bergsma, William (b. Oakland, Calif., 1 Apr. 1921). Pupil of Hanson and Bernard

Rogers. Member of the faculty of the Juilliard School of Music, 1946–63; director of the School of Music at the Univ. of Washington for several years from 1963. Has composed ballets (incl. *Paul Bunyan*, 1938); operas (incl. *The Wife of Martin Guerre*, New York, 1956); a symphony, 1949, and other works for orch.; choral symphonic poem, *A Carol on Twelfth Night*, 1953; *Confrontation* for chorus and instruments, 1963, and other choral works and songs; a violin concerto, 1965; piano works (incl. *Tangents*, 1951); 3 string quartets.

Berio, Luciano (b. Oneglia, Italy, 24 Oct. 1925). Pupil of Ghedini and Dallapiccola. Founded (1955) the Studio di fonologia musicale, Milan, for work on acoustics and electronic music; member of the faculty of the Juilliard School of Music from 1965. Has employed serial, electronic, and aleatory techniques. Has composed a ballet, *Mimomusique*, 1954; *Nones*, 1954, and other orch. works; *Differences* for 5 instruments and stereophonic tape, 1959; *Omaggio a Joyce*, on tape, 1958; *Circles* for soprano, harp, 2 percussion ensembles, poems by e. e. cummings, 1960; *Epiphanie* for soprano and orch., 1961; *Sinfonia* for reciters, chorus, and orch., 1968; other works for voices, electronic instruments, and various ensembles (incl. several for voice and for solo instruments titled *Sequenza*).

Berkeley, Lennox (Randal Francis) (b. Oxford, 12 May 1903). Pupil of N. Boulanger. Professor of composition at the Royal Academy of Music, London, 1946–68. Has composed operas (incl. *Nelson*, London, 1953); an oratorio, *Jonah*, 1935; *Domini est Terra* for chorus and orch., 1938; *4 Sonnets of Ronsard* for tenor and orch., 1963; a ballet, *The Judgement of Paris*, 1938; 3 symphonies and other orch. works; numerous piano works (incl. *6 Preludes*); 3 string quartets and other chamber music.

Berlin school. Collective designation for a group of composers, also known as *Norddeutsche* (North German) *Schule*, who worked in Berlin during the second half of the 18th century. Most of them were connected with the court of Frederick the Great (1712–86), who, with his numerous flute sonatas and other compositions, himself contributed actively to the musical life of his court. The most important members of the group were: J. J. Quantz (1697–1773), J. G. Graun (1703–71), K. H. Graun (1704–59), F. Benda (1709–86), K. P. E. Bach (1714–88), C. Nichelmann (1717–62), F. W. Marpurg (1718–95), J. P. Kirnberger (1721–83), and J. F. Agricola (1720–74). While these men, particularly K. P. E. Bach, made significant contributions in instrumental music, their activity in the field of the *lied (*Berliner Liederschule*) was less important. The situation changed when a younger generation, known as the *Zweite* (Second) *Berliner Liederschule,* turned to the poems of Klopstock and the young Goethe. J. A. P. Schulz (1747–1800), J. F. Reichardt (1752–1814), and C. F. Zelter (1758–1832) are the most important members of this group. The name *Berliner Schule* is sometimes restricted to this latter group.

Berlioz, Hector (-Louis) (b. La-Côte-Saint-André, Isère, 11 Dec. 1803; d. Paris, 8 Mar. 1869). Pupil of Lesueur and Reicha. Awarded the Prix de Rome on his third attempt, 1830. Librarian at the Paris Conservatory from 1839. Contributed articles on music to several journals; wrote his memoirs and a book on orchestration. Works: *Symphonie fantastique,* 1828–30, and its sequel the monodrama *Lélio,* 1831; *Harold en Italie* for viola and orch.; *Roméo et Juliette,* for vocal soloists, chorus, and orch.; *Symphonie funèbre et triomphale* for chorus and orch., 1840; the operas *Benvenuto Cellini,* Paris, 1838, *Les *troyens,* and *Béatrice et Bénédict,* Baden-Baden, 1862; a "dramatic legend" *La *damnation de Faust;* the overtures *Le *carnaval romain, Le corsaire, Les francs juges, Waverly, Le Roi Lear, Rob Roy;* the oratorio *L'*enfance du Christ,* a *Te Deum,* a Requiem, 1837, and other choral works; songs.

Bernardi, Steffano (b. Verona, last quarter of the 16th cent.; d. probably in or near Salzburg, before 1638). *Maestro di cappella* at the Verona Cathedral, 1611–22; at the Salzburg Cathedral, 1628–34. Composed numerous Masses; numerous madrigals; psalms; motets; instrumental works. Wrote a manual on counterpoint.

Berners, Lord (Gerald Hugh Tyrwhitt-Wilson) (b. Bridgnorth, England, 18 Sept. 1883; d. London, 19 Apr. 1950). Composer, painter, diplomat, and author. Largely self-taught, though he received some advice from Stravinsky and Casella. Composed an opera; ballets (incl. *The Triumph of Neptune,* 1926; *A Wedding Bouquet,* 1936); piano pieces; songs.

Bernhard, Christoph (b. Danzig, 1627; d. Dresden, 14 Nov. 1692). Pupil of Schütz and Carissimi. Assistant *Kapellmeister* in Dresden from 1655; cantor at Hamburg, succeeding Thomas Selle, 1664–74; *Kapellmeister* at Dresden, 1681–88. Composed Latin and German sacred works. Wrote treatises on composition and counterpoint.

Bernstein, Leonard (b. Lawrence, Mass., 25 Aug. 1918). Conductor and composer. Pupil of Piston, Hill, and Thompson. Conductor of the New York City Center Orchestra, 1945–48; of the New York Philharmonic, 1958–68. Has composed orch. works (incl. the *Jeremiah Symphony,* 1944; *The Age of Anxiety,* 1949; *Kaddish,* 1963; *Chichester Psalms* with countertenor and chorus, 1965); ballets (*Fancy Free,* 1944; *Facsimile,* 1946; *Dybbuk,* 1974); an opera, *Trouble in Tahiti,* Waltham, Mass., 1952; other stage works (incl. *Candide,* 1956, rev. 1973; *West Side Story,* 1957); *Mass* ("Theater Piece for Singers, Players, and Dancers"), 1971; film score to *On the Waterfront,* 1954; *Songfest* for vocal soloists and orch., 1977; chamber music; piano pieces; songs. Has published several books on music, incl. *The Joy of Music,* 1959, and *The Unanswered Question,* 1976.

Bersag horn. See under Brass instruments.

Berton, Henri-Montan (b. Paris, 17 Sept. 1767; d. there, 22 Apr. 1844). Pupil of Rey and Sacchini. Succeeded Méhul as professor of composition at the Paris Conservatory in 1818. Composed numerous operas (incl. *Aline, reine de Golconde,* 1803); oratorios; cantatas; ballets. Published theoretical works.

Berton, Pierre-Montan ("Le Breton") (b. Maubert-Fontaine, Ardennes, 7 Jan.

1727; d. Paris, 14 May 1780). Pupil of Le-clair. Conductor of the royal orchestra and the Opéra in Paris. Composed operas (incl. *Érosine*, 1765; *Silvie*, 1765; and *Théonis*, 1767, in collaboration with Trial); motets; additions to operas by Lully, Rameau, Gluck, and Campra.

Bertoni, Ferdinando (Gasparo) (b. Salò, near Venice, 15 Aug. 1725; d. Desen-zano, 1 Dec. 1813). Organist and com-poser. Pupil of Padre Martini. Choirmas-ter at the Ospedale dei mendicanti in Venice from 1755; succeeded Galuppi as *maestro di cappella* of San Marco in Venice, 1785. Composed numerous operas (incl. *Orfeo ed Euridice*, 1776); oratorios, cantatas, Masses, psalms, and other sacred vocal music; 6 harpsichord sonatas; chamber music.

Bertrand, Antoine de (b. *c*. 1540?; d. Toulouse, *c*. 1581). Belonged to the hu-manist circle around Cardinal d'Arma-gnac at Toulouse. Composed sacred and secular chansons (incl. settings of Ron-sard), some employing advanced chro-maticism and microtones.

Beruhigt, beruhigend [G.]. Calm, quiet-ing.

Berwald, Franz Adolf (b. Stockholm, 23 July 1796; d. there, 3 Apr. 1868). Violin-ist and composer. Musical director of the Univ. of Uppsala from 1849; member of the faculty of the Stockholm Academy, 1864–67, and of the Stockholm Conser-vatory, 1867–68. Composed operas (incl. *Estrella di Soria*, 1841, prod. Stockholm, 1862; *Drottningen av Gol-conda*, 1865); 6 symphonies (incl. *Sin-fonie sérieuse*, 1842; *Sinfonie capri-cieuse*, 1842; *Sinfonie singulière*, 1845); 5 cantatas; a violin concerto and a piano concerto; 3 string quartets, 5 piano trios, and other chamber music; many other choral and instrumental works.

Bes [G.]. B-double-flat. See Pitch names.

Bésard, Jean-Baptiste (b. Besançon, *c*. 1567; d. probably in southern Germany, *c*. 1625). Lutenist, physician, chemist, and composer. Published anthologies of lute works containing original composi-tions; a pedagogical treatise.

Beschleunigt [G.]. *Accelerando.

Besetzung [G.]. Setting, scoring, distri-bution of parts, e.g., *Besetzung für Chor und kleines Orchester* (setting for chorus and small orchestra).

Bestimmt [G.]. With decision.

Betont [G.]. Stressed, emphasized.

Bewegt [G.]. Animated, with motion.

Bezanson, Philip (b. Athol, Mass., 6 Jan. 1916). Pupil of D. S. Smith, Donovan, and Clapp. Teacher at the Univ. of Iowa, 1954–64, and at the Univ. of Massachu-setts at Amherst from 1964. Has com-posed an opera for television, *Golden Child*, 1960; a piano concerto and other orch. works; a string quartet and other chamber music; vocal works.

Bezifferter Bass [G.]. Figured bass, i.e., *thoroughbass.

Biber, Heinrich Ignaz Franz von (b. War-tenburg, Bohemia, 12 Aug. 1644; d. Salz-burg, 3 May 1704). Violinist and com-poser. Served the Emperor Leopold I; the Bavarian court; the Archbishop of Salzburg from 1763. A pioneer of *scor-datura for violin. Composed numerous violin sonatas; 2 operas; Masses and other sacred works.

Bicinium [L.]. A 16th-century name, used chiefly in Italy and Germany, for a composition (vocal or instrumental) in two parts. In contrast to some *duets, *bi-cinia* are without accompaniment. The Greek synonym *diphona* also has been used.

Bien nourri. See *Nourri*.

Billings, William (b. Boston, 7 Oct.? 1746; d. there, 26 Sept. 1800). A tanner's apprentice, largely self-taught in music. Singing master for lay groups in several Boston churches, incl. the Brattle Street Church and the Old South Church. Com-poser of hymns, anthems, and fugue tunes. Published 6 collections of his works (incl. *The New England Psalm Singer*, 1770; *The Singing Master's As-sistant*, 1776; *The Psalm Singer's Amusement*, 1781).

Billy Budd. Opera in four acts by Britten (libretto by E. M. Forster and E. Cro-zier, after the short novel by H. Mel-ville), produced in London, 1951. Set-ting: aboard *H.M.S. Indomitable*, 1797.

Bina. *Vīna.

Binary and ternary form. Two basic musical forms, consisting of two and three main sections, respectively. In a binary form, both main sections are repeated, and the first section characteristically ends in the dominant (or relative major, if the tonic is minor). Thus, the first section is not self-contained tonally but demands instead continuation and tonal resolution by the second part, which concludes in the tonic. The two sections may be of equal length, or the second may be distinctly longer. In the latter case, the return to the tonic in the second section may coincide with a return to the thematic material of the first section, the greater part of which may then be repeated in such a way as to remain entirely in the tonic. This is known as *rounded binary* form. Most of the dances in the suites of Bach and other composers of the baroque era are in binary form. The minuets, scherzos, and trios of the late 18th and 19th centuries are also usually binary forms, most often rounded. *Sonata form derives from rounded binary form.

In a ternary form (sometimes called *song form), the first and third sections are identical (or very nearly so), and they are self-contained tonally. That is, they begin and end in the tonic. This feature of the first section provides the crucial distinction between ternary form and rounded binary form (including sonata form). The second or middle section generally provides some element of tonal as well as thematic and textural contrast; it may or may not be a wholly self-sufficient musical entity. Examples of ternary form abound in the shorter works of the 19th century, e.g., the nocturnes of Chopin and the piano pieces of Brahms, and they are frequently found in the slow movements of sonatas, e.g., Beethoven, piano sonatas op. 7 and op. 2, no. 1. Taken as a whole, a minuet with trio or a scherzo with trio may also be regarded as a ternary form, since such movements conclude with a repetition of the minuet or scherzo after the trio, though when a minuet or scherzo is repeated after a trio each of its two component sections is played only once.

Binchois, Gilles (b. Mons, Hainaut, c.

1400; d. probably in or near Mons, late Sept. or early Oct. 1460). Served the Earl of Suffolk in Paris from 1424; Philip the Good of Burgundy from 1430. Composed numerous chansons; sacred works, incl. Masses, motets, Magnificats.

Bind. *Tie.

Biniou. See under Bagpipe.

Binkerd, Gordon (b. Lynch, Nebr., 22 May 1916). Pupil of Bernard Rogers and Piston. Member of the faculty of the Univ. of Illinois, 1949–71. Has composed 4 symphonies; *A Christmas Carol* and other choral works; piano pieces; string quartets and other chamber music; songs.

Birtwistle, Harrison (b. Accrington, Lancashire, 15 July 1934). Associated with Davies in the Manchester New Music Group and the chamber ensemble Pierrot Players (reorganized as The Fires of London). Composed *Refrains and Choruses* for wind quintet, 1957; works for orch. (incl. *Chorales,* 1963; *The Triumph of Time,* 1970); *Punch and Judy,* chamber opera, Edinburgh, 1968; *Tragoedia* for winds, strings, and harp, 1965; other works for voices and various ensembles.

Bis [L., twice]. (1) In French and Italian, request for *encore. (2) Indication that notes or passages should be repeated.

Bisbigliando [It., whispering]. A special effect of harp playing, obtained by a quickly reiterated motion of the finger and resulting in a soft tremolo.

Biscroma [It.]. Thirty-second note. See Notes.

Bisdiapason [L.]. The interval or range of two octaves.

Bishop, Henry Rowley (b. London, 18 Nov. 1786; d. there, 30 Apr. 1855). Served in several conducting positions in London, including the Ancient Concerts, 1840–48. Professor of music at Oxford Univ., 1848–53. Composed numerous operas (incl. *Clari, or the Maid of Milan,* London, 1823, containing "Home Sweet Home"); farces; ballets; oratorios; cantatas; several pasticcios after Shakespeare (incl. *A Midsummer Night's*

Dream); arrangements of and additions to others' operas; songs, glees, and other vocal works.

Bitonality, polytonality. The simultaneous use of two (occasionally three or four) different keys in different parts of the musical fabric. This device has been used considerably by 20th-century composers, sometimes with humorous intentions. The combination of C and F♯ triads has become known as the "Petrushka chord" because it occurs in Stravinsky's *Petrushka*, composed in 1911. The main champion of bitonal music has been Darius Milhaud, who also occasionally used three or four keys simultaneously.

Biwa. The Japanese lute. For ill. see Lute.

Bizet, Georges (Alexandre-César-Léopold) (b. Paris, 25 Oct. 1838; d. Bougival, 3 June 1875). Pupil of Halévy. Composed several operas (incl. **Carmen; Les *pêcheurs de perles; Ivan le terrible,* 1865; *Djamileh,* Paris, 1872); incidental music for *L'*arlésienne;* several orch. works (incl. a Symphony in C, 1855; *Roma,* 1868); choral works; numerous piano pieces (incl. *Jeux d'enfants* for 4 hands, 1871); songs.

Bkl. [G.]. Abbr. for *Bassklarinette,* bass clarinet. See Clarinet family.

Blacher, Boris (b. Newchwang [now Yingkow], China, of German-Russian parents, 6 Jan. 1903; d. Berlin, 30 Jan. 1975). Member of the faculty of the Hochschule für Musik in West Berlin from 1945, and its director, 1953–70. Developed a system of variable meters. Composed operas (incl. *Fürstin Tarakanowa,* Wuppertal, 1941; *Abstrakte Oper,* Frankfurt, 1953; *Rosamunde floris,* Berlin, 1960); ballets; incidental music for theater, film, and radio; orch. works (incl. *Concertante Musik,* 1937, and 3 piano concertos); chamber works (incl. *Jazzkoloraturen,* 1929); piano pieces; songs.

Black-key Etude. Chopin's Etude for piano op. 10, no. 5, in G♭ major, in which the right hand plays only on the black keys.

Blackwood, Easley (b. Indianapolis, 21

Apr. 1933). Pianist and composer. Pupil of Messiaen, Hindemith, and N. Boulanger. Member of the faculty of the Univ. of Chicago from 1958. Has composed 3 symphonies; *Chamber Symphony,* 1955; concertos for clarinet, for violin, for flute, for piano; 2 string quartets and other chamber music; works for piano.

Bladder pipe [G. *Platerspiel*]. See under Bagpipe.

Blanche [F.]. Half note. See Notes.

Blasinstrument [G.]. Wind instrument. *Blasmusik,* music for wind instruments.

Blatt [G.]. Sheet; also, reed (**Rohrblatt*). *Blattspiel,* sight reading.

Blech [G.]. Brass, used as a collective designation for *Blechinstrumente,* i.e., brass instruments. *Blechmusik,* music for brass bands.

Blech, Leo (b. Aachen, 21 Apr. 1871; d. Berlin, 24 Aug. 1958). Conductor and composer. Pupil of Humperdinck. Conductor at the Berlin Opera, 1906–23 and 1926–36; in Riga, 1938–41; in Stockholm 1941–49. Composed operas (incl. *Das war ich,* Dresden, 1902; *Versiegelt,* Hamburg, 1908; the fairy tale opera *Alpenkönig und Menschenfeind,* Dresden, 1903, rewritten as *Rappelkopf,* Berlin, 1917); symphonic poems; choral works; piano pieces; songs.

Blind octaves. A device of piano virtuosity. The two hands alternate rapidly with octaves, the passage (usually a trill or a scale) being played with the thumbs and doubled by the little fingers alternately in the higher and lower octave.

Bliss, Arthur (b. London, 2 Aug. 1891; d. there, 27 Mar. 1975). Pupil of Stanford, Vaughan Williams, and Holst. Succeeded Arnold Bax as Master of the Queen's Music. Composed *Rout* for soprano and chamber orch.; an opera, *The Olympians,* London, 1949; cantatas; ballets (incl. *Checkmate,* 1937; *Miracle in*

the Gorbals, 1944; *Adam Zero,* 1946); score for the H. G. Wells film *The Shape of Things to Come;* orch. works (incl. *A Colour Symphony,* 1922, rev. 1932); a piano concerto, 1938; chamber music; piano pieces; songs.

Blitzstein, Marc (b. Philadelphia, 2 Mar. 1905; d. Fort-de-France, Martinique, 22 Jan. 1964). Pupil of Scalero, Schoenberg, and N. Boulanger. Composed operas (incl. *The Cradle Will Rock,* New York, 1937; *No for an Answer,* New York, 1941; *Regina,* Boston, 1949); vocal works (incl. a cantata, *This Is the Garden,* 1957); orch. works (incl. *Airborne Symphony,* 1945; *Freedom Morning,* 1943); chamber music; film scores; an adaptation of the Brecht-Weill *Three-Penny Opera,* 1952.

Bloch, Ernest (b. Geneva, 24 July 1880; d. Portland, Ore., 15 July 1959). Pupil of Jaques-Dalcroze, Ysaÿe, I. Knorr, and Thuille. Conductor and teacher in Geneva, 1904–15; director of the Cleveland Institute of Music, 1920–25; of the San Francisco Conservatory, 1925–30. Settled in Oregon in 1941 and taught summer courses at the Univ. of California at Berkeley until 1952. His pupils incl. Sessions, Porter, Jacobi, Freed, Stevens, and Bernard Rogers. Composed operas (incl. **Macbeth*); *Concerto Grosso* no. 1, 1925, no. 2, 1953; symphonic poems *Hiver-Printemps,* 1905, and *America,* 1926; *Israel,* a symphony, 1912–17; a violin concerto, 1938; *Schelomo,* a rhapsody for cello and orch., 1916; other orch. works; chamber music; piano works; *Avodath Hakodesh,* sacred service for Reformed Temple, 1933.

Block harmony. A succession of identical or similar chords, e.g., parallel triads or seventh chords. See Parallel chords.

Blockflöte [G.]. Block flute, i.e., **recorder. See also under Whistle flute.

Blockx, Jan (b. Antwerp, 25 Jan., 1851; d. there, 26 May 1912). Pupil of Benoit. Member of the faculty of the Antwerp Conservatory from 1886; succeeded Benoit as director of the Royal Flemish Conservatory, 1901. Composed operas (incl. *Herbergprinses,* Antwerp, 1896, performed in French as *Princesse d'Auberge; De Bruid der Zee,* Antwerp, 1901

[*F. La fiancée de la mer*]); a ballet, *Milenka,* 1886; cantatas (incl. *Op den stroom,* 1875); oratorios; orch. works (incl. *Rubens,* 1877); chamber music; piano pieces; songs.

Blomdahl, Karl-Birger (b. Växjö, Sweden, 19 Oct. 1916; d. Kungsängen, 14 June 1968). Pupil of Rosenberg. Member of the faculty of the Royal Academy of Music, Stockholm; 1960–64. Composed operas (incl. *Aniara,* Stockholm, 1959; *Herr von Hancken,* Stockholm, 1965); 3 symphonies; *Sisyphos,* 1954, and *Forma ferritonans,* 1961, for orch.; *Anabase,* 1956, and *I speglarnas sal,* 1952, for orch. and voices; *Altisonans,* 1966, on tape; chamber music.

Blow, John (b. Nottinghamshire, bapt. 23 Feb. 1649; d. Westminster, London, 1 Oct. 1708). Organist at Westminster Abbey, 1668–79, succeeded by his pupil Purcell; returned to the post after Purcell's death, from 1695 to his own death. Master of the children in the Chapel Royal and composer for the King's Private Musick from 1674; master of the choristers at St. Paul's Cathedral, 1687–1703. Composed the masque *Venus and Adonis,* 1684 or 1685; choral odes (incl. *Ode for St. Cecilia; Ode on the Death of Purcell*); numerous anthems; Anglican services; songs; harpsichord pieces.

Blue notes. See Blues.

Bluebeard's Castle [Hung. *A Kékszakállú Herceg Vára*]. Opera in one act by Bartók (libretto by B. Balázs after Maeterlinck), produced in Budapest, 1918. Setting: hall in Bluebeard's castle.

Blues. Most often, a type of jazz based on a repeated harmonic progression consisting of twelve measures of 4/4 time in which measures 1–4 are on the tonic, measures 5–8 on the subdominant, measures 9–10 on the dominant, and measures 11–12 on the tonic. Although its origins among American Negroes around 1900 and before are vocal, the blues can be either vocal or strictly instrumental. Often, though not always, the tempo is moderate or slow, in keeping with the sad or resigned character of many of the sung texts. The texts frequently consist of two statements, the first of which accompanies measures 1–4 and is repeated for measures 5–8. The melodies accompanying the harmonic progression make frequent use of the lowered third and seventh degrees (called *blue notes*), and like other pitches employed, these may be inflected in ways that do not conform to equal temperament. Similarly, the basic harmonic structure may be elaborated upon by means of secondary dominants and the like. Thus, the lowered seventh in the melody often occurs as an element of a seventh chord on the tonic in measure 4, which chord functions as the dominant seventh of the subdominant of measure 5. Published blues occur as early as 1912 with W. C. Handy's *Memphis Blues*. But a substantial part of the tradition is improvisatory. Ma Rainey, Bessie Smith, and Huddie Leadbelly Ledbetter were among the important early exponents of this tradition.

From this particular type of musical structure, the term has been extended to apply to the general style of performance with which it is associated and to the dejected state of mind frequently expressed in its texts. Early uses of the term are also not restricted to the type described above.

Blumen [G.]. The *coloraturas of *Meistersinger.

Boatwright, Howard (b. Newport News, Va., 16 Mar. 1918). Violinist and composer. Pupil of Hindemith. Teacher at Yale Univ., and music director of St. Thomas's Church in New Haven, 1949–64. Member of the faculty of Syracuse Univ. from 1964. Has composed orch. works; sacred music; choral works; songs and other works for voice and instruments; chamber music.

Bocal [F.]. Mouthpiece of a brass instrument.

Bocca chiusa [It.]. Same as *bouche fermée. Bocca ridente* (laughing mouth) indicates, in singing, a smiling position of the lips.

Boccherini, Luigi (b. Lucca, 19 Feb. 1743; d. Madrid, 28 May 1805). Cellist and composer. Chamber composer to the Infante Luís in Madrid, 1769–85; thereafter to King Carlos III in Madrid and simultaneously to Friedrich Wilhelm II of Prussia. Composed 2 operas; sacred and secular cantatas; oratorios; a Mass; chamber symphonies; hundreds of string trios, quartets, and quintets; violin sonatas; cello concertos.

Boehm. See Böhm system.

Boëllmann, Léon (b. Ensisheim, Alsace, 25 Sept. 1862; d. Paris, 11 Oct. 1897). Organist and composer. Pupil of Gigout. Composed *Variations symphoniques* for cello and orch.; a symphony; several piano works; a cello sonata; numerous organ works (incl. *Suite gothique* and the collection *Heures mystiques*); other sacred and secular instrumental and vocal works.

Boëly, Alexandre-Pierre-François (b. Versailles, 19 Apr. 1785; d. Paris, 27 Dec. 1858). Organist and composer. Held several positions as church organist in Paris. Influenced Franck and Saint-Saëns. Composed numerous piano and organ works.

Bogen [G.]. (1) The bow of a violin, etc. (2) The *tie. *Bogenführung*, bowing. For *Bogenklavier, Bogenflügel*, see Sostenente piano.

Bogenform [G.]. Bow form or arch form, i.e., a form with an approximately symmetrical shape such as A B A or A B C B A.

Bohème, La. Opera in four acts by Puccini (libretto by G. Giacosa and L. Illica, based on H. Mürger's novel *Scènes de la vie de Bohème*), produced in Turin, 1896. Setting: Latin Quarter, Paris, 1830. One of the best-known examples of *verismo.

Böhm, Georg (b. Hohenkirchen, Thuringia, 2 Sept. 1661; d. Lüneburg, 18 May 1733). Organist at the Johanneskirche in Lüneburg from 1698. Composed sacred and secular vocal music; works for harpsichord and for organ, incl. suites, partitas, preludes, and fugues.

Böhm system. A system of keying a woodwind instrument that allows the holes to be cut in the proper acoustical position and size and yet be within the spread of the average hand. It was invented about 1830 by the flutist Theobald Böhm (1794–1881) of Munich to supersede earlier methods of keying, in which the holes were not placed exactly from the acoustical point of view but in a sort of compromise position, with greater regard for the hand than for the ear. In spite of its complicated mechanism or action and the fact that it detracts slightly from the tonal quality of the instrument, it has been universally adopted in the manufacture of flutes and has also been applied to oboes, clarinets, and (to a lesser extent) bassoons.

Boieldieu, François-Adrien (b. Rouen, 16 Dec. 1775; d. Jarcy, near Grosbois, 8 Oct. 1834). Pupil of Broche, whose assistant organist he became at the church of Saint-André in Rouen, 1790. Professor at the Paris Conservatory, first of piano, 1798–1803, then of composition, 1817–26; in the interval, served as music director and opera composer for the imperial court at St. Petersburg. Composed numerous operas (incl. *La *dame blanche; Le calife de Bagdad,* Paris, 1800; *La jeune femme colère,* St. Petersburg, 1805; *La fille coupable,* Rouen, 1793; *Ma tante Aurore,* Paris, 1803; *Beniowsky,* Paris, 1800; *Jean de Paris,* Paris, 1812); songs; instrumental works, incl. a harp concerto.

Bois [F.]. Wood. The woodwinds [see Wind instruments].

Boismortier, Joseph Bodin de (b. Thionville, Moselle, 23 Dec. 1689; d. Roissy-en-Brie, 28 Oct. 1755). Spent his youth in Metz; in Perpignan, 1720–22; settled in Paris in 1724. Composed 3 operas (incl. *Don Quichotte chez la duchesse,* 1743); oratorios; motets; secular cantatas; numerous flute sonatas; suites for the musette; other chamber works.

Boîte à musique [F.]. Music box; see under Mechanical instruments. Also, title of pieces imitating the high notes and mechanical motion of a music box.

Boito, Arrigo (b. Padua, 24 Feb. 1842; d. Milan, 10 June 1918). Poet and composer. Studied at the Milan Conservatory. Composed 2 cantatas in collaboration with Faccio; the operas *Mefistofele,* Milan, 1868, and *Nerone,* begun in 1862, unfinished; *La luna diffonde* for 4-part chorus and orch.; *Ode all'arte;* libretti for several operas, incl. Verdi's *Otello* and *Falstaff,* Ponchielli's *Gioconda,*

Faccio's *Amleto;* translations into Italian of several operas, incl. Wagner's *Tristan* and Weber's *Freischütz.* Also published several volumes of poetry; novels; critical articles on theater and music.

Bolcom, William (Elden) (b. Seattle, 26 May 1938). Pianist and composer. Pupil of McKay, Verrall, Milhaud, Rivier, Messiaen, L. Smith. Teacher at the Univ. of Michigan from 1973. A leader in the revival of American popular music of around 1900. Has employed a wide range of techniques and materials including serialism, electronic means, popular music, and improvisation. Works incl. *Dynamite Tonight,* a pop opera, New York, 1963; *Open House* for tenor and chamber orch., 1975; string quartets and other chamber music; piano pieces.

Bolero. A Spanish dance said to have been invented by Sebastián Cerezo, a celebrated dancer of Cádiz, about 1780. Danced by one dancer or a couple, it includes many brilliant and intricate steps, quick movements such as the *entrechat* of classical ballet, and a sudden stop in a characteristic position with one arm held arched over the head (*bien parado*). The music, which employs castanets, is in moderate triple time with rhythms such as those in the accompanying figure. Particularly famous are Chopin's *Bolero* op. 19 for piano and Ravel's *Bolero* for orchestra (1927).

The Cuban bolero is in 2/4 meter, and its most characteristic rhythmic pattern is:

In a moderate or slow tempo, this rhythm is employed in a great deal of Latin American popular music with sentimental texts.

Bologna school. A group of 17th-century instrumental composers who were active in Bologna. Among its members are M. Cazzati (*c.* 1620–77, G. B. Vitali (1632–92), G. B. Bassani (*c.* 1657–1716), G. Torelli (1658–1709), and T. A. Vitali

(1663–1745). The Bologna school was important in the formal development of the trio sonata, solo violin sonata, solo cello sonata, *concerto grosso*, and violin concerto. The most illustrious proponent of the Bologna style was Arcangelo Corelli (1653–1713), who studied and worked at Bologna from 1666 until 1671. The designation "detto il bolognese" appears in his op. 1 (1681) and op. 2 (1685).

Bombarde [F.]; **bombarda** [It.]. (1) Names for the shawm, particularly the bass size of this instrument. In Germany, such corruptions as *Bomhart, Pomhart, Pumhart,* and *Pommer* were used. See Oboe family III. (2) Same as the bombardon [see Brass instruments II (e)]. (3) An organ stop of the solo-reed type [see Organ].

Bombardon. See under Brass instruments II (e).

Bonang. A family of instruments used in Javanese music. There are three sizes, each consisting of a double row of kettles suspended on crossed cords.

Bongos. A pair of small Afro-Cuban drums of differing pitch, fixed to one another, and played with the hands.

Bononcini, Antonio Maria (b. Modena, 18 June 1677; d. there, 8 July 1726). Son and pupil of Giovanni Maria Bononcini and brother of Giovanni Bononcini. Served at the Austrian court, 1704–11, after which he returned to Italy. Composed numerous operas (incl. *Il trionfo di Camilla, regina dei Volsci,* Naples, 1696); oratorios; sacred vocal music.

Bononcini, Giovanni (b. Modena, 18 July 1670; d. Vienna, 9 July 1747). Pupil of his father, Giovanni Maria Bononcini, and of Colonna; brother of Antonio Maria Bononcini. Cellist and composer. Composer to the Viennese court, 1700–11. From 1720, a member of the Royal Academy of Music, London, where he became the rival of Handel, its director. After being shamed in a plagiarism scandal, he withdrew to Paris in 1733 and later to Vienna. Composed numerous operas (incl. *Astarto,* London, 1720; *Astianatte,* London, 1727; the second act of *Muzio Scevola,* the third act being by Handel, London, 1721); oratorios; sere-

natas; chamber works; sacred vocal and instrumental works.

Bononcini, Giovanni Maria (b. Modena, 23 Sept. 1642; d. there, 19 Oct. 1678). Pupil of Uccellini and Colonna. Father of Giovanni and Antonio Maria Bononcini. Violinist and *maestro di cappella* in Bologna and Modena. Composed sets of instrumental works, incl. trio sonatas and dances for varying numbers of instruments; cantatas, madrigals, and other vocal works. Also published a treatise, *Musico prattico,* 1673.

Bonporti, Francesco Antonio (b. Trento, bapt. 11 June 1672; d. Padua, 19 Dec. 1749). Pupil of Corelli. A cleric at the Cathedral of Trento until 1740. Composed numerous chamber works, incl. sonatas for violin and thoroughbass, trio sonatas, dances, *Invenzioni* for violin, motets for soprano, violin, and thoroughbass.

Boogie-woogie. Originally, a special type of piano *blues, first heard in Chicago in the early 1920s. It was revived about 1935, becoming very popular for a number of years. This type of playing is characterized by a constantly repeated bass figure, usually sharply rhythmic, against which the right hand rhapsodizes freely.

Boone, Charles (b. Cleveland, 21 June 1939). Pupil of Krenek and Weiss. Associate of the San Francisco Composers' Forum and the Mills College Performing Group and Tape Music Center. Has composed works for orch.; small ensembles; solo flute; solo clarinet; electronic instruments.

Bordun [G.]; **bordone** [It.]. See *Bourdon.*

Borea [L., It.]; **boree, borre, borry** [O. Eng.]. See Bourrée.

Boris Godunov. Opera in four acts by Mussorgsky (libretto by Mussorgsky after Pushkin's play and Karamzin's *History of the Russian State*), first version composed 1868–69, rev. version produced in St. Petersburg, 1874; rev. by Rimsky-Korsakov, 1896, 1908. Setting: Russia and Poland, 1598–1605.

Bořkovec, Pavel (b. Prague, 10 June 1894; d. there, 22 July 1972). Pupil of Křička, Foerster, and Suk. Professor at the Academy of Musical Art in Prague, 1946–64. Composed operas; a ballet,

The Pied Piper, 1939; 3 symphonies, 2 piano concertos, and other orch. works (incl. *Start*, 1929); 4 string quartets and other chamber works; songs.

Borodin, Alexander Porfirievich (b. St. Petersburg, 12 Nov. 1833; d. there, 28 Feb. 1887). Chemist and composer. Student at the Academy of Medicine in St. Petersburg, 1850–58; professor there from 1864. Associate of Balakirev, Stasov, and Mussorgsky; one of The *Five. Composed the operas *Bogatyry*, Moscow, 1867, and *Prince Igor*; 3 symphonies (the 3rd unfinished); symphonic sketch, *In the Steppes of Central Asia*, 1880; chamber music, incl. 2 string quartets; piano pieces; songs.

Borowski, Felix (b. Burton, England, 10 Mar. 1872; d. Chicago, 6 Sept. 1956). Critic and composer. On the faculty of the Chicago Musical College, 1897–1925, and its president from 1916; professor of musicology at Northwestern Univ., 1937–42. Music editor for the *Chicago Sun* from 1942. Composed the ballet *A Century of the Dance*, 1934; 2 ballet-pantomimes; the opera *Fernando del Nonsensico*, 1935; 3 symphonies and several symphonic poems; chamber music; songs.

Bortniansky, Dmitri Stepanovich (b. Glukhov, Ukraine, 1751; d. St. Petersburg, 10 Oct. 1825). Pupil of Galuppi. Director of vocal music at the St. Petersburg court chapel from 1796; active in reforming singing standards. Composed Italian and French operas; numerous sacred choral works, incl. a Mass according to the Orthodox rite.

Boskovich, Alexander Urija (b. Cluj, Transylvania, 16 Aug. 1907; d. Tel Aviv, 6 Nov. 1964). Pianist, conductor, and composer. Studied at the Vienna Academy of Music and with Dukas and N. Boulanger. Settled in Palestine in 1938. Teacher at the Academy of Music in Tel Aviv, 1945–64. Music critic for the newspaper *Ha'aretz*, 1955–64. Worked with Jewish sacred and folk materials and with serial techniques. Composed orch. works (incl. *Semitic Suite*, 1947); concertos for violin and for oboe; choral works (incl. the cantata *Daughter of Israel*, 1960); chamber music (incl. *Concerto da camera*, 1962).

Bossi, (Marco) Enrico (b. Salò, Brescia, 25 Apr. 1861; d. at sea, en route from the U.S. to Italy, 20 Feb. 1925). Organist, pianist, and composer. Pupil of his father, Pietro Bossi, and of Ponchielli. *Maestro di cappella* at the Como Cathedral, 1881–89; teacher in music schools in Naples, Venice, Bologna, and Rome, 1889–1923. Composed operas; orch. works (incl. *Tema e variazioni*); choral works (incl. *Canticum canticorum; Il Cieco; Il Paradiso perduto; Giovanna d'Arco*); organ pieces; piano pieces; sacred vocal music; chamber music.

Bossi, Renzo (b. Como, 9 Apr. 1883; d. Milan, 2 Apr. 1965). Son of Enrico Bossi. Conductor and composer. Composed operas (incl. *Volpino il calderaio*, after Shakespeare's *Taming of the Shrew*, Milan, 1925); ballets; orch. works (incl. *Pinocchio*); chamber music.

Boston, valse Boston. A term hardly known in America but widely used in Europe (particularly Germany) during the period after World War I for the hesitation waltz, a slow waltz with a sophisticated rhythm, characterized by the frequent suppression of single beats or entire measures in the accompaniment. In postwar Germany it acquired a prominent position as an American importation and was imbued with jazzlike elements. Numerous composers have written Bostons, e.g., Hindemith (1st String Quartet; *1922 Suite für Klavier*); Louis Gruenberg (*Jazzberries*, 1925); Conrad Beck (*Zwei Tanzstücke*, 1929).

Bottesini, Giovanni (b. Crema, 22 Dec. 1821; d. Parma, 7 July 1889). Double-bass virtuoso, conductor, and composer. Toured Cuba, the U.S., England, France, Russia, Germany, Spain, Portugal, Mexico, and Scandinavia as instrumentalist and conductor. Composed operas (incl. *Cristoforo Colombo*, Havana, 1847; *Ero e Leandro*, Turin, 1879); an oratorio, *Gethsemane*, 1887; symphonies and other orch. works; pieces for double bass; chamber music; songs.

Bouché [F.]. See under Horn.

Bouche fermée [F.]; **bocca chiusa** [It.]. Singing without words and with closed mouth or, at least, closed teeth.

Boucourechliev, André (b. Sofia, 28 July

1925). Critic and composer. Studied in Bulgaria, Germany, and France, where he settled. Has been associated with the Studio di fonologia in Milan and the Groupe de recherches musicales of the French Radio. Has composed some works on tape and some employing aleatory procedures in the creation of mobile or open forms (incl. 4 titled *Archipel*).

Bouffons [F.]. In the 15th and 16th centuries, costumed dancers performing the *moresca*. For *Querelle (Guerre) des bouffons*, see War of the Buffons.

Boughton, Rutland (b. Aylesbury, 23 Jan. 1878; d. London, 24 Jan. 1960). Pupil of Stanford and H. W. Davies. Organized stage festivals at Glastonbury to pursue Wagnerian ideals of the universality of the arts. Composed operas (incl. *The Immortal Hour*, Glastonbury, 1914); *Bethlehem*, a choral drama, 1915; orch. and chamber works. Published several writings on music, incl. *Music Drama of the Future*.

Boulanger, Lili (Marie-Juliette) (b. Paris, 21 Aug. 1893; d. Mézy, near Paris, 15 Mar. 1918). Sister of Nadia Boulanger. The first woman to be awarded the Grand Prix de Rome (1913). Composed choral works with orch.; symphonic poems; incidental music to Maeterlinck's *La princesse Maleine;* chamber music; songs (incl. "Pie Jesu").

Boulanger, Nadia (b. Paris, 16 Sept. 1887). Teacher of composers, conductor, and composer. Pupil of Fauré and Widor. Member of the faculty of the École normale de musique in Paris, 1920 –39; of the American Conservatory in Fontainebleau, 1921–50, and its director from 1950. Her pupils incl. Carter, Copland, Harris, Piston, and many other well-known American and European composers. Works incl. *Rhapsodie* for piano and orch.; *La ville morte,* after d'Annunzio; a cantata, *La sirène* (2nd Prix de Rome, 1908).

Boulez, Pierre (b. Montbrison, 26 Mar. 1925). Conductor and composer. Pupil of Messiaen and Leibowitz. Has served as conductor and composer at the Théâtre Marigny, where he also founded the Domaine musical, a concert series devoted to new music; permanent guest conductor of the Cleveland Orchestra; chief conductor of the B.B.C. Orchestra; music director of the New York Philharmonic, 1971–77. Founder and director of the Institut de recherche et de coordination acoustique/musique, established in Paris in 1977. A leader in developing and promoting techniques of total serialism, but subsequently made some use of aleatory procedures. Works incl. *Polyphonie X* for 18 instruments, 1951, rev. 1978; 3 piano sonatas, 1946, 1948, 1957; *Le *marteau sans maître* for alto and 6 instruments, 1955; *Poésie pour pouvoir* for tape and 3 orchestras, 1958; *Structures I* and *II* for 2 pianos, 1952 and 1961; *Sonatine* for flute and piano, 1946; *Pli selon pli* for soprano and orch. on texts by Mallarmé, 1957–62; *Éclat* for orch., 1965–71; *Livre pour quatuor* for string quartet, 1949, later rev. for string orch. as *Livre pour cordes*, 1969; *Rituel* for orch., 1975.

Bourdon [F.]. Generally, a low note of long duration, i.e., a drone or pedal point. As early as *c.* 1280 the medieval Latin term *burdo* was used for the sustained tenor tones of the organum duplum [see under Organum]. The term was also applied to instrumental devices producing such tones, e.g., to the low-pitched bass-courses of the *vielle* and *hurdy-gurdy, which could be sounded continuously against a melody played on the higher strings, to the large pipes of the organ, or to the drones of the bagpipe. In French 17th-century music, the name *bourdon* is given to uniform bass accompaniments similar to that of the drones of a bagpipe, e.g., C–g–c–g C–g –c–g.

Bourgault-Ducoudray, Louis-Albert (b. Nantes, 2 Feb. 1840; d. Vernouillet, 4 July 1910). Pupil of Ambroise Thomas. Professor of music history at the Paris Conservatory, 1878–1908. Composed operas (incl. *Thamara*, Paris, 1891); orch. works; vocal works (incl. a cantata, *Louise de Mezières,* 1862); piano pieces; numerous songs. Collected and published folksongs from Greece, France, and England.

Bourgeois, Loys (Louis) (b. Paris, *c.* 1510; d. there?, *c.* 1561?). Lived in Geneva, 1541–57, where, as a follower of

Calvin, he composed or adapted tunes for all but the last 40 of the psalms in the Geneva Psalter and harmonized some of them. The texts of the psalms were translated into French by Marot and Bèze. He also composed several chansons and published a treatise, *Le droict chemin de musique,* 1550, on solmization.

Bourrée [F.]. A French 17th-century dance, probably from Auvergne, usually in quick duple meter with a single upbeat. Lully used it in his ballets and operas, whence it was transferred to the *suites of the late 17th and early 18th centuries (Pachelbel, J. K. F. Fischer, J. S. Bach).

Boutade [F.]. A dance or ballet in a capricious style. The name is also used for 18th-century instrumental pieces of a similar nature.

Bow [F. *archet;* G. *Bogen;* It. *arco, archetto;* Sp. *arco*]. An implement used in playing the violin and related instruments, consisting of a stick to which horse hair has been attached in such a way that the hair can be drawn across the strings of the instrument so as to produce sound [see also Rosin]. The bow was given its classical and present form by François Tourte (1747–1835). The most important characteristics of his bow [see ill.] are the long, tapering, and slightly inward curving stick, the use of metal or ivory plates for the head (the head serving to hold the hair away from the stick), the use (not for the first time, however) of Pernambuco wood for the stick, careful measurements designed to achieve balance, and the metal ferrule of the frog through which the hair passes evenly spread (though this last invention has also been attributed to Tourte's contemporary John Dodd). The modern violin bow is normally 29 1/2 inches long, with 25 1/2 inches of free hair. Bows for the cello and double bass are shorter.

In the course of the 16th century, the shape of the stick, which at first often resembled the hunting bow in curving distinctly outward from the hair (as do many non-Western bows), became straighter, and in this and the following centuries it became longer as well. The straightening of the stick made necessary

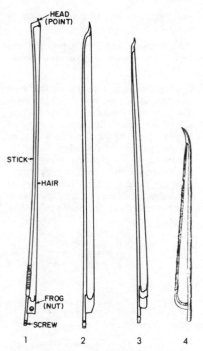

Bows: 1. Tourte, c. 1800. 2. Thomas Smith, 1760–70. 3. Anonymous, 1694. 4. Marin Mersenne, Harmonie universelle, 1635.

the creation of a horn-shaped frog and, subsequently, a distinct head to hold the hair away from the stick. Movable frogs for adjusting the tension of the hair by means of a screw mechanism, as on the modern bow, were first introduced around 1700. In the decades preceding that, this purpose was sometimes served by a metal catch on the frog that could be engaged in one or another of a set of teeth (dentated or *crémaillère* bow). Although throughout the 17th and 18th centuries the stick was either very nearly straight or curved outward from the hair, there is no reason to suppose that it was possible to release the tension on the hair enough to permit playing on all strings of the violin at once, as has sometimes been suggested.

In France until about 1750, it was common to hold the bow with the thumb on the hair next to the frog. The Italian grip, which ultimately prevailed everywhere, held the stick itself between the thumb and fingers at the frog (or sometimes slightly above it).

Bowed harp. Modern name for the *crwth and similar instruments of northern Europe.

Bowing. The technique of using the *bow on stringed instruments (violins, etc.). The mastery of the bow includes a considerable number of different manners of bowing, the most important of which are named and briefly described below. It should be noted that the terms themselves are not much used by players and that the various effects frequently are not indicated exactly by a specific notation but rather are suggested by the character of the music.

(a) *Plain bowing* (*legato*). This consists of two basic strokes: down-bow [F. *tiré;* G. *Abstrich, Herabstrich, Herstrich, Herunterstrich, Niederstrich;* It. *arcata in giù;* Sp. *arco abajo*] and up-bow [F. *poussé;* G. *Aufstrich, Heraufstrich, Hinaufstrich;* It. *arcata in su;* Sp. *arco arriba*]. In down-bow, indicated by a sign [Ex. 1], the arm is moved away from the body, and in up-bow [Ex. 2] the arm moves toward the body. The slur [Ex. 3] indicates the number of notes to be taken in a single stroke.

(b) *Détaché* [F.]. A broad, vigorous stroke in which the notes of equal time value are bowed singly with a slight articulation or detachment from one another owing to the rapid change of bow. This stroke is much used for loud passages of not very great speed. Sometimes it is indicated by lines under (or above) the notes [Ex. 4]. An exceptionally long stroke is called *le grand détaché*.

(c) *Martelé* [F.; It. *martellato*]. Liter-

ally, a "hammered" stroke, an effect obtained by releasing each stroke forcefully and suddenly. It can be played in any section of the bow and is sometimes indicated by an arrowhead [Ex. 5].

(d) *Sautillé* [F.; It. *saltando;* G. *Springbogen;* Sp. *saltillo*]. A short stroke played in rapid tempo in the middle of the bow so that the bow, once set in motion for the stroke, bounces slightly off the string repeatedly. It is indicated by dots [Ex. 6]. The same indication may be used for the *spiccato* [It., detached], in which the bow is dropped on the string and lifted again after each note.

(e) *Jeté* [F.; also known as *ricochet*]. This is done by "throwing" the bow on the string in the upper third of the bow so that it will bounce a series of rapid notes on the down-bow. Notation as in Ex. 7. Usually from two to six notes are taken in one stroke, but up to ten or eleven can be played.

(f) *Louré* [F.] or *portato* [It.]. A stroke useful in slow tempo to separate slightly each of several notes taken in a slur. It is indicated as in Ex. 8 (or with dots instead of dashes). It is used in passages of a *cantabile* character.

(g) *Staccato* [It.]. This is a solo effect and theoretically consists of a number of *martelé* notes taken in the same stroke. It can be executed either up-bow or down-bow at slow to moderately rapid tempo. When the bow is allowed to spring slightly from the string in more rapid passages, *staccato volante* (flying staccato) results. Notation as in Ex. 9.

(h) *Viotti-stroke.* This is attributed to Giovanni Battista Viotti (1755–1824) and consists of two detached and strongly marked notes, the first of which is unaccented and given very little bow, while the second comes on the accent and takes much more bow. Its use is practically limited to the works of Viotti, Kreutzer, and Rode. Notation as in Ex. 10.

(i) *Arpeggio, arpeggiando, arpeggiato* [It.]. A bouncing stroke played on broken chords so that each bounce is on a different string. Indicated as in Ex. 11.

(j) *Tremolo* [It.]. This is primarily an orchestral effect and is produced by moving the bow back and forth, in short and extremely rapid strokes, on one note [Ex. 12]. See Tremolo.

(k) *Sul ponticello* [It.; F. *au chevalet;* G. *am Steg;* Sp. *sobre el puentecillo*]. A nasal, brittle effect produced by bowing very close to the bridge.

(l) *Sul tasto, sulla tastiera* [It.; F. *sur la touche;* G. *am Griffbrett*]. A flutelike effect (also called *flautando*) produced by bowing very slightly over the fingerboard.

(m) *Col legno* [It.]. This is done by striking the string with the stick instead of the hair.

(n) *Ondulé* [F; It. *ondeggiando*]. A form of tremolo ("undulating tremolo") produced by rapid alternation between two strings [see Tremolo]. The term is sometimes also applied to the undulating motion of the bow used in playing arpeggios. See *Ondeggiando.*

Bowles, Paul Frederic (b. New York, 30 Dec. 1910). Composer, folk-music collector, and writer. Pupil of Copland, Thompson, and N. Boulanger. Works incl. operas, ballets, incidental music for theater and films, orch. pieces, and chamber music.

Boyce, William (b. London, 11 Sept. 1711; d. Kensington, 7 Feb. 1779). Organist of the Chapel Royal from 1758. Composed symphonies and overtures; organ voluntaries; trio sonatas; stage works, incl. songs to Shakespeare's plays; anthems; songs. Known especially for *Cathedral Music,* an anthology in 3 volumes of works by British composers, begun by M. Greene.

Braccio [It.]. Arm. For *Viola da braccio* see Viola (2).

Brace [F. *accolade*]. The bracket connecting two or more staves of a score; also, the group of staves thus connected.

Brade, William (b. 1560; d. Hamburg, 26 Feb. 1630). English viol player and composer. Court musician to Christian IV of Denmark; served the Brandenburg house in Berlin and held other positions in Berlin, Hamburg, and elsewhere. Composed numerous instrumental dance suites.

Brahms, Johannes (b. Hamburg, 7 May 1833; d. Vienna, 3 Apr. 1897). Pupil of Eduard Marxsen. Toured Germany as a pianist with the Hungarian violinist Eduard Reményi in 1853. Close associate of Robert and Clara Schumann and J. Joachim. Visited and conducted in Vienna several times (at the Singakademie, 1863–64, and the Gesellschaft der Musikfreunde, 1871–74), finally settling there in 1878. Orch. works incl. 4 symphonies; 2 piano concertos; a violin concerto; *Akademische Festouvertüre; *Tragische Ouvertüre;* 2 serenades; *Haydn Variations.* Chamber works incl. 3 string quartets, 2 string quintets, and 2 string sextets; 3 piano trios, 3 piano quartets, and a piano quintet; a clarinet quintet; a trio for horn, violin, and piano; a trio for clarinet, cello, and piano; 3 violin sonatas; 2 cello sonatas; 2 clarinet sonatas. Choral works incl. *Ein *deutsches Requiem; Rinaldo,* a cantata; *Rhapsodie aus Goethe's "Harzreise im Winter"* (known as The Alto Rhapsody); *Triumphlied; *Schicksalslied; Nänie.* Piano works incl. *Handel Variations* and *Paganini Variations;* 3 sonatas; 3 rhapsodies; intermezzi, ballades, and other short pieces; piano duets, incl. *Liebeslieder* waltzes with vocal quartet; *Hungarian Dances.* Vocal works incl. numerous songs, vocal duets and quartets, and folksong settings for voice and piano.

Brand, Max (b. Lvov, 26 Apr. 1896). Pupil of Schreker. Founded the Mimoplastische Theater for ballet in Vienna; produced, directed, and scored several musical films. Emigrated to the U.S. in 1940. Composed operas (incl. *Maschinist Hopkins,* 1928); ballets; a scenic oratorio, *The Gate,* 1944; a scenic cantata, *The Chronicle,* 1938; orch. works (incl. *The Wonderful One-Hoss Shay,* 1950); twelve-tone studies (incl. *Kyrie Eleison* for chorus, 1940); chamber music; electronic compositions.

Brande [Old G.]. *Branle.

Brandenburg Concertos. Six concertos written 1718–21 by J. S. Bach (who called them *Concerts avec plusiers instruments*) and dedicated to Christian Ludwig, Margrave of Brandenburg. Each consists of three movements, fast–slow–fast, except for the first, which has a Minuet and a Polonaise added at the end. Three of them, nos. 2, 4, and 5, are *concerti grossi,* employing a group of solo instruments against the string orchestra.

Brando [It.]; **brangill** [Old E.]. *Branle.

Branle [F.]. In the 15th century, one of the various dancing steps of the *basse danse,* indicated in the dance notation by the letter *b.* In the 16th century, the branle was an independent popular dance. There were numerous local varieties, many of which were of the follow-the-leader type, similar to the *farandole and the *cotillon. It was accompanied by singing and apparently included some swaying movements of the body or hands. The *branle double* and *branle simple* were in duple meter (the former with phrases of four, the latter, of three measures), whereas the *branle gay* was in triple meter. The *branle à mener* survived in the *amener of the 17th century and, very likely, in the *minuet. In England the dance was known as a "brangill" or "brawl" [see Shakespeare, *Love's Labour's Lost,* Act III, 1].

Brant, Henry (Dreyfus) (b. Montreal, 15 Sept. 1913). Pupil of Goldmark, Antheil, and Riegger. Member of the faculty of Columbia Univ., 1945–52; of the Juilliard School of Music, 1947–54; of Bennington College from 1957. A pioneer among 20th-century composers in the spatial distribution of sound. Composed orch. works (incl. *Antiphony I* for 5 separated groups, 1953); chamber music (incl. *Music for a Five and Dime Store* for violin, piano, and kitchenware, 1931; *Consort for True Violins* for violins of various sizes, 1966); theater and film music.

Brass band. A group of brass instruments. Today, the term refers to a fairly standardized combination of 24 players, consisting of 1 E♭ soprano cornet, 8 B♭ cornets, 1 B♭ Flügelhorn, 3 E♭ tenor horns, 2 B♭ baritone horns, 2 B♭ euphoniums, 2 B♭ tenor trombones, 1 B♭ bass trombone, 2 E♭ bass tubas, and 2 BB♭ bass tubas.

The brass band dates from the time when valves began to be used in brass instruments in the reorganization of Prussian cavalry bands, beginning about 1830 [see Brass instruments]. Since about 1860, their popularity in America has declined. In England, however, they continued to flourish, becoming an integral part of recreational and educational programs offered by industry, religious groups, and schools.

Brass instruments [F. *instruments de cuivre;* G. *Blechinstrumente;* It. *stromenti d'ottone;* Sp. *instrumentos de metal*]. The family of *wind instruments made of brass or other metal in which the player's lips serve as a reed, i.e., lip-vibrated aerophones. The vibrations of the lips are transmitted to a tube by means of a cup- or funnel-shaped mouthpiece. Some earlier members of the family were made of wood, e.g., the *cornett. Of the numerous varied types and sizes, the following are among the most important.

I. *Orchestral instruments.* The brass section of the modern orchestra consists mainly of the French *horn, *trumpet, *trombone, and *tuba. The tuba is related to the horn; both have a pipe whose diameter increases throughout the greater part of its length (conical pipe). In the trumpet and trombone the pipe is to a great extent (about two-thirds) cylindrical and widens only at the end into a relatively small bell. The mouthpieces are more cup-shaped in the trumpet and trombone than in the horn and tuba, which have funnel-shaped mouthpieces. Other instruments occasionally used in the modern orchestra are the Wagner tubas [see Tuba (2)], cornet, and several types discussed under II.

II. *Band instruments.*

(a) Cornet [F. *cornet à pistons;* G. *Kornett;* It. *cornetta;* Sp. *cornetín*]. An instrument similar in shape to the trumpet but shorter and with a relatively longer conical portion and cupped mouthpiece. Pitched in B♭ (sometimes in A), it has a written range from f♯ to c''', sounding a whole tone (or three semitones) lower. The cornet's timbre is similar to that of the trumpet but less brilliant.

(b) Flügelhorn [G.; F. *bugle;* It. *flicorno;* Sp. *fiscorno*]. An instrument similar in design and size to the cornet but with a wider conical bore, usually with three valves. It is usually built in B♭, more rarely in C. Its sound is somewhat similar to that of the horn, but it lacks the latter's mellowness. The instruments named below are larger sizes con-

BRASS INSTRUMENTS

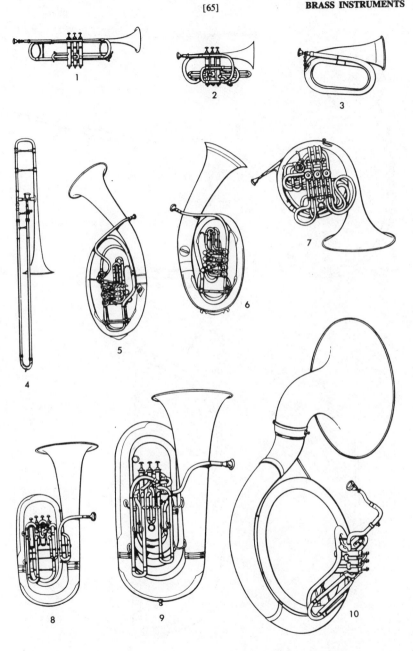

Brass instruments: 1. *Trumpet.* 2. *Cornet.* 3. *Bugle.* 4. *Trombone.* 5. *Wagner tuba.* 6. *Double B-flat baritone.* 7. *French horn.* 8. *B-flat euphonium.* 9. *Double B-flat tuba.* 10. *Sousaphone.*

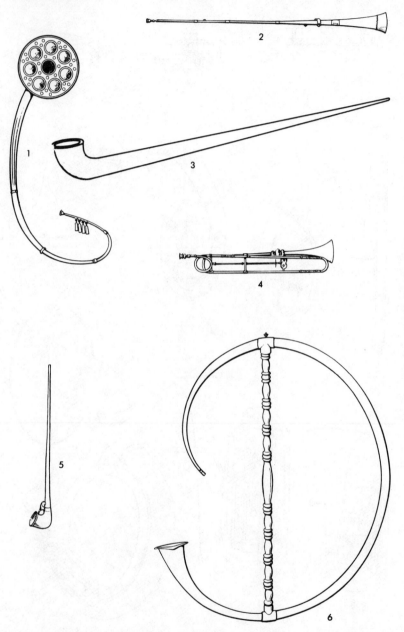

Old brass instruments and related instruments: 1. Lur. 2. Buysine. 3. Alphorn. 4. Slide trumpet. 5. Lituus. 6. Buccina.

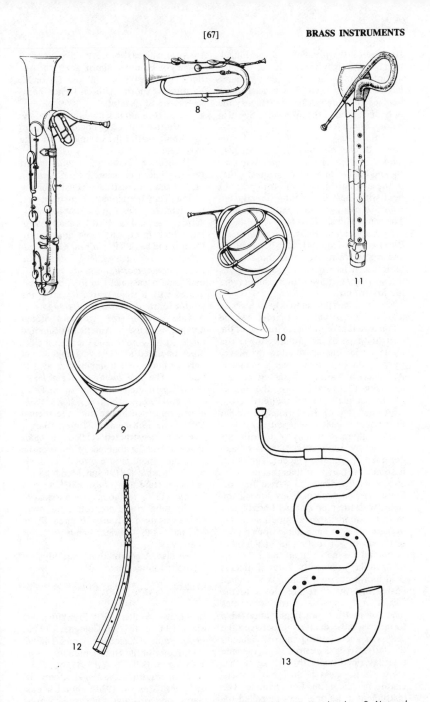

Old brass instruments and related instruments: 7. Ophicleide. 8. Key bugle. 9. Natural horn. 10. Hand horn. 11. Bass horn. 12. Cornett. 13. Serpent.

structed on the principles of the Flügel-horn. They might be regarded as forming a family for which the generic name *bugles* is often used. The largest members of the family are the *tubas, the only ones used in the orchestra. See also below, under (f).

(c) Baritone [F. *bugle ténor;* G. *Tenor-horn;* It. *flicorno tenore;* Sp. *fiscorno tenor*]. This is a larger instrument in C or B♭ and built in one of two shapes, either in the oblong shape of the trumpet, but held with the bell pointing directly upward, or oval, with the bell at an angle. The range is from E to b♭'.

(d) Euphonium [F. *basse à pistons;* G. *Baryton;* Sp. *eufonio*]. Its shape, pitch, and range are the same as those of the baritone. A larger bore, however, gives it a broader, mellower timbre and favors the lower notes.

(e) Helicon. This name is used for bass, and contrabass tubas in a circular shape (similar to that of the horn) instead of the upright shape of the ordinary tuba. The circle is wide enough to allow the player to carry the instrument over a shoulder. An American variety, characterized by a specially designed bell, is the *sousa-phone* (named after John Philip Sousa, who suggested it). In Germany a similar instrument is called a *Bombardon.*

(f) Saxhorn. A family of instruments invented by Adolphe Sax (1814–94) and designed on a uniform model. Their bore is somewhat narrower than that of the instruments described above, resulting in a more brilliant timbre. They are all upright, with the pipe starting horizontally from the funnel-shaped mouthpiece (as in the tubas, etc.) and the pistons on top of the upper horizontal part of the tube. It should be noted that the saxhorns made today frequently differ in details (width of bore, etc.) from Sax's original design and therefore are closer to the Flügelhorn. Indeed, most authorities maintain that it is practically impossible to make a clear distinction between the saxhorns and the Flügelhorns. Usually, the latter term is restricted to the one size described under (b). All agree that there is a hopeless confusion of nomenclature in this group. For example: The instrument in E♭ or F may be called so-pranino saxhorn, soprano saxhorn, so-prano Flügelhorn; in B♭ or C, soprano

saxhorn, alto saxhorn, Alt Flügelhorn; in low E♭ or F, alto saxhorn, saxhorn. Alt-horn, tenor saxhorn; in low B♭ or C, baritone saxhorn, Althorn, tenor horn; in EE♭ or FF, saxtuba.

The *saxtromba* is a modification of the saxhorn that has a less conical bore, approaching that of the trumpet. It is little used today.

III. *Military instruments and related types.* Under this heading brief mention may be made of instruments used for signaling. They are all natural instruments, restricted to tones 2 to 6 of the harmonic series, e.g., g d' g' b' d'' for an instrument built in G. The most common of them is the *bugle* [F. *clairon;* G. *Signal-horn;* It. *cornetta segnale;* Sp. *cuerno de caza, bocina, clarín, corneta*], built in G or B♭ and occasionally in F. A bugle furnished with a single valve lowering the pitch a fourth is known as a *Bersag horn.* A wide variety of sizes, with and without a valve, is in use in American drum and bugle corps. About 1800 the use of side-holes operated by keys was applied not only to horns and trumpets but also to bugles. The *key bugle* or *Kent bugle* (*Kent horn*), named in honor of the Duke of Kent [F. *bugle à clefs,* G. *Klappen-horn*], remained in use until the second half of the 19th century. Later a larger size was constructed; called an *ophi-cleide,* it had the doubled-up shape of the bassoon. Spontini prescribed it in his opera *Olympie* (1819) and Mendelssohn in his overture to *A Midsummer Night's Dream* (1826). Although soon replaced by the tuba in the orchestra, the ophicleide was used in Italian, French, Spanish, and South American bands up to this century.

See also Alphorn; Buccina; Buysine; Cornett; Lituus; Lur.

Bratsche [G.]. *Viola. Bratschist,* viola player.

Braunfels, Walter (b. Frankfurt am Main, 19 Dec. 1882; d. Cologne, 19 Mar. 1954). Pupil of Leschetizky and Thuille. Co-director of the Hochschule für Musik in Cologne, 1925–33 and 1945–50. Composed operas (incl. *Die Vogel,* after Aristophanes, Munich, 1920); choral works; piano concertos and other orch. works; string quartets; piano and organ pieces; songs.

Brautlied [G.]. Bridal song.

Bravura [It.]. Skill. Applied to compositions demanding great skill of the performer, e.g., *aria di bravura.*

Brawl. English term for the *branle.

Breit [G.]. Broad, largo. *Breit gestrichen,* broadly bowed.

Bretón y Hernández, Tomás (b. Salamanca, 29 Dec. 1850; d. Madrid, 2 Dec. 1923). Member of the faculty of the Madrid Conservatory from 1901. Active in reviving the *zarzuela.* Composed operas (incl. *Los amantes de Teruel,* Madrid, 1899; *La Dolores,* Madrid, 1895); *zarzuelas* (incl. *La verbena de la paloma,* Madrid, 1897); an oratorio; orch. works; chamber music.

Breve, brevis [L.]. A note value that, as implied by the name [L. *brevis,* short], originally (early 13th century) was the shortest value in use; see Notation; Mensural notation. Because of the subsequent introduction of six or more degrees of smaller value (*semibrevis, minima,* etc.), it became, in the late 16th century, the longest value commonly used. Today it is occasionally used as the equivalent of two whole notes, written ⊨ or |o| . See also *Alla breve.*

Breviary [L. *breviarium*]. See Liturgical books (2).

Bréville, Pierre Onfroy de (b. Bar-le-Duc, 21 Feb. 1861; d. Paris, 24 Sept. 1949). Music critic and composer. Pupil of T. Dubois and Franck. Member of the faculty of the Schola cantorum. Music critic for several French journals. Composed an opera, *Eros vainqueur,* Brussels, 1910; sacred choral works; incidental music to Maeterlinck's *Les sept princesses;* orch. works; organ pieces; piano pieces; other instrumental works; songs.

Brian, William Havergal (b. Dresden, Staffordshire, England, 29 Jan. 1876; d. Shoreham, Sussex, 28 Nov. 1972). Self-taught as a composer. Worked as a journalist for *The Musical World,* 1904–49. Composed *Gothic Symphony* and 31 other symphonies (7 of which he wrote after the age of 90); concertos and other orch. works; an opera; choral works; songs.

Bridge [F. *chevalet;* G. *Steg;* It. *ponticello;* Sp. *puente*]. (1) In stringed instruments, the wooden support over which the strings are stretched and which, resting on the belly, transmits the vibrations of the strings to the body of the instrument. (2) Short for *bridge passage.*

Bridge, Frank (b. Brighton, 26 Feb. 1879; d. Eastbourne, 10 Jan. 1941). Pupil of Stanford. Violist in the Joachim and English Quartets. Conductor at Covent Garden and elsewhere. His pupils incl. Britten. Composed a children's opera, *The Christmas Rose,* 1919–29; orch. suite, *The Sea,* 1911, and other orch. works; chamber music, incl. string quartets and piano trios; pieces for violin, viola, cello, piano, organ; songs.

Bridge passage. In musical compositions, a passage serving to connect two themes. Frequently it effects a modulation of key, e.g., from the first to the second theme in *sonata form.

Brindisi [It.]. Drinking song, particularly in operas, e.g., in Verdi's *La traviata* ("Libiamo"), Mascagni's *Cavalleria rusticana* ("Viva il vino").

Brio, con; brioso [It.]. With vigor and spirit.

Brisé [F.]. An 18th-century name for the *turn. In modern terminology, indication for *arpeggio playing, or for detached *bowing. See also *Style brisé.*

Bristow, George Frederick (b. Brooklyn, 19 Dec. 1825; d. New York, 13 Dec. 1898). Violinist and organist for several New York orchestras and churches. Teacher in the New York public schools from 1854. Composed operas (incl. *Rip Van Winkle,* New York, 1855); oratorios; cantatas; 6 symphonies and other orch. works; 2 string quartets; pieces for organ, piano, violin; choral pieces; songs.

Britten, (Edward) Benjamin (b. Lowestoft, Suffolk, 22 Nov. 1913; d. Aldeburgh, 4 Dec. 1976). Pupil of Bridge and Ireland. Founded the Aldeburgh Festival, 1948. Toured widely as conductor and pianist. Composed operas (incl. *Peter Grimes; The *Rape of Lucretia; *Albert Herring; *Billy Budd; The *Turn of the Screw; A *Midsummer Night's

Dream; Curlew River, Aldeburgh, 1964; *Death in Venice,* 1973); *Sinfonia da Requiem,* 1940; *The Young Person's Guide to the Orchestra,* variations and fugue on a theme by Purcell, 1946; other orch. works; choral works (incl. *War Requiem,* 1961; *Cantata academica,* 1959; A **Ceremony of Carols*); *Sinfonietta* for chamber orch., 1932, and other chamber works; numerous songs, many written for the tenor Peter Pears.

Broderie [F.]. (1) French term for coloratura (1). Also used in German writings, more in the sense of "delicately embroidered melody," as in 15th-century music. (2) Auxiliary tone [see under Counterpoint].

Broken chord. Figuration consisting of the notes of a chord (triad, seventh chord, etc.), as in the C-major Prelude of *The Well-Tempered Clavier,* Vol. I, or the stereotyped patterns known as the **Alberti bass. *Arpeggio* is often used as a synonym.

Broken consort. See Consort.

Broken octave. See under Short octave.

Brossard, Sébastien de (b. Dompierre, Orne, France, bapt. 12 Sept. 1655; d. Meaux, 10 Aug. 1730). Theorist and composer. *Maître de chapelle* at the Strasbourg Cathedral from 1689; at the Meaux Cathedral from 1698, and canon there from 1709. Composed sacred vocal music; airs; instrumental music. Known especially for his *Dictionnaire de musique,* 1703.

Brott, Alexander (b. Montreal, 14 Mar. 1915). Violinist, conductor, and composer. Pupil of B. Wagenaar. Member of the faculty of McGill Univ. from 1939. Has composed a ballet, *Le corriveau,* 1967; the suite *From Sea to Sea,* 1946, a violin concerto, 1950, and other orch. works; chamber music.

Brouwer, Leo (b. Havana, 1 Mar. 1939). Guitarist and composer. Pupil of Persichetti, Freed, and Wolpe. Member of the faculty at the National Conservatory in Havana, 1961–67; music consultant for Havana Radio and head of the experimental music studio of the Cuban Film Institute. Works incl. *Sonograma I* for prepared piano, 1963, *II* for orch., 1964;

guitar pieces (incl. *Canticum*); *Dos conceptos del tiempo* for 10 players, 1965; numerous film scores and other instrumental works.

Brown, Earle (b. Lunenburg, Mass., 26 Dec. 1926). Trained in the system developed by Schillinger. Associate member (with Cage and Tudor) of the Music for Magnetic Tape project in New York, 1952–55; member of the faculty of the Peabody Conservatory in Baltimore, 1968–70. Works (many employing aleatory processes and "open" forms): *25 Pages* for 1–25 pianos, 1953; *Folio,* 1953; *Available Forms I,* 1961, and *II,* 1962; *Event: Synergy II* for chamber ensemble, 1968; *Corroboree* for 2 or 3 pianos, 1964.

Browning. A 16th- or 17th-century English composition based on the tune "The leaves be greene, the nuts be browne." Most brownings are intricate variations for instrumental ensembles, e.g., Byrd's "Browning" in five parts.

Bruch, Max (b. Cologne, 6 Jan. 1838; d. Friednau, near Berlin, 2 Oct. 1920). Conductor and composer. Pupil of F. Hiller and Reinecke. Taught a master class in composition at the Berlin Academy, 1891–1910. Composed operas (incl. *Die Loreley,* Mannheim, 1863); secular oratorios; orch. works (incl. *Scottish Fantasy* for violin and orch., 1880; 3 violin concertos; *Kol Nidre* for cello and orch., 1880; 3 symphonies); chamber music; piano pieces; songs.

Bruck, Arnold von (b. Bruges?, *c.* 1490; d. Linz, 1554?). Entered the service of Kaiser Ferdinand I in Vienna, *c.* 1510; became *Kapellmeister* there, 1527. Composed motets; psalms; hymns (incl. many arrangements of Lutheran hymns, though he himself was a Catholic); secular polyphony.

Bruckner, Anton (b. Ansfelden, Austria, 4 Sept. 1824; d. Vienna, 11 Oct. 1896). Pupil of Sechter. Cathedral organist at Linz from 1856; member of the faculty of the Vienna Conservatory from 1868, and of Vienna Univ. from 1875. An admirer of Wagner, whom he visited several times in Bayreuth. Composed 9 symphonies (excluding 2 early works that he rejected, one of which he had numbered

"0"), the ninth unfinished; a *Requiem;* several Masses, a *Te Deum,* and other sacred choral and orch. works; choruses for male voices; a string quintet; piano pieces; organ pieces.

Brüll, Ignaz (b. Prossnitz, Moravia, 7 Nov. 1846; d. Vienna, 17 Sept. 1907). Pianist and composer. Close associate of Brahms. Professor of piano at the Horak Institute in Vienna, 1872–78, and its co-director from 1881. Composed operas (incl. *Das goldene Kreuz,* Berlin, 1875; *Der Husar,* Vienna, 1898); a ballet; orch. works, incl. a symphony; 2 piano concertos and a violin concerto; choral works; piano pieces; songs.

Brumel, Antoine (b. *c.* 1460; d. *c.* 1520). Master of the choristers and canon at Notre Dame, Paris, 1498–1500; thereafter in Lyon; from 1505, in service to Alfonso I, Duke of Ferrara. Composed Masses; motets; Magnificats; French chansons.

Brumeux [F.]. Misty, veiled.

Brün, Herbert (b. Berlin, 9 July 1918). Pupil of Wolpe. Member of the faculty of the Univ. of Illinois from 1963, having previously lived in Germany and Israel. Has composed a ballet; *Mobile for Orchestra,* 1958, and other orch. works; chamber music (incl. 3 string quartets; *Gestures for 11,* 1964); electronic works (incl. *Futility 1964; Infraudibles,* produced with computer, 1968).

Bruneau, **(Louis-Charles-Bonaventure-)** **Alfred** (b. Paris, 3 Mar. 1857; d. there, 15 June 1934). Conductor, music critic, and composer. Pupil of Massenet. Close associate of Zola, who wrote some of his librettos (*Messidor,* Paris, 1897; *L'ouragan,* Paris, 1901; *L'enfant roi,* Paris, 1905) and inspired others (incl. *La rêve,* Paris, 1891; *L'attaque du moulin,* Paris, 1893). In addition to operas, he composed ballets (incl. *Les bacchantes,* after Euripides, 1912); orch. works; a Requiem; chamber music; songs.

Brunette [F.]. A 17th- and 18th-century type of French popular song, with or without accompaniment, with idyllic, pastoral, or amorous subjects. It replaced the earlier **bergerette* and **vaudeville.* The name is probably derived from one famous example, "Le

beau berger Tirsis," which has the refrain "Ah petite brunette, ah tu me fais mourir."

Brunswick, Mark (b. New York, 6 Jan. 1902; d. London, 26 May 1971). Pupil of Goldmark, Bloch, N. Boulanger, and Sessions. Music Department chairman at City College of New York, 1946–65. Composed an unfinished opera; a ballet, *Lysistrata,* 1930; *Symphony in B-flat,* 1945; choral symphony, *Eros and Death,* on texts of Lucretius, Sappho, and Hadrian, 1954; chamber music, incl. works for string quartet; piano pieces.

Brustwerk, Brustpositiv [G.]. A special group of smaller organ pipes placed in the middle of the front of the organ, between the large pedal pipes. The group has softer intonation than the *Hauptwerk* (great organ) and is usually played on the second manual.

Buccina [L.]. An ancient Roman brass instrument [see ill. under Brass instruments]. The name reappears in the medieval term **buysine,* in the German word *Posaune* (i.e., trombone), and in the French *buccin* (or *buccine*). The last was a pseudoantique variety of trombone with a bell shaped like a dragon's head, used during the French Revolution for festive occasions.

Buck, Dudley (b. Hartford, Conn., 10 Mar. 1839; d. Orange, N.J., 6 Oct. 1909). Composer and organist. Pupil of Hauptmann and Moscheles at the Leipzig Conservatory. Served as church organist in various American cities. Composed much church music; works for organ; 2 operas.

Buckwheat note. See under Fasola.

Budd, Harold (b. Los Angeles, 24 May 1936). Pupil of de la Vega, Strang, and Dahl. Member of the faculty of the California Institute of the Arts from 1970. Works incl. *Magnus Colorado* for amplified gongs, 1969; mobile works, incl. *Noyo* for piano, vibraphone, and chimes, 1966; *The Candy-Apple Revision,* D♭-major chord for any sound source, 1970.

Buffet [F.]. Organ case.

Buffo [It.]. In Italian 18th-century opera, a comic character, usually a *basso buffo* (e.g., Leporello in Mozart's *Don Giovanni*). Hence, a singer for comic roles. See Comic opera.

Bügelhorn [G.]. German term for the entire family sometimes referred to as *bugles*.

Bugle. A military instrument [see Brass instruments III]. The term is also used generically for the entire group of brass instruments described under Brass instruments II (b)–(e). For the key bugle (Kent bugle), see Brass instruments III.

Bühne [G.]. Stage. *Bühnenfestspiel* (stage festival play) and *Bühnenweihfestspiel* (stage-consecrating festival play) are names used by Wagner, the former for his *Ring* cycle, the latter for *Parsifal*. *Bühnenmusik* means *incidental music for plays, or, in operas, music played on the stage itself, as in the final scene of Mozart's *Don Giovanni*.

Buisine. See *Buysine*. For ill. see under Brass instruments.

Bull, John (b. England, 1562 or 1563; d. Antwerp, 12 or 13 Mar. 1628). Organist of the Chapel Royal from 1591; professor of music at Gresham College, 1596–1607; court musician in Brussels, 1613; organist of Notre Dame Cathedral, Antwerp, 1617 to his death. Composed numerous keyboard pieces; church music.

Bund [G.; pl. *Bünde*]. Fret. For *bundfrei,* see under Clavichord.

Buonamente, Giovanni Battista (d. Assisi, 1643). Court musician in Mantua, 1622; at the Viennese court, 1626; in Prague, 1627; *maestro di cappella* at the Franciscan monastery in Assisi, 1636. Published numerous violin sonatas, trio sonatas, and other instrumental pieces.

Burck, Joachim a (real name Moller) (b. Burg, near Magdeburg, 1546; d. Mühlhausen, Thuringia, 24 May 1610). Organist at the Protestant Church of St. Blasius in Mühlhausen, 1566. Close associate of J. Eccard. Composed *Die deutsche Passion* (a dramatic Passion with German text for Lutheran use); numerous motets; odes; other sacred and secular pieces.

Burden. *Refrain. The term is used par-

ticularly in connection with the 15th-century *carol.

Burdo [L.]. See *Bourdon*.

Burgmüller, (August Joseph) Norbert (b. Dusseldorf, 8 Feb. 1810; d. Aachen, 7 May 1836). Brother of Friedrich Johann Franz Burgmüller. Pupil of Spohr and Hauptmann. Composed 2 symphonies (one unfinished and subsequently orchestrated in part by Schumann) and other orch. works; string quartets and other chamber music; piano pieces; numerous songs.

Burgmüller, Friedrich Johann Franz (b. Regensburg, 4 Dec. 1806; d. Beaulieu, near Paris, 13 Feb. 1874). Brother of August Joseph Norbert Burgmüller. Composed a ballet, *La Peri;* an overture; numerous piano pieces; songs with piano or guitar accompaniment.

Burgundian cadence. See under Cadence.

Burgundian school. The leading Continental school of composers of the early and middle 15th century, represented chiefly by Guillaume Dufay (*c*. 1400–74), and Gilles Binchois (*c*. 1400–60). In older writings, the Burgundian school is called the first Netherlands school [see Netherlands schools]. Today, the term *Burgundian school* is preferred because the musical activity in question centered in the cultural sphere of the duchy of Burgundy, which, under Philip the Good (1419–67) and Charles the Bold (1467–77), included the whole of eastern France as well as Belgium and the Netherlands. Closely related to that of contemporaneous English composers such as John Dunstable, the music of the Burgundian school is remarkably consonant and makes particular use of thirds and sixths. The use of what would in modern terms be called sixth chords is particularly common at *cadences and is the essential feature of the *fauxbourdon,* an important innovation of the period. The leading secular form of the period is the *rondeau,* most often set in three parts and in the equivalent of 3/4 meter. Other composers who can be grouped with Dufay and Binchois in this connection are Hayne von Ghizeghem,

Robert Morton, and Arnold and Hugho de Lantins.

Burian, Emil František (b. Pilsen, Czechoslovakia, 11 June 1904; d. Prague, 9 Aug. 1959). Pupil of Foerster. Founder and director of *D 34*, an avantgarde Prague theater, 1933–40 and 1945–49. Introduced the "voice band," a recitation ensemble. Composed operas (incl. *Maryša*, Brno, 1940); ballets; film scores; theater music; cantatas; orch. works; chamber music; songs.

Burkhard, Willy (b. Leubringen bei Biel, Switzerland, 17 Apr. 1900; d. Zürich, 18 June 1955). Studied in Leipzig with Karg-Elert and in Munich and Paris. Member of the faculty of the Bern Conservatory, 1928–33; of the Zürich Conservatory, 1942–55. Composed an opera; oratorios (incl. *Das Gesicht Jesajas*, 1935), cantatas (incl. *Die Sintflut*, 1955), and other sacred choral works; a symphony and other orch. works; string quartets and other chamber music; organ pieces; piano pieces; songs.

Burla, burlesca [It.]. A composition of a playful character. Bach's A-minor Partita includes a *burlesca*, Schumann's *Albumblätter* a *burla*.

Burlesque, burletta. An English (and later, American) type of stage entertainment of the late 18th and 19th centuries that may be considered the successor of the *ballad opera. Like the latter, it was a "low-brow" entertainment consisting of comic dialogue and songs sung to borrowed melodies.

Burrasca [It.]. A composition descriptive of a tempest or thunderstorm, e.g., the overture of Rossini's *Guillaume Tell*.

Burt, Francis (b. London, 28 Apr. 1926). Pupil of Ferguson and Blacher. Settled in Vienna in 1956. Works incl. an opera, a ballet, a cantata, pieces for orch., chamber music.

Bush, Alan Dudley (b. Dulwich, London, 22 Dec. 1900). Pianist, conductor, and composer. Pupil of Corder and Ireland. Member of the faculty of the Royal Academy of Music from 1925. Director of the Workers' Music Association Singers, 1941–54. Has composed operas (incl. *Wat Tyler*, 1950; *The Sugar Reapers*, 1964; *Joe Hill*, 1968, and several children's operas); 3 symphonies; *Fantasia on Soviet Themes*, 1945, and other orch. works; choral works; works for string quartet and other chamber music; piano pieces; arrangements of English songs.

Busnois, Antoine (d. 6 Nov. 1492?). Chapel singer to Charles the Bold of Burgundy, 1467. Composed numerous chansons; Masses; Magnificats; motets (incl. *In hydraulis,* in which he calls himself a pupil of Ockeghem).

Busoni, Ferruccio (Benvenuto) (b. Empoli, near Florence, 1 Apr. 1866; d. Berlin, 27 July 1924). Pianist, conductor, and composer. Performed and taught in Italy, Germany, Russia, U.S., Belgium, Denmark, Austria, Switzerland; settled in Berlin in 1894. Composed operas (incl. *Turandot*, Zürich, 1917; *Arlecchino*, Zürich, 1917; *Die Brautwahl*, Hamburg, 1912; *Doktor Faust*, completed by Jarnach, Dresden, 1925); *Konzertstück* for piano and orch., 1890, and a piano concerto, 1904; a violin concerto, 1897; works for voice and orch.; chamber music; numerous piano pieces (incl. *Fantasia contrappuntistica*, 1910); numerous transcriptions for piano of works by Bach; songs. Edited Bach's *Well-Tempered Clavier* and Liszt's piano works; published critical, theoretical, and literary works, some of them anticipating important developments in 20th-century music.

Busser, Henri-Paul (b. Toulouse, 16 Jan. 1872; d. Paris, 30 Dec. 1973). Organist and composer. Pupil of Guiraud, Widor, Gounod, and Franck. Organist at Saint-Cloud from 1892; conductor of the Grand Opéra, 1905–39 and from 1947; taught composition at the Paris Conservatory, 1930–48. Composed operas (incl. *Daphnis et Chloë*, Paris, 1897; *Colomba*, Nice, 1921; *Le carrosse du Saint-Sacrement*, 1936, prod. Paris, 1948); a ballet; orch. works; church music; organ pieces; piano pieces; songs.

Bussotti, Sylvano (b. Florence, 1 Oct. 1931). Composer and painter. Pupil of Dallapiccola and Max Deutsch. Has employed graphic notation and aleatory procedures. Works incl. *La passion selon Sade,* "staged concert" for voices, instruments, narrator, 1966; *Five Piano Pieces for David Tudor,* 1959; *Torso,* for voice and orch., 1963; *The Rara Requiem,* 1969; *Due Voci* for soprano, Ondes Martenot, and orch., 1958.

Butterworth, George Sainton Kaye (b. London, 12 July 1885; killed in the battle of Pozières, 5 Aug. 1916). Studied at Oxford and the Royal College of Music. Composed *A Shropshire Lad,* orchestral rhapsody, 1913, and 2 song cycles with the same title (after Housman); other orch. works, incl. *The Banks of Green Willows,* 1914; choral works; piano pieces; arrangements of English folksongs.

Butting, Max (b. Berlin, 6 Oct. 1888; d. there, 13 July 1976). Pupil of Klose and Walter Courvoisier. Music director of the East Berlin Radio from 1948; held various administrative posts in the German Academy of the Arts in East Berlin from 1950 to 1959. Composed 10 symphonies and numerous other works for orch.; 10 string quartets and other chamber music; piano pieces; an opera; songs.

Buus, Jacques (b. probably early 16th cent. in Flanders; d. Vienna, Aug. 1565). Organist at San Marco in Venice from 1541; court organist in Vienna from 1551. Composed ricercars and canzonas for keyboard or instrumental ensemble; motets; madrigals.

Buxtehude, Dietrich (b. Oldesloe, Holstein, *c.* 1637; d. Lübeck, 9 May 1707). Organist and composer. Succeeded Franz Tunder at the Marienkirche in Lübeck, 1668; reorganized the **Abendmusiken* there, 1673. Bach walked from Arnstadt in 1705 to visit Buxtehude and hear the *Abendmusik.* Composed liturgical church music; numerous cantatas, arias, and other vocal works with instruments; chamber music; numerous organ works.

Buysine, buzine, busine, buisine, buzanne [L. *buccina*]. A medieval straight trum-

pet. See *Buccina;* ill. under Brass instruments.

BWV. Abbr. for *Thematisch-Systematisches Verzeichnis der musikalischen Werke von Johann Sebastian Bach* (1950), i.e., the thematic catalog of the works of J. S. Bach, edited by W. Schmieder. The initials stand for *Bach Werke-Verzeichnis.*

Byrd, William (b. probably in Lincolnshire, 1543; d. Stondon, Essex, 4 July 1623). Organist at Lincoln Cathedral, 1563–72; served with Tallis as organist of the Chapel Royal from 1572, though himself a Roman Catholic. Music printer, under a license from Queen Elizabeth I, first in partnership with Tallis and then independently after Tallis's death in 1585. Composed Catholic and Anglican church music, incl. anthems, motets, and Mass Propers (*Gradualia* in 2 vols., 1605, 1607) as well as Ordinaries; instrumentally accompanied songs; madrigals; pieces for viols; pieces for virginals.

Byzantine chant. The ecclesiastical chant of the Christian church in the Byzantine Empire (founded A.D. 330 by Constantine the Great; destroyed 1453, with the fall of Constantinople). Although the language of the Byzantine Church was Greek, Byzantine chant has many features in common with the Latin Gregorian chant, being monophonic, unaccompanied, chiefly diatonic, and devoid of strict meter. But whereas psalmodic and other scriptural texts prevail in Gregorian chant, the texts of Byzantine chant are mostly nonscriptural, although often modeled after psalms or the canticles. The music of the Greek Orthodox Church is a descendant of this tradition.

Some features of Gregorian chant, including its classification of melodies into one or another of eight modes [see Church modes; Echos], derive from Byzantine chant. Byzantine notation, however, relies on quite different principles from those of Western notation.

C

C. (1) See Pitch names; Letter notation; Hexachord. (2) As an abbreviation, *C* may stand for: *con* (*colla, coll'*), i.e., with [**c.a.; *c.b.; *c.o.; *c.s.*]; *cantus* [**c.f.*]; *capo* [**D.C.*]; **ceja*. In modern part songs *C* means *contralto;* in 16th-century **partbooks, cantus*. (3) For C clef, see Clef.

C.a. [It.]. Abbr. for **col arco* (with the bow).

Caamaño, Roberto (b. Buenos Aires, 7 July 1923). Pianist and composer. Pupil of Athos Palma in Buenos Aires. Teacher at the Institute of Sacred Music and at the National Conservatory in Buenos Aires. Artistic director of the Teatro Colón, 1960–64. Has composed orch. works; a piano concerto; choral pieces; string quartets and other chamber music; piano pieces; songs.

Cabaletta [It.]. (1) A short operatic song in popular style, characterized by a rather uniform rhythm in the vocal line and accompaniment. (2) In 19th-century Italian opera, the final stretto close of arias or duets, in which elaborate treatment usually gives way to quick, uniform rhythm.

Cabanilles, Juan Bautista José (b. Algamesí, Valencia, bapt. 6 Sept. 1644; d. Valencia, 20 Apr. 1712). Organist of the Valencia Cathedral from 1665 to his death. Composed *tientos, diferencias,* and other works for organ.

Cabezón, Antonio de (b. Castrojeriz, Burgos, *c.* 1510; d. Madrid, 26 Mar. 1566). Blind from infancy; served as court organist to the Emperor Charles V and Empress Isabel from 1526 and court musician to Prince Philip (later Philip II) from 1543. Composed numerous works for organ, keyboard, harp, and vihuela, incl. *tientos, diferencias,* arrangements of hymn tunes and of motets by Josquin and others.

Caccia [It.]. A form of 14th-century Italian poetry and music. The text often deals with hunting and fishing scenes or with similar realistic subjects (a fire, cries of street vendors, etc.). The musical form is a strict **canon in two parts, the second usually beginning six or more measures after the first, which is followed by a ritornello that sometimes is also canonic. The two "chasing" voices are usually supported by a tenor line in longer note values that does not imitate the canon melody. Some 26 *cacce* survive, by Giovanni da Cascia, Jacopo da Bologna, Landini, and others. See also *Chace.*

Caccini, Giulio (called "Romano") (b. Tivoli, *c.* 1550; buried Florence, 10 Dec. 1618). Singer at the Tuscan court in Florence from 1565 and participant in the Florentine Camerata. Composed the early opera *L'Euridice,* 1600; accompanied monodies, incl. madrigals and strophic arias, published in collections such as his *Le nuove musiche,* 1601.

Cachucha [Sp.]. An Andalusian dance in triple time, similar to the **bolero. It was introduced by the dancer Fanny Elssler in the ballet *Le diable boiteux* (1836).

Cacophony. Harsh, discordant sound.

Cadence [G. *Kadenz;* F. *cadence;* It. *cadenza;* Sp. *cadencia*]. (1) A melodic or harmonic formula that occurs at the end of a composition, a section, or a phrase, conveying the impression of a momentary or permanent conclusion. A cadence is called *perfect* (*final, full*) if it can be satisfactorily and normally used as the close of a composition. According to the standards of classical harmony, the last chord must be the tonic triad (I) [see Scale degrees] and must have the tonic note in the soprano and the bass. For the penultimate chord, there is a choice between the dominant (V) and the subdominant (IV), both in root position. The combination V–I is called an *authentic* cadence [Ex. 1]; the progression IV–I, a *plagal* cadence (or Amen cadence, because it is employed in the singing of

"Amen" at the end of Protestant hymns) [Ex. 2]. The authentic cadence usually occurs in the fuller form IV–V–I (II⁶–V –I) [Ex. 3] or, still more complete, IV–I⁶₄ –V–I (II⁶–I⁶₄–V–I) [Ex. 4]. The last two are sometimes called *mixed* cadences.

The remaining cadences fall into two classes, *imperfect* cadences and *deceptive* (or *interrupted*) cadences. The imperfect cadences are the same as the two elementary perfect cadences except that they have the tonic chord in another arrangement, e.g., with the third or fifth in the soprano [Ex. 5]; or they have the penultimate chord in inversion [Ex. 6]— these are called *inverted* or *medial* cadences, as opposed to a *radical* [L. *radix,* root] cadence—or occur in transposition to the dominant (or more rarely, the subdominant) [Ex. 7–10]. These "transposed" cadences occur almost regularly at the end of the first half of a musical phrase and are therefore termed *half-cadences* (authentic or plagal).

The deceptive cadence [F. *cadence rompue, c. évitée;* G. *Trugschluss;* It. *inganno;* Sp. *cadencia interrumpida*] is an authentic (or, sometimes, plagal) cadence whose tonic chord (I) is replaced by some other chord, most frequently by VI [Ex. 11]. See also Masculine, feminine cadence. Prior to 1450, practically all cadences of polyphonic music were based on the progression II–I in the lowest part (tenor). This cadence appears with various modifications, among which that with two "leading tones," one before the octave and the other before the fifth, is particularly common before and after 1400 [Ex. 12–13]. This is sometimes called a Lydian cadence [see Church modes] or a Burgundian cadence, though it is common a century before the *Burgundian school. It is often accompanied by a melodic figure in the uppermost voice in which the sixth scale degree occurs between the leading tone and the octave [Ex. 14–15]. Both the melodic figure and the cadence as a whole are often called a "Landini cadence," after Francesco Landini (1325–97). Both, however, occur widely in the music of other composers before and after Landini, including Machaut and the Burgundians. See also Phrygian.

(2) A 17th-century French name for the trill.

Cadenza [It.]. Cadence, and thus more generally, the elaboration by a soloist of a cadence. In works for instrumental soloists, i.e., *concerti, this occurs near the end of a movement (especially the first) following a I⁶₄ chord [see Cadence, Ex. 4] sounded by the orchestra. A *fermata* or *pause is usually placed over the chord itself or a rest immediately following. The soloist, usually without accompaniment, then proceeds in an improvisatory and virtuosic style, drawing frequently on thematic material from the movement itself. Often, the cadenza concludes as the soloist trills on the dominant chord (V) and is joined by the orchestra in stating the tonic (I), following which the movement concludes with a brief coda by the orchestra. Although cadenzas were traditionally improvised, composers as early as Mozart have written them for their own works. In Beethoven's Piano Concerto no. 5, op. 73 (Emperor Concerto) and in many later works by other composers, the cadenza is written by the composer as an integral part of the work. Celebrated performers have also composed cadenzas for use with the concertos of Mozart, Beethoven, and others. Similar improvised displays of virtuosity were common in the singing of opera arias in the 18th and 19th centuries.

Cadenzato [It.]. Rhythmical.

Cadman, Charles Wakefield (b. Johnstown, Pa., 24 Dec. 1881; d. Los Angeles, 30 Dec. 1946). Organist, music critic, conductor, and composer. Active in the study and performance of American Indian music. Composed operas (incl. *Shanewis*, New York, 1918); suites, symphonic poems, and other orch. works; cantatas; a piano sonata; violin pieces; numerous songs (incl. "At Dawning"; "Memories"; "From the Land of the Sky Blue Water").

Cage, John (b. Los Angeles, 5 Sept. 1912). Pupil of A. Weiss, Cowell, and Schoenberg. Organized the Project of Music for Magnetic Tape, 1952. Music director of the Cunningham Dance Co. from 1945. Active at Black Mountain College, 1948–52. Introduced performances with prepared piano and pioneered and has worked extensively with aleatory procedures. Works incl. *4' 33"* (4 minutes, 33 seconds) for any instruments, in which no sound is called for, 1952; *Imaginary Landscape* no. 4 for 12 radios, 1951; *Atlas Eclipticalis* for orch., 1961; *Renga* with *Apartment House 1776* for orch., 1976; *Music of Changes* for piano, 1951; *HPSCHD* for 1–7 harpsichords and 1–51 tape machines, 1969, with Hiller; *34' 46.776" for a Pianist*, 1954; *First Construction (in Metal)* for percussion sextet, 1939. Published the books *Silence*, 1961; *A Year from Monday*, 1967.

Caisse [F.]. Drum. See under Percussion instruments II.

Caix d'Hervelois, Louis de (b. Amiens?, *c.* 1680; d. Paris, *c.* 1760). Viola da gamba player and composer. Court musician to the Duke of Orléans. Composed several volumes of pieces for viola da gamba and for flute.

Calando [It.]. Gradually diminishing.

Caldara, Antonio (b. Venice, 1670; d. Vienna, 26 Dec. 1736). Probably a pupil of Legrenzi. Assistant choirmaster to Fux in Vienna from 1716. Composed numerous operas (incl. *L'Atenaidi*); numerous oratorios (incl. *Morte e sepoltura di Cristo*); numerous Masses and other sacred music; cantatas; chamber music.

Calliope. An instrument invented in America in the 1880s and consisting of a number of steam-blown whistles played from a keyboard.

Callithump. *Charivari.

Calm Sea and Prosperous Voyage. See *Meeresstille und glückliche Fahrt.*

Calmando, calmato [It.]. Quieting, quieted.

Calore, con; caloroso [It.]. With warmth.

Calvisius, Sethus (Seth Kalwitz) (b. Gorsleben, Thuringia, 21 Feb. 1556; d. Leipzig, 24 Nov. 1615). Cantor at the Schulpforta, Leipzig, 1582–92; cantor at the Thomasschule and music director of the Thomaskirche and Nikolaikirche there from 1594 to his death. Composed *bicinia;* motets; four-part arrangements of hymns by Luther and others. Also published theoretical treatises.

Cambert, Robert (b. Paris, *c.* 1628; d. London, 1677). Pupil of Chambonnières. Served as superintendent of music to the queen-dowager Anne of Austria (widow of Louis XIII), 1666. Received (with poet Pierre Perrin) in 1669 a patent to present operas and inaugurated what became the Paris Opéra with his *Pomone* (1671). After the patent was transferred to Lully in 1672, he emigrated to London (1673), where he founded (with Grabu) a Royal Academy of Music and served as Master of the King's Music to Charles II. Composed operas (incl. *Pomone*, Paris 1671; *Ariane, ou Le mariage de Bacchus*, 1661; *La pastorale* [his first "comedy with music," now lost], 1659; *Les peines et les plaisirs de l'amour*, 1672); motets; songs.

Cambia, cambiano [It.]. Direction in orchestral scores to change instruments or tuning [see under Muta].

Cambiata. See under Counterpoint.

Cambini, Giuseppe Maria Gioacchino (not Giovanni Giuseppe, as he is sometimes identified) (b. Livorno, 13 Feb. 1746?; d. Bicêtre, Paris, 29 Dec. 1825?). Violinist and composer. Pupil of Padre Martini. According to two of his treatises, he belonged to a string quartet with Manfredi, Nardini, and Boccherini. Participated in the Concert spirituel and the Concert des amateurs from 1773. Composed ballets; operas; oratorios; numerous symphonies and *sinfonie concertanti;* hundreds of string quartets, quintets, and other pieces of chamber music; cantatas; motets and other sacred vocal music; organ preludes; sonatas.

Camera [It.]. In baroque music (1600–1750), *da camera* indicates music for use outside the church, as distinguished from *da *chiesa,* music to be performed in the church. This dichotomy was applied especially to sonatas and concertos, where it entailed a distinct difference of form that is discussed under *Sonata da camera, da chiesa,* and *Concerto grosso.* In modern Italian usage, *musica da camera* means chamber music.

Camerata [It.]. In the 16th century, a name for small academies. Specifically, a group of literary men, musicians, and amateurs who, about 1580, began to gather in the palace of Count Giovanni Bardi at Florence to discuss the possibilities of a new musical style in imitation of the music of the ancient Greek drama [see Nuove musiche; Opera]. Members were the poet Ottavio Rinuccini and the musicians Vincenzo Galilei, Giulio Caccini, and Jacopo Peri. In 1592, when Bardi went to Rome, Jacopo Corsi became the leader of the group.

Camminando [It.]. Walking, pushing on.

Campana [It.]. Bell. Campanology is the art of bell-founding and bell-ringing.

Campanette, campanelle [It.]. *Glockenspiel.

Campion, Thomas (Campian) (b. London, 12 Feb. 1567; d. there, 1 Mar. 1620). Physician, poet, and composer. Composed numerous lute songs to his own texts, incl. *A Book of Ayres, Set Foorth to be sung to the Lute Orpherian and Base Violl,* 1601, and other collections; songs for masques. Also published poetry, criticism, and a treatise on counterpoint.

Campo y Zabaleta, Conrado del (b. Madrid, 28 Oct. 1879; d. there, 17 Mar. 1953). Violinist and composer. Pupil of Serrano and Chapí y Lorente at the Madrid Conservatory, of which he later became director. Composed operas (incl. *El final de Don Álvaro,* 1911; *El Avapiés,* with Ángel Barrios, 1919); symphonic poems and other orch. works; string quartets (incl. *Caprichos románticos,* 1908); a concerto for cello; piano pieces; sacred music.

Campos-Parisi, Hector (b. Ponce, Puerto Rico, 1 Oct. 1922). Pupil at the New England Conservatory and of N. Boulanger and Copland. Active in Puerto Rico as a teacher, writer, and composer. Has composed ballets; chamber music; piano pieces; songs.

Campra, André (b. Aix-en-Provence, bapt. 4 Dec. 1660; d. Versailles, 29 June 1744). *Maître de chapelle* at the Toulouse Cathedral, 1683–94, then at Notre Dame in Paris. Conductor of the Opéra from 1703 and its director from 1730. *Maître de la chapelle royale* from 1722. Composed operas and opera-ballets (incl. *L'Europe galante,* 1697; *Le carnaval de Venise,* 1699; *Tancrède,* 1702); 3 books of *Cantates françoises;* motets; psalms; Masses.

Can. Abbr. for *cantoris;* see Decani and *cantoris.*

Canarie, canario. A French dance of the 17th century, named for the natives of the Canary Islands. It is in quick 3/8 or 6/8 time, usually with a dotted note on each strong beat. Examples are found in the harpsichord suites of Chambonnières and Louis Couperin and in the operas of Lully and Purcell (*Dioclesian,* 1690).

Cancan. A French dance of the late 19th century that developed from the quadrille and became world famous for its vulgarity and lasciviousness. J. Offenbach introduced it into his *Orphée aux enfers* (1874).

Cancel. Natural sign. See Accidentals.

Canción [Sp.]. (1) Song. (2) A type of Spanish poetry of the Renaissance, largely derived from Italian models (particularly the *canzone* stanza), in which 7- and 11-syllable lines alternate freely and which makes use of freely invented rhyme schemes.

Cancionero [Sp.]. A collection of songs. The term is applied to collections of poems alone as well as to collections of poems set to music, whether popular or serious in character.

Cancrizans. In crabwise motion; see Retrograde.

Cannabich, (Johann) Christian (Innocenz Bonaventura) (b. Mannheim, bapt. 28 Dec. 1731; d. Frankfurt, 20 Jan. 1798). Pupil of J. Stamitz and Jommelli. First violinist (from 1757) and director (from 1774) of the Mannheim orchestra. Friend of Mozart, who taught his daughter Rosa and dedicated a sonata to her. Composed numerous ballets; a *Singspiel, Azakia,* Mannheim, 1778; a melodrama, *Electra,* Mannheim, 1781; numerous symphonies; violin concertos; many chamber works.

Canon. (1) A contrapuntal device whereby an extended melody, stated in one part, is imitated strictly and in its entirety in one or more other parts. Usually the imitating part follows at a short distance (one measure), as in the accompanying example by Schubert (Piano Trio op. 100, Scherzo). It is thus the strictest form of *imitation.

Vln. and cello

Piano

The leading part is called the *dux,* the following part (or parts) the *comes.* Several types are commonly distinguished. (a) According to the temporal distance between the parts: canon of one, two, etc., measures. (b) According to the interval of imitation: canon in unison, at the fifth, fourth, etc. (c) According to

special devices: canon by *augmentation* or *diminution* (the *comes* has the melody in doubled or in halved values); canon by *inversion* (the *comes* has the inverted melody); *retrograde canon, crab canon,* or *canon cancrizans* (the *comes* imitates the *dux* in retrograde motion; see Retrograde); *canon al contrario riverso* (the *comes* is the retrograde inversion of the *dux*); *group canon* (the *dux* and, consequently, the *comes* consist of two or more parts each; a famous example of this type is Byrd's motet *Diliges Dominum*); *circle canon* or perpetual canon (i.e., one that leads back to the beginning and that therefore may be repeated several times; most of the popular canons called *rounds belong to this type); *spiral canon* or *canon per tonos* (here the melody ends one tone higher than it started; thus the canon must be played six times, e.g., first in C, then in D, E, F♯, etc.; an example is found in Bach's *Musikalisches Opfer* under the title "Ascendenteque modulatione ascendat gloria regis," i.e., "May the glory of the king rise as the modulation ascends"). A canon is called *mixed* if parts are added (usually in the bass) that do not participate in the imitation (e.g., the canons in Bach's *Goldberg Variations*). The term *canon* is also used for what is more properly called (fugal) *stretto.

(2) In early music, the present-day type of canon occurs under such names as *caccia, *chace (14th century), or *fuga* (16th century), while the term *canon* means any kind of inscription ("rule") giving a clue for the execution of a composition that is intentionally notated incompletely or obscurely (*riddle* or *enigmatic canon*). In *mensuration canons* of the 15th and 16th centuries, for example, a single written part must be read simultaneously in different mensurations or proportions [see Mensural notation].

(3) In the Roman liturgy, the Canon is the central and most solemn part of the Mass, said by the officiating priest after the Sanctus. It begins with the words "Te igitur" [see *LU,* p. 4].

Canonical hours. See under Office, Divine.

Cantabile [It.]. Singable, singing.

Cantata. A composite vocal form prominent in the baroque period, consisting usually of a number of movements, such as arias, recitatives, duets, and choruses, which are based on a continuous text that may be either lyrical or dramatic, and that is not intended to be staged. Owing to the activity of J. S. Bach, the church cantata, i.e., a cantata with devotional subject matter, is particularly well known. However, the secular cantata was the earlier and the more common type throughout the 17th century, especially in Italy.

The cantata appeared shortly after 1600 as an offspring of the monodic style [see Monody]. Early examples, such as those by Alessandro Grandi, are written in the form of strophic arias [see Strophic bass]. By mid-century, however, the works of Luigi Rossi, Giacomo Carissimi, and Marc' Antonio Cesti illustrate the composite form clearly in their free alternation of recitative, arioso, and aria. By about 1700 the *da capo* *aria became a standard element, as in the more than 600 cantatas of Alessandro Scarlatti, where usually two or three such arias are linked by recitatives. Similar forms were adopted in France during the 18th century by André Campra, Louis Nicolas Clérambault, and Jean-Philippe Rameau. In Germany, greater importance was given to sacred texts, and chorus and orchestra became important elements in the form. Franz Tunder and Dietrich Buxtehude were among the important predecessors of J. S. Bach in the composition of cantatas. About 200 sacred cantatas by Bach survive, many of which begin with a choral movement in imitative style, proceed with alternating arias and recitatives, and conclude with a *chorale harmonization for chorus and orchestra. An important type is the *chorale cantata. The form has enjoyed less prominence since the 18th century but continues to be cultivated.

Cante flamenco, cante hondo, cante jondo. See under Flamenco.

Canteloube (de Malaret), (Marie-) Joseph (b. Annonay, near Tournon, 21 Oct. 1879; d. Paris, 4 Nov. 1957). Pianist, writer on music, and composer. Pupil of d'Indy. Composed 2 operas, *Le mas,* 1913, prod. Paris, 1929, and *Vercingétorix,* Paris, 1933; symphonic works; numerous songs and arrangements of folksongs for voice with piano or orch. (incl. *Chants d'Auvergne*).

Canti carnascialeschi [It.]. Late 15th- and early 16th-century part songs designed for the elaborate carnival festivities that took place in Florence under the Medicis, particularly Lorenzo de' Medici (ruled 1469–92), who himself wrote a number of the poems. In style as well as form, the *canti carnascialeschi* are very similar to the **frottole.*

Canticle [L. *canticum*]. In the Roman and Anglican liturgies, a scriptural text similar to a psalm but occurring elsewhere than in the Book of Psalms. Important examples include "Magnificat anima mea Dominum" (My soul doth magnify the Lord, Luke 1:46–55, Canticle of the Blessed Virgin Mary); "Benedictus Dominus Deus Israel" (Blessed be the Lord, Luke 1:68–79, Canticle of Zachary); and "Nunc dimittis" (Lord, now lettest thou thy servant depart, Luke 2:29–32, Canticle of Simeon). They play an important role in the Office of the Gregorian rite, where they are sung with *antiphons and *psalm tones like those of the antiphonal psalms of the Office. See Psalmody III.

Cantiga. A monophonic song of the 13th century from Spain, usually in honor of the Virgin Mary (*cantigas de Santa Maria*). More than 400 *cantigas* were collected for Alfonso X (*el Sabio,* the Wise; 1221–84), King of Castile and Leon. The language of these songs is actually a Galician-Portuguese dialect. The chief form of the *cantiga* is the same as that of the **virelai* [see also *Villancico; Zejel*].

Cantilena [It., L.]. (1) A vocal melody of a lyrical rather than a dramatic or virtuosic nature; also, an instrumental passage of the same kind. (2) In medieval writings the term is loosely used for secular vocal compositions, homophonic as well as polyphonic (*ballades, rondeaux,* etc.). See also *Ballade* style.

Cantillation. Religious chanting in recitative style, especially that of the Jewish service.

Cantino [It.; F. *chanterelle*]. The highest string of lutes, viols, and related stringed instruments. A 16th-century German equivalent is *Sangsaite*.

Cantio sacra [L.; pl. *cantiones sacrae*]. *Motet.

Cantionale [L.]. A publication containing simple, homophonic settings of chorales, etc., for the German Protestant service. Hence the designation *cantional style* [G. *Kantionalstil*], used for chorale settings in a homophonic style, with the melody in the topmost voice.

Cantique [F.]. Canticle. Also, a religious song.

Canto [It.]. Song; melody; soprano. For *c. carnascialesco*, see *Canti carnascialeschi; c. fermo, *cantus firmus; c. piano* [Sp. *canto llano*], *plainsong. See also *Col canto*.

Canto de órgano [Sp.]. Polyphony (as opposed to *canto llano*, plainsong), in the Renaissance and baroque eras.

Cantor. In the Roman Catholic liturgy, a soloist who sings the solo portions of the chants (incipits and verses), as opposed to the *schola* (chorus). In Protestant churches, the director of music (e.g., Bach in Leipzig). In the Jewish service, the solo singer, also called *chazzan*.

Cantus [L.]. Song. In 12th-century polyphony, the original voice part, generally lower than the added one, called *discantus*. In 15th- and 16th-century polyphony, the topmost part (abbr. *C*).

Cantus firmus [L.; pl. *cantus* (or *canti*) *firmi;* It. *canto fermo*]. An existing melody that is made the basis of a polyphonic composition. In terms of their origin, *cantus firmi* can be divided into four groups: (a) plainsong melodies; (b) Protestant chorales; (c) secular melodies; (d) abstract subjects. The *cantus firmus* appears frequently in long notes that contrast with the more florid design of the other parts, though it may also be ornamented. Most polyphony from the Middle Ages and much from the Renaissance is based on *cantus firmi*.

Cantus prius factus [L.]. Same as *cantus firmus.

Canzo, canso [Prov.; F. *chanson*]. This term (or similar ones, such as *canzone, Kanzone, chanson,* as well as the deriva-

tive *Rundkanzone,* round-chanson) has been used for a type of troubadour song characterized by initial repeat, A A B [see *Bar* form; *Ballade* (1)], as opposed to the through-composed song, called a *vers.*

Canzona, canzone [It.; pl. *canzone, canzoni*]. (1) In Italian poetry of the 13th through 17th centuries, a serious lyrical poem, usually in several stanzas of identical form employing a freely invented rhyme scheme and free alternation of 7- and 11-syllable lines. (2) In 18th- and 19th-century music, a lyrical song (e.g., the *canzone* "Voi che sapete" in Mozart's *Le nozze di Figaro*) or an instrumental piece of a similar character (e.g., the slow movement of Tchaikovsky's Symphony no. 4, designated "in modo di canzone"). (3) See *Canzo.* (4) Any of several types of 16th-century Italian secular vocal music, including: (a) settings of one or more stanzas of a poem of the type described under (1) above, which settings (employing *canzoni* by Petrarch and others) occur in the *frottola* repertory (*c.* 1510) and have many of the literary and musical features of the 16th-century *madrigal; (b) later popular forms of the *villanella* type, called *canzoni villanesche* and *canzoni alla napolitana.* (5) An important type of instrumental music of the 16th and 17th centuries that developed from the Franco-Flemish *chansons of Josquin, Janequin, Crécquillon, Sermisy, and others. The immense popularity of these chansons is reflected in the numerous arrangements found in nearly all 16th-century sources of lute and keyboard music. In Italy, where the French chanson was called *canzona francese* (or *c. alla francese*), composers wrote original compositions in the style and form of the French models, either for organ (*canzona d'organo*) or for instrumental ensembles (*canzona da sonar*). This procedure eventually led in the instrumental field to the sonata of the 17th century and in keyboard music to the fugue. Like their vocal models, the instrumental canzonas were characterized by clarity of texture, sectional structure often involving repetition (in schemes such as A B A, A B B, A A B C, etc.), and variety of treatment (imitative or homophonic style, duple or triple meter). They differed from the contemporary *ricercar in their tendency toward a harmonically conditioned counterpoint, in the absence of the various devices of "learned counterpoint," in their more lively rhythm, moving in quarter and eighth notes, and in their frequent use of themes starting with reiteration of a single pitch (a device found in many French chansons by Sermisy and his contemporaries; see Ex.). In the key-

board canzona, composers such as Girolamo Cavazzoni, Andrea Gabrieli, and Claudio Merulo through the 16th and into the 17th century made some use of vocal models alongside freely composed works. In the early 17th century, Giovanni Maria Trabaci's works showed the beginnings of the rise to prominence of the *variation canzona,* in which the various sections are based on free rhythmic and melodic variants of a single theme. This procedure was employed by Frescobaldi, Froberger, and others, including J. S. Bach. Throughout its history, the keyboard canzona retained a sectional form; imitation, one of its characteristic devices, employing lively thematic material, forms its principal link to the fugue. In the ensemble canzona, greater emphasis was placed on variety and contrast among the sections, as in the works of Giovanni Gabrieli and his followers around 1600 and in those of Frescobaldi from the 1620s and 1630s. By c. 1650 the terms *canzona* and *sonata* (from *sonare*) were largely synonymous, with the tradition of multimovement instrumental works established under the latter.

Canzona francese. See under Canzona (5).

Canzonet, canzonetta [It.]. In the late 16th and throughout the 17th century, a short, polyphonic vocal piece in a light vein, much in the character of a dance song [see *Balletto*]. The later *canzonette* usually had instrumental accompaniment. The name was also used for short instrumental pieces as well as for short organ *canzonas.

Caoine [pronounced Keen]. An Irish

dirge of ancient tradition. See also Coronach.

Capitolo [It.]. One of the various subspecies of the *frottola,* consisting of a number of three-line stanzas (rhyme scheme *aba bcb cdc*) sung to the same music. Sometimes the final stanza consisted of four lines, the last of which was sung to a different melody.

Caplet, André (b. Le Havre, 23 Nov. 1878; d. Neuilly-sur-Seine, Paris, 22 Apr. 1925). Pupil of Leroux, Lenepveu, and Vidal. Close associate of Debussy. Worked as an opera conductor in Paris, Boston, and London. Composed an oratorio, *Miroir de Jésus,* 1924; orch. works (incl. *Épiphanie* for cello and orch., 1923; *Le masque de la mort rouge,* after Poe, for harp and orch., 1909); choral works; chamber music; piano pieces; songs.

Capo, capotasto [It.; corrupted forms are *capodastro, capotaster;* G. *Kapodaster;* F. *barré*]. A mechanical contrivance used with fretted instruments such as the guitar and the lute to shorten the vibrating length of all the strings simultaneously. It consists of a small piece of hardwood or metal that can be fixed across the fingerboard. By setting the capotasto across, e.g., the first fret, a piece in C-sharp can be fingered as if it were in C. See also *Barré, grand-barré.*

Cappella [It.]. In the Middle Ages, a small place of worship (chapel). In the 14th century the name was used for groups of clerical singers (*cappellani*), superseding the earlier designation *schola cantorum* and eventually coming to mean church choir. After 1600 *cappella* meant any large group of musicians —vocal, instrumental, or mixed. See also Chapel; *Kapelle; A cappella.*

Capriccio [It.; F. *caprice*]. (1) A title used by various 19th-century composers, among them Mendelssohn and Brahms, for pieces of a humorous or capricious character. (2) In the 17th century, the capriccio is one of the four important prefugal forms [see Ricercar; Canzona (5); Fantasia]. The capriccio is less restrained than the others and frequently involves peculiarities such as the use of special themes, e.g., Frescobaldi s *Capriccio sopra il cucu, Capriccio sopra ut re mi fa sol la, Capriccio sopra la bergamasca.* (3) The term also occurs as a noncommittal title of 16th- and 17th-century publications, often vocal. (4) Opera in one act by R. Strauss (libretto by C. Krauss), produced in Munich, 1942. Setting: near Paris, 1775.

Capriccio espagnol. A symphonic suite in five sections, op. 34, by Rimsky-Korsakov, composed in 1887. Native dance rhythms and melodic figures evoke a Spanish atmosphere.

Capriccio italien. A symphonic poem by Tchaikovsky, op. 45, written in 1880 while the composer was visiting Italy. Italian folksongs provide most of the thematic material.

Capriccioso [It.]. Capricious, i.e., to be played in a capricious style.

Cara, Marco (Marchetto) (d. Mantua, *c.* 1530). At the court of Isabella d'Este in Mantua from 1495. With Tromboncino, among the most important composers of *frottole.*

Card Game, The. See *Jeu de cartes.*

Cardew, Cornelius (b. Winchcombe, England, 7 May 1936). Pupil of Stockhausen (with whom he collaborated on *Carré* for 4 orchestras, 4 choruses, and 4 conductors), Ferguson, and Petrassi. Recent works have primarily employed graphic notation and aleatory procedures. Has composed *Autumn '60* for orch., 1960; *First Movement for String Quartet,* 1962, and other chamber works; *3 Winter Potatoes,* 1965, and other piano works; works for unspecified performing media, incl. *Treatise,* 1967, and *Schooltime Compositions,* 1967.

Cardillac. Opera in three acts by Hindemith (libretto by F. Lion, after E. T. A. Hoffmann), produced in Dresden, 1926; new version in Zürich, 1952. Setting: Paris, 17th century.

Carey, Henry (b. prob. Yorkshire, *c.* 1687; d. London, 4 Oct. 1743). Poet, librettist, playwright, and composer. Pupil of Roseingrave and Geminiani. Composed ballad operas (incl. *A Wonder or the Honest Yorkshire-Man,* London, 1735); *The Musical Century,* a collection

of 100 ballads; cantatas; songs (incl. "Sally in our Alley," words now known by a different tune). His son George Savile Carey (1743–1807) falsely attributed to him the authorship of "God Save the King."

Carillon [F.]. A set of bells (originally four) hung in the tower of a church or in a similar structure and played by means of a keyboard or a clockwork mechanism. A modern carillon consists of 30 to 50 bells with a clapper inside, tuned chromatically from C or G through three or four octaves. The clappers are connected by wires to long wooden keys, arranged like those of a manual and a pedal of an organ. The manual keys are struck with the closed hand, which is protected by a glove.

Carissimi, Giacomo (b. Marino, near Rome, bapt. 18 Apr. 1605; d. Rome, 12 Jan. 1674). Organist at Tivoli Cathedral, 1625–27; *maestro di cappella* at San Rufino Cathedral in Assisi, 1628–29, and at the Church of San Apollinare, Rome, from 1630 to his death. Composed oratorios (incl. *Jephte; Jonas; Judicium Salomonis*); Masses, motets, and other sacred music; secular cantatas and arias.

Carmen [L., song; pl. *carmina*]. (1) A term used by 14th- and 15th-century writers for the upper part (*cantus*) of polyphonic compositions, or for entire compositions, specifically chansons. (2) About 1500, name for instrumental compositions of various types, some of them perhaps arrangements of vocal pieces. (3) [Sp. proper name] Opera in four acts by Bizet (libretto by H. Meilhac and L. Halévy, after a story by Mérimée), produced in Paris, 1875. Setting: Seville and environs, 1820.

Carmina burana. A collection from *c.* 1300 of secular Latin songs, mostly of French origin, preserved at the monastery of Benedictbeuren (from which they take their name) in southwest Germany. They were not, in general, part of the repertory of wandering musicians such as the Goliards. Carl Orff's *Carmina burana* (1937) is a scenic oratorio based on 25 of these poems.

Carnaval: scènes mignonnes sur quatre notes [F., Carnival: Dainty Scenes on

Four Notes]. Work for piano by Robert Schumann, op. 9, composed in 1834–35, and consisting of 20 short pieces bearing programmatic titles. The notes in question are derived from the name of a Bohemian town, Asch, by means of the system of German *pitch names. The results are a four-note group, A, Eb, (from the S interpreted as Es), C, and B ♮ (called H in German), and a three-note group, Ab (from As), C, and B ♮.

Carnaval des animaux, Le [F., The Carnival of the Animals]. A "Grand Zoological Fantasy" for orchestra and two pianos by Saint-Saëns, composed in 1886. In a series of brief pieces named for the different animals, the composer uses various instruments and sections of the orchestra in descriptive fashion.

Carnaval romain, Le [F., The Roman Carnival]. Concert overture by Berlioz, op. 9, composed in 1844. The themes are taken from his opera *Benvenuto Cellini* (produced in Paris, 1838).

Carnival songs. See *Canti carnascialeschi.*

Carol [F. *noël;* G. *Weihnachtslied;* It. *canzone di Natale;* Sp. *villancico, cántico de Navidad*]. In present-day usage, a traditional song for the celebration of Christmas. Occasionally the term is used also for other devotional songs of a joyful character (Easter carol; May carol). Originally the carol was not necessarily associated with Christmas. The numerous examples in 15th-century sources show that the distinguishing characteristic of the carol was not its subject matter but its form, especially the presence of a burden or refrain sung in alternation with a number of uniform stanzas called verses. In the 16th century the carol became more varied in form and style but more uniform in subject matter, the emphasis being on Christmas. See also Noel.

Caron, Firmin (same as Philippe or Jean?) (fl. second half of the 15th cent.). Perhaps from Cambrai and active later in Italy. Named by Johannes Tinctoris *c.* 1476 with Ockeghem, Busnois, and Regis as among the best composers that he had ever heard. Composed Masses, chansons, and settings of some Italian texts.

Carpenter, John Alden (b. Park Ridge, Chicago, 28 Feb. 1876; d. Chicago, 26 Apr. 1951). Pupil of Paine, Elgar, and Bernhard Ziehn. Served as vice-president of his family's shipping business, 1909–36. Composed ballets (incl. the "jazz pantomime" *Krazy Kat,* 1921; *Skyscrapers,* 1926); symphonies, concertos, and other orch. works; chamber music; piano pieces; songs (incl. the cycles *Gitanjali,* 1913, after R. Tagore, and *Water Colors,* 1918, on Chinese poems).

Carpentras (real name Elzéar Genet; called "il Carpentrasso") (b. Carpentras, Vaucluse, before 1475; d. Avignon, 14 June 1548). Served Louis XII, who sent him to Rome where he was a member of the papal chapel, 1513–21, and its *maestro di cappella* from 1518. Settled in Avignon, where he was sent on papal business in 1521. Composed Masses, Lamentations, hymns, Magnificats, motets, and other sacred music; French and Italian secular polyphony.

Carr, Benjamin (b. London, 12 Sept. 1768; d. Philadelphia, 24 May 1831). Organist, music publisher, and composer. Pupil of S. Arnold and C. Wesley. Emigrated to the U.S. in 1793; served as organist at St. Augustine's Church and St. Peter's Church in Philadelphia. Composed stage works; *Dead March for Washington,* 1799; piano pieces (incl. *The Federal Overture,* 1794); songs and ballads.

Carrée [F.]. The double whole note, or *breve.

Carrillo, Julián (b. Ahualulco, San Luis Potosí, Mexico, 28 Jan. 1875; d. Mexico City, 9 Sept. 1965). Composer, conductor, and violinist. Pupil of Melesio Morales, Jadassohn, and Reinecke. Developed the microtonal system *Sonido 13* and special instruments and notation for the performance of his compositions in this system. Director of the National Conservatory of Mexico, 1913 and 1920–24. Works (not all of which employ microtones): operas; symphonies; *Horizontes* for small *Sonido 13* orch. accompanied by a conventionally tuned orch., 1950; other orch. works; chamber music; works for solo instruments; *Missa de la restauración* for Pope John XXIII, in quarter tones for men's voices *a cappella*, 1962.

Carse, Adam von Ahn (b. Newcastle-on-Tyne, 19 May 1878; d. Great Missenden, Buckingham, 2 Nov. 1958). Pupil of Corder and Burnett. Member of the faculty of Winchester College, 1909–22; of the Royal Academy of Music, 1922–40. Composed an opera; a dramatic cantata; symphonies, symphonic poems, suites, and other orch. works; choral works; chamber music; piano pieces; songs. Published several books on music history (particularly on the orchestra and its history) and theory.

Carter, Elliott (Cook) (b. New York, 11 Dec. 1908). Pupil of Piston, Hill, and N. Boulanger. Received encouragement from Ives. Has taught at Juilliard, Columbia, Yale, Cornell, and M.I.T. Has composed an opera; ballets (incl. *Pocahontas*, 1939; *The Minotaur*, 1947); a symphony, 1942; *Variations for Orchestra*, 1955; *Concerto for Orchestra*, 1969; *Double Concerto* for harpsichord, piano, 2 chamber orchestras, 1961; a piano concerto, 1966; *Symphony of Three Orchestras*, 1976; choral works; 3 string quartets (no. 2, 1959, and no. 3, 1973, awarded Pulitzer prizes) and other chamber music (incl. a cello sonata, 1948; a woodwind quintet, 1948; a sonata for flute, oboe, cello, and harpsichord, 1952; a duo for violin and piano, 1974; a brass quintet, 1974); a piano sonata, 1946; *A Mirror on Which to Dwell* for soprano and chamber ensemble, 1976; songs.

Carulli, Ferdinando (b. Naples, 20 Feb. 1770; d. Paris, 17 Feb. 1841). Guitarist and composer. Settled in Paris, 1808. Composed numerous works for guitar, incl. concertos and chamber music.

Casadesus, Robert (Marcel) (b. Paris, 7 Apr. 1899; d. there, 19 Sept. 1972). Pianist and composer. Pupil of Leroux. Member of the faculty of the American Conservatory at Fontainebleau from 1934, and its director, 1947–50. Composed symphonies; concertos for 1 and 2 pianos; chamber music; piano sonatas and other pieces.

Casals, Pablo (Pau) (b. Vendrell, Catalonia, 29 Dec. 1876; d. Puerto Rico, 22 Oct. 1973). Virtuoso cellist and composer. Performed in Europe, U.S., and South America from 1895. Settled in Prades, France, after the Spanish Civil War. Composed cello pieces, incl. *Sardanas* for cello ensemble; *La visión de Fray Martín* for chorus; a Christmas oratorio, *El pesebre;* a Miserere and other sacred vocal works.

Casella, Alfredo (b. Turin, 25 July 1883; d. Rome, 5 Mar. 1947). Pianist, conductor, and composer. Pupil of Leroux and Fauré. Toured widely as performer and teacher in Europe and the U.S. Founded the Società italiana di musica moderna, 1917, and reorganized it with d'Annunzio and Malipiero as the Corporazione delle nuove musiche in 1924. Composed operas; ballets (incl. *La giara,* after Pirandello, 1924); orch. works (incl. *Paganiniana*, 1942; *Italia*, 1910; *Scarlattiana* for piano and orch., 1927); concertos; sacred and secular vocal works; chamber music; piano pieces (incl. *11 pezzi infantili*, 1920). Published several books on music history and theory.

Cassa [It.]. Drum. See Percussion instruments.

Cassation [It. *cassazione;* G. *cassatio*]. A term applied in the late 18th century to a variety of lighter multimovement works, often for mixed ensemble of four strings and 2 horns, and sometimes intended for outdoor performance. Closely related (and sometimes synonymous) terms are *divertimento, *notturno,* and *serenade*. Works bearing the title *cassation* include Mozart's K. 63 (for 2 violins, 2 violas, cello, 2 oboes, 2 horns) and K. 99 (for 2 violins, viola, cello, 2 oboes, 2 horns).

Casse-noisette. See *Nutcracker, The.*

Castanets [F. *castagnettes;* G. *Kastagnetten;* It. *nacchere, castagnette;* Sp. *castañuelas*]. A percussion instrument (clappers) consisting of two shell-shaped pieces of hardwood hinged together with a string that passes over the player's thumb. They are used by Spanish dancers, usually in pairs (one set in each hand). The castanets of the modern orchestra (e.g., in Bizet's *Carmen*) have springs and handles (or a connecting stick) that greatly facilitate playing. For ill. see under Percussion instruments.

Castelnuovo-Tedesco, Mario (b. Florence, 3 Apr. 1895; d. Beverly Hills, Calif., 16 Mar. 1968). Pupil of Pizzetti. Settled in the U.S., 1939. Member of the faculty of the Los Angeles Conservatory from 1942. Composed film scores; operas (incl. *La mandragola,* Venice, 1926); ballets; 3 violin concertos, 2 piano concertos, and a cello concerto; biblical oratorios; cantatas; other choral works, incl. a *Sacred Synagogue Service,* 1943; chamber music; guitar pieces (incl. a concerto, 1939, and *Platero y yo,* with speaker, 1960); piano pieces; songs (incl. the cycle *Coplas,* 1915, and numerous settings of Shakespeare).

Castiglioni, Niccolò (b. 17 July 1932). Pianist and composer. Pupil of Ghedini and Blacher. Has composed operas; orch. works (incl. *Synchronie,* 1963; *A Solemn Music II* with soprano, 1965; *Symphony in C* with chorus, 1969); chamber music (incl. *Gymel* for flute and piano, 1960; *Tropi* for flute, clarinet, violin, cello, and percussion, 1959); vocal works; piano and organ pieces.

Castrato [It.]. Also *evirato.* A male singer, castrated as a boy so as to preserve his soprano or alto range after his chest and lungs had become those of an adult. Castration was practiced in Italy in the 16th through the 18th centuries, and such singers were important in *opera seria.* The most famous were F. Senesino (1680–*c.* 1750), G. Caffarelli (1710–83), and Carlo Farinelli (or Carlo Broschi, 1705–82).

Castro, Juan José (b. Avellaneda, Buenos Aires, 7 Mar. 1895; d. Buenos Aires, 3 Sept. 1968). Pupil of d'Indy. Toured widely as a conductor. Director of the Puerto Rico Conservatory from 1959. Composed operas (incl. *Proserpina y el extranjero,* Milan, 1952; settings of García Lorca's *La zapatera prodigiosa,* 1943, and *Bodas de sangre,* Buenos Aires, 1956); ballets; orch. works (incl. *Corales criollos no. 3*); chamber music; pieces for piano (incl. *Sonatina española*); songs.

Catalani, Alfredo (b. Lucca, 19 June 1854; d. Milan, 7 Aug. 1893). Professor of composition at the Milan Conservatory from 1888, succeeding Ponchielli. Composed operas (incl. *Loreley,* Turin, 1890; *Dejanice,* Milan, 1883; *La Wally,*

Milan, 1892); symphonies; a symphonic poem; piano pieces; songs.

Catch. An English *round of the 17th and 18th centuries. Morley, in his *Plaine and Easie Introduction to Practicall Musicke* (1597), mentions the catch as similar to the canon in construction. Today it is often defined as a circular canon, or round. The texts are frequently humorous and obscene.

Catel, Charles-Simon (b. l'Aigle, Orne, 10 June 1773; d. Paris, 29 Nov. 1830). Pupil of Gossec. Professor of harmony (on which he wrote a standard text) at the Paris Conservatory from 1795. Composed primarily operas (incl. *Les bayadères,* Paris, 1810); also some symphonies and chamber music.

Catholicon. A term (meaning "universal"), coined by Glareanus in his *Dodecachordon* (1547), for compositions so designed that they may be sung in more than one *church mode. The two best-known examples are Ockeghem's *Missa cuiusvis toni* (Mass in any mode) and his *Prennez sur moy fuga,* a triple canon at the distance of a fourth.

Cat's Fugue. Popular name of a fugue by Domenico Scarlatti, so called because the theme consists of wide and irregular skips in ascending motion, as if produced by a cat bounding across a keyboard.

Caturla, Alejandro García. See García Caturla, Alejandro.

Cauda [L. tail]. (1) In *mensural notation, the vertical dash attached to certain notes (*maxima, longa, minima,* etc.) or to *ligatures. (2) In the 13th century, a passage without text appearing in a *conductus as an extended vocalization over the first or the last (or next-to-last) vowel of a line of the text.

Caurroy, Eustache du. See Du Caurroy, François Eustache.

Cavalieri, Emilio de' (Del Cavaliere) (b. Rome, *c.* 1550; d. there, 11 Mar. 1602). Participant in the Florentine Camerata. Active in the development of recitative style. Composed *La *rappresentazione di anima e di corpo,* Rome, 1600, often regarded as the first oratorio; Lamentations; *intermedi.*

Cavalleria rusticana [It., Rustic Chivalry]. Opera in one act by P. Mascagni (libretto by G. Menasci and G. Targioni-Tozzetti, based on G. Verga's play), produced in Rome, 1890. Setting: Sicilian village, late 19th century. It inaugurated the musical movement known as *verismo.

Cavalli, Pier Francesco (real name Caletti-Bruni) (b. Crema, 14 Feb. 1602; d. Venice, 17 Jan. 1676). Singer at San Marco, Venice, under Monteverdi, 1617–35; later organist there and finally *maestro di cappella*, 1668. Invited to Paris, 1660–62, to produce an opera (*Serse*) for the marriage of Louis XIV to Maria Theresa of Austria. Composed numerous operas (incl. *Giasone*, Venice, 1649; *Serse*, Venice, 1654; *Ercole amante*, Paris, 1662); a Requiem and other sacred music.

Cavata [It.]. An inscription or an epigram concisely expressing an important thought. In 18th-century music the term is used occasionally for short epigrammatic ariosos found at the end of a long recitative (*recitativo con cavata*). There are many examples in Bach's choral works, e.g., in the recitativo no. 3 of his cantata *Ein' feste Burg* [see Arioso]. The *cavate* in Traëtta's operas approach the *cavatina*.

Cavatina [It.]. In 18th- and 19th-century operas and oratorios, a short solo song, simpler in style than the aria and without repetition of words or phrases, i.e., a "sentence" set to music [see Cavata]. Examples of this type are the two *cavatine* in Haydn's *The Seasons*, and also the "Porgi amor" and "L'ho perduta" from Mozart's *Le nozze di Figaro*. Other examples are in Karl Heinrich Graun's *Montezuma* (1755), Rossini's *Il barbiere di Siviglia* (1816), Weber's *Der Freischütz* (1821), and Gounod's *Faust* (1859). The name has also been applied to instrumental pieces of a songlike character, e.g., Beethoven, Quartet op. 130, fifth movement.

Cavazzoni, Girolamo (b. Urbino, *c*. 1510; d. Mantua, after 1565). Organist and composer. Son of Marco Antonio Cavazzoni and godson of Cardinal Pietro Bembo. Pioneer in the development of the imitative ricercar for keyboard. Composed ricercars, canzonas, hymns, and Magnificats for organ.

Cavazzoni, Marco Antonio (da Bologna, detto d'Urbino) (b. probably Bologna, *c*. 1490; d. Venice, after 1570). Father of Girolamo Cavazzoni. Served as a musician at the papal chapel in Rome; at San Marco in Venice under Willaert; in Padua; and as organist of the Chioggia Cathedral. Composed numerous keyboard works published under the title *Recerchari, motetti, canzoni*, 1523.

Cavendish, Michael (b. *c*. 1565; d. Aldermanbury, London, 5 July 1628). Held the position of "servant in the bedchamber" to Prince Charles (later King Charles I). Composed lute songs and madrigals.

Cazden, Norman (b. New York, 23 Sept. 1914). Pupil of B. Wagenaar, Piston, and Copland. Collector of Catskill Mountain folk music. Has held several teaching positions in U.S. universities and conservatories, incl. the Univ. of Maine from 1969. Has composed *Dingle Hill*, a musical drama, 1958; symphonies, *3 Ballads*, 1949, and other orch. works; *Concerto for 10 Instruments*, 1937; chamber music, incl. *Elizabethan Suites* nos. 1 and 2, 1965; piano pieces.

Cazzati, Maurizio (b. Guastalla, Italy, *c*. 1620; d. Mantua, 1677). Organist, music publisher, and composer. *Maestro di cappella* at the Accademia della Morte in Ferrara, 1650; at Santa Maria Maggiore in Bergamo, 1653–57; at San Petronio in Bologna, 1657–73; then at the court of Mantua until his death. Composed canzonas, sonatas, and other works for one and two violins with thoroughbass, for ensembles, and for keyboard; cantatas; oratorios; Masses, motets, psalms, and other sacred vocal music; secular vocal music.

C.b. [It.]. Abbr. for *col basso* (with the bass) or *contrabasso* (*double bass).

C.d. [It.]. Abbr. for *colla destra* (with the right hand).

Cebell. See Cibell.

Cecilian movement. A 19th-century movement for the reform of Roman Catholic church music, initiated by K. Proske (1794–1861) and named for St. Cecilia, the patron saint of music. The movement aimed at the reinstatement of Palestrina's *a cappella* music to replace the church music for choir and instruments that had come into use during the 18th century.

Cédez [F.]. Slow down.

Ceja, cejilla [Sp.]. *Barré.

Celere [It.]. Quick, swift.

Celesta. See Percussion instruments.

Cellier, Alfred (b. London, 1 Dec. 1844; d. there, 28 Dec. 1891). Conductor and composer. Composed numerous operas and operettas (incl. *The Mask of Pandora,* text by Longfellow, Boston, 1881; *Dorothy,* London, 1886; *The Mountebanks,* London, 1892); a symphonic suite; songs.

Cello (abbr. for *violoncello*). The bass size of the violin, tuned an octave and a fifth below it: C G d a. It is about twice the length of the violin (48 1/2 in. as against 23 1/2 in.) with the other measurements nearly in proportion, except for higher ribs (5 in. as against 1 1/4 in.). [For ill. see under Violin family.] The cello came into existence along with the violin and the viola. Two instruments by Andrea Amati, made between 1560 and 1570, are the earliest preserved specimens.

Cellone. See under Violin family (i).

Cembal d'amour. *Clavecin d'amour.

Cembalo [It.; G.]. Abbr. of *clavicembalo.* *Harpsichord.

Cenerentola, La [It., Cinderella]. Opera in two acts by Rossini (libretto by J. Ferretti), produced in Rome, 1817. Setting: Italy, 18th century (suggested).

Cent. The unit of an exact, scientific method of measuring musical intervals that was introduced by A. J. Ellis (1814–90) and has been widely adopted in acoustics as well as in ethnomusicology. The semitone of equal *temperament equals 100 cents, and the octave contains 1200 cents. Mathematically, cents are a logarithmic measurement; see Intervals, calculation of.

Cento [L.]; **centon** [F.]; **centone** [It.]. Patchwork. The term and its derivatives, "centonization" and "to centonize," refer to literary and musical works made up of selections from other works. The term *cento* has been used for poems consisting only of refrains, for *quodlibets,* and for 18th-century operas put together by several composers [see Pasticcio]. Melodies are said to be centonized if they are pieced together from preexisting fragments. This procedure is of basic importance in the Tracts of Gregorian chant and to a certain extent also in the Graduals and Responsories.

Cercar la nota [It.]. In vocal technique, a slight anticipation of the following note, e.g., d–(c)–c. It may also occur in the form of a passing note, e.g., e–(d)–c.

Ceremony of Carols, A. A setting for treble voices and harp of nine medieval English carols, composed by Benjamin Britten in 1942. A Latin plainsong processional and recessional enframe the carols, which retain their Middle English texts.

Cererols, Joan (b. Martorell, Catalonia, 9 Sept. 1618; d. Montserrat, 28 Aug. 1676). Entered the Monastery of Montserrat in 1636 and was head of its choir school for many years. Composed psalms, hymns, canticles, Vespers, antiphons, Masses, *villancicos,* and other sacred vocal music, some in polychoral style.

Cerha, Friedrich (b. Vienna, 17 Feb. 1926). Composer and musicologist. Pupil of Uhl. Has conducted and performed (as a violinist) much new music with the ensemble Die Reihe, of which he was the founder. Teacher and director of the electronic music studio of the Vienna Academy of Music from 1960. Has composed orch. works (incl. *Espressioni fondamentali,* 1957; *Spiegel I–VII,* with tape, 1960–68); works for violin and piano; works for various chamber ensembles; piano pieces.

Certon, Pierre (d. Paris, 23 Feb. 1572). Held a clerical position at Notre Dame, Paris, 1529; singer at the Sainte-Chapelle, Paris, from 1532 and master of the choirboys by 1542. Composed Masses, motets, psalms, Magnificats; numerous chansons published by Pierre Attaingnant along with those of Claudin de Sermisy and Clément Janequin.

Cervantes, Ignacio (b. Havana, 31 July 1847; d. there, 29 Apr. 1905). Pupil of Gottschalk, Alkan, and Marmontel. Made use of native Cuban materials. Composed an opera, orch. pieces, and piano pieces (incl. *Danzas cubanas*).

Cervelas, cervelat [F.]. French name for the racket (sausage bassoon); see Oboe family III.

Ces, Ceses [G.]. C-flat, C-double-flat; see Pitch names.

Cesti, Marc' Antonio (baptismal name Pietro) (b. Arezzo, bapt. 5 Aug. 1623; d. Florence, 14 Oct. 1669). After having his first operas produced in Venice, he entered the service of Archduke Ferdinand Carlo in Innsbruck, 1652; later served as singer in the papal choir and assistant *Kapellmeister* at the Viennese court. Composed numerous operas (incl. *Orontea*, Venice, 1649; *La Dori*, Florence, 1661; *Il pomo d'oro*, Vienna, 1668); cantatas; motets.

Cetera, cetra [It.]. (1) *Zither. (2) Cittern [see under Guitar].

C.f. Abbr. for *cantus firmus*.

Chabrier, (Alexis-) Emmanuel (b. Ambert, Puy de Dôme, 18 Jan. 1841; d. Paris, 13 Sept. 1894). Studied law and served in government, 1857–79. Belonged to the circles of Saint-Saëns, Massenet, d'Indy, Duparc, and Franck. Composed operas and operettas (incl. *Gwendoline*, Brussels, 1886; *Le roi malgré lui*, Paris, 1887); a cantata; orch. works (incl. *España*, rhapsody, 1883); piano pieces (incl. *Bourrée fantasque*, 1891); songs.

Chace [F.]. A French composition of the early 14th century in the form of a strict *canon at the unison. Unlike the Italian *caccia, which it seems to have antedated slightly, it does not have a free, supporting tenor. Its texts sometimes concern hunting.

Chaconne and passacaglia. Two closely related forms of baroque music, each a kind of continuous *variation, often in moderately slow triple meter and with a slow *harmonic rhythm, the harmonies changing generally with the measure. Baroque composers used the terms in-discriminately. Modern writers have not succeeded in deciding on acceptable definitions, and the literature is full of contradictory and frequently arbitrary statements about the difference between a chaconne and a passacaglia. The only distinction that is valid is that between continuous variations with and without a *basso ostinato* (*ground). The difference between these two types is illustrated in the accompanying examples. Ex. 1 and 2 show a very usual ground, the descending tetrachord in its diatonic form and in its chromatic modification; Ex. 3 shows the use of a (related) scheme of harmonies, without ground.

The terms derive, respectively, from the Spanish terms *chacona* and *pasacalle*, which first appear in about 1600. The former refers to a dance often associated with the early *saraband. The latter refers to music played on the guitar while walking in the street.

Chadwick, George Whitefield (b. Lowell, Mass., 13 Nov. 1854; d. Boston, 4 Apr. 1931). Pupil of Reinecke, Jadassohn, and Rheinberger. Organist at South Congregational Church, Boston, from 1880; taught at the New England Conservatory from 1882 and was its director from 1897 to his death. Composed operas (incl. *Tabasco*, Boston, 1894); symphonies; overtures; *Symphonic Sketches*, 1908, *Suite symphonique*, 1911, and other orch. works; choral works (incl. *Ode for the Opening of the Chicago World's Fair*, 1892); sacred music; chamber music; organ pieces; piano pieces; songs.

Chalumeau [F.]. (1) A 17th-century name for (a) an early oboe (shawm) [see Oboe family III], (b) an early clarinet [for ill.

see under Clarinet family]. The chalumeau in Gluck's *Orfeo ed Euridice* (1762) is probably a real clarinet (with keys). (2) The lowest register of the modern clarinet.

Chamber music. Instrumental ensemble music performed by one player for each part, as opposed to orchestral music in which there are several players for each part. According to the number of players (or parts), chamber music is often classified as follows: *trio (three players), *quartet (four), *quintet (five), *sextet (six), *septet (seven), *octet (eight). String trios (quartets, etc.) are for stringed instruments only; if one of the strings is replaced by another instrument, names such as piano trio (piano and two strings) or horn quintet (horn and four strings) are used. The violin (cello) sonata, for violin (cello) and piano, is sometimes not considered chamber music on account of the markedly solo character of the parts. In chamber music, emphasis lies on the ensemble, not on the individual player.

The string quartets and related forms (including, at times, the *divertimento) of Haydn and Mozart and their contemporaries established the basic principles of form and style to which many composers of chamber music have since adhered: the form is that of the *sonata in four movements; the style is characterized by individual treatment of the parts and exclusion of virtuosic elements. Beethoven, however, particularly in his late string quartets, significantly expanded the character of these forms. The 20th century has seen the composition of works with clear debts to the tradition of Haydn and Mozart as well as of works in which the relationship to that tradition is very weak or nonexistent. Among the latter are a great many works for very diverse combinations of instruments. Such works often bear abstract titles (e.g., *Composition for 4 Instruments*) or more suggestive literary titles.

Chamber music in its broadest sense already existed in the late Middle Ages and Renaissance. Instrumental pieces in this period were not written for, nor restricted to, specific instruments but were performed on whatever instruments were available—viols, recorders, cor-

nettos, or mixed ensembles [see, e.g., Canzona (5); Ricercar]. The chief type of baroque chamber music is the *trio sonata in its two varieties, the *sonata da chiesa* and the *sonata da camera* [see Sonata da camera]. The solo sonata, particularly for violin with *thoroughbass, was also cultivated in this period.

Chamber opera. An opera of small dimensions, of an intimate character, and for small orchestra (chamber orchestra), e.g., R. Strauss' *Ariadne auf Naxos* (second version, 1916).

Chamber orchestra. An orchestra of about 25 players. Before 1800 most orchestras were of this size, and recent composers have again written for such groups (chamber symphony).

Chamber pitch [G. *Kammerton*]. See under Pitch.

Chamber sonata. The baroque *sonata da camera*.

Chambonnières, Jacques Champion de (b. Paris or Chambonnières, *c.* 1602; d. Paris, between 1670 and 1672). Served as court harpsichordist to Louis XIV and was succeeded by his pupil d'Anglebert. Composed two books of harpsichord pieces.

Chaminade, Cécile (-Louise-Stéphanie) (b. Paris, 8 Aug. 1857; d. Monte Carlo, 13 Apr. 1944). Pianist and composer. Pupil of Godard. Composed orch. works; *Les Amazones* for chorus and orch., 1888; 2 piano trios; numerous piano pieces; songs.

Champagne, Claude (b. Montreal, 27 May 1891; d. there, 21 Dec. 1965). Pupil of Gédalge and Laparra. Taught at McGill Univ., 1932–41; at the Conservatoire de la Province de Québec, 1942–62. He collected and used French-Canadian folksongs. Composed *Suite canadienne* for chorus and orch., 1928; symphonic poems (incl. *Altitude*, 1959) and other orch. works; chamber music; piano pieces; violin pieces; a Mass; songs.

Chance music. See Aleatory music.

Chandos Anthems. Twelve anthems by Handel, composed 1716–18 for the Earl of Carnarvon, later Duke of Chandos, and performed at his palace. There also are a *Chandos Te Deum* and a *Chandos Jubilate.*

Change ringing. The ringing of a set (peal) of church bells by a group of people and in a methodical order, the sequence being prescribed not by a melody but by certain schemes of arithmetic permutation. For instance, in a peal of five bells, the first "change" might be 1 2 3 4 5, the second, 2 1 3 4 5, the third, 2 3 1 4 5, and so on. Certain standard selections are known under traditional names such as "Grandsire Triple," "Treble Bob," etc. Change ringing is still widely practiced in England.

Changing note. See under Counterpoint.

Chanler, Theodore (Ward) (b. Newport, R.I., 29 Apr. 1902; d. Boston, 27 July 1961). Pupil of A. Shepherd, Bloch, and N. Boulanger. Composed a chamber opera, *The Pot of Fat,* Cambridge, Mass., 1955; a violin sonata, 1927; songs (incl. *Epitaphs,* 1937, 1940) on texts by Walter de la Mare; *The Children* for children's chorus or voice and piano, 1945; piano pieces.

Chanson [F.]. (1) Song, whether for one or more voices, with or without accompaniment. The term is applied to the monophonic songs of the *troubadours and *trouvères, to the polyphonic *formes fixes of the 14th and 15th centuries (usually composed for three voice-parts, one vocal and two instrumental, e.g., those by Machaut, Dufay, Binchois, Ockeghem, and Busnois; see also *Ars nova;* Burgundian school), and to the freer forms for four or more voices cultivated in the 16th century [see below under (2)]. With the rise of the monodic style in the early 17th century, the polyphonic chanson largely disappeared. The interest turned to *vaudevilles, pastourelles, *bergerettes,* and *brunettes,* i.e., to the more popular styles that predominated throughout the 18th and 19th centuries [see also *Air de cour*]. The late 19th century saw the beginnings of a new tradition of French art song (to which the term *mélodie* is also applied) in which works of the leading French poets have been set by composers such as Duparc, Fauré, Debussy, Ravel, Roussel, and Poulenc. (2) Specifically, a polyphonic secular vocal work from the 15th or 16th century with a French text but not cast in one of the *formes fixes.* The continuous development of such works begins near the end of the 15th century, and prominent among the early composers were Compère, La Rue, and Josquin (all born *c.* 1450). They initiate a highly contrapuntal style for four or more voices that is cultivated particularly by Flemish composers throughout the 16th century. Beginning in the 1520s, Sermisy, Janequin, Certon, and others cultivate a somewhat different style (often called the "Parisian chanson") in which the texture is more frequently homophonic; in this repertory lie the origins of the *vaudeville* and the *air de cour.*

Chanson balladée [F.]. Alternative name, used chiefly by Machaut, for the *virelai.*

Chanson de geste [F.]. A French epic poem of the Middle Ages, such as the *Chanson de Roland* (11th century). Such poems were extremely long (more than 10,000 lines of nearly equal meter) and were divided into sections of various lengths (20 or 50 lines); each section, called a *laisse,* contained one "thought" of the poem. These poems were perhaps sung to a short melodic formula repeated for every line except the last in each *laisse,* for which a different formula with a more definite close was employed.

Chanson de toile [F.]. A trouvère poem of the early 13th century dealing with the sufferings of a lovesick girl or an unhappy wife.

Chanson mesurée. See *Vers mesuré.*

Chansonnier [F.]. A collection of songs. The term is applied particularly to the 13th-century manuscripts containing the monophonic songs of the *troubadours and *trouvères and to the manuscripts of polyphonic chansons from the 15th century.

Chant. (1) General term for liturgical music similar to plainsong, i.e., monophonic and in free rhythm. In particular, the term applies to the liturgical music of the Christian churches, which falls into two main divisions, Eastern chant and Western chant. To the former belong Armenian, *Byzantine, Coptic, and *Syrian chant; to the latter *Ambrosian, *Gallican, *Mozarabic, *Gregorian, and

*Old Roman chant. Also see Anglican chant; Psalm tones. (2) [F.]. Song, melody.

Chantant, chanté [F.]. Singing, sung, i.e., in a singing style.

Chanter. See under Bagpipe.

Chanterelle [F.]. See Cantino.

Chantey, chanty. See Shanty.

Chapel [F. *chapelle;* G. *Kapelle;* It. *cappella;* Sp. *capilla*]. Derived from It. *cappa,* i.e., cape or cloak, the term originally meant a building where the cloaks or other revered relics of saints were housed. It was later extended to apply to private churches of the nobility, Popes, and bishops, as well as to the staff attached to these churches and, in particular, to the musicians and the singers employed there. The connotation of "private body of musicians" survives in the Chapel Royal of the English kings, an institution that played a valuable part in the development and cultivation of English music. A chapel master (It. *maestro di cappella;* F. *maître de chapelle;* G. *Kapellmeister;* Sp. *maestro de capilla*) is the director of such a body of musicians. See also *Cappella; Kapelle; Maîtrise.*

Chapí y Lorente, Ruperto (b. Villena, near Alicante, 27 Mar. 1851; d. Madrid, 25 Mar. 1909). Composed several operas (incl. *Margarita la Tornera,* Madrid, 1909) and very numerous *zarzuelas* (incl. *La tempestad,* 1882; *La revoltosa,* 1897; *La bruja,* 1887); orch., chamber, and vocal works.

Character notation. See Fasola.

Character piece [G. *Charakterstück*]. A convenient term for a large repertory of short 19th-century compositions, mostly for piano or piano and one solo instrument, designed to convey a definite mood or programmatic idea. Often these pieces have titles that suggest briefness or casualness, e.g., Bagatelle, Impromptu, Moment musical. Many have programmatic titles, such as "Der Dichter spricht" (The Poet Speaks; Schumann) or *Jeux d'eau* (The Play of Water; Ravel). Most 19th-century masters contributed to this field, including Beethoven (*Bagatelles*), Schubert (*Im-*

promptus and *Moments musicaux*), Mendelssohn (*Lieder ohne Worte* [Songs Without Words] and *Kinderstücke* [Children's Pieces]), Chopin (*Nocturnes, Préludes, Études, Impromptus,* etc.), Schumann (*Kinderscenen, Fantasiestücke, Novelletten, Nachtstücke* [Night Pieces], *Bunte Blätter* [Colored Leaves], and *Albumblätter* [Album Leaves]), Brahms (*Balladen, Rhapsodien,* capriccios, and intermezzi), and Debussy (two books of *Préludes pour piano*). Schumann also wrote long and difficult compositions consisting of a number of character pieces to be played in succession and representing a unified idea (character cycle), among them his *Papillons, Davidsbündlertänze, Kreisleriana,* and *Carnaval.* Many of these pieces are written in the ternary form A B A [see Binary and ternary form].

Characteristic note. *Leading tone, note.

Charivari. A French term of unknown origin that signifies a deliberately distorted and noisy performance, such as was given in provincial towns in front of the homes of unpopular or objectionable persons, or as a mock serenade for a newly married couple. An American corruption of the name is "shivaree," a German term is *Katzenmusik* (cat music), an Italian, *scampata.*

Charpentier, Gustave (b. Dieuze, Lorraine, 25 June 1860; d. Paris, 18 Feb. 1956). Pupil of Massenet. Founded a conservatory for the working classes, who were the subject of his most successful work, the opera *Louise.* Also composed other operas; orch. works (incl. the suite *Impressions d'Italie,* 1892); choral works; songs.

Charpentier, Marc-Antoine (b. Paris, 1636?; d. there, 24 Feb. 1704). Pupil of Carissimi. Composer for the Comédie-Française, collaborating with Molière and others, 1672–85; served as *maître de musique* at the Sainte-Chapelle, 1698 to his death. Composed operas (incl. *Médée,* libretto by Corneille, Paris, 1693), overtures, intermezzi, and other music for the theater; secular cantatas; Latin and French oratorios (incl. *Le reniement de Saint-Pierre*); Masses, motets, psalms, and other sacred vocal music; airs; instrumental pieces.

Chasins, Abram (b. New York, 17 Aug. 1903). Pianist and composer. Pupil of R. Goldmark. Taught at the Curtis Institute, 1926–35; music consultant for New York radio station WQXR from 1943 and its director from 1947. Composed 2 piano concertos; works for 1 and 2 pianos; orch. works; chamber music. Has published several books on music.

Chasse, La [F., The Hunt]. Title for pieces imitating hunting horns or some other aspect of the hunt. Examples are the so-called "Hunt" Quartets of Haydn and Mozart and the "Hunt" Symphony of Haydn. Also, modernized spelling for the 14th century *chace.

Chaunter. See under Bagpipe.

Chausson, Ernest (-Amédée) (b. Paris, 20 Jan. 1855; d. Limay, near Mantes, 10 June 1899). Pupil of Massenet and Franck. Composed stage works (incl. *Le roi Arthus*, Brussels, 1903); a symphony in B♭, c. 1890, *Poème* for violin and orch., 1896, symphonic poems, and other orch. works; works for chorus and orch.; chamber music; piano pieces; motets; songs.

Chávez, Carlos (b. Mexico City, 13 June 1899; d. there, 2 Aug. 1978). Pupil of Ponce and J. B. Fuentes. Conducted the Orquestra sinfónica, 1928–48; director of the National Conservatory of Mexico, 1928–35. Composed an opera, *The Visitors*, libretto by C. Kallman, 1953; ballets; 6 symphonies; symphonic ode, *Clio*, 1969; *Discovery* for orch., 1969; a violin concerto, 1948; other orch. works; *Cuatro nocturnos* for voice and orch.; *Tambuco* and *Toccata* for percussion; chamber music, incl. string quartets and *Inventions*, nos. 1–3 (for piano; string trio; harp); piano pieces; songs. Books incl. *Musical Thought*, 1961.

Chef d'orchestre [F.]. Conductor. *Chef d'attaque*, concertmaster.

Cheironomy. See Chironomy.

Chekker. See Échiquier.

Cheng. (1) See Jeng. (2) French spelling for *sheng*, the Chinese mouth organ.

Cherubic hymn. (1) In the Byzantine Mass, the *cherubikon* (*cheroubikon*), sung by the choir at the "Great En-trance" (the symbolic entrance of Christ and the cherubim, i.e., angels). An Ordinary chant, it corresponds to the Proper Offertory of the Roman Mass. (2) Name for the Sanctus of the Mass or, more properly, for its Biblical source, the vision of Isaiah, who heard the angels crying unto each other: "Holy, holy, holy is the Lord of Hosts" (Isaiah 6:3).

Cherubini, Luigi (Carlo Zanobi Salvatore Maria) (b. Florence, 8 or 14 Sept. 1760; d. Paris, 15 Mar. 1842). Pupil of Sarti. Court composer in London, 1784–86. Settled in Paris, 1787, where he served as an inspector of the Conservatory from 1796 and its director, 1822–41; succeeded Martini as superintendent of the Royal Chapel, 1816. Composed numerous operas (incl. *Les *deux journées; Médée*, Paris, 1797; *Lodoïska*, Paris, 1791; *Faniska*, Vienna, 1806); a ballet; cantatas; choruses; Masses, motets, and other sacred music; orch. works; chamber music; piano pieces; pedagogic works, incl. *38 Solfeggi* and a book on counterpoint and fugue.

Chest of viols. A set of six or more viols, usually including two trebles, two tenors, and two basses, which, in the 17th century, was kept in a chest with several partitions. See Consort.

Chest voice. The lower register of a voice [see Register (2)].

Chevalet [F.]. Bridge of violins, etc. See Bowing (k).

Cheville [F.]. Peg of stringed instruments. *Cheviller*, pegbox.

Chevreuille, Raymond (b. Brussels, 17 Nov. 1901). Studied at the Brussels Conservatory, though largely self-taught in composition. Engineer and later director of music programming at Brussels Radio and Television. Has composed 7 symphonies; 3 piano concertos; 3 violin concertos; 2 cello concertos; 6 string quartets; cantatas; radio plays; other orch. and chamber works.

Chiaramente [It.]. Clearly, distinctly.

Chiave [It.]. *Clef.

Chiavette (sing. *chiavetta*), **chiavi trasportati** [It.]. A late 16th-century system of writing vocal music with all the clefs moved down or up a third from their normal position, so that, e.g., the F-clef would appear on line 3 (baritone clef) or on line 5 (subbass clef) rather than on line 4 (bass clef; see Clef, Ex. 3, h–j). Examples of compositions notated in the lowered clefs are quite numerous, while the system with the raised clefs was much more rarely used. Until recently, it was generally thought that they indicated a transposition to the lower or upper third, respectively. Recent studies have shown that this theory is without historical foundation. The clefs were moved mainly in order to avoid the use of ledger lines. Evidence has been found, however, that the lowered clefs occasionally indicated transposition down a fourth or a fifth.

Chiesa [It., church]. In baroque music, *da chiesa* indicates instrumental pieces (sonatas, concertos) or vocal pieces with instrumental accompaniment (cantatas) designed for use in the church, as opposed to similar pieces for secular use, designated *da *camera*. See *Sonata da camera, sonata da chiesa*.

Chifonie [F.]. Medieval (12th–15th cent.) corruption of *symphonia, i.e., *hurdy-gurdy.

Chihara, Paul (b. Seattle, 9 July 1938). Pupil of N. Boulanger, Schuller, Palmer, and Pepping. Member of the faculty of the Univ. of California at Los Angeles from 1966. Works incl. the ballet *Shinju,* 1974; *Forest Music,* 1968, and other pieces for orch.; a viola concerto, 1965; a Magnificat for treble voices, 1966, and other choral works; *Logs XVI* for amplified string bass and magnetic tape, 1969; *Primavera* for string quartet, 1978; music for films.

Child, William (b. Bristol, 1606 or 1607; d. Windsor, 23 Mar. 1697). Organist at St. George's Cathedral, 1632; held several posts in the Chapel Royal from 1660. Composed services, psalms, anthems, canons, catches.

Childhood of Christ, The. See *Enfance du Christ, L'.*

Children's Corner. Set of 6 piano pieces (with English titles) by Debussy, composed 1906–8: "Doctor Gradus ad Parnassum" (humorous allusion to Clementi's **Gradus ad Parnassum);* "Jimbo's Lullaby"; "Serenade for the Doll"; "Snow Is Dancing"; "The Little Shepherd"; "Golliwogg's Cakewalk." They were written for Debussy's daughter, Claude-Emma, referred to as "Chou-chou" in the dedication.

Childs, Barney (b. Spokane, Wash., 13 Feb. 1926). Pupil of Chávez, Copland, and Carter. Has taught both English and music at U.S. colleges. Has worked with aleatory procedures and has made some use of American Indian melodies. Works incl. 2 symphonies; *Concerto* for clarinet, 1970; *Nonet,* 1967; *Quartet* for clarinet and strings, 1953, several string quartets, and other chamber music; *Keet Seel* for chorus *a cappella,* 1970; *When Lilacs Last in the Dooryard Bloom'd,* after Whitman, for vocal soloists, chorus, and band, 1971.

Chimes. See under Percussion instruments I. The term is also used for a set of real bells (*carillon), for the orchestral glockenspiel [see Percussion instruments I], and for various Oriental instruments consisting of a series of tuned sonorous agents (gong chimes, stone chimes).

Chiming. See under Bell.

Ch'in. See Chyn.

Chinese block. A percussion instrument that consists of a hollowed-out wooden block of rectangular cross section. Played with a drumstick, it produces a dry, hollow sound. See also Temple block.

Chinese crescent, Chinese pavilion. See Turkish crescent.

Ching. Korean gong, corresponding to the Chinese *jeng (2).

Chironomy. A term for neumatic signs lacking clear indication of pitch, the implication being that such signs were interpreted to the choir by the conducting precentor, who moved his hands [Gr. *cheir*] in an appropriate manner. The clearest information about this method is found in Byzantine sources, according to which it dates from the time of Kosmas and John Damascene (8th century). See Neumes.

Chisholm, Erik (b. Glasgow, 4 Jan. 1904; d. Rondebosch, South Africa, 8 June 1965). Pupil of Tovey. Served as music critic for Scottish journals, 1930–34. Conducted the Glasgow Grand Opera Society and the Carl Rosa Opera Company. Director of the South African College of Music at Cape Town Univ. from 1945 to his death. Composed operas; ballets; 2 symphonies; concertos for piano and for violin; other orch. works; chamber music.

Chitarra [It.]. *Guitar. The *chitarrina* is a smaller type, used in Naples.

Chitarra battente [It.]. See under Guitar family.

Chitarrone [It.]. See under Lute.

Chiterna [It.]. Same as *cittern, gittern;* see Guitar family.

Chiuso [It.]. In horn playing, same as stopped; see Horn. In 14th-century music, see Ouvert and clos.

Choir. A body of church singers, as opposed to a secular chorus. The name is also used for instrumental groups of the orchestra, e.g., brass choir, string choir, woodwind choir.

Choir organ. Originally, a small organ used to accompany the choir. Today, the third manual of the normal *organ, which is provided with stops useful for accompaniment purposes.

Choir pitch. See under Pitch (3).

Choirbook [G. *Chorbuch*]. The large-sized manuscripts of 15th- and 16th-century polyphonic music that were placed on a stand and from which the whole choir (about 15 singers) sang. For choirbook arrangement, see under Score.

Chopin, Frédéric (François) (b. Zelazowa Wola, near Warsaw, 1 Mar. or 22 Feb. 1810; d. Paris, 17 Oct. 1849). Pianist and composer. Pupil of Elsner. Settled in Paris, 1831, where he taught piano privately and gave concerts. Belonged to the circles of Liszt, Berlioz, Meyerbeer, Bellini, Balzac, Heine; his ten-year liaison with George Sand (Mme. Dudevant) is reflected in her novel, *Lucrezia Floriani.* Composed works for piano solo: mazurkas, variations, nocturnes, etudes, waltzes, ballades, impromptus, polonaises, scherzos, preludes, sonatas (incl. *Sonate funèbre*), and other pieces (incl. *Berceuse, Fantaisie-Impromptu,* and *Barcarolle*); works for piano with orch. (incl. 2 piano concertos), and with cello; a piano trio; Polish songs.

Chor [G.]. A chorus or choir.

Choral [G.]. (1) The plainsong of the Roman Catholic Church, usually called *Gregorianischer Choral* [see Gregorian chant]. (2) The hymn tunes of the German Protestant Church [see Chorale].

Choral, chorale. According to Webster, *cho'ral* (adj.) means of or belonging to a chorus or a choir, while *choral'* (noun) means a hymn tune, a sacred melody. For the latter meaning, the spelling "chorale" is preferred, and the same preference is observed in the present book. Thus, a "choral fantasia" is a fantasia employing a chorus, whereas a "chorale fantasia" is a fantasia based on a hymn tune. Unfortunately, the situation is further complicated by the fact that the word *chorale* usually refers to the hymn tunes of the German Protestant Church, which in German are called *Choral* (accent on the last syllable), while, on the other hand, the equivalent of the English adjective "choral" is the German noun *Chor-* (united to the noun it precedes). Thus, we have the following equivalents: E. choral fantasia = G. *Chorfantasie;* E. chorale fantasia = G. *Choralfantasie.* Similarly, choral cantata = *Chorkantate;* chorale cantata = *Choralkantate.* See also Chorale.

Choral cantata [G. *Chorkantate*]. A cantata that employs a chorus (as most cantatas by Bach do), as opposed to a solo cantata (the usual type of the 17th-century Italian cantata). See also Chorale cantata.

Choral Symphony. Popular name for Beethoven's Symphony no. 9 in D minor, op. 125 (1823–24), which in the last movement uses a chorus (and four soloists) in addition to the orchestra. The formal plan of the symphony is: I. Allegro; II. Scherzo with Trio; III. Adagio; IV. Introduction (with quotations of themes from the preceding movements) and Allegro assai (with chorus on Schiller's poem, "Ode to Joy" [G.

"Freude, schöne Götterfunken"]). The original title is: *Sinfonie mit Schlusschor über Schillers Ode: "An die Freude," für grosses Orchester, 4 Solo- und 4 Chorstimmen.*

Choralbearbeitung [G.]. Generic term for any composition based on a *Choral* (chorale). The term refers chiefly to the various methods of composition used for Protestant chorales from 1600 to 1750 [see Chorale cantata; Chorale fantasia; Chorale prelude; Chorale variations; Organ chorale]. However, it has also been used by German musicologists for compositions based on Gregorian melodies, especially for the organa and *clausulae* of the 12th and 13th centuries.

Chorale [G. *Choral*]. A hymn tune of the German Protestant Church. Martin Luther (1483–1546), an accomplished musician himself, considered the chorale a pillar of his reform movement and played a very active part in building a suitable repertory of texts and melodies. In conformity with his principle of congregational participation, he favored vernacular texts and simple, tuneful melodies. In his search for suitable texts Luther resorted chiefly to Roman Catholic hymns, many of which he (or his collaborators) translated into German, e.g., "Nun komm, der Heiden Heiland" ("Veni redemptor gentium"). The chief sources for his melodies were secular songs for which he or his collaborators provided new (sacred) texts, e.g., "Durch Adams Fall ist ganz verderbt" (from the song "Freut euch, freut euch in dieser Zeit"). Some Gregorian melodies were also retained, and Luther himself composed some new texts and perhaps their melodies as well, e.g., "Ein' feste Burg" ("A mighty fortress"). The first polyphonic settings of chorales in the 16th century, by Johann Walter, were in the style of the motet and placed the chorale melody in the tenor. Later in the century, homophonic settings suitable for congregational performance were composed (by Lucas Osiander and others) with the chorale melody in the uppermost part [see Cantionale]. New chorales continued to be created through the 17th century, and the 17th and 18th centuries saw the creation of numerous organ and choral works based on chorale texts and melodies. The chorale harmonizations of J. S. Bach continue to be used widely and are regarded as models for the writing of tonal harmony in four parts. See also Chorale cantata; Chorale fantasia; Chorale fugue; Chorale motet; Chorale prelude; Chorale variations; Organ chorale.

Chorale cantata [G. *Choralkantate*]. A term applied, usually with reference to Bach's works, to cantatas in which chorale texts (and, as a rule, chorale melodies) are used for movements other than the final one, itself nearly always a harmonized chorale. The following types may be distinguished: (a) those in which chorale texts are used for all the movements; (b) those in which some of the chorale verses are recast in free poetry in order to allow for arialike treatment; (c) those in which chorale texts are used in some movements while the others are free recitatives or arias. The only example of (a) is Bach's early cantata *Christ lag in Todesbanden.* An example of (b) is *Ach Gott vom Himmel,* and examples of (c) are *Wachet auf* and *Ein' feste Burg.*

Chorale fantasia. An organ composition in which a *chorale melody is treated in the free manner of a *fantasia, involving various techniques, such as ornamentation, fragmentation, and echo effects.

Chorale fugue. A term often used as a synonym of *chorale motet* but that might better be used for a different type of chorale composition, nearly always for organ, in which there is imitative treatment only of the initial line of the *chorale melody, which thus becomes the theme of a real fugue. As a result of this restriction, the chorale fugue is much shorter as well as stylistically simpler than the chorale motet. Those by J. S. Bach are often termed *fughetta:*

Chorale motet. A composition in which a *chorale melody is treated in *motet style, i.e., as a succession of imitative sections, each based on one of the successive lines of the chorale. Examples abound in vocal music from Josquin (*Veni sancte spiritus*) to Bach (first movements of cantatas nos. 16, 27, 58, 60, 73, 95, etc.), as well as in organ music, where the chorale motet is one of the principal types of *organ chorale (e.g., Bach's *Nun komm, der Heiden Heiland* and *Wenn wir in höchsten Nöten sein*).

Chorale prelude [G. *Choralvorspiel*]. An organ composition based on a Protestant *chorale and designed to be played before the chorale is sung by the congregation. See Organ chorale.

Chorale variations. Variations on a *chorale melody, nearly always for organ or harpsichord, occasionally for lute. In the late baroque period this form was often called a *partita (Pachelbel, Bach). It was favored especially by the earliest composers of Protestant *organ chorales. All the settings by Sweelinck and nearly all those by Scheidt consist of variations, called *versus*.

Choralis Constantinus. A large cycle of liturgical compositions written by H. Isaac (*c.* 1450–1517) for the cathedral of Constance, completed by his pupil, L. Senfl, and published posthumously by Formschneider (Nuremberg) in three volumes (1550–55). It consists of polyphonic settings of the Proper of the Mass.

Chord. Three or more tones sounded simultaneously, two simultaneous tones usually being designated as an *interval. The most basic chords in the system of tonic-dominant (or triadic) tonality are the major and minor *triads and their *inversions (i.e., *sixth chords and *six-four chords). Other chords that play an important, though subordinate, role are the *seventh chord, the *ninth chord, the augmented sixth chord, and the diminished triad, each of which is regarded in this context as dissonant [see Consonance, dissonance]. In works of the 20th century not based on this system, chords of numerous kinds are used, the concepts of consonance and dissonance being often irrelevant [see also Fourth chord; Tone cluster]. In discussions of such music, the term *simultaneity* is sometimes preferred to *chord*, the latter appearing in such compounds as *trichord, tetrachord, pentachord,* and *hexachord* for collections of 3, 4, 5, and 6 pitches, respectively, which may or may not be sounded simultaneously.

Chordal style. A composition or a passage is said to be in chordal style if its texture consists essentially of a series of chords. In strict chordal style there is a given number of parts, usually four (e.g., a hymn); in free chordal style there is no such restriction (e.g., Chopin's *Prélude* no. 20). See Homorhythmic.

Chordophone. See under Instruments.

Chorister. Boy singer in a choir.

Chorlied [G.]. Choral song, particularly one without accompaniment. Such pieces were composed by Schumann, Mendelssohn, and others.

Chôro [Port.]. Originally, Brazilian term for an ensemble of serenaders, i.e., a kind of popular band consisting of small and large guitars, flutes, trumpets, and percussion instruments. Today the term is very loosely used for many kinds of ensemble music in which one instrument dominates the others and is used for virtuoso improvisation. Villa-Lobos and many other Brazilian composers have used the *chôro* in art music.

Chorton [G.]. See under Pitch (3).

Chorus. (1) A large body of singers, not connected with a church [see Choir]. Also, music for such a body. (2) Medieval Latin name for the *crwth or the *bagpipe. (3) Same as burden, *refrain.

Chou, Wen-chung (b. Chefoo, China, 29 June 1923). Settled in the U.S., 1946. Pupil of Varèse, Luening, McKinley, Slonimsky, and Martinů. Member of the faculty of Columbia Univ. from 1964. Has worked with *I Ching* principles and other Chinese sources. Works incl. *7 Poems of T'ang Dynasty* for tenor and instruments, 1952; *And the Fallen Petals* for orch., 1954; *Riding the Wind* for wind orch., 1964; *Pien* for piano, winds, percussion, 1966; film music.

Christ on the Mount of Olives. See *Christus am Ölberge*.

Christmas Concerto. Corelli's Concerto Grosso in G minor, op. 6, no. 8, entitled "Fatto per la Notte di Natale" (made for Christmas Night). The closing movement is a *pastorale.

Christmas Oratorio [G. *Weihnachts-Oratorium*]. Bach's *Christmas Oratorio*, composed in 1734, consists of six church cantatas, intended to be performed on six different days between Christmas Day and Epiphany. A number of the pieces in the oratorio are borrowed from earlier cantatas. An important forerunner of Bach's work is Schütz's Christmas oratorio, entitled *Historia der freuden- und gnadenreichen Geburth Gottes und Marien Sohnes, Jesu Christi* (1664).

Christophe Colomb [F., Christopher Columbus]. Opera in two parts by D. Milhaud (libretto by P. Claudel), produced in Berlin, 1930. Setting: Spain, end of the 15th century.

Christou, Yannis (b. Heliopolis, Egypt, 9 Jan. 1926; d. near Athens, 8 Jan. 1970). Studied philosophy at Cambridge with Wittgenstein and Russell; psychology in Zürich with Jung; music in England with H. Redlich and in Italy with F. Lavagnino. Settled in Greece in 1956. Employed serial techniques and later adopted aleatory procedures and developed a form of graphic notation. Composed *The Strychnine Lady* for actors, instruments, tapes, etc., 1967; music for Greek plays; oratorios (incl. *Mysterion*, with speakers, actors, choruses, orch., tape, 1966); orch. works (incl. *Enantiodromia*, 1968); *Praxis for 12* for 11 strings and piano, also for string orch. and piano, 1966.

Christus am Ölberge [G., Christ on the Mount of Olives]. Oratorio by Beethoven, op. 85 (libretto by F. X. Huber), first performed in Vienna, 1803.

Chromatic. An adjective applied to (1) the *scale that includes all of the 12 pitches (and thus all of the 12 semitones) contained in an octave (as opposed to the *diatonic scale); (2) harmony and melodies that employ some if not all of the pitches of the chromatic scale in addition to those of the diatonic scale of some particular key, whether or not the harmony or melody in question can be understood within the context of any single key; (3) an instrument capable of playing a chromatic scale, e.g., brass instruments with valves as distinct from natural instruments [but see also Harp]; (4) one of the three genera (the other two being *diatonic and *enharmonic) of an-

cient Greek music, namely the one employing a *tetrachord bounded by a perfect fourth and in which the lower two intervals are both semitones. (5) In the 16th century the Italian word *cromatico*, as in Cipriano de Rore's *Libro de madregali cromatici* (1544), occasionally refers to works that use not semitones but black notes and are thus also described as being *a note nere*.

Chromatic Fantasy and Fugue. A composition (*c.* 1720) for harpsichord by J. S. Bach that uses extended chromatic harmonies in the fantasy and a chromatic progression in the theme of the fugue.

Chromaticism. The use of at least some pitches of the *chromatic scale in addition to those of the *diatonic scale of some particular key. It can occur in limited degrees that do not detract from the sense of key or tonal center, and thus it can function fully within the system of tonic-dominant *tonality. Its increasing use in the later 19th century, however, led eventually to the abandonment of tonality by many composers. This last development may be seen to begin with the mature works of Richard Wagner, in which chromaticism is used in such a way as to produce long passages in which no single key assumes predominance, and to lead to the atonal works [see Atonality] of Arnold Schoenberg and others in the 20th century. There are also important instances of chromaticism in music composed before the system of tonality became fully established, e.g., in 16th-century madrigals by composers such as Luca Marenzio and Carlo Gesualdo.

Chronos, chronos protos [Gr.]. The temporal or rhythmic unit of ancient Greek music. It is not divisible into smaller values.

Chueca, Federico (b. Madrid, 5 May 1846; d. there, 20 June 1908). Composed numerous *zarzuelas* (incl. *La Gran Vía*, Madrid, 1886, with Valverde; *Cádiz; Agua, azucarillos y aguardiente*); also waltzes and other dances.

Church modes [L. *modus, tonus*]. The church modes (ecclesiastical modes) are a system, originating in the Middle Ages, of eight scales, each consisting of the

			Fin.	Amb.	Dom.
I. *Protus auth.*	*Primus tonus*	Dorian	d	d–d′	a
II. " *plag.*	*Secundus t.*	Hypodorian	d	A–a	f
III. *Deuterus auth.*	*Tertius t.*	Phrygian	e	e–e′	c′
IV. " *plag.*	*Quartus t.*	Hypophrygian	e	B–b	a
V. *Tritus auth.*	*Quintus t.*	Lydian	f	f–f′	c′
VI. " *plag.*	*Sextus t.*	Hypolydian	f	c–c′	a
VII. *Tetrardus auth.*	*Septimus t.*	Mixolydian	g	g–g′	d′
VIII. " *plag.*	*Octavus t.*	Hypomixolydian	g	d–d′	c′
IX.	*Nonus t.*	Aeolian	a	a–a′	e′
X.	*Decimus t.*	Hypoaeolian	a	e–e′	c′
XI.	*Undecimus t.*	Ionian	c′	c′–c″	g′
XII.	*Duodecimus t.*	Hypoionian	c′	g–g′	e′

Church modes

tones of the C major scale but starting and closing on d, e, f, or g and limited to the range of about an octave. For each of these four notes, called a final (*finalis*), there exist two modes distinguished by different positions of the octave range (*ambitus*) and called, respectively, authentic and plagal. In the *authentic modes* the ambitus extends from the final to the upper octave; in the *plagal modes,* from the fourth below the final to the fifth above it. The designation, still occasionally encountered, of the authentic modes as "Ambrosian" and of the plagal modes as "Gregorian" is entirely without tonal foundation. The octave range or ambitus of either form of mode may be enlarged by the addition of the *subtonium,* i.e., the tone below its lower limit or by a tone (even two) above. This additional tone below the final is of particular importance in the authentic modes, where it is used for cadences (e.g., in the progressions c–d, d–e, etc.), and in these it is also called the subfinal (*subfinalis*). The eight scales just described are the basis of the tonal classification of Gregorian chant, and beginning in the late 15th century they were used in discussions of polyphonic music as well. In the 16th century, H. Glareanus (*Dodecachordon,* 1547), enlarged the eight-mode system of Gregorian chant to include the two scales on a and the two scales on c′ (essentially our minor and major), thus bringing the number up to twelve. This system, too, was applied to polyphonic music.

The earliest designation (9th century) for the modes was derived from the names *protus, deuterus, tritus,* and *tetrardus* (corruptions of Gr.; first, second,

third, fourth) given to the four basic finals: *protus authenticus* (final d; range d–d′), *protus plagius* (d; A–a), *deuterus authenticus* (e; e–e′), *deuterus plagius* (e; B–b), etc. Slightly later we find the most common (and preferable) designation, in which the modes (originally called *tonus) are numbered in the same order: *primus tonus* (d; d–d′), *secundus tonus* (d; A–a), etc. Early discussions of the modes also stress the importance of *melody type and characteristic opening phrases for each of the modes. [See also Echos.] Another terminology, rarely employed in the Middle Ages but commonly used today, borrows its names from ancient Greek theory: the four authentic modes are called *Dorian, Phrygian, Lydian,* and *Mixolydian;* the prefix *hypo-* is employed for the plagal modes (*Hypodorian,* etc.). To these names Glareanus added *Aeolian* (for a) and *Ionian* (for c′). Zarlino, in his *Istitutioni harmoniche* of 1558, adopted Glareanus' system of twelve modes but placed the Ionian and Hypoionian first, so that the series began with the two modes on c. In modern writings the twelve-mode system is sometimes enlarged to one of fourteen by the addition of *Locrian* and *Hypolocrian,* based on the tone b as the final. These modes are mentioned by Glareanus (under the names Hyperaeolian and Hyperphrygian) but rejected because they involve a diminished fifth (b–f′) above the final.

In addition to the final and ambitus, each mode is usually said to have a third characteristic, called the *dominant,* somewhat in the nature of a secondary tonal center. As a rule, the dominant is a fifth above the final in the authentic modes, a third above it in the plagal modes. However, the tone b, which was not used as a final [see above], was also avoided as a dominant and was replaced by c' (in modes III and VIII). Another change occurred in mode IV, where the dominant g was raised to a. Actually, these dominants are a characteristic less of the modes than of a few special recitation formulas associated with the modes, that is, the eight *psalm tones (also tones for the Magnificat, etc.), in which they are used as the pitch for the monotone recitation. Therefore, what is called dominant should properly be called recitation tone (*repercussio, tenor, tuba;* see accompanying table).

Church sonata. The *sonata da chiesa* of the baroque; see under *Sonata da camera.*

Chyn, guuchyn (*ch'in, ku-ch'in*). A Chinese seven-stringed zither made of hollowed wood, about 4 feet long, 8 inches wide, and 3 inches thick [see ill. accompanying Zither]. The strings, made of silk, are stretched over the entire length of the board. The most common tuning is C D F G A c d. It is often played so as to produce harmonics.

Ciaccona [It.]. *Chaconne.

Cialamello [It.]. Shawm. See under Oboe family.

Cibell, cebell. A 17th-century name for the *gavotte, used by Purcell and others. The name is derived from a song in praise of the goddess Cybele, found in Lully's opera *Athys.*

Ciconia, Johannes (b. Liège, *c.* 1335–40; d. Padua, Dec. 1411). Theorist and composer. Traveled in Italy, 1358–67; held a prebend in Liège, 1372–1401, and was a canon in Padua thereafter. Composed Mass sections, motets, and secular pieces with texts in French and in Italian.

Cifra, Antonio (b. in or near Terracina, 1584; d. Loreto, 2 Oct. 1629). Pupil of Nanino. *Maestro di cappella* at Santa Casa di Loreto, 1609–22 and from 1626; and at San Giovanni in Laterano, Rome, 1623–26. Composed Masses, motets, psalms, church concertos, antiphons, and other sacred music; madrigals; ricercars and canzonas.

Cikker, Ján (b. Banska Bystrica, Czechoslovakia, 29 July 1911). Pupil of Křička and Novák. Teacher at the Prague Conservatory from 1939; at the Bratislava Conservatory from 1951. Has primarily composed operas, incl. *Juro Jánošík,* Bratislava, 1954; *Prince Bajazid,* Bratislava, 1957; *The Resurrection* (after Tolstoy), Prague, 1962; *Mister Scrooge* (after Dickens), Kassel, 1963; also symphonic poems and 2 string quartets.

Cilèa, Francesco (b. Palmi, Calabria, 26 July 1866; d. Varazze, 20 Nov. 1950). Pianist and composer. Studied at the Naples Conservatory. Director of the Palermo Conservatory, 1913–16, and of the Majella Conservatory in Naples, 1916–35. Composed operas (incl. *Adriana Lecouvreur; L'arlesiana,* Milan, 1897); 2 orch. suites; *Poema sinfonico* for solo, chorus, orch., 1913; chamber music; piano pieces; songs.

Cimarosa, Domenico (b. Aversa, near Naples, 17 Dec. 1749; d. Venice, 11 Jan. 1801). Pupil of Sacchini and probably of Piccinni. Composer to the Russian court in St. Petersburg, 1787–91 (succeeding Paisiello); *Kapellmeister* (succeeding Salieri) to the Emperor Leopold at Vienna, 1791–93. Otherwise active principally in Rome and Naples. Composed numerous operas (incl. *Il *matrimonio segreto; Le stravaganze del conte,* Naples, 1772; *Gli Orazi e Curiazi,* Venice, 1794); cantatas; oratorios; Masses, motets, psalms, and other sacred music; keyboard sonatas and other instrumental works; *solfeggi; songs.*

Cimbalom. A large *dulcimer used in Hungarian gypsy and popular music. The effects of the cimbalom are imitated in Liszt's Hungarian Rhapsody no. 11 ("quasi *Zimbalo"*), and the instrument itself is called for in Stravinsky's *Renard* and Kodály's *Háry János* suite. For ill. see under Zither.

Cimbasso [It.]. A narrow-bore tuba in B♭.

Cinelli [It.]. Cymbals.

Cinque-pace [It. *cinque passi;* F. *cinq pas;* Eng. *sinkapass, sink pas, sink-a-pace, sinck a part,* etc.]. The basic five steps of the Renaissance *galliard and *saltarello, consisting of a forward thrust of alternate legs (L R L R) on the first four beats of the measure (coincidentally with each thrust the opposite foot executes a bounce), a leap on the fifth beat, and a resting stance (posture) on the sixth. All movements were gentle for the *saltarello* and pronounced for the galliard.

Cipher, ciphering. The continued sounding of an organ pipe, due to some defect of the mechanism.

Circle of fifths. The circular, clockwise arrangement of the twelve keys in an order of ascending fifths (C, G, d, a, etc.), showing that after twelve such steps the initial key is reached again. In this order, each successive key increases by one the number of sharps in the key signature. If the circle is viewed counterclockwise (i.e., order of descending fifths: c', f, B♭, etc.), the keys follow each other with one more flat in the signature. At one point of the circle the transition from the sharp keys to the flat keys must be made, for instance, at F♯ = G♭ (*enharmonic change). The scheme of signatures might also serve for the minor keys, by starting from A in-

stead of from C. The series of fifths "closes" only in well-tempered tuning [see Temperament]. If Pythagorean (pure) fifths are considered, the 12th of these fifths is higher by the Pythagorean comma (about one-eighth of a tone) than the starting tone. See also Key relationship.

Cis, Cisis [G.]. C-sharp, C-double-sharp; see Pitch names.

Cister, cistre, cither, citole, cittern. See under Guitar family.

Cithara. Medieval spelling of *kithara.

Cl. Abbr. for *clarinet.*

Clair de lune [F.]. A piano piece by Debussy, properly the third movement of his *Suite Bergamasque.*

Clairon [F.]. Bugle. See under Brass instruments III.

Clapp, Philip Greeley (b. Boston, 4 Aug. 1888; d. Iowa City, 9 Apr. 1954). Studied at Harvard and with Schillings in Stuttgart. Held teaching positions at Harvard, Dartmouth, Juilliard; at the Univ. of Iowa from 1919. Composed symphonies and symphonic poems; *A Chant of Darkness* for chorus and orch.; a 2-piano concerto; chamber music; violin sonata; songs.

Claquebois [F.]. *Xylophone.

Clarin trumpet. See Clarino (2).

Clarinet family. A large group of single-reed woodwind instruments [see Reed], in distinction to the oboe family, which includes the double-reed instruments.

    I. *The clarinet.* The clarinet consists of a cylindrical pipe made of wood or ebonite (sometimes of metal) with a bell-shaped opening at one end and a characteristic mouthpiece (beak) at the other. The beak looks as if it were pinched to form a sharp edge at the top and has a single reed (made from a thin piece of cane) fixed to its back. Played by means of holes and keys, the clarinet has the acoustical properties of a "stopped" pipe, thus overblowing at the twelfth rather than the octave. The even-numbered partials in general cannot be obtained by overblowing, a fact that also

Major Keys

Circle of Fifths

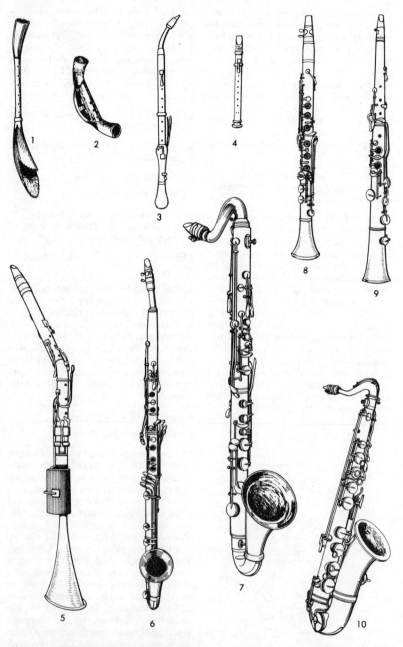

Clarinets: *1. Pibgorn. 2. Hornpipe (Basque). 3. Clarinette d'amour. 4. Chalumeau. 5. Basset horn (old). 6. Basset horn (modern). 7. Bass clarinet. 8. Clarinet. 9. Tarogato. 10. Tenor saxophone.*

affects its *tone color. See Wind instruments.

Owing to the fact that only the odd-numbered partials can be obtained by overblowing (e.g., c–g′–e″), a number of holes and, consequently, a complicated key mechanism are necessary to obtain the tones in between. The *Böhm system for such mechanisms is popular in America but has not been universally adopted. All clarinets have a written range as shown in Ex. 1, although the higher members of the family occasionally exceed its high point and the lower members become somewhat weak in the top octave. The least characteristic and most troublesome portion of their range is, to the average player, at the top of the first twelfth, the so-called "break" or throat register [see Ex. 2]. The register below the break is called *chalumeau* and that above it *clarion* or *clarino*. All clarinets are notated as *transposing instruments.

II. *Present forms.* The most common form is the *clarinet in B♭*, which sounds a whole tone lower than written. Next in importance is the *clarinet in A,* which sounds a minor third lower than written. The bass instrument of the clarinet family is the *bass clarinet in B♭*, whose range is an octave lower than that of the clarinet in B♭ plus an additional semitone provided by a low E♭ key, thereby enabling performance of music written for the now obsolete bass clarinet in A. To avoid too unwieldy a length, the lower end of the instrument is curved upward and ends in a metal bell, while the upper end, likewise of metal, is curved downward to bring the mouthpiece within easier reach for the player.

Additional types are the *clarinet in E♭,* a small instrument pitched a perfect fourth above the clarinet in B♭; the *alto clarinet in E♭,* pitched a fifth below the clarinet in B♭; and the *contrabass clarinet in B♭* (pedal clarinet, double-bass clarinet), pitched an octave below the bass clarinet. These are commonly found in bands and are occasionally called for

in orchestral scores. Other single-reed instruments are the *saxophone and the *tarogato.

III. *Obsolete forms.* Primitive instruments belonging to this family include the *pibgorn* and *hornpipe.* The immediate forerunner of the clarinet was the *chalumeau* (of which there was also a double-reed type), a small, sometimes keyless, cylindrical pipe. The clarinet proper was developed around 1700. During the 19th century a great many other clarinets were built, e.g., the clarinet in C, the clarinet in D (called for in Liszt's *Mazeppa* and Strauss' *Till Eulenspiegel;* now replaced by the clarinet in E♭), the bass clarinet in C or A (Liszt, *Mazeppa*), the *bathyphone* (constructed by E. Skorra, 1839), etc. An older instrument is the *basset horn,* an alto clarinet with a narrower bore, thinner wall, and a range four semitones beyond the low E (which sounds A in the usual F pitch). Originally (*c.* 1770) it was crescent-shaped and in this form was called for by Mozart, singly or in pairs, in *La clemenza di Tito, Die Zauberflöte, Die Entführung aus dem Serail,* the Requiem, and in various instrumental works (e.g., K. 411). About 1800 the crescent shape was replaced by a model that was sharply bent (almost forming a right angle) and, somewhat later, it was given the straight form in which it is constructed today. Beethoven used it only in *Prometheus,* and Mendelssohn wrote two concert pieces for clarinet and basset horn with piano (op. 113, 114). Rare later examples of parts for it, now generally played on the alto clarinet in E♭, are to be found in R. Strauss' *Elektra,* in F. S. Converse's *Iolan or The Pipe of Desire,* and in R. Sessions' Concerto for violin and orchestra. Finally, there is the *clarinette d'amour,* a larger clarinet in G or A♭ with the pear-shaped bell of the oboe d'amore.

Clarino. (1) The high register of the clarinet [see Clarinet family I]. (2) In the 17th and 18th centuries, a virtuoso method of trumpet playing, practiced by trumpeters trained in the art of producing the highest harmonics, i.e., from the third octave onward, where they form a continuous scale. It was this training that enabled the trumpeters of Bach's time to play demanding rapid passages in high position. Clarino, therefore, is less a name for a special instrument (*clarin trumpet*) than a special manner of playing the natural long-tube trumpet of the baroque period. The modern *Bach trumpet* is a short, straight, three-valve instrument, usually pitched in F or D and designed for rendering clarino passages in Bach's music, e.g., Cantata 75 and the second Brandenburg Concerto.

Clarion. An ancient English trumpet in round form. Also an organ stop like the trumpet stop but at 4' pitch.

Clarke, Henry Leland (b. Dover, N.H., 9 Mar. 1907). Musicologist and composer. Pupil of N. Boulanger, Holst, H. Weisse, and Luening. Teacher at the Univ. of California at Los Angeles, 1949–58; at the Univ. of Washington from 1958. Has composed operas (incl. the chamber opera *The Loafer and the Loaf*, 1951); orch. works; choral works (incl. *No Man Is an Island*, 1951); chamber music.

Clarke, Jeremiah (b. *c*. 1673; d. London, 1 Dec. 1707). Organist at St. Paul's from 1695; joint organist (with Croft) of the Chapel Royal from 1704, succeeding Blow. Composed operas; incidental music to several plays; cantatas; odes; services; anthems (incl. "Praise the Lord, O Jerusalem" and "I Will Love Thee"); songs; *The Prince of Denmark's March* (erroneously ascribed to Purcell under the title *Trumpet Voluntary*) and other harpsichord pieces.

Clarke, Rebecca (b. Harrow, England, of a U.S. father, 27 Aug. 1886). Violinist and composer. Pupil of Stanford. Performed in the U.S. and Europe from 1916. Composed chamber music; a psalm for voices and piano and one for chorus *a cappella;* songs.

Clarone [It.]. (1) Bass clarinet. (2) Older name for the basset horn (Mozart); see Clarinet family III.

Clarsech, clairseach, clarseth. The Irish harp [see Harp].

Classical. (1) Popularly, all art music as against popular music. (2) More properly, the music, style, or period of which the works of Haydn, Mozart, and Beethoven are the chief representatives. Thus, the period so identified extends from about 1770 to about 1830. The music of this period, as contrasted with that of the late *baroque (up to about 1750) is characterized by the regular recurrence of relatively short, clearly articulated phrases (often but not always of four measures), often combined in symmetrical patterns, and by textures that are somewhat less polyphonic. In retrospect, the period and its music are sometimes regarded as embodying a spirit of lucid placidity, repose, and simplicity as contrasted with the more subjective, passionate, and exuberant spirit of the period following, usually called the *romantic period. Like most such distinctions in the history of music, especially when the terms employed are borrowed (as these are) from the other arts, this is overly simple and even misleading. Tension and contrast, for example, are important elements in the music of the classical masters, and Mozart himself was regarded in the early 19th century as a romantic composer though he is almost never so described today. Beethoven, on the other hand, is often regarded today as a romantic figure (often for reasons having to do with his personal life), though his music relies in fundamental ways on the norms of style that characterize the works of Haydn and Mozart. His later works do represent a sufficient departure from earlier norms to cause some historians to see the classical period as ending by 1820 or before. For the principal forms of this period, see Sonata; Sonata form; String quartet; Symphony; Concerto. For the period immediately preceding, see Rococo.

Classical Symphony. Prokofiev's First Symphony, op. 25, composed 1916–17, so called because it is written in a "modernized" Mozart-Haydn idiom. It is scored for a typical classical orchestra of strings and pairs of each wind instrument.

Clausula [L.]. (1) A section, characterized by the use of *discant style, of a 12th- or 13th-century *organum (especially as found in the *Magnus liber organi* and related repertories), i.e., a section in which the textless contrapuntal part or parts proceed in a strict rhythm along with the notes of the chant melody on which the organum as a whole is based. The *clausulae* thus contrast with "organal" or melismatic passages, in which individual pitches of the chant melody are sustained against florid contrapuntal parts. *Clausulae* occur in an organum at points where the chant melody is itself melismatic, i.e., where there are many notes for only one or a very few syllables of text. The rhythms employed are those of the rhythmic modes [see Modes, rhythmic]. *Clausulae* are found in the manuscripts of the period both in the organa themselves and as separate compositions evidently intended for substitution in the organa. The earliest *motets are simply *clausulae* in which texts have been added to the contrapuntal parts. (2) Cadence, particularly the cadential formulas of 16th-century polyphonic music. (3) In Ambrosian chant, the terminations (*differentiae*) of the psalm tones.

Clavecin, clavessin [F.]. *Harpsichord.

Clavecin d'amour, cembal d'amour, cembalo d'amore. A *clavichord (not a cembalo, i.e., harpsichord), built by G. Silbermann about 1721, in which the strings are twice the normal length and are struck in the middle. The instrument had no damping cloth woven between the strings, like that required in the ordinary clavichord to damp the shorter section of the string. Therefore both sections of the string sounded the same tone, thus producing a louder sound.

Claves [Sp.]. A pair of solid, hardwood cylinders, each about 7 inches long, used as a percussion instrument in popular music of Cuba and of Latin America in general. One cylinder rests on the fingernails of a loosely formed fist and is struck with the other.

Clavicembalo [It.]. *Harpsichord.

Clavichord [F. *clavicorde;* G. *Klavichord, Clavier;* It. *clavicordo;* Sp. *clavi-*cordio]. A stringed keyboard instrument in use from the 15th through 18th centuries. The clavichord consists essentially of a rectangular case with a keyboard either projecting from or set into one of the longer sides. The part of the case to the right of the keyboard is occupied by the soundboard, and the strings run across the case from right to left. When the player depresses a key, its *tangent* (a brass blade driven into the back end of the key) strikes a pair of strings. The portion of the strings to the left of the tangent is damped by a strip of cloth (listing); the portion to the right (which passes over a bridge that transmits the strings' vibrations to the soundboard) is set into vibration by the blow of the tangent. When the key is released, the tangent falls away from the strings, which are then immediately silenced by the cloth damping. Since the point at which the tangent strikes the strings determines their vibrating length, one can produce several different pitches from a single pair of strings by causing a number of tangents to strike the strings at different points along their length. However, since a single pair of strings can produce only one pitch at a time, keys whose tangents strike the same pair of strings cannot be sounded simultaneously. For this reason, clavichord builders seem from the earliest times to have taken care that only notes forming dissonances with each other would be sounded from the same string. Clavichords in which pairs of strings are struck by more than one tangent are called fretted [G. *gebunden*]; those in which each key has its own pair of strings are called unfretted or fret-free [G. *bundfrei*]. The sound of the clavichord is very soft, though variations in the force with which the keys are struck produce variations in loudness in much the same way as they do on the piano, and the dynamic range of good instru-

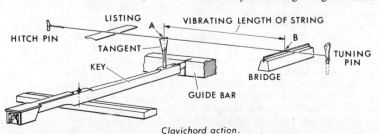

Clavichord action.

ments is quite wide. A special effect unavailable on any other keyboard instrument is the *Bebung, a kind of vibrato achieved by varying the pressure with which a key is held down.

Clavicymbal. *Harpsichord.

Clavicytherium. A *harpsichord with a vertical body.

Clavier. (1) French term for keyboard. (2) German term used in the baroque period (and now also in English) as a generic designation for keyboard instruments such as the harpsichord, clavichord, and organ [see *Clavier-Übung*]. Later it denoted mainly, if not exclusively, the clavichord (K. P. E. Bach). In the 19th century the term was transferred to the piano (in modern German, *Klavier*).

Clavier-Übung [G.]. A title (literally, "keyboard study") used by J. S. Bach for four publications of keyboard music. *Clavier-Übung* I (1731) contains the six partitas; II (1735), the *Italian Concerto and the French overture; III (1739), a number of organ chorales preceded by the Prelude in E♭ and ending with the Fugue in E♭ (*St. Anne's Fugue) and four duets; IV (1742), the *Goldberg Variations. The contents of parts I, II, and IV are specifically for the harpsichord, while that of part III is specifically for the organ. The title was adopted by Bach from earlier publications such as Kuhnau's *Neue Clavier-Übung* (1689, 1692) and Johann Krieger's *Anmuthige Clavier-Übung* (1699).

Clavilux. An instrument invented by Thomas Wilfrid *c.* 1920 for the performance of color music [see Color organ].

Clef [F.; G. *Schlüssel;* It. *chiave;* Sp. *clave*]. A sign written at the beginning of the staff in order to indicate the pitch of the notes. There are three such signs, which respectively represent the tones g', c', and f, hence the names G clef, C clef (of which there are three common forms), and F clef [see Ex. 1]. The G clef, also called *treble clef* or violin clef, is used on the second line of the staff; it indicates that the note on the second line is g'. The F clef, also called *bass clef,* is used on the fourth line; it indicates that the note written on the fourth line is f.

1. The G-clef; three forms of the C-clef; the F-clef.

2. Positions of the clefs on the staff.

3. Position of each clef and middle C(c') in music prior to 1750: a. French violin clef. b. Violin clef, also called G-clef or treble clef. c. Soprano clef or descant clef. d. Mezzo-soprano clef. e. Alto clef or C-clef. f. Tenor clef. g. Baritone clef. h. Baritone clef. i. Bass clef or F-clef. j. Subbass clef.

The C clef is used in two positions, on the third line (*alto clef* or viola clef) or on the fourth line (*tenor clef;* see Ex. 2). The G clef is used for the upper staff of piano music and for all high instruments (e.g., violin, flute); the F clef is used for the lower staff of piano music and for low instruments (e.g., cello, double bass). The alto clef is used for the viola and instruments of a similar range; the tenor clef for the high range of the cello, the bassoon, the tenor trombone, etc. In choral music and in recent publications of early music, the G clef is often used to notate parts (e.g., the tenor) that sound an octave below those of the normal G clef. This is sometimes indicated by means of a subscript 8 or by placing two G clefs next to one another. In some older music, the soprano part is notated with a C clef on the bottom line (*soprano clef*), and before 1750 all three clefs were used in a variety of positions [see Ex. 3]. See also *Chiavette.*

Clemens, Jacobus (real name Jacobus or Jacques Clement, called Clemens non Papa) (b. probably at Middelburg, The Netherlands, between 1510 and 1515; d. Dixmuide?, before 1558). Lived for a time in Ypres; choirmaster at Sankt Donatian in Bruges, 1544. Composed Masses; motets; French chansons; and *Souterliedekens.*

Clementi, Aldo (b. Catania, 25 May 1925). Pupil of Petrassi and Alfredo Sangiorgi; participant in Stockhausen's courses in Darmstadt, 1961–62. Has worked with serial and aleatory techniques. Has composed instrumental and electronic works, incl. *Collage,* nos. 1–3 (no. 2 on tape), 1962; *Informel,* nos. 1–3, 1963; *3 studi* for chamber orch., 1957; *Triplum* for flute, oboe, and clarinet, 1960.

Clementi, Muzio (b. Rome, probably 23 Jan. 1752; d. Evesham, Worcestershire, 10 Mar. 1832). Pianist and composer. Completed his musical education in England from 1766. Toured widely in Europe and Russia as a pianist and composer; met and competed with Mozart in Vienna, 1781, and met Beethoven there in 1807. Cramer, Field, and Meyerbeer were among his pupils. Established in England a piano factory and music publishing house (now Collard and Collard). Composed symphonies; overtures; over 100 piano sonatas and numerous other piano pieces; pedagogic piano works, incl. *Gradus ad Parnassum,* 1817.

Clemenza di Tito, La [It., The Clemency of Titus]. Opera in two acts by Mozart (libretto by Metastasio, rev. by C. Mazzolà, *secco* recitatives composed by F. X. Süssmayr), produced in Prague, 1791, at the coronation of Emperor Leopold II as King of Bohemia, for which it had been commissioned. Setting: ancient Rome.

Clérambault, Louis Nicolas (b. Paris, 19 Dec. 1676; d. there, 26 Oct. 1749). Pupil of Raison, whom he succeeded as organist of the Jacobins of the rue Saint-Jacques, 1720. Composed stage works (incl. *Le soleil vainqueur des nuages,* 1721); an oratorio, motets, and other sacred vocal works; harpsichord pieces; organ pieces; violin sonatas; airs.

Climacus. See table accompanying Neumes.

Clivis. See table accompanying Neumes.

Cloches [F.]. *Bells, especially the tubular bells of the orchestra. See Percussion instruments I (5).

Clock Symphony. Popular name for Haydn's Symphony no. 101 in D major, composed in 1794 in London. The name refers to the ticking motif in the Andante.

Clocking. See under Bell.

Clos [F.]. See Ouvert, clos.

Close. *Cadence.

Close harmony. Chords in close position, i.e., with all the four notes within an octave or a twelfth. See Spacing.

Clutsam keyboard. See under Keyboard.

C.O., c.o. [It.]. Abbr. for *coll' ottava; c.o.b., coll' ottava bassa.* See *Coll' ottava.*

Coates, Eric (b. Hucknall, Nottinghamshire, 27 Aug. 1886; d. Chichester, 21 Dec. 1957). Violist, conductor, and composer. Pupil of Corder. Composed orch. works (incl. *Miniature Suite,* 1911; *Sleepy Lagoon,* 1930; *London Suite,* 1933); instrumental pieces; songs.

Coclico, Adrianus Petit (b. Flanders, 1499 or 1500; d. Copenhagen, after Sept. 1562). Court chapel musician in Königsberg from 1547 and in Copenhagen from 1556. Among the first to use the term *musica reservata.* Composed motets, incl. the collection *Musica reservata, consolationes piae ex psalmis Davidicis,* 1552. Wrote the treatise *Compendium musices,* 1552, in which he claimed to be a pupil of Josquin.

Coda [It.]. A concluding section or passage, extraneous to the basic structure of the composition but added in order to confirm the impression of finality. In movements in sonata form, however, the coda frequently takes on considerable dimensions, occasionally becoming a second development section (e.g., in the first movement of Beethoven's Fifth Symphony). A short coda is sometimes called a *codetta.* However, this term more commonly means a closing passage at the end of an inner section, such as the exposition in sonata form or the first section (A) of a slow movement in ternary form (A B A).

Codetta. (1) See under Coda. (2) In the exposition of a fugue, any short transitional section between two entries of the subject (generally between the second and third).

Coelho, Rui (b. Alcacer do Sol, Portugal, 3 Mar. 1891). Pianist, conductor, critic, and composer. Pupil of Humperdinck, Bruch, Schoenberg, and Vidal. Composed operas (incl. *Belkiss,* Lisbon, 1928); ballets; symphonic poems, suites, and other orch. works; concertos for piano and orch.; oratorios; piano pieces; songs.

Coerne, Louis Adolphe (b. Newark, N.J., 27 Feb. 1870; d. Boston, 11 Sept. 1922). Pupil of Paine and Rheinberger. Taught at several U.S. colleges and universities. Composed operas (incl. *Zenobia,* 1902, prod. Bremen, 1905); a ballet, *Evadne,* 1892; other stage works; orch. works (incl. the symphonic poem *Hiawatha,* 1893); chamber music; piano pieces; organ works; choral works; songs.

Coffee Cantata. A secular cantata by Bach, *Schweigt stille, plaudert nicht* (Be quiet, don't prattle), for solo voices, chorus, and orchestra, composed *c.* 1732.

Cohn, Arthur (b. Philadelphia, 6 Nov. 1910). Conductor and composer. Pupil of R. Goldmark. Has composed orch. works (incl. *4 Symphonic Documents,* 1939; *Kaddish,* 1964); concertos; chamber music (incl. *Music for Ancient Instruments,* 1939; *Quotations in Percussion I,* 1958, and *II,* 1959); piano pieces (incl. *Machine Music* for 2 pianos, 1937).

Col arco [It.]. With the bow (after *pizzicato).

Col canto [It.]. With the song, i.e., the accompanist should follow the tempo of the performer of the melody.

Col legno [It.]. In violin playing, striking the strings with the bow-stick instead of playing with the hair.

Colascione, colachon. See under Lute.

Colasse, Pascal. See Collasse, Pascal.

Cole, Rossetter Gleason (b. Clyde, Mich., 5 Feb. 1866; d. Lake Bluff, Ill., 18 May 1952). Pupil of Bruch. Served as organist and teacher in Wisconsin, Iowa, and Illinois. Composed an opera, *The Maypole Lovers,* 1919–31; *Pioneer Overture,* 1919, and other orch. works; cantatas; instrumental pieces; songs.

Coleman, Charles (Colman) (b. *c.* 1595?; d. London, 9 July 1664). Viol player and composer. In the service of Charles I, 1625; succeeded Henry Lawes as court composer to Charles II, 1662. Participated in the composition of *The First Day's Entertainment* and *The *Siege of Rhodes* (the first English opera); also composed fancies and other instrumental music; airs with thoroughbass accompaniment.

Coleridge-Taylor, Samuel (b. London, 15 Aug. 1875; d. Croydon, 1 Sept. 1912). Pupil of Stanford. Taught at the Royal Academy of Music from 1898. Conductor of the London Handel Society, 1904–12. Made some use of his African musical heritage, his father having been a native of Sierra Leone. Composed operas and operettas; works for vocal soloists, chorus, and orch. (incl. the trilogy *The Song of Hiawatha,* 1898–1900, consisting of *Hiawatha's Wedding Feast, Death of Minnehaha,* and *Hiawatha's Departure*); an oratorio; numerous orch. works (incl. *An African Suite* and a violin concerto); anthems and other vocal works; chamber music; pieces for piano, for organ, for violin.

Colgrass, Michael (Charles) (b. Chicago, 22 Apr. 1932). Percussionist and composer. Pupil of Milhaud, Foss, Riegger, and Weber. Active in New York and Toronto. Works incl. *The Earth's a Baked Apple* for chorus and orch., 1968; *As Quiet As* for orch., 1966; *Virgil's Dream* for 4 actor-singers, 4 mime-musicians, 1967; *Déjà vu,* concerto for 4 percussionists and orch., 1977; *Inventions on a Motive* for percussion quartet, 1955; *Variations* for 4 drums and viola, 1957.

Colinde. See Koleda.

Coll', colla [It.]. "With the." *Colla destra, sinistra,* with the right, left hand. *Colla parte, colla voce* (with the part) is an indication directing the player of the accompaniment to "follow along" with the main part, which is to be performed in free rhythm. *Colla punta d'arco,* with the point of the bow. Also *col,* as in *col arco; *col canto.

Coll' ottava [It.]. With the octave. An indication to duplicate the written notes at the upper octave. Similarly, *coll' ottava* *bassa* calls for duplication at the lower octave.

Collasse, Pascal (Colasse) (b. Rheims, bapt. 22 Jan. 1649; d. Versailles, 18 July 1709). Pupil and assistant of Lully. Court musician in the royal chapel from 1683; later also court chamber musician. Composed operas (incl. *Thétis et Pelée*, 1689); occasional pieces for the court; motets and other sacred vocal music; airs.

Collect. In the Roman Catholic rite, one of the prayers [L. *oratio*] offered by the priest at Mass (after the Gloria; see Mass, with accompanying table), so called because it represents the collected prayers of all present. It is sung to special recitation tones called *toni orationum* [see *LU*, p. 98]. In Anglican rites, the collect is a short prayer to be used for a particular day in liturgical services.

Collegium musicum. Beginning in the 17th century, a musical association formed by amateurs for the performance of serious music. Nowadays the name is used for such associations connected with a university and devoted to the cultivation of old music.

Collingwood, Lawrance Arthur (b. London, 14 Mar. 1887). Pupil of Glazunov, Wihtol, Steinberg, and Tcherepnin at the St. Petersburg Conservatory. Active as an opera conductor in England from 1918. Composed operas (incl. *Macbeth*, London, 1934); a symphonic poem; piano pieces and other instrumental works.

Colman, Charles. See Coleman, Charles.

Colonna, Giovanni Paolo (b. Bologna, 16 July 1637; d. there, 28 Nov. 1695). Pupil of Carissimi, Benevoli, and Abbatini. Organist at San Petronio in Bologna from 1659; *maestro di cappella* there from 1674. Composed operas, oratorios, and much church music, incl. Masses, motets, Lamentations, psalms.

Colophane, colophony. *Rosin.

Color [L.]. See Isorhythm.

Color and music. Although pitch and the optical phenomenon of color have some physical bases that are analogous, attempts to relate specific pitches or keys to specific colors remain entirely subjective. Nevertheless, a few composers, most notably Rimsky-Korsakov, Scriabin, and Arthur Bliss, have attached considerable importance to such relationships. Bliss' *Colour Symphony* (1922; rev. 1932) is based on color associations, and Scriabin's *Prometheus* (op. 60, 1910) prescribes as part of its performance the visual display of colors by means of a special instrument [see Color organ]. The use of *color* and related terms in connection with instrumental timbre is strictly metaphorical and does not necessarily imply connections between particular timbres and colors [see Tone color; Acoustics].

Color organ. Any of several kinds of instruments designed to display colors in conjunction with, or in ways analogous to, musical compositions. Many such instruments devised in the 18th and 19th centuries were based on the idea of an exact correspondence between single sounds and single colors. More recently, this idea has largely given way to notions of a general coordination of musical and optical impressions. The *clavilux* of T. Wilfrid (exhibited in New York in 1922) renounces all direct connections with music and simply manipulates optical phenomena in ways analogous to those in which sound is manipulated in musical compositions. Scriabin's *Prometheus* (op. 60, 1910) calls for a special "clavier à lumières" (keyboard of lights) along with conventional musical instruments.

Coloration. (1) The use of colored (originally red, later black) notes in early notation; see Mensural notation. (2) The use of stereotyped written-out ornaments in music of the 15th and 16th centuries; see Ornamentation; Colorists; Intabulation.

Coloratura [It.]. (1) A rapid passage, run, trill, or similar virtuosic material, particularly in vocal melodies of 18th- and 19th-century operatic arias: *aria di coloratura, aria di bravura, Koloraturarie*. A famous example is the aria of the Queen of the Night in Mozart's *Zauberflöte*. A coloratura soprano is one with the requisite high range and vocal agility for such music. (2) The stereotyped ornamentation formulas of 16th-century keyboard and lute music [see Colorists].

Colorists [G. *Koloristen*]. A group of German composers of the late 16th century, including Elias Nicolaus Ammerbach (1530–97), Bernhard Schmid the older (*c.* 1520–90), Jacob Paix (1556–1617), B. Schmid the younger (b. 1548), and others, who used stereotyped ornamentation formulas (coloraturas) in their lute and keyboard compositions.

Colpo d'arco [It.]. Stroke of the bow (of violins, etc.).

Combattimento di Tancredi e Clorinda, Il [It., The Duel between Tancred and Clorinda]. A work composed by Monteverdi in 1624 and published in his 8th book of madrigals. Partly acted and partly narrated, it is based on a passage from Tasso's *Gerusalemme liberata*.

Combination pedal, stops. See under Organ.

Combination tone, resultant tone [F. *son résultant;* G. *Kombinationston;* It. *tono di combinazione;* Sp. *tono resultante*]. In musical acoustics, a tone of different pitch that is heard when two sufficiently loud tones are sounded simultaneously. Its frequency is the difference (*differential tones*) or the sum (*summation tones*) of the frequencies of the two primary tones or of their multiples. Although the combination tones are frequently referred to as an acoustical phenomenon, they actually are a physiological phenomenon. It is the inner ear (*cochlea*) that produces the aural sensations corresponding to the greater or lesser frequencies. The differential tones, which are more easily recognized than the summation tones, were discovered by G. Tartini in 1714 and described in his *Trattato di musica* of 1754. The tone known as Tartini's tone [It. *terzo suono,* "third tone"] is the first of the combination tones above, determined by the difference of the original frequencies. Tartini's tone can easily be heard on the harmonium, organ, and violin. On the violin, it was recommended by Tartini and other violinists (Leopold Mozart) as a means of controlling the correct intonation of double stops. Practical application of the first differential tone is made in the *acoustic bass of organs.

Combinatoriality. See Serial music.

Come [It.]. As, like. *Come prima, come sopra,* as at first, as above; *come sta,* as it stands, i.e., without improvisations.

Comes [L.]. See *Dux, comes.*

Comic opera. An opera or other dramatic work with a large admixture of music, on a light or sentimental subject, with a happy ending, and in which comic elements are present. The category thus includes a number of types, such as the operetta, vaudeville, *opéra bouffe,* and musical comedy, the distinctions among which are not always clearly marked. Until the middle of the 19th century, comic operas (except for the Italian *opera buffa*) usually contained spoken dialogue; in more recent times this feature has tended to disappear, so that a distinction on this basis is no longer generally valid. It should be noted that not all operas with spoken dialogue are "comic," though in France the name *opéra comique* is traditionally applied to such works, even when they are serious or tragic, e.g., Bizet's *Carmen.* The music of comic opera is almost always more "popular" in style than that of serious opera, generally easier both to perform and to comprehend. In some forms (e.g., musical comedy) it is usually confined to a series of songs of popular character. The scenes and personages of comic opera are apt to be taken from everyday life, or if fantasy is present it is treated in a sentimental or amusing fashion. Frequently there is satire of manners, allusion to current topics, or parody of the serious opera style.

Comic scenes early made their way into serious opera, and the juxtaposition of serious and comic episodes is a general feature of 17th-century librettos. With the abolition of comic episodes in the "reformed" opera librettos of Apostolo Zeno and Pietro Metastasio, the comic opera as a separate genre took on renewed importance, showing, in the 18th century, well-defined national types. The Italian *opera buffa* began early in the century to evolve out of *intermezzi performed between the acts of serious operas. The most famous early example is Pergolesi's *La serva padrona* (1733). Toward the end of the 18th century the Italian comic opera (like that of all other countries) tended to combine with the earlier plots of farcical intrigue some elements of the semiserious, sentimental drama; at the same time its music changed accordingly. Examples of this later type are Piccinni's *La buona figliuola* (1760, libretto by Goldoni), Paisiello's *Nina* (1789), Mozart's *Le nozze di Figaro* (1786), and Cimarosa's *Il matrimonio segreto* (1792).

The French *opéra comique,* beginning before 1715 with popular farces and satires that mingled spoken dialogue with songs to familiar airs (*vaudevilles*), was given a new direction by the example of the Italian buffo opera [see War of the Buffoons] and developed a type known as *comédie mêlée d'ariettes,* i.e., a spoken comedy mingled with newly composed songs, of which important composers were J.-J. Rousseau (*Le devin du village,* 1752), Gluck (*La rencontre imprévue,* Vienna, 1764), and Grétry (*Zémire et Azor,* 1771; *Richard Coeur-de-Lion,* 1784). The romantic quality of the librettos of many of these works and the frequent comment on political and social problems show the influence of Rousseau and the Encyclopedists.

The typical English 18th-century form was the *ballad opera, which was succeeded by similar works using original music by such composers as Thomas Arne (*Love in a Village,* 1762), Charles Dibdin (*The Waterman,* 1774), William Shield (*Rosina,* 1782), and Stephen Storace (*The Haunted Tower,* 1789). With respect to subject matter and treatment, the course of English comic opera in this period parallels the French *opéra comique.*

The corresponding form for this period in Spain is the *tonadilla [see also *Zarzuela; Sainete*]. In Germany, it is the *Singspiel.*

In the 19th century, comic opera lost some of its earlier distinctive character, approaching on the one hand the style, form, and subject matter of serious opera or on the other tending toward the light, purely "entertainment" types, such as *vaudeville,* and *operetta.*

Comma, schisma. Terms for minute differences in pitch that occur in the calculation of intervals if the same note is obtained through different combinations of octaves, perfect fifths, and pure major

thirds. The *ditonic* (or *Pythagorean*) comma is the difference between twelve perfect fifths and seven octaves (23.5 *cents, i.e., about one-fourth of a semitone). The *syntonic* (or *Didymic*) comma (named for Didymus, a Greek theorist, b. 65 B.C.) is the difference between four perfect fifths and two octaves plus a major third (21.5 cents). The *schisma* is the difference between eight perfect fifths plus one major third and five octaves (2 cents). The *diaschisma* is the difference between three octaves and four perfect fifths plus two major thirds (20 cents).

The ditonic comma is also the difference between the two semitones of the *Pythagorean scale, and the syntonic comma that between the two whole tones of *just intonation. The schisma is also the difference between the ditonic and syntonic comma, as well as that between the syntonic comma and diaschisma. The schisma nearly equals the difference between the Pythagorean fifth $(3/2 = 702$ cents) and the fifth of equal temperament (700 cents). This difference is therefore also called schisma. See also Temperament.

Commedia dell' arte [It.]. A type of comical stage presentation that developed in Italy about 1500. It had no music, but its traditional characters—the rich Venetian merchant, his unfaithful wife, the unscrupulous lawyer, the Bolognese doctor, the comic servant, etc.—have often been introduced into musical comedies, from O. Vecchi's *L'Amfiparnaso* (1594; see Madrigal comedy) and G. Pergolesi's *La serva padrona* (1733) to Mozart's *Le nozze di Figaro* (1786) and Stravinsky's *Pulcinella* (ballet, 1920).

Commiato [It.]. See under *Envoi.*

Common chord. The major *triad.

Common meter. See under Poetic meter.

Common time. 4/4 *meter.

Communion [L. *communio*]. In the Roman Catholic rite, the last of the five items of the Proper of the *Mass, sung after (originally during) the distribution of the Host. Originally it was an antiphon with the psalm verse "Gustate et videte" (Taste ye and see) from Psalm 33 (34) or with other psalm verses [see Antiphon (3)]. However, these verses disappeared in the 12th century so that only an antiphon (*antiphona ad communionem*) remained.

Comodo [It.]. Comfortable, easy.

Compass. The range of pitches obtainable from an instrument or voice.

Compère, Loyset (b. *c.* 1450; d. Saint-Quentin, France, 16 Aug. 1518). Perhaps trained at Cambrai. Chapel singer to the Duke of Milan, 1474–75; court singer to Charles VIII of France, 1486; canon of Saint-Quentin thereafter. Composed Masses, motets, Magnificats; numerous chansons; settings of Italian popular songs.

Complement. (1) The difference between the octave and any interval, therefore identical with inverted interval [see Inversion (1)]. (2) In the theory of twelve-tone music [see Serial music], a *hexachord comprised of the six pitch classes not included in a given hexachord.

Completorium [L.]. In the Roman Catholic liturgy, Compline [see Office]. In the Milanese rites, a chant sung at Vespers.

Compline. See under Office.

Composition pedals, stops. See under Organ.

Compostela, school of. A name sometimes applied to the anonymous composers of a small mid-12th-century repertory of monophonic and polyphonic music contained in the Codex Calixtinus and associated with the shrine of Santiago (St. James) de Compostela in northwestern Spain. The repertory includes early examples of *conductus similar to contemporaneous examples from France.

Compound interval. See under Interval.

Compound meter, time. See under Meter.

Compound stop. Same as mixture stop. See Organ.

Computer, musical applications of. Computers have made significant contributions to music and musical research in at least five areas: (1) information retrieval, (2) *style analysis, (3) composition, (4)

sound generation, and (5) acoustic analysis. Their use in composition may involve the process of composing music for conventional instruments, as in Lejaren Hiller's *Illiac Suite for String Quartet* (1957) and Iannis Xenakis' *Metastaseis* for orchestra (1953–54), or the generation and organization of sound by the computer itself (in conjunction with other electronic equipment controlled by the computer) according to the specifications of a composer, as in works by Hiller, Leland Smith, J. K. Randall, and Charles Dodge.

Con [It.]. With. For phrases beginning with this word, see under the noun following.

Concentus. See *Accentus, concentus*.

Concert. A public performance of music, especially one involving a group of musicians (a performance given by a soloist being called a recital). Concerts are a fairly recent institution. Through the end of the 17th century, performances of art music took place in churches, in the homes of princes or wealthy persons who could afford a private orchestra, or in closed circles, such as *academies or *collegia musica*. The first step toward public performance was taken with the foundation of the Teatro San Cassiano in Venice in 1637 [see Opera houses]. The first concerts (nonoperatic) open to the public were organized by John Banister, a London violinist, in 1672. They continued for six years, with a daily afternoon program. In France, public concerts began with the foundation, by A. Philidor, of a series of concerts called the Concert spirituel, which continued from 1725 until the French Revolution (1789). They became the model for similar institutions in Leipzig, Berlin, Vienna, and Stockholm. Among the earliest German concerts were the Gewandhaus Concerts of Leipzig, which started in 1781 under J. A. Hiller and which later attained international recognition under Felix Mendelssohn. The first concerts of record in what is now the United States took place in Boston (1731), Charleston, S.C. (1732), New York (1736), and Philadelphia (1757).

Concert pitch. The pitch at which the piano and other nontransposing instruments play. See Transposing instruments; Pitch.

Concertant [F.]; **concertante** [It.]. As adjectives, the terms are applied beginning in the 18th century to works for two or more performers, including orchestral works, in which one or more of the performers is called upon for soloistic display, as in Mozart's *Sinfonia concertante* K. 364 for violin, viola, and orchestra, and Weber's *Grand duo concertant* op. 48 for clarinet and piano. The form *concertante* has also been used as a noun in connection with pieces of this kind, particularly in the 18th century.

Concertato [It.]. A term used occasionally in the early 17th century in connection with various manifestations of the then novel principle of "contrast" or "rivalry" among groups of instruments or between instruments and voices, e.g., in T. Merula's *Canzoni, overo sonate concertate* (1637). In 17th-century vocal works, *coro concertato* means a small body of singers, in contrast to the full chorus, the *coro ripieno* or the *cappella*. The term has been recommended as a generic designation for the numerous and varied forerunners of the true *concerto.

Concertgebouw [D.]. Concert building, specifically the one constructed in Amsterdam in 1888 that is so called and from which Holland's foremost orchestra takes its name.

Concertina. See under Accordion.

Concertino. (1) In baroque music, the soloist group of the *concerto grosso*. (2) A composition of the 19th or 20th century in the style of a concerto but in free form, usually in a single movement with sections of varying speed and character (G. *Konzertstück*), e.g., Weber's Concertino for Clarinet op. 26.

Concertmaster [Brit. leader; F. *chef d'attaque*; G. *Konzertmeister*; It. *violino primo*; Sp. *concertino*]. The first violinist of an orchestra. He or she is entrusted with violin solo passages and is responsible for coordinating the bowing of the violins and thus the attack of the violins and of the orchestra in general.

Concerto [F., It.; G. *Konzert*; Sp. *concierto, concerto*]. Since the late 18th century, a composition for orchestra and a solo instrument, though in the 17th and 18th centuries also a composition for orchestra and a small group of solo instruments [see *Concerto grosso*]. An essential feature of such works is the contrast between passages dominated by the soloist (usually requiring some display of virtuosity) and passages (called *tutti*) for the orchestra alone. Beginning with the examples by Mozart, the concerto as a form has typically shared a number of features with the *sonata. Nevertheless, it is almost always in only three movements (fast-slow-fast), the minuet or scherzo typical of many sonatas and symphonies being omitted (Brahms' Piano Concerto op. 83 is a rare exception). The first movement is written in a modified *sonata form in which the exposition, instead of being repeated in full, is written out twice, first in a preliminary and abbreviated form with the tonic as the main key throughout and for the orchestra only, then in its full form for the soloist and orchestra and with the proper modulation to the dominant (or relative major). The first orchestral exposition and the subsequent principal passages for the orchestra that make use of the same thematic material are given the name *ritornello* by some writers, and historically they probably derive from the ritornello of the *concerto grosso* rather than from direct adaptations of the principles of the classical sonata form. The development and recapitulation are similar in outline to those of sonata form. Toward the end of the recapitulation there is a *cadenza for the soloist, and less elaborate cadenzas may occur in other movements as well. The final movement is usually a *rondo.

A concerto in a free one-movement form is called a *concertino [G. *Konzertstück*]. Some 20th-century composers (Hindemith, Piston, Bartók, Barber, and others) have written pieces under titles like "concerto for orchestra." These often draw on elements of the baroque concerto, including the use of a group of soloists.

The term *concerto* was first used for vocal compositions supported by an instrumental (or organ) accompaniment, in order to distinguish such pieces from the then current style of unaccompanied (*a cappella*) vocal music. To this category belong the *Concerti ecclesiastici* (church concertos) of Andrea and Giovanni Gabrieli (1587). The use of the name *concerto* for accompanied vocal music persisted throughout the baroque period, e.g., in Schütz's *Kleine Geistliche Concerte* of 1636 and several cantatas by Bach that he called "Concerto."

In purely instrumental music the term came to mean contrasting performing bodies playing in alternation. The baroque instrumental concerto reached its peak in the late 17th and early 18th centuries. The main advance over the previous period is the establishment of a form in three or four different movements, and the adoption of a fuller, more homophonic style, with increasing melodic emphasis on the upper parts. It is in this period that both the *concerto grosso* and the solo concerto emerge, particularly in the works of Torelli, Corelli, and other members of the *Bologna school. Torelli established the standard form of the baroque concerto, in three movements, fast-slow-fast, with the first movement in *ritornello form. This model, cultivated by Vivaldi, Bach, and numerous others, gave way to the classical form described above and embodied in the works of Mozart, Haydn, and Beethoven.

Concerto grosso. The most important type of baroque concerto, characterized by the use of a small group of solo instruments, called *concertino* or *principale*, against the full orchestra, called *concerto grosso, tutti*, or *ripieni. The concertino frequently consists of two violins and a thoroughbass (cello plus harpsichord), i.e., the ensemble most frequently encountered in the baroque *trio sonata. The ripieni are a small string orchestra, later occasionally including wind instruments (trumpets, oboes, flutes, horns).

The earliest known examples of the *concerto grosso* principle occur in two *Sinfonie a più instrumenti* by A. Stradella (1644–82). Some *concerti grossi* by Corelli (1653–1713), although published much later, would seem to be of a date close to Stradella's; they show the patchwork structure of the earlier canzona with quick changes of a considerable number of short "movements" (nos. 1,

2, 5, 7 of the 12 *Concerti grossi* op. 6, 1712). Corelli, Torelli (1658–1709), and others often distinguished between *concerti da chiesa* (church) and *concerti da camera* (chamber), by analogy with the similarly named sonatas of the period. The former typically consist of four movements in the pattern slow-fast-slow-fast (except in Corelli's works, where there are usually more than four movements), at least one movement being fugal in character. The *concerto da camera* consists of an introductory movement followed by a series of dances. Torelli ultimately discarded this distinction and established the standard form in three movements, fast-slow-fast, that was adopted by Vivaldi (1678–1741), Bach [see Brandenburg Concertos], and others, and in which the most common design for single movements is the *ritornello form. The tradition of the *concerto da chiesa* continued to make itself felt, however, e.g., in the concerti of Handel (op. 6, 1740).

Concitato [It.]. Excited, agitated. *Stile concitato,* the agitated, dramatic style of some 17th-century works, e.g., Monteverdi's *Il combattimento di Tancredi e Clorinda*.

Concord, discord. Concord is a combination of sounds that is pleasing to the ear, while discord is an unpleasant combination. The terms are subjective and used for aesthetic rather than technical descriptions.

Concord Sonata. The second of two piano sonatas by Charles Ives, composed 1909–15. Its complete title is "Concord, Mass., 1840–1860." Ives provided a guide to the content by adding titles to the four movements: "Emerson," "Hawthorne," "The Alcotts," and "Thoreau."

Concrete music. *Musique concrète.*

Conducteur [F.]. An abridged orchestral score, usually a reduction for the piano, as distinct from the *grande partition*, or full score.

Conducting. Directing a performing group—orchestra, chorus, opera—in order to bring about complete coordination of all the players and singers. Its basic aspect is beating time, i.e., the

clear indication of the metric pulse by the conductor's right hand, often with the help of a baton. A clear and decisive downstroke will fall on the first beat of each measure, while the remaining motions of the hand depend upon the meter and tempo and may require from two to six or more beats. The accompanying illustration shows the basic diagrams for 2, 3, 4, and 6 beats. In addition, the conductor indicates—mainly with the left hand—the entrances of instruments or voice-parts, shading of dynamics, and other details of performance. Suggestive motion of the whole body and facial expressions may be used to indicate subtle changes of mood.

It was not until the early part of the 19th century that leadership became generally entrusted to an independent conductor standing in front of the group and using a baton. Conductors were at first frequently composers, e.g., Spontini, Spohr, Weber, and Mendelssohn. Previously, the first violinist or a keyboard player most often served as leader.

Conductor's part. An abbreviated score of orchestral works. It usually includes the leading part (chiefly first violin) with the other important instruments cued in. Normally, however, conductors employ full scores.

Conductus [L.; pl. *conductus* or *conducti*]. A Latin strophic song of the 12th or 13th century for one or more voices. An early occurrence of the term in a manuscript for the play of Daniel (*c.* 1140; see Liturgical drama) suggests that such pieces served originally as processionals (L. *conducere,* to lead or bring together). Other early examples occur in the repertory associated with Santiago de *Compostela. Later examples, of which there are many in the *Notre Dame repertory, have texts on a wide variety of subjects both sacred and secular and include occasional references to historical events. Many examples have *melismas (called *caudae*) at the beginnings and ends of lines of text. Otherwise, the texts are most often set syllabically. The rhythmic

interpretation of the syllabic portions is still a subject of controversy. In polyphonic examples (rarely for more than three voices), the text is declaimed simultaneously in all voices, from whence the term "*conductus* style" for some motets and other kinds of pieces of similar character. Unlike other types of contemporaneous polyphony (e.g., *organum, *motet), *conductus,* with rare exceptions, were not based on preexistent melodies.

Cone, Edward T. (Toner) (b. Greensboro, N.C., 4 May 1917). Pianist, critic, and composer. Pupil of Sessions. Member of the faculty of Princeton Univ. from 1947. Has composed a symphony and other orch. works; a cantata, *The Lotus Eaters,* 1939–47; *La figlia che piange* for tenor and chamber orch.; *Excursions* (after Thoreau) for *a cappella* choir, 1955; 2 string quartets, a string sextet, 1966, and other chamber music; piano pieces; songs (incl. the cycle *Philomela* for soprano, flute, viola, and piano, on texts by Robert Bridges). Has published the books *Musical Form and Musical Performance,* 1968, and *The Composer's Voice,* 1974; numerous articles.

Confinalis [L.]. Same as *affinalis* [see *Affinales*].

Conflicting signature. Another term for *partial signature.

Confractorium [L.]. In *Ambrosian, *Gallican, and *Mozarabic chant, an item of the Proper of the Mass associated with the breaking of the communion bread.

Conga. A long, single-headed, Latin-American drum, often with a shell that bulges in the middle. A single drum or a pair tuned to differing pitches is usually played with the hands.

Conjunct, disjunct. Notes are called "conjunct" if they are successive degrees of the scale, "disjunct" if they form intervals larger than a second.

Conjunctura [L.]. A symbol (ligature) of square notation [see under Notation], consisting of a note in the shape of a *longa* followed by two or more diamond-shaped notes called *currentes,* always forming a descending scale passage. Its rhythmic meaning is often ambiguous, though the presence of three or more *currentes* usually implies notes of short duration. It developed from the neume *climacus* [see table accompanying Neumes].

Consecration of the House. See *Weihe des Hauses, Die.*

Consecutives. See under Parallel fifths, octaves.

Consequent. See Antecedent and consequent.

Conservatory [F. *conservatoire;* G. *Konservatorium;* It., Sp., *conservatorio*]. A school specializing in musical training. Originally, a *conservatorio* was a charitable institution for the education of orphans, but at an early time the main emphasis was placed on music. The oldest institutions of this type are the *ospedali* of Venice, so called because they were attached to hospitals, founded as early as the 13th century. The name *conservatorio* originated in Naples in the 16th century.

Console. (1) The case that encloses the keyboard, stops, etc., of an organ. (2) See Piano.

Consonance, dissonance. Popularly, combinations of pitches that are, respectively, pleasing or displeasing. Used in this way, the terms are entirely subjective and of little value, given the changes of taste over the history of music. More narrowly, consonances are those combinations of pitches that have been used in Western tonal music as suitable points of at least momentary repose and not necessarily requiring resolution. Dissonances are those combinations that, in Western tonal music, do not serve as points of repose but require, instead, resolution to some consonance.

Since about the 13th century, the following two-pitch combinations or *intervals and their compounds have been treated as consonances: unison, perfect octave, perfect fifth, major third, minor third, and the *inversions of these last two, namely the major sixth and minor sixth. Major and minor thirds and sixths are called imperfect consonances. The perfect fourth, which is the inversion of

the perfect fifth, functions as a consonance when it is part of a combination of three or more pitches such that the lower of its two pitches is not the lowest sounding pitch of the entire combination. All remaining intervals are dissonances, e.g., seconds and sevenths and their compounds as well as diminished and augmented intervals. Chords, i.e., combinations of three or more pitches, are consonant if they contain only consonant intervals and dissonant if they contain even a single dissonant interval. It follows that the only consonant chords are the major and minor *triads (elements of which may be doubled) and their *inversions except for the second inversion (the *six-four chord), which normally requires resolution because it includes a fourth above the lowest sounding pitch. Repeated attempts over the centuries to derive these concepts from nature (e.g., by means of vibrating string lengths or the harmonic series) have been largely unsatisfactory, and in much music of the 20th century these concepts are irrelevant.

The principles governing the use of consonance and dissonance in tonal music are variously studied and taught under the headings of *harmony [see also Harmonic analysis] or *counterpoint. For a description of some of the principal kinds of dissonance employed in tonal music, see Counterpoint.

Consort. A 16th- and 17th-century English term for instrumental chamber ensembles or compositions written for them. A group including only instruments of the same family was called a *whole consort* (consort of viols, recorders; see Chest of viols), whereas a group consisting of various kinds was called a *broken consort.* Thomas Morley's *First Booke of Consort Lessons* of 1599, written for treble lute, pandora, cittern, bass viol, flute, recorder, and treble viol, contains examples of the broken consort.

Consul, The. Opera in three acts by Gian Carlo Menotti (to his own libretto), produced in New York, 1950. Setting: a European country, the present.

Contes d'Hoffmann, Les [F., The Tales of Hoffmann]. *Opéra fantastique* in three acts with prologue and epilogue by J. Offenbach (libretto by J. Barbier and

M. Carré, based on stories by E. T. A. Hoffmann), produced in Paris, 1881. Setting: Germany and Italy, 19th century. Offenbach died before completing the work, which was orchestrated by E. Guiraud.

Continuo. Abbr. for *basso continuo;* see Thoroughbass. In the scores of baroque composers (e.g., Bach, Handel), the bass part, which was performed by the harpsichord or organ together with a viola da gamba or cello.

Contra [It.]. (1) Abbr. for **contratenor.* (2) As part of other terms, the word has one of two meanings: (a) "against," e.g., in *contrapunctus* [see Counterpoint] or **contratenor,* from which such terms as **contralto, haut-contre* [see Haut], and *basse-contre* are derived; (b) the lower octave. The latter led to the term *contra-octave* for the octave below the great octave [see Pitch names] and, consequently, to names such as *contrabasso* [G. *Kontrabass*], *contrabassoon,* and *contrabass-clarinet* for instruments of the lowest range.

Contra-octave. See under Pitch names.

Contra-violin. See Violin family (b).

Contrabassoon. See Oboe family I (d).

Contra(b)basso [It.]. *Double bass.

Contradanza [It.]. See Contredanse.

Contrafactum [L.]. A vocal composition in which the original text is replaced by a new one, particularly a secular text by a sacred one, or vice versa.

Contrafagotto [It.]. Contrabassoon. See Oboe family I (d).

Contralto [It.]. (1) Same as *alto voice (female). (2) See Violin family (d).

Contrappunto [It.; L. *contrapunctus*]. *Counterpoint. *C. doppio,* double counterpoint. *C. alla mente,* extemporized counterpoint [see *Discantus supra librum*].

Contrapuntal. In the style of *counterpoint.

Contrary motion. See under Motion.

Contratenor [L.; abbr. *contra*]. In compositions of the 14th and 15th centuries,

a third voice-part, added to the basic two-voice texture of discant (*superius*) and tenor. It has about the same range as the tenor, with which it frequently crosses, so that the lowest note may fall now to the tenor, now to the contra. Its contour is usually much less melodic than that of the two other parts, to which it was added for harmonic completeness. With the establishment about 1450 of four-part writing and the consequent separation of ranges, the contratenor split in two parts: the *contratenor altus* (high c.) or, simply, *altus* (alto), and the *contratenor bassus* (low c.) or, simply, *bassus* (bass). This process explains the name *alto (high) for a part that, from the modern point of view, can hardly be considered "high," as well as the use of the term *countertenor* for the male alto.

Contrebasse [F.]. *Double bass. *Contrebasson,* double bassoon [see Oboe family I (d)].

Contredanse [F.; G. *Contratanz* or *Kontretanz;* It., Sp. *contradanza*]. A dance that attained great popularity in France and elsewhere during the late 18th century. It was performed by two (or more) couples facing each other and executing a great variety of steps and motions. The music consists of a long series of eight-measure phrases that may be repeated over and over. It is now generally accepted that the *contredanse* developed and took its name from the English *country dance, which it resembles in various respects. The *contredanse* developed into the *française* and the **quadrille.* Beethoven wrote 12 contredanses for orchestra (1803), one of which (no. 7) he used in the final movement of the Eroica Symphony.

Converse, Frederick Shepherd (b. Newton, Mass., 5 Jan. 1871; d. Westwood, Mass., 8 June 1940). Pupil of Chadwick, Paine, and Rheinberger. Taught at the New England Conservatory, 1899–1901 and 1921–38; at Harvard Univ., 1901–7. Composed operas (incl. *The Pipe of Desire,* Boston, 1906); oratorios; cantatas; *Flivver Ten Million,* orch. fantasy, 1927; symphonies and other orch. works (incl. *California,* 1928; *American Sketches,* 1935); chamber music; piano pieces; songs.

Convertible counterpoint. Same as *invertible counterpoint.

Conzert [G.]. See *Konzert*.

Cooke, Benjamin (b. London, 1734; d. there, 14 Sept. 1793). Pupil of Pepusch, whom he succeeded, 1752, as conductor of the Academy of Ancient Music. Choirmaster (from 1757) and later lay vicar and organist at Westminster Abbey. Composed glees, canons, catches; odes; church music; instrumental pieces.

Cooke, Henry (b. *c*. 1615; d. Hampton Court, London, 13 July 1672). Court singer and composer and master of the children in the Chapel Royal from 1660. His pupils incl. Purcell and Blow. Composed anthems and odes; participated in the production of *The First Day's Entertainment* and *The *Siege of Rhodes* (the first English opera).

Coperario, John (or Coprario; Italianized from Cooper) (b. *c*. 1575; d. London, 1626). Lutenist, viola da gamba player, and composer. Studied in Italy *c*. 1600; returned to England *c*. 1605. Mentioned as one of "the King's Musicians" in 1625. His pupils incl. King Charles I, W. Lawes, and probably H. Lawes. Composed music for masques; fancies, suites, and other works for organ and for viols; anthems; songs. Wrote a treatise, *Rules How To Compose, c.* 1610.

Coperto [It.]. Covered. *Timpani coperti*, kettledrums muted by being covered with a cloth.

Copla [Sp.]. Couplet or stanza of Spanish songs such as the **cantiga* or **villancico*. See *Couplet*.

Copland, Aaron (b. Brooklyn, 14 Nov. 1900). Pupil of R. Goldmark and N. Boulanger. Co-organizer of the Copland-Sessions Concerts 1928–31. Taught at the New School for Social Research, 1927–37; was head of the composition department at the Berkshire Music Center at Tanglewood, 1940–65. Has made use at various times of American folk music, jazz, and serial techniques. Has composed the opera *The *Tender Land;* the ballets *Billy the Kid*, 1938, *Rodeo*, 1942, **Appalachian Spring*, and *Dance Panels*, 1962; orch. works (incl. 3 symphonies; *A Dance Symphony*, 1925; *Lincoln Portrait*, 1942; *El *salón México; *Appalachian Spring*, suite from the ballet, awarded the Pulitzer Prize for 1945; *Symphony* for organ and orch., 1924, of which a revised version without organ is the Symphony no. 1, 1928; *Connotations*, 1962; *Inscape*, 1967); choral works; a piano quartet, 1950, and other chamber music; *Twelve Poems of Emily Dickinson* for voice and piano, 1950; piano pieces (incl. *Variations*, 1930; *Fantasy*, 1957); film scores (incl. *Our Town*, 1940; *The Red Pony*, 1948; *The Heiress*, 1949). Has published the books *What to Listen for in Music*, 1939, rev. 1957; *Our New Music*, 1941, rev. as *The New Music, 1900–1960*, 1968; *Music and Imagination*, 1952.

Coppélia. Ballet by Delibes (choreography by Arthur Saint-Léon, based on a story by E. T. A. Hoffmann), first produced in Paris in 1870.

Copula [L.]. A term used by mid-13th-century theorists to describe a style midway between **discant* and **organum*. With organum it shares the use of sustained tones in the tenor. With discant it shares the use of measured rhythm in the upper part, though the rhythm of this upper part is said by at least one theorist to proceed faster in copula than in discant.

Coq d'or, Le. See *Golden Cockerel, The*.

Cor [F.]. (French) **horn. Cor anglais*, English horn [see Oboe family I (b)]; *cor à pistons*, valve **horn; cor de basset*, basset horn [see Clarinet family III]; *cor de chasse*, hunting horn; *cor des Alpes*, **alphorn; cor d'harmonie*, valve **horn; cor naturel*, natural **horn.

Coranto [It.]. See *Courante*.

Corda [It.]; **corde** [F.]. String. *Corde à vide, corda vuota*, open string (of the violin). See also *Una corda*.

Corder, Frederick (b. London, 26 Jan. 1852; d. there, 21 Aug. 1932). Pupil of Ferdinand Hiller. Taught composition at the Royal Academy of Music from 1888. An admirer of Wagner, several of whose operas he translated into English in collaboration with his wife. Composed operas (incl. *Nordisa*, Liverpool, 1887;

Ossian, 1905) and operettas; orch. works; cantatas; choral works; songs. Published several composition manuals.

Cordero, Roque (b. Panama, 16 Aug. 1917). Pupil of Krenek. Directed the National Institute of Music in Panama, 1953 –64. Conducted the National Orchestra of Panama, 1964–66. Member of the faculty of the Latin-American Music Center at Indiana Univ. from 1966; at Illinois State Univ. from 1972. Has made some use of Panamanian folk materials; adopted twelve-tone techniques. Has composed 3 symphonies; a violin concerto, 1962; *Rapsodia campesina* for orch., 1949; *Mensaje fúnebre* for clarinet and string orch., 1961; *8 miniaturas* for small orch., 1953; 2 string quartets and other chamber music.

Corelli, Arcangelo (b. Fusignano, near Ravenna, 17 Feb. 1653; d. Rome, 8 Jan. 1713). Violinist (from 1675) and director of violins (1685–1709) at San Luigi dei Francesi in Rome. His works are important in the development of the baroque sonata and *concerto grosso.* Composed *concerti grossi;* trio sonatas; sonatas for violin and thoroughbass (incl. *La Follia*).

Cori spezzati [It.]. Properly, *coro spezzato*, i.e., divided choir. See Polychoral style.

Corigliano, John (b. New York, 16 Feb. 1938). Pupil of Luening, Giannini, and Creston. Directed the music department of radio station WBAI, 1962–64; assistant director of musical programs for C.B.S.-TV, 1961–72; on the faculty of Lehman College in New York City from 1972. Has composed works for orch. (incl. *Elegy*, 1966; *Tournaments Overture*, 1967; *The Cloisters*, with voice, 1965); a clarinet concerto, 1977; choral works; incidental music to several plays; *The Naked Carmen*, arrangement of Bizet's *Carmen* for rock and pop groups and Moog synthesizer; a violin sonata, 1963.

Coriolan Overture. Orchestral composition by Beethoven (op. 62, 1807), written as an overture to a play by H. J. von Collin about the same subject as Shakespeare's *Coriolanus.*

Corista [It.]. Orchestral pitch; tuning fork. *C. di camera*, chamber pitch.

Cornamusa [It.]; **Cornemuse** [F.]. *Bagpipe.

Cornelius, Peter (b. Mainz, 24 Dec. 1824; d. there, 26 Oct. 1874). Writer and composer. A member of Liszt's circle in Weimar from 1852 and a close associate of Wagner, whom he met in Vienna in 1859 and accompanied to Munich in 1865. Taught harmony and rhetoric at the Royal Music School there from 1875. Composed operas (incl. *Der Barbier von Bagdad,* Weimar, 1858); song cycles (incl. *Vater-unser-Lieder* and *Weihnachtslieder*); choral works (incl. *Der alte Soldat*). Translated numerous operas and published poetry and essays on music and art.

Cornet [F. *cornet à pistons;* G. *Kornett;* It. *cornetto;* Sp. *cornetín*]. See Brass instruments II and accompanying illustrations. Not to be confused with the *cornett. Also, name of an organ stop.

Cornett [F. *cornet à bouquin;* G. *Zink;* It. *cornetto;* Sp. *corneta*]. A medieval instrument (the earliest known picture of it dates from the 13th century) that, in one form or another, was used until the middle of the 19th century. It consists of a straight or slightly bent tube of wood (occasionally ivory, possibly originally goathorn), which is octagonal in cross section, usually with a cup-shaped mouthpiece and with six finger holes [see ill. under Brass instruments]. Although in some books this instrument is called a *cornet, leading to confusion with an entirely different 19th-century instrument, the two types are usually distinguished by the different spelling. In addition to the normal cornett (*Zink, cornetto*), pitched in a, there is a soprano size (*Kleiner Zink, cornettino*) pitched in e' and a tenor size (*Grosser Zink, cornone*) pitched in d. The above-mentioned instruments have a separate cup-shaped mouthpiece, but there is also a cornett, usually of straight shape, that has a small funnel-shaped opening carved out of the upper end of the tube. This is the *Gerader Zink* (*cornetto diritto*) or *Stiller Zink* (*cornetto muto*). In the 16th century a bass size was added, which, in order to bring the finger holes within easy reach of the hands, is bent in a serpentine shape and therefore is called a *serpent* [see ill. under Brass instruments]. It was particularly favored in French church music, hence the 19th-century name *serpent d'église*, "church serpent." The serpent was still in favor early in the 19th century with composers such as Rossini (*Le siège de Corinth*), Mendelssohn (*Meeresstille und glückliche Fahrt; Paulus*), Wagner (*Rienzi*), and Verdi (*Les vêpres siciliennes*). By this time, however, the instrument had a shape similar to the tuba's. In 1788 J. J. Regibo built one bent back on itself in the shape of a bassoon, and in this form it became known as a *Russian bassoon*. An improved variety of this instrument was the metal *bass horn,* invented about 1800, also called an *English bass horn* [F. *basse-cor*]. All these instruments retained the six finger holes of the old cornetts. The addition of more finger holes operated by keys led to the *chromatic bass horn* and *ophicleide*. [See ill. under Brass instruments.]

Cornett-ton [G.]. See under Pitch (3).

Cornetta [It.]. *Cornet.

Cornetto [It.]. *Cornett or *cornet.

Corno [It.]. *Horn. *Corno a mano,* *natural horn; *corno a macchina* (*a pistoni, cromatico, ventile*), valve *horn; *corno inglese,* English horn [see Oboe family I (b)]; *corno di bassetto,* basset horn [see Clarinet family III]; *corno da caccia,* hunting horn. In Bach's scores *corno* usually means the old *cornett [G. *Zink*]. For Bach's *corno da tirarsi* see under Trumpet (slide trumpet).

Cornyshe, William (b. East Greenwich, *c.* 1468; d. Hylden, Kent, Oct. 1523). Entered the service of Henry VII, 1492; master of the children of the Chapel Royal, 1509. He was a favorite of Henry VIII and, with the Chapel Royal, accompanied him to the Continent on various occasions. Composed sacred music and secular songs.

Coro [It.]. Choir, chorus. *Coro spezzato* (also *coro battente*), see under Polychoral style. In organ music, *gran coro* means full organ.

Coronach, corronach. A funeral dirge of Scotland chanted by the bard (*Seannachie*) on the death of a chief or other prominent personage of the clan. Similar songs prevailed in Ireland (*caoine*). Schubert wrote a "Coronach" for women's chorus (op. 52, no. 4) to a text from Sir Walter Scott's *The Lady of the Lake.*

Coronation Anthems. Four anthems by Handel, composed for the coronation of George II (1727), entitled: 1. "Zadok the Priest"; 2. "The King shall rejoice"; 3. "My heart is inditing"; 4. "Let thy hand be strengthened." Purcell also wrote a coronation anthem, "My heart is inditing," for the coronation of James II (1685).

Coronation Concerto. Mozart's Piano Concerto in D major (K. 537, 1788), so called because he played it (together with another concerto, K. 459) at the coronation of Emperor Leopold at Frankfurt in 1790. The latter is also called Coronation Concerto.

Coronation Mass. Mozart's Mass in C major (K. 317, 1779), composed for the annual coronation of the statue of the Virgin at the shrine of Maria Plain, near Salzburg, Austria.

Correa de Araujo, Francisco (b. Seville, *c.* 1576; d. Segovia, Feb. 1655). Organist at San Salvador in Seville, 1599–1636; in Jaén, 1636–40; and in Segovia, 1640 to his death. Published *Facultad orgánica,* 1626, containing numerous *tientos* and other organ pieces.

Corrente [It.]. See Courante.

Corrette, Michel (b. Rouen, 1709; d. Paris, 22 Jan. 1795). Organist in several church and court positions. Composed Masses; motets; works (incl. concertos) for musette, vielle, flute, oboe, violin, organ, harpsichord, etc.; airs; pedagogical works, incl. methods for violin, harp, and other instruments.

Corteccia, Francesco Bernardo (b. Arezzo, July 1504; d. Florence, 7 June 1571). Served Cosimo I de' Medici in Florence. Composed Mass Propers, motets, hymns, responsories, and madrigals (incl. some for the *intermedi* of a play performed at Cosimo's wedding).

Cortège [F.]. A composition in the character of a solemn procession or a triumphal march.

Cortés, Ramiro (b. Dallas, 25 Nov. 1933). Pupil of Cowell, Stevens, Dahl, Sessions, Donovan, Giannini, and Petrassi. Teacher at the Univ. of Southern California from 1966. Has worked with serial techniques. Works incl. an opera, *Prometheus,* 1960; orch. works (incl. *Meditation; Xochitl,* 1965); a woodwind quintet, 1968, and other chamber music; choral works; piano pieces.

Così fan tutte, ossia La scuola degli amanti [It., Thus Do All (Women), or The School of Lovers]. Comic opera in two acts by Mozart (libretto by L. da Ponte), produced in Vienna, 1790. Setting: Naples, 18th century.

Costa, Michael Andrew Agnus (Michele Andreas Agniello) (b. Naples, 4 Feb. 1808; d. Hove, England, 29 Apr. 1884). Pupil of Zingarelli. Settled in England in 1829. Conducted the London Philharmonic and the Royal Italian Opera from 1846; the Birmingham Festivals from 1849; and the Handel Festivals from 1857. Composed operas (incl. *Don Carlos,* London, 1844); ballets; oratorios; 3 symphonies; a Mass.

Costeley, Guillaume (b. probably in Pont-Audemer, Normandy, *c.* 1531; d. Évreux, 1 Feb. 1606). Served as organist to Charles IX of France. Active in organizing the Confrérie de Sainte-Cécile in Évreux. Composed chansons, incl. some employing advanced chromaticism; a fantasy for organ or spinet; motets.

Cotillon, cotillion. A popular dance of the 18th and 19th centuries, used especially at the close of an entertainment. It includes a large variety of steps and figures that are executed by a leading couple and imitated by all the others. The cotillon has no particular music; any dance music (waltz, polka, mazurka) can be played for it.

Coulé [F.]. A French 18th-century *agrément* in the character of an *appoggiatura. For coulé sur une tierce,* see Appoggiatura, double.

Coulisse [F.]. The slide of a trombone or a slide trumpet.

Council of Trent. A council of the Roman Church, held at Trento (South Tirol, now Italy) 1545–63, where important decisions regarding church music were made. The council abolished all but four *tropes and *sequences. For a time it considered abolishing all music in the service other than plainsong. There is, however, no truth to the frequently repeated story that Palestrina "saved music" by composing his *Missa Papae Marcelli* [see Marcellus Mass]. Palestrina's role in the council was rather inconspicuous and much slighter than that of Jacobus de Kerle and others.

Counterfugue [G. *Gegenfuge*]. A fugue in which the answer (*comes*) is the inverted form of the subject (*dux*), e.g., nos. 5, 6, 7 of Bach's *The Art of Fugue.*

Counterpoint [G. *Kontrapunkt;* F. *contrepoint;* It. *contrappunto;* L. *contrapunctus;* Sp. *contrapunto*]. The term, derived from *punctus contra punctum,* i.e., "note against note" or, by extension, "melody against melody," denotes music consisting of two or more lines that sound simultaneously. *Counterpoint* is practically synonymous with *polyphony* except for differences of emphasis. The latter term is preferred for early music and the former for later periods (16th to 18th centuries). Also, the latter has the connotation of a broad stylistic and historical classification (polyphony vs. *monophony and *homophony), and the former that of systematic study for the purpose of instruction (Palestrina counterpoint, Bach counterpoint, strict and free counterpoint, *species counterpoint, etc.).

Although counterpoint is a feature of all music in which combinations of two or more simultaneously sounding pitches are regularly employed, the term (and its adjective form *contrapuntal*) is often used to distinguish musical *textures in which each of the several lines sounding together retains its character as a line from textures in which one line predominates and the remainder are clearly subservient, retaining little or no distinct character as lines. In this sense, a fugue of Bach is contrapuntal whereas a nocturne of Chopin is not, even though careful analysis might reveal that the two are equally well worked out in linear terms. Similarly, counterpoint, with its emphasis on the linear or horizontal aspect of music, is sometimes contrasted with *harmony, which concerns primarily the vertical aspect of music embodied in the nature of the simultaneously sounding combinations of pitches employed. Counterpoint and harmony, nevertheless, are fundamentally inseparable.

The principles usually taught under the heading of counterpoint (also called the principles of *voice-leading*) describe the types of *motion permitted in individual lines with respect to one another (one of the most important of these principles being the prohibition against motion in *parallel fifths and octaves) and the types of dissonance (and resolution; see Consonance, dissonance) permitted between two or more lines. The principal types of dissonance (sometimes called *nonharmonic tones or embellishing tones) occurring in tonal counterpoint are as follows: (1) *Passing tone* [Ex. 1], which connects two consonant pitches by stepwise motion and normally occurs in a metrically weak position. When it occurs in a strong metrical position [see Accent], it is called an accented passing tone. (2) *Neighboring tone* (or *auxiliary tone*), which consists in a motion to and from a step above (upper neighbor; Ex. 2) or a step below (lower neighbor; Ex. 3) a consonant tone. Upper and lower neighbors are sometimes combined to form double neighbors [Ex. 4 and 5], to which the term *cambiata* [see below] is also sometimes applied [see also *échappée* below]. Single neighboring tones may be either strong or weak metrically. (3) *Suspension* [Ex. 6], normally a dissonant tone occurring in a strong metrical position, having been

sustained (or "suspended" or "prepared") from an initial attack as a consonance and converted to a dissonance as a result of motion in another voice. It is most often resolved downward. (4) *Appoggiatura* [Ex. 7], a metrically strong dissonance, normally arrived at by leap and resolved by descending step. The term is also applied to accented dissonances smiliar to the suspension [Ex. 8], in which case it is said to be a *prepared appoggiatura,* and more loosely to any accented dissonance that is resolved by step. (5) *Anticipation* [Ex. 9], a metrically weak dissonant tone that is immediately harmonized as a consonance. (6) *Échappée* (or *escape tone;* Ex. 10), a metrically weak dissonance approached by step and left by leap in the opposite direction. Such formations can also be understood as *incomplete neighboring tones.* (7) *Cambiata* (or *nota cambiata*), properly a five-note figure [Ex. 11], the second note of which is dissonant and third of which is consonant. The term is also applied, however, to a similar figure moving in an upward direction [Ex. 12] and to several related shorter figures [Ex. 13 and 14] as well as to the *double neighboring tones* described above [Ex. 4 and 5], to which the term *changing notes* is sometimes applied. All of these are common in music of the 15th and 16th centuries. The term *cambiata* has sometimes been further extended to include another figure [Ex. 15], the principal feature of which is that the motion to the dissonance is in the same direction (unlike the motion of the *échappée*) as the motion between the initial and final consonances.

Although all of the above formations serve primarily to introduce dissonance into an otherwise consonant succession, some of them, particularly the first three, may on occasion be entirely consonant. See also Species; Imitation; Fugue.

Countersubject. See under Fugue.

Countertenor. Male *alto, derived from *contratenor altus.*

Country dance. A generic term for English dances of folk origin, of which there are a great variety. They differ in the arrangement of the dancers as well as in the steps and gestures, but all are group

dances. The dancers usually stand in two long lines, men and women facing each other, and move forward and back in figures that change with every eight-measure phrase of the music. There is a definite similarity (if not direct connection) between these English dances, which flourished especially throughout the 17th and 18th centuries, and the French *branles of the 16th century. The melodies written for these dances are all simple tunes with a marked rhythm and in symmetrical eight-measure phrases. The authoritative source for the country dances is Playford's *The English Dancing Master* (1651; reprinted 1957), which contains more than a hundred tunes, each accompanied by directions and figures for the dancers. See *Contredanse*.

Coup d'archet [F.]. Bow stroke.

Coup de langue [F.]. *Tonguing.

Couperin. A family of French musicians whose prominence began in the 17th century with the three brothers Louis, François, and Charles. In the second generation it was represented by François' son Nicolas and Charles' son François "le Grand"; in the third generation by Nicolas' son Armand-Louis; in the fourth by Armand-Louis' sons Pierre-Louis and Gervais-François. Members of the family held the position of organist of Saint-Gervais in Paris until 1826. See the entries following.

Couperin, Armand-Louis (b. Paris, 25 Feb. 1727; d. there, 2 Feb. 1789). Succeeded his father Nicolas as organist of Saint-Gervais, 1748. Served as organist to the King at Versailles, 1770–89. Composed harpsichord and organ pieces; violin sonatas; trio sonatas; motets and other church music.

Couperin, François ("le Grand") (b. Paris, 10 Nov. 1668; d. there, 11 Sept. 1733). Son and pupil of Charles Couperin. Organist of Saint-Gervais from 1685; one of the four organists of the royal chapel from 1693; royal chamber musician and music master to the royal family from 1701. Composed motets and other sacred music for voices with instruments; trio sonatas and other chamber music (incl. the collections *Concerts royaux*, 1722; *Les goûts réunis*, 1724;

Les nations, 1726, containing *L'impériale*); 27 *ordres (suites) for harpsichord publ. in 4 books, each titled *Livre de clavecin*, 1713–30, the entire collection referred to as *Pièces de clavecin;* organ pieces; secular vocal music. Wrote a book on harpsichord playing, *L'art de toucher le clavecin*, 1717, with an appendix containing 8 preludes.

Couperin, Louis (b. Chaumes-en-Brie, *c.* 1626; d. Paris, 29 Aug. 1661). Violinist, organist, and composer. Pupil of Chambonnières, whom he accompanied to Paris. Organist of Saint-Gervais from 1650. Served as a court musician from 1656. Composed pieces for harpsichord, for organ, for violin.

Coupler [G. *Koppel*]. See under Organ.

Couplet [F.]. In French poetry, the stanza of a poem (not two rhyming lines, like the English couplet). The corresponding Spanish term, *copla, denotes the various stanzas of the *villancico, which alternate with the refrain (*estribillo*). In music, *couplet* is used mainly for the various sections of the 17th-century rondeau, which are connected by the reiterated refrain [see Rondeau (2); also Rondo]. In 18th- and 19th-century light opera (*Singspiel,* operetta) *couplet* means a strophic song of a witty character. Properly these should be called *couplets* (stanzas), but the singular form was generally adopted in Germany (Johann Strauss), where it was also used, from about 1890 to 1910, for popular refrain songs of a light and humorous character.

Courante [F.]; **corrente** [It.]. A dance that originated in the 16th century and became, in the mid-17th century, one of the standard movements of the *suite. The earliest known musical example, "La corante du roy" in B. Schmid's tablature of 1577, does not show any differences from the *saltarello. However, a number of "Corantos" of the Fitzwilliam Virginal Book vaguely foreshadow the 17th-century courante with their generally lighter texture and short "running" figures. In the 17th century the dance became stylized as two types, the Italian corrente and the French courante [for a similar case, see under Gigue (2)].

(a) The Italian corrente is in quick triple time (3/4, sometimes 3/8), with continuous running figures in a melody-accompaniment texture. It appears to be the direct outgrowth of the late 16th-century type as exemplified in the Fitzwilliam Virginal Book.

(b) The French courante is in moderate 3/2 or 6/4 time, with a frequent shift from one of these meters to the other (i.e., from the accents 1' 2 3' 4 5' 6 to the accents 1' 2 3 4' 5 6; see Hemiola). Its texture is a free contrapuntal fabric in which the melodic interest frequently shifts temporarily from the upper to one of the lower parts. Examples abound in the works of Chambonnières, L. Couperin, Froberger, D'Anglebert, F. Couperin, and others.

The courantes of Bach's suites are usually of the French type. Especially remarkable for its rhythmic ambiguity is the courante of the English Suite no. 2; in others, the change from 3/2 to 6/4 occurs chiefly in the final measure of each section. The Italian type occurs in the French Suites nos. 2, 4, 5, 6 and in the Partitas nos. 1, 3, 5, 6. Some editors have substituted the name Courante for some or all of the correntes.

Course [F. *choeur;* G. *(Saiten)chor;* It. *coro;* Sp. *orden*]. In stringed instruments, chiefly those of the lute type, a group of strings tuned in unison or in the octave and plucked simultaneously. On 16th-century lutes courses of two strings each were used for the lower strings, as follows: G–g c–c' f–f' a–a d'–d' g' (also G–G c–c f–f a–a d'–d' g'). In order to simplify the terminology, the single string g' is also called a "course," so that the 16th-century lute would have 11 strings in 6 courses. A bass-course is a string (single or double) that runs alongside the fingerboard and therefore does not lie over the frets; hence, it is invariable in pitch. See Lute. Unison courses of two or three strings are used for the higher ranges of the piano.

Cousser, Johann Sigismund. See Kusser, Johann Sigismund.

Covered fifths, octaves. Same as hidden fifths, octaves. See under Parallel fifths, octaves.

Cowell, Henry (Dixon) (b. Menlo Park, Calif., 11 Mar. 1897; d. Shady, N.Y., 10 Dec. 1965). Pianist and composer.

Taught at several U.S. colleges and conservatories, incl. the New School for Social Research 1928–63; Columbia Univ. 1951–65. Actively promoted contemporary American music, for which purpose he founded New Music, publisher of numerous compositions by important American composers. Made some use of Asian musical materials as well as early American models. Developed the piano technique of *tone clusters; pioneered playing directly on the strings of the piano and the use of aleatory procedures; invented the Rhythmicon, a keyboard percussion instrument, in collaboration with Leon Theremin. Composed an opera; 2 ballets; 20 symphonies and other orch. works (incl. *Tales of Our Countryside* for piano and orch., 1939); band pieces; 18 works for various combinations each titled *Hymn and Fuguing Tune,* 1944–64; chamber music; choral works; numerous piano pieces; songs. Published a theoretical work, *New Musical Resources,* 1930.

Cowen, Frederick Hymen (b. Kingston, Jamaica, 29 Jan. 1852; d. London, 6 Oct. 1935). Pupil of Benedict, Goss, Hauptmann, Moscheles, and Reinecke. Conducted several orchestras, incl. the London Philharmonic (1888–92 and 1900–1907) and the Liverpool Philharmonic (1896–1913). Composed operas and other stage music; oratorios (incl. *The Veil,* 1910); cantatas; 6 symphonies and other orch. works; a piano concerto; chamber music; songs.

Crab motion, crab canon [G. *Krebsang, Krebskanon*]. See Retrograde; Canon (1).

Cracovienne [F.]. See *Krakowiak.*

Cramer, Johann Baptist (b. Mannheim, 24 Feb. 1771; d. London, 16 Apr. 1858). Pupil of his father, Wilhelm Cramer (1745–99), and of Clementi and Abel. Toured widely as a concert pianist and teacher. Established a music publishing house in England, 1824 (now J. B. Cramer and Co., Ltd.). Composed numerous piano works, incl. concertos, sonatas, quartets, quintets; and a pedagogic series, *Grosse praktische Pianoforte Schule,* 1815.

Crawford, Ruth Porter (Mrs. Charles

Seeger) (b. East Liverpool, Ohio, 3 July 1901; d. Chevy Chase, Md., 18 Nov. 1953). Pupil of Adolf Weidig and Charles Seeger. Composed orch. pieces; a string quartet and other chamber music; choral works; piano pieces; also made transcriptions of and accompaniments for numerous folksongs.

Creation, The [G. *Die Schöpfung*]. Oratorio by Haydn, composed in 1797. It is based on a poem compiled by Lidley from Milton's *Paradise Lost,* which was suggested to Haydn by the concert-manager Salomon during his second stay in London (1794–95). Upon Haydn's return to Vienna, the text was translated into German by his friend Baron Gottfried van Swieten, and this translation (*Die Schöpfung*) became the basis of the oratorio, which was first performed in Vienna in 1798.

Creation Mass. Popular name for Haydn's Mass in B♭ (1801), used because a theme from his oratorio *The Creation* appears in the "Qui tollis."

Creatures of Prometheus. See *Geschöpfe des Prometheus, Die.*

Crécelle [F.]. *Rattle.

Crécquillon, Thomas (b. prob. Ghent; d. prob. Bethune, *c.* 1557). Court musician to Charles V of Spain from 1540. Composed Masses, motets, Lamentations, French chansons.

Credo [L.]. The third item of the Ordinary of the *Mass. In plainsong, the first phrase, "Credo in unum Deum" (I believe in one God), is sung by the officiating priest, and the chorus enters at "Patrem omnipotentem" (Father almighty). It was the last of five Ordinary chants to be incorporated into the Roman Mass (in 1014 at the insistence of Emperor Henry II). Even today, the Credo melodies are grouped separately from other items [*LU,* pp. 64 ff.]. Early polyphonic settings (14th to 16th centuries) nearly always begin with "Patrem omnipotentem."

Crescendo, decrescendo [It.; abbr. *cresc., decresc.,* or *decr.;* indicated by the signs ≺ and ≻]. The usual terms and signs for increasing or decreasing loudness. For the latter, the word *diminuendo (dim.)* is also used.

Crescent. See Turkish crescent.

Creston, Paul (real name Joseph Guttoveggio) (b. New York, 10 Oct. 1906). Self-taught as a composer. Theater organist for silent films, 1926–30; organist at St. Malachy's Church in New York, 1934–67. Teacher at Central Washington State College from 1967. Has composed 5 symphonies; concertos; other orch. works; choral works; chamber music; works for organ and for piano. Has published books on music theory.

Crist, Bainbridge (b. Lawrenceburg, Ind., 13 Feb. 1883; d. Barnstable, Mass., 7 Feb. 1969). Pupil of Juon and Enesco. After practicing law in Boston (1907–12), he taught singing there and in Washington, D.C. Composed stage works (incl. a Javanese ballet, *Pregiwa's Marriage,* 1920); orch. works (incl. *American Epic, 1620,* 1943); choral works; chamber music; piano pieces; songs.

Croce, Giovanni ("Il Chiozzotto") (b. Chioggia, *c.* 1557; d. Venice, 15 May 1609). Pupil of Zarlino, under whom he served as a chorister at San Marco in Venice from 1565; in 1603 he became *maestro di cappella* there. Composed Masses, motets, Magnificats, Lamentations, and other sacred music; madrigals; *canzonette;* humorous and topical pieces in Venetian dialect (in the collections *Mascharate piacevole e ridicolose,* 1590, and *Triaca musicale,* 1595).

Croche [F.]. Eighth note. See under Notes.

Croft, William (Crofts) (b. Nether Ettington, Warwickshire, bapt. 30 Dec. 1678; d. Bath, 14 Aug. 1727). Chorister in the Chapel Royal under Blow; joint organist there with J. Clarke from 1704. Succeeded Blow as organist of Westminster Abbey, 1708. Composed anthems, a *Burial Service,* and other church music; overtures and other music for plays; choral odes; sonatas for flute and for violin; pieces for harpsichord and for organ; songs.

Croiser les mains. See *Croisez.*

Croisez, croisement [F.]. Indication to cross the hands in piano playing.

Croma [It.]. Eighth note. See under Notes.

Cromatico [It.]. Chromatic. See especially under Chromatic (5).

Cromorne [F.]. Crumhorn. See under Oboe family III.

Crook or shank. See under Wind instruments; Horn; Trumpet.

Cross, Lowell (Merlin) (b. Kingsville, Tex., 24 June 1938). Studied music at Texas Technological College and at the Univ. of Toronto, where he was also a pupil of Marshall McLuhan. On the faculty of Mills College and director of its Tape Music Center, 1968–70; appointed artist-in-residence at the Center for New Performing Arts, Univ. of Iowa, 1971. Works (many involving monochrome and color television, laser devices, and other visual components) incl. a series of works titled *Video II; Video/Laser II* (with Tudor and Carson Jeffries), 1970.

Cross relation [F. *fausse relation;* G. *Querstand*]. Also *false relation*. The succession of a pitch in one voice by a chromatic alteration of that pitch (or its equivalent in another octave) in another voice [see Ex.]. A simultaneous or verti-

cal cross relation is the simultaneous occurrence of two pitches related in this way. Although such relations are normally prohibited by the academic formulations of "classical" 18th- and 19th-century harmony and counterpoint, their use in the music of that period is not infrequent.

Cross rhythm. The simultaneous use of conflicting rhythmic patterns, e.g., three notes against four, or of conflicting accents, e.g., 3/4 meter against 4/4 meter. See Polyrhythm.

Crosse, Gordon (b. Bury, England, 1 Dec. 1937). Studied at Oxford and with Petrassi in Rome. Has composed operas (incl. *Purgatory,* after Yeats); works for children and instruments (incl. *Meet My Folks!,* 1964, and *Ahmet the Woodseller*); orch. pieces; works for small ensembles.

Crot. See Crwth.

Crotales [F.]; **crotalum** [Gr.–L.]. The *crotalum* of Greek and Latin antiquity was a rattle or clapper similar to the castanets, consisting of two wooden or metal shells held in one hand. The French *crotales* usually means a clapper, specifically the castanets. See also under Cymbals.

Crotch, William (b. Norwich, 5 July 1775; d. Taunton, 29 Dec. 1847). Organist and composer. Professor of Music at Oxford Univ. and organist of St. John's College from 1797; head of the Royal Academy of Music from its founding in 1822 until 1832. Composed oratorios (incl. *Palestine,* 1812; *The Captivity of Judah,* 1834); symphonies and other orch. works; organ concertos; anthems; odes (incl. *Mona on Snowdown Calls*); glees; a motet, *Methinks I Hear the Full Celestial Choir;* piano pieces; organ fugues. Published books on theory and composition.

Crotchet. In British terminology, the quarter note. See Notes.

Crouth, crowd, cruit. See Crwth.

Crucible, The. Opera in four acts by R. Ward (libretto by B. Stambler, after A. Miller's play), produced in New York, 1961. Setting: Salem, Mass., 1692.

Crucifixus. A section of the *Credo of the Mass dealing with the Crucifixion. In Mass compositions it frequently appears as a separate movement of sorrowful expression, as in Bach's B-minor Mass.

Crüger, Johann (b. Gross-Breese, near Guben, Prussia, 9 Apr. 1598; d. Berlin, 23 Feb. 1662). Traveled widely from 1613; divinity student at Wittenberg, 1620. Cantor of St. Nicolai's (Lutheran) Church in Berlin, 1622 to his death. Composed numerous chorale melodies, collected and published as *Praxis pietatis melica,* 1644 (incl. "Jesu, meine Freude"; "Nun danket alle Gott"; "Schmücke dich, o liebe Seele"); psalms, motets, and other sacred music. Also published several theoretical works.

Crumb, George (b. Charleston, W.Va., 24 Oct. 1929). Pupil of Blacher and Finney. Teacher at the Univ. of Colorado,

1959–64; at the State Univ. of New York at Buffalo, 1964–65; at the Univ. of Pennsylvania from 1965. Has composed orch. works (incl. *Echoes of Time and the River,* awarded the Pulitzer Prize for 1968; *Starchild,* with voices, 1977); works for voices and instruments (incl. *Ancient Voices of Children,* words by García Lorca, 1970; *Songs, Drones, and Refrains of Death,* words by García Lorca, 1971; several books of *Madrigals*); chamber music (incl. *Vox balaenae* for amplified flute, cello, and piano, 1971; *Black Angels* for electric string quartet, 1970); piano pieces (incl. *Makrokosmos I,* 1972, and *II,* 1973, both for amplified piano; *Makrokosmos III: Music for a Summer Evening* for 2 amplified pianos and percussion, 1974).

Crumhorn. See Oboe family III.

Crwth. A bowed six-stringed instrument probably of ancient Celtic origin. It is conspicuous for its rectangular shape, which is strongly reminiscent of the Greek *kithara.* The oldest illustrations (11th century) show the instrument without a fingerboard and played like a harp. It was used with a bow from the 12th or 13th century, and later a fingerboard was added, whereby it became associated with the violin family [see ill. under Lyra]. The instrument was still used in Wales in the early years of the 19th century. It is also known by the anglicized name *crowd* and the Irish names *crot* and *cruit.* A medieval Latin name, used in the 11th to the 14th centuries, is *chorus.* The medieval form, without fingerboard, is usually called *rotta* or *rotte.*

C.s. [It.]. (1) Abbr. for *colla sinistra,* with the left hand. (2) Abbr. for *con sordino,* with *mute.

Csárdás [Hung.]. A Hungarian dance of the early 19th century. It probably represents a ballroom variant of the old *verbunkos.* It is in rapid 2/4 time, considerably faster than the *friss* (fast) sections of the old *verbunkos.* The slow *lassu* sections were not incorporated into the *csárdás.*

Cue. (1) In orchestral parts including a long rest, a short passage taken from another leading instrument and printed in small notes, in order to alert the player to the approaching entry of his own part. (2) A gesture given by the conductor to one or more singers or players to mark the entry of their parts.

Cui, César Antonovich (b. Vilna, 18 Jan. 1835; d. Petrograd, 26 Mar. 1918). Military officer and composer. Pupil of Moniuszko. Music critic for Russian and European newspapers, 1864–1900. One of "The *Five." Composed operas (incl. *William Ratcliff,* St. Petersburg, 1869); orch. works; choral works; chamber music; a set of 25 songs on poems by Pushkin for voice and soprano, 1899, and other songs; violin pieces (incl. *Kaleidoscope*); piano pieces. Also published several books.

Cuivre [F.]. *Instruments de cuivre* or simply *les cuivres* are the brass instruments of the orchestra. *Cuivré* calls for a forced, harsh tone in playing, especially of the *horn.

Cunning Little Vixen, The [Cz. *Lišky Příhody Bystroušky*]. Opera in three acts by L. Janáček (to his own libretto), produced in Brno, 1924. Setting: fairy tale.

Currentes [L.]. Same as *conjunctura* or, at least, the diamond-shaped notes of the *conjunctura.*

Cursive and tonic. Terms applied to the termination formulas of Gregorian recitatives (psalm tones, Introit tones, responsorial tones), depending on whether they are invariable or subject to modification by the insertion of extra notes for additional unaccented syllables of the text. As transmitted in modern liturgical books, the more ornate terminations (used for the verses of Introits and Responsories) are usually cursive, while the simple ones (for the psalms and canticles) are tonic. The cursive endings consist of five units (single notes or short groups of notes) to which the last five syllables of the text are sung, regardless of their accentual structure. In tonic terminations the accented syllables always fall on the same unit. Medieval practice was more varied and included the use of cursive cadences of varying length for simple tones as well.

Curtain tune. Same as act tune [see Entr'acte].

Curtal(l). See under Oboe family III.

Custer, Arthur (b. Manchester, Conn., 21 Apr. 1923). Pupil of Pisk, Bezanson, and N. Boulanger. Teacher and administrator in several U.S. colleges and music centers. Has composed works for orch. (incl. *Sinfonia de Madrid*, 1961; *Found Objects II*, 1969); works for voices and instrumental ensembles; *Interface I* for string quartet and 2 recording engineers, 1969; *Rhapsodality Brown!* for piano, 1969; chamber music.

Custos [L.]. *Direct.

Cycle. (1) In musical *acoustics, a complete vibration. (2) Any of various systems of equal temperament, i.e., systems whose tonal material is obtained by dividing the octave into a number of equal intervals. The simplest is the twelve-tone division, which is the basis of most Western art music composed since the 17th century. Others are the 53-division Mercator-cycle (after Nicholas Mercator, *c.* 1620–87); the cycle named after Christian Huygens (1629–95), with 31 tones to the octave; and a 19-division cycle discussed by Zarlino and Salinas and expressly called for in a "chromatic" chanson by Costeley in the 16th century.

Cyclic, cyclical. (1) Generally, any musical form including several movements; thus, e.g., the sonata, symphony, suite, and cantata, are cyclic forms. (2) Specifically (and preferably), compositions—usually sonatas or symphonies—in which related thematic material is used in all or in some of the movements, e.g., Schubert's *Fantasie* op. 15 ("Wanderer") and Berlioz' *Symphonie fantas-*

tique. In many Masses of the 15th and 16th centuries, all movements are based on the same tenor or begin with identical opening measures (*cantus firmus* cycle, motto cycle).

Cylinder. See Valve.

Cymbalon. *Cimbalom.

Cymbals. A percussion instrument (idiophone) consisting of two metal plates that are struck together. Single cymbals may also be struck with sticks of various kinds. Cymbals in the form of two small saucers attached to handles or held by means of leather straps were used in ancient Egypt, Greece, and Rome (*crotalum*). Similar instruments have been used by Debussy (*cymbales antiques*) and Ravel (*crotales*). These are small cymbals of thick metal that are tuned to a definite pitch. The normal orchestral cymbals are much larger, of thin metal, and of indefinite pitch; see Percussion instruments.

Cythara. Medieval spelling of *kithara* but used as a generic designation for stringed instruments.

Czardas. *Csárdás.

Czerny, Carl (b. Vienna, 20 Feb. 1791; d. there, 15 July 1857). Pianist and pedagogue. Pupil of Beethoven; his own pupils incl. Liszt. Composed symphonies; overtures; concertos; chamber music; Masses and other sacred music; numerous collections of piano studies and exercises.

Czimbalom. *Cimbalom.

D

D. (1) See Pitch names; Letter notation; Hexachord. (2) In 16th-century *partbooks *D* stands for *discantus* (soprano). (3) In harmonic analysis *D* means *dominant. (4) Abbr. for O. E. Deutsch's catalog of Schubert's works.

Da capo [It.; abbr. *D.C.*]. From the be-

ginning. Indication that the piece is to be repeated from the beginning to the end, to a place marked *fine* (*da capo al fine*), or to a place marked with a specified sign (e.g., *da capo al segno*, or *al* 𝄋, or *al* ⊕). On reaching the sign in the last case, the player is to skip ahead to the next occurrence of the same sign, often marking the beginning of a *coda. This may occur in conjunction with or as an alternative to the direction *da capo e poi la coda* (from the beginning, and then the coda). In the course of the repetition, other internal repetitions are normally omitted, as in the case of the minuet or scherzo with trio. This is sometimes made explicit with the direction *da capo senza repetizione*. See also *Dal segno*.

Da capo aria. See under Aria.

Da Motta, José Vianna. See Viana da Mota, José.

Dactyl, dactylic. See table under Poetic meter.

Dahl, Ingolf (b. Hamburg, 9 June 1912; d. Frutigen, near Bern, Switzerland, 7 Aug. 1970). Pupil of Jarnach and N. Boulanger. Member of the faculty of the Univ. of Southern California from 1945 to his death. Composed orch. works (incl. *The Tower of Saint Barbara,* 1954); chamber music (incl. a piano trio and piano quartet); vocal works; works for piano.

Dal segno [It.; abbr. *D.S.*]. Indication for repetition, not from the beginning [see *Da capo*] but from another place (frequently near the beginning) marked by the sign ⅜.

Dalayrac, Nicolas (originally d'Alayrac) (b. Muret, Haute-Garonne, 8 June 1753; d. Paris, 27 Nov. 1809). Pupil of Grétry. Composed numerous operas (incl. *Nina ou La folle par amour,* Paris, 1786; *Deux petits savoyards,* Paris, 1789; *Adolphe et Clara,* Paris, 1799); chamber music; occasional patriotic and other songs.

Dalcroze. See Jaques-Dalcroze.

Dale, Benjamin James (b. London, 17 July 1885; d. there, 30 July 1943). Pupil of Corder at the Royal Academy of Music, where he later taught composition. Composed orch. works; choral works (incl. *Song of Praise,* 1923; a cantata, *Before the Paling of the Stars,* 1912); chamber music; piano pieces (incl. a sonata in D minor, 1905); violin and viola pieces; songs.

Dall'Abaco, Evaristo Felice. See Abaco, Evaristo Felice dall'.

Dallapiccola, Luigi (b. Pisino, Istria, 3 Feb. 1904; d. Florence, 19 Feb. 1975). Studied at the Cherubini Conservatory in Florence, where he was later a member of the faculty (1931–67, with interruptions); also taught briefly in the U.S. on several occasions. Employed twelve-tone techniques in a way often described as lyrical or characteristically Italian. Composed operas (incl. *Volo di notte,* after St. Exupéry, Florence, 1940; *Il prigioniero,* 1948, prod. Florence, 1950); a ballet; works for solo voice with instruments (incl. *Cinque canti,* 1956; *Sicut umbra,* 1970); choral works (incl. *Canti di prigionia,* 1941; *Canti di liberazione,* 1955; *Requiescant,* 1958); *Partita,* 1933, and other orch. works; chamber music; piano pieces (incl. *Quaderno musicale di Annalibera,* 1952–53; version for orch. titled *Variazioni per orchestra,* 1954); songs.

Dalza, Joan Ambrosio (b. Milan, 2nd half of the 15th cent.; d. after 1508). Lutenist and composer. A volume of his works for lute was published in 1508 by the printer Petrucci, containing dances (incl. *pavane–saltarello–piva* groups), *tastar de corde* (similar to toccatas), and ricercars.

Dame blanche, La [F., The White Lady]. Opera in three acts by Boieldieu (libretto by A. E. Scribe, based on Sir Walter Scott's *Guy Mannering* and *The Monastery*), produced in Paris, 1825. Setting: Scotland, 17th century.

Damnation de Faust, La [F., The Damnation of Faust]. "Dramatic legend" in five acts by Berlioz (libretto by the composer and A. Gandonnière, based on G. de Nerval's version of Goethe's *Faust*). Described by Berlioz as a "concert opera," it was produced in concert form in Paris, 1846; stage version (adapted by R. Gunsbourg) in Monte Carlo, 1893.

Damper [F. *étouffoir;* G. *Dämpfer;* It. *sordino;* Sp. *sordina*]. In pianos and harpsichords, the part of the mechanism that terminates the vibration of the string —hence, the sound—at the moment the key is released. The piano dampers are small pieces of wood, their underside covered with felt, that are placed above the strings, and these can all be simultaneously removed from contact with the strings by means of the damper pedal. See Piano; also Mute.

Dämpfer [G.]. (1) The *dampers of the piano. (2) The *mutes of violins and related instruments. *Dämpfen* (to damp) is also used for the muting of the horn and other instruments.

Damrosch, Walter Johannes (b. Breslau, 30 Jan. 1862; d. New York, 22 Dec. 1950). Conductor and composer. Pupil of his father, Leopold Damrosch, and of Draeseke. Conductor at the Metropolitan Opera House in New York, 1885–91 and 1900–1902; of the New York Philharmonic, 1902–3; of broadcasts with the N.B.C. Symphony Orchestra, 1928–42. Organized the Damrosch Opera Company, 1894. Composed operas (incl. *The Scarlet Letter*, Boston, 1896; *Cyrano*, New York, 1913; *The Man Without a Country*, New York, 1937); choral pieces; incidental music to plays by Euripides and Sophocles; songs.

Dan, Ikuma (b. Tokyo, 7 Apr. 1924). Conductor and composer. Pupil of S. Moroi. Music director and composer for Toho Motion Picture Co. from 1954. Has composed operas (incl. *Yuzuru* [Crane of Twilight], Tokyo, 1952); 5 symphonies; choral works; chamber music; piano pieces; songs; music for radio and for films.

Dance music. The earliest surviving music for dance in the West dates from *c*. 1300 and includes instrumental pieces —some monophonic, some in two parts —of French or English derivation, all of which have the structure of the *estampie or *ductia. To the same type belong some 14th-century Italian dances (all monophonic) called *istampita* or *saltarello*. In the 15th century, dance as courtly entertainment and also as an art form reached its first great peak. All over Europe the stately *basse danse* (*bassadanza*) and the more intricate dances were taught by choreographers of renown, and the dancing master was as esteemed a member of any princely household as the court musician or chapel singer. More than 200 court dances from the 15th and early 16th centuries with all their choreographic details are preserved in contemporary dance instruction books, though the music for these dances is much less precisely documented. The dance treatises themselves contain approximately 100 melodies without accompaniment. In actual performances these melodies served as *cantus firmi* for instrumental improvisation.

The increasingly diverse repertory of dances in the 16th century is reflected in the large variety of dance compositions in the collections of lute, keyboard, and ensemble music of the time. As in the 15th century, the starting point was usually a twin arrangement of a slow-moving main dance followed by a lively jumping dance (*Nachtanz, tripla, *Proportz, Hupfauf, *saltarello*). Among such pairs are the Italian *bassadanza–saltarello* and the Franco-Burgundian *basse danse–pas de breban* (*c*. 1400–1550), and the later Italian *passamezzo–saltarello* (*c*. 1550–1600) and *pavane–*galliard, as well as suitelike combinations such as *basse danse–recoupe–tourdion, pavane–saltarello–*piva*. Also important are the various *branles*.

In the 16th century, new dances appeared that were to play a prominent part in the art music of the 17th century: the (German) *allemande, the (French) *courante, the (Spanish) *saraband, and the (English) *jig or *gigue. About 1650 these dances became the standard movements of the *suite, which until then had employed earlier types such as the *padovana, gagliarda, and intrada. At the same time a host of new dances, considerably more refined, grew up under the auspices of the French court at Versailles, where Louis XIV patronized dance and ballet to an extent unparalleled in history. Most of them were originally peasant dances of the French provinces: the *bourrée (from Auvergne), the *gavotte (from Dauphiné), the *passepied (from Brittany), the *rigaudon (from Provence), the *loure (from Normandy), and, most important of all, the *minuet (from Poitou). Together with certain dances of foreign origin, such as the *anglaise, *hornpipe, *polonaise, and *canarie, they played a prominent part in the ballets and operas of Lully, Purcell, and Rameau, and became, about 1700, the constituents of the optional group of the suite. An important national type of the 17th century is the English *country dance.

The 18th century cultivated particularly the minuet and did not add much to the repertory of dance music until the end of the century. Then appeared the vigorous *écossaise and the swaying *Ländler, the latter of which soon developed into one of the most famous dances of all time, the *waltz. Between 1830 and 1850 a number of dances quickly superseded one another in popularity, e.g., the Polish *mazurka, the *quadrille, the Bohemian *polka, and the *galop. The rise of nationalism led to the discovery by composers of a wealth of national dances, among which the Spanish dances figure prominently, e.g., *bolero, *fandango, *jota. Since the early part of the 20th century, the Americas have produced a great variety of music often associated with dances, including *ragtime, *jazz, *swing, rock, and the conga, mambo, rumba, *tango, and samba, some of which have had an effect on art music. See also Ballet; Suite.

Dandrieu, Jean François (b. Paris, 1682; d. there, 16 Jan. 1738). Probably a pupil of Moreau. Organist at Saint-Merry, Paris, from 1704; at the royal chapel from 1721; at Saint-Barthélemy from 1733. Composed numerous harpsichord pieces; trio sonatas; violin sonatas; organ pieces; songs.

Danican. See under Philidor.

Daniel, John (Danyel) (b. c. 1565; d. 1630). English court musician from 1618; one of the royal "musicians for the lute and voices" from 1625. Composed lute pieces; songs for voice(s) with lute and viol.

Daniel-Lesur. See Lesur, Daniel.

Daniels, Mabel Wheeler (b. Swampscott, Mass., 27 Nov. 1878; d. Boston, 10 Mar. 1971). Pupil of Chadwick and Thuille. Composed stage works; orch. works (incl. *Deep Forest,* 1931); choral works (incl. *A Psalm of Praise,* 1954); chamber music (incl. *Three Observations* for oboe, clarinet, and bassoon, 1943).

Danse macabre [F.]. (1) Dance of death. (2) Symphonic poem by Saint-Saëns, op. 40 (1874), that depicts Death playing the violin and dancing in a graveyard at midnight. The music includes the *Dies irae* from the Requiem Mass.

Dante Symphony. Orchestral work with choral ending by Liszt (1856; full title: *Eine Symphonie zu Dantes Divina commedia*), based on Dante's *Divina commedia*. It is in two movements, entitled "Inferno" (see also under *Dies irae*) and "Purgatorio."

Danza tedesca [It.]. The *Ländler* or the early *waltz (c. 1800).

Danzi, Franz (Ignaz) (b. Schwetzingen, 15 June 1763; d. Karlsruhe, 13 Apr. 1826). Pupil of Abbé Vogler. Court musician in Mannheim and Munich from 1778. Court *Kapellmeister* at Stuttgart, 1807–12, and at Karlsruhe thereafter. Composed numerous operas (incl. *Die Mitternachtsstunde,* 1788) and *Singspiele;* symphonies; concertos; Masses and other sacred music; choral works; chamber music; sonatas; songs.

Daphnis et Chloé [F.]. Ballet by Ravel (choreography by M. Fokine), produced in Paris, 1912. It is based on the classical story. Two suites from the ballet music, arranged by the composer, are frequently played in orchestral concerts.

Daquin, Louis-Claude (b. Paris, 4 July 1694; d. there, 15 June 1772). A child prodigy, he played clavecin before Louis XIV at age 6. Competed successfully with Rameau for the position of organist at Saint-Paul, which he held from 1727 to his death; succeeded Dandrieu as organist of the royal chapel, 1739. Composed the cantata *La rose;* numerous harpsichord pieces (incl. "Le coucou") and organ pieces.

Dargomizhsky, Alexander Sergeievich (b. Tula, 14 Feb. 1813; d. St. Petersburg, 17 Jan. 1869). Lived in St. Petersburg from 1817; close associate of Glinka, whom he met in 1834. Composed operas (incl. *Esmeralda,* Moscow, 1847; *The Triumph of Bacchus,* 1845, prod. Moscow, 1867; *Russalka,* St. Petersburg, 1856; *The Stone Guest,* after Pushkin, completed by Cui, orchestrated by Rimsky-Korsakov, St. Petersburg, 1872); orch. works (incl. *Baba-Yaga*); songs.

Daseian notation. A notational system of the 9th and 10th centuries in which the tones of the scale are represented by signs derived from the *prosodia daseia,* i.e., the aspirate sign in ancient Greek

[Ex. 1]. The signs in Ex. 2 indicate the tetrachord d–e–f–g, while others are derived largely from these by turning them upside down or reversing from right to left.

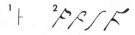

Dastgah. The melody types that are the basis of Persian art music. See Melody types.

Dauer, dauernd [G.]. Duration, enduring or continuing.

Daughter of the Regiment, The. See *Fille du Régiment, La.*

Dauvergne, Antoine (b. Moulins, 3 Mar. 1713; d. Lyons, 12 Feb. 1797). French royal chamber musician from 1741; conductor of the Concert spirituel, 1762–71; conductor of the Grand Opéra, 1769–90. Composed numerous operas (incl. *Les troqueurs,* Paris, 1753); symphonies; trio sonatas; sonatas for violin with thoroughbass.

David, Félicien (-César) (b. Cadenet, Vaucluse, 13 Apr. 1810; d. Saint-Germain-en-Laye, 29 Aug. 1876). *Maître de chapelle* at Saint-Sauveur, Aix-en-Provence, 1829. Traveled in the Middle East, 1833–35. Succeeded Berlioz as member of the Academy and librarian of the Paris Conservatory, 1869. Composed operas (incl. *Lalla-Roukh,* Paris, 1862); symphonic works (incl. *Le désert* with chorus, 1844); choral works; chamber music; cello pieces; piano pieces; songs.

David, Ferdinand (b. Hamburg, 19 Jan. 1810; d. near Klosters, Switzerland, 18 July 1873). Pupil of Spohr and Hauptmann. Violinist in several orchestras and quartets in Germany and Russia. Close associate of Mendelssohn. Taught violin at the Leipzig Conservatory from 1843. Composed an opera, *Hans Wacht,* Leipzig, 1852; symphonies; violin concertos; many violin pieces; string quartets and other chamber music; numerous pedagogical pieces for violin.

David, Johann Nepomuk (b. Eferding, Austria, 30 Nov. 1895). Pupil of J. Marx. Professor of composition at the Leipzig Conservatory from 1934 and its director

from 1939; professor of composition at the Musikhochschule in Stuttgart, 1947–63. Has composed 8 symphonies; concertos; other orch. works; choral works; chamber music; organ works (incl. *Choralwerk,* containing numerous chorale settings); motets; songs.

Davidovsky, Mario (b. Buenos Aires, 4 Mar. 1934). Has taught in Buenos Aires and at City College of the City Univ. of New York. Served as assistant director of the Columbia-Princeton Electronic Music Center. Has composed works for orch. and chamber ensembles; *Contrasts* no. 1 for strings and electronic sounds, 1962; *Synchronisms* nos. 1–7 (no. 6, for piano and electronic sound, was awarded the Pulitzer Prize for 1971); other instrumental and electronic works.

Davidsbündler Tänze [G., Dances of the David-leaguers]. Robert Schumann's cycle of 18 *character pieces for piano, op. 6, composed in 1837. The title refers to an imaginary "League of David" frequently mentioned in Schumann's writings on music, to which he entrusted the task of fighting the musical "Philistines" of his day. Each piece is signed E. or F., for Eusebius and Florestan, imaginary characters representing respectively the pensive introverted and the impulsive extroverted sides of Schumann's own personality. They also appear in his *Carnaval,* together with a "March of the David-leaguers against the Philistines."

Davies, Henry Walford (b. Oswestry, Shropshire, 6 Sept. 1869; d. Wrington, Somerset, 11 Mar. 1941). Pupil of Stanford; pupil and assistant of Parratt, whom he succeeded as organist of St. George's Chapel, Windsor, in 1924. Held several positions as church organist; taught in several British schools (incl. the Royal College of Music, 1895–1903). Succeeded Elgar as Master of the King's Music, 1934. Composed numerous works for soloists, chorus, and orch. (incl. *Everyman,* 1904); orch. works (incl. *Solemn Melody* for organ and strings, 1908); church music; chamber music; songs and part songs; a children's opera.

Davies, Peter Maxwell (b. Manchester, 8 Sept. 1934). Studied at Royal Manchester College of Music and with Petrassi and Sessions. With Birtwistle, founded the Pierrot Players (now the Fires of London), 1967, for the performance of contemporary music. Has composed stage works (incl. the operas *Taverner*, 1970, and *The Martyrdom of St. Magnus*, 1977; *Vesalii icones* for dancer-pianist, cello, instrumental ensemble, 1970); orch. works (incl. 2 *Fantasias* on an *In nomine* of Taverner, 1962 and 1964; *A Mirror of Whitening Light*, 1977); choral works (incl. *O magnum mysterium*, 1960); works for voice and instruments (incl. *8 Songs for a Mad King*, 1969); *L'homme armé* for instruments and tape, 1968; piano pieces.

Davy, Richard (b. *c.* 1467; d. probably at Blickling Hall, Norfolk, *c.* 1516). Organist at Magdalen College, Oxford, 1490. Ordained a priest, 1497; in the service of the Boleyn family from 1501 to his death. Composed a Passion according to St. Matthew; carols; motets.

Daza, Estéban (citizen of Valladolid, Spain; fl. mid-16th cent.). Published a collection of vihuela tablatures under the title *El parnaso*, 1576, containing original works and transcriptions of sacred and secular vocal works.

D.C. Abbr. for *da capo.*

De Koven, Henry Louis Reginald (b. Middletown, Conn., 3 Apr. 1859; d. Chicago, 16 Jan. 1920). Studied at Oxford and with R. Genée and Delibes. Served as music critic for several newspapers in the U.S. Organized (1902) and conducted (1902–4) the Washington, D.C., Philharmonic. Composed numerous operettas (incl. *Robin Hood*, Chicago, 1890; 2 operas (*The Canterbury Pilgrims*, New York, 1917; *Rip Van Winkle*, Chicago, 1920); instrumental works; numerous songs.

De Lara, Isidore (real name Cohen) (b. London, 9 Aug. 1858; d. Paris, 2 Sept. 1935). Studied at the Milan Conservatory and with Lalo in Paris. Composed operas (incl. *Messalina*, Monte Carlo, 1899; *Les trois mousquetaires*, Cannes, 1921); songs.

De Pablo, Luis (b. Bilbao, 28 Jan. 1930). Studied at the Madrid Conservatory and at the Darmstadt summer courses. Has worked with serial, aleatory, theater, and electronic techniques. Works incl. *Tombeau* for orch., 1963; *Heterogéneo* for organ, speakers, and orch., 1968; *Movil 1* for 2 pianos, 1958; *Comentarios* for soprano and instruments, 1956; *We, on tape*, 1969.

De profundis [L.]. Psalm 129 (130): "De profundis clamavi, ad te Domine" (Out of the depths have I cried unto thee O Lord). One of the penitential psalms, it is part of the Roman Catholic Office for the Dead and has frequently been set polyphonically.

Deaconing. See Lining (out).

Dead interval. An interval between the last note of a melodic phrase and the first note of the next, the two notes often separated by a rest.

Death and the Maiden. See *Tod und das Mädchen, Der.*

Death and Transfiguration. See *Tod und Verklärung.*

Debussy, Claude (-Achille) (b. Saint-Germain-en-Laye, 22 Aug. 1862; d. Paris, 25 Mar. 1918). Pupil of Marmontel, Lavignac, Guiraud, and Franck. Close associate of the circle of French symbolist poets incl. Mallarmé. Works: stage works (incl. the opera *Pelléas et Mélisande* and the ballet *Jeux*); the cantata *L'*enfant prodigue*; orch. works (incl. *Prelude à "L'après-midi d'un faune"; Trois *nocturnes; La *mer; *Images*, containing *Ibéria*); chamber music (incl. a string quartet, 1893; sonatas for cello and piano, 1915; for flute, viola, and harp, 1916; and for violin and piano, 1917); piano works (incl. *Suite bergamasque*, containing "Clair de lune": *Pour le piano*, 1896–1901; *Estampes; *Children's Corner; 2 books of *Préludes*, 1910, 1913; 2 books of *Études*, 1915); songs to texts by Verlaine, Villon, Baudelaire, Louÿs, Mallarmé, and others. See Impressionism.

Decani and cantoris [L.]. In Anglican church music, two groups of the choir, one by the dean's stall (right side facing the altar), the other close to the cantor (left side). Late-16th-century composers (Tallis, Farrant, Byrd) often employed the groups antiphonally, separately, or jointly. See Polychoral style.

Decay. The characteristics of the dying away of a sound [see under Acoustics].

Deceptive cadence. See under Cadence.

Déchant [F.]. *Discant. For *déchant sur le livre*, see *Discantus supra librum*. For *déchant de viole*, descant viol, see under Viol.

Decibel. See Bel.

Declamation. That aspect of the musical setting of a text that corresponds to the purely sonorous quality of the text itself. Thus, good declamation normally requires that musical *accent and textual accent coincide, both at the level of individual words and syllables and at the level of phrases and sentences. This norm first became a feature of vocal music during the 16th century.

Decrescendo [It.; abbr. *decr., decresc.*]. See Crescendo, decrescendo.

Deering, Richard (Dering) (b. *c*. 1580; d. London, buried 22 Mar. 1630). Educated in Italy; served as musician to the English court from 1625. Composed vocal works, incl. motets with thoroughbass, canticles, *canzonette;* anthems; instrumental works, incl. pieces for viol.

Degen, Helmut (b. Aglasterhausen, near Heidelberg, 14 Jan. 1911). Pupil of Jarnach and Maler. Taught composition at the Duisburg Conservatory from 1937; has taught at the Hochschulinstitut für Musik in Trossingen from 1947. Has composed stage works (incl. *Die Konferenz der Tiere,* 1950); orch. works and concertos; oratorios and other choral works; chamber music; piano and organ pieces; pedagogic works for strings and for piano.

Degree. See Scale degrees.

Dehors, en [F.]. Emphasized.

Del Tredici, David (Walter) (b. Cloverdale, Calif., 16 Mar. 1937). Pupil of A. Elston, Shifrin, Sessions, Kim, and Milhaud. Member of the faculty of Harvard Univ., 1966–71; teaching associate of Boston Univ. from 1973. Works incl. *Six Songs* (text by James Joyce) for voice and piano, 1959; *Syzygy* for amplified soprano and 18 instruments, 1966; *The Last Gospel,* 1967, and *Pop-pourri,* 1968, for amplified rock group, chorus, and orch.; several works based on *Alice in Wonderland* (incl. *Final Alice* for orch., 1976); piano pieces.

Delannoy, Marcel (-François-Georges) (b. La Ferté-Alais, 9 July 1898; d. Nantes, 14 Sept. 1962). Pupil of Aubert, Gédalge, and Honegger. Composed operas (incl. *Le poirier de misère,* Paris, 1927; *Ginevra,* Paris, 1942); ballets; 2 symphonies; a piano concerto; a string quartet and other chamber music; piano pieces; song cycles.

Delibes, (Clément-Philibert-) Léo (b. Saint-Germain-du-Val, Sarthe, 21 Feb. 1836; d. Paris, 16 Jan. 1891). Pupil of Adam. Church organist from 1853. Second chorusmaster at the Grand Opéra from 1865. Taught composition at the Paris Conservatory from 1881. Composed operas (incl. *Lakmé; Le roi l'a dit,* Paris, 1873; *Jean de Nivelle,* Paris, 1880); operettas; ballets (incl. *Coppélia, La source,* and *Sylvia*); choral works; songs with piano accompaniment.

Delius, Frederick (bapt. Fritz Albert Theodor) (b. Bradford, England, 29 Jan. 1862; d. Grez-sur-Loing, France, 10 June 1934). Pupil of Reinecke and Jadassohn in Leipzig after having lived for a time in Florida. Lived in France from 1888. Because of an illness that led to paralysis and blindness, he dictated his later works to the composer Eric Fenby. Composed operas (incl. *A Village Romeo and Juliet,* Berlin, 1907; *Fennimore and Gerda,* Frankfurt, 1919); symphonic works (incl. *Brigg Fair,* 1907; *On Hearing the First Cuckoo in Spring,* 1912; *North Country Sketches,* 1914); works for chorus and orch. (incl. *Appalachia,* 1902; *Sea Drift,* 1903); concertos; chamber music; songs.

Dello Joio, Norman (b. New York, 24 Jan. 1913). Pupil of Yon, Wagenaar, and Hindemith. Has taught at Sarah Lawrence College and Mannes College of Music. Dean of Fine Arts at Boston Univ. from 1972. Has composed operas (incl. *The Triumph of St. Joan,* 1950; *The Ruby,* 1955; *The Trial at Rouen,* 1956); ballets for Martha Graham, José Limón, and others; orch. works (incl. *Meditations on Ecclesiastes,* Pulitzer Prize, 1957; *Homage to Haydn,* 1969); concertos and concertinos; choral works (incl. a Mass, 1969); chamber music; piano pieces.

Delvincourt, Claude (b. Paris, 12 Jan. 1888; d. Orbetello, Italy, 5 Apr. 1954). Pupil of Widor and Busser. Director of the Versailles Conservatory, 1931–41, and of the Paris Conservatory, 1941 to his death. Composed stage works, incl. the musical comedy *La femme à barbe,* Versailles, 1938; orch. works; vocal works with orch. (incl. *Ce monde de rosée,* 1935); chamber music; piano pieces.

Démancher [F.]. In string playing, to shift the left hand from one position to another.

Demantius, (Johannes) Cristoph (b. Reichenberg, 15 Dec. 1567; d. Freiberg, Saxony, 20 Apr. 1643). Enrolled at Wittenberg Univ., 1593. Cantor at Zittau from 1597 and at Freiberg, 1604–43. Composed sacred works (incl. motets and a German Passion according to St. John); secular works (incl. German polyphonic songs, madrigals, *canzonette, villanelle,* dances); several treatises.

Demi- [F.]. Half. For *demi-jeu,* see *Plein-jeu; demi-pause, demi-soupir,* see Notes; *demi-ton,* semitone; *demi-voix* or *mezza voce,* see Mezzo.

Demisemiquaver. See under Notes.

Denisov, Edison Vasilievich (b. Tomsk, Siberia, 6 Apr. 1929). Pupil of Shebalin. Member of the faculty of the Moscow Conservatory from 1959. Works incl. an opera; *Symphony in D* for 2 string orchestras and percussion, 1964; *Plachi* (Tears) for soprano, piano, and percussion, 1966; *Solntse inkov* (Incan Sun) for soprano and instruments, 1964; *Crescendo e diminuendo* for harpsichord and strings, 1967; chamber music; piano pieces; songs.

Déploration [F.]. See Lament (2).

Derb [G.]. Robust, tough.

Dering, Richard. See Deering, Richard.

Des, deses [G.]. D-flat, D-double-flat. See Pitch names.

Des Marais, Paul (b. Menominee, Mich., 23 June 1920). Pupil of Sowerby, N. Boulanger, and Piston. Member of the faculty of Harvard Univ., 1953–56; of the Univ. of California at Los Angeles from 1956. Has made some use of serial techniques. Works incl. *Epiphanies,* chamber opera with film sequences, 1968; sacred vocal music; instrumental works; 2 piano sonatas; *Le cimetière marin* for voice, keyboard instruments, and percussion, 1971.

Des Prez, Josquin. See Josquin des Prez.

Descant. Anglicized form of L. *discantus* and a variant of *discant.* Throughout the Middle Ages the term was used interchangeably with other terms, such as *descaunt.* In the 17th century it took on special connotations in instrumental practice. *Descant viol* and *descant recorder* are names for the highest-pitched instruments of their families, a fourth or a fifth above the treble size [see Viol; Recorder]. *Descant clef* is an older name for the soprano clef [see Clef]. In modern hymn-singing, an obbligato part that soars above the tune is known as a descant.

Descort [F.]. See under Lai.

Descriptive music. See Program music; Word painting.

Dessau, Paul (b. Hamburg, 19 Dec. 1894). Conducted successively in Cologne, Mainz, and Berlin, 1919–33; left Germany in 1933 and lived in New York from 1939 until he settled in East Berlin in 1948. Member of the faculty of the German Academy of Arts from 1959. Has composed operas (incl. *Das Verurteilung des Lukullus,* libretto by Brecht, Berlin, 1951); music for theater (incl. several plays by Brecht) and films; symphonic works; oratorios; cantatas; chamber music; piano pieces; works for voice and instruments.

Dessus [F.]. Old term corresponding to *treble,* while *par-dessus* corresponds to *descant.* Thus, *dessus de viole,* treble viol; *par-dessus de viole,* descant viol.

Destouches, André-Cardinal (b. Paris, bapt. 6 Apr. 1672; d. there, 7 Feb. 1749). Pupil of Campra. Appointed superintendent of the Paris Opéra by Louis XIV, 1713; its director from 1728. Composed operas (incl. *Issé,* Fontainebleau, 1697; *Omphale,* Paris, 1700; *Callirhoé,* Paris,

1712); secular songs; cantatas; motets and other sacred music.

Destra [It.]. Right (hand).

Détaché [F.]. See under Bowing (b).

Dett, Robert Nathaniel (b. Drummondville, Quebec, 11 Oct. 1882; d. Battle Creek, Mich., 2 Oct. 1943). Pianist, conductor, and composer. Studied at the Oberlin Conservatory, Columbia Univ., Harvard Univ., Eastman School of Music, Howard Univ., the Univ. of Pennsylvania, and with N. Boulanger in Paris. Taught at several U.S. colleges, including Hampton Institute. Composed 2 oratorios (incl. *The Ordering of Moses,* 1937); choral works; songs; piano works (incl. *In the Bottoms Suite,* 1913, containing *Juba Dance*). Published 2 collections of Negro spirituals and folksongs.

Deuterus [Gr.]. See under Church modes.

Deutlich [G.]. Clear, distinct.

Deutsches Requiem, Ein. A work for solo voices, chorus, and orchestra by Johannes Brahms, op. 45, composed 1857–68, after the death of his mother. It consists of seven movements based on German texts freely selected from the Scriptures, instead of the Latin text of the liturgical *Requiem Mass. Its first complete performance was in 1869 in Leipzig.

Deux journées, Les [F., The Two Days; also produced in English as *The Water-Carrier*]. Opera in three acts by Cherubini (libretto by J.-N. Bouilly), produced in Paris, 1800. Setting: Paris and environs, 1617.

Development. (1) The working out of previously stated thematic material, usually by means of the application of techniques such as *sequence and *imitation to relatively short melodic motives (either taken directly from or derived from the material in question) in such a way as to produce a series of modulations and a sense of increased structural tension. (2) The section of a movement in *sonata form that makes use of the techniques of (1) and that serves to return the key of the movement from the dominant (or relative major), in which the exposition

ends, to the tonic, in which the recapitulation begins and the movement as a whole ends.

Devienne, François (b. Joinville, Haute-Marne, France, 31 Jan. 1759; d. Charenton, 6 Sept. 1803). Flutist, bassoonist, and composer. Taught flute at the Paris Conservatory from 1795. Composed operas (incl. *Les visitandines,* Paris, 1792); orch. works; concertos for various wind instruments with orch.; numerous pieces for solo winds and wind ensembles; chamber music; patriotic hymns and songs. Published several theoretical and pedagogic works.

Devil and Daniel Webster, The. Opera in one act by D. Moore (libretto by S. V. Benét, based on his story), produced in New York, 1939. Setting: New Hampshire, the 1840s.

Devil's Trill Sonata. A violin sonata by Tartini, said to have been inspired by a dream in which the devil appeared to him. The long trill for which it is named occurs in the last movement.

Di molto [It.]. Very; e.g., *allegro di molto,* very fast.

Di nuovo [It.]. Again.

Diabelli, Anton (b. Mattsee, near Salzburg, 5 Sept. 1781; d. Vienna, 8 Apr. 1858). Music publisher (who published much of Schubert's music) and composer. Pupil of Michael Haydn. Taught piano and guitar. Composed an opera and operettas; Masses; cantatas; chamber music; dance music; piano pieces; songs; a waltz theme on which Beethoven based his *Diabelli Variations.*

Diabelli Variations. Beethoven's op. 120 (1823), consisting of 33 variations on a waltz by Diabelli (full title: *33 Veränderungen über einen Walzer von A. Diabelli*). They were written in response to a request sent by the Viennese publisher Diabelli to 51 composers that each contribute one variation to a collective set meant to represent contemporary musical composition in Austria. The entire collection was published under the title *Vaterländischer Künstlerverein* (Society of Artists of the Fatherland), in two volumes; the first contained the variations of Beethoven; the second, those of the

50 other composers (incl. Schubert, Moscheles, Kalkbrenner, and Liszt—then 11 years old).

Diabolus in musica [L., the devil in music]. Late medieval name for the *tritone, which in musical theory was regarded as the most dissonant interval. See Mi-fa.

Diacisma, diaschisma. See Comma, schisma.

Dialogues des Carmélites, Les [F., The Dialogues of the Carmelites]. Opera in three acts by F. Poulenc (libretto by G. Bernanos), produced in Milan, 1957. Setting: France, 1789.

Diamond, David (Leo) (b. Rochester, N.Y., 9 July 1915). Pupil of Rogers, Sessions, and N. Boulanger. Lived in Italy, 1953–65. Chairman of the composition department of the Manhattan School of Music, 1965–67. Has composed ballets; 8 symphonies; concertos; *Rounds* for string orch., 1944; other orch. works (incl. *Psalm,* 1936; *Romeo and Juliet,* 1947); 10 string quartets, *Nonet* for 3 violins, 3 violas, and 3 cellos, 1962, and other chamber music; choral pieces; piano pieces; songs.

Diapason. (1) In Greek and medieval theory, the interval that includes "all the tones," i.e., the octave [see *Diapente; Diatessaron;* Interval]. Derived meanings, chiefly used in French terminology, are: (2) range of voice; and (3) concert pitch, usually termed *diapason normal* [see Pitch (3)]; or tuning fork, also called *diapason à branches.* (4) The main foundation stop of the organ, also called *principal;* see Organ.

Diapente [Gr.]. Ancient Greek and medieval name for the fifth. *Epidiapente,* fifth above; *subdiapente* or *hypodiapente,* fifth below; *canon in epidiapente,* canon at the fifth above.

Diaphonia, diaphony. (1) In Greek theory, dissonance, in contrast to *symphonia,* consonance. (2) More commonly, the term is used by Latin theorists of the 9th to 12th centuries to mean two-part polyphony. The term *discantus* [see Discant] is probably the Latin translation of *diaphonia.*

Diaschisma. See Comma, schisma.

Diastematic. See under Neumes.

Diatessaron [Gr.]. Greek and medieval name for the interval of the fourth. *Epidiatessaron,* fourth above; *subdiatessaron, hypodiatessaron,* fourth below. See also *Diapente.*

Diatonic. An adjective applied to (1) the major and minor *scales, which employ particular combinations of both whole tones and semitones (as opposed to the *chromatic scale, which employs only semitones); (2) harmony and melodies that employ only the pitches of a particular diatonic scale; (3) one of the three genera (the other two being *chromatic and *enharmonic) of ancient Greek music, namely the one employing a *tetrachord constructed of a whole tone, a semitone, and a whole tone. See also Pandiatonicism.

Dibdin, Charles (b. Southampton, bapt. 4 Mar. 1745; d. London, 25 July 1814). Composer to Covent Garden, Drury Lane, and Royal Circus (later Surrey) theaters. Composed numerous operas and other stage pieces; "table-entertainments" (a genre of his own invention, written, composed, sung, and accompanied by himself); sea-songs; other songs. Published several books of fiction and nonfiction.

Dichterliebe [G., Poet's Love]. *Song cycle by Robert Schumann, op. 48 (1840), consisting of 16 settings of poems by Heine.

Dido and Aeneas. Opera in three acts by Purcell (libretto by Nahum Tate, after Virgil's poem), produced about 1689 at Josias Priest's boarding school for girls in Chelsea (London). Setting: Carthage, after the fall of Troy.

Diepenbrock, Alfons (Alphonsus Johannes Maria) (b. Amsterdam, 2 Sept. 1862; d. there, 5 Apr. 1921). Self-taught in music. Composed incidental music for plays by Sophocles, Aristophanes, Goethe; choral works (incl. a Mass and a *Te Deum*); works for accompanied voice (incl. *Hymne an die Nacht* for soprano and orch., text by Novalis); songs.

Dieren, Bernard van (b. Rotterdam, 27 Dec. 1884; d. London, 24 Apr. 1936). Close associate of Busoni and Delius.

Settled in London 1909 and worked as a newspaper correspondent. Composed stage works (incl. *The Tailor*, comic opera, 1917); orch. works; works for voices and orch. (incl. *Diaphony*, to sonnets by Shakespeare; *Chinese Symphony*, 1914); chamber music; piano pieces; violin pieces; songs. Published numerous articles and two books.

Dies irae [L.]. A rhymed sequence [see Sequence (2)], probably by Thomas of Celano (d. 1256), sung in the Requiem Mass [*LU*, p. 1810]. Not until the mid-16th century did it become an integral part of the Requiem Mass. More recent composers have usually retained only the text and have written for it free music of a highly dramatic character (Mozart, Cherubini, Verdi). However, the old melody [for the first section, see Ex.] has frequently been incorporated into program compositions having death or damnation as their subject, e.g., Berlioz' *Symphonie fantastique* (last movement: "Dream of a Witches' Sabbath"), Liszt's *Totentanz* and *Dante Symphony*, Saint-Saëns' *Danse macabre*.

Di - es i - rae, di - es il - la, Sol - vet saec - lum

in fa - vil - la, Tes - te Da - vid cum Si - bil - la.

Dièse [F.]. The sharp sign [see Accidentals; Pitch names]. In the 17th century, also used to indicate the major mode, e.g., *mi dièse,* E major.

Diesis [Gr.]. (1) In early Greek theory (Pythagoras), the diatonic semitone of the *Pythagorean scale. This meaning survives in many medieval treatises, in which *diesis* is explained as the *semitonium minus*. (2) In later Greek theory, the quarter tone of the *enharmonic genus. (3) In some 15th-century treatises the term is used for the sharp sign. This meaning survives to the present day in Italian and French terminology [see *Dièse*]. (4) In modern writings on acoustics the term is occasionally used to designate certain theoretical intervals, about a quarter tone in size. The difference between four minor thirds (of just intonation) and the octave is called *great diesis* ($(6/5)^4:2 = 648/625 = 63$ cents), while that between the octave and three major thirds is called *minor diesis* or *enharmonic diesis* ($2:(5/4)^3 = 128/125 = 41$ cents).

Dietrich, Albert Hermann (b. Forsthaus Golk, near Meissen, 28 Aug. 1829; d. Berlin, 20 Nov. 1908). Pupil of Otto, Moscheles, Hauptmann, and Schumann. Conductor in Bonn and Oldenburg. Composed stage music (incl. the opera *Robin Hood,* Frankfurt, 1879); choral works; orch. works (incl. a symphony in D min.); concertos; chamber music; piano pieces; songs. Published a book on Brahms.

Dietrich, Sixtus (b. Augsburg, between 1492 and 1494; d. St. Gall, Switzerland, 21 Oct. 1548). Choirmaster at Constance from 1517; associated with the Lutheran circle at Wittenberg by late 1540. A friend of Glareanus, to whose *Dodecachordon* he contributed examples. Composed Magnificats, antiphons, hymns, motets; sacred German polyphonic songs.

Dieupart, Charles (b. France; d. London, *c.* 1740). Violinist, harpsichordist, and composer. Settled in London, *c.* 1700, where he collaborated in the production of several operas. Published a set of harpsichord suites, parts of which were copied by J. S. Bach and some material from which was incorporated in Bach's *English Suites*.

Diferencia [Sp.]. A 16th-century name for a *variation. The *diferencias* of Luís de Narváez' *Delphín de música* (1538) are among the earliest preserved examples of variations. Cabezón wrote *diferencias* for keyboard instruments. See also *Glosa*.

Difference tone, differential tone. See Combination tone.

Differentiae [L.]. The various endings of a *psalm tone.

Diluendo [It.]. Fading away.

Dimeter. See under Poetic meter.

Diminished intervals. See under Interval.

Diminished seventh chord. See Seventh chord.

Diminished triad. See Triad.

Diminuendo [It.; abbr. *dim.* or *dimin.*]. *Decrescendo* [see Crescendo, decrescendo].

Diminution [L. *diminutio*]. (1) Term in counterpoint and in mensural notation; see Augmentation and diminution. (2) The breaking up of the notes of a melody into quick figures, as is frequently done in variations. See Ornamentation; also Division.

D'Indy, Vincent. See Indy, Vincent d'.

Direct. A mark ($\wedge\!\!\!\wedge$) that in early manuscripts and publications is given at the end of each staff (or only of the page) to warn the player of the first note of the following staff (or page). The Latin name is *custos*.

Dirge. A vocal or instrumental composition designed to be performed at a funeral or at memorial rites. The name is derived from L. *Dirige Domine,* an antiphon from the Office for the Dead [see *LU,* p. 1782].

Dirigent, dirigieren [G.]. Conductor, to conduct.

Dis, disis [G.]. D-sharp, D-double-sharp; see Pitch names. In earlier music, *dis* often stands for E-flat, e.g., in Bach's St. Matthew Passion: "Wiederhole den Choral aus dem Dis" (Repeat the chorale in E-flat). As late as 1805, Beethoven's *Eroica* Symphony was described, at the first performance, as being "in Dis."

Discant [L. *discantus,* perhaps from Gr. **diaphonia*]. (1) In the 12th and 13th centuries, music in which two or more parts proceed note-against-note in strictly measured rhythms (often employing the rhythmic modes [see Modes, rhythmic]), as opposed to *organum, in which one or more measured parts proceed against sustained tones in another part, and to *copula, which shares features of both discant and organum. Thus, discant is the style of the *clausulae in the organa of the *Notre Dame repertory. In the 13th through the 15th centuries, discant comes to be equated with *counterpoint and thus in theoretical treatises forms a subject comprised of the principles of voice-leading and consonance and dissonance. The term "English discant" is sometimes applied to a 15th-century style of three-part writing making extensive use of parallel *sixth chords [see also Sixth-chord style] and in which there is a *cantus firmus in the lowest part. This usage remains a subject of controversy, as does the relationship between this phenomenon and *fauxbourdon. See also *Discantus supra librum.*

(2) The uppermost part (soprano, treble) of a polyphonic composition. The term is used frequently today in connection with 14th- and 15th-century compositions in which a *cantus firmus* appears in the upper part (rather than in the tenor), nearly always in an embellished form (paraphrase). This technique was applied to hymns, Marian antiphons, Masses or Mass sections, etc. See also *Descant.*

Discantus supra librum [L.; F. *déchant sur le livre*]. Designation for methods of improvising polyphony on the basis of a single notated melody found "in the book," i.e., the book of Gregorian chant. The *organum of the 9th and 10th centuries, proceeding largely in parallel fourths or fifths, may be considered an early type of *discantus supra librum,* since its rules enabled a singer to improvise a second voice (*vox organalis*) to the plainsong melody (*vox principalis*). Usually, the term is applied to more elaborate methods of improvised harmonization of the 14th and 15th centuries. One such method is described by an anonymous early 15th-century English writer as *faburden. The notated part or *cantus firmus* (in black notes in the accompanying Ex.) appears in one or another of the three parts most often employed, depending on the particular method used. See also Fauxbourdon; Sixth-chord style.

Discord. See Concord, discord.

Disinvolto [It.]. Jaunty, unconstrained.

Disjunct. See Conjunct, disjunct.

Diskant [G.]. Soprano; see Discant.

Disposition. The arrangement of stops, manuals, pedals, couplers, etc., of an organ.

Dissonance. See Consonance, dissonance.

Dissonant (Dissonance) Quartet. Mozart's String Quartet in C major, K. 465, so called because of the dissonance in the introduction to the first movement.

Distler, Hugo (b. Nuremberg, 24 June 1908; d. Berlin, 1 Nov. 1942). Pupil of H. Grabner. Held several positions as church organist and teacher in Lübeck, Stuttgart, and Berlin. Composed cantatas; an oratorio, *Die Weltalter,* 1942, unfinished; other sacred and secular choral works; a concerto for harpsichord and string orch., 1935; *Konzertstück* for 2 pianos; organ works.

Dital harp. See Harp lute.

Dithyramb [Gr. *dithyrambos*]. A song in honor of the Greek god Dionysus. Modern composers have occasionally used the word as a title for compositions of a free and passionate nature.

Dittersdorf, Karl Ditters von (b. Vienna, 2 Nov. 1739; d. Castle Rothlhotta, near Neuhaus, Bohemia, 24 Oct. 1799). Violinist and composer. Traveled to Italy with Gluck, 1763. *Kapellmeister* (succeeding Michael Haydn) to the Bishop of Grosswardein, Hungary, 1765–69; then to the Prince-Bishop of Breslau. Composed numerous symphonies; concertos for violin and for other instruments; Italian operas and German *Singspiele* (incl. *Doktor und Apotheker,* Vienna, 1786); a ballet; divertimenti; oratorios; cantatas; Masses; string quartets and other chamber music; numerous piano works.

Div. Abbr. for *divisi.*

Divertimento [It.]. A term applied in the second half of the 18th century, especially in Austria, to an enormous variety of nonorchestral, instrumental works. In the period 1750–80 these include lighter types, such as the *cassation, *serenade, and *notturno, as well as more serious types of chamber music, such as the string quartet. After about 1780, the term *divertimento* is more often restricted to lighter instrumental works in a variety of nonorchestral scorings and with varying numbers of movements, most often including one or more minuets, marches, or other dances. These were distinguished from the more serious forms of chamber music in standard combinations identified by the number of participants, e.g., *trio, *quartet, *quintet. See also *Divertissement.*

Divertissement [F.]. (1) A musical potpourri, frequently in the form of pieces extracted from an opera. (2) In French baroque opera, the ballets, dances, entr'actes, etc.—in short, all those pieces that served merely to entertain without being essential to the plot. (3) Same as *divertimento.*

Divided stop. A device of organ building that makes it possible to use different registrations for the upper and lower halves of the manual. It was frequently found in organs of the 17th century, especially in Spain. Contemporaneous terms are half-stop (Purcell or Blow), *registro spezzato* [It.], *registre coupé* or *rompu* [F.], *medio registro* [Sp.], and *meyo (meio) registo* [Port.].

Divisi [It.; abbr. *div.*]. Used in orchestral scores to indicate that an instrumental body, e.g., the first violins, is to be divided into two or more groups, each playing a separate part. See under *A due;* also Gymel (2).

Division. A 17th- and 18th-century term for *figuration, that is, the breaking up of a melody into quick figures and passages [see also Ornamentation; Coloratura (2)]. In particular, the term refers to the predominantly English practice of playing written or improvised variations (usually by a viol or other melodic instrument) over a *ground bass.

Division viol. See under Viol.

Dixieland. A style of jazz developed in New Orleans (and sometimes therefore called New Orleans style) beginning in about 1910 and still widely performed. It draws on both *blues and *ragtime, particularly the strongly syncopated rhythms and "two-beat" meter (i.e., a duple meter in which the first and third of four pulses are emphasized) of the latter. It is characteristically performed by an ensemble (Dixieland band) of trumpet or cornet, clarinet, slide trombone, piano or banjo, double bass (played pizzicato) or tuba, and drums. Among the most important exponents of this style have been trumpeters King Oliver and Louis Armstrong and pianist Jelly Roll Morton. The term *Dixieland* first achieved currency in the names of groups such as the Original Dixieland Jazz Band, which made its first recordings in 1917. This band was led by white musicians who imitated the style of Negro musicians in New Orleans and played an important role in the dissemination of that style.

Dlugoszewski, Lucia (b. Detroit, 16 June 1931). Pupil of Varèse. From 1960, teacher and composer for the Foundation for Modern Dance. Has developed, composed for, and performed on numerous glass, plastic, wood, paper, and metal percussion instruments, incl. the timbre piano. Works incl. *Orchestra Structure for the Poetry of Everyday Sounds,* 1952; *Delicate Accidents in Space* for unsheltered rattle quintet, 1959; *Velocity Shells* for timbre piano, trumpet, invented percussion, 1970; *Space Is a Diamond* for trumpet, 1970; other works for various ensembles, many of them for the dance.

Do, doh. See Pitch names; Solmization; Tonic sol-fa.

Dodecaphonic. Pertaining to twelve-tone technique or compositions [see Serial music].

Dodge, Charles (b. Ames, Iowa, 5 June 1942). Pupil of Bezanson, Milhaud, Schuller, Berger, Beeson, Chou Wen-chung, Luening, and Ussachevsky. Teacher at Columbia Univ., 1967–69 and from 1970. Works incl. *Rota* for orch., 1966; *Changes,* computer-synthesized sounds on tape, 1970; *Folia* for chamber ensemble, 1965; *Speech Songs,* 1973; other works composed with the aid of the computer and for conventional instruments.

Dohnányi, Ernst von (Ernö) (b. Pressburg [Bratislava], 27 July 1877; d. New York, 9 Feb. 1960). Pupil of Koessler and d'Albert. Toured widely as a pianist and conductor in Europe and the U.S. Taught piano at the Hochschule für Musik in Berlin, 1905–15. Director of the Budapest Conservatory and conductor of the Budapest Philharmonic from 1919. Taught at Florida State College in Tallahassee from 1949. Composed the operas *The Tower of Voivod,* Budapest, 1922, and *The Tenor,* Budapest, 1929; the pantomime *Der Schleier der Pierrette,* Dresden, 1910; other stage works; symphonies, concertos, and other works for orch. (incl. *Variations on a Nursery Song* for piano and orch., 1913); a Mass and other sacred music; chamber music; piano pieces (incl. *Ruralia hungarica,* also in an orch. version, 1924); songs.

Doigté [F.]. Fingering. *Doigté fourchu,* cross fingering.

Dolce [It.]. Sweetly, softly.

Dolcino, dolcian. See under Oboe family III.

Dolente, doloroso [It.]. Sorrowful.

Doles, Johann Friedrich (b. Steinbach-Hallenberg, Thuringia, 23 Apr. 1715; d. Leipzig, 8 Feb. 1797). Pupil of J. S. Bach. Cantor in Freiberg, 1744–55, and at the Thomasschule in Leipzig from 1756. Composed Passions and oratorios; Masses; cantatas; psalms; chorale settings; motets; songs; harpsichord and organ works.

Domchor [G.]. The choir of a German cathedral (*Dom*), either Protestant or Roman Catholic.

Domestic Symphony. See *Symphonia domestica.*

Dominant. (1) The fifth *scale degree of the major or minor scale. The *triad and the *seventh chord built on this degree as root are the dominant triad and dominant seventh, respectively. As part of a *cadence, both of these chords are most often resolved to the *tonic triad. When serving as the root of a chord, the fifth scale degree is identified by the numeral V or the letter D (for dominant). *Secondary dominants* are the dominants of degrees other than the tonic and are designated as follows: V of II (or simply V/II; e.g., in the key of C, the fifth above D, namely A), V of III (V/III), etc. (2) For the dominant of the modes, see Church modes.

Domp(e). See Dump.

Domra. A Russian long-necked *lute of the 16th and 17th centuries, the forerunner of the *balalaika.

Don Carlos. Opera in five acts by Verdi (libretto, in French, by F. J. Méry and C. DuLocle, based on Schiller's drama; It. trans. by De Lauzières), produced in Paris, 1867, rev. It. version in Milan, 1884. Setting: Spain, mid-16th century.

Don Giovanni [It., Don Juan]. *Dramma giocoso* in two acts by Mozart (libretto by L. da Ponte), produced in Prague, 1787. Setting: Seville, 17th century. The original title, *Il dissoluto punito*, is rarely used today.

Don Juan. Symphonic poem by R. Strauss, op. 20 (1881–89), based on a dramatic poem by Lenau.

Don Pasquale. Opera in three acts by Donizetti (libretto by the composer and G. Ruffini), produced in Paris, 1843. Setting: Rome, early 19th century.

Don Quixote. (1) Symphonic poem by R. Strauss, op. 35 (1897), based on the novel by Cervantes and composed in the form of an Introduction, Theme with Variations, and Finale. It includes an important part for solo cello and one for solo viola. (2) Ballet by Minkus (choreography by Marius Petipa), produced in Moscow, 1869.

Don Rodrigo. Opera in three acts by A. Ginastera (libretto by A. Casona), produced in Buenos Aires, 1964. Setting: Toledo, Spain, 8th century.

Donato, Baldissera (Donati) (b. *c*. 1530; d. Venice, 1603). Choirmaster of the "small choir" at San Marco, Venice, under Rore, 1562–65; singer there from 1565 under Zarlino, whom he succeeded as *maestro di cappella*, 1590. Composed madrigals, *villanesche*, motets.

Donatoni, Franco (b. Verona, 9 June 1927). Pupil of Pizzetti. Teacher at various times at conservatories in Milan, Turin, and Siena. Has employed serial and aleatory procedures. Has composed orch. works (incl. *Sinfonia* for strings, 1953; *Sezioni*, improvisations, 1960; *Doubles II*, 1970); 4 string quartets and other chamber music; piano pieces (incl. *3 Improvisations*, 1957).

Donizetti, Gaetano (Domenico Maria) (b. Bergamo, 29 Nov. 1797; d. there, 8 Apr. 1848). Pupil of Mayr. Composed numerous operas (incl. the serious operas *Anna Bolena*, Milan, 1830; *Lucrezia Borgia*, Milan, 1833; *Maria Stuarda*, Naples, 1834; *Lucia di Lamermoor; Roberto d'Evereux*, Naples, 1837; *La favorite*, Paris, 1840; *Linda di chamounix*, Vienna, 1842; the comic operas *L'*elisir d'amore, La *fille du régiment, *Don Pasquale*); Masses (incl. a Requiem for Bellini); cantatas; vespers; psalms; motets; string quartets; piano pieces.

Donovan, Richard (Frank) (b. New Haven, Conn., 29 Nov. 1891; d. Middletown, Conn., 22 Aug. 1970). Studied at Yale Univ. and was a pupil of Widor in Paris. Taught at Yale Univ., 1928–60; organist and choirmaster of Christ Church, New Haven, 1928–65; associate conductor of the New Haven Symphony Orchestra, 1936–51. Composed orch. works (incl. *Passacaglia on Vermont Folk Tunes*, 1949); sacred and secular choral works (incl. a Mass, 1955); chamber music; works for voice with instruments (incl. *5 Elizabethan Lyrics*, 1957); piano and organ pieces.

Doppel [G.]. Double. *Doppel-Be*, double flat; *Doppelchor*, double chorus; *Doppelfuge*, double fugue; *Doppelgriff*, double stop; *Doppelkreuz*, double sharp; *Doppelpedal*, double pedal; *Doppelschlag*, turn; *Doppeltriller*, double trill; *Doppelzunge*, double-tonguing. In regard to instruments, the term usually denotes *duplex instruments.

Doppelt so schnell [G.]. Twice as fast.

Dopper, Cornelis (b. Stadskanaal, near Groningen, 7 Feb. 1870; d. Amsterdam, 18 Sept. 1939). Pupil of Jadassohn and Reinecke. Toured America as an opera conductor, 1906–8; then served as assistant conductor of the Concertgebouw Orchestra in Amsterdam, 1908–31. Composed operas and a ballet; symphonic works (incl. *Zuiderzee-Symphonie; Rembrandt-Symphonie; Ciaconna gotica*); concertos; numerous choral works; chamber music; piano pieces; songs.

Doppio [It.]. Double. *Doppio bemolle*, double flat; *doppio diesis*, double sharp;

doppio movimento (*tempo*), double speed; *doppio pedale,* double pedal.

Doret, Gustave (b. Aigle, Switzerland, 20 Sept. 1866; d. Lausanne, 19 Apr. 1943). Pupil of Joachim, Dubois, and Massenet. Traveled widely in Europe as a conductor. Composed operas (incl. *Les Armaillis,* Paris, 1906); incidental music for plays; a cantata; an oratorio; orch. works; chamber music; numerous songs.

Dorian. (1) See under Church modes. (2) The Dorian sixth is the major sixth above the tonic in a minor key (e.g., in C minor, c–a ♮), so called because it appears in the Dorian church mode (d–b, often in the context of melodic patterns such as d f g a b a).

Dorian Toccata and Fugue. A Toccata and Fugue in D minor by Bach for organ, written without the customary B♭ in the key signature and therefore having the appearance of a composition in Dorian mode. Actually, however, the accidentals for D minor are supplied throughout. The use of key signatures with one flat fewer than is used today (e.g., one flat for G minor, two flats for C minor) was a common practice throughout the 17th century.

Dorn, Heinrich Ludwig Egmont (b. Königsberg, 14 Nov. 1804; d. Berlin, 10 Jan. 1892). Pupil of Zelter and B. Klein. Music director at the Cathedral of St. Peter in Riga, 1832–42; succeeded Nicolai as *Kapellmeister* at the Royal Opera in Berlin, 1849–69. Composed operas (incl. *Die Rolandsknappen,* Berlin, 1826; *Die Nibelungen,* Berlin, 1854, independent of Wagner); a ballet, *Amors Macht,* 1830; orch. works; cantatas; a *Missa pro defunctis,* 1851; piano pieces; songs.

Dot [F. *point;* G. *Punkt;* It. *punto;* Sp. *puntillo*]. In present-day musical notation a dot is used: (a) after a note, to indicate augmentation of its value by one-half [see Dotted notes]; (b) above or below a note, to indicate *staccato or *portato. See also *punctus* under Mensural notation.

Dotted notes. A dot placed after a note adds to it one-half of its value. Thus, a dotted half note equals three quarter notes [Ex. 1a]. Two dots after a note add to it one-half plus one-fourth of its value.

Thus, a double-dotted half note equals seven (4 + 2 + 1) eighth notes [Ex. 1b]. In modern practice, dotted notes are used only if their value does not extend over a bar line; otherwise tied notes are used [Ex. 1c]. Brahms revived an older practice when he wrote dotted rhythm as shown in Ex. 1d.

Prior to 1750, the dot was frequently used in a different manner, which has been the subject of much investigation and controversy. The only proper conclusion is that in the baroque period the dot indicated a prolongation of undetermined value depending on various factors, such as the character of the piece, the rhythm of the other parts, the tempo, or the performer's interpretation. Statements to this effect are found in practically all theory books written between c. 1680 and 1750. J. J. Quantz, in his *Versuch einer Anweisung die Flöte traversière zu spielen* (1752), seems to have been the first to use the double dot, thus paving the way for a clearer indication of different degrees of prolongation. The following cases of the freely used dot are noteworthy:

(a) If dotted notes are used in conjunction with triplets, the dotted rhythm may be modified (attenuated) into a triplet rhythm [Ex. 2; Bach, Partita no. 1]. According to contemporary writers, however, this modification was not obligatory but was left to the performer's discretion.

(b) According to French writers of the early 18th century, compositions written in "French style" (i.e., the style of the slow section in Lully's French *overture) call for a more pronounced rhythm than is indicated in writing, so that a dotted note should be performed almost as a *double-dotted* value, as in Ex. 3.

(c) About 1700, dotted rhythm was also applied to passages written in equal notes. See *Inégales*.

Inverted dotting is the reverse of the ordinary dotted rhythm; in other words, a dotted note that is preceded, not followed, by its complementary short value (e.g., ♪ ♩.). This rhythm is generally known as a "Scotch snap," because it is a typical feature of the *strathspey and other Scottish folk tunes.

Double. (1) The French word *double* is a 17th- and 18th-century term for a simple type of variation, consisting chiefly of the addition of embellishments. It occurs especially in certain dances of the suite (Bach, English Suite no. 1: courante with two *doubles*; English Suite no. 6: sarabande with *double*). (2) The English word *double* indicates either instruments of lower pitch or a combination of two instruments in one. The former meaning, which is derived from the double octave, is exemplified by the double bass, double-bass clarinet, double-bass trombone, and double bassoon, and the latter by double horn, double trumpet, and double flageolet. See Duplex instruments. (3) As a verb, to play (or to specify the playing of) a single part simultaneously on two or more different instruments, e.g., to double the flute part with (by) the oboe. The result is a *doubling* and may be called for at a single pitch level or at the interval of one or more octaves.

Doublé [F.]. Term used by the French clavecinists for the *turn.

Double appoggiatura. See Appoggiatura, double.

Double bass [F. *contrebasse*; G. *Kontrabass*; It. *contrabasso*; Sp. *contrabajo*]. The instrument of this name is also called *bass viol* or *contrabass*. The largest member of the *viol family, serving in the orchestra with members of the *violin family (of which family it is now sometimes regarded as a member) somewhat as a 16-foot organ stop and frequently doubling the cellos in the lower octave. The modern instrument has four strings tuned E_1 A_1 D G, notated an octave higher (E A d g). Some instruments have a fifth string, tuned C_1, and some have a mechanical device controlled by levers that extends the range of the E

string down to C_1. The upper limit for orchestral parts is the pitch a (notated a').

More than any other orchestral stringed instrument, the double bass has been subjected to modification and experimentation in shape, size, number and tuning of the strings, etc. It is the only such instrument to which the principles of violin-building have never been fully applied. Thus, to the present day it retains various features of the viol family, e.g., sloping shoulders, flat back, tuning of the strings in fourths rather than fifths. This ancestry is evident also in the names "bass viol" and "double bass," both abbreviated versions of the full name *double-bass viol* [see Viol]. Some players (particularly in Europe) hold the bow in the manner of viol-playing, i.e., with the hand underneath the stick.

The most common instrument of this type in use in late 18th-century Austria seems to have been a five-stringed type, tuned F_1 A_1 D F♯ A, and provided with frets, though writers of the period also mention four- and three-stringed instruments without frets. Three-stringed instruments, tuned A_1 D G or G_1 D A, were common throughout Europe in the 19th century. The modern tuning of the four-stringed instrument originated in the late 18th century and became standard only in the 19th century. The first consistent extensions of the range down to C_1 also took place in the 19th century.

Double-bass clarinet, trombone. See under Clarinet family II; Trombone (d).

Double bassoon. See under Oboe family I.

Double C (D, etc.). Great C (D, etc.). See under Pitch names.

Double cadence [F.]. A compound ornament, frequently introduced at cadences in music of the 17th and 18th centuries and consisting of a *trill (for which the French term is *cadence*) upon each of two successive notes. See Turn.

Double concerto. A concerto for two solo instruments and orchestra, such as Brahms' Concerto for violin and cello, op. 102.

Double corde [F.]. *Double stop.

Double counterpoint. See Invertible counterpoint.

Double-croche [F.]. Sixteenth note. See under Notes.

Double dot, double dotting. See under Dotted notes.

Double flat. See under Accidentals.

Double fugue. A *fugue with two subjects. A genuine double fugue consists of three distinct sections, each complete in itself: a fugue on the first subject (I), a fugue on the second subject (II), and a fugue on both subjects in contrapuntal combination (I + II). Bach employed this structure in the great harpsichord fugue in A minor, in the fugue of the organ toccata in F major, and in the G♯ minor fugue of the *Well-Tempered Clavier,* vol. II. Usually, the term is applied to a much simpler type, i.e., a fugue in which the countersubject has an individual character and is consistently used throughout the piece, combined with the main subject; in other words, fugues represented by the last section only of the genuine double fugue.

Double pedal. In organ playing, the use of both feet simultaneously for rendering intervals or two parts.

Double reed. See Reed.

Double sharp. See under Accidentals.

Double stop. The execution of two or more tones simultaneously on the violin and similar instruments. See Stopping.

Double tonguing. See Tonguing.

Double touch. A modern principle of organ construction that allows the keys of the organ to be depressed in two successive degrees, so that different registrations become available simultaneously on the same manual.

Double trill. A simultaneous trill on two different notes, usually a third apart.

Doubling. See Double (3).

Doucement [F.]. Gently, smoothly, softly.

Douloureux [F.]. Sorrowful.

Dowland, John (b. near Dublin, Dec. 1562; d. London, 21 Jan. 1626). Lutenist to King Christian IV of Denmark, 1598–1606, and to Charles I of England from 1612. Composed several books of *Songs or Ayres,* some polyphonic, with lute accompaniment; *Lachrymae,* a collection of dance pieces for lute, viols, or violins, 1605.

Down in the Valley. Folk drama in one act by K. Weill (libretto by A. Sundgaard), produced at Indiana University, 1948. Setting: America, the present.

Doxology. An expression of the glory of God. In the Roman liturgy, the name of two important texts, the Lesser Doxology: "Gloria Patri et Filio et Spiritui Sancto" (Glory be to the Father and to the Son and to the Holy Ghost); and the Greater Doxology: "Gloria in excelsis Deo" (Glory to God in the highest). The Greater Doxology is the *Gloria of the Mass. The Lesser Doxology is a part of all the Introits and is added as a final verse to all psalms and nearly all canticles [see also Psalm tones]. In Protestant churches, *doxology* usually refers to the metrical verse "Praise God from whom all blessings flow," which is widely sung to the *Old Hundredth tune.

Draeseke, Felix (August Bernhard) (b. Coburg, 7 Oct. 1835; d. Dresden, 26 Feb. 1913). Pupil of Rietz and friend of Liszt and Wagner. Taught at the Lausanne Conservatory, 1863–74, and at the Dresden Conservatory from 1876. Composed operas (incl. *König Sigurd,* 1857; *Gudrun,* Hanover, 1884); orch. works (incl. *Germaniamarsch,* 1861, and the symphonic poems *Julius Caesar,* 1860, and *Frithjof,* 1862); choral works (incl. *Christus,* 1912); concertos; chamber music; songs.

Drag. See under Percussion instruments II.

Draghi, Antonio (b. Rimini, *c.* 1635; d. Vienna, 16 Jan. 1700). Court musician in Vienna from 1658, becoming imperial *Kapellmeister* there in 1682. Works incl. numerous operas; festival plays; serenades; oratorios; cantatas; Masses.

Dragma [Gr.]. A note form of the late 14th century shaped like the *minima* but with a second stem added opposite the first. Its meaning varies. See Notation.

Drame lyrique [F.]; **dramma lirico** [It.]. Modern terms for opera, not necessarily of a lyrical character. The English term *lyrical drama* is used in the same way.

Dramma per musica [It.]. The earliest name for Italian operas (17th century), particularly serious ones (the later *opera seria*). Bach used the term for secular cantatas in dialogue form that were designed for a modest stage performance (*Der Streit zwischen Phöbus und Pan, Kaffeekantate*, etc.).

Drängend [G.]. Pressing on.

Drdla, Franz (František) (b. Saar, Moravia, 28 Nov. 1868; d. Bad Gastein, 3 Sept. 1944). Pupil of Bruckner. Toured Europe and the U.S. as a violinist. Composed operettas; numerous pieces for violin and piano (incl. *Souvenir; Vision; Serenade in A*); chamber music; a violin concerto.

Dreher [G.]. An Austrian dance, similar to the **Ländler*.

Drehleier [G.]. *Hurdy-gurdy.

Drehorgel [G.]. *Street organ.

Dreigroschenoper, Die [G., The Threepenny Opera]. A play with music by Kurt Weill (libretto by Bertolt Brecht), produced in Berlin, 1928. Setting: London, early 18th century. It is a modern *ballad opera, based on the plot of John Gay's *The Beggar's Opera* (1728). The English adaptation by Marc Blitzstein was first produced in 1952.

Dreitaktig [G.]. In phrases of three measures.

Dresden, Sem (b. Amsterdam, 20 Apr. 1881; d. The Hague, 30 July 1957). Pupil of B. Zweers and Pfitzner. Director of the Amsterdam Conservatory, 1924–37; succeeded J. Wagenaar as director of the Royal Conservatory at The Hague, from 1937. Composed an opera, *François Villon*, orch. by J. Mul, prod. Amsterdam, 1958; orch. works; concertos for violin, for oboe, for piano, for flute, for organ; choral works (incl. *Chorus tragicus*, 1928); chamber music; songs.

Driessler, Johannes (b. Friedrichsthal, near Saarbrucken, 26 Jan. 1921). Pupil of Maler. Teacher in Detmold from 1946. Has composed operas; symphonies and

other orch. works; oratorios (incl. *Dein Reich komme*, 1949); cantatas; *a cappella* choruses; chamber music; organ works; piano pieces.

Drone. (1) The low pipes of the *bagpipe. (2) A primitive bagpipe, capable of playing only a few low tones and used to accompany other instruments or voices. (3) In musical composition, long sustained notes, usually in the lowest part (drone bass). See Pedal point; *Bourdon*.

Druckman, Jacob (b. Philadelphia, 6 June 1928). Pupil of B. Wagenaar, Persichetti, Mennin, and Copland. Has taught at the Juilliard School, Bard College, Brooklyn College, and Yale Univ. (from 1976); an associate of the Columbia-Princeton Electronic Music Center from 1967. Has composed orch. works (incl. *Windows*, Pulitzer Prize for 1972; *Mirage*, 1976; *Chiaroscuro*, 1977); music for dance; choral works; works for voice with instruments (incl. *The Sound of Time*, 1965, and *Lamia*, 1974, for soprano and orch.); works for voices and/or instruments with tape (incl. *Animus I, II*, and *III*, 1966–69); string quartets and other chamber music (incl. *Incenters* for 13 players, 1968); *Synapse* on tape.

Drum. Generic name for instruments consisting of skin stretched over a frame or vessel and struck with the hands or a stick (or sticks). Drums therefore are practically identical with the category "membranophones" [see Instruments]. In some primitive cultures, however, there are drums that have no membrane, consisting simply of a tree trunk hollowed out through a narrow longitudinal slit (slit-drum). These are classified as idiophones. The membranophonous drums are among the oldest and most widespread of all instruments. For the modern orchestral drums, see Percussion instruments.

Drum-Roll Symphony. Popular name for Haydn's Symphony no. 103 in E♭ major (*Salomon Symphonies no. 11), composed in 1795, so called because of the drum roll in the opening measure of the Introduction.

Drum Stroke Symphony. See Surprise Symphony.

D.S. [It.]. Abbr. for *dal segno*.

Du Caurroy, François Eustache (b. Beauvais, bapt. 4 Feb. 1549; d. Paris, 7 Aug. 1609). Court musician at the royal chapel in Paris and canon of several provincial churches. One of the principal composers of *musique mesurée* [see *Vers mesuré*]. Also composed Masses, motets, and other sacred music; instrumental pieces; chansons.

Dubensky, Arcady (b. Viatka, Russia, 15 Oct. 1890; d. Tenafly, N.J., 14 Oct. 1966). Violinist at the Moscow Opera, 1910–19. Settled in the U.S., 1921, and played with the New York Philharmonic Orchestra. Composed operas; stage and film music; works for orch. (incl. *Fugue for 18 violins*); chamber music.

Dubois, (Clément-François-) Théodore (b. Rosnay, Marne, 24 Aug. 1837; d. Paris, 11 June 1924). Pupil of Benoit and Thomas. Succeeded Saint-Saëns as organist at the Madeleine in Paris, 1877–96, and was succeeded in this position by Fauré. Taught at the Paris Conservatory from 1871, succeeding Thomas as director, 1896. Composed operas; a ballet, *La farandole*, 1883; numerous orch. works (incl. *Symphonie française*, 1908); oratorios; cantatas; Masses, motets, and other sacred music; secular choral works; chamber music; organ works; piano pieces; songs.

Ducasse, Roger. See Roger-Ducasse.

Ducis, Benedictus (Benedikt Herzog, Hertogh) (b. probably near Constance, c. 1490; d. Schalckstetten, near Ulm, late in 1544). Was in Austria c. 1515 and may have studied in Vienna. Pastor at Schalckstetten, 1535 to his death. Composed motets; psalms; chorale settings; odes.

Ductia. A medieval instrumental form (13th century) that, according to Johannes de Grocheo, is a shorter *stantipes* [see *Estampie*], i.e., with three to four *puncta* instead of five or more.

Dudelsack [G.]. *Bagpipe.

Due [It.]. Two. *Due corde*, two strings, indicates in violin music that the same tone should be sounded on two strings; in piano music, see *Una corda*. See also *A due*.

Duenna, The [Rus. *Obruchenie v monastyre*, Betrothal in a Monastery]. Opera in four acts by Prokofiev (libretto by the composer and M. Mendelssohn, based on R. B. Sheridan's play), produced in Leningrad, 1946. Setting: Seville, 18th century.

Duet [F. *duo*; G. *Duett*, *Duo*; It. *duetto*; Sp. *dúo*]. A composition for two performers of equal importance, with or without accompaniment.

Dufay, Guillaume (b. c. 1400; d. Cambrai, 27 Nov. 1474). Boy chorister at the Cambrai Cathedral, traveling to Italy and the service of the Malatesta family by 1420. Member of the papal chapel in Rome, 1428–33, and in Florence and Bologna, 1435–37. Served the Duke of Savoy, 1434–35 and 1437–39. Canon of the Cambrai Cathedral and resident there 1439–50. Thereafter he was again in Savoy until his final return to Cambrai in 1458. Composed Masses, motets, hymns, and other sacred music; French and Italian secular polyphony.

Dukas, Paul (b. Paris, 1 Oct. 1865; d. there, 17 May 1935). Pupil of Dubois and Guiraud. Close associate of Debussy and d'Indy. Wrote music criticism for several French journals. Professor of composition at the Paris Conservatory from 1927. Composed an opera, *Ariane et Barbe-Bleue*, Paris, 1907; a ballet, *La Péri*, 1912; orch. works (incl. *L'*apprenti sorcier*); choral works; works for voice and piano, horn and piano, and piano solo.

Duke, Vernon. See Dukelsky, Vladimir.

Duke Bluebeard's Castle. See *Bluebeard's Castle*.

Dukelsky, Vladimir (Vernon Duke) (b. Parfianovka, Russia, 10 Oct. 1903; d. Santa Monica, Calif., 16 Jan. 1969). Pupil of Glière. Left Russia, 1920; settled in the U.S., 1929. Composed ballets (incl. *Zephyr et Flore* for Diaghilev, Paris, 1925); operas; symphonies and other orch. works; concertos for piano and for other instruments; choral works; chamber music; piano pieces; many popular songs (incl. "April in Paris").

Dulcimer [F. *tympanon*; G. *Hackbrett*; It. *salterio tedesco*]. (1) Medieval stringed instrument, a variety of *psaltery and almost identical to it in shape, having a flat soundboard, often triangular, with ten or more parallel strings that are struck by small hammers (the psaltery is plucked). Thus the dulcimer and psaltery are related to each other as are their ultimate descendants, the piano and harpsichord. See also Cimbalom; Pantaleon.

(2) A plucked folk instrument of uncertain ancestry but with features derived from the German Scheitholt and the Swedish hummel, played in the Appalachian Mountain region of the U.S. It consists of an elongated sound box of wood, either oval or with a narrow waist, about a yard long and nine inches wide, on which is mounted a narrow fretted fingerboard. In a three-string instrument, one string, tuned g, may be the melody string, while the other two strings, tuned c g, sound as a drone bass to the melody. The player lays the instrument flat, across the knees or on a table. Traditionally the strings are plucked with a goose quill and stopped with a quill or stick. The dulcimer, also called "dulcimore," is generally used to accompany singing and only rarely as a solo instrument.

Dulcina. Same as the dolcino [see Oboe family III].

Dulcitone. A variety of celesta, with tuning forks instead of steel plates. See Percussion instruments.

Dulzian [G.]. Same as the dolcino [see Oboe family III].

Dumka [Rus.; also *dumki, dumky*]. (1) A Slavic (especially Ukrainian) folk ballad, poem, or meditation describing heroic deeds. It is generally thoughtful or melancholy in character. (2) A type of instrumental music involving sudden changes from melancholy to exuberance. Well-known examples are Dvořák's piano trio op. 90 (1891; called *Dumky-Trio*), his *Dumka* (Elegy) op. 35 (1876), and his *Furiant with Dumka* op. 12 (1884).

Dumont, Henri (Henry de Thier) (b. Villers-l'Evèque, near Liège, 1610; d. Paris, 8 May 1684). Organist at the Church of St. Paul, Paris, from 1640. Chamber musician to the Duke of Anjou,

c. 1652, and to Queen Marie-Thérèse from 1660. *Maître de la chapelle royale,* with P. Robert, from 1663. Composed Masses, motets, and other sacred music, some with instruments; chansons; pieces for organ, viols, etc.

Dump, domp. A type of English 16th-century instrumental music. The oldest and most celebrated example is "My Lady Careys Dompe" from *c.* 1525, a series of continuous variations on a tonic-dominant harmony (T T D D). Nearly all the others show a similar structure. These pieces, like the dump mentioned in literary sources, are probably laments [see Lament (2)].

Dunayevsky, Isaak Osipovich (b. Lokhvitza, near Poltava, 30 Jan. 1900; d. Moscow, 25 July 1955). Violinist and composer; one of the chief exponents of "Socialist Realism." Composed operettas; film scores; ballets; orch. works; vocal works; popular songs.

Dunhill, Thomas Frederick (b. London, 1 Feb. 1877; d. Scunthorpe, Lincolnshire, 13 Mar. 1946). Pupil of Stanford. Professor at the Royal Academy of Music from 1905. Composed operas (incl. *The Enchanted Garden,* London, 1927; *Tantivy Towers,* London, 1931); a ballet; orch. works; choral works; chamber music; songs.

Duni, Egidio Romoaldo (b. Matera, Italy, 9 Feb. 1709; d. Paris, 11 June 1775). Pupil of Durante. Court musician at Parma, 1748–57. Settled in Paris, 1757; became director of the Comédie-Italienne there, 1761. Composed serious and comic operas (incl. *Nerone,* Rome, 1735; *Le peintre amoureux de son modèle,* Paris, 1757; *Les deux chasseurs et la laitière,* Paris, 1763); oratorios; Masses and other sacred music; trio sonatas and other instrumental works.

Dunstable, John (b. probably between 1380 and 1390; buried London, 24 Dec. 1453). Mathematician and composer. Served Duke John of Bedford (d. 1435; brother of King Henry V), with whom he probably traveled to France. Composed Masses, motets, hymns, Magnificats, and other sacred music. Several secular pieces are ascribed to him (incl. "O rosa bella," dubiously).

Duo [F., G., Sp.] *Duet.

Duole [G.]; **duolet** [F.]. *Duplet.

Duparc, (Marie-Eugène) Henri (Fouques) (b. Paris, 21 Jan. 1848; d. Mont-de-Marsan, Landes, 12 Feb. 1933). Pupil of Franck and friend of d'Indy. Composed songs; orch. works; a motet; chamber music; piano pieces.

Duple meter, time. See under Meter.

Duplet [F. *duolet;* G. *Duole;* Sp. *dosillo*]. A group of two notes played in the time normally occupied by three notes of the same kind.

Duplex instruments. Instruments, usually of the brass family, that are a combination of two instruments. The two most important members of the class are: (a) The *double euphonium,* which has a wide euphonium bell and a narrow Saxtromba bell, either of which may be used by manipulating a controlling valve to direct the windstream through one or the other of the bells and thus make two different tone qualities available. (b) The *double horn* in F and B♭, which combines two instruments of the same timbre but of different pitch, the change from one to the other being effected by an additional valve.

Duplum. In the organa and *clausulae* of the school of *Notre Dame, the part above the tenor. In 13th-century motets this part was called the *motetus* because here the *duplum* was provided with *mots* [F., words, i.e., text]. *Triplum* and *quadruplum* are the third and fourth parts above the tenor, respectively, frequently of the same range as the *duplum.* See Organum (2).

Dupont, Gabriel (Edouard Xavier) (b. Caen, 1 Mar. 1878; d. Vésinet, near Paris, 2 Aug. 1914). Pupil of Gédalge, Massenet, and Widor. Composed operas (incl. *La cabrera,* Milan, 1904; *Antar,* 1914); orch. works; choral works; chamber music; piano pieces (incl. *Les heures dolentes,* 1905); songs.

Duport, Jean-Louis (b. Paris, 4 Oct. 1749; d. there, 7 Sept. 1819). Cellist in Paris until 1789. Court musician in Berlin during and after the French Revolution. Returned to Paris, 1812, and taught at the Conservatory there. Composed

works for cello solo and for cello with other instruments; published what became a standard pedagogic work for cello.

Dupré, Marcel (b. Rouen, 3 May 1886; d. Meudon, near Paris, 30 May 1971). Pupil of Guilmant and Widor. Toured widely (incl. the U.S. and Australia) as an organist. Taught organ at the Paris Conservatory from 1926, succeeding Delvincourt as director, 1954–56. Succeeded Widor as organist at Saint-Sulpice, 1934. Director of the American Conservatory in Fontainebleau from 1947. Composed works for organ (incl. *Symphonie-Passion,* 1921–24; and *Le chemin de la croix,* 1931–32); works for organ with other instruments; sacred choral works.

Dupuis, Albert (b. Verviers, 1 Mar. 1877; d. Brussels, 19 Sept. 1967). Pupil of d'Indy and Guilmant. Director of the Verviers Conservatory, 1907–47. Composed operas (incl. *La passion,* Monte Carlo, 1916); ballets; 2 symphonies and other orch. works; concertos; choral works; oratorios; chamber music; songs.

Dur, moll [G.]. Major and minor, e.g., *C-dur,* C major; *A-moll,* A minor. The names *Dur* and *Moll* stem from two different forms of the letter b, the *b durum* (so called on account of its angular shape) and the *b molle* (round shape), which originally represented B♮ and B♭, respectively [see Hexachord].

Duramente [It.]. Harshly.

Durante, Francesco (b. Frattamaggiore, near Naples, 31 Mar. 1684; d. Naples, 13 Aug. 1755). Taught at several Italian conservatories; his pupils incl. Duni, Traetta, Piccinni, Pergolesi, Paisiello, Guglielmi, and Sacchini. Composed Masses, psalms, motets, antiphons, hymns, and other sacred music; *solfeggi;* instrumental pieces.

Duration. The time that a sound (or silence) lasts. This can, of course, be measured in seconds or similar units, though for this purpose common musical notation employs *notes of various shapes whose values are fixed with respect to one another. The absolute duration of individual notes in the system is fixed either approximately, through the use of terms such as *allegro* (fast), or precisely, by the specification of the number of occurrences per minute of some particular value. See also Tempo; Tempo marks; Metronome.

Durchbrochene Arbeit [G.]. A technique of writing in which fragments of a melody are given to different instruments in turn.

Durchführung [G.]. In sonata form, the *development; in a fugue, the *exposition.

Durchkomponiert [G.]. *Through-composed.

Durey, Louis (Edmond) (b. Paris, 27 May 1888). Music critic for *L'humanité* and other journals from 1950. A member of "Les *six." Has composed works for voice with instruments (incl. *L'offrande lyrique,* after Tagore, 1914, and *Deux poèmes,* after Ho Chi Minh, both with piano, 1951; settings of Gide, Apollinaire, Rilke, and L. Hughes); choral works; orch. works; chamber music; piano pieces; stage works.

Durezza [It.]. In modern music, *con durezza* means to play with an expression of harshness and determination. In the 17th century, *durezza* meant dissonance.

Durón, Sebastián (b. Brihuega, Spain, bapt. 19 Apr. 1660; d. Cambo, France, 3 Aug. 1716). Organist at the royal chapel in Madrid from 1691. Banished in 1706, after the Spanish War of Succession, he settled in France. Composed operas; *zarzuelas;* a Requiem and other sacred music.

Duruflé, Maurice (b. Louviers, France, 11 Jan. 1902). Pupil of Dukas. Church organist in Paris from 1930; teacher at the Paris Conservatory from 1944. Composed orch. works (incl. *Trois danses,* 1936); choral works (incl. motets and a Requiem); chamber music; organ pieces.

Dušek, František Xaver (b. Chotěborky, Bohemia, 8 Dec. 1731; d. Prague, 12 Feb. 1799). Pianist and composer. Pupil of Wagenseil and friend of Mozart. His numerous works incl. symphonies, piano concertos, quartets and other chamber music, piano sonatas, and songs.

Dušek, Jan Ladislav (Dussek) (b.

Čáslav, Bohemia, 12 Feb. 1760; d. Saint-Germain-en-Laye, 20 Mar. 1812). Pupil of K. P. E. Bach. Traveled widely as a pianist, teacher, and composer, settling in London for about 10 years until 1800. *Maître de chapelle* to Prince Talleyrand in Paris, 1808. Composed numerous piano works, incl. concertos and sonatas; numerous violin sonatas; chamber music.

Dutilleux, Henri (b. Angers, 22 Jan. 1916). Pupil of Busser. Worked for French Radio, 1944–63; president of L'école normale de musique, Paris, from 1969. Has composed ballets; incidental music for plays; film music; symphonies and other orch. works; concertos; works for voice with orch.; chamber music; piano pieces (incl. a sonata, 1948); songs.

Duval, François (b. *c.* 1673; d. Versailles, 27 Jan. 1728). Violinist and composer. Served the Duke of Orléans, *c.* 1700; one of the celebrated *Vingt-quatre violons du roi* of Louis XIV from 1714. Composed several books of violin sonatas with thoroughbass (said to be the first French composer to do so); trio sonatas.

Dux, comes [L.]. In imitative compositions (fugue, canon), the statement and answer of the theme, also called *antecedent and consequent or subject and *answer.

Dvořák, Antonín (b. Mühlhausen, Bohemia, 8 Sept. 1841; d. Prague, 1 May 1904). Violist in Prague, 1862–73; organist at St. Adalbert's Church in Prague from 1873. Taught at the Prague Conservatory from 1890. Artistic director of the National Conservatory in New York, 1892–95. Composed operas (incl. *Rusalka,* Prague, 1901; *Armida,* Prague, 1904; *The Devil and Kate,* Prague, 1899); 9 symphonies (incl. *New World Symphony*); symphonic poems; overtures (incl. *Carnival,* 1891) and other orch. works (incl. Slavonic rhapsodies and dances); concertos for cello, for piano, for violin; choral works with orch. (incl. a *Stabat Mater; Hymnus*) and unaccompanied; 13 string quartets (incl. no. 6 "The American"), 4 piano trios (incl. "Dumky" op. 90), and other chamber music; piano pieces; songs.

Dvorsky, Michel. See Hofmann, Josef.

Dykes, John Bacchus (b. Kingston-upon-Hull, England, 10 Mar. 1823; d. Tice-hurst, Sussex, 22 Jan. 1876). Minor canon and precentor at Durham Cathedral from 1849; vicar of St. Oswald, Durham, from 1862. Composed services; anthems; hymns (incl. "Nearer, My God, to Thee"; "Jesus, Lover of My Soul"); part songs.

Dynamic marks. The words, abbreviations, and signs that indicate degrees of loudness. The most common are: *pianissimo* (*pp*) and **piano* (*p*); *mezzo piano* (*mp*) and **mezzo forte* (*mf*); **forte* (*f*) and *fortissimo* (*ff*); **crescendo* (*cresc.*) and *decrescendo* or *diminuendo* (*decr.*, *dim.*), **sforzato* (*sf*); *forte-piano* (*fp*). Increased loudness on individual pitches or chords for the sake of producing dynamic **accents* may be indicated with

the signs $>$ and $\wedge$, the second calling for greater loudness and sharper attack than the first. See also Expression marks.

Dynamics. (1) That aspect of music relating to degrees of loudness. (2) **Dynamic marks.

Dyson, George (b. Halifax, Yorkshire, 28 May 1883; d. Winchester, 29 Sept. 1964). Taught at several British schools and colleges; director of the Royal College of Music, 1938–52. Composed symphonic works; concertos; an oratorio; choral works (incl. *The Canterbury Pilgrims,* a cantata, 1931); chamber music; church music; piano pieces; pedagogic works.

Dzerzhinsky, Ivan Ivanovich (b. Tambov, Russia, 9 Apr. 1909; d. Leningrad, 1978). Pupil of Gnessin. Has composed operas (incl. *Quiet Flows the Don,* Leningrad, 1935); instrumental works.

E

E. See Pitch names; Letter notation; Hexachord.

Ear training. Training intended to improve musical perception, including the ability to recognize and reproduce melodies, intervals, harmonies, rhythms, and meters. See also Solfège.

East, Michael (Easte, Est, Este) (b. London, *c.* 1580; d. Lichfield, Staffordshire, 1647 or 1648). Master of the choristers, later organist, at Lichfield Cathedral. Composed madrigals; anthems; fancies and other instrumental pieces.

Eaton, John (b. Bryn Mawr, Penn., 30 Mar. 1935). Pupil of Babbitt, Cone, and Sessions. Active as a jazz pianist from 1958. Teacher at Indiana Univ. from 1970. Has composed operas (incl. *Heracles,* Bloomington, Ind., 1971; *Myshkin,* after Dostoievsky, for television, 1970; *Danton and Robespierre,* Bloomington, Ind., 1978); chamber music; works for voice and instruments; *Concert Piece* for tape and jazz ensemble, 1962; *Concert Piece* for Syn-Ket and symphony orch.,

1967; *Mass* for soprano, clarinet, and synthesizers, 1970; *Microtonal Fantasy* for piano, 1965; other works employing the Syn-Ket, a small synthesizer that can be used in live performances.

Eberl, Anton Franz Josef (b. Vienna, 13 June 1765; d. there, 11 Mar. 1807). Associate of Mozart, under whose name some of his works were first published. Toured Europe and Russia as a pianist and teacher. Composed operas; symphonies; piano concertos; chamber music; piano pieces; songs.

Eccard, Johannes (b. Mühlhausen, 1553; d. Berlin, 1611). Pupil of Lassus and probably of Burck. In the service of Jacob Fugger in 1578. Second *Kapellmeister* in Königsberg from 1580 and *Kapellmeister* there from 1604; *Kapellmeister* to the Elector in Berlin from 1608. Composed several collections of sacred music, incl. motets and chorale settings; secular polyphonic songs.

Eccles, John (b. London, *c.* 1668; d. Kingston-on-Thames, 12 Jan. 1735). Violinist and composer. Pupil of his father, Solomon Eccles. Master of the King's Music from 1700. Composed music for *Don Quixote,* 1694 (with Purcell), and other stage works; songs; instrumental pieces; pedagogical works for harpsichord and violin.

Échappée [F.]. See under Counterpoint.

Échappement [F.]. Escapement (of the *piano).

Échelette [F.]. *Xylophone.

Échelle [F.]. *Scale.

Échiquier [F.; also *eschiquier, eschequier, eschaquier, escacherium, exaquir*]. An early stringed keyboard instrument mentioned in various literary sources of the 14th and 15th centuries. It is described as similar to the organ but sounding with strings. The same instrument is probably meant by the English *chekker* and German *Schachtbrett.* Both the etymology of the name and the nature of the instrument are obscure.

Echos [Gr.; pl. *echoi*]. In ancient Syrian and Byzantine chant, a system of tonal classification that corresponds to the system of modes [see Church modes] of Roman chant. There were eight *echoi,* collectively referred to as *oktoechos* (eight *echoi*). They were not simply abstract scale formations but formulas that included the characteristic features (tonic, cadential endings, typical progressions) of melodies. Thus they are *melody types.* The earliest mention of the *oktoechos* is found in a Syrian source of about 515 [see Syrian chant], 300 years before the earliest account of the eight church modes, which were probably derived from the Syrian or Byzantine *echoi,* possibly by amalgamation with the ancient Greek system of octave species (*tonoi*).

Éclatant [F.]. Brilliant, sparkling.

Eclogue. An idyllic poem in which shepherds converse (after the model of Virgil's ten *Bucolic Eclogues*). In the 16th century such poems were frequently written in the form of dramatic plays and performed on the stage, particularly in Spain. These presentations, which probably involved music, are believed to be among the precursors of opera. Modern composers have used the term *eclogue* (eglogue) as a title for compositions of an idyllic, pastoral character.

Eco [It.]. Echo.

École d'Arcueil, L'. A group of 20th-century French musicians (Henri Sauguet, Roger Desormière, Maxime Jacob, Henri Cliquet-Pleyel) named after Arcueil, the working-class suburb of Paris that, after 1898, was the home of Erik Satie, whom they considered their leader. The group was founded in 1923. See also Les *six.*

Écossaise [F.]. A dance that, despite its name, has nothing in common with genuine Scottish dance music [*reel, *strathspey] but belongs to the category of English *country dances. It appeared about 1780 in England and France and was very popular in the early 19th century. Beethoven as well as Schubert wrote collections of *écossaises,* all in quick 2/4 time.

Ecphonetic notation. Term for certain primitive systems of musical notation, consisting only of a limited number of conventional signs designed for the solemn reading of a liturgical text. Originally they were simply signs added to the text in order to clarify its sentence structure, comparable to present-day punctuation marks. Signs also were added to individual syllables or words of importance that were to be emphasized. Ecphonetic signs occur in Syrian, Jewish, Byzantine, Armenian, and Coptic manuscripts from *c.* 600 to 1000 and later. In Jewish chant they developed into fuller musical notation, the *ta'amim,* used to the present day. See also Neumes; Notation.

Effinger, Cecil (b. Colorado Springs, Colo., 22 July, 1914). Oboist and composer. Pupil of B. Wagenaar and N. Boulanger. Teacher at the Univ. of Colorado from 1948. Has composed operas; oratorios, cantatas, and other choral works; symphonies and other works for orch.; band works; string quartets and other chamber music; organ pieces.

Egge, Klaus (b. Gransherad, Norway, 19 July 1906). Music critic and composer. Pupil of Valen. President of the Norwegian Composers' Society from 1945. Has composed a ballet; 5 symphonies; concertos for piano, for violin, for cello; choral works; works for voice with orch.; chamber music; piano pieces; songs.

Egk, Werner (b. Auchsesheim, Bavaria, 17 May 1901). Pupil of Orff. Conductor for the Berlin State Opera, 1937–41. Director of the Berlin Musikhochschule, 1950–53. Has composed operas (incl. *Peer Gynt*, Berlin, 1938; *Die Zaubergeige*, Frankfurt, 1935; *Columbus*, Munich, 1933; *Irische Legende*, Salzburg, 1955); ballets; orch. works; cantatas; an oratorio, *Furchtlosigkeit und Wohlwollen*, 1931; various works for voice with instruments.

Eglogue. *Eclogue.

Egmont. Incidental music, op. 84, composed by Beethoven in 1810 for Goethe's play. The overture is often played alone.

Eguale. See Equale.

Eichheim, Henry (b. Chicago, 3 Jan. 1870; d. Montecito, Calif., 22 Aug. 1942). Violinist and composer. Member of the Boston Symphony Orchestra, 1890–1912. Works, many using oriental instruments and subjects, incl. a ballet; orch. works (incl. *Oriental Impressions*, 1922; *Chinese Legend*, 1925; *Burma*, 1926; *Java*, 1929); chamber music.

Eichner, Ernst Dieterich Adolph (bapt. Arolsen, Germany, 15 Feb. 1740; d. Potsdam, early in 1777). Bassoonist and composer. Prussian court musician in Potsdam from 1773. Composed symphonies; piano concertos and sonatas; chamber music.

Eight-foot. See under Foot (2).

Eighteen-Twelve Overture. A festival overture by Tchaikovsky, op. 49, first performed in 1882 in commemoration of the 70th anniversary of Napoleon's retreat from Moscow (1812).

Eile, mit; eilend [G.]. Hurrying.

Eimert, Herbert (b. Bad Kreuznach, Germany, 8 Apr. 1897; d. Cologne, 15 Dec. 1972). Studied musicology in Cologne, where he also worked as a music critic and for West German Radio and established an electronic music studio. Was co-editor of *Die Reihe*, 1955–62.

Works incl. 2 string quartets and several compositions on tape.

Einem, Gottfried von (b. Bern, 24 Jan. 1918). Pupil of Blacher and David. Teacher at the Akademie für Musik und darstellende Kunst in Vienna from 1963. Has composed operas (incl. *Dantons Tod*, after Büchner, Salzburg, 1947; *Der Prozess*, after Kafka, Salzburg, 1953); ballets (incl. *Prinzessin Turandot*, 1944); orch. works (incl. *Meditations*, 1954); choral works (incl. the cantata *An die Nachgeborenen*, 1975); chamber music; songs.

Einleitung [G.]. Introduction.

Einsatz [G.]. (1) *Attack. (2) Entrance of an orchestral part.

Einstimmig [G.]. Monophonic.

Eintritt [G.]. Entrance, particularly of a fugal subject [see *Einsatz*].

Eis, eisis [G.]. E-sharp, E-double-sharp; see Pitch names.

Eisler, Hanns (b. Leipzig, 6 July 1898; d. Berlin, 6 Sept. 1962). Pupil of Schoenberg and Webern. Associate of Brecht. Lived in the U.S., 1938–48, and composed for films in Hollywood. Left the U.S. owing to the efforts of the House Un-American Activities Committee. Taught at the Akademie der Künste, East Berlin, from 1950. Composed operas and other stage works; much music for films; orch. works; numerous vocal works of all kinds, incl. workers' songs and choruses; piano pieces. Published *Composing for the Films*, 1947.

Eisteddfod. See under Bard.

Ekphonetic. See Ecphonetic notation.

El-Dabh, Halim (b. Cairo, Egypt, 4 Mar. 1921). Settled in the U.S. in 1950 and was a pupil of Fine and Copland. Has worked at the Columbia-Princeton Electronic Music Center. Member of the faculty of Kent State Univ. Has made use of Egyptian musical materials. Works incl. the ballets *Clytemnestra*, 1958, and *Lucifer*, 1974, both for Martha Graham; 3 symphonies and other orch. works; *Leiyla and the Poet*, on tape, 1962.

Élargissant [F.]. Broadening; slowing.

Electronic instruments. Musical instruments in which the tone is produced, modified, or amplified by electronic means. The first such instrument, the Telharmonium of Thaddeus Cahill, was made about 1904, and truly practical types began to appear only in the 1920s. Electronic instruments may be divided into two groups: those in which sound is generated entirely by electronic means and those in which sound is generated by mechanical systems (such as vibrating strings or reeds) and modified electronically. The latter may entail primarily amplification of the sound of otherwise conventional instruments, such as the guitar, piano, or saxophone, or it may entail more elaborate electronic means for both amplification and modification of sounds, as in the case of the strings of an electric violin or guitar; these instruments lack a conventional soundboard or resonating body yet may be capable of wide variations in tone quality. Among the electronic instruments generating sound entirely by electronic means belong various instruments that attempt to imitate in some measure the sounds of conventional instruments, such as the organ or the piano (though some electronic organs and pianos make use of mechanical vibrations), as well as instruments that have been independently conceived. Among historically important examples of the latter are the *Theremin* (invented *c.* 1920), the *Ondes Martenot* (or Ondes Musicales, *c.* 1928; employed by Messiaen, Milhaud, Boulez, and others), and the *Trautonium;* these produce only a single pitch at a time, though the pitch is continuously variable. Of more recent invention and now in widespread use are various types of *synthesizer that permit the creation of immense varieties of sound. Sometimes controlled by a keyboard, the synthesizer may be used to create compositions on tape or, in some cases, for live performances. For all of the instruments described here, the sound is of course transmitted to the listener by means of loudspeakers. See also Electronic music.

Electronic music. Music made by electronic means. This may include music produced on magnetic tape by wholly electronic means such as the *synthe-sizer or the *computer and subsequently reproduced through loudspeakers; music created on synthesizers in live performances; music created by recording and electronically modifying nonelectronic sounds of all kinds (*musique concrète); and music that combines one or more of the foregoing types with live singers or performers on conventional instruments.

Electronic music in Europe grew out of research by the post-Webern generation in the years 1950–54 and was, at least in the beginning, closely tied to *serial music. Its chief pioneers were the composers K. H. Stockhausen, H. Eimert, G. Ligeti, and G. M. Koenig at the West German Radio studio in Cologne, L. Berio and B. Maderna in the Italian Radio studio at Milan, and H. Pousseur at both centers. The *musique concrète* studio of the French Radio in Paris, founded in 1948, although not involved with the concerns of the first electronic composers, nevertheless greatly assisted in the creation of electronic-music studios.

In the U.S., after independent research that in the early 1950s was called "tape music," involving such pioneers as V. Ussachevsky, L. and B. Baron, J. Cage, and others, several studios were formed, notably the Columbia-Princeton Electronic Music Center in New York, directed by Ussachevsky, M. Babbitt, and O. Luening. This center, which includes three studios of complementary equipment, has been open to all directions of research and composition, including serial music.

Two centers making significant use of computers are the Center for Computer Research in Music and Acoustics, headed by J. Chowning, at Stanford University and the Institut de recherche et de coordination acoustique/musique established in Paris in 1977 under the directorship of P. Boulez and with the collaboration of M. Mathews (formerly of Bell Telephone Laboratories, where important work has also been done).

In principle, the creation of works by electronic means permits composers complete freedom with respect to the specification of all parameters of music (pitch, timbre, loudness, duration) independently and with respect to the realization of compositions without the mediation of performers (other than themselves). The limitations of available technology and of the scientific understanding of the nature of sound, however, have prevented the realization in practice of all of the imagined possibilities, though many of these limitations are being overcome, particularly with the aid of digital computers and improved synthesizers. In any case, the combination of human performers and electronically produced sound has continued to interest many composers.

A few works making at least some use of electronic means are: John Cage, *Imaginary Landscape No. 1,* for variable-speed phonograph turntables, piano, cymbal (1939); Vladimir Ussachevsky, *Sonic Contours,* for tape and instruments (1952); Karlheinz Stockhausen, *Gesang der Jünglinge* (1956), *Kontakte* (1960); Edgard Varèse, *Poème electronique* (1958); Pierre Boulez, *Poésie pour pouvoir,* for tape and three orchestras (1958); Milton Babbitt, *Composition for Synthesizer* (1961), *Vision and Prayer,* for soprano and synthesizer-produced tape (1962); J. K. Randall, *Lyric Variations,* for violin and computer-produced tape (1968); Morton Subotnick, *Touch* (1969); Charles Wuorinen, *Time's Encomium* (1969); Charles Dodge, *Changes,* computer-produced tape (1970).

Electropneumatic action. In organs, a system of key action, developed in the late 19th century and widely prevalent today, in which the pipe valves in the wind chest are opened by pneumatic motors actuated by electrical impulses from the keys. See Organ.

Elegie für junge Liebende [G., Elegy for Young Lovers]. Opera in three acts by H. W. Henze (libretto by W. H. Auden and C. Kallman), produced in German in Schwetzingen, 1961, and in English (the original language of the libretto) in Glyndebourne, later that year. Setting: Austrian Alps, early 20th century.

Elegy. A plaintive poem; hence, a musical composition of a mournful character.

Elektra. Opera in one act by R. Strauss (libretto by H. von Hofmannsthal, based on Sophocles' tragedy), produced in Dresden, 1909. Setting: courtyard in the royal palace of Mycenae, after the Trojan War.

Elevation [L. *elevatio;* It. *elevazione*]. (1) The Elevation of the Host in the Roman Catholic Mass, sometimes accompanied by music, e.g., Frescobaldi's "Toccata per l'elevazione" and similar pieces. (2) See Appoggiatura, double.

Eleventh. See under Interval. Eleventh chord, see under Ninth chord.

Elgar, Edward (William) (b. Broadheath, near Worcester, England, 2 June 1857; d. Worcester, 23 Feb. 1934). Pupil of his father, whom he succeeded as organist of St. George's Roman Catholic Church in Worcester, 1885. Succeeded Parratt as Master of the King's Music, 1924. Composed oratorios (incl. *The Dream of Gerontius,* 1900; *The Kingdom,* 1906), cantatas, and other choral works; orch. works (incl. 2 symphonies, 1908, 1911; *Falstaff,* 1913; *Enigma Variations; *Pomp and Circumstance; Cockaigne Overture,* 1901); concertos for cello, for violin; chamber music; stage works; songs.

Elijah [G. *Elias*]. Oratorio by Mendelssohn to words from the Old Testament, produced in the English version at the Birmingham Festival, 1846, and in the German version at Hamburg, 1847.

Elisir d'amore, L' [It., The Elixir of Love]. Opera in two acts by Donizetti (libretto by F. Romani), produced in Milan, 1832. Setting: Italian village, early 19th century.

Eloy, Jean-Claude (b. Mont-Saint-Aignan, near Rouen, 15 June 1938). Pupil of Milhaud and Boulez. Has worked with serial and aleatory techniques. Has composed film music; orch. works (incl. *Étude III,* 1962); works for chamber ensembles (incl. *Équivalences,* 1963); works for voice with instruments; piano pieces.

Elsner, Joseph Anton Franz (not Xaver) (b. Grottkau, Poland, 1 June 1769; d. Elsnerowo, near Warsaw, 18 Apr. 1854). Theater *Kapellmeister* at Lvov from 1792. In Warsaw, founded a school that became the Warsaw Conservatory, which he directed, 1821–30. Chopin was among his pupils. Composed operas and other stage works; ballets; orch. works, incl. 8 symphonies; concertos; Masses and other sacred music; sacred and secular choral works; chamber music; piano pieces; songs.

Elwell, Herbert (b. Minneapolis, 10 May 1898). Music critic and composer. Pupil of Bloch and N. Boulanger. Taught at the Cleveland Institute from 1928. Has composed a ballet, *The Happy Hypocrite,* 1927; works for orch. (incl. *The Forever Young,* with voice, 1954); choral works; works for voice with instruments; 2 string quartets and other chamber music; songs.

Embellishment. (1) *Ornamentation. (2) Auxiliary tone; see Counterpoint.

Embolada [Port.]. A type of Brazilian folk singing that involves alliteration and onomatopoeias sung very fast and requiring enormous skill in diction. Each syllable of the text is set to one note in patterns of rapid sixteenth notes. Villa-Lobos frequently used the term as a title for instrumental pieces written in a fast toccatalike manner.

Embouchure [F.]. (1) The proper position of the lips in the playing of wind instruments (also called "lip," "lipping"). It is sometimes misspelled "embrochure." (2) The mouthpiece of a wind instrument, especially of the brass instruments and the flute.

Emmanuel, Maurice (Marie-François) (b. Bar-sur-Aube, 2 May 1862; d. Paris, 14 Dec. 1938). Pupil of Dubois, Delibes, Gevaert, and Bourgault-Ducoudray; succeeded the latter as professor at the Paris Conservatory, 1907–37. Associate of Guiraud and Debussy. Composed operas and other stage works; 2 symphonies and other orch. works; church music; vocal works; chamber music; piano pieces. Published numerous works of musical scholarship.

Emperor Concerto. Popular name for Beethoven's Piano Concerto no. 5 in E♭, op. 73 (1809).

Emperor Quartet [G. *Kaiserquartett*]. Haydn's String Quartet in C, op. 76, no. 3, so called because the slow movement consists of variations on the "Emperor's Hymn," formerly the national anthem of Austria, which was composed by Haydn (as a four-part chorus) in 1797.

Empfindsamer Stil [G., sensitive style]. The North-German style of the second half of the 18th century, represented by W. F. Bach, K. P. E. Bach, Quantz, G. Benda, Reichardt, and others who, in the period *c.* 1750–80, tried to arrive at an expression of "true and natural" feelings, to some extent anticipating 19th-century romanticism. A basic tenet of this school was to replace the baroque idea of maintaining an "affection" throughout a composition (or a sonata movement) by a constant change of affection or expression, together with changes of dynamics, etc.

Empfindung, mit [G.]. With feeling.

Empressé [F.]. Hurrying.

Ému [F.]. With emotion, with feeling.

En dehors [F.]. See *Dehors.*

Enchaînez [F.]. Same as *segue (1).

Encina, Juan del (real name Juan de Fermoselle) (b. Salamanca, 12 July, 1468; d. León, late 1529). Poet and composer. Court musician to the Duke of Alba from *c.* 1492; in Rome and various Spanish cities from 1500; prior at the Cathedral of León from 1519. Composed *Eglógas* [see Eclogue]; *autos;* numerous *villancicos.*

Enclume [F.]. *Anvil.

Encore [F., again]. In a public performance, the repetition of a piece, or an extra piece played in response to applause by the audience. In French and Italian, also *bis* (twice).

Enescu, George (Enesco, Georges) (b. Liveni-Virnav, now named George Enescu, Rumania, 19 Aug. 1881; d. Paris, 4 May 1955). Pupil of Fauré, Massenet, Dubois, Gédalge, and Thomas. Toured Europe and the U.S. as violinist, conductor, and composer. Yehudi Menuhin was among his pupils. Composed an opera, *Oedip,* Paris, 1932; symphonic works (incl. 3 symphonies, 2 Rumanian rhapsodies, *Poème rumain,* 1898); concertos; choral works; 2 string quartets and other chamber music; 3 violin sonatas; piano pieces.

Enfance du Christ, L' [F., The Childhood of Christ]. Oratorio by Berlioz, op. 25 (1854), for solo voices, chorus, and orchestra.

Enfant et les sortilèges, L' [F., The Child and the Sorceries; sometimes trans. The Bewitched Child]. Opera in one act by Ravel (libretto by Colette), produced in Monte Carlo, 1925. Setting: contemporary French country house.

Enfant prodigue, L' [F., The Prodigal Son]. (1) Cantata (lyric scene) by Debussy (libretto by E. Guinand), composed in 1884 for the Prix de Rome; produced as an opera in London, 1910. (2) Ballet by Prokofiev (choreography by Balanchine), produced in Paris, 1929.

Engel, A. Lehman (b. Jackson, Miss., 14 Sept. 1910). Conductor, writer, and composer. Pupil of R. Goldmark and Sessions. Has composed operas; ballets for Martha Graham and others; incidental music for numerous plays; music for films, television, radio; 2 symphonies and other works for orch.; a violin concerto; choral works; works for voice with instruments; chamber music; piano pieces.

Engelmann, Hans Ulrich (b. Darmstadt, 8 Sept. 1921). Pupil of Fortner, Leibowitz, and Krenek. Teacher at the Musikhochschule in Berlin from 1969. Has worked with serial, aleatory, and electronic techniques. Has composed operas (incl. *Der Fall van Damm,* radio opera, Cologne, 1968); a ballet; *Ophelia,* a theater piece, 1969; a cantata; an oratorio; music for films and the theater; choral works; orch. works; chamber music; *Modelle I* for electronic ensemble; piano pieces; songs. Has published numerous articles.

Engführung [G.]. *Stretto of fugues.

Englert, Giuseppe Giorgio (b. Florence, 22 July 1927). Pupil of Burkhard. Assistant organist at Saint-Eustache, Paris, 1957–62. Teacher at the Centre experimental universitaire de Vincennes, Paris, from 1970. Has employed theatrical and electronic techniques. Works incl. *Miranda,* "musique visuelle"; orch. works; chamber music; vocal works with instruments; works for tape and instruments (incl. *Vagans animula* for organ and tape, 1969).

English discant. See under Discant.

English flute. An 18th-century name for the end-blown flutes (*recorder or flageolet), as distinct from the side-blown type (transverse flute), which was known as the German flute. See Whistle flute.

English horn. See Oboe family I (b).

English Suites. Six *suites for the harpsichord by Bach, composed in Köthen (1720?). Each opens with an extended prelude. The name "English" was not used by Bach himself.

Enharmonic. (1) In modern theory, tones that are actually one and the same degree of the equally tempered chromatic scale but are named and written differently, e.g., $g\sharp$ and $a\flat$, which are thus said to be "enharmonically equivalent." In systems of tuning other than equal *temperament, $g\sharp$ and $a\flat$ and similar pairs may not represent exactly the same pitch. Keyboard instruments that make possible such distinctions (by means of separate keys and pipes or strings for each of the pitches in question) are called "enharmonic instruments." (2) One of the three genera (the other two being *chromatic and *diatonic) of ancient Greek music, namely the one employing a *tetrachord bounded by a perfect fourth and in which the lower two intervals are quarter-tones.

Enigma Variations. Theme with variations for orchestra by Elgar, op. 36 (1899). Each variation depicts a person who is enigmatically indicated by initials or by a nickname.

Enigmatic canon. See under Canon (2). For *enigmatic scale,* see *Scala enigmatica.*

Enna, August (Emil) (b. Nakskov, Denmark, 13 May 1860; d. Copenhagen, 3 Aug. 1939). Composed operas (incl. *Hexen* [The Witch], Copenhagen, 1892; *Cleopatra,* Copenhagen, 1894; *Pigen med Svovlstikkerne* [The Little Match-Girl], Copenhagen, 1897); ballets; 2 symphonies and other orch. works; a violin concerto; choral works.

Enríquez, Manuel (b Ocotlán, Mexico, 17 June 1926). Pupil of Mennin and Wolpe. Assistant choirmaster of the National Symphony Orchestra of Mexico from 1958; teacher at the Mexican National Conservatory from 1968. Has composed film music; symphonies and other orch. works; 2 violin concertos; string quartets and other chamber music; electronic music; *Móvil I* for piano, *II* for violin.

Ensalada [Sp., salad]. A poem that mixes lines from other poems or diverse meters, often in several languages and usually with humorous intent. Also a musical setting of such a poem, particularly a composition that quotes other compositions or melodies. The singing of such works was apparently common in 16th-century Spain, and the principal surviving examples are those by Mateo Flecha the elder and his nephew of the same name, published in 1581.

Ensemble. (1) A group of musicians performing together. One speaks of a "good" or "bad" ensemble with reference to the balance and unification attained in the performance of a string quartet, etc. (2) In opera, a piece for more than two singers or for the soloists together with the chorus. Such pieces often occur at the end of an act (the finale).

Entführung aus dem Serail, Die [G., The Abduction from the Seraglio]. *Singspiel* (comic opera with dialogue) in three acts by Mozart (libretto by G. Stephanie, based on C. F. Bretzner's play), produced in Vienna, 1782. Setting: Turkey, 16th century.

Entr'acte. A piece (usually instrumental) performed between the acts of a play or opera, e.g., Beethoven's compositions for Goethe's play *Egmont,* or Bizet's entr'actes for his opera *Carmen.* Purcell's instrumental entr'actes are known as act tunes or curtain tunes. The term *intermezzo* is sometimes used instead.

Entrada [Sp.]; **entrata** [It.]. See Intrada; Entrée.

Entrée. In Lully's operas and similar works, a marchlike piece that was played for the entrance of a dancing group or important personage. The term is also used for nonoperatic compositions of a similar character, e.g., in Bach's Suite in A for violin and harpsichord [see Intrada]. In French ballet of the 17th and 18th

centuries, an entrée is a subdivision of an act, roughly corresponding to a "scene" in opera [see Quadrille (2)]. The term is also used as equivalent to "act," e.g., in Rameau's *Les indes galantes;* in such works, each entrée has its own plot, unconnected with that of any other entrée.

Entremés [Sp.]. The Spanish variety of the operatic *intermezzo.

Entry. The "entrance" of the theme in the different parts of a *fugue, at the beginning as well as in the later expositions.

Entschieden, entschlossen [G.]. Determined, resolute.

Envelope. The characteristics of the attack and decay of a sound. See under Acoustics.

Envoi, envoy [F.]. In strophic trouvère songs, a short stanza added at the end as a "send-off." The Provençal (troubadour) term is *tornada,* while the Italian is *commiato.* It is also a feature of some *ballades of the 14th and 15th centuries, where it is addressed to one or more of the nobility.

Éoliphone [F.]. *Wind machine (e.g., in Ravel's *Daphnis et Chloé*).

Epidiapente, epidiatessaron. See Diapente; Diatessaron.

Epilogue. Synonym for *coda (in sonatas, etc.).

Épinette [F.]. *Spinet, harpsichord.

Episema [Gr.]. In some 9th- and 10th-century manuscripts, a subsidiary sign in the form of a horizontal dash attached to a neume. It indicates a prolonged note value and therefore is important in the study of *Gregorian chant rhythm.

Episode. A secondary passage or section forming a digression from the main theme. The term is used mainly for a section of a *fugue that does not include a statement of the subject and for the subsidiary sections of the *rondo.

Epistle sonata. A 17th- and 18th-century instrumental piece designed to be played in church before or after the reading of the Epistle. Mozart composed several for organ and violin, etc.

Epithalamium [It. *epitalamio*]. In Greek poetry (Sappho), a poem to be sung by a chorus at weddings; hence music intended for use at weddings.

Epstein, David M. (b. New York, 3 Oct. 1930). Conductor and composer. Pupil of McKinley, Berger, Fine, Babbitt, Sessions, and Cone. Teacher at the Massachusetts Institute of Technology from 1965. Works incl. film music; a symphony, 1958; *Sonority-Variations*, 1968, and other orch. works; *Vent-ures* for symphonic wind ensemble, 1971; choral works; chamber music; piano variations; songs (incl. the cycle *The Seasons,* 1956).

Equal temperament. See under Temperament.

Equal voices. Indication for men's voices only or for women's voices only, as opposed to mixed voices. Less frequently, it indicates soprano voices (or another part) only. See Equale.

Equale [It.; also *aequale, eguale*]. A composition for *equal voices, i.e., all male or all female, or for equal instruments. In particular, a composition for four trombones, written for solemn occasions. Beethoven composed three such pieces (1812), which, arranged for male chorus, were performed at his funeral.

Erb, Donald (James) (b. Youngstown, Ohio, 17 Jan. 1927). Pupil of Gaburo, Heiden, M. Dick, and N. Boulanger. Professor of composition and director of the Electronic Music Studio at the Cleveland Institute of Music from 1966. Has worked with serial and aleatory techniques. Has composed orch. works (incl. *Symphony of Overtures,* 1965; *Music for a Festive Occasion,* with tape, 1976; *Christmasmusic,* 1967); *Klangfarbenfunk I* for orch., rock band, and electronic sounds, 1970; *Cummings Cycle* for chorus and orch., 1963; works for band; chamber music; piano pieces.

Erbach, Christian (b. Gaualgesheim, Hesse, *c.* 1570; d. Augsburg, 14 June 1635). Organist in Augsburg from 1602. Composed motets, settings of Propers of the Mass, and other sacred music; organ works.

Ergriffen [G.]. Deeply moved.

Erickson, Robert (b. Marquette, Mich., 7 Mar. 1917). Pupil of Krenek and Sessions. Has taught at the San Francisco Conservatory, 1957–66, and at the Univ. of California at San Diego from 1967. Has worked with serial, electronic, and improvisatory techniques. Has composed orch. works (incl. *Chamber Concerto,* 1960); vocal works; chamber music; works on tape and for instruments with tape (incl. *Pacific Sirens,* 1968; *General Speech,* 1969); piano pieces.

Erkel, Ferenc (Franz) (b. Gyula, Hungary, 7 Nov. 1810; d. Pest, 15 June 1893). Studied with his father. Conductor at the National Theater, founder and director of the Budapest Philharmonic Concerts, and teacher at the National Musical Academy. Composed operas (incl. *Hunyady László,* the first national Hungarian opera, Budapest, 1844; *Bánk-Bán,* Budapest, 1861); numerous songs; the Hungarian National Hymn, 1845.

Erlebach, Philipp Heinrich (b. Esens, East Frisia, bapt. 25 July 1657; d. Rudolstadt, 17 Apr. 1714). Court *Kapellmeister* at Rudolstadt from 1681. Composed sacred and secular cantatas; motets; suites for orch.; sonatas for violin and for viola da gamba; songs with thoroughbass.

Erlöschend [G.]. Fading away.

Ermattend [G.]. Tiring, weakening.

Ernani. Opera in four acts by Verdi (libretto by F. M. Piave, after V. Hugo's play), produced in Venice, 1844. Setting: Spain and Aix-la-Chapelle, about 1519.

Ernst, ernsthaft [G.]. Serious.

Ernst, Heinrich Wilhelm (b. Brno, 6 May 1814; d. Nice, 8 Oct. 1865). Pupil of Seyfried and Mayseder. Toured widely as a violinist. Knew and was influenced by Paganini. Composed numerous works for violin (incl. *Élégie;* a concerto in F ♯ min.; *Rondo Papageno*); chamber music.

Eroica. Beethoven's Third Symphony in E♭ major, op. 55, composed in 1803–4. It was written in homage to Napoleon, but Beethoven withdrew the planned dedication when Napoleon took the title of emperor, changing the work's title from

"Sinfonia grande: Bonaparte" to "Sinfonia eroica composta per festeggiar il sovvenire d'un gran uomo" (Heroic symphony composed to celebrate the memory of a great man). The last movement is a series of free variations, also including fugal sections, all based on a dancelike theme that Beethoven had used in three earlier compositions: *Contretanz* no. 7 [see *Contredanse*]; *Die *Geschöpfe des Prometheus* (a ballet); *Eroica* Variations.

Eroica Variations. Variations for piano by Beethoven, in E♭ major, op. 35 (1802), so called because the theme is the same as the one he employed later in the last movement of the *Eroica Symphony. Another name is *Prometheus Variations,* after the ballet, *Die *Geschöpfe des Prometheus,* in which the theme occurred for the first time.

Ersterbend [G.]. Dying away.

Erwartung [G., Expectation]. Monodrama in one act by Schoenberg (libretto by M. Pappenheim), completed in 1909 but not produced until 1924, in Prague. Setting: the edge of a forest, timeless.

Erzähler [G.]. Narrator.

Erzlaute [G.]. *Archlute.

Es, eses [G.]. E-flat, E-double-flat; see Pitch names.

Escape note. Same as *échappée;* see under Counterpoint.

Escapement. See under Piano.

Eschequier. *Échiquier.*

Escher, Rudolf (George) (b. Amsterdam, 8 Jan. 1912). Pupil of Pijper. Teacher at the Institute for Musical Science at the State Univ. of Utrecht from 1964. Has composed stage works; symphonies and other orch. works (incl. *Musique pour l'esprit en deuil,* 1943); choral works; works for voice with instruments; chamber music; piano pieces; songs.

Escobar, Luis Antonio (b. Villapinzón, near Bogotá, Colombia, 14 July 1925). Pupil of Nabokov and Blacher. Works incl. operas; ballets (incl. *Preludes,* scored for percussion and piano, choreography by Balanchine, 1960); symphonies; concertos for piano and for flute; choral works; chamber music; piano pieces.

Escobedo, Bartolomé (b. Zamora, Spain, c. 1515; d. Segovia, before Nov. 1563). Singer in the papal choir at Rome, 1536–41 and 1545–48. Succeeded Flecha as *maestro de capilla* of the Castile court, 1548–52; canon at Segovia from 1552. Composed Masses, motets.

Esercizio [It.]. Exercise, *etude.

Eshpai, Andrei Yakovlevich (b. Kozmodemiansk, U.S.S.R., 15 May 1925). Pianist and composer. Pupil of Miaskovsky and Khachaturian. Teacher at the Moscow Conservatory, 1963–70. Has employed folk materials from his native Mari nation and elements of American popular music. Has composed a ballet; symphonies, a concerto for orch., 1967, and other orch. works; a violin concerto; choral works; chamber music; much music for films and television; popular songs.

Eslava y Elizondo, Miguel Hilarión (b. Burlada, Navarre, 21 Oct. 1807; d. Madrid, 23 July 1878). Music director at the Seville Cathedral, 1832–47; master of the royal chapel in Madrid from 1847. Professor at the Madrid Conservatory from 1854 and its director from 1866. Composed 3 Italian operas; published *Lira sacro-hispana,* 1869, a collection of Spanish sacred music of the 16th through 19th centuries, incl. some original works.

Esplá, Oscar (b. Alicante, Spain, 5 Aug. 1886; d. Madrid, 6 Jan. 1976). Pupil of Reger and Saint-Saëns. Professor at the Madrid Conservatory from 1931 and its director 1936–39. Director of the O. Esplá Conservatory in Alicante from 1958. Composed operas, ballets, and other stage works; orch. works (incl. *Don Quijote velando las armas,* 1925); sacred vocal music; chamber music; piano pieces; songs.

Espressivo [It.]. Expressively; abbreviated *espr.*

Estampes [F., Prints]. A set of three piano pieces by Debussy (1903): "Pagodes" (Pagodas); "Soirée dans Grenade" (Evening in Granada); "Jardins sous la pluie" (Gardens in the Rain).

Estampie [F.]; **estampida** [Prov.]; **istanpitta, stampita** [It.]. An important instrumental and dance form of the 13th and 14th centuries consisting of four to seven sections called *puncta,* each of which is repeated: aa bb cc, etc. The form is thus similar to that of the sequence [see Sequence (2)]. Different endings, called **ouvert* and *clos* [It. *aperto* and *chiuso*], are provided for the first and second statement of each *punctum,* as in the modern **prima* and *seconda volta.* Owing to the similarity of name and structure the *estampie* is usually identified with the *stantipes,* a form described by Johannes de Grocheo (*c.* 1300) as consisting of from five to seven *puncta.* Grocheo distinguishes the *stantipes* from the **ductia,* characterizing the latter as having four (or fewer) *puncta.*

Estey organ. See under Harmonium.

Estinto [It.]. Barely audible.

Estribillo [Sp.]. See under *Villancico.*

Et in terra pax. See under Gloria.

Éteint [F.]. Barely audible.

Ethnomusicology. The study of a musical tradition not only in terms of itself but also in relation to its cultural context. Currently the term has two broad applications: (1) the study of all music outside the European art tradition, including survivals of earlier forms of that tradition in Europe and elsewhere; (2) the study of all varieties of music found in one locale or region. Previously, the term *comparative musicology* (G. *vergleichende Musikwissenschaft*) was used. See also Musicology.

Ethos [Gr.]. In ancient Greek music, the "ethical" character of the various scales, e.g., manly and strong, ecstatic and passionate, feminine and lascivious, sad and mournful. Similar characterizations, doubtless influenced by the sometimes imperfectly understood Greek ideas, are found in medieval and later discussions of the **church modes.*

Etler, Alvin (Derald) (b. Battle Creek, Iowa, 19 Feb. 1913; d. Northampton, Mass., 13 June 1973). Oboist and composer. Pupil of Shepherd and Hindemith. Taught at Smith College, 1949–73.

Works (some using serial techniques) incl. orch. works (incl. *Triptych,* 1961); concertos for chamber ensembles with orch.; choral works; 2 string quartets, 2 wind quintets, and other chamber music.

Étouffé [F.]. Damped, muted. *Étouffoir,* piano damper.

Etude [F. *étude,* study]. A piece designed to aid the student of an instrument in developing his technical ability. An etude is usually devoted entirely to one of the special problems of instrumental technique, such as scales, arpeggios, octaves, double stops, or trills. The originator of the modern etude was Muzio Clementi (1752–1832), whose *Préludes et exercices* (1790) and *Gradus ad Parnassum* (1817) mark the beginning of the enormous literature of the 19th-century etude. Outstanding collections of etudes for the piano were written by Cramer, Czerny, Moscheles, and Bertini, and for the violin by Kreutzer, Rode, Paganini, d'Alard, and Bériot. Chopin, in his 27 etudes (op. 10, op. 25, and three single pieces), created the concert etude, which is designed not only for study but also for public performance and which combines technical difficulty with high artistic quality. His example was followed by F. Liszt (*Études d'exécution transcendante,* and others), Scriabin (op. 8, op. 42, op. 65), and Debussy (12 *Études,* dedicated to the memory of Chopin, 1915).

Études d'exécution transcendante [F., Transcendental Etudes]. Twelve concert etudes by Liszt, published in 1852, some composed by 1838. The title refers to their great technical difficulty.

Études symphoniques [F., Symphonic Etudes]. A set of twelve piano pieces by Schumann, op. 13 (1834), in the form of a theme (by Fricken) with variations and a finale.

Etwas [G.]. Some, something, somewhat.

Eugen Onegin [Rus. *Yevgeny Onyegin*]. Opera in three acts by Tchaikovsky (libretto by K. S. Shilovsky and the composer, after a poem by Pushkin), produced in Moscow, 1879. Setting: Russia, about 1820.

Eunuch flute. See Mirliton.

Euouae. In the liturgical books of the Roman rites, the usual abbreviation for "seculorum. Amen" (consisting of the vowels of these two words), the closing words of the "Gloria Patri" [see Doxology]. It is given at the end of Introits and antiphons in order to indicate the proper ending (*differentia*) for the verse (or verses), which leads back to the final repetition of the Introit or antiphon. See Psalm tones. The spelling *Evovae* is frequently found in older books.

Euphonium. See Brass instruments II (d).

Eurhythmics. See Jaques-Dalcroze, Émile.

Euridice, L'. Title of the two earliest extant operas, one by Peri (first perf. 1600), the other by Caccini (publ. 1600; first perf. 1602), both produced at Florence and based on the same libretto (by O. Rinuccini), which relates the story of Orpheus and Eurydice. Setting: ancient Greece.

Evangelisti, Franco (b. Rome, 21 Jan. 1926). Pupil of Krenek and Leibowitz. Has worked with electronic, graphic, and improvisatory techniques. Works incl. *Random or not random* for orch., 1962; *Spazio a 5* for voices and percussion, 1961; *4!* for violin and piano, 1955; *Campi integrati* on tape, 1959; *Proporzioni* for solo flute, 1958.

Evensong. The sung form of the Evening Prayer of the Anglican Church, corresponding to the Roman Catholic Vespers.

Evett, Robert (b. Loveland, Colo., 30 Nov. 1922; d. Takoma Park, Md., 4 Feb. 1975). Pupil of Harris and Persichetti. Music critic and book editor for *The New Republic*, 1952–68; arts and letters editor for the *Atlantic Monthly*, 1968–69. Composed 3 symphonies; concertos for cello, for piano, for harpsichord, for bassoon; choral works, incl. liturgical music; chamber music; piano pieces; songs.

Evirato [It.]. *Castrato.*

Evovae. See *Euouae.*

Exequiae [L.]. Exequies, i.e., music for funeral rites.

Exposition. In the *sonata form, the first section, containing the statement of the themes. In a *fugue, the first as well as subsequent sections containing the imitative presentation of the theme.

Expression marks. Signs or words (sometimes abbreviated) used to indicate aspects of a work (as it is to be realized in performance) other than pitches and rhythms. The most basic types are *tempo marks and *dynamic marks. In addition there are signs for *legato and *staccato, for various kinds of *bowing, for *articulation and *phrasing, for the use of the piano pedals, etc., and finally, numerous terms such as *passionate, dolce,* and *con brio* that are intended to describe the general character or mood of a composition, section, or passage. The use of the term *expression* in this context implies a misleading separation between the rhythms and pitches of a composition on the one hand, as specified relatively unambiguously by the composer, and tempo, dynamics, and the like on the other, with respect to which the performer has greater freedom. Historically informed taste necessarily demands limits on this freedom and an appropriate relationship between the latter and the former. It is certainly a mistake to assume that the expressive powers of music, however great or limited they may be, lie primarily in the province of the execution as distinct from the composition as notated.

Expression marks first appear in the 16th century and are used increasingly throughout the 17th and 18th centuries. Nevertheless, in the music of Bach, for example, they are restricted to the *f*, *p*, and *pp* appearing in only a handful of works.

Expressionism. A term taken over from the history of the visual arts, where it is applied particularly (though not exclusively) to a group of painters (Nolde, Kirchner, Kokoschka, Kandinsky, *et al.*) working in Germany in the period from about 1905 to about 1930. These painters used distortion, exaggeration, symbolism, and abstraction as means of emphasizing their own subjective states and interpretations of their subjects and of conveying these states and interpretations to the viewer. This was in some measure a reaction to *impressionism, in which painters sought to depict their subjects as seen through a highly sensitive but objective eye and without regard for the psychological or emotional aspects of these subjects. The composers most often associated with expressionism were contemporaries of the movement in German painting, particularly Schoenberg (himself a painter), Berg, and Webern. Works often cited are Schoenberg's *Pierrot lunaire* and *Erwartung.* As a description of particular musical techniques (as opposed, e.g., to the literary and philosophical associations of a text or subject for a musical work), the term *expressionism* is of limited usefulness beyond its implication of an avoidance of strictly conventional forms.

Extemporization. See Improvisation.

Eybler, Joseph Leopold (b. Schwechat, near Vienna, 8 Feb. 1765; d. Schön-

brunn, 24 July 1846). Pupil of Albrechtsberger. Friend of Haydn and Mozart. Assistant court *Kapellmeister* in Vienna from 1804 under Salieri, whom he succeeded as *Kapellmeister* in 1824. Composed an opera; symphonies; concertos; oratorios; Masses and other sacred music; chamber music; songs.

Eye music [G. *Augenmusik*]. Music in which some purely graphical aspect of the notation conveys nonmusical meaning to the eye. Such techniques were used particularly in the 15th and 16th centuries, the most common being the use of blackened notes for texts expressing grief or lament as well as for individual words such as *night, dark,* and the like. The term is also applied to examples of *word painting such as the use of ascending or descending motion in conjunction with words such as *up, down, heaven,* or *hell.*

F

F. (1) See Pitch names; Letter notation; Hexachord. (2) Abbr. for **forte; ff (fff),* abbr. for *fortissimo.* (3) For F clef, see Clef. For f-hole, see Sound hole.

F-hole. See Sound hole.

Fa. See Pitch names; Solmization; Hexachord. *Fa fictum* is f'', i.e., the first pitch above the upper limit of the *gamut of medieval and Renaissance theory, which extended from G to e''; f'' is therefore part of *musica ficta.* This pitch is sometimes indicated in early manuscripts and prints by what looks like a modern flat sign, which in this context merely instructed the performer to produce *fa,* i.e., f natural, and not f-flat.

Fa-la, fa-la-la. A type of 16th-century song in which the syllables "fa la la" or similar ones are used as a refrain, e.g., "Now is the month of Maying, When merry lads are playing, Fa la la la . . . , fa la la la . . . " (T. Morley). See *Balletto.*

Fabini, Eduardo (b. Solís de Mataojo, Uruguay, 18 May 1882; d. Montevideo, 17 May 1950). Violinist and composer. Studied in Uruguay and at the Brussels Royal Conservatory. Composed works for orch. (incl. *Campo,* 1922; *La isla de los ceibos,* 1926); chamber music; piano pieces; songs.

Fabordón. Spanish 16th-century corruption of F. *fauxbourdon,* used to denote four-part harmonization of the psalm tones [see *Falsobordone*].

Faburden. (1) A term used in English sources of the 15th and 16th centuries to describe a method of improvised harmonization; see *Discantus supra librum.* It involves the use of a derivative melody that is imagined or "sighted" generally a third above but occasionally in unison with a plainsong and that is transposed and sung down a fifth, thus producing fifths and thirds with the plainsong. The "sighted" parts are sometimes found copied in chant books of the period. (2) In

English organ music of the early 16th century (John Redford, *et al.*), a "verse on the faburden" is a polyphonic setting not of the original plainsong but of the derivative faburden part that is below the plainsong. (3) See *Falsobordone.*

Fackeltanz [G.]. A traditional dance of Prussian court ceremonies of the 19th century, consisting of a slow torchlight procession [G. *Fackel,* torch]. Spontini, Flotow, and Meyerbeer wrote music for such occasions.

Fagott [G.]; **fagotto** [It.; abbr. *Fag.*]. Bassoon. See under Oboe family. *Fagottino* [It.] is the tenor oboe (tenoroon), *fagottone* [It.], the contrabassoon. *Fagottgeige* [G.] is a large 18th-century viol whose strings were overspun with silk and therefore produced a buzzing sound reminiscent of the Fagott.

Fairchild, Blair (b. Belmont, Mass., 23 June 1877; d. Paris, 23 Apr. 1933). Pupil of Paine and Widor. In the U.S. diplomatic service in Turkey and Persia. Lived primarily in Paris from 1903. Composed ballets (incl. *Dame Libellule,* 1921); orch. works, some on Persian subjects; choral works; chamber music; song cycles; piano pieces (incl. *Indian Songs and Dances*).

Fairlamb, James Remington (b. Philadelphia, 23 Jan. 1838; d. Ingleside, N.Y., 16 Apr. 1908). Studied in Paris from 1858. American Consul in Zürich, 1861–65. Church organist in Philadelphia, Jersey City, and New York, 1872–98. Composed operas (incl. *Valérie*); choral works; organ works; songs.

Fall, Leo (b. Olomouc, Moravia, 2 Feb. 1873; d. Vienna, 16 Sept. 1925). Conductor and composer. Studied at the Vienna Conservatory. Composed operettas (incl. *Die Dollarprinzessin,* Vienna, 1907; *Der fidele Bauer,* Mannheim, 1907); *Singspiele* (incl. *Brüderlein fein,* Vienna, 1909); operas.

Falla, Manuel de (b. Cádiz, 23 Nov. 1876; d. Alta Gracia, Argentina, 14 Nov. 1946). Conductor, pianist, and composer. Pupil of Pedrell. Associate of Debussy, Dukas, and Ravel during his stay in Paris, 1907–14. Emigrated to Argentina after the Spanish Civil War. Composed operas (incl. *La vide breve,* Nice,

1913; *El retablo de Maese Pedro,* marionette opera, 1919, prod. Madrid, 1923); ballets (incl. *El *amor brujo,* 1915; *El *sombrero de tres picos,* 1919); orch. works (incl. **Noches en los jardines de España* with piano; *Homenajes,* 1920–39); a concerto for harpsichord and chamber orch., 1926; *Atlántida* for chorus and orch., completed by E. Halffter; songs (incl. *Siete canciones populares españolas,* 1914); piano pieces (incl. *Fantasía bética,* 1919).

Falsa [Sp., Port.]. Dissonance. In 17th-century organ music, *obra* (or *tiento) de falsas* is a composition making deliberate use of dissonances.

Falsa musica. See *Musica ficta.*

False. *False cadence,* same as deceptive **cadence. False fifth (triad),* old term for the diminished fifth (triad) [see Interval; Triad]. *False relation,* see Cross relation.

Falsetto [It.]. The male voice above its normal range, the latter usually called the *full* or *chest voice.* It entails a special method of voice production frequently used by tenors to extend the upper limits of their range. Male **altos or countertenors use only this method of voice production. The falsetto voice has a distinctly lighter quality and is less powerful than the full voice.

Falsobordone [It.; from F. **fauxbourdon*]. A 16th-century term for simple four-part harmonization of psalm tones or other liturgical recitatives (Magnificat, Lamentations, etc.). This style was cultivated particularly in Spain, where it was called *fabordón,* and Italy, and it was most often used in alternation with Gregorian chant.

Falstaff. Opera in three acts by Verdi (libretto by A. Boito, based on Shakespeare's *Henry IV* and *The Merry Wives of Windsor*), produced in Milan, 1893. Setting: Windsor, early 15th century.

Familiar style [It. *stile familiare*]. A style of vocal music in which the voices (usually four) move uniformly in regard to note values as well as to syllables of the text, as in a church hymn. From the point of view of musical texture, familiar style is equivalent to *note-against-note*

style. Other designations include **homorhythmic*.

Fanciulla del West, La [It., The Girl of the Golden West]. Opera in three acts by Puccini (libretto by G. Civinini and C. Zangarini, based on a play by D. Belasco), produced in New York, 1910. Setting: California during the Gold Rush (1849–50).

Fancy (fantasy). A type of 16th- and 17th-century lute, keyboard, and instrumental ensemble music of English origin. The fancy stems from the Italian fantasia [see Fantasia (5)]. In general, fancies are fairly long compositions in which several themes are treated in imitation. Thus, they consist of several thematic sections, which, however, usually overlap, as in a **ricercar*. In the early 17th century the sections are often clearly separated and contrasting in character. Toward the middle of the 17th century the fancy acquired suitelike features by the inclusion of dance movements modeled after the pavane, galliard, allemande, saraband, etc. Composers of fancies included William Byrd (1543–1623), Thomas Morley (1557–1602), John Coperario (*c*. 1575–1626), Alfonso Ferrabosco (*c*. 1575–1628), Orlando Gibbons (1583–1625), Thomas Tomkins (1572–1656), William Lawes (1602–45), John Jenkins (1592–1678), and Henry Purcell (1659–95).

Fandango. A Spanish dance in moderate to quick triple time danced by a couple to the accompaniment of guitar and castanets, in alternation with sung couplets. The fandango appeared in Spain in the early 18th century, and a popular melody was used by Gluck in his ballet *Don Juan* (1761), as well as by Mozart in *Le nozze di Figaro* (1786; finale of Act III, section in 3/4 time).

Fanfare. (1) French term for a brass band, either military or civilian. (2) A short tune for trumpets, used as a signal for ceremonial, military, or hunting purposes. Since fanfares are usually intended for natural instruments [see Natural horn, trumpet], they often include the tones of the major triad only.

Fantasia [It., fantasy; F. *fantaisie;* G. *Fantasie, Phantasie*]. Generally speaking, a composition in which the "free

flight of fancy" prevails over conventions of form or style. Naturally, the term covers a great variety of types, which may be tentatively classified in five groups.

(1) Pieces of a markedly improvisatory character, e.g., Bach's Chromatic Fantasy, Mozart's Fantasia in D minor for piano, and Beethoven's Fantasia op. 77. (2) **Character pieces of the 19th century such as Brahms' *Fantasien* op. 116 and Schumann's *Fantasiestücke* op. 12 and op. 111. (3) Sonatas in freer form, or of a special character; e.g., Beethoven's op. 27, nos. 1 and 2, both entitled "Sonata quasi una fantasia" and deviating in various respects from the conventional sonata form and style; Schubert's *Wanderer Fantasie* op. 15, in which his song "Der Wanderer" is used as the main subject for all the movements [see Cyclic, cyclical]. (4) Free and somewhat improvisatory treatments of existing themes, often from operas, e.g., Liszt's *Réminiscences de "Don Juan"* (1841). (5) In the 16th and 17th centuries, a term for instrumental music that was sometimes used interchangeably with **ricercar*, **tiento*, and even *praeambulum*. Thus, like the ricercar, the fantasia often makes significant use of imitation. The great majority of 16th-century fantasies are for lute, vihuela, guitar, and other stringed instruments, but the keyboard fantasia has a considerably longer development, leading to the **fancies of the English virginalists and important 17th-century examples by Sweelinck, Frescobaldi, and Froberger, each of whom developed unique types. In the 17th century, the ensemble fantasia or fancy was cultivated mainly in England.

Fantasiestück [G.]. See under Fantasia (2).

Fantastic Symphony. See *Symphonie fantastique*.

Fantasy. (1) See Fantasia; Fancy. (2) The **development section (fantasy section) in **sonata form.

Farandole. A Provençal dance performed by men and women who, holding hands, form a long chain and follow the leader through a great variety of figures to music (usually in a moderate 6/8 meter) played on the **pipe and tabor.

The dance has been introduced into opera by Bizet (*L'arlésienne*) and Gounod (*Mireille*).

Farce [It. *farsa*]. (1) Originally, an interpolation, such as a *trope. (2) In plays and operas, chiefly of the 18th century, farcing means the introduction of alien elements, usually of a humorous, comical, or even lascivious nature [see Intermezzo]. This meaning persists in present-day usage, in which a farce is a light comedy, sometimes vulgar, frequently a travesty of a serious model. About 1800, Italian comic operas in one act were called *farsa*, e.g., Rossini's *La cambiale di matrimonio* (1810).

Farewell Sonata. See *Adieux, Les*.

Farewell Symphony. See *Abschieds-Symphonie*.

Farina, Carlo (b. Mantua, *c*. 1600; d. probably in Massa, Tuscany, *c*. 1640). Violinist and composer. Court musician under Schütz in Dresden, 1625–29. His compositions, among the earliest examples of virtuoso violin music, incl. dances and sonatas.

Farinel, Michel (Farinelli) (b. Grenoble, bapt. 23 May 1649; d. there, early 18th cent.). Violinist and composer. Performed in Lisbon, 1668; Paris, 1672; the English court, 1675–79. Composed variations on *Les *Folies d'Espagne*; sacred music.

Farkas, Ferenc (b. Nagykanizsa, Hungary, 15 Dec. 1905). Pupil of Leó Weiner and Respighi. Professor, and later director, at the Cluj (Rumania) Conservatory from 1941; professor at the Academy of Music in Budapest from 1949. Has composed a ballet; film music and incidental music for plays; operas (incl. *The Magic Cupboard*, Budapest, 1942); orch. works; concertos; a cantata; an oratorio; chamber music; piano pieces; songs.

Farmer, John (fl. 1591–99). Organist and master of the choristers at Christ Church Cathedral in Dublin, *c*. 1595. Composed madrigals; settings of psalm tunes, hymns, and canticles; a pedagogical collection of canons.

Farnaby, Giles (b. *c*. 1565; buried London, 25 Nov. 1640). Composed madrigals; motets, psalms, and other sacred music; 52 pieces for virginal in the *Fitzwilliam Virginal Book*.

Farrant, Richard (b. *c*. 1530; d. 1580 or 1581). Organist at St. George's Chapel, Windsor, and member of the Chapel Royal; presented a theater piece before Queen Elizabeth yearly from 1567. Composed a Cathedral Service; anthems (incl. "Hide Not Thou Thy Face" and "Call to Remembrance"); secular songs; keyboard pieces.

Farwell, Arthur (George) (b. St. Paul, Minn., 23 Apr. 1872; d. New York, 20 Jan. 1952). Pupil of Humperdinck, Guilmant, and Pfitzner. Taught in several U.S. colleges, incl. Michigan State Univ., 1927–39. Established the Wa-Wan Press, 1901, for the publication of American music. Composed a stage piece, *Caliban*, New York, 1916; orch. works (incl. *Dawn*, 1901–26; several *Symbolistic Studies*); concertos (incl. one for 2 pianos and one for string orchestra); choral works; chamber music; piano pieces (incl. *American Indian Melodies*); songs; collections and arrangements of American folksongs and American Indian songs.

Fasch, Johann Friedrich (b. Buttelstadt, near Weimar, 15 Apr. 1688; d. Zerbst, 5 Dec. 1758). *Kapellmeister* at Lukaveč, Bohemia, 1721–22, and at Zerbst thereafter. A contemporary of J. S. Bach, who admired his work and made himself copies of several of Fasch's orchestral suites. Composed operas; symphonies, overtures, and orch. suites; concertos; trio sonatas and other chamber music; Masses; motets; an oratorio; several series of church cantatas.

Fasch, Karl Friedrich Christian (b. Zerbst, 18 Nov. 1736; d. Berlin, 3 Aug. 1800). Son of Johann Friedrich Fasch. Appointed accompanist, jointly with K. P. E. Bach, to Frederick the Great in Berlin, 1756. Conductor at the Berlin Opera, 1774–76. Founded the Berlin Singakademie, 1791, which he directed until his death. Composed a Mass; a Requiem; motets; cantatas; oratorios; piano sonatas and other piano works; songs.

Fasola. A system of *solmization, much used in England and in America during the 17th and 18th centuries, in which only four of the six Guidonian syllables are used, the syllables *fa sol la* being applied, e.g., in the key of C major, to the progressions C–D–E and F–G–A, both of which contain two whole steps, the *mi* being used for the seventh degree, B. Before 1800 the fasola method was used in certain American tune books, the letters F, S, L, F, S, L, M being placed on a staff. In 1802 William Little (*The Easy Instructor*) introduced four shapes of note, one for each of the syllables, a method known as buckwheat, four-shape, shape-note, or character notation. The note shapes and syllables could be transposed for use in a variety of keys [see Ex.].

[fa   sol   la   fa   sol   la   mi   fa]

Fastoso [It.]. Pompous.

Fauré, Gabriel (-Urbain) (b. Pamiers, Ariège, 12 May 1845; d. Paris, 4 Nov. 1924). Pupil of Niedermeyer and Saint-Saëns. *Maître de chapelle* at the Madeleine in Paris from 1877 and chief organist there from 1896. Professor at the Paris Conservatory from 1896 and its director (succeeding Dubois) from 1905. Among his pupils were Ravel, Enescu, Schmitt, Aubert, and N. Boulanger. Composed operas (incl. *Prométhée*, Béziers, 1900; *Pénélope*, Monte Carlo, 1913) and incidental music for plays; orch. works; sacred music (incl. *Messe de Requiem*, 1887); secular works for chorus and various vocal ensembles; chamber music; piano pieces; numerous songs (incl. the cycle *La bonne chanson*, 1892).

Faust. Opera in five acts by Gounod (libretto by J. Barbier and M. Carré, based on Goethe's tragedy), produced in Paris, 1859. Revised version with accompanied recitatives and ballet produced in Paris, 1869. Setting: Germany, 16th century.

Faust-Symphonie, Eine [G., A Faust Symphony]. Orchestral work by Liszt (completed in 1857) in three movements described by Liszt as "character sketches": (1) Faust, (2) Gretchen, and (3) Mephistopheles (including a choral setting of the final words of Goethe's drama).

Fauxbourdon [F.]. (1) Historically and properly, a 15th-century French technique of composition in which a plainsong melody transposed to the upper octave is notated together with a contrapuntal part moving along at the lower sixth or occasionally at the octave, while a middle part is extemporized by a singer doubling the melody at the lower fourth throughout. Its first use seems to be in the Communion of Dufay's *Missa Sancti Jacobi*. There has been considerable disagreement over its relationship to the English *faburden and over the derivation of the term itself. See also Discant; *Discantus supra librum; Fabordón; Faburden; Falsobordone*. (2) In modern usage, a general designation for harmonic progressions based on parallel sixth chords, such as occur not only in older music but in the works of Bach, Beethoven, and others. In scholarly writings the designation *sixth-chord style (or six-three writing) is preferable. (3) In present-day English usage, *descant.

Favola d'Orfeo, La. [It., The Fable of Orpheus]. Opera in a prologue and four acts by Monteverdi (libretto by A. Striggio), produced in Mantua, 1607. Setting: ancient Greece.

Fayrfax, Robert (b. Deeping Gate, Lincolnshire, bapt. 23 Apr. 1464; d. St. Albans, 24 Oct. 1521). Gentleman of the Chapel Royal from 1496 and organist at St. Albans' Abbey from *c.* 1498. Composed Masses; motets; Magnificats; secular part songs.

Feierlich [G.]. Solemn.

Feldman, Morton (b. New York, 12 Jan. 1926). Pupil of Riegger and Wolpe. Associate of Cage from 1949 and of Brown, Wolff, and Tudor. Has worked with indeterminacy and graphic notation. On the faculty of the State Univ. of New York at Buffalo. Has composed instrumental works (incl. *Projections I-V*, 1951; *Marginal Intersection*, 1951, and *In Search of an Orchestration*, 1967, for orch.; *Structures* for string quartet, 1951; *First Principles* for large ensemble, 1967); choral works (incl. *The Swallows of Salangan*, 1960); works for voice with instruments; electronic works.

Feldmusik [G.]. A 17th- and 18th-century designation for wind music for open-air performance; such pieces were also called *Feldstücke, Feldsonaten, Feldpartiten,* etc.

Feminine cadence. See Masculine, feminine cadence.

Fennelly, Brian (b. Kingston, N.Y., 14 Aug. 1937). Pupil of Powell, Martino, Perle, and Schuller. Member of the faculty of New York Univ. from 1968. Works incl. a wind quintet, 1967; *Divisions for a Violinist,* 1968; *Evanescences* for chamber ensemble and tape, 1969.

Feo, Francesco (b. Naples, 1691; d. there, 18 or 28 Jan. 1761). Pupil of Pitoni. *Maestro di cappella* at the Conservatory of Sant' Onofrio, 1723–38, and at the Conservatory of the Poveri di Gesù Cristo, succeeding Durante, 1739–43. Pergolesi was among his pupils. Composed operas (incl. *Siface,* Naples, 1723; *Ipermestra,* Rome, 1728); intermezzi; oratorios; Masses; a Requiem.

Ferguson, Howard (b. Belfast, Ireland, 21 Oct. 1908). Pianist and composer. Pupil of R. O. Morris. Professor at the Royal Academy of Music in London, 1948–63. Composed a ballet, *Chauntecleer,* 1948; orch. works; a piano concerto with string orch., 1951; cantatas; chamber music (incl. an octet and 2 violin sonatas); works for voice with instruments (incl. the cycle *Discovery,* 1952); piano pieces.

Fermata [It.]. *Pause.

Fernández, Oscar Lorenzo (b. Rio de Janeiro, 4 Nov. 1897; d. there, 26 Aug. 1948). Conductor, pianist, and composer. Pupil of F. Braga. Co-founder of the Brazilian Conservatory in Rio de Janeiro and its director from 1936. Composed an opera, *Malazarte,* Rio de Janeiro, 1941 (containing a *Batuque*); a ballet; orch. works (incl. a symphony, 1945; *Reisado do pastoreio,* 1930; *Imbapara,* 1928); a violin concerto, 1942; choral works; chamber music (incl. *Trio brasileiro,* 1924); piano pieces; songs.

Ferne, wie aus der [G.]. As if from a distance.

Ferrabosco, Alfonso (the elder) (b. Bologna, bapt. 18 Jan. 1543; d. there, 12 Aug. 1588). Son of the madrigalist Domenico Maria Ferrabosco (1513–74). Visited England several times and was in the service of Queen Elizabeth, 1562–68. Court musician to the Duke of Savoy from 1578. Composed madrigals; motets; instrumental pieces.

Ferrabosco, Alfonso (the younger) (b. London, *c.* 1575; d. there, buried 11 Mar. 1628). Viol player and composer. Son of Alfonso Ferrabosco the elder. Music teacher to the future Charles I from 1612; royal court musician, succeeding Coperario, from 1626. Close associate of Ben Jonson, for six of whose masques he provided music. Also composed ayres with lute and viol accompaniment; fancies, dances, and other works for viols.

Ferrari, Benedetto ("della Tiorba") (b. Reggio Emilia, 1597?; d. Modena, 22 Oct. 1681). Theorbo player, librettist (of the first publicly given opera, F. Manelli's *L'Andromeda,* Venice, 1637), and composer. Court musician in Modena from 1645. Composed operas (incl. *Armida,* Venice, 1639; *Il pastor regio,* Venice, 1640); an oratorio, *Il Sansone;* solo cantatas.

Ferrari, Luc (b. Paris, 5 Feb. 1929). Pupil of Honegger, Messiaen, and Varèse. Co-founder (1958, with Pierre Schaeffer) and director (1961–63) of the Groupe de recherches musicales. Works incl. *musique concrète* (incl. *Visage V,* 1959; *Tautologos II,* 1961; *Presque rien*); orch. works; works for chamber ensembles; *Tautologos III* for any group of instruments, 1969.

Ferroud, Pierre-Octave (b. Chasselay, near Lyon, 6 Jan. 1900; d. in an automobile accident near Debrecen, Hungary, 17 Aug. 1936). Pupil of Ropartz and Schmitt. Composed ballets; the comic opera *Chirurgie,* Monte Carlo, 1928; a symphony in A, 1931, and other symphonic works; chamber music; piano pieces (incl. *Au Parc Monceau*); songs. Also wrote music criticism and a book about Schmitt.

Fes [G.]. F-flat. See Pitch names.

Festa, Costanzo (b. Villafranca, near Turin, *c.* 1480; d. Rome, 10 Apr. 1545). Singer in the papal chapel from 1517 to his death. Composed madrigals (of which he was the first important native Italian composer); Masses, motets, Magnificats, and other sacred music.

Festing, Michael Christian (b. probably London, *c*. 1680; d. probably London, 24 July 1752). Violinist and composer. Pupil of Geminiani. Director of the Italian Opera in London from 1737 and royal chamber musician. Composed violin concertos; violin sonatas with thoroughbass; solo violin pieces; cantatas; songs.

Festoso [It.]. Festive.

Fevin, Antoine de (b. probably Arras, *c*. 1473; d. Blois, late 1511 or early 1512). Court musician to Louis XII. Composed Masses, motets, Magnificats, Lamentations; *bicinia;* French chansons.

FF. Abbr. for *fortissimo.* See *Forte.*

Fiato [It.]. Breath. *Stromenti da fiato,* wind instruments.

Fibich, Zdeněk (Zdenko) (b. Seboriče, near Časlav, Czechoslovakia, 21 Dec. 1850; d. Prague, 15 Oct. 1900). Pupil of Moscheles, Richter, Lachner, and Jadassohn. Assistant conductor of the National Theater in Prague, 1875–78, and director of the Russian Church choir there, 1878–81. Composed operas (incl. *Nevěsta Messinská* [The Bride of Messina], Prague, 1884; *Šarka,* Prague, 1897; *Pad Arkuna* [The Fall of Arkun], Prague, 1900; *Hédy,* Prague, 1896); *Hippodamia,* a trilogy of melodramas, 1890–91; orch. works, incl. 3 symphonies; choral works; chamber music; piano pieces; songs.

Ficher, Jacobo (b. Odessa, Russia, 15 Jan. 1896). Conductor and composer. Pupil of M. Steinberg in St. Petersburg. Settled in Buenos Aires, 1923; has taught at several Argentine schools and conservatories. Has composed chamber operas; ballets; 8 symphonies and other orch. works; concertos for piano and for violin; choral works; chamber music; piano pieces.

Fiddle. (1) Colloquial name for the *violin and stringed instruments resembling it, particularly the folk varieties used to accompany dancing. (2) Any of the primitive ancestors of the violin, including types found in many Oriental cultures.

Fidelio [G.]. Opera in two acts by Beethoven (libretto translated into German by J. Sonnleithner from J. N. Bouilly's libretto for P. Gaveaux's *Léonore, ou L'amour conjugale*), first produced in Vienna in 1805 as *Fidelio, oder Die eheliche Liebe* (this title being used against Beethoven's will) in three acts; rev. 1806 as *Leonore* in two acts (libretto revised by S. von Breuning); final rev. 1814 as *Fidelio* (libretto revised by G. F. Treitschke). Setting: a state prison in Spain, 18th century. See also Leonore Overtures; Melodrama.

Field, John (b. Dublin, 26 July 1782; d. Moscow, 23 Jan. 1837). Pianist and composer. Pupil of Clementi, for whom he worked as a piano salesman. Settled in St. Petersburg, 1803. Composed piano works (incl. concertos, sonatas, polonaises, and the earliest known nocturnes); chamber music.

Fiero [It.]. High-spirited, bold.

Fife. A small transverse flute with six to eight finger holes and usually no key, used chiefly in military bands. It has been replaced in the drum corps by the piccolo. For ill. see under Flute.

Fifteenth. In organs, a foundation stop sounding two octaves (fifteen notes) above normal. Hence, a 2-foot stop.

Fifth. See under Interval; Scale degrees. Also Circle of fifths; Parallel fifths.

Figaro, The Marriage of. See *Nozze di Figaro, Le.*

Figlia del regimento, La. See *Fille du régiment, La.*

Figural, figurate, figured [G. *figuriert*]. The terms are rather indiscriminately used with two different though related meanings. (1) As a translation of L. *musica figurata,* a 15th- and 16th-century term for any polyphonic music as opposed to *musica plana,* plainsong. In particular, the term *figural music* or *style* [G. *Figuralmusik, figurierter Stil*] denotes the highly florid polyphonic style of the early Flemish composers, such as Ockeghem and Obrecht. (2) Applied to 17th- and 18th-century music, the terms mean the use of stereotyped figures or motifs, particularly in variations or in the accompanying parts of organ chorales [see Figuration; Figured chorale].

Figuration. The use of stereotyped figures or *motifs, particularly in variations on a theme.

Figure. See under Motif.

Figured bass. A bass part provided with figures (numerals) to indicate harmonies [see Thoroughbass].

Figured chorale [G. *figurierter Choral*]. A species of *organ chorale (sometimes called a *melody chorale*) in which a certain figure (i.e., a short and characteristic group of notes) is used consistently, in one or several of the contrapuntal parts, against the plain notes of the chorale, which usually is in the soprano. Most of the chorales in Bach's *Orgelbüchlein* belong to this category, e.g., "Alle Menschen müssen sterben," "Der Tag, der ist so freudenreich," "Jesu, meine Freude," and "Ich ruf zu dir."

Figured melody. Ornamented or florid melody.

Figures, doctrine of [G. *Figurenlehre*]. A 17th- and 18th-century theory of musical composition based on the idea that music is an art analogous to rhetoric and thus could be understood as a system of figures like those established in rhetoric by Aristotle and Quintilian.

Filar il tuono [It.]; **filer le son** [F.]. "To draw out the tone." An 18th-century term, properly a synonym of **messa di voce*. Modern writers and singers, however, frequently interpret it as calling for sustained notes, without the crescendo and decrescendo implied by *messa di voce*.

Fille du régiment, La [F., The Daughter of the Regiment; It. *La figlia del reggimento*]. Opera in two acts by Donizetti (libretto by J. F. A. Bayard and J. H. Vernoy de Saint-Georges), produced in Paris, 1840. Setting: Bologna, early 19th century.

Filtz, (Johann) Anton (Filz, Fils, Fieltz) (bapt. Eichstatt, 22 Sept. 1733; d. Mannheim, buried 14 Mar. 1760). Pupil of Stamitz. First cellist in the Mannheim Orchestra from 1754. Composed numerous symphonies; concertos; chamber music.

Fin' al segno [It.]. "As far as the sign," indicating repetition from the beginning to the sign 𝄋.

Final, finalis. See under Church modes.

Finale [It.]. (1) The last movement of a sonata or any of the related forms, usually fast. (2) The last piece of an operatic act, usually longer and more elaborate than the other pieces (arias), since a good deal of the dramatic action is likely to take place at the end of an act. Finales frequently include various sections of contrasting character (e.g., those in Mozart's *Le nozze di Figaro*).

Finck, Heinrich (b. Bamberg, Germany, probably 1444 or 1445; d. Vienna, 9 June 1527). Musician at the Polish court, 1492–1506; court *Kapellmeister* successively in Stuttgart, Augsburg, and Vienna, 1510–27. Composed Masses, motets, and other sacred music; secular German polyphonic songs.

Finck, Hermann (b. Pirna, Saxony, 21 Mar. 1527; d. Wittenberg, 28 Dec. 1558). Great-nephew of Heinrich Finck. Student at Wittenberg Univ. from 1545, teacher there from 1554, and organist there from 1557. Composed German and Latin vocal works. Published a widely used treatise, *Practica musica,* 1556.

Fine [It.]. End, close.

Fine, Irving (Gifford) (b. Boston, 3 Dec. 1914; d. there, 23 Aug. 1962). Pupil of Piston and N. Boulanger. Taught at Harvard Univ., 1947–50, and at Brandeis Univ., 1950 to his death. Composed orch. works (incl. a symphony, 1962, and *Serious Song,* 1955); choral works; chamber music (incl. *Fantasia* for string trio, 1956; a string quartet, 1952); piano pieces; songs (incl. the cycle *Mutability,* 1952).

Fine, Vivian (b. Chicago, 28 Sept. 1913). Pianist and composer. Pupil of Sessions, Weidig, Ruth Crawford (Seeger), and George Szell. Teacher at Bennington College from 1964. Has composed ballets (incl. *The Race of Life,* choreography by Doris Humphrey, 1937; *Alcestis,* choreography by Martha Graham, 1960); a piano concerto; choral works; chamber music; piano pieces; works for voice with instruments (incl. *A Guide to the Life Expectancy of a Rose,* 1956).

Fingal's Cave. See *Hebriden, Die*.

Fingerboard. In stringed instruments, a long strip of hardwood (ebony) fixed to the neck, over which the strings are stretched and against which they are pressed (stopped) by the fingers in order to vary their pitch. The fingerboards of some older instruments such as the lute, guitar, viola da gamba, and lyra were provided with *frets, as are the present-day guitar and ukulele.

Fingering [F. *doigté;* G. *Fingersatz, Applicatur* (obs.); It. *diteggiatura, tocco;* Sp. *digitación*]. The methodical use of the fingers in playing instruments. The modern principles of fingering for keyboard instruments are relatively new, their definite establishment by M. Clementi (1752–1832) being practically simultaneous with the replacement of the harpsichord and clavichord by the piano. The earlier fingering is distinguished from the modern method chiefly by its very sparing use of the thumb and fifth finger in scale passages. For the system of fingering for stringed instruments, see Positions.

Finke, Fidelio Fritz (Friedrich) (b. Josefsthal, Bohemia, 22 Oct. 1891; d. Dresden, 12 June 1968). Pupil of Novák. Teacher at the German Musikakademie in Prague from 1920 and its director from 1927. Director of the State Music Academy in Dresden, 1946–51; professor at the Hochschule für Musik, Leipzig, 1951–58. Composed 2 operas; orch. works; a piano concerto; choral works; chamber music; works for voice with instruments; piano pieces (incl. *Eine Reiterburleske; Romantische Suite*); organ works.

Finlandia. *Symphonic poem by Sibelius, op. 26 (1899), of strongly nationalistic character.

Finney, Ross Lee (b. Wells, Minn., 23 Dec. 1906). Pupil of N. Boulanger, Berg, and Sessions. Taught at Smith College, 1929–48; on the faculty of the Univ. of Michigan, 1949–74. Has worked with serial techniques since about 1950. Has composed 4 symphonies and other orch. works; concertos for violin and for piano; choral works with orch. (incl. *Still Are New Worlds,* 1962); 8 string quartets and other chamber music; piano pieces; organ pieces; songs.

Finzi, Gerald (b. London, 14 July 1901; d. Oxford, 27 Sept. 1956). Pupil of R. O. Morris. Professor at the Royal Academy of Music in London, 1930–33. Composed orch. works (incl. the nocturne *New Year Music*); a cello concerto, 1955; choral works (incl. *Intimations of Immortality* for tenor, chorus, and orch., 1950; *Dies natalis,* cantata for voice and string orch., 1939); songs.

Fiorillo, Federigo (b. Brunswick, Germany, bapt. 1 June 1755; place and date of death unknown). Violinist, conductor, and composer. Pupil of his father, Ignatio Fiorillo (1715–87), a conductor and composer. Participant in the Concert spirituel in Paris, 1785; performed widely in Europe and Russia. Composed violin pieces (incl. *Études pour violon,* a collection of 36 caprices); chamber music; concertos; ballets.

Fioritura [It.]. Embellishment, either written out or improvised. See Ornamentation.

Fipple flute. *Whistle flute.

Firebird, The. See *Oiseau de feu, L'*.

Fireworks Music. Handel's *Music for the Royal Fireworks,* an instrumental suite composed for performance at a fireworks display in London in 1749 celebrating the Peace of Aix-la-Chapelle.

First-movement form. Same as *sonata form.

Fis, fisis [G.]. F-sharp, F-double-sharp. See Pitch names.

Fischer, Johann Christian (b. Freiburg im Breisgau, 1733; d. London, 29 Apr. 1800). Oboist and composer. Court chapel musician in Dresden, 1760–64. In the service of Frederick the Great, *c.* 1767. Settled in England shortly after 1768, where, with his close associates Johann Christian Bach and C. F. Abel, he belonged to the royal chamber orchestra of George III. Composed 10 oboe concertos (one containing a minuet on which Mozart wrote variations for piano); flute sonatas and divertimenti for 2 flutes; chamber music.

Fischer, Johann Kaspar Ferdinand (b. near Schlackenwerth, Bohemia, *c.* 1665; d. Rastatt, 27 Aug. 1746). Served the

Margrave of Baden, 1692–1716. Composed a *Singspiel;* ballets; airs; harpsichord suites; organ pieces (incl. *Ariadne musica,* 1715, a collection of preludes and fugues in 20 keys); sacred music.

Fišer, Luboš (b. Prague, 30 Sept. 1935). Studied in Prague. Has composed an opera, *Lancelot,* Prague, 1961; a musical play, *The Good Soldier Schweik,* Prague, 1962; music for television and films; 2 symphonies and other orch. works (incl. *15 Prints after Durer's Apocalypse,* symphonic suite, 1965); choral works; chamber music; piano sonatas.

Fistula [L.]. Medieval name for the flute and, particularly, organ pipe (*fistula organica*).

Fitelberg, Jerzy (b. Warsaw, 20 May 1903; d. New York, 25 Apr. 1951). Pupil of his father, Grzegorz Fitelberg, a composer and conductor. Settled in the U.S., 1940. Composed orch. works; concertos for violin, for cello, and for piano; vocal works; string quartets and other chamber music.

Fitzwilliam Virginal Book. The largest manuscript collection of English music for the *virginal.* Its nearly 300 pieces date from *c.* 1562 to at least *c.* 1612 and include dances, arrangements of songs and madrigals, preludes, and sets of variations representing nearly all of the principal English keyboard composers of the period.

Five, The. A group of five Russian composers who, about 1875, united their efforts in order to create a truly national school of Russian music. The original name, coined in a newspaper article by Stasov in 1867, was *Moguchaya Kuchka* (The Mighty Handful). They were César A. Cui (1835–1918), Alexander P. Borodin (1833–87), Mily A. Balakirev (1837–1910), Modest P. Mussorgsky (1839–81), and Nikolai A. Rimsky-Korsakov (1844–1908).

Five-three chord. The common *triad, so called because in figured bass it is indicated by the figures $\frac{5}{3}$ calling for the third and fifth scale degrees above the root.

Fixed-do(h). See under Movable do(h).

Flagellant songs. See *Geisslerlieder.*

Flagello, Nicolas (b. New York, 15 Mar. 1928). Conductor, pianist, violinist, oboist, and composer. Pupil of Giannini and Pizzetti. Has taught at the Manhattan School of Music from 1950; at the Curtis Institute, 1964–65. Has composed operas (incl. *The Judgement of St. Francis,* 1959, prod. New York, 1966); orch. works; concertos; choral works; chamber music; songs.

Flageolet. See under Whistle flute. For ill. see under Flute. For flageolet tones, see *Flageolett-Töne;* Harmonics.

Flageolett-Töne. German term for the *harmonics of stringed instruments. The English term *flageolet tones* is rarely used.

Flam. See under Percussion instruments II (side drum).

Flamenco. A south Spanish (Andalusian) type of song performed to the accompaniment of guitars and often danced. It makes considerable use of *Phrygian progressions as well as inflections of pitch that lie outside the system of equal *temperament. Particularly cultivated among the Gypsies of Spain, it owes a great deal to the music of the Arabic-speaking peoples who occupied parts of Spain for almost eight centuries. Although some writers distinguish between *cante hondo (jondo)* and *cante flamenco,* regarding the former as an antecedent of the latter, the two terms are often used synonymously.

Flanagan, William (b. Detroit, 14 Aug. 1926; d. New York, 31 Aug. 1969). Music journalist and composer. Pupil of B. Phillips, Bernard Rogers, Honegger, Berger, Copland, and Diamond. Composed operas (incl. *Bartleby,* after Melville, libretto by J. Hinton and E. Albee, New York, 1961; *The Ice Age,* 1963); film music; incidental music for plays by Albee; orch. works; choral works; chamber music; piano pieces; songs on texts by Melville, A. E. Housman, Howard Moss, and others.

Flat [F. *bémol;* G. *Be;* It. *bemolle;* Sp. *bemol*]. The sign ♭, which indicates the lowering of the pitch of a note by a half-step. See Accidentals; Pitch names. "Flat" is also used to describe incorrect intonation below the correct pitch.

Flatterzunge [G.]. Flutter tonguing. See Tonguing.

Flautando, flautato. See Bowing (1).

Flauto [It.]. *Flute. *Flauto a becco, flauto diritto, flauto dolce,* *recorder; *flauto d'amore,* see Flute II (b); *flautone,* alto flute or bass flute; *flauto piccolo,* piccolo (flute). Until the middle of the 18th century, e.g., in the music of Bach, *flauto* always meant the recorder, the flute being called *flauto traverso* [see Flute II]. In the same period, *flauto piccolo* meant not the transverse piccolo but a small recorder.

Flaviol. A small Spanish flute, played with one hand and used for dance music. See Pipe (1).

Flecha, Mateo (the elder) (b. Prades, Tarragona, Spain, 1481; d. Poblet, Tarragona, 1553). Court musician to the family of Charles V. Composed *ensaladas.*

Flecha, Mateo (the younger) (b. Prades, Tarragona, Spain, 1530; d. Solsona, Lérida, 20 Feb. 1604). Nephew and pupil of Mateo Flecha the elder and of Escobedo. Court musician to Charles V and later to the Empress Maria, wife of Maximilian II, in Vienna. Composed madrigals; *ensaladas;* psalms, motets, and other sacred music; instrumental pieces.

Fledermaus, Die [G., The Bat]. Operetta in three acts by Johann Strauss, Jr. (libretto by C. Haffner and R. Genée, derived from a French farce, *Le reveillon,* by H. Meilhac and L. Halévy after R. Benedix's *Das Gefängnis*), produced in Vienna, 1874. Setting: Bad Ischl, Austria, 1874.

Flemish school. The name sometimes given to several generations of prominent composers of the 15th and 16th centuries who came from the region now composed of the Netherlands, Belgium, and northern France. These masters are also referred to as Netherlandish, Franco-Netherlandish, and Franco-Flemish. If the generation of Dufay and Binchois is regarded as constituting the *Burgundian school, then the Flemish school may be seen as beginning with Johannes Ockeghem in the late 15th century and continuing with Jacob Obrecht, Heinrich Isaac, Josquin

des Prez, Jean Mouton, Adrian Willaert, Nicolas Gombert, Jacob Arcadelt, Clemens non Papa, Cipriano de Rore, Roland de Lassus, and others throughout the 16th century. These musicians held important posts throughout Europe and thus profoundly affected the development of music in countries far from their own homeland. It was they who created and developed the international polyphonic style in which four or more voices occupying separate ranges were treated as equal in importance and in which *imitation became a significant element (beginning with the works of Josquin around 1500). This style was universally employed in *motets and Masses, and it strongly affected the character of secular vocal music such as the *madrigal and the *chanson. See also Netherlands schools.

Flex, flexa. (1) See under Psalm tones. (2) Same as *clivis* (also *punctus flexus*); see table accompanying Neumes.

Flicorno [It.]. An Italian variety of Flügelhorn [see Brass instruments II (b)].

Fliegende Holländer, Der [G., The Flying Dutchman]. Opera in three acts by Richard Wagner (to his own libretto after Heine's *Memoiren des Herrn von Schnabelewopski*), produced at Dresden, 1843. Setting: medieval, legendary time.

Fliessend, fliessender [G.]. Flowing, more flowing.

Flöte [G.]. *Flute.

Flötenuhr [G.]. See under Mechanical instruments.

Flothuis, Marius (Hendrikus) (b. Amsterdam, 30 Oct. 1914). Music critic and composer. Studied musicology at Amsterdam Univ. Artistic director of the Concertgebouw Orchestra from 1955. Has composed orch. works; concertos for flute, for horn, for piano, for violin, for clarinet, for chamber orch.; vocal works; chamber music.

Flotow, Friedrich von (b. Toitendorf, Germany, 27 Apr. 1812; d. Darmstadt, 24 Jan. 1883). Pupil of Reicha. Associate of Grisar, with whom he collaborated on several operas. Lived in Paris from 1828 until the revolution of 1848. Composed ballets (incl. *Lady Henriette*, Paris, 1844); operas (incl. **Martha; Alessandro Stradella*, Hamburg, 1844); chamber music; piano pieces; songs.

Flott [G.]. Briskly, without hesitation.

Flourish. (1) A trumpet call or **fanfare. (2) A somewhat showy, decorative passage, often one added by the performer.

Floyd, Carlisle (b. Latta, S.C., 11 June 1926). Pupil of Bacon. Member of the faculty of Florida State Univ. from 1947. Has composed operas (incl. *Susannah*, Tallahassee, Fla., 1955; *Wuthering Heights*, Santa Fe, 1958; *The Passion of Jonathan Wade*, New York, 1962; *Of Mice and Men*, Seattle, 1970); a ballet; orch. works; choral works; songs.

Flue pipes (stops, work). See under Organ.

Flügel [G., wing]. The grand piano, which is wing-shaped.

Flügelhorn. See under Brass instruments II (b).

Flüssig [G.]. Flowing.

Flute. For the general characteristics of flutes, see under Wind instruments. I. *Present forms.* (a) Flute [F. *flûte*; G. *Flöte*; It. *flauto*; Sp. *flauta*]. The modern flute is a cylindrical tube closed at the upper end. At this end is a side hole (embouchure) across which the player blows (and for which reason it is described as a transverse flute; for the end-blown flute, see Recorder), thus making the column of air inside the tube vibrate. It is generally made of silver, though older instruments were of wood, and gold and platinum are occasionally used. Ex. 1 shows its range; in addition, some instruments seem to have had the low B♭, and the high C♯ and D are occasionally called for. The lowest octave of the fundamental scale is overblown by increased wind pressure to provide the second octave. The remainder of its three-octave range is produced by further overblowing and by cross fingering. The modern flute was largely developed by T. Böhm [see Böhm system].

(b) Piccolo [F. *petite flûte*; G. *kleine Flöte, Pickelflöte*; It. *flauto piccolo, ottavino*; Sp. *flautín*]. A small flute, pitched an octave above the flute. Its

written range is shown in Ex. 2, and it sounds an octave higher. It is sometimes pitched in D♭, E♭, or F.

(c) Alto flute [F. *flûte alto*; G. *Altflöte*; It. *flautone*; Sp. *flauta bajo*], sometimes called bass flute. An instrument built in G, i.e., a perfect fourth lower than the normal flute, with a range from g to c'''. It is notated as a transposing instrument, c' to f''', a fourth above its actual sound.

(d) Bass flute, sometimes called contrabass flute. An instrument built an octave below the standard flute. Another kind of flute is the *Albisiphone* (invented by A. Albisi, 1911). This instrument is held vertically, the extension being shortened by means of a double U-tube between the embouchure and the tuning slide. The mouth part is bent horizontally to form the top of a T. The fingering is that of the regular Böhm system. The compass is from B to f''♯. See also Giorgi flute.

II. *Obsolete forms.* (a) *Terzflöte* [G., third flute]. So called from being built in E♭, a minor third higher than the standard instrument. (b) *Flûte d'amour* [G. *Liebesflöte*; It. *flauto d'amore*; Sp. *flauta de amor*]. A flute built a third lower than the regular flute. The alto flute [see I (c)] is sometimes called by this name.

Throughout the Middle Ages, Renaissance, and early baroque period, the transverse flute was mainly a military instrument (fife) associated particularly with Germany, so it was generally known as the German flute. For artistic purposes, the end-blown flute, or **recorder, was preferred. The transverse flute (*flûte traversière*) became an important solo instrument in the mid-18th century, as shown by the appearance of Quantz's epochal treatise, *Versuch einer Anweisung die Flöte traversière zu spielen* (1752). In the music of Bach and Handel, however, the plain name *flauto* still invariably meant the recorder, the transverse flute being called *flauto traverso* or *traverso*. Lully was probably the first composer to use the flute in the orchestra; it did not become a permanent member until the time of Haydn. Begin-

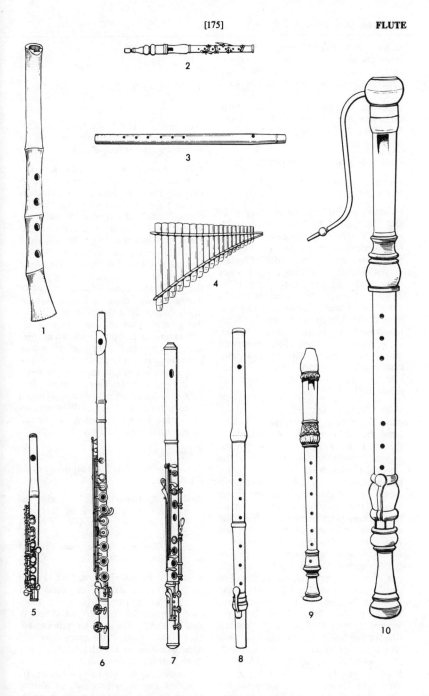

Flutes: 1. Shakuhachi. 2. Keyed flageolet. 3. Fife. 4. Panpipes. 5. Piccolo. 6. Metal flute. 7. Wooden flute. 8. Flute (18th century). 9. Alto recorder. 10. Bass recorder.

ning *c*. 1800, attempts were made to improve the instrument, chiefly to compensate for the position of the side holes, which were cut to conform to the reach of the fingers rather than the laws of acoustics. The final step in this development was the system of *Böhm. See also Fife; Whistle flute (flageolet); Panpipes; *Shakuhachi.*

Flutter tonguing. See Tonguing.

Flying Dutchman, The. See *Fliegende Holländer, Der.*

Foerster, Joseph Bohuslav (b. Prague, 30 Dec. 1859; d. Nový Vestec, Czechoslovakia, 29 May 1951). Organist, conductor, music critic, and composer. Pupil of his father, the organist Josef Förster. Professor at the Hamburg Conservatory from 1901 and in Vienna from 1903. Teacher (from 1918) and rector (1922–31) at the Prague Conservatory. President of the Czech Academy, 1931–39. Composed operas (incl. *Eva,* Prague, 1899; *Jessika,* Prague, 1905); incidental music for plays; symphonies and other orch. works; concertos for violin and for cello; sacred vocal music; chamber music; songs.

Folia, follia, folies d'Espagne. (1) A dance, probably of Portuguese origin, mentioned in Portuguese documents of the late 15th century. In all probability it was a "fool's dance" similar to the *moresca.* No music from this early period survives. (2) A harmonic pattern [see Ex.] related to the *passamezzo antico* and the *romanesca,* used by a great many composers in the 17th and 18th centuries, and by a few in the 19th and 20th centuries, as the skeletal structure for continuous variations. As is true of the *bergamasca* and the *romanesca,* one discant melody became attached to the skeletal bass in the 17th century and is found in many of the compositions written on the pattern. *Folia* variations were written by M. Farinel, A. Scarlatti (for harpsichord), M. Marais (for viola da gamba; *Pièces de viole,* 1681), Corelli (for violin, op. 5, no. 12, 1700), J. S. Bach (*Bauernkantate,* 1742), K. P. E. Bach (for piano, 1778), Grétry (in the opera *L'amant jaloux,* 1778), Cherubini (overture to *L'hôtellerie portugaise,* 1798), Liszt (*Rapsodie espagnole,* 1863),

Carl Nielsen (opera *Maskarade,* 1906), and Rachmaninov (*Variations on a Theme by Corelli,* op. 42, 1932).

Folk music, folksong. The musical repertory and tradition of communities (particularly rural), as opposed to art music, which is the work of individual, formally trained composers. It generally develops anonymously, usually among the uneducated classes, and originally was (and may still be) transmitted orally, thereby becoming subject to modification. Folk music exists in practically every part of the world and constitutes a vast body whose study often requires special methods [see Ethnomusicology]. By far the greatest part of this repertory involves singing and thus is known as folksong. In practice, folk and art music have frequently interpenetrated, particularly in the use of folk materials by composers of art music. This has been a feature of Western art music through much of its history. In some non-Western cultures, the distinction must be treated with greater care still.

Follia. See *Folia.*

Fonds d'orgue [F.]. Foundation stops of the *organ.

Fontane di Roma [It., Fountains of Rome]. Symphonic poem by Respighi (1917) in four movements, each of which depicts a fountain in Rome: Valle Giulia at dawn, Triton in the morning, Trevi at midday, and Villa Medici at sunset.

Foot. (1) In versification, see Poetic meter. (2) In organ building, terms such as eight-foot (written 8-ft. or 8'), four-foot (4'), sixteen-foot (16'), and thirty-two foot (32') are used to differentiate stops that sound at the pitch normally corresponding to a particular key on a manual from others sounding higher or lower octaves or even other intervals. If, e.g., the key c' is touched, an 8'-stop sounds c', but a 4'-stop sounds c'' and a 16'-stop sounds c. The terminology is derived from the fact that, in any normally pitched flue stop, such as 8'-principal, the length of the pipe sounding c measures about 8 feet (the other pipes for higher pitches of the same stop being, of course, correspondingly shorter), whereas, in a stop of the 4'-class, the pipe sounded by the same key is only half as long [see Organ]. These terms are used in a similar way with respect to *harpsichords.

Foote, Arthur (William) (b. Salem, Mass., 5 Mar. 1853; d. Boston, 8 Apr. 1937). Pupil of Paine and Heller. Organist at the First Unitarian Church in Boston, 1878–1910. Taught at the New England Conservatory from 1921. Composed orch. works (incl. *Suite in E major* for strings, 1886); a cello concerto, 1894; choral works (incl. the cantata *The Farewell of Hiawatha,* 1886); church music; 3 string quartets and other chamber music; piano and organ pieces; numerous songs.

Ford, Thomas (b. c. 1580; d. London, buried 17 Nov. 1648). Lutenist and composer. Court musician to Prince Henry from 1611 and to Charles I from 1626. Composed *Musicke of Sundrie Kinds,* a collection containing ayres with lute accompaniment and dance pieces for viols; anthems; catches.

Forefall. See Backfall, forefall.

Forlana, furlana. A dance from northern Italy (Friuli). In dance collections of the 16th century it is similar to the **passamezzo* (in duple meter), whereas in the baroque period it is a gay dance in triple meter (6/4, 6/8) with dotted rhythms and characteristic repeats of motifs. Bach's orchestral suite in C includes a *forlane*.

Form. (1) In the most fundamental sense, the shape of a musical composition as defined by all of its pitches and rhythms. In this sense, there can be no distinction between musical form and musical content, since to change even a single pitch or rhythm that might be regarded as part of the content of a composition necessarily also changes the shape of that composition even if only in detail. (2) From this follows the application of the term *form* to abstractions or generalizations that can be drawn from groups of compositions for purposes of comparing them with one another. Thus, e.g., *sonata form is defined by a loose group of general features shared in varying degrees by a relatively large number of works, no two of which are in fact exactly the same. Only when *form* is used in this sense can one speak of a distinction between form and specifically musical content. Any attempt to define forms of this kind too rigidly will be futile or will at the very least greatly diminish the usefulness of the definition by excluding too many specific compositions. Such definitions ought to be viewed as generalizations made after the fact rather than as recipes followed slavishly by composers. See Binary and ternary form; Rondo; Variation; Sonata; Concerto; Suite; Toccata; Fugue; *Formes fixes; Bar* form; *Bogenform;* Organum; Motet; Mass; Cantata; Oratorio; Opera.

Formant. See under Acoustics.

Formes fixes [F.]. Collective designation for the three chief forms of late medieval French poetry and music: **ballade, *virelai,* and **rondeau.* They were cultivated principally in the 14th and 15th centuries, gradually declining in importance after 1450.

Forqueray, Antoine (b. Paris, Sept. 1672; d. Mantes, 28 June 1745). Viola da gamba player (rival of Marin Marais) and composer. Chamber musician to Louis XIV from 1689. Composed a collection of *Pièces de viole.*

Förster, Emanuel Aloys (b. Niederstein, Silesia, 26 Jan. 1748; d. Vienna, 12 Nov. 1823). Settled in Vienna in 1776 and was admired there as a teacher by Beethoven and others. Composed numerous string quartets; piano sonatas; organ pieces; songs. Published a work on thoroughbass, *Anleitung zum Generalbass,* 1802.

Forte [It.; abbr. *f*]. Loud. *Fortissimo,* abbr. *ff (fff),* very loud; *più forte,* louder; *forte-piano,* abbr. *fp,* loud followed by soft; *mezzoforte,* abbr. *mf,* medium loud.

Forte-piano [It.]. (1) See under *Forte.* (2) Older name for the **piano.*

Fortissimo [It.; abbr. *ff*]. Very loud. See *Forte.*

Fortner, Wolfgang (b. Leipzig, 12 Oct. 1907). Conductor and composer. Pupil of H. Grabner at the Leipzig Conservatory.

Taught at the Evangelical Church Music Institute in Heidelberg, 1931–54; at the Northwest-German Music Academy in Detmold, 1954–57; at the Musikhochschule in Freiburg im Breisgau from 1957. Has worked with twelve-tone techniques. Has composed operas (incl. *Bluthochzeit,* after García Lorca, Cologne, 1957); a ballet, *Die weisse Rose,* 1950; orch. works (incl. a symphony, 1947); concertos for organ, for piano, for violin, for cello; cantatas (incl. *An die Nachgeborenen,* after Brecht, 1948; *The Creation,* 1954) and other vocal works; 3 string quartets and other chamber music; piano pieces (incl. 7 elegies, 1950; *Kammermusik,* 1944).

Forty-eight, The. Popular name for the 48 preludes and fugues of Bach's *Well-Tempered Clavier* I and II (24 in each).

Forza [It.]. Force.

Forza del destino, La [It., The Force of Destiny]. Opera in four acts by Verdi (libretto by F. M. Piave), produced in St. Petersburg, 1862. Setting: Spain and Italy, 18th century.

Forzando, forzato [It.; abbr. *fz*]. Forcing, forced, accented. Same as **sforzando.*

Foss, Lukas (b. Berlin, 15 Aug. 1922). Pianist, conductor, and composer. Pupil of N. Gallon, Scalero, R. Thompson, and Hindemith. Settled in the U.S., 1937. Pianist with the Boston Symphony Orchestra, 1944–50. Professor at the Univ. of California at Los Angeles 1951–62. Conductor of the Buffalo Philharmonic Orchestra, 1963–70; the Brooklyn Philharmonia, 1971–75; the Jerusalem Symphony from 1972. Founder and director of the Center for Creative and Performing Arts of the State Univ. of New York at Buffalo from 1963. Has made use of serial and electronic techniques, indeterminacy, and improvisation in works since about 1960. Has composed operas (incl. *The Jumping Frog of Calaveras County,* Bloomington, Ind., 1950); ballets; incidental music for plays; orch. works (incl. a symphony, 1944; *Baroque Variations,* 1967; *Geod* with voices, 1969); concertos for piano and for oboe; *Cello Concert* for cello, orch., and tape, 1966; vocal and choral works (incl. *Psalms* with orch., 1956; *The Prai-*

rie, cantata, 1942; *Time Cycle,* for soprano and orch., 1960); chamber music (incl. *Echoi,* 1961–63; *Elytres,* 1964); piano pieces.

Foundation stops. Designation for the unison and octave-sounding (8′, 16′, 4′, 2′) ranks of the **organ, especially those of the diapason chorus.

Fountains of Rome. See *Fontane di Roma.*

Four Saints in Three Acts. Opera in four acts by Virgil Thomson (libretto by Gertrude Stein), produced in Hartford, Conn., 1934. Setting: Spain, 16th century.

Four-shape notation. See Fasola.

Fourniture [F.]. A mixture stop of the **organ.

Fourth. See under Interval; Scale degrees.

Fourth chord. Any of various chords consisting of superimposed fourths, e.g., c–f–b♭, c–f♯–b–e′, or of fourths in dissonant combinations with other intervals. These chords play an important role in the harmonic idiom of some modern composers (Scriabin, Casella, Hindemith, Bartók), replacing the traditional harmonies resulting from the superposition of thirds (**triad, **seventh chord, **ninth chord). Scriabin was the first to make deliberate use of fourth chords. Several of his compositions are based on a single fourth-chord combination, e.g., the so-called **mystic chord, c–f♯–b♭–e′ –a′–d″.

FP. Abbr. for *forte-piano* [see under *Forte*].

Française. See under *Contredanse.*

Françaix, Jean (-René) (b. Le Mans, 23 May 1912). Pupil of N. Boulanger. Has composed operas (incl. *La main de gloire,* Bordeaux, 1950); ballets; music for films; orch. works; the oratorio *L'apocalypse de St. Jean,* 1942; a piano concerto, 1937, and a concertino for piano and orch., 1934; vocal works; a wind quintet and other chamber music.

Francesco Canova da Milano (b. Monza, probably 18 Aug. 1497; d. probably 15 Apr. 1543). Lutenist and composer.

Court musician in Mantua *c*. 1510; in the service of Pope Paul III in Rome from 1535. Composed ricercars, fantasies, and other original pieces, as well as transcriptions of motets and chansons for the lute.

Franchetti, Alberto (b. Turin, 18 Sept. 1860; d. Viareggio, 4 Aug. 1942). After study in Turin, he was a pupil of Rheinberger and Draeseke. Directed the Cherubini Conservatory in Florence, 1926–28. Composed operas (incl. *Germania,* Milan, 1902; *Asrael,* Reggio Emilia, 1888; *Cristoforo Colombo,* Genoa, 1892); symphonic works; *Inno* for soloists, chorus, and orch.; chamber music; songs.

Franck, César (-Auguste-Jean-Guillaume-Hubert) (b. Liège, 10 Dec. 1822; d. Paris, 8 Nov. 1890). Organist and composer. Pupil of Reicha. *Maître de chapelle* (beginning in 1858) and organist (from 1859 to his death) at Sainte-Clotilde, Paris. Succeeded his former teacher Benoist as professor of organ at the Paris Conservatory, 1872. His pupils incl. d'Indy, Chausson, Bréville, Duparc, Ropartz, and Vierne (his successor at Sainte-Clotilde). Composed operas (incl. *Hulda,* Monte Carlo, 1894); oratorios (incl. *Les *Béatitudes*); orch. works (incl. a symphony in D minor, 1888; *Variations symphoniques* for piano and orch., 1885); symphonic poems (incl. *Les Éolides,* 1876; *Le chasseur maudit,* 1882; *Psyché* with chorus, 1888); Masses, motets, offertories, and other sacred music; chamber music (incl. a violin sonata, 1886, and a string quartet, 1889); numerous organ works; piano works (incl. *Prélude, choral et fugue,* 1884); songs.

Franck, Melchior (b. Zittau, *c*. 1579 or 1580; d. Coburg, 1 June 1639). *Kapellmeister* at the Coburg court from 1602 to his death. Composed numerous sacred and secular vocal works; instrumental works, incl. intradas and dances.

Franco-Flemish school. See Flemish school.

Franz, Robert (originally Knauth) (b. Halle, 28 June 1815; d. there, 24 Oct. 1892). Pupil of J. C. F. Schneider. Organist at the Ulrichskirche, Halle, from 1841 and conductor of the Singakademie there from 1842. Deafness caused his retirement in 1867. Composed numerous lieder (incl. "Die Widmung"; "Schlummerlied"; "Wonne der Wehmuth"; "Gewitternacht"; "Die Heide ist braun"); sacred choral works; arrangements of works by Bach and Handel.

Frau ohne Schatten, Die [G., The Woman Without a Shadow]. Opera in three acts by R. Strauss (libretto by H. von Hofmannsthal), produced in Vienna, 1919. Setting: fairy tale.

Frauenchor [G.]. Women's chorus.

Frauenliebe und Leben [G., Woman's Love and Life]. A cycle of eight songs by Schumann, op. 42 (1840), based on a group of poems by Adalbert von Chamisso (published under the same title). It was composed shortly after Schumann married Clara Wieck.

Frederick II (The Great) of Prussia (b. Berlin, 24 Jan. 1712; d. Sanssouci, near Potsdam, 17 Aug. 1786). Patron of the arts, flutist, and composer. Pupil of Quantz. Established the Berlin Opera House. As crown prince and as king (from 1740) he employed as court *Kapellmeister* C. H. Graun (from 1735); J. F. Agricola (from 1757); J. F. Reichardt (from 1775). As harpsichordists he employed K. P. E. Bach (from 1740) and C. Nichelmann (from 1744). J. S. Bach visited the Potsdam court in 1747 and composed the *Musical Offering* on a theme proposed by Frederick. His own compositions incl. 121 flute sonatas; 4 concertos for flute and string orch.; marches and other instrumental works; 3 secular cantatas; arias for several operas.

Freed, Isadore (b. Brest Litovsk, 26 Mar. 1900; d. Rockville Center, N.Y., 10 Nov. 1960). His family settled in Philadelphia, 1903. Pupil of Bloch and d'Indy. Taught at Temple Univ., 1937–47; head of the music department at Hartt College of Music, Hartford, Conn., from 1948 to his death. Composed operas; a ballet; 2 symphonies and other orch. works; concertos; choral works; chamber music; piano and organ pieces; songs.

Freeman, Harry Lawrence (b. Cleveland, Ohio, 9 Oct. 1869; d. New York, 24 Mar. 1954). Conductor and composer. Orga-

most characteristic Frescobaldis imitatur wks [handwritten annotation]

nized and directed the Freeman School of Music, 1911–22, and the Freeman School of Grand Opera from 1923. Founded the Negro Opera Company, 1920. Composed numerous operas (incl. *The Octoroon*, 1904; *American Romance*, a jazz opera, 1927; *Voodoo*, 1928); songs.

Frei [G.]. Free, with freedom.

Freischütz, Der [G., The Freeshooter]. Opera in three acts by Weber (libretto by F. Kind), produced in Berlin, 1821. Setting: Bohemia, after the Seven Years' War. *Der Freischütz* marks the beginning of German romantic opera. See also under Melodrama.

Freitas Branco, Luís (b. Lisbon, 12 Oct. 1890; d. there, 26 Nov. 1955). Studied in Lisbon, in Berlin with Humperdinck, and in Paris with Grovlez. Teacher at the Lisbon Conservatory, 1916–39, and prolific writer and critic. Composed 5 symphonies and other works for orch.; choral works; chamber music; piano pieces; songs.

French harp. Older name for the mouth organ or *harmonica.

French horn. The *horn, as opposed to the English horn, which is a member of the *oboe family.

French overture. See under Overture; Suite.

French sixth. See Sixth chord.

French Suites. Six *suites for harpsichord by Bach, composed about 1720 (in Köthen). The name "French" (not by Bach) has little significance since French elements are present here no more than in the other suites of Bach and those of his German predecessors (Pachelbel, Froberger).

Frequency. See under Acoustics.

Frescobaldi, Girolamo (b. Ferrara, early Sept. 1583; d. Rome, 1 Mar. 1643). Organist and composer. Pupil of Luzzaschi. Organist at the Accademia di Santa Cecilia in Rome, 1604; visited Brussels and Antwerp, 1607–8. Organist at St. Peter's, Rome, from 1608 to his death, except for a period as court organist in Florence, 1628–34. His pupils incl. Froberger. Composed numerous works for

organ and for harpsichord, incl. collections of fantasias, ricercars, canzonas, toccatas, partitas, capriccios; other instrumental works; secular vocal works (incl. madrigals); sacred vocal works.

Fret [F. *touche*; G. *Bund*, pl. *Bünde*; It. *tasto*; Sp. *traste*]. A thin strip of material placed across the fingerboard of certain instruments (lute, guitar, viols, balalaika, banjo, and various Indian and Arab instruments) against which the strings are stopped. Formerly frets were made from pieces of catgut that were tied tightly around the neck. In more modern instruments they are narrow strips of wood or metal fixed on the fingerboard.

Frettevole, frettoso, frettoloso [It.]. Hurried.

Fricassée [F.]. *Quodlibet.

Fricker, Peter Racine (b. London, 5 Sept. 1920). Pupil of Seiber and R. O. Morris. Music director of Morley College, London, 1952–64. Member of the music faculty at the Univ. of California at Santa Barbara from 1964. Has composed a ballet, *Canterbury Prologue*, 1951; radio operas; film music; 4 symphonies and other orch. works (incl. *3 Scenes*, 1966); concertos for viola, for piano, for violin; choral works (incl. a Magnificat); works for voice with instruments (incl. *O longs desirs*, cycle for soprano and orch., 1963); chamber music (incl. a wind quartet, 1947); piano pieces (incl. *4 Sonnets*, 1955; *12 Studies*, 1961).

Friss, friszka. See *Csárdás; Verbunkos*.

Froberger, Johann Jakob (b. Stuttgart, bapt. 19 May 1616; d. Héricourt, France, 6 or 7 May 1667). Organist and composer. Pupil of his father, Basilius Froberger (1575–1637), a court musician in Stuttgart, and of Frescobaldi. Court organist in Vienna, 1637, 1641–45, and 1653–57. Toured as organist to Paris, London, and Brussels. Composed numerous harpsichord and organ pieces, incl. toccatas, fantasias, canzonas, fugues, ricercars, capriccios, partitas; harpsichord suites (a genre whose classical form he established).

Frog [Brit. *nut]. That portion of the *bow of a stringed instrument that is held in the player's hand and by means of which the tension of the hair is adjusted.

Fröhlich [G.]. Joyful.

From My Life [Cz. *Z mého života*]. Smetana's name for each of his two string quartets, in E minor (1876) and in D minor (1882), both of them autobiographical. Today the name is used particularly for the E-minor quartet.

From the New World. See *New World Symphony*.

Frosch [G.]. The *frog of the bow of a stringed instrument. See also *Am Frosch*.

Frottola [It.]. (1) Generic name for various types of Italian secular song of the late 15th and early 16th centuries. The *frottole* are often in a simple, essentially chordal style in three or four parts, with the upper part standing out as a melody. Since only the upper part has a text, they were probably performed as accompanied songs, the lower parts being played on instruments (viols, lute, harpsichord, etc.). However, purely vocal performance cannot be ruled out, particularly for the numerous examples written in a strictly *homorhythmic style. The *frottola* developed under the aegis of the courts of northern Italy, particularly at Mantua, where the two most outstanding composers of *frottole*, Marco Cara (d. *c*. 1530) and Bartolomeo Tromboncino (d. after 1535), worked under the patronage of Isabella d'Este. The late *frottole* are important forerunners of the *madrigal.

(2) Specifically, the *frottola* is one of the various poetic-musical types represented in the printer Petrucci's collections of *frottole*. This particular form was also known as a *barzelletta*. Others are the *capitolo, *villota, canzona [see Canzona (4)], oda*, and *strambotto. The *frottola* is a late offspring of the 14th-century *ballata.

Frullato [It.]. Flutter *tonguing.

Fry, William Henry (b. Philadelphia, 10 Aug. 1813; d. Santa Cruz, West Indies, 21 Sept. 1864). Music journalist and composer. Composed 4 operas (incl. *Leonora*, Philadelphia, 1845); symphonic works (incl. *Niagara*, 1854; *Santa Claus*, 1853); cantatas; a *Stabat Mater;* songs.

Frye, Walter (d. before 5 June 1475). English composer. Active in London from at least 1457. Perhaps at Ely for about ten years before that. Perhaps also active on the Continent, most of his works being preserved in Continental sources. Composed Masses and at least one motet; English and French secular polyphony.

Fuenllana, Miguel de (b. Navalcarnero, Madrid, *c*. 1500; d. probably in Valladolid, *c*. 1579). Vihuela virtuoso and composer, blind from birth. Served the Spanish royal court during the 1560s. Published *Libro de musica para vihuela entitulado Orphénica lyra*, 1554, containing original works for vihuela and arrangements for vihuela of vocal works by Franco-Flemish composers.

Fugato. A passage in fugal style that is part of a primarily nonfugal composition. Such passages frequently occur in the *development sections of symphonies, sonatas, and quartets.

Fuge tune, fuging tune. A form of hymn or psalm tune of English origin developed in New England during the late 18th and early 19th centuries. It commonly begins with a homophonic section, usually cadencing in the tonic and followed by a phrase in which the voices enter in succession (the order varies), which is in turn followed by a concluding homophonic phrase. It does not represent a crude attempt to write a real fugue. Among the most gifted of its composers were William Billings (1746–1800), Daniel Read (1757–1836), and Andrew Law (1749–1821).

Fughetta [It.]. A short fugue.

Fugue [F. *fugue;* G. *Fuge;* It., Sp. *fuga*]. A fugue is always written in contrapuntal style, i.e., with a texture consisting of a number of individual voices, usually three or four. It is based on a short melody, called the *subject* or *theme*, which is stated at the beginning by one voice alone and taken up ("imitated") by the other voices in close succession, reappearing throughout the piece in all the voices.

The first statement of the subject is in the tonic, and the second statement (by the second voice to enter) is at some different pitch level, usually the dominant. The third statement returns to the tonic, and the alternation continues until all voices have entered. In relation to one another, the first and second statements (and successive pairs of statements) are referred to as "subject and answer," or "antecedent and consequent," or *dux* (leader) and *comes* (follower). If the answer is an exact transposition of the subject, it is called a *real answer*. If it is modified in certain ways, it is called a *tonal answer* [see Tonal and real].

In each voice the space between one statement of the subject and the next is filled in by a freely invented counterpoint, which, however, is usually unified by recurrent motifs. These motifs are derived either from the subject itself, or, more usually, from its continuation, which forms the counterpoint to the first imitation (second statement) of the subject near the beginning of the fugue. Frequently, but not always, this continuation takes a rather definite form, almost equal to the subject in individuality and importance. When it does it is called a *countersubject;* it too reappears throughout the fugue but less rigidly than the main subject.

A section in which the theme appears at least once in each voice is called an *exposition*. Sometimes this term is restricted to the first exposition, with no special name applied to later sections of similar construction. A section of the fugue that does not include a statement of the subject is called an *episode*. Episodes are based chiefly on short motifs derived from the subject or its continuation (countersubject). The overall structure of a fugue is an alternation of expositions and episodes. The middle expositions usually involve modulations into other keys, such as the relative minor, dominant, or subdominant, with return to the main key in the last exposition. The fugue usually closes with a *coda, which often has a *pedal point.

Because of the wide variety of ways in which the elements of a fugue can be combined, it is preferable to see the fugue as a procedure rather than as a specific *form. Other techniques frequently encountered in fugues are *augmentation and diminution, *inversion, and *stretto. See also Counterfugue; Double fugue. The fugue's most important antecedents are the *ricercar and *canzona of the 16th and 17th centuries.

Reaching a peak in the works of J. S. Bach, the fugue is prominent also in the later works of Beethoven (e.g., piano sonatas op. 106, 110, and the string quartets op. 131, 133).

Fugue tune, fuguing tune. See Fuge tune.

Fuleihan, Anis (b. Kyrenia, Cyprus, 2 Apr. 1900; d. Stanford, Calif., 11 Oct. 1970). Pianist, conductor, and composer. Settled in the U.S., 1915. Professor at Indiana Univ., 1947–52. Director of the Beirut Conservatory, Lebanon, 1953–60. Composed an opera, *Vasco;* orch. works (incl. 2 symphonies; *Three Cyprus Serenades,* 1941; *Symphonie concertante* for string quartet and orch., 1940); concertos for piano, for cello, for viola, for violin, and for theremin; 5 string quartets and other chamber music; choral works; piano pieces; songs.

Fundamental, fundamental tone. The lowest tone, i.e., the bass note of a chord. Also, the first harmonic [see under Acoustics].

Fundamental bass [F. *basse fondamentale*]. In J. P. Rameau's theory, the root or roots of a chord or a succession of chords. Rameau used the *basse fondamentale* in order to demonstrate his then novel theory of chord *inversion.

Fundamentum [L.]. Title used by 15th- and 16th-century German composers for collections of pieces designed to teach composition of keyboard music. The most famous example (for organ) is Conrad Paumann's *Fundamentum organisandi* of 1452.

Fuoco, con [It.]. With fire.

Furiant. A rapid and fiery Bohemian dance, in 3/4 time, with frequently shifting accents. It has been used repeatedly by Dvořák (op. 12, *Dumka and Furiant;* op. 42, *Two Furiants;* also in his chamber music) and by Smetana (*The Bartered Bride; Czech Dances*).

Furlana. See *Forlana.*

Furniture stop. Mixture stop. See under Organ.

Fusa [L.; G. *Fusela, Fusel*]. See under Mensural notation.

Futurism. The term *futurismo* was introduced by the Italian writer Marinetti in 1909 to describe extreme radicalism in literature and in all the arts. His ideas were applied to music at least theoretically by Francesco Pratella in his *Musica futurista* (1912), a work for conventional instruments. A more striking manifestation of futurism was in the work of the painter Luigi Russolo, who advocated an "art of noises" that would treat all sounds as musical material and who composed works for various noisemakers (*intonarumori*) of his own invention.

Fux, Johann Joseph (Fuchs) (b. Hirtenfeld, Austria, 1660; d. Vienna, 13 Feb. 1741). Music theorist and composer. Or-

ganist at the Schottenkirche, Vienna, 1696–1702. *Kapellmeister* at St. Stephen's from 1705 and at the Viennese court (succeeding Ziani) from 1715. Wrote a very influential treatise on counterpoint, *Gradus ad Parnassum*, 1725. Composed 18 operas (incl. *Elisa*, Vienna, 1719; *Costanza e Fortezza*, Prague, 1723); oratorios; numerous orch. suites (incl. the *Concentus musico-instrumentalis*) and other instrumental works; sacred music (incl. *Missa canonica* and numerous other Masses; several Requiems; numerous psalms).

Fz. Abbr. for *forzando, forzato,* same as **sforzando* (*sf, sfz*).

G

G. See Pitch names; Letter notation; Hexachord. For G clef, see Clef.

Gabrieli, Andrea (b. Venice, probably in the period 1510–20; d. there, late 1586). Organist and composer. Pupil of Willaert and chorister under him at San Marco in Venice. Organist at San Geremia di Venezia in the 1550s; court musician in Bavaria, 1562. Second organist at San Marco from 1564 and first organist there (succeeding Merulo) from 1585. Among his pupils were his nephew Giovanni Gabrieli and H. L. Hassler. Composed motets (some polychoral), Masses, psalms, and other sacred vocal music; madrigals and other secular vocal music; choruses for Sophocles' *Oedipus Tyrannus;* works for organ and for instrumental ensembles, incl. canzonas, ricercars, fantasias, toccatas, and *intonationi.*

Gabrieli, Domenico (Gabrielli; "Menghino [diminutive of Domenico] dal violoncello") (b. Bologna, *c.* 1659; d. there, 10 July 1690). Cellist and composer. Pupil of Legrenzi. Member of the orchestra of San Petronio in Bologna from 1680; president of the Bologna Philharmonic Academy, 1683. Composed 12 operas; orato-

rios; cantatas; numerous solo and accompanied cello works, incl. ricercars and sonatas; pieces for string ensembles; motets.

Gabrieli, Giovanni (b. Venice, between 1554 and 1557; d. there, 12 Aug. 1612 or 1613). Organist and composer. Pupil of his uncle, Andrea Gabrieli. Musician at the Munich court under Lassus, 1575–79. Second organist at San Marco in Venice from 1585. His pupils incl. Schütz. Composed sacred vocal works, incl. motets (many of them polychoral and with instruments), Masses, Magnificats; madrigals; works for organ and for instrumental ensembles, incl. *intonationi,* canzonas, ricercars, toccatas, fantasias, and sonatas (incl. *Sonata pian e forte*).

Gaburo, Kenneth (Louis) (b. Somerville, N.J., 5 July 1926). Pupil of Bernard Rogers, Petrassi, and B. Phillips. Teacher at the Univ. of Illinois, 1955–68, and at the Univ. of California at San Diego from 1968. As founder of the New Music Choral Ensemble he has worked with expanded choral resources, including improvisation and elements of theater. Has composed operas; music for plays; *Lingua I–IV*, a six-hour theater, 1970; chamber music (incl. *Antiphony I* for strings and tape, 1957; *4 Inventions* for clarinet and piano, 1954; *Line Studies* for flute, clarinet, trombone, viola, 1957); electronic music; choral works; piano pieces; songs.

Gade, Niels (Wilhelm) (b. Copenhagen, 22 Feb. 1817; d. there, 21 Dec. 1890). Visited Leipzig, 1843–48, where he was Mendelssohn's assistant and later (1847) his successor in conducting the Gewandhaus concerts. Conductor of the Copenhagen Musical Society from 1850 and church organist in Copenhagen from 1851. Co-founder of the Copenhagen Conservatory, 1866. Composed ballets (incl. *Et Folkesagn*, 1853) and other stage works; 8 symphonies; overtures (incl. *Nachklänge von Ossian*, 1840) and other orch. works; a violin concerto, 1880; cantatas (incl. *Zion*, *c.* 1873; *Elverskud*, 1853); chamber music; pieces for piano and for organ; choral works; songs.

Gafori, Franchino (L. Franchinus Gafurius) (b. Lodi, 14 Jan. 1451; d. Milan, 24 June 1522). Music theorist and composer. Accompanied the Doge Prospero Adorno into exile in Naples, 1478, where he became a friend of Tinctoris. *Maestro di cappella* in the Milan Cathedral from 1484 to his death. Composed sacred music, incl. Masses, motets, Magnificats, hymns; several secular compositions. Wrote treatises on music, incl. *Practica musicae*, 1496, and *Theorica musicae*, 1492.

Gagaku [Jap.]. The orchestral music of the Japanese court, founded in the 8th century and preserved to the present day with little change. It also includes vocal pieces, and it may accompany a dance. The term *gagaku* is also used for a type of orchestral music of continental Asia, particularly China and Korea, which is the predecessor of the Japanese *gagaku*.

Gagliano, Marco da (b. Gagliano, Florence, *c.* 1575; d. Florence, 24 Feb. 1642). Founded the Accademia degli Elevati, 1607. *Maestro di cappella* at San Lorenzo in Florence from 1608 and at the Medici court from 1611. Composed operas (*La Dafne*, Mantua, 1608; *La*

Flora, Florence, 1628); Masses, motets, and other sacred music; madrigals.

Gagliard, gaillarde. See Galliard.

Gaita. See Bagpipe.

Gaitilla. A Spanish 17th-century organ stop with a nasal sound, in imitation of the gaita.

Gál, Hans (Johann) (b. Brunn, Vienna, 5 Aug. 1890). Music scholar, conductor, and composer. Taught at the Vienna Conservatory, 1918–29. Director of the Mainz Musikhochschule, 1929–33. Emigrated to England, 1938, and taught at the Univ. of Edinburgh, 1945–65. Has composed operas (incl. *Die heilige Ente*, Düsseldorf, 1923); 3 symphonies and other orch. works; concertos; chamber music; numerous sacred and secular choral works; piano pieces.

Galanterien [G.]. An 18th-century name for short entertaining pieces in homophonic (nonfugal) style, including airs, variations, dances. The term is used particularly for the more recent dances in the optional group of the *suite, such as the bourrée, passepied, gavotte.

Galilei, Vincenzo (b. Santa Maria a Monte, near Florence, *c.* 1520; d. Florence, buried 2 July 1591). Lutenist, theorist, and composer; father of the astronomer Galileo Galilei. Pupil of Zarlino. Served as theorist to the Florentine Camerata. Composed madrigals; songs with lute accompaniment; transcriptions and original pieces for lute. Wrote several important treatises on music theory, incl. the *Dialogo della musica antica et della moderna*, 1581.

Galindo (Dimas), Blas (b. San Gabriel, Jalisco, Mexico, 3 Feb. 1910). Pupil of Chávez, Rolón, Huízar, and Copland. Director of the Conservatorio nacional of Mexico from 1947. Has worked with native Mexican Indian materials. Has composed ballets; 3 symphonies and other orch. works (incl. *Obra para orquesta mexicana* for native instruments, 1938); concertos; cantatas; works for voice and orch.; chamber music; piano pieces; songs.

Gallant style [F. *style galant;* G. *galanter Stil*]. In the 18th century, the light, elegant style of the *rococo, as opposed to the serious, elaborate style of the *baroque. In part it resulted from the transition from a strict contrapuntal style to a freer, more homophonic style. This change is already evident in the harpsichord compositions of J. K. F. Fischer, F. Couperin, Telemann, and G. T. Muffat, as well as in the optional dances (minuets, bourrées, gavottes, etc.; see Galanterien) of Bach's suites.

Galliard [F. gaillarde; It. gagliarda; Sp. gallarda]. A gay, rollicking 16th-century dance of Italian origin. The music is characterized by a predominantly compound duple (6/8) meter interspersed with hemiola (3/4) measures. The dance step of the galliard is similar to that of the 16th-century *saltarello. Both use variations of the same basic five steps (*cinque-pace or cinq pas), the galliard being more vigorous. The music for the two dances is indistinguishable in style. Either dance is frequently coupled with a *pavane or a *passamezzo.

Galliard, Johann Ernst (John Ernest) (b. Zell, Hanover, c. 1680; d. London, 1749). Oboist and composer. Pupil of Steffani. Member of the Hanover court chapel from c. 1698. Musician to Prince George of Denmark in London from 1706. Composed operas (incl. Calypso and Telemachus, London, 1712); music for plays; The Hymn of Adam and Eve, after Milton, 1728; cantatas; anthems; pieces for flute and for cello.

Gallican chant. The French branch or "dialect" of plainsong of the medieval Western Church [see Chant]. It was in use in France until the introduction of the Roman chant and rite in the 8th century. Its liturgical structure has much in common with *Mozarabic and *Ambrosian chant.

Gallus, Jacobus (real name Handl, Händl, Hähnel) (b. Reifnitz, between 15 Apr. and 31 July 1550; d. Prague, 18 July 1591). Member of the Viennese court chapel, 1574. Kapellmeister to the Bishop of Olmütz, 1579–85. Imperial Kapellmeister at Prague from 1585 to his death. Composed sacred music, incl. Masses, motets, Passions.

Galop. A quick round dance of the mid-

19th century (c. 1825–75) with rhythms such as those shown in the illustration. It was executed with many changes of steps and hopping movements. Offenbach parodied it in his Orphée aux Enfers (1858). Liszt wrote a Grand galop chromatique (1838) and a Galop de bal (c. 1840).

Galoubet. See under Pipe (1).

Galuppi, Baldassare (called "il buranello") (b. Burano, near Venice, 18 Oct. 1706; d. Venice, 3 Jan. 1785). Pupil of Lotti. Second maestro di cappella at San Marco in Venice from 1748 and first maestro there, 1762–64. Maestro to the Russian imperial court, 1765–68. Director of the Conservatorio degli incurabili, 1762–64 and from 1768. Composed over 100 serious and comic operas (incl. L'arcadia in Brenta, Venice, 1749; Il filosofo di campagna, Venice, 1754; La diavolessa, Venice, 1755; Ifigenia in Tauride, St. Petersburg, 1768); oratorios; sacred music; numerous harpsichord sonatas and other instrumental works.

Gamba, gambe [G.]. Abbr. for *viola da gamba.

Gambang (saron). An Indonesian idiophone, consisting of a number of wood, bamboo, or metal bars resting on a large trough resonator. For ill. see under Percussion instruments.

Game of Cards, The. See Jeu de cartes.

Gamelan. Generic term for a wide variety of instrumental ensembles of Java and Bali, differing in size, function, and musical style. Each gamelan is a particular set of instruments and may have its own proper name. The instruments employed include varying sizes of hanging gongs (gong ageng, kempul), inverted kettles (kenong, ketuk, *bonang), instruments made of bronze slabs over resonators (*gendèr), and drums, as well as a xylophone (*gambang), an end-blown flute (suling), and a two-stringed, bowed instrument (rebab; see Rabāb) played by the leader. Each orchestral composition or gending consists of a fixed and unique melody that serves as a foundation for improvisation.

Gamma [Gr.]. In medieval theory, the lowest tone of the scale, G (an octave and a fourth below middle C) of the modern scale. In Guidonian terminology it was called *gamma-ut* [see under Hexachord], a term later used for "all the tones from gamma," i.e., the entire scale of the Guidonian system from G to e''. This meaning persists in the Italian *gamma* and the French *gamme* for scale, as well as in the English *gamut* for scale or range.

Gamme [F.]. *Scale. See under Gamma. *Gamme des physiciens* (i.e., of the physicists), the "natural" scale derived from just intonation.

Gamut. See under Gamma.

Gandini, Gerardo (b. Buenos Aires, 16 Oct. 1936). Pianist and composer. Pupil of Ginastera and Petrassi. Has taught at several Argentine schools; associated with the American Opera Center at Juilliard from 1970. Has composed a chamber opera, *La pasión de Buster Keaton*, 1972; orch. works; *Fantasie-impromptu* for piano and orch., 1970; concertinos; works for various instrumental ensembles (incl. *L'adieu* for piano, vibraphone, and percussion, 1967); piano pieces.

Ganze Note, ganze Pause [G.]. Whole note, whole-note rest. See Notes.

Ganzton [G.]. Whole tone. *Ganztonleiter*, whole-tone scale.

Gapped scale. A scale that is derived from a more complete system of tones by omitting some of them. Thus, the pentatonic scale is a gapped scale of the diatonic system, which in turn can be considered a gapped scale of the chromatic system.

Garant, Serge (b. Quebec City, Canada, 22 Sept. 1929). Pupil of Messiaen. Member of the faculty of the Univ. of Montreal from 1966. Has worked with techniques of total serialism. Works incl. *Ennéade* for orch., 1964; *Offrande I* for prerecorded soprano and instruments, 1969; *Cage d'oiseau* for soprano and piano, 1962; piano pieces.

Garbo, con; garbato [It.]. Graceful, elegant.

García, Manuel del Popolo Vicente (b. Seville, 21 Jan. 1775; d. Paris, 9 June 1832). Tenor and composer. Toured as a singer in Spain, France, Italy, England, the U.S., and Mexico. Close associate of Rossini, who wrote several parts for him. Composed numerous operas in Spanish, French, and Italian (incl. *L'amante astuto*, New York, 1825; *La figlia dell'aria*, New York, 1826); numerous ballets.

His three children were also musicians: Manuel Patricio Rodríguez García (b. Zafra, Spain, 7 Mar. 1805; d. London, 1 July 1906) taught singing at the Paris Conservatory and at the Royal Academy of Music in London; his pupils incl. Jenny Lind. Maria Felicità Malibran (b. Paris, 24 Mar. 1808; d. Manchester, 23 Sept. 1836) and Michelle-Ferdinande-Pauline Viardot-García (b. Paris, 18 July 1821; d. there, 18 May 1910) were singers and composers.

García Abril, Antón (b. Teruel, Spain, 19 May 1933). Pupil of Palau and Petrassi. Has taught at the Madrid Conservatory from 1957. Has composed a ballet; music for films, theater, and television; a concerto for strings, 1967; a piano concerto, 1963; vocal works; chamber music; piano pieces; songs.

García Caturla, Alejandro (b. Remedios, Cuba, 7 Mar. 1906; d. there, 12 Nov. 1940). Pupil of Sanjuán and N. Boulanger. Founder and conductor of the Orquesta de Conciertos de Caibarién, Cuba, from 1932. Worked with Afro-Cuban materials. Composed orch. works (incl. *3 danzas cubanas*, 1927; *La rumba*, 1933); choral works (incl. *Yamba-O*, with orch., 1931); works for voice with instruments; chamber music; piano pieces; songs.

Gardiner, Henry Balfour (b. London, 7 Nov. 1877; d. Salisbury, 28 June 1950). Studied at Oxford and with I. Knorr. Composed orch. works (incl. *Shepherd Fennel's Dance*, 1911); *News from Whydah* for chorus and orch., 1912; chamber music; piano pieces; songs.

Gardner, John (Linton) (b. Manchester, 2 Mar. 1917). Pupil of R. O. Morris. Teacher at the Royal Academy of Music from 1956. Has composed incidental music for the theater; operas (*The Moon and Sixpence*, London, 1957; *The Visi-*

tors, Aldeburgh, 1972); a symphony, 1951, and other orch. works; chamber music (incl. *Theme and Variations* for brass, 1951); sacred and secular choral works; piano pieces; songs.

Gaspard de la nuit [F.]. A set of three piano pieces by Ravel (1908) inspired by the collected poems of Bertrand, which were published under the same title (literally, Caspar of the Night, a nickname for Satan): (1) "Ondine," a water nymph; (2) "Le gibet" (gallows); (3) "Scarbo" (a goblin appearing in a hallucination).

Gasparini, Francesco (b. Camaiore, near Lucca, 5 Mar. 1668; d. Rome, 22 Mar. 1727). Pupil of Corelli and Pasquini. *Maestro del coro* at the Conservatorio della Pietà in Venice from *c.* 1700; *maestro di cappella* at the Lateran in Rome from 1725. His pupils incl. B. Marcello and D. Scarlatti. Composed numerous operas (incl. *Ambleto,* Venice, 1705; *Il più fedel fra i vassalli,* Venice, 1703); madrigals; Masses, motets, psalms, oratorios, and other sacred music. Published *L'armonico pratico al cimbalo,* 1708, a method for thoroughbass playing.

Gassmann, Florian Leopold (b. Brüx, Bohemia, 3 May 1729; d. Vienna, 20 Jan. 1774). Pupil of Padre Martini. Court composer in Vienna from 1764 and court *Kapellmeister* there (succeeding J. Reutter) from 1772. His pupils incl. Salieri. Composed numerous operas (incl. *Merope,* Venice, 1757; *Achille in Sciro,* Venice, 1766; *L'amore artigiano,* Vienna, 1767; *La contessina,* Neustadt and Vienna, 1770); an oratorio, *La Betulia liberata;* cantatas; numerous symphonies; chamber music; sacred music.

Gast, Peter (real name Johann Heinrich Köselitz) (b. Annaberg, Germany, 10 Jan. 1854; d. there, 15 Aug. 1918). Pupil of E. F. E. Richter. Close associate of Nietzsche. Composed operas (incl. *Der Löwe von Venedig,* first produced as *Die heimliche Ehe,* Danzig, 1891); a festival play, *Walpurgis,* 1903; orch. works; choral works; chamber music; songs.

Gastoldi, Giovanni Giacomo (b. Caravaggio; d. 1622). Singer at the Mantuan court, 1581. *Maestro di cappella* at Santa Barbara in Mantua, 1582, and in Milan, 1609. Composed *balletti* (the first published compositions of this genre); madrigals; *canzonette;* Masses, motets, psalms, and other sacred music.

Gathering note. In hymn singing, a note sounded by the organist as a signal to the congregation and in order to give the correct pitch of the hymn.

Gatty, Nicholas Comyn (b. Bradfield, near Sheffield, 13 Sept. 1874; d. London, 10 Nov. 1946). Conductor, organist, music critic, and composer. Pupil of Stanford. Composed operas (incl. *Greysteel,* London, 1906; *Duke or Devil,* London, 1909; *The Tempest,* after Shakespeare, London, 1920; *Prince Ferelon,* London, 1921); orch. works; *Ode on Time* for soloists, chorus, and orch., after Milton; chamber music; piano pieces; songs.

Gaubert, Philippe (b. Cahors, France, 3 July 1879; d. Paris, 8 July 1941). Pupil of Lenepveu. Professor of flute at the Paris Conservatory and conductor of its concerts from 1919. Conductor at the Paris Opéra from 1931. Composed operas; ballets; numerous symphonic works; a violin concerto; chamber music; songs; transcriptions for flute. Published several pedagogic works, incl. a *Méthode complète de flûte,* 1923.

Gaultier, Denis (b. probably at Marseille, 1597 or *c.* 1603; d. Paris, 1672). Lutenist and composer. Composed suites of stylized dances, often with fanciful titles, in the collections *La rhétorique des dieux* (the Hamilton codex), 1664–72; *Pièces de luth,* 1669; and *Livre de tablature,* 1672.

Gaveaux, Pierre (b. Béziers, France, 9 Oct. 1760; d. Charenton-le-Pont, near Paris, 5 Feb. 1825). Tenor and composer. Sang professionally in Paris, 1789–1812. Composed numerous musical dramas (incl. *L'amour filial,* Paris, 1792; *Le petit matelot,* Paris, 1796; *Léonore, ou L'amour conjugal,* on the libretto later translated for Beethoven, Paris, 1798; *Le bouffe et le tailleur,* Paris, 1804); a ballet, *L'amour à Cythère,* 1805; motets; romances.

Gaviniès, Pierre (b. Bordeaux, 11 May 1728; d. Paris, 8 Sept. 1800). Violinist and composer. Participant in the Concert spirituel from 1741 and its director (with Gossec and Leduc), 1773–77. Professor of violin at the newly founded Paris Conservatory from 1795 to his death. Composed *Les 24 matinées,* violin studies; violin concertos; sonatas for violin with bass, for violin with cello, and for 2 violins; a comic opera, *Le prétendu,* Paris, 1760; airs, incl. *Romance de Gaviniès.*

Gavotte. A French dance of the 17th century, said to be from the province of Dauphiné, in moderate 4/4 time, with an upbeat of two quarter notes, and with the phrases thus usually ending and beginning in the middle of a measure. Earlier examples, however, are frequently notated without upbeat. Bach often used it as one of the optional dances in his instrumental and keyboard *suites.

Gazzaniga, Giuseppe (b. Verona, 5 Oct. 1743; d. Crema, 1 Feb. 1818). Pupil of Porpora and Piccinni. Court musician in Munich and Dresden; later *maestro di cappella* at the Crema Cathedral, 1791 to his death. Composed numerous operas (incl. *Il finto cieco,* libretto by Da Ponte, Vienna, 1770; *Don Giovanni Tenorio, ossia Il convitato di pietra,* probably known to Mozart and Da Ponte, Venice, 1787); church music; a symphony; 3 piano concertos.

Gebrauchsmusik [G.]. A term originated in the 1920s (by Hindemith?) meaning "music for use," i.e., music intended for practical use by amateurs, in the home or at informal gatherings, as opposed to music written "for its own sake" and intended chiefly for concert performance by professionals.

Gebunden [G.]. *Legato.

Gedackt [Old G.]; **gedeckt** [G.]. Stopped. The former term is used for an organ register consisting of stopped pipes [see Organ], the latter for the modern "stopped" instruments, such as the clarinet [see Wind instruments].

Gédalge, André (b. Paris, 27 Dec. 1856; d. Chessy, 5 Feb. 1926). Theorist and composer. Pupil of Guiraud. Professor at the Paris Conservatory from 1905; his pupils incl. Ravel, Enescu, Ibert, Milhaud, Honegger, Koechlin, and Roger-Ducasse. Composed operas and other stage works; 4 symphonies; a piano concerto; chamber music; songs. Wrote pedagogic works, incl. a *Traité de la fugue,* 1900.

Gedämpft [G.]. Muted, muffled.

Gedehnt [G.]. Stretched out, slow.

Gefühlvoll [G.]. With feeling.

Gehalten [G.]. Held out, sustained.

Geheimnisvoll [G.]. Mysterious.

Gehend [G.]. Moving along, *andante.

Geige [G.]. *Violin; see also under Gigue (1). *Geigenwerk,* see Sostenente piano.

Geisslerlieder [G.]. German 14th-century monophonic songs that were sung during the penitential processions of the flagellants, particularly in the year of the Black Death, 1349. Melodically and structurally they anticipate to some degree the Lutheran chorale.

Geistertrio [G., Ghost Trio]. Popular name for Beethoven's Piano Trio in D major op. 70, no. 1; the name refers to the character of the second movement.

Geistlich [G.]. Sacred, réligious, spiritual. *Geistliche Konzerte* (as composed by Schütz and others) are concerted vocal and instrumental pieces for church use.

Gekkin. A Japanese guitar; see under Guitar family.

Gekoppelt [G.]. Coupled.

Gelassen [G.]. Quiet, calm.

Gelinek, Joseph (Jelinek) (b. Seltsch, Bohemia, 3 Dec. 1758; d. Vienna, 13 Apr. 1825). Pianist and composer. Pupil of Albrechtsberger. Pianist and chaplain to Prince Esterházy from 1795. Composed piano pieces, incl. fantasias, variations, sonatas, dances; violin sonatas.

Gemächlich [G.]. Comfortable, leisurely.

Gemässigt [G.]. Moderate.

Gemell. *Gymel.

Gemendo [It.]. Lamenting.

Gemessen [G.]. Restrained.

Geminiani, Francesco (Saverio) (b. Lucca, *c.* 1680?, bapt. 5 Dec. 1687; d.

Dublin, 17 Sept. 1762). Violinist and composer. Pupil of Corelli and A. Scarlatti. Active as a teacher and performer in London from 1714 and in Dublin from 1733. Composed violin and cello sonatas; trios; *concerti grossi;* transcriptions and arrangements for violin. Published one of the first violin methods, *The Art of Playing on the Violin,* 1730, and other didactic works.

Gemischte Stimmen [G.]. Mixed voices.

Gendèr. A Javanese metallophone, consisting of thin bronze slabs over resonating bamboo tubes.

Genera. Plural of L. **genus.*

General pause [G. *Generalpause*], abbr. *G.P.* In orchestral works, a rest for the entire orchestra.

Generalbass [G.]. **Thoroughbass.*

Genet, Elzéar. See Carpentras.

Genus [L.; pl. *genera*]. Kind, sort; specifically with respect to the **tetrachords* of ancient Greek music, of which there were three kinds: **diatonic, *chromatic,* and **enharmonic.* In the Renaissance, attempts were made to revive all three.

Genzmer, Harald (b. Blumenthal, near Bremen, 9 Feb. 1909). Pupil of Hindemith. Teacher at the Hochschule für Musik in Freiburg-im-Breisgau, 1946–57, and at the Hochschule für Musik in Munich from 1957. Has composed ballets; cantatas; symphonic works; concertos for numerous instruments, incl. the Trautonium; choral works; chamber music; piano and organ pieces; songs.

Georges, Alexandre (properly George) (b. Arras, 25 Feb. 1850; d. Paris, 18 Jan. 1938). *Maître de chapelle* at Sainte-Clotilde, Paris, where Franck was organist; from 1899, organist at Saint-Vincent-de-Paul. Composed operas (incl. *Charlotte Corday,* Paris, 1901; *Miarka,* Paris, 1905); oratorios; a mystery play; symphonic poems; a Mass, 2 Requiems, and other sacred music; chamber music; numerous songs (incl. *Chansons de Miarka,* 1899).

Gerhard, Roberto (b. Valls, Spain, 25 Sept. 1896; d. Cambridge, England, 5 Jan. 1970). Pupil of Pedrell and Schoen-berg. Emigrated to England, 1936. Taught at several English and U.S. schools. Worked with twelve-tone techniques. Composed an opera, *The Duenna,* after Sheridan, 1948, prod. Frankfurt, 1951; ballets (incl. *Don Quixote,* 1950); film music; incidental music for plays; an oratorio, *The Plague,* 1964; 4 symphonies and other orch. works (incl. a *Concerto for Orchestra,* 1965); concertos; chamber music (incl. *Leo* for 10 players, 1969, and other works with titles after signs of the Zodiac); works for voice with instruments (incl. *7 Hai-Ku,* 1922); piano pieces (incl. *Impromptus,* 1950); songs.

German, Edward (real name Edward German Jones) (b. Whitchurch, Shropshire, 17 Feb. 1862; d. London, 11 Nov. 1936). Pupil of Prout. Director of the Globe Theatre, 1888. Composed operas (incl. *Merrie England,* London, 1902); incidental music to plays; 2 symphonies and other orch. works; chamber music; sacred vocal music; piano and organ pieces; songs.

German flute. An 18th-century name for the transverse flute, as distinguished from the English flute, i.e., the recorder.

German Requiem, A. See *Deutsches Requiem, Ein.*

German sixth. See Sixth chord.

Gershwin, George (real name Jacob Gershvin) (b. Brooklyn, 26 Sept. 1898; d. Beverly Hills, Calif., 11 July 1937). Pupil of R. Goldmark, Cowell, and Schillinger. Composed musical comedies; an opera, *Porgy and Bess,* Boston, 1935; orch. works (incl. *Rhapsody in Blue* for piano and jazz orch., 1924; *An American in Paris,* 1928; *Cuban Overture,* 1932; a piano concerto in F, 1925; *Second Rhapsody* for piano and orch., 1931); numerous popular songs; film scores; piano pieces (incl. *3 Preludes,* 1936).

Gervaise, Claude (fl. Paris, mid-16th cent.). Composed chansons; several volumes of *Danceries,* containing 4- and 5-part arrangements of branles, pavanes, etc.

Ges, geses [G.]. G-flat, G-double-flat. See Pitch names.

Gesang [G.]. Song.

Gesangvoll [G.]. Songlike, cantabile.

Geschöpfe des Prometheus, Die [G., The Creatures of Prometheus]. Ballet by Beethoven, op. 43 (choreography by S. Vigano), produced in Vienna, 1801. It is remembered chiefly for its overture and for a theme in the finale that Beethoven used in three other compositions [see under *Eroica; Eroica* Variations].

Geschwind [G.]. Quick, nimble.

Gesteigert [G.]. Increased.

Gestopft [G.]. Stopped. See under Horn.

Gesualdo, Carlo (b. Naples, *c.* 1560; d. there, 8 Sept. 1613). Prince of Venosa; lutenist and composer. A friend of Tasso; probably a pupil of Nenna. Composed madrigals, some employing striking chromaticism; sacred music.

Geteilt [G.]. Divided. See *Divisi*.

Getragen [G.]. Sustained, slow.

Gewandhaus [G.]. See under Concert.

Gewöhnlich [G.]. Usual. An instruction to the player to return to the usual way of playing after a previous instruction to play in a special way, e.g., after an instruction to bow over the fingerboard.

Ghedini, Giorgio Federico (b. Cuneo, Piedmont, 11 July 1892; d. Nervi, near Genoa, 25 Mar. 1965). Pupil of Bossi. Taught at the Liceo musicale in Turin from 1918; at the Parma Conservatory, 1938–41; at the Milan Conservatory from 1941 and director there, 1951–62. Composed operas (incl. *Maria d'Alessandria,* Bergamo, 1937; *Billy Budd,* Venice, 1949; *L'ipocrita felice,* after Beerbohm, Milan, 1956); orch. works (incl. *Architetture,* 1940); concertos (incl. *Concerto dell'Albatro,* after Melville, for 8 solo instruments, orch., and speaker, 1945); sacred and secular vocal music; chamber music; songs; transcriptions of works by Bach, Monteverdi, and others.

Ghent, Emmanuel (b. Montreal, 15 May 1925). Psychiatrist and composer. Studied at McGill Univ. and with Shapey. Settled in New York, where he has taught psychology at New York Univ. and has been associated with the Columbia-Princeton Electronic Music Center

from 1966. Has composed works for various chamber ensembles; electronic music (incl. *Helices,* 1969).

Gherardello da Firenze (Gherardellus de Florentia) (fl. Florence; d. *c.* 1363). A composer of the generation of Landini in the flowering of 14th-century Italian polyphony. Works incl. a Gloria, an Agnus; a *caccia,* 5 *ballate,* and 10 madrigals. See *Ars nova.*

Ghiselin, Johannes (called Verbonnet) (b. *c.* 1455; d. perhaps in Bergen op Zoom, *c.* 1511). Member of the chapel of Ercole I d'Este in Ferrara, 1491–93 and occasionally thereafter. Composed Masses and motets; chansons and other secular polyphony, incl. perhaps an instrumental piece.

Ghost Trio. See *Geistertrio.*

Gianni Schicchi. See under *Trittico.*

Giannini, Vittorio (b. Philadelphia, 19 Oct. 1903; d. New York, 28 Nov. 1966). Pupil of R. Goldmark. Taught at the Juilliard (1939–66) and Manhattan (1941–66) schools of music and at the Curtis Institute (1956–66). Was the first director of the North Carolina School of the Arts. Composed operas (incl. *The Scarlet Letter,* Hamburg, 1938; *The Taming of the Shrew,* 1950, prod. on television, 1953); 4 symphonies and other orch. works; concertos for piano, for 2 pianos, and for organ; sacred and secular vocal music; chamber music; piano pieces; songs.

Gibbons, Christopher (b. London, bapt. 22 Aug. 1615; d. there, 20 Oct. 1676). Son of Orlando Gibbons. Organist at Winchester Cathedral from 1638; from 1660, organist of the Chapel Royal and Westminster Abbey and court organist to Charles II. Composed music for Shirley's masque *Cupid and Death* in collaboration with M. Locke; numerous string fantasies; several anthems.

Gibbons, Orlando (b. Oxford, bapt. 25 Dec. 1583; d. Canterbury, 5 June 1625). Organist of the Chapel Royal, 1605 to his death, and at Westminster Abbey from 1623. Royal chamber musician from 1619. Composed sacred music, incl. full and verse anthems, services, and psalms; madrigals; fantasies and other works for viols; compositions for virginals.

Gibbs, Cecil Armstrong (b. Great Baddow, near Chelmsford, 10 Aug. 1889; d. Chelmsford, 12 May 1960). Studied at Cambridge and at the Royal College of Music, where he later taught (1920–39). Composed operas (incl. *The Blue Peter*, 1924) and other stage works; 3 symphonies and other orch. works; choral works; chamber music; numerous songs.

Gideon, Miriam (b. Greeley, Colo., 23 Oct. 1906). Pupil of Saminsky and Sessions. Has taught at several schools, incl. Brooklyn College, City College of New York, the Jewish Theological Seminary, and the Manhattan School of Music. Has composed an opera, *Fortunato*, and other dramatic works; orch. works; choral works; works for voice with chamber ensemble (incl. *The Condemned Playground*, 1963; *Questions on Nature*, 1964; *Rhymes from the Hill*, 1968); chamber music; piano pieces; songs.

Gigault, Nicolas (b. Paris? 1624 or 1625; d. there, *c.* 1707). Organist at Saint-Nicolas-des-Champs in Paris from *c.* 1652. Composed a collection of works for organ.

Gigelira [It.]. *Xylophone.

Gigout, Eugène (b. Nancy, 23 Mar. 1844; d. Paris, 9 Dec. 1925). Organist, music critic, and composer. Pupil of Saint-Saëns at the École Niedermeyer in Paris, where he later taught, 1863–85 and 1900 –1905. Organist at Saint-Augustin from 1863. Founded an organ school in Paris, 1885. Professor at the Paris Conservatory, succeeding Guilmant, from 1911. Composed numerous organ works (incl. *Album grégorien*); sacred choral works; a piano sonata.

Gigue. (1) Medieval name for stringed instruments, perhaps specifically the rebab [see *Rabāb*]. Probably the German *Geige* [Old. G. *gîge*], violin, is derived from the French *gigue*. (2) In the suites of 1650–1750 the gigue [It. *giga*] is one of the four standard dance movements, usually the final one [see Suite; Dance music]. The gigue evolved from the 16th-century Irish or English *jig, which on the Continent developed differently in France and in Italy. The French type (Gaultier, Chambonnières) is characterized by compound duple time (6/8, 6/4), dotted rhythm, wide intervals (sixths, sevenths, octaves), and fugal writing, usually with the inverted subject [see Inversion (2)] used for the second section. The less common Italian type, the *giga,* is much quicker (presto gigue) and nonfugal, with running passages over a harmonic basis. This type occurs in the works of G. B. Vitali, Corelli, and Zipoli. The gigues in the suites of Froberger, Handel, and Bach are usually of the French type.

Gilbert, Henry Franklin Belknap (pseudonym Frank Belknap) (b. Somerville, Mass., 26 Sept. 1868; d. Cambridge, Mass., 19 May 1928). Pupil of Mac-Dowell. Associate of Farwell, whose Wa-Wan Press published his early works. Composed an opera; orch. works (incl. *The Dance in Place Congo*, 1906; *Comedy Overture on Negro Themes*, 1905; *Negro Rhapsody*, 1913; *Indian Sketches*, 1921); vocal works; piano pieces; songs and arrangements of folksongs.

Gilboa, Yaakov (Jacob) (b. Košice, Czechoslovakia, 2 May 1920). Settled in Tel Aviv, 1938. Pupil of Tal, Ben-Haim, and Stockhausen. Has composed works for voices with instruments (incl. *The Twelve Chagall Windows at Jerusalem,* 1964); works for various small instrumental ensembles; a theater piece; a violin sonata; piano pieces.

Gilchrist, William Wallace (b. Jersey City, N.J., 8 Jan. 1846; d. Easton, Penn., 20 Dec. 1916). Choirmaster at several Philadelphia churches; teacher at the Philadelphia Musical Academy from 1882. Composed 2 symphonies; cantatas; a Christmas oratorio; church music; chamber music; songs.

Gillis, Don (E.) (b. Cameron, Mo., 17 June 1912). Conductor and composer. Program arranger for the National Broadcasting Corporation in New York, 1944–54. Chairman of the arts division of Dallas Baptist College, 1968–72. At the Univ. of South Carolina from 1972. Has composed operas; a ballet; 12 symphonies (incl. No. 5 1/2, *Symphony for Fun,* 1947) and many other orch. works; band works; a cantata; 5 string quartets and other chamber music; piano pieces.

Gilson, Paul (b. Brussels, 15 June 1865;

d. there, 3 Apr. 1942). Pupil of Gevaert. Taught at the Brussels Conservatory, 1899–1909, and at the Antwerp Conservatory, 1904–9. Wrote musical criticism for several journals, incl. *Le soir.* Composed operas (incl. *Prinses Zonneschijn,* Antwerp, 1903); ballets (incl. *La captive,* 1902); symphonic works (incl. *La mer,* 1892); the oratorio *Francesca da Rimini,* 1894; choral works; band works; chamber music; piano pieces; songs. Published several pedagogical works on music theory.

Gimel. *Gymel.

Ginastera, Alberto (b. Buenos Aires, 11 Apr. 1916). Pupil of A. Palma. Organized (1962) and has directed the Center for Advanced Musical Studies at the Torcuato di Tella Institute in Buenos Aires. Has worked with microtonal and twelve-tone techniques since about 1960. Has composed operas (incl. *Don Rodrigo; Bomarzo,* Washington, D.C., 1967; *Beatrix Cenci,* Washington, D.C., 1971; *Barabbas,* New York, 1977); ballets (incl. *Panambí,* 1940); orch. works; concertos; *Cantata para América mágica* for soprano and percussion orch., 1960, *Turbae* for chorus and orch., 1976, the cantata *Bomarzo,* 1964, and other vocal works; string quartets and other chamber music; piano pieces; songs.

Gioconda, La. Opera in four acts by Ponchielli (libretto by A. Boito, based on V. Hugo's play), produced in Milan, 1876. Setting: Venice, 17th century.

Giocoso [It.]. Jocose, humorous.

Gioioso [It.]. Joyous, cheerful.

Giordani, Tommaso (b. Naples, *c.* 1730; d. Dublin, late Feb. 1806). Worked with his family's traveling opera company, touring on the Continent and in England. Conductor and composer at the King's Theatre, London, from 1769, and in Dublin theaters from 1783. Composed operas (incl. *La comediante fatta cantatrice,* London, 1756; *L'eroe cinese,* Dublin, 1766) and other music for the stage; cantatas; an oratorio; chamber music; concertos; piano pieces; songs.

Giordano, Umberto (Menotti Maria) (b. Foggia, 28 Aug. 1867; d. Milan, 12 Nov. 1948). Studied at the Naples Conserva-

tory. Composed operas (incl. *Andrea Chénier; Fedora,* Milan, 1898; *Siberia,* Milan, 1903; *Madame Sans-Gêne,* New York, 1915; *La cena delle beffe,* Milan, 1924); an overture; chamber music.

Giorgi flute. A flute invented by C. T. Giorgi (1888) that has finger holes for each chromatic tone, making cross fingering unnecessary. It was blown at the end rather than across the bore.

Giovanelli, Ruggiero (b. Velletri, 1560; d. Rome, 7 Jan. 1625). Pupil of Palestrina. *Maestro di cappella* at San Luigi de' Francesi in Rome, succeeding Nanino, from 1583, and at St. Peter's, succeeding Palestrina, from 1594. Member of the papal chapel from 1599; *maestro di cappella* there from 1614. Composed Masses, motets, psalms, and other sacred music; madrigals, *canzonette, villanelle.* Prepared a new edition of the Gradual, 1614–15.

Giovanni da Cascia (Johannes de Florentia) (b. probably near Florence; fl. 14th cent.). Organist at Santa Maria del Fiore in Florence. Served the court in Verona, 1329–51. Composed madrigals, *cacce, ballate,* etc.

Giraffe piano [G. *Giraffenklavier*]. An early 19th-century variety of piano, somewhat like the grand piano but with the wing-shaped part of the case put upright, thus vaguely resembling the neck of a giraffe.

Girl of the Golden West. See *Fanciulla del West, La.*

Giro [It.]. *Turn.

Gis, gisis [G.]. G-sharp, G-double-sharp. See Pitch names.

Giselle. Ballet by Adolphe-Charles Adam (choreography by Jean Coralli, based on a story by H. Heine), first produced in Paris, 1841.

Gitana, alla [It.]. In the gypsy style.

Gittern. See under Guitar family.

Giuliani, Mauro (Giuseppe Sergio Pantaleo) (b. Bisceglie, Bari, 27 July 1781; d. Naples, 8 May 1829). Settled in Vienna, 1806, where he became an associate of Hummel and Moscheles. Traveled on the Continent and to London as a guitarist. Composed numerous guitar works, incl. concertos and sonatas.

Giulio Cesare in Egitto [It., Julius Caesar in Egypt]. Opera in three acts by Handel (libretto by N. Haym), produced in London, 1724. Setting: Egypt, 48 B.C.

Giustiniana. See under *Villanella*.

Giusto [It.]. Just, right. *Tempo giusto,* fitting tempo or strict tempo.

Glanville-Hicks, Peggy (b. Melbourne, Australia, 29 Dec. 1912). Music critic and composer. Pupil of Vaughan Williams, Wellesz, and N. Boulanger. Lived in New York, 1942–59, and in Athens from 1959. Has composed ballets; operas (incl. *The Transposed Heads,* Louisville, Ky., 1954; *Nausicaa,* Athens, 1961); orch. works; *Etruscan Concerto* for piano and chamber orch., 1956; choral works; chamber music; songs; film music.

Glass, Philip (b. Baltimore, 31 Jan. 1937). Studied at the Univ. of Chicago and with Persichetti, Bergsma, and N. Boulanger. Has worked with amplified instruments. Works incl. *Music in Similar Motion,* 1969; *Music in Fifths,* 1969; *Music with Changing Parts,* 1970; *Music in 12 Parts,* 1973.

Glass harmonica. An instrument that Benjamin Franklin invented in 1763 and called "armonica." It consists of a series of glass basins of graded sizes fixed on a horizontal spindle, which is made to revolve by a treadle operated by the player's foot. The spindle is fitted into a trough filled with water so that the glasses are kept wet. [For ill. see under Percussion instruments.] The sound is produced by delicate rubbing of the fingers against the glasses. The instrument was extraordinarily popular, particularly in Germany and Austria. Among various compositions for the glass harmonica are Mozart's Adagio in C major (K. 356) for harmonica alone and Adagio and Rondo (K. 617) for harmonica, flute, oboe, viola, and cello, both composed in 1791. They seem to require an instrument equipped with a keyboard mechanism such as that constructed in 1784.

Glazunov, Alexander Konstantinovich (b. St. Petersburg, 10 Aug. 1865; d. Paris, 21 Mar. 1936). Pupil of Rimsky-Korsakov. Teacher at the St. Petersburg Conservatory from 1899 and its director, 1905–28. After 1928 he lived in Paris, touring Europe and North America as conductor of his own works. Composed ballets (incl. *Raymonda,* 1896; *The Seasons,* 1899); orch. works (incl. 8 symphonies; *Stenka Razin,* 1884, and other symphonic poems; overtures; suites); concertos for violin, for piano, for cello, for saxophone; choral works; chamber music (incl. 7 string quartets and 5 *Novelettes* for string quartet); piano pieces (incl. 2 sonatas); organ pieces; songs.

Gleason, Frederick Grant (b. Middletown, Conn., 17 Dec. 1848; d. Chicago, 6 Dec. 1903). Music critic and composer. Pupil of Buck. Church organist in Connecticut; director of the Chicago Auditorium Conservatory, 1900 to his death. Composed operas (incl. *Otho Visconti,* Chicago, 1907); orch. works; chamber music; organ and piano pieces; vocal works; Episcopal services.

Glee. An 18th-century genre of English choral music, unaccompanied, in three or more parts, for solo men's voices (including a male alto), comparatively brief, sectionally constructed, and homophonic (chordal) rather than polyphonic. In the latter part of the century, societies including both amateur and professional members devoted themselves to composing and performing glees. During the first half of the 19th century glee singing was much in vogue, but in time its best qualities merged with the part song. Among the most celebrated glee writers were Benjamin Cooke (1734–93); Samuel Webbe (1740–1816); Stephen Paxton (1735–87); and John Callcott (1766–1821). In American colleges and universities, glee clubs have at times tended toward light entertainment and at times concentrated on more serious music.

Gleichmässig [G.]. Even, regular.

Gli scherzi. See *Scherzi, Gli*.

Glière, Reinhold Moritzovich (b. Kiev, 11 Jan. 1875 [old style 30 Dec. 1874]; d. Moscow, 23 June 1956). Pupil of Taneiev, Arensky, and Ippolitov-Ivanov. Director of the Kiev Conservatory, 1914–20. Teacher at the Moscow Conservatory,

1920–41. His pupils incl. Prokofiev and Miaskovsky. Composed the opera *Shah-Senem*, Baku, 1934; ballets (incl. *The Red Poppy*, 1927); incidental music for plays; orch. works (incl. 3 symphonies, the 3rd titled *Ilya Murometz*, 1911; *The March of the Red Army*, 1924); concertos for cello, for horn, for harp, for violin; 4 string quartets and other chamber music; piano pieces; songs.

Glinka, Mikhail Ivanovich (b. Novosspaskoye, Smolensk, 1 June 1804; d. Berlin, 15 Feb. 1857). Studied first in St. Petersburg and later in Italy and Berlin; traveled widely in Russia and Western Europe. Composed operas (*A *Life for the Czar; *Russlan and Ludmilla*); a ballet; other works for the theater; orch. works (incl. *Kamarinskaya*, 1848; *Jota aragonesa*, 1845; *Summer Night in Madrid*, 1848); choral works; chamber music; piano pieces; songs; church music.

Glissando [It.; abbr. *gliss.*]. (1) The execution of rapid scales by a sliding movement. In piano playing, the nail of the thumb or of the third finger is drawn rapidly over the white keys or the black keys. A similar technique is much used on the harp. (2) On stringed instruments such as the violin and on wind instruments (particularly though not exclusively the slide trombone), a continuous sliding of pitch from one pitch to another. It is frequently notated by a straight or wavy line drawn between two pitches. See also *Portamento.

Globokar, Vinko (b. Anderny, France, 7 July 1934). Trombonist and composer. Studied at the Ljubljana Conservatory, at the Paris Conservatory, and with Leibowitz and Berio. Teacher at the Musikhochschule in Cologne from 1968. Works incl. *Voie* for 3 choruses and 3 orch. groups, 1966; *Etude pour folklora II* for orch., 1968; *Correspondences* for 4 instrumentalists, 1969; *Discours III* for 5 oboes, 1969.

Glocke [G.]. Bell.

Glockenspiel. See Percussion instruments I, 2. The portable glockenspiel of military bands consists of steel bars fixed on a frame in the shape of the ancient Greek lyre; hence the name "bell lyre"

[G. *Lyra*]. In German the word *Glockenspiel* [lit. bell-play] is also used for a set of bells, i.e., a *carillon.

Gloria (in excelsis) [L.]. The second item of the Ordinary of the *Mass, also known as the Greater *Doxology. In plainsong the first phrase, "Gloria in excelsis Deo" (Glory to God in the highest), is sung by the officiating priest, and the chorus enters at "Et in terra pax" (And peace on earth). Early (15th- and 16th-century) polyphonic settings of the Gloria therefore begin with the latter phrase.

Gloria Patri. See Doxology.

Glosa [Sp.]. A 16th-century name used for *diminutions [see also Ornamentation]. Cabezón uses the term for simple figurative variations of harmonized psalm tones (*fabordón y glosas*), while more elaborate variations are called *diferencias*.

Gluck, Christoph Willibald (b. Erasbach, Upper Palatinate, 2 July 1714; d. Vienna, 15 Nov. 1787). Pupil of Sammartini. Traveled widely as a composer, chiefly of operas, working in London, where he met Handel, 1745–46; in Germany; in Vienna; in Paris, where he was the rival of Piccinni, 1773–79. In collaboration with the librettist Ranieri Calzabigi he undertook to reform Italian *opera seria* [see Opera]. Composed numerous operas (incl. *Semiramide riconosciuta; *Orfeo ed Euridice; La rencontre imprévue*, Vienna, 1764; *Alceste; Paride ed Elena*, Vienna, 1770; *Iphigénie en Aulide; Armide*, Paris, 1777; *Iphigénie en Tauride*); ballets (incl. *Don Juan*, Vienna, 1761); orch. works; sacred music (incl. a *De profundis* for chorus and orch.); chamber music; songs.

Glückliche Hand, Die [G., The Lucky Hand]. Monodrama in one act by Schoenberg (to his own libretto), published in 1913, first performed in Vienna, 1924.

Gnessin, Mikhail Fabianovich (b. Rostov-on-the-Don, 2 Feb. 1883; d. Moscow, 5 May 1957). Pupil of Rimsky-Korsakov, Liadov, and Glazunov. Visited Palestine, 1914, to study Jewish music, elements of which were incorporated in a number of his works. He later lived as teacher and composer in Moscow and Leningrad. His pupils incl. Khachaturian. Composed music for plays; operas (incl. *Abraham's Youth*, 1923); orch. works; chamber music; vocal works; piano pieces; arrangements of Jewish folksongs.

G.O. In French organ music, abbr. for *grand orgue*, i.e., great *organ.

Godard, Benjamin (-Louis-Paul) (b. Paris, 18 Aug. 1849; d. Cannes, 10 Jan. 1895). Pupil of Reber. Taught at the Paris Conservatory from 1887. Composed operas (incl. *Jocelyn*, Brussels, 1888); symphonies; concertos for violin and for piano; choral works (incl. *Le Tasse*, 1878); incidental music for plays; chamber music; numerous piano pieces; songs.

Godowsky, Leopold (b. Soshly, near Vilna, 13 Feb. 1870; d. New York, 21 Nov. 1938). Pianist and composer. Pupil of Saint-Saëns. Taught in the U.S., 1890–1900, and at the Vienna Academy of Music, 1909–14. Settled permanently in the U.S., 1914. Composed numerous works for piano (incl. *Triakontameron; 53 Studies on Chopin's Etudes*); chamber music.

Goehr, Alexander (b. Berlin, 10 Aug. 1932). Studied at the Royal Manchester College of Music and was a pupil of Messiaen in Paris. His family settled in England, 1933. Has taught at the New England Conservatory, at Yale Univ., at the Univ. of Leeds from 1971, and at Cambridge Univ. from 1976. Founded the Music Theatre Ensemble. Has composed an opera, *Arden muss sterben*, Hamburg, 1967; *Triptych*, three theater pieces, 1968–70; cantatas (incl. *The Deluge*, 1958); orch. works; chamber music; a violin concerto, 1962; piano pieces; works for voice with instruments.

Goetz, Hermann Gustav (b. Königsberg, Prussia, 7 Dec. 1840; d. Hottingen, near Zürich, 3 Dec. 1876). Organist, music critic, and composer. Pupil of J. Stern and H. von Bülow. Organist and teacher in Switzerland from 1863. Composed operas (incl. *Der Widerspenstigen Zähmung* [The Taming of the Shrew], Mannheim, 1874); incidental music for the the-

ater; a symphony; a piano concerto and a violin concerto; choral works (incl. *Nänie*); chamber music; piano pieces; songs.

Goeyvaerts, Karel (August) (b. Antwerp, 8 June 1923). Pupil of Messiaen and Milhaud. Worked at the Electronic Music Studio of the German Radio in Cologne. Teacher at the Antwerp Music Academy, 1950–57, and at the Antwerp Conservatory from 1966. Has employed serial and electronic techniques. Works incl. a sonata for 2 pianos, 1951; a violin concerto; *Composition No. 5*, on tape, 1953; *Messe Johannes XXIII* for chorus and 10 winds, 1968.

Goldberg Variations. A series of 30 variations by J. S. Bach, commissioned by the Russian Count Kayserling and named after Bach's pupil, Johann Gottlieb Goldberg (c. 1727–56), who was in the count's service as a harpsichordist. Bach published them in the fourth part of the *Clavier-Übung* (1742). The plan is two variations in free style (frequently of a highly virtuosic character) followed by a canonic variation (nos. 3, 6, 9, etc.); the final variation is a *quodlibet.

Golden Cockerel, The [Rus. *Zolotoy Pyetushok;* F. *Le coq d'or*]. Opera-ballet in three acts by Rimsky-Korsakov (libretto by V. I. Byelsky, based on a fairy tale by Pushkin), produced in Moscow, 1909, one year after the composer's death.

Goldmark, Karl (Károly) (b. Keszthely, Hungary, 18 May 1830; d. Vienna, 2 Jan. 1915). Violinist, music critic, choral director, and piano teacher in Budapest and Vienna. Composed operas (incl. *Die Königin von Saba*, Vienna, 1875); symphonies (incl. *Rustic Wedding*), overtures (incl. *Sakuntala*, 1865), and other orch. works; 2 violin concertos; choral works; chamber music; piano pieces; songs.

Goldmark, Rubin (b. New York, 15 Aug. 1872; d. there, 6 Mar. 1936). Nephew of Karl Goldmark. Pupil of Dvořák. Taught composition at the Juilliard School of Music, 1924 to his death. His pupils incl. Copland, Gershwin, Jacobi, and Wagenaar. Composed orch. works (incl. *Hiawatha*, 1900; *Samson*, 1914; *A Negro Rhapsody*, 1923; *Requiem Suggested by*

Lincoln's Gettysburg Address, 1919); chamber music; songs.

Golestan, Stan (b. Vaslui, Rumania, 26 May 1875; d. Paris, 22 Apr. 1956). Pupil of d'Indy, Roussel, and Dukas. Served as critic for *Le Figaro* and teacher at the École normale in Paris. Worked with native Rumanian musical materials. Composed orch. works (incl. *Rhapsodie roumaine*); concertos; chamber music; piano pieces; vocal works (incl. *10 chansons populaires roumaines,* 1909).

Goliard songs. Latin poems of the 10th to 13th centuries written by goliards, wandering students or young ecclesiastics who played an important part in the cultural life of that period.

Gombert, Nicolas (b. probably in Flanders, late 15th cent.; d. *c.* 1556). Pupil of Josquin des Prez. Master of the choirboys to Charles V, *c.* 1526–40. Composed Masses, numerous motets, chansons.

Gomes, Antonio Carlos (b. Campinas, Brazil, 11 July 1836; d. Pará, Belém, Brazil, 16 Sept. 1896). Studied in Rio de Janeiro and Milan. Composed numerous operas (incl. *Il Guarany,* Milan, 1870); a cantata, *Colombo,* 1892, and other vocal works; piano pieces; songs.

Gomólka, Mikolaj (b. Sandomierz, Poland, *c.* 1535; d. after 1591). Chorister in Cracow, 1545, then court instrumentalist there. Returned to settle in Sandomierz, 1566. Composed a collection of settings of Polish translations from the Psalms, *Melodiae ná psalterz polski,* 1580.

Gong. See under Percussion instruments II, 7.

Goossens, Eugene (b. London, 26 May 1893; d. there, 13 June 1962). Conductor and composer. Pupil of Stanford. Conducted the Rochester Philharmonic Orchestra, 1923–31, and the Cincinnati Symphony Orchestra, 1931–46. Director of the New South Wales Conservatory and conductor of the Sydney Symphony Orchestra, 1947–56. Composed a ballet; operas (*Judith,* London, 1929; *Don Juan de Mañara,* London, 1937); incidental music for the theater; an oratorio; orch. works, incl. 2 symphonies; an oboe concerto and a piano concerto; chamber music; choral works; piano pieces; songs.

Gopak, hopak. A lively dance of Byelorussia in duple time. A well-known example is in Mussorgsky's unfinished opera *The Fair at Sorochinsk.*

Górecki, Henryk Mikolaj (b. Czernica, Poland, 6 Dec. 1933). Studied in Katowice. Has worked with serial and aleatory techniques. Has composed orch. works (incl. *Symphonia 1959*); vocal works; chamber music; piano and organ pieces.

Gorgia [It.]. Generic term for the art of improvised ornamentation, particularly as practiced *c.* 1600 in the performance of madrigals, motets, etc. *Gorgheggio* is a modern term for very rapid vocal passages.

Goss, John (b. Fareham, England, 27 Dec. 1800; d. London, 10 May 1880). Organist and composer. Pupil of Attwood, whom he succeeded as organist of St. Paul's Cathedral, 1838–72. Composer to the Chapel Royal from 1865. Composed church services, anthems, and other sacred music; an overture; songs and glees.

Gossec, François-Joseph (b. Vergnies, Belgium, 17 Jan. 1734; d. Paris, 16 Feb. 1829). Boy chorister at the Antwerp Cathedral, 1743–51. Director of the Concert des amateurs from 1769 and of the Concert spirituel in Paris, with Gaviniès and Leduc, 1773–77. Teacher at the Paris Conservatory from its founding in 1795. Composed operas (incl. *Les pêcheurs,* Paris, 1766; *Toinon et Toinette,* Paris, 1767); a ballet, *Mirza,* 1779; sacred choral works (incl. a *Te Deum* requiring hundreds of singers and instrumentalists; a *Messe des morts*); revolutionary hymns (incl. *Chant du 14 juillet*); over 30 symphonies; chamber music; pedagogic works.

Gothic music. A term used to denote music contemporary with or culturally related to the Gothic era in architecture, sculpture, and painting. It is usually understood to embrace the period from 1150 (Perotinus) to 1450 (Dufay), that is, before the beginning of the *Renaissance.

Gotovac, Jakov (b. Split, Yugoslavia, 11 Oct. 1895). Pupil of J. Marx. Conductor and chorus master of the Croatian National Theater, Zagreb, 1923–58. Has composed operas (incl. *Morana,* Brno, 1930; *Ero the Joker,* Zagreb, 1935); incidental music for the theater; orch. works (incl. *Symphonic Kolo,* 1926); choral works (incl. *Koleda,* 1925); songs.

Götterdämmerung. See *Ring des Nibelungen, Der.*

Gottschalk, Louis Moreau (b. New Orleans, 8 May 1829; d. Rio de Janeiro, 18 Dec 1869). Toured widely in Europe and North and South America as a pianist and conductor of his own works. Composed 2 operas; works for orch. (incl. *La nuite des tropiques; Escenas campestres cubanas*); numerous piano pieces (incl. *Bamboula*); songs.

Goudimel, Claude (b. Besançon, *c.* 1514; d. Lyon, late Aug. 1572, in the St. Bartholomew massacre). Associate of the Parisian publisher Du Chemin. Composed 2 settings of the psalter translations of Marot and de Bèze, 1564 and 1565; Masses, motets, and other sacred music; sacred and secular chansons; settings of the odes of Horace.

Gould, Morton (b. Richmond Hill, N.Y., 10 Dec. 1913). Conductor, pianist, and composer. Worked for the Columbia Broadcasting System from 1943. Has composed ballets (incl. *Interplay,* 1943; *Fall River Legend,* 1947); musical comedies; orch. works (incl. *Symphony of Spirituals,* 1976, and other symphonies; *Foster Gallery,* 1940; *Venice,* 1966; *Jekyll and Hyde Variations,* 1955; *Declaration,* with chorus and speakers, 1956); concertos; band works (incl. *Derivations,* 1956); chamber music; piano pieces; film scores.

Gounod, Charles François (b. Paris, 17 June 1818; d. there, 18 Oct. 1893). Pupil of Halévy, Lesueur, Paër, and Reicha. Conductor of the Orphéon choral society in Paris, 1852–60. Organized and directed Gounod's Choir in London, 1872–74. Composed operas (incl. **Faust; Philémon et Baucis,* Paris, 1860; *Mireille,* Paris, 1864; *Roméo et Juliette,* Paris, 1867; *Le médecin malgré lui,* Paris, 1858); incidental music for the the-

ater; orch. works; much sacred music (incl. motets, Masses; Requiems; *La rédemption,* a trilogy for soloists, chorus, and orch., 1881); chamber music; piano and organ pieces; numerous songs.

Goyescas. Two sets of piano pieces by Enrique Granados (1911), inspired by etchings of Francisco Goya (1746–1828). Granados also wrote an opera *Goyescas* (1916) that includes material from the piano pieces.

G.P. In orchestral scores, abbr. for *general pause or the German equivalent, *Generalpause.* In French organ music, abbr. for *grand positif,* i.e., great and choir *organ coupled.

G.R. In French organ music, abbr. for *grand récitatif,* i.e., great and swell *organ coupled.

Gr. Fl. [G.]. Abbr. for *Grosse Flöte,* the ordinary flute.

Gr. Tr. [G.]. Abbr. for *Grosse Trommel,* bass drum.

Grabovsky, Leonid Alexandrovich (b. Kiev, 28 Jan. 1935). Pupil of Liatoshinsky. Has taught at the Kiev Conservatory and composed for film studios there. Works incl. *4 Ukranian Songs* for chorus and orch., 1959; pieces for orch.; chamber music; piano pieces.

Grace. Term used by early English musicians for any musical ornament, whether written out in notes, indicated by sign, or improvised by the performer.

Grace note. A note printed in small type to indicate that its time value is not counted in the rhythm of the bar and must be subtracted from that of an adjacent note. Large groups of grace notes sometimes represent an exception to this rule in that together they fill up the time value of a single note that has been omitted from the score (as in works by Chopin and others), in which case the rhythm of the grace notes is flexible and not subject to a strict beat. See also Appoggiatura; Appoggiatura, double; Ornamentation.

Gradatamente [It.]. Gradually.

Gradevole [It.]. Pleasant, pleasing.

Gradual [L. *graduale*]. (1) The second item of the Proper of the *Mass. The Graduals are responsorial chants (whence the term *responsorium graduale*), consisting of respond and verse [for the full form, see Psalmody II]. They have highly florid melodies, usually including long melismas in the respond as well as in the verse. (2) The *liturgical book containing the musical items of the Mass, as distinguished from the *antiphonal. Originally the gradual was called *antiphonale missarum*.

Gradus ad Parnassum [L., Steps to Parnassus (a mountain sacred to Apollo and the Muses)]. Title of a treatise on counterpoint by J. J. Fux (1725) and a collection of piano etudes by M. Clementi (1817).

Graener, Paul (b. Berlin, 11 Jan. 1872; d. Salzburg, 13 Nov. 1944). Teacher at the Royal Academy of Music in London, 1897–1902. Director of the Mozarteum in Salzburg, 1910–13. Teacher at the Leipzig Conservatory, 1920–24. Director of the Stern Conservatory in Berlin, 1930–34. Composed operas (incl. *Friedemann Bach*, 1931); orch. works (incl. *Schmied Schmerz*, symphony; *Variationen über ein russisches Volkslied*); concertos; choral works; chamber music; songs.

Grainger, Percy (Aldridge) (b. Brighton, Australia, 8 July 1882; d. White Plains, N.Y., 20 Feb. 1961). Pupil of I. Knorr. Close associate of Grieg. Toured England, South Africa, and Australia as a pianist from 1900; settled in the U.S., 1914. Taught at the Chicago Musical College, 1919–31, and at New York Univ., 1932–33. Active in collecting and arranging British folksongs, incorporating them in many of his works. He worked on the development of an electronic instrument for the realization of "free music" employing microtones and free rhythms. Composed orch. works (incl. *Shepherd's Hey*, 1913); band works (incl. *Lads of Wamphray*, 1905); choral works; chamber music (incl. *Handel in the Strand*, 1913; *Free Music* for string quartet, 1935); piano pieces; songs.

Gram, Hans (fl. late 18th cent.). Studied in Stockholm. Settled in Boston before 1790; served as organist of the Brattle Street Church. Composed *The Death Song of an Indian Chief*, for voice with orch., publ. 1791; *Sacred Lines for Thanksgiving Day;* co-edited *The Massachusetts Compiler*, a work on psalmody.

Gran cassa, gran tamburo [It.]. Bass drum.

Granados, Enrique (b. Lérida, Spain, 27 July 1867; d. at sea, 24 Mar. 1916). Pianist and composer. Pupil of Pedrell. Composed operas (incl. *Goyescas*, New York, 1916; *María del Carmen*, Madrid, 1898); symphonic poems and other orch. works (incl. *Intermezzo* from *Goyescas*, 1911); chamber music; piano pieces (incl. *Danzas españolas*, 1898; *Goyescas*, 1911); songs (incl. the collections *Tonadillas en estilo antiguo* and *Canciones amatorias*).

Grand [F.]. *Grand jeu, grand orgue*, great *organ; grand opéra*, an *opera (always serious) with fully composed text, as distinct from *opéra comique*.

Grandezza, con; grandioso [It.]. With grandeur, grandiose.

Grandi, Alessandro (b. Sicily, *c*. 1577; d. Bergamo, 1630). *Maestro di cappella* at the Accademia della morte in Ferrara, 1597–1604, and at the Accademia dello Spirito Santo there from 1604. Second *maestro di cappella* at San Marco, Venice, from 1620. *Maestro di cappella* at Santa Maria Maggiore in Bergamo, from 1627. Composed motets, psalms, and other sacred works; secular works, incl. madrigals and a collection of *Cantade et arie* (1620) containing strophic bass arias.

Graun, Johann Gottlieb (b. Wahrenbrück, near Dresden, 1702 or 1703; d. Berlin, 27 Oct. 1771). Brother of Karl Heinrich Graun. Pupil of Tartini. *Konzertmeister* from 1726 in Merseburg; court *Konzertmeister* to the Crown Prince Frederick (later Frederick the Great) from 1732 in Rheinsburg and from 1741 (to the King) in Berlin. Composed numerous symphonies, overtures, violin concertos, and *concerti grossi;* harpsichord concertos; cantatas and other vocal works; trio sonatas, string quartets, and other chamber music; sacred music; songs.

Graun, Karl Heinrich (b. Wahrenbrück, near Dresden, 1703 or 1704; d. Berlin, 8 Aug. 1759). Brother of Johann Gottlieb Graun. Court musician in Brunswick from 1725. Chamber musician to the Crown Prince Frederick from 1735 at Rheinsburg and *Kapellmeister* to Frederick (now King) from 1740 in Berlin, where he organized an opera company with singers he brought from Italy. Composed operas (incl. *Montezuma,* on Frederick's libretto, 1755); sacred works (incl. *Der Tod Jesu,* Passion oratorio, 1755; a *Te Deum*); sacred and secular cantatas; instrumental works, incl. concertos for harpsichord and for flute, a *concerto grosso,* trio sonatas, and other chamber music; organ pieces.

Graupner, Christoph (b. Kirchberg, Saxony, 13 Jan. 1683; d. Darmstadt, 10 May 1760). Pupil of Heinichen and Kuhnau. Vice *Kapellmeister* in Darmstadt from 1709 and *Kapellmeister* there from 1712 to his death. Composed operas (incl. *Dido,* Hamburg, 1707; *La costanza vince l'inganno,* Darmstadt, 1719); secular cantatas; overtures; symphonies; concertos; chamber music; numerous sacred works, incl. an enormous quantity of church sonatas.

Graupner, Johann Christian Gottlieb (b. Verden, near Hanover, 6 Oct. 1767; d. Boston, 16 Apr. 1836). Oboist in Haydn's orchestra in London, 1791. Settled in the U.S., *c.* 1795. In Boston, he ran a music store, taught, organized the Boston Philharmonic Society, built and repaired instruments, and worked as a theater oboist. In 1815, co-founder of what later became the Handel and Haydn Society. Works incl. an oboe concerto.

Grave [It.]. Grave, solemn.

Gravicembalo [It.]. Italian 17th-century name for the harpsichord, possibly for one of large size used especially for orchestral accompaniment. The name may be a corruption of *clavicembalo,* or it may refer to the presence of a "grave" 16-foot stop.

Great Fugue. See *Grosse Fuge.*

Greater perfect system. In the music theory of ancient Greece, the diatonic pitches from A through a', made up of

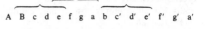

two pairs of conjunct *tetrachords separated by a tone, plus an added bottom tone (A), as in the accompanying table.

Grechaninov, Alexander Tikhonovich (b. Moscow, 25 Oct. 1864; d. New York, 3 Jan. 1956). Pupil of Arensky and Rimsky-Korsakov. Teacher at the Gnessin Music School in Moscow until 1922. Settled in Paris, 1925; in New York, 1939. Composed operas (incl. *Dobrinya Nikitich,* Moscow, 1903); incidental music for plays; orch. works, incl. 5 symphonies; vocal works, many of them sacred (incl. *Missa Oecumenica* for soloists, chorus, and orch., 1944); chamber music; piano pieces; songs.

Green, Ray (b. Cavendish, Mo., 13 Sept. 1909). Pupil of Bloch. Music director and manager for the May O'Donnell Dance Company in New York, 1940–61. Founder of the publishing firm American Music Edition, 1951. Has composed symphonies and other orch. works; a violin concerto; numerous band pieces; dance scores for May O'Donnell, Martha Graham, José Limón; choral works; chamber music; piano pieces; songs.

Greene, Maurice (b. London, *c.* 1695; d. there, 1 Dec. 1755). Choirboy under J. Clarke at St. Paul's Cathedral, London, and organist there from 1718. Organist and composer to the Chapel Royal from 1727. Taught at Cambridge Univ. from 1730. Master of the King's Music from 1735. Composed 2 oratorios, *Jephthah,* 1737, and *The Force of Truth,* 1744; dramatic pastorals; works for organ and for harpsichord; church music (incl. *Forty Select Anthems,* 1743); canons, catches, glees, sonnet settings (incl. *Spenser's Amoretti,* 1739), and other songs.

Gregorian chant. The liturgical chant of the Roman Catholic Church. It is named after Pope Gregory I (reigned 590–604), to whom tradition has assigned an important role in its formulation. Much of the repertory as it has been preserved, however, seems to have been formed in France during the 8th and 9th centuries, whence the terms *Frankish* and *Franco-Roman* chant. A somewhat different and perhaps equally old repertory of specifically Roman origin is now usually called *Old Roman.

Like the liturgical chant of the other branches of Western Christendom (*Ambrosian, *Gallican, and *Mozarabic), the Gregorian chant is entirely *monophonic, though the practice of accompanying it on the organ is widespread even if not universally approved. The nature of its rhythm is the subject of considerable controversy. One view holds that all notes are essentially of equal duration except for occasional prolongation of individual notes and that the rhythm of the chant is thus free and is independent even of textual accent. This is the view formulated and propagated by the monks of *Solesmes in various official liturgical books. Also among those who advocate an essentially free rhythm are the *accentualists* (some of whom were also from Solesmes), who attach greater significance to textual accent as an organizing force in performance of the melodies. The second principal point of view is that of the *mensuralists,* who identify at least two fixed durational values and thus interpret the chant as having a stricter rhythm. Evidence for this position is found in the notation of some medieval sources, though interpretations of that evidence differ widely.

The chant is preserved in a variety of *liturgical books, the two principal types being those that contain music for the services of the *Office and those that contain music for the *Mass. Each book is arranged according to the structure of the liturgical year, which includes occasions of two general classes: (1) feasts of the Lord, i.e., Sundays and other holy days such as Christmas and Easter that commemorate events in the life of Jesus (known as the Proper of the Time or *Temporale*) and (2) the feasts of individual Saints (known as the *Sanctorale*), some of whom are assigned specific services (the Proper of the Saints) and for some of whom services are used that are designated for general categories of Saints (Apostles, Martyrs, Confessors, etc., comprising the Common of Saints).

The principal source of texts for the chant is the Book of Psalms, though other passages of Scripture are also employed. Thus, the principal musical forms are described as belonging to three types of *psalmody, even when specific texts are nonpsalmodic (i.e., not taken from the Book of Psalms). Other musical forms are used for the nonpsalmodic texts of the Ordinary of the *Mass and for the poetic texts of the *hymns and sequences [see Sequence (2)].

In general, three musical styles are identified in the chant: (1) *syllabic,* in which each syllable of text receives a single note, which category includes much of the antiphonal psalmody of the Office; (2) *group* or *neumatic,* in which there are relatively frequent groups of two to four notes on a single syllable, which category includes the antiphonal psalmody of the Mass; and (3) *melismatic,* in which melismas, i.e., groups of as many as ten or twenty notes for a single syllable, are a prominent feature, which category includes the responsorial psalmody of the Mass. Tonally, the melodies in all styles are classified according to the system of the eight *church modes. This system, together with certain other features of the chant and rite of the Roman Church, was imported from Eastern Christendom, particularly from the Greek or *Byzantine rite. The various methods of psalmody, on the other hand, almost certainly have their origins in the practice of Psalm singing in the Jewish synagogue.

Grétry, André Ernest Modeste (b. Liège, 11 Feb. 1741; d. Montmorency, near Paris, 24 Sept. 1813). Settled in Paris, 1767. Composed numerous operas (incl. *L'ingénu, ou Le huron,* Paris, 1768; *Le tableau parlant,* Paris, 1769; *Zémire et Azor,* Fontainebleau, 1771; *Richard Coeur-de-Lion,* Paris, 1784); hymns and other sacred music; instrumental music. Wrote numerous essays on a wide range of subjects.

Grieg, Edvard Hagerup (b. Bergen, Norway, 15 June 1843; d. there, 4 Sept. 1907). Pupil of Moscheles, E. F. E. Richter, Hauptmann, Reinecke, and Gade. Settled in Christiania (Oslo), 1866; organized and directed the Norwegian Academy of Music there from 1867. Composed orch. works (incl. incidental music to Ibsen's *Peer Gynt,* 1876; the *Peer Gynt Suites* nos. 1 and 2, 1888 and 1891; the *Holberg Suite,* 1885, arranged from the piano pieces of the same name; *Sigurd Jorsalfar Suite,* 1872, from incidental music to Bjørnson's play; symphonic dances, 1898); a piano concerto, 1868; choral works (incl. *Landjaenning,* 1872; *Album* for male voices, 1877); chamber music; piano pieces (incl. 10 books of *Lyric Pieces;* arrangements of songs and dances); numerous songs.

Griffbrett [G.]. Fingerboard of a stringed instrument. See *Am Griffbrett.*

Griffes, Charles Tomlinson (b. Elmira, N.Y., 17 Sept. 1884; d. New York, 8 Apr. 1920). Pupil of Humperdinck. Taught music at the Hackley School for boys in Tarrytown, New York. Composed stage works (incl. *Sho-Jo,* ballet, 1917); orch. works (incl. *The Pleasure Dome of Kubla Khan,* tone poem, 1919; *Poem for Flute and Orchestra,* 1919); vocal works; chamber music (incl. *2 Sketches on Indian Themes* for string quartet, 1922); piano pieces (incl. *The White Peacock,* 1917, also for orch.); songs.

Grigny, Nicolas de (b. Saint-Pierre-le-Vieil, near Reims, 8 Sept. 1672; d. Reims, 30 Nov. 1703). Organist at Saint-Denis in Paris, 1693–95, and at the Reims Cathedral from 1697. Composed a Mass and hymns for organ published as *Premier livre d'orgue,* 1711; J. S. Bach made himself a copy of this work.

Grisar, Albert (b. Antwerp, 26 Dec. 1808; d. Asnières, near Paris, 15 June 1869). Pupil of Reicha and Mercadante. Composed numerous operas (incl. *Le mariage impossible,* Brussels, 1833; *Les porcherons,* Paris, 1850; *Bonsoir, Monsieur Pantalon,* Paris, 1851).

Grofé, Ferde (Ferdinand Rudolph von) (b. New York, 27 Mar. 1892; d. Santa Monica, Calif., 3 Apr. 1972). Pianist and arranger for Paul Whiteman's Band from 1920. Composed orch. works (incl. *Grand Canyon Suite,* 1931); an arrangement of Gershwin's *Rhapsody in Blue* and other arrangements; piano pieces.

Groppo [It.]. See *Gruppetto.*

Gross [G., masculine singular; other endings depending on case and gender]. Large, great. *Grosse flöte,* the ordinary flute. *Grosses Orchester,* full orchestra.

Grosse Trommel, bass drum. *Grosse Sext (Terz),* major sixth (third); *Grosse Quinte (Quarte),* perfect fifth (fourth). *Grosse Oktave,* great octave.

Grosse caisse [F.]. Bass drum.

Grosse Fuge [G., Great Fugue]. Beethoven's fugue for string quartet, op. 133. It was composed in 1825 as the last movement of his String Quartet op. 130 but later was published as a separate composition.

Ground, ground bass [It. *basso ostinato*]. A short melodic phrase (normally four to eight measures) that is repeated over and over as a bass line, with varying music for the upper parts. The resulting composition is also called a "ground." The bass melody is not always entirely "fixed"; it may recur with modifications or in another key. It may vary from such simple formations as a descending tetrachord (e.g., a–g–f–e, one note to the measure) to a full-length melody. The ground is a characteristic form of baroque music and was cultivated especially in England, frequently with improvisation of the upper parts [see Division]. It belongs to the general category of continuous *variations. See also Chaconne and passacaglia; Ostinato; Strophic Bass.

Groven, Eivind (b. Lardal, Norway, 8 Oct. 1901). Studied at Oslo Conservatory. Has composed 2 symphonies and other orch. works; a piano concerto; choral works; works for voice with instruments; arrangements of Norwegian folksongs.

Grovlez, Gabriel (-Marie) (b. Lille, 4 Apr. 1879; d. Paris, 20 Oct. 1944). Conductor and composer. Pupil of Lavignac, Gédalge, and Fauré. Taught piano at the Schola cantorum in Paris; held many positions as conductor, including one at the Paris Opéra, 1914–34. Composed operas (incl. *Le Marquis de Carabas,* 1925); ballets; symphonic works; vocal works; chamber music; piano pieces; songs.

Gruenberg, Louis (b. Brest Litovsk, 3 Aug. 1884; d. Los Angeles, 9 June 1964). Pianist and composer. Lived in the U.S. from infancy. Pupil of Busoni. Taught at the Chicago Musical College, 1933–36.

Employed elements of jazz in some works. Composed operas (incl. *The Emperor Jones*, New York, 1933); film scores; an oratorio; 5 symphonies and other orch. works (incl. *The Hill of Dreams*, 1921); concertos for piano and for violin; *Daniel Jazz* for tenor and 8 instruments, 1925; chamber music; piano pieces.

Gruppen [G., Groups]. Composition by Stockhausen for three orchestras with three conductors, composed in 1955–57. Its use of spatial deployment of sound sources, a technique first explored by Stockhausen in the electronic work *Gesang der Jünglinge* for five groups of loudspeakers, was widely imitated.

Gruppetto, gruppo, groppo [It.]. (1) Italian 16th-century names for an ornament like a *trill. See Ornamentation. (2) *Turn.

Gsp. Abbr. for **glockenspiel.*

Guárdame las vacas [Sp., Watch over the cows for me]. The subject of several sets of 16th-century Spanish variations (L. de Narváez, 1538; A. Mudarra, 1546; Enríquez de Valderrábano, 1547; A. de Cabezón). It is identical to the **romanesca.*

Guarnieri, Camargo Mozart (b. Tietê, Brazil, 1 Feb. 1907). Pupil of Koechlin. Taught at the São Paulo Conservatory, 1927–38. Has composed operas; cantatas; 4 symphonies and other orch. works (incl. *Dansa Brasileira*); 2 violin concertos, 5 piano concertos; chamber music; piano pieces; choral works; songs.

Guédron, Pierre (Guesdron) (b. second half of the 16th cent.; d. late 1621 or early 1622). Singer in the French royal chapel, 1590. Composer of the king's chamber music from 1601 and superintendent thereof from 1613. Composed ballets; 6 books of *airs de cour.*

Guerre des bouffons [F.]; **guerra dei buffoni** [It.]. See War of the Buffoons.

Guerrero, Francisco (b. Seville, probably 4 Oct. 1528; d. there, 8 Nov. 1599). Pupil of his brother Pedro Guerrero and of Morales. *Maestro de capilla* of the Jaén Cathedral from 1546; singer at the Seville Cathedral from 1548 and *maestro de capilla* from 1574. Made an extended visit to Italy from 1582 and a pilgrimage to Palestine, 1588–89. Composed Masses, motets, Magnificats, psalms; Passions according to St. Matthew and St. John; a collection of *Canciones y villanescas espirituales* on Spanish texts, some of which were originally secular compositions.

Guglielmi, Pietro Alessandro (b. Massa Carrara, 9 Dec. 1728; d. Rome, 18 Nov. 1804). Pupil of his father, Jacob Guglielmi, and of Durante. Lived in London, 1768–72. *Maestro di cappella* of St. Peter's in Rome from 1793. Composed operas (incl. *Il ratto della sposa*, Venice, 1765; *La sposa fedele*, Venice, 1767; *La bella pescatrice*, Naples, 1789); oratorios; cantatas; sacred music; instrumental pieces. His son Pietro Carlo Guglielmi (*c.* 1763–1817) was also a composer.

Guidonian hand. A sketch of the human hand with the notes from G to e″ in various places, used in the Middle Ages and Renaissance as an aid for memorizing the gamut [see Gamma] and its *solmization syllables. In the accompanying sketch the tones are indicated by the modern pitch names instead of the composite solmization names (Gamma ut, A re, B mi, etc.; see Hexachord) that are used in the early treatises. The Guidonian hand is not present in the works of Guido d'Arezzo (*c.* 990–1050), for whom it is named, nor is the complete system of solmization. The hand is found for the first time in treatises of the late 13th century.

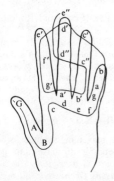

Guillaume Tell [F., William Tell]. French opera in four acts by Rossini (libretto by E. Jouy and H. Bis after Schiller's play), produced in Paris, 1829. Setting: Switzerland, early 14th century.

Guilmant, Félix Alexandre (b. Boulogne-sur-mer, 12 Mar. 1837; d. Meudon, near Paris, 29 Mar. 1911). Pupil of his father, the organist Jean-Baptiste Guilmant, and of Lemmens. Organist at several Paris churches. Co-founder (with d'Indy and Bordes) of the Schola cantorum, 1894. Taught at the Paris Conservatory from 1896. Composed numerous organ works, some with orch.; Masses, motets, and other sacred music; edited organ works of old masters.

Guimbarde [F.]. *Jew's-harp.

Guiraud, Ernest (b. New Orleans, 23 June 1837; d. Paris, 6 May 1892). Pupil of his father, Jean-Baptiste Guiraud, and of Marmontel and Halévy. Taught at the Paris Conservatory from 1876; his pupils incl. Debussy, Gédalge, and Loeffler. Composed operas (incl. *Piccolino*, Paris, 1876); a ballet; orch. works; recitatives for Bizet's *Carmen*. He completed the orchestration of Offenbach's *Contes d'Hoffmann*.

Güiro. Latin American percussion instrument consisting of a notched gourd that is scraped with a stick.

Guitar [F. *guitare*; G. *Gitarre*; It. *chitarra*; Sp. *guitarra*]. A plucked stringed instrument, similar to the *lute but with a flat back and built-up, inward-curved ribs, somewhat like those of the violin. [For ill. see Guitar family.] The modern guitar has metal frets and six strings tuned E A d g b e'. The music is notated on a single staff with treble clef, one octave higher than it sounds. When used to provide a simple chordal accompaniment to a dance or a song, especially folksong, the chords are often indicated in a manner similar to that of 16th-century *tablatures.

In 16th-century Spain at least three types of guitar were in use: (1) the six-course *vihuela*, an instrument equal in artistic importance to the contemporaneous lute and for which seven books of tablature were published (one each by L. Milán, L. de Narváez, A. Mudarra,

Enríquez de Valderrábano, D. Pisador, M. de Fuenllana, and E. Daza), containing a great many fantasias, variations (*diferencias*), duets, songs (*villancicos, romances*), a few dances, and many intabulations; (2) the four-course *guitarra*, a popular instrument for which Mudarra and Fuenllana composed a few pieces; and (3) the five-course *guitarra española*, whose vogue at the end of the century and throughout the 17th century was in part responsible for the eclipse of the lute and whose music usually consisted of chordal accompaniment only. In the late 17th century, the instrument came into vogue in French court circles.

Boccherini used the guitar in some of his chamber music, as did Paganini and some other composers of the 18th and 19th centuries. Fernando Sor (1778–1839) was the first internationally famous Spanish virtuoso and composer for the guitar. Francisco Tárrega (1852–1909), perhaps the greatest of all guitar players, initiated the present-day revival of the instrument.

Guitars of various kinds are in use for folk and popular music. These include nonelectric (sometimes called acoustic) instruments similar to the classical instrument but often of slightly different shape or design, employing, e.g., f-shape sound holes instead of a single round hole. The first electric guitars resulted from the application of amplifying devices to instruments of the traditional type. The increasing sophistication of the related electronics, however, which now make possible a wide range of tone color and loudness, has rendered largely unnecessary the resonant body of the traditional instrument. Hence, modern electric guitars display a variety of body shapes, usually smaller than those of the traditional instrument and often concave at the point where the body and fingerboard are joined, so as to facilitate playing on the highest frets. See also Guitar family.

Guitar family. This category is here understood to include instruments that have the general characteristics of the *lute family but have the flat body of the guitar. Like the lute, the guitar is of Arabic origin. It appears in various shapes in 13th-century miniatures from Spain.

Guitar family: 1. Yuehchyn. 2. Bandurria. 3. Banjo. 4. Ukulele. 5. Balalaika. 6. Chitarra battente. 7. Cittern. 8. Guitar.

Several such instruments existed in the 16th and 17th centuries under different names. The most important of these was the *cittern* (also *cithren, cister, cistre, cither, cithara, cetera, cistola, citole*), which had an oval belly and back, similar to that of the lute, and wire strings. The *Cythringen* (*Cithrinchen*) was a smaller instrument of this type. In the 18th century the cittern was much used in England under the name *English guitar*. Derived from the cittern are the **bandurria* and its larger variety, the *bandolon*. The names of these instruments come from that of the 16th-century **bandora* (sometimes called *pandora*). The *gittern*, which had gut strings, is another early member of the guitar family, but the name *quinterne* (probably from *guitterne*) was applied to other instruments as well. A Portuguese guitar, much used in the Azores, is the *machete,* which is the ancestor of the modern *ukulele.* The *chitarra battente* is an Italian form of guitar. Of the various guitar instruments of Russia only the **balalaika* survives today. A circular guitar with a short neck is used in China under the name *yuehchyn* [see accompanying ill.] and in Japan under the name *gekkin.* The Japanese *shamisen* (*samisen*), though sometimes considered a guitar, is more closely related to the lute.

Guridi (Bidaola), Jesús (b. Vitoria, Spain, 25 Sept. 1886; d. Madrid, 7 Apr.

1961). Pupil of d'Indy, Grovlez, and Jongen. Organist at Bilbao, 1909–39; taught at the conservatory there from 1927 and at the Madrid Conservatory, 1944–60. Worked with Basque folk materials. Composed *zarzuelas* (incl. *El caserío*, 1926); 2 operas (*Mirentxu*, 1910; *Amaya*, 1920); orch. works (incl. *10 melodías vascas*); choral works, several on Basque themes; chamber music; piano pieces; organ pieces; church music; songs.

Gurlitt, Cornelius (b. Altona, near Hamburg, 10 Feb. 1820; d. there, 17 June 1901). Pupil of J. P. E. Hartmann. Associate of Reinecke and Gade. Organist at the Altona Cathedral, 1864–98. Taught at the Hamburg Conservatory, 1879–87. Composed operas; an oratorio; orch. works; choral works; chamber music; song cycles; numerous piano pieces for 2 and 4 hands (incl. the collections *Jugend-Album* and *Miniaturen*).

Gurney, Ivor Bertie (b. Gloucester, 28 Aug. 1890; d. Dartford, Kent, 26 Dec. 1937). Pupil of Stanford and Vaughan Williams. Composed songs, piano pieces, violin pieces. Also published several volumes of poetry.

Gurrelieder [G.]. A song cycle ("Great Cantata") by Schoenberg to poems (originally in Danish) by J. P. Jacobsen, for five solo voices, three four-part male choruses, one eight-part mixed chorus, narrator, and large orchestra, begun 1900–1901 but not finished until 1911.

Gusle. A primitive one-stringed instrument played with a bow. It is used almost exclusively to accompany and support the chanting of the epic poems of the southern Slavs (Serbs, Montenegrins, Macedonians, and, less frequently, Bulgarians). Pear-shaped, it is covered with skin and has a long neck ending with a decorative carving, usually in the shape of an animal's head. [For ill. see Violin family.]

Gusli. Russian instrument similar to the *zither, unrelated to the Balkan *gusle.

Gusto, con [It.]. With style, with zest.

Gutchë, Gene (real name Romeo E. Gutsche) (b. Berlin, 3 July 1907). Pupil of D. Ferguson and Clapp. Settled in the U.S., 1925. Has worked with twelve-tone and microtonal techniques. Has composed orch. works (incl. 6 symphonies; *Ghenghis Khan*, symphonic poem, 1963; *Gemini*, 1966); concertos for various instruments; choral works; 4 string quartets; piano sonatas.

Gymel, gimel, gemell [from L. *gemellus*, twin]. (1) A late medieval term for two-part polyphony based on thirds, sixths, and tenths. A number of English compositions from *c*. 1300 are in this style. (2) In English musical sources of the 15th century, an indication that a part is temporarily divided into two.

Gypsy scale. See Scale.

Gyrowetz, Adalbert (Mathias) (b. Budweis, Bohemia, 19? Feb. 1763; d. Vienna, 19 Mar. 1850). Pupil of Paisiello. *Kapellmeister* at the Vienna Opera, 1804–31. Traveled widely on the Continent and in England. Composed Italian and German operas (incl. *Der Augenarzt*, 1811; *Agnes Sorel*, 1806); *Singspiele* (incl. *Robert, oder Die Prüfung*, 1813); ballets; numerous symphonies; concertos; string quartets and other chamber music; Masses and other sacred music; piano pieces; songs.

H

H. German for B natural. See Pitch names; Letter notation. Abbr. for *horn* (in orchestral scores).

Haas, Joseph (b. Maihingen, Germany, 19 Mar. 1879; d. Munich, 31 Mar. 1960). Pupil of Reger. Taught at the Stuttgart Conservatory, 1911–21, and in Munich schools, 1921–50. Composed operas (incl. *Tobias Wunderlich*, Kassel, 1937); oratorios (incl. *Die heilige Elisabeth*, 1931); cantatas, Masses, and other sacred and secular choral works; works for orch.; chamber music; piano and organ pieces; song cycles.

Hába, Alois (b. Vizovice, Moravia, 21 June 1893; d. Prague, 18 Nov. 1973). Pupil of Novák and Schreker. Taught at the State Conservatory in Prague, 1923–51. Worked with microtonal and twelve-tone techniques and with Moravian and Slovak folk materials. Composed operas (incl. *Matka* [The Mother], Munich, 1931); orch. works (incl. *The Path of Life*, symphonic fantasy, 1935); 2 violin concertos; choral works; chamber music; pieces for piano and for guitar.

Habanera [Sp.]. A Cuban dance named after the city of Havana but perhaps of Spanish origin, and widely popular in Europe and Latin America in the second half of the 19th century. An example by Sebastián Yradier was adapted by Bizet in *Carmen*. Other examples are by Albéniz, Debussy, Chabrier, Falla, and Ravel. In a moderate 2/4 meter, its most characteristic rhythms are shown in the accompanying example.

Hackbrett [G.]. *Dulcimer.

Hadley, Henry Kimball (b. Somerville, Mass., 20 Dec. 1871; d. New York, 6 Sept. 1937). Pupil of Chadwick. Toured widely as a conductor in Europe, Japan, and South America; conductor of several U.S. orchestras, incl. the San Francisco Symphony and the New York Philhar-monic. Composed operas (incl. *Azora, Daughter of Montezuma*, Chicago, 1917; *Cleopatra's Night*, New York, 1920); orch. works (incl. *5 symphonies; The Culprit Fay*, 1909); choral works; chamber music; piano pieces; anthems and songs.

Hadley, Patrick Arthur Sheldon (b. Cambridge, England, 5 Mar. 1899; d. Norfolk, 17 Dec. 1973). Pupil of Vaughan Williams and R. O. Morris. Taught at Cambridge Univ., 1938–62. Composed music for Greek tragedies and Shakespeare's plays; choral works with orch. (incl. *The Trees So High*, 1931); works for solo voice with orch. (incl. *Scene from the Cenci*, 1951); chamber music.

Haffner Serenade and **Haffner Symphony.** Mozart's Serenade in D (K. 250), composed in 1776, and his Symphony in D (K. 385), composed in 1782, both for festive occasions in the family of Sigmund Haffner in Salzburg.

Hahn, Reynaldo (b. Caracas, Venezuela, 9 Aug. 1875; d. Paris, 28 Jan. 1947). Pupil of Lavignac, Dubois, and Massenet. Music critic for *Le Figaro* from 1934 and musical director of the Paris Opéra from 1945. Composed operas and operettas (incl. *La carmélite*, Paris, 1902; *Ciboulette*, Paris, 1923); incidental music for the theater; ballets; pantomimes; orch. works; choral works; piano pieces; numerous songs.

Haieff, Alexei (b. Blagoveschensk, Siberia, 25 Aug. 1914). Emigrated to the U.S., 1931. Pupil of R. Goldmark, F. Jacobi, and N. Boulanger. Teacher at the State Univ. of New York at Buffalo, 1962–68; at the Univ. of Utah, 1968–71. Has composed ballets (incl. *Divertimento*, 1944, not originally for ballet); 3 symphonies; concertos; vocal works; chamber music; piano pieces; songs.

Halb, halbe [G.]. Half. *Halbe Note (Pause)*, half note (rest). *Halbsopran*, mezzosoprano. *Halbton*, semitone.

Halévy, Jacques-François (-Fromental-Élias) (b. Paris, 27 May 1799; d. Nice, 17 Mar. 1862). Pupil of Cherubini and Berton. Teacher at the Paris Conservatory from 1827 and *chef du chant* at the Paris Opéra from 1830. His pupils incl. Gounod and Bizet. Composed numerous operas (incl. *La juive*, Paris, 1835; *L'éclair*, Paris, 1835; *La reine de Chypre*, Paris, 1841; *Les mousquetaires de la reine*, Paris, 1846); ballets; vocal and instrumental works; settings of the Hebrew psalms.

Half. *Half-close*, imperfect *cadence. *Half-fall*, see Appoggiatura. *Half-shift*, the first shift on the violin, i.e., second *position. *Half-step*, *semitone. *Half-stop*, see Divided stop. *Half-tube* instruments, see Wind instruments.

Halffter, Cristóbal (b. Madrid, 24 Mar. 1930). Nephew of Ernesto and Rodolfo Halffter. Conductor and composer. Pupil of Conrado del Campo. Taught at the Madrid Conservatory, 1962–66; its director, 1964–66. Has worked with serial techniques. Has composed an opera, *Don Quijote*, 1970; vocal works (incl. *Simposion*, 1966; *Misa ducal*, 1956; the cantata *Yes, Speak Out Yes* for soprano, baritone, 2 choruses, 2 orchestras, 2 conductors, 1970); instrumental works (incl. *Sinfonía* for 3 instrumental groups; *Secuencias* for orch., 1964; *Espejos* for percussion and tape, 1963; *Anillos* for orch., 1968; a cello concerto, 1974).

Halffter, Ernesto (b. Madrid, 16 Jan. 1905). Brother of Rodolfo Halffter. Pupil of Falla, Ravel, and Esplá. Director of the Seville Conservatory, 1931–36. Teacher at the Instituto Español in Lisbon, 1942–52. Has composed operas; ballets (incl. *Sonatina*, 1928); orch. works (incl. *Sinfonietta*, 1924; *Dos bocetos sinfónicos*); a guitar concerto, 1969; vocal works; chamber music; piano pieces.

Halffter, Rodolfo (b. Madrid, 30 Oct. 1900). Brother of Ernesto Halffter. Pupil briefly of Falla. Music critic for the Madrid paper *La voz*, 1934–36. Settled in Mexico, 1939. Has worked with twelvetone techniques. Has composed an opera, *Clavileño*, 1936; ballets (incl. *Don Lindo de Almería*, 1940); orch. works; concertos for violin and for piano; choral

works; chamber music; piano pieces (incl. *3 hojas de álbum*, 1953); a *Giga* for guitar, 1930; songs.

Hallelujah. From the Hebrew, meaning "Praise the Lord." For its use in Gregorian chant, see Alleluia. In choral compositions of the 17th and 18th centuries the word frequently serves as the text for an extensive movement. Famous examples are the Hallelujah choruses in Bach's cantata *Christ lag in Todesbanden* and in Handel's *Messiah*.

Hallén, Johan Andreas (b. Göteborg, 22 Dec. 1846; d. Stockholm, 11 Mar. 1925). Conductor, critic, and composer. Pupil of Reinecke and Rheinberger. Taught at the Stockholm Conservatory, 1909–19. Composed operas (incl. *Harald der Wiking*, Leipzig, 1881; *Waldemarsskatten*, Stockholm, 1899); symphonic poems (incl. *Die Toteninsel*, 1899) and other orch. works; choral works (incl. a *Missa Solemnis*); chamber music; songs.

Halling. A fast, lively Norwegian folk dance in 2/4 or 4/4 meter. It is a strenuous solo dance for men in which one person in the middle of the room holds a man's hat on a long pole. Several men in turn try to kick the hat off the pole. Grieg has used the dance in several of his *Lyric Pieces*.

Hallström, Ivar (b. Stockholm, 5 June 1826; d. there, 11 Apr. 1901). Librarian to the future King Oscar II from 1850. Director of Lindblad's music school from 1861. Among the first composers to make use of Swedish folksongs. Composed operas (incl. *Den bergtagna* [The Enchanted One], Stockholm, 1874; ballets; cantatas; choral works; piano pieces; songs; arrangements of folksongs.

Hambraeus, Bengt (b. Stockholm, 29 Jan. 1928). Organist, musicologist, and composer. Worked for the Swedish Broadcasting Corp., 1957–72. Teacher at McGill Univ. in Montreal from 1972. Works incl. *Responsorier* for soloists, chorus, and instruments, 1964; *Rota* for 3 orchestras and tape, 1962; *Constellations I–III* for organ and tape, 1961.

Hamerik, Asger (Hammerich) (b. Copenhagen, 8 Apr. 1843; d. Frederiksberg, 13 July 1923). Pupil of Gade, J. P. E. Hartmann, H. von Bülow, and Berlioz. Director of the Peabody Conservatory in Baltimore, 1871–98. Composed operas; symphonies and other orch. works; cantatas; choral works; songs.

Hamilton, Iain (Ellis) (b. Glasgow, 6 June 1922). Teacher at London Univ. from 1955; at Duke Univ. in North Carolina, 1962–71; at the City Univ. of New York from 1971. Has worked with serial techniques. Has composed a ballet, *Clerk Saunders*, 1951; operas (incl. *The Catiline Conspiracy*, Stirling, Scotland, 1974); music for films; orch. works (incl. 2 symphonies; *Sinfonia* for 2 orchestras, 1959; *Voyage* for horn and orch., 1970); concertos for clarinet, for jazz trumpet, for violin, and for piano; vocal works (incl. *Epitaph for This World and Time* for 3 choirs, 3 organs, 1970); chamber music; piano pieces; *Threnos: In Time of War* for organ, 1966.

Hammerklavier [G.]. Early 19th-century name for the piano. Beethoven used the term in the titles for his sonatas op. 101 and 106 (the latter is widely known as the Hammerklavier Sonata).

Hammerschmidt, Andreas (b. Brüx, Bohemia, 1611 or 1612; d. Zittau, 8 Nov. 1675). Organist at Freiberg, 1635–39, and at the Johanniskirche in Zittau from 1639 to his death. Composed sacred works, incl. Lutheran services, motets, "sacred madrigals," "dialogues," concerted pieces; secular music, incl. odes, madrigals, dances for viols with thoroughbass.

Hand organ. Term for two *mechanical instruments similar in construction but different in purpose: the English barrel organ, formerly used in small churches, and the street organ of the organ grinders.

Handel, George Frideric (Händel, Georg Friedrich) (b. Halle, 23 Feb. 1685; d. London, 14 Apr. 1759). Pupil of Zachow. Close associate of Mattheson. Second violinist and composer for the German opera in Hamburg from 1703. Visited Italy, 1706–10, where he met Corelli and Alessandro and Domenico Scarlatti. Succeeded Steffani as *Kapellmeister* to the Elector of Hanover, 1710. Settled in London, 1712. Soon thereafter (1714) his patron the Elector became King George I of England. Succeeded Pepusch as chapel master to the Duke of Chandos, 1717. Directed the newly established Royal Academy of Music from 1720, producing Italian operas. This institution failed in 1728, owing in part to the success of *The *Beggar's Opera*. In the years 1729–34, Handel produced Italian operas in partnership with J. J. Heidegger. After 1737, when his third Italian opera enterprise failed and he suffered a stroke, he turned increasingly to the composition of oratorios. In 1741–42 he visited Dublin, where he produced *Messiah*. Unsuccessful surgery for his failing eyesight, begun in 1751, led to total blindness in his last years.

Works: numerous operas (incl. [for London except as noted] *Almira*, Hamburg, 1705; *Rodrigo*, Florence, 1707; *Agrippina*, Venice, 1709; *Rinaldo*, 1711; *Radamisto*, 1715; *Ottone*, 1723; **Giulio Cesare*, 1724; *Tamerlano*, 1724; *Rodelinda*, 1725; *Orlando*, 1733; *Ariodante*, 1735; *Alcina*, 1735; *Serse*, 1738, his only comic opera; *Deidamia*, 1741); oratorios (incl. *Esther*, 1732; *Deborah*, 1733; **Saul*, 1739; **Israel in Egypt*, 1739; **Messiah*, 1742; *Samson*, 1743; *Semele*, 1744; *Belshazzar*, 1745; **Judas Maccabaeus*, 1747; *Joshua*, 1748; *Susanna*, 1749; *Theodora*, 1750; **Jephtha*, 1752); secular choral works (incl. **Acis and Galatea*, 1720; *Alexander's Feast*, 1736; *Ode for St. Cecilia's Day*, 1739); orch. works (incl. **Water Music, c.* 1717, and **Fireworks Music*, 1749; 12 organ concertos; 18 *concerti grossi*); sacred music (incl. the **Chandos Anthems*, 1716–18, and other anthems; the *Utrecht Te Deum and Jubilate*, 1713; the *Dettingen Te Deum*, 1743; psalms; motets; 2 Passions); instrumental chamber music; vocal chamber music (incl. many Italian cantatas for one and two voices with instruments); 3 sets of *Lessons* and other harpsichord works; odes, arias, songs.

Handel Variations. Twenty variations (and a fugue) for piano by Brahms, op. 24 (1861), based on a theme by Handel (the "Air" from his harpsichord suite in B♭). The fugue is based on a theme freely derived from the initial notes of the tune.

Handl, Jacob. See Gallus, Jacobus.

Handtrommel [G.]. Tambourine. See Percussion instruments II, 4.

Hänsel und Gretel. Opera in three acts by Humperdinck, produced in Weimar, 1893. The libretto, written by his sister, Adelheid Wette, is based on one of Grimm's *Fairy Tales.* Setting: the Hartz Mountains, Germany.

Hanson, Howard (b. Wahoo, Nebr., 28 Oct. 1896). Conductor and composer. Pupil of Oldberg. Director of the Eastman School of Music in Rochester, New York, 1924–64, and conductor of its American music festivals. His pupils incl. Bergsma, Mennin, and Palmer. Has composed a ballet; an opera, *Merry Mount,* New York, 1934; 6 symphonies (no. 2, *Romantic,* 1930; no. 4, *The Requiem,* received the Pulitzer Prize for 1944); symphonic poems and other orch. works; concertos; choral works (incl. *Lament of Beowulf,* with orch., 1926; *Drum Taps,* with baritone and orch., after Whitman, 1935); a cantata, *Song of Human Rights,* 1963; chamber music; piano pieces; songs.

Harbison, John (b. Orange, N.J., 20 Dec. 1938). Conductor and composer. Pupil of Sessions and Kim. Jazz instrumentalist, 1952–65. Teacher at the Massachusetts Institute of Technology from 1969. Has composed *Sinfonia* for violin and double orch., 1963; *Shakespeare Series,* for soprano and piano, 1965; *Confinement* for 12 players, 1965; *Cantata Sequence* for soprano and instruments, 1968; *Parody-Fantasia* for piano, 1968; a piano trio, 1969; *Bermuda Triangle* for tenor saxophone, amplified cello, and electronic organ, 1970; *The Flower Fed Buffaloes* for baritone, chorus, and instruments, 1976.

Hardingfele, Hardanger fiddle. A Norwegian folk instrument shaped somewhat like the violin but slightly smaller and with a flatter bridge. [For ill. see under Violin family.] It has four gut strings above four or five metal sympathetic strings in various tunings, such as a d' a' e'' or a e' a' c''♯ for the former, b d' e' f'♯ a' or c'♯ d' e' f'♯ a' for the latter. It is used to accompany folk dances such as the *halling, ganger,* and *springar.*

Harfe [G.]. *Harp.

Harmonic. See under Acoustics; Harmonics.

Harmonic analysis. The study of the *chords or *harmonies that make up a composition and their relation to one another in that context. An important part of such study is the identification of individual chords with respect to the *scale degrees on which they are formed and the particular disposition of the individual pitches of which they consist. The scale degree of the *root of a chord is usually designated by a roman numeral. The pitch content (e.g., *triad, *seventh chord) and particular disposition (e.g., *root position, *inversion) are designated by the presence or absence of one or more arabic numerals, which indicate the intervals formed above the lowest sounding pitch, as in a *thoroughbass. Thus, V_5^6 denotes a seventh chord formed on the fifth scale degree of the tonic key disposed with the third of the chord as the lowest sounding pitch. In the key of C, for example, such a chord would consist of the pitches b, d', f', and g' (or their equivalents in other octaves, so long as the lowest sounding pitch is a B), the g' forming a sixth with the b and the f' forming a fifth with the b. In addition to identifying chords in this way, harmonic analysis seeks to elucidate the principles according to which chords succeed one another and thus the function of chords with respect to one another. Although such analysis is particularly applicable to the tonal music of the 18th and 19th centuries, any analysis even of this music that fails to take some account of the principles of *counterpoint must necessarily remain incomplete. See also Altered chords; Modulation; Harmonic rhythm.

Harmonic minor (scale). See Major, minor.

Harmonic rhythm. The rhythmic pattern created by the durations of successive *harmonies in a composition. Harmonic rhythm may be spoken of as fast or slow, depending on the rate at which harmonies change. This may be entirely independent of *tempo. That is, a piece with a fast tempo may have a slow harmonic rhythm as a result of employing single harmonies in various ways for several measures in succession.

Harmonic series. See under Acoustics.

Harmonica. (1) The *glass harmonica. (2) The mouth harmonica or mouth organ [F. *harmonica à bouche;* G. *Mundharmonika;* It. *armonica a bocca;* Sp. *armónica*]. A popular instrument that consists of a small, flat metal box with slitlike openings on one of its long sides. Each slit leads to a pair of reeds inside the box, one of which works by means of pressure and the other by means of suction. The player places the instrument against the lips and, moving it back and forth according to the notes desired, blows into or inhales against the slits. For ill. see under Wind instruments. (3) In French and German the name is also used for a variety of instruments of the xylophone type, i.e., consisting of tuned strips of wood (*harmonica de bois, Holzharmonika*), steel (*harmonica à lames d'acier, Stahlharmonika,* i.e., *glockenspiel*), stone (*harmonica à lames de pierre,* e.g., the Chinese *bianchinq*), etc. The *Ziehharmonika* [G.] is the *accordion.

Harmonics [G. *Flageolett-Töne;* F. *sons harmoniques*]. (1) See under Acoustics. (2) In the playing of stringed instruments (including the harp and guitar), high tones of a flutelike timbre, sometimes called *flageolet tones,* produced by causing a string to vibrate in segments corresponding to a mode of vibration other than the fundamental and thus suppressing altogether the pitch that is produced when the string vibrates along its entire length [see Acoustics]. Harmonics are produced by touching the string lightly at a node for the desired mode of vibration at the same time that the string is bowed or plucked. Thus, if a string is bowed or plucked while being touched lightly at a point one-third of the distance from one end, it will produce the harmonic with a pitch an octave and a fifth higher than that of the open string. This may be notated by placing a small circle above the desired pitch. For instruments of the violin family, natural harmonics are those produced on open strings. Artificial harmonics are those produced on stopped strings and are often notated by a normal note-shape, indicating the pitch for which the string is to be stopped, in combination with a lozenge placed a fourth above, indicating the point at which the

sounds

notated

string is to be touched lightly so as to produce the harmonic having a pitch two octaves higher than that of the stopped pitch [see the Ex., where the lower staff shows the notation and the upper staff the sounded pitch]. The introduction of harmonics has been variously ascribed to Domenico Ferrari (1722–80), a pupil of Tartini, and to Jean de Mondonville (1711–72).

Harmonie [F., G.]. Harmony. In French usage the term also means the wind section of the orchestra, or a special wind band. *Cor d'harmonie,* French horn.

Harmonie der Welt, Die [G., Harmony of the World]. (1) A symphony by Hindemith, composed in 1951. The three movements were derived from the composer's opera of the same title before the opera was finished and performed. (2) Opera in five acts by Hindemith (to his own libretto), produced in Munich, 1957. Setting: Central Europe, between 1608 and 1630.

Harmoniemesse [G., Wind-band Mass]. Haydn's Mass in B♭ composed in 1802, so called because of its generous use of wind instruments.

Harmonious Blacksmith. Popular name attached in the 19th century to the air with variations from Handel's Harpsichord Suite No. 5, in E, from his first set of suites (1720).

Harmonium. A keyboard instrument that sounds when thin metal tongues are set in vibration by a steady current of air, which, except in modern instruments, is provided by a pair of pedal-operated bellows. The metal tongues act as free *reeds. It can produce "expressive" gradations of sound by means of the expression stop, which puts the pressure in the bellows under direct control of the player's feet. The harmonium was developed in the 19th century from Grenié's *orgue expressif* (1810). The first real harmonium was made by A. Debain in 1840.

The *expression stop* was invented by Mustel in 1854 (*Mustel organ*). An important variety of harmonium is the *American organ,* in which the wind is not forced out through the reeds by compression but is drawn in by evacuation. It produces a softer, more organlike tone. Modern instruments have an electric wind supply, leaving the feet of the player free to operate a pedal-keyboard. The principle of the American organ was invented in Paris about 1835 and was put into practical form by Estey of Brattleboro, Vt. (*Estey organ,* 1856), and by Mason and Hamlin of Boston (1861).

Harmony. That aspect of music consisting of simultaneously sounded pitches (i.e., *chords) as opposed to simultaneously sounded melodies or lines, the latter termed *counterpoint. Visualized in terms of musical notation, harmony is the vertical element in musical *texture and counterpoint the horizontal element. The two are fundamentally inseparable, but harmony is often taught as a separate subject [see Harmonic analysis]. The term sometimes connotes pleasant sound, but properly it is applied to any collection of pitches sounded either simultaneously or in such a way as to cause them to function as a simultaneity. It may also be used with reference to an abstraction of some such pitch collection as distinct from the particular chords (of which there may be many) that are examples of it. Thus, one might say that C major is the harmony of a certain measure in which the pitches of the C-major triad are presented in a variety of ways. As with other aspects of music, tastes in harmony have varied widely with time and place, though there have been numerous attempts to show that the particular harmonic style of Western music of the 18th and 19th centuries is ordained in nature [see Acoustics].

Harold en Italie [F., Harold in Italy]. A program symphony by Berlioz, op. 16, written in 1834 at the request of Paganini, who wanted a work that would feature an exceptional viola he had just acquired. The symphony, which has a prominent viola part, is in four movements, after portions of Byron's *Childe Harold.*

Harp [F. *harpe;* G. *Harfe;* It., Sp. *arpa*]. Generic name for chordophones in which the plane of the strings is perpendicular to the soundboard (not parallel as in, e.g., the zither and piano). Such instruments are nearly always plucked. The *double action* (or double pedal) *harp* used in modern orchestras was introduced about 1810 by Sébastien Érard. It has a large triangular frame that consists of an upright pillar, a hollow, tapered back (with the soundboard), and a curved neck. The strings are attached to the neck and extend down to the soundboard. It has a range of six octaves and a fifth, with seven strings to the octave, tuned normally in the key of $C\flat$ major, i.e., from $C_1\flat$ to $g''''\flat$. At the foot of the instrument are seven pedals, one controlling all the C strings, one all the D strings, etc. Each pedal can be depressed to two notches—"double action"—thus shortening the strings so as to raise their pitches by one semitone at each notch. Thus, the C pedal in high position gives the tone $C\flat$, in the first notch the tone C, and in the second notch the tone $C\sharp$. Operation of single pedals makes all the major and minor keys available, though the essentially diatonic design of the instrument imposes certain limitations on the combinations of pitches that can be played. The *chromatic harp* was introduced in 1897 by the Parisian firm of Pleyel. It abandons the pedal mechanism, substituting a string for each semitone of the octave. Despite certain advantages, it has not been generally accepted and has only a small repertory of music.

Harps are among the oldest instruments. In Mesopotamia they are documented as far back as *c.* 3000 B.C., and a great variety of forms existed there as well as in Egypt. In spite of many Biblical references to King David's "playing the harp," his instrument, the *kinnor,* was not a harp but a lyre, similar perhaps to the Greek kithara. In Europe, harps made their first appearance perhaps as early as the 9th century in Ireland, which still uses the Irish harp (*clarsech*) as its heraldic symbol. The earliest extant sources for harp music are from 16th-century Spain. The harp was occasionally used in Italian opera of the early 17th century (Monteverdi, *Orfeo,* 1607), and

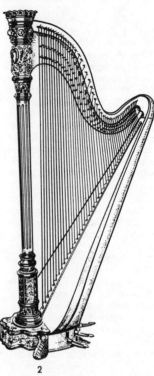

1. Irish harp. 2. Harp.

then it almost disappeared from the orchestra until the 19th century, when it assumed a regular position there.

Harp lute. (1) An early 19th-century instrument combining features of the guitar (rather than the lute) and harp. Similar constructions were the *Ditar harp* and *Harp-lute guitar*. (2) A small harp built by Pleyel in the early 20th century and used by Falla in his *El retablo de Maese Pedro*.

Harp Quartet. Popular name for Beethoven's String Quartet in E♭ op. 74 (1809), so called on account of some pizzicato arpeggios in the first movement.

Harpsichord [F. *clavecin;* G. *Cembalo* (*Clavicimbel, Kielflügel*); It. *clavicembalo;* Sp. *clavicémbalo*]. A stringed keyboard instrument in use from the 16th through 18th centuries and similar in shape to the modern grand piano, the strings being roughly parallel to the long

side of the case. Each string is plucked by a plectrum of crow quill (which, like other materials used originally, is now often replaced by synthetic materials of various kinds) mounted in the pivoted tongue of a fork-shaped jack, which stands on the rear end of the key lever. Depressing the key raises the jack until the horizontally projecting plectrum plucks the string. Upon release of the key, the jack falls back until the underside of the plectrum touches the string, causing the tongue to rotate on its pivot. As the jack continues to fall the plectrum is tilted upward and back until its point passes below the string. A spring of boar's bristle mounted at the rear of the jack then returns the tongue to its original position so that the jack is again ready to pluck. A damper made of woven woolen cloth is inserted into a slot sawed in one tine of the forked jack, its bottom edge just above the level of the plectrum. When the key is at rest the damper touches the string, but the slightest depression of the key raises the damper, leaving the string free to vibrate. Thus the string of the harpsichord, like the pipe of an organ, can continue sounding only so long as the player holds a key down.

Each rank of jacks is carried in a pair of mortised battens mounted vertically one over the other. The lower batten (lower guide) is fixed, but the upper batten (slide or register) is movable, usually by means of hand stops. Thus each rank of jacks can be moved slightly toward or away from its choir of strings, engaging or disengaging the plectra. In this way *stops* or ranks of jacks can be silenced or added to the ensemble.

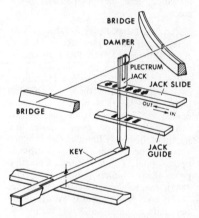

BRIDGE
DAMPER
PLECTRUM
JACK
JACK SLIDE
OUT
IN
BRIDGE
KEY
JACK
GUIDE

Harpsichord action.

The typical 18th-century harpsichord has three choirs of strings, two of which are tuned to 8′ pitch and one an octave higher at 4′ pitch [see Foot]. (Very rarely a fourth choir at 16′ pitch might be added.) Such a harpsichord would ordinarily have three ranks of jacks, one for each choir. Frequently there are two keyboards, the upper of which might have only one 8′ stop. The lower manual usually sounds the other 8′ stop and the 4′ stop. The upper manual normally can be coupled to the lower, making all three stops available from the lower keyboard.

The choirs of strings are used singly or in various combinations to provide variations in loudness and timbre, much as the stops of the organ are employed, since the force with which the key is struck has no effect on loudness. Sometimes a special rank of jacks is provided to pluck the upper manual choir of 8′ strings at its extreme end to produce a nasal timbre (*lute stop*). Buff leather pads are used to partially damp one choir of strings, giving a harplike effect (*buff stop*).

Many modern harpsichords do not resemble their antique prototypes in the most essential details. Especially during the first years of the 20th-century revival of the harpsichord, there was a tendency to employ concepts of design and aesthetic more germane to the piano or organ than to the harpsichord. The ability of the harpsichord to vary its timbre has been exploited more than in earlier centuries, and for many years nearly all harpsichords seen in concert halls had several pedals provided to change the stops. The 16′ stop for a time was almost universally fitted to concert instruments despite the fact that in early times it was found only in Germany during the 18th century, and even there only rarely. Most of these modern instruments were constructed far more heavily (sometimes with metal frames) than the early instruments, with longer treble strings and shorter bass strings, often overspun in the manner of the bass strings of the piano. Plectra were of leather instead of the quill almost invariably found in early times. All of these changes tended to produce a more sustained but weaker tone of less harmonic complexity than that typical of antique instruments.

Since about 1950, many makers in several countries have returned to the early principles, and harpsichords are now being made that closely resemble those for which the keyboard music of the Renaissance and baroque was composed. At present the field is still being contested by the proponents of the modern and antique styles of instrument.

Throughout the baroque period the harpsichord was the chief instrument for the realization of *thoroughbass accompaniment, always in chamber music and occasionally (in place of the organ) in church music. There is also an extensive solo literature from this period. By the late 18th century, the instrument was superseded by the piano. See also Pedal harpsichord; Virginal.

Harris, Roy (Leroy) (b. Lincoln County, Okla., 12 Feb. 1898). Pupil of Farwell and N. Boulanger. Teacher and composer-in-residence at several U.S. schools and colleges, incl. the Univ. of California at Los Angeles, 1961–73. Has composed 14 symphonies and other orch. works; ballets; concertos; band pieces; vocal works (incl. *Abraham Lincoln Walks at Midnight*, chamber cantata, 1953; a Mass and other sacred choral works); chamber music; piano pieces.

Harrison, Lou (b. Portland, Oreg., 14 May 1917). Conductor, writer, music critic, instrument builder, and composer. Pupil of Cowell and Schoenberg. Has taught at several U.S. colleges, including Mills College, 1936–40, and San Jose State College in California, from 1967. Has worked with serial and aleatory techniques as well as Asian instruments and musical materials and instruments of his own invention. Has employed Esperanto for the titles and texts of some works. Has composed operas; ballets (incl. *Solstice*, 1950); incidental music for plays; orch. works (incl. 2 suites for string orch.; *Symphony on G*, 1948–61; *Concerto in Slendro*, 1961; *Pakifika Rondo* for chamber orch. of Western and Asian instruments, 1963); choral works; songs.

Harsányi, Tibor (b. Magyarkanizsa, Hungary, 27 June 1898; d. Paris, 19 Sept. 1954). Pianist and composer. Pupil of Kodály. Worked with Hungarian folk materials. Composed ballets; a chamber opera and a radio opera; music for films; orch. works (incl. *Suite hongroise*, 1937); choral works; a violin concerto and a piano concerto; chamber music; piano pieces; songs.

Hart, Fritz Bennicke (b. Brockley, Kent, 11 Feb. 1874; d. Honolulu, 9 July 1949). Pupil of Stanford. Director of the Melbourne Conservatory, 1915–35. Conductor of the Honolulu Orchestra from 1932 and teacher at the Univ. of Hawaii, 1936–42. Composed operas; a symphony and other orch. works; chamber music; choral works; songs.

Hartig, Heinz Friedrich (b. Kassel, 10 Sept. 1907; d. Berlin, 16 Sept. 1969). Pupil of Gál. Taught at the Berlin Hochschule from 1948. Worked with serial techniques. Composed ballets; a chamber opera, *Escorial*, 1961; incidental music for the theater; orch. works (incl. *Variationen über einen siebentönigen Klang*, 1962); concertos; choral works (incl. *Perché* for chorus and guitar, 1958); chamber music; piano pieces; songs.

Hartley, Walter Sinclair (b. Washington, D.C., 21 Feb. 1927). Pianist and composer. Pupil of Hanson and Bernard Rogers. Has taught at the State Univ. College at Fredonia, N.Y., from 1969. Works incl. *Concerto for 23 Winds*, 1957; *Sinfonia* no. 3 for brass choir, 1963, no. 4 for winds, 1965; string quartets; vocal works (incl. *A Psalm Cycle* for voice, flute, and piano, 1967); piano pieces.

Hartmann, Johan Peder Emilius (Johann Peter Emil) (b. Copenhagen, 14 May 1805; d. there, 10 Mar. 1900). Jurist, organist, and composer. Succeeded his father, August Wilhelm Hartmann, as organist of the Copenhagen Garnisonkirche, 1824; organist at the Copenhagen Cathedral from 1843 to his death. Co-director (with Gade and Paulli) of the newly founded Copenhagen Conservatory from 1867. Composed operas (incl. *Liden Kirsten*, Copenhagen, 1846); ballets (incl. *Valkyrien*, 1861); melodramas (incl. *Guldhornene*, 1834); orch. works; vocal works; chamber music; piano and organ pieces; songs.

Hartmann, Karl Amadeus (b. Munich, 2 Aug. 1905; d. there, 5 Dec. 1963). Pupil of Haas, Scherchen, and Webern. Worked with twelve-tone techniques. Works incl. a chamber opera; 8 symphonies; several concertos, incl. one for piano, winds, and percussion, 1953; vocal works (incl. *Gesangsszene* for baritone and orch., 1963, unfinished).

Harty, (Herbert) Hamilton (b. Hillsborough, Ireland, 4 Dec. 1879; d. Hove, near Brighton, 19 Feb. 1941). Church organist in Belfast and Dublin. Conductor of the Halle Orchestra in Manchester, 1920–33. Toured widely in Europe, the U.S., and Australia as a conductor. Composed orch. works (incl. *Comedy Overture*, 1907; *With the Wild Geese*, symphonic poem, 1910; *Irish Symphony*,

1924); a violin concerto, 1909; vocal works (incl. *The Mystic Trumpeter*, after Whitman, for baritone, chorus, and orch., 1913); chamber music.

Harwood, Basil (b. Woodhouse, Gloucestershire, 11 Apr. 1859; d. London, 3 Apr. 1949). Organist and composer. Pupil of Reinecke and Jadassohn. Choral director at Oxford Univ., 1900–1909. Composed choral works; sacred music, incl. services, motets, and anthems; organ works (incl. *Dithyramb; Paean*); songs.

Hasse, Johann Adolph (b. Bergedorf, near Hamburg, bapt. 25 Mar. 1699; d. Venice, 16 Dec. 1783). Tenor with the Hamburg Opera, 1718, and with the Brunswick Opera, 1719–22. Pupil of Porpora and A. Scarlatti in Naples from 1722. Court *Kapellmeister* in Dresden from 1731. Traveled widely in Europe producing operas; lived in Vienna, 1764–73. Composed numerous operas (incl. *Cleofide*, Dresden, 1731; *Artaserse*, London 1734; *Ruggiero*, Milan, 1771); cantatas; oratorios; Masses, psalms, motets, and other sacred music; instrumental works, incl. concertos, chamber music, keyboard sonatas.

Hassler, Hans Leo (b. Nuremberg, bapt. 26 Oct. 1564; d. Frankfurt, 8 June 1612). Pupil of A. Gabrieli. Court organist in Augsburg, 1586–1600. Chief musician of Nuremberg from 1601. Titular imperial chamber organist in Prague from 1602. Organist to the Elector of Saxony in Dresden from 1608. Composed sacred music, incl. Masses, motets, psalms, Lutheran chorales; secular music, incl. madrigals, *canzonette*, instrumental dances; keyboard ricercars.

Hässler, Johann Wilhelm (Hasler) (b. Erfurt, 29 Mar. 1747; d. Moscow, 29 Mar. 1822). Pianist and composer. Nephew and pupil of Kittel. Performed in Erfurt, Berlin, Potsdam, Dresden (where he competed with Mozart), and London (under Haydn). Imperial court *Kapellmeister* in St. Petersburg, 1792–94; teacher in Moscow thereafter. Composed piano works; organ works; songs.

Hastig [G.]. With haste, hurrying.

Hastings, Thomas (b. Washington, Conn., 15 Oct. 1784; d. New York, 15 May 1872). Settled in New York, 1832, where he worked with Lowell Mason at the Normal Institute and led the chorus of the Bleeker Street Presbyterian Church. Composed numerous hymn tunes, incl. "Rock of Ages"; "Retreat"; "Zion"; "Ortonville." Published anthologies of hymns, etc.

Haubenstock-Ramati, Roman (b. Cracow, 27 Feb. 1919). Pupil of A. Malawski and J. Koffler. Music director of Radio Cracow, 1947–50. Has lived in Tel Aviv, 1950–56, and in Vienna from 1957. Has taught at several schools in Europe, Israel, Brazil, and the U.S. Has worked with serial, aleatory, and electronic techniques and with graphic notation. Has composed an opera, *Amerika*, after Kafka, Berlin, 1966; *Tableaux*, 1967–71, and other orch. works; works for various instrumental ensembles (incl. several titled *Jeux* for percussionists); vocal works with instruments (incl. *Mobile for Shakespeare*, 1959); electronic works.

Haubiel, Charles (Trowbridge) (b. Delta, Ohio, 30 Jan. 1892). Pupil of Scalero. Has taught at several U.S. colleges, including Juilliard, 1921–29, and New York Univ., 1922–47. Founded the Composers' Press, 1935. Works incl. *Brigands Preferred*, musical satire, 1925; orch. works (incl. *Portraits*, 1934; *Karma*, 1928); cantatas; chamber music; choral works; piano pieces; songs; Mexican folk opera, *Sunday Costs Five Pesos*, 1950.

Hauer, Josef Matthias (b. Wiener-Neustadt, near Vienna, 19 Mar. 1883; d. Vienna, 22 Sept. 1959). Conductor and composer. Early experimenter with twelve-tone techniques [see Trope (2)]. Composed 2 operas; cantatas (incl. *Der Menschen Weg*, 1953); a chamber oratorio, *Wunlungen*, 1928; orch. suites; concertos for violin and for piano; chamber music; choral works; *Nomoi*, 1912, and other piano works; songs; numerous instrumental pieces entitled *Zwölftonspiel*.

Haupt- [G.]. Chief, principal. *Hauptstimme*, principal part (usually soprano); *Hauptwerk*, great organ; *Hauptsatz*, first theme (or section) in the sonata form [see under *Satz*].

Hauptmann, Moritz (b. Dresden, 13 Oct. 1792; d. Leipzig, 3 Jan. 1868). Music theorist and composer. Pupil of Morlacchi and Spohr. Violinist in the court orchestra at Kassel, 1822–42. Cantor at the Thomasschule in Leipzig from 1842 and teacher at the newly founded conservatory there from 1843. His pupils incl. F. David, Joachim, H. von Bülow, Jadassohn, and Sullivan. Composed numerous sacred works incl. Masses and psalms; an opera, *Mathilde*, Kassel, 1826; instrumental pieces; numerous songs. Published several works on music history and theory, incl. *Die Natur der Harmonik und der Metrik*, 1853.

Hausegger, Siegmund von (b. Graz, 16 Aug. 1872; d. Munich, 10 Oct. 1948). Pupil of his father, Friedrich Hausegger. Held conducting positions in Graz, Munich, Frankfurt, Hamburg, and Berlin. Composed operas; orch. works (incl. *Dionysische Phantasie*, 1899; *Barbarossa*, 1900; *Natursymphonie*, 1911); choral works; a Mass; songs.

Haut, haute [F.]. High. *Haute-contre*, high tenor, male *alto. In France in the 18th and early 19th centuries, singers so designated were not falsettists. *Hautdessus*, high treble, soprano.

Hautbois, hautboy [F.]. *Oboe.

Haydn, (Franz) Joseph (b. Rohrau, Austria, 31 Mar. 1732; d. Vienna, 31 May 1809). Boy chorister at the Vienna Cathedral from 1740. After his voice changed, he served as accompanist for Porpora's singing lessons. In this position he met Wagenseil, Gluck, and Dittersdorf. Court musician at Lukaveč, near Pilsen, from 1758. Vice *Kapellmeister* to the Esterházy family from 1761 and *Kapellmeister* to them from 1766 at Eisenstadt and later at Esterház. In 1790 the court chapel was dissolved upon the death of Prince Nikolaus Esterházy; Haydn remained titular *Kapellmeister* but moved to Vienna. He made two very successful visits to England in 1790–92 and 1794–95. Beethoven had some lessons from him in 1792.

Instrumental works: at least 104 symphonies (incl. *Le *matin;* the **Abschieds-Symphonie;* the *Paris Symphonies; the *Salomon Symphonies); *Sinfonia concertante* for oboe, violin, bassoon, cello, and orch.; numerous concertos for piano, for violin, for cello, for horn, and for other instruments; marches, dances, and other orch. works; an instrumental Passion, *Die Sieben Worte Christi am Kreuz,* later arranged for string quartet and as an oratorio [see Seven Last Words]; numerous divertimenti; 68 (not 83) string quartets; numerous works for baryton; piano trios; other chamber music; numerous piano sonatas and other piano works; pieces for mechanical clocks.

Vocal works: numerous operas, most for performance at Esterház (incl. *La cantarina,* 1767; *L'infedeltà delusa,* 1773; *La vera costanza,* 1776; *Il mondo della luna,* 1777; *Orlando Paladino,* 1782; *Armida,* 1784); Singspiele and marionette operas; 4 oratorios (incl. *Die Schöpfung* [The *Creation], 1798; *Die Jahreszeiten* [The *Seasons], 1801; *Die Sieben Worte des Erlösers am Kreuze* [The *Seven Last Words]); cantatas; choruses; sacred music (incl. 14 Masses; 2 Te Deums; a *Stabat Mater*); songs; vocal duets, trios, and quartets; numerous canons and rounds; numerous arrangements of Scotch, Irish, and Welsh songs; the hymn "Gott erhalte Franz den Kaiser," which served as the Austrian national anthem until 1920 and 1929–46.

Haydn, (Johann) Michael (b. Rohrau, Austria, 14? Sept. 1737; d. Salzburg, 10 Aug. 1806). Brother of Franz Joseph Haydn. Boy chorister at the Vienna Cathedral. *Kapellmeister* at Grosswardein, Hungary, from 1757. Music director to the Archbishop Sigismund at Salzburg from 1763; succeeded Leopold Mozart as piano teacher at the Kapellhaus there and was organist at the Cathedral there from 1781 to his death. Composed sacred music, incl. Masses, Requiems, oratorios, etc.; operas and other stage works; secular vocal works; numerous symphonies, concertos, and other orch. works; chamber music, incl. string quartets and quintets; organ preludes; songs.

Haydn Quartets. Familiar name of six string quartets by Mozart (K. 387, 421, 428, 458, 464, 465), composed 1782–85 and all dedicated to Haydn. They are listed as nos. 14 to 19 in the complete series of Mozart's string quartets.

Haydn Variations. A set of eight variations and a finale by Brahms on a theme titled "St. Anthony's Chorale" that is employed in a *divertimento* formerly attributed incorrectly to Haydn. Brahms' work was published in 1873 in two versions, one for orchestra (op. 56a) and one for two pianos (op. 56b).

Haym, Nicola Francesco (b. Rome, *c*. 1679; d. London, 11 Aug. 1729). Violinist in the orchestra of Cardinal Ottoboni, 1694–1700. Went to England shortly thereafter and was household musician to the Duke of Bedford until 1711. Collaborated with Dieupart on the production of Italian opera in London, arranging several operas of Bononcini and A. Scarlatti and inserting some new numbers of his own composition. Also wrote some libretti for Handel. Composed sonatas for 2 violins with thoroughbass; sonatas for flute and for oboe; church music.

Hayne van Ghizeghem (fl. second half of the 15th cent.). Flemish composer and singer at the Burgundian court under Charles the Bold. Composed French chansons.

Hb. [F.]. Abbr. for *hautbois,* oboe.

Head voice. Higher register of a voice; cf. *chest voice. See Register (2).

Hebriden, Die, or **Fingals Höhle** [G., The Hebrides, or Fingal's Cave]. Concert overture by Mendelssohn (in B minor, op. 26, 1830, rev. 1832). The composition was inspired by a visit to the famous cave in Scotland during his first tour through the British Isles.

Heckelphone. See Oboe family II (e).

Heftig [G.]. Violent.

Hegar, Friedrich (b. Basel, 11 Oct. 1841; d. Zürich, 2 June 1927). Conductor and composer. Pupil of Hauptmann, F. David, and Rietz. Held many conducting positions in Zürich, including that with the Choral Society there, 1865–1901. A co-founder (1876) and director (to 1914) of the Zürich Conservatory. Composed many choral works (incl. *Manasse,* 1885, with soloists and orch.); orch. works; concertos; chamber music; songs.

Heiden, Bernhard (b. Frankfurt, 24 Aug. 1910). Conductor and composer. Pupil of Hindemith. Emigrated to the U.S., 1935. Professor of composition at Indiana Univ. from 1946. Has composed an opera, *The Darkened City,* Bloomington, Ind., 1963; a ballet; film music; 2 symphonies and other orch. works; choral works; chamber music; sonatas and other piano works.

Heiller, Anton (b. Vienna, 15 Sept. 1923). Organist, conductor, and composer. Teacher at the Vienna Academy of Music from 1945. Has composed Masses and much other sacred music; secular vocal works; a toccata for 2 pianos, 1943; organ pieces; other instrumental works.

Heinichen, Johann David (b. Krössuln, near Weissenfels, 17 Apr. 1683; d. Dresden, 16 July 1729). Lawyer, music theorist, and composer. Pupil of Kuhnau. Produced several operas during a visit to Italy, 1710–16. *Kapellmeister* to the Elector of Saxony in Dresden from 1717. Composed operas; sacred music, incl. Masses, cantatas, oratorios, hymns, psalms; secular cantatas; orch. works; chamber music. Published theoretical works, incl. *Neu erfundene und gründliche Anweisung . . . zu vollkommener Erlernung des General-Basses,* 1711 (revised as *Der Generalbass in der Composition,* 1728).

Heinrich, Anthony Philip (Anton Philipp) (b. Schönbüchel, Bohemia, 11 Mar. 1781; d. New York, 3 May 1861). Emigrated to the U.S., 1810; settled in Kentucky, 1817. Conductor in Philadelphia from 1821. After extensive visits to Europe, 1826–37, he settled in New York. Composed large-scale orch. works (incl. *The Columbiad, or Migration of American Wild Passenger Pigeons; Pushmataha: A Venerable Chief of a Western Tribe of Indians*); smaller instrumental works; choral works; piano pieces; songs.

Heise, Peter Arnold (b. Copenhagen, 11 Feb. 1830; d. Stokkerup, near Copenhagen, 12 Sept. 1879). Pupil of Hauptmann. Music teacher and organist at Sorö, Denmark, 1858–65. Visited Italy several times, where he was a close associate of Sgambati. Settled in Copenhagen, 1865. Composed 2 operas (incl. *Drot og Marsk* [King and Marshall], Copenhagen, 1878); a symphony; choral works (incl.

Tornerose, 1874); chamber music; piano pieces; numerous songs.

Heiter [G.]. Cheerful.

Heldenleben, Ein [G., A Hero's Life]. Symphonic poem by R. Strauss, op. 40, completed 1898. It includes quotations of themes from other works by Strauss.

Heldentenor [G.]. A tenor voice of great brilliancy and volume, well suited for operatic parts of the "hero," particularly in the works of Wagner.

Helicon. See Brass instruments II (e).

Hellendaal, Pieter (b. Rotterdam, Mar. 1721 or 1718, bapt. 1 Apr. 1721; d. Cambridge, 19 Apr. 1799). Violinist, organist, and composer. Pupil of Tartini. Settled in England, 1752. Organist at Pembroke College, Cambridge, from 1762 and at St. Peter's College there from 1777. Composed violin pieces; cello pieces; keyboard pieces (incl. *Celebrated Rondo*); *Six Grand Concertos,* 1758; glees and catches; a *Collection of Psalms for the Use of Parish Churches.*

Heller, Stephen (b. Budapest, 15 May 1813; d. Paris, 14 Jan. 1888). Pianist and composer. Lived in Augsburg, 1830–38; then settled in Paris. Friend of Berlioz. Composed numerous piano pieces, incl. etudes, ballades, sonatas, sonatinas, waltzes, mazurkas, nocturnes, variations.

Hellermann, William (David) (b. Milwaukee, 15 July 1939). Classical guitarist and composer. Pupil of Giannini, Chou Wenchung, Luening, Ussachevsky, Wolpe, Stockhausen, Ligeti, and Carter. Teacher at Columbia Univ. from 1967. Has composed orch. works (incl. *Time and Again,* 1969); chamber music; vocal works; pieces for piano and for solo guitar; electronic works (incl. *Passages 13 —The Fire* for trumpet and tape, 1971).

Hellinck, Lupus (b. *c.* 1496; d. Bruges, probably 14 Jan. 1541). Boy chorister at St. Donatian in Bruges, 1506–11; choirmaster there from 1523 to his death. Composed sacred music, incl. Masses and motets; settings of Protestant chorale tunes; secular polyphony.

Helm, Everett (Burton) (b. Minneapolis, 17 July 1913). Musicologist and com-

poser. Pupil of Malipiero, Vaughan Williams, and Piston. Has taught at several schools in the U.S. and abroad. Music journalist from 1948. Has composed an opera, *The Siege of Tottenburg,* for broadcast in Germany, 1956; a *Singspiel;* a ballet; *Adam and Eve,* a mystery, 1952; orch. works; concertos for various instruments; string quartets and other chamber music; choral works; songs.

Helps, Robert (b. Passaic, N.J., 23 Sept. 1928). Pianist and composer. Pupil of Sessions. Has taught at Princeton Univ. and the Manhattan School of Music. Works incl. a symphony, 1955, and other orch. works; 2 piano concertos; chamber music; vocal works; piano pieces (incl. *Recollections; Portrait; Image; Solo; Saccade* for 4 hands).

Hemidemisemiquaver. See under Notes.

Hemiola, hemiolia [Gr.]. In early theory the term had two meanings, both implying the ratio 3:2. (1) If applied to pitches, *hemiola* meant the fifth, since the lengths of two strings sounding this interval are in the ratio 3:2. (2) In treatises on *mensural notation (15th, 16th centuries) the term is applied to time values that are in the relationship 3:2; in modern terms, three half notes against two dotted half notes:

$$\frac{6}{4}|\,d.d.|ddd| \ \text{or} \ \frac{3}{4}|d.|d.|dd|dd|$$

This change from 6/4 to 3/2 or vice versa is found very frequently in the works of Dunstable, Dufay, and other 15th-century composers, as well as in the music of the baroque period. It is a typical trait of the *courante. See also Proportions.

Henkemans, Hans (b. The Hague, 23 Dec. 1913). Psychiatrist, pianist, and composer. Pupil of Pijper. Has toured as a concert pianist in Europe and South Africa. Has composed a symphony; *Passacaglia und Gigue* for piano and orch., 1942; concertos; vocal works with orch. (incl. *Villonnerie,* 1965); chamber music; piano pieces; songs.

Henry, Pierre (b. Paris, 9 Dec. 1927). Pupil of N. Boulanger and Messiaen. With Pierre Shaeffer, a co-founding member of the Groupe de recherches de musique concrète from 1949. Works (on tape) incl. *Le Voyage,* 1963, and other ballets; an opera, *Orphée 53,* 1953; *Symphonie pour un homme seul,* 1950, rev. 1966, in collaboration with Shaeffer; *Apocalypse de Jean,* 1968; *Variations pour une porte et un soupir,* 1963; film and stage music.

Henschel, George (Isidor Georg) (b. Breslau, 18 Feb. 1850; d. Aviemore, Scotland, 10 Sept. 1934). Singer, conductor, and composer. Pupil of Moscheles, Kiel, and Reinecke. Conducted the Boston Symphony, 1881–84; founded (1886) and conducted the London Symphony Concerts; held several other conducting and singing positions. Friend of Brahms, of whom he wrote a memoir. Composed operas (incl. *Nubia,* Dresden, 1899); incidental music to *Hamlet;* orch. works; sacred choral works (incl. a Requiem and a *Stabat Mater*); numerous songs.

Hensel, Fanny Cäcilia (née Mendelssohn) (b. Hamburg, 14 Nov. 1805; d. Berlin, 14 May 1847). Pianist and composer. Sister of Felix Mendelssohn. Works incl. numerous songs; part songs; piano pieces (incl. *Lieder ohne Worte*); chamber music.

Henselt, (Georg Martin) Adolf von (Hänselt) (b. Schwabach, Bavaria, 9 May 1814; d. Warmbrunn, Silesia, 10 Oct. 1889). Pianist and composer. Pupil of Hummel and Sechter. Friend of Liszt. Lived in Russia, 1838–78, as imperial pianist and piano teacher. Composed numerous works for piano (incl. a concerto; etudes; *Poème d'amour; Frühlingslied*); orch. works; chamber music; vocal works.

Henze, Hans Werner (b. Gütersloh, Germany, 1 July 1926). Pupil of Fortner and Leibowitz. Settled in Italy, 1956. Has worked at one time or another with twelve-tone, microtonal, and electronic techniques. Has composed operas (incl. *Das Wundertheater,* Heidelberg, 1949; *Boulevard Solitude,* Hanover, 1952; *Ein Landarzt* for radio, 1953; *Der König Hirsch,* Berlin, 1956; **Elegie für junge Liebende* [Elegy for Young Lovers]; *The Bassarids,* Salzburg, 1966); ballets (incl. *Undine,* 1958); other stage works; 6 symphonies and other orch. works; concertos for violin, for piano, and for double bass; vocal works (incl. *El cimarrón*

for voice, flute, guitar, percussion, 1970); chamber music.

Herbeck, Johann (Franz) von (b. Vienna, 25 Dec. 1831; d. there, 28 Oct. 1877). Court *Kapellmeister* in Vienna, 1866–71; director of the court opera there, 1871–75; conductor of several choral societies there. Composed numerous sacred and secular choral works and songs; several symphonies and other orch. works; chamber music.

Herbert, Victor (b. Dublin, 1 Feb. 1859; d. New York, 26 May 1924). Cellist with several European orchestras, including the court orchestra in Stuttgart from 1881. Emigrated to the U.S., 1886. Conducted the Pittsburgh Symphony Orchestra, 1898–1904; organized the Victor Herbert N.Y. Orchestra, 1904; conducted and performed with several other orchestras. Composed numerous operettas (incl. *Babes in Toyland,* Chicago, 1903; *Mlle. Modiste,* Trenton, N.J., 1905; *Naughty Marietta,* Syracuse, N.Y., 1910; *Sweethearts,* Baltimore, 1913); operas (incl. *Natoma,* Philadelphia, 1911); music for the theater; film music; orch. works; 2 cello concertos; choral works; chamber music; piano pieces; songs.

Herbst, Johannes (b. Kempton, Swabia, 23 July 1735; d. Salem, N.C., 15 Jan. 1812). Moravian minister and composer. Emigrated to the U.S., 1786, in the course of his ministry. Composed numerous choral anthems and hymns.

Hermannus Contractus (Herman the Lame) (b. Saulgau, Swabia, 18 July 1013; d. in the Reichenau Monastery, 24 Sept. 1054). Music theorist, mathematician, astronomer, and composer. Educated at the Reichenau Monastery from 1020; entered the Benedictine Order, 1043. Composed the Gregorian Marian antiphon *Alma Redemptoris Mater* and other liturgical chants. Wrote important treatises on music, science, and history.

Herold,   Louis-Joseph-Ferdinand (b. Paris, 28 Jan. 1791; d. Thernes, near Paris, 19 Jan. 1833). Son of Franz-Joseph Herold, a pianist and composer who had been a pupil of K. P. E. Bach. Pupil of his father and of Méhul. Accompanist and later chorus master at the Italian opera in Paris, 1820–27; répétiteur at the Grand Opéra from 1827. Composed operas (incl. *Marie,* Paris, 1826; *Zampa,* Paris, 1831; *Le pré aux clercs,* Paris, 1832); ballets; orch. works; vocal works; chamber music; piano pieces.

Hero's Life, A. See *Heldenleben, Ein.*

Herrmann, Bernard (b. New York, 29 June 1911; d. Los Angeles, 24 Dec. 1975). Conductor and composer. Pupil of P. James, Grainger, Stoessel, and B. Wagenaar. Held various positions with the Columbia Broadcasting System in New York from 1933, including director of the C.B.S. Symphony Orchestra, 1940–55. Has composed an opera; film scores (incl. *Citizen Kane,* 1940); ballets; orch. works (incl. *For the Fallen,* 1943); a violin concerto; cantatas (incl. *Moby Dick,* 1940); choral works.

Herrmann, Hugo (b. Ravensburg, 19 Apr. 1896; d. Stuttgart, 7 Sept. 1967). Pupil of Schreker. Church organist in Detroit and member of the Detroit Symphony Orchestra, 1923–25. Director of the Trossingen Musikschule, 1935–62. Composed operas (incl. *Vasantasena,* 1930) and other stage works; 5 symphonies and other orch. works; concertos for organ, harpsichord, accordion, and other instruments; sacred music; choral works; chamber cantatas; instrumental chamber music; pieces for accordion, for harmonica, for piano, and for organ.

Hertel, Johann Wilhelm (b. Eisenach, 9 Oct. 1727; d. Schwerin, 14 June 1789). Son and pupil of Johann Christian Hertel (1699–1754), a violinist and composer. Court musician at Strelitz from 1744; *Kapellmeister* at the Schwerin court from 1754. Composed symphonies; concertos; stage works; oratorios; cantatas; sonatas for piano and for flute; psalms; odes; songs.

Hertz, abbr. *Hz.* In *acoustics, a measure of frequency equal to one cycle per second and named after the German physicist Heinrich R. Hertz.

Hervé (real name Florimond Ronger) (b. Houdain, near Arras, 30 June 1825; d. Paris, 3 Nov. 1892). Pupil of Auber. Held several positions as church organist in Paris. Conducted several theater orches-

tras there; opened the Folies-Concertantes (Folies Nouvelles) there, 1855, for the production of light operas. Composed numerous operettas (incl. *L'oeil crevé,* Paris, 1867; *Chilpéric,* Paris, 1868; *Le petit Faust,* Paris, 1869; *Mam'zelle Nitouche,* Paris, 1883); an opera; ballets (incl. *Sport,* 1887).

Hervorgehoben [G.]. Emphasized.

Herz, Henri (Heinrich) (b. Vienna, 6 Jan. 1803; d. Paris, 5 Jan. 1888). Pupil of Hünten and Reicha. Toured widely as a concert pianist; taught piano at the Paris Conservatory from 1842. Established a successful piano factory in Paris. Composed numerous piano works, some with orch., incl. etudes, concertos, sonatas, variations, fantasies, nocturnes. Also published a method for piano.

Herzogenberg, (Leopold) Heinrich von (b. Graz, 10 June 1843; d. Wiesbaden, 9 Oct. 1900). Pianist and composer. Co-founder (with Holstein and P. Spitta, 1874) and conductor (1875–85) of the Bachverein in Leipzig. Teacher at the Hochschule für Musik in Berlin from 1885. Composed 2 symphonies and a symphonic poem; a cantata; oratorios; choral works; chamber music; organ fantasies; piano pieces.

Heseltine, Philip Arnold (pen name Peter Warlock) (b. London, 30 Oct. 1894; d. there, 17 Dec. 1930). Writer, critic, and composer. Friend and admirer of Delius. Founded the journal *The Sackbut,* 1920, and made numerous transcriptions of early music. Composed orch. works (incl. *Capriol Suite*); choral works (incl. *Corpus Christi*); chamber music; numerous songs (incl. the cycle *The Curlew*).

Hesitation waltz. See Boston, *valse Boston.*

Heterophony. An improvisational type of polyphony, namely, the simultaneous use of slightly or elaborately modified versions of the same melody by two (or more) performers, e.g., a singer and an instrumentalist, the latter adding a few extra tones or ornaments to the singer's melody. In addition to other polyphonic procedures, heterophony plays an important role in many genres of primitive, folk, and non-Western art music.

Heure espagnole, L' [F., The Spanish Hour]. Opera in one act by Ravel (libretto by Franc-Nohain, based on his own comedy), produced in Paris, 1911. Setting: Toledo, Spain, 18th century.

Hewitt, James (b. Dartmoor, England, 4 June 1770; d. Boston, 1 Aug. 1827). Organist, violinist, publisher, concert manager, and composer. Emigrated to the U.S., 1792. Organist at Trinity Church, Boston, from 1812. Composed several ballad operas (incl. *Tammany,* New York, 1794); incidental music for plays; overtures; piano pieces (incl. *The Battle of Trenton;* sonatas); songs.

Hewitt, John Hill (b. New York, 11 July 1801; d. Baltimore, 7 Oct. 1890). Son of James Hewitt. Composed ballad operas; cantatas; an oratorio; choruses; numerous songs.

Hexachord. (1) In medieval theory, a group of six tones in the intervallic sequence *t t s t t,* (*t = tonus,* whole tone; *s = semitonus,* half tone), e.g., c d e f g a. In the diatonic (i.e., the equivalent of the modern C major) scale there are two—and only two—pitch classes on which such hexachords can be formed, C and G. If, however, B♭ is added, there is a third pitch class on which such a hexachord can be formed, namely, F. The hexachord on C was called the *hexachordum naturale;* that on G the *hexachordum durum,* because it included the *b durum* (written with a square shape), i.e., B♮ (B natural); that on F the *hexachordum molle,* because it included the *b molle* (written with a round shape), i.e., B♭ (B-flat).

As an aid for memorizing, Guido d'Arezzo (*c.* 990–1050) designated the six tones of the hexachord by the vocables [L. *voces, voces musicales*] ut, re, mi, fa, sol, la. These are the initial syllables of the first six lines of a hymn to St. John [see *LU,* p. 1504], whose melody has the feature of beginning one tone higher with each successive line. These syllables were used as a "movable *solmization*," being applied to each of the seven hexachords (one for each of the C's, F's, and G's on which a complete hexachord could be formed) within the complete gamut from G to e″. Thus, the tone d was *sol* (fifth) in the hexachord on

G, and *re* (second) in that on c. To indicate the various "functions" of a given tone, compound names were devised so as to include the tone's pitch letter as well as all its syllables, e.g., D sol re (Desolre), thus indicating that the tone d may appear either as a *sol* or a *re.* The accompanying table gives the complete nomenclature (D. for *durum;* N. for *naturale;* M. for *molle*). To a certain extent the compound names served to differentiate octaves, e.g., C fa ut (c), C sol fa ut (c'), and C sol fa (c″). In order to accommodate melodic progressions exceeding the compass of one hexachord, two (or more) hexachords were interlocked by a process of transition called *mutation.* The system appeared in its full form (with three hexachords, compound pitch names, mutation, *Guidonian hand, etc.) shortly before 1300.

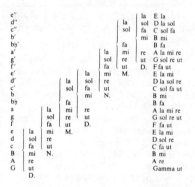

(2) Any six pitches; but particularly, in the theory of twelve-tone music [see Serial music], either of the two collections of six pitch classes that make up a twelve-tone row.

Hexameter. See under Poetic meter.

Heyden, Sebald (b. Bruck, near Erlangen, probably 8 Dec. 1499; d. Nuremberg, 9 July 1561). Cantor of the Spitalschule in Nuremberg from 1519 and rector there from 1521. Rector at the Sebaldschule from 1525 to his death. Composed a Passion, psalms, and other Protestant church music (incl. the chorale "O mensch, bewein dein Sünde gross"). Also published a theoretical work, *Musicae, i.e., artis canendi libri II,* 1537.

Hidalgo, Juan (b. Las Moralejas?, Spain, c. 1612; d. Madrid, buried 31 Mar. 1685). Harpist and composer. Member of the royal chapel in Madrid from 1631 to his death. Earliest known composer of *zarzuelas* (incl. *Los celos hacen estrellas,* 1644?; *Celos aun del aire matan,* 1662, text by Calderón de la Barca). Also composed sacred and secular vocal music, incl. *villancicos.*

Hidden fifths, octaves. See under Parallel fifths, octaves.

Hill, Alfred (b. Melbourne, 16 Dec. 1870; d. Darlinghurst, New South Wales, 30 Oct. 1960). Violinist and composer. Performed with the Gewandhaus Orchestra in Leipzig under Brahms, Tchaikovsky, and Grieg. Taught at the Sydney Conservatory. Employed Maori musical materials in some works. Composed operas (incl. *The Weird Flute);* film music; orch. works (incl. *Maori Symphony);* cantatas on Maori themes; choral works; chamber music; violin pieces; piano pieces; songs.

Hill, Edward Burlingame (b. Cambridge, Mass., 9 Sept. 1872; d. Francestown, N.H., 9 July 1960). Pupil of Paine, Chadwick, F. F. Bullard, and Widor. Taught at Harvard Univ., 1908–40; his pupils incl. Thomson, Finney, and L. Bernstein. Composed orch. works (incl. *Lilacs,* 1927; 3 symphonies; *The Fall of the House of Usher,* symphonic poem, 1920); a violin concerto; choral works; chamber music; piano pieces; 2 pantomimes with orch.

Hiller, Ferdinand (b. Frankfurt, 24 Oct. 1811; d. Cologne, 10 or 11 May 1885). Conductor, critic, and composer. Associate of Mendelssohn, Chopin, Liszt, and Berlioz. Traveled as conductor and composer to Italy, Paris, London, and Germany. Settled in Cologne, 1850, where he organized the Cologne Conservatory and directed it until his death. Composed operas (incl. *Die Katakomben,* Wiesbaden, 1862); oratorios (incl. *Die Zerstörung Jerusalems,* 1840); cantatas; orch. works; piano concertos; choral works; chamber music; piano pieces; songs.

Hiller, Johann Adam (Hüller) (b. Wendisch-Ossig, near Görlitz, 25 Dec. 1728; d. Leipzig, 16 June 1804). Pupil of Homilius. Conductor, from 1763, of a Leipzig concert series that became the Gewandhaus Concerts. Founded a singing school in Leipzig, 1771. Succeeded Doles as music director of the Thomasschule there, 1789–1801. Composed *Singspiele* (incl. *Der Teufel ist los,* Leipzig, 1766, after C. Coffey's ballad opera *The Devil to Pay; Die Jagd,* Weimar, 1770); a symphony; cantatas; church music; string quartets; keyboard works; lieder (incl. *Lieder für Kinder,* 1769).

Hiller, Lejaren (b. New York, 23 Feb. 1924). Chemist, computer scientist, and composer. Pupil of Sessions and Babbitt. Member of the chemistry faculty of the Univ. of Illinois, 1953–58, and of the music faculty there from 1958. From 1968, co-director (with Foss) of the Center for the Creative and Performing Arts in Buffalo and teacher at the State Univ. of New York there. Has worked with electronic and computer techniques and visual effects. Has composed stage works; symphonies; chamber music (incl. *Illiac Suite for String Quartet,* 1957, generated by computer, with L. Isaacson); piano pieces; electronic works with instruments (incl. *Machine Music* for piano, percussion, and tape, 1964; *HPSCHD* for 1–7 harpsichords and 1–51 tapes, 1968, in collaboration with Cage).

Hilton, John (the elder) (d. Cambridge, Mar. 1608). Countertenor at Lincoln Cathedral, 1584. Organist at Trinity College, Cambridge, from 1594. Composed anthems, organ pieces, a madrigal.

Hilton, John (the younger) (b. Oxford or Cambridge, 1599; d. London, buried 21 Mar. 1657). Possibly the son of the preceding. Organist at St. Margaret's, Westminster, from 1628. Composed 2 services; anthems and other sacred vocal music; instrumental works; ayres (incl. a collection of *Ayres, or FaLa's for 3 Voyces);* catches, rounds, canons.

Himmel, Friedrich Heinrich (b. Treuenbrietzen, Brandenburg, 20 Nov. 1765; d. Berlin, 8 June 1814). Pupil of Naumann. Traveled widely in Europe and Russia. Court *Kapellmeister* in Berlin from 1795. Composed operas and *Singspiele* (incl. *Fanchon das Leiermädchen,* Berlin,

1804; *Der Kobold,* Vienna, 1813); an oratorio; a cantata; orch. works; piano concertos; sacred and secular vocal music; chamber music; piano pieces; songs (incl. "An Alexis"; "Vater, ich rufe dich").

Hinaufstrich [G.]. See Bowing (a).

Hindemith, Paul (b. Hanau, near Frankfurt, 16 Nov. 1895; d. Frankfurt, 28 Dec. 1963). Pupil of Sekles and A. Mendelssohn. Concertmaster of the Frankfurt Opera, 1915–23. Taught at the Berlin Hochschule für Musik, 1927–35. Worked on musical programs for the Turkish government, 1935–37. Settled in the U.S., 1940, and taught at Yale Univ. until 1953, when he settled in Switzerland, teaching at the Univ. of Zürich until 1956. Composed operas (incl. *Cardillac; Neues vom Tage,* Berlin, 1929, rev. 1954; *Mathis der Maler; Die *Harmonie der Welt*); ballets (incl. *Nobilissima visione,* 1938); orch. works (incl. *Philharmonic Concerto,* 1932; *Mathis der Maler,* symphony, 1934; *Symphony in E-flat,* 1940; *Symphonic Metamorphosis on Themes of Carl Maria von Weber,* 1943; *Hérodiade,* for chamber orch.; *Die Harmonie der Welt,* symphony, 1951); *Symphony in B-flat* for band, 1951; concertos and other works for solo instruments and orch. (incl. *Trauermusik* for viola and strings, 1936); vocal works with orch. (incl. the oratorio *Das Unaufhörliche,* 1931; *When Lilacs Last in the Dooryard Bloom'd,* with chorus, 1946; *Apparebit repentina dies* for chorus and brass, 1947); choral works; chamber music (incl. a number of works with title *Kammermusik;* sonatas for each orch. instrument with piano); works for voice and piano (incl. *Das Marienleben* for soprano and piano, 1922–23, rev. 1936–48); piano works (incl. *Ludus tonalis,* 1942); numerous didactic pieces and pieces intended for use by a wide musical public. He published several books, incl. *Unterweisung im tonsatz,* 3 vols., 1937, 1938, 1970 (vols. I and II publ. in English as *The Craft of Musical Composition,* 1941, rev. 1945); *A Composer's World,* 1952.

Hingston, John (d. London, buried 17 Dec. 1683). Pupil of Orlando Gibbons. Organist, teacher, and composer to Charles I, Cromwell, and Charles II. Purcell succeeded him as court organ tuner and repairer. Composed organ voluntaries; fancies and dances for viols.

Hinsterbend [G.]. Fading away.

Hirmos (Heirmos). In early Byzantine music (9th–12th centuries), a melody composed for the first stanza of a hymn and repeated with subsequent stanzas.

His [G.]. B-sharp. See Pitch names.

Histoire du soldat, L' [F., The Soldier's Tale]. A play with music and dance by Stravinsky (libretto by C. F. Ramuz), produced in Lausanne, 1918. Setting: fairy tale. It is somewhat like a *ballet d'action,* combining ballet performance with a story told in dialogue by the characters and a narrator. The music consists of a number of pieces, including Marche, Tango, Valse, Ragtime, and Choral, composed for an ensemble of six instruments and percussion.

History of music. The table on page 224 illustrates the approximate dates of the principal forms of Western music and of the periods most often identified by historians of music [see also separate entries]. Agreement about the designations and the chronological limits of periods is in many cases quite limited, the terms and concepts often having been borrowed from other branches of history, particularly art and literature.

Hob. Abbr. to signify A. van Hoboken's catalog of Haydn's works.

Hoboe. Old spelling for *oboe.

Hocket [L. *hoketus, oketus, ochetus;* F. *hocquet, hoquet;* It. *ochetto*]. In medieval polyphony (13th and 14th centuries), the rapid alternation of two or more voices with single notes or short groups of notes, one part sounding while the others rest. Numerous motets of the period include passages of this type. In some pieces hocket technique is used consistently between the two upper parts.

Hoddinott, Alun (b. Bargoed, Wales, 11 Aug. 1929). Pupil of Benjamin. Has taught at colleges in Cardiff from 1951. Has composed 4 symphonies and other

General Periods		Musical Periods	Monophonic Music	Part Music, Vocal

Chronological chart of music history:

General Periods: Early Middle Ages (600–1100), Romanesque, Early Gothic, Late Gothic, Renaissance, Baroque, Rococo, Classical, Romantic, Modern

Musical Periods: St. Martial, Notre Dame, Ars antiqua, Ars nova, Burgundian school, Flemish school, Venetian school, Nuove musiche, Roman school, Bologna school, Neapolitan school, Mannheim school, Berlin school, Viennese classics, Nationalism, Impressionism, Expressionism, Neoclassicism, Musique concrète, Electronic music, Aleatory music, Serial techniques

Monophonic Music: Gregorian chant, Sequence, Trope, Liturgical drama, Troubadours, Trouvères, Minnesingers, Laude, Cantigas, Meistersinger, Prelude, Toccata, Canzona, Variation, Fugue (Ricercar), Suite, Sonata (baroque), Concerto (baroque), Symphony, Concerto (modern), String quartet, Sonata (modern), Character piece, Symphonic poem

Part Music, Instrumental

Part Music, Vocal: Organum, Clausula, Conductus, Motet, Rondeau, Virelai, Ballade, Madrigal, Caccia, Ballata, Mass, Chanson, Frottola, Madrigal, Aria, Chorale, Opera, Anthem, Cantata, Oratorio, Catch, Lied, Glee, English, French song

: Indicates sporadic continuation

orch. works; concertos for several instruments; 2 *concerti grossi;* choral works; chamber music; piano and organ pieces; songs.

Hodkinson, Sydney (P.) (b. Winnipeg, Manitoba, Canada, 17 Jan. 1934). Clarinetist, conductor, and composer. Pupil of Bernard Rogers, L. Mennini, Carter, Sessions, Babbitt, Bassett, Finney, and Castiglioni. Has taught at several U.S. schools and colleges, incl. the Univ. of Michigan, 1968–72, and the Eastman School of Music, from 1973. Has worked with serial and aleatory techniques and elements of theater. Has composed orch. works (incl. *Caricatures*, 1966; *Valence* for chamber orch., 1970); vocal works (incl. *Ritual* for chorus, 1970); works for various instrumental ensembles.

Høffding, (Niels) Finn (b. Copenhagen, 10 Mar. 1899). Pupil of K. Jeppesen and J. Marx. Taught at the Copenhagen Conservatory, 1931–69; co-founded (1932) the Copenhagen Folkemusikskole. Has composed operas (incl. *The Emperor's New Clothes*, Copenhagen, 1928; the concert opera *Pasteur*, Copenhagen, 1938); 4 symphonies and other orch. works (incl. *Evolution*, symphonic fantasy, 1939); a concerto for oboe and strings; vocal works; chamber music; songs.

Hoffmann, E. T. A. (Ernst Theodor Amadeus) (b. Königsberg, 24 Jan. 1776; d. Berlin, 25 June 1822). Writer, jurist, and composer. Conducted theater orchestras in Bamberg, Leipzig, and Dresden. Wrote numerous works of literature; wrote essays on music under the name *Kapellmeister* Johann Kreisler. Composed operas (incl. *Undine*, Berlin, 1816); *Singspiele;* other stage works; sacred vocal music; a symphony; chamber music; piano pieces; songs.

Hoffmann, Richard (b. Vienna, 20 Apr. 1925). Settled in the U.S., 1947. Pupil and later secretary of Schoenberg. Teacher at Oberlin College from 1954. Works incl. *Orchestra Piece*, 1961; concertos for piano, for cello, and for violin; choral works; chamber music (incl. a string trio, 1963); piano pieces; organ works (incl. *Fantasy and Fugue in Memoriam Arnold Schoenberg*, 1951); songs.

Hoffmeister, Franz Anton (b. Rottenburg, Württemberg, 12 May 1754; d. Vienna, 9 Feb. 1812). Music publisher and composer. The firm he established in 1784, which eventually became the house of C. F. Peters, published works of Mozart, Beethoven, Haydn, Albrechtsberger, Dittersdorf, *et al.* Hoffmeister composed operas; symphonies, overtures, and other orch. works; concertos; chamber music (incl. numerous string quartets and trios); numerous pieces for flute; piano sonatas; songs.

Hofhaimer, Paul (b. Radstadt, near Salzburg, 25 Jan. 1459; d. Salzburg, 1537). Court organist at Innsbruck from 1480; in the service of the Emperor Maximilian I there from 1490. Cathedral organist in Salzburg from 1524. Composed organ pieces; *Harmoniae poeticae* (settings of Horatian odes); polyphonic lieder.

Hofmann, Josef (Casimir) (b. Podgorze, near Cracow, 20 Jan. 1876; d. Los Angeles, 16 Feb. 1957). Pupil of his father, the pianist Casimir Hofmann, and of Anton Rubinstein. Toured widely as a pianist in Europe, Russia, and the U.S. Director of the Curtis Institute in Philadelphia, 1926–38. Some of his works were published under the pen name Michel Dvorsky. Composed symphonic works; several piano concertos; *Chromaticon* for piano and orch., 1916; numerous piano pieces.

Hoftanz [G.]. A 16th-century German variety of the French **basse danse.*

Hoiby, Lee (b. Madison, Wis., 17 Feb. 1926). Pupil of Menotti. Has composed operas (incl. *Natalia Petrovna*, after Turgenev, New York, 1964; *Summer and Smoke*, after Williams, St. Paul, Minn., 1971); ballets (incl. *After Eden*, 1966); incidental music for plays; orch. works; a piano concerto, 1958; *The Tides of Sleep*, symphonic song for low voice and orch., 1961; choral works; chamber music; piano pieces.

Holborne, Anthony (d. London?, 1602). Cittern player and composer in the service of Queen Elizabeth I. Composed cittern and lute pieces; dances and other pieces for instrumental ensembles. His brother William Holborne (d. after 1602) was also a composer.

Holbrooke, Joseph (Josef) (b. Croydon, Surrey, 5 July 1878; d. London, 5 Aug. 1958). Pianist, conductor, and composer. Pupil of Corder. Composed operas (incl. the trilogy *The Cauldron of Anwyn*, 1912–29); ballets; 5 symphonies; symphonic poems (incl. several after works of Poe, e.g., *The Raven*, 1900; *The Bells*, with chorus, 1906); suites and other orch. works (incl. variations on *Three Blind Mice*); concertos for violin, for piano, and for saxophone; choral works; chamber music; piano pieces; clarinet pieces; songs.

Hold. *Pause.

Holden, Oliver (b. Shirley, Mass., 18 Sept. 1765; d. Charlestown, Mass., 4 Sept. 1844). Minister, carpenter, and composer. Established a music store in Charlestown, 1790. Represented Charlestown in the Mass. House of Representatives, 1818–33. Composed odes, psalms, hymns. Published several collections of sacred music.

Höller, Karl (b. Bamberg, 25 July 1907). Pupil of Haas and Hausegger. Teacher at the Musikhochschule in Frankfurt from 1937; at the Musikhochschule in Munich from 1949 and its president from 1954. Has composed a symphony and other orch. works; concertos for violin, for cello, and for organ; a *Kammerkonzert* for harpsichord and chamber orch.; sacred and secular vocal works; chamber music; organ pieces; piano pieces; music for films.

Holliger, Heinz (b. Langenthal, Switzerland, 21 May 1939). Oboist and composer. Pupil of Veress and Boulez. Professor of oboe at the Musikhochschule in Freiburg im Breisgau from 1966. Works have been composed for him by Berio, Henze, Krenek, Penderecki, Pousseur, Stockhausen, and others. His own works incl. a cantata and other vocal works with and without instruments; chamber music; *Siebengesang* for oboe, orch., voices, and amplifiers, 1967; music for winds; piano pieces.

Holmboe, Vagn (b. Horsens, Denmark, 20 Dec. 1909). Music critic and composer. Pupil of K. Jeppesen, Toch, and Høffding. Teacher at the Royal Danish Conservatory from 1950. Has collected Rumanian and Danish folk music. Has composed operas and other stage works; 10 symphonies and other orch. works; 13 chamber concertos; choral works; 10 string quartets and other chamber music; piano pieces.

Holmès, Augusta Mary Anne (pseudonym Hermann Zenta) (b. Paris, 16 Dec. 1847; d. there, 28 Jan. 1903). Pianist and composer. Pupil of Franck. Composed operas (incl. *La montagne noire*, Paris, 1895); symphonic works (incl. *Irlande*, symphonic poem, 1882); vocal works (incl. *In exitu*); piano pieces; numerous songs.

Holst, Gustav Theodore (von) (b. Cheltenham, 21 Sept. 1874; d. London, 25 May 1934). Pupil of Stanford. Trombonist with several orchestras. Music teacher at St. Paul's Girls' School from 1905; Morley College from 1907; and the Royal College of Music, 1919–23. Close associate of Vaughan Williams. Composed operas (incl. *Sāvitri*, 1908, prod. London, 1916; *The Perfect Fool*, London, 1923); choral ballets; orch. works (incl. *The *Planets; Egdon Heath*, 1927); choral works, some with orch. (incl. *First Choral Symphony*, 1924; *The Hymn of Jesus*, 1917; *Hymns from the Rig-Veda* for female voices and harp, 1910); works for voice with orch.; 2 suites for military band, 1909, 1911; chamber music; piano pieces; songs.

Holstein, Franz von (b. Brunswick, 16 Feb. 1826; d. Leipzig, 22 May 1878). Pupil of M. Hauptmann. Co-founder with Herzogenberg and P. Spitta of the Leipzig Bachverein. Composed operas (incl. *Der Haideschacht*, Dresden, 1868; *Die Hochländer*, Mannheim, 1876); overtures; choral works; chamber music; piano pieces; songs.

Holyoke, Samuel (Adams) (b. Boxford, Mass., 15 Oct. 1762; d. East Concord, N.H., 7 Feb. 1820). Founded the Groton Academy (later the Lawrence Academy), 1793; taught music in Salem, Mass., from 1800. Composed hymns and other sacred vocal music; airs; marches. Published several collections of sacred music.

Holz- [G.]. Wood. *Holzblasinstrumente*, woodwinds. *Holzbläser*, player of woodwinds. *Holzharmonika, Holzstabspiel,* xylophone. *Holzschlegel,* wooden drumstick. *Holztrompete,* wooden trumpet, such as the *alphorn.

Holzbauer, Ignaz Jakob (b. Vienna, 17 Sept. 1711; d. Mannheim, 7 Apr. 1783). Court *Kapellmeister* at Stuttgart from 1751 and at Mannheim from 1753. Visited Italy several times. Composed a German opera, *Günther von Schwarzburg,* Mannheim, 1776; 12 Italian operas; pantomimes; oratorios (incl. *La Betulia liberata,* 1760); Masses, motets, and other sacred music; numerous symphonies; concertos; divertimentos; string quartets and other chamber music.

Homer, Sidney (b. Boston, 9 Dec. 1864; d. Winter Park, Fla., 10 July 1953). Pupil of Chadwick and Rheinberger. Composed numerous songs (incl. "A Banjo Song"; "The Song of the Shirt"; "General William Booth Enters into Heaven"); some instrumental pieces.

Homilius, Gottfried August (b. Rosenthal, Saxony, 2 Feb. 1714; d. Dresden, 2 June 1785). Pupil of J. S. Bach. Organist of the Frauenkirche in Dresden from 1742 and music director of the three principal churches there from 1755. Composed Passions; a Christmas oratorio; cantatas; motets; numerous chorales and other sacred works; songs; organ pieces.

Homme armé, L' [F., The Armed Man]. A 15th-century melody [see Ex.] used as a *tenor of polyphonic Masses by numerous 15th- and 16th-century composers, including Dufay, Busnois, Caron, Ockeghem, Obrecht, Tinctoris,

Josquin, Brumel, La Rue, Pipelare, Senfl, Orto, Morales, Palestrina, and, in the 17th century, Carissimi.

Homophony. Music in which one voice leads melodically, being supported by an accompaniment in chordal or a slightly more elaborate style. Also music in which all the voices move in the same rhythm. Hence, *homophonic* is synonymous with *homorhythmic;* homophonic style is also "strict chordal style" and "familiar style." See also Polyphony.

Homorhythmic. A type of polyphonic (or part) music in which all the voices move in the same rhythm, thus producing a succession of intervals (in two-part writing) or of chords (in three- or four-part writing). The best-known examples are the four-part harmonizations of hymn or chorale melodies. Other terms applied to such music are *chordal style, *familiar style, *homophonic, isometric, note-against-note,* or even *harmonic style.*

Honegger, Arthur (b. Le Havre, 10 Mar. 1892, of Swiss parents; d. Paris, 27 Nov. 1955). Pupil of Hegar, Gédalge, Widor, and d'Indy. One of the group called "Les *six." Composed operas (incl. *Antigone,* Brussels, 1927) and operettas; ballets; incidental music for plays; music for films and for radio; oratorios (incl. *Jeanne d'Arc au bûcher,* 1938, after Claudel); dramatic psalm, *Le *roi David,* 1921; 5 symphonies; numerous suites and other orch. works (incl. *Pacific 231,* 1924; *Rugby,* 1928); choral works; concertos; chamber music; piano pieces; songs.

Hook, James (b. Norwich, 3 June 1746; d. Boulogne, 1827). Held several positions as church and theater organist in London and as a piano teacher. Composed operas and other dramatic works; incidental music for plays; oratorios; instrumental works, incl. keyboard sonatas and concertos; odes; numerous songs.

Hopak. See Gopak.

Hopkins, Edward Jerome (b. Burlington, Vt., 4 Apr. 1836; d. Athenia, N.J., 4 Nov. 1898). Music journalist, pedagogue, and composer. Organized several "Free Singing and Opera Schools," 1886. Composed dramatic works (incl.

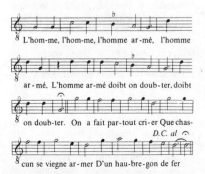

L'hom-me, l'hom-me, l'homme ar-mé, l'homme

ar-mé, L'homme ar-mé doibt on doub-ter, doibt

on doub-ter. On a fait par-tout cri-er Que chas-

D.C. al

cun se viegne ar-mer D'un hau-bre-gon de fer

Taffy and Old Munch, children's fairy tale, 1880); choral works; songs; pedagogic works. Compiled 2 collections of church music.

Hopkins, Edward John (b. London, 30 June 1818; d. London, 4 Feb. 1901). Chorister in the Chapel Royal, 1826–33. Held several positions as church organist, including that at Temple Church in London, 1843–98. Composed anthems (incl. "Out of the Deep"); hymns; services; other sacred music; secular songs.

Hopkinson, Francis (b. Philadelphia, 21 Sept. 1737; d. there, 9 May 1791). Lawyer, statesman (a signer of the Declaration of Independence), writer, and composer. Composed *7 Songs for the harpsichord or forte piano,* 1788 (containing "My days have been so wondrous free"), in which he claimed to be the first native composer of the U.S.; a cantata; songs.

Hoquet, hoquetus. See Hocket.

Horn [F. *cor;* G. *Horn;* It. *corno;* Sp. *trompa*]. The modern orchestral instrument called the French horn (in order to distinguish it from the English horn, a member of the *oboe family) is a *brass instrument with a funnel-shaped mouthpiece and a narrow conical bore wound into a spiral and ending in a large, flaring bell. It has three *valves (usually rotary) and is therefore also called a valve horn [F. *cor-à-pistons, cor chromatique;* G. *Ventilhorn;* It. *corno ventile, corno a macchina;* Sp. *trompa de pistón*] to distinguish it from the early (before *c.* 1815) valveless instruments (*natural horn). See ill. under Brass instruments. See also Wind instruments.

Normally the horn is pitched in F, and the series of its natural tones is F_1 F c f a c' f' g' a', etc. Owing to the narrow bore, however, the lowest tone of this series (pedal tone) is practically unobtainable, so that the series starts with F. Operating the valves makes a complete chromatic scale from B_1 to f'' available. The horn is notated as a transposing instrument, written a fifth higher than it sounds. The double horn combines an instrument in F with one in B♭, changes from one to the other being effected by an additional valve [see Duplex instruments].

Horn playing requires several special methods of tone production. The most important of these is stopping [F. *bouché;* G. *gestopft;* It. *chiuso;* Sp. *tapada*], achieved by inserting the hand into the bell. On the natural (valveless) horn the missing tones of the natural series were produced by inserting the hand flat into the bell and closing it 1/4, 1/2, or 3/4. This gave a continuous scale mostly of diatonic tones, which, however, was not very satisfactory since the stopping changed the timbre. A horn played in this way is called a *hand horn* [It. *corno a mano*]. Nowadays stopping is used only to obtain a special effect. Blocking the bell with the hand and sharply increasing the wind pressure cause the tone to rise approximately a semitone. Stopped tones are indicated thus: +. The *mute* [F. *sourdine;* G. *Dämpfer;* It., Sp. *sordina*] is a pear-shaped piece of metal, wood, or cardboard that is inserted into the bell in order to produce yet another timbre (muted horns). Modern mutes are nontransposing; the older ones, smaller and shaped slightly differently, raised the pitch. Muting may also be done with the player's hand. "Brassy" tones [F. *cuivré;* G. *schmetternd*] are obtained by increasing wind pressure and can be produced open, stopped, or muted.

In the 18th century, horns were provided with crooks, additional lengths of tubing by means of which the pitch of the instruments could be changed. A horn in F could thus be made into a horn in E or E♭.

Horn, Charles Edward (b. London, 21 June 1786; d. Boston, 21 Oct. 1849). Conductor, opera singer, and composer. Son and pupil of the organist and composer Karl Friedrich Horn (1762–1830). Emigrated to the U.S., 1832. Conductor of the Handel and Haydn Society in Boston from 1848. Composed operas; oratorios (incl. *The Remission of Sin*); a cantata, *Christmas Bells;* glees; songs.

Horn fifths [G. *Hornquinten*]. See under Parallel fifths.

Hornpipe. (1) An obsolete wind instrument of the clarinet family. (2) A dance popular in England from the 16th through 19th centuries which, at least in its later development, was performed as a solo dance by sailors. The numerous hornpipes of the 17th and 18th centuries are usually in moderate 3/2 time (later in 4/4 time) with a characteristic "Scotch snap" rhythm [see under Dotted notes]. Examples are found in the theatrical works of Purcell and in Handel's *Concerto grosso* no. 7.

Horst, Louis (b. Kansas City, 12 Jan. 1884; d. New York, 23 Jan. 1964). Music director of the Ruth St. Denis and Denishawn dance companies, 1915–25. Associated with the Martha Graham Dance Company, 1926–48. Composed numerous dance scores, some of them choreographed by Graham, incl. *El penitente*, 1940; *Frontier*, 1935; *Celebration*, 1934; *Primitive Mysteries*, 1931.

Hosanna, Osanna. A Hebrew word expressing triumph and glorification. In the phrase "Hosanna in excelsis" it occurs in the Sanctus of the Ordinary of the *Mass.

Hotteterre, Jacques Martin ("le romain") (b. Paris, *c.* 1680; d. there, *c.* 1761). Flutist and composer. Member of a large family of musicians. Served as instrumentalist in the Musique de la Grande Écurie from 1705. Composed numerous pieces for flute (incl. sonatas, suites, minuets); pieces for musette; songs. Published several manuals on the transverse flute and other instruments.

Hovhaness, Alan (Scott) (b. Somerville, Mass., 8 Mar. 1911). Pupil of Converse and Martinů. Teacher at the Boston Conservatory, 1948–52, and organist at the Boston Armenian Church. Has traveled widely in India, Russia, and the Far East. Has worked with Armenian and Oriental materials and with aleatory techniques. His very numerous works incl. operas and other stage works; 25 symphonies and other orch. works (incl. *And God Created Great Whales*, 1970, with whale sounds on tape); choral works (incl. *Triptych*, 1953); chamber music; piano pieces; songs.

Howe, Mary (b. Richmond, Va., 4 Apr. 1882; d. Washington, D.C., 14 Sept. 1964). Pianist and composer. Pupil of Strube and N. Boulanger. Composed orch. works (incl. *Rock*, 1955); choral works (incl. *Prophecy 1792*, 1943; *Chain Gang Song*, 1925); chamber music; songs.

Howells, Herbert Norman (b. Lydney, Gloucestershire, 17 Oct. 1892). Pupil of Stanford and Parry. Held several positions as church organist from 1905. Teacher at the Royal College of Music from 1920; music director of Morley College from 1925; music director (succeeding Holst) of St. Paul's Girls' School in London from 1935; teacher at the Univ. of London from 1952. Has composed orch. works; concertos for piano and for cello; sacred music, incl. Masses, anthems; choral works (incl. *Sine nomine*, with orch., 1922; *Hymnus paradisi*, 1938); chamber music; organ pieces; piano pieces; clavichord pieces; songs.

Hptw. [G.]. Abbr. for *Hauptwerk*, i.e., great *organ.

Hr. Abbr. for *Horn.

Hrisanide, Alexandru (b. Petrila, Rumania, 15 June 1936). Pianist, critic, and composer. Pupil of N. Boulanger. Teacher at the Bucharest Academy of Music, 1959–62, and at the Bucharest Conservatory from 1962. Has worked with twelve-tone and aleatory techniques and with Rumanian folk materials. Has composed orch. works (incl. *Passacaglia*, 1959); pieces for various chamber ensembles (incl. *Volumes-Inventions* for cello and piano, 1963; *Mers-Tefs II* for 1–4 violins, 1960–70); choral works; piano pieces.

Hubay, Jenö (originally Huber) (b. Budapest, 15 Sept. 1858; d. there, 12 Mar. 1937). Violinist and composer. Pupil of Joachim and of Vieuxtemps, whom he succeeded as professor at the Brussels Conservatory, 1882. Professor at the Budapest Conservatory from 1886 and its director, 1919–34. Organized the Hubay String Quartet. Composed operas (incl. *A Cremonai hegedüs* [The Violin Maker of Cremona], Budapest, 1894); a ballet; 4 symphonies and other orch. works; 4 violin concertos; *Csardajelenet* (Scenes from the Csarda) for violin and orch.; choral works; chamber music; violin pieces; songs.

Huber, Hans (b. Eppenberg, near Olten, Switzerland, 28 June 1852; d. Locarno, 25 Dec. 1921). Pianist and composer. Pupil of Richter and Reinecke. Director of the Allgemeine Musikschule in Basel, 1896–1918. Composed operas (incl. *Ku-*

drun, Basel, 1896; *Die schöne Bellinda,* Bern, 1916); 8 symphonies and other orch. works; 4 piano concertos; a violin concerto; choral works; chamber music; piano pieces; organ pieces; pedagogic works; songs.

Huber, Klaus (b. Bern, 30 Nov. 1924). Pupil of Burkhard and Blacher. Has taught at the Zürich Conservatory from 1950; at the Lucerne Conservatory from 1960; at the Basel Conservatory from 1961; at the Musikhochschule in Freiburg im Breisgau (succeeding Fortner) from 1973. Has composed orch. works (incl. *Tenebrae,* 1967); a cantata, *Des Engels Anredung an die Seele,* 1957; sacred and secular vocal works; chamber music; organ pieces (incl. *In te Domine speravi,* 1966).

Hudson, George (fl. 17th cent.; d. London, before 1673). Violinist and composer. Court musician to Charles II from 1660. Composed music for *The *Siege of Rhodes;* ayres; pieces for viols; other instrumental works.

Hüe, Georges-Adolphe (b. Versailles, 6 May 1858; d. Paris, 7 June 1948). Pupil of Reber and Paladilhe. Succeeded Saint-Saëns as member of the Académie, 1922. Composed operas (incl. *Les pantins,* Paris, 1881) and other stage works; orch. works; works for violin and orch. and for flute and orch.; choral works (incl. *Rübezahl* with orch., 1886); songs.

Hufnagelschrift [G.]. See *Nagelschrift.*

Huguenots, Les [F., The Huguenots]. Opera in five acts by Meyerbeer (libretto by E. Scribe), produced in Paris, 1836. Setting: Paris and Touraine, 1572.

Hullah, John Pyke (b. Worcester, 27 June 1812; d. London 21 Feb. 1884). Church organist at Croydon from 1836 and at Charter House, London, from 1858. Established a singing school in London, 1841; also taught singing at King's College there, 1844–74. Composed operas (incl. *The Village Coquettes,* after Dickens, London, 1836); songs. Published several anthologies of vocal music and books on voice, music theory, and music history.

Hume, Tobias (d. London, 16 Apr. 1645). Army officer, viola da gamba player, and composer. Composed songs and instrumental works, incl. the collections *The First Part of Ayres . . . With Pavines, Galliards and Almaines,* 1605; *Captain Humes Poeticall Musicke,* 1607.

Humel, Gerald (b. Cleveland, 7 Nov. 1931). Pupil of Elwell, Siegmeister, Blacher, Rufer, Finney, Howells, and Gerhard. Settled in Berlin, 1960. Conductor of the Ensemble der Gruppe Neue Musik Berlin from 1967. Has worked with twelve-tone techniques. Has composed operas; ballets (incl. *Die Folterungen der Beatrice Cenci,* 1971); a symphony and other orch. works; chamber music.

Humfrey, Pelham (b. 1647; d. Windsor, 14 July 1674). Boy chorister in the Chapel Royal under Cooke from 1660, with Blow and Turner. Court lutenist from 1666. Succeeded Cooke as master of the children of the Chapel Royal, 1672. Composer to the royal orchestra from 1673. Composed incidental music for *The Tempest;* sacred and secular songs; a service, anthems, and other church music.

Hummel, Johann Nepomuk (b. Pressburg, 14 Nov. 1778; d. Weimar, 17 Oct. 1837). Pianist and composer. Pupil of his father, Johannes Hummel, and of Mozart, Albrechtsberger, Salieri, and Haydn. Second *Kapellmeister* (under Haydn) to Prince Esterházy, 1804–11. Court *Kapellmeister* at Stuttgart from 1816 and at Weimar from 1819 to his death. Composed operas (incl. *Mathilde von Guise,* Vienna, 1810); ballets; pantomimes; 7 piano concertos; Masses and other sacred music; cantatas; chamber music; numerous piano pieces. Published a piano method, *Anweisung zum Pianofortespiel,* 1828.

Humoreske [G.]; **humoresque** [F.]. A 19th-century name for instrumental compositions of a humorous, fanciful, or simply good-humored nature. Schumann used it for a long composition (op. 20) in which the expression frequently changes from one extreme to another.

Humperdinck, Engelbert (b. Siegburg, near Bonn, 1 Sept. 1854; d. Neustrelitz, 27 Sept. 1921). Pupil of Hiller, Gernsheim, Lachner, and Rheinberger. Assistant to Wagner in Bayreuth, 1880–82. Taught at the Barcelona Conservatory, 1885–87, and at Hoch's Conservatory in Frankfurt, 1890–96. Composed operas (incl. *Hänsel und Gretel; Königskinder,* New York, 1910, based on incidental music of 1897); incidental music for plays; other stage works; orch. works; choral works; piano pieces; songs.

Hungarian Dances [G. *Ungarische Tänze*]. A collection of 21 dances by Brahms, for piano four-hands, published in four volumes (1852–69). Some were arranged for orchestra by Brahms. Some of them employ genuine Hungarian melodies, but others are freely invented in the Hungarian Gypsy style.

Hungarian Rhapsodies [F. *Rhapsodies hongroises*]. A group of about 20 piano compositions by Liszt, in the character of free fantasies based on Hungarian themes. Most of them open with a slow introduction and continue with a fast, dancelike movement in imitation of the Hungarian *csárdás*.

Hunnenschlacht, Die [G., The Battle (Slaughter) of the Huns]. Symphonic poem by Liszt (1857), inspired by a painting by Kaulbach.

Hunt Quartet. (1) Popular name for Mozart's String Quartet in B♭ major, K. 458 (no. 3 of the *Haydn Quartets), also called *La chasse,* with reference to the hunting-horn motif in the opening theme. (2) Popular name for Haydn's String Quartet in B♭ major, op. 1, no. 1, first published in 1762.

Hunt Symphony. Haydn's Symphony in D major, no. 73 (1781), also called *La chasse,* with reference to the last movement, which was originally composed to depict a hunting scene in his opera *La fedeltà premiata* (1780).

Hünten, Franz (b. Coblenz, 26 Dec. 1792; d. there, 22 Feb. 1878). Pianist and composer. Pupil of Cherubini and Reicha. Lived in Paris as a piano teacher, 1819–35 and 1839–48. Composed numerous piano pieces, incl. fantasies, variations, rondos, waltzes; chamber music; songs; a piano method and other didactic works.

Hupfauf [G.]. See under Dance music.

Hurdy-gurdy [F. *vielle (à roue);* G. *Drehleier;* It. *ghironda;* Sp. *zanfoña*]. A medieval stringed instrument, shaped somewhat like a lute or viol, whose strings are put in vibration not by a bow but by a rotating rosined wheel operated by a handle at the lower end of the body. The instrument usually had two to four unfingered bass-strings that were allowed to sound continuously, producing a drone harmony (c–g–c'), and two melody strings (tuned in unison) running over the fingerboard, which were stopped by tangents connected with a keyboard. The instrument was very popular from the 10th to 14th centuries; later, as a street musician's instrument, it was disdained. However, in the 17th century, together with the *musette, it became fashionable in French society. Haydn wrote five concertos and seven *notturnos* for two hurdy-gurdies. He called the instrument *lyra* or *lira organizzata,* a name that has been erroneously interpreted as *lira da braccio.* The name "lyra" as well as the use of a crank has also led to confusion with the *street organ, to which the name is also applied. See ill. under Violin family.

Huré, Jean (b. Gien, Loiret, 17 Sept. 1877; d. Paris, 27 Jan. 1930). Pianist, organist, and composer. Founded the École normale de musique in Paris, 1910. Church organist at Saint-Augustin, succeeding Gigout, from 1925. Composed stage works; 3 symphonies; pieces for saxophone and orch.; sacred and secular vocal music; chamber music.

Hurlebusch, Conrad Friedrich (b. Brunswick, 1695 or 1696; d. Amsterdam, 17 Dec. 1765). Organist and composer. Court *Kapellmeister* at Stockholm, 1723 –25. Organist at the Oude Kerk in Amsterdam from 1743. Composed operas; cantatas; orch. works; concertos; pieces for harpsichord, for organ, and for other instruments; odes; psalms.

Hurlstone, William Yeates (b. London, 7 Jan. 1876; d. there, 30 May 1906). Pianist and composer. Pupil of Stanford. Teacher at the Royal College of Music from 1905. Composed orch. works (incl. *Variations on a Swedish Air; The Magic Mirror*); a piano concerto; chamber music (incl. *Fantasy String Quartet*); choral works; piano pieces; songs.

Hurtig [G.]. Quick, nimble.

Husa, Karel (b. Prague, 7 Aug. 1921). Pupil of Řídký, Honegger, and N. Boulanger. Has conducted many European and U.S. orchestras. Member of the faculty of Cornell Univ. from 1954. Has composed the ballet *Monodrama*, 1975; orch. works (incl. Symphony no. 1, 1953; *Mosaïques*, 1961; *Music for Prague 1968* for band or orch.; *Two Sonnets from Michelangelo*, 1972; *The Steadfast Tin Soldier* with narrator, 1974); *Apotheosis of This Earth* for symphonic band, 1970, version for orch. and chorus, 1973; *American Te Deum* for chorus and wind ensemble, 1976, version for chorus and orch., 1978; a concerto for saxophone and winds, 1967, and one for trumpet and winds, 1973; chamber music (incl. *Evocations of Slovakia* for clarinet, viola, and cello, 1951; String Quartet no. 3, awarded the Pulitzer Prize for 1969; *Landscapes* for brass quintet, 1977); choral works; piano pieces.

Huss, Henry Holden (b. Newark, N.J., 21 June 1862; d. New York, 17 Sept. 1953). Pianist and composer. Pupil of Rheinberger. Composed orch. works; works for piano and orch. (incl. *Rhapsody* and a concerto in B); vocal works (incl. *Ave Maria* for chorus); chamber music; piano pieces; songs.

Hüttenbrenner, Anselm (b. Graz, 13 Oct. 1794; d. Ober-Andritz, near Graz, 5 June 1868). Pianist and composer. Pupil of Salieri. Friend of Schubert and Beethoven. Artistic director of the Steiermärkischer Musikverein in Graz, 1825–39. Composed operas; symphonies, overtures, and other orch. works; Masses and other sacred music; 2 string quartets and other chamber music; piano pieces; numerous songs (incl. "Erlkönig") and quartets for male voices.

Hydraulos [F. *orgue hydraulique;* G. *Wasserorgel*]. The organ of the ancient Greece and Rome, invented by Ktesibios of Alexandria (*c.* 300–250 B.C.). It differed from the pneumatic organ mainly in the wind supply, which was provided by water instead of bellows. The water was enclosed in a separate container and served to conduct hydraulic pressure provided by hand pumps.

Hymn. A song of praise, usually to a god or a hero. Two hymns to Apollo of *c.* 150 B.C. are among the most complete remnants of Greek music. In the early Christian era, the term *hymn* was applied to all songs in praise of the Lord; later it was restricted to newly written poems, as distinguished from the scriptural psalms and canticles.

The Eastern churches (Syrian, Byzantine, Armenian) gave hymns a much more prominent part in the service than they ever attained in the Western church. The earliest preserved Christian hymn melody is the Oxyrhynchos Hymn of *c.* A.D. 300. St. Hilary, Bishop of Poitiers (d. *c.* 367), is credited with having written the first Latin hymns, in imitation of the Syrian and Greek hymns of the early Eastern churches. St. Ambrose (*c.* 340–97) introduced a type of hymn that, because of its clarity and regularity, became immensely popular and gained a firm foothold in the Milanese as well as the Roman rites [see Ambrosian hymns]. The earliest sources of hymn melodies, however, date from the 11th or 12th century. There are only a few scattered examples of polyphonic hymns from before 1400, but in the course of the 15th and 16th centuries such hymn settings became quite common.

The Germans began to sing hymns in their native language as early as *c.* 1300. These became the point of departure for the ensuing development of the German Protestant hymn [see Chorale]. Echoes of Continental hymn singing reached the British Isles by about 1540 with the publication of collections containing English translations from the German, including such tunes used in Germany as "Ein' feste Burg." Music editions of the Sternhold and Hopkins metrical psalms date from 1560, and all of these collections, apart from containing the 150 psalms set in meter, also had a few hymns or metrical prayers appended.

After the Psalters published by John Day (1522–84), significant collections with new tunes were published by Thomas East (1591, 1592), Thomas Ravenscroft (1621), and John Playford (1671, 1677). The new style of hymn texts by Isaac Watts (1674–1748) and

Charles Wesley (1707–88) inspired many new tunes. English *tune books of the 18th century included John Wesley's *A Collection of Tunes . . . sung at the Foundery* (1742). Composers such as J. B. Dykes in the mid-19th century wrote tunes with four-part harmony that were miniature part songs. These, introduced in successive editions of *Hymns Ancient and Modern* (1861–1950), completely changed the character of hymn singing. Other musical editions of the period were Arthur Sullivan's *Church Hymns with Tunes* (1874) and Joseph Barnby's *The Hymnary* (1872). Important collections of the 20th century are *The English Hymnal* (1906) and *Songs of Praise* (1925).

In America, apart from a few tunes bound in the back of successive editions of *The Bay Psalm Book,* the first tune book to be published was James Lyons' *Urania* (1761), followed shortly by Francis Hopkinson's *A Collection of Psalm Tunes* (1763) and Josiah Flagg's *A Collection of the Best Psalm Tunes* (1764; on plates engraved by Paul Revere). By 1800, more than 130 such collections had been published along the Atlantic coast. Today, each major Protestant denomination has its own hymnal, sharing nearly half its hymns and tunes with other denominations.

Hyper-, hypo- [Gr.]. Prefixes denoting higher and lower pitches, respectively. *Hyper-* (*hypo-*) *diatessaron* is the upper (lower) fourth; *hyper-* (*hypo-*) *diapente,* the higher (lower) fifth. In Greek theory, terms such as Hyperdorian and Hypodorian signify modes (more properly, octave species) that start a fifth above and below the initial tone of the original octave, e.g., Dorian on e, Hyperdorian on b, Hypodorian on A. In the medieval system of *church modes the prefix *hypo-* denotes modes whose range (*ambitus*) is a fourth below that of the corresponding primary (authentic) mode [see Church modes].

Hz. Abbr. for *Hertz.*

I

Iamb, iambic. See under Poetic meter; Modes, rhythmic.

Iberia [L.]. Twelve piano pieces, in four sets of three each, by Albéniz, published 1906–9. Each is based on a Spanish theme or locale. For Debussy's *Ibéria,* see under *Images.*

Ibert, Jacques (b. Paris, 15 Aug. 1890; d. there, 5 Feb. 1962). Pupil of Gédalge and Vidal. Director of the French Academy in Rome, 1937–55. Director of the Paris Opéra and the Opéra-Comique, 1955–56. Composed operas (incl. *Angélique,* Paris, 1927) and other stage works; ballets (incl. *Le chevalier errant,* after Cervantes, 1935); orch. works (incl. *Escales* [Ports of Call], 1922; *Ballade de la geôle de Reading,* after Wilde, 1920); concertos, incl. one for saxophone and chamber orch.; vocal works; chamber music; piano pieces (incl. *Le petit âne blanc*); music for films.

Ichiyanagi, Toshi (b. Kobe, Japan, 4 Feb. 1933). Pupil of Ikenouchi, Copland, Foss, and Cage. Has collaborated in performances with Cage and Tudor. Has employed Oriental and Western instruments as well as electronic means. Works incl. *Distance,* a theater work; *The Field* for bamboo flute and orch.; *Sapporo* for any number of players up to 15 and any number of instruments; *Extended Voices* for chorus; several pieces titled *Music for Piano;* several works on tape.

Ictus [L.]. In prosody, a stress or accent. The term was introduced in music by the monks of *Solesmes as an integral part of their rhythmic interpretation and performance of *Gregorian chant. The ictus serves primarily to mark off those groups of two and three notes that form the basis of their rendition of the chant. Ictus has nothing to do with speech or grammatical accent.

Idée fixe. Berlioz' name for the principal subject of his *Symphonie fantastique*. It occurs in all the movements [see Cyclic, cyclical].

Idiomatic style. A style appropriate for the instrument for which particular music is written.

Idiophone. See under Instruments.

Idomeneo. Opera in three acts by Mozart (libretto by G. B. Varesco), produced in Munich, 1781. Setting: Crete in legendary times.

Ikenouchi, Tomojiro (b. Tokyo, 21 Oct. 1906). Pupil of Busser in Paris. Teacher at the Univ. of Nihon, 1938–48, and at the National College of Music and Graphic Arts in Tokyo from 1946. Has composed orch. works (incl. *Mago Uta*); string quartets and other chamber music.

Im Takt. See *Takt*.

Images [F.]. Title used by Debussy for two cycles of compositions. (1) Six piano pieces in two sets of three each: I (1905), II (1907). (2) Three symphonic poems (*Images pour orchestre*, 1906–11): *Rondes de printemps* (Dances of Spring), *Ibéria, Gigues*. The second, *Ibéria*, consists of three movements: "Par les rues et par les chemins" (In the Streets and Alleys), "Les parfums de la nuit" (The Perfumes of the Night), and "Le matin d'un jour de fête" (The Morning of a Festival Day).

Imbrie, Andrew W. (Welsh) (b. New York, 6 Apr. 1921). Pupil of Sessions and N. Boulanger. Teacher at the Univ. of California at Berkeley from 1949. Has composed an opera; orch. works (incl. 3 symphonies and a symphonic poem, *Legend*, 1959); 2 violin concertos, 1953, 1957; a piano concerto, 1973; a flute concerto, 1977; choral works; 4 string quartets and other chamber music; piano pieces.

Imitation. The restatement in close succession of a melody (theme, motif) in different parts (lines) of a contrapuntal texture [see Counterpoint]. Such restatements are frequently at a pitch level different from that of the initial statement. This device is most consistently employed in the *canon, in which an entire voice-part is imitated in another (canonic imitation). Imitation of themes (subjects) is an essential feature of the *fugue (fugal imitation) as well as the 16th-century *motet and the various prefugal forms, the *ricercar, *canzona, *fantasia, and *capriccio. While in a fugue the imitation is normally restricted to one theme, the earlier forms usually have several. Although its history begins with the school of *Notre Dame, c. 1200, imitation finds its first systematic realization in the 14th century, in the Italian *caccia and French *chace, which are extended two- and three-part canons. The works of Obrecht, Isaac, and Josquin show more and more deliberate use of imitation, which c. 1500 became an essential element of musical style. The development reached its climax with Nicolas Gombert (d. c. 1556), whose motets are pervaded by imitation [see also Point (3)]. Throughout the 16th century and the baroque period, imitation remained a basic element of contrapuntal writing. In the rococo period (c. 1725–75) came a sharp reaction against the fugal style of the baroque era [see Gallant style]. However, free use of imitation became prominent again in Haydn's and Mozart's later symphonies and quartets and remained an important technique of composition, particularly in the development section of symphonies, quartets, sonatas, etc.

Imperfect. See Cadence; Consonance; dissonance; Mensural notation.

Impressionism. A term borrowed from the history of painting, where it is associated with the works of a group of late 19th-century French painters (principally Monet, Manet, Renoir, and Degas), and applied primarily to the music of Debussy (who himself disapproved of its use in this way). A concern of the painters in question was the nature of light and its perception rather than the symbolic, literary, or emotive value of the thing perceived. Avoiding strongly formal designs, the painters preferred instead (partly owing to the influence of contemporary photography) casual scenes or poses. These features of their work have suggested analogies with some works of Debussy in which there seems to be a similar avoidance of traditional musical forms including clearly delineated melodies and in which greatly expanded resources of instrumental tone color and harmony are employed, including free treatment of dissonance, *parallel chords, and pitch collections such as the *whole-tone scale that weaken or eliminate the role of single pitches as tonal centers operating over long spans. Use of the analogy has also been encouraged by those compositions of Debussy whose titles suggest pictorial associations reminiscent of the works of the impressionist painters: "Clouds," "The Sunken Cathedral," "Reflections in the Water," etc. The purely musical organization of such compositions, however, cannot be regarded as lacking in formal clarity, much less as "dreamy" or "vague," and others of his compositions lack such pictorial associations altogether. Thus, like other borrowed terms of its kind, *impressionism* can be quite misleading and may inhibit a proper understanding of the whole range of Debussy's art.

Other composers whose works are sometimes associated with Debussy's under this rubric include Ravel, Dukas, Roussel, Delius, Griffes, Falla, and Respighi.

Impromptu [F.]. Title for short pieces by Schubert (who is probably not responsible for its use with his op. 90, D. 899, and op. 142, D. 935), Chopin (op. 29, 36, 51, 66), and others, suggesting an offhand or extemporized style. In style and form, however, these are not markedly different from some other types of *character pieces.

Improperia [L., reproaches]. In the Roman Catholic liturgy, chants for Good Friday Mass. They consist of three passages from the Prophets, each of which is followed by the *Trisagion. Palestrina set them in *falsobordone* style for double chorus.

Improvisation, extemporization. The art of creating music spontaneously in performance. In practice, the resulting music is often based on some subject or theme and may, in such cases, take the form of a set of variations. Fugues or entirely free forms may also result, however. In earlier periods of Western art music, improvisation was much more widely practiced than it is today, masters such as Bach, Handel, Mozart, and Beethoven having been as famous for their improvising as for their written compositions. In the concert music of today, it survives chiefly among organ virtuosos, though it is also a feature of some contemporary music [see Aleatory music]. Introduction of improvised details into the performance of written compositions was an essential feature of *ornamentation as early as the Middle Ages and was of particular importance in the 17th and 18th centuries. It remained prominent in the 19th century in some forms of vocal music (principally Italian opera) and in the *cadenza of concertos. It is also an essential feature of the realization of the *thoroughbass of baroque music. Improvisation in the broadest sense plays a fundamental role in *jazz, some types of popular music, and the art music of many non-Western cultures.

In nomine [L.]. Title of a large number of English instrumental pieces (for viols, lute, or keyboard) of the 16th and 17th centuries based on a *cantus firmus* that begins d f d d d c f g f g a. This *cantus firmus* is quite similar to the melody of the Vespers antiphon of Trinity Sunday *Gloria tibi Trinitas,* and the seemingly wrong designation is explained by the fact that this type of composition originated with and developed from the *In nomine* ("Benedictus qui venit in nomine Domini") from the Sanctus of Taverner's *Missa Gloria tibi Trinitas.* This section (like many others in this Mass) employs the melody of *Gloria tibi Trinitas* as a *cantus firmus.* The *In nomine* was the most favored type of *cantus firmus* composition in England after *c.* 1550, replacing the *Felix namque,* cultivated mainly before that date.

Incalzando [It.]. Pressing, hurrying.

Incidental music. Music to be used in connection with a play. It may consist of occasional songs, marches, dances, and background music for monologues and dialogues, as well as instrumental music before and after each act. Nearly all of Purcell's dramatic music is incidental music for plays. Later examples are Beethoven's music to Goethe's *Egmont* and to Kotzebue's *Die Ruinen von Athen,* Mendelssohn's music to *A Midsummer Night's Dream,* Bizet's music to Daudet's *L'arlésienne* (1872), and Grieg's music to Ibsen's *Peer Gynt* (1875).

Incoronazione di Poppea, L' [It., The Coronation of Poppea]. Opera in three acts by Monteverdi (libretto by G. F. Busenello), produced in Venice, 1642. Setting: Rome during Nero's reign, A.D. 62.

Indeterminacy. See Aleatory music.

India, Sigismondo d' (b. Palermo, *c.* 1580; d. probably in Modena, shortly before 19 Apr. 1629). Director of chamber music at the Turin court, 1611–23; court musician in Modena, 1623–24; musician to Cardinal Maurizio of Savoy in Rome, 1624–26. Composed madrigals; arias; *villanelle;* a Mass; motets; cantatas.

Indy, (Paul-Marie-Théodore-) Vincent d' (b. Paris, 27 Mar. 1851; d. there, 2 Dec. 1931). Pupil of Franck. Close associate of Duparc. Organist at Saint-Leu-la-Forêt from 1872. Chorusmaster of the Colonne Orchestra from 1873. Co-founder, with Bordes and Guilmant, of the Schola cantorum, 1894, and its director from 1911. Teacher at the Paris Conservatory from 1912. Traveled widely as a conductor in Europe, Russia, and the U.S. Composed stage works (incl. *Le chant de la cloche,* dramatic poem, 1912; the operas *Fervaal,* Brussels, 1897, and *L'étranger,* Brussels, 1903); orch. works (incl. *Wallenstein,* symphonic trilogy, 1873–81; *Jour d'été à la montagne,* 1905; *Symphonie sur un chant montagnard français* with piano, 1886; **Istar*); chamber music; choral works; songs; piano and organ pieces; didactic works; numerous arrangements of folksongs. Also published numerous writings on music.

Inégales [F.; abbr. for *notes inégales*]. The practice of performing certain evenly written notes "unequally," with alternation of longer and shorter values. This manner crystallized in France during the 17th century into a distinct convention that, elaborately codified, lasted with little apparent change until the late 18th century. Inequality in a pair of notes was definitely long-short only and applied generally to the fastest prevailing notes: in duple meter to the fourfold subdivision of the metrical unit such as the sixteenth note in 4/4, the eighth note in 2/4; in triple meters to twofold subdivisions: the eighth note in 3/4, the sixteenth note in 3/8; to shorter notes, if they occurred, but never to longer ones. It applied to melodies that moved by and large in stepwise progression; it was limited to French music written in the French style, hence excluding works patterned after foreign models such as Italianate sonatas or concertos. The composer could cancel inequality by such words as *détaché* or *marqué,* or by dots or dashes above the notes. The degree of unevenness was left up to the performer, varying from a slight lilt (*louré*) to a more pronounced inequality (*pointé* or *piqué*) that could approach, but only rarely reached, the full meaning of a dot. The only known non-French reference in the 18th century is a passage in Quantz' treatise of 1752, where this advocate of a "mixed style" endorses the *inégales* convention. The passage has become the mainstay of a widely accepted theory that the *inégales* were a universal "baroque practice" that applied to German masters, including Bach, as well as to the French.

Inflection, inflexion. See under Monotone.

Ingegneri, Marc'Antonio (b. Verona, *c.* 1547; d. Cremona, 1 July 1592). *Maestro di cappella* of the Cremona Cathedral from 1581. Monteverdi was his pupil. Composed madrigals; Masses, motets, hymns, responsories, Lamentations.

Inghelbrecht, Désiré-Émile (b. Paris, 17 Sept. 1880; d. there, 14 Feb. 1965). Conductor and composer. Friend and admirer of Debussy. Conductor of the Ballets Suedois, 1920–23, and of the Paris Opéra between 1924 and 1933. Composed an opera; ballets (incl. *El Greco,* 1920); orch. works; choral works (incl. *Le cantique des créatures de Saint François,* with orch., 1919); chamber music; piano pieces; songs.

Initium [L.]. The two or three opening notes of a *psalm tone.

Innig [G.]. Heartfelt, tender.

Inno [It.]. *Hymn.

Instrumentation. *Orchestration.

Instruments. Generic name for all mechanisms producing musical sounds and hence for all musical media with the exception of the human voice. Western instruments usually are grouped in three categories: *stringed instruments, *wind instruments,* and *percussion instruments.* In the more general classification scheme now in use for the sake of including non-Western instruments as well, the members of the first group are called *chordophones* [Gr. *chordos,* string; *phonos,* sound]; the second, *aerophones* [Gr. *aeros,* air, wind]; the third, which are extremely numerous in non-Western music, are divided into two classes, *idiophones* [Gr. *idios,* self], instruments that consist simply of some material (metal, wood) capable of producing sound, and *membranophones* [L. *membranum,* skin], instruments in which a stretched skin is the sound-producing agent. To these four classes a fifth has recently been added, the *electrophones,* in which the acoustical vibrations are produced by electronic means [see Electronic instruments]. Each of these categories is further subdivided.

Intabulation [G. *Intabulierung;* It. *intavolatura*]. A keyboard or lute *arrangement of vocal music, common from the 14th through the 16th centuries. The term (from L. *tabula,* table) refers to the change from the original notation in single parts to the scorelike (tabular, vertical) notation used for the *tablatures of the solo instruments. Intabulations frequently alter the vocal originals through the rearrangement or omission of original parts and through the introduction of substantial amounts of written ornamentation.

Interlude. Music played between sections of a composition or of a dramatic work [see Entr'acte; Intermezzo]. Also music played (sometimes improvised) between lines or stanzas of a hymn or between parts of a liturgical service.

Intermedium [L.]; **intermède** [F.]; **intermedio** [It., Sp.]. See Intermezzo (1).

Intermezzo. (1) A light theatrical entertainment introduced between the acts of a serious play or opera. Also interpolations consisting only of instrumental music, sometimes termed *entr'actes. The 16th-century *intermedi* of stage plays are among the forerunners of the *opera, and the 18th-century intermezzi of operas were the predecessors of the *opera buffa* [see Comic opera]. In the latter part of the 17th century most of the Italian operas performed at Paris were furnished with *intermèdes* (ballets and vocal music) by French composers. (2) One of the numerous titles of 19th-century *character pieces, suggestive of the somewhat casual origin of a piece, as if it were composed between works of greater importance (Schumann, Brahms).

Interrupted cadence. See under Cadence.

Interval. The distance (in terms of pitch) between two pitches. For purposes of Western tonal music, intervals are named according to (1) the number of diatonic *scale degrees comprised, as represented in the letter names of the two pitches, and (2) the number of semitones (the smallest interval in the Western system) between the two pitches. The former is expressed as a number, determined by counting the letters of the alphabet beginning with that of the lower pitch and including that of the higher (remembering that only the first seven letters are used and then repeated). Thus, c–c is a prime or unison, c–d a second, c–e a third, c–f a fourth, c–g a fifth, c–a a sixth, c–b a seventh, c–c' an octave. Intervals larger than an octave can be named similarly (ninth, tenth, eleventh, etc.), though they are also known as *compound* intervals, since they can be thought of as consisting of an octave plus a smaller interval (e.g., a tenth is the same as an octave plus a third). For most purposes, compound intervals function as do their corresponding simple intervals (e.g., a tenth functions much as does a third, both being consonant [see Consonance, dissonance]). The number of semitones between the two pitches is indicated by a qualifying adjective

	Diminished	Minor	Major	Augmented
Second	c♯–d♭ (0)	c–d♭ (1)	c–d (2)	c–d♯ (3)
Third	c♯–e♭ (2)	c–e♭ (3)	c–e (4)	c–e♯ (5)
Sixth	c♯–a♭ (7)	c–a♭ (8)	c–a (9)	c–a♯ (10)
Seventh	c♯–b♭ (9)	c–b♭ (10)	c–b (11)	c–b♯ (12)

		Perfect		
Fourth	c♯–f (4)	c–f (5)		c–f♯ (6)
Fifth	c♯–g (6)	c–g (7)		c–g♯ (8)
Octave	c♯–c′(11)	c–c′ (12)		c–c♯′ (13)

(perfect, major, minor, diminished, or augmented), as illustrated in the table above, where the number of semitones in each case is given in parentheses.

This table shows that the fourth, fifth, and octave above the tonic in a major scale (c–f, c–g, c–c′, as illustrated here with the scale of C major) are called *perfect*. The remaining intervals above the tonic (c–d, c–e, c–a, c–b) are called *major*. A perfect interval if reduced by a semitone becomes diminished. A major interval if reduced by a semitone becomes minor, and a minor interval if reduced by a semitone becomes diminished. Both perfect and major intervals become augmented if increased by a semitone. Interval types that contain the same number of semitones but have different names (e.g., the diminished third and the major second) are enharmonically equivalent [see Enharmonic] (though specific examples of each will be enharmonically equivalent only if the specific pitches in question are enharmonically equivalent). Two intervals that form an octave when added together are complements of one another, and the *inversion of an interval is its complement. Thus, the inversion of a major sixth (e.g., c–a) is a minor third (a–c′), and these two intervals complement each other in that they form an octave

when added together (c–a + a–c′ = c–c′).

Intervals, calculation of. The size of an interval can be expressed as the ratio of the frequencies of its two component pitches. And since the frequency of a vibrating string varies inversely with its length [see Acoustics], the inverse of the ratio of frequencies is the ratio of the two string lengths required to produce a given interval. Thus, the ratio of the frequency of a′ (440) to that of a an octave below (220), and thus the ratio for an octave, is 2/1. And the length of string required to produce a′ (assuming strings of equal mass and tension) will be 1/2 that required to produce a.

In the system of equal *temperament, the ratios for all semitones are the same. Since there are twelve semitones in each octave and since the ratio for the octave is 2/1, it follows that the ratio for the semitone is $\sqrt[12]{2}/1$, or 1.05946/1. Ratios for other intervals can be expressed as $i^n/1$, where $i = \sqrt[12]{2}$ and n = the number of semitones in the desired interval. For purposes of comparing intervals of various sizes, it is convenient to adopt a logarithmic scale in which every semitone, as it occurs in equal temperament, comprises 100 cents, and thus the octave comprises 1200 cents. The accompany-

	P	E	J
Semitone	256/243 = 90	i = 100	16/15 = 112 (C-D♭); 135/128 = 92 (C-C♯)
Whole tone	9/8 = 204	i² = 200	9/8 = 204 (C-D); 10/9 = 182 (D-E)
Minor third	32/27 = 294	i³ = 300	6/5 = 316
Major third	81/64 = 408	i⁴ = 400	5/4 = 386
Fourth	4/3 = 498	i⁵ = 500	4/3 = 498
Aug. fourth	729/512 = 612	i⁶ = 600	45/32 = 590
Dim. fifth	1024/729 = 588	i⁶ = 600	64/45 = 610
Fifth	3/2 = 702	i⁷ = 700	3/2 = 702
Minor sixth	128/81 = 792	i⁸ = 800	8/5 = 814
Major sixth	27/16 = 906	i⁹ = 900	5/3 = 884
Minor seventh	16/9 = 996	i¹⁰ = 1000	16/9 = 996 (D-C); 9/5 = 1018 (E-D)
Major seventh	243/128 = 1110	i¹¹ = 1100	15/8 = 1088 (C-B); 256/135 = 1108 (C-C♭)
Octave	2 = 1200	i¹² = 1200	2 = 1200

ing table compares in this way the intervals of three important systems: the *Pythagorean scale (P), equal *temperament (E), and *just intonation (J). For the first and last of these, the ratios of frequencies (and thus of string lengths, in terms of which the discussions of early theorists are carried on) are given as well. The ratios 3/2, 4/3, 5/4, and 6/5 for the perfect fifth, perfect fourth, major third, and minor third, respectively, are those derived from the harmonic or overtone series [see Acoustics] and are said to be acoustically pure. The table illustrates the difference between these intervals and those of equal temperament.

Intolleranza 1960. Opera-oratorio by L. Nono (libretto by the composer after A. M. Ripellino), produced in Venice, 1961. Setting: the present.

Intonation. (1) In ensemble performance, the degree of accuracy with which pitches are produced. (2) In Gregorian chant, the opening notes of a *psalm tone or other recitation tone. (3) See Just intonation.

Intonatione. A 16th-century Italian name for a prelude, designed chiefly for liturgical use to establish the tone of the chant that follows. The best-known examples are those by A. and G. Gabrieli.

Intrada, entrada [It.]. A 16th- and 17th-century name for an opening piece, of festive or marchlike character. Intradas in duple or triple meter figure prominently among the dance types of the German orchestral suites of the early 17th century. Mozart (*Bastien und Bastienne*) and Beethoven (*Wellingtons Sieg*) used the name for short overtures.

Introit [L. *introitus*]. The initial chant of the Proper of the *Mass. It is an antiphonal chant [see under Antiphon (3)] and is usually in a moderately ornate style. For the form of the Introit, see Psalmody III.

Invention. A title used for Bach's 15 keyboard pieces in two parts to which he gave the title "Inventiones," and 15 pieces in three parts, to which he gave the title "Sinfoniae," all composed in a contrapuntal style in the years 1720–23. The designation was used by G. B. Vitali for pieces involving special tricks and by

F. A. Bonporti for suites (partitas) in a work (op. 10) published under different titles at various times (1712, 1725).

Inversion. (1) *Harmonic inversion.* An *interval is inverted by transferring its lower pitch into the higher octave or its higher pitch into the lower octave, e.g., the inversion of d–a is a–d' or A–d. By inversion, a fifth changes into a fourth, a third into a sixth, etc. (for intervals smaller than an octave, the sum of the numbers indicated in the names of the two intervals is always nine: 5 + 4 = 9; 3 + 6 = 9; the sum of the semitones in two such intervals is always twelve). Both intervals together form an octave [see Complement]. Major intervals when inverted become minor, augmented intervals become diminished, and a perfect interval produces another perfect interval. A *triad or other chord is inverted by transferring its lowest pitch to a higher octave, e.g., changing g–b–d' into b–d'–g'. A chord has, therefore, as many inversions as it has pitch classes excluding the *root.

(2) *Melodic inversion.* A melody (subject) is inverted when each ascending interval is changed into the corresponding descending interval, and vice versa. By this process, an ascending fifth c–g changes into a descending fifth c–F, the ascending progression c'–d'–e' into the descending progression c'–b–a. Inversion is said to be *strict* (or real) if the original and inverted intervals contain exactly the same number of semitones. Thus the strict inversion of c'–d'–e' is c' –b♭–a♭. It is *tonal* if it utilizes the degrees of the scale of the appropriate key. Thus in C major c'–d'–e' becomes c'–b –a, preserving the tonality. See also Invertible counterpoint.

Inverted mordent [G. *Schneller*]. An 18th-century ornament calling for alternation of the written note with the note immediately above it, to be performed as a short, rapid trill beginning on the beat. The inverted mordent was not one of the French *agréments,* having been introduced after 1750 by K. P. E. Bach, who always indicated it by two small grace notes [Ex. 1]. Later composers often designated the inverted mordent with a short wavy line [Ex. 2], which originally indicated a somewhat different ornament

called the *Pralltriller*. The *Pralltriller* is a rapid trill of four notes, beginning with the upper auxiliary, as was customary with trills in that period. This trill was used only on the lower side of a descending second and tied to the preceding note, sometimes giving the erroneous impression that the *Pralltriller* begins with the main note. The *Schneller*, on the other hand, can occur only on a detached note, that is, the upper note of a descending second, so that the position of the sign shown in Ex. 2 usually indicates whether a *Schneller* [Ex. 3] or a *Pralltriller* [Ex. 4] is meant.

After 1800 the *Pralltriller* dropped out of use so that the sign shown in Ex. 2 always indicates the *Schneller*. Simultaneously, however, the name *Schneller* dropped out of use and the ornament illustrated in Ex. 3 became known as the *Pralltriller*, the current German term for the inverted mordent. The former restriction regarding its position on the first note of a descending second has, of course, been long abandoned. About 1830 (e.g., in works of Hummel and Moscheles), the inverted mordent began to be performed before the main note.

Invertible counterpoint. Counterpoint so designed that it can also be performed with the lower part transposed (usually by an octave) to lie above the upper part or with the upper part transposed to lie below the lower part. This is an application of the principle of harmonic inversion [see Inversion (1)]. If applied to two parts, the method is called *double counterpoint*, if to three (four) parts, triple (quadruple) counterpoint.

Occasionally double counterpoint is treated in a more elaborate manner, involving transposition at intervals other than the octave. Particularly remarkable is its application in J. S. Bach's *Canonic Variations on "Vom Himmel hoch"* and *The *Art of Fugue*.

Invitation to the Dance. See *Aufforderung zum Tanz*.

Invitatory [L. *invitatorium*]. In the Roman Catholic rites, the opening chant of Matins [see Office], consisting of Psalm 94 (*psalmus invitatorius*) "Venite, exsultemus Domino" (Psalm 95 of the King James Version: "O come let us sing unto the Lord"), sung with varying *antiphons. The psalm is sung to a number of tones considerably more elaborate than the ordinary *psalm tones, and the antiphons are equally elaborate. In the Anglican rites the "Venite" with proper antiphons forms a part of every Morning Prayer.

Ionian. See under Church modes.

Iphigénie. Two operas by Gluck, *Iphigénie en Aulide* (F., Iphigenia in Aulis; libretto by F. L. G. Lebland du Roullet, after Racine's tragedy), produced in Paris, 1774, and *Iphigénie en Tauride* (F., Iphigenia in Tauris; libretto by N. F. Guillard, produced in Paris, 1779. Both are based on dramas by Euripides. Setting: ancient Greece.

Ippolitov-Ivanov, Mikhail Mikhailovich (b. Gatchina, near St. Petersburg, 19 Nov. 1859; d. Moscow, 28 Jan. 1935). Pupil of Rimsky-Korsakov. Associate of Arensky and Grechaninov. Teacher at the Moscow Conservatory from 1893 and its director from 1906. Conductor of the Bolshoi Theater in Moscow from 1925. Composed operas (incl. *The Last Barricade*, 1934); orch. works (incl. *Caucasian Sketches*, 1895); choral works; numerous songs.

Ireland, John (Nicholson) (b. Inglewood, Bowden, Cheshire, 13 Aug. 1879; d. Washington, England, 12 June 1962). Pupil of Stanford. Organist at St. Luke's Church in Chelsea, 1904–26. Teacher at the Royal College of Music, 1923–39. His pupils incl. Britten. Composed orch. works (incl. *London Overture*, 1936); a piano concerto, 1930; Anglican services and other church music; choral works (incl. *These Things Shall Be* for baritone, chorus, and orch., 1937); chamber music; piano pieces; organ pieces; numerous songs.

Irish harp. See ill. under Harp.

Isaac, Heinrich (b. *c*. 1450; d. Florence, 26 Mar. 1517). Musician to Lorenzo de' Medici in Florence, 1480–92, and then to the Emperor Maximilian I in Vienna and elsewhere. Composed Masses, motets, psalms, and other sacred music (incl. the *Choralis Constantinus*); secular vocal works with texts in German, French, and Italian.

Isometric. See under Homorhythmic.

Isorhythm. A technique of some 14th- and early 15th-century music consisting of the repetition of a pattern of durations in one or more parts, but most often in the tenor. The rhythmic pattern or *talea* may or may not coincide in length with a succession of pitches or *color* that is also repeated. Statements of the *talea* may employ *augmentation and diminution. An example is found in the tenor of G. de Machaut's motet *Hé mors—Fine amour —Quare non sum mortuus*.

Isouard, Nicolo (Nicolò de Malte) (b. Malta, 6 Dec. 1775; d. Paris, 23 Mar. 1818). Pupil of N. Sala and Gugliemi in Naples. Church organist in Malta, 1795–98. Settled in Paris, 1799. Composed operas (incl. *Cendrillon*, Paris, 1810; *Michel-Ange*, Paris, 1802; *Le billet de loterie*, Paris, 1811; *Joconde*, Paris, 1814; *Jeannot et Colin*, Paris, 1814); cantatas; Masses, motets, and other sacred music.

Israel in Egypt. Oratorio by Handel (to a scriptural text), first performed in 1739.

Istampita, istanpitta. See *Estampie*.

Istar Variations. Seven orchestral variations by d'Indy, op. 42 (1896), which start with the most complex variation and end with the theme in octaves.

Istesso tempo, L' [It.]. The same tempo. Thus, an indication that, even though the meter changes, the duration of the beat remains unaltered.

Italian Concerto. A composition for solo harpsichord by Bach, published in 1735 as part of the *Clavier-Übung*, and so called because it is in the form and style of the Italian instrumental concertos of the early 18th century.

Italian sixth. See Sixth chord.

Italian Symphony. Mendelssohn's Symphony no. 4 in A major, op. 90 (1831–33), begun in Italy and containing allusions to Italian folk music, particularly in the last movement, entitled "Saltarello."

Italiana in Algeri, L' [It., The Italian Woman in Algiers]. Opera in two acts by Rossini (libretto by A. Anelli), produced in Venice, 1813.

Ives, Charles (Edward) (b. Danbury, Conn., 20 Oct. 1874; d. New York, 19 May 1954). Pupil of his father, George Ives (a band leader), and of Horatio Parker. Held several positions as church organist. Partner in the insurance agency of Ives and Myrick, 1907–30. An early proponent of polytonality, complex rhythms, tone clusters, and what much later came to be called aleatory procedures. A number of his works include quotations of hymns or other music. Composed orch. works (incl. 5 symphonies, of which the third, "The Camp Meeting," 1904–11, was awarded the Pulitzer Prize for 1947; *Central Park in the Dark*, 1906, and *The Unanswered Question*, 1908, both for chamber orch.; *A Symphony: Holidays*, 1904–13; *Orchestral Set* no. 1 "Three Places in New England," 1903–14; *Orchestral Set* no. 2, 1915); choral works (incl. *Harvest Home Chorales*, 1902); 2 string quartets, a piano trio, 5 violin sonatas, and other chamber music; *Variations on America* for organ, 1892; piano pieces (incl. the *Concord Sonata*; pieces for 2 pianos tuned a quarter tone apart, 1924); numerous songs. Published writings on music, incl. *Essays Before a Sonata*, 1920.

Ivey, Jean Eichelberger (b. Washington, D.C., 3 July 1923). Studied at the Peabody Conservatory, the Eastman School of Music, and the Univ. of Toronto. Teacher at the Peabody Conservatory and director of its electronic music studio from 1969. Has composed works for orch.; chamber music; electronic works, some with instruments and/or voices (incl. *Hera, Hung from the Sky* for mezzo soprano, winds, percussion, piano, tape).

J

Jácara [Sp., Port.]. A popular ballad or dance tune. Also (17th century) a picaresque comic interlude inserted into stage plays and describing the antics of some objectionable person. In time it developed into the *tonadilla*.

Jachet of Mantua (real name Jacobus Collebaude) (b. Vitré, France, c. 1495; d. Mantua, 1559). *Maestro di cappella* in Mantua, 1539–58. Composed Masses, motets, Passions, and other sacred vocal works.

Jack. See under Harpsichord.

Jackson, William (b. Exeter, 29 May 1730; d. there, 5 July 1803). Organist and composer. Pupil of Travers. Organist and choirmaster at Exeter Cathedral from 1777 to his death. Composed operas (incl. *The Lord of the Manor*, London, 1780); madrigals; odes (incl. *Ode to Fancy*); hymns, anthems, and services; harpsichord sonatas.

Jacob, Gordon (Percival Septimus) (b. London, 5 July 1895). Conductor and composer. Pupil of Stanford, Vaughan Williams, and Howells. Teacher at the Royal College of Music, 1926–54. Has composed ballets; music for films and for plays; orch. works (incl. 2 symphonies; *Passacaglia on a Well-known Theme*, 1931; *Variations on an Original Theme*, 1936); concertos for viola, for piano, for oboe, for bassoon, for violin, and for horn; choral works; arrangements for orch. of Schumann's *Carnaval* and other works, for ballet; chamber music (incl. *Divertimento* for harmonica and string quartet); songs.

Jacobi, Frederick (b. San Francisco, 4 May 1891; d. New York, 24 Oct. 1952). Pupil of Juon, Bloch, and R. Goldmark. Teacher at the Juilliard School of Music, 1936–50. Worked with American Indian and Jewish materials. Composed an opera, *The Prodigal Son*, 1944; 2 symphonies and other orch. works (incl. *Indian Dances*, 1927); concertos for piano,

for violin, and for cello; string quartets and other chamber music (incl. *Hagiographa* for string quartet and piano, 1938); vocal works; piano pieces.

Jacopo da Bologna (Jacobus de Bononia) (fl. Italy, 14th cent.). Court musician at Verona, probably c. 1340–45, and at Milan, probably c. 1345–55. Composed madrigals, a *caccia*, a motet, a *lauda*. See *Ars nova*.

Jadassohn, Salomon (b. Breslau, 13 Aug. 1831; d. Leipzig, 1 Feb. 1902). Theorist and composer. Pupil of Liszt and Hauptmann. Teacher at the Leipzig Conservatory from 1871. Composed 4 symphonies and other orch. works; 2 piano concertos; choral works; chamber music; piano pieces; songs. Published numerous writings on music theory, incl. *Harmonielehre*, 1883, publ. in English as *A Manual of Harmony*, 1893.

Jagd- [G.]. Hunt. *Jagdhorn*, hunting horn; *Jagdmusik*, hunting music.

Jahreszeiten, Die. See *Seasons, The*.

Jam. Jazz musicians' term for group improvisation. At a jam session, musicians choose a familiar tune or chord progression and improvise on it, both together and as soloists.

James, Philip (b. Jersey City, N.J., 17 May 1890; d. Southampton, N.Y., 1 Nov. 1975). Pupil of Scalero and R. Goldmark. Conductor of the New Jersey Symphony Orchestra, 1922–29, and the Bamberger Little Symphony, 1929–36. Teacher at New York University, 1923–55. Composed stage works; orch. works (incl. 2 symphonies; *Bret Harte*, overture, 1936; *Station WGZBX*, suite, 1932; *Song of the Night*, symphonic poem, 1931); sacred and secular choral works; chamber music; piano pieces; organ pieces; songs.

Janáček, Leoš (b. Hukvaldy, Moravia, 3 July 1854; d. Ostrava, 12 Aug. 1928). Director of the Brno Organ School, 1881

–1919. Conductor of the Czech Philharmonic, 1881–88. Teacher at the Brno Conservatory, 1919–25. Composed operas (incl. *Jenufa; *Kát'a Kabanová; The *Cunning Little Vixen; The Makropulos Case*, Brno, 1926; *From the House of the Dead*, 1928, prod. Brno, 1930); choral works (incl. *Glagolitic Mass [Festival* or *Slavonic Mass]*, 1927); a cantata, *Amarus*, 1898; orch. works (incl. *Taras Bulba*, 1918; *Sinfonietta*, 1926); chamber music; piano pieces; organ pieces; song cycles; arrangements of folk songs.

Janequin, Clément (b. Châtellerault, *c.* 1485; d. Paris, probably late Jan., 1558). Chaplain of the Angers Cathedral from 1527; active in Bordeaux *c.* 1529; curate at Unverre from 1548. Singer at the royal chapel in Paris from 1555 and composer to the King thereafter. Composed numerous polyphonic chansons (incl. the descriptive works *Le chant des oiseaux, La chasse, La guerre*); Masses, motets, and other sacred music.

Janizary music. Music of the Janizary, the military bodyguard of the Turkish sovereigns (*c.* 1400–1826), or pieces written in imitation thereof. The characteristic instruments of the Janizary were big drums, cymbals, triangles, and the *Turkish crescent. About 1800, this type of music was extremely popular in Europe. Haydn imitated it in his "Military" Symphony (no. 100); Mozart in his *Entführung aus dem Serail* and the Rondo "alla Turca" oɩ ..is Piano Sonata in A (K. 331); Beethoven in *Die Ruinen von Athen* (also in his Variations op. 76) and, most effectively, in the finale of his Ninth Symphony (tenor solo: "Froh wie Deine Sonnen fliegen"). The harpsichords and pianos of the late 18th century were frequently provided with a Janizary stop, which produced a rattling noise.

Janko keyboard. See under Keyboard.

Jaques-Dalcroze, Émile (b. Vienna, of French parents, 6 July 1865; d. Geneva, 1 July 1950). His family settled in Geneva in 1873. Pupil of R. Fuchs, Fauré, Bruckner, and Delibes. Teacher at the Geneva Conservatory, 1892–1910. Developed *eurhythmics*, a system of teaching music, particularly rhythm, through gestures and founded an institute for its propagation at Hellerau, Germany, 1911. This was succeeded in 1915 by another institute under his direction in Geneva that became the headquarters for a world-wide movement. Composed operas and other stage works; orch. works; choral works; chamber music; piano pieces; numerous songs. Published numerous writings on music and eurhythmics.

Jarnach, Philipp (b. Noisy, France, of a Catalan father and a German mother, 26 July 1892). Pupil of Lavignac. Close associate of Busoni. Teacher at the Cologne Conservatory, 1927–49, and director of the Hochschule für Musik in Hamburg from 1950. Has composed orch. works (incl. *Musik mit Mozart*, symphonic variations, 1935); choral works; chamber music (incl. *Musik zum Gedächtnis der Einsamen* for string quartet, 1952); piano pieces; songs.

Järnefelt, (Edward) Armas (b. Vyborg, now U.S.S.R., 14 Aug. 1869; d. Stockholm, 23 June 1958). Pupil of Wegelius, Busoni, and Massenet. Conductor of the Royal Opera in Stockholm, 1907–32; of the Finnish Opera in Helsinki, 1932–36; of the Helsinki Municipal Orchestra, 1942–43. Composed orch. works (incl. *Berceuse; Praeludium*); cantatas; choral works; piano pieces; songs.

Jazz. A kind of music that emerged in the southern United States, particularly in the city of New Orleans, around the end of the 19th century. The term itself, the origins of which are obscure, gained currency around 1915 and has since been applied to diverse and continually changing styles. Among the progenitors of these styles were Gospel singing, *spirituals and other types of singing current among black slaves, the music of brass bands, string bands, and minstrel shows, and probably rhythms of African drumming brought to the U.S. by slaves. Throughout the history of jazz, its tonal language has been essentially that of Western Europe, combined, however, with characteristic inflections of pitch [see under Blues]. Other characteristics of much jazz are steady though often strongly syncopated rhythms, established by a "rhythm section" most often consisting of drums, double bass (played pizzicato) or tuba, and piano; improvisation by soloists and groups within the framework of some harmonic pattern, often that of a popular song; and effects of timbre and intonation different from those employed in the tradition of Western concert music. The first two prominent substyles of jazz (antedating the term itself) were *ragtime and *blues. Others, in approximately chronological order, have been *Dixieland (or New Orleans style), Chicago style (which followed closely on Dixieland), *swing, *be-bop, *progressive jazz, and, most recently, free jazz (in which the use of steady rhythms and fixed harmonic patterns is largely abandoned). Music that attempts to combine the traditions of jazz with those of concert music is given the name *third-stream.

Jelinek, Joseph. See Gelinek, Joseph.

Jemnitz, Alexander (Sándor) (b. Budapest, 9 Aug. 1890; d. Balatonföldvár, Hungary, 8 Aug. 1963). Conductor, music critic, and composer. Pupil of Koessler, Straube, Schoenberg, and Reger. Teacher at the Béla Bartók Conservatory in Budapest from 1945. Composed a ballet; orch. works; choral works; chamber music; sonatas for unaccompanied solo instruments, incl. cello, harp, double-bass, and trumpet; piano pieces; organ pieces; song cycles.

Jena Symphony. A symphony discovered at Jena, Germany, in 1909. Once acclaimed as an early work of Beethoven, it was not generally accepted as such. It may have been composed by Friedrich Witt (1770–1836).

Jeng (also spelled cheng, tseng). (1) A Chinese stringed instrument similar to the *chyn but without frets. (2) A shallow, basin-shaped Chinese gong corresponding to the Korean ching.

Jenkins, John (b. Maidstone, Kent, 1592; d. Kimberly, Norfolk, 27 Oct. 1678). Lutenist, viol player, and composer. Court musician to Charles I and Charles II. Composed ayres; rounds and canons; fancies for viols and sonatas for violins with thoroughbass.

Jensen, Adolf (b. Königsberg, 12 Jan. 1837; d. Baden-Baden, 23 Jan. 1879). Pupil of Gade. Composed an opera; can-

tatas; orch. works; choral works; piano pieces (incl. *Wanderbilder; Idyllen; Erotikon*); numerous songs (incl. the cycles *Dolorosa* and *Gaudeamus*).

Jenufa [Cz.; orig. title *Její Pastorkyna*, Her Foster-daughter]. Opera in three acts by Janáček (libretto by the composer after G. Preissová), produced in Brno, 1904. Setting: village in Moravia.

Jephtha. (1) Handel's last oratorio (English text by Thomas Morell), produced in London, 1752. (2) Oratorio by Carissimi (Latin text from the Scriptures), composed about 1650.

Jeté [F.]. See Bowing (e).

Jeu [F.]. In music for *organ, stop; *jeu de fonds*, foundation stop; *jeu de mutation*, mutation stop; *jeu à bouche*, flue stop; *jeu d'anche*, reed stop. *Jeu de timbres*, *glockenspiel. For *jeu-parti*, see Tenso.

Jeu de cartes [F., Card Game]. Ballet "in three deals" by Stravinsky (choreography by George Balanchine) produced in New York, 1937.

Jeune France, La. A group of French composers, formed in 1936, consisting of Yves Baudrier (b. 1906), André Jolivet (1905–74), Daniel Lesur (b. 1908), and Olivier Messiaen (b. 1908).

Jeux [F., Games]. Ballet by Debussy (choreography by Vaslav Nijinsky, scenery and costumes by Léon Bakst), produced in Paris, 1913.

Jew's harp or **trump** [F. *guimbarde;* G. *Maultrommel*]. A primitive instrument consisting of an elastic strip of metal, one end of which is attached to a small horseshoe-shaped frame of metal or wood. The frame is held between the teeth, and the elastic strip is plucked with the fingers, causing it to vibrate in the player's mouth. Although the instrument as such produces only one sound, different harmonics can be obtained by changing the position of lips, cheeks, and tongue. The instrument is ancient and widespread. Its name is unexplained.

Jig. (1) An English popular dance of the 16th century, the forerunner of the *gigue. (2) A type of English stage entertainment (also spelled "jigg"), a kind of low comedy nearly always dealing with indecent subjects, that was popular in England from the late 16th to the early 18th centuries. A forerunner of the *ballad opera, it consisted of verses sung to well-known tunes, interspersed with lively dances.

Jirák, Karel Boleslav (b. Prague, 28 Jan. 1891; d. Chicago, 30 Jan. 1972). Pupil of Novák and Foerster. Conductor of the Hamburg Opera, 1915–18. Teacher at the Prague Conservatory, 1920–30. Music director of the Czechoslovak Radio, 1930–45. Teacher at Roosevelt College in Chicago from 1947. Composed operas; symphonies and other orch. works; a piano concerto; choral works; chamber music; piano pieces; song cycles.

Joachim, Joseph (b. Kittsee, near Pressburg, 28 June 1831; d. Berlin, 15 Aug. 1907). Violin virtuoso, conductor, and composer. Pupil of Hauptmann and F. David. Concertmaster of the Weimar court orchestra from 1849; court violinist at Hanover from 1853. Director of the Lehranstalt für ausübende Tonkunst in Berlin from 1868. Organized the Joachim Quartet, 1869. Composed works for violin and orch. (incl. *Hungarian Concerto,* 1857); works for violin and piano, viola and piano; cadenzas to violin concertos of Beethoven and Brahms; songs.

Jodel. See Yodel.

Johnson, Hunter (b. Benson, N.C., 14 Apr. 1906). Pupil of Bernard Rogers and Casella. Has taught at Cornell Univ., 1948–53; the Univ. of Illinois, 1958–65; and the Univ. of Texas, 1966–71. Has composed ballets (incl. *Letter to the World,* 1940, and *Deaths and Entrances,* 1943, both for Martha Graham); a symphony and other orch. works; a piano concerto; chamber music; a piano sonata; songs.

Johnson, Robert (b. London, probably *c.* 1580; d. *c.* 1634). Lutenist to the Chapel Royal from 1604. Composed settings of songs from Shakespeare's plays; music for masques; ayres, songs, catches, and other vocal works; instrumental pieces for lute, virginals, viols.

Johnston, Ben(jamin) (b. Macon, Ga., 15 Mar. 1926). Pupil of Milhaud, Phillips, Luening, Ussachevsky, Partch, and Cage. Teacher at the Univ. of Illinois from 1951. Has worked with serial and aleatory techniques and with microtonal and other nonstandard tuning systems. Has composed a dance-opera, *Gertrude, or Would She Be Pleased to Receive It?,* 1956; *Gambit for Dancers and Orchestra* for Merce Cunningham, 1959; *Quintet for Groups* for orch., 1966; *Sonata for Microtonal Piano,* 1965; 4 string quartets; works for jazz band.

Jolas, Betsy (b. Paris, 5 Aug. 1926). Studied at Bennington College and in Paris with Milhaud and Messiaen. Has worked for the French Radio-Television Network from 1955. Has composed music for films and theater; orch. works (incl. *4 Plages,* 1967); vocal works (incl. *Quatuor II* for coloratura soprano and string trio, 1964); pieces for various instrumental ensembles.

Jolivet, André (b. Paris, 8 Aug. 1905; d. there, 20 Dec. 1974). Pupil of Varèse and Le Flem. Founded the group "La jeune France" with Messiaen, Lesur, and Baudrier, 1936. Conductor (from 1943) and music director (1945–59) of the Comédie-Française. Teacher at the Paris Conservatory, 1965–70. Composed music for radio, films, and theater; an opera; 2 ballets; cantatas; 5 symphonies and other orch. works; concertos for Ondes Martenot, for flute, for trumpet, for piano, for harp, for bassoon; choral works (incl. *Les trois complaintes du soldat,* 1940); chamber music; piano and organ pieces.

Jommelli, Niccolò (b. Aversa, near Naples, 10 Sept. 1714; d. Naples, 25 Aug. 1774). Friend of the librettist Pietro Metastasio and pupil of Padre Martini. Director of the Conservatorio degli incurabili in Venice, 1743–47. Assistant *maestro di cappella* at St. Peter's in Rome to 1753. *Kapellmeister* at Stuttgart, 1753–70. Composed numerous operas (incl. *L'errore amoroso,* Naples, 1737; *Merope,* Venice, 1741; *Demofoonte,* Padua, 1743; *Didone abbandonata,* Rome, 1747; *Olimpiade,* Stuttgart, 1761; *Fetonte,* Ludwigsburg, 1768); intermezzi; oratorios; secular cantatas; a *Miserere* and other sacred works; orch. and chamber works.

Jones, Charles (b. Tamworth, Ontario, 21 June 1910). Pupil of B. Wagenaar and Copland. Teacher at Mills College, 1939 –44; at the Aspen Music School from 1951; and at the Juilliard School of Music, 1954–61. Has composed a ballet; 4 symphonies and other orch. works; cantatas (incl. *The Seasons*, 1959); 6 string quartets and other chamber music; vocal works; piano and harpsichord pieces.

Jones, Daniel (Jenkin) (b. Pembroke, Wales, 7 Dec. 1912). Studied at the Royal Academy of Music in London. Has composed an opera, *The Knife*, London, 1963; incidental music for plays; 4 symphonies, tone poems, and other orch. works (incl. *Symphonic Prologue*, 1950; *Five Pieces for Orch.*, 1939); sacred choral works; string quartets and other chamber music; a sonata for kettledrums; piano pieces; songs.

Jones, Robert (b. *c*. 1577; d. after 1615). Lutenist and composer. Directed a school in London for "Children of the Revels to the Queen." Composed ayres with lute accompaniment; madrigals; anthems.

Jongen, Joseph (-Marie-Alphonse-Nicolas) (b. Liège, 14 Dec. 1873; d. Sartlez-Spa, 12 July 1953). Pupil of Radoux. Teacher at the Liège Conservatory from 1902; at the Brussels Conservatory from 1920 and its director, 1925–39. Composed a ballet; orch. works (incl. *Fantaisie sur deux noëls wallons,* 1902); concertos for violin, for cello, for harp, and for piano; *Symphonie concertante* for organ and orch., 1926; choral works; chamber music; piano and organ pieces; songs.

Jongleur. See Minstrel.

Jonny spielt auf [G., Johnny Strikes Up the Band]. Opera in two parts by E. Krenek (to his own libretto), produced in Leipzig, 1927. Setting: the present.

Josquin des Prez (b. probably at Beaurevoir, near Saint-Quentin, France, *c*. 1440; d. Condé-sur-l'Escaut, 27 Aug. 1521). Singer in the Milan Cathedral, 1459–72, in the service of the Sforzas from sometime thereafter until 1479, and 'n the papal choir in Rome, 1486–99. *Maestro di cappella* at the court in Fer-

rara, 1503–4. Provost of the Church of Notre Dame in Condé from 1504 until his death. His sacred polyphony, particularly in its use of pervading imitation, established norms of style that remained in force through much of the 16th century. Composed Masses and motets; French chansons; *frottole;* instrumental pieces.

Josten, Werner (b. Elberfeld, now Wuppertal, Germany, 12 June 1885; d. New York, 6 Feb. 1963). Pupil of Jaques-Dalcroze and R. Siegel. Teacher at Smith College, 1923–49. Composed ballets (incl. *Batouala*, 1931); orch. works (incl. a *Symphony in F*, 1936, and a *Rhapsody*, 1957); 2 *Sacred Concertos* for piano and string orch., 1925; vocal works; chamber music; songs.

Jota [Sp.]. A dance of Aragon (northeast Spain) in rapid triple time, performed by one or more couples and accompanied by castanets. One of the most popular melodies was used by Liszt in his *Rhapsodie espagnole* no. 16 (*Folies d'Espagne et jota aragonese*) and by Glinka in his orchestral overture *Jota aragonesa*. Other examples occur in Falla's *El sombrero de tres picos* and in compositions by Saint-Saëns and Albéniz.

Jubilus. In the Gregorian *Alleluias, the melisma sung to the final vowel of the first word, *Alleluia*. The melisma of the jubilus often recurs at the end of the verse.

Judas Maccabaeus. Oratorio by Handel (libretto by T. Morell), produced in London, 1747.

Juon, Paul (Pavel Feodorovich) (b. Moscow, 6 Mar. 1872; d. Vevey, Switzerland, 21 Aug. 1940). Pupil of Taneiev, Arensky, and Bargiel. Teacher at the Hochschule für Musik in Berlin, 1906–34. Composed orch. works; 3 violin concertos; *Episodes concertantes* for piano trio and orch.; chamber music; piano pieces; songs.

Jupiter Symphony. Popular name for Mozart's last symphony, in C major, no. 41 (K. 551), composed in 1788.

Just intonation. A system of intonation and tuning in which all the intervals are derived from the natural (pure) fifth and

	c	d	e	f	g	a	b	c'
c = 1:	1	%	¾	⅘	½	⅔	1%	2
c = 24:	24	27	30	32	36	40	45	48
Intervals:		%	¹⁰⁄₉	¹⁶⁄₁₅	%	¹⁰⁄₉	%	¹⁶⁄₁₅

the natural (pure) third [see Acoustics; Intervals, calculation of]. In the accompanying table, the first line of figures shows the ratios for the intervals formed between c and each of the other pitches of the C major scale in this system; the second line of figures expresses these relationships in whole numbers; the third line of figures shows the ratios (easily derived from the whole numbers of the second line) for the intervals between adjacent pitches in the C major scale. See also Temperament.

K

K. or **K.V.** Abbr. for *Köchel-Verzeichnis*, i.e., the chronological list of all the works of Mozart made by L. von Köchel (publ. 1862, rev. by Einstein, 1937, 1947; by Giegling, Weinmann, and Sievers, 1964).

Kabalevsky, Dmitri Borisovich (b. St. Petersburg, 30 Dec. 1904). Pupil of Miaskovsky. Teacher at the Moscow Conservatory from 1932. A number of his works are on Soviet social and political themes. Has composed operas (incl. *The Family of Taras*, Moscow, 1947, rev. 1950; *Colas Breugnon*, Leningrad, 1938); ballets; incidental music for plays; music for films; symphonies and other orch. works (incl. *The Comedians*, 1940); concertos for piano, for violin, for cello; choral works; chamber music; piano pieces; songs.

Kabeláč, Miloslav (b. Prague, 1 Aug. 1908). Pupil of Jirák. Music director for Radio Prague from 1932. Teacher at the Prague Conservatory, 1958–62. Has composed 8 symphonies and other orch. works (incl. *Mysterium času* [The Mystery of Time], 1957); choral works; cantatas; works for solo voice with instruments; chamber music; piano and organ pieces.

Kadosa, Pál (b. Léva, Hungary, now Levice, Czechoslovakia, 6 Sept. 1903). Pianist and composer. Pupil of Kodály. Teacher at the Fodor Music School in Budapest, 1927–43, and at the Budapest Academy of Music from 1946. Has composed an opera, *Huszti Kaland* (Adventure in Huszt), 1950; 8 symphonies and

other orch. works; concertos for piano, for violin, and for viola; cantatas (incl. *De amore fatali*, 1940); choral works; string quartets and other chamber music; piano pieces; songs.

Kaffeekantate [G.]. See Coffee Cantata.

Kagel, Mauricio (Raúl) (b. Buenos Aires, 24 Dec. 1931). Conductor and composer. Teacher at the Darmstadt summer courses, 1960–66; director of the Institute for New Music, Cologne, from 1969. Has worked with aleatory and audiovisual techniques, including elements of the theater, and with *musique concrète* and other electronic techniques. Has composed a string sextet, 1953; *Tower Music* for taped instruments, *musique concrète*, and projections, 1953; *Der Schall* for 5 players, 1968; *Pas de cinq*, theater piece, 1965; *Improvisation ajoutée* for 3 organists, 1962; *Transición I* and *II* for piano, percussion, and tape, 1958–60; several films.

Kaiserquartett [G.]. See Emperor Quartet.

Kalevala. The Finnish national epic, dating from the 13th and 14th centuries. Several symphonic poems by Sibelius (and other Finnish composers) are based on legends from this epic, e.g., **Lemminkäinen's Homecoming, *Pohjola's Daughter, *Swan of Tuonela, *Tapiola.*

Kalinnikov, Vassili Sergeievich (b. Voin, near Mtzensk, 13 Jan. 1866; d. Yalta, Crimea, 11 Jan. 1901). Conductor and composer. Composed 2 symphonies and other orch. works; a cantata, *Joann Da-*

maskin; a ballade, *Russalka,* for soloists, chorus, and orch.; chamber music; piano pieces; songs.

Kalkbrenner, Friedrich Wilhelm Michael (b. near Kassel between 2 and 8 Nov. 1785; d. Deuil, near Paris, 10 June 1849). Pianist and composer. Pupil of his father, the composer Christian Kalkbrenner, and of Albrechtsberger. Settled in Paris, 1824, as a partner in the Pleyel piano firm. Composed 4 piano concertos; numerous works for chamber ensembles with piano; pieces for piano solo, incl. sonatas, fantasies, variations; numerous piano etudes.

Kalliwoda, Johann Wenzel (b. Prague, 21 Feb. 1801; d. Karlsruhe, 3 Dec. 1866). Violinist and composer. Pupil of Pixis and F. D. Weber. Court *Kapellmeister* in Donaueschingen from 1822. Composed 2 operas; numerous orch. works, incl. 7 symphonies; violin concertos; choral works; Masses; chamber music; violin pieces; piano pieces; songs.

Kallstenius, Edvin (b. Filipstad, Wärmland, Sweden, 29 Aug. 1881; d. Stockholm, 22 Nov. 1967). Music critic and composer. Studied at the Leipzig Conservatory. Music librarian for Stockholm Radio, 1927–46. Composed orch. works (incl. 5 symphonies; *Sinfonietta dodicitonica,* 1956); works for solo instrument with orch.; vocal works; 7 string quartets and other chamber music; piano pieces; songs.

Kálmán, Emmerich (Imre) (b. Siófok am Plattensee, Hungary, 24 Oct. 1882; d. Paris, 30 Oct. 1953). Pupil of Koessler. Lived in Vienna to 1938 and in the U.S., 1940–49. Composed numerous operettas (incl. *Ein Herbstmanöver,* Vienna, 1909, prod. in N.Y. as *The Gay Hussars,* 1909; *Die Csardasfürstin,* Vienna, 1915, prod. in the U.S. as *The Riviera Girl; Gräfin Mariza,* Vienna, 1924; *Die Zirkusprinzessin,* Vienna, 1926, prod. in English as *The Circus Princess*); other stage works; instrumental pieces.

Kalomiris, Manolis (b. Smyrna, 26 Dec. 1883; d. Athens, 3 Apr. 1962). Studied in Athens, Constantinople, and Vienna. Teacher at the Kharkov Conservatory, 1906–10, and at the Athens Conservatory, 1910–19. Director of the Hellenic Conservatory in Athens, 1919–26; founder and director (from 1926) of the National Conservatory there. Composed operas (incl. *Protomastoras,* libretto by Kazantzakis, Athens, 1916, rev. 1940); symphonies and tone poems; a piano concerto, a *Rhapsody* for piano and orch., and other works for soloists and orch.; vocal works; chamber music; piano pieces; songs. Published numerous textbooks.

Kamānja, kemânğe. An Arab stringed instrument. For ill. see under Violin family.

Kamienski, Maciej (Mathias) (b. Sopron [Ödenburg], Hungary, 13 Oct. 1734; d. Warsaw, 25 Jan. 1821). Composed the first Polish operas (incl. *Nedza uszczesliwiona* [Comfort in Misfortune], Warsaw, 1778; *Zoska,* Warsaw, 1781); a cantata; Masses; instrumental and vocal polonaises.

Kaminski, Heinrich (b. Tiengen, Austria, 4 July 1886; d. Ried, Bavaria, 21 June 1946). Pupil of Wolfrum, Kaun, and Juon. Teacher at the Berlin Academy, 1930–33. Composed 2 operas, *Jürg Jenatsch,* Dresden, 1929, and *Das Spiel vom König Aphelius,* 1946, prod. Göttingen, 1950; orch. works (incl. a *concerto grosso* for double orch., 1922); sacred and secular choral works (incl. a Magnificat, 1925); chamber music; organ and piano pieces; songs.

Kammer- [G.]. Chamber. *Kammerton,* chamber pitch [see Pitch (3)]; *Kammermusik,* chamber music; *Kammerkantate,* chamber cantata; etc.

Kanon. (1) German for *canon.* (2) A type of medieval Byzantine poetry. (3) In ancient Greek music, name for the *monochord.*

Kantele. A Finnish folk instrument. For ill. see under Zither.

Kanun (*qānūn*). Arabic name for a *psaltery shaped like a trapezoid and mounted with numerous strings (as many as 64 in the 14th century). For ill. see under Zither.

Kapelle [G.]. *Chapel, usually with the connotation of "private or small orchestra," e.g., *Hofkapelle* (court orchestra),

Militärkapelle (military band). *Kapell-meister*, originally an honorable title (Bach served as *Kapellmeister* to Prince Ernst of Köthen from 1717 to 1723), is now an old-fashioned provincialism for *Dirigent* (conductor).

Kapr, Jan (b. Prague, 12 Mar. 1914). Pupil of Řídký and of Křička. Music director of Czechoslovak Radio in Prague, 1939–46. Teacher at the Janáček Academy in Brno from 1961. Has worked with twelve-tone and aleatory techniques. Works incl. an opera; a ballet; 7 symphonies and other orch. works; concertos; vocal works; 7 string quartets and other chamber music; piano pieces; songs; music for films.

Karel, Rudolf (b. Pilsen, 9 Nov. 1880; d. in the Teresin concentration camp, 6 Mar. 1945). Pupil of Dvořák. Teacher at the Prague Conservatory, 1923–41. Composed operas (incl. *Ilsea's Heart*, Prague, 1924; *Godmother Death*, Brno, 1933); orch. works (incl. *Scherzo Capriccio*, 1904); an oratorio; choral works; chamber music; piano pieces; songs.

Karelia. Orchestral overture (op. 10) and Suite (op. 11) by Sibelius, composed in 1893. Karelia is the southern province of Finland, where the composer lived at the time.

Karg-Elert, Sigfrid (b. Oberndorf am Neckar, 21 Nov. 1877; d. Leipzig, 9 Apr. 1933). Organist and composer. Pupil of Reinecke and Jadassohn. Teacher at the Magdeburg Conservatory from 1902 and at the Leipzig Conservatory from 1919. Composed organ works (incl. 66 chorale improvisations; 20 chorale preludes and postludes); pieces for harmonium; orch. works; chamber music; choral works; lieder. Also published many theoretical and pedagogic writings.

Kasemets, Udo (b. Tallinn, Estonia, 16 Nov. 1919). Pupil of Krenek. Settled in Canada, 1951. Has worked with serial and aleatory techniques, graphic notation, and elements of theater. Works incl. *Calceolaria*, time/space variations on a floral theme, 1966; *T^t*, a computer-controlled multi-media piece, 1968; *Cumulus* for instrument(s) and 2 tape recorders, 1964; other works for various instrumental and vocal ensembles.

Kastalsky, Alexander Dmitrievich (b. Moscow, 28 Nov. 1856; d. there, 17 Dec. 1926). Choral conductor and composer. Pupil of Tchaikovsky and Taneiev. Teacher at the Synodal School in Moscow from 1887; at the Moscow Philharmonic Institute, 1912–22; at the Moscow Conservatory from 1923. Composed an opera; incidental music for plays; patriotic and sacred choral works; arrangements of folksongs; piano pieces.

Kastner, Jean Georges (Johann Georg) (b. Strasbourg, 9 Mar. 1810; d. Paris, 19 Dec. 1867). Theorist and composer. Pupil of Berton and Reicha. Composed *Livres-Partitions* (symphony-cantatas with accompanying essays, incl. *Les danses des morts*, 1852; *Parémiologie musicale de la langue française*, 1862); operas; orch. works; choral works; piano pieces; songs. Published manuals and treatises on orchestration, music theory, etc., and numerous articles in journals.

Kát'a Kabanová. Opera in three acts by Janáček (libretto by V. Červinka, after a story by A. N. Ostrovsky), produced in Brno, 1921. Setting: Kalinow, a small town on the Volga, about 1860.

Katerina Ismailova. See *Lady Macbeth of Mtsensk.*

Kaun, Hugo (b. Berlin, 21 Mar. 1863; d. there, 2 Apr. 1932). Studied in Berlin. Lived in Milwaukee, 1887–1901, after which he returned to Berlin. Composed operas; 3 symphonies and other orch. works; piano concertos; sacred and secular choral works; 4 string quartets and other chamber music; piano pieces; organ pieces; songs.

Kay, Ulysses (Simpson) (b. Tucson, Ariz., 7 Jan. 1917). Pupil of Hanson, Bernard Rogers, Hindemith, and Luening. Teacher at Lehman College, City Univ. of New York, from 1968. Has composed a ballet; operas (incl. *The Juggler of Our Lady*, 1956); music for films and theater; orch. works (incl. *Markings*, 1966; a symphony, 1967); numerous choral works; chamber music; piano pieces; songs.

Kazoo. See Mirliton.

Keats, Donald (b. New York, 27 May

1929). Pupil of Q. Porter, Hindemith, Luening, Moore, Cowell, Jarnach, and Argento. Teacher at Antioch College from 1957. Has composed a ballet; 2 symphonies; choral works (incl. *The Hollow Men,* 1955); 2 string quartets and other chamber music; piano pieces; songs.

Keiser, Reinhard (b. Teuchern, bapt. 12 Jan. 1674; d. Hamburg, 12 Sept. 1739). Director and manager of the Hamburg Opera from 1703; canon and cantor at the Hamburg Cathedral from 1728. Composed numerous operas and *Singspiele* (incl. *Störtebecker und Goedje Michel,* Hamburg, 1701; *Octavia,* Hamburg, 1705; *Croesus,* Hamburg, 1711; *Prinz Jodelet,* Hamburg, 1726); oratorios; cantatas; psalms, motets, and other sacred vocal music; several instrumental pieces.

Kelemen, Milko (b. Podravska Slatina, Yugoslavia, 30 Mar. 1924). Pupil of Šulek, Messiaen, and Fortner. Teacher at the Zagreb Music Academy from 1955 and at the Schumann Conservatory in Düsseldorf from 1969. Has worked with folk materials and with serial and aleatory techniques. Has composed operas (incl. *König Ubu*); ballets; orch. works (incl. *Composé* for 2 pianos, 3 orchestras, 1967; *Surprise* for string orch., 1967; *Changeant* for cello and orch., 1968); concertos; cantatas; choral works; chamber music; piano pieces; songs; music for films.

Kelley, Edgar Stillman (b. Sparta, Wis., 14 Apr. 1857; d. New York, 12 Nov. 1944). Critic and composer. Studied in Chicago and Stuttgart. Taught in Berlin, 1902–10, and at the Cincinnati Conservatory from 1910 to his death. Composed a comic opera, *Puritania,* Boston, 1892; incidental music for plays (incl. *Ben Hur,* 1900); symphonies and other orch. works (incl. *Aladdin,* "Chinese suite," 1894); choral works (incl. *The Sleeper,* after Poe); chamber music; piano pieces; songs.

Kelly, Michael (b. Dublin, 25 Dec. 1762; d. Margate, 9 Oct. 1826). Tenor and composer. Pupil of M. Arne and of various teachers in Naples. Opera singer in Vienna in the early 1780s and associate of Mozart there; in London, singer at

Drury Lane from 1787 and director of the King's Theatre from 1793. Composed stage works; songs. Published 2 vols. of *Reminiscences,* 1826.

Kelly, Robert (b. Clarksburg, W. Va., 26 Sept. 1916). Pupil of Scalero and Elwell. Teacher at the Univ. of Illinois at Urbana from 1946. Has composed an opera, *The White Gods,* Urbana, Ill., 1966; 3 symphonies; concertos; band music; choral works; *Chorale and Fugue* for antiphonal brass choirs and timpani, 1951; *Diacoustics* for piano and percussion ensemble, 1970; chamber music; songs.

Kelterborn, Rudolph (b. Basel, 3 Sept. 1931). Conductor and composer. Pupil of Handschin, Burkhard, and Fortner. Teacher at the Northwest-German Music Academy in Detmold, 1960–68, and at the Zürich Musikhochschule from 1968. Has worked with serial techniques. Has composed 2 operas; a symphony and other orch. works; string quartets and other chamber music; piano pieces; works for voice with instruments.

Kennan, Kent (Wheeler) (b. Milwaukee, Wis., 18 Apr. 1913). Pupil of Pizzetti, H. Johnson, Hanson, and Bernard Rogers. Teacher at the Univ. of Texas at Austin from 1940. Has composed a symphony, 1938, and other orch. works; works for solo instrument with orch. (incl. *Il campo dei fiori* for trumpet, 1937; *Night Soliloquy* for flute, strings, and piano, 1936); choral works; chamber music (incl. a sonata for trumpet and piano, 1956); piano and organ pieces; songs.

Kent bugle, Kent horn. Key bugle; see under Brass instruments III.

Kerle, Jacobus de (b. Ypres, 1531 or 1532; d. Prague, 7 Jan. 1591). Organist and composer. Lived in Orvieto, Augsburg, and Cambrai; chaplain to the imperial court at Prague from 1583. Composed *Preces speciales pro salubri generalis concilii successu,* for the *Council of Trent; Masses, hymns, psalms, motets, and other sacred music; madrigals and other secular works.

Kerll, Johann Kaspar (von) (b. Adorf, Saxony, 9 Apr. 1627; d. Munich, 13 Feb. 1693). Organist and composer. Pupil of Carissimi, Valentini, and probably Frescobaldi. Court *Kapellmeister* at Munich from 1656; court organist at Vienna from 1680. Composed operas; a Jesuit drama, *Pia et fortis mulier;* Masses, a Requiem, and other sacred vocal music; organ pieces (incl. *Modulatio organica super Magnificat,* 1689); other instrumental pieces; secular vocal works.

Kerr, Harrison (b. Cleveland, 13 Oct. 1897). Pupil of N. Boulanger. Teacher at the Univ. of Oklahoma, 1949–68. Has composed an opera; a *Sinfonietta* for chamber orch., 1968, 3 symphonies, and other orch. works; choral works; 2 string quartets, a piano trio, and other chamber music; *Dance Sonata* for 2 pianos, percussion, and dancers, 1938; works for voice and instruments; piano pieces.

Kesselpauke, Kesseltrommel [G.]. Kettledrum.

Kettledrum. See under Percussion instruments.

Keussler, Gerhard von (b. Schwanenburg, Latvia, 5 July 1874; d. Niederwartha, near Dresden, 21 Aug. 1949). Conductor and composer. Pupil of Reinecke, Jadassohn, and Klengel. Conductor in Prague, Hamburg, and Australia; teacher at the Berlin Academy from 1934. Composed operas; a melodrama; 2 symphonies and other orch. works; oratorios; songs.

Key. (1) [F. *touche;* G. *Taste;* It. *tasto;* Sp. *tecla*] On keyboard instruments, any of the parts of the action that are depressed by the player's fingers [see Keyboard]. In woodwinds the term applies to comparable devices, i.e., the levers covering the side holes [F. *clef;* G. *Klappe;* It. *chiave;* Sp. *llave*].

(2) [F. *ton;* G. *Tonart;* It., Sp. *tono*] In a tonal composition, the main pitch or "tonal center" to which all of the composition's pitches are related; by extension, the entire tonal material itself in relation to its center. Thus, *key* is practically synonymous with *tonality,* since one may describe a composition as being in the key of, e.g., C. There is, however, a distinct difference between *key* and *scale;* numerous notes extraneous to the scale can be used in the key, e.g., as chromatic variants or in connection with modulations. There are 24

keys, one *major and one minor on each of the 12 pitch classes of the chromatic scale. See Key signature.

Key bugle. See under Brass instruments III.

Key relationship. The degree of relationship between two keys (i.e., tonalities) is primarily a function of the number of pitches that they hold in common. The most closely related keys are those adjacent to one another on the *circle of fifths. Their *key signatures differ by a single flat or sharp, and thus they share six of their seven pitches. Conversely, distant keys are those that are distant from one another on the circle of fifths. Other important relationships are those between *parallel* keys, i.e., major and minor keys with the same tonic, and between *relative* keys, i.e., major and minor keys with the same key signature. The relative minor of any major key or scale, while sharing its key signature and pitches, takes as its tonic the sixth scale degree of that major key or scale; e.g., the relative minor of E♭ major is C minor. See also Major, minor; Modulation.

Key signature. The sharps or flats appearing at the beginning of each staff to indicate the *key of a composition. A given signature indicates one of two keys, a *major key or its relative minor key, depending on which of two pitch classes is treated as the tonic by means, e.g., of prominent cadences at the conclusion of the work and elsewhere. For each key signature the tonic for the major key and the tonic for the minor key are shown in the accompanying example by a white and a black note, respectively. Thus, e.g., the key signature consisting of three sharps may indicate either A major or F♯ minor. Although there are only 12 pitch classes in each oc-

tave, there can be more than 12 key signatures if a notational distinction is made between *enharmonic keys, e.g., C♯ and D♭. See also Circle of fifths.

Key trumpet. See under Trumpet.

Keyboard. The whole set of *keys in pianos, organs, harpsichords, and other such instruments, known as keyboard instruments. The modern piano keyboard usually includes 88 keys for seven full octaves, from C_1 to c'''''', and a quarter octave added at the lower end of the compass (down to the A below C_1). (The organ has 61; the harpsichord varies.) In each octave there are seven white and five black keys [see ill.; in harpsichords the colors are reversed.]. This arrangement reflects the importance of the *diatonic scale fundamental to Western tonal music, the white keys, starting from C and proceeding to the right, presenting the following pattern of whole tones (t) and semitones (s): t t s t t t s. The semitones occur between E and F and between B and C, respectively, where no black key intervenes between two adjacent white keys. This pattern is the basis of *major and minor scales.

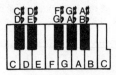

In the 17th century, keyboards had an average compass of four octaves, with all the chromatic notes except for the lowest range. Bach's harpsichord had more than five octaves. Broadwood, in 1794, made the first piano keyboard with six octaves, from C_1 to c''''; this was the compass of the Broadwood instrument used by Beethoven from 1817 on. Various attempts have been made within the last century to improve the keyboard. The *Janko keyboard* (patented 1882) had six rows of short keys arranged somewhat like a typewriter keyboard. In the *Clutsam keyboard* (1907) the keys were arranged in a slightly curved instead of a straight line, taking into account the fact that the player's arms move in arcs. This arrangement has been widely adopted

for organ pedals. Moór's *Duplex Coupler Grand Piano* imitates the two manuals of the harpsichord. The upper of the two keyboards gives the tones of the higher octave and can be coupled with the lower.

Keynote. *Tonic.

Khachaturian, Aram Ilich (b. Tiflis, 6 June 1903; d. Moscow, 1 May 1978). Pupil of Gnessin and Miaskovsky. Teacher in Moscow at the Conservatory and the Gnessin Institute from 1951. Employed a variety of folk materials. Composed ballets (incl. *Gayane,* 1942, containing "Sabre Dance"; *Spartacus,* 1956); orch. works (incl. 3 symphonies; *Masquerade* suite, 1944); concertos and concerto-rhapsodies for violin, for cello, and for piano; choral works (incl. *Poem of Stalin,* with orch., 1938); chamber music; piano pieces; music for theater and films.

Khovanshchina. Opera in five acts by Mussorgsky (to his own libretto), produced in St. Petersburg, 1886. Setting: Moscow and environs, 1682–89.

Khrennikov, Tikhon Nikolaievich (b. Yelets, Russia, 10 June 1913). Pupil of Shebalin. Teacher at the Moscow Conservatory from 1963. A leader as secretary of the Composers' Union in denouncing Prokofiev and other "formalists" in 1948 and thereafter. Has worked with folk materials. Has composed operas (incl. *Mother,* Moscow, 1957); a ballet; orch. works; concertos; piano pieces; songs; music for theater and films.

Kielflügel [G.]. Old name for harpsichord.

Kienzl, Wilhelm (b. Waizenkirchen, Austria, 17 Jan. 1857; d. Vienna, 3 Oct. 1941). Critic and composer. Pupil of Krejčí. Associate of Wagner. Opera conductor in Amsterdam, Hamburg, and Munich. Composed operas (incl. *Der Evangelimann,* Berlin, 1895); incidental music for plays; orch. works; choral works; chamber music; numerous piano pieces; numerous songs.

Kilar, Wojciech (b. Lvov, 17 July 1932). Studied in Katowice, Cracow, and Darmstadt, and with N. Boulanger in

Paris. Has composed symphonies and other works for orch. (incl. *Little Overture*, 1955; *Générique*, 1963; *Springfield Sonnet*, 1965); *Herbsttag*, cantata for alto and string quartet after Rilke, 1959; *Riff 62* for clarinets, saxophones, trumpets, trombones, violins, double basses, piano, and percussion, 1962; works for chamber ensembles.

Kilpinen, Yrjö (Henrik) (b. Helsinki, 4 Feb. 1892; d. there, 2 Mar. 1959). Pupil of Juon, though largely self-taught. Composed orch. works; chamber music; choral works; piano pieces; numerous songs to German, Finnish, and Swedish texts (incl. *Fjeldliedern; Kanteletar*).

Kim, Earl (b. Dinuba, Calif., 6 Jan. 1920). Pupil of Schoenberg and Sessions. Teacher at Princeton Univ., 1952–67, and at Harvard Univ. from 1967. Has composed *Dialogues* for piano and orch., 1959; *Exercises en Route* for soprano, chamber ensemble, dancers, actors, film, begun in 1962; piano pieces; a violin sonata; a cello sonata; *Earthlight* for violin, soprano, piano, and lights, 1973; songs.

Kimball, Jacob, Jr. (b. Topsfield, Mass., 22 Feb. 1761; d. there, 6 Feb. 1826). Lawyer and composer. Works incl. anthems, hymns, psalm tunes, fuguing pieces.

Kin. Japanese name for a small **koto*.

Kindermann, Johann Erasmus (b. Nuremberg, 29 Mar. 1616; d. there, 14 Apr. 1655). Organist and composer. Pupil of J. Staden and possibly of Cavalli. Church organist in Nuremberg from 1636. Composed organ and other instrumental pieces; sacred and secular songs with instrumental accompaniment; numerous chorale harmonizations.

Kinderscenen [G., Scenes from Childhood]. A composition by Schumann, op. 15 (1838), consisting of 13 short and simple **character pieces for piano. The familiar "Träumerei" (Dreams) is no. 7 in the group.

Kindertotenlieder [G., Children's Death Songs]. A cycle of five songs with orchestra or piano by Mahler (poems by Rückert), composed 1901–4.

King David. See *Roi David, Le*.

Kinnor. See under Harp.

Kirbye, George (b. *c*. 1565?; d. Bury St. Edmonds, Suffolk, Oct. 1634). House musician to a noble English family. Composed madrigals and motets.

Kirchen- [G.]. Church. *Kirchenjahr*, church year; *Kirchenkantate*, church cantata; *Kirchenmusik*, church music; *Kirchenschluss*, plagal *cadence; *Kirchensonate*, church sonata (**sonata da chiesa*); *Kirchenton*, *church mode; *Kirchenlied*, church song, either a Protestant *chorale or a Roman Catholic *hymn written in German.

Kirchner, Leon (b. Brooklyn, 24 Jan. 1919). Pupil of Stravinsky, Bloch, Sessions, Schoenberg, and Toch. Pianist and composer. Teacher at Mills College, 1954–60, and at Harvard Univ. from 1961. Has composed an opera, *Lily*, after Saul Bellow, New York, 1977; orch. works (incl. *Sinfonia*, 1952); 2 piano concertos; vocal works; chamber music (incl. String Quartet no. 3, with tape, awarded the Pulitzer Prize in 1967); piano pieces.

Kirchner, Theodor Fürchtegott (b. Neukirchen, near Chemnitz, 10 Dec. 1823; d. Hamburg, 18 Sept. 1903). Pupil of I. Knorr. Associate of Mendelssohn and Schumann. Teacher in Zürich, 1862–72. Director of the Royal Music Academy in Würzburg, 1873–75; teacher at the Royal Conservatory in Dresden, 1883–90. Composed numerous piano pieces; choral works; chamber music; organ pieces; songs.

Kiriac, Dumetru Georgescu (b. Bucharest, 18 Mar. 1866; d. there, 8 Jan. 1928). Pupil of d'Indy, Dubois, Pessard, Widor, and Vidal. Teacher at the Bucharest Conservatory from 1900. Worked with folk materials. Composed sacred and secular choral works; piano pieces; songs; arrangements of folksongs.

Kirnberger, Johann Philipp (b. Saalfeld, Thuringia, bapt. 24 Apr. 1721; d. Berlin, 26 or 27 July 1783). Theorist and composer. Pupil of J. S. Bach. Violinist to Frederick the Great at Potsdam from 1751. Composed orch. works; chamber music; sonatas, fugues, and other keyboard pieces; choral works; cantatas;

motets; songs. Published important theoretical writings, incl. *Die Kunst des reinen Satzes in der Musik*, 1774, 1779.

Kistler, Cyrill (b. Gross-Aitingen, near Augsburg, 12 Mar. 1848; d. Kissingen, 1 Jan. 1907). Pupil of Wüllner, Rheinberger, and Lachner. Music teacher in Bad Kissingen from 1885. Composed operas (incl. *Kunihild*, Sonderhausen, 1884; *Eulenspiegel*, Würzburg, 1889); orch. works; choral works; pieces for organ or harmonium; songs. Published several works on music theory and pedagogy.

Kit [F. *pochette; G. Taschengeige;* It. *sordino*]. A tiny fiddle to be carried in the pocket, used by dancing masters in the 17th and 18th centuries. There were two types, one a diminutive violin, the other a descendant of the medieval *rebec. See ill. under Violin family.

Kithara. The foremost instrument of ancient Greece, consisting of a square wooden soundbox and two curved arms connected by a crossbar. A number of strings, varying from 5 (8th century B.C.) to 7 (7th century B.C.) and finally 11 or more (5th century B.C.), were stretched between the soundbox and the crossbar. They were plucked with a plectrum. See ill. under Lyra.

Kittel, Johann Christian (b. Erfurt, bapt. 18 Feb. 1732; d. there, 17 Apr. 1809). Organist and composer. Pupil of J. S. Bach. Church organist in Erfurt from 1756. Published *Neues Choralbuch*, a collection of chorale melodies, 1803. Composed sonatas and other pieces for keyboard; organ pieces, incl. preludes and hymns.

Kittl, Johann Friedrich (Jan Bedřich) (b. Castle Worlik, Bohemia, 8 May 1806; d. Lissa, Poland, 20 July 1868). Pupil of Tomášek. Associate of Wagner, Liszt, and Berlioz. Director of the Prague Conservatory, 1843–64. Composed operas (incl. *Die Franzosen vor Nizza*, Prague, 1848, libretto by Wagner, originally *Bianca und Giuseppe*); orch. works (incl. *Jagdsinfonie*, 1837, and other symphonies); choral works; chamber music; piano pieces; songs.

Kjerulf, Halfdan (b. Oslo, 17 Sept. 1815; d. Grefsen, near Oslo, 11 Aug. 1868).

Pupil of Richter and Gade. Composed choral works; piano pieces and piano arrangements of folksongs and dances; numerous songs, many on Norwegian subjects.

Kl. [G.]. Abbr. for *Klarinette*, clarinet.

Kl. Fl. [G.]. Abbr. for *kleine Flöte*, piccolo. See Flute.

Kl. Tr. [G.]. Abbr. for *kleine Trommel*, side drum. See under Percussion instruments.

Klagend [G.]. Lamenting.

Klami, Uuno (Kalervo) (b. Virolahti, Finland, 20 Sept. 1900; d. Helsinki, 29 May 1961). Studied in Helsinki and with Ravel in Paris. Composed symphonies and other orch. works (incl. *Kalevala Suite*, 1932, rev. 1943; *Nummisuutarit*, overture, 1936); concertos for piano and for violin; choral works; chamber music; songs; incidental music for plays.

Klangfarbenmelodie [G., tone-color melody]. A term suggested by Schoenberg in his *Harmonielehre* (1911) in a discussion of the possibility of composing "melodically" with varying tone colors on a single pitch level as well as with varying pitch, duration, and intensity. The term attempts to establish timbre as a structural element comparable in importance to pitch, duration, etc. Schoenberg's concern with timbre as a structural element became evident in the *Five Orchestral Pieces* op. 16 (1909, rev. 1949), especially the third of these. The concept of melodic writing with successive points of tone color was extensively explored by Schoenberg's pupil Anton Webern, e.g., in the first of his *Five Pieces for Orchestra* op. 10 (1913).

Klappe [G.]. Key of wind instruments. *Klappenhorn, -trompete,* key bugle, key trumpet.

Klar [G.]. Clear, distinct.

Klarinette [G.]. *Clarinet.

Klaviatur [G.]. *Keyboard.

Klavier [G.]. *Piano. *Klavierauszug*, piano arrangement; *Klavierstück*, piano piece; *Klavierspiel*, piano playing. In historical studies *Klavier* is the generic designation for stringed keyboard instruments, as distinct from the organ. Sometimes the term means "manual" (*Orgel mit 2, 3, Klavieren*). Prior to the introduction of the piano, i.e., until about 1775, *Klavier* (then usually spelled *Clavier*) meant the harpsichord and/or clavichord. Hence, titles such as *Clavier-Übung or *Das Wohltemperierte Clavier* do not reveal which instrument was intended. To K. P. E. Bach and his contemporaries *Clavier* usually meant the clavichord. See also Clavier.

Klebe, Giselher (Wolfgang) (b. Mannheim, 28 June 1925). Pupil of Wolfurt, Rufer, and Blacher. Teacher at the Northwest-German Music Academy in Detmold from 1957. Has worked with twelve-tone techniques. Has composed operas (incl. *Die Räuber,* Düsseldorf, 1957); ballets; orch. works (incl. 4 symphonies; *Rhapsodie,* 1953); choral works; chamber music; works for voice with instruments.

Kleine Nachtmusik, Eine [G., A Little Night Music, or Serenade]. A celebrated composition for string ensemble by Mozart (K. 525), composed in 1787. It is in four movements, similar to those of a symphony.

Klenau, Paul (August) von (b. Copenhagen, 11 Feb. 1883; d. there, 31 Aug. 1946). Conductor and composer. Pupil of Malling, Bruch, Thuille, and Schillings. Composed operas (incl. *Gudrun auf Island,* Hagen, Westphalia, 1924, a revision of *Kjartan und Gudrun,* 1918; *Rembrandt van Rijn,* Berlin, 1937); the ballet-pantomime *Klein-Idas Blumen,* 1916; 7 symphonies and other orch. works, several after Dante; choral works; chamber music; piano pieces; works for voice and instruments.

Klengel, August Stephan Alexander (b. Dresden, 29 June 1783; d. there, 22 Nov. 1852). Pianist, organist, and composer. Pupil of Clementi, whom he accompanied to St. Petersburg, remaining there 1805–11. Organist of the Dresden court chapel from 1816. Composed numerous piano works (incl. *Canons et fugues dans tous les tons majeurs et mineurs*); 2 piano concertos.

Klengel, Julius (b. Leipzig, 24 Sept. 1859; d. there, 27 Oct. 1933). Cellist and composer. Brother of Paul Klengel. Pupil of Jadassohn. First cellist in the Gewandhaus Orchestra in Leipzig, 1881 –1924; teacher at the Leipzig Conservatory from 1881. Composed chamber music; cello concertos; pieces for cello and piano and for cello ensembles; cello exercises, etc.

Klengel, Paul (b. Leipzig, 13 May 1854; d. there, 24 Apr. 1935). Conductor, violinist, pianist, and composer. Brother of Julius Klengel. Pupil of F. David and Reinecke. Teacher at the Leipzig Conservatory from 1907. Composed chamber music; violin pieces; piano pieces; songs.

Klingen [G.]. To sound.

Klose, Friedrich (b. Karlsruhe, 29 Nov. 1862; d. Ruvigliana, Lugano, 24 Dec. 1942). Pupil of Bruckner. Teacher at the Akademie der Tonkunst in Munich, 1907 –19. Composed an opera, *Ilsebill,* Munich, 1905; an oratorio, *Der Sonne-Geist,* 1918; symphonic poems and other orch. works; choral works (incl. a Mass in D minor); chamber music; organ pieces; songs.

Klusák, Jan (b. Prague, 18 Apr. 1934). Pupil of Řídký and Bořkovec. Has composed an opera, *Proces* (The Trial), after Kafka, 1964; music for films; 3 symphonies and other orch. works (incl. *Invention I* for chamber orch., 1961); choral works; chamber music; works for solo instruments; works on tape.

Knab, Armin (b. Neu-Schleichach, Germany, 19 Feb. 1881; d. Wörishofen, 23 June 1951). Teacher at the Hochschule für Musik-Erziehung in Berlin, 1934–43. Composed numerous songs; stage works, incl. musical fairy tales; an oratorio; sacred cantatas and folksong cantatas; numerous choral works; instrumental pieces.

Knaben Wunderhorn, Des [G., The Youth's Magic Horn]. A group of German folksong texts collected and published by Achim von Arnim and Clemens Brentano (*c.* 1820). Mahler composed settings of a number of these texts: nine songs with piano (1892), ten songs with piano or orchestra (1892–99), and three songs as parts of symphonies (including

"Urlicht," which was incorporated into the *Resurrection Symphony).

Knarre [G.]. *Rattle.

Knecht, Justin Heinrich (b. Biberach, Swabia, 30 Sept. 1752; d. there, 1 Dec. 1817). Organist and music director in Biberach from 1771. Composed operas and other stage works; *Portrait musicale de la nature* for 15 instruments; pieces for piano, organ, flute; Masses, psalms, and other sacred music.

Kneifend [G.]. Plucking, i.e., *pizzicato.

Kniegeige [G.]. *Viola da gamba.

Knipper, Lev Konstantinovich (b. Tiflis, 3 Dec. 1898; d. Moscow, 30 July 1974). Pupil of Glière and Jarnach. Composed operas; ballets; 14 symphonies and other orch. works; concertos; choral cantatas; chamber music; piano pieces; music for films; songs and folksong arrangements.

Knorr, Ernst-Lothar von (b. Eitorf, near Cologne, 2 Jan. 1896; d. Heidelberg, 30 Oct. 1973). Director of the Hochschulinstitut für Musikerziehung in Trossingen from 1944; of the Hanover Music Academy from 1952; of the Heidelberg Hochschule für Musik und Theater from 1969. Composed a concerto for 2 orchestras; works for accordion ensembles; choral works, with orch. and *a cappella;* chamber music; pieces for organ, for piano, for accordion, for recorder; songs.

Knorr, Iwan (Otto Armand) (b. Mewe, Germany, 3 Jan. 1853; d. Frankfurt, 22 Jan. 1916). Pupil of Moscheles, E. F. E. Richter, Reinecke, and Jadassohn. Teacher at the Hoch Conservatory in Frankfurt from 1883 and its director from 1908. Composed operas; orch. works (incl. *Variationen über ein ukrainisches Volkslied*, 1890); chamber music; vocal works. Published textbooks on harmony and fugue.

Knyaz Igor. See *Prince Igor.*

Koch, (Sigurd Christian) Erland von (b. Stockholm, 26 Apr. 1910). Conductor and composer. Teacher at the Royal Music Academy in Stockholm from 1953. Has composed a ballad opera, *Lasse Lucidor,* 1943; ballets; 3 symphonies and other orch. works; *Musica malinconica* for string orch., 1952; con-

certos; choral works; chamber music; piano pieces; songs.

Köchel-Verzeichnis. See under K.

Kodály, Zoltán (b. Kecskemét, Hungary, 16 Dec. 1882; d. Budapest, 6 Mar. 1967). Pupil of Koessler. Associate of Béla Bartók, with whom he collaborated in the collection of national folksongs. Teacher at the Budapest Academy of Music from 1907. Composed operas (incl. *Háry János,* Budapest, 1926; *Székely fonó,* [The Spinning Room], Budapest, 1932; *Czinka Panna,* Budapest, 1948); orch. works (incl. *Suite from Háry János,* 1927; *Marosszék Dances,* 1930; *Dances of Galánta,* 1933); a concerto for orch.; numerous sacred and secular choral works (incl. *Psalmus hungaricus,* 1923); chamber music; works for voice with piano; piano pieces; songs; didactic pieces. Published numerous writings on folk music and music education.

Koechlin, Charles (b. Paris, 27 Nov. 1867; d. at his villa Le Canadel, Var, 31 Dec. 1950). Pupil of Gédalge, Massenet, and Fauré. Composed ballets and other stage works; orch. works (incl. *7 Stars Symphony,* 1933; *Le buisson ardent,* symphonic poem, 1938, 1945; *Les Bandar-Log,* symphonic poem after Kipling, 1940); works for solo instrument and orch.; choral works; string quartets and other chamber music; piano pieces (incl. *Paysages et marines,* c. 1916); organ pieces; songs; music for films. Published books on counterpoint, harmony, orchestration, Debussy, and Fauré.

Koellreutter, Hans Joachim (b. Freiburg, Germany, 2 Sept. 1915). Conductor and composer. Pupil of Hindemith. Settled in Brazil, 1938, and taught at the Brazilian Conservatory in Rio de Janeiro, 1938–52. Founded several music schools in Brazil. Has worked with twelve-tone techniques. Has composed orch. works; works for voice and instruments; chamber music; works for various instrumental ensembles, incl. Indian and Japanese instruments; songs.

Koessler, Hans (b. Waldeck, Germany, 1 Jan. 1853; d. Ansbach, 23 May 1926). Organist and composer. Pupil of Rheinberger and Wüllner. Teacher at the Dresden Conservatory from 1877 and at the Budapest Academy of Music, 1882–1908 and 1920–25. Composed an opera, *Der Münzenfranz*, Strasbourg, 1903; an oratorio; 2 symphonies and other orch. works; concertos; choral works (incl. *Psalm XLVI; Sylvesterglocken*, with orch.); chamber music; songs.

Köhler, (Christian) Louis (Heinrich) (b. Brunswick, 5 Sept. 1820; d. Königsberg, 16 Feb. 1886). Pupil of Sechter and Seyfried. Settled in Königsberg, 1845, and established a piano school there. Composed operas; a ballet; orch. works; cantatas and other vocal works; numerous piano studies. Published *Systematische Lehrmethode für Klavierspiel und Musik*, 1856, and other theoretical and pedagogic writings.

Kohn, Karl (b. Vienna, 1 Aug. 1926). Pianist and composer. Settled in the U.S., 1939. Pupil of Piston, Fine, and R. Thompson. Teacher at Pomona College in California from 1950. Has composed orch. works; *Concerto mutabile* for piano and orch., 1963; choral works; chamber music; piano and organ pieces; songs.

Kohs, Ellis (Bonoff) (b. Chicago, 12 May 1916). Pupil of B. Wagenaar and Piston. Teacher at the Univ. of Southern California from 1950. Has composed an opera, *Amerika*, after Kafka, 1969; incidental music for the theater; 2 symphonies and other orch. works; works for solo instrument and orch.; choral works; chamber music; piano and organ pieces; works for voice with instruments.

Kolb, Barbara (b. Hartford, Conn., 10 Feb. 1939). Pupil of Franchetti, Foss, and Schuller. Teacher at Wellesley College from 1975. Has composed vocal works (incl. *Chansons bas* for voice, harp, percussion, 1965); works for instrumental ensembles (incl. *Trobar Clus* for 12 instruments, 1970); piano pieces; works with tape.

Koleda, kolenda. A Bohemian, Rumanian, or Polish song for Christmas and other feasts, comparable to the English *carol.

Kontra- [G.]. *Kontrabass*, double bass; *-fagott*, contrabassoon; *-bassklarinette*, double-bass clarinet.

Kontretanz [G.]. **Contredanse.*

Kontski, Antoine de (Katski, Antoni) (b. Cracow, 27 Oct. 1817; d. Ivanovich, Russia, 7 Dec. 1889). Pianist and composer. Member of a large musical family. Pupil of Field and Sechter. Traveled widely in Russia, Europe, the U.S., Japan, and China. Composed 2 light operas; orch. works; Masses; oratorios; 2 piano concertos; piano pieces (incl. *Le reveil du lion*).

Konzert [G.]. Concert or concerto. *Konzertmeister*, concertmaster.

Konzertstück [G.]. See Concertino (2).

Koppel [G.]. Coupler. See under Organ.

Koppel, Hermann (David) (b. Copenhagen, 1 Oct. 1908). Pianist and composer. Teacher at the Royal Academy of Music in Copenhagen from 1949. Has composed an opera, *Macbeth* (1968); a ballet; music for theater, films, and radio; 7 symphonies and other orch. works; 4 piano concertos, a clarinet concerto, a cello concerto; an oratorio; *3 Psalms of David* for tenor, boys chorus, orch., 1949; chamber music; piano pieces; songs.

Korn, Peter Jona (b. Berlin, 30 Mar. 1922). Settled in the U.S., 1941. Pupil of Rubbra, Wolpe, Toch, Eisler, Schoenberg, and Rózsa. Music director of the New Orchestra in Los Angeles, 1948–56; director of the Richard Strauss Conservatory in Munich from 1967. Has composed an opera, *Heidi*, 1963; 3 symphonies and other orch. works; a saxophone concerto and other works for solo instrument and orch.; choral works; chamber music; songs.

Kornauth, Egon (b. Olomouc, Moravia, 14 May 1891; d. Vienna, 28 Oct. 1959). Pupil of R. Fuchs, Schreker, and Franz Schmidt. Founded and conducted an orchestra in Sumatra, 1926–28. Teacher at the Mozarteum in Salzburg from 1945. Composed orch. works; choral works; chamber music; piano pieces; songs.

Kornett [G.]. See under Cornet. Not to be confused with Eng. **cornett* (G. *Zink*).

Korngold, Erich Wolfgang (b. Brno, 29 May 1897; d. Hollywood, Calif., 29 Nov. 1957). Pupil of R. Fuchs and Zemlinsky. Settled in the U.S., 1934, and worked for

Warner Brothers. Close associate of the film director Max Reinhardt. Composed operas (incl. *Die tote Stadt,* Hamburg, 1920); other stage works; music for films and theater; orch. works; concertos; chamber music; piano pieces; songs.

Kósa, György (b. Budapest, 24 Apr. 1897). Pianist and composer. Pupil of Kodály, Bartók, Siklós, and Dohnányi. Teacher at the Budapest Academy of Music, 1927–62. Has composed operas; ballets; incidental music for plays; 8 symphonies and other orch. works; oratorios; cantatas; choral works; chamber music; piano pieces; songs.

Köselitz, Johann Heinrich. See Gast, Peter.

Koto [Jap.]. A Japanese stringed instrument, usually classified as a zither. It has a rectangular wooden body and 7 to 13 silk strings. It is placed horizontally on the floor and is plucked with the fingers, sometimes assisted by artificial nails. [See ill. under Zither.] There are two types of *koto: sō* (or Chinese **jeng*), with movable bridges; and *kin* (or Chinese **chyn*) without such bridges and usually with 7 strings.

Kotoński, Wlodzimierz (b. Warsaw, 23 Aug. 1925). Studied at the Warsaw Conservatory and with Szeligowski. Has worked with electronic techniques at the Groupe de recherches musicales in Paris and at the studio of the West German Radio in Cologne. Has taught electronic music at the State Higher School of Music (formerly Conservatory) in Warsaw from 1967. Has composed *Musique en relief* for four orchestral groups, 1959; *Die Windrose* for orch., 1976; *Chamber Music for 21 Instruments and Percussion,* 1958; a trio for flute, guitar, and percussion, 1960; *Canto per complesso da camera,* 1961; *Pezzo per flauto e pianoforte,* 1962; *Musica per fiati e timpani,* 1963; *A battere* for percussion, guitar, harpsichord, viola, and cello, 1966; *Aeolian Harp* for soprano and four instruments, 1973; *Microstructures—musique concrète,* 1963, and other works on tape; works employing elements of theater (incl. *Multiplay* for brass sextet, 1971).

Kotzwara, Franz (Kočvara, František)

(b. Prague; d. London, 2 Sept. 1791). Lived mostly in London and Dublin. Composed *The Battle of Prague* for piano, violin, cello, and drum; other instrumental works.

Koutzen, Boris (b. Uman, near Kiev, 1 Apr. 1901; d. Mt. Kisco, N.Y., 10 Dec. 1966). Violinist and composer. Pupil of Glière. Settled in the U.S., 1923. Teacher at the Philadelphia Conservatory from 1925 and at Vassar College from 1944. Composed operas; orch. works (incl. *Valley Forge,* symphonic poem, 1940); a violin concerto, 1946, and other works for solo instruments with orch.; chamber music; piano pieces.

Kovařovic, Karel (b. Prague, 9 Dec. 1862; d. there, 6 Dec. 1920). Conductor and composer. Pupil of Fibich. Opera conductor at the National Theater in Prague, 1900–1920. Composed operas (incl. *The Dog-Heads,* Prague, 1898; *On the Old Bleaching Ground,* Prague, 1901); ballets; orch. works; a piano concerto; choral works; chamber music; piano pieces; songs.

Koven, Reginald de. See De Koven, Henry Louis Reginald.

Koželuch, Leopold Anton (Kotzeluch) (b. Welwarn, Bohemia, 26 June 1747; d. Vienna, 7 May 1818). Pianist and composer. Pupil of his cousin J. A. Koželuch and of Dušek. Court musician in Vienna from 1778. Succeeded Mozart as court composer in 1792. Composed ballets; pantomimes; operas; oratorios; cantatas; symphonies and other orch. works; concertos; choral works; chamber music; piano pieces; songs.

Kraft, Anton (b. Rokitzán, near Pilsen, 30 Dec. 1749; d. Vienna, 28 Aug. 1820). Cellist and composer. Pupil of Haydn. Cellist in the chapel of Prince Esterházy, 1778–90; court cellist in Vienna, 1796–1820. Composed works for cello, incl. sonatas, grand duos for 2 cellos or cello and violin.

Kraft, Leo (b. Brooklyn, 24 July 1922). Pupil of Rathaus, R. Thompson, and N. Boulanger. Teacher at Queens College in New York from 1947. Has composed orch. works; choral works; string quartets and other chamber music; *Dialogues* for flute and tape, 1968; piano pieces;

works for voice with instruments (incl. *Spring in the Harbor* for soprano, flute, cello, piano, 1969).

Kraft, Nicolaus (b. Esterház, Hungary, 14 Dec. 1778; d. Eger, 18 May 1853). Cellist and composer; son of Anton Kraft. Court cellist in Vienna from 1809 and in Stuttgart from 1814. Composed several works for cello.

Kraft, William (b. Chicago, 6 Sept. 1923). Pupil of Luening, Lockwood, Beeson, Cowell, and Ussachevsky. Principal percussionist of the Los Angeles Philharmonic from 1962 and one of its guest conductors. Has taught at the Univ. of Southern California and the California Institute of the Arts. Has composed music for theater and films; orch. works (incl. *Contextures: Riots Decade '60, I*, 1968, and *II*, 1974); a concerto for 4 percussion soloists and orch., 1964; a piano concerto, 1972; chamber music; works for percussion ensembles; vocal works.

Kräftig [G.]. Strong, vigorous.

Krakowiak [F. *Cracovienne*]. A Polish dance named after the city of Cracow (Krakow). The music is in 2/4 time and employs simple syncopated patterns. In vogue in the early part of the 19th century, it was danced by large groups, with shouting, improvised singing, and striking together of the heels. Chopin wrote a "Krakowiak" for piano and orchestra (op. 14).

Kramer, Arthur Walter (b. New York, 23 Sept. 1890; d. there, 8 Apr. 1969). Publisher, critic, and composer. Managing director of the Galaxy Music Corp., 1936–56. Composed orch. works (incl. *Two Sketches*, 1916); *Symphonic Rhapsody* for violin and orch., 1912; choral works (incl. *In Normandy*, 1925); chamber music; piano pieces; songs.

Kraus, Joseph Martin (b. Miltenberg am Main, near Mainz, 20 June 1756; d. Stockholm, 15 Dec. 1792). Pupil of Abbé Vogler. Court *Kapellmeister* in Stockholm from 1788. Composed operas (incl. *Soliman II*, Stockholm, 1789); a ballet; orch. works; a violin concerto; chamber music; sacred and secular vocal music (incl. a funeral cantata for Gustaf III, 1792); piano pieces.

Krebs, Johann Ludwig (b. Buttelstedt, near Weimar, bapt. 12 Oct. 1713; d. Altenburg, 1 Jan. 1780). Pupil of J. S. Bach. Held several positions as court and church organist. Composed keyboard pieces, incl. suites and preludes; trio sonatas and other chamber music; organ works, incl. fugues and chorale variations; sacred vocal works.

Krebs, Karl August (real name Mied[c]ke) (b. Nuremberg, 16 Jan. 1804; d. Dresden, 16 May 1880). Conductor and composer. Pupil of Seyfried. Director of the Hamburg Opera, 1827–50, and *Kapellmeister* at the Dresden court, succeeding Wagner, 1850–72. Composed operas (incl. *Agnes Bernauer*, Hamburg, 1833, rev. Dresden, 1858); sacred music; piano pieces; songs (incl. "An Adelhaid"; "Die süsse Bell").

Krein, Alexander Abramovich (b. Nizhni-Novgorod, 20 Oct. 1883; d. Staraya Russa, near Moscow, 21 Apr. 1951). Studied at the Moscow Conservatory. Teacher at the People's Conservatory in Moscow, 1912–17. Composed operas; ballets; incidental music for plays of the Jewish Drama Theater in Moscow; music for films; orch. works; choral works (incl. *Kaddish*, 1921; *U.S.S.R.*, 1925); chamber music (incl. *Hebrew Sketches* for clarinet and string quartet, 1909, 1910); songs.

Krein, Grigory Abramovich (b. Nizhni-Novgorod, 18 Mar. 1879; d. Komarovo, near Leningrad, 6 Jan. 1955). Brother of Alexander Krein. Pupil of Juon, Glière, and Reger. Composed orch. works; works for solo instrument and orch. (incl. *Hebrew Rhapsody* for clarinet and orch.); chamber music; piano pieces.

Krein, Julian (b. Moscow, 5 Mar. 1913). Son of G. A. Krein. Pianist and composer. Pupil of his father and of Dukas. Teacher at the Moscow Conservatory, 1934–47. Has composed a ballet; orch. works; chamber music; piano pieces; songs.

Kreisler, Fritz (b. Vienna, 2 Feb. 1875; d. New York, 29 Jan. 1962). Violin virtuoso and composer. Pupil of Delibes and Bruckner. Settled in New York, 1940. Composed 2 operettas; a violin concerto; songs; violin pieces (incl. *Caprice Vien-*

nois; Tambourin Chinois). Some of his own violin pieces he at first attributed to earlier composers such as Vivaldi, Couperin, and Dittersdorf.

Kreisleriana. Schumann's cycle of eight piano pieces op. 16 (1838). The title refers to the whimsical and fantastic figure of the "Kapellmeister Kreisler," invented by the German novelist E. T. A. Hoffmann.

Krejčí, Iša (František) (b. Prague, 10 July 1904; d. there, 6 Mar. 1968). Pupil of Novák, Jirák, and Křička. Conductor of the Prague National Theater from 1958 to his death. Composed operas (incl. *Revolt at Ephesus*, after Shakespeare's *Comedy of Errors*, Prague, 1946); a ballet; orch. works; works for solo instrument and orch.; chamber music; vocal works; piano pieces.

Krenek, Ernst (Křenek) (b. Vienna, 23 Aug. 1900). Pupil of Schreker. Settled in the U.S., 1938, and has taught briefly at various institutions, incl. Vassar College, 1939–42, and Hamline Univ., 1942 –47. Has worked with serial and electronic techniques. Has composed operas (incl. **Jonny spielt auf; Karl V,* Prague, 1938; *Der goldene Bock,* Hamburg, 1964); ballets; other stage works; 5 symphonies and other orch. works; works for solo instrument with orch.; sacred and secular vocal works (incl. *Lamentatio Jeremiae prophetae,* 1941; *Reisetagebuch aus den österreichischen Alpen,* song cycle, 1929; *Sestina* for soprano, violin, guitar, clarinet, trumpet, percussion, 1957); electronic works; 7 string quartets and other chamber music; piano pieces. Published numerous literary works, incl. memoirs and a book on Ockeghem.

Kreutzer, Konradin (Conrad Kreuzer) (b. Messkirch, Baden, 22 Nov. 1780; d. Riga, 14 Dec. 1849). Pupil of Albrechtsberger. Court conductor in Stuttgart from 1812 and in Donaueschingen, 1817– 22. Composed operas and *Singspiele* (incl. *Das Nachtlager von Granada,* Vienna, 1834; *Konradin von Schwaben,* Stuttgart, 1812); an oratorio; a cantata; choral works; chamber music; piano pieces; songs.

Kreutzer, Rodolphe (b. Versailles, 16 Nov. 1766; d. Geneva, 6 Jan. 1831). Pupil of A. Stamitz. Violinist in the French royal chapel, 1782–92; violinist at the Paris Opéra from 1801 and its director from 1816. Teacher at the Paris Conservatory from 1795. Beethoven's *Kreutzer Sonata* was dedicated to him. Kreutzer composed numerous operas (incl. *Lodoïska,* Paris, 1791); ballets; orch. works; 19 violin concertos; 15 string quartets and other chamber music; numerous violin pieces (incl. *40 études ou caprices*).

Kreutzer Sonata. Popular name for Beethoven's Violin Sonata op. 47 (1803), dedicated to the French composer and violin virtuoso Rodolphe Kreutzer (1766 –1831) but originally composed for the English violinist George Bridgetower (*c.* 1780–1860), whom Beethoven accompanied at the first performance in 1803.

Kreuz [G., cross]. Sharp. See Accidentals.

Křička, Jaroslav (b. Kelč, Moravia, 27 Aug. 1882; d. Prague, 23 Jan. 1969). Teacher at the Prague Conservatory, 1919–45. Composed operas (incl. *White Ghost,* Brno, 1929) and other stage works; music for films; orch. works; a violin concerto; choral works; chamber music; piano pieces; songs.

Krieger, Adam (b. Driesen, Neumark, Prussia, 7 Jan. 1634; d. Dresden, 30 June 1666). Pupil of Scheidt. Court organist in Dresden from 1658. Composed lieder for one to five voices with instrumental accompaniment (incl. the collection *Neue Arien,* 1657, 1667); cantatas (incl. *An den Wassern zu Babel sassen wir und weineten*).

Krieger, Edino (b. Brusque, Brazil, 17 Mar. 1928). Conductor and composer. Pupil of Koellreutter, Copland, Mennin, and Berkeley. Has worked with twelvetone techniques and with Brazilian folk materials. Has composed music for theater and films; chamber music; vocal works; orch. works; piano pieces.

Krieger, Johann (Krüger) (b. Nuremberg, bapt. 1 Jan. 1652; d. Zittau, 18 July 1735). Organist and composer. Brother and pupil of J. Philipp Krieger, whom he succeeded as court organist at Bayreuth,

1672. Municipal organist at Zittau from 1681 to his death. Composed organ and other keyboard works, incl. preludes, fugues, and dances; sacred and secular vocal works.

Krieger, Johann Philipp (von) (b. Nuremberg, bapt. 27 Feb. 1649; d. Weissenfels, 7 Feb. 1725). Brother of Johann Krieger. Court organist at Bayreuth from 1670; *Kapellmeister* at Weissenfels and Halle from 1680 to his death. Composed operas and *Singspiele;* cantatas; sacred and secular vocal works; trio sonatas, suites for wind instruments or strings, and other chamber music; keyboard pieces.

Krommer, Franz Vincenz (Kramář, František Vincenc) (b. Kamenice, Moravia, 27 Nov. 1759; d. Vienna, 8 Jan. 1831). Violinist and composer. Imperial *Kapellmeister* in Vienna from 1818. Composed symphonies; concertos for clarinet and for other instruments; a Mass and other sacred music; chamber music; piano pieces.

Krummhorn [G.]. Crumhorn; see under Oboe family III. Also, an organ stop.

Kubelík, (Jeronym) Rafael (b. Býchory, near Kolín, Czechoslovakia, 29 June 1914). Conductor and composer. Studied at the Prague Conservatory. Conductor of the Czech Philharmonic from 1936, and of the Chicago Symphony Orchestra, 1950–53. Music director of the Covent Garden Opera from 1955 and briefly of the Metropolitan Opera from 1972. Has composed operas (incl. *Veronika,* Brno, 1947); a cantata; choral symphonies; a violin concerto; a cello concerto; 2 Requiems; chamber music; piano pieces; songs.

Kubik, Gail (b. South Coffeyville, Okla., 5 Sept. 1914). Pupil of Bernard Rogers, Sowerby, Piston, and N. Boulanger. Has taught at several U.S. colleges and universities, incl. Scripps College from 1970. Has composed a ballet; a folk opera, *Mirror for the Sky,* New York 1947; film scores (incl. *Gerald McBoing-Boing,* 1950); symphonies and other orch. works (incl. *Symphonie concertante,* awarded the Pulitzer Prize for 1952); choral works; chamber music; piano pieces; songs; television and radio scores.

Kücken, Friedrich Wilhelm (b. Bleckede, near Luneburg, 16 Nov. 1810; d. Schwerin, 3 Apr. 1882). Conductor and composer. Pupil of Sechter and Halévy. *Kapellmeister* in Stuttgart, 1851–61. Composed 2 operas (incl. *Der Prätendent,* Stuttgart, 1847); polonaises for chorus and orch.; instrumental pieces; songs (incl. "Ach wie wärs möglich dann"; "Wer will unter die Soldaten").

Kuencheu. A 16th-century development of Chinese musical drama, often referred to as the classical Chinese opera. Still heard fairly frequently today, it is characterized by a sophisticated singing style and prominent use of dance, which is closely integrated with song. The orchestra, which uses the flute as the melody instrument, is generally mellow. It has had a great influence on the *Peking opera, which was established about 1850 and which today is more popular. Both types make use of melodic fragments that are used in different songs. The *kuencheu,* however, makes use of a greater number of different melodies.

Kuhlau, Daniel Friedrich Rudolph (b. Ülzen, Germany, 11 Sept. 1786; d. Copenhagen, 12 Mar. 1832). Court musician in Copenhagen from 1813. Composed operas and other stage works (incl. *Elverhøj* [The Fairies' Mound], Copenhagen, 1828); chamber music, much of it for flute; sonatinas and other piano pieces; male quartets; songs.

Kuhnau, Johann (b. Geising, Saxony, 6 Apr. 1660; d. Leipzig, 5 June 1722). Organist, theorist, and composer. Organist at the Thomaskirche in Leipzig from 1684. Music director of the Thomaskirche and Nikolaikirche and cantor of the Thomasschule from 1701, in which positions he was succeeded by J. S. Bach. Music director of the Univ. of Leipzig from 1701. Composed suites and sonatas for harpsichord, incl. the descriptive *Biblische Historien,* 1700; church cantatas and other sacred music.

Kuhreigen [G.]. *Ranz des vaches.*

Kujawiak. A Polish dance from the province of Kujawy. It is a rapid *mazurka. Chopin's mazurkas op. 33, no. 3, and op. 41, no. 2, are *kujawiaks.*

Kullak, Theodor (b. Krotoszyn, Poland, 12 Sept. 1818; d. Berlin, 1 Mar. 1882). Pupil of Czerny, Sechter, and Nicolai. Royal court pianist in Berlin from 1846; established a school there, the Neue Akademie der Tonkunst, in 1855. Composed piano pieces, incl. dances, caprices, impromptus, pedagogic pieces, and salon pieces; chamber music; songs.

Kunst der Fuge, Die. See *Art of Fugue, The.*

Kupferman, Meyer (b. New York, 3 July 1926). Clarinetist and composer. Self-taught in composition. Teacher at Sarah Lawrence College from 1951. Has made some use of twelve-tone techniques and elements of jazz. Has composed operas (incl. *The Judgement,* 1967); ballets; music for films; 4 symphonies and other orch. works; a concerto for cello and jazz band, 1962; chamber music; a series of pieces titled *Cycle of Infinities* for various instrumental ensembles begun in 1961; choral works; piano pieces; songs.

Kurka, Robert (b. Cicero, Ill., 22 Dec. 1921; d. New York, 12 Dec. 1957). Pupil of Luening and Milhaud. Taught at City College of New York and at Queens College. Composed an opera, *The Good Soldier Schweik,* New York, 1958; 2 symphonies and other orch. works; works for solo instrument and orch.; choral works; string quartets and other chamber music; piano pieces.

Kurtág, György (b. Lugos, Rumania, 19 Feb. 1926). Pupil of Farkas, Kadosa, Veress, Leó Weiner, Milhaud, and Messiaen. Teacher at the Budapest Academy of Music from 1967. Has worked with serial techniques. Has composed a viola concerto; chamber music; piano pieces; vocal works (incl. *Bornemisza Péter mondásai* [The Sayings of Peter Bornemisza] for soprano, piano, and orch., 1968).

Kurz [G.]. Short. *Kurz Oktave,* *short octave. *Kurzer Vorschlag,* short *appoggiatura.

Kusser, Johann Sigismund (Cousser) (b. Pressburg, bapt. 13 Feb. 1660; d. Dublin, late Nov. 1727). Pupil and friend of Lully. Director of the Hamburg Opera, 1694–95; of the Stuttgart Opera, 1698–1704. Settled in Dublin, 1706. Composed operas (incl. *Porus,* Brunswick, 1693; *Erindo,* Hamburg, 1694); instrumental works (incl. a set of suites for strings titled *Composition de musique suivant la methode française,* 1682); serenatas and other vocal works.

Kuula, Toivo (Timoteus) (b. Vaasa, Finland, 7 July 1883; d. Vyborg, 18 May 1918). Pupil of Wegelius, Järnefelt, Bossi, and Labey. Conductor of the Vyborg Orchestra from 1916 to his death. Composed orch. works; a cantata; a *Stabat Mater;* choral works; chamber music; organ pieces; piano pieces; songs.

K.V. See K.

Kvapil, Jaroslav (b. Fryšták, Czechoslovakia, 21 Apr. 1892; d. Brno, 18 Feb. 1958). Pupil of Janáček and Reger. Teacher at the Brno Conservatory from 1920 and at the Janáček Academy of Music in Brno from 1947. Composed an opera and other stage works; an oratorio; 4 symphonies and other orch. works; works for solo instrument and orch.; chamber music; piano pieces; songs.

Kyrie [Gr.]. The first item of the Ordinary of the Roman Catholic *Mass. Its full text is: "Kyrie eleison; Christe eleison; Kyrie eleison" (Lord, have mercy, etc.). Each of these three invocations is sung three times, usually with the melodies repeated according to the scheme: aaa bbb ccc' (c' indicates an extension or variant of c), or aaa bbb aaa'.

L

L. Abbr. for *left* or [G.] *links;* L.H., left hand or [G.] *linke Hand.*

La. See Pitch names; Solmization; Hexachord.

La Guerre, Élisabeth-Claude Jacquet de (b. Paris, *c.* 1664; d. there, 27 June 1729). Harpsichordist, organist, and composer. Composed an opera, *Céphale et Procris,* Paris, 1694; a ballet; sacred and secular cantatas; violin sonatas; trio sonatas; suites and other keyboard pieces; airs.

La Montaine, John (b. Oak Park, Ill., 17 Mar. 1920). Pupil of Hanson, Bernard Rogers, B. Wagenaar, and N. Boulanger. Pianist with the N.B.C. Symphony Orchestra, 1950–54. Has composed a trilogy of Christmas pageant-operas; orch. works (incl. a symphony; *From Sea to Shining Sea,* 1961); a piano concerto (awarded the Pulitzer Prize for 1959); *Birds of Paradise* for piano and orch.; choral works; works for voice with instruments; chamber music; piano and organ pieces; songs.

La Rue, Pierre de (b. probably at Tournai, *c.* 1460; d. Courtrai, 20 Nov. 1518). Singer at the Siena Cathedral, 1482–85; chapel singer at the Burgundian court in Brussels and Malines, 1492–1516. Canon at Courtrai from 1516. Composed Masses, a Requiem, motets, chansons.

La Tombelle, (Antoine-Louis-Joseph) Fernand de (Fouant de) (b. Paris, 3 Aug. 1854; d. Château de Fayrac, Dordogne, 13 Aug. 1928). Organist and composer. Pupil of Guilmant, Dubois, and Saint-Saëns. Assistant organist at the Madeleine in Paris, 1885–98; teacher at the Schola cantorum, 1896–1904. Composed operettas; oratorios; cantatas; orch. works; sacred choral works; chamber music; organ and piano works; songs.

Labarre (Berry), Théodore (-François-Joseph) (b. Paris, 24 Mar. 1805; d. there, 9 Mar. 1870). Harpist and composer. Pupil of Fétis and Boieldieu. Conductor of the Opéra-Comique, 1847–49; teacher at the Paris Conservatory, 1867–70. Composed 4 operas (incl. *Pantagruel*); ballets; harp pieces; songs. Published a harp method.

L'Abbé, Joseph Barnabé Saint-Sevin (real name Saint-Sevin) (b. Agen, France, 11 June 1727; d. Paris, 25 July 1803). Violinist and composer. Pupil of Leclair. Violinist at the Concert spirituel, 1741–55, and at the Paris Opéra, 1742–62. Composed violin works, incl. sonatas, symphonies for 3 violins and thoroughbass, and airs. Published a manual, *Les principes du violon,* 1761.

Labey, (Jean) Marcel (b. Le Vesinet, Seine-et-Oise, 6 Aug. 1875; d. Nancy, 25 Nov. 1968). Conductor and composer. Pupil of Lenormand and d'Indy. Vice-director of the Schola cantorum in Paris from 1931 and director of the César Franck School from 1935. Composed an opera; 4 symphonies and other orch. works; chamber music; piano pieces; songs.

Labial pipes. Same as flue pipes. See Organ.

Labunski, Felix Roderick (b. Ksawerynow, Poland, 27 Dec. 1892). Brother of Wiktor Labunski. Studied at the Warsaw Conservatory and in Paris with N. Boulanger and Dukas. Settled in the U.S., 1936. Taught at the Cincinnati College-Conservatory of Music, 1945–64. Has composed a ballet; orch. works (incl. a suite for strings, 1942; *Canto di aspirazione,* 1963); sacred and secular vocal works; chamber music; piano pieces; organ pieces.

Labunski, Wiktor (b. St. Petersburg, 14 Apr. 1895; d. Lenexa, Kans., 26 Jan. 1974). Brother of Felix Labunski. Studied at the St. Petersburg Conservatory. Pianist and composer. Settled in the U.S., 1928. Teacher at the Kansas City Conservatory from 1937 and its director from 1941. Composed a symphony; works for piano and orch.; piano pieces.

Lacerda, Osvaldo (b. São Paulo, Brazil, 23 Mar. 1927). Pupil of Guarnieri, Giannini, and Copland. Has taught at several Brazilian schools and conservatories. Has composed orch. works; choral works; chamber music; sacred music; works for voice with instruments; piano pieces (incl. a series of *Brasilianas*); pedagogic works.

Lachner, Franz Paul (b. Rain, Bavaria, 2 Apr. 1803; d. Munich, 20 Jan. 1890). Brother of Ignaz and Vincenz Lachner. Pupil of Sechter and close associate of Schubert. Conductor at the Kärtnertor Theater in Vienna, 1827–34; at the Mannheim Opera, 1834–36. *Kapellmeister* at the Munich court from 1836 and general music director there, 1852–65. Composed operas (incl. *Catarina Cornaro,* Munich, 1841) and other stage works; symphonies, suites, and other orch. works; oratorios; cantatas; choral works; Masses, a Requiem, and other sacred music; chamber music; piano pieces; organ pieces; songs.

Lachner, Ignaz (b. Rain, Bavaria, 11 Sept. 1807; d. Hanover, 24 Feb. 1895). Brother of Franz and Vincenz Lachner. Organist, conductor, and composer. Worked with his brother Franz in Vienna, 1825–31. Music director at the Stuttgart court from 1831; in Munich, 1842–53; and at the Frankfurt court, 1861–75. Composed operas (incl. *Die Regenbrüder,* Stuttgart, 1839); *Singspiele;* ballets; symphonies; Masses; chamber music; piano pieces.

Lachner, Vincenz (b. Rain, Bavaria, 19 July 1811; d. Karlsruhe, 22 Jan. 1893). Brother of Franz and Ignaz Lachner. Organist, conductor, and composer. Court *Kapellmeister* at Mannheim, 1836–72; teacher at the Karlsruhe Conservatory from 1873. Composed four-part male choruses; orch. works; psalms; chamber music; piano pieces; songs.

Lacombe, Louis Trouillon (b. Bourges, France, 26 Nov. 1818; d. Saint-Vaast-la-Hougue, 30 Sept. 1884). Pianist and composer. Pupil of P. Zimmerman at the Paris Conservatory and of Czerny, Sechter, and Seyfried in Vienna. Composed operas; a melodrama; a cantata, *Sapho,* 1878; orch. works; choral works; chamber music; numerous piano pieces; songs.

Lacombe, Paul (b. Carcassonne, France, 11 July, 1837; d. there, 5 June 1927). Associate of Bizet and Saint-Saëns. Composed 3 symphonies and other orch. works; chamber music; numerous piano pieces; songs.

Lacrimoso [It.]. Tearful, mournful.

Laderman, Ezra (b. Brooklyn, 29 June 1924). Pupil of Luening, Moore, and Wolpe. Teacher at Sarah Lawrence College from 1960; at the State Univ. of New York at Binghamton from 1966. Has composed operas (incl. *Galileo Galilei,* television opera-oratorio, 1967); other stage works; music for films; symphonies and other orch. works; a cantata, *And David Wept,* prod. on television, 1971; string quartets and other chamber music; piano pieces; songs.

Ladmirault, Paul-Émile (b. Nantes, 8 Dec. 1877; d. Kerbili-en-Camoël, Morbihan, France, 30 Oct. 1944). Pupil of Gédalge and Fauré. Teacher, later director, at the Nantes Conservatory. Composed 2 operas; a ballet; orch. works (incl. *Suite bretonne,* 1903); choral works (incl. *Choeurs des âmes de la forêt* with orch., 1903); sacred works; chamber music; piano pieces; songs.

Lady Macbeth of Mtsensk [Rus. *Lady Macbeth Mtsenskago Uyezda*]. Opera in four acts by Shostakovich (libretto by A. Preis and the composer, based on a novel by N. S. Lyeskov), produced in Moscow, 1934. Setting: a village in Russia, 1840. The opera was officially condemned by the Soviet government in 1936 as "bourgeois and formalistic." It was revised after the official decree was rescinded (1958) and was produced under the title *Katerina Ismailova* (1962).

Lage [G.]. *Position, with reference to (1) violin playing (e.g., *erste* or *zweite Lage,* i.e., first or second position); (2) chords (*enge* or *weite Lage,* i.e., close or open position) [see Spacing]; (3) ranges of voices and instruments (*hohe* or *tiefe Lage,* i.e., high or low range) [see Voices, range of].

Lagnoso [It.]. Lamenting.

Lai, lay. A form of medieval French poetry and music developed mainly in northern France during the 13th century by the *trouvères. The *lai* was also culti-vated in southern France, but only two or three *troubadour (Provençal) *lais* are preserved with music. The development of the musical form ended with Machaut, who wrote 18 *lais*. The poems consist of 60, 100, or more lines divided into irregu-lar stanzas of 6 to 16 or more lines. The schemes of meter and rhyme to be found in the stanzas vary greatly. The stanzas occur, however, in pairs, within each of which the two stanzas are identical in rhyme and meter. Examples from the 14th century normally include 12 such pairs, the first and last of these also being identical in rhyme and meter.

The musical structure of the *lai* is es-sentially that of the sequence [see Se-quence (2)]. Thus, the same music is used for both stanzas of each pair, yield-ing the form AA BB CC. . . . A stanza of a *lai*, however, is normally much longer than a versicle of a sequence. In some cases, music for the first half of a stanza is repeated for the second half, re-sulting in a fourfold repetition of music for a pair of stanzas. Another name for the *lai* is *descort* ("disorder"). The Ger-man counterpart of the *lai* is the 14th-century *Leich*.

Laisse. See under *Chanson de geste.*

Laisser [F.]. To allow, to leave. *Laissez vibrer,* allow to vibrate, e.g., a cymbal or the strings of a harp.

Lajtha, László (b. Budapest, 30 June 1891; d. there, 16 Feb. 1963). Teacher at the Budapest National Conservatory, 1919–49. Worked with Hungarian folk music. Composed an opera; 2 ballets; music for films; 9 symphonies and other orch. works; a violin concerto; sacred and secular choral works; chamber music; piano pieces; works for voice and piano; arrangements of folksongs.

Lakmé. Opera in three acts by Delibes (libretto by E. Gondinet and P. Gille), produced in Paris, 1883. Setting: India, 19th century.

Lakner, Yehoshua (b. Bratislava, Czechoslovakia, 24 Apr. 1924). Studied in Israel and with Copland and B. A. Zimmermann. Teacher at the Israel Music Academy from 1950; theater com-poser in Zürich from 1963. Has com-posed music for plays; *Ballet for Rina*

Schönfeld for flute, cello, piano, and per-cussion, 1962; orch. works; vocal works; *musique concrète;* piano pieces; other instrumental works.

Lalande, Michel-Richard de (Delalande) (b. Paris, 15 Dec. 1657; d. Versailles, 18 June 1726). Held several positions as church organist in Paris from 1679 and was superintendent of the royal chapel in Versailles from 1683. Composed ballets and divertissements; incidental music for the theater; 42 motets for chorus and orch.; instrumental pieces, incl. *sym-phonies des noëls* and *symphonies pour les soupers du roi.*

Lalo, (Victor-Antoine-) Édouard (b. Lille, 27 Jan. 1823; d. Paris, 22 Apr. 1892). Violinist, violist, and composer. Studied in Lille and at the Paris Conservatory. Composed operas (incl. *Le Roi d'Ys,* Paris, 1888); 2 ballets; 3 symphonies and other orch. works (incl. *Symphonie espagnole* for violin and orch., 1873; *Rhapsodie norvégienne,* 1881); con-certos for violin, for cello, and for piano; sacred vocal music; chamber music; songs.

Lambert, Constant (b. London, 23 Aug. 1905; d. there, 21 Aug. 1951). Conduc-tor, music journalist, and composer. Pupil of R. O. Morris and Vaughan Wil-liams. Music director of Sadler's Wells Ballet Co., 1931–47. Composed ballets (incl. *Romeo and Juliet* for Diaghilev, 1926; *Horoscope,* 1937; *Tiresias,* 1951); music for films; orch. works; choral works (incl. *The Rio Grande,* with orch., 1927; *Summer's Last Will and Testa-ment,* with orch., 1935); piano pieces; songs.

Lament. (1) In Scottish and Irish music, a piece for bagpipes or a song used at clan funerals or other mournful occa-sions. (2) General designation for com-positions commemorating the death of a famous person. The medieval Latin term for these is *planctus.* From the 14th to 17th centuries laments, called *déplora-tions, tombeaux, plaintes,* or *apothé-oses,* were often written for great com-posers by their pupils.

Lamentations. Music set to the Lamenta-tions of Jeremiah. In the Roman Catholic rite the Lamentations are sung, in place of the three lessons, during the first nocturn of Matins on Thursday, Friday, and Saturday of Holy Week (*Tenebrae), in a simple recitation tone [*LU*, pp. 631, 692, 754]. A characteristic feature of the text is the enumeration of the verses by Hebrew letters, aleph, beth, etc. From the late 15th through the 17th centuries the text was often composed polyphonically, usually in a simple homorhythmic style, except for the Hebrew letters, which often received a more elaborate treatment. The Sistine Choir still uses the settings of Palestrina and Allegri. A recent setting is Stravinsky's *Threni* (1958).

Lampe, John Frederick (Johann Friedrich) (b. Saxony, 1703; d. Edinburgh, 25 July 1751). Bassoonist in the King's Theatre Orchestra in London from 1725. Composed stage works (incl. *The Dragon of Wantley*, in collaboration with Carey, London, 1737); instrumental pieces (incl. *The Cuckoo Concerto; Medley Overture*); hymns; ballads, airs, songs.

Lampugnani, Giovanni Battista (b. Milan, 1706; d. after 1784). Director of the King's Theatre in London from 1743. *Maestro al cembalo* at La Scala in Milan from 1755. Composed numerous operas (incl. *L'amor contadino*, Venice, 1760); contributions to pasticcios; symphonies; concertos; trio sonatas.

Lancio, con [It.]. With vigor.

Landi, Stefano (b. Rome, *c*. 1590; d. there, *c*. 1655). Singer and composer. Pupil of Nanino. *Maestro di cappella* at Santa Maria dei Monti in Rome from 1624 and singer in the Cappella Giulia at St. Peter's from 1629. Composed a pastoral opera, *La morte d'Orfeo*, Venice, 1619; a sacred opera, *Il Sant'Alessio*, Rome, 1632; Masses; psalms; madrigals; arias.

Landini, Francesco (Landino) (b. Fiesole, *c*. 1335?; d. Florence, 2 Sept. 1397). Organ virtuoso and composer, blind from childhood. Organist at the church of San Lorenzo in Florence. Composed *ballate*, madrigals, *cacce*. See *Ars nova*.

Landini cadence. See under Cadence.

Ländler [G.]. An Austrian dance in triple meter very much like a slow *waltz. It was very popular in the early 19th century, before the waltz came into vogue. Mozart (K. 606), Beethoven (11 *Mödlinger Tänze*, 1819), and Schubert (e.g., op. 171, D. 790) wrote collections of *Ländler*. See Dance music.

Landowski, Marcel (b. Pont l'Abbé, France, 18 Feb. 1915). Conductor and composer. Pupil of Busser. Music director of the Comédie-Française, 1962–65; of the French Ministry of Cultural Affairs from 1966. Has composed operas; a ballet; an oratorio; music for films; 3 symphonies and other orch. works; works for solo instrument and orch.; vocal works; chamber music.

Landré, Guillaume (Louis-Frédéric) (b. The Hague, 24 Feb. 1905; d. Amsterdam, 6 Nov. 1968). Jurist and composer. Pupil of Pijper. Composed operas (incl. *De Snoek*, Amsterdam, 1938); 4 symphonies and other orch. works; concertos for violin, for cello, and for clarinet; choral works; chamber music; songs.

Lange-Müller, Peter Erasmus (b. Frederiksborg, near Copenhagen, 1 Dec. 1850; d. Copenhagen, 26 Feb. 1926). Composed operas (incl. *Spanske Studenter*, Copenhagen, 1883) and other stage works (incl. the melodrama *Renoessance*, Copenhagen, 1901); incidental music for plays; 2 symphonies and other orch. works; a violin concerto; choral works; chamber music; numerous songs.

Langgaard, Rued Immanuel (b. Copenhagen, 28 July 1893; d. Ribe, Denmark, 10 July 1952). Organist of the Ribe Cathedral from 1940. Composed operas; 16 symphonies and other orch. works; choral works (incl. *Music of the Spheres*, with orch.); chamber music; piano and organ pieces; songs.

Langlais, Jean (François) (b. La Fontenelle, 15 Feb. 1907). Organist and composer, blind from infancy. Pupil of Dupré and Dukas. Organist at Sainte-Clothilde in Paris from 1945; teacher at the Schola cantorum there from 1961. Has composed orch. works; 2 concertos for organ and string orch.; a suite for cello and orch.; cantatas and other choral works; numerous organ works; Masses, motets, and other church music; songs.

Langsam [G.]. Slow.

Lanier(e), Nicholas (Laneare, Lanyere) (b. London, bapt. 10 Sept. 1588; d. Greenwich, 24 Feb. 1666). Lutenist, singer, painter, and composer. Master of the King's Music under Charles I and Charles II. Composed music for masques (incl. Jonson's *Lovers Made Men,* 1617, perhaps the first English work in recitative style); a cantata, *Hero and Leander;* a funeral hymn for Charles I; a pastoral on the birth of Prince Charles, text by Herrick; ayres and dialogues.

Lantins, Arnold de (probably born near Liège; fl. 15th cent.). Singer in the papal chapel in Rome, 1431–32. Composed a Mass and Mass sections; motets; French chansons.

Lantins, Hugho de (b. probably near Liège; fl. 15th cent.). Possibly related to Arnold de Lantins. Composed Mass Ordinary sections; motets; French and Italian secular polyphony.

Lanza, Alcides (b. Rosario, Argentina, 2 June 1929). Pianist, conductor, and composer. Pupil of Ginastera, Messiaen, Malipiero, Copland, Maderna, and Ussachevsky. On the staff of the Columbia-Princeton Electronic Music Center, 1965–70. Teacher at McGill Univ. in Montreal from 1971. Has composed orch. works; a piano concerto; vocal works; works for various instrumental ensembles; electronic music, some including conventional instruments; piano pieces; mixed-media works.

Laparra, Raoul (**Louis-Félix-Émile-Marie**) (b. Bordeaux, 13 May 1876; d. Suresnes, Hauts-de-Seine, near Paris, 4 Apr. 1943). Music critic and composer. Pupil of Gédalge, Massenet, and Fauré. Composed operas (incl. *La habanera,* Paris, 1908; *L'illustre Fregona,* after Cervantes, Paris, 1931); orch. works; *Un dimanche basque* for piano and orch.; chamber music; piano pieces; songs.

Lara, Isidore de. See De Lara, Isidore.

Largamente [It.]. Broadly.

Largando. *Allargando.*

Larghetto [It.]. The diminutive of *largo,* therefore somewhat faster than this

tempo. Also, title for pieces in such a tempo.

Largo [It.]. (1) Very slow in tempo. See Tempo marks. (2) Title for pieces in this tempo, e.g., a famous composition by Handel, originally the aria "Ombra mai fù" ("Shade never was") from his opera *Serse* (*Xerxes*) but usually played in an arrangement for organ or other instruments.

Lark Quartet. Popular name for Haydn's String Quartet in D major op. 64, no. 5, so called because of the high passage played by the first violin at the opening of the first movement.

Larsson, Lars-Erik (b. Akarp, near Lund, Sweden, 15 May 1908). Studied at the Royal Academy of Music in Stockholm and with Berg in Vienna. Teacher at the Royal Academy of Music in Stockholm, 1947–59. Has composed an opera; incidental music for plays; 3 symphonies and other orch. works; concertos for cello, for violin, and for saxophone; 12 concertinos for solo instruments and string orch.; choral works; a *Missa brevis;* chamber music; piano pieces; songs.

Laserna, Blas de (b. Corella, Navarre, 4 Feb. 1751; d. Madrid, 8 Aug. 1816). Composer to Madrid theaters. Works incl. operas; *zarzuelas;* incidental music for plays; *tonadillas; sainetes.*

Lassen, Eduard (b. Copenhagen, 13 Apr. 1830; d. Weimar, 15 Jan. 1904). Court *Kapellmeister* at Weimar, 1858–95; conductor of the Weimar Opera, 1860–95, succeeding Liszt. Composed operas (incl. *Landgraf Ludwigs Brautfahrt,* Weimar, 1857); a ballet; incidental music for plays; cantatas; 2 symphonies and other orch. works; sacred vocal music; songs.

Lassu. See under *Verbunkos; Csárdás.*

Lassus, Roland de ([L.] Orlandus Lassus; [It.] Orlando di Lasso) (b. Mons, *c.* 1532; d. Munich, 14 June 1594). *Maestro di cappella* at San Giovanni in Laterano in Rome, 1553–54. Musician at the Bavarian court in Munich from 1556 and *Kapellmeister* there from *c.* 1564 to his death. His pupils incl. Lechner, Eccard, Aichinger, and G. Gabrieli. Composed approximately 150 Italian madrigals; approximately 150 French chansons; approximately 90 German lieder; over 50 Masses; over 500 motets; *Psalmi Davidis penitentiales;* Magnificats; Passions; hymns; other sacred works; instrumental pieces.

Lauda [It.; pl. *laude;* the less correct forms *laude* (sing.), *laudi* (pl.), are also used]. Hymns of praise and devotion in the Italian language. Their origin and early development were closely connected with St. Francis of Assisi (*c.* 1182 –1226) as well as with the many penitential fraternities of the 13th and 14th centuries. The *laude* of the 13th century are monophonic songs similar in some ways to French troubadour music. Their textual structure is that of a refrain poem, and a few are cast in the form of the French **virelai* (or the Italian **ballata*). The original manuscripts give no indications for rhythm. The *lauda* poetry flourished in the 15th century, but only few remnants of the music—some monophonic, some in two parts—have survived. A new period of *lauda* compositions began with the printer Petrucci's two books of *Laude* (1507, 1508), containing works by some of the **frottola* composers (Tromboncino, Cara, Fogliano). These are all polyphonic, in three or four parts, and in a simple chordal style borrowed from the *frottola*. In the second half of the 16th century Fra Serafino Razzi inaugurated a vast literature of *laude* in the popular styles of the **villanella* and **canzonetta*.

Laudon Symphony. Haydn's Symphony no. 69 in C (*c.* 1778), composed in honor of the Austrian field marshal Baron von Laudon (1717–90).

Lauds. The second of the canonical hours. See under Office.

Lauf [G.; pl. *Läufe*]. A rapid passage, particularly in scales. For *Laufwerk,* see under Mechanical instruments.

Launeddas. A Sardinian triple clarinet thought to be of Oriental origin. It consists of three pipes made of cane and provided with single reeds. The two outer pipes are melody pipes with five or six holes, while the center pipe is an unchangeable **bourdon*.

Laute [G.]. **Lute.*

Lavallée, Calixa (b. Verchères, Quebec, 28 Dec. 1842; d. Boston, 21 Jan. 1891). Pianist and composer. Studied at the Paris Conservatory. Settled in Boston, 1880, and taught at the Petersilea Conservatory there. Composed operas (incl. *The Widow,* Boston, 1881); an oratorio; a symphony; choral works; piano sonatas; salon music; music of the Canadian national song, "O Canada."

Lavolta. See Volta (1).

Lavry, Marc (b. Riga, 22 Dec. 1903; d. Haifa, 20 Mar. 1967). Conductor and composer. Settled in Palestine, 1935. Music director for Israeli Radio, 1948– 58. Composed operas; oratorios; orch. works; works for solo instrument and orch.; choral works; harp pieces.

Law, Andrew (b. Milford, Conn., Mar. 1749; d. Cheshire, Conn., 13 July 1821). Preacher, singing teacher, and composer. Composed hymn tunes. Published compilations of church music and pedagogic works.

Lawes, Henry (b. Dinton, Wiltshire, 5 Jan. 1596; d. London, 21 Oct. 1662). Brother of William Lawes. Probably a pupil of Coperario. Court musician under Charles I and Charles II. Contributed music to The **Siege of Rhodes.* Composed masques (incl. Milton's *Comus,* 1634); psalms; settings of poems by Milton, Herrick, and others; anthems; songs.

Lawes, William (b. Salisury, bapt. 1 May 1602; d. Chester, 1645). Brother of Henry Lawes. Pupil of Coperario. Chamber musician to Charles I. Composed stage works; anthems; psalms; catches; canons; songs; part songs (incl. "Gather ye rosebuds while ye may"); instrumental pieces (incl. the collection *Royall consort*).

Lay. **Lai.*

Layolle, François de (Antonio Francesco Romolo di Agniolo di Piero Aiolle) (b. Florence, 4 Mar. 1492; d. Lyon?, *c.* 1540). Singer in Florence, 1505–7. Music teacher of Benvenuto Cellini. Settled in Lyon in 1518. Composed Masses and motets; madrigals; chansons.

Layton, Billy Jim (b. Corsicana, Tex., 14 Nov. 1924). Pupil of McKinley, Q. Porter, and Piston. Teacher at Harvard Univ., 1960–66, and at the State Univ. of New York at Stony Brook from 1966. Has composed orch. works (incl. *Dance Fantasy,* 1964); *3 Dylan Thomas Poems* for chorus and brass sextet, 1956; chamber music (incl. a string quartet, 1956, and *5 Studies* for violin and piano, 1952); piano pieces.

Lazarof, Henri (b. Sofia, 12 Apr. 1932). Pupil of Ben-Haim, Petrassi, and Shapero. Teacher at the Univ. of California at Los Angeles from 1962. Has composed orch. works; works for solo instrument and orch. (incl. a violin concerto, 1960, and a cello concerto, 1968); vocal works; string quartets and other chamber music; *Quantetti* for piano and 3 prerecorded pianos on tape, 1964; other works for various ensembles.

Lazzari, Sylvio (Josef Fortunat Silvester) (b. Bolzano, Italy, 30 Dec. 1857; d. Suresnes, near Paris, 10 June 1944). Pupil of Franck and Guiraud. Composed operas (incl. *Le sautériot,* Chicago, 1918; *La lépreuse,* Paris, 1912); a pantomime; incidental music for Goethe's *Faust;* orch. works (incl. *Rhapsodie espagnole*); a *Rhapsodie* for violin and orch.; vocal works; chamber music; piano pieces; songs.

Le Flem, Paul (b. Lézardrieux, Côtes-du-Nord, France, 18 Mar. 1881). Music critic and composer. Pupil of d'Indy and Roussel. Teacher at the Schola cantorum from 1923 and singing director at Saint-Gervais from 1925. Composed operas (incl. *Le rossignol de Saint-Malo,* Paris, 1942); music for films and radio; incidental music for plays; orch. works; choral works; chamber music; piano pieces; harp pieces; songs.

Le Jeune, Claude (b. Valenciennes, *c.* 1530; d. Paris, 25 Sept. 1600). Associated with Antoine de Baïf's Académie de poésie et musique for the cultivation of **musique mesurée.* Court composer to Henry IV from *c.* 1595. Composed *Le printemps,* publ. 1603, a collection of *musique mesurée;* psalm settings (incl. the collection *Dodécachorde,* 1598); Italian madrigals; French chansons; Latin motets.

Le Maistre, Matthaeus (b. Roclenge-sur-Geer, near Liège, *c.* 1505; d. Dresden,

before Apr. 1577). Succeeded J. Walter as *Kapellmeister* at the Dresden court, 1554–68. Composed Masses, motets, Magnificats; sacred and secular polyphonic lieder.

Le Roy, Adrien (b. Montreuil-sur-Mer, *c.* 1520; d. Paris, 1598). Lutenist and composer; founding partner with Robert Ballard of a music-printing firm. Composed pieces for lute, guitar, cittern; chansons and *airs de cour;* intabulations of vocal works; wrote and published theoretical and pedagogic works.

Leader. Conductor (in America) or concertmaster (in England).

Leading motive, motif. **Leitmotiv.*

Leading tone, note [F. *note sensible;* G. *Leitton;* It. *sensibile;* Sp. *sensible*]. The seventh degree of the scale, a semitone below the tonic, so called because of the frequency with which it "leads up" (resolves upward) to the tonic. In the major scale, the seventh degree naturally lies a semitone below the tonic. In the pure minor scale (and in various of the **church modes*), the seventh degree is a whole tone below the tonic and is therefore raised a semitone by means of an accidental when it is to function as a leading tone [see Major, minor; *Musica ficta; Scale degrees*].

Lebègue, Nicolas-Antoine (b. Laon, 1631; d. Paris, 6 July 1702). Organist at Saint-Merry in Paris from 1664; organist at the royal chapel there from 1678 to his death. Composed organ and harpsichord pieces; airs for 2 and 3 voices with *continuo;* a *Méthode pour toucher l'orgue.*

Lebendig, lebhaft [G.]. Lively.

Lechner, Leonhard (b. Etschtal, Austrian Tirol, *c.* 1553; d. Stuttgart, 9 Sept. 1606). Boy chorister under Lassus. Chapel singer in Stuttgart from 1587 and *Kapellmeister* there from 1595. Composed a Passion according to St. John; Masses, motets, Magnificats, psalms; sacred and secular polyphonic lieder; arrangements of *villanelle* by Regnart.

Leclair, Jean-Marie ("l'aîné") (b. Lyon, 10 May 1697; d. Paris, 22 or 23 Oct. 1764). Brother of Jean-Marie Leclair "le cadet." Violinist and composer. Settled in Paris, 1723. Participant in the Concert spirituel, 1728–34. Musician to the royal court in Paris, 1734–36. Composed an opera; concertos; chamber music (incl. trio sonatas and 48 sonatas for violin and *continuo*).

Leclair, Jean-Marie ("le cadet") (b. Lyon, 23 Sept. 1703; d. there, 30 Nov. 1777). Brother of Jean-Marie Leclair "l'aîné." Violinist and composer. Composed motets, ariettas, and other vocal works; violin sonatas and other instrumental pieces.

Lecocq, (Alexandre) Charles (b. Paris, 3 June 1832; d. there, 24 Oct. 1918). Pupil of Halévy. Composed comic operas and operettas (incl. *La fille de Mme. Angot*, Brussels, 1872; *Giroflé-Girofla*, Brussels, 1874); ballets; instrumental pieces; sacred and secular vocal works; piano pieces; songs.

Ledger lines. Short lines above or below the staff, used to indicate pitches above or below those of the staff itself. The use of ledger lines can be avoided by appropriate choices of *clef. See example under Notation.

Lee, Dai-Keong (b. Honolulu, 2 Sept. 1915). Pupil of Sessions, Jacobi, and Copland. Has composed operas; ballets; symphonies and other orch. works (incl. *Golden Gate Overture*, 1942; *Pacific Prayer*, 1942); a violin concerto; choral works; chamber music; piano pieces; songs; music for films.

Lee, Noël (b. Nanking, China, of American parents, 25 Dec. 1924). Pupil of Piston, Fine, and N. Boulanger. Has traveled widely as a concert pianist. Has composed a ballet; orch. works; chamber music; numerous piano pieces; song cycles.

Leere Saite [G.]. Open string.

Lees, Benjamin (b. Harbin, Manchuria, of Russian parents, 8 Jan. 1924). Pupil of Stevens, Dahl, and Antheil. Has lived in the U.S. since infancy. Has taught at the Peabody Conservatory, Queens College in New York, and the Manhattan School of Music. Has composed operas; 3 symphonies and other orch. works; *Etudes* for piano and orch., 1974, and concertos for orch., for piano, for violin, for oboe, and for string quartet with orch.; vocal

works (incl. *Visions of Poets,* cantata, 1961); chamber music; piano pieces.

Leeuw, Ton (Antonius Wilhelmus Adrianus) de (b. Rotterdam, 16 Nov. 1926). Pupil of Messiaen and Badings. Teacher at the Amsterdam and Utrecht Conservatories and at the Univ. of Amsterdam from 1959; director of the Amsterdam Conservatory from 1972. Has composed operas (incl. *De Droom*, Amsterdam, 1965); ballets; orch. works; *Haiku II* for soprano and orch., 1968; the oratorio *Hiob*, 1956; electronic music, with and without voices and instruments; string quartets and other works for instrumental ensembles, incl. a series of pieces titled *Spatial Music;* piano pieces; songs.

Lefébure-Wély, Louis James Alfred (b. Paris, 13 Nov. 1817; d. there, 31 Dec. 1869). Pupil of Halévy and Adam. Organist in Paris at the Madeleine, 1847–57, and at Saint-Sulpice from 1863. Composed an opera; a cantata; 3 symphonies; 3 Masses and other sacred music; chamber music; piano pieces (incl. *Les cloches du monastère* and 50 etudes); organ and harmonium pieces; songs.

Lefebvre, Charles-Édouard (b. Paris, 19 June 1843; d. Aix-les-Bains, 8 Sept. 1917). Teacher at the Paris Conservatory from 1895. Composed operas; orch. works; choral works; works for voice with orch.; psalms and other sacred music; chamber music; pieces for piano and other solo instruments; songs.

Legato [It.]. To be played without any perceptible interruption between the notes, often indicated with a *slur [Ex. 1], as opposed to *non legato* [Ex. 2], *portato* [Ex. 3; or with dashes instead of dots], and *staccato* [Ex. 4]. *Legatissimo*, indicated by the word and not with notational symbols, is either a more forceful indication of legato or a sort of super-legato in which the preceding note is held for a short moment together with the following one [Ex. 5].

Leger lines. *Ledger lines.

Leggero, leggiero [It.]. Light, nimble, quick. This can occur in both *staccato and *legato passages.

Legley, Victor (b. Hazebrouck, French Flanders, 18 June 1915). Violist and composer. Pupil of Absil. Teacher at the Brussels Conservatory from 1949 and at the Chapelle Musicale Reine Elisabeth from 1955. Has composed an opera; a ballet; 5 symphonies and other orch. works; concertos for violin, for viola, for harp, and for piano; string quartets and other chamber music; sonatas for various solo instruments; songs.

Legno [It.]. Wood. *Col legno,* tapping the strings with the stick of the bow instead of bowing them. *Stromenti di legno,* woodwind instruments.

Legrenzi, Giovanni (b. Clusone, near Bergamo, bapt. 12 Aug. 1626; d. Venice, 26 May 1690). *Maestro di cappella* at the Accademia dello Spirito Santo in Ferrara, 1657–65. Director of the Conservatorio de' mendicanti in Venice from 1672; *maestro di cappella* at San Marco there from 1685. Composed operas (incl. *Totila,* 1677; *Il Giustino,* 1683); oratorios; sacred concertos; Masses, psalms, motets, and other sacred vocal works; trio sonatas and other chamber music.

Lehár, Franz (b. Komorn, Hungary, 30 Apr. 1870; d. Bad Ischl, Austria, 24 Oct. 1948). Pupil of Foerster and Fibich. Held several positions as military bandmaster, 1890–1902. Composed operettas (incl. *Die *lustige Witwe* [The Merry Widow]; *Der Graf von Luxemburg,* Vienna, 1909; *Zigeunerliebe* [Gypsy Love], Vienna, 1910; *Paganini,* Vienna, 1925); other stage works; orch. works; marches; dances (incl. *Gold und Silber*); music for films; piano pieces; songs.

Lehmann, Hans Ulrich (b. Biel, Switzerland, 4 May 1937). Pupil of Boulez and Stockhausen. Teacher at the Basel Musik-Akademie from 1964; at the Univ. of Zürich from 1969; and at the Zürich Conservatory from 1972. Has composed orch. works (incl. *Quanti I* for flute and chamber orch., 1962); chamber music; vocal works (incl. *Rondo* for soprano and orch., 1967).

Leibowitz, René (b. Warsaw, 17 Feb. 1913; d. Paris, 28 Aug. 1972). Conductor and composer. Pupil of Schoenberg and Webern. Conductor for French Radio, 1946–54. Worked with and taught twelve-tone techniques. His pupils incl. Boulez. Composed operas; a music drama; symphonies and other orch. works; works for solo instrument with orch.; choral works; string quartets and other chamber music; piano pieces; songs.

Leich [G.]. The 14th-century German counterpart of the French *lai.

Leidenschaftlich [G.]. Passionate.

Leier [G.]. Usually, the lyre [see Lyra (1)]. In earlier usage, the *hurdy-gurdy (*Drehleier, Radleier, Bettlerleier*). Schubert's song "Der Leiermann" portrays a player of the hurdy-gurdy (not of the street organ, called *Leierkasten*).

Leierkasten [G.]. *Street organ.

Leifs, Jón Thorleifsson (b. Solheimar, Iceland, 1 May 1899; d. Reykjavik, 30 July 1968). Studied at the Leipzig Conservatory. Music director of the Icelandic Radio from 1935. Worked with native Icelandic materials. Composed orch. works; choral works; chamber music; piano pieces; songs.

Leigh, Walter (b. London, 22 June 1905; d. near Tobruk, Libya, 12 June 1942). Studied at Cambridge and with Hindemith in Berlin. Music director of the Cambridge Festival Theatre, 1931–32. Composed operas (incl. *Jolly Roger,* London, 1933); a pantomime, *Aladdin,* 1931; a revue; incidental music for plays; music for films and radio; orch. works; vocal works; chamber music; piano pieces; songs.

Leighton, Kenneth (b. Wakefield, Yorkshire, 2 Oct. 1929). Pianist, conductor, and composer. Studied at Oxford and with Petrassi in Rome. Teacher at the Univ. of Edinburgh from 1956. Has composed stage works; a symphony and other orch. works; concertos for string orch., for piano, for violin, for cello; choral works (incl. a Mass; sacred cantatas); string quartets and other chamber music; piano and organ pieces.

Leise [G.]. (1) Soft. (2) Medieval congregational hymns in the German language, so called because of their refrain, kyrie *eleis*(on), which was abbreviated to *kirleis* or *leis*. Several Protestant chorales belong to this category, e.g., "Nun bitten wir den heiligen Geist" and "Christ ist erstanden."

Leiter [G.]. (1) Scale (*Tonleiter*). (2) Leader of an orchestra.

Leitmotiv, leitmotif [G., leading motif]. A term coined by Wagner's friend H. von Wolzogen to denote those musical *motifs used in Wagner's later works in association with particular characters, situations, ideas, etc. Wagner transforms and combines such motifs for dramatic purposes in ways that produce a continuous symphonic texture. Dramatically, they may serve simply to identify persons, events, and the like, or they may provide foreshadowing or reminiscence of such elements in the drama. Much less far-reaching examples of the use of recurrent music for dramatic purposes are found as early as the late 18th century. An important antecedent of Wagner's works in this and other respects is Weber's *Der *Freischütz*.

Leitton [G.]. *Leading tone.

Lekeu, (Jean-Joseph-Nicholas-) Guillaume (b. Heusy, near Verviers, Belgium, 20 Jan. 1870; d. Angers, France, 21 Jan. 1894). Pupil of d'Indy and Franck. Composed orch. works; choral works; chamber music; a violin sonata; piano pieces; songs; fragments of an opera.

Lemare, Edwin Henry (b. Ventnor, Isle of Wight, 9 Sept. 1865; d. Los Angeles, 24 Sept. 1934). Organist and composer. Pupil of G. A. and W. C. MacFarren. Held several positions as church and municipal organist in England and the U.S. Composed numerous sacred and secular organ works.

Lemmens, Nicolas Jacques (b. Zoerle-Parwijs, Belgium, 3 Jan. 1823; d. Linterpoort, near Malines, 30 Jan. 1881). Organist and composer. Pupil of Fétis. Teacher at the Brussels Conservatory from 1849. Opened a school of religious music at Malines, 1879. Among his pupils were Guilmant and Widor. Com-

posed 2 symphonies; choral works; sacred vocal works; organ works; pieces for piano and for harmonium; songs. Wrote an *École d'orgue*.

Lemminkäinen's Homecoming. Symphonic poem by Jean Sibelius, op. 22, no. 4 (1893–95), describing (after a story from the *Kalevala) the hero's journey home from Pohjola [see *Pohjola's Daughter*].

Leningrad Symphony. A title sometimes used for Shostakovich's Symphony no. 7, op. 60, composed in 1941, when Leningrad was besieged by the Germans.

Lenormand, René (b. Elbeuf, France, 5 Aug. 1846; d. Paris, 3 Dec. 1932). Founded a society for the cultivation of songs of all nations. Composed an opera; orch. works; works for solo instrument with orch.; piano pieces; numerous songs. Published a manual on harmony.

Lent [F.]. Slow.

Lento [It.]. Slow. See under Tempo marks.

Leo, Leonardo (Lionardo Oronzo Salvatore de Leo) (b. San Vito degli Schiavi, near Brindisi, 5 Aug. 1694; d. Naples, 31 Oct. 1744). Organist of the Cappella reale in Naples from 1717; assistant *maestro di cappella* there from 1737 and *maestro* in 1744. Organist and teacher at the Conservatorio di Sant' Onofrio, 1725–34, and from 1739. His pupils incl. Piccinni and Traetta. Composed serious operas (incl. *Demofoonte*, Naples, 1735; *L'Olimpiade*, Naples, 1737) and comic operas (incl. *Amor vuol sofferenze*, Naples, 1739); oratorios; Masses, motets, Magnificats, and other sacred works (incl. a *Miserere* for double chorus); cantatas; cello concertos; harpsichord pieces; fugues for organ.

Leoncavallo, Ruggiero (b. Naples, 8 Mar. 1858; d. Montecatini, 9 Aug. 1919). Studied at the Naples Conservatory. Traveled widely in Europe and the Near East as a café pianist and piano teacher. Composed operas (incl. *I *pagliacci; I Medici*, Milan, 1893, the first part of an unfinished trilogy on the Italian Renaissance; *La bohème*, Venice, 1897; *Zaza*, Milan, 1900); operettas; a ballet; orch. works; piano pieces; songs.

Leonin (Leoninus) (fl. Paris, late 12th cent.). A master of the *Notre Dame school. Composed organa included in the *Magnus liber organi.*

Leonore Overtures. The overtures Beethoven wrote for his opera *Fidelio,* prior to the final overture, known as the Fidelio Overture (or, incorrectly, as Leonore Overture no. 4). Leonore no. 2 was written for the first production in 1805. No. 3 is a revision of no. 2 and was written for a revival of the opera in 1806. No. 1, op. 138, was written in 1806 and 1807 with a view to a production of the opera in Prague that never materialized. The name refers to the original title of the opera, *Leonore.* The *Fidelio* overture was written for the revival of the opera in 1814.

Leroux, Xavier-Henry-Napoléon (b. Velletri, Papal States, 11 Oct. 1863; d. Paris, 2 Feb. 1919). Pupil of Dubois and Massenet. Teacher at the Paris Conservatory from 1896 to his death. Composed operas (incl. *La Reine Fiammette,* Paris, 1903; *Le chemineau,* Paris, 1907); a Mass; motets; songs.

Leschetizky, Theodor (Leszetycki) (b. Lancut, Poland, 22 June 1830; d. Dresden, 14 Nov. 1915). Pianist and composer. Pupil of Czerny and Sechter. Teacher at the St. Petersburg Conservatory from 1862 and in Vienna from 1878. Paderewski was among his pupils. Composed an opera, *Die erste Falte,* Prague, 1867; numerous piano pieces (dances, nocturnes, romances, salon pieces, etc.).

Lessard, John Ayres (b. San Francisco, 3 July 1920). Pupil of N. Boulanger. Teacher at the State Univ. of New York at Stony Brook from 1963. Has composed orch. works; works with solo instrument and orch.; chamber music (incl. a wind octet, a partita for wind quintet, a string trio, and a piano trio); vocal works; piano and harpsichord pieces; songs.

Lesson [L. *lectio*]. (1) In the Roman Catholic rites, a reading from the Scriptures or other sources, e.g., the writings of the church fathers. (2) A 17th- and 18th-century name for a type of English instrumental piece, particularly for harpsichord or organ. The term does not imply any special form or style, nor necessarily a pedagogical purpose.

Lesueur, Jean-François (Le Sueur) (b. Drucat-Plessiel, near Abbeville, France, 15 Feb. 1760; d. Paris, 6 Oct. 1837). *Maître de chapelle* at several churches; at the court of Napoleon from 1804, succeeding Paisiello. Inspector at the Paris Conservatory, 1795–1802, and teacher there from 1818 to his death. Among his pupils were Berlioz and Gounod. Composed operas (incl. *La caverne,* Paris, 1793; *Paul et Virginie,* Paris, 1794; *Télémaque,* Paris, 1796; *Ossian, ou Les bardes,* Paris, 1804); oratorios; secular cantatas; revolutionary hymns; Masses, motets, and other sacred music. Published pedagogic and theoretical writings.

Lesur, Daniel (Jean-Yves) (Daniel-Lesur) (b. Paris, 19 Nov. 1908). Organist and composer. Pupil of G. Caussade, J. Gallon, and Tournemire. Teacher at the Schola cantorum from 1935 and its director, 1957–62. Music director of French Television from 1962. Associate of Messiaen, Jolivet, and Baudrier in the organization of "La *jeune France." Has composed an opera, *Andrea del Sarto,* Marseille, 1969; ballets; orch. works (incl. the symphonic poem *Andrea del Sarto,* 1949); sacred and secular choral works; chamber music; piano and organ pieces.

Letelier (Llona), Alfonso (b. Santiago, Chile, 4 Oct. 1912). Pupil of Allende. Cofounder (1940) and director (to 1953) of the Escuela moderna de música in Santiago; teacher at the National Conservatory there from 1947. Dean of the faculty of Fine Arts of the Univ. of Chile, 1952–62. Has composed orch. works; a guitar concerto and other works for solo instrument and orch.; an oratorio; choral works; works for voice and orch. (incl. *Los sonetos de la muerte,* 1947); a Mass; chamber music; piano pieces; songs.

Letter notation. The use of letters for the indication of tones is restricted today to theoretical and instructive purposes; see Pitch names. In earlier periods letters were also used for writing down music, e.g., in ancient Greece, in Arab and Persian music of the 13th century, and in German organ *tablature. Letters are also used in French lute tablature, but here they indicate finger positions, not pitches. In the Middle Ages there were several systems of letter notation based on the Roman alphabet.

Levalto. See Volta (1).

Levare, levate [It.]. To take off (organ stops, mutes). *Si levano i sordini,* take off the mutes.

Levatio [L.]; **elevazione, levazione** [It.]. *Elevation.

Lévy, Ernst (b. Basel, 18 Nov. 1895). Pianist and composer. Pupil of H. Huber and Pugno. Teacher at the Basel Conservatory, 1916–20, and at several U.S. institutions, 1941–66, incl. the New England Conservatory, Bennington College, the Univ. of Chicago, the Massachusetts Institute of Technology, and Brooklyn College. Returned to Switzerland, 1966. Has composed 14 symphonies and other orch. works; a cello concerto; choral works; string quartets and other chamber music; works for voice with instruments; keyboard works; songs.

Levy, Marvin David (b. Passaic, N.J., 2 Aug. 1932). Pupil of P. James and Luening. Has composed operas (incl. *Mourning Becomes Electra,* after O'Neill, New York, 1967); a Christmas oratorio; a *Sacred Service* for synagogue, 1964; orch. works; a piano concerto; chamber music.

Lewis, Robert Hall (b. Portland, Oreg., 22 Apr. 1926). Trumpet player and composer. Pupil of Bernard Rogers, Hanson, N. Boulanger, Krenek, Apostel, and Schiske. Teacher at the Peabody Conservatory in Baltimore, 1958–62, 1964–66, and since 1972. Has composed 2 symphonies and other orch. works; works for brass and other instrumental ensembles; vocal works; string quartets and other chamber music; works for various instruments without accompaniment; piano pieces.

L.H. Abbr. for *left hand* or [G.] *linke Hand.*

Lhéritier, Jean (b. diocese of Thérouanne, between 1480 and 1490; d. probably after 1552). Pupil of Josquin des Prez, according to a contemporary. *Maestro di cappella* at San Luigi dei

Francesi in Rome, 1521–22, and to the papal legate at Avignon by 1540. Composed a Mass, motets, and Magnificats; a chanson.

Liadov, Anatol Konstantinovich (b. St. Petersburg, 11 May 1855; d. at his estate Polynovka, district of Novgorod, 28 Aug. 1914). Pupil of his father, Konstantin N. Liadov, and of Rimsky-Korsakov. Teacher at the St. Petersburg Conservatory from 1878 to his death. Among his pupils were Prokofiev and Miaskovsky. Composed orch. works (incl. *Baba Yaga,* 1904; *8 Russian Folksongs,* 1906; *Kikimora,* 1909; *Enchanted Lake,* 1909); vocal works; chamber music; incidental music for plays; piano pieces (incl. *Birulki,* 1876); arrangements of Russian folksongs.

Liapunov, Sergei Mikhailovich (b. Yaroslavl, Russia, 30 Nov. 1859; d. Paris, 8 Nov. 1924). Pianist and composer. Pupil of Taneiev. Teacher at the St. Petersburg Conservatory from 1910. Settled in Paris, 1923. Composed 2 symphonies, 2 symphonic poems, and other orch. works; concertos for piano and for violin; a cantata; choral works; piano pieces (incl. *Études d'exécution transcendante; Fêtes de Noël*); songs and arrangements of Russian folksongs.

Liatoshinsky, Boris Nikolaievich (b. Zhitomir, Russia, 3 Jan. 1895 [old style 22 Dec. 1894]; d. Kiev, 15 Apr. 1968). Pupil of Glière. Teacher at the Kiev Conservatory from 1920 and at the Moscow Conservatory from 1935. Composed operas (incl. *Shchors,* Kiev, 1938); music for films; 3 symphonies and other orch. works; choral works; string quartets and other chamber music; piano pieces; songs and arrangements of Ukrainian folksongs.

Liber usualis [L.]. See under Liturgical books.

Libretto [It.]. The text of an opera, oratorio, etc.

Licenza, con alcuna [It.]. With some freedom or license, e.g., in performance or in composition.

Lidholm, Ingvar (Natanael) (b. Jönköping, Sweden, 24 Feb. 1921). Conductor and composer. Pupil of Rosenberg and Seiber. Teacher at the Royal Academy of Music in Stockholm from 1965. Has composed a television opera, *Holländarn*, after Strindberg, 1967; a ballet; orch. works (incl. *Ritornello*, 1955; *Poesis*, 1963); choral works; chamber music; a piano sonata; songs.

Liebermann, Rolf (b. Zürich, 14 Sept. 1910). Pupil of Vogel. Director of the orchestra of the Swiss Broadcasting Corp. from 1950; manager of the Hamburg State Opera from 1959. Has composed operas (incl. *Penelope*, Salzburg, 1954) and other stage works; orch. works (incl. *Furioso*, 1947); a concerto for jazz band and orch., 1954; cantatas; music for films; piano pieces; songs.

Liebesgeige; -oboe [G.]. *Viola d'amore; oboe d'amore [see Oboe family II (a)].

Liebeslieder [G., Love Songs]. Two groups of 18 (op. 52, 1869) and 15 (*Neue Liebeslieder*, op. 65, 1875) short pieces by Brahms. Each is in the character of a waltz for vocal quartet and piano duet. Brahms arranged some of these works for voices and small orchestra. The texts are taken from Daumer's *Polydora*, except for the last song in op. 65, which is by Goethe.

Lied [G.; pl. *Lieder*]. *Song. The term is particularly applied to the German art song of the 19th century as represented in the works of composers such as Schubert, Schumann, Brahms, and Wolf. As a generic term, it is also applied to the following German repertories among others: the monophonic songs of the *Minnesinger and *Meistersinger (*c.* 1250–1550); the polyphonic songs of the 15th and 16th centuries, as represented in various 15th-century collections [see *Liederbuch*] and in the works of composers such as Heinrich Isaac, Paul Hofhaimer, and Ludwig Senfl; the accompanied solo songs of the baroque period by composers such as Adam Krieger; and the more lyrical and sometimes folklike songs of the late 18th and early 19th centuries composed by members of the second *Berlin school and others.

Lied von der Erde, Das [G., The Song of the Earth]. A symphonic song cycle by Mahler (who called it a symphony), for mezzo-soprano, tenor, and orchestra, set to German translations (by Hans Bethge) of old Chinese poems: 1. "Das Trinklied vom Jammer der Erde" (The Drinking Song of Earth's Woe); 2. "Der Einsame im Herbst" (The Lonely One in Autumn); 3. "Von der Jugend" (Of Youth); 4. "Von der Schönheit" (Of Beauty); 5. "Der Trunkene im Frühling" (The Toper in Spring); 6. "Der Abschied" (The Farewell). The work was completed in 1908 and first performed in Munich in 1911, after the composer's death.

Lieder eines fahrenden Gesellen [G., Songs of a Wayfarer]. Four songs for contralto and orchestra by Mahler (composed 1883–85), set to his own poems.

Lieder ohne Worte [G., Songs Without Words]. Forty-eight piano pieces by Mendelssohn, published in eight groups of six each (op. 19b, 30, 38, 53, 62, 67, 85, 102; 1830–45) and each written in the form and style of a song, i.e., with a melody and a simple, uniform accompaniment. The individual titles given in modern editions ("Spring Song," "Hunting Song," "Spinning Song") are not authentic, except for the three called *Venezianisches Gondellied*, nos. 6, 12, and 29, the *Duetto*, no. 18, and the *Volkslied*, no. 23.

Liederbuch [G.]. A term commonly applied to 15th- and 16th-century collections of German songs, particularly the Lochamer Liederbuch (*c.* 1450), which is the most important source of early German folksong (some monophonic, some in three-voice composition), and the Glogauer Liederbuch (*c.* 1480), which contains vocal pieces and instrumental dances and canons.

Liedercyclus, Liederkreis [G.]. *Song cycle.

Liedertafel [G.]. A men's singing society, founded by Zelter in 1809, whose members first sat around a table [G. *Tafel*] for refreshments. Various similar societies sprang up during the 19th century.

Lieto [It.]. Gay, joyful.

Lieutenant Kije. A Russian film with music by Prokofiev (op. 60, 1933). The composer arranged a suite from this music that bears the same title.

Lievo [It.]. Light, easy.

Life for the Czar, A [Rus. *Zhizn za Tsarya*]. Opera in four acts and an epilogue by Glinka (libretto by G. F. Rosen), produced in St. Petersburg, 1836. Setting: Russia, 1612–13. An alternate title in current use in Russia is *Ivan Susanin*. It was the first popular opera in the Russian language.

Ligature. (1) Any notational sign of the 13th to 16th centuries that combines two or more notes in a single symbol. Such signs developed in the late 12th century as square-shaped modifications of the *neumes [see also Notation]. Although in plainsong and related bodies of monophonic music these signs are but graphic modifications of the neumes, they adopted definite rhythmic meanings in polyphonic music. The first step in this direction was in the modal notation of the school of *Notre Dame, in the early 13th century. Here, ligatures are the ordinary notational signs for all the parts, single notes being used only for special reasons (e.g., long notes of the tenor). The rhythmic values of ligatures in this repertory depend entirely on their grouping, according to the rhythmic *modes. The rise of the *motet (*c.* 1225) greatly diminished the use of ligatures in the upper parts because these parts had full texts whose syllables were sung, as a rule, to single notes. The final step in the development of the ligatures came *c.* 1250 with Franco of Cologne, who assigned an unambiguous rhythmic significance to each of the various shapes. His rules remained unaltered throughout the ensuing period of *mensural notation.

The rhythmic values of ligatures in Franco's system are determined with reference to the standard shapes for two-note ascending and descending ligatures, illustrated in the first line of the accompanying table. These standard shapes have the value Breve (*B*) followed by Long (*L*). They are described by theorists such as Franco as having both *propriety* (a reference to the shape of the note that begins the ligature) and *perfection* (a reference to the shape of the note that ends the ligature). If the shape of the beginning note is modified (in descending ligatures by the removal of the tail, in ascending ligatures by the addition of a tail, as in line 2 of the table), the ligature is without propriety, and thus the value of the beginning note becomes *L*. If the shape of the note ending the ligature is altered (in descending ligatures by the use of an oblique shape, in ascending ligatures by placing the ending note to the right of the note preceding instead of directly above it, as in line 3 of the table), the ligature is without perfection, and thus the value of the ending note becomes *B*. (If in an ascending ligature the ending note is both turned to the right *and* supplied with a tail, its value is *L*.) Any ligature (whether ascending or descending) that begins with an upward tail, as in line 5 of the table, is a ligature of opposite propriety, and its first two notes are both semibreves (*S*). If a ligature consists of more than two notes, the values of the beginning and ending notes are determined according to these same principles, the question of ascent or descent being determined with reference to the immediately preceding or following note. All intervening notes have the value *B*, as illustrated in lines 6 and 7 of the table.

	Descending	Ascending	Value
1	♭	♯	B L
2	♭	♯	L L
3	♭	♯	B B
4	♭	♯	L B
5	♭ or ♭	♭ or ♯	S S
6	♭♯		S S B B
7	♭♯		B B B B

(2) In modern notation, a *slur connecting two or more notes, indicating that all are to be sung to a single syllable. (3) In instruments of the clarinet family, the adjustable metal band that attaches the reed to the mouthpiece.

Ligeti, György (b. Diciosânmartin, Transylvania, 28 May 1923). Pupil of Veress and Farkas. Teacher at the Budapest Music Academy, 1950–56; at the International Courses for New Music in Darmstadt from 1959; at the Royal Academy of Music in Stockholm from 1961; at the Staatliche Hochschule für Musik in Hamburg from 1973. Has composed the mime-dramas *Aventures*, 1962, and *Nou-*

velles aventures, 1965; orch. works (incl. *Atmosphères,* 1961; *Lontano,* 1967; *Melodien,* 1971; *San Francisco Polyphony,* 1974); a cello concerto, 1966; *Poème symphonique* for 100 metronomes, 1962; vocal works (incl. a *Requiem,* 1965; *Lux aeterna,* 1966); electronic works (incl. *Artikulation,* 1958); a chamber concerto for 13 players, 1970; string quartets and other chamber music; organ and piano pieces; songs.

Lining (out). In American and English psalm and hymn singing of the 18th and 19th centuries, the practice of having each line read by the minister or some other person before it is sung by the congregation. In England it was known as "deaconing."

Linke Hand [G.]. Left hand.

Linley, Thomas, Jr. (b. Bath, 7 May 1756; d. Grimsthorpe, 5 Aug. 1778). Eldest son of Thomas Linley, Sr. Violinist and composer. Pupil of his father and of Boyce and Nardini. Composed an opera; incidental music for the theater; vocal works; violin pieces.

Linley, Thomas, Sr. (b. Badminton, 17 Jan. 1733; d. London, 19 Nov. 1795). Pupil of Paradisi. Musical director of the Drury Lane Theatre in London from 1776. Composed music for stage works (incl. an opera, *The Royal Merchant,* after Beaumont and Fletcher, London, 1767; *The Duenna,* libretto by Sheridan, to which Linley contributed 7 numbers, London, 1775); *6 Elegies* for 3 voices; *12 Ballads;* cantatas; madrigals.

Linz Symphony. Mozart's Symphony in C, no. 36 (K. 425), composed at Linz, Austria, in 1783 and first performed there by the private orchestra of Count Thun.

Lip. See Embouchure.

Lipatti, Dinu (b. Bucharest, 19 Mar. 1917; d. Chêne-Bourg, canton Geneva, 2 Dec. 1950). Pianist and composer. Pupil of Dukas, N. Boulanger, and Stravinsky. Teacher at the Geneva Conservatory from 1944. Composed a symphonic suite, *Satrarii,* 1933, and *3 Rumanian Dances* for orch., 1945; a concertino for piano and orch., 1935; cadenzas to the piano concertos of Mozart and Haydn; chamber music; piano pieces (incl. a sonatina for the left hand alone); songs.

Lira. A 15th- and 16th-century type of violin having a wide neck with front pegs, drone strings, and a slightly pear-shaped body. The *lira da braccio* was held in the arm, the larger *lira da gamba* (*lirone*) between the knees. See ill. under Violin family. For Haydn's *lira organizzata,* see Hurdy-gurdy.

Liscio [It.]. Smooth, even.

Lissenko, Nikolai Vitalievich (b. Grinki, near Kremenchug, Russia, 22 Mar. 1842; d. Kiev, 6 Nov. 1912). Pupil of E. F. E. Richter, Reinecke, and Rimsky-Korsakov. Active in the collection of Ukrainian folksongs. Composed operas (incl. *Taras Bulba,* 1890; *Natalka-Poltavka,* 1890); cantatas; orch. works; numerous songs and arrangements of Ukrainian folksongs; piano pieces.

L'istesso tempo. See *Istesso tempo, L'*.

Liszt, Franz (Ferencz) (b. Raiding, Hungary, 22 Oct. 1811; d. Bayreuth, Germany, 31 July 1886). Pianist and composer. Pupil of Czerny, Salieri, Reicha, and Paër. Concertized widely in Europe. Associate of Wagner from 1841. *Kapellmeister* at the Weimar court, 1848–59. Lived in Rome from 1861. Made an abbé by Pope Pius IX in 1866. President of the newly founded Hungarian Academy of Music at Budapest from 1875. The first composer to employ the term *symphonic poem.* Works: an opera, *Don Sanche, ou Le chateau d'amour,* Paris, 1825; orch. works (incl. *Dante Symphony,* 1856; *Eine *Faust-Symphonie,* 1857); the symphonic poems *Ce qu'on entend sur la montagne,* 1848, *Tasso,* 1849, *Les *préludes,* 1848–54, *Mazeppa,* 1851, *Die *Hunnenschlacht,* 1857, and 8 others; works for piano and orch. (incl. 2 concertos, 1830–49 and 1839–49, and *Totentanz,* completed 1849; all three works revised at various times); sacred and secular choral works (incl. the oratorios *Die Legende von der Heiligen Elisabeth* [The Legend of St. Elisabeth], 1857–62, and *Christus,* 1855–66); chamber music; numerous works for piano (incl. *Études d'exécution transcendante,* publ. 1852; *Années de pèlerinage,* 1836–77; *Hungarian Rhapsodies,* 1839–85); songs.

Litany. In the Roman Catholic Church, a series of solemn supplications addressed to God, the Virgin, or the Saints. Litanies open with the *Kyrie eleison, continue with numerous exclamations such as "Mater Christi, ora pro nobis," sung responsively to a short inflected monotone, and close with the *Agnus Dei. The Anglican litany has the same basic structure as the Roman Catholic litanies. It consists of petitions interspersed with responses such as "Spare us, good Lord," "Good Lord, deliver us."

Literes Carrión, Antonio (b. Artá, Majorca, *c.* 1675; d. Madrid, 18 Jan. 1747). Cellist, violinist, and composer. Instrumentalist in the royal chapel in Madrid from 1693. Composed operas; numerous zarzuelas (incl. *Accis y Galatea,* 1708); psalms, Magnificats, and other sacred works.

Litolff, Henry Charles (b. London, 6 Feb. 1818; d. Bois-Colombes, near Paris, 6 Aug. 1891). Pianist, music publisher, and composer. Pupil of Moscheles. *Kapellmeister* in Warsaw, 1841–44. Traveled widely as a pianist. Composed operas (incl. *Die Braut vom Kynast,* Brunswick, 1847); an oratorio; orch. works (incl. the overture *Robespierre,* 1870); works for solo instrument with orch. (incl. several "concerto-symphonies" for piano and orch.); piano trios and other chamber music; numerous piano pieces; songs.

Liturgical books. The most important books of the Roman Catholic rites are the following: (1) The *missale* (missal) contains all the texts for the Mass, i.e., the prayers, lessons, and the texts of the Mass chants. (2) The *breviarium* (breviary) is the corresponding collection of all the texts for the Office. (3) The *graduale* (gradual) contains the Mass chants, with their music. (4) The *antiphonale* or *antiphonarium* (antiphonal, antiphonary, or antiphoner) contains the Office chants (except Matins), with their music. (5) The *Liber usualis* is a modern combination of the four books just mentioned, with some additions and many omissions. It includes the spoken texts as well as the musical items for both the Mass and the Office, arranged in their proper order. (6) The *kyriale* (kyrial) contains only the chants of the Ordinary of the Mass (beginning with the Kyrie).

(7) The *vesperale* (vesperal) contains the service of Vespers and usually that of Compline as well. (8) The *processionale* (processional) is a collection of the chants (mostly responsories and antiphons) sung during processions (within the church) before Mass. (9) The *sacramentarium* (sacramentary), a very early type (6th to 8th century), contains only the texts spoken by the priest or the officiating bishop, mainly the prayers and the variable Prefaces for the Canon of the Mass [see Canon (3)]. In this period the readings from the Scriptures and Gospels were also in separate books, the *lectionarium* (lectionary) and the *evangelarium* (evangeliary or evangelistary). (10) The *tonarium* or *tonale* (*tonary) is a medieval book in which the chants are arranged according to the eight church modes. (11) The *cantatorium* (cantatory), a 9th- to 10th-century prototype of the gradual, contains only the solo chants of the Mass, i.e., Graduals, Alleluias, and Tracts. (12) The *troparium* (*troper) is a medieval book containing *tropes. (13) The *pontificale* (pontifical) contains the services used in functions where a bishop or prelate officiates, e.g., consecration of a church, ordination of priests. (14) The *Liber responsorialis,* a modern compilation, contains mostly *responsories.

Antiphonale originally was the name for a gradual as well as for an antiphonary. The earliest graduals and antiphonals (8th to 10th centuries) contain only the texts of the chants. See also Solesmes.

Liturgical drama. Medieval plays (chiefly of the 12th and 13th centuries) representing Biblical stories (in Latin) with action and, occasionally, monophonic music. They are usually thought to have developed during the 10th and 11th centuries from *tropes in dialogue form to the Introits for Christmas and Easter. One of the earliest examples is the trope *Hodie cantandus est* (possibly by Tuotilo, d. *c.* 915) to the Christmas Introit *Puer natus est.* A more fully developed type—in fact, a real play—is the 10th-century trope *Quem queritis* to the Introit *Resurrexi* for Easter Sunday. Some recent research suggests, however, that this dialogue was never an Introit trope in the usual sense but that it, and thus liturgical drama in general, had its origins in a separate ceremony preceding the Mass. Later plays, mostly of French origin, deal with the story of Daniel, the massacre of the innocents (containing the "lament" of Rachel), the wise and foolish virgins (the 12th-century play, *Sponsus*), etc. Favorite subjects for other plays were the miracles of various saints, particularly St. Nicholas (the so-called miracle plays).

From the 14th to 16th centuries, liturgical drama developed into the mysteries or mystery plays [corruption of L. *ministerium*, service], coming under secular sponsorship and using the vernacular. These were dramatic representations based on Biblical subjects such as the life of Jesus, the Acts of the Apostles, and the Creation, elaborately staged and in some instances continuing over a period of 20 days or longer. They used music only incidentally, for processions, fanfares, and dances, occasionally including plainsong or popular songs. In Italy they were known as *sacre rappresentazioni*, in Spain and Portugal as *autos*. It is chiefly from these plays that European drama developed.

Liturgy. The officially authorized service of a Christian church, particularly of the Roman Catholic Church. See Gregorian chant; Mass; Office; Liturgical books; also Liturgical drama.

Lituus. (1) A Roman trumpet, possibly of Etruscan origin; see ill. under Brass instruments. (2) A 17th-century Latin name for the *cornett or the crumhorn [see Oboe family III]. (3) In the 18th century, the term could apply either to the natural horn or the natural trumpet. The two *litui* in Bach's Cantata no. 118 are evidently natural brass instruments pitched in B♭.

Liuto [It.]. *Lute.

Livret [F.]. *Libretto.

Locatelli, Pietro Antonio (b. Bergamo, 3 Sept. 1695; d. Amsterdam, 30 Mar. 1764). Violin virtuoso and composer. Pupil of Corelli. Composed *12 Concerti grossi*, 1721; *L'arte del violino*, containing concertos and caprices for 2 violins, viola, cello, and *continuo*, 1733; trio sonatas; flute sonatas; violin sonatas; other instrumental works.

Locke, Matthew (b. Exeter, *c.* 1630; d. London, Aug. 1677). Composer to Charles II from 1661, succeeding Coperario. Organist to Queen Catherine. Composed music for *The Tempest* and other plays; music for Shirley's masque *Cupid and Death*, in collaboration with C. Gibbons, 1653; music for *The *Siege of Rhodes*, 1656; anthems, services, and other church music; instrumental works; ayres and other secular vocal works.

Lockwood, Normand (b. New York, 19 Mar. 1906). Pupil of Respighi and N. Boulanger. Teacher at Oberlin College, 1932–45, at Columbia Univ., 1945–53, and at the Univ. of Denver from 1961. Has composed operas; music for plays; orch. works; concertos for oboe and for piano; oratorios; choral works (incl. *Out of the Cradle Endlessly Rocking*, 1939); works for voice and instruments; chamber music; piano pieces; organ pieces.

Loco [It.; abbr. *loc.*]. Place. Used to indicate return to the normal octave after *all' ottava* or similar designations.

Locrian. See under Church modes.

Loeffler, Charles Martin (Tornow) (b. Mulhouse, Alsace, 30 Jan. 1861; d. Medfield, Mass., 19 May 1935). Violinist and composer. Pupil of Joachim and Guiraud. Emigrated to the U.S., 1881. Second concertmaster of the Boston Symphony Orchestra, 1882–1903. Composed 2 operas; orch. works (incl. *A Pagan Poem*, 1906; *Memories of My Childhood*, symphonic poem, 1925); works for solo instrument with orch.; choral works; chamber music; songs; *Violin Studies for the Development of the Left Hand*, 1936.

Loeillet, Jean-Baptiste (John) (b. Ghent, bapt. 18 Nov. 1680; d. London, 19 July 1730). Harpsichordist, flutist, and composer. Settled in London in 1705 and played oboe in the Queen's Theatre there. Composed sonatas for recorder, for flute, and for other instruments with thoroughbass; trio sonatas; harpsichord pieces.

Loewe, (Johann) Karl (Gottfried) (b. Löbejün, near Halle, 30 Nov. 1796; d.

Kiel, 20 Apr. 1869). Singer and composer. Pupil of Türk. Schoolmaster and organist at Stettin from 1820 and municipal music director there from 1821. Composed operas; oratorios; choral works; orch. works; chamber music; piano pieces; numerous songs (incl. "Erlkönig," "Edward," "Herr Oluf," "Elvershöh"); motets; pedagogic works.

Logroscino, Nicola Bonifacio (b. Bitonto, Italy, bapt. 22 Oct. 1698; d. Palermo, *c.* 1765 or 1767). Teacher at the Conservatorio dei figliuoli dispersi in Palermo from 1747. Composed serious and comic operas; church music.

Lohengrin. Opera in three acts by Wagner (to his own libretto, based on W. von Eschenbach and medieval legends), produced in Weimar, 1850. Setting: Antwerp, early 10th century.

Lombardic style [It. *stile lombardo*]. Unexplained name for inverted dotting; see Dotted notes.

London, Edwin (b. Philadelphia, 16 Mar. 1929). Pupil of Clapp, Bezanson, Milhaud, and Dallapiccola. Teacher at Smith College, 1960–68, and at the Univ. of Illinois from 1969. Has composed a mime opera, *Santa Claus,* text by e. e. cummings, 1960; works for band; choral works; electronic works; *Portraits of 3 American Ladies,* a mixed-media work, 1967; chamber music.

London Symphony. (1) Haydn's Symphony no. 104 in D. See Salomon Symphonies. (2) Ralph Vaughan Williams' Symphony no. 2, composed in 1913.

Longa, long. See under Mensural notation.

Loomis, Harvey Worthington (b. Brooklyn, 5 Feb. 1865; d. Boston, 25 Dec. 1930). Pupil of Dvořák. Worked with American Indian musical materials. Composed operas, melodramas, musical pantomimes; incidental music for plays; choral works; piano pieces (incl. 2 volumes of *Lyrics of the Red Man,* 1904); songs, many for children; a violin sonata.

Lopatnikoff, Nikolai Lvovich (b. Reval, Estonia, 16 Mar. 1903). Studied in St. Petersburg, Helsinki, and with Toch in Berlin. Settled in the U.S., 1939. Teacher at the Carnegie-Mellon Univ. in Pittsburgh, 1945–68. Has composed an opera, *Danton,* 1933; 4 symphonies and other orch. works; concertos for piano and for violin; 3 string quartets and other chamber music; piano pieces (incl. *Contrasts; Dialogues*).

Lopes Graça, Fernando (b. Tomar, Portugal, 17 Dec. 1906). Pianist, music critic, and composer. Studied at the Lisbon Conservatory and with Koechlin in Paris. Teacher at the Academy of the Friends of Music in Lisbon, 1941–54. Has composed orch. works; 2 piano concertos; choral works; chamber music; piano pieces; songs and arrangements of folksongs. Has published many books on music.

Lorenzani, Paolo (b. Rome, 1640; d. there, 28 Oct. 1713). Pupil of Benevoli. Court and church musician in Paris from 1678. *Maestro di cappella* at St. Peter's in Rome from 1694 to his death. Composed operas; motets; Italian airs and other vocal music.

Lortzing, (Gustav) Albert (b. Berlin, 23 Oct. 1801; d. there, 21 Jan. 1851). Actor, singer, conductor, and composer. Composed operas (incl. *Zar und Zimmermann,* Leipzig, 1837; *Hans Sachs,* Leipzig, 1840; *Der Wildschütz,* Leipzig, 1842; *Undine,* Magdeburg, 1845; *Der Waffenschmied,* Vienna, 1846); incidental music for plays; an oratorio; songs.

Lotti, Antonio (b. Venice, *c.* 1667; d. there, 5 Jan. 1740). Pupil of Legrenzi. Organist at San Marco in Venice from 1692 and *maestro di cappella* there from 1736. Composed operas; oratorios; cantatas; Masses, motets, and other sacred vocal works; a collection of *Duetti, terzetti e madrigali;* instrumental pieces.

Loudness. The perceived characteristic of a sound that is a function of its intensity, i.e., of the physical energy that the sounding body transmits to the surrounding medium. *Volume* is most often used to mean the same thing. The human ear is not equally sensitive to changes in intensity throughout the range of audible frequencies, it being least sensitive at high and low extremes of frequency. This phenomenon is sometimes called the Fletcher-Munson effect, and some phonograph amplifiers are equipped with a "loudness" control (as distinct from the "volume" control) that attempts to compensate for it by permitting some control of the relative intensities of various ranges of frequencies independent of the intensity (or "volume") with which the sound as a whole is reproduced.

Louise. Opera in four acts by Gustave Charpentier (to his own libretto), produced in Paris, 1900. Setting: Paris, *c.* 1900. See *Verismo.*

Lourd [F.]. Heavy.

Loure [F.]. (1) A 16th- and 17th-century name for bagpipe. (2) A 17th-century dance from Normandy (originally accompanied by the instrument loure?) in moderate 6/4 time and with dotted rhythms leaning heavily on the strong beats. Examples are in Lully's opera *Alceste* of 1677 and in Bach's French Suite no. 5.

Louré [F.]. See Bowing (f).

Lourié, Arthur Vincent (b. St. Petersburg, 14 May 1892; d. Princeton, N.J., 13 Oct. 1966). Studied at the St. Petersburg Conservatory. Lived in Paris, 1923–40, and in the U.S. from 1941. Composed an opera; an opera-ballet; symphonies and other orch. works; sacred music; works for voice and instruments; piano pieces.

Love for Three Oranges, The [Rus. *Lyubov k trem Apelsinam*]. Farcical opera in four acts by Prokofiev (to his own libretto, based on a tale by C. Gozzi), produced (in French) in Chicago, 1921. Setting: fairy tale. Numerous set pieces from it, particularly the March and the Scherzo, have become standard concert works.

Lualdi, Adriano (b. Larino, Campobasso, 22 Mar. 1885; d. Milan, 8 Jan. 1971). Music critic and composer. Pupil of Wolf-Ferrari. Head of the music department of the Italian government from 1928. Director of the Conservatory of San Pietro a Maiella in Naples, 1936–46, and of the Florence Conservatory, 1947–56. Composed operas (incl. *La figlia del re,* after Sophocles, Turin, 1922) and other stage works; an oratorio; symphonic poems and other orch. works; vocal works; chamber music; songs.

Lübeck, Vincent (b. Padingbüttel, near Dorum, Germany, Sept. 1654; d. Hamburg, 9 Feb. 1740). Organist at St. Cosmae et Damiani in Stade, 1675–1702, and at the Nikolaikirche in Hamburg from 1702 to his death. Composed cantatas; organ works, incl. chorale preludes, preludes, and fugues.

Lucas, Leighton (b. London, 5 Jan. 1903). Dancer, conductor, and composer. Member of the Diaghilev Russian Ballet, 1918–21. Chorus and orchestra conductor in England from 1922. Teacher at the Royal Academy of Music in London from 1955. Has composed ballets and other stage works; orch. works; works for solo instrument and orch.; choral works; chamber music; piano pieces; songs; music for films.

Lucia di Lammermoor. Opera in three acts by Donizetti (libretto by S. Cammarano, after Sir Walter Scott), produced in Naples, 1835. Setting: Scotland, end of the 17th century.

Lucier, Alvin (b. Nashua, N.H., 14 May 1931). Pupil of Boatwright, Porter, Berger, Fine, Shapero, Foss, and Tudor. Teacher at Brandeis Univ. from 1962 and at Wesleyan Univ. from 1970. Has composed electronic works (incl. *Music for Solo Performer,* amplified brain waves with percussion, 1965; *North American Time Capsule* for voices and vocorder, 1967; *Chambers* for sound environments, 1968); *Signatures* for orch., 1970; music for the theater; *Action Music for Piano,* 1962.

Ludford, Nicholas (b. *c.* 1485; d. London, *c.* 1557). Musician at St. Stephen's, Westminster, from shortly after 1510. Composed Masses, motets, and a Magnificat.

Luening, Otto (b. Milwaukee, 15 June 1900). Pupil of Jarnach and Busoni. Teacher at Bennington College from 1934; at Barnard College from 1944; at Columbia Univ. from 1949. Co-director of the Princeton-Columbia Electronic Music Center from 1959 (with Babbitt, Ussachevsky, and Sessions). Has composed an opera, *Evangeline,* 1927–48, and other stage works; orch. works (incl. 2 *Symphonic Fantasias,* 1924, 1939–49; *Kentucky Concerto,* 1951; *Music for Orchestra,* 1952; *Synthesis,* with tape,

1952); choral works; 3 string quartets, 3 sonatas for violin alone, and other chamber music; works for voice with instruments; piano pieces; songs; works on tape (incl. *Fantasy in Space* for flute on tape, 1952; *Diffusion of Bells,* composed with Halim El Dabh, 1962) and works for tape with instruments (incl. *Theater Piece No. 2* for tape, voice, brass, percussion, and narrator, choreography by Doris Humphrey and José Limón, 1956; *Gargoyles,* with violin, 1961).

Luftpause [G.]. See Pause (3).

Luigini, Alexandre (Clément-Léon-Joseph) (b. Lyon, 9 Mar. 1850; d. Paris, 29 July 1906). Pupil of Massenet. Conductor in Lyon and teacher at the Lyon Conservatory from 1877. Conductor of the Opéra-Comique in Paris from 1897 to his death. Composed ballets (incl. *Ballet egyptien,* 1875); comic operas; orch. works; chamber music; piano pieces.

Lully, Jean-Baptiste (Lulli) (b. Florence, 28 Nov. 1632; d. Paris, 22 Mar. 1687). Educated in Paris from 1646, where he was a pupil of Roberday and Gigault. Composer to King Louis XIV from 1653; director of the royal chamber music from 1661, and music master to the royal family from 1662. [See also *Vingt-quatre violons du roi.*] Director of the Académie royale de musique (which later became the Grand Opéra) from 1672. Composed operas (incl. *Cadmus et Hermione,* Paris, 1673; *Alceste,* Paris, 1674; *Thésée,* Saint-Germain, 1675; *Atys,* Saint-Germain, 1676; *Bellérophon,* Paris, 1679; *Phaéton,* Versailles, 1683; *Amadis de Gaule,* Paris, 1684; *Roland,* Versailles, 1685; *Armide,* Paris, 1686); comedy-ballets (incl. *Le bourgeois gentilhomme,* with Molière, 1670); ballets; incidental music for the theater; sacred vocal works; instrumental pieces; songs.

Lulu. Unfinished opera in three acts by Alban Berg (to his own libretto, based on two plays by F. Wedekind), produced in Zürich, 1937. Setting: Germany, Paris, London, 19th century.

Lungo, lunga [It.]. Long. *Lunga pausa,* long rest.

Lupi, Johannes (Leleu, Lupus) (b. Cambrai, *c.* 1506; d. there, 20 Dec. 1539). Boy chorister at the Cambrai Cathedral;

maître de chapelle there from 1527. Composed Masses, motets, psalms.

Lupo. A family active as composers and instrumentalists in the English court during the 16th and 17th centuries. Members of this family, principally one or more Thomas Lupo, composed instrumental pieces, incl. fantasies and dances for strings and virginals; motets; anthems; songs.

Lur [Dan.; pl. *lurer*]. A prehistoric Nordic trumpet of bronze, preserved (especially in Denmark) in about 50 examples dating from the 12th to 6th centuries B.C. The instruments are in the shape of a long twisted S, ending in a flat ornamental disk, and are usually found in pairs turned in opposite directions, resembling a pair of mammoth tusks. See ill. under Brass instruments.

Lusingando [It.]. Flattering, coaxing.

Lustig [G.]. Merry, cheerful.

Lustige Witwe, Die [G., The Merry Widow]. Operetta in three acts by F. Lehár (libretto by V. Léon and L. Stein), produced in Vienna, 1905. Setting: Paris, early 20th century.

Lustigen Weiber von Windsor, Die [G., The Merry Wives of Windsor]. Opera in three acts by Otto Nicolai (libretto by S. H. Mosenthal, after Shakespeare's play), produced in Berlin, 1849. Setting: Windsor, 15th century.

Lute [F. *luth;* G. *Laute;* It. *lauto, liuto, leuto;* Sp. *laúd;* L. *testudo* or *chelys,* i.e., "turtle," a humanist misnomer referring to the tortoise shell of the ancient Greek *lyra*]. A plucked stringed instrument with a round body in the shape of a halved pear, a flat neck with 7 or more frets, and a separate pegbox set nearly perpendicular to the neck. The instruments of the 16th century had 11 strings in 6 *courses, tuned (in theory) G c f a d' g' or A d g b e' a', with the two lowest courses doubled, sometimes in the higher octave, and the three following courses doubled in the unison. (In practice the 16th-century lute was tuned to a convenient pitch, depending on the music to be played.) In the 17th century an increasing number of bass-courses (up to six) were added, running alongside

Lutes: 1. Pyiba.   2. Biwa.   3. Tanbur.   4. 'Ūd.   5. Shamisen.   6. Sitar.   7. Colascione.

Lutes: 8. Mandola. 9. Mandolin. 10. Lute. 11. Orpharion. 12. Bandora (pandora).
13. Theorbo. 14. Chitarrone.

the fingerboard and therefore being unalterable in pitch. They were normally tuned F E D C, etc. About 1640 another system of tuning, introduced by the lutenist and lute-composer Denis Gaultier (d. 1672), was generally adopted, A d f a d' f'; called *nouveau ton,* it persisted through the end of the 18th century.

There are two main types of early lute, the long lute, with a neck much longer than the body, and the short lute, with a neck slightly shorter than the body. The former is by far the older instrument. It appears on Mesopotamian figurines dating from about 2000 B.C. From Babylon it spread to Egypt (*c.* 1500 B.C.) and Greece, where it was called a *pandoura.* This lute had a small body covered with parchment through which the long handle penetrated. The later development of the long lute took place in Persia, where it was called a *setār* ("three strings"), *cartār* ("four strings"), or *panctār* ("five strings"), according to the number of strings, and in Arabia, where it was named **ṭunbūr.* The Indian **sitar* derives from the Persian instrument. A European offshoot of the Arabian long lute was the *colascione* of the 16th and 17th centuries and the Russian **domra* (*dombra*). The Japanese *shamisen* (*samisen*) has a nearly square body with rounded corners. It is covered with skin and has a long neck and three silk strings tuned in fourths or fifths.

The short lute appears first on Persian clay figures from about 800 B.C. and on Indian reliefs from the first centuries A.D. About the latter time we find it in China, under the name **pyiba* [Jap. *biwa*]. In these early instruments the neck is formed by the tapering body. The Arabic *'ūd* is a short lute described in detail in Arabic theoretical treatises beginning in the 10th century. This instrument seems to have had frets at this time, though its modern descendant (still widely used in Arabic-speaking countries) does not have them. The *'ūd* (Arab. *al 'ūd,* Sp. *laúd,* whence *lute,* etc.) is the immediate ancestor of the European lute, having been introduced to Europe through Spain in about the 13th century. The first European instruments seem to have had four strings and no frets. The lute's rise to great prominence and the development of the classical form described above occurred in the 15th century.

Numerous varieties of lute were used during the 16th and 17th centuries. The *mandola* or *mandore* had a long pegbox slightly curved and with a head-scroll reminiscent of the violin's. A diminutive form of this instrument is the **mandolin.* The *angelica* was a 17th-century variety with 17 different strings tuned to the tones of the diatonic scale, so that stopping was largely avoided. During the 17th century the increasing demand for bass instruments led to the construction of archlutes [G. *Erzlaute;* It. *arciliuto;* Sp. *archilaúd*], i.e., double-neck lutes with a second pegbox that carried the bass courses. There was a "short" archlute, the *theorbo,* and a "long" archlute, the *chitarrone.*

All the instruments named above have the round back characteristic of the lute. For instruments with a flat back, see under Guitar family.

Lute harpsichord [G. *Lautenclavicymbel*]. A harpsichord with gut strings instead of the usual metal strings. The tone was very much like that produced by the gut strings of the lute. Such harpsichords are mentioned by S. Virdung in 1511. In 1740, Bach had such an instrument made for his own use.

Lutherie [F.]. The art of making lutes or stringed instruments in general. *Luthier,* the maker of such instruments, today of violins, etc.

Lutoslawski, Witold (b. Warsaw, 25 Jan. 1913). Studied at the Warsaw Conservatory. Has worked with serial and aleatory techniques and with folk music. Has composed 3 symphonies and other orch. works (incl. *Concerto for Orchestra,* 1954; *Funeral Music,* 1958; *Venetian Games,* 1961; *Livre pour orchestre,* 1968; *Mi-parti,* 1976); works for voice and orch. (incl. *Paroles tissées* for tenor and chamber orch., 1965; *Les espaces du sommeil* for baritone and orch., 1975); choral works (incl. *3 Poems of Henri Michaux,* with orch., 1963); a cello concerto, 1970; chamber music (incl. a string quartet, 1964); piano pieces; songs; incidental music for plays; music for films and for radio.

Luttuoso [It.]. Mournful.

Lutyens, (Agnes) Elisabeth (b. London, 9 July 1906). Studied at the Royal College of Music in London and at the École normale de musique in Paris. Has worked with twelve-tone techniques. Has composed operas; *3 Symphonic Preludes,* 1942; concertos for viola and for horn; choral works; works for voice and instruments (incl. *And Suddenly It's Evening* for tenor and chamber ensemble, 1967); 6 chamber concertos for various ensembles; 6 string quartets and other chamber music; piano and organ pieces; incidental music for the theater; music for films and for radio.

Luzzaschi, Luzzasco (b. Ferrara, *c.* 1545; d. there, 11 Sept. 1607). Pupil of Rore. Court organist at Ferrara from 1571. Frescobaldi was among his pupils. Composed motets; madrigals, incl. some with instrumental accompaniment for 3 celebrated women singers in Ferrara; works for organ.

Lvov, Alexei Feodorovich (b. Reval, Russia, 5 June 1798; d. Romano, near Kaunas, Russia, 28 Dec. 1870). Violinist and composer. Pupil of his father, Feodor Petrovich Lvov, whom he succeeded as director of the imperial court chapel in St. Petersburg in 1837. Composed 3 operas (incl. *Starosta Boris,* St. Petersburg, 1854); 2 operettas; a violin concerto; sacred vocal works; violin pieces; "God Save the Tsar," which served as the Russian national anthem, 1833–1917.

Lybbert, Donald (b. Cresco, Iowa, 19 Feb. 1923). Pupil of Carter, Luening, and N. Boulanger. Teacher at Hunter College in New York from 1954. Has composed operas; *Concert Overture for Orchestra,* 1958; works for various instrumental ensembles (incl. *Praeludium* for brass and percussion, 1963); vocal works (incl. *Lines for the Fallen* for soprano, 2 pianos tuned a quarter tone apart, 1968); piano pieces; songs.

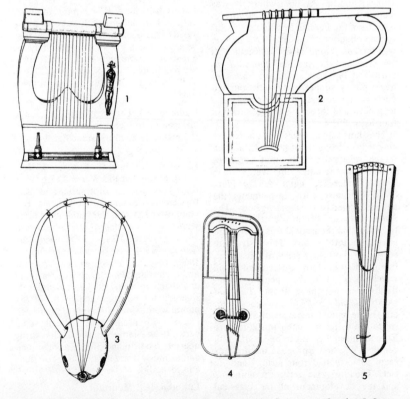

Lyres: 1. Kithara (Greek). 2. Kithara (Egypt, Mesopotamia). 3. Lyra. 4. Crwth. 5. Rotta.

Lydian. See under Church modes. For Lydian cadence, see Cadence.

Lyon, James (b. Newark, N.J., 1 July 1735; d. Machias, Maine, 12 Oct. 1794). Graduate of Princeton Univ., 1759. Pastor in Nova Scotia from 1765 and in Machias, Maine, from 1771. Composed psalm tunes and settings of psalms and other poems.

Lyra. (1) An ancient Greek stringed instrument, similar to the *kithara but of simpler construction, smaller, and with the soundbox usually made of tortoise shell [see ill.]. It was played with a plectrum. Instruments of the same design appear on Egyptian wall paintings from *c*. 1500 B.C. The name "lyre" was adopted for several instruments only remotely like the Greek lyra, namely: (2) A medieval fiddle similar to the rebec (hence the name *lira* for a 16th-century violin). (3) The *hurdy-gurdy, particularly in the names *lyra rustica* (peasant's lyra) and *lyra mendicorum* (beggar's lyra). (4) In modern German usage, the military *glockenspiel, on account of the shape of its frame, which is similar to the Greek lyra. The "Lyra" called for in several compositions by Haydn is not the *lira da braccio* but the *hurdy-gurdy. See also Kithara; Crwth; *Rotta*.

Lyra piano [G. *Lyraflügel*]. An early 19th-century variety of upright piano, with a case shaped like a Greek lyre.

Lyra viol. See under Viol. For ill. see under Violin family.

Lyra-way. See under Viol.

Lyre. See Lyra.

Lyric Suite. Suite in six movements for string quartet by Alban Berg (1926), parts of which were later arranged for orchestra (1928).

M

M. In organ music, *manual* or *manualiter*. In keyboard music, **main* or **mano*, hand. See also Metronome; Dynamic marks.

Ma [It.]. But. *Ma non troppo*, but not too much.

Ma mère l'oye [F., *Mother Goose* (*Suite*)]. Suite by Ravel based on fairy tales by C. Perrault (1678–1703). Originally written (1908) for piano duet, it was scored for orchestra by Ravel and produced as a children's ballet in 1915.

Má Vlast [Cz., My Fatherland]. Cycle of six symphonic poems by Smetana, composed 1874–79, based on various subjects pertaining to his country: 1. *Vyšehrad* (the old citadel of Prague); 2. *Vltava* (the river Moldau); 3. *Šárka* (an Amazon of Czech legend); 4. *Z českých luhův a hájuv* (From Bohemia's Meadows and Forests); 5. *Tábor* (an ancient city); 6. *Blaník* (a mountain near Prague where, according to legend, the old heroes slumber, ready to rise again).

Ma'ayani, Ami (Hai) (b. Ramat Gan, Israel, 13 Jan. 1936). Pupil of Ben-Haim and Ussachevsky. Has composed orch. works; concertos for harp, for violin, for cello, for 2 pianos; vocal works; chamber music; electronic works; pieces for harp; film scores.

Macbeth. (1) Opera in three acts and a prologue by E. Bloch (libretto by E. Fleg, after Shakespeare's play), produced in Paris, 1910. Setting: Scotland, 11th century. (2) Opera in four acts by Verdi (libretto by F. M. Piave, after Shakespeare's play), produced in Florence, 1847; rev. version (in French) in Paris, 1865. Setting: Scotland, 11th century.

MacCunn, Hamish (b. Greenock, Scotland, 22 Mar. 1868; d. London, 2 Aug. 1916). Pupil of Parry and Stanford. Teacher at the Royal Academy of Music in London, 1888–94. Conductor of the Carl Rosa Opera Company from 1898 and of the Savoy Theatre from 1900.

Composed operas (incl. *Jeanie Deans,* Edinburgh, 1894; *Diarmid,* London, 1897); incidental music for plays; overtures (incl. *The Land of the Mountain and Flood,* 1887) and other orch. works; choral works; chamber music; piano pieces; songs.

MacDowell, Edward Alexander (b. New York, 18 Dec. 1861; d. there, 23 Jan. 1908). Pianist and composer. Studied at the Paris Conservatory and with Raff at the Frankfurt Conservatory. Professor at Columbia Univ., 1896–1904. Composed orch. works (incl. *Indian Suite,* 1895); works for solo instrument and orch. (incl. 2 piano concertos, 1885 and 1890); choral works; numerous piano pieces (incl. 4 sonatas and the sets *Woodland Sketches* [containing "To a Wild Rose"], 1896; *Sea Pieces,* 1898; *Fireside Tales,* 1902; *New England Idyls,* 1902); songs.

Macero, Teo (b. Glens Falls, N.Y., 30 Oct. 1925). Pupil of Brant. Saxophonist and composer. Producer, composer, conductor, and arranger for Columbia Records from 1955. Has composed dance scores; a musical, *Dylan,* 1964; orch. works; film scores; music for television.

Macfarren, George Alexander (b. London, 2 Mar. 1813; d. there, 31 Oct. 1887). Student at the Royal Academy of Music, teacher there from 1834, and its director from 1876; teacher at Cambridge Univ. from 1875. Composed operas (incl. *Robin Hood,* London, 1860; *Helvellyn,* London, 1864); oratorios; 9 symphonies and other orch. works (incl. *Chevy Chase,* overture, 1836); cantatas; concertos for violin, for cello, and for flute; sacred music; chamber music; piano pieces; songs.

Macfarren, Walter Cecil (b. London, 28 Aug. 1826; d. there, 2 Sept. 1905). Pianist and composer. Brother and pupil of George Alexander Macfarren. Teacher at the Royal Academy of Music, 1846–1903. Composed orch. works; vocal works; chamber music; piano pieces; songs.

Machaut, Guillaume de (b. probably at Machaut, Champagne, *c.* 1300; d. Rheims, Apr. 1377). Poet and musician.

Served King John of Bohemia from *c.* 1323. Canon at Notre Dame in Rheims from 1337. After 1346, served at the court of King Charles V of France. Composed a Mass; motets; a hocket; *ballades, rondeaux, virelais,* and *lais.*

Machete. See under Guitar family; Ukulele.

Mackenzie, Alexander Campbell (b. Edinburgh, 22 Aug. 1847; d. London, 28 Apr. 1935). Studied at the Royal Academy of Music. Violinist, composer, and teacher in Edinburgh, 1865–79. Director of the Royal Academy of Music in London, 1888–1924. Composed operas (incl. *The Cricket on the Hearth,* 1900, prod. London, 1914); orch. works (incl. *Scottish Rhapsody* no. 1 and no. 2, 1880, 1881); works for solo instrument with orch. (incl. a *Scottish Concerto* for piano, 1897); cantatas; chamber music; piano pieces; hymns, anthems; part songs; occasional odes; songs.

MacMillan, Ernest (Alexander) Campbell (b. Mimico, Ontario, 18 Aug. 1893; d. Toronto, 6 May 1973). Conductor and composer. Studied at the Univ. of Toronto and at Edinburgh Univ. Director of the Toronto Conservatory, 1926–42; dean of the music faculty of the Univ. of Toronto, 1927–52. Conductor of the Toronto Symphony Orchestra, 1931–56. Composed orch. works; choral works (incl. *England,* after Swinburne, 1917); chamber music; songs and settings of Indian and Canadian folksongs. Edited folksongs and published several textbooks.

Maconchy, Elizabeth (b. Broxbourne, Hertfordshire, 19 Mar. 1907). Pupil of Vaughan Williams. Has composed operas; ballets (incl. *The Little Red Shoes,* 1935); other stage works; a symphony, 1948, and other orch. works; works for solo instrument and orch. (incl. a concertino for clarinet and strings, 1945); choral works; 9 string quartets and other chamber music; piano and harpsichord pieces; songs.

Macque, Giovanni de (Jean) (b. Valenciennes, *c.* 1550; d. Naples, Sept. 1614). Pupil of Monte. Chorister at the Vienna court chapel *c.* 1563. Organist at San Luigi dei Francesi in Rome from 1568 and at Santa Annunziata in Naples from

1590. Organist of the Cappella reale in Naples from 1594 and *maestro di cappella* there from 1599. Among his pupils were Trabaci and L. Rossi. Composed motets; madrigals; keyboard pieces, incl. canzonas, capriccios, partitas, toccatas.

Madama Butterfly. Opera in three acts by Puccini (libretto by G. Giacosa and L. Illica, based on a story by John L. Long and D. Belasco's dramatization), produced in Milan, 1904. Setting: near Nagasaki, Japan, about 1900.

Maderna, Bruno (b. Venice, 21 Apr. 1920; d. Darmstadt, 13 Nov. 1973). Conductor and composer. Pupil of Malipiero. Settled in Germany in 1951. Works (some employing serial and electronic techniques) incl. operas (incl. *Satyrikon,* The Hague, 1973); *Aria da Hyperion* for soprano, flute, orch., with stage action, 1964; the theater piece *Hyperion,* 1964; *Oedipe-Roi,* ballet, 1970; orch. works (incl. *Composizione in 3 tempi,* 1954); concertos for piano, for 2 pianos, for flute, and for oboe; vocal works; works for chamber ensembles (incl. *Serenata II* for 11 instruments, 1957); works on tape (incl. *Notturno,* 1956; *Continuo,* 1958; *Dimensioni II,* 1960).

Madetoja, Leevi Antti (b. Oulu, Finland, 17 Feb. 1887; d. Helsinki, 6 Oct. 1947). Music critic and composer. Pupil of Järnefelt, Sibelius, d'Indy, and R. Fuchs. Teacher at the Helsinki Conservatory, 1916–39, and at the Helsinki Univ., 1926–47. Composed 2 operas, *Pohjalaisia,* Helsinki, 1924, and *Juha,* Helsinki, 1935; a ballet; incidental music for plays; 3 symphonies and other orch. works (incl. *Kullervo,* symphonic poem, 1913); choral works; chamber music; piano pieces; songs.

Madrigal. Name for two different types of Italian vocal music, one of the 14th century, the other of the 16th century (to which the term more often refers). The etymology of the term is in dispute.

I. *The 14th-century madrigal.* As a poetic form the madrigal consists of two or, more rarely, three strophes of three lines each, which are followed by a final strophe of two lines, called a *ritornello. In each strophe, two lines rhyme. The lines

are usually 7 or 11 syllables long. The subject of the madrigal is often amatory and pastoral. Music for these texts was composed usually in two voice-parts, though sometimes in three, in a form that closely follows that of the poetry, the same music (A) being provided for the strophes, and different music (B) for the ritornello, so that the two-stanza (8-line) madrigal has the musical form A A B, and the three-stanza (11-line) madrigal the form A A A B. Madrigals were composed chiefly in the first half of the 14th century, e.g., by Jacopo da Bologna and Giovanni da Cascia, whereas in the second half of the century the madrigal was largely abandoned in favor of the **ballata.* Landini, for instance, wrote only 12 madrigals but 140 *ballate.* The style of the 14th-century madrigal is best described as an ornamented *conductus style, contrasting sharply with the genuinely polyrhythmic style of contemporary French music (Machaut).

II. *The 16th-century Italian madrigal.* As a literary type, the madrigal of the 16th century is a freely arranged succession of 7- and 11-syllable lines, often inspired by the poetry of Petrarch. As a musical composition, it is an outgrowth of the *frottola* and, more specifically, of the canzona [see Canzona (4)], and its texts include a variety of forms in addition to that of the madrigal proper.

The development of the madrigal in Italy is usually divided into three phases. (a) *The early madrigal* (publications beginning *c.* 1530): Philippe Verdelot, Costanzo Festa (the first Italian composer of madrigals), Jacob Arcadelt. The style is, in spite of considerable imitation, prevailingly homophonic; the writing is in three or four parts; the expression is quiet and restrained. (b) *The classic madrigal* (publications 1550–80): Adrian Willaert (properly intermediate between the early and classical types), Cipriano de Rore, Andrea Gabrieli, Roland de Lassus, Philippe de Monte, Palestrina. Here the writing is in four to six (usually five) parts, and the style is more genuinely polyphonic and imitative, approaching that of the contemporary motet, the expression being more intense and closely allied to the text in meaning as well as in pronunciation. A collateral type of this period is the *madrigale spi-*

rituale, intended for devotional use. (c) *The late madrigal* (publications 1580–1620): Luca Marenzio, Carlo Gesualdo, Claudio Monteverdi. Here, the development leads to a highly elaborate type of music, employing new extremes of chromaticism at times, *word painting, coloristic effects, declamatory monody, virtuosity of the vocal soloist, and dramatic effects. Particularly important is the transition to the new monodic style. This transition is apparent in the madrigals of Monteverdi, whose books I, II, III, and IV (1587, 1590, 1592, 1603) are purely polyphonic, whereas in the following books (V, 1605; VI, 1614) the style becomes increasingly soloistic, and the accompaniment often requires *basso continuo;* book VII, called *Concerto* (1619), is entirely in *stile rappresentativo* with *basso continuo*. Giulio Caccini's *Le nuove musiche* of 1601 contains "madrigals" for solo voice that are through-composed, in contrast to his strophic "arias."

Outside Italy, the madrigal was cultivated chiefly in England, though it had an important impact on the secular polyphony of France, Germany, and Spain as well. William Byrd (1543–1623) and Thomas Morley (1557–1602) represent the earlier period of the English madrigal, whose style corresponds to a certain extent to that of the second Italian school. The younger Englishmen, notably Thomas Weelkes and John Wilbye, leaned further toward Italy and exploited to a limited degree the innovations of Marenzio and Gesualdo.

Madrigal comedy. Modern designation for late 16th-century works in which an entire play [It. *commedia*] was set to music in the form of madrigals and other kinds of polyphonic vocal music. Among the first and most famous examples is *L'Amfiparnaso* by Orazio Vecchi (performed in Modena, 1594; printed 1597). Vecchi's preface makes it clear that his work was not to be acted, and this was probably the case with other examples as well.

Madrigalism. A term commonly used for *word painting and related devices, such as are found particularly in Italian madrigals of the late 16th century.

Maegaard, Jan (b. Copenhagen, 14 Apr. 1926). Music critic and composer. Pupil of K. Jeppesen. Teacher at the Copenhagen Conservatory from 1954 and at the Univ. of Copenhagen from 1959. Has composed orch. works (incl. *2 Tempi*, 1961); vocal works (incl. *Antigone* for chorus and orch., 1966); chamber music; piano pieces. Has written a study of Schoenberg's music.

Maestoso [It.]. Majestic.

Maestro [It., master]. Now an honorary title for distinguished teachers, composers, and conductors.

Maestro de capilla [Sp.]. See under Chapel.

Maestro di cappella [It.]. See under Chapel.

Magadis. An ancient Greek harp, which seems to have had ten pairs of strings, each pair consisting of a fundamental and its octave. The term "magadizing" is sometimes used to describe singing in octaves.

Maggiore [It.]. Major mode. See Major, minor.

Magic Flute, The. See *Zauberflöte, Die*.

Magnard, (Lucien-Denis-Gabriel-) Albéric (b. Paris, 9 June 1865; d. Baron, Oise, 3 Sept. 1914). Pupil of Dubois, Massenet, and d'Indy. Composed operas (incl. *Guercoeur*, 1904; *Bérénice*, Paris, 1911); 4 symphonies and other orch. works; chamber music; piano pieces; songs.

Magnificat. The *canticle of the Virgin, "Magnificat anima mea Dominum" (My soul doth magnify the Lord), Luke 1:46–55. It consists of 12 verses, including the *Doxology at the end. In the Roman Catholic rites it is sung at the Office of Vespers by alternating choruses to one of eight *toni*, recitation chants similar to the *psalm tones [see *LU*, pp. 207 ff.], in connection with an antiphon (Magnificat antiphon) that is usually somewhat more elaborate in style than the psalm antiphons. From the 15th through the 18th centuries the Magnificat was frequently set for voices or for organ [see Verset]. After 1450 it became customary to compose only alternate verses, the others being sung in plainsong. The well-known setting of J. S. Bach is in the style of some of his cantatas.

Magnus liber organi [L., Great Book of *Organum]. Title of the collection of two-voice organa for the entire ecclesiastical year written *c*. 1175 by Leonin, with additions and modifications by his successor Perotin (*c*. 1200; see *Ars antiqua; Notre Dame*, school of). The full title was *Magnus liber organi de gradali et antiphonario pro servitio divino multiplicando*. The complete collection includes 59 pieces for the *Mass ("de gradali") and 34 pieces for the *Office ("de antiphonario"), all composed "to enrich the divine service."

Mahler, Gustav (b. Kalischt, Bohemia, 7 July 1860; d. Vienna, 18 May 1911). Studied at the Vienna Conservatory with R. Fuchs. Attended Bruckner's lectures at the Univ. of Vienna. Held conducting positions at the Prague Opera, 1885–86; at the Royal Opera in Budapest, from 1888; at the Hamburg Municipal Opera, 1891–97; at the Vienna Court Opera, 1897–1907; at the Metropolitan Opera in New York, from 1907; with the New York Philharmonic Society, 1909–11. Works: 9 symphonies and an unfinished 10th (incl. the *Resurrection Symphony*); works for voice and orch. (incl. *Lieder eines fahrenden Gesellen*, 1883–85; *Lieder aus "Des *Knaben Wunderhorn,"* with piano or orch., 1892–99; *Kindertotenlieder*, 1901–4; *Das *Lied von der Erde*, 1908); *Das Klagende Lied* for soloists, chorus, and orch., 1880–99; songs with piano.

Maid as Mistress, The. See *Serva padrona, La*.

Maillart, (Louis) Aimé (b. Montpellier, 24 Mar. 1817; d. Moulins, 26 May 1871). Pupil of Halévy. Composed 6 operas (incl. *Les dragons de Villars*, Paris, 1856); cantatas; sacred music.

Main [F.]. Hand. *Main droite (gauche)*, right (left) hand. *À deux (quatre) mains*, for two (four) hands.

Maître de chapelle. See under Maîtrise; Chapel.

Maîtrise [F.]. The choir school and choir of a French church. These institutions, which date from the 15th century if not earlier, were under the direction of a "maître de chapelle" and provided board as well as education, both general and musical.

Majeur [F.]. Major mode. See Major, minor.

Majo, Gian Francesco di (de) (b. Naples, 27 Mar. 1732; d. there, 17 Nov. 1770). Pupil of his father, the composer Giuseppe Majo, and of Padre Martini. Organist of the Cappella reale in Naples from 1747. Composed about 20 operas (incl. *Cajo Fabricio*, Naples, 1760; *Ifigenia in Tauride*, Naples, 1764; *Alessandro*, Naples, 1767); cantatas; arias; Masses; oratorios.

Major, Jakab Gyula (originally Mayer) (b. Kassa, Hungary, now Košice, Czechoslovakia, 13 Dec. 1858; d. Budapest, 30 Jan. 1925). Pianist, conductor, and composer. Pupil of Liszt and Volkmann. Composed operas; 5 symphonies and part of a 6th; other orch. works (incl. *Balaton*, symphonic poem); concertos for piano, for violin, and for cello; chamber music; piano pieces; songs.

Major, minor [F. *majeur, mineur;* G. *dur, moll;* It. *maggiore, minore;* Sp. *mayor, menor*]. Terms used (1) to distinguish *intervals, e.g., major second (C–D), and minor second (C–D♭); (2) for two types (or *modes) of *scale, *triad, or key. The major scale comprises the arrangement of tones (t) and semitones (s) shown in Ex. 1 and is the same both ascending and descending. In the *pure minor* scale, the third, sixth, and seventh *scale degrees are, by comparison with the major scale, lowered one semitone each, both ascending and descending [Ex. 2]. In the *harmonic* minor, the third and sixth remain lowered both ascending and descending, and the seventh or leading tone is raised to a semitone below the tonic [Ex. 3]. This results in an augmented second (t+) between the sixth and seventh degrees, an awkward melodic progression that is avoided in the *melodic* minor. Here the third is lowered and the sixth and seventh are raised when ascending, whereas the third,

sixth, and seventh are all lowered when descending [Ex. 4]. A triad formed on the tonic of a major scale is major, since the lower of its two thirds is major while the upper is minor. A triad formed on the tonic of a minor scale is minor, since the lower of its two thirds is minor while the upper is major. Correspondingly, a major key is one that employs a major scale and whose tonic triad is therefore major, and a minor key is one that employs a minor scale and whose tonic triad is therefore minor. Both major and minor scales and triads can be formed on any of the twelve *pitch classes.

The definite establishment of the major and minor modes as the tonal basis of Western music took place during the 17th century, though clear steps in this direction were taken in both the music and the theoretical writings of the 16th century.

Malagueña [Sp.]. Term for three different types of southern Spanish folk music, all localized in the provinces of Málaga and Murcia: (1) Usually a local variety of the *fandango. (2) A type of highly emotional song, in free style and rhythm. (3) An older type of dance music, based on the ostinatolike repetition of the harmonies VIII–VII–VI–V (in minor), played in parallel triads and with an improvised melody above.

Maldere, Pierre van (Malderre) (b. Brussels, 16 Oct. 1729; d. there, 1 Nov. 1768). Violinist and composer. Concert master of the royal chapel at Brussels from 1749. Conductor of the Brussels Opera, 1763–66. Composed operas; symphonies; trio sonatas; violin sonatas; other instrumental works.

Maleingreau, Paul (**Eugène-Constant-Charles-Joseph-Marie**) **de** (properly Malengreau) (b. Trélon-en-Thiérache, near Chimay, Belgium, 23 Nov. 1887; d. Brussels, 9 Jan. 1956). Organist and composer. Pupil of Tinel and Gilson. Teacher at the Brussels Conservatory from 1913. President of the Froissart Academy from 1946. Composed 2 symphonies and other orch. works; sacred vocal music; chamber music; organ works; piano pieces; songs.

Maler, Wilhelm (b. Heidelberg, 21 June 1902; d. Hamburg, 29 Apr. 1976). Pupil of Haas and Jarnach. Teacher at the Rheinische Musikschule in Cologne, 1925–44; at the National Academy of Music there from 1928; at Bonn Univ. from 1931; at the Northwest-German Music Academy in Detmold from 1946. Director of the Hamburg Musikhochschule from 1959. Has composed cantatas; an oratorio; a *concerto grosso* and other orch. works; concertos for harpsichord, for violin, and for piano trio; choral works; chamber music; piano pieces; arrangements of German folksongs.

Malinconico [It.]. Melancholy.

Malipiero, Gian Francesco (b. Venice, 18 Mar. 1882; d. Treviso, 1 Aug. 1973). Pupil of Bossi. Director of the Venice Conservatory, 1939–52. Composed operas (incl. the trilogies *L'Orfeide*, 1918–22, and *Il misterio di Venezia*, 1925–28; *I capricci di Callot*, Rome, 1942; *Venere prigionera*, Florence, 1957); ballets; 11 symphonies and other orch. works (incl. *Pause del silenzio*, 1917–26); concertos for violin, for cello, for piano; choral works; works for voice with instruments; 7 string quartets and other chamber music; piano pieces; songs. Wrote several books and edited the complete works of Monteverdi.

Man. Abbr. for *manual.

Manchicourt, Pierre de (b. Béthune, Pas-de-Calais, c. 1510; d. Madrid, before late Jan. 1562). *Maître de chapelle* at Notre Dame in Tournai, 1539–54; at the Antwerp Cathedral from 1557; at the Flemish chapel of Philip II in Madrid from 1561. Composed Masses, motets, madrigals, chansons.

Mancinelli, Luigi (b. Orvieto, 5 Feb. 1848; d. Rome, 2 Feb. 1921). Cellist, conductor, and composer. Director of the Liceo musicale in Bologna from 1881. Conductor at the Royal Theater in Madrid from 1888; at the Metropolitan Opera in New York from 1894; at the Teatro Colón in Buenos Aires from 1906. Composed operas (incl. *Ero e Leandro,* Madrid, 1897); orch. works (incl. *Intermezzi sinfonici*); 3 Masses; oratorios and other vocal works.

Mancini, Francesco (b. Naples, 16 Jan. 1672; d. there, 22? Sept. 1737). Pupil of Provenzale. Organist of the court chapel in Naples from 1704. *Maestro di cappella* of the Conservatorio Santa Maria di Loreto in Naples from 1720. Succeeded Scarlatti as director of the Cappella reale in Naples, 1725. Composed operas (incl. *Gli amanti generosi,* Naples, 1704, prod. as *Hydaspes,* London, 1710); intermezzi; *serenate;* Masses, motets, oratorios, and other sacred music; instrumental works (incl. concertos for flute and string orch.; keyboard pieces).

Mandola, mandora. See under Lute.

Mandolin. The most recent instrument of the lute family. In general use chiefly in southern Italy. The Neapolitan mandolin has four double courses (eight steel strings) tuned g d' a' e''. It is played with a plectrum of tortoise shell or other flexible material. The tones are rendered as a sustained tremolo, which is produced by a quick vibrating movement of the plectrum. See ill. under Lute.

Manfred. (1) Overture and incidental music by Schumann, op. 115 (1848–49), to Byron's poem of the same name. (2) Symphony by Tchaikovsky, op. 58 (1885), based on Byron's poem.

Manfredina. See *Monferrina.*

Manfredini, Francesco Maria (b. Pistoia, *c.* 1680; d. there, *c.* 1748). Violinist and composer. Pupil of Torelli. *Kapellmeister* in Munich from 1711 and at the Pistoia Cathedral from 1727. Composed *concerti grossi;* sinfonias; trio sonatas; vocal works, incl. oratorios.

Manica [It.]. Shift of *position in violin playing.

Manico [It.]. *Fingerboard of the violin, etc.

Manieren [G.]. An 18th-century term for ornaments of restricted melodic range, approximately equivalent to *agréments.*

Männerchor [G.]. Men's chorus.

Mannheim school. A group of German composers of the mid-18th century, centered at Mannheim and associated with the orchestra of Karl Theodor (1724–99), Elector of Pfalzbayern (Palatinate). Johann Stamitz (1717–57), who joined the orchestra in 1741 and soon became its conductor, inaugurated a novel style of orchestral music and performance. Conspicuous features of the new style were melodic prominence of the violins in an essentially homophonic, noncontrapuntal texture; abandonment of imitation and fugal style; presto character of the quick movements; use of dynamic devices such as extended crescendos and unexpected fortes and fortissimos; rests for the entire orchestra in the course of a movement (i.e., general pauses); figures that quickly rise over a wide range, usually in broken chords, the so-called *Raketen* [G., rockets, Roman candles]; orchestral effects such as the tremolo and broken chords in quick notes; replacement of thoroughbass accompaniment by written out orchestral parts. Johann Stamitz' activity was continued by Ignaz Holzbauer (1711–83; came to Mannheim in 1753), Franz Xaver Richter (1709–89; came to Mannheim in 1747), and a younger generation including Anton Filtz (1733–60), Franz Beck (1723–1809), Christian Cannabich (1731–98), and Johann Stamitz' sons Karl Stamitz (1745–1801) and Anton Stamitz (1754–1809). Recent scholarship has greatly diminished the strength of earlier claims regarding the importance of the Mannheim school in the creation of the *classical style in the symphony and chamber music that culminated in the works of Haydn and Mozart.

Mano [It.; pl. *mani*]. Hand. *Mano destra* (*sinistra*), right (left) hand.

Manon. Opera in five acts by Massenet (libretto by H. Meilhac and P. Gille, based on Prévost's novel, *Histoire de*

Manon Lescaut), produced in Paris, 1884. Setting: France, early 18th century.

Manon Lescaut. Opera in four acts by Puccini (libretto in Italian by M. Praga, P. Oliva, and L. Illica, based on Prévost's novel), produced in Turin, 1893. Setting: France and Louisiana, early 18th century. (Also, an opera by Auber.)

Manual. On the organ, any of the keyboards provided for the hands, as opposed to the pedal. Similarly, the keyboards of the harpsichord. *Manualiter* [L.] means playing with the hands only.

Manzoni, Giacomo (b. Milan, 26 Sept. 1932). Music critic and composer. Studied at the Milan Conservatory and the Darmstadt summer courses. Teacher at the Milan Conservatory from 1962 and at the Bologna Conservatory from 1965. Has composed 2 operas (incl. *Atomtod,* Milan, 1965); orch. works; vocal works; chamber music; piano pieces; works on tape.

Manzoni Requiem. The name sometimes given to Verdi's *Requiem,* which was first performed on the first anniversary of the death of the Italian novelist and poet Alessandro Manzoni in 1874.

Maqām [Arab.; pl. *maqāmāt*]. See under Melody type.

Maraca. A gourd or calabash shell shaker filled with dry seeds, typical of the Caribbean countries but known throughout Latin America. It is usually used in pairs.

Marais, Marin (b. Paris, 31 May 1656; d. there, 15 Aug. 1728). Viola da gamba player and composer. Pupil of Lully. Instrumentalist of the French court, 1679–1725; director of the orchestra of the Paris Opéra, 1695–1710. Composed operas (incl. *Alcyone,* Paris, 1706); chamber music (incl. *La gamme,* 1723, a collection of trios for violin, viola da gamba, and harpsichord); 5 books of pieces for viola da gamba.

Marazzoli, Marco (b. Parma, *c.* 1602 or *c.* 1608; d. Rome, 26 Jan. 1662). Singer, harpist, and composer. Singer in the Papal Chapel, 1637–40. Composed operas (incl. *Chi soffre, speri,* an early

comic opera, with V. Mazzocchi, Rome, 1637; *Dal male il bene,* with A. M. Abbatini, Rome, 1653); cantatas; oratorios; *canzonette;* arias, etc.

Marbeck, John (Merbecke) (b. Windsor, between 1500 and 1510; d. there?, *c.* 1585). Chorister and later lay clerk, organist, and chaplain at St. George's Chapel in Windsor. Works incl. *The Book of Common Praier Noted,* 1550, the first adaptation of liturgical chant to the English ritual authorized in 1549; other sacred music.

Marcando, marcato [It.]. Marked, stressed.

Marcello, Alessandro (pseudonym Eterio Stinfalico) (b. Venice, *c.* 1684; d. there. *c.* 1750). Poet, singer, painter, and composer. Brother of Benedetto Marcello. Composed orch. concertos and concertos for flute, for violin, for oboe; violin sonatas; solo cantatas; etc.

Marcello, Benedetto (b. Venice, 9 Aug. 1686; d. Brescia, 24 or 25 July 1739). Poet and composer. Brother of Alessandro Marcello. Pupil of Gasparini and Lotti. Served on the Council of Forty in Venice from 1711. Composed *Estro poetico-armonico,* settings for voices and instruments of 50 psalms paraphrased by G. Giustiniani, 1724–26; stage works; oratorios; madrigals; *canzone,* arias, etc.; chamber cantatas; concertos; sonatas. Published *Il teatro alla moda,* 1720, a satire on operatic manners.

Marcellus Mass. A famous Mass by Palestrina, named after Pope Marcellus II (*Missa Papae Marcelli*) and once thought to have played a decisive role at the *Council of Trent. The work is exceptional among Palestrina's Masses in that it makes substantial use of homorhythmic (note-against-note) texture, resulting in a clearly intelligible declamation of the text.

March. Music originally designed to promote orderly marching of a large group, especially of soldiers. Marches are generally in duple meter and in simple, strongly marked rhythm and regular phrases. The standard form, derived from the minuet-with-trio, is that of a march repeated after one or several trios of a more melodious character: M T M, or M T M T M. Military marches may be divided into four categories: (1) funeral march; (2) slow march—75 beats or steps per minute, 2 steps per bar; (3) quick march—108 to 128 beats per minute; (4) double-quick march—140 to 160 beats per minute. In the United States the standard military march is the quick march, the finest examples having been written by John Philip Sousa. Marches and marchlike music also occur in art music—particularly in operas, but also in symphonies, sonatas, and the like, e.g., the second movements of Beethoven's Piano Sonata op. 101 and Symphony no. 3 (*Eroica*). Schubert composed a number of marches for piano four-hands.

Marchand, Louis (b. Lyon, 2 Feb. 1669; d. Paris, 17 Feb. 1732). Church organist in Paris from 1689 and organist of the royal chapel there, 1706–14. Composed an opera; a cantata; French and Italian airs; 3 *Cantiques spirituels* on texts by Racine; works for harpsichord and for organ.

Marcia [It.]. *March. *Marcia funebre,* funeral march. *Alla marcia,* in the manner of a march.

Marco, Tomás (b. Madrid, 12 Sept. 1942). Music critic and composer. Pupil of Stockhausen. Has composed works for orch.; works for chamber and other instrumental ensembles (incl. *Ensemble,* in collaboration with Stockhausen, 1967); works for guitar and for piano; mixed-media pieces.

Marenzio, Luca (b. Coccaglio, near Brescia, 1553 or 1554; d. Rome, 22 Aug. 1599). Probably a pupil of G. Contini. In the service of Cardinals Madruzzo, Luigi d'Este, and Aldobrandini in Rome at various times. Served Sigismund III, King of Poland, 1596–98. Composed sacred and secular madrigals; *villanelle;* motets; other sacred and secular vocal works.

Mariachi [Sp.]. Mexican ensemble of folk musicians, composed of two or more violins, guitars of various sizes, and often a harp and one or two trumpets. Also, a member of such a group.

Marimba. An African and Central and South American *xylophone, consisting of a number of wooden plates of different size and thickness. Underneath the plates are resonators made of gourds. The instrument has been modernized (first by Sebastián Hurtado of Guatemala c. 1895) and is now made with bars of hardwood of uniform thickness and with tuned tubular metal resonators, encompassing up to six or seven octaves. It is played with rubber- or felt-headed mallets, often by two to five players. For ill. see under Percussion instruments. The marimba is especially popular in Central America and is considered the national instrument of Guatemala.

Marimbaphone. Several varieties of marimba, designed and made by J. C. Deagan of Chicago between 1915 and 1920.

Marine trumpet. See Tromba marina.

Marini, Biagio (b. Brescia, c. 1597; d. Venice, 20 Mar. 1665). Violinist and composer. Probably a pupil of Monteverdi. Court and church violinist in Neuberg (1623–45), Dusseldorf, Venice, Milan, and other Italian cities. Composed some of the earliest Italian violin sonatas; other instrumental pieces; madrigals, *canzonette,* and other secular vocal works.

Markevich, Igor (b. Kiev, 27 July 1912). Conductor and composer. Pupil of N. Boulanger and Rieti. Conducted the Concerts Lamoureux in Paris, 1957–61, and has toured widely. Has composed the ballets *Rebus,* 1931, and *L'envoi d'Icare,* 1933; orch. works (incl. a concerto grosso, 1930; *Le nouvel âge,* 1938); works for piano and orch.; oratorios; choral works; chamber music; works for voice with instruments.

Markiert [G.]. Marked, stressed.

Markig [G.]. Vigorous.

Marqué [F.]. Marked, stressed.

Marriage of Figaro, The. See *Nozze di Figaro, Le.*

Marsch [G.]. *March.

Marschner, Heinrich August (b. Zittau, Saxony, 16 Aug. 1795; d. Hanover, 14 Dec. 1861). Opera director in Dresden, with Morlacchi and Weber, from 1823 and in Leipzig from 1826. Court *Kapell-*

meister at Hanover, 1831–59. Composed operas (incl. *Der Vampyr*, Leipzig, 1828; *Der Templar und die Jüdin*, after Scott's *Ivanhoe*, Leipzig, 1829; *Hans Heiling*, Berlin, 1833); other stage works; orch. works; choral works; chamber music; sacred vocal works; piano pieces; songs.

Marteau sans maître, Le [F. The Hammer Without a Master]. Composition by Boulez in nine movements for alto, alto flute, viola, guitar, xylophone, and percussion, composed in 1953–55 (rev. 1957) on a cycle of texts of the same name by René Char.

Martelé [F., hammered]. A special method of violin bowing; see Bowing (c). *Martellando, martellato* [It.] means either the *martelé* of the violin or a somewhat similar technique of piano playing in which the hands act like hammers.

Martha. Opera in four acts by F. von Flotow (libretto by F. W. Riese), produced in Vienna, 1847. Setting: Richmond, England, about 1710.

Martin, Frank (b. Geneva, 15 Sept. 1890; d. Naarden, the Netherlands, 21 Nov. 1974). Teacher at the Institut Jaques-Dalcroze in Geneva, 1928–38, and at the Cologne Hochschule für Musik, 1950–57. Has worked with twelve-tone techniques and with folksong materials. Has composed 2 operas; ballets; incidental music for plays; 5 oratorios (incl. *Le vin herbe*, 1941); orch. works (incl. *Petite symphonie concertante*, 1945); several *Ballades* for solo instrument with piano or orch.; concertos for violin, for cello, for harpsichord, for piano; choral works; chamber music; works for accompanied voice; piano pieces.

Martín y Soler, (Atanasio Martín Ignacio) Vicente (Tadeo Francisco Pelegrín) (called Martini lo Spagnuolo) (b. Valencia, 2 May 1754; d. St. Petersburg, 11 Feb. 1806). Court composer to Catherine the Great at St. Petersburg from 1788. Composed operas (incl. *Una cosa rara*, Vienna, 1786; *Il burbero di buon cuore*, Vienna, 1786); ballets; pasticcios; cantatas; *canzonette*, arias, other small vocal works; instrumental pieces.

Martini, Giambattista (Giovanni Battista) ("Padre Martini") (b. Bologna, 24 Apr. 1706; d. there, 3 Aug. 1784). *Mae-*

stro di cappella at San Francesco in Bologna from 1725 and ordained a priest in 1729. His pupils incl. Mozart, Jommelli, and Johann Christian Bach. Composed oratorios; Masses and other church music; intermezzi; canons; vocal chamber music; keyboard sonatas. Wrote various treatises, incl. *Storia della musica.*

Martino, Donald (James) (b. Plainfield, N.J., 16 May 1931). Clarinetist and composer. Pupil of Bacon, Babbitt, Sessions, and Dallapiccola. Teacher at Yale Univ., 1959–69, and then at the New England Conservatory. Has worked with serial techniques. Has composed works for orch. (incl. *Mosaic for Grand Orchestra*, 1967; *Ritorno*, 1976); a piano concerto, 1965; works for chamber ensembles (incl. *Notturno* for flute, clarinet, violin, cello, percussion, and piano, awarded the Pulitzer Prize for 1974); pieces for clarinet (incl. *B,a,b,b,it,t*, 1966) and for piano; choral works (incl. *Paradiso Choruses* for soloists, chorus, orch., tape); songs.

Martinon, Jean (b. Lyon, 10 Jan. 1910; d. Paris, 1 Mar. 1976). Violinist, conductor, and composer. Pupil of Roussel and d'Indy. Conductor of the Chicago Symphony Orchestra, 1963–69. Composed stage works; 4 symphonies and other orch. works; 2 violin concertos and a cello concerto; choral works (incl. *Psaume CXXXVI: Chant des captifs*, with orch., 1943); string quartets and other chamber music; piano pieces; songs.

Martinů, Bohuslav (b. Polička, Czechoslovakia, 8 Dec. 1890; d. Liestal, near Basel, 28 Aug. 1959). Pupil of Suk and Roussel. Settled in New York, 1941; returned to Europe, 1953. Composed operas (incl. *Juliette*, Prague, 1938; *The Marriage*, N.B.C.-TV, 1953; *The Greek Passion*, after Kazantzakis, 1955–58); ballets; an oratorio, *The Prophecy of Isaiah*, 1959; 6 symphonies and other orch. works; works for solo instruments with orch.; choral works; 7 string quartets and much other chamber music; piano pieces.

Martirano, Salvatore (b. Yonkers, N.Y., 12 Jan. 1927). Pupil of Bernard Rogers, Dallapiccola, and Elwell. Teacher at the Univ. of Illinois at Urbana from 1968.

Has composed a chamber opera; *Prelude for orch.*, 1950; *A Cappella Mass* for chorus, 1953; *O O O O That Shakespeherian Rag* for chorus and instruments, 1958; works for instrumental ensembles, some with tape; *Cocktail Music* for piano, 1962; works for accompanied voice; theater pieces, incl. *L's GA*, 1968.

Martucci, Giuseppe (b. Capua, Italy, 6 Jan. 1856; d. Naples, 1 June 1909). Conductor, pianist, and composer. Studied in Naples. Director of the Bologna Conservatory, 1886–1902, and of the Naples Conservatory from 1902. Composed 2 symphonies and other orch. works; 2 piano concertos; an oratorio; a Mass; 2 piano trios and other chamber music; piano pieces; songs.

Marx, Joseph (Rupert Rudolph) (b. Graz, 11 May 1882; d. there, 3 Sept. 1964). Music critic and composer. Teacher at the Vienna Academy from 1914, at the Hochschule für Musik in Vienna, 1924–27, and at the Univ. of Graz from 1947. Composed orch. works; works for piano and orch.; string quartets and other chamber music; choral works; numerous songs.

Marx, Karl (b. Munich, 12 Nov. 1897). Pupil of Orff and Hausegger. Teacher at the Akademie der Tonkunst in Munich from 1924; at the Hochschule für Musikerziehung in Graz from 1939; and at the Stuttgart Hochschule für Musik, 1946–66. Has composed orch. works; concertos for piano and for violin; cantatas; choruses; chamber music; organ works; songs.

Mascagni, Pietro (b. Livorno, 7 Dec. 1863; d. Rome, 2 Aug. 1945). Pupil of A. Soffredini and Ponchielli. Director of the Rossini Conservatory in Pesaro, 1895–1902. Composed operas (incl. **Cavalleria rusticana; L'amico Fritz,* Rome, 1891; *Iris,* Rome, 1898; *Isabeau,* Buenos Aires, 1911); orch. works; vocal works (incl. *Poema Leopardiano,* 1898); chamber music; songs.

Mascherata. See under *Villanella.*

Masculine, feminine cadence. A cadence or ending is called "masculine" if its final pitch or chord occurs on a metrically strong beat [see Measure] and "feminine" if it is postponed to fall on a weak beat.

Masked Ball, A. See *Ballo in maschera, Un.*

Mason, Daniel Gregory (b. Brookline, Mass., 20 Nov. 1873; d. Greenwich, Conn., 4 Dec. 1953). Grandson of Lowell Mason. Pupil of Paine, Whiting, P. Goetschius, Chadwick, and d'Indy. Teacher at Columbia Univ., 1910–42. Composed 3 symphonies and other orch. works (incl. the overture *Chanticleer,* 1928); vocal works; chamber music (incl. a string quartet on Negro themes, 1919); piano pieces; songs. Published several books on music.

Mason, Lowell (b. Medfield, Mass., 8 Jan. 1792; d. Orange, N.J., 11 Aug. 1872). Organist, conductor, and composer. Church organist in Boston from 1827. Co-founder (1832) of the Boston Academy of Music. Published anthologies of sacred and secular songs, incl. some of his own hymn tunes; pedagogic works.

Masque, mask. A stage production of the 16th and 17th centuries, designed for the entertainment of the nobility and combining poetry, vocal and instrumental music, dancing, and acting, lavishly applied to the presentation of mythological and allegorical subjects. The masque originated in Italy and France, where members of the court played an active part in their preparation as well as performance. It was introduced into England during the 16th century and remained in great favor during the 17th century. The best-known writer of masques was Ben Jonson, who from 1605 to 1631 provided them for the court. Composers of music for masques were Thomas Campion (1567–1620), Alfonso Ferrabosco the younger (c. 1575–1628), Robert Johnson (c. 1580–c. 1634), John Coperario (c. 1575–1626), Nicholas Laniere (1588–1666), Henry Lawes (1596–1662), who wrote the music to Milton's masque *Comus,* produced in 1634, and William Lawes (1602–45). See also Ballet.

Mass [F. *messe;* G. *Messe;* It. *messa;* L. *missa;* Sp. *misa*]. The most solemn service of the Roman Catholic Church, representing the commemoration and mystical repetition of the Last Supper. The name is derived from the words "Ite, missa est (congregatio)"—literally, "Depart, the congregation is dismissed" —sung at the end of the service [see, e.g., *LU*, p. 19]. The discussion following refers to the full form known as High Mass (*Missa solemnis;* for *Missa brevis* and *Missa lecta* see under *Missa*). Liturgically, the Mass falls into two parts, the Mass of the Catechumens and the Mass of the Faithful; the former ends with the Gospel, while the latter extends from the Offertory to the end. (The Credo, a later addition, belongs to neither.)

I. *The Mass in Gregorian chant.* The Mass consists of a number of items whose texts vary from day to day (*Proper* of the Mass, *proprium missae*) and of others having the same text in every Mass (*Ordinary* of the Mass, *ordinarium missae*). Another classification can be made according to whether an item is recited to a *monotone or spoken, or whether it is sung to a distinct melody. The former category is entrusted to the celebrant priest and his assistants, the latter to the choir (*schola*). The following table shows the normal structure of the Mass, with the items classified under four categories: Ia, Proper sung; Ib, Ordinary sung; IIa, Proper recited or spoken; IIb, Ordinary spoken. The items of the rubric Ib, the

sung Ordinary of the Mass, are what is usually known to music students as the "Mass," since these are the items included in polyphonic Masses beginning in the 14th century and in the elaborate choral-orchestral Masses of the 18th and 19th centuries.

II. *The polyphonic Mass.* Important collections of Mass music containing settings of items from the Proper include the *Magnus liber organi* (12th–13th cent.), the *Trent Codices (15th cent.), Heinrich Isaac's *Choralis Constantinus* (16th cent.), and William Byrd's *Gradualia* (publ. 1605–7). For the most part, however, the history of the polyphonic Mass is the history of settings of some or all of the sung items of the Ordinary. The 14th century saw numerous settings of single items and pairs of items and the first complete Mass cycles, i.e., settings of the complete Ordinary (though after the 14th century the *Ite missa est* is typically omitted) as a single, multimovement work. Most notable among the 14th-century cycles is that by Guillaume de Machaut. The first systematic attempts (by Power and other English composers) to give the cycles as a whole some musical unity occurred in the 15th century.

The principal types of Mass composition of the 15th and 16th centuries are the following: (1) *Plainsong Mass,* sometimes called a paraphrase Mass, in which

Sung		Recited or Spoken	
Ia Proper	Ib Ordinary	IIa Proper	IIb Ordinary
1. Introit			
	2. Kyrie		
	3. Gloria		
		4. Collect	
		5. Epistle	
6. Gradual			
7. Alleluia or Tract			
		8. Gospel	
	9. Credo		
10. Offertory			
		11. Secret	
		12. Preface	
	13. Sanctus		
			14. Canon
	15. Agnus Dei		
16. Communion			
		17. Post-Communion	
	18. Ite missa est or Benedicamus Domino		

each movement is based on (or paraphrases) the appropriate liturgical melody. (2) *Cantus firmus* Mass, in which a single melody (either sacred or secular) provides the principal thematic material for all of the movements. The melody in question may be stated literally, in long note-values, and in a single voice (usually the tenor), or it may be freely elaborated by all of the voices of the polyphonic texture (in which case the term "paraphrase Mass" is sometimes employed instead). (3) *Motto Mass,* in which all movements begin with the same music (or motto). (4) *Parody Mass. (5) Freely invented Mass, in which no preexistent music forms the basis of the polyphonic texture. Such Masses often bear the name of the *church mode in which they are composed or are simply titled *Missa sine nomine* (Mass without a name), since where preexistent material is used, the Mass generally takes the name of that material. In all of these types, each of the five principal movements usually consists of several discrete sections. Virtually all of the composers of polyphonic music of this period contributed to the Mass repertory.

After 1600, Mass composition loses its former importance. In general, there is a tendency toward the use of larger performing resources (including the orchestra), the division of the longer movements (i.e., the Gloria and Credo) into greater numbers of independent sections, and the use of forms such as the aria that are derived from secular music. Among composers who have contributed to the Mass repertory since the 17th century are Bach, Haydn, Mozart, Beethoven, Schubert, Liszt, Bruckner, and Stravinsky. See also Requiem Mass.

Massé, Victor (properly Félix-Marie) (b. Lorient, Morbihan, France, 7 Mar. 1822; d. Paris, 5 July 1884). Pupil of Zimmermann and Halévy. Chorusmaster at the Paris Opéra from 1860. Teacher at the Paris Conservatory, 1866–80. Composed operas (incl. *Galatée,* Paris, 1852; *Les noces de Jeannette,* Paris, 1853; *Les saisons,* Paris, 1855; *Paul et Virginie,* Paris, 1876); songs.

Massenet, Jules (Émile-Frédéric) (b. Montaud, near Saint-Étienne, Loire, 12 May 1842; d. Paris, 13 Aug. 1912). Pupil of Reber and Ambroise Thomas. Teacher at the Paris Conservatory, 1878 –96. His pupils incl. G. Charpentier, Koechlin, Leroux, and Enescu. Composed operas (incl. *Manon; Esclarmonde,* Paris, 1889; *Werther; Thaïs,* Paris, 1894); ballets (incl. *Le Cid,* 1885); incidental music for plays; oratorios; choral works; orch. works; a piano concerto; a fantasy for cello and orch.; chamber music; piano pieces; numerous songs.

Mässig [G.]. Moderate, moderately.

Mastersingers. See Meistersinger.

Mastersingers of Nuremberg, The. See *Meistersinger von Nürnberg, Die.*

Mata, Eduardo (b. Mexico City, 15 Sept. 1942). Conductor and composer. Pupil of R. Halffter, Chávez, and Orbón. Director of the Ballet clásico de Méjico from 1964 and teacher at the National Conservatory from 1971. Conductor of the Dallas Symphony from 1977. Has worked with aleatory and serial techniques. Has composed a ballet (on tape); 3 symphonies and other orch. works; chamber music (incl. several pieces with the title *Improvisación*); vocal works; piano pieces.

Mather, Bruce (b. Toronto, 9 May 1939). Pupil of Morawetz, Beckwith, Weinzweig, Milhaud, Messiaen, Leland Smith, and Harris. Teacher at McGill Univ. in Montreal from 1966. Has composed orch. works (incl. *Symphonic Ode,* 1964; *Ombres,* 1967); a piano concerto; works for various instrumental ensembles; piano pieces; works for voice with instruments (incl. *Orphée,* 1963; *Madrigal II, 1968, III,* 1971).

Mathis der Maler [G., Mathias the Painter]. Opera in seven tableaux by Hindemith (to his own libretto), finished in 1934 and produced in Zürich, 1938. Setting: in and near Mainz, Germany, *c.* 1525. Three extracts (the overture, the scene at the painter's deathbed, and a crowd scene from the second act) were combined into a three-movement symphony.

Matin, Le [F., The Morning]. Popular name for Haydn's Symphony no. 6 in D, which, together with *Le midi* (Noontime), no. 7 in C, and *Le soir* (The Evening), no. 8 in G, forms a well-known group of Haydn's earliest symphonies, all having been composed about 1761.

Matins. The first of the canonical hours, consisting of the *Invitatory followed by three *nocturns. See Office.

Matrimonio segreto, Il [It., The Secret Marriage]. Opera in two acts by Cimarosa (libretto by G. Bertati, after the play *The Clandestine Marriage* by G. Colman and D. Garrick), produced in Vienna, 1792. Setting: Italy, 18th century.

Matsudaira, Yoritsune (b. Tokyo, 5 May 1907). Pupil of Tcherepnin. Has worked with Japanese musical materials and twelve-tone techniques. Has composed orch. works (incl. *Ancient Japanese Dance,* 1953); works for piano and orch.; vocal works (incl. *Metamorphosis* on an old Japanese melody, for soprano and orch., 1954); chamber music; piano pieces; songs.

Matsushita, Shin-ichi (b. Osaka, 1 Oct. 1922). Teacher at Osaka City Univ. from 1965. Has composed orch. works (incl. *Correlazioni per 3 gruppi,* 1960); works for various instrumental ensembles; electronic works; vocal works with instruments and/or tape; piano pieces.

Matteis, Nicola (b. probably in Naples; d. after 1700). Violinist and composer. Settled in London, *c.* 1672. Composed violin pieces with thoroughbass; an *Ode for St. Cecilia's Day;* songs; a manual on guitar thoroughbass. His son Nicholas (Nicola) (b. England, probably 1670; d. Shrewsbury, *c.* 1749 or Vienna, 23 Oct. 1737) was Charles Burney's teacher and a member of the Vienna court chapel from 1700 who composed violin pieces.

Mattheson, Johann (b. Hamburg, 28 Sept. 1681; d. there, 17 Apr. 1764). Singer, conductor, music theorist, and composer. Singer at the Hamburg Opera from 1695; composer and conductor there from 1699 and associate of Handel. Music director and cantor of the Hamburg Cathedral, 1715–28. Composed operas (incl. *Cleopatra,* Hamburg, 1704); oratorios and cantatas; a Mass; a Passion; chamber music; keyboard pieces; songs. Published many treatises, incl. *Der vollkommene Capellmeister,* 1739.

Matton, Roger (b. Granby, Quebec, 18 May 1929). Pupil of Champagne, N. Boulanger, and Messiaen. Teacher at Laval Univ. in Quebec from 1957. Has composed orch. works (incl. *Mouvements symphoniques* nos. 1 and 2, 1960, 1962); concertos for 2 pianos and for saxophone; choral works; chamber music; piano works (incl. *Suite on Gregorian Themes,* 1950).

Mauduit, Jacques (b. Paris, 16 Sept. 1557; d. there, 21 Aug. 1627). Lutenist and composer. Associate of Jean-Antoine de Baïf in the Académie de poésie et musique, working with *musique mesurée.* Composed a Requiem; Masses and other sacred works; ballets; *chansonettes mesurées* (on texts by Baïf); instrumental fantasies; songs.

Mavra. Opera in one act by Stravinsky (libretto by B. Kochno, based on Pushkin's story "The Little House of Kolomna"), produced in Paris, 1922. Setting: living room in a Russian village long ago.

Maw, Nicholas (b. Grantham, Lincolnshire, 5 Nov. 1935). Pupil of Berkeley and N. Boulanger. Fellow at Trinity College, Cambridge, 1966–69. Has worked with serial techniques. Has composed operas (incl. *The Rising of the Moon,* Glyndebourne, 1970); a *Sinfonia* for orch., 1966; *Scenes and Arias* for 3 women's voices and orch., 1962–69; choral works; chamber music (incl. *Chamber Music* for piano and winds, 1962); songs.

Maxfield, Richard (Vance) (b. Seattle, 2 Feb. 1927; d. Los Angeles, 27 June 1969). Pupil of Sessions, Babbitt, Krenek, Dallapiccola, Maderna, Copland, and Cage. Taught at the New School for Social Research in New York and at San Francisco State College. Worked with electronic and serial techniques. Composed an opera; ballets; instrumental works; numerous electronic works, some with instruments.

Maxima. See under Mensural notation.

Maxwell Davies, Peter. See Davies, Peter Maxwell.

Mayer, William (b. New York, 18 Nov. 1925). Pupil of Sessions, F. Salzer, and Luening. Associated with the Columbia-Princeton Electronic Music Center from 1969. Has composed operas; a ballet; orch. works (incl. *Overture for an American*, 1958); *Octagon* for piano and orch., 1966; works for brass ensembles; choral works (incl. *Brief Candle* for small chorus and chamber orch., 1965); chamber music; piano pieces; songs and other works for accompanied voice.

Mayr, Johann Simon (b. Mendorf, Bavaria, 14 June 1763; d. Bergamo, 2 Dec. 1845). Studied in Ingolstadt, Bergamo, and with Bertoni in Venice. *Maestro di cappella* at Santa Maria Maggiore in Bergamo from 1802 and director of the Musical Institute there from its founding in 1805. Donizetti was among his pupils. Composed numerous operas (incl. *Saffo*, Venice, 1794; *Lodoiska*, Venice, 1796; *Adelaide di Guesclino*, Venice, 1799; *Ginerva di Scozia*, Trieste, 1801; *Medea in Corinto*, Naples, 1813); oratorios; cantatas; liturgical music; instrumental pieces.

Mayuzumi, Toshiro (b. Yokohama, 20 Feb. 1929). Pupil of Ikenouchi and of T. Aubin in Paris. Has composed an opera; ballets (incl. *Bugaku*, 1962, choreography by George Balanchine); an oratorio; orch. works (incl. *Mandala Symphony*, 1960; *Samsara*, symphonic poem, 1962); works for various instrumental ensembles; vocal works; works on tape (incl. *Campanology*, 1959); film scores.

Mazeppa. Symphonic poem by Liszt, composed 1851, based on a poem by Victor Hugo describing the insurrection (1708) and death of the Ukrainian Cossack chief Mazeppa. The music incorporates elements from Liszt's *Mazeppa Etude* for piano, one of the **Études d'exécution transcendante* (1851).

Mazurka. A family of Polish folk dances. The mazurka is in triple meter and is performed at several speeds from moderately slow to quite rapid. One type is the **kujawiak* (not to be confused with **krakowiak*), so named because it originated in the province of Kujawy. Another is the **obertas*. Characteristic of these dances is the heavy accenting of normally weak beats. The mazurka spread throughout Europe in the 18th and 19th centuries, first as a dance and later as a source for art music. For the latter, Chopin's piano mazurkas dominate the literature.

Mazzocchi, Domenico (b. Città Castellana, Italy, bapt. 8 Nov. 1592; d. Rome, 21 Jan. 1665). Lawyer, priest, and composer. Pupil of Nanino. Contributed to the development of modern notation for dynamics. Composed operas (incl. *La catena d'Adone*, Rome, 1626); oratorios; liturgical music; madrigals and other vocal works.

Mazzocchi, Virgilio (b. Città Castellana, Italy, bapt. 22 July 1597; d. there, 3 Oct. 1646). Brother of Domenico Mazzocchi. Music theorist and composer. *Maestro* of the Cappella Giulia in Rome from 1629 to his death. Composed operas (incl. *Chi soffre, speri*, an early comic opera, in collaboration with Marazzoli, Rome, 1637); incidental music to tragedies of Seneca; oratorios; psalms; other vocal works.

McBride, Robert (Guyn) (b. Tucson, Ariz., 20 Feb. 1911). Clarinetist, oboist, and composer. Pupil of Luening. Teacher at Bennington College, 1935–46, and at the Univ. of Arizona from 1957. Has composed ballets (incl. *Jazz Symphony*, 1953; *Brooms of Mexico*, for soprano and chamber ensemble, 1970); orch. works (incl. *March of the Be-bops*, 1948; *Panorama of Mexico*, 1960; *Hill Country Symphony*, 1964); choral works; chamber music; piano pieces; songs; music for films.

McDonald, Harl (b. near Boulder, Colo., 27 July 1899; d. Princeton, N.J., 30 Mar. 1955). Pianist, conductor, and composer. Studied at the Univ. of Southern California, Redlands Univ., and the Leipzig Conservatory. Business manager of the Philadelphia Orchestra, 1939–55. Composed 4 symphonies and other orch. works; concertos for violin, for 2 pianos, and a suite for harp and orch.; choral works, some with orch.; chamber music. Published *New Methods of Measuring Sound*, 1935.

McDowell, John Herbert (b. Washington, D.C., 21 Dec. 1926). Actor, director, choreographer, and composer. Pupil of Luening, Beeson, and Goeb. Has composed operas; numerous dance scores, some for orch. and some on tape; a cantata, *Good News from Heaven*, 1956, and other choral works; chamber music; songs; theater pieces (incl. *Tumescent lingam* for oboe, chorus, tape, rock group, 101 people, 1 dog, film, lights, 1971); much other music for television, films, and theater.

McEwen, John Blackwood (b. Hawick, Scotland, 13 Apr. 1868; d. London, 14 June 1948). Pupil of Corder and Prout. Teacher at the Royal Academy of Music in London, 1898–1936, and its director from 1924. Composed 5 symphonies and other orch. works; a viola concerto; choral works; 17 string quartets and other chamber music; piano pieces; songs. Published several books on music theory and aesthetics.

McKinley, Carl (b. Yarmouth, Maine, 9 Oct. 1895; d. Boston, 24 July 1966). Pupil of Hill, N. Boulanger, and R. Goldmark. Teacher at the New England Conservatory from 1929. Composed *Masquerade, an American Rhapsody*, 1926, and other works for orch.; choral works; a string quartet and other chamber music; piano pieces; organ pieces; songs.

McPhee, Colin (b. Montreal, 15 Mar. 1901; d. Los Angeles, 7 Jan. 1964). Pupil of Strube, Le Flem, and Varèse. Lived in Bali, 1934–39, and made a study of its music. Taught at the Institute for Ethnomusicology at the Univ. of California at Los Angeles, 1958–64. Composed symphonies and other orch. works (incl. the toccata *Tabuh-Tabuhan*, 1936; *Nocturne*, 1958); a *Concerto for Wind Orchestra*, 1959; choral works; chamber music (incl. *Concerto* for piano and wind octet, 1929; *Balinese Ceremonial Music* for flute and 2 pianos, 1942); published *Music in Bali*, 1966.

M.d. Abbr. for *main droite* [F.] or *mano destra* [It.], i.e., right hand.

Mean-tone system. See under Temperament.

Meane, mene. In 15th- to 17th-century English music, a middle part of a polyphonic composition. See also Sight.

Measure [F. *mesure;* G. *Takt;* It. *misura;* Sp. *compás*]. A group of beats or pulses (units of musical time) marked off in musical notation by *bar lines. The number of beats contained in a measure and the particular note-value used to represent each beat determine the *meter or time of the measure. Most Western art music from the 17th through the 19th centuries (and most Western popular music of the 20th century) employs regularly recurring groups of beats of this kind in which the first beat is regarded as the strong beat of the measure. This type of stress or *accent results from the tonal structure of the music and does not necessarily require a coincident dynamic accent created by increased loudness. Momentary contradictions of the regular pattern of measures constitute *syncopation.

Mechanical instruments. Devices designed to produce musical performance mechanically, i.e., without an actual performer. Prior to the end of the 19th century such an apparatus was always based on a barrel-and-pin mechanism. The hand, or a mechanical clockwork, turned a cylinder bearing pins acting against levers or similar devices, which in turn operated the hammers of a keyboard instrument, the clappers of a set of bells, the mouthpieces of organ pipes, etc. As early as the 14th century, carillons were operated by such a mechanism. In the 16th century the same principle was applied to harpsichords and organs. Mozart wrote several compositions for the mechanical organ, an Adagio in F minor and an Allegro in F major (K. 594), a Fantasia in F minor (K. 608), and an Andante in F major (K. 616). The only instrument of the barrel-and-pin type that attained considerable practical importance was the English *barrel organ* of the 18th and 19th centuries. This was a small organ connected with an arrangement of interchangeable barrels, each containing a number of the most popular psalm and hymn tunes. See also *Orgue (Orgue de Barbarie).*

Toward the end of the 18th century various small instruments called *Flötenuhr* (flute-clock) were made by P. Niemecz, librarian to Prince Esterházy. They combined an ordinary clock with a set of small pipes and bellows operated by a clockwork. For these instruments (also called *Laufwerk*) Haydn wrote a number of pieces.

"Music boxes" [F. *boîte à musique, tabatière à musique;* G. *Spieldose*], whose high, thin tones have frequently been imitated in piano pieces, e.g., by A. Liadov, T. Leschetizky, and, with irony, by Stravinsky in *Petrushka* (Valse), apply the barrel-and-pin principle to a piece of metal similar to a comb, each tooth of which produces a different pitch, depending on its length.

In the early 19th century a number of instruments were built for the mechanical reproduction of entire orchestras, e.g., J. N. Maelzel's *Panharmonicon* (1804), for which Beethoven originally wrote the "Sieges-Symphonie" of his *Wellingtons Sieg* (1813), the *Appollonicon* built by Flight and Robson (1817), the *Orchestrion* of Friedrich Theodor Kaufmann (1851), and numerous others, whose descendants are still found in taverns throughout Europe, playing the same role as the American jukebox.

An important advance over the barrel-and-pin mechanism was the perforated paper-roll of the late 19th century. A roll of cardboard is pierced with small openings corresponding in position and length to the pitch and duration of the tones of the composition to be reproduced. This passes over a cylinder furnished with numerous small apertures (similar to those of the mouth harmonica), which are connected by pipes to the action of a piano. As often as an opening in the cardboard passes over the cylinder, a stream of air is pushed (or drawn) through the corresponding pipe, setting the hammer in motion. This principle has been applied with a considerable degree of accomplishment in instruments such as the *player piano,* the *Welte-Mignon,* the *Pianola,* and the *Phonola.* The player-rolls are sometimes reproductions of performances by famous virtuosos.

Medesimo tempo [It.]. The same tempo.

Medial cadence. See under Cadence.

Mediant. See under Scale degrees.

Mediation [L. *mediatio*]. See under Psalm tones.

Medieval music. See Middle Ages.

Medio registro [Sp.]. *Divided stop.

Medium, The. Opera in two acts by Gian Carlo Menotti (to his own libretto), pro- duced in 1946 at Columbia University. Setting: outside a large city, the present.

Medley. *Potpourri.

Medtner, Nikolai Karolovich (b. Moscow, 5 Jan. 1880; d. London, 13 Nov. 1951). Pianist and composer. Pupil of Arensky and Taneiev. Teacher at the Moscow Conservatory at various times until he left Russia in 1921, settling first in Berlin and later in London. Composed 3 piano concertos; numerous piano pieces (incl. 3 *Improvisations,* 1902; 34 *Fairy Tales,* 1905–29); numerous songs; chamber music.

Meeresstille und glückliche Fahrt [G., Calm Sea and Prosperous Voyage]. Orchestral overture by Mendelssohn (op. 27, 1828), based on two short poems by Goethe. The same poems were set by Beethoven as a cantata for chorus and orchestra (op. 112, 1815).

Méfano, Paul (b. Basra, Iraq, 6 Mar. 1937). Pupil of Milhaud, Messiaen, Boulez, Stockhausen, and Pousseur. Works incl. *Incidences* for piano and orch., 1960; *Paraboles* for soprano, piano, and chamber ensemble, 1964; *Interferences* for horn, piano, and chamber ensemble, 1966; *Aurélia* for 3 choruses, 3 orchestras, and 3 conductors, 1968; *Old Oedip* for narrator, actress, contact amplifiers, ring modulator, and tape, 1970.

Mehr- [G.]. More, several. *Mehrchörig,* polychoral; *Mehrsätzig,* in several movements; *Mehrstimmig,* in more than one part, i.e., polyphonic; *Mehrstimmigkeit,* polyphony.

Méhul, Étienne-Nicolas (b. Givet, near Mézières, France, 22 June 1763; d. Paris, 18 Oct. 1817). Studied in Paris and became an inspector in the newly founded Paris Conservatory in 1795. Composed operas (all for Paris, incl. *Euphrosine, ou Le tyran corrigé,* 1790; *Stratonice,* 1792; *Ariodant,* 1799; *Une folie,* 1802; *Uthal,* 1806; *Joseph,* 1807); ballets; choral works; works for orch.; chamber music; piano pieces.

Meistersinger [G., mastersinger]. A member of a literary and musical movement of the 15th and 16th centuries cultivated by the guilds of German craftsmen that represents the middle-class continuation of the aristocratic *minnesingers of the 12th to 14th centuries. Among the Meistersinger were Conrad Nachtigall, Hans Sachs (1494–1576), Georg Hager (1552–1634), Hans Folz (all in Nuremberg), Sebastian Wilde (in Augsburg), and Adam Puschmann (1532–1600, in Breslau). In the 16th century the movement spread over most of Germany, but it declined rapidly during the 17th century. Certain schools existed throughout the 18th century; that of Ulm was dissolved in 1839. Characteristic of the movement were the rigid rules that regulated the composition of songs and the procedure of weekly meetings (on Sunday, after church), the establishment of competitions and prizes, the promotion of members into various classes (*Schüler, Schulfreund, Singer, Dichter, Meister,* i.e., pupil, friend, singer, poet, master), etc. The rules were set down in the so-called *Tabulatur* (tablature). The musical repertory of the Meistersinger, as it is preserved, consists of a large number of melodies, written in a more or less free rhythm. Practically all of them are in *Bar* form, the traditional form of the minnesingers.

Meistersinger von Nürnberg, Die [G., The Mastersingers of Nuremberg]. Opera in three acts by Wagner (to his own libretto, based on Goethe, E. T. A. Hoffmann, and others), produced in Munich, 1868. Setting: Nuremberg, 16th century.

Melisma. A vocal passage sung to one syllable. The term is used particularly with reference to *Gregorian chant but may also be applied to other vocal styles.

Mellers, Wilfrid Howard (b. Leamington, England, 26 Apr. 1914). Music historian and composer. Studied at Cambridge and the Univ. of Birmingham and with Wellesz and Rubbra. Has taught at Cambridge, the Univ. of Birmingham, the Univ. of Pittsburgh, and the Univ. of York (from 1964). Works incl. an opera; *Alba* for flute and orch., 1962; *Life Cycle* for 3 choirs and 2 orchestras, 1968; *Yeibichai* for chorus, orch., jazz trio, soprano, scat singer, tapes, 1969; vocal chamber music; a string trio, 1945, and other instrumental chamber music; piano pieces. His books incl. *Man and His Music,* 1957, *Music in a New-Found Land,* 1964, and *Caliban Reborn,* 1967.

Mellophone. A brass instrument, similar to an althorn [see under Brass instruments II (f)] but in circular form, pitched in E♭ and F. It is sometimes used in bands in place of the French horn, which it resembles.

Mélodie [F.]. Solo song with accompaniment, corresponding to the German lied. See *Chanson.*

Melodrama. A stage production intermediate between play and opera, consisting of spoken text and music. The genre became very popular in the second half of the 18th century. The first full melodrama was J.-J. Rousseau's *Pygmalion* (1762), followed by Georg Benda's *Ariadne auf Naxos* (1775) and *Medea* (1775). In all of these works, spoken text and music alternate, and music sometimes serves as a background for pantomime gestures. Well-known examples of melodramatic style are the gravedigging scene in Beethoven's *Fidelio* and the incantation scene in Weber's *Der Freischütz.*

Melody. A succession of single pitches perceived as such, in contrast to *harmony, which consists of pitches sounded simultaneously or perceived primarily as constituting a simultaneity. With reference to Western tonal music, the concept typically implies an orderly succession that establishes some *key and leads to a clearly recognizable conclusion in that key. The *motion from one pitch to another in tonal melodies is largely by leap of some consonant interval or by step, and such melodies most often strongly imply certain accompanying harmonies. The tonal structure of such melodies is also intimately related to their rhythmic and metrical structure, with the result that in Western tonal music, melody, rhythm, *meter, and harmony are fundamentally inseparable.

In much (though not all) music of the 18th and 19th centuries, melody is the most prominent feature of the musical *texture, and in this period larger forms (e.g., *sonata form) are often conceived as successions of melodies. The continued popularity of the music of this period has sometimes found expression in the unjustified criticism of music from other periods and cultures as being not sufficiently melodic or devoid of melody altogether. In such a criticism, *melody* serves as an evaluative term that takes as its standard the narrowly defined class of tonal melodies described above. The musics of some non-Western cultures, however, as well as some music from the Western Middle Ages (notably liturgical chant), comprise melodies embodying tonal principles quite different from those of tonic-dominant *tonality, in some cases without any accompanying harmony. Similarly, in much Western music of the 20th century, the nature of melody is simply different from that of earlier periods.

A composition consisting of a melody without accompaniment is *monophonic. One consisting of several melodies of comparable importance performed simultaneously is *polyphonic. One consisting of a melody with clearly subordinate accompaniment in a similar rhythm is *homophonic.

Melody type. A term used in some writings on non-Western and early European music for traditional melodies, melodic formulas, stereotyped figures, tonal progressions, ornamentations, rhythmic patterns, etc., that serve as models for the creation of new melodies. To the category of melody types belong the ancient Greek *nomos,* the *echos* of Byzantine and Armenian church music, the Syrian *risqolo,* the Javanese *paṭet,* the Indian *rāga,* the Arabian *maqām,* the Persian *dastgah,* and, in Europe, the Russian *popievki* and the *Weisen* or *Töne* of the Meistersinger.

Scholars formerly considered the *rāgas, maqāmāt, echoi,* etc., as the "modes" of Hindu, Arab, Byzantine, etc., music. Actually, these and other "types" prescribe not only a scale with a given ambitus and center tone—as does a mode—but also typical motifs and tone progressions. The medieval system of eight *church modes probably developed from an earlier system of melody types, possibly from the Byzantine *echos.* Early medieval discussions of the church modes do in fact stress the importance of characteristic melodic patterns for each of the modes.

Mélophone. A free-reed instrument shaped like a guitar or hurdy-gurdy, about 32 inches long, with a broad neck and bellows housed in the body. The player activates the bellows by pushing and pulling a metal handle with the right hand, while the left hand depresses the desired keys, placed on the neck in 7 rows of 12 keys each. The instrument was invented in the 1830s in Paris. See ill. under Wind instruments.

Melopiano. See under Sostenente piano.

Membranophone. See under Instruments.

Mendelssohn, Fanny. See Hensel, Fanny Cäcilia.

Mendelssohn (Bartholdy), (Jakob Ludwig) Felix (b. Hamburg, 3 Feb. 1809; d. Leipzig, 4 Nov. 1847). Pianist, conductor, and composer. Pupil of Zelter and Moscheles. Initiated a widespread revival of interest in the music of J. S. Bach by conducting a performance of the *St. Matthew Passion* at the Berlin Singakademie in 1829. Made a series of highly successful visits to England beginning in 1829. Conductor of the Leipzig Gewandhaus Orchestra, 1835–43. Organized the Leipzig Conservatory in 1843. Works: operas (incl. *Die Hochzeit des Camacho,* Berlin, 1827); incidental music to plays (incl. Shakespeare's *A *Midsummer Night's Dream,* 1843); oratorios (incl. *St. Paul,* 1836, and *Elijah,* 1846); the symphony-cantata *Lobgesang,* 1840, also known as the Symphony no. 2; sacred and secular choral works; 5 symphonies (incl. the *Scotch,* the *Italian,* and the *Reformation*); overtures (incl. *A *Midsummer Night's Dream; Die *Hebriden* [The Hebrides, or Fingal's Cave]; *Meeresstille und glückliche Fahrt; Die schöne Melusine,* 1833; *Ruy Blas,* 1839); 2 piano concertos, 1831 and 1837; a violin concerto, 1844; 6 string quartets, 2 string quintets, a sextet for strings and piano, 2 piano trios, 3 piano quartets, a string octet (1825), a violin sonata, 2 cello sonatas, and other chamber music; piano pieces (incl. 3 sonatas; *Rondo capriccioso;* preludes and fugues; 8 books of *Lieder ohne Worte* [Songs Without Words]); organ pieces (incl. preludes and fugues; 6 sonatas); songs and vocal duets.

Mene. See Meane; also Sight.

Mennin, Peter (real name Mennini) (b.

Erie, Pa., 17 May 1923). Pupil of Lockwood, Bernard Rogers, and Hanson. Director of the Peabody Conservatory, 1958–62, and president of the Juilliard School from 1962. Has composed 8 symphonies, *Canto*, 1963, and other works for orch.; concertos for cello and for piano; the cantata *The Christmas Story*, 1949, and other choral works; 2 string quartets and other chamber music; piano pieces; songs.

Meno [It.]. Less. *Meno mosso*, less quickly.

Menotti, Gian Carlo (b. Cadegliano, Italy, 7 July 1911). Studied at the Verdi Conservatory in Milan and with Scalero at the Curtis Institute in Philadelphia. Teacher at the Curtis Institute, 1948–55. Founder of the Festival of Two Worlds at Spoleto, Italy, and since 1977 also in Charleston, S.C. Has composed operas (incl. *Amelia Goes to the Ball*, Philadelphia, 1937; *The Old Maid and the Thief*, radio broadcast, 1939; *The *Medium; The *Telephone; The *Consul; *Amahl and the Night Visitors; The Saint of Bleeker Street*, New York, 1954, awarded the Pulitzer Prize; *The Last Savage*, Paris, 1963; *Help, Help, the Globolinks*, Hamburg, 1968; *The Most Important Man in the World*, New York, 1971); ballets (incl. *Sebastian*, 1944; *The Unicorn, the Gorgon, and the Manticore*, 1956); a piano concerto, 1945, and a violin concerto, 1952; piano pieces; songs. Has written librettos for his own works and for others (incl. Barber's *Vanessa*); plays; film scripts; song texts.

Mensural music (mensurable, mensurate). Translation of L. *musica mensurata* (*cantus mensurabilis*), which in early theory (13th–16th centuries) contrasts with *musica plana*, i.e., plainsong. Mensural music is polyphonic music in which every note has a strictly determined value, as distinct from Gregorian chant, with its free rhythm. See Mensural notation.

Mensural notation. The system of musical notation that was established *c*. 1250 by Franco of Cologne and others and remained in use until 1600. This period actually embraces a variety of systems differing in many particulars [see under

Notation]. The following discussion concerns the final stage of the development (*c*. 1450–1600), called *white mensural notation*, with reference to the white shapes of the larger note values used instead of the earlier black shapes.

The notational signs fall into two classes; single notes and *ligatures. The single notes are *maxima* (Mx), *longa* (L), *brevis* (B), *semibrevis* (S), *minima* (M), *semiminima* (Sm), *fusa* (F), and *semifusa* (Sf). Table 1 shows the single notes and corresponding rests, together with the modern forms derived from them.

For the transcription into modern notation it is advisable not to use the exact equivalents (S = whole note, etc.) but smaller values that conform more closely to the actual temporal duration of the old signs. In the subsequent description a reduction of 4:1 is used so that the S is rendered as a quarter note.

Mensuration is the general term for the temporal relationships between the note values, comparable to the different meters of the modern system. Special terms are: *modus* (relationship between L and B), *tempus* (B and S), and *prolatio* (S and M). While in modern notation a note (unless dotted) is invariably equal to two notes of the next smaller value, in mensural notation the chief notes, namely L, B, and S, may equal either two or three of the next smaller value. This dichotomy is indicated by the terms *imperfect* and *perfect*, respectively. Omitting the *modus*, which is usually imperfect, there result four combinations of *tempus* and *prolatio* (e.g., *tempus perfectum cum prolatione imperfecta*), which constitute the four main mensurations of mensural notations and are indicated by special signs. They are the equivalent of four basic meters of modern notation, as shown in Table 2.

A perfect note, equal to three of the next smaller value, may be *imperfected*, i.e., made equal to two of the next

2

Tempus	Prolatio	Sign.	Value of B	Value of S	Example
I. Imperfect	Imperfect				
II. Perfect	Imperfect				
III. Imperfect	Perfect				
IV. Perfect	Perfect				

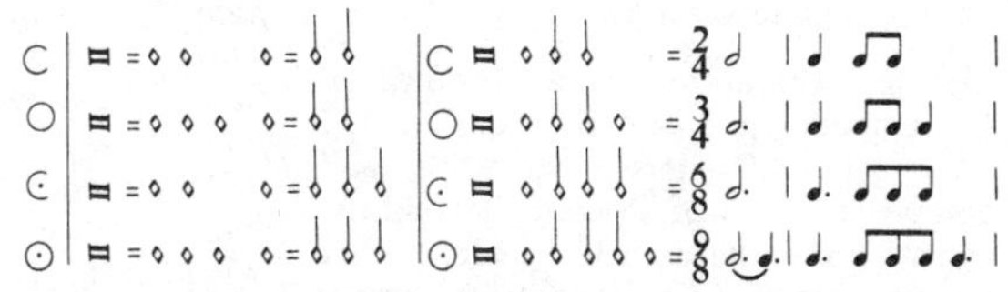

smaller value, if it is followed immediately by a single note or rest of the next smaller value (and under certain other circumstances as well). A note may be *altered,* i.e., made equal to twice its normal value, if it is the second of two notes of the same type occurring between two notes of the next higher value when the mensuration of the latter is perfect. The dot or *punctus* is used primarily to show that the note preceding is equal to three of the next lower value. Thus, in perfect mensurations it serves primarily to prevent imperfection (and alteration), whereas in imperfect mensurations it has the effect of adding to a note half of its value. *Coloration* is the substitution of black for normally white notes (or, in earlier black notation, the substitution of red for black) and serves primarily to introduce a group of three notes of some particular value in the time that would otherwise be occupied by a group of two notes of that value. This rhythmic relationship is also called **hemiola*. See also Notation; Proportions.

Mensuration. See Mensural notation.

Mensuration canon. See under Canon.

Mente, alla [It.]. Improvised.

Menuet [F.]; **Menuett** [G.]. *Minuet.

Mer, La [F., The Sea]. Three "symphonic sketches" by Debussy, composed 1903–5: *De l'aube à midi sur la mer* (From Dawn to Noon on the Sea); *Jeux de vagues* (Play of the Waves); *Dialogue du vent et de la mer* (Dialogue of the Wind and the Sea).

Mercadante, (Giuseppe) Saverio (Raffaele) (b. Altamura, near Bari, Italy, bapt. 17 Sept. 1795; d. Naples 17 Dec. 1870). Pupil of Zingarelli, whom he succeeded as director of the Naples Conservatory in 1840. *Maestro di cappella* at the Novara Cathedral from 1833 and in Lanliano from 1839. Composed operas (incl. *Elisa e Claudio,* Milan, 1821; *Il giuramento,* Milan, 1837; *La vestale,* Naples, 1840); Masses and other sacred music; orch. works; much chamber music; numerous songs.

Mercure, Pierre (b. Montreal, 21 Feb. 1927; d. en route from Paris to Lyon, 29 Jan. 1966). Bassoonist and composer. Pupil of Champagne, N. Boulanger, Dallapiccola, Pousseur, Maderna, Nono, and Berio. Producer of music programs for the French television network of the Canadian Broadcasting Corporation. Worked with aleatory and electronic techniques. Works incl. *Kaleidoscope* for orch., 1947–49; *Cantate pour une joie* for soprano, chorus, and orch., 1956; the ballet *Incandescence,* 1961, and other works on tape, some with instruments and some employing concrete sounds; film scores; chamber music.

Merikanto, Aarre (b. Helsinki, 29 June 1893; d. there, 28 Sept. 1958). Son of the composer Oskar Merikanto (1868–1924). Pupil of Reger and Vassilenko. Teacher at the Sibelius Academy in Helsinki from 1937. Composed an opera; a ballet; 3 symphonies, 5 symphonic poems, and other works for orch.; concertos for piano, for violin, for cello; chamber music; piano pieces; songs.

Merry Widow, The. See *Lustige Witwe, Die.*

Merry Wives of Windsor, The. See *Lustigen Weiber von Windsor, Die.*

Merula, Tarquinio (b. probably Cremona, *c.* 1590; d. there, 10 Dec. 1665). Organist at the court of Sigismund III of Poland, 1624. *Maestro di cappella* at the Cremona Cathedral from 1628 and from 1652; at the Bergamo Cathedral from 1639. Composed *concerti spirituali,* Masses, and other sacred works for voices with instruments; madrigals; instrumental canzonas; church and chamber sonatas; keyboard pieces.

Merulo, Claudio (real name Merlotti) (b. Correggio, bapt. 8 Apr. 1533; d. Parma, 5 May 1604). Organist, publisher, and composer. Pupil of Donato. Second organist at San Marco in Venice from 1557 and first organist, succeeding Padovano, from 1566. Court organist at Parma from 1586 and cathedral organist there from 1587. Composed ricercars, toccatas, and canzonas for organ and for instrumental ensembles; Masses, motets, and other sacred music; madrigals.

Mescolanza [It.]. *Medley.

Messa di voce [It.]. A special vocal technique of 18th-century *bel canto, consisting of a gradual crescendo and decrescendo over a sustained tone. The term should not be confused with *mezza voce. See also *Filar il tuono.

Messager, André (Charles-Prosper) (b. Montluçon, France, 30 Dec. 1853; d. Paris, 24 Feb. 1929). Pupil of Gigout, Saint-Saëns, and Fauré. Organist at Saint-Sulpice, succeeding Fauré, from 1874. Conductor at the Opéra-Comique, 1898–1903; artistic director at Covent Garden in London, 1901–7; co-director of the Paris Opéra, 1908–19. Composed operas and operettas (incl. *La basoche,* Paris, 1890; *Les p'tites Michu,* Paris, 1897; *Monsieur Beaucaire,* Birmingham, 1919); ballets; incidental music to plays; orch. works; chamber music; piano pieces; songs.

Messe [F., G.]. *Mass. *Messe des morts* [F.], *Requiem Mass.

Messiaen, Olivier (b. Avignon, 10 Dec. 1908). Pupil of J. and N. Gallon, G. Caussade, Emmanuel, Dupré, and Dukas. Organist at the Church of the Trinity in Paris from 1931. Founded "La jeune France" with Jolivet, Baudrier, and Lesur, 1936. Teacher at the Paris Conservatory from 1942 (of composition from 1966). His pupils include Boulez, Barraqué, Amy, Henry, Stockhausen, and Xenakis. Has employed techniques derived from a wide variety of materials, incl. liturgical chant, Oriental rhythms, and bird calls. Has composed orch. works (incl. *Turangalîla-symphonie,*

1948; *Chronochromie,* 1960); choral works (incl. *5 rechants,* 1948; *La transfiguration de Notre Seigneur Jésus-Christ,* with orch., 1965–69); works for instrumental ensembles (incl. *Quatuor pour la fin du temps* for violin, clarinet, cello, piano, 1941; *Oiseaux exotiques* for piano, 2 clarinets, percussion, small wind orch., 1955; *Couleurs de la cité céleste* for piano, winds, percussion, 1964); works for piano (incl. *20 regards sur l'Enfant Jésus,* 1944; *4 études de rhythme:* "Île de Feu I," "Mode de valeurs et d'intensités," "Neumes rythmiques," "Île de Feu II," 1949–50; *Catalogue d'oiseaux,* 1956–58); *Visions de l'Amen* for 2 pianos, 1943; works for organ (incl. *Apparition de l'Église éternelle,* 1931; *L'ascension,* 1933, also for orch.; *La nativité du Seigneur,* 1935; *Messe de la Pentecôte,* 1965; *Le livre d'orgue,* 1951); songs.

Messiah. Oratorio in three parts by Handel (libretto by C. Jennens, based on various books of the Bible), produced in Dublin, 1742, later revised, and published in 1767.

Mesto [It.]. Sad, mournful.

Mesure [F.]. *Measure or *meter.

Metamorphosis. See Transformation of themes.

Meter. The pattern of fixed temporal units, called beats [see Beat (1)], by which the timespan of a piece of music or a section thereof is measured. Meter is indicated by *time signatures. For instance, 3/4 meter (or 3/4 time) means that the basic values are quarter notes and that these recur in groups of three. Such metric groupings are indicated by *bar lines that mark off *measures. According to whether there are two, three, or four units to the measure, one speaks of duple (2/2, 2/4, 2/8), triple (3/2, 3/4, 3/8), and quadruple (4/2, 4/4, 4/8) meter, 4/4 also being called "common" meter. All these are simple meters. For 4/4 and 2/2 the signs C and ₵ are also used [see *Alla breve*]. *Compound meters* are simple meters multiplied by three: compound duple (6/2, 6/4, 6/8), compound triple (9/4, 9/8), and compound quadruple (12/4, 12/8, 12/16). *Quintuple meter (5/4) is usually either 2/4 + 3/4 or 3/4 + 2/4, depending on where the secondary accent lies. See also Accent; Poetic meter; Rhythm; Time signatures.

Metrical psalms. See under Psalter.

Metronome. An apparatus that sounds regular beats at adjustable speed and is used to indicate accurately an exact tempo. The instrument in general use today was invented c. 1812 by Dietrich Nikolaus Winkel of Amsterdam but is named after Johannes N. Maelzel, who usurped and exploited Winkel's invention. The Maelzel Metronome (M.M. or M.) is based on the principle of a double pendulum, i.e., an oscillating rod with a weight at each end, the one at the upper end being movable along a scale. By adjustment of this weight away from or toward the axis, the oscillations can be made slower or faster, respectively. An indication such as M.M. 80 means that the pendulum makes 80 oscillations (and sounds 80 times) per minute. In a piece marked M.M. $\mathrel{\rlap{/}{\bigcirc}} = 80$, the duration of the half note will be $\frac{60}{80} = \frac{3}{4}$ second.

Mettez [F.]. Draw (an organ stop).

Meulemans, Arthur (b. Aerschot, Belgium, 19 May 1884; d. Brussels, 29 June 1966). Pupil of Tinel. Founded and directed an organ and song school in Hasselt, 1917–30. Conductor of the orchestra of Brussels Radio, 1930–42. Composed 3 operas; 14 symphonies and other orch. works; concertos for violin, for cello, for piano, for flute, for oboe, etc.; Masses, oratorios, cantatas, and other choral works; 4 string quartets and other chamber music; piano pieces; songs.

Meyerbeer, Giacomo (real name Jakob Liebmann Beer) (b. Tasdorf, near Berlin, 5 Sept. 1791; d. Paris, 2 May 1864). Pupil of Clementi, Zelter, and Abbé Vogler. Visited Italy in 1815 on the advice of Salieri. General music director at the court in Berlin under Wilhelm IV from 1842. Composed operas (incl. *Il crociato in Egitto,* Venice, 1824; *Robert le Diable,* Paris, 1831; *Les *Huguenots; Le prophète,* Paris, 1849; *L'étoile du nord,* Paris, Opéra-Comique, 1854; *L'*africaine;* all but the first of these on librettos by Eugène Scribe); incidental music for the theater; sacred and secular

choral works; songs; instrumental pieces.

Meyerowitz, Jan (b. Breslau, 23 Apr. 1913). Pupil of Zemlinsky, Casella, and Respighi. Settled in the U.S., 1946. Teacher at Brooklyn College, 1954–61, and at the City College of New York from 1962. Has composed operas (incl. *The Barrier,* libretto by Langston Hughes, New York, 1950); *The Glory Round His Head* for soloists, chorus, and orch., 1953, and other choral works; cantatas on texts of Hughes, e. e. cummings, Robert Herrick, Emily Dickinson; orch. works (incl. the symphony *Midrash Esther,* 1954; *6 Pieces,* 1965); chamber music; piano pieces; songs.

Mezzo, mezza [It.]. Half. *Mezzo forte* (abbr. *mf*), half loud, moderately forte. *Mezza voce,* with "half voice," i.e., with restrained volume of tone [see, however, *Messa di voce*]. *Mezzo legato,* half legato. *Mezzo-soprano,* see Voices, range of.

MF [It.]. Abbr. for *mezzo forte,* half loud.

M.g. [F.]. Abbr. for *main gauche,* left hand.

Mi. See Pitch names; Solmization; Hexachord; Mi-fa.

Mi contra fa. See Mi-fa.

Mi-fa. In the theory of *hexachords used in the Middle Ages and Renaissance, a combination of *solmization syllables designating any of several dissonant intervals against which singers and composers were warned by theorists. Because each of the syllables could designate several pitches, the combination *mi-fa* could represent *tritones (called the *diabolus in musica* and to which the warning to avoid *mi contra fa* was particularly directed), minor seconds (as well as their inversions and compounds [see Interval]), and *cross relations.

Miaskovsky, Nikolai Yakovlevich (b. Novogeorgievsk, near Warsaw, 20 Apr. 1881; d. Moscow, 9 Aug. 1950). Pupil of Glière, Liadov, and Rimsky-Korsakov. Teacher at the Moscow Conservatory from 1921 until his death. Composed 27 symphonies and other orch. works; choral works (incl. the cantata *Kirov Is With Us*, 1942); a violin concerto, 1938; 13 string quartets and other chamber music; 9 sonatas and other piano pieces; songs.

Michael, David Moritz (b. Kienhausen, near Erfurt, Germany, 27 Oct. 1751; d. Neuwied, Germany, 1825). Wind player, violinist, and composer. Active in the Moravian communities in Nazareth and Bethlehem, Pennsylvania, 1796–1814. Works incl. suites for wind instruments.

Microtone. An interval smaller than a semitone. Long a structural feature of Asian music, the use of microtones in Western music, although far from new, has been far less extensive. The enharmonic system of Greek music, which gained temporary importance in the 5th century B.C., included *quarter tones. In the 16th century, the system was revived by N. Vicentino [see Arcicembalo], and various works employing microtones survive from this period. At the end of the 17th century, Christiaan Huygens proposed a division of the octave into 31 equal parts, permitting transpositions of the diatonic scales in *just intonation.

Since the late 19th century, microtones have again become widely used. In 1895, the Mexican Julián Carrillo wrote a string quartet using quarter tones [see *Sonido trece*]. Between 1903 and 1914 Charles Ives wrote a *Quarter-tone Chorale* for strings. In 1907, Busoni was considering the use of third tones (*Entwurf einer neuen Ästhetik der Tonkunst* [1906?]). Ives used quarter tones in at least two other works, *3 Quarter-tone Pieces* for two pianos tuned a quarter tone apart and his Fourth Symphony. Similar techniques were explored by Hans Barth (*Concerto for Quarter-tone Piano and Strings*, 1930), I. Vyshnegradsky (*Dithyramb*, 1926; Prelude and Fugue, 1929), and Alois Hába, whose extensive list of compositions includes works using both quarter tones and sixth tones. Both Carrillo and Harry Partch have written a considerable number of pieces using even smaller intervals.

Techniques of this kind can no longer be regarded as particularly unusual or experimental even in works for conventional instruments, much less in works employing electronic instruments that make readily possible the creation of a wide variety of microtones.

Middle Ages, music of the. The music of the period preceding the *Renaissance, roughly from 600 to 1450. See History of music; Gregorian chant; *Ars antiqua; Ars nova;* Burgundian school.

Middle C. The C near the middle of the piano keyboard, i.e., c' [see Pitch names]. It is represented on the first ledger line below the treble staff, or on the first ledger line above the bass staff.

Midi, Le [F.]. See under *Matin, Le.*

Midsummer Night's Dream, A. (1) Incidental music by Mendelssohn, op. 61, to Shakespeare's play, first performed in 1843. The overture, op. 21, was composed in 1826. (2) Opera in three acts by Britten (libretto by the composer and P. Pears, after Shakespeare's play), produced in Aldeburgh, England, 1960. Setting: a wood near Athens and Theseus' palace in Athens, legendary times.

Mignon. Opera in three acts by A. Thomas (libretto by J. Barbier and M. Carré, based on Goethe's *Wilhelm Meisters Lehrjahre*), produced in Paris, 1866. Setting: Germany and Italy, 18th century.

Mignone, Francisco (b. São Paulo, Brazil, 3 Sept. 1897). Studied in São Paulo and Milan. Teacher at the National Conservatory in São Paulo from 1929 and at the School of Music of the Univ. of Brazil in Rio de Janeiro, 1934–67. Has made extensive use of native Brazilian musical materials. Has composed operas (incl. *O contractador dos diamantes*, Rio de Janeiro, 1924); ballets (incl. *Yara*, 1946); an oratorio; orch. works (incl. *Congada*, 1922, from the opera *O contractador; Festa das Igrejas*, 1942); *4 fantasias brasileiras* for piano and orch., 1931–37, and *Seresta* for cello and orch., 1939; choral works; chamber music; numerous piano pieces; numerous songs.

Migot, Georges (Elbert) (b. Paris, 27 Feb. 1891; d. there, 5 Jan. 1976). Painter, writer, and composer. Pupil of Widor, d'Indy, Gédalge, Gigout, and Guilmant. Curator of the Museum of Ancient Instruments at the Paris Conservatory, 1949–61. Has composed operas (incl. *Le* *rossignol en amour,* 1926); ballets (incl. *Hagoromo,* 1921); oratorios (incl. *Saint-Germain d'Auxerre,* 1947) and other choral works, some with soloists and orch.; orch. works; works for solo instruments with orch. (incl. *La jungle* for organ, 1928); 12 "symphonies" for various combinations of instruments, 1919–62; chamber music; piano pieces; harpsichord pieces; organ pieces; songs.

Mihalovich, Ödön Péter József de (Edmund von) (b. Fericsancze, Hungary, 13 Sept. 1842; d. Budapest, 22 Apr. 1929). Pupil of Mosonyi, Hauptmann, and Cornelius. Succeeded Liszt as director of the Hungarian Academy of Music, 1887–1919. Composed operas (incl. *Hagbart und Signe,* Dresden, 1882; *Toldi szerelme* [Toldi's Love], Budapest, 1893); 4 symphonies and other orch. works; choral works; piano pieces; songs.

Mihalovici, Marcel (b. Bucharest, 22 Oct. 1898). Studied in Bucharest and with d'Indy in Paris. Settled in France in 1919 and taught at the Schola cantorum, 1959–62. Has composed operas (incl. *Les jumeaux,* Brunswick, Germany, 1963); ballets; incidental music for plays by Cocteau, Eliot, Beckett, and others; 5 symphonies and other orch. works; choral works; string quartets, violin sonatas, and other chamber music; piano pieces; songs.

Mikrokosmos. A collection of 153 piano pieces in six volumes by Bartók, published in the period 1926–37 and arranged in order of difficulty from very elementary works to very difficult ones.

Milán, Luís de (b. c. 1500; d. after 1561). Member of the court at Valencia. Published *Libro de musica de vihuela de mano intitulado El maestro,* 1536, containing *tientos,* fantasias, and pavanes for vihuela, along with *villancicos, romances,* and sonnets for voice accompanied by vihuela, the first of a series of such publications by Spanish composers; *El cortesano,* 1561, a book on courtly life.

Milanese chant. See Ambrosian chant.

Milford, Robin (Humphrey) (b. Oxford, 22 Jan. 1903; d. Lyme Regis, Dorsetshire, 29 Dec. 1959). Pupil of Holst,

Vaughan Williams, and R. O. Morris. Composed a children's opera; ballets (incl. *The Snow Queen,* 1946); oratorios (incl. *Pilgrim's Progress,* 1932) and other choral works; orch. works (incl. *Double Fugue,* 1927; *Concerto grosso,* 1936); a violin concerto, 1937; chamber music; piano pieces; organ pieces; songs.

Milhaud, Darius (b. Aix-en-Provence, France, 4 Sept. 1892; d. Geneva, 22 June 1974). Pupil of Leroux, Gédalge, Widor, and d'Indy. Lived in Brazil, 1917–18, as secretary to Paul Claudel, the French ambassador. Member of "Les *six.*" Emigrated to the U.S., 1940, and thereafter taught alternately at Mills College and the Paris Conservatory. Remarkably prolific, he employed a wide variety of musical materials, though his name is most often associated with the technique of polytonality. Composed operas (incl. the trilogy *L'Orestie,* 1913–24, on Claudel's translation of Aeschylus; the "opera-bouffe" *Esther de Carpentras,* 1925, prod. Paris, 1938; **Christophe Colomb; Maximilien,* Paris, 1932; *Bolivar,* 1943, prod. Paris, 1950; *David,* Jerusalem, 1954); ballets (incl. *L'homme et son désir,* 1918; *Le boeuf sur le toit,* 1919, based on popular Brazilian dance tunes, and for which Cocteau wrote the scenario subsequently, prod. 1920; *La création du monde,* 1923); incidental music for the theater; choral works; symphonies and other orch. works (incl. *Saudades do Brasil,* 1921, also for piano); concertos for various instruments, incl. percussion; string quartets (nos. 14 and 15 playable together) and other chamber music; piano pieces; works for 2 pianos (incl. *Scaramouche,* 1939); songs; music for films.

Military band. See under Symphonic band.

Military Polonaise. Familiar name for Chopin's most popular polonaise, op. 40, no. 1, in A major (publ. 1840).

Military Symphony. Popular name for Haydn's Symphony in G, no. 100 (no. 8 of the **Salomon Symphonies*), composed 1794. The second movement, Allegretto, employs triangles, cymbals, and bass drum in imitation of Turkish music [see Janizary music] and also contains a trumpet fanfare.

Millöcker, Karl (b. Vienna, 29 Apr. 1842; d. Baden, near Vienna, 31 Dec. 1899). Conductor of the Theater an der Wien, 1869–83. Composed numerous operettas (incl. *Der Bettelstudent*, Vienna, 1882, prod. in New York as *The Student Beggar*, 1883).

Mills, Charles (b. Asheville, N.C., 8 Jan. 1914). Pupil of Copland, Harris, and Sessions. Has composed music for films and television; 3 symphonies and other orch. works; concertos for flute and for piano; choral works; 5 string quartets and other chamber music (incl. *Concerto sereno* for woodwind octet, 1948); works for jazz ensemble; piano pieces; songs.

Milner, Anthony (Francis Dominic) (b. Bristol, England, 13 May 1925). Writer on music and composer. Pupil of R. O. Morris and Seiber. Has taught at Morley College, London, 1946–62; the Royal College of Music from 1961; the Univ. of London from 1965. Has composed oratorios (incl. *The Water and the Fire*, 1961); cantatas (incl. *St. Francis*, 1956) and other choral works (incl. a Mass, 1951, and a *Festival Te Deum*, 1967); orch. works (incl. a symphony, 1968, and *Variations for Orchestra*, 1958); chamber music; songs (incl. the cycle *Our Lady's Hours*, 1957).

Mimaroglu, Ilhan Kemaleddin (b. Istanbul, 11 Mar. 1926). Writer on music and composer. Pupil of Beeson, Chou Wenchung, Ussachevsky, Wolpe, and Varèse. Associate of the Columbia-Princeton Electronic Music Center, 1965–67. Teacher at Columbia Univ. from 1970. Has composed works for small instrumental ensembles; piano pieces; vocal works; electronic works (incl. *Agony; Wings of the Delirious Demon*).

Mimodrame [F.]. Older name for *panto-mime.

Mineur [F.]. Minor.

Minim [L. *minima*]. (1) British name for the half note. (2) See Mensural notation.

Minkus, (Aloysius) Ludwig (or Léon) (b. Vienna, 23 Mar. 1826; d. after 1891). Music supervisor at the Bolshoi Theater in Moscow, 1866–72; composer to the imperial ballet in St. Petersburg from 1872. Composed ballets (incl. *La fiam-metta*, 1863; *Don Quixote*, 1869; *La bayadère*, 1877).

Minnesinger [G. *Minnesänger*]. German poet-musicians of noble birth who flourished from the 12th to 14th centuries. Inspired by the French *trou-badours (not the *trouvères), the minnesingers became the leading representatives of German music during the Middle Ages. The start of the movement is usually traced to the marriage of Frederick Barbarossa to Beatrix of Burgundy in 1156. Among the most well-known minnesingers were Walther von der Vogelweide (d. 1230), Neidhardt von Reuenthal (*c.* 1180–1240), Tannhäuser (mid-13th cent.), Heinrich von Meissen, called Frauenlob (d. 1318), Wizlav von Rügen (d. 1325), Hermann Münch von Salzburg (*c.* 1350–1410), and Oswald von Wolkenstein (*c.* 1377–1445). The works embodying the minnesinger tradition are exclusively monophonic songs (though the two last-named composers also wrote some polyphony), the rhythms of which are still not entirely agreed upon, with both narrative and lyrical texts on sacred as well as secular subjects. The principal forms employed are the *Bar and the *Leich* [see under *Lai*].

Minor. See Major, minor.

Minstrel. (1) Originally, the professional musician (instrumentalist) of the Middle Ages, especially one employed in a feudal household. In the 11th and 12th centuries *jongleurs* were employed by the troubadours and trouvères [see Troubadour]. In the 14th century the name *jongleur* was replaced by *ménestrier*, probably in order to distinguish a class of higher social standing and professional repute. The *ménestriers* became organized in guilds known as *ménestrandise*, similar to those of the medieval craftsmen. In England, a class of acrobat-musicians was known as "gleemen," and in Germany as *Gaukler*. The term *minstrel* appeared in the early 14th century. Guilds and fraternities were gradually formed, whose history can be traced at least to the beginning of the 17th century. The German counterparts of these guild musicians were the *Stadtpfeifer*. (2) More generally, a popular musical entertainer of any period. (3) In the United States, a white entertainer dressed and made up as a black, singing songs and telling jokes in imitation of North American Negroes. After about 1830 and the first entertainment of this kind by Thomas Rice, numerous troupes of such entertainers were formed to produce minstrel shows, most of the music for which was composed by white men, among them Stephen Foster.

Minuet [F. *menuet;* G. *Menuett;* It. *minuetto;* Sp. *minué, minuete*]. A French country dance from Poitou introduced at the court of Louis XIV about 1650. It quickly spread throughout Europe, completely superseding the older types (courantes, pavanes) and establishing a new period of dance and dance music. Lully introduced the minuet into his ballets and operas, and G. Muffat, J. Pachelbel, and J. K. F. Fischer used it in their suites (*c.* 1700). Many of these minuets already show the *alternativement* arrangement of two minuets, M_1 M_2 M_1, which is the origin of the minuet and trio movement of the sonata [see Trio (2)]. The operatic sinfonias of Alessandro Scarlatti (1660–1725) and others usually close with a minuet, as do many of the symphonies and sonatas of the pre-Haydn period. The minuet with trio as the next to last movement is found in practically all the symphonies of the *Mannheim school [see Sonata].

The minuet is in 3/4 meter; originally, it was in moderate tempo. In the symphonies of Haydn and Mozart the minuet became faster, and humorous or whimsical in character, like the *scherzo, which replaces the minuet in some works of Beethoven. See also Dance music and, for the internal structure of the minuet, Binary and ternary form.

Minute Waltz. Popular name for Chopin's Waltz in Db, op. 64, no. 1, derived from the fact that it lasts approximately one minute when played at a very rapid tempo.

Miracle play. See under Liturgical drama.

Mirliton [F.]. An instrument consisting of a pipe closed at one end by a membrane. Directing the natural voice against the membrane alters the tone and

makes the timbre quite nasal. In the 17th century the instrument was known as the *flûte-eunuque* (eunuch flute). The musical toy common today shaped approximately like a cigar and known as a kazoo is a kind of mirliton.

Miroglio, Francis (b. Marseille, 12 Dec. 1924). Studied at the Marseille Conservatory, with Milhaud at the Paris Conservatory, and with Maderna at Darmstadt. Has employed serial and aleatory procedures in the creation of mobile forms, some in alternate versions. Works incl. *Espaces* for large orch., 1962, and other works with the same title for diverse ensembles; *Phases,* in versions for 4 different chamber ensembles, 1965; *Insertions* for harpsichord, 1969.

Mirror composition. One that can be performed in *inversion with respect to the intervals of each part as well as the relationship of all of the parts to one another (thus, as if it were being performed from a mirror held below the notation) or one that can be performed in *retrograde (i.e., backwards, as if from a mirror held at the end of the notation). Canons and fugues are sometimes composed according to these principles. Well-known examples occur in Bach's The *Art of Fugue.

Miserere [L.]. Psalm 50 (51): "Miserere mei, Deus, secundum magnam misericordiam tuam" (Have mercy upon me, O God, according to thy loving kindness). In the Roman Catholic rites it is sung as the first psalm of Lauds on Maundy Thursday, Good Friday, and Holy Saturday [see Tenebrae]; also at Lauds of the Office for the Dead and during the Burial Service. It is one of the penitential psalms and has been composed polyphonically as such, but also independently. The celebrated composition by Gregorio Allegri (*c.* 1582–1652) that remained in use at the papal chapel until 1870, alongside Palestrina's *Improperiae and *Lamentations, is in a plain *falsobordone* style.

Missa [L.]. *Mass. Missa solemnis* (solemn Mass, High Mass) is the Mass in its full form, with all the items (except for lections, etc.) sung, while in the *Missa lecta* (read Mass, Low Mass) there is no music, except perhaps hymn singing. *Missa cantata* (sung Mass) is, from the musical point of view, identical with the High Mass but is celebrated in a less elaborate manner. Beethoven's *Missa Solemnis* (op. 123, composed 1818–23), like most polyphonic Masses, consists of settings of the five sung parts of the Mass Ordinary. The *Missa brevis,* short Mass, sometimes consists of settings of only the Kyrie and Gloria. *Missa pro defunctis,* Mass for the Dead, *Requiem Mass. *Missa Papae Marcelli,* see Marcellus Mass. *Missa L'homme armé,* see *Homme armé, L'.*

Missal [L. *missale*]. See under Liturgical books.

Misura [It.]. Measure, beat. *Alla misura,* in strict time; *senza misura,* without strict time.

Mit [G.]. With. For phrases beginning with this word, see under the noun following.

Mixed voices. A combination of men's and women's voices [see Equal voices].

Mixolydian. See under Church modes.

Mixture stop. See under Organ.

Miyoshi, Akira (b. Tokyo, 10 Jan. 1933). Studied at Tokyo Univ. and at the Paris Conservatory. Has taught at Tokyo Univ. of the Arts since 1966. Has composed *Concerto for Orchestra,* 1964, and other orch. works; concertos for piano, for violin, for marimba; *Red Death I* for orch. and tape, 1969; string quartets and other chamber music; piano pieces.

M.M. See under Metronome.

Mobile forms. See Aleatory music.

Modal. Pertaining to a mode, either a *church mode (e.g., modal harmony; see Modality) or the rhythmic modes [see Modes, rhythmic] of the 13th century (e.g., modal notation, modal interpretation, modal rhythm).

Modality. The use of harmonic and melodic formations based on the *church modes, as opposed to those based on the major and minor modes (*tonality). In particular, the term refers to the use of modal idioms in the prevailingly tonal music of the 19th and 20th centuries.

Mode. (1) The selection of tones, arranged in a scale, that form the basic tonal substance of a composition. In a narrower sense, any of the *church modes. See also Melody type; Scale. (2) See Modes, rhythmic; also *Modus.*

Moderato [It.]. In moderate speed, i.e., between andante and allegro.

Modes, rhythmic. Certain simple rhythmic patterns in ternary meter, consistently repeated in a 12th- and 13th-century system of rhythm. Usually six modes are distinguished, as shown below. The Greek names (added in parentheses) were not used until relatively late (W. Odington, *c.* 1290). In musical compositions, the patterns were reiterated a number of times, depending on the length of the phrase—in medieval terminology, the *ordo.* The *ordo* indicated the number of times a rhythmic pattern was repeated without interruption. The modes are the rhythmic basis of the *organa, *clausulae,* and *motets of the 13th century, which are therefore said to be written in *modal notation.* Some scholars have argued for the application of these rhythms to the *conductus and to medieval monophonic music such as that of the trouvères and troubadours. In practice, certain modifications of the normal patterns were admitted, such as occasional omission of a weak beat or breaking up of one note into two or three.

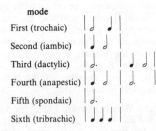

Modulation. Change of key within a composition. A modulation is often effected by means of a *pivot chord,* i.e., a chord common to both the initial and the new key. For instance, in Ex. 1, the third chord is the pivot chord, being I in the old key (C) and IV in the new key (G). In Ex. 2, the same chord adopts the function of VII in D (properly, D minor), while in Ex. 3, V of C is reinterpreted as III of E (properly, E minor).

Usually three types of modulation are distinguished: diatonic, chromatic, and enharmonic. A diatonic modulation is made through a chord that is diatonic in both keys. Ex. 1–3 belong to this category. A chromatic modulation is made through a chord that is chromatically altered in one or both keys, a very common example being the modulation through the Neapolitan sixth [Ex. 4]. Enharmonic modulation involves the enharmonic change of one or several notes. This is frequently achieved through the diminished seventh [Ex. 5]. If the new key is touched upon only momentarily, leading quickly into a third key, the modulation is sometimes said to be *false* or *passing* [but see also Tonicization].

As described here, modulation is a phenomenon of tonic-dominant *tonality inasmuch as it relies on the existence of a set of tonal centers or keys that are clearly defined in themselves and in relation to one another. Even within this system, modulations vary widely in character, depending in part on the relationship of the two keys in question [see Key relationship], the ways in which the modulations are prepared by preceding musical events in a particular composition, their duration, and the relative emphasis given to the key that is reached. Thus, the nature of modulation has changed as musical language has changed. Modulations can be said to occur also in some pretonal works (e.g., in some works of the Renaissance) that in general employ a more limited system of keys.

Modulator. See Tonic sol-fa.

Modus [L.]. (1) *Church mode; see also Tonus. (2) *Mode, rhythmic. (3) In *mensural notation, *modus major* (*modus maximarum*) denotes the relationship between the *maxima* and the *longa*, and *modus minor* (*modus longarum*), or simply *modus*, that between the *longa* and the *brevis*. In English books, Morley's translations "greater mood" and "lesser mood" are frequently used in this sense.

Moeran, Ernest John (b. Heston, Middlesex, 31 Dec. 1894; d. Kenmare, Ireland, 1 Dec. 1950). Pupil of Ireland. Composed a symphony in G minor, 1937, and other orch. works; concertos for violin and for cello; choral works; chamber music; piano pieces; numerous songs and arrangements of folksongs.

Moeschinger, Albert (Jean) (b. Basel, 10 Jan. 1897). Studied in Bern, Leipzig, and Munich. Teacher at the Bern Conservatory, 1937–43. Has composed an opera; incidental music for the theater; ballets; 4 symphonies and other orch. works; concertos for piano, for violin, for clarinet, for trumpet; choral works (incl. a Mass and motets); string quartets and other chamber music; piano pieces; organ pieces; songs.

Moevs, Robert (Walter) (b. La Crosse, Wis., 2 Dec. 1920). Pupil of Piston and N. Boulanger. Teacher at Harvard Univ., 1955–63, and at Rutgers from 1964. Works incl. *14 Variations for Orchestra*, 1952; *Et occidentem illustra* for chorus and orch., 1964; *A Brief Mass*, 1968, and other sacred choral works; *Musica da camera*, 1965, and other chamber music; piano pieces; songs.

Mohaupt, Richard (b. Breslau, 14 Sept. 1904; d. Reichenau, Austria, 3 July 1957). Pianist, conductor, and composer. Lived in New York, 1939–55. Composed operas; ballets; a symphony and other orch. works (incl. *Stadtpfeifermusik*, 1946); concertos for piano, for violin; choral works; chamber music; piano pieces; songs.

Moldau, The. English title of the second (*Vltava*) of Smetana's symphonic poem cycle *Má Vlast*.

Moll [G.]. Minor, e.g., *G moll*, G minor. See *Dur*.

Moller, John Christopher (d. New York, 21 Sept. 1803). German organist and composer, active in New York from 1790; organist at Zion Church in Philadelphia from 1793; and manager of the New York City Concerts from 1796. Works incl. chamber music; harpsichord and piano pieces, some with violin or cello; a piano method.

Molter, Johann Melchior (b. Tiefenort, Werra, Germany, 10 Feb. 1696; d. Karlsruhe, 12 Jan. 1765). *Kapellmeister* at the court of the Margrave of Baden in Durlach, 1722–33, and in Karlsruhe from 1743. Composed numerous symphonies, overtures, and concertos; operas; cantatas; a Passion; sonatas.

Molto [It.]. Very. *Molto allegro (adagio)*, very quick (slow).

Moments musicals [F., Musical Moments, correctly *Moments musicaux*]. Title of Schubert's six piano pieces op. 94, D. 780 (1828?). See under Character piece.

Mompou, Federico (b. Barcelona, 16 Apr. 1893). Studied in Barcelona and in Paris (where he lived 1911–14 and 1921–41). Has made use of native Spanish musical materials. Has composed works for piano (incl. *Scènes d'enfants*, 1915–18; *Canción y danza* nos. 1–12, 1919–62); songs and other works for voice and piano (incl. *Combat del somni*, 1942–51; *Llueve sobre el río*, text by Juan Ramón Jiménez, 1945); choral works; *Suite compostelana* for guitar.

Moncayo, José Pablo (b. Guadalajara, Mexico, 29 June 1912; d. Mexico City, 16 June 1958). Pupil of Chávez, Candelario Huízar, and Copland. Conductor of the National Symphony Orchestra of Mexico and teacher at the National Conservatory from 1949. Works incl. an opera, *La mulata de Córdoba*, Mexico City, 1948; ballets; *Huapango*, 1941, and *Homenaje a Cervantes* for orch.; chamber music; piano pieces.

Mondonville, Jean-Joseph Cassanéa de (b. Narbonne, France, bapt. 25 Dec. 1711; d. Belleville, near Paris, 8 Oct. 1772). Violinist and composer. Participant in the Concert spirituel from 1734 and its director, 1755–62. Intendant of the music of the chapel at Versailles,

1745–58. Composed operas (incl. *Titon et l'Aurore*, Paris, 1753); oratorios; motets; sonatas for violin with thoroughbass (incl. the collection *Les sons harmoniques*, 1736); keyboard sonatas with violin accompaniment.

Mondscheinsonate [G.]. *Moonlight Sonata.

Monferrina. A country dance from Piedmont (north Italy) in 6/8 time that became fashionable in England *c.* 1800, where it usually was called *monfrina*, *monfreda*, or *manfredina*.

Moniuszko, Stanislaw (b. Ubiel, Minsk, Russia, 5 May 1819; d. Warsaw, 4 June 1872). Studied in Warsaw and Berlin. Church organist in Vilna from 1840 until 1858, when he settled in Warsaw and became a teacher at the conservatory there. Composed operas (incl. *Halka*, the first Polish national opera, Vilna, 1848, rev. Warsaw, 1858; *The Raftsman*, Warsaw, 1858; *The Countess*, Warsaw, 1860; *The Haunted Manor*, Warsaw, 1865); ballets; Masses and other sacred and secular choral works; a symphonic poem; 2 string quartets; numerous songs.

Monn, Mathias (Johann) Georg (Mann) (b. Vienna, 9 Apr. 1717; d. there, 3 Oct. 1750). Organist at the Karlskirche in Vienna. Composed symphonies; concertos; Masses; string quartets and other chamber music; harpsichord sonatas.

Monochord. A device consisting of a single string stretched over a long wooden resonator to which a movable bridge is attached so that the vibrating length of the string can be varied. The monochord was widely used in antiquity (under the name *kanon) and in the Middle Ages for the investigation and demonstration of the laws of musical acoustics, a purpose for which it is still used today.

Monocordo. In violin playing, the performance of a piece or passage on a single string.

Monodrama. A dramatic work for a single singer or actor, e.g., Berlioz' *Lélio* and Schoenberg's *Erwartung*.

Monody. Occasionally a term for *monophonic music or for accompanied solo song in general but more properly a par-

accompanied solo song about 1600 in reaction to ‌ style of the 16th century characterized by recitative- of the voice-part and by thor- companiment. Some of the nples of true monody were a Caccini's Le *nuove mu-*.

monophonic. Music consist- le melodic line without addi- or accompaniment, as op- lyphony, *homophony, etc.].

ic, polythematic. Terms de- mpositions based on one , a fugue) or several themes ata or a movement in sonata form). They are applied particularly to the imitative forms of the 16th and 17th centuries, such as the fantasia and ricer- car.

Monotone. The recitation of a liturgical text on an unchanged pitch, as in psalms, prayers, lessons (reading from the Scrip- tures). Usually, monotonic declamation is modified by *inflections,* i.e., a few as- cending or descending tones at the begin- ning, middle, or end of the phrase of the text. See Psalm tones.

Monsigny, Pierre-Alexandre (b. Fau- quembergues, near Saint-Omer, France, 17 Oct. 1729; d. Paris, 14 Jan. 1817). Studied music as a child but supported himself first as a government clerk and later as *maître d'hôtel* to the Duke of Orléans. Subsequently took lessons in composition. Inspector at the Paris Con- servatory, 1800–1802, succeeding Pic- cinni. Composed operas (incl. *Le roi et le fermier,* Paris, 1762; *Rose et Colas,* Paris, 1764; *Le déserteur,* Paris, 1769).

Monte, Philippe de (Filippo di Monte) (b. Malines, Belgium, 1521; d. Prague, 4 July 1603). Lived in Italy, c. 1540–54, and at various times thereafter. Visited England in 1555 as a member of the choir of Philip II of Spain. *Maestro di cappella* to the Emperor Maximilian II in Vienna and Prague. Composed Masses, motets, madrigals, chansons.

Montéclair, Michel Pinolet de (b. Ande- lot, France, bapt. 4 Dec. 1667; d. near Saint-Denis, 27 Sept. 1737). Double bass

player at the Paris Opéra from 1707. Composed the opera-ballet *Les fêtes de l'été,* Paris, 1716; the biblical opera *Jephté,* Paris, 1732; cantatas; motets; trio sonatas and other instrumental pieces; airs. He published a violin method, 1712, and two treatises on music.

Montemezzi, Italo (b. Vigasio, near Verona, 4 Aug. 1875; d. there, 15 May 1952). Studied at the Milan Conserva- tory. Lived in the U.S., 1939–49. Com- posed operas (incl. *L'amore dei tre re,* Milan, 1913; *La nave,* Milan, 1918); 2 symphonic poems; a cantata; an elegy for cello and piano.

Monteverdi, Claudio (Giovanni Antonio) (b. Cremona, bapt. 15 May 1567; d. Ven- ice, 29 Nov. 1643). Boy chorister at the Cathedral of Cremona under Ingegneri. Musician to Vincenzo Gonzaga, Duke of Mantua, c. 1590, and his *maestro di cap- pella* from 1602 until Vincenzo's death in 1612. *Maestro di cappella* at San Marco in Venice from 1613. Composed operas (incl. *La *favola d'Orfeo; L'Arianna,* of which only the "Lament" survives, Mantua, 1608; *Il ritorno d'Ulisse in pa- tria,* Venice, 1641; *L'*incoronazione di Poppea;* and approximately 10 others now lost); the ballet-opera *Il ballo delle ingrate,* Mantua, 1608; 9 books of madri- gals (the fifth, 1605, being the first to in- clude a *basso continuo;* the 8th, *Madri- gali guerrieri et amorosi,* 1638, includes *Il *combattimento di Tancredi e Clorinda*); Masses, motets, Vespers, Magnificats, and other sacred works.

Montezuma. Opera by Sessions, first produced in Berlin, 1964. Setting: Mex- ico, 1519–20.

Montsalvatge, Xavier (b. Gerona, Spain, 11 Mar. 1912). Pupil of Pahissa. Teacher at various institutions in Barcelona from 1960 and music critic for the newspaper *La vanguardia* there from 1962. Has composed operas (incl. *El gato con botas,* 1948); ballets; orch. works (incl. *Sinfonía mediterránea,* 1949; *Desinte- gración morfológica de la "Chacona" de Bach,* 1963); *Concierto breve* for piano and orch., 1953; chamber music; piano pieces; *5 canciones negras* for so- prano and piano or orch., 1950, and other songs.

Mood. See *Modus* (3).

Moonlight Sonata [G. *Mondscheinsonate*]. Popular name for Beethoven's *Sonata quasi una fantasia* op. 27, no. 2 (1801), in C♯ min. for piano.

Moór, Emanuel (b. Kecskemét, Hungary, 19 Feb. 1863; d. Vevey, Switzerland, 20 Oct. 1931). Pianist, conductor, and composer. Studied in Budapest and Vienna. Invented the Moór-Duplex piano with two manuals, tuned an octave apart, that can be coupled. Composed operas; symphonies and other orch. works; concertos for piano, for violin, for cello; string quartets, violin sonatas, and other chamber music; piano pieces; numerous songs.

Moore, Douglas (Stuart) (b. Cutchogue, N.Y., 10 Aug. 1893; d. Greenport, N.Y., 25 July 1969). Conductor and composer. Pupil of Parker, d'Indy, N. Boulanger, and Bloch. Teacher at Columbia Univ. from 1926. Composed operas (incl. *The *Devil and Daniel Webster; Giants in the Earth*, New York, 1951, awarded the Pulitzer Prize; *Ballad of Baby Doe; Gallantry*, New York, 1958; *The Wings of the Dove*, New York, 1961; *Carry Nation*, Lawrence, Kans., 1966); orch. works (incl. *Pageant of P. T. Barnum*, 1924; *Symphony in A*, 1945; *Farm Journal*, 1947); choral works; chamber music; songs.

Morales, Cristóbal de (b. Seville, *c*. 1500; d. Málaga, between 4 Sept. and 7 Oct. 1553). *Maestro de capilla* at the Cathedral of Ávila from 1526. Member of the papal choir in Rome, 1535–45. *Maestro de capilla* at the Cathedral of Toledo, 1545–47; at the Cathedral of Málaga, 1551 until his death. Composed Masses, motets, Magnificats, Lamentations, and other sacred works; a few secular vocal works.

Moran, Robert (Leonard) (b. Denver, Colo., 8 Jan. 1937). Pupil of Apostel, Milhaud, and Haubenstock-Ramati. Director of the New Music Ensemble in San Francisco, 1966–72. Has worked with mixed media and graphic notation. Works incl. *Interiors* for chamber ensemble, or orchestra, or percussion ensemble, 1964; *Hallelujah* for 20 marching bands, drum and bugle corps, choruses, carillons, organs, rock groups, blimp, spotlights, automobile horns, etc., for performance by the 75,000 inhabitants of Bethlehem, Pennsylvania, 1970.

Morawetz, Oskar (b. Svetla, Czechoslovakia, 17 Jan. 1917). Pupil of Křička. Settled in Canada in 1940. Teacher at the Royal Conservatory in Toronto, 1946–56, and at the Univ. of Toronto from 1952. Has composed symphonies and other orch. works; a piano concerto, 1962; *From the Diary of Anne Frank* for soprano and orch., 1970; choral works; string quartets and other chamber music; piano pieces; songs.

Morceau [F.]. Piece, composition.

Mordent [G.; F. *mordant* (Old F. *pincé, pincement*); It. *mordente;* Sp. *mordiente*]. A musical ornament, primarily of the baroque period, consisting of the alternation of the written note with the note immediately below it. It is indicated by one of the signs given in Ex. 1 (the third sign is used only in music for bowed instruments). In performance the mordent always occupies part of the value of the written note and should not be introduced before it. The alternations of the written note and the auxiliary may be either single or double [Ex. 2] (there is a special sign for the latter [Ex. 3], but it is not often used). The choice between these executions is generally left to the performer, whose decision is based chiefly on the duration of the written note. Contemporary authorities recommend that if two mordents occur in close succession, one should be made single and the other double. See also Inverted mordent.

Moreau, Jean-Baptiste (b. Angers, France, 1656; d. Paris, 24 Aug. 1733). After holding posts in Angers, Langres, and Dijon, went to Paris in 1686 and entered the service of Louis XIV. Composed divertissements, incl. *Les bergers de Marly,* 1687; musical interludes for Racine's *Esther,* 1698, and *Athalie,* 1691; music for several of Racine's *Cantiques spirituels;* a *Te Deum.*

Morel, François d'Assise (b. Montreal, 14 Mar. 1926). Pupil of Champagne. Has composed *Antiphonie,* 1953, *Rituel de l'espace,* 1958, and other works for orch.; string quartets and other works for instrumental ensembles of various sizes; works for jazz ensemble; piano pieces; songs; music for theater and films.

Morendo [It.]. Dying, fading away.

Moresca [It.]; **morisca** [Sp.]. A pantomimic dance of the 15th and 16th centuries that was executed in Moorish costume and other grotesque disguises, the dancers having their faces blackened and small bells attached to their legs. It was easily the most popular dance for the ballets and mummeries of the Renaissance. The two types were a solo dance and a dance of two groups that represented a sword fight between Christians and Moslems. Dances of this kind are still known today in Spain, Corsica, and Guatemala. In England they survived under the name "Morris dance." For the vocal *moresca,* see under *Villanella.*

Morlacchi, Francesco (b. Perugia, 14 June 1784; d. Innsbruck, 28 Oct. 1841). Pupil of Zingarelli. Director of the Italian opera from 1810 and later *Kapellmeister* at the court in Dresden. Composed operas (incl. *Le Danaidi,* Rome, 1810; *Tebaldo ed Isolina,* Venice, 1822); oratorios; cantatas; Masses and other sacred works.

Morley, Thomas (b. 1557; d. Oct. 1602). Pupil of Byrd. Organist at St. Paul's Cathedral, London, in 1591. Gentleman of the Chapel Royal from 1592. Granted a patent to publish music in 1598 and brought out collections (some including works of his own) of madrigals and other secular vocal works, incl. *The Triumphs of Oriana,* 1601; a collection of consort lessons; a collection of lute songs; and his own treatise, *A Plaine and Easie Introduction to Practicall Musicke,* 1597. Composed madrigals, canzonets, balletts, anthems, services, motets, lute songs.

Moroi, Makoto (b. Tokyo, 17 Dec. 1930). Son of Saburo Moroi. Pupil of Ikenouchi. Has employed the bamboo flute and other native Japanese instruments. Works incl. a symphony with optional tape, 1968; *Développements raréfiants* for soprano and instruments, incl. Ondes Martenot, 1957; a piano concerto, 1966.

Moroi, Saburo (b. Tokyo, 7 Aug. 1903). Studied at Tokyo Univ. and at the Berlin Hochschule für Musik. Superintendent of music in the Japanese Ministry of Education, 1946–64. Director of the Senzokugakuen Music Academy from 1967. Has composed 5 symphonies and other orch. works; concertos for piano, for cello, for violin; an oratorio; chamber music; piano pieces.

Moross, Jerome (b. Brooklyn, 1 Aug. 1913). Studied at New York Univ. and at the Juilliard School. Has composed operas and ballet-operas (incl. *Susanna and the Elders,* 1940); a symphony, 1941, *A Tall Story,* 1938, and other orch. works; choral works; chamber music; piano pieces; music for films and television.

Morris, Harold (b. San Antonio, Tex., 17 Mar. 1890; d. New York, 6 May 1964). Pianist and composer. Studied at the Univ. of Texas, at the Cincinnati Conservatory, and with Scalero. Teacher at the Juilliard School, 1922–39, and at Columbia Univ., 1939–46. Composed orch. works (incl. 3 symphonies; *Poem,* after Tagore, 1918); a piano concerto, 1931, and a violin concerto, 1939; chamber music; piano pieces.

Morris, R. O. (Reginald Owen) (b. York, 3 Mar. 1886; d. London, 14 Dec. 1948). Pupil of C. Wood. Teacher at the Royal College of Music in London from 1920, except for the years 1926–28, when he taught at the Curtis Institute in Philadelphia. Composed a symphony in D, 1934; chamber music; songs. Published criticism in *The Nation* and several textbooks on music theory.

Morris dance. See under *Moresca.*

Mortari, Virgilio (b. Passirana di Lainate, near Milan, 6 Dec. 1902). Pupil of Pizzetti and Bossi. Teacher at the Benedetto Marcello Conservatory in Venice, 1933–40, and at the Santa Cecilia Conservatory in Rome from 1940. Has composed operas (incl. *La figlia del diavolo,* Milan, 1954); a ballet; orch. works; a piano concerto; works for voices and instruments; chamber music; arrangements of works by Galuppi, Pergolesi, Monteverdi, Mozart.

Mortelmans, Lodewijk (b. Antwerp, 5 Feb. 1868; d. there, 24 June 1952). Pupil of Benoit and Blockx. Teacher at the Antwerp Conservatory from 1902 and its director, 1924–33. Composed an opera; symphonic poems and other orch. works; choral works; piano pieces; songs with Flemish texts.

Mortensen, Finn (Einar) (b. Oslo, 6 Jan. 1922). Pupil of Egge and Niels Viggo Bentzon. Teacher at the Oslo Conservatory from 1970. Has composed orch. works (incl. a symphony, 1953; *Evolution*, 1961); a piano concerto, 1963; chamber music; piano pieces.

Morton, Robert (d. 1475). English composer. Singer at the Burgundian court from 1457 and chaplain there from 1470. Composed French chansons.

Moscheles, Ignaz (b. Prague, 23 May 1794; d. Leipzig, 10 Mar. 1870). Pianist and composer. Pupil of Albrechtsberger and Salieri. Associate of Beethoven, Hummel, and Meyerbeer. Piano teacher and associate of Mendelssohn. Traveled widely as a virtuoso pianist. Settled in London in 1821 and was a teacher at the Royal Academy of Music there until 1846, when he joined the staff of the Leipzig Conservatory at Mendelssohn's invitation, remaining there until his death. Composed 8 piano concertos and other works for piano and orch.; chamber music with piano; numerous piano pieces (incl. *Sonate caractéristique; Sonate mélancolique;* etudes and other didactic works).

Moses und Aron. Unfinished opera in three acts by Schoenberg (to his own libretto), acts 1 and 2 completed in 1932; composition resumed, but not completed, in 1951. Produced in Hamburg, 1954, concert performance; Zürich, 1957, stage performance. Setting: Mt. Sinai, biblical times.

Mosonyi, Mihály (real name Michael Brand) (bapt. Boldogasszonyfalva, Hungary, now Frauenkirchen, Austria, 4 Sept. 1815; d. Budapest, 31 Oct. 1870). Double bass player and composer. Associate of Liszt. Composed operas (incl.

Szép Ilonka [Fair Ilonka], Budapest, 1861); 2 symphonies and other orch. works (incl. *Funeral Music for Széchenyi,* 1860); 5 Masses and other sacred and secular choral works; 6 string quartets and other chamber music; songs.

Moss, Lawrence (b. Los Angeles, 18 Nov. 1927). Pupil of Kirchner and Dahl. Teacher at Mills College, 1956–59; at Yale Univ. 1960–69; at the Univ. of Maryland from 1969. Has composed operas (incl. *The Brute,* 1960; *The Queen and the Rebels,* 1965); orch. works (incl. *Scenes for Small Orchestra,* 1961); chamber music (incl. *Timepiece* for violin, piano, percussion, 1970; *Auditions* for woodwind quintet and tape, 1971); piano pieces; songs (incl. *3 Rilke Songs,* 1963).

Mosso [It.]. Moved, agitated.

Mossolov, Alexander Vasilievich (b. Kiev, 11 Aug. 1900; d. Moscow, 12 July 1973). Pianist and composer. Pupil of Glière and Miaskovsky. Collected and arranged folksongs. Composed operas; 6 symphonies and other orch. works (incl. *Zavod* [The Factory, or The Iron Foundry], 1927); concertos for piano, for cello, for harp; *Kirghiz Rhapsody,* for soprano, chorus, and orch. 1933; choral works; chamber music; songs.

Moszkowski, Moritz (b. Breslau, 23 Aug. 1854; d. Paris, 4 Mar. 1925). Pianist and composer. Studied at the Dresden Conservatory and at the Kullak Academy in Berlin, where he later taught. Settled in Paris, 1897. Composed an opera; a ballet; orch. works; concertos for piano and for violin; chamber music; piano pieces (incl. 2 books of *Spanish Dances* for one or two pianos; etudes).

Motet. The most important form of polyphonic music during the Middle Ages and Renaissance. It is impossible to formulate a general definition that covers all the phases of its development during the more than five centuries of its existence (*c.* 1220–1750). In general, however, a motet is an unaccompanied choral composition based on a Latin sacred text.

The medieval motet originated in the early 13th century, possibly as early as 1200, through the addition of a full text to the upper parts of *clausulae. Owing to the addition of mots [F., words], the upper part (duplum) with text was called the motetus, a name that was adopted for the entire composition. The tenor of such a motet (like that of a clausula) is practically always a melismatic (vocalized) passage taken from a Gregorian chant (usually a Gradual, Alleluia, or responsory) and identified by the word or syllable with which it occurs in the original plainsong. The only change is in rhythm, from the free rhythm of plainsong to a strict modal pattern [see Modes, rhythmic]. The first step in the development of the 13th-century motet probably was to supply individual clausulae with a text that paraphrases or comments upon the word in the tenor. Frequently, however, not only unrelated Latin texts but also French secular texts were employed. Another important step was the addition of a third voice-part (triplum), in either Latin or French (a Latin triplum was used only in connection with a Latin motetus). There also exist a few motets from this period in four parts. A special type is the conductus motet in three (occasionally four) parts, in which the upper parts have a single text and identical rhythms, as in a *conductus. Motets with two (three) different texts are called double (triple) motets. The Latin double motet may be regarded as the classical type of 13th-century motet. While most of the earlier motets are based on clausulae, those of a later date (after 1250?) consist of freely invented parts added to the tenor. The rhythmic structure of the early motets is based largely on the rhythmic *modes, the upper parts frequently employing a quicker pattern (first, second, sixth mode) than the tenor (third, fifth mode). This rhythmic differentiation of the parts increases over the course of the 13th century, the motets of Petrus de Cruce from the end of the century employing quite small note values in the uppermost parts.

In the 14th century the motet lost its dominant position [see Ars nova] but grew in length, elaboration, and rhythmic variety. A feature of special interest is the introduction of the *isorhythmic principle. Practically all the motets of Machaut (c. 1300–77) are isorhythmic,

and a number of them apply this principle not only to the tenor but also, with a certain amount of freedom, to the upper parts. The final stage of the development is represented by the strictly panisorhythmic motet (in which all parts are strictly isorhythmic), used a few times by Machaut but predominantly by his successors until c. 1430.

Beginning in the 15th century, the two characteristics of the medieval motet, polytextuality and a cantus firmus tenor, were temporarily abandoned in favor of free composition with the same text in all the parts. The earliest examples of this type are by J. Ciconia (c. 1335–1411). In the works of Dunstable and Dufay, free motets appear side by side with the last representatives of the isorhythmic type. They are usually in three voice-parts, with only the upper part (sometimes the two upper parts) carrying the text. This style, which resembles that of the contemporaneous secular chanson, was also employed for the setting of hymns and other liturgical melodies, the melody in question being paraphrased in the uppermost part. The later 15th century brought the motet back to prominence as a musical form second in importance only to the Mass. The motet now became a choral setting of a Latin religious text, in four to six or more voice-parts. Its texture became much more unified, all the parts being vocal and having approximately the same degree of rhythmic animation. In not a few motets, however, one part (usually the tenor) is made to stand out from the others by having a cantus firmus in slower motion, sometimes in long-held values, e.g., one note to the measure. Such cantus firmus motets often have a different text for the main voice. Examples occur in the works of Obrecht and Josquin.

The most striking changes in the style of the motet—changes that profoundly affected all kinds of polyphony in the 16th century—occurred in the decades around 1500. The total range of the voice parts was expanded, particularly in the works of Ockeghem, where the lower parts of the bass range were exploited more fully than they had been previously. Of greatest importance, however, was the introduction of *imitation as a fundamental feature of polyphonic composition. The first composer to make such systematic use of imitation (sometimes called "pervading imitation") was Josquin, though it was in the works of Gombert that the regular succession of overlapping *points of imitation (a new point for each phrase of text) became the norm. This new style, largely the creation of Franco-Flemish composers, was soon taken up by composers throughout Europe, but particularly by the Italians, who assumed the leadership in the field of motet composition in the second half of the century.

The later 16th century saw a continuing refinement of this polyphonic style by composers such as Palestrina, who is often regarded as the leading composer of a *Roman school, as well as the cultivation of novelties such as the *polychoral style and instrumental accompaniment associated primarily with a *Venetian school, which, to be sure, also had its origins in the work of northern composers such as Willaert and Rore.

Although the tradition of the Roman school (under the rubric *stile antico,* i.e., "old style") was cultivated well into the 18th century, the years following 1600 brought considerable change to the motet as well as to other kinds of music. A wide variety of resources was employed, often including one or more soloists and instrumental accompaniment; texts were frequently in the vernacular (as they had been in England as early as the late 16th century; see Anthem) rather than Latin; and other terms for works of similar type came into use (e.g., *Concerti ecclesiastici*). In Germany, however, the motet, of which J. S. Bach wrote several examples, remained primarily a choral work, with a text in the vernacular. Since 1750 the motet has been much less widely cultivated.

Motetus [L.]. (1) *Motet. (2) In the medieval motet, the voice above the tenor; see Motet; *Duplum.*

Mother Goose Suite. See *Ma mère l'oye.*

Motif, motive [F. *motif;* G. *Motiv;* It., Sp. *motivo*]. A short melodic and/or rhythmic figure of characteristic design that recurs throughout a composition or a section as a unifying element. A motif is distinguished from a theme or subject by being much shorter and generally fragmentary. In fact, motifs are often derived from themes, the latter being broken up into shorter elements. As few as two notes may constitute a motif, if they are sufficiently characteristic melodically and/or rhythmically. The technique of motifs is particularly important in sonatas and symphonies, whose *development sections often are largely based on motifs derived from the various themes of the exposition. See also Leitmotiv; Motto.

Motion. (1) The pattern of changing pitch levels (high-low) in a melody, as distinguished from rhythm, which is the pattern of different durations (long-short). Motion may be ascending or descending, in the narrow steps of the scale (conjunct) or in the wider steps of a chord (disjunct). (2) The term is also used to describe the relative changes of pitch in two or more simultaneous voice-parts. Two such parts are said to be in *parallel* motion if the interval separating them remains the same [Ex. 1]; in *similar* motion if they move in the same direction but the interval separating them changes [Ex. 2]; in *contrary* motion if they move in opposite directions [Ex. 3]; in *oblique* motion if one part remains stationary while the other moves [Ex. 4].

Moto [It.]. Motion. *Andante con moto,* somewhat faster than andante.

Motta, José Vianna da. See Viana da Mota, José.

Motte, Diether de la (b. Bonn, 30 Mar. 1928). Pupil of Maler and, at the Darmstadt summer courses, of Fortner and Messiaen. Teacher at the Evangelical School for Church Music in Düsseldorf, 1950–59; at the Hamburg Musikhochschule from 1962. Has composed an opera; a concerto for orch., 1965, a symphony, 1964, and other orch. works; concertos for piano and for flute; choral works; chamber music; piano pieces; organ pieces; works on tape.

Motto [It.]. (1) In 15th- and 16th-century

Masses, an opening motif (also called a "head-motif") used in each of the movements [see Mass]. (2) In 17th- and 18th-century arias, a preliminary statement of the initial motif of the melody. Usually, this initial motif appears twice, first sung and then echoed by the instruments. Such a composition is called a *motto aria* [G. *Devisenarie*].

Motu proprio [L.]. Generally, a papal decree concerning the administration of the Church. Particularly, a decree issued by Pope Pius X in 1903 that contained new regulations for the music in the Roman Catholic service. The most important points were a return to Palestrina's music as the model for polyphonic church music; restoration of Gregorian chant according to the principles of the monks of *Solesmes; suppression of instrumental music except for special occasions and reduction of organ playing to a modest role.

Mount of Olives, The. See *Christus am Ölberge*.

Mouret, Jean-Joseph (b. Avignon, 11 Apr. 1682; d. Charenton, 22 Dec. 1738). Conductor at the Paris Opéra, 1714–18; at the Comédie-Italienne, 1716–37; director of the Concert spirituel, 1728–33. Composed operas and opera-ballets; motets and other sacred works; instrumental works (incl. 2 *Suites de symphonies;* concertos; fanfares).

Mouth organ. See Harmonica (2).

Mouthpiece [F. *embouchure;* G. *Mundstück, Schnabel;* It. *bocchino, bochetta;* Sp. *boquilla*]. The part of a wind instrument that is inserted into the mouth or applied to the lips. Four main types can be distinguished: (a) Cupped mouthpiece, used for the *brass instruments. (b) Single-reed mouthpiece, used for the *clarinet family [see also Reed]. (c) Double-reed mouthpiece, used for the *oboe family (usually not considered a "mouthpiece" but included here for the sake of completeness and comparison; see Reed). (d) Fipple mouthpiece, used for *recorders [see Whistle flute].

Mouton, Jean (b. Holluigue, now Haut-Wignes, near Boulogne, France, *c.* 1459; d. Saint-Quentin, 30 Oct. 1522). Said to have been a pupil of Josquin. Held posi-

tions at Nesle, Amiens, and Grenoble and then entered the service of Queen Anne of Brittany. Following her death in 1514, served Francis I. Composed Masses, motets, chansons.

Mouvement [F.]. (1) Movement. (2) Tempo.

Movable do(h). Generally, any system of *solmization so designed that the syllables can be used in transposition for any key, as distinguished from fixed do(h), in which the syllables correspond to invariable pitches. See also Tonic sol-fa.

Movement [F. *mouvement;* G. *Satz;* It. *movimento;* Sp. *movimiento*]. Any of the various complete and comparatively independent divisions of the sonata, symphony, concerto, string quartet, suite, cantata, etc. In performance, successive movements are usually separated by a brief pause (during which the audience customarily does not applaud). Composers occasionally specify, however, that a movement is to succeed another without pause [see *Attacca*], as in the case of the third and fourth movements of Beethoven's Symphony no. 5.

Moyzes, Alexander (b. Klåštor pod Znievom, Czechoslovakia, 4 Sept. 1906). Son of the composer Mikuláš Moyzes (1872–1944). Pupil of his father, of Karel, and of Novák. Teacher at the Bratislava Conservatory from 1929; at the newly founded Academy of Music in Bratislava from 1949. Has composed an opera; 9 symphonies and other orch. works; cantatas and other choral works; concertos for violin, for flute; chamber music; piano pieces; songs, some with orch.; arrangements of folksongs.

Mozarabic chant. The *chant of the medieval Christian Church of Spain. The name refers to the Mozarabs, the Christians living in Spain while it was under Muhammedan rule. Another name for it is *Visigothic chant,* referring to the Visigoths, who conquered Spain in the 5th century. St. Leander (d. 599), St. Isidore (*c.* 570–636), and St. Ildefonsus (d. 667) played an important role in the development of the chant, which remained in use, untouched by Gregorian reforms, until about the 11th century, when it was supplanted by the Roman Catholic rite.

The Mozarabic liturgy has many details in common with the *Gallican. The music of the Mozarabic rite has been preserved in a number of manuscripts dating from the 9th to 11th centuries—written, unfortunately, in a neumatic notation that cannot be deciphered. Only about 20 chants survive in a legible script.

Mozart, (Johann Georg) Leopold (b. Augsburg, bapt. 14 Nov. 1719; d. Salzburg, 28 May 1787). Father of W. A. Mozart. Violinist in the orchestra of the Archbishop of Salzburg from 1743; court composer there from 1757; vice *Kapellmeister* there from 1763. Composed operas; oratorios; cantatas; Masses and other sacred choral works; symphonies; concertos; chamber music; organ pieces; piano pieces; songs. Published a violin method, *Versuch einer gründlichen Violinschule,* 1756.

Mozart, Wolfgang Amadeus (bapt. Johannes Chrysostomus Wolfgangus Theophilus [translated Gottlieb or Amadeus]) (b. Salzburg, 27 Jan. 1756; d. Vienna, 5 Dec. 1791). Pupil of his father, Leopold Mozart, and of Padre Martini. A child prodigy, made his first public performances as a keyboard player (at first on the harpsichord and later on the piano) in Munich and Vienna in 1762, sometimes with his sister Maria Anna (nicknamed Nannerl). He traveled to Germany, France, England, and Italy, his first published compositions appearing during a stay in Paris in 1763. *Konzertmeister* to the Archbishop of Salzburg from 1769 and court organist there from 1779. Settled in Vienna in 1781, where he was chamber composer to the Emperor from 1788.

Works: operas (incl. *Bastien und Bastienne; Mitridate,* Milan, 1770; *Ascanio in Alba,* Milan, 1771; *Lucio Silla,* Milan, 1772; *La finta giardiniera,* Munich, 1775; *Il re pastore,* Salzburg, 1775; *Idomeneo; Die *Entführung aus dem Serail; Der Schauspieldirektor,* Vienna, 1786; *Le *nozze di Figaro; *Don Giovanni; *Così fan tutte; Die *Zauberflöte; La *clemenza di Tito);* Masses (incl. the *Coronation Mass; a Requiem, left unfinished at his death and completed by Süssmayr); motets and other sacred vocal works; about 50 sym-phonies, of which 41 have been numbered in series (incl. *Paris; *Haffner; *Linz; *Prague; no. 39, K. 543, in E♭; no. 40, K. 550, in G min.; *Jupiter); marches, dances, and other orch. works; 25 piano concertos, one for 2 pianos, one for 3 pianos; 6 violin concertos; a *Concertone* for 2 violins; 4 horn concertos; 2 flute concertos; a clarinet concerto; a bassoon concerto; a *sinfonia concertante* for violin and viola and one for oboe, clarinet, bassoon, and horn; sonatas for organ and orch. and for organ and strings; serenades, divertimentos, cassations, and other works for various instrumental ensembles (incl. *Eine *kleine Nachtmusik); 5 string quintets; 23 string quartets and an adagio and fugue for string quartet; 2 piano quartets; 7 piano trios; 4 flute quartets; an oboe quartet; a clarinet quintet; a horn quintet; a quintet for piano and winds; a trio for clarinet, viola, and piano; 42 violin sonatas; 17 piano sonatas, a fantasia and fugue, 3 fantasias, and 15 sets of variations for piano; 5 sonatas and an andante with variations for piano four-hands; a sonata and a fugue for 2 pianos; pieces for mechanical instruments; arias, duets, and trios for voices with orch.; unaccompanied vocal canons.

MP [It.]. Abbr. for *mezzo piano,* half soft.

M.s. [It.]. Abbr. for *mano sinistra,* left hand.

Mudarra, Alonso (b. c. 1508; d. Seville, 1 Apr. 1580). Vihuelist and composer. Raised in the service of the Dukes of the Infantado in Guadalajara. Canon of the Seville Cathedral from 1547. Published *Tres libros de musica en cifra para vihuela,* 1546, a collection of dances, variations, *tientos, glosas,* and fantasies for vihuela; *villancicos, canciones,* sonnets, *romances,* and other poetry for voice and vihuela; transcriptions for vihuela of works by Josquin and others; and a few pieces for guitar with four strings.

Muffat, Georg (b. Megève, Savoy, bapt. 1 June 1653; d. Passau, 23 Feb. 1704). Pupil of Corelli and Pasquini. Organist to the Archbishop of Salzburg from 1678. *Kapellmeister* at Passau from 1690. Composed an opera; orch. suites; *con-*

certi grossi; sonatas; toccatas and other pieces for organ.

Muffat, Gottlieb (Theophil) (b. Passau, bapt. 25 Apr. 1690; d. Vienna, 9 Dec. 1770). Son of Georg Muffat. Pupil of Fux. Second court organist at Vienna from 1717 and first court organist there, 1741–63. Composed toccatas, fugues, and other pieces for organ; a collection of harpsichord pieces containing a discussion of ornamentation.

Müller, Georg Gottfried (b. Gross Hennersdorf, Saxony, 22 May 1762; d. Lititz, Pa., 19 Mar. 1821). Moravian minister, violinist, and composer. Settled in the U.S. in 1784; active thereafter in the Moravian community in Lititz. Composed church music.

Müller, Wenzel (b. Tyrnau, Moravia, 26 Sept. 1767; d. Baden, near Vienna, 3 Aug. 1835). Pupil of Dittersdorf. Conductor at the Brno Theater from 1783; at the Leopoldstadt Theater in Vienna from 1786. Composed numerous *Singspiele* and other stage works (incl. *Das neue Sonntagskind,* Vienna, 1793; *Die Teufelsmühle am Wienerberg,* Vienna, 1799).

Multimetric. A metric scheme wherein the meter changes frequently. It is common in the works of Stravinsky and other 20th-century composers.

Multiphonics. On woodwind instruments, two or more pitches produced simultaneously by means of special fingering and blowing techniques often called for in contemporary music.

Mumma, Gordon (b. Framingham, Mass., 30 Mar. 1935). Studied at the Univ. of Michigan. Co-founder of the Cooperative Studio for Electronic Music in Ann Arbor, Michigan, and co-director of the ONCE group there. Composer and performer in the Merce Cunningham Dance Co. from 1966. Has employed aleatory and live electronic procedures, the latter termed *cybersonics.* Works incl. *Gestures II* for 2 pianos, 1958–62; several works titled *Mograph* for various numbers of pianos and pianists, 1962–64; *Mesa* for bandoneon and cybersonic console, 1966; *Digital Process* for acoustical and electronic instruments, digital control circuitry, tape, motion-picture projectors, 1967–69.

Mundharmonika [G.]. Mouth organ. See Harmonica (2).

Mundy, John (b. *c.* 1550; d. Eton, buried 30 June 1630). Pupil of his father, William Mundy (*c.* 1529–91), who was a Gentleman of the Chapel Royal from 1564 and a composer of Masses, motets, anthems, and services. John was organist at St. George's Chapel, Windsor, from 1585. Composed services, anthems, motets, psalms, madrigals, keyboard pieces.

Munter [G.]. Merry, cheerful.

Muradeli, Vano Ilich (b. Gori, Georgia, Russia, 6 Apr. 1908; d. Tomsk, Siberia, 14 Aug. 1970). Studied at the Tiflis Conservatory and with Miaskovsky in Moscow. Composed operas (incl. *The Great Friendship,* Moscow, 1947, the performance of which led to the condemnation of modern musical trends by the Communist Party in 1948); 2 symphonies and other orch. works; choral works (incl. *Stalin's Will Has Led Us,* etc.); piano pieces; songs; music for films.

Murky. A name of unknown origin given to pieces with a bass accompaniment in broken octaves (murky bass). This accompaniment was widely used in the second half of the 18th century.

Murrill, Herbert Henry John (b. London, 11 May 1909; d. there, 25 July 1952). Organist, choral conductor, and composer. Studied at the Royal Academy of Music with Bush and at Oxford. Member of the music staff of the British Broadcasting Corporation from 1936 and head of music there from 1950. Composed a jazz opera, *Man in Cage,* London, 1930; a ballet; incidental music for plays; orch. works; 2 cello concertos; choral works; piano pieces; organ pieces; songs; music for films.

Musette. (1) The French *bagpipe of the 17th and 18th centuries, popular in aristocratic circles. It had two chanters, a number of drones, and arm-operated bellows. (2) Dancelike pieces of a pastoral character with a long-held drone, such as could easily be played on the instrument described above. Well-known examples are found in Bach's English Suites nos. 3 and 6, where they are marked "gavotte." (3) French name for the flageolet, an instrument similar to the recorder [see Whistle flute].

Musgrave, Thea (b. Edinburgh, 27 May 1928). Conductor and composer. Studied at the Univ. of Edinburgh with Gál and in Paris with N. Boulanger. Teacher at the Univ. of California at Santa Barbara from 1970. Has composed operas (incl. *The Decision*, 1964, prod. London, 1967; *The Voice of Ariadne*, Aldeburgh, 1974; *Mary Queen of Scots*, Edinburgh, 1977); the ballets *A Tale for Thieves*, 1953, and *Beauty and the Beast*, with tape, 1969; orch. works (incl. *Festival Overture*, 1965; *Concerto for Orchestra*, 1967); choral works (incl. *The 5 Ages of Man*, with orch., 1963); a clarinet concerto, a horn concerto, and a viola concerto; several chamber concertos for various combinations of instruments (incl. *Night Music* for 2 horns and chamber orch., 1969); a string quartet, 1958, and other chamber music (incl. *Soliloquy* for guitar and tape, 1969); piano pieces; songs, some with guitar.

Music box. See under Mechanical instruments.

Music drama. *Opera of the Wagnerian type.

Musica [L.]. Music. The term was used in early writings in the following ways: *Musica divina* or *sacra*, church music; *musica vulgaris*, secular music; *musica mensurabilis*, *mensural (measured, i.e., polyphonic) music; *musica plana*, *plainsong; *musica figurata*, *figural music; **musica ficta* or *falsa*, music involving chromatic tones. Widely adopted during the Middle Ages was Boethius' division of music into three parts: *musica mundana* (harmony of the universe), *musica humana* (harmony of the human soul and body), and *musica instrumentalis* (music as sound, including both vocal and instrumental music).

Musica ficta, musica falsa [L., fictive or false music]. In music before 1600, those pitches that were not part of the *gamut [see Gamma; Hexachord] extending from G to e''; thus, f'' [see Fa] and all chromatic pitches except b♮ and b♭'. *Mu-

sica falsa* is the earlier term, having been introduced sometime before the 13th century, when theorists objected to its use on the grounds that such pitches were not really false but instead were necessary. *Musica ficta* became the standard term in the 14th century, and it is the one used in modern writings to refer generally to the problem of *accidentals in the music of the Middle Ages and Renaissance, particularly those accidentals thought to be implied but not actually specified in the sources of the time. Although there is some doubt about the extent to which accidentals were left unspecified in earlier periods, writers in the 15th and 16th centuries as well as recent scholars agree that the sources of this period do not supply all of the necessary accidentals, leaving some to be supplied by performers. (Only in *tablatures for fretted instruments is there no ambiguity about accidentals.) There is, however, distinctly less agreement on the principles according to which such accidentals are to be supplied, let alone on innumerable specific passages in the repertory where the most commonly accepted principles cannot be unambiguously applied. Among such principles are the prohibition against *mi-fa both as a linear succession within a single voice-part and as an interval between two or more voice-parts, and the rule of counterpoint that calls for a raised *leading tone at many if not most cadences. In modern scholarly editions, accidentals supplied by the editors are placed above the notes to which they apply in order to distinguish them from accidentals supplied in the sources. See also Partial signature.

Musica reservata, riservata [L.]. A term first used by Adrian Coclico in his *Compendium musices* (1552) to describe the music of Josquin and his followers as opposed to that of the preceding period (Ockeghem, Obrecht, Isaac). In the same year Coclico also published a collection of motets under the title *Musica reservata*. The literal meaning of the term has been much disputed. The word *reservata* has been explained as referring to the greater "reserve" (restraint) of the newer style in the use of figurations and ornamental design; or as pointing to some "reserved" secrets of musical technique (perhaps of improvisation, expression of the text by musical motifs, chromaticism not indicated by accidentals); or as indicating the "reserved" (exclusive) character of music written for audiences of high cultural standing. In later writings the term *musica reservata* occurs as a designation for expressive interpretations of the text (S. Quickelberg, *c*. 1560, with reference to Lassus), for a continuous flow of the melodic line (anon. treatise of Besançon, 1571), etc. Thus, no single definite meaning can be assigned to it.

Musical comedy. See under Operetta.

Musical glasses. See Glass harmonica.

Musical Joke, A. See *Musikalischer Spass, Ein.*

Musical Offering. See *Musikalisches Opfer.*

Musicology. The scholarly study of music. It is sometimes divided into three main fields: historical, comparative, and systematic musicology. The first deals with the history of music. The second comprises what is now generally known as *ethnomusicology, the study of folk music and non-Western music. The third field includes acoustics, some aspects of physiology and psychology, aesthetics, sociology, pedagogy, and theory (melody, rhythm, harmony, counterpoint, etc.). In practice, musicology is somewhat more loosely defined and includes criticism of a kind similar to that practiced by students of literature as well as a great many subjects that are closely allied to the performance of music from all periods [see Performance practice]. Among the principal contributions of the discipline has been the preparation of reliable editions.

Musikalischer Spass, Ein [G., A Musical Joke]. A sextet (*divertimento) by Mozart, K. 522 (1787), for strings and two horns that caricatures the work of undistinguished composers and performers of the period.

Musikalisches Opfer [G., The Musical Offering]. One of J. S. Bach's last works, composed and published in 1747 and dedicated to Frederick the Great of Prussia. It contains a number of contrapuntal pieces, all based on a theme of the King's invention upon which Bach had extemporized during his visit to Potsdam in 1747. The dedication copy bears the inscription "Regis Iussu Cantio Et Reliqua Canonica Arte Resoluta" (Upon the King's Demand, the Theme and Additions Resolved in Canonic Style), which forms the acrostic RICERCAR, emphasizing the learned character of the work. The work consists of thirteen compositions: no. 1, *Ricercar a 3;* nos. 2–7, six *Canons;* no. 8, *Fuga canonica;* no. 9, *Ricercar a 6;* no. 10, *Canon a 2 quaerendo invenietis;* no. 11, *Canon a 4;* no. 12, *Trio;* no. 13, *Canone perpetuo.*

Musikwissenschaft [G.]. *Musicology.

Musique concrète [F., concrete music]. Music produced from recorded sounds of all kinds, not merely those of conventional musical instruments. The sounds are normally subjected to some sort of electronic modification. The concept and term were introduced in 1948 by Pierre Schaeffer on the basis of his work at the French Radio in Paris. In his view, the concept excludes sounds that are electronically synthesized. More recently, much *electronic music has combined the use of such "concrete" sounds with wholly synthesized sounds as well as with live performers.

Musique mesurée [F.]. See *Vers mesuré.*

Mussorgsky, Modest Petrovich (b. Karevo, Pskov, Russia, 21 Mar. 1839; d. St. Petersburg, 28 Mar. 1881). One of "The *Five." Studied at the school of, and joined, the Imperial Guard. Held civil service posts, 1863–67 and from 1869. Received advice from Rimsky-Korsakov, in whose revised versions many of Mussorgsky's works were first published and performed. Composed operas (incl. *Boris Godunov; *Khovanshchina; Fair at Sorochinsk, completed by Cui, prod. Moscow, 1913); orch. works (incl. *Night on Bald Mountain); choral works; piano pieces (incl. *Pictures at an Exhibition); songs (incl. the cycles The Nursery, 1868–72, and Songs and Dances of Death, 1875–77).

Mustel organ. See under Harmonium.

Muta, mutano [It., imperative, 3rd person pl.]. Change, e.g., of instrument and/or tuning. Thus, in a timpani part, "muta in G/d" means that the tuning of the timpani should be changed to G and d. In a flute part, "muta in flauto piccolo" means that the player should change to the piccolo.

Mutation. (1) The change from soprano or alto to tenor or bass that takes place in a boy's voice during adolescence, usually between the ages of 14 and 16. (2) The term is occasionally used for the *shift in violin playing. (3) See under Hexachord.

Mutation stops. See under Organ.

Mute [F. *sourdine;* G. *Dämpfer;* It. *sordino;* Sp. *sordina*]. A device for softening or muffling the tone of a musical instrument. In violins, etc., the mute is a clamp with three (occasionally two or five) prongs that is placed on the bridge. Brass instruments are muted by inserting a pear-shaped piece of wood or metal into the bell. The French horn, however, is usually muted by inserting the player's hand. Kettledrums were formerly muted by placing a cloth over the parchment; today sponge-headed drumsticks are generally used instead. In grand pianos, the sound is muted by the left pedal (soft pedal, *una corda* pedal), which causes the whole keyboard with the action and hammers to shift a little to the right [G. *Verschiebung,* shift], so that the hammers strike only one or two strings instead of two or three (hence the Italian term *una corda,* one string); see Piano. In upright pianos a similar effect is achieved by reducing the ambit of the hammers by use of a pedal.

The term *mute* is often identified or confused with *damper. Properly, a damper is a device that prevents or stops the vibrations that produce sound. The Italian word *sordino* is applied to the muting of violins as well as to the dampers of the piano; muting the piano is called playing *una corda.* Thus, the indication *senza sordini* in the first movement of Beethoven's Moonlight Sonata means "without dampers," i.e., "with the right-hand pedal." See *Una corda.*

Müthel, Johann Gottfried (b. Mölln, Germany, 17 Jan. 1728; d. Bienenhof, near Riga, 14 July 1788). Friend of J. S. and K. P. E. Bach. Court organist at Schwerin from 1747. Organist at the court at Riga from 1753 and at St. Peter's Lutheran Church there from 1755. Composed works for organ and for harpsichord or piano; a cantata and other vocal works; chamber music.

M.v. [It.]. Abbr. for *mezza voce;* see under *Mezzo.*

My Country (Fatherland). See *Má Vlast.*

Mysliveczek, Joseph (b. Ober-Sárka, near Prague, 9 Mar. 1737; d. Rome, 4 Feb. 1781). Studied in Prague and went to Italy in 1763. Composed operas (incl. *Bellerofonte,* Naples, 1767); oratorios; cantatas; Masses and a Requiem; symphonies; concertos; chamber music; keyboard sonatas.

Mystery play. See under Liturgical drama.

Mystic chord. A chord invented by Scriabin, consisting of a series of five fourths: c–f♯–b♭–e′–a′–d″. It forms the harmonic basis of his *Prometheus* (1910), op. 60, and the Seventh Piano Sonata, op. 64. See Fourth chord.

N

Nabokov, Nicolas (b. Lubcha, Minsk, Russia, 17 Apr. 1903; d. New York, 6 Apr. 1978). Pupil of Rebikov, Busoni, and Juon. Settled in the U.S. in 1933; taught at various institutions, incl. Wells College, 1936–40; St. John's College, 1940–44; the Peabody Conservatory, 1947–52; State Univ. of New York at Buffalo, 1970–71; New York Univ., 1972–73. Secretary General of the Congress for Cultural Freedom, 1951–66. Cultural adviser to the mayor of Berlin, 1963–66. Composed the operas *The Holy Devil* (also titled *Rasputin's End*), Louisville, Ky., 1958, and *Love's Labour's Lost,* libretto by W. H. Auden and C. Kallmann, 1970, prod. Brussels, 1973; ballets (incl. *Ode,* for the Ballets Russes, 1928; *Don Quixote,* choreography by George Balanchine, 1965); 3 symphonies and other orch. works; concertos for piano, for flute, for cello; an oratorio, *Job,* 1933; works for voice and orch.; chamber music; piano pieces; songs.

Nabucco or **Nabucodonosor** [It., Nebuchadnezzar]. Opera in four acts by Verdi (libretto by T. Solera), produced in Milan, 1842. Setting: Jerusalem and Babylon, 568 B.C.

Nacaire [F.]. *Naker.

Nacchera [It.]. (1) *Naker. (2) In present-day usage, *nacchere* (pl. form) means *castanets.

Nachdrücklich [G.]. Emphatic, expressive.

Nachlassend [G.]. Relaxing, slackening.

Nachschlag [G.]. (1) In modern German terminology, the two terminating notes that are usually played at the end of a *trill. (2) In 17th- and 18th-century music, an ornament consisting of one or several short notes attached to the preceding main note. The ornamenting notes constitute a melodic movement away from the preceding note and are to be performed as a part of it, i.e., *before* the next main note. If the pitch of the or-

namental note and the next main note are the same the ornamental note may be called an *anticipation* [see Counterpoint (5)]. Thus the Nachschlag is the exact opposite of the *appoggiatura, which is a melodic movement toward, and a part of, the following main note. The accompanying example shows the simplest method of notating the Nachschlag, together with the correct rendition.

In French music of the 17th and 18th centuries the most common form of Nachschlag is the *agrément* variously called *accent, aspiration,* or *plainte,* which consists of adding to the end of a sustained note a short note a half-tone or a whole tone higher. Its 17th-century English equivalent is called the *springer.*

Nachspiel [G.]. *Postlude.

Nachtanz [G.]. After-dance. In the instrumental music of the 16th century, a quick dance in triple meter that immediately followed a slower dance in duple meter [see Dance music; *Proportz*].

Nachtmusik [G., night music]. *Serenade.

Nachtstück [G., night piece]. (1) *Nocturne. (2) A piece specifically evocative of the night.

Nagelgeige [G.]. *Nail violin.

Nagelschrift, Hufnagelschrift [G.]. A German variety of *neumes used during the 14th and 15th centuries, so named because the characters resemble the type of nail used with horseshoes [G. *Nagel,* nail; *Huf,* hoof]. Another name is *Gothic neumes.*

Nail violin, nail harmonica. An instrument consisting of a flat, round wooden soundboard with a set of nails or U-shaped iron pins of various lengths driven around the rim. The nails are made to vibrate with a violin bow. It was invented by J. Wilde, *c.* 1740.

Naked fifth. *Open fifth.

Naker [Arab. *nagarah;* F. *nacaire;* It. *nacchera*]. A small kettledrum of Arabic origin used in the Middle Ages, usually in pairs.

Nanino, Giovanni Maria (Nanini) (b. Tivoli, *c.* 1545; d. Rome 11 Mar. 1607). Pupil of Palestrina. *Maestro di cappella* at Santa Maria Maggiore in Rome, succeeding Palestrina, 1571–75; at San Luigi dei Francesi, 1575–77. Member of the papal choir from 1577 and *maestro di cappella* at the Sistine Chapel from 1604. Composed motets, psalms, Lamentations, and other sacred music; canons; madrigals, *canzonette.*

Napoletana. See under *Villanella.*

Napravnik, Eduard (b. Býšt, near Hradec Králové, Bohemia, 24 Aug. 1839; d. St. Petersburg, 23 Nov. 1916). Pupil of Kittl. Conductor of the imperial opera in St. Petersburg from 1869 until his death. Composed operas (incl. *Dubrovsky,* St. Petersburg, 1895); 4 symphonies and other orch. works; a piano concerto; choral works; chamber music; piano pieces; songs.

Nardini, Pietro (b. Livorno, 12 Apr. 1722; d. Florence, 7 May 1793). Violinist and composer. Pupil of Tartini. Court musician at Stuttgart, 1762–65. *Maestro di cappella* at the court in Florence from 1769. Composed concertos, sonatas, duets, and solos for violin; string quartets and other chamber music.

Nares, James (b. Stanwell, Middlesex, bapt. 19 Apr. 1715; d. London, 10 Feb. 1783). Pupil of Croft and Pepusch. Organist and composer to the Chapel Royal, succeeding Greene, 1756–80, and master of the children there from 1757. Composed a dramatic ode, *The Royal Pastoral;* services, anthems, and other church music; catches, canons, glees; organ pieces. Wrote methods for keyboard playing and for singing.

Narváez, Luís de (b. Granada, *c.* 1505?; d. after 1555?). Vihuelist and composer. In the service of the Comendador of

León in 1538. Master of the children in the chapel of Prince Philip (the future Philip II) in 1548. Published *Los seys libros del Delphín de música de cifra para tañer vihuela,* 1538, containing original fantasies and variations, and transcriptions of sacred and secular vocal works by Josquin and others for vihuela; *villancicos, canciones, romances,* and variations for voice and vihuela.

Nationalism. In music, a movement beginning in the second half of the 19th century that is characterized by a strong emphasis on national elements and resources of music. It is based on the idea that the composer should make his work an expression of national and ethnic traits, chiefly by drawing on folk melodies and dance rhythms and by choosing scenes from his country's history or life as subjects for operas and symphonic poems. Although this idea also characterizes much of German musical romanticism beginning in the early 19th century, and although French and Italian music of the 19th and early 20th centuries often have clearly identifiable national elements, nationalism so called is usually regarded as a phenomenon in the music of "peripheral" nations seeking to throw off the domination of international styles, particularly those of German origin.

Nationalism found its first full realization in Glinka's opera *A Life for the Czar* (1836). About 1860 the movement gained fresh impulse in Bohemia, Norway, and Russia, with Smetana's *The Bartered Bride* (1866), Grieg's first book of *Lyric Pieces* (op. 12; e.g., "Folk Song," "Norwegian Melody"), and Borodin's *Prince Igor* (1869–87). In Russia, the group known as The *Five formed a strong bulwark of nationalism against the internationally inclined Tchaikovsky and Rubinstein. Mussorgsky's *Boris Godunov* (1874) in particular is a landmark in the nationalist movement. In Bohemia, Smetana's work was carried on to some extent by Dvořák and more wholeheartedly by Janáček (the opera *Jenufa,* 1894–1903). Toward the end of the 19th century the movement spread to Spain, where it found ample nourishment in the immense wealth of Spanish dance rhythms and melodies. Albéniz, Granados, and Falla are the outstanding representatives. In Finland, Sibelius first was an ardent supporter of nationalism but later turned to "absolute" music, which, nonetheless, remained largely Finnish in character. In England the national movement was championed by Elgar and Vaughan Williams, in Hungary by Bartók and Kodály, and in Rumania by George Enescu. Outstanding nationalist composers of Latin America are Brazil's Heitor Villa-Lobos and Mexico's Carlos Chávez.

In the United States the nationalist movement started with H. F. Gilbert, some of whose compositions have a flavor derived largely from Negro music (*Negro Rhapsody*, 1913). Frederick Converse drew inspiration from the American landscape (*California*, 1928; *American Sketches*, 1935). Among later composers Harris, Gershwin, and Copland can be cited in this context.

Natural. (1) A note that is neither sharp nor flat, e.g., G natural as opposed to G-sharp or G-flat. (2) The sign ♮, which indicates the natural note in cases where the note would otherwise be altered, whether by the signature or a previous *accidental.

Natural horn, trumpet. A horn or trumpet consisting only of a pipe, with neither side holes operated by keys nor additional tubing operated by *valves. Such instruments can produce only the natural tones (i.e., those of the harmonic series [see under Acoustics]), aside from certain artificial chromatic alterations produced by stopping (stopped notes; see under Horn). Natural instruments were used until the end of the 18th century, when the first keyed instruments were invented (key trumpets, key bugle). See Horn; Trumpet; Brass instruments III.

Naumann, Johann Gottlieb (b. Blasewitz, near Dresden, 17 Apr. 1741; d. Dresden, 23 Oct. 1801). Pupil of Tartini, Padre Martini, and Hasse. Court composer in Dresden from 1764 and *Kapellmeister* there from 1776. Composed operas (incl. *Le nozze disturbate*, Venice, 1773; *Cora och Alonzo*, in Swedish, Stockholm, 1782); oratorios, cantatas, Masses, and other sacred works (incl. a *Vater unser*); symphonies; sonatas for violin and for piano; songs.

Navarro, Juán (b. Marchena, Spain, c. 1530; d. Palencia, 25 Sept. 1580). *Maestro de capilla* in Ávila, 1565–66; in Salamanca, 1566–74; in Ciudad Rodrigo, 1574–78; in Palencia from 1578. Composed motets, Magnificats, and other sacred works; polyphonic settings of secular Spanish texts.

Nāy [Arab.]. An end-blown flute widely used among Arabic-speaking peoples.

Naylor, Edward Woodall (b. Scarborough, England, 9 Feb. 1867; d. Cambridge, 7 May 1934). Pupil of his father, John Naylor (1838–97), who was also an organist and composer. Studied at Cambridge and the Royal College of Music. Organist and lecturer at Emmanuel College, Cambridge, from 1902. Composed an opera, *The Angelus*, London, 1909; orch. works; services, anthems, and other choral works; chamber music. Published several books on music. His son Bernard (b. 1907) is also a composer.

Neapolitan school. A term somewhat loosely applied to a school of composition in the 18th century that is thought to have originated in Naples and to have been cultivated particularly in that city or by composers who studied there. It included a great many composers of greater or lesser importance, e.g., F. Provenzale (1627–1704), A. Scarlatti (1660–1725), N. Porpora (1686–1768), L. Vinci (1690–1730), F. Feo (1691–1761), L. Leo (1694–1744), N. Logroscino (1698–c. 1765), G. B. Pergolesi (1710–36), G. Latilla (1711–91), D. Pérez (1711–78), D. Terradellas (1713–51), N. Jommelli (1714–74), P. Anfossi (1727–97), T. Traetta (1727–79), P. Guglielmi (1728–1804), N. Piccinni (1728–1800), A. Sacchini (1730–86), G. Tritto (1733–1824), G. Paisiello (1740–1816), and D. Cimarosa (1749–1801). A. Scarlatti's German pupil J. A. Hasse (1699–1783) also belongs to this group.

Most of these composers were known chiefly for their operas, and, because many of them were born in or near Naples and received their musical education in one of the famous *conservatorii* of that city, the general type of opera they represent has frequently been called Neapolitan. The composers mentioned, however, were active in many different parts of Europe, and the Italian *opera *seria* of the 18th century was not peculiar to Naples but was rather a general type, cultivated all over Italy and extending to other countries.

Neapolitan sixth. See under Sixth chord.

Nebra, José de (b. Catalayud, Zaragoza, 6 Jan. 1702; d. Madrid, 11 July 1768). Second organist at the royal chapel in Madrid from 1724; vice *maestro de capilla* there from 1751. Composed *zarzuelas* (incl. *De los encantos del amor la música es el mayor*, Madrid, 1725); music for plays (incl. Calderón's *La vida es sueño*); numerous sacred works (incl. a Requiem for Queen Barbara).

Neck. The projecting portion of a violin, lute, guitar, or related stringed instrument, by which the instrument is held and to which the *fingerboard is attached.

Neefe, Christian Gottlob (b. Chemnitz, Germany, 5 Feb. 1748; d. Dessau, 26 Jan. 1798). Pupil of J. A. Hiller. Court organist in Bonn from 1782 and Beethoven's teacher there. Conductor of the opera in Dessau from 1796. Composed *Singspiele* and other stage works (incl. *Die Apotheke*, Berlin, 1771; *Adelheit von Veltheim*, Frankfurt, 1780); choral works (incl. settings of Klopstock's *Oden*, 1776); a piano concerto; piano pieces; songs.

Neighboring tone. Same as an auxiliary tone; see under Counterpoint.

Nelhybel, Vaclav (b. Polanka, Czechoslovakia, 24 Sept. 1919). Conductor and composer. Studied in Prague and in Fribourg, Switzerland. Music director of Radio Free Europe in Munich, 1950–57. Settled in the U.S., 1957. Has composed operas; ballets; orch. works (incl. *Étude symphonique*, 1949; *3 Modes*, 1952); choral works; string quartets and other chamber music; piano pieces.

Nelson, Ron J. (b. Joliet, Ill., 14 Dec. 1929). Choral conductor and composer. Pupil of Hanson, Bernard Rogers, L. Mennini, Barlow, Honegger, and T. Aubin. Teacher at Brown Univ. from 1963. Has composed an opera, *The Birthday of the Infanta*, 1956; an oratorio, *What is Man?*, 1964, a *Triumphal Te Deum*, 1962, and other choral works; orch. works.

Nelson Mass. Mass by Haydn in D minor, said to have been written in 1798 while Lord Nelson was engaged in the Battle of the Nile. The Mass is sometimes called "The Imperial."

Nenna, Pomponio (b. Bari, Italy, *c*. 1550; d. Rome or Naples, *c*. 1618). Perhaps Gesualdo's teacher. Composed 8 books of madrigals; responsories and other sacred works.

Neoclassicism. A movement of 20th-century music that is characterized by adoption of features of the music of the 17th and 18th centuries. It represents a general reaction against the unrestrained emotionalism of late romanticism. Particularly distinct is the influence of Bach, which makes itself felt in an emphasis on contrapuntal texture; in the revival of early forms such as the suite (not the ballet-suite of the late 19th century), toccata, passacaglia, ricercar, *concerto grosso,* and ground; in the reduction of orchestral resources and colors; in the abandoning of program music; and in a general tendency toward an objective and detached style. The term *neoclassicism* is usually restricted, furthermore, to music whose harmonic language is derived from tonality. Thus, for example, *serial works that make use of traditional forms (suite, variation, symphony, etc.) are not usually described as neoclassical. The music of Scarlatti, Pergolesi, Monteverdi, F. Couperin, and Lully has left imprints on contemporary works, particularly those by French and Italian composers who supplemented the "back to Bach" movement with the motto "clarté latine" (Latin clarity).

The term is often applied to the music of Stravinsky from *Pulcinella* (1920) to *The *Rake's Progress* (1951) and beyond that to this period of music history in general. For the period as a whole, however, the term is clearly inadequate, and the movement should not be seen as the last step in a rigid succession that leads from *impressionism through *expressionism to neoclassicism and that accounts for all that is important in 20th-century music.

Nepomuceno, Alberto (b. Fortaleza, Brazil, 6 July 1864; d. Rio de Janeiro, 16 Oct. 1920). Studied in Rome, Berlin, and

Paris (with Guilmant). Director of the National Institute of Music in Rio de Janeiro, 1902–16. Employed native Brazilian musical materials. Composed operas (incl. *Artemis,* Rio de Janeiro, 1898; *Abul,* Buenos Aires, 1913); orch. works (incl. *Suite brasileira,* 1897, containing a *Batuque*); choral works; string quartets, a piano trio, and other chamber music; piano pieces; songs.

Neri, Massimiliano (b. Brescia?, early 17th cent.; d. Bonn?, after 1666). First organist at San Marco in Venice from 1644. Organist to the Elector of Cologne from 1664. Composed church and chamber sonatas and canzonas for instrumental ensembles; motets.

Netherlands schools. A designation introduced by R. G. Kiesewetter in 1826 for the long series of 15th- and 16th-century musicians of the Low Countries. He distinguished a first, second, and third Netherlands school, which were headed respectively by Dufay (*c.* 1400–74), Ockeghem (*c.* 1425–97) and Obrecht (1451–1505), and Josquin (*c.* 1440–1521). Today, these terms have been largely discarded, chiefly because only one of the so-called Netherlands masters, Obrecht, came from the Netherlands proper, all the others coming from the southern Lowlands (Belgium), from northern France (Cambrai), or from Burgundy (Dijon). A more appropriate name for the first Netherlands school is **Burgundian school;* the musicians from Ockeghem to Lassus can be grouped best in various generations of the *Flemish school.

Neubauer, Franz Christoph (Neubaur) (b. Melník, Bohemia, 21 Mar. 1750; d. Bückeburg, Germany, 11 Oct. 1795). Violinist and composer. Active in Munich and Vienna. Succeeded Johann Christoph Friedrich Bach as court *Kapellmeister* at Bückeburg. Composed an opera; 12 symphonies; concertos for piano, for flute, for cello; Masses and cantatas; 10 string quartets and other chamber music; songs.

Neukomm, Sigismund (von) (b. Salzburg, 10 July 1778; d. Paris, 3 Apr. 1858). Pupil of Michael and Joseph Haydn. Conductor of the German Opera at St. Petersburg from 1806. Settled in Paris in 1809;

was an associate there of Monsigny, Gossec, Grétry, and Cherubini; entered Talleyrand's service, succeeding J. L. Dušek. Court music director to the Emperor Dom Pedro in Rio de Janeiro, 1816 –21, after which he returned to the service of Talleyrand until 1826. Resided alternately in London and Paris thereafter. Composed 10 operas; orch. works; oratorios (incl. *Mount Sinai* and *David*); Masses and other sacred music; chamber music; numerous pieces for piano and for organ; numerous songs.

Neuma. (1) See Neumes. (2) Medieval term for extended melismatic passages of plainsong, sung to one syllable or simply a vowel. (3) In the later Middle Ages the name *Neuma* was given to instructive melodies devised to show the special characteristics of each mode [see *Noeane*].

Neumatic style. See under Gregorian chant.

Neumes. The notational signs of the Middle Ages (8th–14th centuries) that were used for writing down plainsong. The term means chiefly the signs used for the music of the Roman Catholic Church (Gregorian chant) but is also used for other systems of a similar character, such as the Byzantine, Mozarabic, or Armenian neumes. This article describes only the first type.

Neumatic notation consists of a large number of signs for single tones as well as for groups of two, three, or more tones. The accompanying table shows examples of some of the most important neumes as they occur in the manuscripts of St. Gall (9th–10th centuries), together with the modern forms used in present-day liturgical books (Solesmes edition, Vatican edition) and a rendition in ordinary notation.

The most generally accepted theory about the origin of the neumes considers them an outgrowth of accents in the Greek language, signs that indicated not so much accentuation in the modern sense as an inflection of the voice. See Ecphonetic notation.

In the earliest sources (9th–10th centuries) the neumes are written so as to give only the general outline of the melodic motion and not the actual intervals.

Punctum	— ●	■	♪
Virga	/ /	¶	♪
Podatus or Pes	♫	▪	♫
Clivis or Flexa	∩	♭	♫
Scandicus	/	♯	♫♪
Climacus	/.	¶∙∙	♫♪
Torculus	∿	♠	♫♪
Porrectus	∕	⋈	♫♪
Scandicus flexus	∩	♯♭	♫♫♪
Porrectus flexus	⋒	⋈	♫♫♪
Torculus resupinus	∕	⋈	♫♫♪
Pes subpunctis	/.	▪∙∙	♫♫♪

Thus, the *podatus* may mean an ascending second, third, fifth, etc. Evidently these signs served only as a mnemonic aid for the singer, who knew the melodies by heart, or for the choir leader, who may have interpreted them to his choir by appropriate movements of the hand. These neumes are called *chironomic, staffless, oratorical, or in campo aperto* ("in the open," i.e., without clear orientation). About A.D. 1000 we find the earliest traces of a more careful arrangement of the neumatic signs so as to give some tentative indication of pitch. Particularly the 11th-century manuscripts of Italy, written in the so-called Longobardian or Beneventan character, are remarkable for their early use of "heighted" (*intervallic, diastematic*) neumes, i.e., neumes that are written on a staff, either imagined or actually indicated by one, two, or finally four lines. Slightly later than the Beneventan neumes are the Aquitanian neumes, whose shapes approximated, and finally

led to, the square-shaped characters of the 13th century. These were quickly adopted everywhere except in Germany, where a peculiar variety, the Gothic neumes, remained in use as late as the 16th century. The square-shaped neumes are still used today in the liturgical books of the Roman Catholic Church. The accompanying illustration shows the eight "simple" neumes in five different styles: I. Messine neumes (Monastery of Metz, 9th–10th cent.); II. Beneventan neumes (Monastery of Benevento in southern Italy, 11th–12th cent.); III. Aquitanian neumes (southern France, 12th–13th cent.); IV. Square neumes from Salisbury, England (Sarum use; 13th cent.); V. Gothic neumes, also called *Nagelschrift* (German manuscripts, 14th–15th cent.).

I	II	III	IV	V
∙ ∼	∙ ∼	∙	♦	♦
∕	¶ ¶	♩	¶	♪
√	♩	✓	♬	♪
⅄	∫	⅄:	♭	♬
∴	∫	⌁	▪	♪♪
∴	♪♩	⋮ ⊥	¶∙∙	♪∙∙
∕	∕∖	⅃ ∕∖	♠	⌐♪
⋎	⋎	⋎∷	⋈	♫♭

The chironomic neumes as such cannot be deciphered; they can only be compared with those of the later sources that have preserved the old melodies in a clearer system of notation. The question of the rhythmic meaning of neumatic notation is even more difficult than that of pitch and has been the subject of painstaking research and of sharp controversies that still continue [see Gregorian chant; Romanus letters]. The neumatic signs in their final shape (square shapes of the 13th century) were also adopted for the notation of secular monophonic melodies (e.g., of the troubadours and trouvères) and polyphonic music (organa, *clausulae* of the school of Notre Dame). In both cases they present problems of rhythmic interpretation entirely different from those of the neumes in Gregorian chant. See Ligature; Notation.

Nevin, Arthur Finley (b. Edgeworth, Pa., 27 Apr. 1871; d. Sewickley, Pa., 10 July 1943). Brother of Ethelbert Nevin. Studied at the New England Conservatory and in Berlin. Studied American Indian folklore. Composed operas (incl. *A Daughter of the Forest*, Chicago, 1918); orch. works; choral works; chamber music; piano pieces; songs.

Nevin, Ethelbert Woodbridge (b. Edgeworth, Pa., 25 Nov. 1862; d. New Haven, Conn., 17 Feb. 1901). Brother of Arthur Nevin. Studied in Pittsburgh, Boston, Dresden, and Berlin. Composed a pantomime; piano pieces (incl. "Narcissus"); songs (incl. "The Rosary," "Mighty Lak' a Rose").

New music. A term translated from [G.] *neue Musik* and used with reference to novel developments in 20th-century music. Introduced *c*. 1926, it has precedents in the terms **nuove musiche* of 1600 and the **ars nova* of *c*. 1300.

New World Symphony. Dvořák's Ninth Symphony (usually called no. 5) in E minor, op. 95 (1893). It was written while Dvořák resided in the United States.

Newsidler, Hans (b. Pressburg, 1508; d. Nuremberg, 2 Feb. 1563). Lutenist and composer. Father of Melchior Newsidler. Settled in Nuremberg, 1530. Composed pieces for the lute, incl. preludes, fantasies, dances, and transcriptions of sacred and secular vocal works.

Newsidler, Melchior (b. Nuremberg, 1531; d. Augsburg, 1591 or 1592). Lutenist and composer. Son of Hans Newsidler. Lived in Augsburg from 1551 or 1552. Court musician at Innsbruck, 1580–81. Composed pieces for the lute, incl. fantasies, dances, and transcriptions of sacred and secular vocal works.

Nichelmann, Christoph (b. Treuenbrietzen, Brandenburg, 13 Aug. 1717; d. Berlin, 20 July 1762). Pupil of J. S. Bach, perhaps of Wilhelm Friedemann Bach, and of Quantz and Graun. Second harpsichordist at the court of Frederick the Great in Berlin, 1745–56. Composed operas and other stage works; concertos,

sonatas, and other works for harpsichord; songs. Published a treatise on melody.

Nicodé, Jean-Louis (b. Jerczik, near Poznan, Poland, 12 Aug. 1853; d. Langebrück, near Dresden, 5 Oct. 1919). Pianist and composer. Pupil of Kullak and others at the Kullak Academy in Berlin. Teacher at the Dresden Conservatory, 1878–85. Composed choral works (incl. *Das Meer* for soloist, chorus, organ, orch., 1889); orch. works (incl. a symphony and symphonic variations); 2 cello sonatas; piano pieces; songs.

Nicolai, (Carl) Otto (Ehrenfried) (b. Königsberg, 9 June 1810; d. Berlin, 11 May 1849). Pupil of Zelter. Organist at the Prussian embassy in Rome from 1833. *Kapellmeister* at the Kärntnertor Theater in Vienna, 1837–38; at the court in Vienna, 1841–47; at the royal opera in Berlin and of the Domchor there from 1847. Composed operas (incl. *Il templario*, Turin, 1840; *Die *lustigen Weiber von Windsor* [The Merry Wives of Windsor]); sacred and secular choral works; 2 symphonies and other orch. works; chamber music; piano pieces; songs.

Niedermeyer, Louis (Abraham) (b. Nyon, Switzerland, 27 Apr. 1802; d. Paris, 15 Mar. 1861). Pupil of Moscheles, Förster, and Zingarelli. Settled in Paris in 1823 and established the École Niedermeyer for the study of church music. Composed operas; much sacred music, incl. Masses, motets, hymns; organ pieces; piano pieces; songs (incl. "Le lac").

Nielsen, Carl (August) (b. Nørre-Lyndelse, Denmark, 9 June 1865; d. Copenhagen, 3 Oct. 1931). Pupil of Gade. Violinist in Copenhagen orchestras, 1886–1905. Conductor of the Copenhagen Opera, 1908–14, and of the Copenhagen Musical Society, 1915–27. Composed operas (incl. *Maskarade*, Copenhagen, 1906); incidental music for the theater; 6 symphonies and other orch. works; concertos for flute, for violin, for clarinet; choral works (incl. *Hymnus amoris*, with soloists and orch., 1896); string quartets, a wind quintet, and other chamber music; piano pieces; organ pieces; songs.

Nielsen, Riccardo (b. Bologna, 3 Mar.

1908). Pupil of C. Gatti and Casella. Director of the Liceo musicale G. Frescobaldi in Ferrara from 1954. Has worked with twelve-tone techniques. Has composed a radio opera, *La via di Colombo,* 1953; choral works; a symphony and other orch. works; chamber music; piano pieces; songs.

Niemann, Walter (b. Hamburg, 10 Oct. 1876; d. Leipzig, 17 June 1953). Scholar, critic, and composer. Pupil of Humperdinck and Reinecke. Composed orch. works, chamber music, and numerous piano pieces. Published numerous works of scholarship.

Nigg, Serge (b. Paris, 6 June 1924). Pupil of Messiaen and Leibowitz. An official of the French ministry of cultural affairs from 1967. Worked with and abandoned twelve-tone techniques. Has composed ballets (incl. *L'étrange aventure de Gulliver à Lilliput,* 1958); orch. works (incl. symphonic poems and *Jérôme Bosch Symphony,* 1960); concertos for piano, 1954, for violin, 1957, and for flute, 1961; choral works; chamber music; piano pieces; songs.

Night on Bald Mountain. Symphonic poem in variation form by Mussorgsky, inspired by the witches' Sabbath in Gogol's story, "St. John's Eve." Composed in 1867, it was repeatedly revised and eventually incorporated into his unfinished opera, *Fair at Sorochinsk.* Today it is performed in an orchestral arrangement by Rimsky-Korsakov.

Nightingale, The [Rus. *Salavei*]. Opera in three acts by Stravinsky (libretto by the composer and S. Mitusov after H. C. Andersen's fairy tale), produced in Paris (in French, as *Le rossignol*), 1914. Setting: fairy tale (China). Adapted for the ballet *Le chant du rossignol,* produced in Paris in 1920 (choreography by Leonide Massine, scenery and costumes by Henri Matisse).

Nights in the Gardens of Spain. See *Noches en los jardines de España.*

Nilsson, Bo (b. Skellefteå, Sweden, 1 May 1937). Self-taught in music. Has employed serial and electronic techniques. Works incl. *Frequenzen* for clarinet, flute, percussion, vibraphone, xylophone, guitar, double bass, *c.* 1956;

Quantitäten for piano, 1958; *Gruppen für Bläser* for piccolo, oboe, clarinet, 1959; *Reaktionen* for 4 percussionists, 1960; *Versuchungen* for orch. in 3 groups, 1963, and other orch. works; works for voice and instruments; choral works.

Nin Culmell, Joaquín María (b. Berlin, 5 Sept. 1908). Pianist, conductor, and composer. Son of Joaquín Nin y Castellanos. Pupil of J. and N. Gallon, Dukas, and Falla. Teacher at Williams College, 1940–50, and at the Univ. of California at Berkeley from 1950. Has composed a ballet, *El burlador de Sevilla,* 1957–65; orch. works (incl. *Diferencias,* 1962; *3 Old Spanish Pieces,* 1960); a piano concerto, 1946; a piano quintet, 1937, and other chamber music; piano pieces; songs; arrangements of Spanish and Cuban folksongs.

Nin (y Castellanos), Joaquín (b. Havana, 29 Sept. 1879; d. there, 24 Oct. 1949). Pianist and composer. Pupil of Moszkowski and d'Indy. Teacher at the Schola cantorum, 1906–8, residing in Berlin, Paris, and Havana thereafter. Composed a mimed drama; a ballet; *Suite espagnole* and other works for violin and piano; *Chants d'Espagne* and other works for cello and piano; *Danza ibérica, Message à Claude Debussy,* and other piano pieces. Published books on aesthetics, and editions of early Spanish keyboard and violin music.

Ninth chord. A *chord consisting of some pitch plus the pitches a third, fifth, seventh, and ninth above it. It is sometimes formed on the fifth scale degree of a key and as such can be interpreted as a dominant harmony in that key (dominant ninth chord), e.g., in C major: g–b–d'–f' –a'. The principle of superimposed thirds that leads from the *triad to the *seventh chord and to the ninth chord can be carried still further, resulting in the eleventh chord (g–b–d'–f'–a'–c'') and thirteenth chord (g–b–d'–f'–a'–c'' –e''). Usually, these chords occur in a reduced form with the higher pitches in a variety of positions. Such chords can most often be interpreted as resulting from various techniques of counterpoint.

Nivers, Guillaume Gabriel (b. probably near Paris, 1632; d. Paris, 30 Nov. 1714). Perhaps a pupil of Dumont and Chambonnières. Organist at Saint-Sulpice in Paris from 1654 to his death. Chapel organist to the king from 1678 and *maître de musique* to the queen from 1681. Composed organ pieces; motets and other church music. Published treatises on chant and on composition.

No drama. See *Noh.*

Noble, Thomas Tertius (b. Bath, England, 5 May 1867; d. Rockport, Mass., 4 May 1953). Pupil of Stanford. Organist at Ely Cathedral, 1892–98; at St. Thomas's Episcopal Church in New York, 1912–47. Composed a comic opera; orch. works; anthems, services, and other church music; chamber music; organ pieces; piano pieces; songs.

Nobre, Marlos (b. Recife, Brazil, 18 Feb. 1939). Pianist, conductor, and composer. Pupil of Koellreutter, Guarnieri, Ginastera, Messiaen, Dallapiccola, and Ussachevsky. Has employed Brazilian musical materials and serial techniques. Has composed orch. works (incl. *Mosaico,* 1970); *Concerto breve,* 1969, and other works for piano and orch.; *Rhythmic Variations* for piano and Brazilian percussion instruments, 1963; a string quartet, a piano trio, and other chamber music; songs and other vocal works (incl. *Ukrínmakrinkrín* for soprano and instruments, 1964).

Noces, Les [F., The Wedding]. Ballet by Stravinsky (choreography by B. Nijinska), produced in Paris, 1923. It is scored for chorus, soloists, four pianos, and seventeen percussion instruments (including four timpani) and consists of four scenes.

Noches en los jardines de España [Sp., Nights in the Gardens of Spain]. Suite for piano and orchestra by Manuel de Falla, finished in 1915. The three movements are (translated titles): (1) In the Generalife; (2) Distant Dance; (3) In the Gardens of the Sierra de Cordoba.

Nocturn [L. *horae nocturnae*]. Any of the three parts into which the Office of Matins is divided, each consisting of three psalms with antiphons and three lessons with responsories. See Office.

Nocturne. Most often, a romantic *character piece for piano with an expressive melody over a broken-chord accompaniment. The first nocturnes were written by the Irishman John Field (1782–1837), from whom Chopin adopted the idea and the name. See *Notturno; Nachtstück.*

Nocturnes. Three symphonic poems by Debussy, composed 1893–99: *Nuages* (Clouds); *Fêtes* (Festivals); *Sirènes* (Sirens), with women's voices. Debussy's use of the term *nocturne* is borrowed from the painter Whistler.

Node. See Acoustics.

Noeane, noeagis, etc. Combinations of syllables, perhaps in imitation of Greek words, that appear in various Latin treatises of the 9th and 10th centuries in connection with short melodies called *neuma* (pl. *neumata*) and designed to illustrate the characteristics of the various *church modes.

Noel [F. *noël*]. A popular Christmas song, particularly of French origin [see Carol]. The term first appeared in polyphonic works of the 15th century, and a number of English carols of this period begin with the word "Nowell." Melodies called *noëls* (and, later, polyphonic settings of such melodies) were published in France beginning in the 16th century. From the 17th to 19th centuries innumerable noels were published (frequently as sheet music), in which semireligious texts were set to secular melodies, dancing songs, drinking songs, *vaudevilles,* etc. In the 17th century the name was applied to organ pieces designed to be played during the Christmas service. Most of these are simple variations on popular Christmas melodies.

Noh [Jap.]. A genre of Japanese theater performed by a group of soloists, a chorus, and three or four instrumentalists. It originated in the 14th century. A *noh* play is normally in one or two acts and is classified according to subject as god play, battle play, woman's play, secular play, or demon's play. Usually a *kyōgen,* a comic intermezzo, is performed between acts or between two *noh* plays. The entire text of *noh* is either sung or recited while that of *kyōgen* is spoken. The instrumental ensemble in *noh* consists of a bamboo flute, two drums shaped like hourglasses, and a barrel-shaped drum played with two wooden sticks.

Noire [F.]. Quarter note. See under Notes.

Nola, Giovanni Domenico del Giovane da (b. Nola, near Naples, c. 1510; d. Naples, 5 May 1592). Organist at the church of the Annunziata in Naples and *maestro di cappella* there, 1563–88. Composed *villanesche,* madrigals, motets.

None. The sixth of the canonical hours. See Office.

Nonet [G. *Nonett;* It. *nonetto;* Sp. *noneto*]. Chamber music for nine instruments.

Nonharmonic tones. The collective name sometimes given to a variety of dissonances that are conceived as ornaments to an underlying succession of consonant harmonies. They are also sometimes called *embellishing tones.* Such tones occur routinely in most Western tonal music and give rise to some quite conventional harmonies, e.g., the dominant *seventh chord. See under Counterpoint.

Nonnengeige [G.]. *Tromba marina.

Nono, Luigi (b. Venice, 29 Jan. 1924). Pupil of Malipiero and Maderna. Has taught at the Darmstadt summer courses. Has worked with serial and electronic techniques and with speech sounds. Has composed the opera *Intolleranza 1960;* a ballet; *Il canto sospeso* for soloists, chorus, orch., 1956, and other choral works, some with tape; orch. works; *Incontri* for chamber orch., 1955; *Polifonica–Monodia–Ritmica* for winds, piano, percussion, 1951; *La fabbrica illuminata* for soprano and tape, 1964; *Contrappunto dialettico alla mente,* on tape, 1968.

Nordheim, Arne (b. Larvik, Norway, 20 June 1931). Critic and composer. Studied at the Oslo Conservatory. Has composed a ballet, *Katharsis,* scored for orch. and tape, 1962; orch. works (incl. *Epitaffio,* with tape, 1963); works for string quartet; songs; *Solitaire,* 1968, and other works on tape, some employing both electronic and concrete sounds.

Nordoff, Paul (b. Philadelphia, 4 June 1909; d. Herdecke, Germany, 18 Jan. 1977). Pupil of R. Goldmark. Taught at the Philadelphia Conservatory, 1938–43, and Bard College, 1949–58. Worked in the field of music therapy from 1961. Composed operas (incl. *The Masterpiece,* Philadelphia, 1951); ballets; orch. works (incl. *Winter Symphony,* 1954); 2 piano concertos and a violin concerto; choral works; 2 string quartets, a piano quintet, and other chamber music; songs.

Nordraak, Rikard (b. Christiania, Norway, 12 June 1842; d. Berlin, 20 Mar. 1866). Pupil of Kullak. Close associate of Grieg. Composed the Norwegian national anthem, *Ja, vi elsker;* incidental music for plays; piano pieces; songs.

Nørgård, Per (b. Gentofte, Denmark, 13 July 1932). Pupil of Holmboe, Høffding, and N. Boulanger. Teacher at the Royal Danish Conservatory, 1960–65, and at the Jydske Conservatory in Aarhus since then. Has employed serial techniques and graphic notation. Has composed operas (incl. *Labyrinth,* Copenhagen, 1967); a ballet; oratorios (incl. *Babel* for clown, rock singer, cabaret singer, conductor, chorus, orch., 1966); orch. works (incl. *Fragment 6* for 6 orch. groups, 1961); chamber music; piano pieces; songs; *The Enchanted Forest,* on tape, 1968.

Norma. Opera in two acts by Bellini (libretto by F. Romani), produced in Milan, 1831. Setting: Gaul during the Roman occupation, c. 50 B.C.

Noskowski, Zygmunt (Sigismund) (b. Warsaw, 2 May 1846; d. there, 23 July 1909). Studied in Warsaw with Moniuszko and in Berlin. Teacher at the Warsaw Conservatory from 1888. Second conductor of the Warsaw Philharmonic Society from 1904 and of the Warsaw Opera from 1906. Composed operas (incl. *Livia Quintilla,* Lvov, 1893) and other stage works; 3 symphonies and other orch. works; (incl. the symphonic poem *Step,* 1896); choral works; 3 string quartets and other chamber music; piano pieces; songs.

Nota cambiata. See under Counterpoint.

Notation. The method or methods used for writing down music. A fully developed system of notation must be designed so as to indicate the two main properties of a musical sound: its pitch and its duration. The method now in general use is based on the note, a sign that indicates pitch by its position on a *staff provided with a *clef, and duration by a variety of shapes, such as hollow or black heads with or without stems, flags, etc. [see Notes]. Additional symbols of modern notation are *accidentals, *key signatures, *time signatures, *dynamic marks, *tempo marks, *expression marks, the *tie, the *slur, etc. The modern system of notation dates from the early 17th century. Previously, systems of notation had been used that differ more or less radically from the present one regarding either the indication of rhythm (as in *mensural notation) or that of pitch (as in the *tablatures).

Classical Greek music was notated by means of letters, but this method left no immediate traces in the musical notation of the Christian era [for a 9th-century revival, see Daseian notation]. The ensuing development is rooted instead in the symbols of Greek and Hebrew speech recitation, the grammatical accents [see Accent (3) (4)] of the 2nd century B.C., and similar signs known generically as *ecphonetic notation. These developed (c. 800?) into a more elaborate system of stenographic symbols vaguely indicating the outlines of melodic movement, the *neumes. Owing to their failure to clearly indicate pitch as well as rhythm, the neumes are not a fully developed notation but only a mnemonic aid for oral transmission of the chant. As early as the 9th century various methods were designed to remedy the indefiniteness of the neumes, chiefly by the addition of letters [see Letter notation; Romanus letters]. Modifications during the 11th century led to shapes that corresponded more accurately to the rise and fall of the melody, the *diastematic neumes*. This evolution was stabilized by the adoption of staff lines, first one, then two, and finally four. About 1200, the neumes acquired the square shapes still used in the liturgical books of the Roman Catholic Church. See Neumes.

These square shapes were soon adopted for the notation of monophonic secular melodies as well as for polyphonic music, where those combining

I. Greek accents: 1. Accentus acutus; 2. Acc. gravis; 3. Acc. circumflexis; 4. Hypothetical. II. Neumes: 5. Virga; 6. Punctum; 7. Podatus; 8. Clivis. III. Black mensural notation (1250): 9. Longa; 10. Brevis; 11. Semibrevis; 12. Descending ligature; 13. Ascending ligature. IV. Additional signs of the 14th century: 14. Minima; 15. Semiminima. V. White mensural notation (1450): 16. =9; 17. =10; 18. =11; 19. =14; 20. =15; 21. Fusa; 22. =12; 23. =13. VI. Modern notation (after 1600): 24. Breve or double-whole note; 25. Whole note; 26. Half note; 27. Quarter note; 28. Eighth note.

two or more pitches were known as *ligatures. The introduction of the square shapes was accompanied, shortly before 1200, by the establishment of definite rhythmic values on the basis of the rhythmic modes [see Modes, rhythmic]. The resulting system is known as *square* or *modal notation*. There followed, during the 13th and 14th centuries, an extremely rapid development, with frequent changes and innovations: the introduction of two note values, called *longa* and *brevis* (c. 1225), which became necessary for the notation of the texted parts of the *motet; about 1250, the introduction of a smaller note value, called a *semibrevis*, two or three of which could be used in place of a *brevis;* about 1260, the unequivocal rhythmic interpretation of the ligatures, independent of the modes (Franco of Cologne; usually considered the beginning of *mensural notation); about 1280, the introduction of more than three *semibreves* (up to seven) in place of a *brevis* (Petrus de Cruce). Shortly after 1300, the exclusive use of modal rhythm (and hence of ternary

Commonly used notational symbols [see separate entry for each].

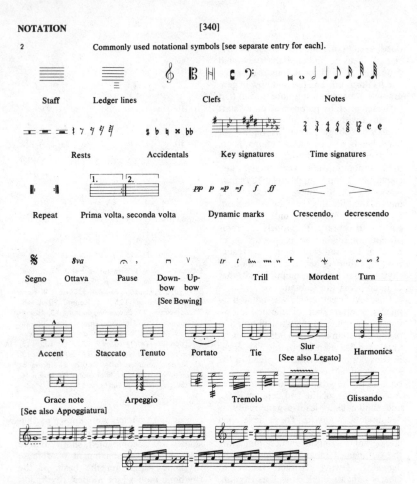

Staff   Ledger lines   Clefs   Notes

Rests   Accidentals   Key signatures   Time signatures

Repeat   Prima volta, seconda volta   Dynamic marks   Crescendo, decrescendo

Segno   Ottava   Pause   Down- Up-   Trill   Mordent   Turn
                            bow   bow
                            [See Bowing]

Accent   Staccato   Tenuto   Portato   Tie   Slur   Harmonics
                                                    [See also Legato]

Grace note   Arpeggio   Tremolo   Glissando
[See also Appoggiatura]

meter) that prevailed throughout the 13th century [see *Ars antiqua*] was abandoned, and the basic principles of rhythm and notation were revised and expanded by Philippe de Vitry and others. The new system, expounded in his treatise *Ars nova* (1322 or 1323), recognized duple and triple rhythms as equally important and applied this dichotomy to all the note values in the different mensurations: *modus* (*longa-brevis*), *tempus* (*brevis-semibrevis*), and *prolatio* (*semibrevis-minima*) [see Mensural notation]. The notational principles of this period remained virtually unchanged until the end of the 16th century, the only modification being the change, *c.* 1450, from black notes (black mensural notation) to white notes (white mensural notation). Simultaneously with

Vitry's system, however, there developed a different system in Italy (Italian notation) that retained to a greater extent the principles of the late 13th century (particularly the Petronian groups of *semibreves*, i.e., those of Petrus de Cruce). After 1350 the Italian system incorporated features of the contemporary and more progressive French system, thus leading to a system (sometimes called "mixed notation") that was used by Francesco Landini and other composers of the second half of the 14th century. Toward the end of this century, a further development (sometimes called "mannered notation") was employed by some French and Italian composers, incorporating a wide variety of note shapes (e.g., the **dragma*) that made possible the notation of quite complex rhythms.

In the first half of the 15th century, this complexity was largely abandoned. There resulted what might be called the "classical" system of mensural notation (c. 1450–1600), characterized by the use of white instead of black notes (white mensural notation). This is the notation used by the Flemish masters Ockeghem, Obrecht, and their numerous successors. In the latter part of the 16th century, triple mensuration (*tempus perfectum, prolatio perfecta*) as well as the ligatures were largely discarded, together with other special methods of mensural notation (*proportions). Thus, the system of notation became virtually that of the present day (in which each note or rest, unless modified by special signs, is equal to two of the next smaller value), particularly after the general acceptance of *bar lines and score arrangement [see Score; Partbooks]. Throughout the 17th century, however, remnants of the older system lingered on, particularly the use of blackened notes (coloration) and some proportional signs [see Time signatures]. Of these the *alla breve sign is the only one that has survived. Ex. 1 illustrates the development of the main notational signs in six periods. Ex. 2 illustrates the principal elements of musical notation now in use and concerning which there are separate entries in this book.

Side by side with the system of mensural notation there existed, particularly in the period 1450–1600, special notational methods known as *tablatures. These were used for writing down keyboard and lute music (generally solo music; mensural notation was used for ensemble music).

Numerous modifications of and substitutes for the musical notation now most widely used have been suggested. The search for alternatives has been accelerated by 20th-century composers' use of greatly expanded pitch and rhythmic resources that cannot be adequately notated with conventional notation. Composers of *aleatory music have frequently made use of extremely diverse kinds of graphic representations of their works. Such graphic notation varies greatly in the extent to which it gives precise instructions to the performer. It may make little or no use of conventional notational signs and may be accompanied by written instructions for its realization.

See also Accidentals; *Chiavette;* Clef; Daseian notation; Ecphonetic notation; Letter notation; Ligatures; Mensural notation; *Musica ficta; Nagelschrift;* Neumes; Notes; Partbooks; Partial signature; *Plica;* Proportions; Romanus letters; Score; Staff; Tablature; Tie; Time signatures; Tonic sol-fa.

Note-against-note style. See Homorhythmic.

Note nere [It.]. See Chromatic (5).

Note sensible [F.]. *Leading tone.

Notes. The signs with which music is written on a staff. In British usage *note* also means the pitch indicated by a note [see Tone (2)], as well as the key by means of which the pitch is produced on the piano.

The accompanying illustration shows the note values with their American names, with rests of equivalent value shown in brackets. British, French, German, Italian, and Spanish terms are given below. The German names for the rests are *ganze* (*halbe, viertel,* etc.) *Pause;* Italian: *pausa di semibreve* (*bianca,* etc.); French: *pause, demi-*

o [▬]	whole note
♩ [▬]	half note
♩ [𝄽]	quarter note
♪ [𝄾]	eighth note
♪ [𝄿]	sixteenth note
♪ [𝅀]	thirty-second note
♪ [𝅁]	sixty-fourth note

Whole note: Brit. semibreve; F. ronde; G. Ganze (Note); It. semibreve; Sp. redonda. Half note: Brit. minim; F. blanche; G. Halbe (Note); It. bianca; Sp. blanca. Quarter note: Brit. crotchet; F. noire [soupir]; G. Viertel; It. nera; Sp. negra. Eighth note: Brit. quaver; F. croche; G. Achtel; It. croma; Sp. corchea. Sixteenth note: Brit. semiquaver; F. double-croche; G. Sechzehntel; It. semicroma; Sp. semicorchea. Thirty-second note: Brit. demisemiquaver; F. triple-croche; G. Zweiunddreissigstel; It. biscroma; Sp. fusa. Sixty-fourth note: Brit. hemidemisemiquaver; F. quadruple-croche; G. Vierundsechzigstel; It. semibiscroma; Sp. semifusa.

pause, soupir, demi-soupir, quart de soupir, huitième de soupir, seizième de soupir; Spanish: *silencio de redonda (blanca, negra, corchea, semicorchea, fusa, semifusa).* Each note or rest in this system, unless modified by special signs, is equal in duration to two of the next smaller value.

Notes inégales [F.]. See *Inégales.*

Notker Balbulus (b. probably Jonschwil, Thurgau, Switzerland, *c.* 840; d. St. Gall, 6 Apr. 912). Monk at the monastery of St. Gall. One of the earliest composers of sequences.

Notre Dame, school of. Designation for a school of French polyphonic music of *c.* 1200, whose leading composers—the only ones known by name—were Leonin (second half of the 12th cent.) and Perotin (*c.* 1160–*c.* 1220). The name is based on the surmise that both masters were connected with the famous cathedral of Paris, whose cornerstone was laid in 1163, though the traditions of other churches in Paris are also represented in the repertory. The repertory of the school of Notre Dame consists of a collection of two-part organa known as the **Magnus liber organi,* additional organa in two, three, and four parts, and numerous **clausulae,* **conductus,* and **motets.* See *Ars antiqua.*

Notturno [It.]. (1) **Nocturne.* (2) In the late 18th century, a term applied to a variety of lighter multimovement works, often for mixed ensemble of 4 strings and 2 horns, intended for performance in the evening. Examples include Haydn's Hob. II:25–32 for 2 *lire organizzate* (**hurdy-gurdies), 2 clarinets, 2 horns, 2 violas, and bass, and Mozart's K. 269a, for strings and 2 horns. Other designations frequently used interchangeably with *notturno,* though without implying evening performance, are **cassation,* **divertimento,* and **serenade.*

Nourri, bien [F.]. *Bien nourri,* with a rich sound.

Novák, Vítězslav (b. Kamenice, Czechoslovakia, 5 Dec. 1870; d. Skuteč, Czechoslovakia, 18 July 1949). Pupil of Dvořák. Teacher at the Prague Conservatory from 1909. Composed operas (incl. *The Imp of Zvíkov,* Prague, 1915; *Karlštejn,* Prague, 1916); ballets (incl.

Signorina Gioventù, 1928); symphonic poems and other orch. works; choral works, some with orch.; 3 string quartets and other chamber music; piano pieces; songs.

Nowak, Lionel (b. Cleveland, 25 Sept. 1911). Pupil of Porter, Sessions, and Elwell. Teacher at Converse College, 1942 –46; at Syracuse Univ., 1946–48; at Bennington College from 1948. Has composed dance scores for Doris Humphrey, José Limón, and others; *Concert Piece* for kettledrums and string orch., 1961; choral works; chamber music; piano pieces; songs.

Nowell. **Noel.*

Nozze di Figaro, Le [It., The Marriage of Figaro]. Opera in four acts by Mozart (libretto by L. da Ponte, after Beaumarchais' play *La folle journée ou Le mariage de Figaro,* sequel to his *Le barbier de Séville,* the source of Rossini's *Il *barbiere di Siviglia),* produced in Vienna, 1786. Setting: castle near Seville, 18th century.

Number opera. An opera written in single "numbers," i.e., separate pieces such as arias, duets, ensembles, and ballets, interspersed with recitative or spoken dialogue. This type of opera prevailed until about the second quarter of the 19th century, when Wagner began to strive for the continuous musical texture that was to characterize his own works and those of many other composers during the second half of the century. As in other respects, here, too, Weber provided a model for Wagner. Italian opera, on the other hand, continued to make significant use of individual numbers through much of this period.

Nunc dimittis. See under Canticle.

Nuove musiche, Le [It., The New Musics]. (1) Title of a publication of 1601 by Giulio Caccini (*c.* 1550–1618), containing arias and madrigals in the then new style of monodic **recitative* with **thoroughbass accompaniment [see Monody]. (2) The term is used for music of the whole period around the year 1600, which marks the beginnings of the opera, oratorio, cantata, and the baroque period in general.

Nut. (1) A slightly raised ridge fastened

to the upper end of the neck of a stringed instrument, serving to raise the strings over the fingerboard. (2) [Brit.] *Frog.

Nutcracker, The [F. *Casse-noisette*]. Ballet by Tchaikovsky (choreography by M. Petipa, based on a story by E. T. A. Hoffmann), completed in 1892 and produced that year in St. Petersburg. The orchestral suite op. 71a drawn from the ballet was also first performed in 1892.

Nystroem, Gösta (b. Silvberg, Sweden, 13 Oct. 1890; d. Särö, Sweden, 9 Aug. 1966). Painter, critic, and composer. Pupil of Hallén and d'Indy. Composed an opera; a ballet; incidental music for plays of Shakespeare; oratorios; 6 symphonies and other orch. works; concertos for piano, for violin, for viola, and a *sinfonia concertante* for cello and orch.; chamber music; piano pieces; songs.

O

Obbligato [It.]. Obligatory, usually with reference to an instrument (*violino obbligato*) or part that must not be omitted; the opposite is *ad libitum*. Unfortunately, through misunderstanding or carelessness, the term has come to mean a mere accompanying part that may be omitted if necessary. As a result, one must decide in each individual case whether obbligato means "obbligato" or "ad libitum"; usually it means the former in early music and the latter in more recent pieces.

Obertas [Pol.]. A Polish round dance in quick triple meter and performed very vigorously, like a wild waltz. Chopin's Mazurka op. 56, no. 2, is in the character of an *obertas*. Another name, more commonly used today, is *oberek*.

Oberwerk [G.]. Swell organ. See Organ.

Oblique motion. See Motion.

Oboe family. A large group of *wind instruments having a double reed [see Reed; Mouthpiece], in contrast to the *clarinet family, comprising the wind instruments with a single reed. Strictly speaking, the oboe, English horn, bassoon, etc., constitute families of their own, since each of these instruments existed in various sizes. All these instruments (with the exception of some old types) have a conical bore, in contrast to the cylindrical bore of the clarinets.

I. *Present-day forms.* (a) Oboe [F. *hautbois*]. The oboe is a conical pipe

made of wood (usually in three sections: top joint, lower joint, and bell) with a double reed fixed to the upper end. It seems to have originated in the mid-17th century.

Normal ranges: a. Oboe. b. English horn. c. Bassoon. d. Contrabassoon.

(b) The English horn [F. *cor anglais;* G. *englisches Horn;* It. *corno inglese;* Sp. *corno inglés*]. An alto oboe, pitched a fifth below the oboe. To facilitate the handling of this rather long instrument, the double reed may be carried on a small metal tube attached to the upper end and bent back toward the player's mouth. Its bell is pear-shaped, with a rather small opening, which accounts for its soft, somewhat nasal timbre. It is treated as a transposing instrument, the parts sounding a fifth lower than written. Early instruments of this size were curved like an animal's horn, a fact that explains half of its name; it is not known why it is called "English." The English horn is thought to have gradually replaced the older *oboe da caccia* in the early part of the 19th century.

(c) Bassoon [F. *basson;* G. *Fagott;* It. *fagotto;* Sp. *fagot*]. The bass of the oboe family. Owing to its great length, the tube is bent back on itself, first descend-

1. *Double bassoon or contrabassoon.* 2. *Bassoon.* 3. *English horn.* 4. *Oboe.* 5. *Heckel-phone.* 6. *Sarrusophone.*

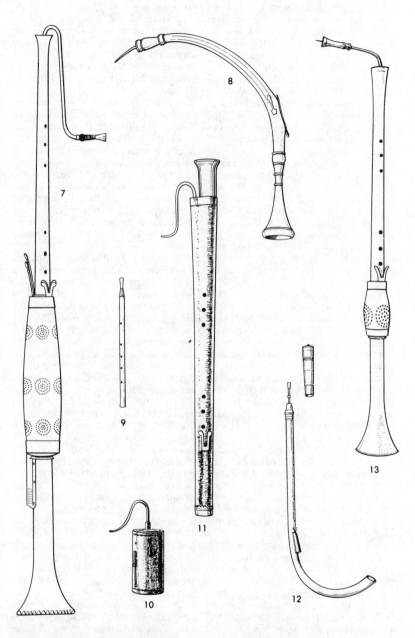

7. Shawm (bass). 8. Oboe da caccia. 9. Aulos. 10. Racket. 11. Curtal, double. 12. Crumhorn (tenor). 13. Shawm (tenor).

ing and then ascending. The instrument consists of five sections: the *crook* (bocal), a narrow, curved metal tube to which the reed is attached; the *wing* or *tenor joint*, which forms the descending section of the pipe; the *butt* or *double joint*, the bottom section, in the shape of a U; the *bass* or *long joint*, which forms the ascending pipe; and the *bell*. The modern bassoon developed from the curtal [see III below] in the 17th century.

(d) Contrabassoon or double bassoon [F. *contrebasson;* G. *Kontrafagott;* It. *contrafagotto;* Sp. *contrafagot*]. This instrument is pitched an octave below the bassoon. Its modern form, which was developed by Heckel (*c.* 1880), has a tube more than sixteen feet long that is doubled on itself four times. Unlike the bassoon bell, the bell of this instrument points down instead of up. The part is notated an octave above the actual sound (in Wagner's *Parsifal* it is written at its true pitch). Both the lowest and highest tones of its range are rather unsatisfactory and therefore infrequently used.

II. *Rare and obsolete forms.* The oboes of the 18th and early 19th centuries were much more strident and piercing in sound than the modern instruments.

(a) Oboe d'amore. A mezzo-soprano instrument pitched a minor third below the ordinary oboe and having the characteristic pear-shaped bell of today's English horn. The name probably refers to its sound, which was "sweeter" than that of the other oboes of the day. It was invented *c.* 1720.

(b) Oboe da caccia. Probably an alto oboe in F, with an expanding bell or, more frequently, a pear-shaped bell that rendered the sound less strident. The instrument was built in the shape of a curved hunting horn and may have been the model for the old, curved form of the English horn. See also Taille.

(c) Tenoroon. A small bassoon pitched a fifth above the ordinary bassoon. Invented and used in the first half of the 19th century, it is now obsolete.

(d) Quartfagott, Quintfagott. According to M. Praetorius (*De organographia,* 1619), instruments pitched, respectively, a fourth and a fifth below the ordinary bassoon. In the 18th and 19th centuries

the names were used for small bassoons pitched a fourth or a fifth above the ordinary bassoon, like the tenoroon described above.

(e) Heckelphone. A baritone oboe invented by Heckel in 1904 and pitched an octave below the oboe. Built in a straight shape with a bulb-shaped bell, it has a bore much wider than the oboe's. In spite of its full, rich sound it has been little used.

(f) Sarrusophone. A whole family of double-reed brass instruments, invented by the French bandmaster Sarrus (patented 1856) and made in eight sizes, from sopranino to subcontrabass. The only sarrusophone used in the orchestra is a contrabass size in C that has the same compass as the contrabassoon and has been preferred to it by numerous French composers. The smaller sizes are obsolete, but the larger ones continue to be used in some wind bands, especially in Italy.

III. *History.* Double-reed instruments are ancient and widespread, much more so than single-reed instruments (clarinets). Ancient forms are usually paired (double oboe), the longer pipe probably being used to provide a drone or, perhaps, some tones missing in the shorter one. Sumerian double oboes are documented as far back as 2800 B.C., and similar instruments were common in Egypt, Israel (*halil*), Greece (*aulos), and Rome (*tibia*).

The early European ancestor of the oboe is the *shawm,* which was used until the 17th century. In France it was called *bombarde, chalemie;* in Germany, *Pommern (Bomhart, Pumhart),* except for the highest member of the group, which was known as *Schalmei;* in Italy, *piffaro;* in Spain, *chirimía.* The earliest reference to such an instrument is in French literary sources of the 13th century. Probably introduced from the Near East in the 12th century, it consisted of a single piece of wood curving in a bell. By the 16th century shawms existed in all sizes, ranging from sopranino to double bass, the name *shawm* being reserved for the soprano instrument while the lower-pitched instruments were called *bombard.* The bombards (all straight tubes) were soon abandoned in favor of shortened instruments, employing folded tubes, called *curtals* [F. *basson, fagot;* G. *Dulzian, Fagott;* It. *dolcino, fagotto;* Sp. *bajón*]. These instruments were forerunners of the modern bassoon but were made from a single block of wood with two parallel bores, one descending and one ascending. *Crumhorns* [F. *cromorne, tournebout;* G. *Krummhorn;* It. *storto;* Sp. *orlo*] are depicted in paintings of the 15th and 16th centuries as held by angels. Their tube was nearly cylindrical, curved upward like a J, and a pierced cap (wind cap) covered the reed, which was thus not touched by the player's lips. The cap served as a wind chamber, so that the reed was set in vibration much as are the reed pipes of the organ. Thus the sound was as unchangeable as that of an organ pipe; overblowing was impossible. The instrument was used until about the mid-17th century. The *racket* [G. *Rackett, Rankett*] is a short, thick cylinder of solid wood pierced lengthwise by ten cylindrical channels connected so as to form a continuous tube. Praetorius described four sizes of racket.

Obrecht, Jacob (b. probably Bergen op Zoom, the Netherlands, 22 Nov. probably 1451; d. Ferrara, 1505). *Maître de chapelle* at the Cambrai Cathedral, 1484 –85. Subsequently worked at St. Donatien in Bruges, 1485–91 and 1498–1500; at Notre Dame in Antwerp, 1492–96 and 1501–4; in Bergen op Zoom, 1496–98. Visited Ferrara in 1487 and returned to the court there in 1504. Composed about 25 Masses, 20 motets, 30 secular pieces with texts in French, Dutch, and Italian.

Obukhov, Nicolas (b. Moscow, 22 Apr. 1892; d. Paris, 13 June 1954). Pupil of Tcherepnin, Steinberg, and Ravel. Settled in Paris in 1918. Developed the *croix sonore* (an electronic instrument), a new system of notation, and a twelve-tone technique independent of Schoenberg. Composed *Le livre de vie* for soloists, chorus, 2 pianos, and orch., a mystical work to which he devoted a major part of his life; pieces for *croix sonore*.

Ocarina. A popular instrument in the shape of an egg, a bird, or a sweet potato (the last name commonly used in the U.S.), with a mouth-hole and a number of finger holes. It is classified as a globular flute, a type with an interesting ancestry in China and Africa.

Ockeghem, Johannes (b. probably Dendermonde, Flanders, *c*. 1425; d. Tours, 6 Feb. 1497). Perhaps a pupil of Binchois. Singer at Notre Dame in Antwerp, 1443– 44; in the chapel choir of Duke Charles I of Bourbon by 1448. Chaplain and composer, successively, beginning in about 1452, to Charles VII, Louis XI, and Charles VIII of France; *maître de chapelle* from 1465. Composed 10 Masses, Mass sections, a Requiem, 9 motets, and about 20 chansons.

Octave. See Interval; Intervals, calculation of.

Octave equivalence. That feature of musical perception by which all pitches separated by one or more perfect octaves (i.e., pitches whose frequencies are related by powers of 2) are regarded as belonging to the same class [see *Pitch class] or as being in some sense equivalent. This is reflected in the system of Western *pitch names, in which the seven letters employed are repeated for each octave.

Octave species. The particular arrangement of tones and semitones occurring in any given octave of the diatonic *scale. This arrangement is different for the octaves bounded by each of the seven diatonic scale degrees. For example, starting on c and proceeding upward along the white keys of the piano, tones (t) and semitones (s) occur in the order t t s t t t s, whereas proceeding upward from d they occur in the order t s t t t s t. This is significant for the *church modes as well as for *tonality. The concept also played an important role in the theory of ancient Greek music.

Octet. Music for eight instruments, whether all strings (Mendelssohn), all winds (Beethoven, op. 103; Stravinsky), or mixed (Schubert, Spohr).

Octobasse. See Violin family (j).

Octoechos. *Oktoechos;* see *Echos.*

Ode. (1) In poetry (ancient Greek and Latin as well as modern), a poem in free meter and verse structure, frequently addressed to a deity. Odes are usually set in a free form similar to that of the cantata, including several movements or sections for chorus, soloist, and orchestra. Dryden's "Ode for St. Cecilia's Day" (set by Handel) and Schiller's "Ode to Joy" (set by Beethoven, Ninth Symphony) are well-known examples. In the 16th century the Horatian odes were frequently set to music in strict chordal style and in a rhythm dictated by the poetic meter. (2) In Byzantine chant, one of the nine sections of the *kanon*, each written in imitation of a scriptural canticle.

Ode to Napoleon Buonaparte. Composition by Schoenberg, op. 41b (1942), based on Byron's poem, scored for string orchestra, piano, and a reciting voice.

Odhecaton. Title (complete form: *Harmonice musices Odhecaton A*) of a collection of "100 songs" (actually only 96) published by the Italian printer Ottaviano de' Petrucci in 1501. The earliest printed collection of polyphonic music, it includes an important repertory of secular polyphony of the period *c.* 1470–1500, particularly by Franco-Flemish composers.

Oedipus Rex [L., King Oedipus]. Opera-oratorio in two acts by Stravinsky (libretto in Latin by J. Cocteau and J. Daniélou, based on Sophocles' tragedy), produced in Paris, 1927. Setting: ancient Thebes.

Oeuvre [F.]. *Opus.

Offenbach, Jacques (b. Cologne, 20 June 1819; d. Paris, 5 Oct. 1880). Settled in Paris and was a pupil there of Halévy. Conductor at the Théâtre Français, 1850–55. Established and managed the Théâtre Bouffes-Parisiens, 1855–62. Manager of the Théâtre de la Gaîté, 1873–75. Composed the opera *Les *contes d'Hoffmann;* operettas (incl. *Orphée au enfers; La *belle Hélène; La vie parisienne,* 1866; *La Périchole,* 1868).

Offertory [L. *offertorium*]. In the Roman Catholic liturgy, the fourth item of the Proper of the *Mass, accompanying the placing on the altar of the elements (bread and wine). Originally it was a psalm with *antiphon (*antiphona ad offerendum*); today only the antiphon remains. Unlike the other antiphonal chants of the Mass (Introit, Communion), the Offertory acquired a highly developed melismatic style, thus becoming a responsorial chant.

Office, Divine [L. *officium*]. In the Roman Catholic liturgy, the services of the canonical or daily hours (as distinct from that of the Mass), such services including *psalms, *canticles, *antiphons, *responsories, *hymns, *versicles, lessons (lections, readings), and prayers. The Office comprises eight services or hours: (1) *Matins* [L. *matutinum*], held during the night, usually between midnight and dawn; (2) *Lauds* [*laudes*], immediately following Matins, originally at sunrise; (3) *Prime* [*ad primam*], *c.* 6 a.m.; (4) *Terce* [*ad tertiam*], *c.* 9 a.m.; (5) *Sext* [*ad sextam*], *c.* noon; (6) *None* [*ad nonam*], *c.* 3 p.m.; (7) *Vespers* [*vesperae*], sunset; (8) *Compline* [*completorium*], immediately after Vespers or before retiring. The Mass follows Terce except on ordinary weekdays, when it follows Sext, or on fast days, when it follows None. From the musical point of view the most important Offices are Matins, Vespers, Lauds, and Compline.

Ohana, Maurice (b. Casablanca, 12 June 1914). Studied at the Sorbonne and was also a pupil of Lesur and Casella. Settled in France. Works incl. operas; ballets; *Llanto por Ignacio Sánchez Mejías* for speaker, baritone, chorus, chamber orch., 1950; a guitar concerto, 1950–56, and *Tres gráficos* for guitar and orch., 1950–57; *Études chorégraphiques* for 6 percussionists, 1955; *Tombeau de Claude Debussy* for soprano, zither in third-tones, piano, chamber orch., 1961.

Oiseau de feu, L' [F., The Firebird]. Ballet by Stravinsky, produced at the Ballets Russes (choreography by Fokine, scenery and costumes by Golovine and Bakst) in Paris in 1910. Three versions of a suite taken from the ballet have been made by the composer, the last (1945) the same as with the first (1911), but for a smaller orchestra.

Oketus. See Hocket.

Oktave [G.]. Octave. Applied to instruments, it means sizes an octave above the normal size (e.g., *Oktavflöte*, piccolo flute), or below it (e.g., *Oktavfagott*, contrabassoon). *Oktavgattung, *octave species.

Oktoechos. See *Echos.*

Old Hundredth. An old hymn tune that was used in Bèze's *Genevan Psalter* (1551) for the 134th Psalm, in Knox's *Anglo-Genevan Psalter* (1556) for the 3rd Psalm, and in Sternhold and Hopkins' *Psalter* (1562) for the 100th Psalm (hence the name).

Old Roman chant. A repertory of chant discovered *c.* 1890 and preserved in five manuscripts (the earliest dated 1071), all of which were written in Rome. Liturgically, it is very similar to Gregorian chant in both the structure of Mass and Office and the texts prescribed for the various services. The melodies are essentially different, although occasionally their outlines agree with those of the corresponding Gregorian melodies. It is now thought that the Old Roman and Gregorian repertories represent different locales rather than different periods, the Old Roman being connected with Rome and the Gregorian with the Frankish kingdom and empire of Pepin and Charlemagne.

Oldberg, Arne (b. Youngstown, Ohio, 12 July 1874; d. Evanston, Ill., 17 Feb. 1962). Studied in Chicago, Vienna, and with Rheinberger in Munich. Teacher at Northwestern Univ., 1899–1941. Composed 5 symphonies and other orch. works; *St. Francis of Assisi* for baritone and orch., 1954; 2 piano concertos and a violin concerto; chamber music; piano pieces.

Oliphant. A medieval instrument for signaling, made from an elephant's tusk, often beautifully carved.

Oliver, Henry Kemble (b. Beverly, Mass., 24 Nov. 1800; d. Salem, Mass., 12 Aug. 1885). Church organist in Salem and Boston. Treasurer of the commonwealth of Massachusetts, 1861–65. Composed hymn tunes, motets, and other church music. Published several collections of church music.

Oliveros, Pauline (b. Houston, 30 May 1932). Pupil of Erickson. Co-founder, with Subotnick and Sender, of the San Francisco Tape Music Center, 1961, and

its director when it was moved to Mills College in 1966. Has worked with group improvisation, electronic techniques, and mixed media. Teacher at the Univ. of California at San Diego from 1967. Works incl. *Outline* for flute, percussion, string bass, 1963; *Aeolian Partitions*, theater piece for chamber ensemble, 1969; *Beautiful Soop*, on tape, 1967; *Festival House*, for orch., chorus, mimes, film, lighting, 1968; *Phantom fathom*, mixed-media events, 1972.

Ondeggiando [It.]; **ondulé** [F.]. In violin playing, an undulating movement of the bow [see Bowing (n)]. It is used for arpeggiolike figures, for an alternation between two or more pitches, and also on one pitch in order to produce a slight fluctuation of intensity. In earlier music (*c.* 1650–1750; Purcell, Stamitz) the third of these effects, which is a kind of *tremolo, was rather common, being indicated by a wavy line [see Tremolo].

Ondes Martenot [F.]. See under Electronic instruments.

O'Neill, Norman (b. London, 14 Mar. 1875; d. there, 3 Mar. 1934). Pupil of Somervell and I. Knorr. Music director of the Haymarket Theatre in London, 1909 –31. Teacher at the Royal Academy of Music from 1924. Composed much incidental music for the theater; ballets; orch. works; chamber music; piano pieces; songs.

Ongarese, all' [It.]. In Hungarian style.

Onion flute. Eunuch flute. See Mirliton.

Onslow, (André) George(s) (Louis) (b. Clermont-Ferrand, 27 July 1784; d. an English father and a French mother; d. there, 3 Oct. 1853). Pupil of Dušek in London and Reicha in Paris. Composed 3 comic operas, all produced in Paris; 4 symphonies and other orch. works; 34 string quintets, 36 string quartets, 6 piano trios, and other chamber music; piano pieces.

Op. Abbr. for *opus.

Open fifth, open triad. A fifth or triad without the third, e.g., c–g–c'.

Open forms. See Aleatory music.

Open harmony. See under Spacing.

Open notes. (1) On wind instruments, the tones produced without depressing any key or valve or covering any finger hole. (2) On stringed instruments, the tones produced on the *open strings.

Open pipe. See under Wind instruments.

Open strings. The unstopped strings of violins, lutes, etc. Their use is sometimes prescribed by a zero where a fingering numeral (1–4) might otherwise occur.

Opera [It.; F. *opéra;* G. *Oper;* Sp. *ópera*]. A drama that is primarily sung, is accompanied by an orchestra, and is presented on the stage. The text of such a work, called a *libretto, is sometimes based on one or more purely literary antecedents. The music frequently begins with an *overture and consists of a combination of *arias, *duets, *ensembles, and *recitatives [see Number opera]. *Ballet may also be an important feature. Throughout much of the history of opera, recitative served to carry forward the dramatic action, while the more lyrical or reflective moments of the drama were set musically as arias, duets, or ensembles. Ensembles occurring at the ends of acts, however, are often designed to bring about musical and dramatic climaxes simultaneously. In some kinds of works, spoken dialogue replaces recitative [see Ballad opera; *Singspiel;* Comic opera; Operetta; Melodrama].

Although music played an important role in ancient Greek theater and was an important part of medieval *liturgical drama as well, the history of opera proper does not begin until about 1600 with the work of the Florentine *camerata and the development of the recitative style of accompanied *monody. The earliest operas, all performed at Florence, were *Dafne,* poem by Rinuccini, music by J. Peri (1597; music lost); *Euridice,* poem by Rinuccini, music by G. Caccini (perf. 1602); *Euridice,* poem by Rinuccini, music by Peri and Caccini (1600). These works consist mostly of recitative over a thoroughbass whose harmonies were realized by a small instrumental ensemble. The first major monument in the history of opera, however, was Monteverdi's *La favola d'Orfeo* (Mantua, 1607; poem by A. Striggio), which shows a much greater richness in the variety and complexity of its musical forms as well as in its instrumentation.

In the third decade of the 17th century the center of operatic interest shifted to Rome. D. Mazzocchi's *La catena d'Adone* (1626) and Landi's *Il Sant' Alessio* (1632) show the gradual differentiation between recitative and aria styles. The Roman operas are distinguished by extensive use of vocal ensembles. This school was also the first to produce *comic opera.

The first public *opera house was opened in Venice in 1637, and the ensuing transformation of opera from a courtly entertainment for invited guests to a public spectacle for a general audience had important consequences for both music and libretto. Composers at Venice in this period included Monteverdi, with *Il ritorno d'Ulisse in patria* (1641) and *L'incoronazione di Poppea* (1642), and P. F. Cavalli, with *Giasone* (1649) and *Serse* (1654). Also important during this period was M. A. Cesti, active in various cities, whose *Il pomo d'oro* was produced in Vienna in 1668. These works show a clear distinction between recitative and aria, the latter having crystallized into standard forms (strophic, ostinato-bass, *da capo*), and they make use of lavish staging, greater numbers of characters, plot complications including comic episodes, and virtuoso soloists, the vocal ensemble being less prominent than in the first half of the century.

By the end of the 17th century, Italian opera was firmly established in its native land as a leading musical institution, and the forms of music and drama that it had developed by then remained basic to the further evolution of opera both in Italy and in other countries over the next two centuries. In addition to the Venetians A. Sartorio and G. Legrenzi, notable composers of the latter part of the century were A. Stradella, F. Provenzale (one of the first composers of opera at Naples), C. Pallavicino, and A. Steffani, the latter two active in South German centers.

French national opera was founded by Robert Cambert (*Pomone,* 1671) and J.-B. Lully (*Cadmus et Hermione,* 1673;

Armide, 1686). Although Italian opera was performed in Paris between 1645 and 1662 (notably the first performance of Luigi Rossi's *Orfeo* in 1647), the French were slow to adopt the form. Nevertheless, Lully was able to combine some features of classical French tragedy (Corneille, Racine), French ballet, and the pastorale to create a form of opera that he called *tragédie lyrique*. These works made use of special kinds of recitative and overture, and, as compared with Italian operas, they employed more ballets, instrumental music, choruses, and short simple *airs rather than elaborate arias. This type of opera remained essentially unchanged in the hands of Lully's successors, including Rameau (*Hippolyte et Aricie*, 1733; *Castor et Pollux*, 1737), whose operas represent the high point of this form in France before Gluck.

English opera developed from the *masque. John Blow's *Venus and Adonis* (*c*. 1684), although entitled "a masque," is the first genuine opera by a single composer to be produced in England. Its most important precedent (sometimes called the first English opera) is *The Siege of Rhodes* (1656; music now lost), which made use of "recitative musick" by Matthew Locke, Henry Lawes, and others. The greatest figure in English opera before the 20th century is Henry Purcell, whose *Dido and Aeneas* (*c*. 1689) shows some French influence.

The early history of opera in Germany is dominated by Italian composers and works. The first important native school of opera was created at Hamburg in the latter part of the 17th century. Its principal composer was R. Keiser (*Croesus*, 1711), whose works have some Italian features and directly influenced Handel. After Keiser, German opera declined and by the middle of the 18th century had entirely disappeared.

The prevailing type of 18th-century Italian serious opera (*opera seria*) was cultivated in all countries (except France) by native and Italian composers alike. Because many of its early composers worked chiefly at Naples, this type of opera is sometimes called Neapolitan [see Neapolitan school], but Naples was one center among many. *Opera seria* was based largely on the dramatic ideals of A. Zeno and P. Metastasio, who sought to reform the 17th-century libretto by purging it of comic and fantastic episodes and creating a unified, three-act dramatic structure with characters and subjects drawn principally from ancient history or legend (seldom mythology). The functions of recitative and aria were strictly separated, and each aria was permitted to express only a single affection [see Affections, doctrine of]. The arias were almost exclusively in the *da capo* form, and a number of stereotypes developed for a variety of dramatic situations [see Aria]. Along with the importance of the aria came the importance of the virtuosi (including the *castrati) who sang them. Though A. Scarlatti is sometimes called the founder of the *opera seria*, the most characteristic features of the genre were not fully realized until about 1720, with the works of N. A. Porpora, L. Vinci, L. Leo, and J. A. Hasse. The greatest representative of Italian opera of the period was G. F. Handel, who produced many such works in London between 1711 and 1740 (*Giulio Cesare*, 1724; *Tamerlano*, 1724; *Rodelinda*, 1725). Later composers of *opera seria* include N. Piccinni, G. Sarti, A. Sacchini, A. Salieri, Gluck (early works), J. C. Bach, and Mozart (*Idomeneo*, 1781).

Attempts to reform *opera seria*, particularly the rigidity of its form and the excesses of singers to which it lent itself, were features of the works of N. Jommelli and T. Traetta. Gluck (in collaboration with the librettist R. Calzabigi) is usually credited with the greatest achievements in this attempted reform. Of his "reform" operas, only *Orfeo ed Euridice* (1762) and *Alceste* (1767) were originally composed in Italian, however, and both were later revised and adapted to French texts. His other late operas (*Iphigénie en Aulide*, 1774; *Armide*, 1777; *Iphigénie en Tauride*, 1779) on French poems were designed for and performed at Paris, and they embodied many of the features that had been characteristic of French opera from the time of Lully and Rameau: comparative subordination of music to drama, avoidance of mere vocal display, flexibility of musical forms, closer approximation of style between recitative and aria, general simplicity both of subject and treatment, and the use of choral and ballet scenes. See also Comic opera.

The climax of later 18th-century Italian opera is reached in the works of Mozart (*Le nozze di Figaro*, 1786; *Don Giovanni*, 1787; *Così fan tutte*, 1790), though these three Italian masterpieces were of the comic or semicomic variety, drawing directly on the tradition of *opera buffa* [see Comic opera]. These works are particularly notable for the sharpness and subtlety of their characterization, the integration of vocal and instrumental factors, and the adaptation of the classical symphonic style in their ensemble finales. Mozart's *Die Entführung aus dem Serail* (1782) and *Die Zauberflöte* (1791) are important examples of **Singspiel*, though the latter elaborates the form considerably and is an important forerunner of 19th-century German romantic opera.

The influence of Gluck was evident in a school of large-scale "heroic" opera centering at Paris, represented by such works as A. Sacchini's *Dardanus* (1784) and *Oedipe à Colone* (1786), A. Salieri's *Les Danaïdes* (1784), Cherubini's *Médée* (1797), G. Spontini's *La vestale* (1807), and E.-N. Méhul's *Joseph* (1807). The continuation of this school was the 19th-century "grand opera," of which the most famous examples are D. Auber's *La muette de Portici* (1828), G. Rossini's *Guillaume Tell* (1829), J. Halévy's *La juive* (1835), G. Meyerbeer's *Robert le Diable* (1831), *Les Huguenots* (1836), and *Le prophète* (1849), R. Wagner's *Rienzi* (1842), and H. Berlioz' *Les troyens* (2nd part prod. 1863; whole work, 1890). Works of this type sought to overwhelm the public with a succession of brilliant numbers, massive crowd scenes, and lavish sets. In contrast to this style was opera with more realistic, often melodramatic subjects, a characteristic form being the "rescue opera" (Cherubini's *Les deux journées*, 1800; Beethoven's *Fidelio*, 1805, 1806, 1814).

In Italy the leading composers were Rossini (best known for his comic opera *Almaviva*, better known as *Il barbiere di Siviglia*, 1816), Bellini (*Norma*, 1831), Donizetti (*Lucrezia Borgia*, 1833; *Lucia di Lammermoor*, 1835), and Verdi (*Rigoletto*, 1851; *Il trovatore*, *La traviata*, 1853; *La forza del destino*, 1862; *Aida*, 1871; *Otello*, 1887; *Falstaff*, 1893). The crowning point of typical Italian opera, characterized by melodramatic plots, melodies of a popular character, and concentration on vocal numbers designed to produce an immediate effect [see Number opera], is reached in Verdi's works of the 1850s. *Aida*, a work in the "grand opera" tradition, shows unmistakable signs of the changes in style that were to be fully realized in *Otello* and *Falstaff:* improved literary quality of the libretto, continuity of presentation, a more flexible rhythm, more varied harmony, and closer approach to equality between vocal and instrumental elements—though still retaining the classical Italian qualities of clarity, dramatic simplicity, and profound comprehension of the expressive possibilities of the solo voice.

In France, interest in "grand opera" in the early 19th century was shared with the *opéra comique*, a form and style inherited from the preceding period and that gradually developed into the lyric opera of Gounod (*Faust*, 1859) and A. Thomas (*Mignon*, 1866), both showing Italian influence. Later 19th-century French opera is represented by Bizet (*Carmen*, 1875), Delibes (*Lakmé*, 1883), Chabrier (*Gwendoline*, 1886, obviously indebted to Wagner's *Tristan und Isolde*, 1865), Massenet (*Manon*, 1884), D'Indy (*Fervaal*, 1897), and other composers discussed below.

In Russia a national school of opera was definitively launched with the performance of Glinka's *A Life for the Czar* in 1836. Its chief representative was Mussorgsky, who in *Boris Godunov* (1874) created a work that combined nationalist subject matter and musical material with originality and great dramatic power. Other composers of Russian opera are Borodin (*Prince Igor*, 1890) and Rimsky-Korsakov (*The Snow Maiden*, 1882; *Sadko*, 1898). Tchaikovsky's works in operatic form (*Yevgeny Onyegin*, or *Eugen Onegin*, 1879; *The Queen of Spades*, 1890) are in the romantic style but are not nationalist.

The background of romantic opera in Germany is found in the *Singspiel* of the late 18th and early 19th centuries. An important early composer is L. Spohr

(*Faust*, 1816; *Jessonda*, 1823). Weber's *Der Freischütz* (1821) and *Euryanthe* (1823) established the fundamental characteristics of the school: (1) romantic treatment of subjects derived from national legend and folklore; (2) a deep feeling for nature and the use of natural phenomena as an essential element in the drama; (3) the acceptance of supernatural agencies as a means of dramatic development; and (4) nationalism. The operas of Marschner (*Der Vampyr*, 1828; *Hans Heiling*, 1833) continue the general type established by Weber, whose influence is strongly evident in Wagner's *Der fliegende Holländer* (1843) and even *Lohengrin* (1850).

Wagner's next two operas after *Der fliegende Holländer* are steps in the evolution toward the *music drama*. *Tannhäuser* (1845) still retains the old-fashioned division into "numbers" and has some unessential display scenes, but in *Lohengrin* (composed 1846–48) music and drama are more closely unified, and the vocal line begins to be emancipated from the older periodic rhythm, approaching the free melodic style of the late works. Wagner employed the early years of his exile (1849–64) in completing the libretto and part of the music of *Der Ring des Nibelungen* and in writing various essays, of which the most important is *Oper und Drama* (1851). In this work he developed the theoretical basis for the music drama, whose practical application appears in the four dramas of the *Ring* (first complete perf. at Bayreuth, 1876), in *Tristan und Isolde* (composed 1857–59, perf. 1865), in *Die Meistersinger von Nürnberg* (composed 1862–67, perf. 1868), and in *Parsifal* (composed 1877–82; perf. 1882).

These works are all based on a concept of the music drama as a universal art form (*Gesamtkunstwerk*) in which all the constituent arts are transfigured, sacrificing their individual identities and some of their special characteristics for the larger possibilities of development opened up by the new association. Myth, in Wagner's view, is the ideal subject, and only music is capable of conveying the intensity of feeling to which the ideas of the myth expressed in poetry give rise. The vocal line is flexible (nonperiodic rhythm) and free (no formal divisions into recitative, aria, etc.); it implies a polyphonic substructure that is realized by the orchestra and that embodies the inner action of the drama (the feelings) as the words embody its outer action (the precise ideas with which the feelings are associated). The orchestral music is continuous throughout an act (no perfect cadences; the continual shifting of the tonal center); the music is unified by *leitmotifs—short musical themes, each connected with a particular person, thing, or idea (or all three, as in the case of Siegfried's horn call), and recurring, varying, or developing musically in accord with the recurrence, variation, or development of the corresponding object in the drama. The influence of Wagner's musical language, especially its extended use of chromaticism, was felt in all fields of composition.

Wagner's musical style and his ideal of continuous melody influenced many composers of opera in the late 19th and early 20th centuries, particularly Richard Strauss (*Salome*, 1905; *Der Rosenkavalier*, 1911). At the same time, the music drama provoked a reaction in favor of so-called realism in subject matter joined with compression and simplicity of musical treatment. This reaction took such forms as the "realism" of Bizet (*Carmen*, 1875), the *verismo* of Mascagni (*Cavalleria rusticana*, 1890), Leoncavallo (*I pagliacci*, 1892), and Puccini (*La bohème*, 1896; *Tosca*, 1900), and the "naturalism" of Bruneau (*Messidor*, 1897) and Charpentier (*Louise*, 1900). Another reaction to 19th-century styles was *impressionism, of which the most important operatic example is Debussy's *Pelléas et Mélisande* (1902). Dukas' *Ariane et Barbe-Bleue* (1907) and Bartók's *Bluebeard's Castle* (composed 1911, perf. 1918), both based on a Maeterlinck drama, were strongly influenced by Debussy. Maurice Ravel's *L'heure espagnole* (1911) and Fauré's *Pénélope* (1913) are also operas in the French impressionist style. In Italian opera immediately before World War I, both French and German influences began to replace the *verismo* style (I. Montemezzi, *L'amore dei tre re*, 1913).

In the period following World War I, the established opera houses still leaned heavily on the standard repertory from

Mozart to Puccini. Despite such works as Alban Berg's atonal *Wozzeck* (1925) and Schoenberg's uncompleted masterpiece *Moses und Aron* (acts I and II completed 1932, radio perf. 1954), many composers retained traditional subjects, forms, and musical styles (R. Strauss, *Die Frau ohne Schatten,* 1919). Among the most significant operas of the 1920s are Janáček's *Kát'a Kabanová* (1921) and *The Cunning Vixen* (1924) and Prokofiev's *The Love for Three Oranges* (1921). Jazz influenced Krenek's *Jonny spielt auf* (1927) and Weill's *Die Dreigroschenoper* (1928). The only serial opera that has found public acceptance is Berg's *Lulu* (1937). Schoenberg's *Moses und Aron* (less successful because of enormous staging difficulties) exemplifies an important tendency in this period to combine the characteristics of opera and oratorio with works of serious ethical purpose with huge musical and stage resources. Other examples of this tendency are Arthur Honegger's *Jeanne d'Arc au bûcher* (1938), Paul Hindemith's *Mathis der Maler* (1938), and Darius Milhaud's *Christophe Colomb* (1930). Other operas of the 1930s are Virgil Thomson's *Four Saints in Three Acts* (1934), an opera in a simple musical style set to a text by Gertrude Stein, and Shostakovich's *Lady Macbeth of Mtsensk* (1934).

Since World War II, numerous works in traditional styles have achieved some public success: G. C. Menotti's *The Medium* (1946), *The Consul* (1950), *Amahl and the Night Visitors* (1951), and *The Last Savage* (1963); S. Barber's *Vanessa* (1958); W. Walton's *Troilus and Cressida* (1954); and A. Copland's *The Tender Land* (1954). In a somewhat more venturesome vein are Britten's *Peter Grimes* (1945), *The Turn of the Screw* (1954), *A Midsummer Night's Dream* (1960), and *Curlew River* (1964). Operas on a very large scale are Prokofiev's *War and Peace* (1955), Hindemith's *Die Harmonie der Welt* (1957), Milhaud's *David* (1954), and Ginastera's *Don Rodrigo* (1964). Along with the tendency toward the fusion of opera and oratorio came an opposite trend toward opera as straightforward dramatic entertainment, serious or comic, in a neoclassical revival of the 18th-century principle of the *number

opera; the outstanding example is Stravinsky's *The Rake's Progress* (1951). Another important work of this type is Poulenc's *Les dialogues des Carmélites* (1957). Serial techniques were used by Luigi Nono for *Intolleranza 1960* (1961).

In the United States *The Ballad of Baby Doe* (1956) by Douglas Moore and *Susannah* (1955) by Carlisle Floyd are examples of folk operas. Gershwin's *Porgy and Bess* (1935) draws on folk materials from American Negro culture as well as elements of jazz and has remained a unique synthesis of these materials with the traditions of opera and a unique popular success. Other American operas are *Montezuma* (first perf. in Berlin, 1964) by Roger Sessions, *The Crucible* (1961) by Robert Ward, *The Mother of Us All* (1947) by Virgil Thomson, and *The Wings of the Dove* (1961) by Douglas Moore.

See also Comic opera; Operetta; Ballad opera; *Singspiel;* Libretto; *Opera seria; Verismo;* Number opera; Aria; Madrigal comedy; Masque; Liturgical drama; Recitative; *Bel canto; Pasticcio; Leitmotiv.*

Opéra bouffe [F.]. See Comic opera.

Opera buffa [It.]. See Comic opera.

Opéra comique [F.]. See Comic opera.

Opera houses. The first public opera house was the Teatro San Cassiano in Venice, opened in 1637; previously, opera performances had been given in private homes and for invited guests only. There followed the establishment of opera houses in London (1656), Paris (1669), Rome (1671), and Hamburg (1678). After 1700, opera houses became common in all the musical centers of Europe.

Opera seria [It.]. An 18th-century Italian opera based on a "serious" plot and divided into three acts, as opposed to the *opera buffa,* the *comic opera consisting of two acts. Handel's operas are examples of *opera seria.* See Opera.

Operetta. In the 18th century, a short opera; in the 19th and 20th centuries, a theatrical piece of light and sentimental character in simple and popular style, containing spoken dialogue, music, and dancing. The modern operetta originated in Vienna with Franz von Suppé (c. 30 operettas from 1860 to his death in 1895) and in Paris with Jacques Offenbach (c. 90 operettas from 1855 to his death in 1880). Johann Strauss the Younger raised the Viennese operetta to international fame with about 16 operettas written between 1871 and 1897, among which *Die Fledermaus* (1874) has remained in the repertory to the present day. The Viennese tradition was continued by Franz Lehár with *Die lustige Witwe* (The Merry Widow, 1905). In England Arthur Sullivan wrote operettas (mostly to librettos by W. S. Gilbert) that represent the first high point in English dramatic music since Purcell.

In the United States, operettas were written by Victor Herbert, composer of *Mlle. Modiste* (1905) and *Naughty Marietta* (1910); and by H. L. Reginald de Koven, remembered chiefly for his *Robin Hood* (1890). Other works are *The Doctor of Alcantara* (1862) by J. Eichberg, *The Firefly* (1912) by Rudolf Friml, *The Student Prince* (1924) by Sigmund Romberg, and G. W. Chadwick's *Tabasco* (1894). During the late 1920s the sentimental operetta began to change (e.g., Jerome Kern's *Showboat,* 1927) into what is now called a *musical comedy, musical play,* or simply *musical.* Political and social satire appeared in *Of Thee I Sing* by George Gershwin (1931; first musical to win a Pulitzer Prize) and Richard Rodgers' *Pal Joey* (text by L. Hart, 1940). Although Irving Berlin's musicals continued the traditional vein (*Annie Get Your Gun,* 1946), a more unified format developed in the 1940s, exemplified by Richard Rodgers' *Oklahoma!* (1943; Pulitzer Prize 1944) and *South Pacific* (1949) and by Cole Porter's *Kiss Me Kate* (1948). Leonard Bernstein's *Candide* (1956) is noteworthy for its musical content, and his *West Side Story* (1957) for the emphasis on choreography. *My Fair Lady* (1956) by Frederick Loewe (lyrics by Alan Jay Lerner) will probably remain a model of the genre. See also Comic opera.

Ophicleide. See under Brass instruments III.

Opus [L., work; F. *oeuvre;* abbr. *op.*]. Used with a number to indicate the chronological position of a composition within a composer's entire output. Opus numbers are usually applied in the order of publication rather than of composition, however. Bach never numbered his compositions, and with both Haydn and Mozart the opus numbers are applied so inconsistently and haphazardly (frequently by the publisher rather than the composer) that they are practically useless. Beethoven was the first to use opus numbers with some consistency, at least for his more important works.

Oratorio. A narrative or dramatic work, usually sacred, employing arias, recitatives, ensembles, choruses, and orchestral music, but not intended to be staged. Many such works employ a narrator [It. *testo*]. The term itself [It., prayer hall] is taken from the name of the place where 16th-century Italian lay congregations met for prayer, readings from the Scriptures, and the singing of **laude.* In its early history and style, the oratorio is closely related to opera.

Emilio de' Cavalieri's *La rappresentazione di anima e di corpo* (1600) is often regarded as the first oratorio, though it is among the works of G. Carissimi (1605–74) that the first oratorios properly so called are found (*Jephte, Jonas, Judicium Salomonis*). Most of Carissimi's oratorios employ Latin texts. Texts in the vernacular (*oratorio volgare*) were also common, however.

The first important German oratorios are by Heinrich Schütz (1585–1672) (*Historia der Auferstehung* [Easter Oratorio]; *Historia von der Geburt Christi* [Christmas Oratorio]). Though often clearly related to the oratorio in form, **Passion music is sometimes regarded as a separate category, and it is to this category that J. S. Bach's principal contributions to the genre were made [see also Christmas Oratorio].

The most celebrated oratorios in English are by G. F. Handel (*Israel in Egypt, Judas Maccabaeus, Jephtha, Messiah*), who turned to the form after a decline in the fortunes of Italian opera in England. In musical style, Handel's oratorios differ from his operas primarily in that the oratorios make greater use of the chorus. Important examples from the period following are Haydn's *The Crea-*

tion and *The Seasons*. Composers of oratorios in the 19th century include Mendelssohn (*Elijah*), Berlioz (*L'enfance du Christ*), Liszt (*Die Legende von der heiligen Elisabeth*), and Franck (*Les Béatitudes*). A flowering of the oratorio in England beginning late in the 19th century included works by Parry (*Job*), Elgar (*The Dream of Gerontius*), and Walton (*Belshazzar's Feast*). Twentieth-century contributions to the repertory have included Honegger's *Le Roi David* and Stravinsky's *Oedipus Rex*, though the latter embodies a fusion of oratorio and *opera that characterizes a number of 20th-century works.

Orbón, Julián (b. Avilés, Spain, 7 Aug. 1925). Studied at the conservatory in Oviedo, Spain, and after emigrating to Cuba, with Ardévol and Copland. Has taught in Cuba and Mexico. Settled in New York, 1963. Has composed a symphony and other orch. works (incl. *Danzas sinfónicas,* 1956, and *Partita* no. 3, 1966); a *concerto grosso* for string quartet and orch., 1958; vocal works; a string quartet and other chamber music; pieces for guitar and for piano.

Orchestra. A large ensemble of instruments, as distinct from a small ensemble (with one player to the part) used for chamber music or from an ensemble consisting primarily of wind instruments, called a *band. The modern symphony orchestra consists of about 100 instruments divided into four main sections: strings, woodwinds, brass, and percussion.

Ensembles of strings (with the occasional addition of winds) first became common in the 17th century. By the late 18th century the standard orchestra included 2 flutes, 2 oboes, 2 clarinets, 2 bassoons, 2 horns, 2 trumpets, 2 kettledrums, and strings (first and second violins, violas, cellos, and double basses, though with fewer players on each part than was the norm in the 19th century).

The orchestra generally called for in compositions of the late 19th century (Wagner, Brahms, Bruckner, Tchaikovsky, R. Strauss) consists of:

Strings: violin I (18); violin II (16); viola (12); cello (10); double bass (8); harp (2). *Woodwinds:* flute (3); piccolo (1); oboe (3); English horn (1); clarinet (3); bass clarinet (1); bassoon (3); double

bassoon (1). *Brass:* horn (6); trumpet (4); trombone (4); tuba (1). *Percussion:* kettledrums (4); glockenspiel, snare drum, bass drum, chimes, xylophones, celesta, cymbals, etc., according to requirements of particular works. To these may be added organ, piano, saxophones, mandolins, and other special instruments. In the early decades of the 20th century, composers often wrote for considerably larger groups.

Orchestration. The art of specifying the use of particular instruments in a composition, especially a composition for a large instrumental ensemble. Sometimes called scoring, it requires a detailed knowledge of the characteristics of individual instruments and of their effects in combination with others. Although the term implies the existence of a process separate from that in which the pitches and rhythms of a composition are chosen, these two aspects of composition are often not entirely separable.

Before 1600 the use of particular instruments was rarely specified in ensemble music. Among the principal factors affecting tastes in orchestration since that time has been continuing technological change in the design and construction of instruments, particularly brasses and woodwinds, whose capabilities were greatly increased during the 19th century. Among the most influential composers with respect to orchestration have been Berlioz, Wagner, R. Strauss, Rimsky-Korsakov, and Mahler. Following World War I, the use of large orchestras such as those specified by Mahler declined in favor of smaller ensembles of diverse kinds. Nevertheless, composers of the 20th century have continued to expand instrumental resources greatly, in part thanks to novel techniques used on traditional instruments (e.g., *multiphonics) and in part through the use of altogether new means of sound production. In the works of some composers of *serial music, orchestration (i.e., the specification of tone color) becomes a structural element [see *Klangfarbenmelodie*]. See also Orchestra.

Orchestrion. See under Mechanical instruments.

Ordinary and **Proper** [L. *ordinarium, proprium*]. In the Roman Catholic rites, the Ordinary is the portion of the service that remains the same for every day of the liturgical year, while the Proper includes all the variable texts and chants. The distinction is particularly important with the *Mass. See also Proper.

Ordoñez, Carlos d' (b. Vienna, 19 Apr. 1734; d. there, 6 Sept. 1786). Violinist and composer. Employed as an Austrian civil servant. Composed *Singspiele;* over 60 symphonies; concertos; over 30 string quartets and other chamber music.

Ordre [F.]. In F. Couperin's *Pièces de clavecin* (1713–30), name for his suite-like collections of pieces in the same key. An *ordre* usually begins with a few pieces in the style of an allemande, courante, and saraband but also includes a great many other pieces with fanciful or descriptive titles. See Suite.

Orfeo. See *Favola d'Orfeo, La* (Monteverdi); *Orphée aux Enfers; Orfeo ed Euridice;* Orpheus and Eurydice.

Orfeo ed Euridice. Opera in three acts by Gluck (libretto by R. di Calzabigi), produced in Vienna, 1762 (produced in Paris as *Orphée,* 1774, with French text). Setting: Greece, legendary times.

Orff, Carl (b. Munich, 10 July 1895). Pupil of Kaminski. Co-founder of the Güntherschule, 1924, where he developed and used techniques of music education involving movement and the use of xylophones and other percussion instruments. Teacher at the Hochschule für Musik in Munich, 1950–60. Has composed operas (incl. *Der Mond,* Munich, 1939, rev. 1950; *Die Kluge,* Frankfurt, 1943; *Antigonae,* Salzburg, 1949; *Oedipus der Tyrann,* Stuttgart, 1959; *Prometheus,* Stuttgart, 1968); the scenic oratorio *Carmina burana;* the scenic cantatas *Catulli carmina,* 1943, and *Trionfo di Afrodite,* 1951, which together with *Carmina burana* form the trilogy *Trionfi;* an Easter cantata and a nativity play; pedagogic works (incl. *Schulwerk,* 1930–35, rev. 1950–54).

Organ [F. *orgue;* G. *Orgel;* It. *organo;* L. *organum;* Sp. *órgano*]. A keyboard instrument, operated by the player's hands and feet, that consists of a series of pipes standing on a wind chest. The wind chest is fitted with valves con-

nected to the keys, either by a direct mechanical linkage (known as a *tracker action) or by electrical and/or pneumatic intermediaries. Means also are provided for delivering a constant supply of air under pressure to the chest. Traditionally the wind was supplied by feeders or bellows; since about 1915 the source of supply has been an electric rotary blower, in which case the bellows serve merely as a reservoir whose top is weighted or sprung to ensure a steady pressure. The simplest organ consists of one set of pipes, each pipe corresponding to one key of the keyboard. However, to make available a variety of tone colors for the performer, organs usually have several sets (*ranks) of pipes, known as *stops or *registers, which can be brought into play or retired ("stopped") at will.

An organ meeting the minimum requirement for a proper rendition of the literature will have two keyboards (*manuals), each controlling a separate division of five or six stops, and a keyboard for the feet (pedal) commanding two to five stops. Organs having four manuals and pedal with fifty to one hundred stops are common, however, and even five to seven manuals have been employed. The divisions, or "organs," connected with the various manuals are called *pedal organ, great organ, swell organ, choir organ, positive organ, solo organ,* and *echo organ.* (Foreign names such as *Hauptwerk, Rückpositiv* [G.] and *récit* [F.] are occasionally used.) Their allotment to the different manuals varies a great deal (except, of course, for the pedal organ), and so does the selection of pipes connected with each of them.

Practically every organ possesses devices that make the various divisions available on keyboards other than their own. These are the so-called *couplers.* For instance, coupler swell-to-great makes the swell organ available on the manual for the great organ, so that stops from both can be sounded simultaneously. Similarly, any manual can be coupled to the pedal. Suboctave couplers and superoctave couplers connect one manual with the lower or higher octave of another manual or of itself. [See also Divided stop.]

Changes in *registration are sometimes desired at moments when the player's hands are too occupied on the keyboard to manipulate a number of stops. To facilitate such changes, special controls are provided in the form of thumb buttons or toe studs, called *combination* (or *composition*) *stops* or *pedals*. Each of these so-called *pistons* controls an *ad libitum* selection of stops, which the player can arrange in advance and then instantly bring into play by a single touch on the piston.

The normal compass of the modern organ manual is 61 notes or five complete octaves extending from C to c''''. That of the pedal keyboard is 32 notes or two and one-half octaves extending from C to g'. The actual pitch range of the organ is much greater than the compass of its keyboards, owing to the fact that there are, in addition to the pipe ranks of normal pitch (comparable to that of the piano), others whose pitch is one or two octaves lower or higher. The normal pitch is called *unison* and is indicated by the symbol 8' [read "eight-foot"; see Foot (2)], the suboctave pitch is 16', and there are three superoctave pitches, designated 4', 2', and 1'. Thus the real compass of the instrument extends over nine complete octaves.

In addition to the various octave pitches, called *foundation stops,* there are the so-called *mutation stops,* whose pitch corresponds to one of the harmonics of the unison pitch. For instance, a mutation stop 2 2/3' is tuned to the third harmonic (twelfth) and hence will sound g' if the key for c is depressed. Such stops are not to be played alone (which would result in transposition) or with a unison stop of about the same loudness (which would result in parallel fifths) but together with a unison stop of considerably greater force, in which case the mutation stop ceases to be heard individually and merely serves as an artificial harmonic, thus modifying the timbre of the unison stop. Finally there are *mixture stops* (also called *compound stops*), i.e., stops that combine a selection of unison and mutation ranks. These serve the same purpose as the mutation stops and must also be drawn together with a sufficiently strong unison stop.

By the 15th century it was customary to place the wind chests, pipes, and mechanism of the organ in a large wooden cabinet, known as the organ case, closed on all sides but the front. The keyboards and stop controls were centered in front at floor level, while the *show pipes* (open diapason, principal, prestant, montre) stood in the opening above the keyboards and together with decorative carvings formed a perforated screen through which the sound from pipes inside the cabinet could pass. For sound projection the close-fitting cabinet acted as a band-shell, giving the organ good attack even in highly reverberant buildings. In the 17th century, when organs grew to the point of having several divisions, each division was likely to be given its own tone cabinet in the overall complex of the organ case, and at least one division, the *Rückpositiv* or chair organ, was nearly always separately situated at the gallery railing below the main body of the instrument and behind the player. The principle according to which an organ is thus visibly divided into cabinets, each relating to a keyboard, is known as the **Werk* principle, a system of organization that became unfashionable during the 19th century but that has been revived in the 20th. A tone cabinet that survived the abandonment of the *Werk* principle is the *expression chamber* or *swell box,* in effect a cabinet whose opening is covered by a set of Venetian shutters that can be opened or closed in varying degrees by a foot pedal. Though artificial, this is for the organ the only possible means for varying dynamics, other than the stepwise addition or subtraction of stops.

There are two distinct classes of organ pipe: flue and reed. The *flue pipe* closely resembles the ordinary tin whistle [see Whistle flute], in which a vibrating air sheet sets up vibrations in the column of air surrounded by the pipe. The type of *reed pipe* used almost exclusively in the organ is known as the *beating reed* and must not be confused with the free reed employed in the harmonium or reed organ [see Reed]. The beating reed consists of a vibrating brass tongue, slightly curved, which rolls down over a long opening in the side of a brass tube, or *shallot,* connected to the lower end of a resonator or horn, usually conical or cylindrical, whose upper end is open to the air.

There are two fundamental kinds of flue pipe: *principal* (or *diapason*) and *flute*. The basic difference between them is the way they are voiced, i.e., adjusted at the mouth, and one speaks of a pipe as being voiced to operate in principal mode or in flute mode. In principal mode the wind sheet vibrates in such a way as to develop in about equal strength the first and second harmonics, while in flute mode only the first harmonic (fundamental) is emphasized. The most common variety of organ flute is the *stopped flute* [G. *gedackt*, F. *bourdon*], whose large-scale cylindrical bodies are made of wood or metal with a stopper or plug in the upper end. *Open flutes* include the *nighthorn* and *block flute*. String-toned stops such as the *cello, viola, salicional,* and *gamba* have a high harmonic development, causing the tone to be thin and cutting. String tone is actually an extreme form of principal tone. *Spitzflute* and *gemshorn* ranks are hybrids that commonly have pipe bodies in the form of an inverted cone.

There are three kinds of reed pipe: *chorus reeds, semichorus reeds,* and *solo* or *orchestral reeds*. Chorus reeds belong chiefly to the trumpet family and appear in the modern organ on both manual and pedal divisions at subunison, unison, and octave pitches. *Posaunes, trombones, trumpets, cornopeans,* and *clarions* are in this category. Although their names suggest orchestral tones, they differ in quality considerably from their orchestral prototypes. The trumpet family has conical resonators of full length, i.e., 8′ C has a resonator of approximately 8 feet in length.

Semichorus reeds come to us largely from the baroque period and are not imitative, although their names may suggest an orchestral background. The *cromorne, schalmei,* and *rankett* are typical examples. The term *semichorus* is used because these reeds may function as chorus reeds, solo stops, or merely timbre creators in combination with other voices. The resonators of this class of reed are often cylindrical and short. They may be half-, quarter-, or even an eighth-length.

The solo or orchestral reeds are imitative of various orchestral instruments, such as the *bassoon, English horn, clari-*

net, and *oboe*. They are used largely as solo stops.

If the organ is regarded as a wind instrument that, besides having multiple pipes of fixed pitches, is mechanically supplied with air under pressure and played from a keyboard, then it dates from *c*. 250 B.C., when the Greek engineer Ktesibios of Alexandria is supposed to have invented the *hydraulos. The pneumatic (as opposed to hydraulically regulated) organ made its first recorded appearance *c*. A.D. 120. In England the organ was known as early as the 7th century, and a large organ is recorded as having been erected at Winchester Cathedral under the Bishop Elphege (d. 951). It supposedly had 400 pipes and 26 bellows, was played by two organists on two keyboards of 20 keys each, and had an exceedingly powerful sound.

The hydraulos and all recorded early pneumatic organs up to as late as 1100 had a very crude key mechanism consisting of slides that were simply pulled out or pushed in to open the pipes. The modern barred wind chest (as in the *tracker action) had its inception in the 14th century, and from that time on the key control was achieved by opening a spring-loaded valve (pallet) that admitted wind from a common supply into a note-channel communicating with all the pipes for any given note.

During the 14th century, along with the development of large but still cumbersome church organs, there appeared a parallel development of a smaller, more refined, and more tractable instrument called a *positive*. This instrument was a self-contained organ small enough to be moved like a piece of furniture. It had one keyboard, no pedals, and no exceptionally large or loud pipes, since it was often used in small rooms or for accompaniment. The use of separate *stops, whereby the player could select different ranks of pipes to play while others remained mute, seems to have begun in Italy during the first half of the 15th century.

While the Gothic church organ and the positive organ are the true ancestors of the modern organ, two other instruments developed during the 14th and 15th centuries also deserve mention. These were the *portative organ*, or organetto, and the *regal*. Both were quite small, the former having a set of ordinary pipes of high pitch and a short-compass keyboard, the latter producing sound by means of beating or free reeds. The regal was actually the ancestor of the modern reed organ or *harmonium. Both the portative and the regal could be carried by means of a strap around the neck, so that the player could work the bellows with the left hand and play on the keyboard with the right.

In the 16th century, national schools of organ building began to develop, and these took distinct forms during the 17th and early 18th centuries, continuing separate evolutions until well into the 19th century. The 20th century has seen a considerable return to the classical principles of organ building of the 17th and 18th centuries.

Organ chorale. A polyphonic composition for organ based on a *chorale melody (excluding simple harmonizations such as those suitable for accompanying congregational singing), often intended to serve as an introduction to congregational singing (in which case it is called a *chorale prelude*). Although the term is commonly used only for the polyphonic settings of German Protestant chorales, the earlier organ settings of hymns of the Roman Catholic Church may also be included. In the works of Bach, the following types can be distinguished: (a) *cantus firmus chorale*, in which the chorale melody is presented in long notes, usually in the bass; (b) *chorale motet*, in which each line of the chorale is treated in imitation, resulting in a succession of "fugues"; (c) *chorale fugue*, in which the first line or the initial phrase of the chorale is treated as a fugue subject; (d) *melody chorale*, in which the chorale appears as a continuous melody in the soprano, accompanied by contrapuntal parts that usually proceed in definite figures (e.g., most of the chorales from the *Orgelbüchlein; see Figured chorale); (e) ornamented chorale*, in which the chorale is used in the soprano with elaborate ornamentation; (g) *chorale fantasia*, in which free treatment of the chorale melody prevails; (h) *chorale variations* (*partitas*), which consist of a number of variations (corresponding to the number of stanzas of the text) on the chorale mel-

ody. Naturally, these methods of treatment frequently overlap.

Organ Mass [G. *Orgelmesse*]. Polyphonic composition of the Mass, nearly always the Ordinary, for organ. The Codex Faenza of *c*. 1400 contains a single Kyrie as well as two Kyrie-Gloria sets, all based on the corresponding plainsong items and composed according to a structural principle encountered in nearly all organ Masses—alternation of organ music and plainsong [see Alternation]. Similar settings of the Gloria, Credo, and Kyrie are preserved in German sources of the 15th century. In the 16th century in Germany, France, England, and Italy, complete organ Masses including all five items (though sometimes without the Credo) were composed, each item employing the alternation principle. In the 17th century the organ Mass was cultivated mainly in Italy and France. Bach wrote what has been called a "German organ Mass" in his *Clavier-Übung*, pt. III.

Organ point. See Pedal point.

Organ stops. See under Organ.

Organetto [It.]. A 14th-century name for the *portative organ.

Organistrum [L.]. Medieval name for the *hurdy-gurdy.

Organum [L.]. (1) Organ. Early writers, including St. Augustine (A.D. 354–430), use the term to refer to instruments in general as well as to the particular instrument still known by that name.

(2) The earliest type of preserved polyphonic music, from the 9th century (the treatise *Musica enchiriadis*) through the 13th century, particularly important examples having been composed about 1200 (by Leonin and Perotin; see also Notre Dame, school of; *Magnus liber organi*). Such pieces consist of a liturgical (plainsong) part, called the tenor, and one or more contrapuntal parts (*duplum, triplum, quadruplum,* respectively, terms which are applied both to the individual contrapuntal parts and to the two-, three-, and four-part texture as a whole). The following types can be distinguished:

I. *Parallel organum* (*c*. 900–1050). To the main part, called the *vox principalis*, is added a *vox organalis* at the lower fifth or fourth, note against note [Ex. 1]. Either or both parts can be duplicated at the octave, so that the sound d–a is amplified to A–d–a, d–a–d′, D–d–a, d–a–a′, d–a–d′–a′, etc. (*composite organum*). In organum at the fourth, the parallelism of the parts is usually observed only in the middle of the phrase, while at the beginning and end the parts move in oblique motion, starting and ending in unison [Ex. 2].

1. Parallel organum at the fifth ("Musica enchiriadis"). 2. Converging organum at the fourth (ibid.). 3. Free organum (Milanese treatise). 4. Contrary organum (Cotton). 5. Melismatic organum (Compostela). 6. Measured organum (Notre Dame; two rhythmic versions).

II. *Free and contrary organum* (*c*. 1050–1150). In the second half of the 11th century, contrary motion began to be used side by side with parallel motion (in fourths, fifths, occasionally even thirds) and oblique motion. This type

may be called free organum. In addition to theoretical sources (*Ad organum faciendum*, in Milan [Ex. 3]; short treatise of Montpellier) there are long compositions written in this style, especially the famous *Ut tuo propitiatus* and five Alleluias from Chartres. John Cotton, in his *Musica* of *c*. 1100, emphasizes the importance of contrary motion [Ex. 4].

III. *Melismatic organum* (mid-12th century). This type is characterized by the use of groups of notes in the added part against a single note of the tenor, the length of such a group varying from a few notes to long melismas. Examples of pure melismatic organum occur particularly in the Codex Calixtinus from *Compostela [Ex. 5]. The organa of *St. Martial often have sections in organal style side by side with others in a note-against-note style called *discant.

IV. *Measured organum* (before and after 1200). In the organa of the school of Notre Dame, the alternation of organal and discant sections became a standard practice and was usually applied so that the syllabic or neumatic sections of the plainsong were composed in a profuse style (up to 40 or more notes against one note in the tenor) and its melismatic sections in a concise style (one to three notes against one). Of the greatest importance was the introduction of measured rhythm, according to the rhythmic *modes. In the earliest Notre Dame organa, all in two parts and presumably composed by Leonin [see *Magnus liber organi*], modal rhythm is clearly present in the discant sections, though less clearly in the others, the rhythmic interpretation of which is in dispute [Ex. 6]. This type of organum is referred to by theorists as *organum duplum, organum purum,* or *organum per se.* Modal rhythm became fully established in the works of Perotin, who wrote numerous organa in three parts (*organum triplum*) as well as two *organa quadrupla.*

In the repertory of *Notre Dame, polyphonic treatment and, therefore, the term *organum* was restricted to settings of certain types of plainsong, mainly responsorial chants (i.e., Graduals, Alleluias, and responsories) and the *Benedicamus Domino.* Only the soloists' sections of such chants were used as the basis for polyphonic composition. For example, in a Gradual only the incipit of the respond and the entire verse, except for its conclusion, were composed polyphonically, the remaining portions being supplied by the choir in plainsong [for the structure of the Graduals, see Psalmody II].

Orgel [G.]. Organ. *Orgelmesse*, *organ Mass. *Orgelpunkt*, *pedal point. *Orgelwalze*, barrel organ [see Mechanical instruments].

Orgelbüchlein [G.]. Original title of a manuscript by J. S. Bach that contains 45 *organ chorales but was intended to include many more, since numerous pages are empty except for the name of the chorale. All the compositions are short settings, mostly of the melody-chorale type [see under Organ chorale]. The collection was probably made toward the end of Bach's stay in Weimar (1708–17). According to the title inscription, it was designed "to instruct a beginning organist how to set a chorale in diverse manners and also how to acquaint himself with the pedal, this being treated fully *obbligato.*"

Orgue [F.]. Organ. *Orgue de Barbarie*, the barrel organ of the Italian organ grinder, consisting of one or two rows of small organ pipes in a small portable case, operated by turning a handle. *Orgue expressif*, *harmonium. *Orgue positif*, positive organ [see Organ].

Ornamentation. The practice, common in varying degrees from the Middle Ages through the 19th century, of embellishing musical works through additions to or variations of their essential rhythm, melody, or harmony. Often, substantial liberty for the performer is implied, though this liberty operates within certain conventions for each period. Although the concept may seem to imply the existence of unadorned compositions representing the pure intentions of their composers, ornamentation, particularly in the 17th and 18th centuries, is often an indispensable feature of a musical work, even when its details are not fully specified by the composer. Ornamentation may be (1) left entirely to the improvisation of the performer(s); (2) indicated by some sort of written sign; (3) written out in notes. Before about 1600 the first type pre-

vailed, except in lute and keyboard music, where ornaments were often written out or indicated by special symbols. The principal technique of improvised ornamentation was diminution, that is, the substitution of running passages in shorter notes for longer notes [see Augmentation and diminution]. There are accounts of the technique from the 16th century, and it is found written out in some instrumental works from Spain (*glosas*) and England (*divisions). The generic term for ornamentation in Italy in this period is *gorgia*. In addition to diminution, 16th-century treatises name certain small melodic formulas that consist of either the repetition of a single note or the rapid alternation of two (or three) adjacent notes. To the former type belongs the Italian *trillo* (an accelerated *tremolo); to the latter (*trills), the *tremolo*, *groppo*, and *ribattuta*, as well as the Spanish *redoble* and *quiebro* and the English *relish. The use of such ornaments, termed *affetti*, was promoted by Italian musicians of the 17th century such as Caccini.

It was in France, however, with the name *agréments*, that these ornaments finally became stereotyped and were systematized to an extent that made it possible to indicate them by signs or abbreviations and to establish definite rules for introducing them extemporaneously. The correct interpretation of these signs constitutes a considerable problem in performing music of the 17th and 18th centuries, owing to the fact that the nomenclature and signs used for the individual *agréments* lacked uniformity and consistency. The *agréments*, in general, may be divided into the following categories: (1) appoggiatura (also double appoggiatura); (2) trill; (3) turn; (4) mordent; (5) *Nachschlag;* (6) arpeggio; (7) vibrato. [See the separate entries for each; see also Notation.] During this period singers probably never executed a solo part as it was written. And in instrumental music, composers such as Corelli, Handel, and Tartini often made their written parts mere sketches of what the player should do. The performer's importance is suggested by the fact that Bach was once criticized for writing out in notes ornaments of the sort that performers were accustomed to supplying themselves.

Although improvised ornamentation persisted in certain kinds of vocal music, composers since the late 18th century have largely inclined toward notating their works as precisely as possible, even where the intended effect may have an improvisatory character like that of the ornamentation of earlier periods. The works of Chopin, for example, include numerous instances of what might be called ornaments that are written out in small grace notes.

Ornstein, Leo (b. Kremenchug, Russia, 11 Dec. 1892). Pianist and composer. Emigrated to the U.S. in 1907. Concertized widely in the U.S. and Europe until about 1935, often playing his own and other strikingly modern works. Founded and taught at the Ornstein School of Music in Philadelphia, 1940–55. Has composed orch. works (incl. *The Fog*, 1915; a symphony, 1934); a piano concerto, 1925; choral works; a string quartet, a quintet for piano and strings, and other chamber music; numerous piano pieces (incl. *3 Moods*, 1913; 4 sonatas; *6 Water Colors*, *c*. 1935; many pieces for children); songs.

Orpharion. An instrument of the lute family that was in use *c*. 1600. Shaped like the *bandora but smaller, it had six or more double courses and was tuned like the lute, G c f a d' g'.

Orphée aux enfers [F., Orpheus in the Underworld]. Operetta in two acts by Offenbach (libretto by H. Crémieux and L. Halévy), produced in Paris, 1858. A version in four acts was produced in Paris in 1874. Setting: Greece, legendary times.

Orpheus and Eurydice. Among the numerous operas based on this story are Monteverdi's *La *favola d'Orfeo* (1607), Gluck's *Orfeo ed Euridice* (1762), Offenbach's parody *Orphée aux enfers* (1858), and Krenek's *Orpheus und Eurydike* (1926).

Orpheus in the Underworld. See *Orphée aux enfers*.

Orr, Robin (Robert Kemsley) (b. Brechin, Scotland, 2 June 1909). Studied at the Royal College of Music, at Cambridge, and with Casella and N. Boulanger. Organist at St. John's College,

Cambridge, 1938–50. Teacher at the Royal College of Music, 1950–56; at the Univ. of Glasgow, 1956–65; at Cambridge from 1965. Has composed operas (incl. *Full Circle*, Perth, Scotland, 1968); *Symphony in One Movement*, 1963, and other orch. works; incidental music for the theater; anthems and other choral works; chamber music; songs.

Orrego-Salas, Juan (b. Santiago, Chile, 18 Jan. 1919). Pupil of Allende, Santa Cruz, Thompson, and Copland. Teacher alternately at the National Univ. and the Catholic Univ. in Santiago, 1942–61; at Indiana Univ. from 1961. Has composed an opera-oratorio, *El retablo del rey pobre*, 1952; ballets; a Mass, 1969, and other choral works; 4 symphonies and other orch. works; a piano concerto, 1950, and a concerto for piano trio and orch., 1962; chamber music; piano pieces; songs.

Ortiz, Diego (b. Toledo, *c*. 1525; d. after 1570). *Maestro de capilla* to the Duke of Alba at the Spanish court in Naples, 1555–70. Published a *Tratado de glosas sobre cláusulas y otros géneros de puntos en la música de violones*, 1553, containing variations and other pieces for viola da gamba; motets and other sacred music.

Orto, Marbriano de (b. Ortho, near Laroche, now Belgium; d. Nivelles, Belgium, buried Feb. 1529). Singer in the papal choir in Rome, 1484–94. Served Philip the Fair of Burgundy from 1505, accompanying him to Spain. In the service of the future Emperor Charles V in 1515. Composed Masses, motets, and other sacred music; chansons.

Osanna. *Hosanna.

Osiander, Lucas (b. Nuremberg, 16 Dec. 1534; d. Stuttgart, 17 Sept. 1604). Theologian, organ builder, and composer. Pastor at various churches in Württemberg. Published *50 geistliche Lieder und Psalmen mit 4 Stimmen* . . . , 1586, a collection of chorale harmonizations in which the chorale melody is for the first time consistently placed in the uppermost part.

Ossia [It., or]. Indication for an alternate version, usually one that is easier to execute.

Osterc, Slavko (b. Verzej, Yugoslavia, 17 June 1895; d. Ljubljana, 23 May 1941). Pupil of Jirák, Novák, and Hába. Teacher at the Ljubljana Conservatory, 1927–39; at the Music Academy there, 1939–41. Made some use of quarter-tones. Composed 6 operas; ballets (incl. *The Masque of the Red Death,* after Poe, 1930); orch. works. (incl. *Mouvement symphonique,* 1938, and *Passacaglia-Chorale,* 1939); choral works; chamber music; organ pieces; piano pieces.

Ostinato [It., obstinate]. A melodic and/or rhythmic figure that is persistently repeated throughout a composition or a section of one. Examples occur as early as the Middle Ages. The use of a bass part constructed in this way [It. *basso ostinato;* see Ground; Chaconne and passacaglia] was common in the 17th and early 18th centuries. The technique (not restricted to the bass part) has also been employed extensively by some composers of the 20th century.

Ostrčil, Otakar (b. Smichov, near Prague, 25 Feb. 1879; d. Prague, 20 Aug. 1935). Pupil of Fibich. Conductor of the Prague National Theater from 1920. Composed 5 operas (incl. *The Bud,* Prague, 1911; *Johnny's Kingdom,* Brno, 1934); a symphony and other orch. works; cantatas; chamber music; songs, some with orch.

Otello [It., Othello]. Opera in four acts by Verdi (libretto by A. Boito after Shakespeare), produced in Milan, 1887. Setting: Cyprus, late 15th century.

Ôtez, ôter [F.]. Take off (a stop or the violin mutes).

Othmayr, Caspar (b. Amberg, Germany, 12 Mar. 1515; d. Nuremberg, 4 Feb. 1553). Studied at Heidelberg Univ. Rector of the monastery school at Heilsbronn, near Ansbach, from 1545. Canon at St. Gumbert's in Ansbach from 1547 and provost there from 1548. Composed polyphonic secular songs; sacred works in German and in Latin.

Ottava [It.]. Octave, abbr. *8va* or *(8)*. *All'ottava, ottava alta, ottava sopra,* or simply *8va* written above the notes indicates that the notes should be played one octave higher than written; *ottava bassa, ottava sotto,* or *8va* written below the notes (usually in the bass part) calls for the lower octave. *Coll'ottava* means doubling in the higher (or lower) octave.

Ottavino [It.]. The piccolo *flute.

Ottoni, stromenti d'ottone [It.]. *Brass instruments.

Ours, L' [F., The Bear]. Popular name for Haydn's Symphony no. 82, in C (1786), the first of the *Paris Symphonies.

Ouseley, Frederick Arthur Gore (b. London, 12 Aug. 1825; d. Hereford, 6 Apr. 1889). Studied at Oxford, where he was professor of music from 1855. Ordained a priest in 1849. Composed 2 oratorios; services and anthems, some with orch.; other choral works; chamber music; organ pieces; songs. Published treatises on harmony, counterpoint, and related subjects.

Ouvert, clos [F., open, closed]. In the *ballades, *estampies, and *virelais of the 14th century, *ouvert* and *clos* [L. *apertum, clausum;* It. *aperto, chiuso*] indicate different endings for repeated sections, corresponding to the modern *prima volta, seconda volta,* or first and second endings.

Ouverture [F.]. *Overture.

Overblowing. See under Wind instruments.

Overton, Hall (Franklin) (b. Bangor, Mich., 23 Feb. 1920; d. New York, 24 Nov. 1972). Jazz pianist and composer. Pupil of Persichetti, Riegger, and Milhaud. Teacher at the New School for Social Research in New York, 1962–66; at the Juilliard School, 1960–72. Composed operas (incl. *Huckleberry Finn,* New York, 1971); a ballet, *Nonage,* 1951; 2 symphonies and other orch. works; 3 string quartets and other chamber music; piano pieces; songs.

Overtones. See under Acoustics.

Overture. An instrumental composition intended as an introduction to an opera, oratorio, or similar work.

The operatic overture. The earliest operas, which usually began with a prologue, had no overture, or at most a flourish of instruments such as the "Toccata" of Monteverdi's *Orfeo* (1607). Among the first more elaborate overtures are the three **Sinfonie* that precede the three acts of S. Landi's *Il Sant' Alessio*, each in the form of a *canzona with several short sections. The "canzona" overture was a favorite type in the Venetian opera, where it is usually in the form of an introductory slow movement in duple rhythm followed by a fast movement in triple rhythm (Cavalli, *Giasone*, 1649). Other overtures, hardly different in form, are called "Sonata" (e.g., Cesti, *Il pomo d'oro*, 1668). The Venetian type of overture was the model for Lully's famous French overture (earliest example in his ballet *Alcidiane*, 1658), which became the first standard type. It consists of a slow introduction with dotted rhythm, followed by an allegro in imitative style on a short, canzonalike subject, though the imitative treatment is not strictly maintained. Sometimes the second movement of the French overture ends with a broad adagio passage, and in some later examples this closing passage is extended into a third movement, as in Bach's so-called French Overture (really a French overture followed by a *suite).

In the late 17th century Alessandro Scarlatti introduced another type. Termed the Italian overture (earliest example in *Dal male il bene*, overture, *c.* 1696), it consists of three sections, allegro, adagio, and allegro, an early adumbration of the three movements of the sonata. These sections are in simple homorhythmic style except the first, which introduces some imitative treatment for the entrances of the voices. The usual name for this type is **sinfonia*. During the first half of the 18th century the French and the Italian types existed side by side. Cases of Italian operas and oratorios with a French overture are not rare (e.g., Handel). The French overture disappeared *c.* 1750.

An important feature of the ensuing development of the overture was em-phasis on its closer connection with the opera itself, mainly by incorporation into the overture of material from the opera. This procedure was used in Cesti's *Il pomo d'oro* and Rameau's *Castor et Pollux* (1737) but did not become accepted practice until after 1750. The overture to Gluck's *Iphigénie en Tauride* is perhaps the first to prepare for the mood of the first scene. Famous examples of using the overture to set the emotional background for the plot are those to Haydn's *Creation*, Mozart's *Don Giovanni* and *Die Zauberflöte*, Beethoven's *Leonore* Overtures (not the final *Fidelio* overture), Weber's *Der Freischütz*, and practically all the overtures by Wagner and his successors. Wagner abandoned the sonatalike structure of the overture in favor of a free *Vorspiel* (prelude) leading into the first scene. His precedent has been followed by most modern composers of opera. In strong contrast to this romantic type is the overture to the 19th-century *grand opéra* of French derivation (Rossini, Boieldieu, Auber, Meyerbeer), which usually is a potpourri of the most prominent melodies of the opera.

The concert-overture. This 19th-century genre is an independent orchestral composition written along the same lines as the operatic overture, either as a single movement in sonata form or in the manner of the free *Vorspiel*. Well-known examples are Mendelssohn's *Die Hebriden*, Berlioz' *Le carnaval romain,* and Brahms' *Akademische Festouvertüre*. In this category may also be included the overtures written as introductions to spoken plays and frequently performed as concert pieces, such as Beethoven's overture to Goethe's *Egmont* and Mendelssohn's overture to *A Midsummer Night's Dream*.

Oxford Symphony. Haydn's Symphony no. 92, in G, composed in 1788. It was performed at Oxford in 1791, when Haydn received an honorary degree from the university.

P

P. Abbr. for **piano;* for *pedal* (in organ and piano music); or for [F.] *positif,* i.e., choir organ.

Pablo, Luis de. See De Pablo, Luis.

Pacato [It.]. Calm.

Paccagnini, Angelo (b. Castano Primo, near Milan, 17 Oct. 1930). Conductor and composer. Studied at the Verdi Conservatory in Milan and with Berio at the Studio di fonologia in Milan, of which he became director in 1968. Composer for Italian Radio, 1955–65. Teacher of electronic music at the Verdi Conservatory from 1969. Has composed stage and radio operas (incl. *Mosè,* for radio, 1963); a ballet; orch. works (incl. *Gruppi concertanti,* 1960); choral works; a string quartet and other chamber music; piano pieces; works on tape (incl. *Sequenze e strutture,* 1962; *Stimmen,* 1969).

Pachelbel, Johann (b. Nuremberg, bapt. 1 Sept. 1653; d. there, 3 Mar. 1706). Organist at St. Stephen's Cathedral in Vienna (1674), Eisenach (1677), Erfurt (1678), Stuttgart (1690), Gotha (1692), and St. Sebald's in Nuremberg (1695). Composed numerous organ works, incl. fugues, toccatas, fantasies, Magnificats, chorale settings, and variations; harpsichord suites; trio sonatas; cantatas.

Pacific 231. Symphonic poem ("Mouvement symphonique") by Honegger (1924), named for an American type of locomotive and suggesting its motion from start to full speed to stop.

Pacini, Giovanni (b. Catania, Italy, 17 Feb. 1796; d. Pescia, Italy, 6 Dec. 1867). Studied in Bologna and Venice. Founded a school of music in Viareggio, transferring it later to Lucca. Composed numerous operas (incl. *Saffo,* Naples, 1840); oratorios; cantatas; Masses and other sacred vocal works; a *Dante* symphony; string quartets and other chamber music; arias.

Pacius, Fredrik (Friedrich) (b. Hamburg, 19 Mar. 1809; d. Helsinki, 8 Jan. 1891). Pupil of Spohr and Hauptmann. Court violinist in Stockholm, 1828–34. Teacher at the Univ. of Helsinki from 1835. Composed operas (incl. *Kung Carls Jakt* [King Charles' Hunting Party], on a Swedish text, Helsinki, 1852); orch. works; a violin concerto; choral works; cantatas; songs, incl. *Vårt land,* which became the Finnish national anthem and was adapted to Finnish words (*Maamme laulu*).

Paderewski, Ignace Jan (b. Kurylówka, Podolia, now U.S.S.R., 18 Nov. 1860; d. New York, 29 June 1941). Studied in Warsaw, Berlin, and with Leschetizky in Vienna. Toured the world with extraordinary success as a pianist. Held diplomatic and other posts in the Polish government, 1918–20. Lived in California at various times from 1913. Composed an opera, *Manru,* Dresden, 1901; a symphony, 1903–7; a piano concerto, 1888; a sonata for violin and piano, 1880; numerous piano pieces (incl. *Humoresques de concert,* containing a minuet in G); songs.

Padiglione [It.]. The bell of a wind instrument. *Padiglione cinese,* Chinese crescent [see Turkish crescent].

Padilla, Juan de (b. probably in Spain, *c.* 1595; d. Puebla, Mexico, Apr. 1664). In Puebla from *c.* 1620 and *maestro de capilla* there from 1629. Composed Masses, motets, and other sacred music; *villancicos.*

Padovana, padoana. (1) In the first half of the 16th century, a generic term for dances of the **pavane-*passamezzo* species. (2) Toward the middle and in the second half of the 16th century, usually a quick dance in quadruple compound meter (12/8) resembling a **piva.*

Padovano, Annibale. See Annibale Padovano.

Paean. A song in praise of Apollo or a song of praise in general.

Paër, Ferdinando (b. Parma, 1 June 1771; d. Paris, 3 May 1839). Opera conductor in Vienna, 1797–1802. Court *Kapellmeister* at Dresden from 1802. *Maître de chapelle* to Napoleon from 1807. Conductor at the Italian Opera in Paris, 1812 –27. Conductor of the royal chamber music in Paris from 1832. Composed operas (incl. *Camilla,* Vienna, 1799; *Leonora,* Dresden, 1804; *Le maître de chapelle,* Paris, 1821); oratorios; cantatas; Masses and motets; orch. works; piano pieces.

Paganini, Niccolò (b. Genoa, 27 Oct. 1782; d. Nice, 27 May 1840). After study in Parma, began a career as a violin virtuoso in 1798, traveling throughout Europe. Court violinist at Lucca, 1805–8. His use of harmonics, double-stops, and left-hand pizzicato advanced violin technique considerably. Composed numerous works for violin, incl. *24 Capricci* for unaccompanied violin, concertos, variations, sonatas (some with guitar accompaniment); quartets for violin, viola, cello, and guitar; other chamber music; guitar pieces.

Paganini Etudes. Six concert etudes for piano by Liszt, based on Paganini's *Capricci* for violin (except no. 3, which is taken from Paganini's *La campanella*). Schumann also wrote twelve etudes on themes from Paganini's *Capricci.*

Paganini Variations. Variations (in two sets) for piano by Brahms, op. 35 (1866), on a theme by Paganini, the same that Liszt had used in no. 6 of his *Paganini Etudes.

Pagliacci, I [It., The Players]. Opera in two acts and a prologue by Leoncavallo (to his own libretto), produced in Milan, 1892. Setting: Montalto Calabria, Aug. 15, 1865.

Pahissa, Jaime (b. Barcelona, 7 Oct. 1880; d. Buenos Aires, 27 Oct. 1969). Architect, critic, and composer. Settled in Buenos Aires in 1935. Composed operas (incl. *La presó de Lleida* [The Prison of Lerida], Barcelona, 1906, rev. as *La Princesa Margarida,* Barcelona, 1928; *Gala Placidia,* Barcelona, 1913); a ballet; orch. works (incl. *Monodía,* 1925; *Suite intertonal,* 1926); choral works; chamber music; piano pieces; songs.

Published several books on music, incl. a life of Falla.

Paik, Nam June (b. Seoul, Korea, 20 July 1932). Studied at the Univ. of Tokyo and with Fortner, Stockhausen, and Cage. Has worked at the electronic music studio of the West-German Radio Network in Cologne, the State Univ. of New York at Stony Brook, WGBH-TV in Boston, and the California Institute of the Arts (since 1970). Has worked with mixed media and video techniques. Works incl. *hommage à john cage* for 2 pianos (destroyed during the performance), 3 tape recorders, projections, actions involving eggs, toy cars, motorbike, 1959; 5 symphonies; pieces for cellist Charlotte Moorman (incl. *Opera sextronique,* 1967, performed topless); *Electronic Opera No. 1,* prepared with others at WGBH-TV, 1968.

Paine, John Knowles (b. Portland, Maine, 9 June 1839; d. Cambridge, Mass., 25 Apr. 1906). Organist and composer. Studied in Berlin. Teacher at Harvard Univ. from 1862, and from 1875 until his death held a professorship of music there, the first such post in the U.S. His pupils incl. Carpenter, Converse, Foote, Hill, and D. G. Mason. Composed an opera, *Azara,* 1901, performed in concert version, 1907; an oratorio, a Mass, cantatas, and other works with soloists, chorus, and orch.; 2 symphonies and 2 symphonic poems; a string quartet, a piano trio, and other chamber music; piano pieces; organ pieces; songs.

Paisiello, Giovanni (b. Taranto, Italy, 9 May 1740; d. Naples, 5 June 1816). Pupil of Durante at the Conservatorio di Sant' Onofrio in Naples, where he subsequently taught, 1759–63. Court music director to Catherine the Great in St. Petersburg, 1776–84. *Maestro* of the royal chamber music and later *maestro di cappella* in Naples, 1787–99, and from 1803. *Maître de chapelle* to Napoleon, 1802–3. Composed about 100 operas (incl. *Socrate immaginario,* Naples, 1775; *Il *barbiere di Siviglia; Il Rè Teodoro in Venezia,* Vienna, 1784; *La molinara,* Naples, 1788; *Nina,* Naples, 1789); numerous Masses, motets, and other sacred music; 12 symphonies; 6 piano concertos; 12 piano quartets, 6 string quartets, and other chamber music; piano pieces.

Paladilhe, Émile (b. Montpellier, 3 June 1844; d. Paris, 6 Jan. 1926). Pupil of Halévy. Composed operas (incl. *Patrie,* Paris, 1886); 2 Masses and other sacred works; a symphony; choral works; chamber music; piano pieces; organ pieces; numerous songs.

Palau, Manuel (b. Valencia, 4 Jan. 1893; d. there, 18 Feb. 1967). Pianist, conductor, and composer. Studied at the Valencia Conservatory, of which he was director from 1952, and in Paris with Koechlin and Ravel. Worked extensively with Spanish folksongs. Composed *zarzuelas* (incl. *Beniflors,* Valencia, 1920); ballets; 3 symphonies and other orch. works (incl. *Gongoriana; Homenaje a Debussy; Concierto levantino* for guitar and orch., 1949); choral works; chamber music; piano pieces; numerous songs.

Palester, Roman (b. Sniatyn, Poland, now U.S.S.R., 28 Dec. 1907). Studied at the conservatories in Lvov and Warsaw. Settled in Paris in 1947. Has composed an opera, *The Living Stones,* 1944; 2 ballets (incl. *Song of the Earth,* 1937); 4 symphonies and other orch. works; concertos for violin, for alto saxophone, and for piano; sacred and secular choral works; string quartets and other chamber music; piano pieces; music for the theater, radio, and films.

Palestrina. Opera in three acts by H. Pfitzner (to his own libretto), produced in Munich, 1917. Setting: Rome and Trent, 1563.

Palestrina, Giovanni Pierluigi da (b. Palestrina, near Rome, *c.* 1525; d. Rome, 2 Feb. 1594). Chorister at Santa Maria Maggiore in Rome in the years around 1537. Organist and singer at the cathedral in Palestrina from 1544. *Maestro* of the Cappella Giulia at St. Peter's in Rome, 1551–55, and from 1571 until his death. Member of the papal choir (Cappella Sistina), from which he was ultimately excluded because he was married, in 1555. *Maestro di cappella* at St. John Lateran, succeeding Lassus, 1555–60. *Maestro* of the Cappella Liberiana at Santa Maria Maggiore, 1561–66. Master

of music at the Roman Seminary, 1566–71. Also *maestro* of the concerts at the villa of Cardinal Ippolito d'Este at Tivoli in 1564 and 1567–71. Composed 105 Masses; over 250 motets; Magnificats, Offertories, hymns, litanies, Lamentations, psalms; sacred and secular madrigals.

Palestrina style. See Roman school.

Pallavicino, Benedetto (b. Cremona, probably 1551; d. Mantua, 6 May 1601). Singer at the court in Mantua from 1582 and *maestro di cappella* there from 1596, succeeding Wert and preceding Monteverdi. Composed Masses, motets, and other sacred music; numerous madrigals.

Pallavicino, Carlo (Pallavicini) (b. Salò, near Brescia, *c.* 1630; d. Dresden, 29 Jan. 1688). *Kapellmeister* at the Dresden court, 1666–73 and from 1685. *Maestro di cappella* at the Ospedale degli incurabili in Venice, 1674–85. Composed operas (incl. *Penelope la casta,* Venice, 1685; *La Gerusalemme liberata,* Venice, 1687); oratorios and cantatas; church music; secular vocal chamber music.

Palmer, Robert (Moffett) (b. Syracuse, N.Y., 2 June 1915). Pupil of Bernard Rogers, Hanson, Copland, and Harris. Teacher at the Univ. of Kansas, 1940–43; at Cornell Univ. from 1943; at the Univ. of Illinois, 1955-56. Has composed an oratorio, *Nabuchodonosor,* 1960–64, and other choral works; a cantata, *Of Night and the Sea,* 1957; 2 symphonies and other orch. works (incl. *Variations, Chorale, and Fugue,* 1947–54; *Organon II* for strings, 1975); a concerto for piano and strings, 1968–70; *Choric Song and Toccata* for winds, 1968–69; 4 string quartets, a piano quintet, 2 piano quartets, a piano trio, a wind quintet, a quintet for clarinet, piano, and strings, and other chamber music; piano pieces; songs.

Palmgren, Selim (b. Björneborg, Finland, 16 Feb. 1878; d. Helsinki, 13 Dec. 1951). Pianist and composer. Studied at the Helsinki Conservatory and with Busoni in Berlin. Teacher at the Eastman School of Music, 1923–26; at the Helsinki Conservatory from 1927; at the Sibelius Academy in Helsinki from 1936.

Composed 2 operas (incl. *Daniel Hjort*, Åbo, 1910, in Swedish, later translated into Finnish); ballets; orch. works; 5 piano concertos; choral works; numerous piano pieces; numerous songs.

Pandean pipes. *Panpipes.

Pandiatonicism. In 20th-century music, the use of the diatonic scale instead of the chromatic scale as a tonal basis, but without conventional harmonic limitations.

Pandora. *Bandora.

Pandoura, pandura. A long-necked lute of ancient Greece and Rome [see Lute].

Panharmonicon. See under Mechanical instruments.

Panpipes, pandean pipes. A primitive wind instrument consisting of a number of tuned pipes (vertical flutes) of different size that are bound or glued together, usually in the form of a raft. The pipes, usually stopped at one end, are blown across the top. [See ill. under Flute.] The panpipes are among the oldest instruments. They were used in ancient Greece, where they were called *syrinx*, attributed to the god Pan, and played by shepherds. They are also found in China, Rumania, and South America.

Pantaleon. An enlarged *dulcimer invented *c*. 1697 by Pantaleon Hebenstreit, who also was a virtuoso on this instrument. It reportedly had 186 strings and was played by means of two small hammers. Toward the end of the 18th century the name was used for a piano with down-striking action.

Pantomime. A dramatic performance in which the actors do not speak or sing, action being revealed instead by facial expression, movements, and gestures, often with musical accompaniment. Pantomime was extremely popular in the 18th century with the stock characters Harlequin, Pantaloon, Clown, and the Old Man and his Pretty Daughter taken from the Italian *commedia dell'arte*. More recent works making use of pantomime include André Wormser's *L'enfant prodigue* (1890), R. Strauss' *Josephslegende* (1914), Stravinsky's *L'histoire du soldat* (1918), and Bartók's *The Miraculous Mandarin* (1919).

Panufnik, Andrzej (b. Warsaw, 24 Sept. 1914). Studied at the Warsaw Conservatory and the Vienna Academy. Conductor of the Cracow Philharmonic, 1945–46, and of the Warsaw Philharmonic, 1946–47. Settled in England in 1954 and was conductor of the Birmingham Symphony Orchestra, 1957–59. Has composed 3 ballets; orch. works (incl. *Sinfonia rustica*, 1948, rev. 1955; *Heroic Overture*, 1952, rev. 1965; *Sinfonia sacra*, 1963); a piano concerto, 1962; 3 cantatas (incl. *Universal Prayer*, after Pope, 1968); choral works; chamber music; piano pieces; songs.

Papaioannou, Iannis (Andreas) (b. Kavalla, Greece, 6 Jan. 1911). Studied at the Hellenic Conservatory in Athens, where he has taught since 1954, and with Honegger. Has worked with serial techniques. Has composed 5 symphonies, 5 symphonic poems, and other orch. works; a ballet; a piano concerto and a concertino for piano and strings; choral works; a string quartet and other chamber music, some with guitar; piano pieces; *3 Byzantine Odes* and other works for voice and instruments.

Papillons [F., Butterflies]. Fanciful title used by Schumann for a set of twelve short piano pieces (op. 2, 1829–31).

Papineau-Couture, Jean (b. Outremont, near Montreal, 12 Nov. 1916). Studied in Montreal and with Q. Porter and N. Boulanger. Teacher at the Univ. of Montreal from 1951. Has composed incidental music for puppet shows; orch. works (incl. *Poème*, 1952; *Oscillations*, 1969); a violin concerto, 1951, and a piano concerto, 1965; choral works (incl. *Psaume CL* for soloists, chorus, and instruments, 1954); *5 pieces concertantes* for various ensembles, incl. orch.; string quartets and other chamber music (incl. *Suite* for violin, 1956); piano pieces; works for voice and piano and for voice and orch.

Paradies, Pietro Domenico (Paradisi) (b. Naples, 1707; d. Venice, 25 Aug. 1791). Pupil of Porpora. Lived in London as a harpsichord teacher from 1746. Composed operas (incl. *Fetonte*, London, 1747); harpsichord sonatas.

Parallel chords. The successive sounding of a fixed chordal combination, consonant or dissonant, through various degrees of the scale. In classical harmony this device is admissible only for the sixth chord and diminished seventh chord, being strictly prohibited for triads, seventh chords, etc., on account of the *parallel fifths that would result. The technique has been widely used in the 20th century, however, and it is usually regarded as a characteristic feature of *impressionism [Ex. 1, Debussy, *Danse sacrée*, 1904; Ex. 2, Stravinsky, *Petrushka*].

Parallel (consecutive) fifths, octaves. The duplication of the melodic progression of a part (e.g., c–d) by another part at the distance of a fifth (g–a) or octave (c'–d'). Such voice-leading [see Ex. 1, 2] is considered faulty and is strictly prohibited in classical tonal counterpoint. Its avoidance is a basic feature of contrapuntal style from the 15th through 19th centuries.

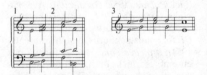

A fifth (or octave) that is reached not in parallel but in similar motion is referred to as a *hidden* (*covered*) *fifth* (or octave). This kind of voice-leading is usually admissible, except for certain extreme cases, e.g., when large intervals are involved in both voices. Particularly common (and entirely legitimate) is the progression illustrated in Ex. 3. This is called *horn fifths* because it is characteristic of the writing for natural horns.

Parallel key. See Key relationship.

Parallel motion. See Motion.

Paralleltonart [G.]. Relative (not parallel) key. See Key relationship.

Parameter. A mathematical term introduced into discussions of contemporary music (*serial music, *electronic music) to denote separate variables such as pitch, duration, loudness, timbre.

Paraphrase. A free rendition or elaboration. In music the term may mean: (1) a textual paraphrase, i.e., a free rewriting of a text; (2) a reworking and free arrangement of well-known melodies, such as Liszt's concert paraphrases of Wagnerian operas; (3) in early music (14th–16th centuries), a free elaboration of a plainsong melody, comparable to the ornamentation of chorale melodies found in many organ chorales by Buxtehude and Bach. The term *paraphrase Mass* has been applied to 15th-century Masses (usually single Mass items) having a paraphrased plainsong in one voice-part, as well as to 16th-century Masses in which a paraphrased plainsong (usually a hymn melody, though also appropriate melodies from the Ordinary) or portions thereof are used in all the voices, producing *points of imitation.

Pardessus de viole. See *Dessus*.

Paris Symphonies. Six symphonies by Haydn, nos. 82–87, composed 1785–86 for the *Concerts de la Loge Olympique* in Paris. Three of them have individual names: *L'ours* (no. 82), *La poule* (no. 83), *La reine* (no. 85).

Paris Symphony. Mozart's Symphony in D (K. 297), written in 1778 during his stay in Paris and performed there at the Concert spirituel.

Parish-Alvars, Elias (b. Teignmouth, England, 28 Feb. 1808; d. Vienna, 25 Jan. 1849). Harpist and composer. Pupil of Labarre. Associate of Mendelssohn in Leipzig. Settled in Vienna in 1847 and became a chamber musician to the emperor. Composed numerous works for harp, incl. 2 concertos.

Parker, Horatio (William) (b. Auburndale, Mass., 15 Sept. 1863; d. Cedarhurst, N.Y., 18 Dec. 1919). Pupil of

Chadwick and Rheinberger. After holding several positions as church organist and choirmaster in New York and Boston, he became professor of music at Yale in 1894, remaining there until his death. Founded and conducted the New Haven Symphony Orchestra. Composed operas (incl. *Mona,* New York, 1912; *Fairyland,* Los Angeles, 1915); a masque, *Cupid and Psyche,* New Haven, 1916; several overtures, a symphony, a symphonic poem, and other orch. works; oratorios (incl. *Hora novissima,* 1893); cantatas; sacred and secular choral works; string quartets and other chamber music; piano pieces; organ pieces; songs.

Parlando, parlante [It.]. In singing, an indication that the voice must approximate speech. In instrumental music, a style of playing suggestive of speech or song.

Parlato [It.]. Same as *parlando, but also used to distinguish the spoken sections in comic opera (ballad opera, *Singspiel*) from those that are sung.

Parody. (1) In present-day usage, a satirical imitation, such as may be created in music either by replacing the original text with a comic one or by changing the composition itself in a comic manner. (2) In early practice, replacement of the text, with or (more often) without the implication of caricature, e.g., parodies of Lully's operas. This can be termed **contrafactum* to distinguish it from the "musical" parody described below. (3) Before 1600 and occasionally in the 17th century, a serious reworking of a musical composition, with additions to or essential modifications of the original. The most important use of this technique was in the Mass [see Parody Mass].

Parody Mass [L. *missa parodia*]. An important type of 15th- and 16th-century Mass composition that incorporates material derived from various voice-parts or from entire sections of another polyphonic composition (motet, chanson, madrigal). This borrowing of polyphonic segments distinguishes the parody Mass from the *cantus firmus* Mass, which employs only one voice-part (tenor or *superius*) of its model. Whereas in the *cantus firmus* Masses there is a fairly uniform practice of employing the borrowed melody as the tenor of each Mass

item, in the parody Masses many varied methods are used, in regard to both amount and treatment of borrowed material. See also Paraphrasè (3).

Parris, Robert (b. Philadelphia, 21 May 1924). Pupil of Mennin, Ibert, Copland, and Honegger. Wrote criticism for the *Washington Post,* 1958–61. Teacher at George Washington Univ. from 1963. Has composed a symphony; concertos for 5 kettledrums, 1955, for viola, 1956, for violin, 1959, for trombone, 1964; choral works; 2 string quartets and other chamber music (incl. *The Book of Imaginary Beings,* 1972); works for voice and instruments.

Parry, Charles Hubert Hastings (b. Bournemouth, England, 27 Feb. 1848; d. Knight's Croft, Rustington, 7 Oct. 1918). Studied at Eton and Oxford and with W. S. Bennett and G. A. Macfarren. Choragus of Oxford Univ. from 1883. Director of the Royal College of Music, succeeding Grove, from 1894 to his death. Professor of music at Oxford, 1900–1908, succeeding Stainer. Composed an opera, *Guinevere,* 1886; oratorios (incl. *Judith,* 1888; *Job,* 1892); choral works (incl. *Blest Pair of Sirens,* with orch., 1887; *Jerusalem,* 1916); anthems, motets, hymns, and other church music; 3 string quartets, 3 piano trios, and other chamber music; piano pieces; organ pieces; numerous songs. Published numerous books and articles on music.

Parsifal. Opera in three acts by Wagner (to his own libretto), produced at Bayreuth, 1882. Setting: in and near Montsalvat, Spanish Pyrenees, Middle Ages.

Parsons, Robert (b. Exeter; d. Newark-on-Trent, 25 Jan. 1570). Gentleman of the Chapel Royal in London from 1563. Composed services, anthems, and motets; madrigals; *In nomine* settings and other instrumental pieces.

Part. (1) In orchestral or chamber music, the music for a particular instrument, such as violin, flute, piano. (2) In contrapuntal music, a single melodic line of the contrapuntal web (fugue in three, four parts). The modern names for such parts, also called voices, are soprano, alto, tenor, and bass. (3) A section of a composition, as in three-part song form.

Part song. A choral composition in homophonic style, i.e., with the top part the sole carrier of the melody. It applies chiefly to choral works of the 19th century, such as were written by Schumann, Mendelssohn, Parry, Stanford, Elgar, and many others. See also Glee. Sometimes the term is used quite differently, i.e., for truly polyphonic songs of the Renaissance.

Partbooks. Manuscript or printed books of the 15th and 16th centuries that each contain the music for an individual voice of a polyphonic composition [see also under Score].

Partch, Harry (b. Oakland, Calif., 24 June 1901; d. San Diego, 6 Sept. 1974). Largely self-taught in music. Developed a tonal system using 43 tones to the octave and invented numerous musical instruments for the performance of his music and a method for notating it. Was influenced by a variety of Western and non-Western musics and employed elements of theater. Works incl. *The Bewitched*, 1955; *Revelation in the Courthouse Park*, 1960; *Delusion of the Fury*, 1963–66; *And on the Seventh Day Petals Fell in Petaluma*, 1963–64, rev. 1966.

Parte [It.]. (1) *Part. See also *Coll', colla*. (2) In the 17th century, variation [see under Partita].

Parthie, partia, partie [G.]. In the 17th and 18th centuries, *suite [see Partita (2)]. The French word *partie* means voice-part (*fugue à 3 parties*) or section, movement (*sonate en 4 parties*).

Partial. See under Acoustics.

Partial signature. The composite key signature of a polyphonic composition in which the signatures for individual voice-parts differ (also called *conflicting signature*). Such signatures were common before 1500, the most common combinations being a single flat in the lowest part or the lowest two parts and no flats (or sharps) in the uppermost part or parts. There has been considerable disagreement over the explanation for such signatures.

Partie [G., F.]. See under *Parthie*.

Partita [It.]. (1) In the late 16th and early 17th centuries, a variation. For a set of such variations, the plural *partite* was used (sometimes also sing. *parte* and pl. *parti*). In Germany, the terms were sometimes applied to chorale variations, e.g., those by Georg Böhm on "Freu dich sehr o meine Seele" and Bach on "O Gott, du frommer Gott." (2) In the 18th century and since, most often a *suite, e.g., the six Partitas in Bach's *Clavier-Übung* I (1731).

Partition [F.]; **Partitur** [G.]; **partitura** [It., Sp.]. *Score.

Partos, Ödön (b. Budapest, 1 Oct. 1907; d. Tel Aviv, 6 July 1977). Pupil of Kodály and Hubay. Settled in Israel in 1938 and was principal violinist of the Israel Philharmonic from then until 1956. Director of the Rubin Academy of Music in Tel Aviv from 1951 and teacher at Tel Aviv Univ. from 1961. Has composed works for chorus and orch. (incl. *Psalm*, 1965); orch. works (incl. *Ein gev*, 1952; *Images*, 1960); concertos and other works for violin and viola with orch.; string quartets and other chamber music.

Pasatieri, Thomas (b. New York, 20 Oct. 1945). Pupil of Giannini, Persichetti, and Milhaud. Has composed operas (incl. *The Trial of Mary Todd Lincoln*, National Educational Television, 1972; *The Seagull*, after Chekhov, Houston, 1974); vocal works; piano pieces.

Paspy. Another name for *passepied*.

Pasquini, Bernardo (b. Massa di Valdinievole, Tuscany, 7 Dec. 1637; d. Rome, 21 Nov. 1710). Pupil of Cesti. Organist at Santa Maria Maggiore in Rome, 1665–67; at the Oratorio di SS. Crocifisso, 1664–85. Chamber musician to Prince Giambattista Borghese. Composed operas (incl. *Dov'è amore è pietà*, Rome, 1679); oratorios; cantatas; arias; harpsichord pieces.

Passacaglia [It.]; **passacaille** [F.]. See Chaconne and passacaglia.

Passage. A term loosely used for a short section of a composition. More specifically, *passages* or *passage work* refers to sections that contain a display of virtuosity rather than important musical ideas, e.g., scale passages, arpeggio passages.

Passaggio [It.]. (1) Transition, modulation. (2) *Passage work. (3) In the 16th-century art of diminution [see Ornamentation], a generic term for improvised ornaments, usually other than plain scale passages or trill-like figurations.

Passamezzo, pass'e mezzo. An Italian dance of the 16th and early 17th centuries similar to a *pavane; indeed, in musical style the common pavane cannot be distinguished from a *passamezzo*. The dance steps must also have been similar. A large proportion of *passamezzi*, a few pavanes, and at least one-fifth of all 16th-century dances (including *saltarelli*, galliards, *padovane*, etc.) are composed on one of two harmonic patterns known as the *passamezzo antico* [Ex. 1] and the *passamezzo moderno* (*commune, novo*; Ex. 2). No particular discant melody was associated with the two harmonic patterns.

Passecaille [F.]. Passacaglia [see under Chaconne and passacaglia].

Passepied [F.]. A gay, spirited dance in rather quick 3/8 or 6/8 meter that was very popular at the French court under Louis XIV and Louis XV. It is said to have come from Brittany. Examples occur in French operas (e.g., Campra, *L'Europe galante*, 1697) and in the suites of German composers (J. K. F. Fischer; J. S. Bach, English Suite no. 5).

Passing tone. See under Counterpoint.

Passion music. A musical setting of the text of the Passion (*Passio Domini nostri Jesu Christi*) according to one of the four Evangelists (Matthew, Mark, Luke, John). In the Middle Ages the Passions were sung in plainsong, in a manner de-

signed to contrast the participants of the story: Jesus, the Jews (*turba Judaeorum*), and the narrator (*Evangelista, Chronista*). Three different pitch levels and speeds of recitation were used: low and solemn for the words of Jesus, medium and in normal speed for those of the Evangelist, high and with pronounced agitation for the Jews. The earliest polyphonic settings known today are English, *c.* 1450. Here only the *turba* sections and the words of individuals, such as John, Peter, Pilate, are polyphonically composed, those of Christ and the Evangelist being sung in plainsong. Because of the dramatic contrast of plainsong with polyphony, this type of Passion is called a *dramatic Passion* (also "scenic," "responsorial"). Other examples are those by Davy (*c.* 1490), Sermisy (1534), Lassus (1575 and later), Guerrero (1585), Asola, Victoria, and Byrd (1607). The polyphonic portions are usually simple settings (often in *falsobordone* style) of the plainsong melody, which is carried in the tenor. In some Italian Passions of the 16th century, the words of Jesus are also composed, plainsong being used only for the Evangelist. In Germany, the Reformation led to adoption of the vernacular and, occasionally, to modifications of the traditional plainsong. The earliest Passion of this type is by Johann Walter (St. Matthew, 1550).

Side by side with this tradition was another, musically more elaborate treatment—the composition of the entire text of the Passion in motet style (*motet Passion*; also *through-composed Passion*). The earliest known example is one by Longaval (*c.* 1510; formerly attributed to Obrecht), whose text is derived from all four Gospels. Others are by Galliculus (1538), Cipriano de Rore (1557), Joachim a Burck (1568), Jacobus Gallus (1587), and Leonhard Lechner (1594). The liturgical plainsong is usually preserved as a *cantus firmus* in the earlier of these polyphonic settings, while later composers adhered less strictly to this principle and occasionally abandoned it altogether.

The 17th century saw the application to the Passion of all the dramatic innovations of the baroque era, such as *stile recitativo*, the aria, and the orchestra, together with a freer treatment of the authentic text, which was either paraphrased or broadened by free poetic interpolations, thus approaching the *oratorio (*oratorio Passion*). An early work indicative of these new tendencies is the Passion according to St. John by Thomas Selle (1643). The great figure in this period is Heinrich Schütz, who late in life (*c.* 1665–72) wrote three Passions (Matthew, Luke, and John) in an austere and archaic style. Technically they belong to the dramatic type of the 16th century, since they employ *a cappella* polyphony for the *turbae* and unaccompanied recitation for the rest of the text, but Schütz replaced the traditional plainsong by a "neo-Gregorian" recitative of his own invention.

After 1700 the authentic text of the Bible was abandoned in favor of rhymed paraphrases in the sentimental and allegorical style of the day. Particularly popular were C. F. Hunold-Menante's *Der blutige und sterbende Jesus* (composed by Keiser, 1704) and Brockes' *Der für die Sünden der Welt gemarterte und sterbende Jesus*. The latter was set to music by many composers, among them Keiser, Telemann, Handel, and Mattheson. Bach's St. John Passion (1724) and St. Matthew Passion (1727) use the biblical text as a basic narrative, set in recitative or (for the *turbae*) in short choruses. Poetic texts (by Brockes for the St. John Passion, by Picander for the St. Matthew Passion) are used for the arias and large choruses.

The ensuing history of the Passion includes such works as Telemann's *St. John Passion* (1741); Passion oratorios by Caldara (1730), Jommelli (1742), and Paisiello (1784), all based on a text by Metastasio (*La passione di Jesù Cristo*); two passions by K. P. E. Bach (1787, 1788); and oratorios dealing with the Passion story, such as Haydn's *Die sieben Worte am Kreuz* (*c.* 1796; see Seven Last Words), Beethoven's *Christus am Ölberge* (1803), and Spohr's *Des Heilands letzte Stunden* (1835). Compositions of the *Stabat Mater* and the *Seven (Last) Words are also in this category. Twentieth-century examples include works such as the *Markus-Passion* of Kurth Thomas, the *Choralpassion* of Hugo Distler, and the *St. Luke Passion* of Krzysztof Penderecki.

Pasticcio [It.]. (1) A musical work consisting of contributions by two or more composers. Examples are the opera *Muzio Scevola* (1721), to which Amadei (sometimes called Pippo), G. B. Bononcini, and Handel contributed one act each, and the oratorio *Die Schuldigkeit des ersten Gebotes*, written by Mozart, Adlgasser, and Michael Haydn. (2) An operatic medley of the 18th century.

Pastoral Symphony. Beethoven's Symphony no. 6, in F major, op. 68, published in 1809 under the title "Sinfonie Pastorale, No. 6." Beethoven's inscriptions for the five movements are (in translation): (1) Awakening of Cheerful Feelings on Arrival in the Country; (2) Scene by the Brook; (3) Merrymaking of the Country Folk; (4) Storm; (5) Song of the Shepherds, Joy and Gratitude after the Storm.

Pastorale. (1) An instrumental or vocal piece written in imitation of the music of shepherds and their shawms and pipes. With reference to the biblical shepherds who attended the birth of Jesus, the pastorale took on the character of idyllic Christmas music. Typical features are 6/8 or 12/8 meter in moderate time, suggestive of a lullaby, and dotted rhythms. Among the many examples of this type of composition are Bach's Pastorale for organ, the Sinfonia that opens the second part of his Christmas Oratorio, the Sinfonia pastorale in Handel's *Messiah*, and the last movement of Beethoven's *Pastoral Symphony. See also *Siciliana.

(2) In the 16th century, a dramatic performance with an idyllic plot. These were among the most important forerunners of *opera.

Patetico [It.]. With great emotion.

Pathétique. (1) Popular name for Beethoven's Piano Sonata in C minor op. 13 (1799). Tchaikovsky chose the name *Symphonie pathétique* for his last symphony, no. 6, in E minor, op. 74 (1893). (2) [F.]. With great emotion.

Pathetisch [G.]. With great emotion.

Patter song. A song whose text, usually humorous, is sung very rapidly.

Pauke [G.]. Kettledrum [see under Percussion instruments].

Paumann, Conrad (b. Nuremberg, between 1410 and 1415; d. Munich, 24 Jan. 1473). Blind organist and composer, also a performer on the harp, lute, flute, and other instruments. Organist at St. Sebald, Nuremberg, from 1446. Court organist at Munich from 1451 until his death. Wrote the *Fundamentum organisandi*, 1452, a treatise on composing for the organ containing preludes, exercises, and settings of German songs.

Pause. (1) [F. *point d'orgue;* G. *Fermate;* It. *fermata;* Sp. *calderón*] The sign ⌒, also known as a "hold" or *fermata*, indicating that the note (or rest) over which it appears is to be prolonged. As a rule, a duration approximately (but not exactly) twice the normal value will prove appropriate. (2) The foreign terms *pause* [F.], *Pause* [G.], and *pausa* [It.] always mean a rest. (3) A brief pause such as might be required to take a quick breath, sometimes therefore called a breathing pause [G. *Atempause, Luftpause*], and indicated with an apostrophe.

Pavane, pavenne [F.; It., Sp. *pavana;* all originally anglicized *pavan, paven, pavin*]. A 16th-century court dance of Italian provenance. The word is derived from *Pava*, a dialect form of *Padua;* music and literature as well as dances from Pava or in the Paduan style were described as *alla pavana*. The dance remained in vogue for most of the century, although its popularity abated somewhat in the last quarter of the period. It was restored and revitalized in idealized musical form by the English virginalists Byrd, Bull, Gibbons, Tomkins, Morley, Farnaby, Philips, Dowland, and others. Under the title *paduana* it flourished briefly in Germany in the early 17th century, where it was used as the introductory movement of the German suite. More recent examples, actually recreations of the earlier idealized dance form, have been written by Saint-Saëns ("Pavane," in *Étienne Marcel*), Ravel ("Pavane de la belle," in *Ma Mère l'oye* and *Pavane pour une infante défunte*), and Vaughan Williams ("Pavane" in *Job*).

The pavane is a slow, processionlike dance, for the most part employing a continuous repetition of basic step patterns: two single and one double step forward followed by two single and one double backward. Most dances of the genre are in a simple quadruple meter (4/4 or 4/2). Musically they resemble the **passamezzo;* indeed, it is often difficult to distinguish the music of a *passamezzo* from that of a pavane. Usually the pavane is followed by one of the faster dances, the **saltarello,* **galliard,* **padovana,* or **piva.*

Pavillon [F.]. The bell of wind instruments. *Pavillon chinois,* the Chinese or **Turkish crescent.

Paz, Juan Carlos (b. Buenos Aires, 5 Aug. 1901; d. there, 25 or 26 Aug. 1972). Critic and composer, largely self-taught in music. Founded the Grupo renovación in 1930 and the Agrupación nueva música in 1937. Employed a variety of techniques in the course of his career, including twelve-tone techniques. Composed orch. works (incl. *Movimiento sinfónico,* 1930; *Rítmica ostinata,* 1942; *Continuidad,* 1960–61); *Music* for piano and orch., 1963; several pieces titled *Composición dodecafónica* and other chamber music; organ pieces; piano pieces; songs.

Peasant Cantata. See *Bauernkantate.*

Pêcheurs de perles, Les [F., The Pearl Fishers]. Opera in three acts by Bizet (libretto by E. Cormon and M. Carré), produced in Paris, 1863. Setting: Ceylon, in the past.

Pedal. (1) In musical instruments, an action operated by the feet. See Organ; Piano; Pedal harpsichord; Harp. (2) Short for **pedal point.*

Pedal clarinet. Older name for the contrabass clarinet [see under Clarinet family].

Pedal harpsichord. A harpsichord that is equipped with a pedal board, similar to that of the organ, so that the bass can be played with the feet. Several 16th- and 17th-century Italian harpsichords are extant that once had pedal boards pulling down the keys of the manual by means of cords. Many traces of French pedalboard harpsichords of the 17th and 18th centuries exist, some of which included a separate instrument lying on the floor under the harpsichord. Toward the end of the 18th century, French makers began to place pedal boards operating a piano action under their harpsichords.

Pedal piano [G. *Pedalflügel, Pedalklavier;* F. *piano à pedalier*]. A piano equipped with a pedal board, similar to that of the organ, so that the bass can be played with the feet. The *Pedalflügel,* which had but fleeting success, is known chiefly through the series of "Studien" and "Skizzen" that Schumann wrote for it (op. 56, 58). There are also compositions for this instrument by Alkan and Gounod.

Pedal point [F. *point d'orgue;* G. *Orgelpunkt;* It. *pedale;* Sp. *bajo de órgano*]. A long-held note, normally in the bass, continuing to sound as harmonies change in the other parts. Sometimes the word *pedal* alone is used. A pedal point may be described as a tonic pedal, dominant pedal, subdominant pedal, etc. (long note on the tonic, dominant, subdominant, etc., of the key). The terms *inverted pedal* and *internal pedal* denote pedal points that appear not in the bass but in the soprano or in a middle part. See Drone; *Bourdon.*

Pedal tone. See under Wind instruments.

Pedalflügel [G.]. *Pedal piano.

Pedalier [F.]. (1) The pedal board of the organ, or a similar apparatus attached to a piano. (2) See Pedal piano.

Pedrell, Felipe (b. Tortosa, Spain, 19 Feb. 1841; d. Barcelona, 19 Aug. 1922). Musicologist and composer. Worked principally in Barcelona, except for the years 1895–1903, when he taught at the Madrid Conservatory. His pupils incl. Granados, Falla, and Gerhard. He was a leader in bringing to light Spain's musical past and in urging a new national music. Composed 10 operas (incl. the trilogy *Los Pirineos,* Barcelona, 1902; *La Celestina,* 1904); sacred and secular choral works, some with orch.; orch. works (incl. *Excelsior* and *I trionfi*); chamber music; piano pieces; songs. Published numerous writings on music and editions of early music, incl. the complete works of Victoria.

Peer Gynt Suite. Two orchestral suites by Grieg, op. 46 (1888) and 55 (1891), arranged from his incidental music to Ibsen's play *Peer Gynt.*

Peerson, Martin (b. March, Cambridgeshire, *c.* 1572; d. London, Dec. 1650). Organist and master of the children at St. Paul's Cathedral, London, from 1626. Composed church music in English and Latin; fantasies and other pieces for viols; airs for one or more voices with instruments; pieces for virginals.

Peeters, Flor (b. Thielen, Belgium, 4 July 1903). Organist and composer. Pupil of Mortelmans. Teacher at the Lemmens Institute in Malines, 1923–52; at the Royal Conservatory in Antwerp from 1948 and its director, 1952–68. Has composed Masses and other sacred choral works with organ accompaniment; numerous organ pieces (incl. an organ concerto, 1944; *Hymn Preludes for the Liturgical Year,* 1959–64); piano pieces; songs. Has written an organ method, *Ars organi,* 1952, in 3 vols., and has published numerous editions of early organ music.

Peiko, Nikolai Ivanovich (b. Moscow, 25 Mar. 1916). Pupil of Miaskovsky. Teacher at the Moscow Conservatory, 1942–59; at the Gnessin Conservatory from 1954. Has composed an opera; 3 ballets (incl. *Zhanna d'Ark,* 1955); 6 symphonies and other orch. works; string quartets and other chamber music; piano pieces; songs; music for films.

Peine entendu, à [F.]. Barely audible.

Peking opera. Established in about 1850, it remains the most popular Chinese musical art form, having largely superseded the *kuencheu.* It relies chiefly on the repeated use of a very few melodies, though with sharply contrasting rhythms and tempos, and makes use of highly stylized singing and acting.

Pelissier, Victor (fl. Philadelphia and New York, 1792–1811). French composer, arranger, and horn player for the Old American Company in New York from 1793. Composed operas (incl. *Edwin and Angelina, or The Banditti,* New York, 1796); incidental music to plays; pantomimes; a few instrumental pieces.

Pelléas et Mélisande. Opera in five acts by Debussy (to his own libretto, after Maeterlinck's play of the same name), produced in 1902. Setting: a mythical kingdom, Allemonde, in the Middle Ages.

Pellegrini, Vincenzo (b. Pesaro, late 16th cent.; d. Milan, 23 Aug. 1630). *Maestro di cappella* at the Milan Cathedral from 1611 until his death. Composed Masses, Magnificats, and other sacred vocal works, some with instruments; canzonas for organ.

Peñalosa, Francisco de (b. Talavera de la Reina, Toledo, c. 1470; d. Seville, 1 Apr. 1528). Singer in the chapel of King Ferdinand the Catholic in 1498. Canon of the Seville Cathedral in 1506. *Maestro de capilla* to the Infante Don Fernando of Aragón from 1511. In the service of Pope Leo X in Rome from 1517. Composed Masses, motets, and other sacred works; *villancicos*.

Penderecki, Krzysztof (b. Debica, Poland, 23 Nov. 1933). Studied at the Music Academy in Cracow, taught there from 1958, and was its director from 1972. Teacher at the Yale School of Music from 1975. Has employed serial techniques and a wide variety of methods of sound production, including the use of convential instruments in unconventional ways. Works incl. an opera, *The Devils of Loudun*, Hamburg, 1969; *The Psalms of David* for chorus and percussion, 1958; *Stabat Mater* for three choruses, 1962; *St. Luke Passion* for narrator, soloists, and orch., 1965; *Utrenja* (Morning Prayer) for soloists, 2 choruses, and percussion, 1970; *To the Victims of Hiroshima—Threnody* for 52 strings, 1960; *Fluorescences* for orch., 1961; *Emanationen* for 2 string orchs., 1959; *De natura sonoris* for orch., 1967; a string quartet, 1960.

Pennillion [sing. *pennill*]. An ancient form of Welsh musical performance executed by a harper and a singer (*bards), the former playing a well-known harp air and the latter extemporizing words and a somewhat different melody to suit the harper's tune and harmonies.

Pentachord. (1) A five-tone segment of the diatonic scale, especially that comprising the first five scale degrees in any key. (2) More generally (and in discussions of 20th-century music) any collection of five pitches.

Pentatonic scale. A scale that has five tones to the octave. Among the numerous scales of this kind the following are of special importance: (a) The *tonal* [G. *anhemitonisch*] *pentatonic scale*, i.e., a five-tone scale that has no semitones. Properly speaking, there is only one such scale (aside from transpositions): c d . f g a . c'. This scale occurs in the music of some non-Western cultures as well as in some Western folk music. (b) The *semitonal* [G. *hemitonisch*] *pentatonic scale* results from omitting the second and the sixth or the second and the fifth degrees of the diatonic scale: c . e f g . b c', or c . e f . a b c'. Since these scales include two major thirds (*ditonus*) they are also called *ditonic*. The second form is of special interest since this is the scale that, in descending motion, prevailed in ancient Greece: e' . c' b a . f e. Semitonal pentatonic scales frequently occur in modern Japanese music. (c) A pentatonic scale with equidistant steps is the Javanese *sléndro*.

Pentland, Barbara (b. Winnipeg, Manitoba, Canada, 2 Jan. 1912). Pianist and composer. Pupil of Jacobi, B. Wagenaar, and Copland. Teacher at the Toronto Conservatory, 1942–49; at the Univ. of British Columbia, 1949–63. Has composed a chamber opera, *The Lake*, 1954; a ballet; 4 symphonies and other orch. works; a violin concerto, 1942, and a piano concerto, 1956; 3 string quartets and other chamber music; piano pieces.

Pépin, Clermont (b. St. Georges de Beauce, Quebec, 15 May 1926). Pupil of Champagne, Scalero, Honegger, Jolivet, and Messiaen. Teacher at the Quebec Province Conservatory and its director from 1967. Has composed ballets; 2 symphonies and other orch. works; 2 piano concertos; *Les quasars* for chorus and orch., 1967; 4 string quartets and other chamber music; piano pieces; songs.

Pepping, Ernst (b. Duisburg, Germany, 12 Sept. 1901). Studied at the Berlin Hochschule für Musik, where he has taught since 1953. Also a teacher at the Berlin Church Music School from 1934. Has composed Masses and numerous other sacred choral works; 3 symphonies and other orch. works; concertos for piano and for organ; piano pieces; organ pieces (incl. preludes and postludes on 18 chorales, 1968); songs.

Pepusch, Johann Christoph (John Christopher) (b. Berlin, 1667; d. London, 20 July 1752). Prussian court musician, 1681–97. Settled in London, 1700, where he became a violinist at the Drury Lane Theatre. Co-founder of the Academy of Ancient Music, 1710. Organist and composer to the Duke of Chandos, 1712–18. Music director of the Lincoln's Inn Fields Theatre from 1713. Organist of the Charter House from 1737 until his death. Arranged music for ballad operas, incl. *The *Beggar's Opera.* Composed masques; cantatas; odes and motets; concertos; sonatas. Published a *Treatise on Harmony,* 1730 and 1731.

Peragallo, Mario (b. Rome, 25 Mar. 1910). Pupil of Casella. Artistic director of the Accademia filarmonica romana, 1950–54. Has composed operas (incl. *La gita in campagna,* Milan, 1954); a scenic madrigal, *La collina,* after Edgar Lee Masters, 1947; a concerto for orch. and other orch. works; concertos for piano and for violin; choral works; chamber music; piano pieces; organ pieces; songs.

Percussion instruments. Generic name for instruments that are sounded by shaking or by striking one object with another. In the general classification of instruments they are divided into two categories, *membranophones* and *idiophones* [see Instruments]. Membranophones are by far the oldest of all instruments and exist in enormous variety all over the world. The percussion instruments of the orchestra can be divided into two groups, those that produce a sound of definite pitch and those that do not.

I. *Of definite pitch.* 1. Kettledrum [G. *Pauke;* F. *timbale;* It. *timpano,* pl. *timpani;* Sp. *timbal*]. A basin-shaped shell of copper or brass over which is stretched a head of calfskin or plastic whose tension can be adjusted by screws fixed to the shell, thereby changing the pitch. The instrument is played with two sticks, each consisting of a wooden handle and a head, usually of hard felt covered with a layer of soft felt, although for special effects different materials may be used. Traditionally, kettledrums were used in pairs, one small and one large, tuned to the tonic and dominant of the key of the composition. A third drum was added in the early 19th century. Today a number of kettledrums of different sizes are used, four being most common. Various methods of tuning the drums mechanically by a controlling pedal (pedal drums or pedal timpani; G. *Pedalpauke*) or other device have been invented. Such instruments, which allow the pitch to be changed quickly, are required in, e.g., *Salome* by R. Strauss or Bartók's *Music for Strings, Percussion, and Celesta,* where glissandos are performed by the kettledrums.

2. Glockenspiel or orchestral bells [E.; G.; F. *carillon;* It. *campanelle, campanette;* Sp. *campanólogo*]. A series of tuned steel bars of varying length, usually without resonators, arranged in two rows, like a piano keyboard, and struck with two, three, or four small-headed mallets. The instrument is generally made in a chromatic range of 2 1/2 octaves, written as in Ex. 1 but sounding two octaves higher. A portable version mounted on a frame shaped like a lyre and usually with a range of only two octaves is also called a *bell lyre.* See also I, 4, below, and the separate entry Glockenspiel.

1. Glockenspiel. 2. Xylophone (not largest size). 3. Celesta.

3. Xylophone. An instrument resembling the glockenspiel in basic construction, except that its bars are wooden. The largest size has a range of 3 1/2 octaves, written as in Ex. 2 but sounding one octave higher.

4. Celesta. An instrument invented in 1886 that looks like a small upright piano. Its tone is produced by the striking of steel bars, similar to those of a glockenspiel, with hammers connected to a keyboard by a simplified piano action. Music for the celesta is notated on two staves, like piano music, with a written range as in Ex. 3, sounding an octave

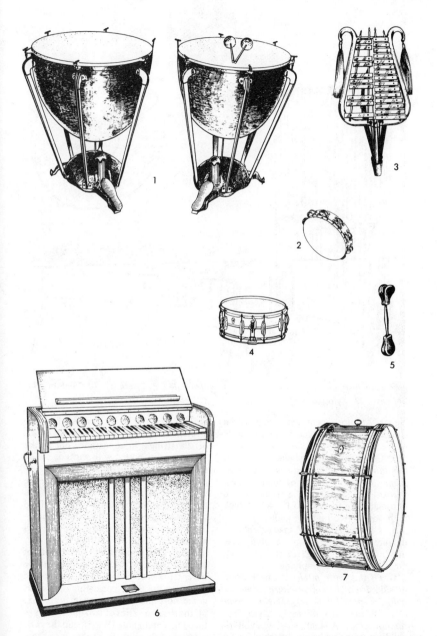

Percussion instruments (orchestra and band): 1. Kettledrums (pedal). 2. Tambourine. 3. Bell lyre. 4. Snare drum. 5. Castanets (orchestral type). 6. Celesta. 7. Bass drum.

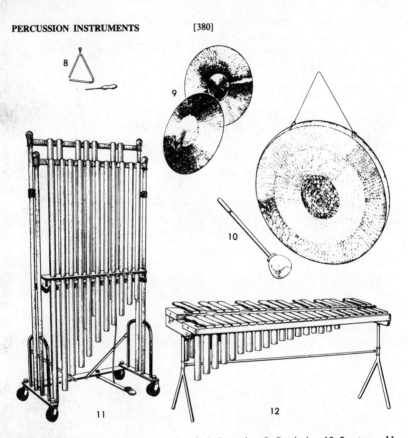

Percussion instruments (orchestra and band): 8. Triangle.   9. Cymbals.   10. Tamtam.   11. Chimes.   12. Xylophone.

higher. A more recent instrument with a similar sound, produced by tuning forks instead of bars, is the *dulcitone*.

5. Chimes or tubular bells [F. *cloches tubulaires*; G. *Röhrenglocken*; It. *campana tubolare*]. A set of metal tubes, vertically suspended in a frame, tuned chromatically from c′ to f″, and struck with one or two rawhide mallets.

6. Other percussion instruments of definite pitch are the *anvil, crotales [see under Cymbals], gong [see II, 7, below], *marimba, and *vibraphone.

II. *Of indefinite pitch.* 1. Snare drum or side drum [F. *caisse claire, tambour militaire, petit tambour*; G. *kleine Trommel*; It. *tamburo militare, cassa*; Sp. *tambor, caja*]. A small, shallow cylindrical drum with two heads stretched over a shell of metal. The upper head, which is struck with two drumsticks, is called the

batter head; the lower, across which are stretched the taut snares (a group of gut or silk strings, in appearance not unlike violin strings, bound with wire), is called the *snare head*. The brilliant tone quality of the side drum results largely from the vibrations of the snarehead against the snares. The instrument may be muffled (*coperto*) by placing a cloth on the batter head. By loosening the snares a dull sound is obtained. In addition to the *roll,* a rapid and continuous succession of strokes that produces a tremolo, three other strokes commonly used on the side drum are the *flam,* consisting of a short grace note preceding a main note [Ex. 4], the *drag,* a series of two quick strokes fused to a main note [Ex. 5], and the *ruff,* a series of three quick strokes fused to a main note [Ex. 6].

2. Tenor drum [F. *caisse roulante*; G.

PERCUSSION INSTRUMENTS

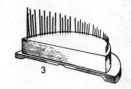

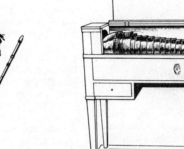

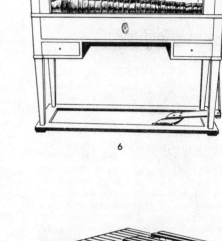

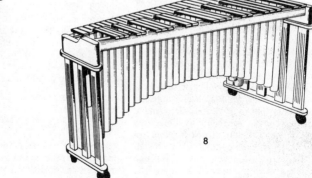

Other percussion instruments: 1. Gangsa gambang (saron). 2. Sistrum. 3. Nail violin. 4. Pipe and tabor. 5. Jew's-harp (shown three times actual size in relation to others). 6. Glass harmonica. 7. Turkish crescent. 8. Marimba.

4. Flam.   5. Drag.   6. Ruff.

Rührtrommel; It. *casa rullante;* Sp. *redoblante*]. A drum with a wooden shell that is deeper (in relation to its diameter) and larger than the side drum. It has no snares. A drum of this type provided with snares is called a *field drum*.

3. Bass drum [F. *grosse caisse;* G. *grosse Trommel;* It. *gran cassa* or *cassa grande;* Sp. *bombo*]. A large, two-headed cylindrical drum that varies considerably in size, in both width and diameter. It is played with a single large, padded stick. A roll can be performed by two timpani sticks or by a two-headed *tampon.

4. Tambourine [F. *tambour de Basque;* G. *Schellentrommel, Tamburin;* It. *tamburino, tamburo basso;* Sp. *pandereta*]. A small, shallow, single-headed drum into whose wooden shell loosely hanging "jingles" (circular metal disks) are inserted, usually in pairs. The instrument is played: (a) by striking the head with knuckles, fingers, closed fist, back of hand, or player's knee, which gives detached sounds and simple rhythmical figures; (b) by grasping the shell firmly and shaking it, which gives a roll of the jingles; (c) by rubbing the thumb along the edge of the head, which gives a tremolo of the jingles; and (d), with the instrument flat, head up, on the player's lap, by playing near the rim with fingers or drumsticks.

5. Triangle [F.; G. *Triangel;* It. *triangolo;* Sp. *triángulo*]. A small cylindrical bar of steel bent in the shape of an equilateral triangle, open at one end, struck with a short metal rod.

6. Cymbals [F. *cymbales;* G. *Becken;* It. *piatti, cinelli;* Sp. *platillos*]. Large circular brass plates of various sizes, made slightly convex so that only the edges touch when they are struck together. In the center of each cymbal is a deep saucerlike depression with a hole through which a strap is attached, enabling the player to hold it. Cymbals are played (a) by clashing them together with a brushing movement—the ordinary way of playing single notes; (b) by clashing the two cymbals against each other in quick repetition by means of a rotating motion, called a "two-plate roll"; (c) by striking a single cymbal (suspended on a stand) with a hard snare-drum stick or a soft timpani stick; (d) by suspending one cymbal and performing a roll on it with two hard snare-drum sticks or two soft timpani sticks; (e) by fastening one cymbal to the top of the bass drum and clashing the other against it, while the player uses his other hand to play the bass drum. See also Cymbals.

7. Tamtam. A broad circular disk of metal, slightly convex, with the rim turned down, giving it the appearance of a shallow plate with low vertical sides. It is hung vertically and struck in the center with a soft-headed beater. The term *gong* is often used synonymously, though it properly refers to instruments with a wider rim, a central boss, and, usually, definite pitch.

8. Other percussion instruments of indefinite pitch, more rarely used in orchestral scores, are the *castanets, *rattle or ratchet, wood block or *Chinese block, *temple block, *thunder machine, *wind machine, *maracas, *claves, *güiro, *timbales, *tom-tom, *bongos, and *conga.

For nonorchestral percussion instruments, see Gambang; Glass harmonica; Jew's-harp; Nail violin; Pipe (1); Sistrum; Turkish crescent.

Perdendo, perdendosi [It.]. Dying away.

Pérez, Davide (b. Naples, 1711; d. Lisbon, 30 Oct. 1778). Pupil of Mancini. *Maestro di cappella* at the Palermo Cathedral, 1739–48; at the royal chapel in Lisbon from 1752. Composed operas (incl. *Solimano,* Lisbon, 1757); Masses, motets, and other sacred vocal works; some secular vocal works.

Perfect. See Cadence; Interval; Mensural notation.

Perfect pitch. See Absolute pitch.

Performance practice. Those aspects of performance that are not unambiguously specified in musical notation. Its study seeks to make possible historically authentic performances, i.e., performances that might approximate those given in the period when the music was composed. The term has sometimes been restricted to refer to the music of the Middle Ages and Renaissance, in which the original notation often does not specify such fundamental matters as accidentals [see *Musica ficta*], tempo, dynamics, and instrumentation. The music of every period, however, is subject to its own conventions of performance. This is now widely recognized with respect to 17th- and 18th-century music, where *ornamentation, for example, plays a particularly important role that relies on convention. Less widely recognized is the importance of performance practice in relation to music from the late 18th and the 19th centuries. This is due in part to the mistaken beliefs that musical notation in the 19th century was always unambiguous, requiring little or nothing of the performer except the carrying out of the composer's orders, and that present-day standards of taste are part of an unchanging tradition fully applicable to the music of that period.

Pergolesi, Giovanni Battista (b. Jesi, near Ancona, Italy, 4 Jan. 1710; buried Pozzuoli, 17 Mar. 1736). Pupil of Durante and Feo. *Maestro di cappella* to the Prince of Stigliano in Naples, 1732–34. Active in Rome in 1734, after which he returned to Naples. Composed operas (incl. *La *serva padrona; L'Olimpiade*, Rome, 1735); oratorios; cantatas; Masses and other sacred music (incl. a *Stabat Mater*, 1736); concertos; trio sonatas; harpsichord pieces.

Peri, Jacopo (b. Rome, 20 Aug. 1561; d. Florence, 12 Aug. 1633). Singer and composer. Pupil of Malvezzi. Church organist in Florence, 1579–88. Director of the music at the court in Florence from 1601. Prominent member of the Florentine *camerata. Composed operas (incl. the first opera, *Dafne*, libretto by O. Rinuccini, Florence, 1597, music now lost; *Euridice*, libretto by Rinuccini, Florence, 1600); music for *intermedi* and ballets; madrigals and other secular vocal works, some with instruments.

Period. A division of time, i.e., a group of measures comprising a natural division of the melody; usually regarded as comprising two or more contrasting or complementary phrases and ending with a cadence.

Perkins, John MacIvor (b. St. Louis, 2 Aug. 1935). Pupil of Berger, Fine, Shapero, N. Boulanger, Gerhard, and Rubbra. Teacher at the Univ. of Chicago, 1962–65; Harvard Univ., 1965–70; Washington Univ. in St. Louis, from 1970. Has composed a chamber opera; orch. works (incl. *Music for Orchestra*, 1964); chamber music (incl. *Music for 13 Players*, 1964); choral works; piano pieces; songs.

Perkowski, Piotr (b. Oweczacz, Ukraine, 17 Mar. 1902). Studied at the Warsaw Conservatory, privately with Szymanowski, and with Roussel in Paris. Teacher at the Warsaw Conservatory, 1947–51 and 1955–72; at the Wroclaw Conservatory, 1951–54. Has composed a radio opera; ballets (incl. *Balladyna*, 1961–64); symphonies and other orch. works (incl. *Nocturne*, 1955); concertos for piano and for violin; numerous piano pieces, incl. Polish dances; songs.

Perle, George (b. Bayonne, N.J., 6 May 1915). Pupil of W. La Violette and Krenek. Teacher at the Univ. of Louisville, 1949–57; Univ. of California at Davis, 1957–61; Queens College in New York, from 1961. Has worked with twelve-tone techniques. Has composed 2 symphonies and other orch. works (incl. *3 Movements for Orchestra*, 1960); *Songs of Praise and Lamentation* for chorus and orch., 1975; a cello concerto, 1966; 6 string quartets, a string quintet, and other chamber music; piano pieces (incl. *6 Preludes*, 1946; *Toccata*, 1969); songs. Has published the book *Serial Composition and Atonality*, 1962, and numerous articles.

Perosi, Lorenzo (b. Tortona, Italy, 21 Dec. 1872; d. Rome, 12 Oct. 1956). Studied at the Milan Conservatory and with F. X. Haberl. Choirmaster at San Marco in Venice from 1894. Ordained a priest in 1896. *Maestro di cappella* of the Sistine Chapel in Rome, 1898–1915 and from 1923. Composed oratorios (incl. a trilogy, *La passione di Cristo*, 1897); numerous Masses, motets, and other sacred vocal works; orch. works, incl. a series named after Italian cities; concertos for piano and for violin; chamber music; numerous organ pieces.

Perotin (Perotinus magnus) (b. *c.* 1160; d. *c.* 1220; fl. Paris, *c.* 1180–1205). A master of the *Notre Dame school. Composed organa for three and four parts; *clausulae,* some for substitution in the *Magnus liber organi; conductus;* motets.

Perpetuum mobile [L.]. A term used by Paganini (*Moto perpetuo,* op. 11), Weber (last movement of Piano Sonata op. 24), and others to denote pieces that proceed from beginning to end in the same rapid motion, e.g., sixteenth notes in presto. Pieces of this type, although not labeled as such, occur also in Chopin's Etudes.

Perséphone. *Melodrama by Stravinsky after a poem of A. Gide, first performed in Paris in 1934.

Persichetti, Vincent (b. Philadelphia, 6 June 1915). Pianist, conductor, and composer. Studied at Combs College, the Philadelphia Conservatory, and the Curtis Institute. Teacher at the Philadelphia Conservatory, 1941–61; at the Juilliard School from 1947. Has composed 9 symphonies and other orch. works; a piano concerto, 1962; an English horn concerto, 1977; an oratorio, *The Creation,* 1970, and other sacred and secular choral works; works for band; 4 string quartets and other chamber music, incl. a series of serenades for various combinations of instruments; 11 sonatas and other piano pieces; organ pieces; numerous songs. Published the book *Twentieth-Century Harmony,* 1961.

Pes [L.]. (1) Same as *podatus;* see table accompanying Neumes. (2) Name for the tenor in English 13th- and 14th-century manuscripts, particularly also for the two lower parts of *"Sumer is icumen in."

Pesante [It.]. Heavy, heavily.

Pescetti, Giovanni Battista (b. Venice, *c.* 1704; d. there, 20 Mar. 1766). Pupil of Lotti. Director in London of the Covent Garden Theatre, 1739, and the King's Theatre, 1740, returning to Italy *c.* 1747. Second organist at San Marco in Venice from 1762. Composed operas (incl. *Diana and Endymion,* London, 1739); an oratorio; sacred works; harpsichord sonatas.

Peter, Johann Friedrich (John Frederik) (b. Heerendijk, Holland, of German parents, 19 May 1746; d. Bethlehem, Pa., 13 July 1813). Settled in the U.S. in 1770 and was active in the Moravian communities in Nazareth, Bethlehem, and Lititz, Pa., and Salem, N.C., the latter during the years 1779–89, after which he returned to Bethlehem as church organist. Composed more than 80 anthems with instrumental accompaniment; 6 string quintets, 1789. His brother Simon (1743–1819), active as a Moravian pastor in North Carolina, 1784–1819, also composed a few anthems.

Peter and the Wolf. An orchestral fairy tale for children by Prokofiev (op. 67, completed in 1936), for a small orchestra and narrator. Each character (cat, duck, Peter, etc.) is associated with a specific instrument and melodic phrase.

Peter Grimes. Opera in three acts by Britten (libretto by M. Slater, based on G. Crabbe's poem, *The Borough*), produced in London, 1945. Setting: the Borough, a fishing village on the east coast of England, about 1830.

Peterson-Berger, Olof Wilhelm (b. Ullånger, Sweden, 27 Feb. 1867; d. Frösö, Sweden, 3 Dec. 1942). Studied in Stockholm and Dresden. Music critic for *Dagens nyheter* in Stockholm, 1896–1930. Stage director for the Royal Opera in Stockholm, 1908–10. Employed Swedish folksongs. Composed operas (incl. *Arnljot,* Stockholm, 1910); 5 symphonies and other orch. works; a violin concerto; choral works; chamber music; piano pieces (incl. collections titled *Frösöblomster,* 1896, 1900, 1914); songs. Published a book on Wagner and translated some of his literary works into Swedish.

Petrassi, Goffredo (b. Zagarolo, near Rome, 16 July 1904). Studied at the Accademia di Santa Cecilia in Rome, where he taught from 1939. Has made some use of twelve-tone techniques. Has composed 2 operas (*Il cordovano,* Milan, 1949; *La morte dell'aria,* Rome, 1950); ballets; 7 concertos for orch. and other orch. works; concertos for piano, 1939, and for flute, 1960; sacred and secular choral works; chamber music (incl. *Estri* for 15 instruments, 1967); piano pieces; songs; music for films.

Petridis, Petro (b. Nigde, Asia Minor, of Greek parents, 23 July 1892). Critic and composer. Largely self-taught as a composer, though he studied briefly with Roussel. Has employed elements of folk music and Byzantine chant. Has composed an opera; a ballet; oratorios (incl. *St. Paul,* 1951); 5 symphonies and other orch. works; 2 piano concertos, a cello concerto, a violin concerto, and a concerto for 2 pianos; chamber music; piano pieces; numerous songs.

Petrov, Andrei Pavlovich (b. Leningrad, 2 Sept. 1930). Studied at the Leningrad Conservatory. Subsequently became an editor of *Muzgiz* and first secretary of the Leningrad branch of the Union of Soviet Composers. Has made use of jazz. Has composed the opera *Peter I, c.* 1974; ballets (incl. *Creation of the World,* prod. 1971); orch. works (incl. *Poem for Strings, Organ, 4 Trumpets and Percussion,* 1966); music for films and the theater.

Petrus de Cruce (fl. late 13th century). Composer and theorist. Composed motets, preserved in a French manuscript, that employ small note-values of a kind not found earlier and not accounted for in the prevailing system of mensural notation usually attributed to Franco of Cologne.

Petrushka. Ballet by Stravinsky (choreography by M. Fokine), produced in Paris, 1911, by Diaghilev's Ballets Russes. The work is often heard in the form of an orchestral suite.

Pettersson, (Gustaf) Allan (b. Västra Ryd, Sweden, 19 Sept. 1911). Pupil of Blomdahl, Leibowitz, and Honegger. Violist in the Stockholm Philharmonic, 1939–51. Has composed 13 symphonies and 3 concertos for string orch.; chamber music; songs.

Petyrek, Felix (b. Brno, 14 May 1892; d. Vienna, 1 Dec. 1951). Pianist and composer. Pupil of Schreker. Teacher at the Athens Conservatory, 1926–30; at the Stuttgart Hochschule für Musik, 1930–39; at the Vienna Academy from 1949. Composed 2 operas; 2 pantomimes;

orch. works; choral works; chamber music; piano pieces (incl. *6 Grotesken*); pieces for 2 pianos, incl. a concerto; songs.

Peu, un [F.]. A little, somewhat.

Peuerl, Paul (Peurl, Bäwerl, Beurlin) (b. *c.* 1570; d. after 1625). Organist in Steyer, Austria, 1609–25. Composed instrumental pieces, incl. canzonas and the earliest variation suites, published in his collection *Newe Padouan, Intrada, Däntz und Galliarda,* 1611; secular polyphony.

Pevernage, Andreas (b. Harelbeke, near Courtrai, Belgium, 1543; d. Antwerp, 30 July 1591). Choirmaster at the Cathedral in Bruges in 1563; at Notre Dame in Courtrai, 1564–85; at the Antwerp Cathedral from 1585. Composed numerous Masses and motets; numerous chansons and other secular polyphony.

Pezel, Johann Christoph (Petzold, Pezelius, Betzel, etc.) (b. Calau, Lusatia, Germany, 1639; d. Bautzen, 13 Oct. 1694). Violinist, trumpeter, and composer. Municipal musician in Leipzig from 1664; in Bautzen from 1681. Composed music for brass and other instrumental ensembles; airs with instrumental accompaniment; a Mass and other sacred works.

Pezzo [It.]. Piece, composition.

Pf. (1) Designating an instrument in orchestral scores, etc., abbr. for *pianoforte* (*piano*). (2) As a dynamic sign, it is an abbr. meaning "piano followed by forte."

Pfitzner, Hans (Erich) (b. Moscow, of German parents, 5 May 1869; d. Salzburg, 22 May 1949). Pupil of I. Knorr. Teacher at Stern's Conservatory in Berlin, 1897–1907. Conductor of the orchestra and the opera in Strasbourg and director of the conservatory there, 1908–16. Teacher at the Berlin Academy, 1920–29; at the Munich Academy, 1929–34. Composed 5 operas (incl. **Palestrina*); 2 symphonies and other orch. works; concertos for piano, for violin, for cello; choral works; 3 string quartets, a piano trio, and other chamber music; piano pieces; numerous songs.

Phantasie [G.]. See Fantasia. *Phanta-siestücke,* fantasy pieces; *Phantasie-bilder,* fantasy pictures; *phantasieren,* to improvise.

Phantasy. A title specified for English chamber works written for the Cobbett Competitions, established in 1906. According to the rules of the competition, the work had to be in one movement. More than forty such compositions were written between 1905 and 1930. Ralph Vaughan Williams, W. H. Hurlstone, Frank Bridge, John Ireland, and Thomas Dunhill were among the contributors.

Philidor, François André Danican (Danican-Philidor) (b. Dreux, France, 7 Sept. 1726; d. London, 31 Aug. 1795). Most famous member of a family (real name Danican) of French musicians. Champion chess player and composer. Pupil of Campra. Composed comic operas (incl. *Le maréchal ferrant,* Paris, 1761; *Tom Jones,* Paris, 1765); serious operas (incl. *Ernelinde, princesse de Norvège,* Paris, 1767); church music; vocal and instrumental chamber music. His brother Anne (1681–1728), a flutist and composer, founded the Concert spirituel in 1725.

Philippot, Michel (Paul) (b. Verzy, France, 2 Feb. 1925). Studied at the Paris Conservatory and with Leibowitz. Sound engineer for the French Radio-Television Network, 1949–59, and its music director from 1964. Director of the Groupe de recherches musicales, 1959–61. Works incl. 3 pieces of *musique concrète* on tape titled *Étude,* 1952–62, and 2 titled *Ambiance,* 1962; *Composition* for piano, 1958; *Composition* for double orch., 1959; *Transformations triangulaires* for 12 instruments, 1962.

Philips, Peter (b. London?, 1560 or 1561; d. Brussels, 1628). Chorister at St. Paul's Cathedral, London, in 1574. Organist at the English College in Rome, 1582–85. In the service of Lord Paget in Rome and elsewhere on the Continent, 1585–90. Organist to Archduke Albert in the royal chapel in Brussels from 1597. Composed Masses, motets, and other sacred works, some with thoroughbass; madrigals; pieces for virginals; pieces for viols.

Phillips, Burrill (b. Omaha, Nebr., 9 Nov. 1907). Pupil of Stringham, Bernard Rogers, and Hanson. Teacher at the Eastman School, 1933–49; Univ. of Illinois, 1949–64. Has composed ballets (incl. *Play Ball,* 1938); a chamber opera; orch. works (incl. *Selections from McGuffey's Reader,* 1934; *Tom Paine Overture,* 1947); a piano concerto, 1942, and a concerto for viola, clarinet, piano, and orch., 1952; choral works; 2 string quartets, a quartet for oboe and strings, 1967, and other chamber music (incl. *Canzona III* for poet and 7 instruments, 1970); piano pieces; organ pieces; songs; music for films.

Phinot, Dominicus (Dominique Finot) (fl. France, perhaps Lyon, and Italy; d. between 1557 and 1560). Highly praised by his contemporaries, he composed Masses, about 90 motets, some for two choruses, and other sacred works; about 25 chansons.

Phoebus and Pan. See *Streit zwischen Phöbus und Pan.*

Phonola. See under Mechanical instruments.

Phrase, phrasing. A section of a musical line somewhat comparable to a clause or sentence in prose is called a phrase; a related term is *period.* Phrases may be a function of harmony and rhythm as well as melody. They are typically defined by arrival at a point of at least momentary stability such as is created by a *cadence.* When one phrase is so constructed as to require further resolution by a second phrase (usually of similar character), the first is called the *antecedent* and the second the consequent phrase. In tonal music [see Tonality], particularly of the late 18th and early 19th centuries, phrases often (but by no means always) consist of multiples of two measures, four-measure phrases being particularly common. That aspect of performance that is concerned with the phrase structure of a composition is called phrasing and is carried out by means of *articulation.* In musical notation, phrases are sometimes indicated by means of arcs or *slurs (also called phrase marks).

Phrygian. (1) See under Church modes.

(2) A Phrygian cadence [Ex.] is one in which the tonic is approached from the semitone above. The term is sometimes extended to include (half-) cadences on the dominant in the minor mode in which the dominant is approached by semitone from the lowered sixth (submediant) above [see Scale degrees].

Piacere, a [It.]. See *A piacere*.

Piacevole [It.]. Pleasing, agreeable.

Pianamente [It.]. Smoothly, softly.

Piangendo [It.]. Crying, plaintive.

Pianino [G.]. Upright piano.

Piano [It.]. (1) Soft; abbr. *p. Pianissimo,* abbr. *pp,* very soft. Sometimes *ppp* and *pppp* are used to indicate further degrees of softness. See Dynamic marks.

(2) Also the pianoforte. A stringed instrument whose strings are struck by hammers activated by keys. It was originally called a *pianoforte* [It. soft-loud; also *forte-piano*] because, in contrast to the earlier harpsichord, the loudness of its sound could be varied by the touch of the fingers. Today the abbreviated name *piano* is more commonly used. The modern instrument described here initially is the "grand" piano, in which the strings are contained in a horizontal, wing-shaped case with one curved side and with the keyboard set perpendicular to the strings, the whole supported on three legs.

The piano has a pitch range—usually more than seven octaves, from A_2 to c'''''—and a dynamic range that are exceeded only by the organ's. The complexity of the piano arises from the fact that the soft felt hammer cannot merely be lifted toward the string like the tangent of the *clavichord or carried past the string like the plucking mechanism of the *harpsichord but must be thrown up and must immediately rebound from the string so that it will not damp out the vibrations it initiates. Since the hammer must be thrown instead of being lifted, it must move faster than the key that activates it, requiring a lever system (called

an *action*) between it and the key. If the action is to give the performer good dynamic control, the distance over which the hammer is thrown after the motion of the key is arrested must be kept small. On the other hand, the hammer must fall far enough away from the string after striking it so that there will be no possibility of its bouncing back up and accidentally restriking the string. This requirement is met by the provision of a device that catches the hammer as it falls (a *backcheck*) and, more important, by an *escapement,* by means of which the lever that lifts the hammer is moved aside just before the hammer's impact on the string. The hammer then falls back farther than it was thrown upward, even while the key is still held down. An action meeting all of these requirements still does not permit rapid repetition of a note, especially when playing softly. This need can be met not only by the *repetition action* or *double escapement,* developed in 1821 by Sébastien Érard (1752–1831). In this action, the hammer falls to an intermediate position and can be thrown upward again before the key returns all the way to its original resting position.

In addition to activating the hammers, the keys of a piano must also control felt-covered *dampers,* lifting them as a note is struck and allowing them to fall back to silence the strings when the keys are released. Generally, three strings per note are provided in the treble, two wound strings in the tenor, and one wound string in the bass. The aggregate tension imposed by these strings, which approaches 18 tons, is borne by a cast-iron frame.

The modern piano is equipped with two or (especially in America) three pedals, the damper or "loud" pedal at the right, the *una corda* or "soft" pedal at the left, and (if present) the sostenuto pedal in the center. On being depressed, the *damper pedal* raises all the dampers, allowing all the strings to vibrate regardless of what keys are being depressed; this produces a characteristic coloring of the tone and permits legato performance of notes that do not lie beneath the hand. On *grand* pianos the *una corda pedal* shifts the entire keyboard and action to the right so that each hammer strikes

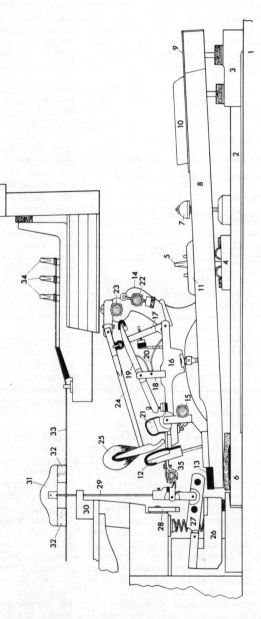

Cross section of grand piano action: 1. Keybed. 2. Keyframe. 3. Front rail. 4. Balance rail. 5. Balance rail stud. 6. Back rail. 7. Key stop rail. 8. White key. 9. Key covering. 10. Black key. 11. Key button. 12. Backcheck. 13. Underlever key cushion. 14. Action hanger. 15. Support rail. 16. Support. 17. Fly. 18. Support top flange. 19. Balancer. 20. Repetition spring. 21. Hammer rest. 22. Regulating rail. 23. Hammer rail. 24. Hammershank. 25. Hammer. 26. Underlever frame. 27. Underlever. 28. Damper stop rail. 29. Damper wire. 30. Damper guide rail. 31. Damper head. 32. Damper felts. 33. String. 34. Tuning pin. 35. Sostenuto rod.

Courtesy of Steinway & Sons

only two of its three unison strings in the treble and only one of its two strings in the tenor. In addition to a reduction in volume, this pedal also produces a characteristic tone color. The *sostenuto pedal* operates to sustain only those tones whose dampers are already raised by the action of the keys. Thus, it permits the sustaining of single notes (e.g., a pedal point in the bass) while both hands are occupied elsewhere and also provides the means of producing various coloristic effects.

Although interest in providing the harpsichord with some sort of hammer mechanism seems to have been fairly widespread in the first years of the 18th century—perhaps owing to the phenomenal success of Pantaleon Hebenstreit (1669–1750) and his large dulcimer, the *pantaleon—the piano was created essentially single-handedly by Bartolomeo Cristofori (1655–1730) of Florence, shortly before 1709. Cristofori's *gravicembalo col piano e forte* was conceived, as its name implies, as a new variety of harpsichord, whose hammer action could provide continuous gradations of loudness instead of the ordinary harpsichord's "terrace dynamics." The perfection of Cristofori's piano action of 1720, which included both an escapement and hammer check, was such that it was not significantly improved upon for nearly a century, and no instruments even comparable in quality, except for direct copies like those of Gottfried Silbermann (1683–1753), were made until the 1770s. The point of departure for most of the German builders seems to have been the clavichord rather than the harpsichord, and the German piano of the 18th century is, in both conception and tone quality, far more like a loud clavichord than a dynamically flexible harpsichord. Most of the mid-18th-century German pianos were in fact built in the "square" form of the clavichord (in contrast to Cristofori's and Silbermann's, which were wing-shaped "grands"). The German builders employed a very simple action, radically different from Cristofori's, whose action appears to have dropped from sight only to be essentially reinvented in England in the last quarter of the 18th century. In the typical German action, the hammer is pivoted in a fork at the back of the key rather than hinged from a rail fixed above the keys as in Cristofori's design. Most of the early German actions lacked an escapement, which was first incorporated by Johann Andreas Stein (1728–92) *c*. 1770. This so-called Viennese action yielded a touch lighter and shallower than that of Cristofori's instrument and greatly facilitated performance of the sparkling passagework characteristic of piano music before Beethoven's time.

The English piano appears to have descended from Cristofori's in a highly indirect fashion, the first pianos in England having been built by a German expatriate, Johann Zumpe, *c*. 1765. Zumpe's square pianos employed an escapementless action that resembled Cristofori's only in having the hammers hinged from an overhead rail; this action was provided with an escapement, probably *c*. 1772 by Americus Backers, John Broadwood, and Robert Stodart, and later was to be the point of departure for Érard. Thus, the English action is the ancestor of that found in all modern pianos. It required a touch heavier than that of the delicate Viennese action, but it proved capable of giving greater volume and a wider dynamic range to the performer.

The history of the piano after the perfection of the double-escapement action is largely concerned with the development of metal bracing that could withstand the ever-increasing tension imposed by the thicker strings required for increased loudness and brilliance. The greatest single advance was the invention in 1825 of the one-piece cast-iron frame by Alpheus Babcock, who also was the first to conceive of *cross-stringing,* an arrangement in which the strings of treble and middle registers fan out over most of the soundboard while the bass strings cross over them, forming a separate fan at a higher level. These two features were given what is essentially their present form in the grand piano exhibited in 1855 by Steinway and Sons of New York.

Of the horizontal piano designs, the clavichord-shaped "square" and the wing-shaped "grand," only the latter has continued to be built in the 20th century. Modern grand pianos range in size from the 9-foot "concert grand" down to 5-

foot, 2-inch "baby grands." (These sizes are the normal extremes; there are instruments as long as 11 feet and shorter than 5 feet.) Pianos with their strings arranged in a vertical plane have been built since the middle of the 18th century. The earliest examples appear to have been either "pyramid" pianos, in which the strings were housed in a case that formed a tall isosceles triangle above the keyboard, or "giraffe" pianos, which were essentially grand pianos set on end. The 19th century saw the introduction of "cabinet" pianos with tall rectangular cases, as well as the diagonally strung "cottage" piano of Robert Wornum (1811), which is the true ancestor of the modern upright. Large upright pianos more than 4 feet high have been largely superseded by lower instruments: the *studio upright* (about 46 inches high), the *console* (about 40 inches high), and the *spinet* (about 36 inches high). The spinet frequently differs from the others in having a special action that operates from below the keys. See also Keyboard; Pedal piano; Sostenente piano; Electronic instruments.

Piano concerto. A *concerto for solo piano and orchestra.

Piano duet. A composition for two pianists playing on either one or two instruments. Compositions to be played on a single instrument are also described as "for four hands" [F. *à quatre mains;* G. *vierhändig;* It. *a quattro mani;* Sp. *a cuatro manos*].

Piano quartet. See under Quartet.

Piano-violin. See Sostenente piano.

Pianola. See under Mechanical instruments.

Piatti [It.]. *Cymbals.

Piatti, Alfredo Carlo (b. Bergamo, 8 Jan. 1822; d. Crocetta di Mozzo, near Bergamo, 18 July 1901). Cellist and composer. Studied at the Milan Conservatory. Traveled widely as a cellist in Europe, Russia, and the British Isles. Particularly active in England, 1846–49 and 1859–98. Composed works for cello, incl. 2 concertos and 6 sonatas for cello and piano.

Pibgorn, pibcorn. An early member of the clarinet family, also called a hornpipe.

Pibroch. A type of Scottish bagpipe music consisting of highly ornamented variations on a theme called an *urlar.*

Picardy third [F. *tierce de Picardie*]. The major third above the tonic as used for the final chord of a composition in a minor key. This practice originated *c.* 1500, but the extent to which it was used prior to 1550 is difficult to assess, this being largely a problem of *musica ficta.* In the second half of the 16th century the practice became fairly common. The Picardy third continued to be used until the end of the baroque period (*c.* 1750). The term probably derives from the Old French *picart* (fem. *picarde,* sharp, pointed) rather than from the name Picardie of a region in France, despite the form given it by Rousseau and most writers since.

Piccinni, Niccolò (Nicola) (b. Bari, Italy, 16 Jan. 1728; d. Passy, near Paris, 7 May 1800). Pupil of Leo and Durante. Second organist at the Cappella reale in Naples, 1771–76. Settled in Paris in 1776. Was held up by its partisans as the principal representative of the Italian style in opera in opposition to the French style of Gluck. Composed about 140 Italian and French operas (incl. *La buona figliuola,* Rome, 1760; *L'Olimpiade,* Rome, 1768; *Roland,* Paris, 1778; *Didon,* Fontainebleau, 1785); oratorios; sacred music; 2 symphonies; arias.

Piccolo [It.]. Small. Abbr. for *piccolo flute;* see Flute.

Pickelflöte [G.]. Older name for the piccolo flute. The modern German name is *kleine Flöte.*

Pickup. See Upbeat.

Pictures at an Exhibition. Collection of descriptive piano pieces by Mussorgsky, composed in 1874. Each piece illustrates a picture by the Russian painter Victor A. Hartmann (d. 1873) shown at a memorial exhibition of his paintings in 1874. The work is often heard in an orchestral version by Ravel.

Pieno [It.]. Full; *organo pieno,* full organ; *a voce piena,* with full voice.

Pierné, (Henri-Constant-) Gabriel (b. Metz, France, 16 Aug. 1863; d. Ploujean, near Morlaix, 17 July 1937). Pupil of Franck and Massenet. Organist at Sainte-Clothilde in Paris, 1890–98, succeeding Franck. Conductor of the Concerts Colonne, 1910–34. Composed operas (incl. *La fille de Tabarin,* Paris, 1901); ballets (incl. *Cydalise et le chèvre-pied,* 1919); oratorios (incl. *La croisade des enfants,* 1905); orch. works; a piano concerto, 1887, and a *Konzertstück* for harp and orch., 1901; chamber music; piano pieces (incl. *Album pour mes petits amis,* 1887, containing the "Marche des petits soldats de plomb"); organ pieces; songs.

Pierrot lunaire [F., Pierrot in the Moon-light]. Cycle of 21 short pieces for a "singing narrator" (**Sprechstimme*) and chamber ensemble by Schoenberg, op. 21 (1912), based on poems by A. Giraud in a German translation by O. E. Hartleben.

Pierson, Heinrich Hugo (originally Henry Hugh Pearson) (b. Oxford, 12 April 1815; d. Leipzig, 28 Jan. 1873). Pupil of Attwood and, after going to Germany in 1839, of Tomášek, Reissiger, and Rinck. Associate of Mendelssohn. Professor of music at Edinburgh, 1844–46, after which he settled again in Germany. Employed the pseudonym Edgar Mansfeldt for some works. Composed operas (incl. *Leila,* Hamburg, 1848); oratorios (incl. *Jerusalem,* 1852); incidental music to the second part of Goethe's *Faust,* 1854, overtures to plays of Shakespeare, and other orch. works; choral works; songs.

Piffero [It.]. Old term for various popular wind instruments, such as the shawm, fife, and bagpipe, all of which were used by shepherds. Hence, the name *pifferari* for the peasants who, in the 18th century, went to Rome every Christmas morning to play there in imitation of the biblical shepherds.

Pijper, Willem (Frederik Johannes) (b. Zeist, the Netherlands, 8 Sept. 1894; d. Leidschendam, 18 Mar. 1947). Critic and composer. Pupil of J. Wagenaar. Teacher at the Amsterdam Conservatory, 1925–28. Director of the Rotterdam Conservatory, 1930–47. Composed operas (*Halewijn,* Amsterdam, 1933, and another that remained unfinished); 3 symphonies and other orch. works; concertos for piano, for cello, for violin; choral works; 4 string quartets, 2 piano trios, and other chamber music; piano pieces; songs.

Pilkington, Francis (b. *c.* 1562; d. Chester, 1638). Held various posts at Chester Cathedral from 1602 and was curate at various churches in Chester and its environs from 1616. Composed madrigals; ayres with lute accompaniment; lute pieces.

Pincé [F.]. (1) See Mordent. (2) Term for plucked instruments (lute, harp, etc.) and for **pizzicato.*

Pini di Roma [It., Pines of Rome]. Symphonic poem by Respighi (1924), depicting four musical "landscapes" near Rome (the Villa Borghese, a catacomb, the Janiculum [a hill named after the god Janus], and the Appian Way).

Pinkham, Daniel (b. Lynn, Mass., 5 June 1923). Conductor, harpsichordist, organist, and composer. Pupil of Piston, Copland, Barber, Honegger, and N. Boulanger. Music director of King's Chapel, Boston, from 1958. Teacher at the New England Conservatory from 1959. Has composed a chamber opera, *The Garden of Artemis,* 1948; 2 symphonies and other orch. works (incl. *Catacoustical Measures,* 1963; *Signs of the Zodiac,* with speaker, 1965); a piano concertino, 1949, and a violin concerto, 1968; a *Christmas Cantata,* 1958, and other sacred and secular choral works, some with orch.; chamber music; organ pieces; electronic works for tape with instruments.

P'ip'a. **Pyiba.*

Pipe. (1) A small instrument of the recorder type that was held and played with the left hand only, while the right hand played the tabor, a small drum. [For ill. see under Percussion instruments.] The playing of the pipe and tabor [Prov. *galoubet* and **tambourin;* Sp. *flaviol* and *tamboril;* Cat. *fluviol* and *tambori*] was popular as early as the 13th century. It was the usual accompaniment to the **farandole* and the English morris dance [see under *Moresca*], and it is still used for the Spanish **sardana.* (2) Generic name for various groups of instruments: all the *wind instruments; the woodwinds; the flutes; the pipes of the organ; primitive instruments in the shape of a single tube.

Pipelare, Matthaeus (b. c. 1450; d. c. 1512). Active in Antwerp. Master of the choristers of the Illustrious Confraternity of Our Lady in 's-Hertogenbosch, 1498–1500. Composed Masses, motets, and chansons.

Pique Dame [F.]. See Queen of Spades, The.

Pisador, Diego (b. Salamanca, c. 1509; d. after 1557). Published Libro de musica de vihuela, 1552, containing fantasias and diferencias, intabulations for vihuela with voice of sacred and secular works by Josquin and others, and settings of romances, villancicos, and other poetry.

Pisk, Paul Amadeus (b. Vienna, 16 May 1893). Musicologist and composer. Pupil of Schreker and Schoenberg. Settled in the U.S. in 1936. Has taught at the Univ. of Redlands, 1937–50; the Univ. of Texas, 1950–63; Washington Univ. in St. Louis, 1963–72. Has composed a ballet, American Suite, 1948, and other stage works; orch. works (incl. Passacaglia, 1948; 3 Ceremonial Rites, 1958); choral works; chamber music; piano pieces; songs.

Pistocchi, Francesco Antonio Mamiliano (b. Palermo, 1659; d. Bologna, 13 May 1726). Singer at San Petronio in Bologna, 1670–75; at the court in Parma, 1686–95. Court Kapellmeister in Ansbach, 1696–99. Returned to San Petronio in 1701 and in 1705 founded a singing school in Bologna. Successful as an opera singer in both Germany and Italy. Composed operas; oratorios; church music; arias, duets, and trios.

Piston. Piston valve [see Valve].

Piston, Walter (Hamor) (b. Rockland, Maine, 20 Jan. 1894; d. Belmont, Mass., 12 Nov. 1976). Studied at Harvard and with N. Boulanger and Dukas in Paris. Teacher at Harvard Univ., 1926–60. His pupils incl. Adler, Berger, Bernstein, Carter, Fine, Layton, Shapero, and R. Ward. Composed a ballet, The Incredible Flutist, 1938; 8 symphonies (no. 3,

1947, and no. 7, 1960, awarded Pulitzer prizes), a concerto for orch., 1933, and other orch. works; a concertino for piano and chamber orch., 1933, 2 violin concertos, 1939 and 1960, a viola concerto, 1957, a concerto for 2 pianos, 1959, a clarinet concerto, 1967, Variations for cello and orch., 1967, Fantasy for violin and orch., 1973, and a concerto for string quartet and orch., 1974; choral works; 5 string quartets, 2 piano trios, and other chamber music; organ pieces; piano pieces. Published books on harmony, counterpoint, and orchestration.

Pitch. (1) [F. hauteur; G. Tonhöhe; It. intonazione; Sp. entonación]. The perceived highness or lowness of a sound. It is a function primarily of frequency, though at some extremes of frequency, intensity may also affect the perception of pitch [see Acoustics].

(2) [F. ton; G. Ton; It., Sp. tono]. Any single point on the entire continuum of pitch, e.g., the pitch c' [see Pitch names].

(3) [F. diapason; G. Kammerton, Stimmung; It. diapason; Sp. diapasón]. The *absolute pitch of one specific note, standardized for the purpose of obtaining identical pitches on all instruments. The present-day standard of pitch is a' = 440 cycles per second. This standard was adopted in 1939 by an international conference held in London under the auspices of the International Standards Association. It replaced the old standard of 435 that had been fixed by the Paris Academy in 1859 (diapason normal) and confirmed, under the term "international pitch," at a conference held in Vienna in 1885.

Before these agreements there was a confusing variety of pitches. Throughout the baroque period different pitch levels were used for different ensembles: Kammerton (chamber pitch) for domestic instrumental music; Chorton (choir pitch, organ pitch) for church organs and, consequently, for sacred choral music; Cornett-ton for the brass instruments used by town musicians. These and other pitch levels of the period are represented in the first column of Table 1 by pitch names (disregarding microtonic deviations). In this scheme, the present standard of pitch (a' = 440 cycles per second) could be represented approximately by C. Thus, *hoch Kammerton*, which must be regarded as the standard instrumental pitch from *c*. 1700 to *c*. 1820, can be seen to lie about a semitone below modern pitch. Works of this period therefore sounded about a semitone lower than they do when performed at the present standard of pitch. The absolute pitch of these pitch levels, however, varied with time and place. Table 2 is a list of some characteristic data covering the period from *c*. 1700 to 1850 (where the first column gives the approximate modern equivalent of C, and the second column gives the frequency of a').

1

	Praetorius (*De Organographia,* 1619)	Common designation after Praetorius
B♭	*Tertia minore*	*Tief Kammerton*
B	*Chorton*	*Hoch Kammerton*
C♯	*Kammerton*	*Chorton*
D	*Cornett-ton*	*Cornett-ton*

2

	Pitch	Date	Source
B♭	396	1716	Strasbourg, Silbermann organ
B	422	1751	Handel's tuning fork
	422	1780	Mozart's tuning fork
	427	1811	Paris, *Grand opéra*
C	440	1834	Scheibler (Stuttgart pitch)
	446	1856	Paris, *Grand opéra*

Pitch aggregate. A collection of pitches, which may or may not be sounded simultaneously. The term is used primarily in discussions of 20th-century music.

Pitch class. A pitch without reference to the octave or register in which it occurs. There are twelve pitch classes employed in Western tonal music, each of which is represented in each octave of the entire range of pitches. The term is used particularly (though not exclusively) with respect to *serial music. See also Octave equivalence.

Pitch names. The accompanying table gives the English, German, French, Italian, and Spanish names for the pitch classes of an octave. Note that in German a sharp is denoted by the suffix *-is* and a flat by the suffix *-es*, a double-sharp by *-isis* and a double-flat by *-eses*.

Irregular formations in German are *B* for B-flat, instead of *Hes; Es*, E-flat, instead of *Ees; As*, A-flat, instead of *Aes*. The English B is called *H* in German, and the English B-flat is *B* in German.

English:	C	D	E		F	G	A	B
German:	C	D	E		F	G	A	H
French:	ut	ré	mi		fa	sol	la	si
Italian:	do	re	mi		fa	sol	la	si
Spanish:	do	re	mi		fa	sol	la	si

English:	C-sharp	C-flat
German:	cis	ces
French:	ut dièse	ut bémol
Italian:	do diesis	do bemolle
Spanish:	do sostenido	do bemol

English:	C-double-sharp	C-double-flat
German:	cisis	ceses
French:	ut double-dièse	ut double-bémol
Italian:	do doppio diesis	do doppio bemolle
Spanish:	do doble sostenido	do doble bemol

Unfortunately there is no uniform practice for indicating different octaves. The second table shows the system employed in this dictionary and widely used elsewhere (1), together with two others, (2) and (3).

Contra Great Small One - line Two - line

Three - line   Four - line

	1.	2.	3.
1.	C_1	C	c	c'	c''	c'''	c''''
2.	CCC	CC	C	c	c'	c''	c'''
3.	C_2	C_1	C	c	c^1	c^2	c^3

For other systems of pitch designation, see Solmization; Letter notation.

Pitch pipe. A device, now often employing one or more reeds after the fashion of a harmonica [see Harmonica (2)], used to set the pitch for a choir or to tune stringed instruments.

Pitoni, Giuseppe Ottavio (b. Rieti, Italy, 18 Mar. 1657; d. Rome, 1 Feb. 1743). *Maestro di cappella* at Assisi, 1674; at Rieti, 1676; at the Collegio di San Marco in Rome, 1677 until his death, though during this period he also served concurrently at San Giovanni in Laterano, 1708

-19, St. Peter's, 1719, and other Roman churches. Composed Masses and much other sacred music, often for two or more choirs (incl. a motet, *Dixit*, for four choirs, still sung at St. Peter's during Holy Week).

Più [It.]. More. *Più allegro*, more quickly; *piuttosto allegro*, rather quick.

Più tosto. See *Tosto*.

Piva. (1) An Italian term for the bagpipe. (2) The fastest measure (*misura*) or step unit of the *bassadanza* (**basse danse*). It consisted of a series of rapid steps (*passetti presti*) embellished by leaps and turns. (3) One of the fastest dances of the early 16th century. Some surviving examples of music appear as the third dance of a suite, following a **pavane* and a **saltarello;* the *piva* is in compound quadruple meter (12/8).

Pivot chord. See under Modulation.

Pixis, Johann Peter (b. Mannheim, 10 Feb. 1788; d. Baden-Baden, 22 Dec. 1874). Pianist and composer. Settled in Paris, 1825, and as a teacher in Baden-Baden, 1845. Composed operas; numerous works for piano (incl. a contribution to the *Hexaméron*, with Liszt, Czerny, Chopin, Thalberg, and Herz).

Pizzetti, Ildebrando (b. Borgo Strinato, near Parma, 20 Sept. 1880; d. Rome, 13 Feb. 1968). Studied at the Parma Conservatory and taught there, 1907–9. Teacher at the conservatory in Florence from 1908; its director, 1917–24. Director of the Verdi Conservatory in Milan, 1924–36. Teacher at the Accademia di Santa Cecilia in Rome, 1936–58, and its director, 1948–51. Composed operas (incl. *Fedra*, after D'Annunzio, Milan, 1915; *Debora e Jaele*, Milan, 1922; *Fra Gherardo*, Milan, 1928; *Lo straniero*, Rome, 1930; *Orsèolo*, Florence, 1935; *Vanna Lupa*, Florence, 1949; *Ifigenia*, radio broadcast, 1950; *Cagliostro*, Milan, 1953; *La figlia di Iorio*, after D'Annunzio, Naples, 1954; *Assassinio nella cattedrale*, after T. S. Eliot, Milan, 1958); incidental music to plays; orch. works (incl. *Concerto dell' estate*, 1928); concertos for cello and for violin; choral works; chamber music; piano pieces; songs (incl. "I pastori," after D'Annunzio).

Pizzicato [It.; abbr. *pizz.*]. For violins and other bowed stringed instruments, indication that the string is to be plucked with a finger, usually with the right hand, though sometimes with the left.

Placido [It.]. Calm, tranquil.

Plagal cadence. See Cadence.

Plagal mode. See Church modes.

Plainchant. See Plainsong; Gregorian chant.

Plainsong. Term derived from *cantus planus*, a 13th-century name for **Gregorian chant*. It is used synonymously with the latter but also is employed as a generic term for the ancient style of monophonic and rhythmically free melody that is common to various Western liturgies (Gregorian, **Ambrosian*, **Gallican*, **Mozarabic chant*) as well as those of the East (Byzantine, Syrian, Armenian chant).

Plainte [F.]. (1) See Lament (2). (2) A baroque ornament, either a **portamento* (in 17th-century viol music) or a **Nachschlag*.

Planets, The. Programmatic suite for orchestra, organ, and women's chorus by Holst (1914–16), describing in successive movements the astrological nature of seven planets.

Planquette, (Jean-) Robert (b. Paris, 31 Mar. 1848; d. there, 28 Jan. 1903). Studied at the Paris Conservatory. Composed operettas (incl. *Les cloches de Corneville*, Paris, 1877, produced in England and the U.S. as *The Chimes of Normandy; Rip Van Winkle*, London, 1882).

Plaqué [F.]. Indication for notes of a chord to be played simultaneously, as opposed to **arpeggio*.

Platti, Giovanni Benedetto (b. Padua, 9 July 1697; d. Würzburg, 11 Jan. 1763). Singer, harpsichordist, and composer. In service at the court in Würzburg, 1724–49. Composed keyboard sonatas; church music; concertos; chamber music.

Player piano. See under Mechanical instruments.

Plectrum. A small piece of horn, tortoise shell, wood, ivory, metal, etc., used to pluck certain stringed instruments, such as the Greek lyre and the modern mandolin and zither. Similarly, that part of the harpsichord jack that plucks the string.

Plein-jeu [F.]. Full organ. Also, name for pieces written for the full organ. *Demi-jeu,* half organ, i.e., softer registration.

Pleskow, Raoul (b. Vienna, 12 Oct. 1931). Pupil of Rathaus, Luening, and Wolpe. Teacher at C. W. Post College from 1959. Has composed *2 Movements for Orchestra,* 1968; chamber music (incl. *Movement for 9 Players,* 1967; *3 Movements for Quintet,* 1971); piano pieces; songs.

Pleyel, Ignaz Joseph (b. Ruppersthal, near Vienna, 18 June 1757; d. near Paris, 14 Nov. 1831). Pianist, piano manufacturer, and composer. Pupil of Vanhal and Haydn. Second *Kapellmeister* at the Strasbourg Cathedral from 1783 and first from 1789 until he went to London in 1791. Settled in Paris in 1795 as a music seller and founded the well-known piano factory bearing his name in 1807. Composed 2 operas; over 60 symphonies; concertos for violin, for cello, for piano; sacred and secular choral works; over 60 string quartets and much other chamber music; piano pieces; songs.

Plica [L.]. A notational sign of the 13th century calling for an ornamental tone to be inserted following the note to which it is connected. The sign for the *plica* is an upward or downward dash that can be attached to single notes (*longa, brevis*) as well as to the final note of a ligature (*ligatura plicata*). The direction of the dash indicates whether the added tone is higher or lower (usually at the interval of a second or, more rarely, a third, depending on the position of the next note). According to 13th-century theorists it was sung in a special manner, though its particular nature is unclear. In modern editions, the added tone is often indicated with a small note similar in appearance to a grace note, with which, however, it should not be confused.

Pneuma. See *Neuma* (2).

Pneumatic action. See Organ.

Pochette [F.]. *Kit.

Poco, un poco [It.]. Little; a little, somewhat. Derivative forms are *pochetto, pochettino, pochissimo.*

Podatus. See table accompanying Neumes.

Poetic meter. Poetic meter, with its regular patterns of accented (strong) and unaccented (weak) syllables or, in ancient Greek terminology, of *thesis* and **arsis,* is very similar to musical meter with its various schemes of accented and unaccented notes. The terminology of ancient Greek poetry therefore is frequently used for corresponding schemes of musical rhythm. The chief patterns (called *feet*) of the Greek system are shown in the accompanying table. This terminology is used in music particularly for the 13th-century system of rhythmic modes [see Modes, rhythmic].

Iamb	⌣ — ⌣ —
Trochee	— ⌣ — ⌣
Dactyl	— ⌣ ⌣ — ⌣ ⌣
Anapest	⌣ ⌣ — ⌣ ⌣ —
Spondee	— — — —
Tribrach	⌣ ⌣ ⌣ ⌣ ⌣ ⌣

The sign ⌣ *indicates a short syllable, the sign* — *a long one. Each of the examples here includes two feet.*

According to the number of feet contained in a line of verse, one distinguishes *dimeter* (two feet), *trimeter* (three), *tetrameter* (four), *pentameter* (five), and *hexameter* (six). In classical verse, in the case of an iambic or trochaic foot, however, the numbering proceeds in pairs of feet (*dipody,* i.e., two feet). Thus a line including four iambs is called iambic dimeter (not tetrameter). In hymnody certain standard meters have special names, e.g., *common meter,* indicated thus: 8 6 8 6 (the figures indicating the number of syllables in each line). Here each line may be considered an iambic dimeter, the lines "8" complete, the lines "6" katalectic, i.e., with one *arsis* and *thesis* missing at the end.

In applying metrical schemes to words (versification), there are two principles that determine on which syllables the *thesis* falls and on which the *arsis*, one ancient and one modern. In ancient poetry the division of lines into feet was quantitative, based on the principle of short and long syllables, whereas in modern poetry the division is accentual, based on the principle of weak and strong syllables.

Poglietti, Alessandro (b. probably Tuscany; d. Vienna, July 1683). Court organist in Vienna from 1661. Composed an opera; church music; 12 ricercars for organ; suites (incl. *Il rossignolo*) and other pieces for harpsichord.

Pohjola's Daughter. Symphonic poem by Sibelius, op. 49 (1906), based on a story from the *Kalevala.

Poi [It.]. Then, afterward. *Poi la coda,* "then the coda."

Point. (1) The upper end of the violin bow. (2) Point of perfection, of division, etc.; see *Punctus.* (3) In motets and other polyphonic works of the 16th century, *point of imitation* means a section of the polyphonic texture in which a single subject, setting a small division in the text, is treated in imitation. Such works may consist of a succession of overlapping points of imitation, the imitative statements of a new subject beginning before statements of the preceding subject conclude.

Point d'orgue [F.]. (1) The *pause and its sign. (2) *Pedal point. (3) A *cadenza in a concerto, so called because its beginning is customarily indicated by a pause sign placed above the preceding chord of the composition proper.

Pokorný, Franz Xaver (František Jiři) (b. Mestec Králové [Königstadt], Bohemia, 20 Dec. 1728; d. Regensburg, 2 July 1794). Pupil of Stamitz, Holzbauer, and Richter. Musician at the court of Thurn and Taxis, 1766 until his death. Composed over 100 symphonies; over 50 concertos; chamber music.

Polacca [It.]. Generic name for Polish dances, usually the *polonaise.

Poldini, Ede (b. Budapest, 13 June 1869; d. Corseaux, Switzerland, 28 June 1957). Studied at the Budapest Conservatory and in Vienna. Settled in Vevey, Switzerland, in 1908. Composed 4 comic operas (incl. *The Vagabond and the Princess,* Budapest, 1903); a ballet; numerous piano pieces (incl. *Poupée valsante*).

Polka. A Bohemian dance in quick duple meter with characteristic rhythms [Ex.]. It originated *c.* 1830 in Bohemia and soon spread to the European salons. The polka was introduced into art music by Smetana (*The Bartered Bride; From My Life; Bohemian Dances*), Dvořák, and others.

Polo. An Andalusian (south Spanish) dance in moderate 3/8 meter with frequent syncopations of the *hemiola type [see Ex.] and rapid *coloraturas sung to words such as "Ay," "Olé." Two famous polos were written by Manuel García (1775–1832), "Yo soy el contrabandista" and "Cuerpo bueno," the latter of which was used by Bizet in the prelude to Act IV of *Carmen.* A modern example is found in Falla's *Seven Spanish Popular Songs,* no. 7.

Polonaise [F.]. A Polish national dance of a stately and festive character. The music is always in moderate triple meter, usually consists of phrases without upbeat and with feminine ending, and often includes measures containing a short repeated rhythmic motif. About 1800 it acquired its classic form, which, in addition to these features, is characterized by the specific rhythmic patterns shown in the accompanying example. Early examples are by J. S. Bach (French Suite no. 6; Orchestral Suite no. 2). Well-known 19th-century examples are by Beethoven (op. 89), Schubert (*Polonaises* for four hands, op. 61, 75), Weber (op. 21, 72), Liszt (*Deux Polonaises*, 1851), Mussorgsky (in *Boris Godunov*), Tchaikovsky (in *Eugen Onegin*), and above all, Chopin.

Polychoral style. Term used for compositions in which the ensemble (chorus with or without the orchestra) is divided into several (usually two or three) distinct groups performing singly (in alternation) as well as jointly. Italian terms are *coro battente* and *coro spezzato* (broken choir), the latter of which also implies separate placement of the groups. Willaert used the technique in his *salmi spezzati* (broken psalms) found in publications of 1550 and 1557. The polychoral style was also cultivated by A. Gabrieli (*c*. 1520–86) and G. Gabrieli (*c*. 1557–1612), and it is a characteristic feature of the *Venetian school.

Polymeter. The simultaneous use of two or more meters. The term is sometimes applied, however, to the successive use of different meters in one or more parts.

Polyphony, polyphonic [F. *polyphonie;* G. *Mehrstimmigkeit;* It. *polifonia;* Sp. *polifonía*]. Music that simultaneously combines several musical lines of individual design, each of which retains its identity as a line to some degree, in contrast to *monophonic music, which consists of a single melody, or *homophonic music, which combines several lines of similar, rhythmically identical design [see also Counterpoint; Heterophony].

Polyrhythm. The simultaneous use of contrasted rhythms in different parts of the musical *texture. Generally the term is restricted to cases in which rhythmic variety is introduced as a special effect, often called *cross rhythm. The technique is prominent in some music of the late 14th century as well as in some music of the 20th century.

Polytextuality. The simultaneous use of different texts in various parts of a composition. It is a characteristic trait of the early *motet, from *c*. 1225 to 1400.

Polythematic. See Monothematic, polythematic.

Polytonality. See Bitonality, polytonality.

Pommer, Pomhart [G.]. Corruptions of *bombarde [see Oboe family III].

Pomp and Circumstance. Five concert marches for orchestra by Elgar, op. 39 (nos. 1 to 4 composed 1901–7, no. 5 in 1930). The title is taken from a phrase in Shakespeare's *Othello,* Act III: "pride, pomp and circumstance of glorious war."

Pomposo [It.]. Pompous.

Ponce, Manuel (María) (b. Fresnillo, Mexico, 8 Dec. 1882; d. Mexico City, 24 Apr. 1948). Studied at the National Conservatory in Mexico City and with Bossi and Dukas. Taught at various times at the National Conservatory and the National University in Mexico City. Worked with native Mexican musical materials. Composed orch. works (incl. *Chapultepec,* 1929; *Suite en estilo antiguo,* 1935); *Concierto del sur* for guitar and orch., 1941, 2 piano concertos, and a violin concerto; a piano trio and other chamber music; numerous piano pieces; 5 sonatas and other guitar pieces; numerous songs (incl. "Estrellita").

Ponchielli, Amilcare (b. Paderno Fasolaro, Cremona, 31 Aug. 1834; d. Milan, 16 Jan. 1886). Studied at the Milan Conservatory. *Maestro di cappella* at the Bergamo Cathedral, 1881–86. Teacher at the Milan Conservatory from 1883. Composed operas (incl. *I promessi sposi,* Milan, 1872; *La *gioconda,* Milan, 1876, containing the "Dance of the Hours"); ballets; church music; occasional vocal pieces.

Poniridy, Georges (Giorgios Poniridis) (b. Chalkedon, near Istanbul, 8 Oct. 1892). Conductor, violinist, critic, and composer. Pupil of Gilson, d'Indy, and Roussel. Head of the music department of the ministry of education in Athens, 1943–59. Has composed a musical tragedy, *Lazaros,* 1960–70; a ballet; incidental music to classical Greek plays; symphonies and other orch. works; concertos for piano and for violin; chamber music; piano pieces; songs and arrangements of Greek folksongs.

Ponticello [It.]. The *bridge of stringed instruments. *Sul ponticello,* see Bowing (k).

Poot, Marcel (b. Vilvoorde, near Brussels, 7 May 1901). Critic and composer. Pupil of Mortelmans, Gilson, and Dukas. Teacher at the Brussels Conservatory, 1938–66, and its director from 1949. Has composed 3 operas; ballets; 4 symphonies and other orch. works; a piano concerto, a *concerto grosso* for piano quartet and orch., and other works for solo instrument and orch.; 2 oratorios; chamber music; piano pieces; songs.

Popov, Gavriil Nikolaievich (b. Novocherkask, Russia, 12 Sept. 1904; d. Repino, near Leningrad, 17 Feb. 1972). Studied at the St. Petersburg Conservatory. Composed operas; music for films; 6 symphonies and other orch. works; choral works; a violin concerto; chamber music; piano pieces.

Popper, David (b. Prague, 9 Dec. 1843; d. Baden, near Vienna, 7 Aug. 1913). Studied at the Prague Conservatory. First cellist of the court orchestra in Vienna, 1868–73. Toured widely as a soloist. Composed 4 concertos and numerous other works for cello.

Porgy and Bess. Opera in three acts by George Gershwin (libretto by D. B. Heyward, adapted from D. B. and D. Heyward's play, *Porgy,* with lyrics by Ira Gershwin), produced in New York, 1935. Setting: Charleston, S.C., in the recent past. The music features the styles of blues, jazz, and Negro spirituals.

Porpora, Nicola (Antonio Giacinto) (b. Naples, 17 Aug. 1686; d. there, 3 Mar. 1768). *Kapellmeister* to the Landgrave of Hesse-Darmstadt, 1711–25. Handel's rival as composer to the Opera of the Nobility in London, 1733–36. Successful singing teacher at various institutions in Naples and Venice and at various times throughout his career. Singing teacher of the Electoral Princess in Dresden, 1747–51. Lived in Vienna, 1751–58, where Haydn was his pupil. Composed about 50 operas (incl. *Didone abbandonata,* Reggio, 1725; *Arianna in Nasso,* London, 1733), some on librettos by Metastasio, who was also his pupil; oratorios; cantatas; Masses and numerous motets; violin sonatas and other chamber music.

Port de voix [F.]. (1) In modern French,

same as **portamento.* (2) One of the most important French *agréments* of the 17th and 18th centuries. Essentially it is an upward-resolved suspension or appoggiatura, generally expressed by a sign or a particular notation [see Appoggiatura (2)]. Usually, however, both appoggiatura and resolution are repeated, so that the ornament consists of four notes, the last three forming a *pincé* (**mordent).

Porta, Costanzo (b. Cremona, *c.* 1529; d. Padua, 19 May 1601). Pupil of Willaert. *Maestro di cappella* at Osimo, near Ancona, 1552–65; at San Antonio in Padua, 1565–67 and 1595–1601; at the Ravenna Cathedral, 1567–74 and 1580–89; at Loreto, 1574–80; at the Padua Cathedral, 1589–95. Composed Masses, motets, hymns, and other sacred music; madrigals.

Portamento [It.]. (1) A special manner of singing in which the voice glides gradually from one tone to the next through all the intermediate pitches. A similar effect called a **glissando* can be obtained on the violin and trombone. See also Portato. (2) An anticipation [see Counterpoint (5)] or **appoggiatura.*

Portative organ. A small portable organ of the late Middle Ages (12th–15th cent.). It was held with the left arm and resting on the left knee, in such a way that the keyboard was nearly at a right angle to the upper body. Thus it could be played only with the right hand (the small bellows being operated by the left hand) and was only a melody instrument. An Italian 14th-century name is *organetto.*

Portato [It.]. A manner of performance halfway between legato and staccato [see Legato]. In string playing, notes so played are taken in a single bow stroke. The use of the term **portamento* for this is misleading and should be avoided.

Portée [F.]. Staff.

Porter (portez) la voix. See *Port de voix* (1).

Porter, Walter (b. *c.* 1588 or *c.* 1595; buried London, 30 Nov. 1659). Pupil of Monteverdi. Singer in the Chapel Royal from 1618. Master of the choristers at

Westminster Abbey, 1639–44. Composed motets for 2 voices with thoroughbass; madrigals and ayres for 2 to 5 voices with instruments and thoroughbass.

Porter, (William) Quincy (b. New Haven, Conn., 7 Feb. 1897; d. Bethany, Conn., 12 Nov. 1966). Violinist, violist, and composer. Pupil of Parker, D. S. Smith, d'Indy, and Bloch. Teacher at the Cleveland Institute of Music, 1922–28 and 1931–32; Vassar College, 1932–38; the New England Conservatory, 1938–46, and its director from 1942; Yale Univ., 1946–65. Composed 2 symphonies and other orch. works (incl. *New England Episodes,* 1958); concertos for viola, 1948, for harpsichord, 1959, and a *Concerto concertante* for 2 pianos and orch., awarded the Pulitzer Prize for 1954; 10 string quartets and other chamber music; piano pieces; organ pieces; songs.

Portugal, Marcos Antonio da Fonseca (Portogallo; real name Ascenção) (b. Lisbon, 24 Mar. 1762; d. Rio de Janeiro, 7 Feb. 1830). Lived in Italy, 1792–99, as a successful opera composer. Director of the San Carlos Theater in Lisbon, 1800–1810. *Maestro di cappella* to the Portuguese court in Lisbon from 1800 until it fled to Brazil in 1807 and in Brazil from 1810 until the court returned to Lisbon in 1821. Composed 35 Italian operas (incl. *La confusione nata della somiglianza,* Florence, 1793; *Il filosofo seducente,* Venice, 1798; *Fernando nel Messico,* Venice, 1798) and 21 Portuguese operas; over 100 sacred works.

Portuguese hymn. The hymn "Adeste fideles" (O come, all ye faithful), so called because it was frequently used *c.* 1800 at the Portuguese chapel in London.

Pos. Abbr. for *position,* or [F.] *positif,* or [G.] *Posaune.*

Posaune [G.]. *Trombone.

Positif [F.]. *Choir organ.

Position. (1) With reference to chords (close, open position), see Spacing. (2) On the violin, etc., positions are the places on the fingerboard to which the left hand moves (shifts) in order to obtain higher or lower tones. Thus, on the G

string the first position covers the fifth from g to d', g being the open string, and the four successive notes, a, b, c', d', being stopped by the four fingers. The second position starts with the first (index) finger on b and ends with the fourth (little) finger on e', third position starts on c', etc. Moving from one position into another is known as *shifting.* The second position is also known as the *half-shift.* (3) On the trombone, any of the points at which the slide is held in order to produce the pitches of the chromatic scale.

Positive organ [F. *orgue positif;* G. *Positiv*]. A medium-sized medieval organ that was not built into the walls of the church but was a self-contained instrument that could be moved. It had one manual, no pedal, and only flue pipes, often in two rows (4' and 2'). A famous illustration is found on Van Eyck's Altar of Ghent. Later the name was used for a special section of the church organ in which there were flue stops (principal, etc.) suitable for the accompaniment of the choir; hence, synonymous with *choir organ, Positif* [F.], *Rückpositiv* [G.]. See Organ.

Postlude. An organ piece played at the conclusion of a service.

Potpourri [F.]. A medley of popular tunes, operatic arias, patriotic songs, etc., which are played in succession, connected by a few measures of introduction or modulation.

Potter, Philip Cipriani Hambley (b. London, 2 Oct. 1792; d. there, 26 Sept. 1871). Pianist and composer. Pupil of Attwood, Crotch, and Förster. Teacher at the Royal Academy of Music in London from 1822; its director, 1832–59. Composed 9 symphonies and 4 overtures; 3 piano concertos; chamber music; piano pieces (incl. *The Enigma,* a set of variations).

Poule, La [F., The Hen]. Popular name for Haydn's Symphony no. 83 in G minor (1785), no. 2 of the *Paris Symphonies.

Poulenc, Francis (b. Paris, 7 Jan. 1899; d. there, 30 Jan. 1963). Pianist and composer. Pupil of Koechlin. Member of

"Les *six." Performed frequently as an accompanist to Pierre Bernac and other singers. Composed operas (incl. *Les mamelles de Tirésias*, after Appollinaire, Paris, 1947; *Les *dialogues des Carmélites; La voix humaine*, after Cocteau, Paris, 1959); ballets (incl. *Les biches*, for the Ballets Russes, 1923); orch. works; concertos for harpsichord (*Concert champêtre*), 1928, for 2 pianos, 1932, for organ, 1938, for piano, 1949, and *Aubade* for piano and 18 instruments, 1929; sacred and secular choral works (incl. a Mass in G, 1937; *Figure humaine*, 1943; a *Stabat Mater*, 1950; a Gloria, 1959; several motets; works for voice with instruments; chamber music, often with winds; numerous piano pieces (incl. *Mouvements perpétuels*, 1918); numerous songs and song cycles; music for plays and for films.

Poussé, poussez [F.]. Up-bow; see Bowing (a).

Pousseur, Henri (b. Malmedy, Belgium, 23 June 1929). Pupil of Souris and Boulez and an associate of Stockhausen and Berio. Has taught in Darmstadt, Basel, Cologne, at the State Univ. of New York at Buffalo, and in Paris. Has employed serial, aleatory, and electronic techniques. Works incl. *Quintette à la mémoire de Webern*, 1955; *Mobile* for 2 pianos, 1958; *Scambi*, 1957, on tape; *3 visages de Liège*, 1961, on tape; *Votre Faust*, an "operatic fantasy" for actors, singers, instrumentalists, and tapes, 1961–67; *Madrigal III* for clarinet, violin, cello, piano, percussion, 1962.

Powell, John (b. Richmond, Va., 6 Sept. 1882; d. Charlottesville, Va., 15 Aug. 1963). Pianist and composer. Studied at the Univ. of Virginia and in Vienna. Collected and made use of folksongs. Composed an opera; *Rapsodie nègre* for piano and orch., 1918, after Conrad's *Heart of Darkness;* orch. works (incl. *Virginia Symphony*, 1951); 2 piano concertos and a violin concerto; choral works, incl. arrangements of folksongs; chamber music; piano pieces; songs and arrangements of folksongs.

Powell, Mel (b. New York, 12 Feb. 1923). Pianist, jazz arranger, and composer. Pupil of B. Wagenaar, Schillinger, Toch, and Hindemith. Teacher at Yale Univ., 1957–69, where he founded the electronic music studio. Dean of music at the California Institute of the Arts from 1969. Works incl. a divertimento for flute, oboe, clarinet, bassoon, trumpet, 1955; *Stanzas* for orch., 1957; *Filigree Setting* for string quartet, 1959; *Haiku Settings* for voice and piano, 1961; *Analogs 1–4*, 1966, on tape; *Immobiles 1–4* for tape and/or orch., 1967.

Power, Leonel (d. Canterbury, 5 June 1445). Probably master of the choristers at Canterbury, where he is known to have been in 1423 and 1441–45. Composed Masses (incl. *Missa Alma redemptoris Mater*, the earliest musically unified setting of the Mass Ordinary), Mass movements, and motets.

PP. Abbr. for *pianissimo*. See *Piano* (1).

P.R. In French organ music, abbr. for *Positif-Récit*, i.e., choir organ and swell organ coupled.

Praeludium [L.]. *Prelude.

Praetorius, Hieronymus (b. Hamburg, 10 Aug. 1560; d. there, 27 Jan. 1629). Succeeded his father, Jacobus Schulze, as organist of the Church of St. James in Hamburg in 1586. Composed Masses, motets in Latin and German, often for two or more choirs, Magnificats, and chorale settings.

Praetorius, Michael (b. Kreuzberg, Thuringia, 15 Feb. 1571 or 1572; d. Wolfenbüttel, 15 Feb. 1621). Pupil of G. Gabrieli. Served the Duke of Brunswick from 1589, at his residence in Wolfenbüttel from 1594, becoming court *Kapellmeister* there in 1604. Composed Masses and over 1,000 other sacred works, incl. motets in Latin and German and settings of chorales, sometimes in elaborate polychoral style and with instruments; secular polyphony; instrumental dances; organ pieces. Wrote an important treatise in three parts, one of which contains detailed discussion and illustrations of instruments, *Syntagma musicum*, 1614–19.

Prague Symphony. Mozart's Symphony no. 38 in D (K. 504), composed in 1786 in Vienna and first performed (1787) in Prague. It has no minuet.

Pralltriller [G.]. See under Inverted mordent.

Pratella, Francesco Balilla (b. Lugo, Italy, 1 Feb. 1880; d. Ravenna, 17 May 1955). Pupil of Mascagni. Director of the Istituto musicale in Lugo, 1910–26; of the Liceo musicale G. Verdi in Ravenna, 1927–45. An advocate of *futurism in some of his numerous writings on music. Composed operas; orch. works (incl. *Musica futurista,* 1912; *L'eroe,* 1915); chamber music; piano pieces; organ pieces; songs.

Pratt, Silas Gamaliel (b. Addison, Vt., 4 Aug. 1846; d. Pittsburgh, 30 Oct. 1916). Organist, conductor, and composer. Pupil of Kullak, Dorn, and Liszt. Founder and director of the Pratt Institute of Music and Art in Pittsburgh from 1906. Composed operas (incl. *Zenobia, Queen of Palmyra,* Chicago, 1883); orch. works (incl. *The Prodigal Son,* 1885); *America,* a scenic cantata with stereopticon projections, 1894.

Préambule [F.]; **preambulum** [L.]. *Prelude.

Precentor. (1) The director of music in a cathedral or monastic church. (2) Deacon, elder, or "chorister" in the Puritan churches of New England in the 17th and 18th centuries who "lined out" the psalm and hymn tunes. See Lining.

Preces [L., prayers]. In the rites of the Latin and Anglican churches, supplications in the form of *versicles and responses. They play an important role in the *Gallican and *Mozarabic rites. The *litanies belong to the same type of chant. In the Anglican prayer books, the portion of Morning and Evening Prayer that begins with the versicle "O Lord, open Thou our lips." There are polyphonic settings by Tallis, Morley, and others.

Precipitando [It.]. Rushing, impetuous.

Prelude [L. *praeludium;* F. *prélude;* G. *Präludium, Vorspiel;* It., Sp. *preludio*]. A piece of music designed to be played as an introduction, e.g., to a liturgical ceremony or, more usually, to another composition, such as a fugue or suite. This connotation, which prevails throughout the entire early history (beginning *c.* 1450) of the prelude, was lost in the 19th century, Chopin, Scriabin, and Debussy having used the word as one of numerous noncommittal titles for piano pieces [see Character piece]. With few exceptions the prelude has been restricted to instrumental solo music, particularly that for keyboard instruments and the lute.

The preludes of the 15th and the early 16th centuries are mostly short pieces (ten to twenty measures long) in a free keyboard style made up of *passages and chords, in marked contrast to the strict contrapuntal style of much contemporary vocal music.

About 1650, composers began to combine the prelude with other compositions. The prelude as an introduction to suites or a suitelike series of pieces was used by Louis Couperin, who created a unique type of prelude, completely free in rhythm and, therefore, notated without the conventional note values. Handel preferred a prelude in a free, improvisatory style for his suites, whereas Bach's introductory pieces to suites and partitas are full-sized *concerto grosso* movements, overtures, toccatas, or sinfonias. The combination of prelude with fugue that became classic with Bach can be traced to organ preludes of the early 17th century, which, after a section in free style, continue and close with a short fugal section. For a closely related form of keyboard music, see Toccata. For the chorale prelude, see Organ chorale.

The 19th-century prelude is represented by the preludes of Chopin, whose principal successors in the genre were Scriabin (90 preludes), Debussy (24 in two books), and Rachmaninov (op. 23). These are essentially pianistic character pieces. Except for those of Debussy, each is usually based on a short figure or motif.

Prélude à "L'après-midi d'un faune" [F., Prelude to "The Afternoon of a Faun"]. Symphonic work by Debussy based on a poem by Mallarmé and completed and first performed in 1894. In 1912 it was choreographed and danced by Vaslav Nijinsky for Sergei Diaghilev's Ballets Russes in Paris.

Préludes, Les. Symphonic poem by Liszt (1848–1854), based on a poem by Lamartine.

Preparation. A harmonic device in which the impact of a dissonant tone in a chord is softened by first sounding it as a consonant tone in the preceding chord. See under Counterpoint (3), (4).

Prepared piano. A piano whose sound is altered by devices such as metal clips or metal bolts attached to the strings; strips of paper, rubber, felt, etc., inserted across the strings; altered tuning on the unison strings, etc. The prepared piano was introduced by John Cage.

Près [F.]. Near. *Près de la touche,* in music for stringed instruments, an instruction to bow near the fingerboard. *Près de la table,* in music for the harp, an instruction to pluck the strings at a point near the soundboard.

Pressante [It.]; **pressez** [F.]. Urgent, hurrying.

Presto [It.]. Very fast, faster than allegro. *Prestissimo* denotes the greatest possible speed. See Tempo marks.

Prick song. A 16th- and 17th-century English term for a written or printed composition, distinguishing it from the oral tradition of plainsong, folksong, popular dance music, etc., as well as from improvised music; or, more generally, a term for any measured music, as distinct from plainsong.

Prima donna [It.]. Beginning in the 18th century, the singer of the principal female role of an opera. In the 19th century the term came to imply a conceited, jealous, capricious operatic star, a meaning also extended to her male counterpart, both in performing and conducting.

Prima (seconda) prattica [It.]. Early 17th-century terms used (first by Monteverdi?) to distinguish the polyphonic style of the 16th century from the monodic style of the 17th. Synonyms are *stile antico* and *stile moderno*. See *Seconda prattica.*

Prima vista [It.]. Playing without previous study. See Sight-reading.

Prima volta, seconda volta [It.]. The different endings for the first and second performances of a section that is repeated. In scores the endings are often identified by the numbers 1 and 2 in conjunction with horizontal brackets. See also *Ouvert, clos;* Repeat.

Primary triad (chord). See under Triad.

Prime. (1) The *interval of a unison. (2) The third of the canonical hours. See Office. (3) In *serial music, the original form of a tone row.

Primo, secondo [It.]. First, second; used to designate the two parts in a duet or in a section of an orchestra that is divided, e.g., first and second violins.

Prince Igor [Rus. *Knyaz Igor*]. Opera in four acts by Borodin (to his own libretto) composed between 1869 and 1887, the year of his death, completed by Rimsky-Korsakov and Glazunov, produced in St. Petersburg, 1890. Setting: semilegendary Russia, 1185.

Principal. In German organs, the "open diapason," in 8', 16', 32', and 4' [see Foot]. In American and British organs, a 4'-open diapason only, or an 8'-open diapason on the pedal. See Organ.

Prodaná Nevĕsta. See *Bartered Bride, The.*

Prodigal Son, The. See *Enfant prodigue, L'.*

Program music. Music inspired by a program, i.e., a nonmusical idea, which is usually indicated in the title and sometimes described in explanatory remarks or a preface. Thus, program music is the opposite of *absolute music. Although examples of program music are found in nearly all periods from at least the 14th century, it reached its greatest prominence in the 19th century. See also Symphonic poem.

Progressive jazz. A style of jazz that became current in the 1950s largely as an extension of *be-bop. It made use of a "cool" instrumental sound instead of the sharper and more piercing timbres of some earlier styles and made use of more running passages in equal note-values instead of accented syncopations and dotted rhythms. Its principal exponents included saxophonist Stan Getz, trumpeter Miles Davis, and pianist Thelonius Monk.

Prokofiev, Sergei Sergeievich (b. Sontzovka, Ukraine, 23 Apr. 1891; d. Moscow, 5 Mar. 1953). Pianist and composer. Studied with Glière, Rimsky-

Korsakov, Wihtol, Liadov, and Tcherep-
nin. Toured widely as a pianist in
Japan, the U.S., and Europe from 1918.
Lived principally in Paris, 1920–32.
Settled in Moscow in 1933, where
some of his works were subsequently
criticized by Soviet officialdom for ex-
cessive "formalism." Works: operas
(incl. *The Gambler,* after Dostoievsky,
1916–27, prod. Brussels, 1929; *The
*Love for Three Oranges; The Flaming
Angel,* 1922–25, rev. 1927; *Semyon
Kotko,* Moscow, 1940; *The *Duenna
[Betrothal in a Monastery]; *War and
Peace,* after Tolstoy, 1943, rev. 1952,
prod. Leningrad, 1946 and 1955; *The
Story of a Real Man,* privately performed in Leningrad, 1948); ballets (incl.
Chout [The Buffoon], 1920; *Le pas
d'acier,* choreography by Massine, 1927;
The Prodigal Son, choreography by Balanchine, 1929; *Romeo and Juliet,* 1936;
Cinderella, 1944; *The Stone Flower,*
1950); incidental music for plays (incl.
Boris Godunov, 1936; *Eugene Onegin,*
1936; *Hamlet,* 1938); music for the films
**Lieutenant Kije,* 1933, *The Queen of
Spades,* 1938, *Alexander Nevsky*
(directed by S. Eisenstein; the music
subsequently recast as a cantata), 1938,
Ivan the Terrible, 1945; 7 symphonies
(incl. the *Classical*), overtures, suites
(incl. *Scythian Suite,* 1914), and other
orch. works (incl. **Peter and the Wolf*);
5 piano concertos, 2 violin concertos,
and a cello concerto; choral works, some
on Soviet subjects; 2 string quartets, 2
violin sonatas, a flute sonata, a cello sonata, and other chamber music; 10 piano
sonatas and other piano pieces; songs.

Prolation [L. *prolatio*]. See Mensural notation. In the early 14th century the term
meant either all the mensurations
(*modus, tempus,* and *prolatio*) or the
four combinations of *tempus* and *prolatio* (Vitry's "quatre prolacions"). The
latter meaning exists in Ockeghem's
Missa prolationum, so called because
each of the four voices sings in a different mensuration (in modern terms, 2/4,
3/4, 6/8, 9/8).

Prometheus. (1) Ballet by Beethoven; see
Geschöpfe des Prometheus, Die. (2) A
symphonic poem by Scriabin, *Prometheus: The Poem of Fire* (op. 60,
1910), for large orchestra, piano, organ,

choruses, and *color organ. It was performed with color organ in New York in
1915. The music is based on the so-called
*mystic (Promethean) chord.

Proper [L. *proprium*]. In the Roman
Catholic litugy, a term used in two ways:
(1) In the classification of feasts, the
Proper of Saints (*Proprium Sanctorum;
Sanctorale*) includes the feasts in honor
of specific Saints, while the Common of
Saints (*Commune Sanctorum*) includes
those in honor of lesser Saints grouped in
categories such as Martyrs or Virgins.
The feasts of the Lord are set apart as
Proper of the Time (*Proprium de Tempore; Temporale*), "time" meaning the
time or life of the Lord. (2) In the classification of chants for any of the above-
mentioned feasts, some are classed as
Proper and others as Ordinary; see Ordinary and Proper.

Proportions. In *mensural notation, the
diminution or (more rarely) augmentation of the normal note values in arithmetic ratios. For example, the sign $\frac{4}{3}$ indicates that, in the subsequent passage,
each note is reduced to three-fourths of
its normal value (the so-called *integer
valor*). In other words, four notes of the
new passage are equal in duration to
three notes of the preceding passage
[Ex.].

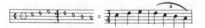

The most important proportions are
proportio dupla, tripla, and *sesquialtera,*
which call, respectively, for a diminution
of the note vales in the ratios of 1:2, 1:3,
and 2:3. The first is usually indicated by
a vertical dash drawn through the sign of
mensuration, ₵, ⊘, and the others by figures. The reduction indicated by *sesquialtera* could also be produced by
*coloration. Regarding *proportio tripla,*
see *Proportz.* See also Time signatures;
Alla breve.

Proportz, Proportio [G.]. In the German
dance literature of the 16th century, a
**Nachtanz* in quick triple time that fol-
lows a main dance in slower duple time.
The two dances have the same melody in
different meters. This is actually implied
in the name, which indicates the applica-

tion of a *proportion to the original melody. Nominally this proportion was *proportio tripla* (another name for such a *Nachtanz* was *Tripla*); actually, however, it was *proportio sesquialtera*. Therefore, three notes of the *Proportz* equal in duration two notes of the main dance.

Prosa [L.]; **prose** [F.]. Medieval name, retained to the present day in France, for the *sequence. Originally, it seems to have been used specifically for the sequence texts, as opposed to their music; hence the designations *sequentia cum prosa* or *prosa ad sequentium* found in some early French manuscripts.

Prosula [L.]. Medieval term for certain kinds of textual insertions adapted to the melismas of certain liturgical chants, resulting in syllabic settings. See also Trope (3).

Protus [Gr.]. See under Church modes.

Prout, Ebenezer (b. Oundle, Northamptonshire, 1 Mar. 1835; d. London, 5 Dec. 1909). Organist, critic, and composer. Studied at the Univ. of London. Teacher at various institutions, incl. the Royal Academy of Music, from 1879, the Guildhall School of Music in London, from 1884, and Dublin Univ., from 1894. Composed 4 symphonies and 2 overtures; 2 organ concertos; cantatas; church music; 2 string quartets and other chamber music. Wrote several widely used textbooks on music theory.

Provenzale, Francesco (b. Naples, 1627; d. there, 6 Sept. 1704). *Maestro di cappella* at the Conservatorio di Santa Maria di Loreto in Naples, 1663–74, and director of the Conservatorio della Pietà de' Turchini there, 1673–1701. Conductor at the Tesoro di San Gennaro in Naples, 1686–99. Vice *maestro di cappella* at the Cappella reale in Naples from 1690. One of the earliest members of the *Neapolitan school of opera composers. Composed operas (incl. *Lo schiavo di sua moglie*, Naples, 1671); oratorios; cantatas; motets and other sacred music.

Prussian Quartets. A set of three string quartets by Mozart, in D, B♭, and F (K. 575, 589, 590), composed in 1789–90 and dedicated to Friedrich Wilhelm II, King of Prussia, who in 1789 had invited him

to Berlin. The cello parts are unusually elaborate, obviously intended to please the King, who played this instrument. (2) The name is also used for Haydn's string quartets op. 50, nos. 1–6, for which the title page of the Artaria first edition (1787) bears a dedication to Friedrich Wilhelm II.

Ps. Abbr. for *Psalm. In German scores, abbr. for *posaune,* i.e., trombone.

Psalm [F. *psaume;* G. *Psalm;* It., Sp. *salmo*]. A sacred poem or song. Specifically, one of the 150 such poems contained in the Book of Psalms in the Bible. The numbering system in the Latin version of the Bible, used in the Roman Catholic services, differs slightly from that of the English version. The English nos. 9 and 10 correspond to no. 9 of the Vulgate (Latin version), and the English no. 147 corresponds to nos. 146 and 147 of the Vulgate. Therefore, for all the psalms between nos. 10 and 147 the English number is one digit higher than the Vulgate's. References in this dictionary are to the Latin number, with the English number (if needed) added in parentheses (or brackets), e.g., Psalm 49 (50).

The Hebrew psalms are poems based mostly on the principle of accentuation. Each psalm consists of a number of verses (marked ℣ in the liturgical books of the Roman Catholic Church); and each verse is made up of two (sometimes three) parts. The psalms were used as texts for the music of many Christian churches, except for the Lutheran, whose music is based on *chorale texts. For the psalm music of the Roman Catholic Church, see Psalmody; Psalm tones; for that of the Anglican Church, see Anglican chant; for that of the Reformed churches, see Psalter.

Psalm tones. In Gregorian chant, the recitation melodies used for singing (complete) psalms during the Office [see Psalmody III]. There are eight such tones, one for each church mode, all in the character of an inflected *monotone. The main note of the recitation, called the *tenor* (*repercussio, tuba,* reciting note), is always the fifth degree of the mode [see Church modes]. In accordance with the usually binary structure of the psalm verses, the psalm tone falls into halves, the first half consisting of intonation (or *initium*), tenor, and mediation, and the second of tenor and termination. If the first half is too long to be sung in one breath, there is another slight inflection at the breathing point, the *flex.* The accompanying example (verse 1 of Ps. 1; see *LU,* p. 923) shows all of these details.

Ps. 1 **(tone 1, termination D)**
intonation   tenor   flexa tenor mediatio

Be - a - tus vir . . . impio - rum, + et . . . to - rum

tenor   terminatio

non ste - tit   et . . . - lenti - ae non se - dit,

Each psalm is sung with an enframing *antiphon. The antiphon determines not only the psalm tone, which must be in the same mode as the antiphon, but also its termination—for which a number of different formulas called *differentiae* (differences) are provided—which must lead back smoothly to the initial note of the antiphon, as sung after the last verse of the psalm. Since the "Gloria patri . . . seculorum amen" [see Doxology] invariably serves as a last verse in the singing of a psalm, the liturgical books give the *differentia* with the syllables *E u o u a e (i.e., the vowels of the words *seculorum Amen*). The canticles of the Office are sung in a similar way.

An exceptional psalm tone is the *tonus peregrinus,* which has different tenors for its first and second halves. It is used for the psalm *In exitu Israel [LU,* p. 160].

Although each of the great *responsories of the Office is normally accompanied by only a single verse, this verse is usually sung to one of a set of eight tones similar in design to the antiphonal tones but somewhat more elaborate.

Psalmody. The psalms are by far the most important texts used in *Gregorian chant. In the early days of Christian worship the service consisted of only psalm singing, and despite the many fundamental changes that took place in ensuing centuries, the psalms retained their dominant position in the Roman liturgy. The forms for the different items of the chant

stem from three original types of psalm singing: direct psalmody, responsorial psalmody, and antiphonal psalmody. The last two terms originally meant two different methods of performance, alternation between soloist and chorus (responsorial) and alternation between two half-choruses (antiphonal). However, this distinction is no longer applicable [see Responsorial singing], and the terms now have only historical and stylistic significance, the responsorial types being the more elaborate of the two.

I. *Direct psalmody* means singing a psalm (or a number of verses thereof) without any textual addition or modification. This method survives in two types of chant, one for the Mass and the other for the Office of the Dead. The former is the *Tract. The latter is known as *psalmus directaneus (in directum, indirectum)* and consists in the singing of a psalm to a psalm tone but without an antiphon [see under III below]. For this method, which is rarely used, special psalm tones called *tonus in directum* are provided.

II. *Responsorial psalmody* was directly taken over from the Jewish service. Originally, the entire psalm was sung by a soloist (*cantor*), with the chorus (congregation; only later the church choir or *schola*) responding after each verse with a short affirmative phrase such as Amen or Alleluia. (A direct model for this exists in Ps. 135 [136], in which each verse ends with the sentence, "For His mercy endureth forever.") Originally the cantor's singing consisted of a simple recitation in the style of an inflected monotone, but there developed, probably in the 4th to the 6th centuries, more elaborate methods that finally led to a highly melismatic style. A similar development took place within the responds, which eventually grew considerably longer, both in text and music. The increase in length of verses and respond necessitated a drastic reduction in the number of sections. Instead of an entire psalm, single verses were selected to be sung, varying in number from four to one. The respond was also cut, so that it was not repeated in full after every verse but in a reduced form, its initial half (or third) being omitted. It is in these reduced forms that responsorial psalmody entered the Gregorian repertory. The most important examples are the *responsory, the short responsory (*responsorium breve*), the *Gradual, and the *Alleluia.

III. *Antiphonal psalmody* originally consisted of the psalms sung by two alternating half-choruses. This method was introduced into the Western church by St. Ambrose (A.D. 340?–97) in imitation of Syrian models. The method was at an early time enriched by the addition of a short sentence called an *antiphon and sung by the whole chorus (perhaps originally by the congregation) after every two verses. A scheme similar in structure to that of the early responsorial psalmody resulted. As in responsorial psalmody, the full scheme survives only in special chants, such as the *Invitatory at the beginning of Matins.

There are four standard types of chant that are considered derivatives of antiphonal psalmody: the Office psalms and canticles, and the *Introit, *Offertory, and *Communion of the Mass. The Office psalms are complete psalms sung to one of eight *psalm tones (the same tone for each verse) and introduced and closed by a short antiphon. In the Introit, a single verse and the Lesser *Doxology are sung to a psalm tone, preceded and followed by the Introit itself. The Offertory and Communion are no longer sung with verses.

Psalter. Name for the Book of Psalms translated into the vernacular (English, French, Dutch Psalter), frequently in rhymed versions (metrical Psalter) and provided with music for congregational singing. Collections of prose psalms set to *Anglican chant are also known as psalters.

The earliest and most influential of the psalters was the French or Genevan Psalter, begun in Strasbourg in 1539 and completed, with metrical versions by Marot and Bèze and music by Bourgeois, in Geneva in 1562. Bourgeois adapted existing melodies, some of them from secular sources, and composed others to fit the various meters. In conformity with the Protestant trend toward musical simplification, the settings are almost uniformly one note to a syllable. The Dutch Psalter is represented by the *Souterliedekens. In 1566 the French Psalter was adopted in the Netherlands, replacing the Dutch versions. During the persecutions under Queen Mary in mid-16th century, many English Protestants fled to Geneva. As a result, the so-called Anglo-Genevan Psalter and the Scottish Psalter of 1564 show the influence of the French style. The English Psalter pursued a different course with regard to both verse and music. Among the better-known English psalters are the "Old Version" of Sternhold and Hopkins, completed and published by Day in 1562; Ravenscroft (1621); Playford (1671; another in 1673); and the "New Version" of Tate and Brady (1696). The English type of psalm tune consists of a number of shorter notes between two longer ones. Another group of refugees came under the influence of the French form, this time in Amsterdam, where Henry Ainsworth in 1612 brought out a psalter for the benefit of the English "Separatists." Thence it traveled to America with the Pilgrims in 1620. Although the highly influential *Bay Psalm Book appeared in 1640, Ainsworth's Psalter was not entirely displaced for many years thereafter.

Psaltery. A class of ancient and medieval instruments (also called *zithers) consisting of a flat soundboard over which a number of strings are stretched. They are plucked with the fingers or a plectrum. See ill. under Zither. This manner of playing distinguishes the psaltery from the *dulcimer, which is struck with hammers. In the general classification of instruments, the term is used for a group that includes the *harpsichord, a keyed psaltery.

Puccini, Giacomo (Antonio Domenico Michele Secondo Maria) (b. Lucca, 22 Dec. 1858; d. Brussels, 29 Nov. 1924). Descendant of a long line of musicians. Studied at the Istituto musicale in Lucca and with Ponchielli at the Milan Conservatory. Composed operas (incl. *Le villi*, Milan, 1884; *Edgar*, Milan, 1889; *Manon Lescaut; La *bohème; *Tosca; *Madama Butterfly; La *fanciulla del West; La rondine*, Monte Carlo, 1917; *Trittico; *Turandot*); some church music, choral works, orch. works, chamber music, organ pieces, songs.

Pugnani, Gaetano (b. Turin, 27 Nov. 1731; d. there, 15 July 1798). Pupil of Somis. Traveled widely as a violinist in Europe and Russia. Played at the Concert spirituel in Paris, 1754. Director of the King's Theatre in London, 1767–70. Teacher and conductor in Turin from 1770. His pupils incl. Viotti. Composed operas; an oratorio; cantatas; 9 violin concertos; 12 sinfonias for strings and winds; 18 violin sonatas and other chamber music.

Pugno, (Stéphane) Raoul (b. Montrouge, near Paris, of an Italian father, 23 June 1852; d. Moscow, 3 Jan. 1914). Pupil of A. Thomas. Concertized widely as a pianist. Organist at Saint-Eugène in Paris from 1871 and *maître de chapelle* there, 1878–92. Teacher at the Paris Conservatory, 1892–1901. Composed operas and other stage works (incl. *La ville morte*, completed after his death by N. Boulanger); ballets; an oratorio; piano pieces; songs.

Pui. See *Puy.*

Pujol, Juan Pablo (b. Barcelona, *c.* 1573; d. there, May 1626). *Maestro de capilla* at the Tarragona Cathedral, 1593–95; at the Cathedral of Nuestra Señora del Pilar in Zaragoza, 1596–1612; at the Barcelona Cathedral from 1612 until his death. Composed Masses, motets, and other sacred music; secular polyphony.

Pulcinella. Ballet by Stravinsky, commissioned by Diaghilev and produced in Paris, 1920. The music is a modern setting of numerous passages from anonymous works formerly thought to be by Pergolesi.

Punctum [L.]. (1) See under Neumes. (2) *Punctus.* See under Mensural notation. (3) In the **estampies* of the 13th and 14th centuries, any of the various sections that are repeated (pl. *puncta*).

Punctus [L.]. See under Mensural notation.

Punta, punto [It.]. Point. *A punta d'arco,* with the point of the bow (of the violin); *punto d'organo,* the **pause and its sign.

Purcell, Daniel (b. London, *c.* 1660; buried there, 26 Nov. 1717). Brother of Henry Purcell. Organist at Magdalen College, Oxford, 1688–95; at St. Andrew's, Holborn, from 1713. Composed music for over 40 plays; odes; anthems and other church music; solo cantatas; songs; sonatas for flute and for violin.

Purcell, Henry (b. London?, 1659; d. Dean's Yard, Westminster, 21 Nov. 1695). Chorister at the Chapel Royal under Cooke and Humfrey from 1669. Pupil of Blow. Composer to the King's violins from 1677. Organist at Westminster Abbey, succeeding Blow, from 1679. An organist of the Chapel Royal from 1682 and keeper of the King's wind instruments from 1683. Composed stage works (all prod. in London, incl. the opera **Dido and Aeneas; Dioclesian,* after Beaumont and Fletcher, 1690; *King Arthur,* libretto by Dryden, 1691; *The Fairy Queen,* after Shakespeare's *Midsummer Night's Dream,* 1692; *The Indian Queen,* libretto by Dryden and Howard, 1695; *The Tempest,* after Shakespeare, 1695?); incidental music for numerous plays by Dryden, Congreve, and others; about 15 full and 50 verse anthems, 3 services, and other sacred works; about 25 odes (several for St. Cecilia's day, incl. *Hail, Bright Cecilia*) and welcome-songs for soloists, chorus, and orch.; secular cantatas; catches; numerous songs and vocal duets with thoroughbass; a "chacony" in G min., 2 *In nomine* settings, and about a dozen fantasias for strings; trio sonatas and other chamber music; suites and other harpsichord pieces; organ voluntaries. Wrote a treatise, *The Art of Descant,* published by Playford in 1683.

Purfling. The inlaid border of violins, etc. Besides its ornamental value, it helps prevent chipping of the edges.

Puritani di Scozia, I [It., The Puritans of Scotland]. Opera in three acts by Bellini (libretto by C. Pepoli, based on a play by F. Ancelot and X. B. Saintine), produced in Paris, 1835. Setting: near Plymouth, during the English Civil War.

Puy, pui. Name for medieval French societies that sponsored literary and musical festivals, held regularly with competitions and prizes. They are documented as far back as the 11th century (earliest troubadours) and existed as late as the 16th century.

Pyiba, pyipar (*p'i-pa, p'i-p'a*). A Chinese pear-shaped short lute with a rather flat body and four strings [see ill. under Lute], usually tuned A d e a.

Pylkkänen, Tauno (Kullervo) (b. Helsinki, 22 Mar. 1918). Pupil of Madetoja and Palmgren. Worked for the Finnish Radio, 1942–61; as a music critic for the newspaper *Uusi Suomi*, 1942–69; as artistic director of the Finnish National Opera, 1960–69. Has composed operas (incl. the radio opera *The Wolf's Bride*, 1950); symphonic poems and other orch. works; a cello concerto; choral works; a string quartet and other chamber music; songs.

Pythagorean hammers. Pythagoras (6th cent. B.C.) is said to have discovered the basic laws of music by listening to the sound of four smith's hammers, which produced agreeable consonances. They turned out to weigh 12, 9, 8, and 6 pounds, respectively. From these figures he derived the octave (12:6 = 2:1), fifth (12:8 = 9:6 = 3:2), fourth (12:9 = 4:3), and whole tone (9:8) [see Intervals, calculation of].

Pythagorean scale. A scale, said to have been invented by Pythagoras (*c*. 550 B.C.), that derives all the tones from the interval of the pure fifth [see Acoustics]. The tones of the diatonic scale are obtained as a series of five successive upper fifths and one lower fifth. For the calculation of the frequencies and intervals, see Intervals, calculation of. The Pythagorean semitone was called *limma* (left over) or *diesis* (difference) because it was obtained by subtracting two whole tones from the fourth. The difference between the whole tone and the semitone was called *apotome* (cut off). In the Greek scale it appears as the interval between B-flat and B natural. It is slightly larger than the *diesis*. In medieval theory these two semitones were distinguished as *semitonium majus* (*apotome*) and *semitonium minus* (*diesis*). Their difference (or that between the whole tone and two *dieses*) is the Pythagorean comma (= 23 cents).

Q

Qānūn. *Kanun.

Quadrille [F.]. (1) A French dance of the early 19th century performed by two or four couples moving in a square. It consisted of five figures (*Le pantalon, L'été, La poule, La trénise* and *La pastourelle, Finale*), the music for which, alternating between 6/8 and 2/4 meter, was chosen from popular tunes, operatic arias, and even sacred music. The dance was very popular during the Napoleonic era and remained fashionable until it was replaced by the *polka. (2) In 17th- and 18th-century French ballet (Campra, Lully), the group of dancers (4, 6, 8, or 12) who performed the figures of an *entrée.

Quadrivium. In the medieval system of education, the four "mathematical arts" —arithmetic, geometry, music, and astronomy—as opposed to the *trivium* of the "rhetorical arts," grammar, logic, and rhetoric. In this scheme music was considered not an art in the modern sense but a science allied with mathematics and physics (acoustics).

Quadruple counterpoint. See Invertible counterpoint.

Quadruple-croche [F.]. Sixty-fourth note. See under Notes.

Quadruple meter, time. See under Meter.

Quadruplet. A group of four notes played in the time normally occupied by three notes of the same kind.

Quadruplum. See under Duplum.

Quagliati, Paolo (b. Chioggia, Italy, *c*. 1555; d. Rome, 16 Nov. 1628). Organist at Santa Maria Maggiore in Rome from 1601 until his death. Composed a dramatic work, *Carro di fedeltà d'amore,* Rome, 1606; motets and other sacred music; madrigals and *canzonette;* secular pieces for 1 and 2 voices with instruments; ricercars and canzonas.

Quantz, Johann Joachim (b. Oberscheden, near Göttingen, 30 Jan. 1697; d. Potsdam, 12 July 1773). Flutist and composer. Pupil of Zelenka, Fux, and Gasparini. Member of the Dresden town orchestra, 1716; of the royal Polish orchestra from 1718. Flute teacher to Frederick the Great (then crown prince) from 1728. Court chamber musician and composer to Frederick the Great in Berlin and Potsdam from 1741 until his death. Composed hundreds of concertos and other pieces for one or more flutes; hymns; other vocal and instrumental works. Published a flute method with valuable information about performance practice, *Versuch einer Anweisung die Flöte traversière zu spielen,* 1752.

Quarrel of the Buffoons. See War of the Buffoons.

Quart, Quarte [G.]. The interval of the fourth. As a prefix in the names of instruments, it indicates that the instrument is a fourth higher (*Quartflöte,* a flute; *Quartgeige,* see under Violin family) or a fourth lower (*Quartfagott;* see Oboe family II [d]) than the normal instrument.

Quartal harmony. Harmony based on the *fourth, as distinguished from the common *tertian harmony, based on the third.

Quarter note. See under Notes.

Quarter tone. An interval equal to one-half semitone, there being twenty-four quarter tones to the octave. See Microtone.

Quartet [F. *quatuor;* G. *Quartett;* It. *quartetto;* Sp. *cuarteto*]. A composition for four instruments or voices. Also, the four performers organized to play or sing such compositions. By far the most important combination is the *string quartet. A number of piano quartets (for piano, violin, viola, and cello) have been written, incl. 2 by Mozart, 4 by Beethoven, 3 by Mendelssohn, 2 by Schumann, 3 by Brahms, 2 by Dvořák, 2 by Fauré, 1 by Chausson, 1 by Copland.

Quartfagott, Quartflöte, Quartgeige [G.]. See under Quart.

Quasi [It.]. As if, almost.

Quattro [It.]. Four. *Quattro mani,* four hands; *quattro voci,* four voices.

Quatuor [F.]. *Quartet.

Quaver. Eighth note. See under Notes.

Queen, The. See *Reine, La.*

Queen of Spades, The [Rus. *Pikovaya Dama*]. Opera in three acts by Tchaikovsky (libretto by M. Tchaikovsky, rev. by the composer, based on a story by Pushkin), produced in St. Petersburg, 1890. Setting: St. Petersburg, end of the 18th century.

Quer- [G.]. Cross, transverse. *Querflöte* (transverse) flute; *Querpfeife,* fife; *Querstand,* *cross relation.

Querelle des bouffons [F.]. See War of the Buffoons.

Queue [F.]. Tail or stem, e.g., of a note. *Piano à queue,* grand piano.

Quiebro. See under Ornamentation.

Quilter, Roger (b. Brighton, 1 Nov. 1877; d. London, 21 Sept. 1953). Studied at Eton and with I. Knorr in Frankfurt. Composed light operas; incidental music for plays; orch. works; choral works; chamber music; piano pieces; songs and song cycles, especially settings of Shakespeare.

Quinta pars, quinta vox [L.]. Fifth part (voice) in a polyphonic composition. The term does not imply any particular range for the voice-part in question.

Quintanar, Hector (b. Mexico City, 15 Apr. 1936). Conductor and composer. Pupil of Galindo, Chávez, and R. Halffter. Studied electronic music in New York, Paris, and Mexico City. Has directed the Composers' Workshop of the National Conservatory in Mexico City from 1965. Has composed symphonies and other orch. works (incl. *Sideral II,* 1969); choral works; chamber music; electronic works, some with instruments.

Quintet [F. *quintette,* formerly *quintuor;* G. *Quintett;* It. *quintetto;* Sp. *quinteto*].

Music for five players. The string quintet is usually for two violins, two violas, and cello (the the repertory includes 12 by Boccherini, 6 by Mozart, 3 by Beethoven, 2 by Mendelssohn, 2 by Brahms, 1 by Bruckner, 1 by Vaughan Williams). The combination of two violins, viola, and two cellos was cultivated by Boccherini (113) but survived only in Schubert's famous Quintet in C, op. 163. A piano (clarinet, etc.) quintet is usually a composition for piano (clarinet, etc.) and string quartet. The literature of piano quintets includes Schumann's op. 44, Brahms' op. 34, and compositions by Dvořák, Franck, Reger, Pfitzner, Fauré, Elgar, Hindemith, Bloch (in quarter tones), and Shostakovich. Schubert's op. 114, D. 667, known as the Trout Quintet, is for piano, violin, viola, cello, and double bass.

Quintfagott [G.]. See under Oboe family II (d).

Quinton [F.]. According to some authorities, a violin with five (instead of four) strings, tuned g d′ a′ d″ g″; according to others, a French 17th-century viol (*pardessus de viole*) with five (instead of six) strings, tuned g c′ e′ a′ d″.

Quintuor [F.]. Old name for *quintet.

Quintuple meter. The *measure of five beats. See Meter. Examples are found in Chopin's Sonata op. 4, Tchaikovsky's Symphony no. 6, Wagner's *Tristan,* Act III, Scene 2, and in much 20th-century music.

Quintuplet. A group of five notes played in the time normally occupied by four notes of the same kind.

Quodlibet [L.]. A humorous type of music in which well-known melodies or texts are combined in an intentionally incongruous manner. The following types can be distinguished: (1) The polyphonic *quodlibet,* in which different melodies or snatches of melodies are used simultaneously in different voice-parts of a polyphonic composition. The best-known example of this type is the final variation of Bach's *Goldberg Variations, in which two popular melodies of his day, "Ich bin so lang nicht bei dir g'west" (Long have I been away from thee) and "Kraut und Rüben" (Cabbage and turnips), are combined within the harmonic frame of the theme. (2) The successive *quodlibet,* a simpler type in which various melodies are quoted in succession, as in a *potpourri. (3) The textual *quodlibet,* a piece that contains a mixture of borrowed texts without borrowed musical material. As in the musical *quodlibet,* the texts may occur simultaneously or successively. Other terms for *quodlibet* are *cento* or *centone, fricassée* [F.], and *incatenatura* [It.].

R

R. In early orchestral music, *ripieno;* in French organ music, *récit;* in Gregorian chant (℞), *responsory.

Rääts, Jaan (b. Tartu, Estonia, 15 Oct. 1932). Studied at the Tallin Conservatory. Music director for Estonian Radio, 1955–66, and subsequently for Estonian Television. Has composed 7 symphonies; concertos for violin, for cello, for piano; choral works; string quartets; a nonet; piano pieces.

Rabāb. Arabic name for various bowed stringed instruments found in Islamic countries. They occur in a number of shapes, e.g., elongated boat, halved pear, trapezoid, rectangle, and usually have three strings. With the spread of Islam the rabāb was carried both eastward, to Malaya and Indonesia (early 15th century), where it is called *rebab,* and westward, via Spain into Europe (8th or 9th cent.), where it was known as *rabec, rabeca, rebec, rebelle, ribibe, ribible* (Chaucer), *rubeba, rubèbe* (Machaut), *rybybe,* etc. Jerome of Moravia, in his *Tractatus de musica* (*c.* 1280), describes the rubeba as having two strings tuned a fifth apart and played with a bow. The most common European form was in the shape of an elongated pear, and its most common name was *rebec*. In the 16th century it is described as having three strings. In France it was used as late as the 18th century by street fiddlers, who were forbidden to use the violin. See ill. under Violin family.

Rabaud, Henri Benjamin (b. Paris, 10 Nov. 1873; d. there, 11 Sept. 1949). Pupil of Gédalge and Massenet. Conductor at the Paris Opéra from 1908; its director, 1914–18. Director of the Paris Conservatory, 1920–41, succeeding Fauré. Composed operas (incl. the comic opera *Mârouf, savetier du Caire,* Paris, 1914); 2 symphonies and other orch. works (incl. *La procession nocturne,* 1898); an oratorio and other choral works; chamber music; piano pieces; songs; music for films and the theater.

Rachmaninov, Sergei Vassilievich (b. Oneg, Novgorod district of Russia, 1 Apr. 1873; d. Beverly Hills, Calif., 28 Mar. 1943). Pianist, conductor, and composer. Pupil of Taneiev and Arensky. Opera conductor at the Bolshoi Theater, 1904–6. First toured the U.S. in 1909. Emigrated to Switzerland in 1917; to the U.S. in 1935. Composed 3 operas (incl. *Aleko,* after Pushkin, Moscow, 1893); 3 symphonies and other orch. works (incl. *The Isle of the Dead,* 1907); 4 piano concertos and a *Rhapsody on a Theme by Paganini* for piano and orch., 1934; choral works (incl. *The Bells,* after Poe, 1910); chamber music; piano pieces (incl. *5 morceaux de fantaisie,* 1892, containing the prelude in C♯ min.; 2 sets of *Études-tableaux,* 1911, 1917; 2 sets of preludes, 1904, 1910); songs.

Racket. See under Oboe family III.

Raddolcendo [It.]. Becoming sweeter, softer.

Raddoppiare [It.]. To double, usually at the lower octave.

Radical bass. *Fundamental bass.

Radleyer [G.]. *Hurdy-gurdy.

Radziwill, Antoni Henryk, Prince (b.

Vilna, 13 June 1775; d. Berlin, 8 Apr. 1833). Singer, cellist, and composer. Governor of Posen. Associate and patron of Beethoven (who dedicated the *Namensfeier* overture to him) and Chopin. Composed incidental music to Goethe's *Faust,* 1806–30; songs, duets, and vocal quartets.

Raff, (Joseph) Joachim (b. Lachen, Lake of Zürich, 27 May 1822; d. Frankfurt, 25 June 1882). Close associate of Liszt, some of whose works he assisted in orchestrating. Director of the Hoch Conservatory in Frankfurt from 1877 until his death. Composed operas (incl. *König Alfred,* Weimar, 1851); 11 symphonies and other orch. works; concertos for violin, for cello, for piano; choral works; 8 string quartets and other chamber music; piano pieces; songs.

Raffrenando [It.]. Slowing down.

Rāga. See under Melody type.

Ragtime. A style of American popular music that reached its peak *c.* 1910–15. It is characterized by a marchlike duple meter with a highly syncopated melody. It was principally the creation of pianists such as Ben Harvey and Scott Joplin, though it was also performed by bands. See also Jazz.

Raimondi, Pietro (b. Rome, 20 Dec. 1786; d. there, 30 Oct. 1853). Studied at the Conservatorio della Pietà de' Turchini in Naples. Director of the royal theaters there, 1824–32. Teacher at the Palermo Conservatory, 1832–52. *Maestro di cappella* at St. Peter's in Rome from 1852. Composed about 60 operas; about 20 ballets; 8 oratorios (incl. the trilogy *Giuseppe,* the three parts of which could be performed simultaneously); Masses and numerous other sacred works; numerous elaborate fugues.

Raindrop Prelude. Popular name for Chopin's Prelude in D♭ op. 28, no. 15.

Rainier, Priaulx (b. Howick, Natal, 3 Feb. 1903). She studied at the South African College of Music in Cape Town, at the Royal Academy of Music in London with McEwen, and in Paris with N. Boulanger. Teacher at the Royal Academy of Music, 1942–63. Has composed orch. works (incl. *Incantation* for clarinet and orch., 1933); a cello concerto, 1964; choral works; string quartets and other chamber music; piano pieces; songs.

Raison, André (b. before 1650; d. Paris, 1719). Organist of the Jacobins and at the church of Sainte-Geneviève in Paris, 1666–c.1716. Teacher of Clérambault. Published 2 books of organ pieces, incl. Masses, Magnificats, etc.

Raitio, Väinö (b. Sortavala, now U.S.S.R., 15 Apr. 1891; d. Helsinki, 10 Sept. 1945). Studied in Helsinki, Moscow, Berlin, and Paris. Teacher at the Viborg Conservatory, 1926–32. Composed 5 operas; 2 ballets; a symphony and several symphonic poems; a piano concerto and a double concerto for violin and cello; choral works; chamber music; songs.

Rake's Progress, The. Opera in three acts by Stravinsky (libretto by W. H. Auden and C. Kallman, inspired by the set of prints by Hogarth), produced in Venice, 1951. Setting: England, 18th century.

Rákóczi March. A Hungarian national air, composed by Janos Bihari in 1809, in homage to Prince Ferencz Rákóczi (1676 –1735), who led the Hungarians in a revolt against Austria. The melody was used by Berlioz in La damnation de Faust and Marche hongroise, as well as by Liszt in Rhapsodie hongroise no. 15.

Ralentir [F.]. To slow down.

Rallentando [It.; abbr. rall.]. Same as *ritardando.

Rameau, Jean-Philippe (bapt. Dijon, 25 Sept. 1683; d. Paris, 12 Sept. 1764). Church organist at Avignon, 1702; Clermont-Ferrand, 1702–5; Paris, 1705–8; Dijon, 1708–14; Clermont-Ferrand, 1715 –22. Settled in Paris in 1723, where he taught harpsichord and theory. Composer of the King's chamber music from 1745. Composed operas (incl. Hippolyte et Aricie, Paris, 1733; Castor et Pollux, Paris, 1737; Dardanus, Paris, 1739; Zoroastre, Paris, 1749); ballets (incl. Les indes galantes, Paris, 1735; Les fêtes d'Hébé, Paris, 1739; Platée, Versailles, 1745; Zaïs, Paris, 1748); church music; cantatas; chamber music; harpsichord pieces. Published several important theoretical treatises, incl. Traité de l'harmonie, 1722. See also War of the Buffoons.

Ramin, Günther (b. Karlsruhe, 15 Oct. 1898; d. Leipzig, 27 Feb. 1956). Studied at the Leipzig Conservatory. Organist of the Thomaskirche in Leipzig from 1918. Cantor at the Thomasschule there from 1940; of the Gewandhaus chorus there, 1945–51. Composed organ pieces; choral works; chamber music.

Randall, J. (James) K. (b. Cleveland, 16 June 1929). Studied with Elwell and Haieff and at Columbia, Harvard, and Princeton. Teacher at Princeton Univ. from 1958. Works incl. Improvisation on a Poem of e. e. cummings, for voice and instruments, 1961; Mudgett: Monologues by a Mass Murderer, 1965; Lyric Variations for violin and computer-produced tape, 1967.

Rands, Bernard (b. Sheffield, England, 2 Mar. 1935). Pupil of Smith-Brindle, Vlad, Dallapiccola, Berio, Boulez, and Maderna. Teacher at Univ. College, Bangor, N. Wales, 1961–66; subsequently at the Univ. of California at San Diego. Works incl. 3 espressioni for piano, 1960; Action for 6 for flute, viola, cello, harp, 2 percussionists, 1963; Formants I for harp, 1965; Per esempio for orch., 1967; works with tape.

Range. See Voices, range of.

Rangström, (Anders Johan) Ture (b. Stockholm, 30 Nov. 1884; d. there, 11 May 1947). Critic, conductor, and composer. Studied in Stockholm and with Pfitzner in Munich. Composed operas (incl. Kronbruden [The Crown Bride], after Strindberg, Stuttgart, 1919); 4 symphonies and several symphonic poems; choral works; chamber music; piano pieces; about 60 songs.

Rank. In organs, a complete set of pipes of the same type, controlled by one *stop knob or tablet. A mixture stop, however, has several ranks, according to the number of pipes combined in the production of a single tone. See Organ.

Rankett [G.]. Racket. See under Oboe family III.

Rankl, Karl Franz (b. Gaaden, near Vienna, 1 Oct. 1898; d. Salzburg, 6 Sept.

1968). Pupil of Schoenberg and Webern. Held conducting posts at various times in Berlin, Graz, Prague, London (Covent Garden, 1946–51), Glasgow, and Australia. Composed an opera, *Deirdre of the Sorrows*, 1951; 8 symphonies and other orch. works; an oratorio and other choral works; chamber music; songs.

Ranta, Sulho (Veikko Juhani) (b. Peräseinäjoki, Finland, 15 Aug. 1901; d. Helsinki, 5 May 1960). Critic and composer. Studied at the Helsinki Conservatory and in Vienna and Paris. Teacher at the Viborg Conservatory, 1925–32; at the Sibelius Academy in Helsinki, 1934–56. Composed a ballet; symphonies, symphonic poems, and other orch. works; a cantata, *Kalevala*, 1935, and other choral works; chamber music; piano pieces; songs.

Ranz des vaches [F.; G. *Kuhreigen, Kuhreihen*]. A type of Swiss mountain melody sung or played on the *alphorn by herdsmen to summon their cows. The *ranz des vaches* has been repeatedly used in operas about Swiss subjects, e.g., in the overtures of Grétry's and Rossini's *Guillaume Tell*.

Rape of Lucretia, The. Opera in two acts by Britten (libretto by R. Duncan after A. Obey's play), produced in Glyndebourne, 1946. Setting: Rome, 510 B.C.

Raphael, Günter (Albert Rudolph) (b. Berlin, 30 Apr. 1903; d. Herford, Germany, 19 Oct. 1960). Studied at the Hochschule für Musik in Berlin. Teacher at the Leipzig Conservatory, 1926–34; at the Duisburg Conservatory, 1949–53; at the Mainz Conservatory, 1956–58; at the Cologne Music Academy from 1957. Composed 5 symphonies and other orch. works; concertos for violin, for cello, for organ, and concertinos for saxophone and for flute; sacred choral works; string quartets and other chamber music; piano pieces; organ pieces.

Rappresentazione di anima e di corpo, La [It., The Representation of Soul and Body]. Stage work by Emilio de' Cavalieri, produced in Rome, 1600. It is often regarded as the first *oratorio.

Rapsodie espagnole [F., Spanish Rhapsody]. Descriptive suite for orchestra by Ravel, composed in 1907. Its four movements are: (1) Prélude à la nuit; (2) Malagueña; (3) Habanera; (4) Feria.

Rasch [G.]. Quick.

Raselius, Andreas (b. Hahnbach, near Amberg, Upper Palatinate, *c.* 1563; d. Heidelberg, 6 Jan. 1602). Studied at Heidelberg Univ. Cantor at the Gymnasium in Regensburg, 1584–1600. Court *Kapellmeister* to the Elector Palatine Frederick IV in Heidelberg from 1600. Composed German and Latin motets; chorale settings; Magnificats. Published a treatise, *Hexachordum seu quaestiones musicae practicae*, 1589.

Rasgado, rasgueado [Sp.]. In guitar playing, strumming the strings with a finger to produce an arpeggio.

Rasumovsky Quartets. Beethoven's string quartets op. 59, nos. 1–3, composed in 1805–6 and dedicated to the Russian Count Rasumovsky. In nos. 1 and 2 Beethoven used a "Thème Russe" taken from a collection published in 1790.

Rathaus, Karol (b. Tarnopol, Poland, 16 Sept. 1895; d. New York, 21 Nov. 1954). Pupil of Schreker in Vienna and Berlin. Settled in the U.S. in 1938. Teacher at Queens College in New York from 1940 until his death. Composed an opera, *Fremde Erde*, Berlin, 1930; ballets; 3 symphonies and other orch. works; a piano concerto, 1939; choral works; 5 string quartets and other chamber music; piano pieces; songs.

Ratsche [G.]. Cog *rattle.

Rattenando, rattenuto [It.]. Holding back.

Rattle. (1) Also called a *ratchet*. An instrument of the percussion family consisting of a wooden cogwheel that revolves against a flexible strip of wood or metal. (2) In the classification of instruments, a generic term for shaken idiophones [see Instruments]. These are among the oldest and most widely distributed instruments.

Ravel, (Joseph) Maurice (b. Ciboure, Basses-Pyrénées, France, 7 Mar. 1875; d. Paris, 28 Dec. 1937). Pupil of Gédalge and Fauré at the Paris Conservatory. Left the Conservatory in 1905 amid a public protest provoked by his being declared ineligible to compete for the Prix de Rome a fourth time, having failed to win it in earlier attempts. After 1932 he was unable to compose because of a brain disease. Works: operas (*L'*heure espagnole*; *L'*enfant et les sortilèges*); ballets (*Daphnis et Chloé; Adélaïde, ou Le langage des fleurs*, orch. version of *Valses nobles et sentimentales*; *Ma mère l'oye*; *La *valse*); orch. works (incl. *Menuet antique*, 1895, originally for piano; the overture *Shéhérazade*, 1898; *Pavane pour une infante défunte*, 1899, originally for piano; *Alborada del gracioso*, 1905, originally for piano; *Rapsodie espagnole*, 1907; *Le tombeau de Couperin*, 1914–17, originally for piano; an orchestral version of Mussorgsky's *Pictures at an Exhibition*, 1922; *Bolero*, 1927); *Tzigane* for violin and orch., 1924, originally for violin and piano; a piano concerto in G, 1931, and a piano concerto for left hand in D, 1931; 3 cantatas; *3 chansons* for chorus, 1915; the song cycle *Shéhérazade* for voice and orch., 1903; *3 poèmes de Stéphane Mallarmé* for voice, piano, string quartet, 2 flutes and 2 clarinets, 1913; *Chansons madécasses* for voice, flute, cello, and piano, 1925–26; chamber music (a string quartet in F, 1902–3; *Introduction et allegro* for harp, string quartet, flute, and clarinet, 1905–6; a piano trio, 1914; a sonata for violin and cello, 1920–22; *Berceuse sur le nom de Fauré* for violin and piano, 1922; a violin sonata, 1923–27; *Tzigane* for violin and piano, 1924); piano pieces (incl. *Pavane pour une infante défunte*, 1899; *Jeux d'eau*, 1901; *Sonatine*, 1905; *Miroirs*, 1905; *Gaspard de la nuit*, 1908; *Valses nobles et sentimentales*, 1911; *Le tombeau de Couperin*, 1917; *Ma mère l'oye* for piano four-hands, 1908); songs with piano accompaniment (incl. *Épigrammes de Clément Marot*, 1898; *Histoires naturelles*, 1906; *5 mélodies populaires grecques*, 1907; *Chants populaires*, 1910; *2 mélodies hébraïques*, 1914; *3 chansons*, 1915, originally for chorus; *Don Quichotte à Dulcinée*, 1932).

Ravenscroft, John (d. London?, before 1708). Violinist and composer. Probably a pupil of Corelli. Known to have been in Rome in 1695. Composed trio sonatas.

Ravenscroft, Thomas (b. after 1590; d. c. 1633). Music editor, theorist, and composer. Chorister at St. Paul's Cathedral, London. Studied at Cambridge. Music master at Christ's Hospital, London, 1618–22. Published *The Whole Booke of Psalmes*, 1621, containing four-part harmonizations by other composers and himself; collections of catches and other music of popular character (incl. *Pammelia*, 1609, the first printed collection of catches); a theoretical treatise, 1614.

Ravvivando [It.]. Quickening.

Rawsthorne, Alan (b. Haslingden, Lancashire, 2 May 1905; d. Cambridge, 24 July 1971). Studied at the Royal Manchester College of Music. Teacher at the School of Dance Mime at Dartington Hall, 1932–34. Composed a ballet, *Madame Chrysanthème*, 1957; 3 symphonies and other orch. works (incl. *Symphonic Studies*, 1939); concertos for violin, for cello, for piano, for 2 pianos, for clarinet, for oboe; 3 string quartets and other chamber music; piano pieces; songs; music for films and radio.

Raxach, Enrique (b. Barcelona, 15 June 1932). Studied in Barcelona and at the Utrecht Conservatory. Became a Dutch citizen in 1969. Works incl. *Métamorphose I*, 1956, and *II*, 1958, for orch.; *Inside Outside* for orch. and tape, 1969; 2 string quartets and other chamber music.

Razor Quartet. Popular name for Haydn's String Quartet no. 61 (op. 55, no. 2), in F minor, composed in 1788.

Re. See under Pitch names; Solmization; Hexachord.

Read, Daniel (b. Attleboro, Mass., 16 Nov. 1757; d. New Haven, Conn., 4 Dec. 1836). Surveyor, comb-maker, singing-school master, and composer. Composed numerous hymn tunes and published several collections, incl. *The American Singing Book*, 1785, and *The Columbian Harmonist*, 1793–95.

Read, Gardner (b. Evanston, Ill., 2 Jan. 1913). Pupil of Bernard Rogers, Hanson, Pizzetti, Sibelius, and Copland. Teacher at Boston Univ. from 1948. Has composed an opera, *Villon*, 1967; incidental music for plays; 4 symphonies and other orch. works (incl. *Sketches of the City*,

1933; *Prelude and Toccata,* 1937; *Pennsylvania,* 1947); a cello concerto, 1945; *The Prophet,* 1960, and other choral works, some with orch.; chamber music; piano pieces; organ pieces; songs. Has published 2 books, incl. one on modern notation, and numerous articles.

Real answer, real fugue. See Tonal and real.

Rebab. See Rabāb.

Rebec. See Rabāb. For ill. see under Violin family.

Reber, Napoléon Henri (b. Mulhouse, Alsace, 21 Oct. 1807; d. Paris, 24 Nov. 1880). Pupil of Reicha and Lesueur. Teacher at the Paris Conservatory from 1851, succeeding Halévy as professor of composition in 1861. Composed several comic operas and a grand opera; a ballet, *Le diable amoureux,* 1840; 4 symphonies; chamber music; piano pieces; songs. Published a *Traité d'harmonie,* 1862.

Rebikov, Vladimir Ivanovich (b. Krasnoyarsk, Siberia, 31 May 1866; d. Yalta, 4 Aug. 1920). Studied at the Moscow Conservatory and in Berlin and Vienna. Worked with the whole-tone scale and parallel motion and composed musico-psychographical dramas (incl. *The Abyss,* 1910) calling for a union of feeling and music in the performer. Also composed operas (incl. *The Storm,* Odessa, 1894); ballets (incl. *Yelka* [The Christmas Tree] for singers and dancers, Moscow, 1903); numerous piano pieces (incl. *Mélomimiques*). Published numerous articles on aesthetics.

Recapitulation. See under Sonata form.

Récit [F.]. A 17th-century term, derived from **récitative,* for a vocal solo piece, usually in aria style; e.g., *récit de basse,* bass aria. In organs, the term is used similarly, i.e., for a solo organ stop and for the entire solo organ (*clavier de récit*); also as a title for an organ piece with a distinct melodic part (as opposed to earlier, contrapuntal organ music).

Recital. A public performance by one or two players (as opposed to *concert,* used for a group of three or more). The term was first used for performances by Liszt in London in 1840.

Recitative [F. *récitative;* G. *Rezitativ;* It., Sp. *recitativo*]. A vocal style designed to imitate and emphasize the natural inflections of speech. It is usually employed with more or less narrative prose texts, particularly in operas, where it serves to carry the action from one **aria* (ensemble, chorus) to another. The earliest operas (Peri's, Caccini's *Euridice,* 1600) were written throughout in a declamatory style (also called *stile rappresentativo*) quite different from the later **parlando.* During the 17th century this *recitativo arioso* [see Arioso] developed in a number of directions. Taking on more distinct phrasing, melodic character, and definite form, it grew into the aria. With the development of the aria as a distinct type, the recitative gradually became faster and less melodic. It was not until the 18th century, however, that this parlando style was generally introduced into opera. It was known as *recitativo secco* [It. *secco,* dry—with reference to its lack of expressiveness]. This type remained in use throughout Italian 18th-century *opera seria* and in the operas of Mozart and Rossini.

Whereas both the early 17th-century recitative and the *recitativo secco* were sung to thoroughbass accompaniment only, a fuller accompaniment (including strings) was introduced for recitatives of special importance. The use of ensemble accompaniment naturally led to a more strictly measured recitative, dramatic rather than declamatory, the *recitativo accompagnato* or *stromentato* (accompanied recitative). It assumed considerable importance in 18th-century opera, where it was usually reserved for the climactic scenes of the drama and served to introduce the most brilliant arias of the work. Although the distinction between aria and recitative continued to be a feature of much opera throughout the 19th century, the distinction was largely abandoned by Wagner and his followers.

Reciting note. See under Psalm tones.

Recorder [F. *flûte à bec;* G. *Blockflöte;* It. *flauto diritto;* Sp. *flauta de pico*]. The most important type of whistle (or fipple) flute, i.e., end-blown, with a "whistle" mouthpiece [see Whistle flute]. Its tone quality is soft and slightly reedy, in part produced by a wide, tapering conical bore. The recorder attained virtually its final form in the late Middle Ages; by the 16th century it formed a complete family of instruments from treble to bass that played an important part in the music of the late Renaissance. By the early 18th century only three or four sizes of recorder remained in use. Parts for recorder were marked "flauto" by J. S. Bach and most of his contemporaries, the transverse flute being called the "German flute," "flûte traversière," or "flauto traverso." Bach and Handel occasionally made use of a "flauto piccolo" or "flautino," a small recorder usually an octave higher in pitch than the flauto. After 1750 the recorder gradually passed out of use.

In the early 20th century, a revival took place, begun by Arnold Dolmetsch in England. Modern instruments are generally made in four sizes: soprano (British, descant), range c''–d''''; alto (British, treble), f'–g'''; tenor, c'–d'''; bass, f–g''. See ill. under Flute.

Recoupe [F.]. See under *Basse danse.*

Recueilli [F.]. Meditative, contemplative.

Reda, Siegfried (b. Bochum, Germany, 27 July 1916; d. Mülheim, 13 Dec. 1968). Organist and composer. Pupil of Pepping and Distler. Director of the Institute for Protestant Church Music at the Folkwangschule in Essen from 1946 until his death. Composed much sacred choral music, incl. collections for use throughout the church year; numerous organ pieces (incl. 3 concertos; 3 "chorale concertos"; *Marienbilder,* 1952; a sonata, 1963).

Redford, John (d. London, 1547). Organist, poet, dramatist, and composer. One of the six vicars-choral at St. Paul's Cathedral, London, and master of the choristers there from about 1534. Composed organ pieces based on plainsong melodies; 3 motets. Wrote the play *Wyt and Science.*

Redoble [Sp.]. See under Ornamentation.

Réduction [F.]. Reduction, arrangement. *Réduction pour le piano,* arrangement for piano.

Reed [F. *anche;* G. *Zunge, Blatt, Rohrblatt;* It. *ancia;* Sp. *lengüeta*]. A thin piece of cane, metal, or other material that is fixed at one end and is free to vibrate at the other. The reed is the sound-producing agent in various musical instruments, chiefly the woodwinds, bagpipes, harmonium, accordion, harmonica, and the reed stops of the organ.

There are two principal types of reed, *idiophonic* and *heterophonic.* Idiophonic reeds are usually made of metal and can produce the sound of one pitch only, this being determined by their length and thickness (as is true of a tuning fork). Such reeds are used in the *harmonium, *accordion, *harmonica, Chinese *sheng, *regal, and in organ reed stops. In the last they are combined with a pipe that serves to reinforce the sound. Heterophonic reeds are made of a flexible, light material, usually cane. They can produce a wide range of pitches when attached to a pipe whose sounding length determines the pitches. In instruments such as the oboe or the clarinet, the sounding length of the pipe can be varied by covering different holes, so that a whole scale can be obtained from the reed. There are two main kinds of heterophonic reed, *single reeds* (clarinet, saxophone) and *double reeds* (oboe, bassoon). With the former, one reed vibrates against a slot of the pipe; with the latter, two reeds, separated by a slight opening, vibrate against each other.

Another distinction is that between *free* and *beating reeds.* In the former type, used in the harmonium, the reeds move in and out of a slot just wide enough to let the reed pass "freely"; in the latter type, used chiefly in the organ, the opening of the slot is somewhat smaller than the reed so that the reed "beats" against the frame [see Organ]. The reed of the clarinet is a beating reed.

Reed, H. (Herbert) Owen (b. Odessa, Mo., 17 June 1910). Pupil of Bernard Rogers, Hanson, Martinů, and Harris. Teacher at Michigan State Univ. from 1936. Has composed a folk opera, *Michigan Dream,* 1955; a ballet-pantomime, *The Masque of the Red Death,* after Poe, 1936; a symphony, 1939, and other orch. works (incl. *The Turning Mind,* 1968); a cello concerto, 1949; band works; choral works (incl. the oratorio *A Tabernacle for the Sun,* 1963); a string quartet and other chamber music; piano pieces; songs. Has published several textbooks.

Reel. A dance performed by two or more couples facing each other and executing figures of eight. It is common in northern Europe and North America, the American variety being known as the "Virginia reel." The music consists of four or eight measures in moderately quick duple meter that are repeated over and over. See under Strathspey.

Reformation Symphony. Mendelssohn's Symphony no. 5, op. 107, in D minor, composed in 1830 for the tercentennial of the Augsburg Conference, where Luther openly declared the establishment of the German Reformed (i.e., Protestant) Church.

Refrain. In poetry, one or two lines recurring at the end of each stanza of a strophic poem. The musical equivalent is the *burden.* In a musical composition, each repetition of the refrain is set to the same melody, so that *refrain* refers to both textual and musical repetition. The refrain is often called the *chorus,* since it is often sung by the full chorus while the stanzas (verses) are solo. Examples of forms incorporating refrains are the **ballade, *virelai, *rondeau, *ballata,* and **villancico.*

Regal. A small portable organ, probably invented *c.* 1450 and much used during the 16th and 17th centuries. It had reed pipes only [see Reed].

Reger, Max (Johann Baptist Joseph Maximilian) (b. Brand, Bavaria, 19 Mar. 1873; d. Leipzig, 11 May 1916). Pianist, organist, and composer. Pupil of H. Riemann in Sonderhausen and Wiesbaden. Toured as a pianist after 1901. Teacher at the Wiesbaden Conservatory, 1895–96; at the Munich Academy, 1905–6; at the Leipzig Conservatory, 1907 until his death. Court *Kapellmeister* in Meiningen, 1911–15. Composed orch. works (incl. *Symphonischer Prolog zu einer Tragödie*); a violin concerto and a piano concerto; numerous choral works, some for liturgical use; 5 string quartets, 2 piano trios, and other chamber music; numerous organ works, incl. preludes,

fugues, chorale fantasies; piano pieces, incl. some for piano four-hands.

Regina caeli laetare [L., Rejoice, Queen of Heaven]. One of the four antiphons B.V.M. See Antiphon (2).

Regis, Johannes (b. Antwerp or Cambrai, *c.* 1430; d. Soignies?, *c.* 1485). Active in Soignies in 1458. Master of the choristers at Notre Dame in Antwerp in 1463. Later Dufay's secretary in Cambrai. In Mons in 1474 and canon at Soignies from 1481. Highly praised along with Busnois and Ockeghem in two contemporary treatises by Johannes Tinctoris. Composed Masses, motets, chansons.

Regisseur [F., G.]. The artistic or stage director of an opera.

Register. (1) In organs, the full set of pipes controlled by one stop; hence, practically identical with organ *stop. A register may include one or (in mixture stops, etc.) several *ranks. (2) In the human voice, the different portions of the range, which are distinguished, according to their place of production and sound quality, as "head register," "chest register," etc. (3) A portion of the total range of pitches (e.g., of some particular instrument). Thus, "upper register," "lower register," etc. (4) More narrowly, and especially with reference to *serial music, the particular range of pitches within which a given *pitch class is represented at a given time.

Registration [G. *Registrierung*]. The art of using and combining organ registers. While modern organ composers frequently indicate the registration of their compositions (at least in a general way), such indications are rare in early organ music.

Regnart, Jakob (Jacques Regnard) (b. Douai, *c.* 1540; d. Prague, 16 Oct. 1599). One of a family of musicians (incl. the composer François Regnart, 1540–*c.* 1600). Singer at the imperial chapel in Vienna, 1564–68. Vice *Kapellmeister* at the court in Prague, 1576–80 and from 1598. Vice *Kapellmeister* to the Archduke Ferdinand in Innsbruck, 1582–84, and *Kapellmeister,* 1585–96. Composed Masses, motets, and other sacred works; Italian *canzone* and German polyphonic lieder in the style of the Italian *villanella.*

Reich, Steve (b. New York, 3 Oct. 1936). Studied at Cornell Univ., the Juilliard School, and with Berio and Milhaud at Mills College. Has worked at the San Francisco Tape Music Center and has studied African drumming in Ghana. Has developed a technique of superimposing rhythmic patterns and shifting them slowly in and out of phase with one another. Works incl. *It's Gonna Rain*, 1965, on tape; *Phase Patterns* for 4 electric organs, 1970; *Drumming* for bongo drums, marimbas, glockenspiels, and voices, 1971; *Music for 18 Musicians*, 1976.

Reicha, Anton (Antonín Josef) (b. Prague, 26 Feb. 1770; d. Paris, 28 May 1836). Flutist and colleague of Beethoven in the orchestra in Bonn from 1788. Piano teacher in Hamburg, 1794–99. Associate of Beethoven, Haydn, Albrechtsberger, and Salieri in Vienna, 1801–8, after which he settled in Paris. Teacher at the Paris Conservatory from 1818. His pupils incl. Berlioz, Liszt, Gounod, and Franck. Composed operas (incl. *Cagliostro*, Paris, 1810); 2 symphonies and other orch. works; sacred choral works; 24 wind quintets, ·20 string quartets, and other chamber music; piano pieces. Published several theory treatises, incl. *Traité de haute composition musicale*, 1824, 1826.

Reichardt, Johann Friedrich (b. Königsberg, 25 Nov. 1752; d. Giebichenstein, near Halle, 27 June 1814). *Kapellmeister* to Frederick the Great and Frederick William II of Prussia, 1775–94. *Kapellmeister* to Jerome Bonaparte in Kassel briefly in 1808, after which he visited Vienna and settled finally in Giebichenstein. Composed Italian operas; *Singspiele* (incl. *Jéry und Bätely*, text by Goethe, Berlin, 1801); symphonies; piano concertos; chamber music; songs, incl. about 60 to texts of Goethe; piano pieces. Published numerous articles and books on music.

Reinagle, Alexander (b. Portsmouth, England, bapt. 23 Apr. 1756; d. Baltimore, 21 Sept. 1809). Singer, pianist, conductor, and composer. Pupil of R. Taylor. Settled in the U.S. in 1786, where he managed concerts in New York and Philadelphia and was active in the production of plays and comic operas in New York, Philadelphia, and Baltimore. Composed incidental music to plays; piano pieces, incl. some for piano four-hands; songs.

Reine, La [F., The Queen]. Nickname for Haydn's Symphony no. 85, in Bb (no. 4 of the *Paris Symphonies), composed *c.* 1786.

Reinecke, Carl (Heinrich Carsten) (b. Altona, near Hamburg, 23 June 1824; d. Leipzig, 10 Mar. 1910). Pupil of his father and associate of Mendelssohn and Schumann. Court pianist in Copenhagen, 1846–48. Teacher at the Cologne Conservatory from 1851. Conductor in Barmen, 1854–59; in Breslau, 1859–60; of the Gewandhaus concerts in Leipzig, 1860–95. Teacher at the Leipzig Conservatory, 1860–1902. His pupils incl. Grieg. Traveled widely as a pianist. Composed operas (incl. *König Manfred*, Wiesbaden, 1867); numerous choral works, some with orch.; 3 symphonies and other orch. works; concertos for piano (4), for harp, for flute, for violin, for cello; 6 string quartets, 6 piano trios, and other chamber music; numerous piano pieces; songs. Published numerous articles and books.

Reiner, Karel (b. Žatec, Czechoslovakia, 27 June 1910). Pianist and composer. Pupil of Suk and Hába. Has worked as a journalist and as head of the music department of the Folk Art Center in Prague, 1951–61. Has made some use of twelve-tone and quarter-tone techniques. Has composed an opera, a ballet, and other music for the stage; a symphony, 1960, a *Suite concertante*, 1967, and other orch. works; concertos for piano, for violin, for bass clarinet; choral works; piano pieces; songs; music for films.

Reinken, Jan Adams (Johann Adam Reincken) (b. Wildeshausen, Oldenburg, 26 Apr. 1623; d. Hamburg, 24 Nov. 1722). Assistant organist to Scheidemann from 1658 and his successor as organist from 1663 at the Katharinenkirche in Hamburg. J. S. Bach made several trips to hear him play. Composed organ pieces, incl. fugues, toccatas, and chorale settings, of which relatively few survive; trio sonatas.

Reissiger, Karl Gottlieb (b. Belzig, near Wittenberg, 31 Jan. 1798; d. Dresden, 7 Nov. 1859). Studied at the Thomasschule in Leipzig, in Vienna, and with Winter in Munich. Director of the opera in Dresden from 1826, succeeding Marschner and Weber. Composed operas (incl. *Die Felsenmühle*, Dresden, 1831); symphonies and other orch. works; Masses and other church music; chamber music; piano pieces; songs.

Reizenstein, Franz (b. Nuremberg, 7 June 1911; d. London, 15 Oct. 1968). Pianist and composer. Pupil of Hindemith and Vaughan Williams. Settled in London in 1934. Teacher at the Royal Academy of Music there from 1958 and at the Royal Manchester College of Music from 1964. Composed a radio opera (*Anna Kraus*, British Broadcasting Corporation, 1952) and other works for radio, films, and television; an oratorio, *Genesis*, 1958, and a cantata, *Voices of Night*, 1951; *Jolly Overture*, 1952, and other orch. works; concertos for piano, for cello, for violin; chamber music; piano pieces.

Related key, relative keys. See Key relationship.

Relative pitch. (1) The pitch of a tone (e.g., E) in relation to a standard tone or given key (e.g., C). It may be expressed as an interval (major third) or by means of solmization syllabiles (mi). (2) The ability to identify the *interval between two sounded pitches and to identify and/or reproduce any pitch in relation to the sound of any other. See also Absolute pitch.

Relish. An ornament used in performing early English music for lute, viol, and keyboard. The term *single relish* was used for any ornament formed by the alternation of two adjacent notes. The *double relish*, a complex ornament similar to the French *double cadence*, consists essentially of a trill upon each of two successive notes.

Remettez [F.]. In *organ music, indication to take off a stop.

Renaissance, music of the. The music of the period *c.* 1450–1600. As with similar terms (e.g., *baroque*) borrowed from general history or from the history of an-

other art, the term *Renaissance* can be fitted to the history of music only with some difficulty. There is general agreement that 1600 is an important dividing point in the history of music, owing to the beginnings of *opera, the *recitative style of singing, and the *thoroughbass. But that these developments should be taken as marking the end of a period called the Renaissance is much less clear, since, for example, they took place in the name of reviving classical antiquity, a phenomenon associated in general history with the Renaissance itself. Defining the beginning of a Renaissance in the history of music proves even more difficult, since there is no sharp dividing line that is congruent with the accepted uses of the term in other branches of history. The most widely held view cites the music of Dunstable, Dufay, and Binchois as marking an important change in the middle of the 15th century. In this view, the music of these composers is novel primarily in its increased use of consonances. The extent of the novelty, however, has been disputed. A clearer turning point occurs around 1500 in the music of Josquin and others, in which the use of *imitation in four or more parts became the norm that was to characterize much of the following century. It is at about this time too that some elements of humanism begin to have an impact on music. However, the year 1500 is almost a century later than what is usually regarded as the beginning of the Renaissance in the visual arts. Thus, although the term Renaissance may be useful in identifying a period in the history of music with reference to the history of Western culture in general, it may be misleading if applied to the history of music uncritically. See Burgundian school; Flemish school; table accompanying History of music.

Renforcer [F.]. To reinforce, to increase in loudness.

Repeat. The signs ||: at the beginning and :|| at the end of a section, which call for the repetition of that section. If the latter sign alone appears, the repetition is to start from the beginning of the composition. In some cases, separate endings (called first and second endings or *prima volta* and *seconda volta*) are provided for the two statements of the passage. These may be identified by the numbers 1 and 2 in conjunction with horizontal brackets.

Répétiteur [F.]. Coach, particularly of singers in an opera company.

Répétition [F.]; **ripetizione** [It.]. Rehearsal. *Répétition générale* [F.], dress rehearsal.

Replica [It.]. *Repeat. Senza replica indicates omission of the repeats, as, e.g., of the sections of the minuet or scherzo after the trio.

Reports. A 17th-century English term for *points of imitation.

Reprise [E., F., G.]. (1) Repetition. The term is used particularly in connection with *sonata form, but unfortunately with two different meanings. Originally, it referred to the repetition of the exposition before the development, usually indicated by the *repeat sign. Today, however, the term usually means the recapitulation, i.e., the repetition of the exposition after the development section. (2) In 17th-century French music, the second section of pieces in *binary form.

Requiem Mass. The Mass for the Dead (*Missa pro defunctis*), so called because it begins with the Introit *Requiem aeternam dona eis Domine* (Give them eternal rest, O Lord). The liturgical structure of this Mass is essentially like that of any other *Mass, except that the joyful portions of the Ordinary (Gloria and Credo) are omitted and the Alleluia is replaced by a Tract, after which the sequence *Dies irae* is added. In polyphonic settings, the Mass for the Dead differs from the normal Mass chiefly by including not only the items of the Ordinary (Kyrie, Sanctus, Agnus Dei), but also, and in fact more prominently, those of the Proper (Introit, Gradual, etc.). Nevertheless, the selection of items for polyphonic treatment has varied considerably. A large number of 16th-century settings exist, among them those by La Rue, Morales, Guerrero, Palestrina, Lasso, and Victoria. In all of these works, the *Dies irae* is not composed but sung in plainsong, as are the opening intonations of the various other items,

while the composed sections use the liturgical melodies more or less freely as *cantus firmus*. Composers of the 17th century, e.g., Biber and Kerll, were particularly attracted by the dramatic words of the *Dies irae*. Among the 18th-century settings for chorus and orchestra, Jommelli's and, above all, Mozart's Requiem are outstanding. Among 19th-century composers of the Requiem are Cherubini, Berlioz, Dvořák, Bruckner, Verdi, Saint-Saëns, and Fauré. Brahms' *Ein *deutsches Requiem* (op. 45, 1868) is based on German texts freely chosen from the Scriptures rather than on the liturgical texts. Important 20th-century examples are Duruflé's Requiem op. 9 (1947) and Britten's *War Requiem* op. 66 (1961).

Reservata. See *Musica reservata*.

Resolution. A progression from a dissonant tone (or harmony) to one that is consonant [see Consonance, dissonance]. In classical tonal *counterpoint, dissonant tones are normally resolved by stepwise *motion.

Resonance. The transmission of vibrations from one vibrating body to another. This phenomenon takes place only when the two bodies are capable of vibrating at the same frequency (or a harmonic thereof). If, e.g., two tuning forks of the same frequency (i.e., same pitch) are placed close together and one of them is struck with a hammer, the other will immediately vibrate and emit the same sound. In the case of vibrating strings, the possibilities for resonance are considerably wider, owing to the presence of harmonics [see under Acoustics]. On the piano, e.g., the string C sets up resonant vibrations in the strings c, g, c', e', etc. Another name for this effect is *sympathetic vibration.* See also Sympathetic string.

Important to musical instruments are the "general resonators," bodies that react with sounds of any frequency or pitch. To this group belong the soundboard of the piano and the belly and back of the violin, which co-vibrate and reinforce any sound produced on the strings.

Resonator. Any acoustical implement, usually in the shape of a hollow vessel, that serves to reinforce sounds by *resonance.

Respighi, Ottorino (b. Bologna, 9 July 1879; d. Rome, 18 Apr. 1936). Violinist, violist, pianist, and composer. Pupil of Martucci, Rimsky-Korsakov, and Bruch. Teacher at the Accademia di Santa Cecilia in Rome from 1913 and its director, 1924–26. Composed operas (incl. *Belfagor,* Milan, 1923; *La fiamma,* Rome, 1934; *Lucrezia,* Milan, 1937); ballets (incl. *Belkis,* 1932); orch. works (incl. *Fontane di Roma,* 1917; *Pini di Roma,* 1924; *Rossiniana,* from Rossini's piano pieces, 1925; *Impressioni brasiliane,* 1927; *Gli uccelli,* 1927; *Feste romane,* 1929); concertos for piano and for violin; choral works; chamber music; piano pieces; songs.

Respond. *Responsory, *response, or the main section of a responsorial chant (corresponding to the antiphon section of antiphonal chants) as opposed to the verse. See Psalmody II.

Response. (1) In Anglican churches, the choral or congregational reply to the versicles (in the *preces and suffrages), the petitions (in the *litany), and the Commandments of the Decalogue. (2) In the Reformed churches, a short piece such as "Hear our prayer, O Lord" or a manifold Amen, sung by the choir, usually after a pastoral prayer.

Responsorial singing. In Gregorian chant, the performance of a chant by one or more soloists (*cantor, cantores*) in alternation with the choir (*schola*), as opposed to performance by two alternating half-choruses, known as *antiphonal singing. Originally each method was restricted to particular portions of the liturgy, the responsorial to the elaborate chants (responsories, Graduals, Alleluias, Offertories) and the antiphonal to the simpler ones (psalms, Introits, Communions); see Psalmody II, III. Today all these chants are sung responsorially, antiphonal performance being used only for certain nonpsalmodic chants, e.g., the Kyrie, Gloria, or the bilingual Sanctus on Good Friday.

Responsory [L. *responsorium*]. In the Roman Catholic rites, a type of chant sung principally at Matins as a musical postlude to a lesson. These long, elaborate chants consist of respond, one or more verses, and the Doxology. The verses and the Doxology are sung to one or another of eight *psalm tones. These responsories are known as great responsories (*responsoria prolixa*), as distinguished from the much simpler short responsories (*responsoria brevia*), which are sung after the short lesson (the so-called chapter) of the daytime hours. See Psalmody II. For *responsorium graduale,* see Gradual.

Ressortir [F.]. To emphasize.

Rest [F. *pause, silence;* G. *Pause;* It. *pausa;* Sp. *silencio*]. A silence or a notational symbol used to indicate it. For the symbols used in specifying the durations of rests, see Notes.

Resultant bass. Organ pipes in which the acoustical phenomenon of resultant (differential) tones is used to produce the lowest registers; also called acoustic bass. See Combination tone.

Resultant tone. *Combination tone.

Resurrection Symphony. Mahler's Symphony no. 2, in C minor, completed in 1894. The fourth movement is a setting for alto solo and orchestra of "Urlicht" (Primordial Light, a song from *Des Knaben Wunderhorn*); the fifth and last movement is a setting of Klopstock's poem "Auferstehung" (Resurrection), for soprano solo, chorus, and orchestra.

Retrograde. Backward, i.e., beginning with the last note and ending with the first. Synonymous terms are *crab motion, cancrizans* [L.], *Krebsgang* [G.], *al rovescio,* and *recte et retro* [It.]. Retrograde motion is a feature of some *canons as early as the 14th century. Together with *inversion and retrograde inversion (i.e., the retrograde of the inversion) it is an important technique of *serial music.

Reubke, Julius (b. Hausneindorf, Germany, 23 Mar. 1834; d. Pillnitz, 3 June 1858). Pianist and composer. Pupil of Kullak and Liszt. Composed an organ sonata on the 94th Psalm; piano pieces; songs.

Reusner, Esajas (b. Löwenberg, Silesia, 29 Apr. 1636; d. Berlin, 1 May 1679). Lutenist to Countess Radziwill in Breslau from 1651; at the court in Brieg from 1655; to the Elector of Brandenburg in Berlin from 1674. Composed suites for the lute; arrangements of sacred melodies for lute; suites for strings and continuo.

Reutter, Hermann (b. Stuttgart, 17 June 1900). Pianist and composer. Studied at the Munich Academy. Teacher at the Stuttgart Musikhochschule, 1932–36, 1952–56, and its director, 1956–66. Teacher at the Hochschule für Musik in Frankfurt, 1936–45; at the Munich Academy, 1966–74. Has composed operas (incl. *Die Brücke von San Luis Rey*, after Thornton Wilder, Frankfurt Radio, 1954; *Die Witwe von Ephesus*, Cologne, 1954); ballets (incl. *Die Kirmes von Delft*, 1937); an oratorio, *Der grosse Kalendar*, 1933, and other choral works; orch. works; 7 piano concertos; chamber music; piano pieces; organ pieces; about 200 songs.

Reutter, Johann Adam Joseph Karl Georg von (b. Vienna, bapt. 6 Apr. 1708; d. there, 11 Mar. 1772). Pupil of his father, Georg von Reutter, whom he succeeded as *Kapellmeister* at St. Stephen's Cathedral in Vienna in 1738, and of Caldara. Second court *Kapellmeister* in Vienna from 1747; acting first *Kapellmeister* there from 1751, assuming the full title in 1769. Composed about 30 operas; oratorios; about 80 Masses and numerous other sacred works; symphonies; chamber music; keyboard pieces.

Revolutionary Etude. Popular name for Chopin's Etude in C minor op. 10, no. 12, written in 1831.

Revueltas, Silvestre (b. Santiago Papasquiaro, Mexico, 31 Dec. 1899; d. Mexico City, 5 Oct. 1940). Violinist, conductor, and composer. Studied in Mexico City and at the Chicago Musical College. Assistant conductor to Carlos Chávez (with whom he also gave violin-piano recitals) of the Orquesta sinfónica de México, 1929–35. Teacher at the National Conservatory in Mexico City, 1929–35. Composed ballets; orch. works (incl. *Esquinas*, 1930; *Sensemayá*, 1938); film scores (incl. *Redes*, 1935); 3 string quartets and other chamber music; songs.

Reyer, (Louis-Étienne-) Ernest (real name Rey) (b. Marseille, 1 Dec. 1823; d. Le Lavandou, near Hyères, 15 Jan. 1909). Librarian of the Paris Opéra from 1866. Music critic for the *Journal des Débats* and other periodicals and, as such, a defender of Berlioz and Wagner. Composed operas (incl. *Sigurd*, Brussels, 1884; *Salammbô*, Brussels, 1890); *Le Sélam*, a "symphonie orientale" in 4 parts, 1850; a ballet-pantomime, *Sacountala*, 1858; sacred and secular choral works; piano pieces; songs.

Reynolds, Roger (Lee) (b. Detroit, 18 July 1934). Pupil of Finney and Gerhard. A co-founder of the ONCE Group in Ann Arbor, Michigan. Has worked at the electronic music studio of the West German Radio in Cologne. Teacher at the Univ. of California at San Diego from 1969. Has worked with mixed media and graphic notation. Works incl. *The Emperor of Ice Cream* for 8 singers, piano, percussion, double bass, staging, 1962; *Quick Are the Mouths of Earth* for chamber ensemble, 1965; *Blind Men* for chorus, brass, percussion, piano, 1966; *Threshold* for divided orch., 1967; *Ping* for flute, piano, harmonium, bowed cymbal, tamtam, film, slides, tape, electronic equipment, 1968; *From Behind the Unreasoning Mask* for trombone, percussion, and tape, 1975.

Reznicek, Emil Nikolaus von (b. Vienna, 4 May 1860; d. Berlin, 2 Aug. 1945). Pupil of Reinecke and Jadassohn. Conductor of the court theater in Mannheim, 1896–99; of the Warsaw Opera, 1907–8; of the Berlin Komische Oper, 1909–11. Teacher at the Scharwenka Conservatory in Berlin from 1906. Composed operas (incl. *Donna Diana*, Prague, 1894; *Ritter Blaubart*, Darmstadt, 1920); 5 symphonies and other orch. works; a violin concerto; a string quartet and other chamber music; piano pieces; songs.

RF., rfz. [It.]. Abbr. for *rinforzando*.

Rhapsodie aus Goethe's "Harzreise im Winter." Composition by Brahms, op. 53 (1869), for contralto, men's chorus, and orchestra, based on a fragment from Goethe's *Harzreise im Winter* (Winter Journey through the Hartz Mountains). Also known as Brahms' Alto Rhapsody.

Rhapsody. Originally, a section of a Greek epic (e.g., the *Iliad*) or a free medley of such sections sung in succession. Musicians, principally in the 19th century, have used the term with different meanings, chiefly for free fantasies of an epic, heroic, or national character (Liszt, *Hungarian Rhapsodies;* Raff; Lalo; Dvořák; Bartók). Brahms' two Rhapsodies for piano op. 79, however, are single-movement works in sonata form.

Rheinberger, Josef (Gabriel) (b. Vaduz, Liechtenstein, 17 Mar. 1839; d. Munich, 25 Nov. 1901). Organist, conductor, and composer. Studied at the Munich Conservatory and with Lachner. Teacher, from 1859 until his death, at the Munich Conservatory, where he attracted numerous students from Europe and America, incl. Humperdinck, Chadwick, and Parker. Composed operas and other music for the stage; a symphony and other orch. works; numerous sacred and secular choral works; a piano concerto and 2 organ concertos; chamber music; 20 sonatas and other pieces for organ; piano pieces; songs.

Rheingold, Das. See *Ring des Nibelungen, Der.*

Rhenish Symphony. Schumann's Symphony no. 3 in E♭, op. 97, composed in 1850 after a trip along the Rhine.

Rhodes, Phillip (b. Forest City, N.C., 6 June 1940). Pupil of Hamilton, Martino, M. Powell, Schuller, and Perle. Teacher at Amherst College, 1968–69; at the Univ. of Louisville, 1969–71; at Carleton College from 1972. Has composed an opera-oratorio, *From "Paradise Lost";* a ballet, *About Faces;* sacred and secular choral works; *The Lament of Michal* for soprano and orch., 1970; works for band; *Autumn Setting* for soprano and string quartet, 1969; a string trio and other chamber music.

Rhythm. That aspect of music concerned with the organization of time. As such it is a function primarily of the *durations* of the sounds and silences of which music consists, though emphases created by means of *loudness* [see also Accent] as well as *harmony* and melodic *motion* also affect rhythm. Most Western music organizes time by means of regularly recurring pulses or beats that are in turn arranged in regularly recurring groups consisting of multiples of two or three pulses. The number of pulses per group and the internal organization of individual groups determine the *meter* of a composition. The rate at which pulses or groups of pulses proceed is the *tempo.* Although metrical regularity is a fundamental feature of much Western music, certain kinds of departures from regularity do occur frequently, e.g., *syncopation,* *hemiola,* and a wide variety of rhythmic patterns that may serve to contradict momentarily some metrical scheme. Such departures, however, derive their meaning from the prevailing regularity within which they occur. Similarly, the rhythm of much Western music is dependent upon a largely regular or steady tempo, but momentary departures from the prevailing tempo, whether specified by the composer or introduced by the performer [see Rubato] in appropriate ways, are also an essential feature of much Western music.

Rhythmic organization of the type described began to be an important part of Western music at least as early as the 13th century, when musical *notation* first included the means to notate rhythm unambiguously. Repertories from earlier periods, e.g., *Gregorian* and other types of liturgical chant, may have been characterized by substantially greater rhythmic freedom, principally the lack of a regular metrical structure. This lack is also a feature of much music of the 20th century and of the music of various non-Western musical cultures. The term "free rhythm" is sometimes used in these contexts, though such music often relies on some fundamental unit of duration employed to mark off a regular pulse.

Although all music consisting of sounds and silences ordered in time is by definition rhythmic, the term *rhythmic* usually implies the use of particularly striking rhythmic patterns. See also Modes, rhythmic; Isorhythm; Polyrhythm.

Rhythmic modes. See Modes, rhythmic.

Riadis, Emilios (real name Khu) (b. Salonica, 13 May 1885; d. there, 17 July

1935). Studied at the Munich Conservatory and with G. Charpentier and Ravel. Teacher at the Salonica Conservatory from 1915 until his death. Composed operas; orch. works; a *Byzantine Mass* and other works for the Greek Orthodox rite; chamber music; piano pieces; numerous songs and song cycles, incl. settings of Greek folksongs.

Ribattuta [It.]. See under Ornamentation.

Ribeba [It.]. *Jew's-harp.

Ricci, Luigi (b. Naples, 8 July 1805; d. Prague, 31 Dec. 1859). Brother of Federico Ricci, 1809–77, a composer with whom he collaborated on some works. Pupil of Zingarelli. *Maestro di cappella* at the Trieste Cathedral and director of the Trieste Opera from 1836. Composed about 30 operas (incl. *Crispino e la comare,* with Federico, Venice, 1850); numerous sacred and secular vocal works.

Ricercar(e), ricercata, recercada [It.]. Terms used during the 16th and 17th centuries for various types of instrumental music that differ considerably in style and purpose. By far the most important of these is the imitative ricercar. It should be noted, however, that 16th-century prints and manuscripts often present the term *ricercar* interchangeably with **fantasia, *tiento,* and *preamble.* The word *study* is a reasonably good equivalent.

The *imitative* (contrapuntal) *ricercar* is, to a certain extent, the instrumental counterpart of the (vocal) motet. Its chief characteristic is imitative treatment of one or more themes, the themes sometimes being slow and lacking rhythmic as well as melodic individuality. Such pieces were written for instrumental (occasionally even vocal) ensembles and for the organ. The earliest ensemble pieces called "ricercar" are found in the *Musica nova* of 1540 (Willaert, Julio da Modena) and in publications by Jacques Buus (1547, 1549), Guiliano Tiburtino (1549; also including eight by Willaert), Willaert (1551, 1559), and Annibale Padovano (1556). Stylistically, these are very similar to motets, being written in a continuous texture with numerous overlapping points of imitation, frequent crossing of voice-parts, and an absence of ornamentation and passagework. These ricercars could be sung (in *vocalization) as well as played on instruments such as viols, recorders, and cornetts. The ensemble ricercar was cultivated until about 1620.

The history of the imitative ricercar for keyboard begins with the four in Girolamo Cavazzoni's *Intavolatura cioè recercari canzoni himni magnificati* of 1542–43. These show many of the stylistic and structural peculiarities that make the organ ricercar a type in its own right rather than a "textless motet." Characteristic of the organ ricercar are a relatively small number of themes, each extensively treated in a lengthy section that comes to a full stop; free-voice writing; cadential *coloraturas; and passages in *toccata style. Andrea Gabrieli wrote a number of ricercars in which the tendency towards elaborate treatment of a small number of themes becomes even more apparent. Five of these ricercars are monothematic; others are based on two or three themes. In addition, Gabrieli made extensive use of contrapuntal devices such as augmentation, diminution, inversion, double counterpoint, and combination of different themes, bestowing on the ricercar the character of learnedness that was later to be associated with it. In Italy the organ ricercar was also cultivated by Merulo, Trabaci, Frescobaldi, Fontana, and Pasquini. German composers of ricercars were Hassler, Froberger, Krieger, and Pachelbel. Bach ended the development with his famous ricercar from the **Musikalisches Opfer,* 1747.

Numerous 16th- and 17th-century compositions bearing the name ricercar differ in style and form from the type described above. They may be characterized as studies. The earliest (also the earliest pieces of any kind called "ricercar") are the lute ricercars in the publisher Petrucci's *Intabulatura de lauto* (1507–8). Unrelated to the motet, they are short pieces in free lute style, consisting chiefly of sequential passages and chords, much like a prelude. Counterpoint is at a minimum, and imitation is usually absent. In the later literature for the lute, the style more and more approaches that of the imitative ricercar. The practice of incorporating preexistent polyphonic music resulted in the parody ricercar [see Parody (3)].

The earliest organ pieces called "ricercar" are found in Marco Antonio Cavazzoni's *Recerchari, motetti, canzoni* (1523). Like the lute pieces, they have no connection with the motet. They are long compositions showing a mixture of chordal elements, passagework, and sporadic imitation of short motifs. In spite of their length they apparently served somewhat as preludes, each of the two ricercars being followed by a piece in the same key. Four ricercars by Giacomo Fogliano and those by Claudio Veggio show increased use of imitation and represent the transition to the imitative ricercar of Girolamo Cavazzoni.

Theorists such as Silvestro Ganassi (*Regola Rubertina*, 1542–43) and Diego Ortiz (*Tratado de glosas*, 1553) use the term *ricercar* for instructive pieces designed to demonstrate the skillful playing of the viola da gamba.

Richafort, Jean (b. Hainaut, *c.* 1480; d. probably Bruges, 1547 or 1548). Said by Ronsard to have been a pupil of Josquin. Chapel master at St. Rombaut in Malines, 1507–9. Served Mary of Hungary, regent of the Netherlands, 1531. Chapel master at St. Gilles in Bruges, 1542–47. Composed Masses, a Requiem, motets, Magnificats, chansons.

Richter, Ernst Friedrich Eduard (b. Gross-Schönau, Saxony, 24 Oct. 1808; d. Leipzig, 9 Apr. 1879). Teacher at the Leipzig Conservatory from its founding in 1843. Conductor of the Singakademie, 1843–47. Organist at various Leipzig churches, becoming cantor at the Thomaskirche in 1868. Composed an oratorio; cantatas; Masses and other sacred choral works; chamber music; piano pieces; organ pieces; songs. Published several theory textbooks, incl. *Lehrbuch der Harmonie*, 1853 and in many later editions and translations.

Richter, Franz Xaver (František) (b. Holleschau, Moravia, 1 Dec. 1709; d. Strasbourg, 12 Sept. 1789). *Kapellmeister* to the Prince-Abbot at Kempten from 1740. Violinist and singer at the Mannheim court from 1747 and later chamber composer there. *Kapellmeister* at the Strasbourg Cathedral from 1769 until his

death. Composed about 70 symphonies; 6 harpsichord concertos; an oratorio, Passions, cantatas; numerous Masses and other church music; trio sonatas and other chamber music.

Ricochet [F.]. See Bowing (e).

Řídký, Jaroslav (b. Františkov, near Liberec, Czechoslovakia, 25 Aug. 1897; d. Poděbrady, 14 Aug. 1956). Pupil of Jirák, Křička, and Foerster. First harpist of the Prague Philharmonic, 1924–38, and occasionally its conductor. Teacher at the Prague Conservatory, 1929–49, and at the Prague Music Academy thereafter. Composed 7 symphonies and other orch. works; concertos for violin, for cello, for piano; cantatas; 5 string quartets and other chamber music; piano pieces; arrangements of folksongs.

Ridotto [It.]. Reduced, i.e., arranged (for piano, etc.).

Ridout, Godfrey (b. Toronto, 6 May 1918). Pupil of Willan. Teacher at the Royal Conservatory in Toronto from 1939 and at the Univ. of Toronto from 1948. Has composed a ballet, *La prima ballerina*, 1966; *Esther* for soloists, orch., and chorus, 1951; *In Memoriam Anne Frank*, 1965; *Cantiones mysticae* for soprano and orch., 1953; *Fall Fair*, 1961, and other orch. works; chamber music; piano pieces; organ pieces; songs.

Riegger, Wallingford (b. Albany, Ga., 29 Apr. 1885; d. New York, 2 Apr. 1961). Cellist, conductor, and composer. Studied at the Institute of Musical Art in New York, and in Berlin. Taught briefly in the 1920s at Drake Univ., the Institute of Musical Art, and Ithaca Conservatory, after which he settled in New York. Made some use of twelve-tone techniques. Used numerous pseudonyms for choral arrangements and pedagogic pieces. Composed dance scores for Doris Humphrey, Martha Graham, and others, for various combinations of instruments (incl. *New Dance* scored for 2 pianos, 1935, choreography by Humphrey); 4 symphonies and other orch. works (incl. *Dichotomy*, 1932; *Dance Rhythms*, 1955); a concerto for piano and woodwind quintet, 1952; works for piano with orch. and for violin and orch.; *La belle dame sans merci* for

4 voices and chamber orch., 1923; choral works; 3 string quartets and other chamber music; piano pieces; songs.

Rienzi. Opera in five acts by Wagner (full title, *Cola Rienzi, der Letzte der Tribunen;* libretto by the composer, based on Bulwer-Lytton's novel), produced in Dresden, 1842. Setting: Rome, about 1350.

Ries, Ferdinand (b. Bonn, 28 Nov. 1784; d. Frankfurt, 13 Jan. 1838). Pupil of Beethoven and Albrechtsberger. Traveled widely in Europe and Russia as a pianist. Lived in London, 1813–24; primarily in Frankfurt after 1830, except for 1834–36, when he was town music director at Aachen. Composed operas; oratorios; 6 symphonies; 9 piano concertos; 14 string quartets and other chamber music; 52 sonatas and other piano pieces; songs. Published *Biographische Notizen über L. van Beethoven,* 1838.

Rieti, Vittorio (b. Alexandria, Egypt, of Italian parents, 28 Jan. 1898). Pupil of Respighi, Casella, and Malipiero, though largely self-taught. Lived primarily in Paris from 1925. Settled in the U.S. in 1940. Teacher at the Peabody Conservatory, 1948–49; Chicago Musical College, 1950–53; Queens College in New York, 1955–60; New York College of Music, 1960–64. Has composed operas; ballets (incl. *Le bal,* 1929, and *Night Shadow,* after Bellini's *La sonnambula* and *I puritani,* 1946, both with choreography by G. Balanchine); 5 symphonies and other orch. works; concertos for piano (3), for 2 pianos, for cello (2), for violin, for harpsichord, for string quartet; choral works; 4 string quartets and other chamber music; piano pieces; songs; music for the theater and films.

Rietz, (August Wilhelm) Julius (b. Berlin, 28 Dec. 1812; d. Dresden, 12 Sept. 1877). Pupil of Zelter. Conductor of the Düsseldorf Opera from 1835, succeeding Mendelssohn, and town music director soon thereafter. Opera conductor in Leipzig, 1847–54. Teacher at the Leipzig Conservatory and conductor of the Gewandhaus concerts from 1848. Court *Kapellmeister* at Dresden from 1860. Composed operas; incidental music for the theater; 2 symphonies and other orch. works; concertos; sacred and secular choral works; chamber music; songs. Edited the complete works of Mendelssohn and contributed to the collected editions of the works of Mozart, Beethoven, and Bach.

Rigaudon, rigadoon. A Provençal dance of the 17th century used in the operatic ballets of Lully, Campra, and Rameau, and also introduced in the optional group of the *suite (Pachelbel, Bach).

Rigo [It.]. Staff.

Rigoletto. Opera in three acts by Verdi (libretto by F. M. Piave, after Victor Hugo's drama *Le roi s'amuse*), produced in Venice, 1851. Setting: Mantua and environs, 16th century.

Riisager, Knudåge (b. Port Kunda, Estonia, 6 Mar. 1897; d. Copenhagen, 26 Dec. 1974). Studied in Copenhagen, in Paris with Roussel and Le Flem, and in Leipzig. President of the Danish League of Composers, 1937–62. Director of the Royal Danish Conservatory, 1956–67. Composed an *opera buffa;* ballets (incl. *Qarrtsiluni* for orch., 1938, ballet, 1942; *Etudes,* after Czerny, 1947; *Månerenen* [The Moon Reindeer], 1956; *Fruen fra Havet* [The Lady from the Sea], 1959); 6 symphonies and other orch. works; choral works; string quartets and other chamber music; piano pieces; songs.

Rilasciando [It.]. Slowing down.

Riley, Terry (Mitchell) (b. Colfax, Calif., 24 June 1935). Soprano saxophonist and composer. Pupil of Erickson and Shifrin and has studied Indian music. Teacher at Mills College from 1972. Has employed aleatory and electronic processes. Works incl. *In C* for any number of instruments, 1964; *Poppy Nogood and the Phantom Band* for soprano saxophone, tape, time-lag and feedback system, 1968; *A Rainbow in Curved Air* for electronic keyboard instruments, 1969; music for films.

Rimsky-Korsakov, Nikolai Andreievich (b. Tikhvin, near Novgorod, 18 Mar. 1844; d. Liubensk, near St. Petersburg, 21 June 1908). Studied at the Russian Naval School and became a naval officer. Pupil of Balakirev and was one of "The *Five." Teacher at the St. Petersburg Conservatory from 1871 until his death. Assistant director of the court chapel in St. Petersburg, 1883–94. Conducted concerts of Russian music in Paris (1889, 1907) and Brussels (1890, 1900). His pupils incl. Glazunov, Ippolitov-Ivanov, Miaskovsky, Prokofiev, Respighi, Steinberg, and Stravinsky. Composed operas (incl. *The Maid of Pskov*, St. Petersburg, 1873, rev. 1895; *Snow Maiden*, St. Petersburg, 1882; *Mlada*, St. Petersburg, 1892; *Christmas Eve*, after Gogol, St. Petersburg, 1895; *Sadko*, Moscow, 1898; *Mozart and Salieri*, after Pushkin, Moscow, 1898; *The Legend of the Invisible City of Kitezh*, St. Petersburg, 1907; *The *Golden Cockerel* [F. *Le coq d'or*]); orch. works (incl. 3 symphonies, no. 2 titled *Antar*, 1868; *Capriccio espagnol*, 1887; the suite *Scheherazade*, 1888; the overture *Russian Easter Festival*, 1888; suites from various of his operas); a piano concerto in C♯ min., 1883, and a concerto for trombone and band, 1878?; choral works with and without accompaniment, incl. Russian folksongs; chamber music; piano pieces; numerous songs; collections of folksongs. Orchestrated and/or completed Dargomizhsky's *The Stone Guest*, Borodin's *Prince Igor*, and Mussorgsky's *Khovanshchina* and *Boris Godunov*. Published his memoirs and a treatise on orchestration, as well as other books and articles.

Rinaldo di Capua (b. Capua or Naples, *c*. 1710; d. Rome, after 1770). Active principally in Rome, where the English writer on music Charles Burney met him in 1770. Composed about 30 operas (incl. *La zingara*, Paris, 1753); cantatas.

Rinck, Johann Christian Heinrich (b. Elgersburg, Saxe-Gotha, 18 Feb. 1770; d. Darmstadt, 7 Aug. 1846). Pupil of Kittel. Organist at Giessen from 1790. Organist at Darmstadt from 1805; court organist there from 1813; and chamber musician to the Grand Duke Ludwig I there from 1817. Made successful concert tours as an organist. Composed numerous organ works; Masses, motets, chorales, and other sacred music; chamber music; piano pieces.

Rinforzando [It.; abbr. *rf, rfz, rinf*.]. A sudden accent on a single note or chord; practically synonymous with *sfor-zando*. In early orchestral music (J. Stamitz) the term is used for a short but strong crescendo.

Ring des Nibelungen, Der [G., The Ring of the Nibelung]. Tetralogy by Richard Wagner, consisting of four operas: *Das Rheingold* (The Rhine Gold, 1853–54; designated by Wagner as *Vorspiel*, i.e., prologue); *Die Walküre* (The Valkyrie, 1854–56); *Siegfried* (1856–71); and *Götterdämmerung* (The Twilight of the Gods, 1873–74). The libretto is by Wagner, based on legends from the Scandinavian Edda and the Nibelungenlied. The first performance of the entire *Ring* took place in Bayreuth, 1876, for the dedication of the Bayreuth Festspielhaus. Setting: Germanic mythology.

Ripieno [It.]. In 17th- and 18th-century orchestral music, particularly in the *concerto grosso*, the "reinforcing section" of the orchestra, comparable to the "rear section" of the violins, etc., in the modern orchestra. Therefore, *ripieni* indicates the full orchestra (*tutti, concerto grosso*) as distinguished from the soloists (*concertino*). *Senza ripieni* (without *ripieni*) calls for the leading orchestra players only, i.e., a smaller ensemble used for the accompaniment of the soloists. A *ripienista* is an orchestral player.

Riposato [It.]. With a feeling of repose.

Riprendere [It.]. To take up (the original tempo).

Ripresa [It.]. (1) *Repeat or repetition (also of a performance, opera, etc.). (2) Recapitulation (in *sonata form). (3) In the 14th-century *ballata (and its descendant, the *frottola), the refrain. (4) In 16th- and 17th-century music, a varied repeat of a dance or a closing section of a dance or a tune.

Risqolo. See under Melody type.

Ritardando [It.; abbr. *rit., ritard.*]. Gradually slowing in speed, also indicated by *rallentando. Ritenuto* properly calls for immediate reduction of speed.

Rite of Spring, The. See *Sacre du printemps, Le.*

Ritenuto [It.]. See under *Ritardando*.

Ritmo [It.]. *Rhythm. For Beethoven's indication "ritmo di tre [quattro] battute," see *Battuta*.

Ritornello [It., literally, little return]. (1) In the 14th-century *caccia and *madrigal, the couplet at the end of the poem, which usually expresses the "thought" derived from the preceding "description." In musical composition, it is treated as a separate section, usually involving a change of meter. The ritornello is not in this context a refrain. (2) In 17th- and 18th-century operas and cantatas, a short instrumental passage occurring at the end of an aria, often having been stated first at the beginning and, in some cases, repeated various times in the course of the aria (e.g., between strophes of a strophic-bass *aria). (3) See Ritornello form; Concerto. See also Ritournelle.

Ritornello form. The typical form of the first and frequently also the last movement of the baroque concerto, particularly the *concerto grosso*. Such movements consist of alternating tutti and solo sections, the tutti sections being based on recurring material while the solo sections vary. The music of the tutti sections therefore constitutes a ritornello. See also Concerto.

Ritournelle [F.]. A 17th-century dance in quick triple time, by far the most common dance type in the ballets of Lully. Like the ritornello [see Ritornello (2)], it serves as the conclusion of a song.

Ritter, Alexander (b. Narva, Estonia, of German parents, 27 June 1833; d. Munich, 12 Apr. 1896). Poet, violinist, and composer. Pupil of Ferdinand David and E.F.E. Richter. Close associate of Liszt, von Bülow, Cornelius, Raff, and, later, of R. Strauss. Composed 2 operas (incl. the fairy-tale opera *Der faule Hans*, Munich, 1885); symphonic poems (incl. *Seraphische Phantasie; Erotische Legende*); a string quartet; piano pieces; songs.

Riverso, rivolto [It.]. *Inversion (of intervals, chords, or parts); also *retrograde motion. See *Rovescio*.

Rivier, Jean (b. Villemomble, France, 21 July 1896). Studied at the Paris Conservatory, where he later taught, 1948–66.

Has composed an opera; 7 symphonies and other orch. works; concertos for piano, for violin, for oboe, for brass, timpani, and strings; a Requiem and other choral works with orch.; string quartets and other chamber music; piano pieces; songs; music for radio and films.

Roberday, François (bapt. Paris, 21 Mar. 1624; d. Auffargis, Seine-et-Oise, 13 Oct. 1680). Organist at the Church of the Petits-Pères in Paris. Chamber musician to the Queen Mother Anne of Austria and to Queen Marie-Thérèse (mother and wife, respectively, of Louis XIV). His pupils incl. Lully. Composed a collection of *Fugues et caprices* for organ.

Robertson, Leroy (Jasper) (b. Fountain Green, Utah, 21 Dec. 1896; d. Salt Lake City, 25 July 1971). Pupil of Chadwick, Converse, and Bloch. Teacher at Brigham Young Univ. from 1925; at the Univ. of Utah, 1948–63. Composed an oratorio, *The Book of Mormon*, 1953, and other choral works; orch. works (incl. *Punch and Judy Overture*, 1946; *Trilogy*, 1947); concertos for violin, for cello, for piano; a string quartet and other chamber music; piano pieces; organ pieces; songs.

Rochberg, George (b. Paterson, N.J., 5 July 1918). Pupil of G. Szell, H. Weisse, Scalero, and Menotti. Teacher at the Curtis Institute, 1948–54; at the Univ. of Pennsylvania from 1960. Publications director for the Theodore Presser Company, 1951–60. Has worked with twelve-tone techniques, though he turned away from these in the 1960s toward collage, the quotation of works of others (including the classical masters), and tonality. Has composed 3 symphonies, no. 3 titled "A 20th-century Passion" with vocal soloists and chorus, 1968, and other orch. works (incl. *Night Music*, 1949; *Time-Span*, 1960, rev. 1962; *Music for the Magic Theater*, 1965; *Imago mundi*, 1974); a violin concerto, 1975; *Apocalyptica* for band, 1964, and *Black Sounds* for winds and percussion, 1965; *3 Psalms* for chorus; 3 string quartets (no. 2 with soprano, 1961), a piano trio, 1963, and other chamber music; *12 Bagatelles*, 1952 (orch. version *Zodiac*, 1965), and other piano pieces; songs with piano and with instruments.

Rococo. In painting, architecture, and other visual and decorative arts, an 18th-century style in which light, ornate decoration (especially in the form of scrolls, shells, etc.), and emphasis on elegance and refinement replace the massive structures of the baroque. Its counterpart in 18th-century music, to which the term should be applied only with caution, is usually said to be the *gallant style, which, with its emphasis on delicacy and prettiness, is in marked contrast to the impressive grandeur of the *baroque style. The main flowering of the rococo in this view was from 1725 to 1775. However, the movement began considerably earlier in France, where François Couperin (1668–1733) represents the musical counterpart of the first major rococo painter, Watteau (1684–1721). From France it spread to Germany (Telemann, 1681–1767; Mattheson, 1681–1764) and Italy (D. Scarlatti, 1685–1757). Rococo elements are still present in the works of K. P. E. Bach, Haydn, and Mozart, according to most authors who employ the term. See Gallant style; *Empfindsamer Stil.*

Rode, (Jacques-) Pierre (-Joseph) (b. Bordeaux, 16 Feb. 1774; d. Château-Bourbon, near Damazan, 25 Nov. 1830). Pupil of Viotti. Traveled widely in Europe and Russia as a violinist. Teacher at the Paris Conservatory from 1795. Violinist to Napoleon in 1800; to Czar Alexander I, 1804–8. Beethoven (*Romance,* op. 50) and Boccherini wrote pieces for him. Composed 13 violin concertos; *24 caprices en forme d'études;* duos for violins; string quartets. Wrote a *Méthode du violon* with Baillot and Kreutzer.

Rodrigo, Joaquín (b. Sagunto, near Valencia, Spain, 22 Nov. 1902). Studied in Valencia and with Dukas in Paris. Associate of Falla. Teacher of music history at the Univ. of Madrid from 1946. Has composed a *zarzuela;* ballets; orch. works; concertos (incl. *Concierto de Aranjuez* for guitar and orch., 1939; *Concierto heroico* for piano and orch., 1942; *Concierto de estío* for violin and orch., 1943; *Concierto galante* for cello and orch., 1949; *Concierto-serenata* for harp and orch., 1952; *Fantasía para un gentilhombre* for guitar and orch., 1954; *Concierto andaluz* for 4 guitars and orch.,

1967; *Concierto-madrigal* for 2 guitars and orch., 1968); choral works; chamber music; piano pieces; songs.

Rodríguez de Hita, Antonio (b. probably Castile, 1724; d. Madrid, 21 Feb. 1787). *Maestro de capilla* at the Palencia Cathedral in 1757. Music director at the Convent of the Incarnation in Madrid from 1757 until his death. Composed works for the stage in collaboration with the dramatist Ramón de la Cruz (incl. the opera *Briseida,* Madrid, 1768; and the zarzuelas *Las segadoras de Vallecas,* Madrid, 1768, and *Las labradoras de Murcia,* Madrid, 1769); church music.

Roger-Ducasse, Jean-Jules Aimable (b. Bordeaux, 18 Apr. 1873; d. Le-Taillan-Médoc, near Bordeaux, 19 July 1954). Pupil of Fauré and Gédalge. Teacher at the Paris Conservatory, 1929–45, succeeding Dukas as professor of composition in 1935. Composed a comic opera and a mimed drama; orch. works; choral works; chamber music; piano pieces; songs; pedagogic works.

Rogers, Benjamin (b. Windsor, May 1614; d. Oxford, buried 21 June 1698). Organist at Christ Church, Dublin, 1639–41; at Eton College *c.* 1660; at Magdalen College, Oxford, 1664–85. Composed much church music, incl. services and anthems; a *Hymnus Eucharisticus;* glees; airs for violins and organ and other instrumental pieces; organ pieces.

Rogers, Bernard (b. New York, 4 Feb. 1893; d. Rochester, 24 May 1968). Studied at the Institute of Musical Art in New York and with Farwell, Bloch, N. Boulanger, and Bridge. Teacher at the Eastman School of Music, 1929–67. Composed operas (incl. *The Warrior,* New York, 1947; *The Veil,* Bloomington, Ind., 1950); 5 symphonies and other orch. works; choral works (incl. *The Passion,* with soloists and orch., 1942); chamber music. Published a book on orchestration.

Rogowski, Ludomir Michal (b. Lublin, Poland, 3 Oct. 1881; d. Dubrovnik, Yugoslavia, 13 Mar. 1954). Studied in Warsaw with Noskowski and in Leipzig and Munich. Active as a conductor, living alternately in Poland and France until he retired to Dubrovnik in 1927. Composed operas; ballets (incl. *Bajka*, 1922; *Kupala*, 1925); 7 symphonies and other orch. works; works for violin and orch.; choral works, incl. arrangements of Slavonic melodies; chamber music; piano pieces; songs; music for radio.

Rohrblatt [G.]. The *reed of the clarinet, oboe, and related instruments called *Rohrblattinstrumente*.

Rohrstimmen, Rohrwerk [G.]. The reeds of the organ.

Roi David, Le [F., King David]. Opera ("dramatic psalm") in two parts by Honegger (libretto by R. Morax), produced in Mézières, Switzerland, 1921, and produced as an oratorio in New York, 1925. In the latter form, the orchestra is considerably enlarged, and a narrator relates the dramatic events between musical selections.

Roland-Manuel, Alexis (real name Roland Alexis Manuel Lévy) (b. Paris, 22 Mar. 1891; d. there, 1 Nov. 1966). Critic and composer. Pupil of Roussel, d'Indy, and Ravel. Teacher at the Paris Conservatory from 1947. Composed operas; ballets; orch. works; a piano concerto; choral works; chamber music; songs; music for films. Published 3 books on Ravel and monographs on Honegger and Falla.

Roldán, Amadeo (b. Paris, of Cuban parents, 12 July 1900; d. Havana, 2 Mar. 1939). Studied at the Madrid Conservatory and with del Campo. Settled in Havana in 1921, where he played violin in and conducted the Philharmonic Orchestra and taught in the conservatory. Employed Afro-Cuban musical materials. Composed ballets (incl. *La rebambaramba*, scenario by A. Carpentier, 1928); orch. works (incl. *3 toques*, 1931); a mystery play; *Motivos de son* for voice and 9 instruments, text by N. Guillén, 1934; a series of *Rítmicas*, some for percussion only, 1930; choral works; chamber music.

Roll. On a drum, a rapid succession of strokes produced by the alternation of two sticks, analogous to a *tremolo.

Rolle [G.]. An 18th-century term (used by D. G. Türk) for the *turn.

Rolle, Johann Heinrich (b. Quedlinburg, Germany, 23 Dec. 1716; d. Magdeburg, 29 Dec. 1785). Violist at the court of Frederick the Great in Berlin from 1741. Church organist in Magdeburg from 1746 and town music director there from 1752. Composed an opera and a *Singspiel;* Passions, oratorios, cantatas, and other sacred music, including several complete cycles for the liturgical year; harpsichord concertos; chamber music; songs.

Rollschweller [G.]. The *swell pedal of the organ.

Rolón, José (b. Ciudad Guzmán, Jalisco, Mexico, 22 June 1883; d. Mexico City, 3 Feb. 1945). Pupil of Moszkowski, N. Boulanger, and Dukas. Founded and taught in a music school in Guadalajara, 1907–27. Teacher at the National Conservatory in Mexico City, 1930–38. Composed orch. works (incl. *Zapotlán*, 1895, rev. 1925; a symphony, 1919; *El festín de los enanos*, 1925; *Cuauhtémoc*, 1929); a piano concerto, 1935; string quartets and other chamber music; piano pieces; songs.

Roman, Johan Helmich (b. Stockholm, 26 Oct. 1694; d. Haraldsmåla, near Kalmar, Sweden, 20 Nov. 1758). Pupil of Ariosti and Pepusch in London, where he played in the Italian opera orchestra at the King's Theatre. Assistant conductor at the court in Stockholm from 1721 and conductor, 1729–35 and 1737–45. Composed a Swedish Mass, motets, hymns, psalms; orch. sinfonias and suites (incl. *Drottningholms-Musiquen*); violin concertos; trio sonatas, flute sonatas, and other chamber music; keyboard pieces.

Roman Carnival, The. See *Carnaval romain, Le*.

Roman chant [L. *cantus romanus, cantilena romana*]. The liturgical chant of the Roman Catholic Church, i.e., *Gregorian chant. See also Old Roman chant.

Roman de Fauvel. An early 14th-century French literary work into one source for which some motets and monophonic songs were interpolated, including works by Philippe de Vitry.

Roman school. A term used with reference to the style of *a cappella* church music established in Rome by Palestrina (c. 1525–94) and continued, with incorporation of the polychoral elements of the *Venetian style, by a long line of strongly conservative musicians, mostly in Rome, among them G. M. Nanino (c. 1545–1607), F. Soriano (1549–1621), R. Giovannelli (1560–1625), F. Anerio (c. 1560–1614), G. Allegri (c. 1582–1652), D. Mazzocchi (1592–1665), V. Mazzocchi (1597–1646), F. Foggia (c. 1604–88), O. Benevoli (1605–72), E. Bernabei (c. 1620–87), T. Bai (c. 1660–1714), G. Pitoni (1657–1743), and A. Caldara (1670–1736). This style, known in the 17th century and later as the *stile antico* (old style), was often cultivated alongside more progressive forms of concerted sacred and secular music [see *Motu proprio*]. It was revived in the 19th century, and Pope Pius X urged its adoption as the standard of liturgical polyphony. Now also known as the Palestrina style, it is, as codified by K. Jeppesen and others, in large measure the basis for instruction in "modal" or "16th-century" counterpoint.

Romance [F., Sp.]; **Romanze** [G.]; **romanza** [It.]. (1) The Spanish *romances* are poems in four-line stanzas dealing primarily with historical or legendary subjects. Their origin can be traced to the 14th century. The *Cancionero musical de palacio* (Palace Songbook, c. 1500) contains polyphonic settings of several. To the present day, the *romance* is extensively cultivated in Spanish folk music.

(2) The French *romance* is a short strophic song of lyrical character, usually dealing with love but also with historical events.

(3) The German *Romanze* is primarily a short instrumental composition of a lyrical character (movements in Haydn's symphony *La Reine* and Mozart's Piano Concerto in D minor, K. 466; Beethoven, *Romance*, op. 40, 50; Schumann, *Albumblätter*, no. 11). In Schumann's *Drei Romanzen* op. 28, only the second is in an idyllic style, the other two being highly dramatic. Vocal *Romanzen* occur mostly in operas, a famous example being Pedrillo's "Romanza" in Mozart's *Die Entführung aus dem Serail*.

Romanesca. A bass line, widely used for

the composition of *arie per cantar* [see Aria (2)] and instrumental variations from the middle of the 16th through the early 17th centuries [Ex.]. Its prove-

nance is uncertain; extant sources indicate that musicians in both Italy and Spain played a significant role in its early history. Because singers in *arie per cantar* improvised discant tunes to the bass pattern, many different discant melodies are found in extant versions of the *romanesca*. Often associated in note-against-note fashion with this bass line, however, is a melody (usually elaborated) consisting of the pitches d' c' b♭ a d' c' b♭ a g. See also *Guárdame las vacas*.

Romanian letters. See Romanus letters.

Romantic, romanticism [F. *romantisme;* G. *Romantik;* It., Sp. *romanticismo*]. An important movement of the 19th century, continuing until c. 1910. Foreshadowed in the late works—particularly the piano sonatas—of Beethoven (1770–1827), it found its first champions in Weber (1786–1826) and Schubert (1797–1828) and its fullest realization in the works of six composers, all born within a single decade: Berlioz (1803–69), Mendelssohn (1809–47), Schumann (1810–56), Chopin (1810–49), Liszt (1811–86), and Wagner (1813–83). Berlioz, Mendelssohn, Schumann, and Chopin worked primarily from 1820 to 1850, a period often designated as early romanticism. Liszt and Wagner, who lived much longer, produced their most important works after 1850, as did Franck (1822–90), Bruckner (1824–96), Smetana (1824–84), Brahms (1833–97), Mussorgsky (1839–81), Tchaikovsky (1840–93), Dvořák (1841–1904), and Grieg (1843–1907). They represent the middle period of romanticism, from about 1850 to 1890. The last phase of this movement, known as late (or neo-) romanticism, from c. 1890 to 1910, is represented by a large number of composers born between 1850 and 1880, among them Elgar (1857–1934), Puccini (1858–1924), Mahler (1860-1911), R. Strauss (1864–1949), Sibelius (1865–1957), and Reger (1873–1916). Some romantic composers, like Grieg, Dvořák, and Albéniz, are identified especially with *nationalism in music.

The romantic movement in the arts began in literature during the second half of the 18th century; it was essentially a reaction against the intellectual, formalistic classical tradition and a call for return to simplicity and naturalism, with greater stress on human instincts and feelings than on intellect. In music, romanticism was largely a Germanic phenomenon. It was characterized by emphasis on subjective, emotional qualities and greater freedom of form. This is not to imply that nonromantic music lacks emotional appeal; nor that the romanticists were not conscious of form. Shortly after 1900 there began a reaction against romanticism gaining such impetus that antiromanticism became the most tangible element of the early modern era [see, e.g., Neoclassicism]. Nevertheless, some composers in mid-century, in America notably Barber and Hanson, espoused elements of romanticism. And the turning away from the more austere aspects of *serial music beginning in the late 1960s (e.g., by Rochberg) has also been labeled "neoromanticism" by some commentators.

In the province of musical forms, three outstanding contributions of romanticism are the *character piece for piano, the art song for voice and piano, and the *symphonic poem for orchestra. Romantic composers contributed much to the development of harmony and of orchestral colors. Finally, they did much to break down some of the barriers separating the arts. For example, their combined use of literature and music is seen in such terms as *symphonic poem* or *tone poem,* in the choice of literary subjects for program pieces, and, most clearly, in Wagner's concept of the opera as a *Gesamtkunstwerk* [see Opera]. Important devices in such music are the *leitmotiv and *transformation of themes.

Romantic Symphony. (1) Popular name for Bruckner's Symphony no. 4, in E♭ major, composed in 1874 (rev. 1878, 1880). (2) Hanson's Symphony no. 2, composed 1928–30.

Romanus letters, Romanian letters [G. *Romanus-Buchstaben*]. A system of let-

ters said to have been invented by a legendary 8th-century papal singer named Romanus and used in various neumatic manuscripts from St. Gall, Metz, and Chartres. The letters were to be used with the neumes in order to clarify details of pitch, rhythm, or performance not indicated by the neumes themselves. Only a few attained practical significance, chiefly those concerning temporal values: *c* (*celeriter,* quick), *t* (*tenere,* slow), and *m* (*mediocriter*). They play a central part in present-day discussions of Gregorian rhythm [see Gregorian chant].

Romanze [G.]. See *Romance.*

Romberg, Andreas Jakob (b. Vechta, near Münster, 27 Apr. 1767; d. Gotha, 10 Nov. 1821). Cousin of Bernhard Romberg, with whom he played in the court orchestra in Bonn, 1790–93, and made concert tours. Violinist at the Concert spirituel in Paris, 1784. Lived in Hamburg, 1801–15. Court *Kapellmeister* at Gotha, succeeding Spohr, from 1815. Composed operas; 10 symphonies (incl. a *Toy Symphony*); 23 violin concertos; choral works (incl. a setting of Schiller's *Das Lied von der Glocke*); 33 string quartets and other chamber music.

Romberg, Bernhard (b. Dinklage, 11 Nov. 1767; d. Hamburg, 13 Aug. 1841). Cousin of Andreas Jakob Romberg, with whom he played in the court orchestra in Bonn, 1790–93, and toured as a cellist. Professor of cello at the Paris Conservatory, 1801–3. Court *Kapellmeister* in Berlin, 1815–19. He also lived briefly in Vienna and traveled to Russia and England. Composed operas; 9 concertos, 3 concertinos, and other works for cello and orch.; 11 string quartets and other chamber music. Published a cello method.

Romeo and Juliet. Among the compositions based on Shakespeare's play are: (1) Dramatic symphony by Berlioz, op. 17 (1839), for solo voices, chorus, and orchestra; (2) opera by Gounod (1867); (3) symphonic poem (Fantasy Overture) by Tchaikovsky (1869, rev. 1870, 1880); (4) ballet by Prokofiev, op. 64 (1935).

Romero, Mateo (real name probably Matthieu Rosmarin; called "El Maestro Capitán") (b. Liège, 1575; d. Madrid, 10

May 1647). Singer in the royal chapel in Madrid from 1593. *Maestro de capilla* there, 1598–1633. Composed Masses, motets, and other church music; secular polyphony, incl. settings of texts by Lope de Vega.

Ronde [F.]. Whole note. See under Notes. Also, a round dance.

Rondeau. (1) An important form of medieval French poetry and music. In its simplest, 13th-century form, it consists of eight short lines, line 1 being identical with lines 4 and 7, and line 2 with line 8. Lines 1 and 2 therefore form a refrain that recurs in part in the middle and complete at the end. Music is composed for the refrain only (line 1 = a, line 2 = b) and is repeated according to the scheme A B a A a b A B (capital letters indicate the refrain). In the 14th and 15th centuries the refrain (and correspondingly the entire poem) was expanded from two lines to three (2 plus 1, *rondeau tercet*), four (2 plus 2, *quatrain*), or five (3 plus 2, *cinquain*), but the musical structure remained the same (i.e., in the five-line refrain, lines 1–3 = a, and lines 4–5 = b). The *rondeau* is one of the three **formes fixes*. Polyphonic settings, usually for voice and two instrumental parts, were composed by Adam de la Hale (*c*. 1240–87), Machaut (*c*. 1300–77) and his successors, and in the 15th century by Dufay, Binchois, Hayne van Ghizeghem, Busnois, Ockeghem, and many others. Of the *formes fixes,* the *rondeau* was the only one widely used after 1400, though the **bergerette* also enjoyed some prominence.

(2) An instrumental form of the 17th century, consisting of a reiterated *refrain (R) and different *"couplets": R A R B R C . . . R. Whether this form is an outgrowth of the medieval *rondeau* is doubtful. It is the form used most by the French clavecinists (Chambonnières, L. Couperin, D'Anglebert, F. Couperin, Rameau), as well as in contemporary orchestral and operatic music (Lully). The refrain as well as each couplet is a well-marked strain of 8 or 16 measures. Each couplet usually emphasizes a different key, e.g., the first, tonic; the second, dominant; the third, relative minor; etc. In the late 18th century, the 17th-century *rondeau* developed into the *rondo form.

Rondellus [L.]. (1) Medieval name (used by W. Odington, *c*. 1300) for a triple or duple *voice exchange. (2) Modern (or medieval?) name for a type of Latin song that is structurally similar to the medieval **rondeau.*

Rondo, rondo form, rondo-sonata form. A form frequently used in classical sonatas, symphonies, and concertos for the final movement. It developed from the *rondeau of the French clavecinists, the number of "couplets" being reduced to three, the same material used for the first and third couplets, and the middle couplet sometimes assuming the character of a development section. The following scheme results: R A R B R A' R. In this form the rondo is similar in some ways to *sonata form, inasmuch as A and A' loosely correspond to the exposition and recapitulation, and B to the development. The recurrent section is usually called the *rondo,* and the intermediate sections *episodes* or *diversions.*

The term *rondo form* is also used, particularly by British writers, for the ternary form A B A [see Binary and ternary form] and the five-part form A B A B A (or A B A C A). These are called, respectively, "first" and "second" rondo form, in distinction to the "third" rondo form discussed above.

Röntgen, Julius (b. Leipzig, 9 May 1855; d. Utrecht, 13 Sept. 1932). Pianist, conductor, and composer. Pupil of Reinecke, Hauptmann, E. F. E. Richter, and F. P. Lachner. Settled in Amsterdam in 1878. Co-founder of the Amsterdam Conservatory in 1884 and its director, 1914–24. Associate of Brahms and Grieg. Composed 3 operas; 12 symphonies and other orch. works; concertos for piano and for other instruments; choral works; much chamber music; piano pieces; organ pieces; songs.

Root. The fundamental or generating note of a triad or *chord. If the pitches of a chord are arranged as a series of superimposed thirds [see Interval], the lowest pitch is the root. A chord sounded with the root as the lowest pitch (even if the remaining pitches are not sounded as superimposed thirds) is said to be in root position. Otherwise, the chord is in *inversion. In *harmonic analysis, the root of a chord is represented by a roman numeral that designates it as a particular *scale degree in the prevailing key.

Root, George Frederick (b. Sheffield, Mass., 30 Aug. 1820; d. Bailey's Island, Maine, 6 Aug. 1895). Organist and composer. Studied in Boston and Paris. Joined the publishing firm of Root and Cady (established by his elder brother) in Chicago in 1859. Composed popular songs (incl. "Battlecry of Freedom"); numerous cantatas.

Rootham, Cyril Bradley (b. Bristol, 5 Oct. 1875; d. Cambridge, 18 Mar. 1938). Pupil of his father and of Stanford and Parratt. Organist at St. John's College, Cambridge, from 1901 until his death. Composed an opera, *The Two Sisters,* Cambridge, 1922; 2 symphonies and other orch. works; choral works (incl. *Brown Earth,* with orch., 1921); string quartets and other chamber music; piano pieces; organ pieces; songs.

Ropartz, (Joseph-) Guy (-Marie) (b. Guingamp, Côtes-du-Nord, 15 June 1864; d. Lanloup-par-Plouha, Côtes-du-Nord, 22 Nov. 1955). Pupil of Dubois, Massenet, and Franck. Director of the Nancy Conservatory, 1894–1919. Conductor of the Strasbourg Municipal Orchestra and director of the Conservatory there, 1919–29. Composed stage works (incl. the opera *Le pays,* Nancy, 1912); 5 symphonies and other orch. works, incl. several on Breton themes; works for oboe, for violin, and for cello with orch.; Masses, motets, and other sacred choral works; 5 string quartets and other chamber music; piano pieces; organ pieces; songs; pedagogic works.

Rore, Cipriano de (b. Malines or Antwerp, 1516; d. Parma, Sept. or Oct. 1565). Pupil of Willaert in Venice. Served Ercole II, Duke of Ferrara, 1547–58. *Maestro di cappella* to Duke Ottavio Farnese in Parma, 1561–62. *Maestro di cappella* at San Marco in Venice, succeeding Willaert, 1563–64. Composed Masses, motets, and other sacred music; madrigals, in which he established 5 parts as the polyphonic norm and introduced innovative chromaticism and dissonance; ricercars and fantasies for instruments.

Rorem, Ned (b. Richmond, Ind., 23 Oct. 1923). Pupil of Sowerby, B. Wagenaar, Copland, Thomson, and Honegger. Has lived in Morocco, 1949–51, Paris, 1951–57, and New York, since 1957. Composer-in-residence at the State Univ. of New York at Buffalo, 1959–61; at the Univ. of Utah, 1966–67. Has composed operas (incl. *Miss Julie,* after Strindberg, 1965; *Bertha,* libretto by Kenneth Koch, 1969); 3 symphonies and other orch. works (incl. *Air Music,* awarded the Pulitzer Prize in 1976); 3 piano concertos; choral works; chamber music; piano pieces; numerous songs and song cycles, for which he is best known, some with piano and some with instruments, on texts by Herrick, Whitman, Roethke, Moss, Koch, Plath, and others. Has published several volumes of reminiscences.

Rosalia. See under Sequence.

Rosamunde. Incidental music by Schubert, D. 797, for a play by Helmina von Chézy, produced in Vienna, 1823.

Rose. Ornamental decoration in the circular sound hole of instruments such as lutes, guitars, and early harpsichords, often serving as the maker's trademark. See Sound hole.

Roseingrave, Thomas (b. Winchester, 1690; d. Dunleary, Ireland, 23 June 1766). Studied with his father, the organist Daniel Roseingrave (1650–1727), and at Trinity College, Dublin. Traveled in Italy from 1710, where he met A. and D. Scarlatti. Returned to London *c.* 1718 and was organist of St. George's, Hanover Square, 1725–37. Returned to Dublin *c.* 1749. Composed an opera; cantatas; anthems; pieces for organ and for harpsichord; pieces for flute with thoroughbass; songs.

Rosenberg, Hilding (Constantin) (b. Bosjökloster, Sweden, 21 June 1892). Pupil of Stenhammar. Teacher at Richard Andersson's Music School in Stockholm, 1916–30. Conductor of the Royal Swedish Opera in Stockholm, 1932–34. Vice President of the Royal Music Academy in Stockholm, 1951–54. Has composed operas (incl. *Resan till America,* Stockholm, 1932; *Marionetter,* 1933, Stockholm, 1939); ballets; 6 symphonies and other orch. works; concertos for violin, for trumpet, for cello, for viola, for piano; oratorios and other choral works; 12 string quartets and other chamber music; piano pieces; organ pieces; songs; music for the theater and for films.

Rosenkavalier, Der [G., The Knight of the Rose]. Opera in three acts by R. Strauss (libretto by H. von Hofmannsthal), produced in Dresden, 1911. Setting: Vienna, mid-18th century.

Rosenmüller, Johann (b. Ölsnitz, Saxony, c. 1619; d. Wolfenbüttel, 10 Sept. 1684). Assistant master at the Thomasschule in Leipzig from 1642. Organist at the Nikolaikirche there, 1651–55. Composer at the Ospedale della pietà in Venice, 1678–82. *Kapellmeister* at the court in Wolfenbüttel from 1682. Composed *sonate da camera,* dance music, and other works for instrumental ensembles; Mass sections, cantatas, and other sacred vocal works.

Rosenthal, Manuel (Emmanuel) (b. Paris, 18 June 1904). Studied at the Paris Conservatory, where he has taught since 1962, and with Ravel and Huré. Has toured widely as a conductor. Has composed operas and operettas; ballets (incl. *Gaîté parisienne,* after Offenbach, choreography by Massine, 1938); orch. works; the oratorio *Saint-François d'Assise,* 1939, and other sacred choral works; chamber music; songs.

Rosetti, Francesco Antonio. See Rössler, Franz Anton.

Rosin, resin. A preparation made from gum of turpentine that is applied to the hair of the violin bow in order to give it the necessary grip on the strings.

Rosseter, Philip (b. 1568?; d. London, 5 May 1623). Lutenist and composer. Member of the Chapel Royal from 1604. Associate of Campion. Composed ayres with lute accompaniment; consort lessons.

Rossi, Luigi (Aloysius de Rubeis) (b. Torremaggiore, Foggia, Italy, 1598; d. Rome, 19 Feb. 1653). Singer, organist, and composer. Pupil of Macque. Organist at San Luigi dei Francesi in Rome, 1633. Musician to the Medici in Florence, 1635; to the Barberini in Rome

from 1641 and to them at the French court from 1646. Composed operas (incl. *Il palazzo incantato,* Rome, 1642; *Orfeo,* Paris, 1647); oratorios; numerous cantatas; motets; arias and duets.

Rossi, Michelangelo (b. Genoa, c. 1602; d. Rome, 7 July 1656). Organist, violinist, and composer. Pupil of Frescobaldi. Served Cardinal Maurizio di Savoia in Rome from 1624. In service to the Duke of Modena in 1638. Composed operas (incl. *Erminia sul Giordano,* Rome, 1633); toccatas and other pieces for organ or harpsichord.

Rossi, Salomone (Salamone, called "Ebreo," Jew) (b. Mantua, 1570; d. there, c. 1630). Violinist and composer. Served at the court in Mantua, c. 1587–1628. Composed music for the stage; madrigals, some with thoroughbass (1602), and other secular vocal music; music for the synagogue; canticles, psalms, hymns, and *laude;* trio sonatas, among the earliest such pieces, publ. in his *Sinfonie e gagliarde,* 1607.

Rossignol, Le. See *Nightingale, The.*

Rossini, Gioacchino (Antonio) (b. Pesaro, 29 Feb. 1792; d. Passy, near Paris, 13 Nov. 1868). Studied singing, cello, and counterpoint with various teachers in Bologna, entering the Liceo communale there in 1807. In 1810 he left Bologna to fulfill a commission in Venice, and in the years following composed operas for Venice, Milan, and Rome. From 1815 until 1823, he was under contract to the impresario Barbaja to produce an opera each year for each of two theaters in Naples. After visits to Vienna in 1822 and London in 1823–24, he settled in Paris, first as director of the Théâtre-Italien and then as composer to the King. This stay culminated in the production of *Guillaume Tell,* after which he composed no further operas. Lived in Bologna, 1836–48; in Florence, 1848–55; in Paris, 1855 until his death. Composed operas (incl. *La cambiale di matrimonio,* Venice, 1810; *L'inganno felice,* Venice, 1812; *Tancredi,* Venice, 1813; *L'*italiana in Algeri; Il *barbiere di Siviglia; Otello,* Naples, 1816; *La *Cenerentola; La gazza ladra,* Milan, 1817; *Mosè in Egitto,* Naples, 1818; *La donna del lago,* Naples, 1819; *Semiramide; Le siège de

Corinthe, a revision of *Maometto II,* Paris, 1826; *Moïse,* a revision of *Mosè in Egitto,* Paris, 1827; *Le Comte Ory,* Paris, 1828; **Guillaume Tell*); a *Stabat Mater,* 1842, a *Petite Messe solennelle,* 1863, and other sacred works; cantatas; orch. works; string quartets and other chamber music; piano pieces; numerous songs and arias.

Rössler, Franz Anton (František Antonín Rösler, also known as Francesco Antonio Rosetti) (b. Niemeš, Bohemia, *c.* 1750; d. Schwerin, Germany, 30 June 1792). Double-bass player and composer. Player in the orchestra of Prince Öttingen-Wallenstein from 1773 and his *Kapellmeister* from 1785. *Kapellmeister* to the Duke of Mecklenburg-Schwerin from 1789. Composed operas; oratorios; Requiems and other sacred vocal works; about 90 symphonies and other orch. works; concertos for various instruments; string quartets and other chamber music; keyboard pieces.

Rota [L.]. (1) Medieval name for a **round,* particularly **"Sumer is icumen in."* (2) See Rotta (1).

Rotta, rotte, rota. (1) A medieval instrument mentioned in numerous literary sources (8th to 14th cent.). Most likely it was a **psaltery.* Possibly the name is a variant of *cruit* [see Crwth]. For ill. see under Lyra. (2) In 14th-century Italian dances, the *rotta* is an after-dance that is a rhythmic variant of the main dance.

Roulade [F.]. A vocal melisma or a highly ornamented melody.

Round. Common name for a circle **canon,* i.e., a canon in which each singer returns from the conclusion of the melody to its beginning, repeating it *ad libitum.* See also Catch.

Roundelay. A 14th-century anglicization of the French term *rondelet,* i.e., **rondeau* (1).

Rousseau, Jean-Jacques (b. Geneva, 28 June 1712; d. Ermenonville, near Paris, 2 July 1778). Philosopher and composer. An active participant in musical disputes, particularly the **"War of the Buffoons."* Composed operas (incl. *Le devin du village,* Fontainebleau, 1752); the melodrama *Pygmalion,* 1762; arias,

romances; duets; some instrumental works. His writings on music incl. *Dissertation sur la musique moderne,* 1743; articles on music in the *Encyclopédie,* revised and published as the *Dictionnaire de musique,* 1767; *Lettre à M. Grimm,* 1752; *Lettre sur la musique française,* 1753.

Roussel, Albert (Charles Paul Marie) (b. Turcoing, Département du Nord, France, 5 Apr. 1869; d. Royan, 23 Aug. 1937). French naval officer in the Orient and elsewhere until 1894, after which he studied with Gigout and d'Indy. Teacher at the Schola cantorum, 1902–14. His pupils incl. Le Flem, Satie, Varèse, and Martinů. Composed operas (incl. the opera-ballet *Padmâvâtî,* 1914–18, prod. Paris, 1923); ballets (incl. *Le festin de l'araignée,* 1912; *Bacchus et Ariane,* 1930; *Aenéas,* 1935); 4 symphonies and other orch. works (incl. *Suite en fa,* 1926; *Pour une fête de printemps,* 1920); a piano concerto, 1927, and a concertino for cello, 1936; choral works (incl. *Évocations,* with soloists and orch., 1910–12); chamber music; piano pieces; songs.

Rovescio [It.]. Retrograde motion or inversion. For example, the "Menuetto al rovescio" in Haydn's Sonata no. 4 for piano and violin (identical to the 3rd movt. of his Symphony no. 47 ["al roverso"] and also used in his Piano Sonata no. 26, Breitkopf and Härtel edition) is to be played backward, in **retrograde* motion. That in Mozart's Serenade K. 388 uses imitation in the inversion.

Row. Tone row. See Serial music.

Rowley, Alec (b. London, 13 Mar. 1892; d. Weybridge, Surrey, 12 Jan. 1958). Organist, pianist, and composer. Pupil of Corder. Teacher at Trinity College of Music from 1920. Composed a pantomime; orch. works; 2 piano concertos and an oboe concerto; choral works; chamber music; piano pieces, incl. some for children; organ pieces; songs.

Rózsa, Miklós (b. Budapest, 18 Apr. 1907). Studied at the Leipzig Conservatory. Lived in Paris from 1932; in London from 1935; in Hollywood from 1940, where he composed for films until 1962. Teacher at the Univ. of Southern California, 1945–65. Has composed the ballet *Hungaria*, 1935; a symphony and other orch. works; concertos for violin, for piano, for cello; choral works; chamber music; piano pieces; songs; music for films (incl. *Ben Hur*).

Rózycki, Ludomir (b. Warsaw, 6 Nov. 1884; d. Katowice, 1 Jan. 1953). Pupil of Noskowski and Humperdinck. Teacher at the Lvov Conservatory (and conductor of the Lvov opera), 1908–12; at the Warsaw Music Academy from 1930; at the Katowice Music Academy from 1945. Lived in Berlin, 1914–20. Composed operas (incl. *Eros und Psyche*, Breslau, 1917; *Casanova*, Warsaw, 1923); ballets (incl. *Pan Twardowski*, Warsaw, 1921); symphonic poems and other orch. works; concertos for piano and for violin; choral works; chamber music; piano pieces; songs.

Rubato [It.]. (1) An elastic, flexible tempo allowing slight accelerandos and ritardandos according to the requirements of musical expression. Two types can be distinguished, one that affects the melody only and another that affects the whole musical texture. (2) About 1800 the term *rubato* was used to indicate modifications of dynamics rather than tempo, e.g., accents on normally weak beats, such as the second and fourth in a 4/4 measure.

Rubbra, (Charles) Edmund (b. Northampton, England, 23 May 1901). Pianist and composer. Pupil of Holst, Vaughan Williams, R. O. Morris, C. Scott. Teacher at Oxford Univ., 1947–68. Has composed an opera; 10 symphonies and other orch. works; works for viola, for cello, and for piano with orch.; sacred and secular choral works; 3 string quartets, a piano trio, and other chamber music; piano pieces; songs.

Rubeba, rubible. See Rabāb.

Rubinstein, Anton Grigorievich (b. Vykhvatinetz, Podolia, 28 Nov. 1829; d. Peterhof, near St. Petersburg, 20 Nov. 1894). Brother of Nicholas Rubinstein (1834–81), a pianist and conductor who directed the Moscow Conservatory from 1866 until his death. Toured Europe and the U.S. as a pianist. Court pianist at St. Petersburg from 1858. Founder, 1862,

and director, 1862–67 and 1887–91, of the Imperial Conservatory in St. Petersburg. Composed 19 operas (incl. *The Demon*, St. Petersburg, 1875); 6 symphonies and other orch. works; 5 piano concertos and other works for piano and orch.; concertos for violin and for cello; choral works; 10 string quartets, 5 piano trios, and other chamber music; numerous piano pieces; numerous songs.

Rückpositiv [G.]. A division of an organ separated from the main portion of the instrument and usually located on the gallery railing at the organist's back. It was almost always played from the lowest keyboard of the main console, although in some organs of the 16th century it had its own keyboard, requiring the organist to turn completely around in order to play it. Other names for it are *positif* [F.], *Rugwerk* [D.], and *chaire* or *chair* [Eng.]. It was very common in German, Dutch, French, and English organs up to the early 19th century and is now being revived in England and America. Also see Positive organ; Organ.

Rudhyar, Dane (real name Daniel Chennevière) (b. Paris, 23 Mar. 1895). Student of theosophy and astrology. Largely self-taught as a composer. Emigrated to the U.S. in 1916. Works incl. the dance poems *Poèmes ironiques* and *Vision végétale*, performed in New York, 1917; *To the Real*, 1920–28, and *Soul Fire*, 1922, for orch.; chamber music; piano pieces (incl. *4 Pentagrams*, 1924–26; *Paeans*, 1927; *Granites*, 1932). He is also a painter and has written numerous books, incl. one on Debussy, and articles.

Rue, Pierre de la. See La Rue, Pierre de.

Ruffo, Vincenzo (b. Verona, *c.* 1510; d. Sacile, Udine, 9 Feb. 1587). *Maestro di cappella* at the Verona Cathedral from 1554; at the Milan Cathedral, 1563–72; at the Pistoia Cathedral, 1573–77; at the Sacile Cathedral, 1580. Composed Masses, motets, Magnificats, and other sacred music; madrigals; instrumental pieces.

Ruggiero. A bass line of Italian provenance, popular from the mid-16th through the early 17th centuries [see

Ex.]. A singer usually improvised a discant tune to the harmonic pattern represented by the bass. Many such melodies survive, as well as many instrumental settings of the *ruggiero.*

Ruggles, Carl (Charles Sprague) (b. Marion, Mass., 11 Mar. 1876; d. Bennington, Vt., 24 Oct. 1971). Painter and composer. Pupil of Paine. Friend of Ives in later life. Founder in 1912 and conductor until 1917 of the Winona Symphony Orchestra in Minneapolis, living thereafter in Arlington, Vt., and New York. He destroyed his early works, incl. the opera *The Sunken Bell.* Surviving works are *Toys* for voice and piano, 1919; *Men and Angels* for brass, 1920, rev. 1939; *Men and Mountains* for orch., 1921–24; *Portals* for strings, 1925–26; *The Sun-Treader* for orch., 1927–32; *Evocations* for piano, 1937–43; *Organum* for orch., 1945–49; *Exaltation,* a hymn, 1958.

Rührtrommel [G.]. Tenor drum; see Percussion instruments II, 2.

Ruinen von Athen, Die [G., The Ruins of Athens]. Incidental music by Beethoven, op. 113, for a play by Kotzebue, produced in Budapest, 1812. It contains an overture and a Turkish march (the latter adapted from a Theme with Variations for piano, op. 76, composed 1809).

Russian Bassoon. See under Cornett.

Russian Quartets. (1) Haydn's String Quartets op. 33. See *Scherzi, Gli.* (2) *Rasumovsky Quartets.

Russlan and Ludmilla [Rus. *Ruslan i Lyudmila*]. Opera in five acts by Glinka (libretto by V. F. Shirkov and V. A. Bakhturin, based on a poem by Pushkin), produced in St. Petersburg, 1842. Setting: Russia, legendary times.

Russolo, Luigi (b. Portogruaro, Italy, 1 May 1885; d. Cerro, 4 Feb. 1947). Painter and composer. Associate of Marinetti in the futurist movement. Invented and gave performances with various kinds of noisemakers (*intonarumori*). [See Futurism.] Works incl. *Convegno d'aeroplani e d'automobili,* London, 1914. Published a book, *L'arte dei rumori,* 1913 (trans. as *The Art of Noise,* 1967), and other writings on related topics.

Rust, Friedrich Wilhelm (b. Wörlitz, near Dessau, 6 July 1739; d. Dessau, 28 Feb. 1796). Violinist and composer. Pupil of K. P. E. Bach. Court music director to Prince Leopold III of Anhalt-Dessau from 1775 until his death. Composed stage works; cantatas; numerous sonatas and other pieces for piano; instrumental pieces; songs. His grandson Wilhelm Rust (1822–92) was also a violinist and composer, cantor of the Thomasschule in Leipzig, and an editor of volumes of Bach's works in the Bach-Gesellschaft edition.

Rute [G.]. A kind of birch brush called for by R. Strauss and others to obtain a special effect on the bass drum.

Rutini, Giovanni Maria Placido (b. Florence, 25 Apr. 1723; d. there, 22 Dec. 1797). Pupil of Padre Martini. *Maestro al cembalo* at Prague in 1748; at St. Petersburg, 1758–62. In the service of the Duke of Modena, 1766–74; of the Grand Duke of Florence from 1774. Composed about 20 operas; sacred vocal works; cantatas; chamber music; harpsichord sonatas, in which he has been regarded by some as an important forerunner of Mozart.

Ruyneman, Daniel (b. Amsterdam, 8 Aug. 1886; d. there, 25 July 1963). Studied at the Amsterdam Conservatory. Worked with Javanese instruments and textless choral sounds. Composed operas; *Symphony 1953* and other orch. works; concertos for piano, for violin; *Sonata for Choir,* without text, 1931; chamber music (incl. *Hieroglyphs* for 3 flutes, 2 mandolins, 2 guitars, celesta, cup bells or vibraphone, piano, 1918); piano pieces; songs to Dutch and Chinese texts.

Rzewski, Frederic (Anthony) (b. Westfield, Mass., 13 Apr. 1938). Pianist and composer. Pupil of R. Thompson and

Spies. Co-founder of the Musica elettronica viva studio in Rome, where he lived until moving to New York in 1971. Works incl. piano pieces; *Composition for 2* for any 2 instruments, 1964; *Self-portrait* for one person, any sounds, 1964; *Nature morte* for chamber ensemble, 1965; *Zoologischer Garten* on tape,

1965; *Spacecraft* for improvising group, 1965; *Portrait* for actor, lights, projections, tapes, 1967; *Coming Together* and *Attica* for narrator and instruments, 1972; *The People United Will Never Be Defeated* for piano, 1975; *Song and Dance* for flute, bass clarinet, double bass, and vibraphone, 1978.

S

S. (1) Abbr. for *segno*, *sinistra*, *subito*. (2) In liturgical books, abbr. for *schola*, i.e., choir. (3) In harmonic analysis, abbr. for *subdominant*. (4) In 16th-century *partbooks, abbr. for *superius*. (5) Abbr. for W. Schmieder's catalog of Bach's works; see *BWV*.

Saccadé [F.]. Abrupt, jerky.

Sacchini, Antonio Maria Gasparo Gioacchino (b. Florence, 14 June 1730; d. Paris, 6 Oct. 1786). Pupil of Durante. Choirmaster from 1768 and director, 1770–72, succeeding Traetta, of the Conservatorio dell' ospedaletto in Venice. Produced operas in London, 1772–82, and in Paris from 1782. Composed operas (incl. *Semiramide*, Rome, 1763; *Dardanus*, Versailles, 1786; *Oedipe à Colonne*, Versailles, 1786); Masses and other sacred works; oratorios; cantatas; symphonies; chamber music; harpsichord sonatas.

Sackbut, sagbut, saqueboute, sacabuche. Names for the medieval *trombone.

Sackgeige [G.]. *Kit.

Sackpfeife [G.]. *Bagpipe.

Sacre du printemps, Le [F., The Rite of Spring]. Ballet by Stravinsky (choreography by Vaslav Nijinsky), produced in Paris, 1913.

Saeta [Sp.]. An Andalusian folksong sung during Lent or the Feast of the Nativity to accompany street processions and other outdoor devotional or penitential activities.

Saeverud, Harald (Sigurd Johan) (b. Bergen, Norway, 17 Apr. 1897). Critic, composer, and conductor. Studied in Bergen and Berlin. Has composed a ballet; incidental music to Ibsen's *Peer Gynt;* 9 symphonies (no. 7 with chorus) and other orch. works; concertos for cello, for oboe, for bassoon, for piano, for violin; a string quartet and other chamber music; piano pieces, incl. some modeled on Norwegian folk dances.

Sainete [Sp.]. A type of Spanish comedy originating in the late 18th century, portraying scenes from everyday life and sometimes set to music or including a few musical numbers.

St. Anne's Fugue. Popular name for Bach's organ fugue in E♭, from the *Clavier-Übung* III (1739), so called because its theme is similar to the beginning of an English hymn tune called "St. Anne" (usually sung to the verses beginning "O God, our help in ages past").

Saint-Georges, Joseph Boulogne (b. Guadeloupe, *c*. 1739; d. Paris, 9 or 10 June 1799). Violinist and composer. Perhaps a pupil of Leclair and Gossec. Composed an opera; symphonies; violin concertos and a *symphonie concertante* for 2 violins and orch.; string quartets and other chamber music, incl. violin sonatas with thoroughbass; keyboard pieces.

St. John Passion. See under Passion music.

St. Martial, school of. The attribution generally given to a diverse repertory produced both in and around the Abbey of St. Martial in Limoges from the 10th through the 12th centuries. This repertory includes *tropes, *sequences, monophonic songs called *versus, and polyphony. The latter includes examples of melismatic *organum that are important antecedents of the *Notre Dame repertory, as well as later works that closely parallel some developments at Notre Dame.

St. Matthew Passion. See under Passion music.

St. Paul. Oratorio by Mendelssohn, op. 36, produced in Düsseldorf, 1836.

Saint-Saëns, (Charles-) Camille (b. Paris, 9 Oct. 1835; d. Algiers, 16 Dec. 1921). Conductor, organist, pianist, writer, and composer. Pupil of Halévy. Was a child prodigy as a pianist. Organist at Saint-Merry in Paris, 1853–57; at the Madeleine, 1858–77. Teacher at the École Niedermeyer, 1861–65. His pupils incl. Messager, Fauré, and Gigout. Composed operas (incl. La princesse jaune, Paris, 1872; *Samson et Dalila; Henry VIII, Paris, 1883; Ascanio, Paris, 1890; Phyrné, Paris, 1893); incidental music for plays; a ballet; 3 symphonies (no. 3 with organ, 1886), symphonic poems (incl. Le rouet d'Omphale, 1871; Phaëton, 1873; *Danse macabre; La jeunesse d'Hercule, 1877), and other orch. works (incl. Le *carnaval des animaux); numerous works for solo instrument with orch. (incl. concertos for piano [5], for cello [2], for violin [3]; Introduction et rondo capriccioso for violin and orch., 1870; Africa for piano and orch., 1891; Caprice andalou for violin and orch., 1904); sacred and secular choral works; 2 string quartets, 2 piano trios, and other chamber music (incl. Havanaise for violin and piano, 2 violin sonatas, and 2 cello sonatas); piano pieces; organ pieces; numerous songs.

Saite [G.]. String. Saitenchor, *course of strings. Saiteninstrument, stringed instrument.

Salieri, Antonio (b. Legnago, near Verona, 18 Aug. 1750; d. Vienna, 7 May 1825). Pupil of Pescetti and Gassmann; later received advice and assistance from Gluck. Succeeded Gassmann as court composer in Vienna in 1774. Court Kapellmeister there, 1788–1824. His pupils incl. Beethoven, Schubert, and Liszt. Composed about 40 operas in Italian, French, and German (incl. Les Danaïdes, Paris, 1784; La grotta di Trofonio, Vienna, 1785; Tarare, Paris, 1787); oratorios; cantatas; Masses and other sacred works; symphonies; concertos; chamber music; harpsichord sonatas.

Salmanov, Vadim Nikolaievich (b. St. Petersburg, 4 Nov. 1912). Pupil of Akimenko, Gnessin, and Shostakovich. Teacher at the Leningrad Conservatory from 1952, succeeding Shostakovich. Has composed a ballet; 3 symphonies and other orch. works; concertos for piano, for violin; an oratorio and other choral works; chamber music; piano pieces; music for films.

Salmo [It., Sp.]. *Psalm, psalm composition.

Salome. Opera in one act by R. Strauss (libretto by H. Lachmann, translated from Oscar Wilde's play), produced in Dresden, 1905. Setting: Terrace of Herod's palace, Galilee, about A.D. 30.

Salomon Symphonies. Haydn's last twelve symphonies, nos. 93 to 104, written 1791–95 in London for the concerts managed by Johann Peter Salomon. They are also known as *London Symphonies, although the name London Symphony specifically applies to no. 104 (also sometimes called the Salomon Symphony). Included in this group are the *Surprise (no. 94), *Military (no. 100), *Clock (no. 101), and *Drum-Roll (no. 103). The numbering of the complete series of Haydn's symphonies is not in agreement with the numbering within this group; nos. 94 and 104 of the complete series are nos. 3 and 7 (rather than 2 and 12) of the Salomon Symphonies.

Salón México, El. Descriptive piece for orchestra by Copland, composed 1933–36, inspired by the composer's visit to Mexico in 1932. It uses several popular Mexican melodies such as might be heard in a dance hall (El salón México).

Saltarello. A gay, sprightly dance of Italian provenance. Four pieces bearing this name survive from the 14th century, all in the form of the *estampie and with varying meters. In the 15th century [F. *pas de breban* (Brabant); Sp. *alta danza*], one of the faster measures (*misura*) or step units of the *bassadanza* (**basse danse*). In the 16th century [F. *sauterelle, tordion, tourdion;* G. *Hupfauf, *Proportz, Sprung, *Nachtanz*], the music of the *saltarello* is indistinguishable from that of the **galliard*. The difference between the two is in the style of dancing as suggested by their respective names: *saltarello*, a small leap; galliard, vigorous. A galliard or a *saltarello* is usually coupled either with a **pavane* or a **passamezzo*, and the coupled dances are composed on the same musical material (harmonic patterns and melodies). The *saltarello* continued in vogue until late in the 19th century. Indeed, its basic steps are still used in folk dances.

Saltato, saltando [It.]. Same as *sautillé* [see Bowing (d)].

Salterio [It., Sp.]. **Psaltery, *dulcimer.

Salve Regina [L., Hail, Queen]. One of the Marian antiphons [see Antiphon (2)].

Salzedo, Carlos (b. Arcachon, France, 6 Apr. 1885; d. Waterville, Maine, 17 Aug. 1961). Studied at the conservatories in Bordeaux and Paris. Traveled widely as a concert harpist. Settled in New York in 1909. Associate of Varèse. First harpist at the Metropolitan Opera in New York, 1909–13. Teacher at the Juilliard School; at the Curtis Institute from 1924. Composed works for harp with orch., harp ensembles, harp with other instruments, and harp solo. Wrote a harp method and developed various novel sonorities on the harp.

Salzman, Eric (b. New York, 8 Sept. 1933). Pupil of Luening, Ussachevsky, Beeson, Sessions, Babbitt, and Petrassi. Music critic for *The New York Times,* 1958–62; for the *New York Herald Tribune,* 1962–66. Music director for WBAI-FM in New York, 1962–63 and 1968–71. Artistic director of Quog Music Theatre in New York from 1970. Has worked with a variety of electronic techniques and elements of theater. Works incl. *Voices,* an "a cappella" radio opera, 1971; *Inventions for Orchestra,* 1958; *Foxes and Hedgehogs* for voices, instruments, and sound systems, 1967; *Queens*

Collage, 1966, on tape; *The Nude Paper Sermon* for actor, Renaissance instruments, chorus, electronic equipment, 1969; the "pageant" *Noah,* composed with M. Sahl, 1978. Has published *Twentieth-Century Music: An Introduction,* 1967, 1974.

Samazeuilh, Gustave (Marie Victor Fernand) (b. Bordeaux, 2 June 1877; d. Paris, 4 Aug. 1967). Critic and composer. Pupil of Chausson, d'Indy, and Dukas. Associate of R. Strauss. Composed orch. works (incl. *Étude symphonique,* 1907; *L'appel de la danse,* 1946); choral works with orch.; chamber music; piano pieces; songs. Published numerous writings on music, incl. a book on Dukas and a book of reminiscences.

Saminsky, Lazare (b. Vale-Hotzulovo, near Odessa, 8 Nov. 1882; d. Port Chester, N.Y., 30 June 1959). Conductor, writer, and composer. Pupil of Rimsky-Korsakov and Liadov. Settled in the U.S. in 1920. Music director of Temple Emanu-El in New York, 1924–58. Made extensive use of Jewish materials. Composed operas (incl. *The Vision of Ariel,* 1916; *The Gagliarda of a Merry Plague,* New York, 1925; *The Defeat of Caesar Julian,* 1933–38); ballets (incl. *The Lament of Rachel,* 1913, rev. 1920); 5 symphonies and other orch. works; synagogue services; choral works; piano pieces; songs.

Samisen. Shamisen. See Lute.

Sammartini, Giovanni Battista (San Martini) (b. Milan, 1700 or 1701; d. there, 15 Jan. 1775). Organist and composer. Brother of Giuseppe Sammartini. *Maestro di cappella* for several Milanese congregations from 1728. Teacher of Gluck. Composed 3 operas; 77 symphonies, of which he was an early exponent; *concerti grossi;* church music; cantatas; much chamber music; harpsichord sonatas.

Sammartini, Giuseppe (San Martini) (b. Milan, *c.* 1693; d. London, before 24 June 1751). Brother of Giovanni Battista Sammartini. Settled in London in 1727, where he was oboist at the King's Theatre and later director of chamber concerts to the Prince of Wales. Composed masques and other stage works; *concerti* *grossi* and solo concertos; vocal works; trio sonatas, violin sonatas, and other chamber music.

Samson et Dalila [F., Samson and Delilah]. Opera in three acts by Saint-Saëns (libretto by F. Lemaire, based on the Bible), produced in Weimar, 1877. Setting: Gaza, Palestine, 1150 B.C.

Sánchez de Fuentes, Eduardo (b. Havana, 3 Apr. 1874; d. there, 7 Sept. 1944). Pupil of Cervantes. Composed operas (incl. *Dolorosa*, Havana, 1910; *Kabelia*, Havana, 1942); orch. works; choral works; chamber music; piano pieces; songs (incl. "Tú"). Also collected and wrote about Cuban folksongs.

Sanctorale [L.]. In the Roman rite, generic name for the feasts of the Saints, as opposed to the *Temporale, the feasts of the Lord. See Gregorian chant; Proper.

Sanctus [L.]. The fourth item of the Ordinary of the *Mass. The text consists of three sections, the Sanctus, the Pleni sunt caeli, and the Benedictus. Polyphonic compositions usually fall into three corresponding sections, or at least two, Sanctus and Benedictus.

Sanders, Robert L. (b. Chicago, 2 July 1906; d. Delray Beach, Fla., 26 Dec. 1974). Conductor, organist, and composer. Studied in Chicago, in Rome with Respighi, and in Paris. Dean of the School of Music at Indiana Univ. from 1938; teacher at Brooklyn College, 1947–73. Composed music for dance (incl. *L'Ag'ya*, 1944); *Little Symphony* nos. 1 and 2 and other orch. works; band works; choral works; chamber music; piano pieces; organ pieces; songs.

Sanft [G.]. Soft, gentle.

Santa Cruz (Wilson), Domingo (b. La Cruz, Chile, 5 July 1899). Pupil of Soro and del Campo. Teacher at the National Conservatory in Santiago, 1928–53. Has played a leading role in the development of musical institutions and culture in Chile. Has composed 4 symphonies and other orch. works (incl. *5 piezas* for strings, 1937); *Cantata de los ríos de Chile* for chorus and orch., 1941, and other choral works; 3 string quartets and other chamber music; piano pieces; numerous songs.

Santa María, Tomás de (b. Madrid, between 1510 and 1520; d. Valladolid, 1570). Organist at the Convent of San Pablo in Valladolid. Published a *Libro llamado Arte de tañer fantasia assi para tecla como para vihuela*, 1565, a treatise on playing fantasies on the keyboard or vihuela, containing original works for keyboard.

Santoro, Claudio (b. Manaos, Brazil, 23 Nov. 1919). Violinist and composer. Pupil of Koellreutter and N. Boulanger. Made use of twelve-tone techniques, but has abandoned these. Has held various teaching and governmental posts in Brazil. Teacher at the Heidelberg-Mannheim Music Academy from 1970. Has composed a marionette opera; ballets; 8 symphonies and other orch. works (incl. *Brasiliana*, 1954); 3 piano concertos and 2 violin concertos; *Ode à Stalingrado*, 1947, and other choral works; 6 string quartets and other chamber music; piano pieces; numerous songs; numerous scores for radio, television, and films.

Saraband [F. *sarabande;* Sp. *zarabanda*]. A 17th- and 18th-century dance in slow triple meter and dignified style, usually without upbeat, frequently with an accent or prolonged tone on the second beat and with feminine endings of the phrases. It is a standard dance of the *suite. The saraband probably came from Mexico, and it appeared in Spain in the early 16th century. Originally it was evidently a wild and even lascivious love dance, for it is described and severely attacked as such by various writers, among them Cervantes.

Sārangī. See under Violin; see ill. under Violin family.

Sarasate, Pablo de (Pablo Martín Melitón Sarasate y Navascuez) (b. Pamplona, 10 Mar. 1844; d. Biarritz, 20 Sept. 1908). Violin virtuoso and composer. Studied at the Paris Conservatory. Composed works for violin and orch. (incl. *Zigeunerweisen*); jotas and other dances for violin and piano; fantasies on operas, incl. *Carmen*.

Sardana. The national dance of Catalonia, usually in quick 6/8 meter and danced in a circle to the accompaniment of the *pipe and tabor.

Saron. See *Gambang.* For ill. see under Percussion instruments.

Sarro, Domenico Natale (Sarri) (b. Trani, Naples, 24 Dec. 1679; d. Naples, 21 Jan. 1744). Vice *maestro* of the Cappella reale in Naples from 1725 and *maestro,* 1737–44. Composed numerous operas (incl. *Didone abbandonata,* Naples, 1724, the first setting of Metastasio's libretto); oratorios; cantatas; sacred music; instrumental pieces.

Sarrusophone. See Oboe family II (f).

Sarti, Giuseppe (b. Faenza, bapt. 1 Dec. 1729; d. Berlin, 28 July 1802). Said to have been a pupil of Padre Martini. Conductor at the court in Copenhagen, 1755 –65 and 1770–75. Director of the Conservatorio dell' ospedaletto in Venice, 1775 –79. *Maestro di cappella* of the Milan Cathedral from 1778. Court musician to Catherine the Great in St. Petersburg, succeeding Paisiello, from 1784, and later to Prince Potemkin and Emperor Paul. Composed operas (incl. *Giulio Sabino,* Venice, 1781; *Fra due litiganti il terzo gode,* Milan, 1782); oratorios; cantatas; Masses, motets, and other sacred music; symphonies; violin sonatas; harpsichord sonatas.

Sarum use. The ritual used in the Cathedral of Salisbury, England, which differed in certain details from the Roman liturgy. It prevailed during the later Middle Ages throughout much of England, until it was abolished by decree in 1547.

Sassofono [It.]. *Saxophone.

Satie, Erik (-Alfred-Leslie) (b. Honfleur, near Le Havre, 17 May 1866; d. Paris, 1 July 1925). Studied at the Paris Conservatory and with Guilmant, and beginning in 1905, after intermittent work as a cabaret pianist, earned a degree in counterpoint at the Schola cantorum under d'Indy and Roussel. A Rosicrucian in the 1890s and a close associate at various times of Debussy, Ravel, Cocteau, and prominent members of the artistic world. His unconventional music and attitudes influenced a number of composers, including the *"École d'Arcueil," "Les *six," and, according to Cocteau and Satie himself, Debussy and Ravel. Composed ballets (incl. *Parade,* in collaboration with Cocteau, for the Ballets Russes, choreography by Leonide Massine, Paris, 1917; *Mercure,* with Picasso and Massine, Paris, 1924; *Relâche,* Paris, 1924); other stage works (incl. the comedy *Le piège de Méduse,* Paris, 1913); *Socrate,* a symphonic drama for 4 sopranos and small orch., 1919; works for voice(s) with piano; numerous piano pieces (incl. *3 sarabandes,* 1887; *3 gymnopédies,* 1888, nos. 1 and 3 orchestrated by Debussy; *3 gnossiennes,* 1890; *3 Préludes* from *Le fils des étoiles,* 1891, for the play by Péladan; *3 morceaux en forme de poire* for piano four-hands, 1893; *En habit de cheval* for piano four-hands, 1911; *Sports et divertissements,* 1914).

Satz [G.]. (1) Movement (of a sonata, symphony, etc.); e.g., *erster Satz,* first movement. *Hauptsatz* and *Seitensatz* (*Nebensatz*) denote the first and second theme, respectively, within a movement. (2) Style, manner of writing; e.g., *strenger (freier) Satz,* strict (free) style.

Sauguet, Henri (real name Henri-Pierre Poupard) (b. Bordeaux, 18 May 1901). Pupil of Canteloube and Koechlin. Associate of Satie and member of the *"École d'Arcueil." Composed operas (incl. *Le plumet du colonel,* Paris, 1924; *La chartreuse de Parme,* Paris, 1939; *La gageuse imprévue,* Paris, 1944); 25 ballets (incl. *La chatte,* for Sergei Diaghilev, choreography by George Balanchine, 1927); orch. works; 3 piano concertos and works for violin and for cello with orch.; choral works; string quartets and other chamber music; piano pieces; songs; *musique concrète;* much music for films and radio.

Saul. Oratorio by Handel, produced in London, 1739.

Sauterelle [F.]. See *Saltarello.*

Sautillé [F.]. See Bowing (d).

Saxhorn. See Brass instruments II (f).

Saxophone [G. *Saxophon;* It. *sassofono;* Sp. *saxófono*]. A family of hybrid instruments invented by Adolphe Sax of Brussels *c.* 1840 (patented 1846). They are played with a single beating reed, as are the clarinets, but are conical in bore, as are the oboes. Their key arrangement also resembles that of the oboes, but

Scala [It.]. *Scale.

Scala enigmatica. An "enigmatic" scale, c db e f♯ g♯ a♯ b c', used by Verdi in his "Ave Maria" (1898).

Scale [F. *gamme;* G. *Skala, Tonleiter;* It. *scala, gamma;* Sp. *escala, gama*]. The underlying tonal material of some particular music, arranged in an order of rising pitches. Since the tonal material varies greatly in different periods as well as in different cultures, there are numerous scales. The basic scale of European art music is the *diatonic scale*. It consists of five whole tones (t) and two semitones (s) in the following arrangement: t t s t t t s (e.g., c d e f g a b c'). This scale is usually referred to as a *major scale* (in this illustration, the C major scale) as distinguished from the pure *minor scale*, in which the arrangement of intervals is t s t t s t t (e.g., c d eb f g ab bb c'). Other forms of the minor scale are illustrated in the accompanying table and described under Major, minor. Both major and minor scales may be transposed to start on any one of the twelve *pitch classes. Thus there are twelve major scales and twelve minor scales, one in each *key. The *chromatic scale* consists of all twelve pitches in any octave [see Interval; Octave equivalence] and so contains only semitones. The diatonic scale is thus a selection of the pitches of the chromatic scale. Numerous selections other than major and minor are possible and occasionally have been employed, particularly the *whole-tone scale*, the so-called *gypsy scale*, and the *pentatonic scale*, as illustrated in the accompanying table. These three scales, like the major and minor scales, may be transposed to start on any pitch, but in the whole-tone scale, only two different pitch collections are possible, regardless of starting point—the one shown in the table and the one consisting of the pitches lying between those shown (i.e., c♯ d♯ f g a b c♯').

In the 20th century, attempts have been made to broaden the tonal material of Western music by the introduction of *quarter tones (resulting in a quarter-tone scale of twenty-four tones to the octave) and other intervals smaller than the semitone. Such intervals, in combination with others, played an important role in

their mouthpiece is like that of the clarinets. The body of the instrument is of metal, as in the brass instruments. [For ill. see under Clarinet family.] The complete family numbers eight instruments: (1) sopranino in Eb; (2) soprano in Bb; (3) alto in Eb; (4) tenor in Bb; (5) baritone in Eb; (6) bass in Bb; (7) contrabass in Eb; (8) subcontrabass in Bb. All are treated as transposing instruments, written in the treble clef with the written chromatic compass shown in the accompanying example. The sopranino sounds a minor third higher than written, the soprano a major second lower than written, etc. Nos. 3 to 5 are the most popular of the group.

Sax(o)tromba. A group of valved brass instruments devised by Adolphe Sax (patented 1845) with a bore intermediate between that of the trombone and saxhorn. They are seldom used today.

Saxtuba. A circular valved brass instrument invented by Adolphe Sax (1852).

Saygun, Ahmed Adnan (b. Izmir, Turkey, 7 Sept. 1907). Pupil of Le Flem and d'Indy. Has held various conducting and teaching positions in Istanbul and Ankara. Has studied and made use of Turkish folk materials. Has composed operas (incl. *Tas Bebek* [The Puppet], Ankara, 1934; *Kerem,* Ankara, 1953); symphonies and other orch. works; concertos for piano, for violin; choral works; string quartets and other chamber music; piano pieces; arrangements of folksongs.

Saynète [F.]. *Sainete.

Scacchi, Marco (b. Rome, *c.* 1602; d. Gallese?, near Rome, before 1685). Musician at the court in Poland from 1623 and conductor of the royal chapel there, 1628–48. Composed operas; an oratorio; Masses and motets; madrigals. Wrote several treatises, incl. *Breve discorso sopra la musica moderna,* 1649, in which he proposed the widely adopted division of musical styles into those appropriate for church, chamber, and theater.

Chromatic	c c♯ d d♯ e f f♯ g g♯ a a♯ b c'
Major	c d e f g a b c'
Minor, melodic	
ascending	c d e♭ f g a b c'
descending	c d e♭ f g a♭ b♭ c'
Minor, harmonic	c d e♭ f g a♭ b c'
Whole tone	c d e f♯ g♯ a♯ c'
Gypsy	c d e♭ f♯ g a♭ b c'
Pentatonic	c d f g a c'

the music of classical antiquity, and attempts to revive their use were made in the Renaissance. See also Microtone; Church modes; Intervals, calculation of; Temperament; Tonality.

Scale degrees. The tones of the major or minor scale, each of which is numbered in order ascending from the tonic and given a name. These names and numbers, which are an important part of *harmonic analysis, are *tonic (I), supertonic (II), mediant (III), *subdominant (IV), *dominant (V), submediant or superdominant (VI), and subtonic or *leading tone (VII).

Scalero, Rosario (b. Moncalieri, near Turin, 24 Dec. 1870; d. Settimo Vittone, near Turin, 25 Dec. 1954). Studied in Genoa, London, and Vienna. Teacher in France and Italy from 1896; at the Mannes School in New York from 1919; at the Curtis Institute in Philadelphia from 1928. His pupils incl. Barber, Menotti, and Foss. Composed orch. works; a violin concerto; sacred choral works; chamber music; piano pieces.

Scaling, scale. The proportion of diameter to length in an *organ pipe or, more generally, in a *rank of pipes.

Scandello, Antonio (b. Bergamo, 17 Jan. 1517; d. Dresden, 18 Jan. 1580). Cornetto player and composer. Court musician in Dresden from 1549. Assistant *Kapellmeister* to Le Maistre there from 1566 and his successor from 1568. Composed a Passion according to St. John and a setting of the Resurrection story; Masses, motets, and other Latin sacred music; *canzoni alla napoletana;* sacred and secular German polyphony.

Scandicus. See table accompanying Neumes.

Scarlatti, (Giuseppe) Domenico (called "Mimmo") (b. Naples, 26 Oct. 1685; d. Madrid, 23 July 1757). Pupil of his father, Alessandro Scarlatti, and of Gasparini. Organist and composer at the Cappella reale in Naples in 1701. *Maestro di cappella* to the Queen of Poland in Rome, 1709–14; at St. Peter's in Rome, 1714–19; of the royal chapel in Lisbon and teacher of the Princess Maria Barbara from 1720. Went to Spain in Maria Barbara's service when she married the heir to the Spanish throne in 1729. Composed operas; sacred music; oratorios and cantatas; about 600 sonatas (under the title *Esercizi per gravicembalo*) and other harpsichord pieces.

Scarlatti, (Pietro) Alessandro (Gaspare) (b. Palermo, 2 May 1660; d. Naples, 22 Oct. 1725). Probably a pupil of Carissimi. *Maestro di cappella* to Queen Christina of Sweden in Rome, 1679–83; to the Viceroy at Naples, 1684–1703. Assistant *maestro* at Santa Maria Maggiore in Rome, 1703–7, and *maestro* there, 1707–8. *Maestro* of the Cappella reale in Naples from 1708. His pupils incl. Hasse, Geminiani, and his son Domenico Scarlatti. He is sometimes regarded, though not altogether appropriately, as the founder of the so-called *Neapolitan school and the creator of *opera seria*. Composed about 115 operas (incl. many now lost and *Statira,* Rome, 1690; *La caduta de' Decemviri,* Naples, 1697; *Eraclea,* Naples, 1700; *Mitridate Eupatore,* Venice, 1707; *Tigrane,* Naples, 1715; *Il trionfo del onore,* a comic opera, Naples, 1718; *Griselda,* Rome, 1721); oratorios; numerous cantatas, many for one voice and thoroughbass; numerous Masses, motets, and other sacred works; madrigals; *concerti grossi;* chamber music; harpsichord pieces.

Scena [It.]. (1) Stage. (2) A scene in an opera, which typically includes one or more arias. (3) A dramatic accompanied *recitative, often immediately preceding an aria. (4) A concert vocal work similar in character to an operatic scene.

Scenario. A skeleton libretto of a play or an opera that indicates the characters and the number and general nature of the scenes.

Schaeffer, Pierre (b. Nancy, 14 Aug. 1910). Has held various positions with the French Radio and Television Network in Paris, including that of director of research from 1960. Teacher at the Paris Conservatory from 1968. Introduced *musique concrète* in 1948. Has composed *musique concrète* (incl. *Étude aux chemins de fer*, 1948; *Symphonie pour un homme seul*, in collaboration with Henry, 1950, rev. 1966; *Études aux objets*, 1959, rev. 1966, 1967); works for instruments with tape.

Schafer, R. Murray (b. Sarnia, Ontario, 18 July 1933). Studied at the Royal Conservatory of Music in Toronto and with Weinzweig at the Univ. of Toronto. Teacher at Simon Fraser Univ. from 1966 and founder of the electronic music studio there. Has worked with electronic and aleatory procedures. Works incl. 2 operas; *Requiems for the Party Girl* for soprano and 9 instruments, 1966; *Son of Heldenleben* for orch. and tape, 1968; *No Longer than Ten (10) Minutes* for orch., 1970.

Schäffer, Boguslaw (Julien) (b. Lvov, 6 June 1929). Studied at the State College of Music in Cracow, where he has taught since 1963. Has worked with Polish folk music, serial techniques, and graphic notation. Works incl. *Nocturne* for strings, 1953; *Tertium datur*, a graphic score for harpsichord and orch., 1958; *Monosonata* for 6 separated string quartets, 1959; *Equivalenze sonore* for percussion, 1959; *Communicazione audiovisiva*, theater piece, 1970; works on tape.

Schalkhaft [G.]. Roguish.

Schall [G.]. Sound, chiefly acoustical. *Schallbecken*, cymbals. *Schalloch*, sound hole. *Schallplatte*, record. *Schalltrichter*, bell of a wind instrument; *schalltrichter auf*, an instruction to hold the bell of a wind instrument up when playing. *Schallwellen*, acoustical waves.

Schalmei [G.]. See under Oboe family III.

Scharwenka, (Franz) Xaver (b. Samter, Posen, 6 Jan. 1850; d. Berlin, 8 Dec. 1924). Pupil of Kullak at Kullak's Academy in Berlin, where he taught from 1868. Co-founder with his brother Philipp of the Scharwenka Conservatory in Berlin in 1881. Lived in New York, 1891 –98, where he also established a Schar-

wenka Conservatory, returning thereafter to Berlin. Traveled widely as a pianist. Composed an opera; a symphony; 4 piano concertos; 2 piano trios and other chamber music; numerous piano pieces; songs; pedagogic works.

Scharwenka, (Ludwig) Philipp (b. Samter, Posen, 16 Feb. 1847; d. Bad Nauheim, 16 July 1917). Studied with Dorn at the Kullak Academy in Berlin, where he taught from 1870. Co-founder with his brother Xaver of the Scharwenka Conservatory in Berlin in 1881. Composed orch. works (incl. the symphonic poem *Traum und Wirklichkeit*); a violin concerto; choral works (incl. *Sakuntala*, with orch.); 2 string quartets, 3 piano trios, and other chamber music; numerous piano pieces (incl. *Album polonais*); songs.

Schat, Peter (b. Utrecht, 5 June 1935). Pupil of van Baaren, Seiber, and Boulez. Has worked with serial and electronic techniques and with elements of theater. Works incl. *Mozaiken* for orch., 1959; *Entelechie no. 1* for 5 groups of instruments, 1961; *Labyrinth*, theater piece, 1960–65; *Collages* for 31-tone organ, 1962; *Reconstructie*, an opera composed with L. Andriessen, van Vlijman, and others, 1969.

Scheherazade. Symphonic suite by Rimsky-Korsakov, op. 35 (1888), based on some tales from the *Arabian Nights* and named for the woman who tells the stories. In 1910 it was presented in Paris as a ballet by the Russian Ballet under Fokine. See also *Shéhérazade* (Ravel).

Scheibe, Johann Adolph (b. Leipzig, bapt. 5 May 1708; d. Copenhagen, 22 Apr. 1776). *Kapellmeister* to the Margrave of Brandenburg-Kulmbach from 1739. Conductor of the court opera in Copenhagen, 1744–48. Composed a Danish opera, *Thusnelda*, Copenhagen, 1749; oratorios; cantatas; much church music; 150 flute concertos and 30 violin concertos; much chamber music; songs. Published various writings on music, incl. a periodical, *Der critische Musicus*.

Scheidemann, Heinrich (b. Hamburg, *c.* 1596; d. there, early 1663). Pupil of Sweelinck and of his father, Hans Scheidemann, whom he succeeded as organist of the Katharinenkirche in Hamburg by 1629. He was himself succeeded by his pupil Reinken. Composed organ pieces, incl. preludes, fugues, and chorale settings; harpsichord pieces; chorale melodies.

Scheidt, Samuel (b. Halle, Germany, bapt. 3 Nov. 1587; d. there, 24 Mar. 1654). Pupil of Sweelinck. Organist at the Moritzkirche in Halle, 1603–8. Court organist to the Margrave of Brandenburg at Halle from 1609. Composed organ pieces (incl. chorale settings and the collection *Tabulatura nova* in 3 vols., 1624, containing fantasies, toccatas, fugues, variations on sacred and secular melodies, dances, and Mass movements, hymns, and other liturgical pieces; the title refers to the novel use of a score of four staves in place of the older German organ tablature); sacred vocal works, some with instruments; pieces for instrumental ensemble, incl. dances.

Schein, Johann Hermann (b. Grünhain, Saxony, 20 Jan. 1586; d. Leipzig, 19 Nov. 1630). Court *Kapellmeister* in Weimar in 1615. Cantor of the Thomasschule at Leipzig, succeeding Calvisius, from 1616 until his death. Composed the collection *Cantional oder Gesangbuch Augsburgischer Confession,* 1627, containing harmonizations of old and original chorales; other sacred vocal music, some with thoroughbass "composed in the Italian style," 1618; Italian-style secular polyphony in German; *Banchetto musicale,* 1617, a collection of dance suites for instrumental ensemble.

Schelle, Johann (b. Geising, Saxony, bapt. 6 Sept. 1648; d. Leipzig, 10 Mar. 1701). Chorister under Schütz at Dresden. Cantor at the Thomasschule in Leipzig from 1677. Composed sacred vocal music in Latin and German; cantatas; secular vocal music.

Schellen [G.]. Tambourine. See under Percussion instruments. *Schellenbaum,* *Turkish crescent. Schellentrommel,* tambourine.

Schelling, Ernest (Henry) (b. Belvidere, N.J., 26 July 1876; d. New York, 8 Dec. 1939). Pupil of Moszkowski, Leschetizky, H. Huber, and Paderewski. A child prodigy as a pianist and later toured

Russia, Europe, and the Americas. Conducted the Baltimore Symphony, 1936–38, and other orchestras in the U.S. and Europe. Composed orch. works (incl. *A Victory Ball,* 1923; *Morocco,* 1927); a violin concerto, 1916, and *Impressions from an Artist's Life* for piano and orch., 1915; chamber music; piano pieces; songs.

Schenk, Johann Baptist (b. Wiener Neustadt, Austria, 30 Nov. 1753; d. Vienna, 29 Dec. 1836). Pupil of Wagenseil. Beethoven studied with him secretly in Vienna while also studying with Haydn. Composed *Singspiele* (incl. *Der Dorfbarbier,* Vienna, 1796; *Die Jagd,* Vienna, 1799); church music; symphonies; concertos; string quartets and other chamber music; songs.

Schenker analysis. A system of musical analysis developed by Heinrich Schenker (1868–1935). It is based on a theory of *tonality that interprets tonal compositions as superimposed layers of elaboration on a fundamental tonal structure [G. *Ursatz*], the simplest of which is a descending fundamental line [G. *Urlinie*] consisting of the third, second, and first *scale degrees accompanied by the progression I-V-I in the bass. Among the most common types of elaboration identified are passing tones and neighboring tones [see under Counterpoint]. The principal stages of elaboration are described as the foreground, which is the composition itself, and the middle ground, which lies between the foreground and the fundamental structure. Although the theory was primarily intended to account for the coherence of tonal music, its techniques of analysis have also been applied to earlier and later repertories.

Scherzando [It.]; **Scherzhaft** [G.]. Playful.

Scherzi, Gli. Popular name for Haydn's six string quartets op. 33, so called because the minuets bear the inscription "Scherzo" or "Scherzando" and accordingly are faster than the usual minuets of the period [see under Scherzo]. They are also known as the Russian Quartets (because they were dedicated to the Grand Duke Pavel Petrovich, who visited Vienna in 1781) and as the Maiden Quartets [G. *Jungfern-Quartette*] because the title page of the 1782 edition shows a female figure.

Scherzo [It., joke]. (1) A movement, usually the third, of sonatas, symphonies, and quartets (rarely concertos), that was first used consistently by Beethoven to replace the *minuet. Like the minuet, the scherzo is followed by a *trio, after which the scherzo is repeated. The distinguishing features of the scherzo are rapid tempo in 3/4 meter, vigorous rhythm, and elements of surprise. The demarcation between minuet and scherzo is by no means always clear. For the structure of the scherzo, see Binary and ternary form.

(2) In the baroque period, *scherzo* was used for vocal pieces in a lighter vein (Monteverdi, *Scherzi musicali,* 1607) as well as for instrumental pieces of a somewhat fanciful character.

Schibler, Armin (b. Kreuzlingen, Switzerland, 20 Nov. 1920). Pupil of Burkhard, Leibowitz, Fortner, Krenek, Messiaen, and Rubbra. Teacher at the Zürich Kanton Gymnasium from 1944. Has composed operas (incl. *Der spanische Rosenstock,* Bern, 1950; *Die Füsse im Feuer,* Zürich, 1955); ballets; 3 symphonies and other orch. works; concertos for piano, for violin, and for other instruments and groups of instruments; the oratorio *Media in vita,* 1958, and other choral works; string quartets and other chamber music; piano pieces; songs.

Schicksalslied [G., Song of Destiny]. Setting by Brahms for chorus and orchestra, op. 54 (1871), of a poem from Hölderlin's *Hyperion.*

Schidlowsky, León (b. Santiago, Chile, 21 July 1931). Studied in Chile and Germany. Has taught at the National Conservatory in Chile and at the Israel Academy of Music in Tel Aviv. Has worked with serial techniques, aleatory procedures, and graphic notation. Has composed *Nueva York,* 1965, and other orch. works; *La noche de cristal* for tenor and orch., 1961; *Eróstrato* for percussion, 1963; *Cantata negra,* 1957, and other works for voice with instruments; *Naci-*

miento, a work of *musique concrète,* 1956.

Schiettamente [It.]. Openly, simply.

Schildt, Melchior (b. Hanover, 1592 or 1593; d. there, 18 May 1667). Pupil of Sweelinck. Court organist at Copenhagen, 1626–29. Succeeded his father, Antonius Schildt, as organist of the Marktkirche in Hanover, 1629 until his death. Composed pieces for organ and for harpsichord; a cantata.

Schillinger, Joseph (b. Kharkov, 31 Aug. 1895; d. New York, 23 Mar. 1943). Pupil of Tcherepnin and Wihtol in St. Petersburg. Taught in Kharkov and Leningrad. Settled in New York in 1928, where he taught at the New School for Social Research and Teachers' College of Columbia Univ. Taught privately and by correspondence his own system of composition based on mathematical principles, published posthumously as *The Schillinger System of Musical Composition,* 1946. His pupils incl. Gershwin. Composed orch. works (incl. *First Airphonic Suite* for Theremin and orch., 1929); chamber music; piano pieces; songs.

Schillings, Max von (b. Düren, Germany, 19 Apr. 1868; d. Berlin, 24 July, 1933). Conductor and composer. Associate of R. Strauss. Assistant stage director at Bayreuth from 1892. General music director in Stuttgart, 1908–18. Intendant of the Berlin State Opera, 1919–25. Composed operas (incl. *Ingewelde,* Karlsruhe, 1894; *Der Pfeifertag,* Schwerin, 1899; *Mona Lisa,* Stuttgart, 1915); incidental music; melodramas; orch. works; a violin concerto; choral works; chamber music; piano pieces; songs.

Schiske, Karl (Hubert Rudolph) (b. Györ [Raab], Hungary, 12 Feb. 1916; d. Vienna, 16 June 1969). Studied at the Univ. of Vienna. Teacher at the Vienna Academy of Music from 1952. Composed 5 symphonies and other orch. works; concertos for piano and for violin; the oratorio *Vom Tode,* 1946, and other choral works; string quartets and other chamber music; piano pieces; songs.

Schisma. See Comma, schisma.

Schlag [G.]. Beat. *Schlaginstrumente, Schlagzeug,* percussion instruments.

Schlegel [G.]. Drumstick.

Schleifer [G.]. See under Appoggiatura, double.

Schleppend [G.]. Dragging, heavy.

Schlick, Arnolt (b. probably Heidelberg, *c*. 1455; d. there, *c*. 1525). Blind organist and lutenist. Organist to the Count Palatine at Heidelberg from *c*. 1485. Toured Germany and Holland as an organist. Composed a collection of pieces in tablature, incl. arrangements for organ of sacred vocal works; settings of songs for voice and one or more lutes; pieces for lute. Published a book on organ building.

Schlummerlied [G.]. Slumber song.

Schluss [G.]. Conclusion, *cadence. *Schlusssatz,* final movement.

Schlüssel [G.]. *Clef.

Schmelzer, Johann Heinrich (b. probably Scheibbs, Lower Austria, *c*. 1623; d. Prague, between 4 Feb. and 20 Mar. 1680). Violinist at the court in Vienna, 1649–70. Assistant *Kapellmeister* there from 1671 and *Kapellmeister* from 1679. Composed ballets, incl. some for operas of Draghi and for Cesti's *Il pomo d'oro,* and trumpet fanfares for the horse ballet; violin sonatas, trio sonatas, and other chamber music; sacred vocal music. His son Anton Andreas Schmelzer (1653–1701) also composed ballets for the court in Vienna.

Schmetternd [G.]. Blaring. An instruction to players of the *horn to produce a brassy tone.

Schmidt, Franz (b. Pressburg, 22 Dec. 1874; d. Perchtoldsdorf, near Vienna, 11 Feb. 1939). Pupil of Bruckner, R. Fuchs, and Leschetizky. Cellist in the Vienna court opera orchestra, 1896–1911. Teacher at the Vienna Conservatory from 1901. Director of the Vienna Academy of Music, 1925–27. Rector of the Vienna Hochschule für Musik, 1927–31. Composed operas (incl. *Notre Dame,* 1902–4, prod. Vienna, 1914); 4 symphonies; 2 piano concertos for left hand

alone; the oratorio *Das Buch mit sieben Siegeln,* 1937, and other choral works; 2 string quartets and other chamber music; organ pieces.

Schmitt, Florent (b. Blâmont, France, 28 Sept. 1870; d. Neuilly, near Paris, 17 Aug. 1958). Critic, pianist, and composer. Pupil of Dubois, Massenet, and Fauré. Settled in Paris in 1906. Director of the Lyon Conservatory, 1921–24. Composed ballets (incl. *La tragédie de Salomé,* 1907); incidental music; orch. works (incl. *Le palais hanté,* after Poe, 1904); choral works (incl. *Psalm XLVII* with orch., 1904); works for solo instrument and for solo voice with orch.; chamber music; piano pieces, incl. some for piano four-hands; songs; music for films (incl. *Salammbô,* 1925).

Schnabel [G.]. The *mouthpiece of the clarinet and recorder.

Schnabel, Artur (b. Lipnik, Austria, 17 Apr. 1882; d. Morschach, Switzerland, 15 Aug. 1951). Pupil of Leschetizky. A child prodigy as a pianist and highly successful as a performer thereafter. Teacher at the Berlin Hochschule für Musik, 1925–33. Lived in New York from 1939. Composed a symphony and a rhapsody for orch.; a piano concerto; string quartets and other chamber music; piano pieces; songs.

Schnarre [G.]. *Rattle. *Schnarrtrommel,* snare drum. *Schnarrwerk,* old term for reed section of the organ.

Schnebel, Dieter (b. Lahr, Germany, 14 Mar. 1930). Studied music in Freiburg im Breisgau; music and theology in Tübingen. Became a Lutheran clergyman in 1957. Has worked with serial techniques, a wide variety of vocal sounds, graphic notation, audience participation, and mixed media. Works incl. *Versuche I– III* for stringed instruments and percussion, 1953; *für stimmen für* for 12 vocal groups, 1958; *concert sans orchestre* for pianist and audience, 1964; *ki-no* for projectors and listeners, 1967.

Schneider, (Johann Christian) Friedrich (b. Alt-Walterdorf, near Zittau, 3 Jan. 1786; d. Dessau, 23 Nov. 1853). Pupil of his father, Johann Gottlob Schneider. Organist at the Thomaskirche in Leipzig from 1813 and music director of the city theater there from 1817. Court *Kapellmeister* at Dessau from 1821. Composed operas; oratorios (incl. *Das Weltgericht*, 1820); Masses and other sacred works; 23 symphonies and other orch. works; 7 piano concertos; numerous choral works; chamber music; piano pieces; numerous songs.

Schnell [G.]. Fast.

Schneller [G.]. See Inverted mordent.

Schnitke, Alfred. See Shnitke, Alfred.

Schobert, Johann (Jean) (b. Silesia?, *c.* 1740; d. Paris, 28 Aug. 1767). Harpsichordist and composer, in the service of Prince de Conti in Paris from *c.* 1760. The slow movement of Mozart's Concerto K. 39 is based on one of his works. Composed a comic opera; harpsichord sonatas and concertos; violin and harpsichord sonatas; other chamber music with harpsichord.

Schoeck, Othmar (b. Brunnen, Switzerland, 1 Sept. 1886; d. Zürich, 8 Mar. 1957). Pupil of Hegar and Reger. Conducted various choral organizations in Zürich, 1909–17; symphony concerts at St. Gall, 1917–44. Composed operas (incl. *Penthesilea*, Dresden, 1927); orch. works; concertos for violin, for cello, for horn; choral works, some with orch.; 2 string quartets and other chamber music; piano pieces; numerous songs and song cycles (incl. *Gaselen* for baritone with instruments, 1923; *Élégie* for voice and chamber orch., 1924; *Lebendig begraben* for baritone and large orch., 1926; *Notturno* for baritone and string quartet, 1933).

Schoenberg, Arnold (Franz Walter) (originally Schönberg) (b. Vienna, 13 Sept. 1874; d. Los Angeles, 13 July 1951). Studied violin and cello as a child and counterpoint with Zemlinsky. Teacher at the Stern Conservatory in Berlin in 1902, returning in 1903 to Vienna, where he was an associate of Mahler. Teacher at the Vienna Academy from 1910 and founder with his students in 1918 in Vienna of the Society for Private Musical Performances. Teacher at the Prussian Academy of Fine Arts in Berlin, 1925–33. Settled in the U.S. in 1933,

teaching at the Univ. of Southern California, 1935–36, and at the Univ. of California at Los Angeles, 1936–44. His European pupils incl. Berg, Webern, and Wellesz; American pupils incl. Kirchner, Kim, and Cage. Developed and began to compose with the twelve-tone technique by 1923. He was also a painter and an associate of Kandinsky. Works: operas (incl. **Erwartung; Die *glückliche Hand; Von Heute auf Morgen*, Frankfurt, 1930; **Moses und Aron*); orch. works (incl. **Verklärte Nacht; Pelleas und Melisande*, symphonic poem after Maeterlinck, 1903; *5 Orchesterstücke*, 1909, rev. 1949; *Variations*, 1928; *Begleitmusik zu einer Lichtspielszene*, 1930; *Chamber Symphony [Kammersymphonie]*, orch. version, 1935; *Chamber Symphony* no. 2, 1939; *Theme and Variations*, also for band, 1943); a violin concerto, 1936, and a piano concerto, 1942; choral works (incl. **Gurrelieder;* the oratorio *Die Jakobsleiter*, 1913, unfinished; *Kol Nidre*, with reciter and orch., 1939; *A Survivor from Warsaw*, with reciter and orch., 1947); **Ode to Napoleon Buonaparte;* chamber music (incl. an early string quartet in D and 4 numbered string quartets: no. 1 in D min., 1905, no. 2 in F♯ with soprano, 1908, rev. 1921, no. 3, 1926, no. 4, 1936; the string sextet **Verklärte Nacht; Kammersymphonie* for 15 instruments, 1906, arranged for orch., 1935; a serenade for septet and bass voice, 1923; a wind quintet, 1924; **Pierrot lunaire;* a string trio, 1946; *Fantasia* for violin and piano, 1946); piano pieces (incl. *3 Klavierstücke* op. 11, 1909; *6 kleine Klavierstücke* op. 19, 1911; *5 Klavierstücke* op. 23, 1923; *Suite* op. 25, 1923, the first piece composed throughout with the twelve-tone method; *Klavierstück* op. 33a, 1929; *Klavierstück* op. 33b, 1932); songs (incl. *Das Buch der hängenden Gärten*, 1908; 2 sets with orch., 1904 and 1914); *Variations on a Recitative* for organ, 1940. He published *Harmonielehre*, 1911, abridged English trans., 1947; *Style and Idea*, 1950; and other writings.

Schola (cantorum) [L.]. Originally, the papal choir and singing school, possibly organized (or reorganized) by St. Gregory (590–604) but first mentioned in 780 by Paul Diacre (Paulus Diaconus).

Loosely, the choir in any performance of Gregorian chant. The name has also been adopted by certain institutions outside the Church, of which that founded in Paris in 1894 by d'Indy, Bordes, and Guilmant is the most important. Originally planned as an institution for church music, it developed c. 1900 into a general music school with an intensive training program based on Gregorian chant and counterpoint. The name *schola* has come to imply the conservative and academic trends in French music, represented by Franck and his spiritual successors.

Schöne Müllerin, Die [G., The Fair Maid of the Mill]. Cycle of 20 songs by Schubert, op. 25, D. 795, composed in 1823 to poems by Wilhelm Müller.

Schöpfung, Die [G.]. *The *Creation.*

Schöpfungsmesse [G.]. *Creation Mass.*

Schottische [G.]. A mid-19th-century round dance similar to a slow polka, not to be confused with the much faster *écossaise.* It was also known in England as the "German polka."

Schreker, Franz (b. Monaco, of Austrian parents, 23 Mar. 1878; d. Berlin, 21 Mar. 1934). Pupil of R. Fuchs in Vienna. Teacher at the Akademie der Tonkunst there from 1912. Director of the Hochschule für Musik in Berlin, 1920–32. His pupils incl. Krenek, Rathaus, and Hába. Associate of Schoenberg and Berg. Composed operas (incl. *Der ferne Klang,* Frankfurt, 1912; *Der Schatzgräber,* Frankfurt, 1920); ballets (incl. *Der Geburtstag der Infantin,* after Wilde, 1908); orch. works; choral works; chamber music; piano pieces; songs, some with orch.

Schrittmässig [G.]. Measured.

Schröter, Johann Samuel (b. Guben, Germany, 1750 or 1752; d. London, 2 Nov. 1788). Pianist, harpsichordist, and composer. Succeeded J. C. Bach as music master to Queen Charlotte in London, 1782. Composed keyboard concertos and sonatas; chamber music. His sister Corona Schröter (1751–1802) was a singer and composer.

Schubart, Christian Friedrich Daniel (b. Obersontheim, Swabia, 24 Mar. 1739; d.

Stuttgart, 10 Oct. 1791). Organist, poet, and composer. Music director of the Stuttgart Theater and court poet there from c. 1787. Composed songs and piano pieces. His literary works incl. the poem "Die Forelle" set by Schubert.

Schubert, Franz Peter (b. Liechtenthal, Vienna, 31 Jan. 1797; d. Vienna, 19 Nov. 1828). Chorister in the Vienna court chapel and pupil of Salieri at the attached school, where he also played violin in the orchestra. Teacher at the elementary school in Liechtenthal, where his father also taught, 1814–16, while continuing studies with Salieri. Lived in Vienna from 1818. Teacher to the Esterházy family in Hungary in the summers of 1818 and 1824. Works: stage works (incl. *Der Zwillingsbrüder,* a *Singspiel,* Vienna, 1820; the operas *Alfonso und Estrella,* 1822, prod. Weimar, 1854, and *Fierrabras,* after Calderón, 1823, prod. Karlsruhe, 1897; the melodrama *Die Zauberharfe,* Vienna, 1820; incidental music to *Rosamunde*); 8 symphonies (incl. the *"Tragic," the *"Unfinished," and the "Great" in C maj., 1828, usually referred to as no. 9; others sketched and/or lost, incl. "no. 7"); 7 overtures; 6 Latin Masses, a German Mass, and other sacred and secular choral works; string quartets, of which 15 are traditionally numbered in series (incl. *Der *Tod und das Mädchen*); other chamber music (incl. a string trio in B♭ maj., 1817; the *"Trout" Quintet; an octet in F maj. for clarinet, horn, bassoon, 2 violins, viola, cello, and double bass, 1824; piano trios in B♭ maj. and E♭ maj., both 1827; a quintet in C maj. for 2 violins, viola, and 2 cellos, 1828; 3 sonatinas, 1816, a sonata in A maj., 1817, a *Rondo brillant* in B min., 1826, and a *Phantasie* in C maj., 1827, for violin and piano; a sonata in A min. for arpeggione and piano, 1824); piano pieces (incl. 22 sonatas; the *Wanderer-Fantasie;* minuets, waltzes, *Ländler, *Écossaises, Moments musicaux* [originally *Moments musicals*], *Impromptus,* and other short pieces; a sonata in B♭ maj., 1818, a sonata in C maj. ["Grand Duo"], 1824, marches, and other pieces for piano four-hands); *Der Hirt auf dem Felsen* for voice, piano, and clarinet or cello, 1828; over 600 songs (incl. the cycles *Die *schöne*

*Müllerin, Die *Winterreise,* and *Schwanengesang;* and the individual songs "Erlkönig," 1814; "Gretchen am Spinnrade," 1814; "Der Wanderer," 1816; "Die Forelle," 1817; "Der Tod und das Mädchen," 1817).

Schübler Chorales. Collection of six chorale preludes for organ by Bach, published about 1747 by Schübler. Four of them are based on arias from cantatas.

Schuller, Gunther (b. New York, 22 Nov. 1925). Principal horn player with the Cincinnati Symphony, 1943–45; with the Metropolitan Opera Orchestra in New York, 1945–59. Teacher at the Manhattan School of Music, 1950–63; at Yale Univ., 1964–67. President of the New England Conservatory in Boston, 1967–77. Has worked with serial techniques and elements of jazz. For the combination of jazz with the traditions of concert music he coined the term "third stream." Has composed operas (incl. *The Visitation,* Hamburg, 1966); orch. works (incl. *Spectra,* 1958; *7 Studies on Themes of Paul Klee,* 1959; a symphony, 1965; *American Triptych,* 1969); concertos for horn, 1944, for cello, 1945, for piano, 1962, for double bass, 1968; *Concertino* for jazz quartet and orch., 1959; *Variants* for the Modern Jazz Quartet and orch., commissioned for dance by George Balanchine, 1960; works for band; works for jazz ensembles; chamber music; songs. Published *Horn Technique,* 1962, and *Early Jazz: Its Roots and Musical Development,* 1968.

Schulz, Johann Abraham Peter (bapt. Lüneburg, 31 Mar. 1747; d. Schweut, 10 June 1800). Pupil of Kirnberger. Conductor of the French theater in Berlin, 1776–78. Court *Kapellmeister* in Rheinsberg, 1780–87; in Copenhagen, 1787–95. Composed stage works (incl. *Le barbier de Séville,* Rheinsberg, 1786, and several works in Danish); church music; oratorios; cantatas; chamber music; piano pieces; songs (incl. the collections *Gesänge am Clavier,* 1779, and *Lieder im Volkston,* 1782).

Schuman, William (Howard) (b. New York, 4 Aug. 1910). Studied at Columbia Univ. and with Haubiel and Harris. Teacher at Sarah Lawrence College, 1935–45. Director of publications for G.

Schirmer, Inc., 1945–52. President of the Juilliard School, 1945–62; of Lincoln Center for the Performing Arts in New York, 1962–69. Has composed the opera *The Mighty Casey,* Hartford, Conn., 1953; dance scores (incl. *Night Journey,* 1947, and *Judith,* 1948, for Martha Graham; *Undertow,* for Anthony Tudor, 1945); 10 symphonies and other orch. works (incl. *New England Triptych,* 1956; *In Praise of Shahn,* 1969); concertos for piano, 1942; for violin, 1947, rev. 1954, 1959; *A Song of Orpheus,* fantasy for cello and orch., 1961; *Concerto on Old English Rounds* for viola, women's chorus, and orch., 1973; works for band; choral works (incl. Secular Cantata no. 2, *A Free Song,* 1943, awarded the first Pulitzer Prize in music); *The Young Dead Soldiers,* text by Archibald MacLeish, for soprano, horn, 8 woodwinds, and 9 strings, 1976; 4 string quartets and other chamber music; piano pieces; songs.

Schumann, Clara Josephine (*née* Wieck) (b. Leipzig, 13 Sept. 1819; d. Frankfurt, 20 May 1896). Wife of Robert Schumann. Traveled widely as a concert pianist. Teacher at Hoch's Conservatory in Frankfurt, 1878–92. Composed a piano concerto; a piano trio and *3 Romances* for piano and violin; piano pieces; songs. Edited her husband's works.

Schumann, Robert (Alexander) (b. Zwickau, Saxony, 8 June 1810; d. Endenich, near Bonn, 29 July 1856). Pupil of Friedrich Wieck (father of his future wife, Clara) and Dorn. An injury to his right hand, sustained while using a mechanical device to strengthen it, ended his career as a pianist. Co-founder in 1834 and editor, 1835–44, of the *Neue Zeitschrift für Musik.* Teacher at the Leipzig Conservatory, 1843–44. Lived in Dresden, 1844–50, where he taught privately, conducted the Liedertafel from 1847, and organized the Chorgesang-Verein in 1848. Town music director at Düsseldorf, 1850–53. Interned in an asylum in Endenich from 1854 until his death. Works: the opera *Genoveva,* Leipzig, 1850; incidental music to Byron's *Manfred;* 4 completed symphonies (incl. no. 1 in B♭ maj., 1841, *Spring;* no. 3 in E♭ maj., *Rhenish*); overtures; works for solo instrument with orch. (incl. a piano concerto in A min., 1841–45; a *Konzertstück* [Introduction and Allegro] in G maj., 1849, and an Introduction and Allegro in D min., 1853, for piano and orch.; a cello concerto in A min., 1850; a *Fantasia* for violin and orch. in C maj., 1853; a violin concerto in D min., 1853); choral works, some with orch. (incl. *Scenen aus Goethe's Faust*, 1844–53); chamber music (incl. 3 string quartets, 3 piano trios, *Fantasiestücke* for piano trio, 2 piano quartets, and 2 completed violin sonatas); numerous piano pieces (incl. 3 sonatas; 3 "Sonatas for the Young"; *Abegg* Variations; *Papillons; *Davidsbündler Tänze; *Carnaval; Fantasiestücke*, 1837, 1851; *Études symphoniques; *Kinderscenen; *Kreisleriana; Humoreske*, 1839; *Novelletten*, 1838; *Faschingsschwank aus Wien: Fantasiebilder*, 1839; *Album für die Jugend*, 1848); pieces for piano four-hands; numerous songs (incl. the cycles *Frauenliebe und Leben* and *Dichterliebe*).

Schürmann, Georg Kaspar (b. Idensen, near Hanover, c. 1672; d. Wolfenbüttel, 25 Feb. 1751). Church and opera singer in Hamburg, 1693–97. *Kapellmeister* to the Duke of Brunswick at Wolfenbüttel in 1697 and from 1707. Court *Kapellmeister* in Meiningen, 1703–6. Composed about 40 operas (incl. *Ludovicus Pius, oder Ludwig der Fromme*, Brunswick, 1726); church music.

Schütz, Heinrich (Henricus Sagittarius) (b. Köstritz, near Gera, Thuringia, 14 Oct. 1585; d. Dresden, 6 Nov. 1672). Choirboy at the court chapel in Kassel and then pupil of G. Gabrieli, 1609–12, returning to Kassel as court organist. Entered the service of the Elector of Saxony in Dresden in 1615, becoming *Kapellmeister* in 1617. While holding this position, he visited Italy, 1628–29, and served as court conductor in Copenhagen, 1633–35, 1637–38, and 1642–44. Composed the first German opera, *Dafne*, 1627, now lost; *Psalmen Davids*, 1619, polychoral settings of the Psalms in German with instruments; *Symphoniae sacrae* (3 parts publ. 1629, 1647, 1650), sacred concerted works in Latin and German; other Latin and German sacred music; *Musikalische Exequien*, 1636; an Easter oratorio; a *Christmas oratorio;

Passions according to Matthew, Luke, and John, 1666; *Die 7 Wörte Christi am Kreuz;* Italian madrigals.

Schwanda the Bagpiper. See *Švanda Dudák.*

Schwanengesang [G., Swan Song]. Schubert's last songs, D. 957 (composed 1828), to seven poems by Rellstab, six by Heine, and one by Seidl, published posthumously by Haslinger (Vienna), who chose the title.

Schwantner, Joseph (b. Chicago, 22 Mar. 1943). Pupil of Bernard Dieter, Anthony Donato, and Alan Stout. Teacher at the Eastman School of Music from 1970. Works, mostly for chamber ensembles, incl. *Consortium I*, 1970; *In aeternum*, 1973; *Canticle of the Evening Bells*, 1974; *Elixir*, 1975; *Wild Angels of the Open Hills* for soprano, flute, and harp, 1977.

Schwärmer [G.]. See under Tremolo.

Schwartz, Elliot (b. Brooklyn, 19 Jan. 1936). Pianist and composer. Pupil of Beeson, Luening, Creston, Brant, Chou, Wolpe, and Varèse. Teacher at the Univ. of Massachusetts, 1960–64; at Bowdoin College from 1964. Works incl. *Island* for orch., 1970; *Texture* for chamber orch., 1966; *Concert Piece for 10 Players*, 1965; *Interruptions* for wind quintet with tape loop, 1964; *Music for Soloist and Audience* for any instrument(s), 1970.

Schweigen [G.]. To be silent.

Schweitzer, Anton (b. Coburg, bapt. 6 June 1735; d. Gotha, 23 Nov. 1787). Studied in Italy and became director of the ducal theater in Weimar in 1766. Court conductor in Gotha from 1778. Composed *Singspiele* and operas (incl. *Die Dorfgala*, Weimar, 1772; *Alceste*, Weimar, 1773, libretto by Wieland; *Rosamunde*, Mannheim, 1780, libretto by Wieland); the first German melodrama, *Pygmalion*, after Rousseau, Weimar, 1772; ballets; symphonies; cantatas; instrumental pieces.

Schweller [G.]. *Swell.

Schwellkasten [G.]. *Swell box. *Schwellwerk*, swell organ.

Schwindend [G.]. Diminishing (in loudness).

Schwungvoll [G.]. Animated, spirited.

Sciolto [It.]. Easy, unconstrained.

Scordatura [It.]. Abnormal tuning of a stringed instrument in order to obtain unusual chords, facilitate difficult passages, or change the tone color. Scordatura was frequently used in the lute music of the 16th and 17th centuries and in the violin music of the 17th century, particularly by Heinrich von Biber. In later music for strings (from Mozart on) the most common instance of scordatura is tuning the lowest string a semitone or whole tone lower in order to increase the range, or a tone higher in order to increase the brilliance of the sound. Occasionally all four strings are tuned up a tone.

Score [F. *partition;* G. *Partitur;* It., Sp. *partitura*]. A notation showing all the parts of an ensemble (orchestra or chamber music) arranged one underneath another on different staves (full score, orchestral score). A vocal score is the score of a vocal work (e.g., opera, oratorio) that shows the vocal parts on separate staves but the instrumental parts in a piano *reduction. A piano score is the reduction of an orchestral score to a version for piano, on two staves.

Since about the mid-19th century it has been the practice to lay out an orchestral score in the following order, starting at the top of the page: woodwind, brass, percussion, strings. If a harp is used, it is placed immediately above the strings, but should voices and organ also be included, they are written between the harp and the strings. In general, the instruments of each group are arranged in order of descending pitch.

Before *c.* 1225, score arrangement was the principal format for writing down polyphonic music. All of the organa, *conductus,* and *clausulae* of the *Notre Dame repertory were notated in this fashion, as was much of the *St. Martial repertory. With the development of the motet (*c.* 1225), the score was discarded in favor of part arrangement, in which the parts are notated separately on one or, usually, two facing pages of a book. This method saved space, since there was a great difference in length between the texted upper parts of the motet and the textless tenor with its few and long notes written in ligatures. A similar arrangement of music in four parts was used in the *choirbooks of the 15th and 16th centuries. The choirbook arrangement persisted until the mid-16th century but was gradually superseded by arrangement in *partbooks, i.e., a separate book for each voice-part. This method was particularly advantageous for printing and, in fact, was almost exclusively employed in the printed books of 16th-century ensemble music, both vocal and instrumental. Solo music (organ, lute), on the other hand, when not written in *tablature, was always written or printed in a scorelike arrangement. About 1600 the development of orchestral music and the acceptance of the *thoroughbass led to the general adoption of the score.

Scoring. (1) *Orchestration. (2) The particular combination of instruments specified in the *score of a composition.

Scorrendo, scorrevole [It.]. Flowing, gliding.

Scotch snap. See under Dotted notes.

Scotch (Scottish) Symphony. Mendelssohn's Symphony no. 3 in A minor, op. 56, inspired by a visit to Scotland in 1829. It was begun in Italy in 1830 and finished in Berlin in 1842.

Scott, Cyril Meir (b. Oxton, Cheshire, 27 Sept. 1879; d. Eastbourne, 31 Dec. 1970). Studied in Liverpool and with I. Knorr in Frankfurt. Settled in Liverpool in 1898. Composed operas (incl. *The Alchemist,* Essen, 1925); a ballet; 3 symphonies and other orch. works; concertos for piano, for violin, for cello, for harpsichord, for oboe; choral works (incl. *La belle dame sans merci,* 1916); chamber music; piano pieces (incl. *Lotus Land,* 1905; *Danse nègre,* 1908; *Impressions of the Jungle Book,* after Kipling, 1912); numerous songs. Wrote poetry and several books on music and philosophy.

Scriabin, Alexander Nikolaievich (b. Moscow, 6 Jan. 1872; d. there, 27 Apr. 1915). Pianist and composer. Pupil of Taneiev and Arensky. Teacher at the Moscow Conservatory, 1898–1903.

Traveled in Europe and the U.S. and lived at various times in Switzerland and Brussels. Made use in later works of the whole-tone scale and other novel sonorities, incl. the *mystic chord, and of lighting effects. Composed 5 symphonies (no. 3, *The Divine Poem,* 1903; no. 4, *The Poem of Ecstasy,* 1908; no. 5, **Prometheus: The Poem of Fire,* 1910); a piano concerto, 1897; piano pieces (incl. mazurkas, several sets of preludes, etudes, impromptus, and 10 sonatas).

Scucito [It.]. Unconnected, *non *legato.*

Sculthorpe, Peter (Joshua) (b. Launceston, Tasmania, Australia, 29 Apr. 1929). Studied at the Univ. of Melbourne and with Rubbra and Wellesz at Oxford. Teacher at the Univ. of Sydney from 1963. Has employed elements of Asian music. Has composed *Sun Music Ballet,* 1968; orch. works (incl. several pieces titled *Sun Music; Music for Japan,* 1970); choral works; chamber music; piano pieces; music for the theater, films, radio, and television.

Sea Symphony. Vaughan Williams' Symphony no. 1 (1910), for solo voices, chorus, and orchestra, based on texts from Walt Whitman's *Leaves of Grass.*

Searle, Humphrey (b. Oxford, 26 Aug. 1915). Pupil of Ireland, R. O. Morris, Jacob, and Webern. Producer for the British Broadcasting Corp., 1938–40 and 1946–48. Teacher at the Royal College of Music in London from 1965. Has worked with twelve-tone techniques. Has composed operas (incl. *The Diary of a Madman,* after Gogol, Berlin, 1958; *The Photo of the Colonel,* after Ionesco, Frankfurt, 1964; *Hamlet,* Hamburg, 1968); ballets (incl. *Noctambules,* 1956); 5 symphonies and other orch. works; 2 piano concertos; choral works (incl. *The Shadow of Cain,* text by Sitwell, 1952); chamber music; piano pieces; songs; music for television, films, and theater. Has published books on Liszt, on 20th-century counterpoint, and on ballet music.

Seasons, The. (1) Oratorio by Haydn, composed 1798–1801, with a German libretto (original title *Die Jahreszeiten*) by G. van Swieten, based on an English poem by J. Thomson. Its four parts portray spring, summer, fall, and winter. (2) Collective title (original, "Le quattro stagioni") of the first four concertos of Antonio Vivaldi's *Il cimento dell' armonia e dell' inventione,* op. 8, for violin, strings, and *continuo.* Each concerto is based on a descriptive sonnet.

Sebastiani, Johann (b. near Weimar, 30 Sept. 1622; d. Königsberg, 1683). *Kapellmeister* at Königsberg, 1663–79, having served there from about 1650. Composed a Passion according to St. Matthew for voices and instruments and employing chorales, publ. 1672; concerted church music; sacred and secular lieder; occasional pieces.

Secco recitative. See under Recitative.

Sechter, Simon (b. Friedberg, Bohemia, 11 Oct. 1788; d. Vienna, 10 Sept. 1867). Pupil of Koželuch. Teacher at the Vienna Institute for the Blind from 1810. Court organist in Vienna from 1824 until his death. Teacher at the Vienna Conservatory from 1851. His pupils incl. Bruckner. Composed an opera; much church music; 4 oratorios; string quartets; organ pieces, incl. many preludes and fugues; piano pieces, incl. fugues and other examples of complex counterpoint; songs. Wrote a treatise on composition and other theoretical works.

Sechzehntel [G.]. Sixteenth note. See under Notes.

Second. See under Interval; Scale degrees.

Seconda prattica [It.]. Term used *c.* 1600 for the then novel style of *monody and its associated freer treatment of dissonance for the setting of texts, as opposed to the *prima prattica,* the polyphonic style of the 16th century, which was viewed as subordinating text to music.

Seconda volta [It.]. See under *Prima volta.*

Secondary dominants. See under Dominant (1).

Seeger, Ruth Crawford. See Crawford, Ruth Porter.

Seelenamt [G.]. *Requiem Mass.

Seelenvoll [G.]. Soulful.

Segno [It.]. A sign (𝄋) used to indicate the beginning or end of a section to be repeated. In the former case, the indication *dal segno, dal S.*, or *D.S.* appears at the end of the section. In the latter case, *al segno* (to the sign), *sin' al segno* (until the sign), or *fin' al segno* (end at the sign) appears; this may occur in conjunction with the instruction *da capo*, from the beginning.

Segue [It., follows]. (1) Indication to the performer to proceed to the following movement or section without a break (e.g., *segue l'aria, segue la coda*). (2) Continue in the same manner, e.g., with a certain pattern of broken chords that is written out in full only at the beginning.

Seguidilla. A dance of southern Spain with a text based on a four-line poem (usually 7 5 7 5), whose lines are freely repeated or broken up in actual performance as well as interspersed with passages played on the guitar. The music is in moderately fast triple meter.

Sehnsucht [G.]. Longing. *Sehnsuchtvoll,* with longing.

Sehr [G.]. Very, much.

Seiber, Mátyás György (b. Budapest, 4 May 1905; d. Johannesburg, 25 Sept. 1960). Pupil of Kodály. Teacher at Hoch's Conservatory in Frankfurt, 1928–33. Settled in London, 1935. Teacher at Morley College there from 1942. Worked with twelve-tone techniques and jazz. Composed an opera and other stage works; orch. works; works for flute, for clarinet, for horn, and for violin with orch.; choral works (incl. a *Missa brevis,* 1924; the cantata *Ulysses,* after Joyce, 1947); 3 string quartets and other chamber music (incl. *Permutazioni a 5,* 1958); piano pieces; songs and arrangements of folksongs; music for films.

Seises [Sp.]. A group of six (or more) choir boys who perform dances with singing and clapping of castanets before the high altar of the Cathedral of Seville (formerly also in other churches of Spain) on great festival days. The *seises* were established in the 15th century.

Seixas, (José Antonio) Carlos de (b. Coimbra, 11 June 1704; d. Lisbon, 25 Aug. 1742). Organist at the royal chapel in Lisbon from 1720 until his death, under D. Scarlatti for part of this time. Composed a harpsichord concerto; sinfonias for strings; church music; numerous pieces for harpsichord, incl. sonatas, fugues, and dances; pieces for organ.

Sekles, Bernhard (b. Frankfurt, 20 Mar. 1872; d. there, 8 Dec. 1934). Pupil of I. Knorr. Teacher at Hoch's Conservatory in Frankfurt from 1896 and its director, 1923–33. His pupils incl. Hindemith. Composed operas (incl. *Sheherazade,* Mannheim, 1917); ballets; orch. works (incl. *Aus den Gärten Semiramis*); a Passacaglia and Fugue for organ and orch.; choral works; chamber music; piano pieces; songs.

Selby, William (b. England, 1738; d. Boston, Dec. 1798). Settled in the U.S. *c.* 1771. Organist at Trinity Church, Newport, R.I., in 1774; at King's Chapel in Boston from 1777. Composed anthems, songs, instrumental pieces.

Selle, Thomas (b. Zörbig, Saxony, 23 Mar. 1599; d. Hamburg, 2 July 1663). Cantor at the Johanneum and music director of the five principal churches in Hamburg from 1641. Composed Passions, incl. one according to St. John, 1642; concerted church music; sacred and secular songs with thoroughbass; secular polyphony.

Semi- [L.]. Half. *Semibiscroma, semibreve (semibrevis), semicroma, semifusa, semiminima, semiquaver,* see Notes; also Mensural notation. *Semichorus,* half-chorus. *Semidiapente,* diminished fifth [see Interval]. *Semiditonus,* the minor third. *Semiditas,* in mensural notation (*proportions*), same as *proportio dupla.*

Semiramide. (1) *Semiramide riconosciuta,* opera in three acts by Gluck (libretto by Metastasio), produced in Vienna, 1748. (2) Opera in two acts by Rossini (libretto by G. Rossi, based on Voltaire), produced in Venice, 1823. Setting (for both): Babylon, legendary times.

Semiseria [It.]. An 18th-century term for an *opera seria* that contained a number of comic scenes.

Semitone. One-half of a whole tone, the

smallest *interval in traditional Western music. (Smaller intervals are called *microtones.) See Intervals, calculation of; Temperament.

Semplice [It.]. Simple, unaffected.

Sempre [It.]. Always; e.g., *sempre legato,* legato throughout.

Senallié, Jean Baptiste (Senaillé) (b. Paris, 23 Nov. 1687; d. there, 15 Oct. 1730). Violinist and composer. Pupil of his father, whom he succeeded as a member of the *Vingt-quatre violons du roi* in 1713, and of Vitali. Performer at the Concert spirituel, 1728–30. Composed 50 violin sonatas with thoroughbass.

Sender, Ramon (b. Madrid, 29 Oct. 1934). Studied with Carter, Erickson, and at Mills College. Co-founder and co-director of the San Francisco Tape Music Center, 1962–66. Has worked with mixed media. Works incl. *4 Sanskrit Hymns* for 4 sopranos, instruments, and tapes, 1961; *Time Fields* for any 6 instruments, 1963; *World Food I–XII* for drone tapes, 1965.

Senfl, Ludwig (b. Basel, *c.* 1486; d. Munich, between 2 Dec. 1542 and 10 Aug. 1543). Pupil and associate of Isaac. Singer in the chapel of Maximilian I from 1507, succeeding Isaac as imperial chamber composer in 1517. Musician at the Bavarian court chapel in Munich from 1523. Composed Masses, motets, Magnificats, and other sacred music (incl. the completion of Isaac's *Choralis Constantinus*); polyphonic settings of odes of Horace; polyphonic German lieder.

Sennet (also written *Sennate, Synnet, Cynet,* etc.). In the stage dirctions of Elizabethan plays, a term meaning that music is to be played. The term is probably derived from *sonata.* For a similar term, see Tucket.

Sensible [F.]. The *leading tone.

Sentito [It.]. Expressive.

Senza [It.]. Without. *Senza tempo, senza misura,* without strict measure. For *senza sordini,* see under Mute.

Septet. Music for seven players, usually strings and winds mixed. Besides Beethoven's well-known Septet op. 20, there are septets by Spohr, Hummel, Saint-Saëns, and Ravel.

Septuor [F.]. *Septet.

Septuplet. A group of seven notes played in the time of four or six.

Sequence. (1) The repetition in a single voice-part of a short musical phrase at another pitch. A sequence is called *melodic* (or *monophonic*) when the repetition occurs in the melody only. It is called *harmonic* (or *polyphonic*) if similar repetitions also occur in the other parts. If the repetitions are made without accidentals (change of key) the sequence is *tonal* or *diatonic.* Such repetition necessarily implies that some of the intervals become larger or smaller by a semitone (e.g., minor instead of major third, diminished instead of perfect fifth). If, on the other hand, the intervals of the model are preserved exactly, the sequence is *real* [see Tonal and real]. In practice most sequences are of a mixed type called *modulatory* or *chromatic.* The sequence is an important device for effecting *modulations. In music of the late 18th century, the term *rosalia* is applied to particularly unimaginative or mechanical sequences.

(2) A type of medieval chant associated with the Roman rite [see Gregorian chant], syllabic in style, and consisting of a single line or versicle of music and text followed by a succession of pairs of versicles (the two elements in any pair being identical in poetic structure and employing the same melody) and concluded with another single versicle. The form is thus x aa bb cc dd . . . y. The origins of the sequence are the subject of some debate. The earliest examples, beginning in about the 10th century, seem to have resulted from the adaption of a text (L. *prosa,* F. *prose,* the latter having been retained to apply to both text and music) to a preexistent melisma (L. *sequentia*) sung following the Alleluia. The earliest known writer of sequences was Notker Balbulus (*c.* 840–912), a monk of St. Gall who describes the process of fitting texts to melodies as an aid to the memory learned from a French monk. In the following centuries, the musical and poetic structure of the sequence became increasingly regular,

the final stage in this development being reached in the 12th century in the works of Adam of St. Victor, who employed regular rhyme schemes throughout and who omitted the single versicles at beginning and end. The *Council of Trent (1545–63) prohibited the use of all but four sequences: Wipo of Burgundy's Easter sequence *Victimae paschali laudes* (the only remnant of the older type); the sequence for Whitsunday, *Veni sancte spiritus* (Golden Sequence, attributed to Innocent III, late 12th cent.); Thomas Aquinas' sequence for Corpus Christi, *Lauda Sion* (*c.* 1261); and Thomas of Celano's sequence for the *Requiem Mass, *Dies irae* (*c.* 1200). In 1727 a fifth sequence was adopted for liturgical use, Jacopone da Todi's celebrated *Stabat Mater*. Similar to the sequence in form are the *estampie* and the *lai*. The sequence should not be confused with the *trope.

Sequentia [L.]. See under Sequence.

Serebrier, José (b. Montevideo, Uruguay, 3 Dec. 1938). Conductor and composer. Pupil of Giannini and Copland. Settled in the U.S. in 1950. Composer-in-residence with the Cleveland Orchestra, 1968–70. Has composed orch. works (incl. *Elegy for Strings,* 1954; a symphony, 1956; *Partita,* 1958); *Colores mágicos* for harp and chamber orch. with projections, 1971; choral works; chamber music; piano pieces; songs.

Serenade. In the 18th century, originally a vocal or instrumental piece performed outdoors in the evening for the benefit of some particular listener. As a title for instrumental works of the period, the term was closely related to *cassation, *notturno,* and *divertimento. It may apply to lighter multimovement works in a variety of scorings, including mixed strings and winds, often intended for soloistic (i.e., with a single player on each part) as opposed to orchestral performance. Since the 18th century (and in discussions of 18th-century music since that time), the term has been most often applied to lighter multimovement works for winds or for scorings intended for orchestral performance. Examples include Mozart's *Haffner Serenade (K. 250) and K. 388, and Brahms' op. 11 and op. 16.

Serenata [It.]. (1) *Serenade. (2) A short 18th-century operatic work written to celebrate the birthday of a royal person (particularly at the Viennese court) and performed (in the evening?) in a reception room with costumes and modest scenery. Well-known examples are Handel's *Acis and Galatea* (1720) and his earlier *Aci, Galatea e Polifemo* (Naples, 1708).

Serial music. Music in which the organization particularly of pitch, but also that of other parameters such as *duration, *timbre, *register, and *dynamics, is based on a particular ordering (or series) of the twelve *pitch classes (or, in the cases of other parameters, a series of durations, etc.). When applied to pitch, the technique and the resulting music are described as *twelve-tone* or *dodecaphonic*. The term *serial* is now often restricted to music in which parameters other than pitch are also serialized. According to the conventions of this technique, the particular series (or the *row* or *set*) of the twelve pitch classes on which a composition is based has four principal forms: the original or prime form, the *inversion of the original form (produced by inverting the intervals separating adjacent elements of the row), the *retrograde of the original form, and the retrograde of the inversion. Each of these principal forms of the row can be transposed to begin on any of the twelve pitch classes, with the result that for each row there is a total of forty-eight forms. A further convention of this method of organizing pitch is that no member of a row can be repeated until all eleven others have been sounded. Any number of elements of the row can be stated simultaneously, however, so long as the convention of repetition is not violated. These conventions typically result in the avoidance of any sense of tonal center [see Tonality; Atonality]. Composers employing these techniques have also usually avoided symmetry and periodicity of the kinds encountered in tonal music. An important aspect of the study and practice of organizing pitch in this way is the analysis of rows in terms of the two *hexachords* (i.e., groups of six pitch classes comprising pitch classes 1–6 and 7–12 of the row) of which each consists. Those properties of a row (and its component hexachords) that enable pairs of its forms to be combined in such a way that the first hexachord of one member of a pair has no pitch classes in common with the first hexachord of the other member of the pair determine the *combinatoriality* of the row.

Twelve-tone technique was developed by Arnold Schoenberg and first used in parts of his op. 23 and op. 24 and throughout his op. 25 (composed 1920–23). [See also Trope (2).] Particularly important in the further development of the technique were Anton Webern, Alban Berg, and later Milton Babbitt, the latter having contributed greatly to a fuller exploitation of the technique's potential as well as to the development of techniques for serializing non-pitch parameters of music and to the adaptation of all of these techniques to electronic music. Other composers of serial music include Boulez, Stockhausen, Krenek, and Dallapiccola. Composers as different from these as Stravinsky and Copland have occasionally made use of serial techniques; thus a variety of styles is possible within this framework.

Sermisy, Claudin de (b. *c.* 1490; d. Paris, 13 Sept. 1562). Musician at the Sainte-Chapelle in Paris in 1508, becoming a canon there in 1533. Singer in the private chapel of Louis XII from 1508, becoming *sous-maître* under Francis I and continuing to serve under Henry II from 1547. Composed Masses and motets; numerous chansons.

Serocki, Kazimierz (b. Torun, Poland, 3 Mar. 1922). Pianist and composer. Studied in Lodz and with N. Boulanger in Paris. Was one of the founders of the Warsaw Autumn festival in 1956. Has worked with Polish folksongs and, more recently, with serial and aleatory procedures. Has composed symphonies (no. 2 with soloists and chorus) and other orch. works (incl. *Symphonic Frescoes,* 1964); works for trombone, for piano, for 2 pianos, and for organ with orch.; choral works (incl. *Niobe* with narrators and orch., 1966); chamber music; piano pieces; songs.

Serov, Alexander Nikolaievich (b. St. Petersburg, 23 Jan. 1820; d. there, 1 Feb. 1871). Critic and composer. Largely self-taught in composition. An advocate of

Wagner in his writings. Composed operas (incl. *Judith,* St. Petersburg, 1863; *Rogneda,* St. Petersburg, 1865; *Malevolent Power,* completed posthumously by N. T. Soloviev and prod. in St. Petersburg, 1871); incidental music for plays; orch. works; church music; piano pieces.

Serpent. See under Cornett; see ill. under Brass instruments.

Serva padrona, La [It., The Maid as Mistress]. *Comic opera in two acts by Pergolesi (libretto by G. A. Federico), produced in Naples, 1733, as an *intermezzo between the three acts of his serious opera, *Il prigionier superbo* (The Haughty Prisoner). Setting: Naples, 1733.

Service. A group of musical settings of the *canticles and other items (Kyrie, Creed, etc.) from the Book of Common Prayer of the Church of England. A morning service consists of Venite exultemus, *Te Deum, and Benedictus, or the alternatives Benedictus es [see under Benedictus Dominus Deus Israel], Benedicite, and Jubilate. The evening service includes the Magnificat and the Nunc dimittis, or the alternatives Cantate Domino and Deus misereatur. The Communion service begins with the Decalogue (or Responses after the Commandments) and/or the *Kyrie, and continues with settings of the Creed, *Sanctus, *Benedictus qui venit, *Agnus Dei, and *Gloria in excelsis. Each canticle is traditionally referred to by the original Latin incipit, although all are sung in English. A complete service includes most of the items listed above, usually composed in the same key and therefore commonly referred to by simply the name of the composer and the key, e.g., Ouseley in B minor. In the 20th century, particularly in the United States, many of the canticles have been composed singly rather than as complete or partial services. The terms "short service" and "great service," used chiefly in the 16th and early 17th centuries, refer to the shorter, syllabic style of the former and the richer, contrapuntal style of the latter, with its repetition of textual phrases.

Sesqui- [L.]. Prefix used to denote fractions whose numerator is larger by one than the denominator, e.g., *sesquialtera:* 3/2. In early music theory these terms were used for either ratios of string lengths (i.e., intervals) or ratios of time values (i.e., *proportions). The former meaning occurs also in the organ stop "sesquialtera," originally a mixture stop combining the octave with the fifth but usually also including other harmonics, such as the third in various octaves. Another term for sesquialtera is *hemiola.

Sessions, Roger (Huntington) (b. Brooklyn, 28 Dec. 1896). Studied at Harvard, with Parker at Yale, and with Bloch. Teacher at Smith College, 1917–21; the Cleveland Institute of Music, 1921–25; Princeton Univ., 1935–45 and 1953–65; Univ. of California at Berkeley, 1945–51; the Juilliard School from 1965. His pupils incl. Babbitt, Cone, Finney, Imbrie, Kirchner, Kim, and Martino. Has worked with twelve-tone techniques. Has composed 2 operas, *The *Trial of Lucullus* and *Montezuma;* incidental music to *The Black Maskers,* 1923; 8 symphonies, a *Divertimento for Orchestra,* 1960, a *Rhapsody for Orchestra,* 1970, and other orch. music; concertos for violin, 1935, for piano, 1956, and for viola and cello, 1971; *Idyll of Theocritus* for soprano and orch., 1954; choral works (incl. a Mass, 1955, and the cantata *When Lilacs Last in the Door-yard Bloom'd,* 1970); 2 string quartets and other chamber music; piano pieces (incl. 3 sonatas and *From My Diary,* 1939); organ music; songs. Has written *The Musical Experience of Composer, Performer, and Listener,* 1950; *Harmonic Practice,* 1951; and *Questions about Music,* 1970.

Sestetto [It.]. *Sextet.

Set. See under Serial music.

Seter, Mordecai (b. Novorossisk, Russia, 26 Feb. 1916). Pupil of Stravinsky, Dukas, and N. Boulanger. Teacher at the Israel Music Academy in Tel Aviv from 1952. Has worked with Middle-Eastern Jewish liturgical and folk materials and with serial techniques. Has composed ballets (incl. *Judith,* for Martha Graham, 1962); orch. works (incl. *The Daughter of Jephtah,* 1965); choral works (incl. a *Sabbath Cantata,* 1947, and *Jerusalem,* 1966); chamber music; piano pieces.

Seven (Last) Words, The. The seven last words of Christ (compiled from the four Gospels) have been used as a text for *Passion music, e.g., by Heinrich Schütz (*Die Sieben Worte, c.* 1645), Haydn (1785), and Gounod (*Les sept paroles du Christ sur la croix,* 1855). Haydn's composition, commissioned by the Bishop of Cadiz, was not originally a choral setting of the text but a series of seven instrumental "sonatas," each to be played after the recitation of one of the "words." As such, its title was *Instrumentalmusik über die Sieben letzten Worte unseres Erlösers am Kreuze oder Sieben Sonaten mit einer Einleitung und am Schluss ein Erdbeben* (Instrumental music on the seven last words of our Savior on the cross, or Seven sonatas with an introduction and at the end an earthquake). It appeared in four versions: for orchestra (op. 47, 1785); for string quartet (op. 48, 1787); for harpsichord or piano (op. 49, 1787), a version not actually made by Haydn but approved by him; an oratorio version appearing by 1796, choral parts having first been added in 1792 by Joseph Friebert to his own text, which text was later revised by Haydn and Baron Gottfried van Swieten.

Seventh. See under Interval; Scale degrees.

Seventh chord. A *chord consisting of some pitch plus the pitches a third, fifth, and seventh above it. In a given key there are seven such chords, one on each degree of the scale, e.g., in C major: c–e –g–b (I⁷), d–f–a–c' (II⁷), e–g–b–d' (III⁷), etc. By far the most important of these is the one on the fifth degree, the so-called dominant seventh: g–b–d'–f' (V⁷). While each of the seven "diatonic" seventh chords contains major as well as minor thirds (in various arrangements), there also is a seventh chord consisting of minor thirds only, the *diminished seventh chord.* It usually appears on the seventh degree of the scale, e.g., b–d'– f'–ab' in C (major or minor). The normal resolution of this chord is into the tonic triad (c'–e'–g'). Because it functions much as does a harmony built on the *dominant, it is frequently called a dominant ninth chord (g–b–d'–f'–ab') with the root (g) omitted. See Harmonic analysis; Ninth chord; Scale degrees.

Séverac, (Joseph-Marie) Déodat de (b. Saint-Félix-de-Caraman, Languedoc, 20 July 1873; d. Céret, 24 Mar. 1921). Pupil of Magnard, d'Indy, and Guilmant. Composed operas (incl. *Coeur du moulin,* Paris, 1909); incidental music for plays; orch. works; sacred and secular choral works; chamber music; piano pieces (incl. *Le chant de la terre,* 1900; *En Languedoc,* 1904); organ pieces; songs and arrangements of folksongs.

Sext. (1) The fifth canonical hour; see Office. (2) German term (also *Sexte*) for the interval of the sixth.

Sextet [F. *sextette, sextuor;* G. *Sextett;* It. *sestetto;* Sp. *sexteto*]. Music for six performers, in various combinations, e.g., two violins, two violas, and two cellos (Brahms, op. 18, op. 36; Dvořák, op. 48); string quartet and two horns (Beethoven, op. 81b); two clarinets, two horns, two bassoons (Beethoven, op. 71).

Sextolet [F.; G. *Sextole;* It. *sestina;* Sp. *seisillo*]. A group of six notes played in the time normally occupied by four notes of the same kind; indicated by a 6, sometimes together with a slur.

Seyfried, Ignaz Xaver (b. Vienna, 15 Aug. 1776; d. there, 27 Aug. 1841). Pupil of Mozart, Koželuch, Haydn, Winter, and Albrechtsberger. Conductor at Schikaneder's theater in Vienna from 1797 and at the new Theater an der Wien, 1801–27. Composed operas, *Singspiele* (incl. *Die Ochsenmenuette,* after Haydn, Vienna, 1799), melodramas, ballets, and other stage works; church music; oratorios; symphonies; chamber music.

Sfoggiando [It.]. Ostentatiously.

Sforzando, sforzato [It.; abbr. *sf, sfz*]. Forcing, i.e., with a sudden strong accent on a single note or chord. *Sfp, sforzando* followed immediately by *piano.*

Sgambati, Giovanni (b. Rome, 28 May 1841; d. there, 14 Dec. 1914). Pianist, conductor, and composer. Pupil of Liszt. Established, in connection with the Accademia di Santa Cecilia, and taught at the Liceo musicale (so named in 1876) in Rome from 1868 until his death. Concertized widely in Europe and Russia. Composed 2 symphonies and other orch. works; a piano concerto; a Requiem and other church music; chamber music; numerous piano pieces, incl. some pedagogic works; songs.

Shake. Older name for the *trill.

Shakuhachi [Jap.]. A Japanese vertical bamboo flute with four finger holes in front and one in back. For ill. see under Flute.

Shamisen [Jap.]. See under Lute.

Shank. See under Wind instruments.

Shanty, chanty, chantey. Names for work songs of English and American sailors, sung while pulling ropes or performing other work requiring concerted effort.

Shape-note. See Fasola.

Shapero, Harold (Samuel) (b. Lynn, Mass., 29 Apr. 1920). Pupil of Slonimsky, Piston, Krenek, Hindemith, and N. Boulanger. Teacher at Brandeis Univ. from 1952. Has composed orch. works (incl. a *Symphony for Classical Orchestra,* 1947; *Credo for Orchestra,* 1955); *Partita* for piano and small orch., 1960; *Hebrew Cantata,* 1954; a string quartet, 1940, and other chamber music; 3 sonatas and other piano pieces; pieces for piano and synthesizer.

Shapey, Ralph (b. Philadelphia, 12 Mar. 1921). Violinist, conductor, and composer. Pupil of Wolpe. Teacher at the Univ. of Pennsylvania, 1963–64; at the Univ. of Chicago from 1964, and conductor there of the Contemporary Chamber Players. Has composed orch. works (incl. *Rituals,* 1959); a violin concerto, 1959; the oratorio *Praise,* 1976; *Songs of Ecstasy* for soprano, piano, percussion, and tape, 1967; *Incantations* for soprano and 10 instruments, 1961; 7 string quartets and other chamber music (incl. *Evocation* for violin, piano, and percussion); piano pieces; songs.

Shaporin, Yuri Alexandrovich (b. Glukhov, Ukraine, 8 Nov. 1887; d. Moscow, 9 Dec. 1966). Studied at the St. Petersburg Conservatory. Teacher at the Moscow Conservatory from 1939 until his death. Composed operas (incl. *The De-*

cembrists, 1930–50, prod. Moscow, 1953); incidental music to plays; orch. works; cantatas (incl. *A Tale of the Battle for the Russian Land,* 1944); choral works; piano pieces; songs; music for films.

Sharp [F. *dièse;* G. *Kreuz;* It. *diesis;* Sp. *sostenido*]. The sign ♯, which indicates the raising of the pitch of a note by a half-step. "Sharp" also designates incorrect intonation on the higher side of the appropriate pitch. See Accidentals; Pitch names.

Shawm [F. *chalemie;* G. *Schalmei;* It. *piffaro*]. See under Oboe family III.

Shchedrin, Rodion Konstantinovich (b. Moscow, 16 Dec. 1932). Pianist and composer. Pupil of Shaporin. Teacher at the Moscow Conservatory, 1964–69. Has composed operas (incl. *Not Love Alone,* 1961; *Dead Souls,* Moscow, 1977); ballets (incl. *Humpback Horse,* 1959; *Carmen Ballet,* after Bizet, 1967; *Anna Karenina,* 1972); 2 symphonies and other orch. works (incl. *The Chimes,* 1967); 3 piano concertos; choral works; piano pieces; songs.

Shebalin, Vissarion Yakovlevich (b. Omsk, Russia, 11 June 1902; d. Moscow, 29 May 1963). Pupil of Miaskovsky. Teacher at the Moscow Conservatory from 1928 and its director, 1942–48. Composed operas (incl. *The Taming of the Shrew,* after Shakespeare, Moscow, 1955); ballets; 5 symphonies and other orch. works (incl. *Lenin,* with soloists and chorus, 1933); concertos for violin and for cello; the cantata *Moscow,* 1946, and other choral works; 9 string quartets and other chamber music; piano pieces; songs.

Shéhérazade. Song cycle for voice and orchestra by Ravel (to poems by T. Klingsor, inspired by the *Arabian Nights*), composed in 1903 and containing three songs: "Asie," "La flûte enchantée," and "L'indifférente." See also *Scheherazade* (Rimsky-Korsakov).

Sheng. A Chinese mouth organ. See ill. under Wind instruments.

Shepherd, Arthur (b. Paris, Idaho, 19 Feb. 1880; d. Cleveland, 12 Jan. 1958). Conductor, critic, and composer. Pupil

of P. Goetschius and Chadwick. Teacher at the New England Conservatory, 1908 –17; at Western Reserve Univ., 1927– 50. Composed orch. works (incl. 4 overtures, 2 symphonies, and *Fantasy on Down East Spirituals,* 1946); works for piano and for violin with orch.; choral works; 3 string quartets and other chamber music; piano pieces; songs.

Shepherd, John (b. *c.* 1520; d. London?, 1563?). Master of the choristers at Magdalen College, Oxford, 1542–43 and from 1545. Gentleman of the Chapel Royal, 1552–54 and 1557. Composed Latin and English church music; instrumental pieces; part songs.

Sheriff, Noam (b. Ramat-Gan, Israel, 7 July 1935). Conductor and composer. Pupil of Blacher and Ben-Haim. Teacher at the Jerusalem Academy of Music, 1966–67; at the Academy of Music in Tel Aviv from 1967. Has worked with Oriental and Jewish materials and with serial techniques. Has composed works for orch. (incl. *Chaconne,* 1968) and chamber orch. (incl. *Heptaprisms,* 1965); music for dance (incl. *Cain,* on tape, 1969); choral works; chamber music; piano pieces.

Shield, William (b. Whickham, Durham, 5 Mar. 1748; d. Brightling, Sussex, 25 Jan. 1829). Violinist and composer. Pupil of Avison. Violist at the Haymarket Theatre, 1773–91. Composer to the Covent Garden Theatre, 1778–97. Master of the King's Music from 1817. Composed about 40 stage works (incl. the comic opera *Rosina,* London, 1782); string quartets and other chamber music; songs. Published 2 theoretical treatises.

Shifrin, Seymour (b. Brooklyn, 28 Feb. 1926). Pupil of Schuman, Luening, and Milhaud. Teacher at the Univ. of California at Berkeley, 1952–66; at Brandeis Univ. from 1966. Has composed orch. works (incl. a *Chamber Symphony,* 1954; *3 Pieces,* 1958); choral works; 5 string quartets and other chamber music (incl. *Serenade for 5 Instruments,* 1954; *Satires of Circumstance* for mezzo-soprano and 6 instruments, 1964); piano pieces (incl. *Responses,* 1977); songs.

Shift, shifting. Movement from one *position to another in violin playing.

Shinohara, Makoto (b. Osaka, Japan, 10 Dec. 1931). Pupil of Ikenouchi, Messiaen, and Stockhausen. Has worked at the Electronic Music Studio of Utrecht Univ. and at the Columbia-Princeton Electronic Music Center. Works incl. *Visions II* for orch., 1970; *Alternance* for percussion, 1961; chamber music; *Mémoires,* on tape, 1966; *Tendance* for piano, 1969.

Shivaree. U.S. corruption of **charivari.*

Shnitke, Alfred (b. Engels, U.S.S.R., 24 Nov. 1934). Studied at the Moscow Conservatory, where he has taught since 1961. Has worked at the Moscow Electronic Music Studio. Has composed *The Yellow Sound,* after Kandinsky, for 9 instruments, tape, chorus, pantomime, and projections, 1973; the oratorio *Nagasaki,* 1958; orch. works; 2 violin concertos, a piano concerto, and a concerto for oboe, harp, and strings, 1970; a string quartet, a violin sonata, and other chamber music; piano pieces; songs; electronic works; music for films, theater, and television. Has written on the music of Shostakovich and other topics.

Shofar. An ancient Jewish instrument made from a ram's horn and used to the present day in Jewish rites for the celebration of the New Year.

Short octave. A special arrangement of the keys in the lowest octave of early organs, harpsichords, etc. The fact that the lowest chromatic tones (C ♯, D ♯, F ♯, G ♯) were almost never needed in keyboard music prior to *c.* 1700 naturally led to the omission of the corresponding pipes or strings. On the keyboard, instead of omitting the four corresponding keys, the keys for the remaining eight tones were arranged in a "shortened" octave that extended downward only to the key normally occupied by E. The keys for the tones F, G, A, B♭, and B were usually left in their normal position, and the three remaining keys (normally E, F ♯, G ♯) were allotted to the tones C, D, and E in one way or another. An advantage of this arrangement was that it enabled playing certain widely spaced chords, e.g., E–B–e–g ♯, with the left hand alone. A later (19th century) arrangement on pianos was the *broken octave.* Here the lowest octave was com-

plete with twelve keys, except that C ♯ was replaced by the more useful note A₁ from below.

Short service. See under Service.

Shostakovich, Dmitri Dmitrievich (b. St. Petersburg, 25 Sept. 1906; d. Moscow, 9 Aug. 1975). Studied composition with Steinberg, and piano at the St. Petersburg Conservatory. Teacher at the Leningrad Conservatory, 1937–41 and 1945–48; at the Moscow Conservatory, 1943–48; at both institutions beginning in the 1960s. Composed operas (incl. *The Nose,* after Gogol, Leningrad, 1930; **Lady Macbeth of Mtsensk*); ballets (incl. *The Golden Age,* 1920); incidental music to plays; 15 symphonies, of which nos. 1 (1925), 5 "A Composer's Answer to Just Criticism" (1937), 7 "Leningrad" (1941), 10 (1953), and 13 (1962), with chorus and texts by Yevtushenko, attracted particular attention; other orch. works; 2 concertos each for piano, for violin, and for cello; choral works; chamber music (incl. 15 string quartets, 2 piano trios, a piano quintet, and sonatas for violin, for cello, and for viola); piano pieces (incl. 2 sonatas, 1926 and 1942, and 24 preludes and fugues, 1951); numerous songs (with texts from Jewish folk poetry, 1948; Pushkin, 1936; Shakespeare, Burns, and Raleigh, 1942; Tsvetaeva, 1973; and Michelangelo, 1974); much music for films. He reorchestrated Mussorgsky's *Boris Godunov* and *Khovanshchina.*

Si. See under Pitch names; Solmization.

Sibelius, Jean (Johann Julius Christian) (b. Tavastehus, Finland, 8 Dec. 1865; d. Järvenpää, 20 Sept. 1957). Studied in Helsinki with Wegelius, in Berlin, and with R. Fuchs and K. Goldmark in Vienna. Teacher at the Helsinki Conservatory, 1892–97. Many of his best-known works were based on the **Kalevala* or other Finnish subjects. He stopped composing in 1929. Composed an opera, *Jungfruburen* (The Maid in the Tower), Helsinki, 1896; incidental music for plays (incl. Järnefelt's *Kuolema,* 1903, containing the *Valse triste;* Maeterlinck's *Pelléas et Mélisande,* 1905; Strindberg's *Svanevhit,* 1908; Knudsen's *Scaramouche,* pantomime, 1913; Hofmannsthal's *Jedermann,* 1916; Shakespeare's *The Tempest,* 1926); 7 symphonies; symphonic poems (incl. *Kullervo* with soloist and chorus, 1892; *En Saga,* 1892, rev. 1901; *4 Legends from the Kalevala: Lemminkäinen and the Maidens,* 1895, *Lemminkäinen in Tuonela,* 1895, *The *Swan of Tuonela,* 1893, *Lemminkäinen's Homecoming,* 1895; *Finlandia; *Pohjala's Daughter; The Oceanides,* 1914; *Tapiola*); overtures and other orch. works (incl. the overture and the suite *Karelia*); choral works, some with orch.; a violin concerto, 1903, rev. 1905, and 6 *Humoresques* for violin and orch., 1917; chamber music (incl. 2 string quartets; *Voces intimae* for string quartet, 1909; 2 piano trios; 2 piano quartets; 2 sonatas and a number of smaller pieces for violin and piano); about 20 sets of piano pieces; numerous songs.

Siciliana, siciliano. A 17th- and 18th-century dance of Sicilian origin, in moderate 6/8 or 12/8 meter, usually with a flowing broken-chord accompaniment and a soft, lyrical melody with dotted rhythms—very similar to, if not identical with, the *pastorale.

Sicilianos, Yorgo (b. Athens, 29 Aug. 1922). Pupil of M. Varvoglis in Athens and of Pizzetti, Piston, Blacher, and Persichetti. Has worked for the Hellenic Broadcasting Network. Teacher at Pierce College in Athens from 1967. Has worked with serial techniques. Has composed ballets (incl. *Bacchantes,* 1959); incidental music for the theater, incl. plays of Euripides; orch. works (incl. a symphony, 1958, and a concerto for orch., 1954); a cello concerto, 1963; choral works; string quartets and other chamber music; piano pieces.

Side drum. Snare drum; see Percussion instruments II, 1.

Siefert, Paul (b. Danzig, bapt. 28 June 1586; d. there, 6 May 1666). Pupil of Sweelinck. Organist at Königsberg, 1611–16; in the chapel of Sigismund III of Poland, 1616–23; at St. Mary's in Danzig from 1623. Composed settings of the Psalms and other sacred works; organ pieces.

Siege of Rhodes, The. The first English opera. Libretto in five entries by W. Davenant, with music (now lost) by Henry Lawes, Henry Cooke, Matthew Locke, George Hudson, and Charles Coleman. Produced in London, 1656.

Siegfried. See *Ring des Nibelungen, Der.*

Siegfried Idyll. A composition for small orchestra by Wagner, composed in 1870 and first performed in his home at Triebschen (hence also called *Triebschen Idyll*) on the birthday of his wife, Cosima. The title refers to their son, Siegfried, then just over one year old. It is based on themes from Wagner's opera *Siegfried* but also includes the cradle song "Schlaf, Kindchen, schlaf" (Sleep, baby, sleep).

Siegmeister, Elie (b. New York, 15 Jan. 1909). Conductor and composer. Studied at Columbia Univ. and with Riegger and N. Boulanger. Teacher at Hofstra College from 1949. Active as a collector and performer of folksongs. Has composed 4 operas (incl. *The Plough and the Stars,* libretto by Sean O'Casey, St. Louis, 1963); a musical, *Sing Out, Sweet Land,* 1944, and other works for the theater; 5 symphonies and other orch. works (incl. *Ozark Set,* 1944; *Prairie Legend,* 1947); concertos for flute and for clarinet; choral works; string quartets, violin sonatas, and much other chamber music; piano pieces; numerous songs. Has published a theory textbook and other writings.

Sight. In English 15th-century treatises, a term indicating the ranges and permissible intervals of the voice-parts added above a plainsong, primarily in connection with improvised counterpoint. In some circumstances, the added voice is called a *meane.*

Sight-reading, -singing [F. *à livre ouvert;* G. *vom-Blatt-Spiel;* It. *prima vista*]. Reading or performing music at first sight, i.e., without preparatory study.

Signature. A sign placed at the beginning of a composition to indicate the key [see Key signature] or meter [see Time signature].

Silva, Andreas de (b. between 1475 and 1480). Perhaps a Spaniard, though said by Galilei to have been French or Fleming. Singer and composer in the papal chapel in Rome, 1519–20. Served at the court in Mantua in 1522. Composed Masses, motets, and other sacred works; madrigals.

Silvestrov, Valentin Vasilievich (b. Kiev, 30 Sept. 1937). Pupil of Liatoshinsky. Teacher at Kiev Univ., 1963–65, and at the Music Studio of the Society of the Ukraine, 1965–69. Has worked with twelve-tone techniques. Has composed works for orch. and for chamber orch. (incl. 2 symphonies; *Monodia,* 1965); *Hymn* for 5 instrumental groups, 1967; chamber music; piano pieces; songs; music for films.

Similar motion. See Motion.

Simile, simili [It.]. Indication to continue "in the same way," e.g., with the same kind of bowing, or with the same type of broken-chord figure, etc.

Simon Boccanegra. Opera in three acts and a prologue by Verdi (libretto by F. M. Piave, rev. by A. Boito, based on a play by A. Gutiérrez), produced in Venice, 1857; rev. version in Milan, 1881. Setting: Genoa and environs, mid-14th century.

Simpson, Christopher (b. *c.* 1605; d. Scampton, Lincolnshire, 1669). Viola da gamba player and composer. Music tutor to the son of Sir Robert Bolles. Composed fancies, suites, etc., for viola da gamba and for viol consort. Published *The Division Violist or an Introduction to the Playing upon a Ground,* 1659 and later eds., with examples; *The Principles of Practicle Musick,* 1665 and later eds.

Sims, Ezra (b. Birmingham, Ala., 16 Jan. 1928). Pupil of Porter, Milhaud, and Kirchner. On the staff of the music library at Harvard Univ. from 1958. Has worked with *musique concrète,* tape collage, and microtonal techniques. Has composed music for the theater and for dance, some on tape; vocal works; string quartets (no. 3 with quarter tones, 1962) and other chamber music.

Simultaneity. Any two or more pitches sounded simultaneously. The term is used particularly with reference to 20th-century music and as an alternative to *chord.

Sin' al fine (segno) [It.]. Until the end (the sign). See *Segno.*

Sinding, Christian August (b. Kongsberg, Norway, 11 Jan. 1856; d. Oslo, 3 Dec. 1941). Pianist and composer. Studied in Norway and with Jadassohn and Reinecke in Leipzig. Teacher at the Eastman School of Music, 1921–22. Composed 2 operas; 4 symphonies and other orch. works; a piano concerto, 3 violin concertos, and other works for violin and orch.; choral works; 3 piano trios and other chamber music; numerous piano pieces (incl. *Frühlingsrauschen* [Rustle of Spring], 1896); numerous songs and arrangements of folksongs.

Sinfonia. (1) [It.]. *Symphony. (2) A name chosen by Bach for his three-part *inventions. (3) In the baroque period (1600–1750), name for orchestral pieces of Italian origin, designed to serve as an introduction to an opera or operatic scene, an orchestral suite, or a cantata. Bach also wrote a sinfonia for harpsichord, in his Partita no. 2. No fixed form or style attaches to these pieces. Not until *c.*1690 did the operatic *sinfonia* become standardized (by A. Scarlatti) into what is usually called the "Italian overture" [see Overture], one of the ancestors of the modern symphony.

Sinfonia concertante [It.]. Term used by Mozart and others for a symphony with one or more solo instruments.

Sinfonietta [It.]. A small symphony, usually scored for a small orchestra.

Sinfonische Dichtung [G.]. *Symphonic poem.

Singing saw. An ordinary handsaw, held between the knees and set in vibration by either a violin bow or drumsticks. Its special effect is a continuous modification of pitch obtained by bending the free end of the blade with the left hand.

Singspiel [G.]. About 1700, the German equivalent for *dramma per musica* (drama with music), i.e., opera, including both serious and comic operas (e.g., Keiser's *Croesus,* 1711). Later (*c.* 1750) the term was restricted to comic operas with spoken dialogue, written on the models of the English *ballad opera or the French *opéra comique.* Charles Coffey's ballad operas *The Devil To Pay* (1731) and *The Merry Cobbler* (1735) were translated by C. F. Weisse (*Der*

Teufel ist los and *Der lustige Schuster*) and then set to new music by J. C. Standfuss (*c.* 1750). J. A. Hiller (1728–1804) wrote operas to the same two librettos and many others (*Lisuart und Dariolette,* 1766; *Die Jagd,* 1770), representing the high point of the Leipzig *Singspiel.* From Leipzig the movement spread elsewhere, chiefly to Berlin and Vienna. Most of the members of the *Berlin school wrote *Singspiele,* notably Georg Benda (*Der Dorfjahrmarkt,* 1775). In Vienna, where as early as 1751 the young Haydn wrote *Der krumme Teufel* (lost), the *Singspiel* reached its artistic peak in Mozart's *Die *Entführung aus dem Serail* (1782). Also see Opera; Comic opera.

Sinigaglia, Leone (b. Turin, 14 Aug. 1868; d. there, 16 May 1944). Studied in Turin, Vienna, and with Dvořák in Prague. Composed orch. works (incl. *Danze piemontesi,* 1905); a violin concerto and a *Rapsodia piemontese* for violin and orch.; chamber music; piano pieces; songs, incl. 6 books of folksongs from the Piedmont, with piano accompaniment.

Sinistra [It.]. Left (hand).

Sink-a-pace, sinqua-pace. *Cinque-pace.

Sistine choir (chapel). The present name of the papal choir of 32 singers who provide the music for services in which the Pope officiates. It developed from the ancient *schola cantorum* and received its present name from the *Cappella Sixtina,* the chapel built by Pope Sixtus IV (1471–84). Since 1480 another choir has existed, the *Cappella Giulia* (endowed by Pope Julian II), that performs at St. Peter's and has often been mistakenly called the Sistine choir.

Sistrum. An ancient Egyptian rattle used in the worship of Isis. For ill. see under Percussion instruments.

Sitar. An Indian long-necked lute of Persian origin with movable frets and from three to seven strings in addition to approximately a dozen thin *sympathetic strings. It is related to the vīna. See ill. under Lute.

Six-four chord. The second *inversion of the triad, e.g., for the C major triad, g–c′ –e′, indicated I⁶₄ in the key of C in mod-

ern *harmonic analysis, and ⁶₄ in figured-bass parts [see Thoroughbass], the intervals formed with the lowest sounding pitch being a sixth and a fourth.

Six, Les [F.]. A name applied in 1920 to a group of six French composers—Louis Durey, Arthur Honegger, Darius Milhaud, Germaine Tailleferre, Georges Auric, and Francis Poulenc—who *c.* 1916 formed a loose association based on their acceptance of the aesthetic ideas of Erik Satie. See also École d'Arcueil, L'.

Sixth. See under Interval; Scale degrees.

Sixth chord. The first *inversion of the triad, e.g., for the C major triad, e–g–c′, indicated I⁶ in the key of C in modern *harmonic analysis, and 6 or ⁶₃ in figured-bass parts [see Thoroughbass]. Also called a six-three chord because the intervals formed with the lowest sounding pitch are a sixth and a third. The *Neapolitan sixth, f–a♭–d♭′ in C major, is usually described as the first inversion of the triad on the lowered supertonic, d♭–f –a♭. Among the numerous chromatic variations on the chord of the sixth, those containing an augmented sixth, e.g., a♭–f♯′, deserve special mention.

There are four common ones: the augmented sixth, the augmented six-five-three, the augmented six-four-three, and the doubly augmented six-four-three. The first three are sometimes called (without historical reason) "Italian," "German," and "French" sixth, respectively. Their derivations and common resolutions are shown in the example (+ and ++ indicate augmented and doubly augmented intervals). See also Added sixth.

Sixth-chord style. Designation for passages formed of consecutive *sixth chords. Such passages are often called "fauxbourdon," but this term should be restricted to one particular manifestation of sixth-chord style, described under Fauxbourdon. Rapid sixth-chord progressions occur in the works of Bach, Mozart, Beethoven, Brahms, and others. However, sixth-chord style plays a much more important role in the music of the late Middle Ages (*c*. 1300–1450). The earliest instances are found in English manuscripts of *c*. 1300. Short progressions in sixth chords are quite common in the works of Landini, especially in *cadences. The sixth-chord style reached its culmination in the compositions of Dunstable, Dufay, and Binchois.

Sjögren, (Johan Gustaf) Emil (b. Stockholm, 16 June 1853; d. there, 1 Mar. 1918). Studied in Stockholm, Berlin, and Vienna. Organist at St. John's Church in Stockholm from 1891 until his death. Composed an overture; choral works; 5 violin sonatas and a cello sonata; piano pieces (incl. 2 sonatas and *Erotikon*, 1883); about 200 songs, with texts by Ibsen and others.

Skalkottas, Nikos (b. Chalcis, Euboea, Greece, 8 Mar. 1904; d. Athens, 19 Sept. 1949). Violinist and composer. Studied at the Athens Conservatory, at the Berlin Hochschule für Musik, and with Weill, Jarnach, and Schoenberg. Worked with twelve-tone techniques. Composed ballets and other music for the stage; orch. works (incl. *36 Greek Dances*, 1936; *Symphonic Suite* no. 2, 1944); works for solo instrument(s) with orch., incl. 3 piano concertos; choral works; 4 string quartets and other chamber music; piano pieces; songs.

Skilton, Charles Sanford (b. Northampton, Mass., 16 Aug. 1868; d. Lawrence, Kans., 12 Mar. 1941). Studied at Yale Univ., with Buck in New York, and with Bargiel in Berlin. Teacher at the Univ. of Kansas from 1903. Studied and made use of American Indian music. Composed operas (incl. *Kalopin*, 1930); orch. works (incl. *Suite Primeval*, part 1 of which, *2 Indian Dances*, 1915, was originally for string quartet; *Shawnee Indian Hunting Dance*, 1930); choral works; chamber music.

Skolie [G.]. Name used by Schubert and others for a drinking song.

Skrowaczewski, Stanislaw (b. Lvov, 3 Oct. 1923). Pupil of N. Boulanger and Honegger. Conductor of the Katowice Philharmonic, 1948–54; of the Warsaw Philharmonic, 1957–59; of the Minneapolis (since 1970 called the Minnesota) Orchestra from 1960. Has composed a ballet; 4 symphonies and other orch. works; choral works; a concerto for English horn; string quartets and other chamber music; piano pieces; songs.

Slancio, con [It.]. With dash.

Slargando [It.]. Slowing down.

Slavenski, Josip (b. Čakovec, Croatia, 11 May 1896; d. Belgrade, 30 Nov. 1955). Pupil of Kodály and Novák. Teacher at the Belgrade Academy of Music from 1949. Worked with microtonal and electronic techniques. Composed orch. works (incl. *Balkanophonia*, 1929); a violin concerto; choral works (incl. *Symphonie des Orients*, with soloists and orch., 1934); chamber music; piano pieces; music for films and the theater.

Sleeping Beauty, The. Ballet by Tchaikovsky (choreography by M. Petipa), completed in 1889 and produced in St. Petersburg in 1890.

Sléndro. See under Pentatonic scale.

Slentando [It.]. Slackening, slowing down.

Slide. (1) In violin playing, a slight *portamento used to pass quickly from one note to another, usually at the distance of a third or a fourth. (2) The movable portion of the *trombone. See also Wind instruments; Trumpet. (3) An ornament consisting of two or more notes approaching the main note by conjunct motion; see Appoggiatura, double.

Slide trumpet. See under Trumpet.

Slonimsky, Nicolas (Leonidovich) (b. St. Petersburg, 27 Apr. 1894). Pianist, conductor, musicologist, and composer. Pupil of Steinberg. Settled in the U.S. in 1923, where he has taught at various institutions, incl. the Univ. of California at Los Angeles, 1964–67. Has composed orch. works; chamber music; piano pieces (incl. *Studies in Black and White*, 1928); songs. Has published *Music since 1900*, 1937 and later eds.; *Lexicon of Mu-*

sical Invective, 1953, 1969; and other writings.

Slonimsky, Sergei Mikhailovich (b. Leningrad, 12 Aug. 1932). Nephew of Nicolas Slonimsky. Studied in Moscow with Shebalin and at the Leningrad Conservatory, where he has taught since 1958. Has studied and made some use of folk materials. Has composed the opera *Virineia,* Leningrad, 1967, rev. 1976; the chamber opera *Master and Margarita,* 1973; the ballet *Ikar,* 1969; orch. works (incl. a symphony, 1958; *Choreographic Miniatures,* 1963; *Concerto Buffo,* 1965); a concerto for orchestra, 3 electric guitars, and solo instruments, 1974; vocal works with orch.; chamber music (incl. *Antiphonies* for string quartet, 1968); piano pieces (incl. *Coloristic Fantasy,* 1972); organ pieces; songs; music for films.

Slur. (1) A curved line placed above or below a group of notes to indicate that they are to be rendered *legato,* e.g., with one stroke of the violin bow or with one breath (sometimes to a single syllable) in singing. When the notes under the slur have either dashes or *staccato dots, the meaning of the combined signs is *portato. A slur connecting two notes of equal pitch is properly called a *tie or bind. See also Phrase, phrasing. (2) An ornament resembling the French *tierce coulée* [see Appoggiatura, double].

Sly Vixen, The. See *Cunning Little Vixen, The.*

Smalley, Roger (b. Swinton, near Manchester, 26 July 1943). Pupil of Fricker and Stockhausen. Artist-in-residence at King's College, Cambridge, from 1967. Co-founder, with Souster, of the ensemble Intermodulation, 1970, devoted to the performance of live electronic works. Works incl. a *Missa Parodia,* 1967; *Strata* for 15 string players, 1970; *Beat Music* for 55 players, with electronics, 1971.

Smareglia, Antonio (b. Pola, Istria, 5 May 1854; d. Grado, near Trieste, 15 Apr. 1929). Studied engineering in Vienna and music at the Milan Conservatory. Teacher at the Tartini Conservatory in Trieste from 1921. Composed operas (incl. *Il vassallo di Szigeth,*

Vienna, 1889; *Nozze istriane,* Trieste, 1895); orch. works; sacred vocal works; piano pieces; songs.

Smetana, Bedřich (Friedrich) (b. Litomyšl, Czechoslovakia, 2 Mar. 1824; d. Prague, 12 May 1884). Pianist, conductor, and composer. A child prodigy, he studied in Prague, where Kittl aided him. Opened a piano school in Prague in 1848 with Liszt's help and encouragement. Conductor of the Philharmonic Society in Göteborg, Sweden, 1856–61; of the National Theater in Prague, 1866–74. Totally deaf from 1874. Composed operas (all first produced in Prague, incl. *The *Bartered Bride; Dalibor,* 1868; *Libussa,* completed 1872, prod. 1881; *The Kiss,* 1876; *The Secret,* 1878); symphonic poems (*Richard III,* 1858; *Wallenstein's Camp,* 1859; *Haakon Jarl,* 1861; *Má Vlast,* containing *The Moldau; The Prague Carnival,* 1883) and other orch. works; choral works; chamber music (incl. 2 string quartets *From My Life;* a piano trio, 1855; 2 pieces for violin and piano, 1878); piano pieces (incl. the concert etude *Am Seegestade,* 1862); songs.

Sminuendo [It.]. *Diminuendo, decrescendo.* See Crescendo, decrescendo.

Smit, Leo (b. Philadelphia, 12 Jan. 1921). Pianist and composer. Pupil of Nabokov. Teacher at the Univ. of California at Los Angeles, 1957–63; at the State Univ. of New York at Buffalo from 1963. Has composed an opera, *The Alchemy of Love,* libretto by Fred Hoyle, 1969; ballets (incl. *Virginia Sampler,* 1947); 2 symphonies and other orch. works; a piano concerto, 1968; choral works (incl. *Copernicus,* text by Hoyle, 1973); chamber music (incl. *In Woods* for oboe, harp, percussion, 1978); piano pieces; songs.

Smith, David Stanley (b. Toledo, Ohio, 6 July 1877; d. New Haven, Conn., 17 Dec. 1949). Pupil of Parker, Thuille, and Widor. Teacher at Yale Univ., 1903–46. Conductor of the New Haven Symphony, 1920–46. Composed 4 symphonies and other orch. works (incl. the overture *Prince Hal,* 1912; *Epic Poem,* 1935); *Requiem* for violin and orch., 1939; choral works (incl. *Visions of Isaiah,* with soloists and orch., 1927); 10

string quartets and other chamber music; piano pieces; songs.

Smith, Hale (b. Cleveland, 29 June 1925). Studied at the Cleveland Institute of Music. Has worked as a jazz arranger and as an editor for music publishers. Teacher at C. W. Post College, 1968–70; at the Univ. of Connecticut from 1970. Has composed orch. works (incl. *Rituals and Incantations,* 1974); choral works (incl. *In Memoriam—Beryl Rubinstein,* 1953); works for band; chamber music; piano pieces (incl. *Evocation*); songs to texts of Langston Hughes and others.

Smith, Julia (Frances) (b. Denton, Tex., 25 Jan. 1911). Pianist, writer, and composer. Pupil of R. Goldmark, Jacobi, B. Wagenaar, and Bauer. Teacher at Juilliard, 1940–42; at Hartt College of Music, 1941–46. Has composed 6 operas (incl. *Daisy,* Miami, 1973); orch. works (incl. *Folkways Symphony,* 1948); a piano concerto, 1939, rev. 1970; works for band; choral works; a string quartet, 1964, and other chamber music; piano pieces; songs. Has published a book on Copland, 1955, and other writings.

Smith, Leland (b. Oakland, Calif., 6 Aug. 1925). Pupil of Milhaud, Sessions, and Messiaen. Teacher at the Univ. of Chicago, 1952–58; at Stanford Univ. from 1958. Works incl. an opera, *Santa Claus,* libretto by e. e. cummings, 1957; orch. works; chamber music; *Machines of Loving Grace* for computer, bassoon, and narrator, 1970.

Smith, Russell (b. Tuscaloosa, Ala., 23 Apr. 1927). Pupil of Luening, Moore, and Copland. Editor for Ricordi in New York, 1961–65. Teacher at various institutions, most recently at the State Univ. in New Orleans. Has composed an opera, *The Unicorn in the Garden,* after Thurber, 1956; a ballet; orch. works; 2 piano concertos; an Anglican *Service in G,* 1954; chamber music; piano pieces; organ pieces; songs; music for television and films.

Smith, William Overton (b. Sacramento, Calif., 22 Sept. 1926). Clarinetist and composer. Studied with Milhaud and Sessions and at the Juilliard School and the Paris Conservatory. Teacher at the Univ. of Southern California, 1955–57

and 1958–60; at the Univ. of Washington from 1966. Has composed works for jazz ensembles, some with orch. (incl. a concerto for jazz clarinet and orch.; a concertino for trumpet and jazz instruments); chamber music (incl. a string quartet and several works with clarinet); *Quadrodram* for clarinet, trombone, piano, percussion, dancer, film, 1970.

Smith-Brindle, Reginald (b. Bamber Bridge, Lancaster, England, 5 Jan. 1917). Studied at the Univ. College of North Wales and with Pizzetti and Dallapiccola. Worked for Italian Radio, 1956–61. Teacher at Bangor Univ., 1967–70; at the Univ. of Surrey from 1970. Has composed a chamber opera, *Antigone,* 1969; orch. works (incl. *Symphonic Variations,* 1957; *Apocalypse,* 1970); works for voice with instruments; chamber music; music for films. Has published books and articles on music.

Smorzando [It.]. Dying away.

Smyth, Ethel Mary (b. Rectory, Middlesex, 22 Apr. 1858; d. Woking, Surrey, 8 May 1944). Pupil of Reinecke and Jadassohn in Leipzig and Herzogenberg in Berlin. Leader in the women's suffrage movement in England. Composed operas (incl. *The Wreckers,* prod. first in German, as *Standrecht,* Leipzig, 1906; a comic opera, *The Boatswain's Mate,* London, 1916); orch. works; choral works (incl. a Mass in D, 1893; *The Prison,* 1930); chamber music; piano pieces; organ pieces; songs. Published autobiographical and other books.

Snare drum. See Percussion instruments II, 1.

Snello [It.]. Nimble, agile.

Soave [It.]. Gentle, sweet.

Sobolewski, (Friedrich) Eduard de (b. Königsberg, 1 Oct. 1808; d. St. Louis, 17 May 1872). Violinist, conductor, critic, and composer. Pupil of C. M. von Weber. Opera conductor in Königsberg, 1830–35 and 1847–54, and in Bremen from 1854. Settled in Milwaukee in 1859, later moving to St. Louis, where he founded and conducted an orchestra until his death. Composed operas (incl. *Komala,* Weimar, 1858; *Mohega,* Milwaukee, 1859); 2 symphonies and other orch.

works; oratorios and other choral works; songs.

Söderman, Johan August (b. Stockholm, 17 July 1832; d. there, 10 Feb. 1876). Studied in Stockholm and with Richter. Chorus master at the Royal Opera in Stockholm from 1860 and second *Kapellmeister* there, 1862–68. Composed operettas; incidental music to about 80 plays; ballades for soloist, chorus, and orch. (incl. *Tannhäuser; Die Wallfahrt nach Kevlaar*, after Heine, 1866); other choral works (incl. a *Missa solemnis*, 1875); chamber music; piano pieces; songs.

Soggetto [It.]. Subject or theme. In 18th-century theory the term is used in a more special sense, for a fugal theme of a traditional character, similar to the subjects of the 16th-century *ricercar. It is thus distinguished from the *andamento*, a longer theme, which usually falls into two phrases, and from the *attacco*, a short motif such as is used in motets or in the episodic sections of fugues. The subjects of the fugues in C♯ minor and G major from Bach's *Well-Tempered Clavier*, vol. I, illustrate the difference between a *soggetto* and an *andamento*.

Soggetto cavato [It., carved subject]. In 16th-century theory, a musical subject derived by "carving out" vowels (*cavato dalle vocali*) from a sentence and transforming them into a melody by means of the *solmization syllables of the Guidonian hexachord. An example is Josquin's Mass *Hercules Dux Ferrarie* (dedicated to Hercules, Duke of Ferrara), whose main subject is *e u e u e a i e;* or, in corresponding solmization syllables, *re ut re ut re fa mi re;* or, in modern notes, d c d c d f e d.

Soir, Le. See under *Matin, Le.*

Sol. See Pitch names; Solmization; Hexachord.

Sol-fa. See Tonic sol-fa.

Soldier's Tale, The. See *Histoire du soldat, L'*.

Soleá [Sp.; pl. *soleares*]. An Andalusian folksong, with stanzas of three eight-syllable lines, the first and the third in rhyme. It is plaintive in character and is basically a form of *cante jondo* [see Flamenco].

Soler, Antonio ("Padre") (b. Olot de Porrera, Gerona, Spain, bapt. 3 Dec. 1729; d. the Escorial, 20 Dec. 1783). Studied as a boy at the school at the monastery of Montserrat. Later probably a pupil of D. Scarlatti. Organist and choirmaster at the monastery of the Escorial from 1753 until his death. Composed much church music; music for stage works; 6 concertos for 2 organs; chamber music; numerous sonatas and a fandango for keyboard.

Solesmes. The Benedictine monks of Solesmes (a village near Le Mans, France) have become famous for their work of restoring Gregorian chant; their edition was officially adopted in 1904 under the name "Editio Vaticana" to replace the corrupt versions of the "Editio Medicea" (17th cent.) and the similar "Ratisbon edition" of the late 19th century. The Solesmes interpretation of Gregorian rhythm has also won official Church recognition.

Solfège [F.]; **solfeggio** [It.]. (1) Vocal exercises sung to a vowel (*a, o, u*) or to the syllables of *solmization (*ut*, [*do*], *re, mi,* etc.). (2) Instruction in the rudiments of music, i.e., the study of intervals, rhythm, clefs, signatures, etc., usually employing solmization and having as its goal the ability to translate symbols (notation) into sound (real or imagined) immediately and accurately.

Solfegietto [It.]. Title used by some composers in the meaning of "little study."

Sollberger, Harvey (b. Cedar Rapids, Iowa, 11 May 1938). Flutist, conductor, and composer. Pupil of Bezanson, Beeson, and Luening. Teacher at Columbia Univ., 1965–71; at the Manhattan School of Music from 1972. Co-director, with Wuorinen, of the Group for Contemporary Music since 1962. Has worked with serial techniques. Works incl. *Chamber Variations for 12 Players and Conductor*, 1964; *Impromptu* for piano, 1968; *Musica transalpina* for soprano, baritone, and 6 players, 1964–70; *Divertimento for Flute, Cello, and Piano*, 1970; a string quartet, 1973; *Riding the Wind*, 1974.

Solmization. General term for systems of designating the degrees of the scale by syllables instead of letters. The syllables mostly used today are: *do* (or *doh*), *re, mi, fa, sol, la, si* (*ti*). There are two current methods of applying these syllables to the scale degrees, known as "fixed do" and "movable do." In the former, the syllables are applied to "fixed" notes, e.g., *do* = C; *re* = D; etc. In the latter, they are applicable to any major scale so that *do, re, mi,* etc., denote tonic, supertonic, mediant, etc. (e.g., in D major: D, E, F♯, etc.). A modern system of "movable do" is the *tonic sol-fa, which is widely used in England.

The modern system of solmization originated with Guido d'Arezzo (*c*. 990–1050), who introduced the syllables *ut re mi fa sol la* as names for the tones c through a. Later they were also used for the two other hexachords [see Hexachord]. The medieval system remained unaltered until the end of the 16th century, when increasingly wider use of chromatic tones and transposed keys rendered it less and less suitable. About 1600, French musicians began to use the Guidonian syllables in a fixed position, *ut* for C, etc. In order to complete the octave, the syllable *si* was introduced, and *c*. 1650 the syllable *ut* was replaced by *do* in most countries except France. In the United States a simplified system of solmization known as *fasola was widely used during the 18th century.

Solo. (1) A piece executed by one performer, either alone (e.g., Bach's Sonatas for violin solo), or with accompaniment by piano, organ, orchestra, etc. (2) In orchestral scores, a passage played by a single player and intended to stand out. (3) In concertos, designation for the soloist, in distinction from the orchestra (tutti). (4) In the early concerto (Bach, Handel), the orchestral part for passages to be played *senza ripieni* [see *Ripieno*].

Sombrero de tres picos, El [Sp., The Three-Cornered Hat]. Comedy-ballet by Falla (choreography by Massine; décor by Picasso; based on a novel by Alarcón), produced in London, 1919.

Somers, Harry (Stewart) (b. Toronto, 11 Sept. 1925). Pupil of Weinzweig and Milhaud. Has worked with twelve-tone techniques, sometimes juxtaposing these with tonal procedures, and with elec-

tronic techniques. Has composed 2 operas (incl. *Louis Riel,* with tape, Toronto, 1967); 3 ballets (incl. *The House of Atreus,* 1964); orch. works (incl. 2 symphonies; *Passacaglia and Fugue,* 1954; *Stereophony,* 1962); a piano concerto; choral works; 3 string quartets and other chamber music; piano pieces; songs and other works for voice with instruments; music for radio, television, and films.

Somervell, Arthur (b. Windermere, England, 5 June 1863; d. London, 2 May 1937). Pupil of Stanford, Parry, and Bargiel. Teacher at the Royal College of Music, 1894–1901, and Inspector of Music to the Board of Education thereafter. Composed a symphony and other orch. works; concertos and other works for solo piano and for solo violin with orch.; church music; choral works (incl. the oratorio *The Passion of Christ,* 1914; the cantata *Christmas,* 1926); chamber music; piano pieces; songs (incl. the cycles *Maud* and *A Shropshire Lad*); 4 children's operettas; pedagogic works.

Somis, Giovanni Battista (b. Turin, 25 Dec. 1686; d. there, 14 Aug. 1763). Violinist and composer. Pupil of Corelli. Royal violinist and director of the royal orchestra in Turin from 1707 until his death. Soloist at the Concert spirituel in Paris, 1733. Composed trio sonatas and other chamber music; violin sonatas.

Sommer, Vladimír (b. Dolní Jeřetín, Czechoslovakia, 28 Feb. 1921). Critic and composer. Pupil of Bořkovec. Teacher at Charles Univ. in Prague from 1960. Has composed 3 symphonies (incl. no. 1, *Vocal Symphony,* with speaker and chorus, 1958, rev. 1963) and other orch. works; concertos for violin, for piano, and for cello; choral works; string quartets and other chamber music; songs; music for television, films, and theater.

Son [F.]. Sound. *Son bouché,* stopped note (of a *horn); *son ouvert,* open (natural) note of a wind instrument.

Sonata. A composition for piano (piano sonata), or for violin, cello, flute, etc., usually with piano accompaniment (violin sonata, cello sonata, etc.), that consists of three or four separate sections called movements. Almost all features of the sonata are also found in other types of instrumental music, i.e., the symphony, chamber music (quartet, trio, quintet, etc.), and, with some modifications, the concerto. The main difference lies in the performing bodies: the symphony can be considered a "sonata" for orchestra, the quartet a "sonata" for four strings.

The normal scheme for the movements of a sonata (and symphony, etc.) is Allegro–Adagio–Scherzo (or Minuet) –Allegro. A slow introduction sometimes precedes the opening Allegro. While Allegro (Allegro molto, Presto) and Adagio (Largo, Lento) merely mean "quick" and "slow," the Scherzo or Minuet has a dancelike character. This movement is sometimes not included, particularly in Mozart's sonatas as well as in most concertos. Notable exceptions to the normal scheme are Beethoven's *Moonlight Sonata* op. 27, no. 2 (designated by Beethoven as *Sonata quasi una fantasia*), consisting of Adagio, Allegretto (a scherzo movement), and Presto; his op. 111, consisting of Maestoso (an introduction), Allegro, and Arietta (an Adagio in variation form); and Liszt's Sonata in B minor.

The first movement (Allegro) is almost always in the so-called *sonata form; the second (Adagio) is often in sonata form or ternary form but may be in *binary or variation form; the third movement is normally in ternary form, Minuet (Scherzo)–Trio–Minuet (Scherzo); the last movement (Allegro, Presto) is in sonata form or *rondo form (occasionally in variation form).

The history of the sonata as a form is not identical with the history of the name. Originally, *sonata* simply meant "sound-piece" and was used for various types of instrumental music. The most fundamental aspect of the classical sonata—the contrast provided by its different movements—can be traced to instrumental compositions of the late 16th century that fall into a number of short sections in contrasting styles. During the first half of the 17th century a large number of compositions for instrumental ensemble called "canzone da sonar" or, occasionally, "sonate," were published. These pieces fall into five or more short

sections in contrasting styles, frequently alternating fairly long sections in imitative style with shorter ones in homophonic texture and slower tempo [see Canzona (5)]. Beginning about 1635, the sections tended to decrease in number and increase in length, thus acquiring the character of "movements."

After 1650 a fairly standard structure developed, mainly in Venice under Legrenzi (1626–90). It consisted of an initial Allegro movement in fugal style, a homophonic second movement in dancelike triple meter, and a final movement similar to the first and often based on identical or related material. Often this three-part scheme was enlarged to four or five movements by the addition of short "Adagios" before and/or after the middle movement. The "symmetrical" structure Allegro–Adagio–Dance–Adagio–Allegro was used also by G. B. Vitali (1632–92). Arcangelo Corelli (1653–1713) used, in his *Sonate a tre*, op. 1, op. 3 (1681, 1689), a new four-movement plan, Adagio (or Grave)–Allegro–Adagio–Allegro, that was generally adopted as the standard form of the *sonata da chiesa* [see *Sonata da camera, sonata da chiesa*]. In op. 5 (1700) Corelli returned to the earlier six-movement form, retaining an Adagio at the beginning. Numerous pieces of the *sonata da chiesa* structure (i.e., with a scheme of four movements, slow–fast–slow–fast) were written by non-Italian composers, such as Bach, Handel, and Jean-Marie Leclair (1697–1764), while the Italians of this period frequently preferred longer or shorter schemes. Thus, Veracini's (1690 –1768) violin sonatas have five to eight movements; Tartini's (1692–1770) usually have three: slow–fast–very fast; and Locatelli's (1695–1764) almost always have three: Andante–Allegro–Minuet (or Aria con variazioni).

These baroque sonatas may be divided into four categories: those written in one part, in two parts (*a due*), in three parts (*a tre*), and in four or more parts. The most famous examples in one part are Bach's unaccompanied sonatas (sometimes also called *suites because they include dances; see *Sonata da camera*) for violin and for cello. The sonatas "a due" usually call for three performers, one for the melody (most commonly violin) and two for the realization of the thorough-bass. This type (often called "violin sonata" or even "solo violin sonata") was cultivated as early as 1617 by Marini (*Affetti musicali*) in a strikingly virtuosic style, employing trills, rapid runs, double-stops, etc. The "sonata a tre" or *trio sonata*, the most important type of all, was performed by one, two, or four players, practically never by three [see Trio sonata], while the "sonata a quatro" and "a cinque" probably were for small orchestral ensembles.

The earliest known keyboard compositions written in distinct movements are three *Canzone francese* by Giovanni Salvatori published in 1641. A publication by Gregorio Strozzi of 1687 contains three pieces called "Sonata" in three or four movements, the first of which bears the remark, "detta da altri impropriamente Canzona francese" (improperly called by others canzona francese). Five years later, Johann Kuhnau (1660–1722) published, with his *Neuer Clavier-Übung*, pt. II (1692), a "Sonata aus dem B" that earned him the somewhat undeserved title of "inventor of the piano sonata." Bernardo Pasquini (1637–1710) used the term "sonata" as a generic description for a variety of keyboard compositions.

The emergence of the Viennese *classical sonata* of Haydn, Mozart, and Beethoven marks one of the most striking developments in music history. The change from the baroque sonata to the classical sonata is not simply a change from a four-movement scheme, Adagio–Allegro–Adagio–Allegro, to a three-movement scheme, Allegro–Adagio–Allegro, or another four-movement scheme, Allegro–Adagio–Scherzo–Allegro. Fundamental changes of style and structure within the movements are involved as well. Further, the repertory now divided into the solo sonata, chamber sonata (quartet, quintet), and orchestral sonata (symphony), each of which follows a separate line of development. [For the others, see String quartet; Symphony.]

The three-movement plan Allegro–Adagio–Allegro was standardized in the Italian overture of Alessandro Scarlatti [see Overture]. Bach employed this form in all but the first of his *Brandenburg Concertos*, in the "Italian Concerto,"

and in the six organ sonatas, which are among the first sonatas written in this form. The Italian composers of harpsichord sonatas (G. B. Sammartini, 1701–75; B. Galuppi, 1706–85; P. D. Paradies, 1707–91; G. M. Rutini, 1723–97) wrote some sonatas in two movements, e.g., Allegro–Andante, or vice versa (Paradies) or Allegro–Minuet (Sammartini). Domenico Scarlatti wrote more than 550 one-movement sonatas, which, in his first publication, *Esercizi per Gravicembalo* (1738), were called "esercizio." Some, if not all, of these pieces were intended to be combined in two- or three-movement sonatas. The "classical" scheme Allegro–Adagio–Allegro was used consistently in the piano sonatas of K. P. E. Bach (Prussian Sonatas, 1742; Württemberg Sonatas, 1744), Haydn (except some of the earliest), and Mozart. The four-movement scheme Allegro–Adagio–Minuet–Allegro was used by Johann Stamitz (1717–57) of the *Mannheim school. Although Haydn and Mozart generally adopted it for their string quartets and symphonies, Beethoven was the first to use it in his sonatas, replacing the Minuet with a Scherzo. In the mid-18th-century sonata (Sammartini, G. M. Rutini) practically all the movements are in *binary form with both sections repeated. For the relationship of this form to the first-movement sonata form, see Sonata form. The slow movements in the sonatas of K. P. E. Bach are usually in a free form. Haydn seems to have been the first to make extensive use of the rondo form for the final movement.

The late sonatas of Beethoven expand the form in various ways. Thereafter the approaches of composers to the sonata have been diverse and relatively infrequent. Schubert, Schumann, Chopin, Liszt, and Brahms all contribute examples, however. The diversity of forms bearing this title in the 20th century has been even greater, though some composers have occasionally taken the 18th-century classical sonata as a model [see Neoclassicism].

Sonata da camera, sonata da chiesa [It.]. Baroque terms meaning chamber or court sonata and church sonata, respectively. Originally, the contrasting terms indicated place of performance, not a specific type or form. Between 1670 and 1690 the two terms gradually became associated more with multimovement forms than single pieces. Arcangelo Corelli standardized the *sonata da chiesa* as a piece in four movements, slow–fast–slow–fast (op. 1, op. 3), and the *sonata da camera* as a suite consisting of an introduction and three or four dances, e.g., Allemande–Sarabande–Gigue (op. 2, op. 4).

Sonata form. The form most often embodied in the first movements of *sonatas, and hence of symphonies, string quartets, and other forms of chamber music, from the period of Haydn and Mozart up until the early 20th century and the decline of *tonality. Although it is sometimes also known as *first-movement form* or *sonata-allegro form,* it is frequently encountered in the second (slow) and final movements of sonatas, symphonies, and chamber works as well. The first movements of *concertos of the same period usually exemplify a modification of sonata form.

Sonata form is fundamentally a two-part design closely related to the *binary form common in music of the baroque period. The first major section, which may be preceded by an introduction (often in slow tempo if the remainder of the movement is fast), begins in the tonic and modulates to the dominant (or another closely related key such as the relative major if the tonic is minor). In works of the classical period, the first section is repeated in the vast majority of cases, though modern performances often do not include this repeat. Most often the two principal tonal areas are each associated with distinctive and sometimes contrasting thematic material, referred to as the *first theme* (or theme group) and *second theme* (or theme group). The modulatory passage connecting the two principal tonal areas is sometimes called the *bridge.* The whole of this first section is known as the *exposition* (or statement).

The second major section consists first of a modulatory passage, often of substantial length and complexity, whose goal is a return to the tonic from the dominant or other key in which the first section ended. Because this modulation or series of modulations typically elaborates upon the thematic material from the exposition, it is usually known as the *development* (or fantasia section). The return to the original tonic coincides with a restatement of the first theme (or theme group) and thus marks the beginning of what is called the *recapitulation* (or restatement). Following the restatement of the first theme, the second theme is also restated, but this time in the tonic, thus necessitating a modification of the bridge passage so as to avoid the modulation embodied in the exposition. The recapitulation is sometimes followed by a *coda to conclude the movement. In some works of the classical period, this second major section (consisting of both development and recapitulation) is also repeated, though this repetition is usually not specified in movements of significant length, especially when the second major section is substantially longer than the first.

As with other types of musical *form, sonata form cannot be regarded as a formula rigidly followed by composers. Any useful definition must acknowledge sonata forms in which a single theme is used for both principal tonal areas of the exposition, as well as examples in which there are more than two important tonal areas and/or theme groups. Historically, however, the crucial feature of sonata form is the tension created by the tonal contrast in the first section and the resolution of this tension by means of a return to both the original tonality and the

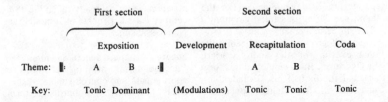

original theme in the second section. This is so despite the usefulness of analyzing what is primarily the thematic aspect of sonata form in terms of the three-fold division into exposition, development, and recapitulation, a view that came into prominence in the first part of the 19th century and that has dominated discussions of the form since.

Because the essential features of sonata form were so closely bound up with the principles of tonic-dominant tonality, it is understandable that the nature of the form changed substantially as tonality weakened or was discarded. Thus, nontonal works are sometimes cited as examples of sonata form when they offer only the barest analogy to notions of exposition, development, and recapitulation.

The accompanying diagram illustrates the principal features of classical sonata form.

Sonata-rondo. See Rondo.

Sonatina. A diminutive sonata, with fewer and shorter movements than the normal type and also usually simpler, designed for instruction (Clementi, Kuhlau). However, such composers as Busoni, Ravel, Bartók, Chávez, and Milhaud have written sonatinas of considerable technical difficulty and artistic merit.

Song. A short composition for solo voice, usually but not necessarily accompanied, and written in a fairly simple style designed to enhance rather than overshadow the text. It is as old and as widespread as the phenomenon of singing itself. In Western art music it is to be distinguished principally from a musically more elaborate form of solo vocal music, found in operas, oratorios, and cantatas, known as the *aria.

Important early repertories usually placed under the heading of song are those of the *goliards, *troubadours, *trouvères, *minnesingers, and *Meistersinger, as well as the Spanish *cantigas and the Italian *laude. See also Chanson.

Although in the Renaissance the principal forms of vocal music were polyphonic (e.g., *madrigal, *chanson), accompanied solo song played a role in the

Italian *frottola, the French *air de cour, the vihuela-accompanied song of Spain, and the lute-accompanied song of England (see Ayre). The great flowering of accompanied song (*monody) in the years around 1600 thus had ample precedent.

The German *lied of the early 19th century, particularly as represented in the works of Schubert, marks a high point in the history of song. Its emphasis on an equal partnership between music and poetry of quality spread to other countries and has continued to provide an aesthetic model despite the radical changes in musical style that have occurred since. See also Song cycle; Song form.

Song cycle [G. *Liederkreis*]. A group of related songs designed to form a musical entity. Examples include Beethoven's *An die ferne Geliebte,* op. 98 (composed in 1816 to words by A. Jeitteles); Schubert's *Die schöne Müllerin* (1823; words by W. Müller) and *Die Winterreise* (1827; also by Müller); Schumann's *Frauenliebe und Leben* (1840; poems by Chamisso) and *Dichterliebe* (1840; poems by Heine); Brahms' *Magelone* (1861–68; poems by Tieck); Fauré's *La bonne chanson* (1892–93; poems by Verlaine); Debussy's *Chansons de Bilitis* (1897; poems by Pierre Louÿs); Hindemith's *Das Marienleben* (1922–23, rev. 1948; poems by Rilke).

Song form. The simple ternary form A B A, actually much more common in instrumental (particularly piano) music than songs. See Binary and ternary form.

Song of Destiny. See *Schicksalslied.*

Song of the Earth. See *Lied von der Erde, Das.*

Songs of a Wayfarer. See *Lieder eines fahrenden Gesellen.*

Songs Without Words. See *Lieder ohne Worte.*

Sonido trece [Sp., thirteenth sound]. Name given by the Mexican composer and theorist Julián Carrillo (1875–1965) to his method of using microtones. In most of the compositions he wrote after 1922 Carrillo employed 1/3, 1/4, 1/8, or 1/16 tones.

Sonnambula, La [It. The Sleepwalker]. Opera in two acts by Bellini (libretto by F. Romani), produced in Milan, 1831. Setting: a Swiss village, early 19th century.

Sonnenquartette. See Sun Quartets.

Sonore [F.]; **sonoro** [It.]. Sonorous.

Sopra [It.]. Above. *Come sopra*, as above. *M.d.* (or *M.s.*) *sopra*, right (or left) hand above the other (in piano playing). See also *Sotto*.

Soprano. The highest female voice; see Voices, range of. Soprano soloists are classified as dramatic, lyric, or coloratura. Voices of similar range are the unchanged boy's voice ("boy soprano") and the "male soprano," i.e., either a *falsetto or, formerly, a *castrato. The term is also used for certain instruments to denote the highest member of a family, e.g., soprano recorder.

Soprano clef. See under Clef.

Sor, Fernando (Joseph Fernando Macari Sors) (b. Barcelona, bapt. 14 Feb. 1778; d. Paris, 10 July 1839). Guitar virtuoso and composer. Studied at the school attached to the monastery of Montserrat. Traveled to France, England, and Russia beginning in 1813, settling finally in Paris in 1828. Composed operas; ballets; orch. works; church music; piano pieces; numerous pieces for guitar, incl. sonatas, variations, and studies. Wrote a guitar method.

Sorabji, Kaikhosru Shapurji (Leon Dudley Sorabji) (b. Chelmsford, Essex, of a Parsi father and a Spanish-Sicilian mother, 14 Aug.? 1892). Pianist and composer. Self-taught. Around 1950 prohibited further public performance of his works. Has composed 3 symphonies and other orch. works; 3 organ symphonies; 5 piano concertos; choral works; chamber music; numerous works for piano (incl. 5 sonatas; *Opus clavicembalisticum*, 1930); songs. Has published several books on music, incl. critical essays.

Sorcerer's Apprentice, The. See *Apprenti sorcier, L'*.

Sordino [It.]. (1) See Mute. (2) Old name for the *kit and also the *clavichord.

Soriano, Francesco (Suriano) (b. Soriano, Italy, 1549; d. Rome, 19 July 1621). Chorister at San Giovanni in Laterano in Rome. Pupil of Nanino and Palestrina. *Maestro di cappella* at various churches in Rome, incl. Santa Maria Maggiore, San Luigi dei Francesi, and San Giovanni in Laterano; at the court in Mantua, 1583–86; finally at St. Peter's in Rome, 1603–20. Composed Masses, motets, and other sacred works; madrigals and *villanelle*. Collaborated with Anerio on the Medicean edition of the Roman Gradual (publ. 1614–15).

Soro, Enrique (b. Concepción, Chile, 15 July 1884; d. Santiago, 2 Dec. 1954). Pianist, conductor, and composer. Studied with his father, the Italian composer José Soro, and at the Milan Conservatory. Teacher at the National Conservatory in Santiago from 1907 and its director, 1919–28. Member of the board of directors of the Instituto de extensión musical of the Univ. of Chile from 1942 until his death. Composed orch. works (incl. *Sinfonía romántica*, 1920; *Aires chilenos*, 1942; *Suite en estilo antiguo*, 1943); a piano concerto, 1919; choral works; chamber music; numerous piano pieces; songs.

Sospirando [It.]. Sighing, plaintive.

Sostenente (sostinente) piano. Generic name for a keyboard instrument that produces a sustained sound like that of the violin or organ. There are four principal means of obtaining such an effect: (1) by currents of air directed against the strings; (2) by repeating hammers; (3) by a bowing mechanism; (4) by means of electricity. The first method was used in Jean Schnell's *Anémocorde* [see also Aeolian harp]. The second, in which rapidly striking hammers produce a tremolo, was invented by Hawkins in 1800, improved in the *Melopiano* of *c.* 1873 (Caldara and Brossi), and patented in a new form by E. Moór in 1931 and by Cloetens in 1932. The third is realized in a number of instruments generically called *piano-violin* [G. *Bogenklavier, Streichklavier, Geigenwerk*], all descendants of the *hurdy-gurdy. Usually, the "bow" consists of one or more wheels bearing rosined strings and set in rotation by a pedal mechanism, while the strings are pressed against the wheel by a key mechanism. The first successful instrument of this type was Hans Heyden's *Geigenwerk* (*c*. 1575). In 1817 H. R. Mott of England patented a "Sostinente Piano Forte" in which rollers acting on silk threads transmitted vibrations to the strings. For the fourth category, see Electronic instruments.

Sostenuto, sostenendo [It.]. Sustaining the tone to or beyond nominal value and thus sometimes with the implication of slackening the tempo. *Andante sostenuto* calls for a slow andante.

Sostenuto pedal. See under Piano.

Sotto [It.]. Under. *Sotto voce* (under the voice), i.e., with subdued sound. *M.d.* (*M.s.*) *sotto*, right (left) hand underneath the other (in piano playing); see also *Sopra*.

Soubrette [F., a lady's maid]. A light operatic soprano, often playing a somewhat comical role, e.g., Zerlina in Mozart's *Don Giovanni*.

Sound hole [F. *ouïe;* G. *Schalloch;* It. *occhi;* Sp. *abertura acústica*]. An opening in one of various shapes cut in the *table of stringed instruments. Such an opening permits freer movement of the central part of the table, thus helping it reinforce the tones produced by the strings. In instruments of the violin family, which have two such holes, one on either side of the strings, these are in the shape of an *f* (*f*-holes). In viols, which also have two, the holes are in the shape of a sickle or half-moon (C-holes). The apertures of lutes and guitars are usually a single circle in the center of the table [see Rose].

Sound post [F. *âme;* G. *Seele, Stimmstock;* It. *anima;* Sp. *alma*]. In violins, etc., a small pillar of wood set between the table and back. It serves both to counter the heavy pressure of the bridge on the table (its original purpose) and, chiefly, to convey the vibrations of the table to the back of the instrument and to bring the various vibrating sections into conformity.

Soundboard [F. *table d'harmonie;* G. *Resonanzboden;* It. *piano armonico, tavola armonica;* Sp. *caja armónica*]. In instruments such as the piano and harp-sichord, the wooden surface over which the strings are stretched, which serves as a resonator. In harps, the strings are attached to the soundboard and stretched perpendicular to it. See also Table.

Soupir [F.]. Quarter rest. See under Notes.

Soupirant [F.]. Sighing, plaintive.

Sourd [F.]. Muffled, muted.

Sourdine [F.]. *Mute.

Souris, André (b. Marchienne-au-Pont, Belgium, 10 July 1899; d. Paris, 12 Feb. 1970). Conductor, critic, and composer. Pupil of Gilson. Conductor of the Radio Orchestra in Brussels, 1937–46. Teacher at the Brussels Conservatory from 1949 until his death. Founder in 1947 of the journal *Polyphonies* and an advocate of surrealism. Composed orch. works (incl. *Symphonies,* 1939); *Hommage à Babeuf* for winds, 1934; *Avertissement* for speakers and percussion, 1926; choral works; vocal and instrumental chamber music; music for radio and films.

Sousaphone. See under Brass instruments II (e).

Souster, Tim (Andrew James) (b. Bletchley, Buckinghamshire, 29 Jan. 1943). Studied at Oxford Univ. and with Stockhausen, Berio, and Richard Rodney Bennett. Composer-in-residence at King's College, Cambridge, 1969–71. Co-founder, with Smalley, of the ensemble Intermodulation, 1970, for live performance of electronic works. Works incl. *Titus Groan Music* for wind quintet, tape, and electronic equipment, 1969; *Pelvic Loops,* on tape, 1969; *Chinese Whispers* for percussion and 3 synthesizers, 1970; *Triple Music II* for 3 orchs., 1970; *Music for Eliot's "Waste Land"* for piano, electric organ, soprano saxophone, 3 synthesizers, 1970.

Souterliedekens [D.]. A 16th-century Netherlands collection of 159 monophonic psalm tunes, published in 1540 in Antwerp and reprinted in more than 30 editions. The publication is the earliest complete translation (rhymed) of the psalms into the vernacular [see Psalter]. The melodies were not newly composed but were taken from popular or folk melodies of the period, mostly Dutch, and the editor indicated with each melody the beginning of the original secular text, thus preserving and identifying numerous early folk melodies. Polyphonic settings were made by Clemens non Papa and others.

Sowerby, Leo (b. Grand Rapids, Mich., 1 May 1895; d. Port Clinton, Ohio, 7 July 1968). Studied in Chicago, where he later taught at the American Conservatory, 1925–62, and was organist at St. James' Episcopal Cathedral, 1927–62. Director of the College for Church Musicians at the National Cathedral in Washington from 1962 until his death. Composed 5 symphonies and other orch. works; concertos for piano, for cello, for organ, for violin; choral works (incl. *The Canticle of the Sun*, with orch., 1944, awarded a Pulitzer Prize; the oratorio *Christ Reborn,* 1950); chamber music; piano pieces; numerous organ pieces; numerous songs; arrangements of folksongs.

Sp. [G.]. Abbr. for *Spitze* (point), indicating in violin music the point of the bow, and in organ music the toe of the foot.

Spacing. Arrangement of the notes of a chord. When the three upper voices are as close as possible, the spacing is described as "close position" or "close harmony" [Ex. 1 and 2], though sometimes these terms are reserved for positions in which all four voices lie within a twelfth [Ex. 3 and 4]. The other arrangements, common in vocal music, are called "open position" or "open harmony" [Ex. 5 and 6].

Spagna [It.]. A famous *basse danse* melody, entitled "Il Re di Spagna" (The King of Spain), preserved as a monophonic melody in the *basse danse* manuscripts of the 15th century and used frequently as the basis of polyphonic compositions.

Spalding, Albert (b. Chicago, 15 Aug. 1888; d. New York, 26 May 1953). Vio-

linist and composer. Studied in Florence, Bologna, Paris, and New York. Toured widely in the U.S. and Europe. Composed works for violin with orch., incl. concertos; chamber music, incl. numerous pieces for violin; piano pieces; songs.

Spanisches Liederbuch [G., Spanish Song Book]. A collection of 44 songs by Hugo Wolf, composed 1889–90, to German translations, by E. Geibel and Paul Heyse, of Spanish poetry of the 16th and 17th centuries.

Spanish Rhapsody. See *Rapsodie espagnole.*

Spanish Song Book. See *Spanisches Liederbuch.*

Speaker key. In wind instruments, a key that facilitates the production of tones by overblowing. It opens a small hole that causes the air column to vibrate in one-half or one-third of its entire length. The oboe usually has two such keys, used to overblow different portions of the scale at the octave, while the clarinet has only one, producing the twelfth.

Speaking stop. In organs, any stop that produces sounds, as distinct from others that merely operate couplers, etc.

Species. In *counterpoint, the five basic techniques (enumerated by J. J. Fux in his *Gradus ad Parnassum,* 1725, and the basis of much instruction in counterpoint since) for adding a contrapuntal voice above or below a given *cantus firmus* (c.f.) [see Ex.]: (1) note against note; (2) two notes against each note of the c.f.; (3) four notes against each note of the

c.f.; (4) notes in syncopated position including suspensions; and (5) florid counterpoint, consisting of a combination of the other species and progressions in eighth notes.

Speech song. **Sprechstimme.*

Spelman, Timothy Mather (b. Brooklyn, 21 Jan. 1891; d. Florence, 21 Aug. 1970). Studied at Harvard with Hill and at the Munich Conservatory. Lived in Florence, 1918–35 and from 1947. Composed operas and other stage works; orch. works (incl. *Saints' Days,* 1925); choral works (incl. *Pervigilium veneris,* 1931); chamber music; piano pieces; songs.

Sperdendosi [It.]. Fading away.

Speyer, Wilhelm (b. Frankfurt, 21 June 1790; d. there, 5 Apr. 1878). Violinist and composer. Studied in Offenbach and Paris. Associate of Spohr and Mendelssohn. Composed choral works; much chamber music, incl. string quartets and violin pieces; piano pieces; hundreds of songs (incl. the ballades "Der Trompeter," "Die drei Liebchen," and "Rheinsehnsucht").

Spezzato [It.]. Split, broken. *Coro spezzato,* divided chorus [see Polychoral style]; *registro spezzato,* divided register [see Divided stop].

Spianato [It.]. Smooth, even.

Spiccato [It.]. See under Bowing (d).

Spiegelman, Joel (Warren) (b. Buffalo, N.Y., 23 Jan. 1933). Pupil of Shapero, Fine, Berger, and N. Boulanger. Teacher at Brandeis Univ., 1961–66; at Sarah Lawrence College from 1966. Founder of the New York Electronic Ensemble in 1970. Works incl. *2 Movements* for orch., 1957; *Kousochki* for piano four-hands; *The 11th Hour,* ballet on tape, 1969; a Jewish sacred service, with tape, 1969; *Daddy* for actress, soprano, flute, oboe, synthesizer, conga drums.

Spieloper [G.]. Term for German 19th-century *comic opera (e.g., works by Lortzing and Marschner).

Spies, Claudio (b. Santiago, Chile, 26 Mar. 1925). Pupil of N. Boulanger, Sha-

pero, Fine, Hindemith, and Piston. Teacher at Harvard Univ., 1954–57; Vassar College, 1957–58; Swarthmore College, 1958–70; Princeton Univ. from 1970. Adopted twelve-tone techniques in the late 1950s. Has composed orch. works (incl. *Music for a Ballet,* 1955); choral works (incl. *Animula blandula, vagula,* 1964); works for voice with piano or other instruments; chamber music (incl. *Tempi* for 14 instruments, 1962; *Viopacem* for viola and harpsichord or piano, 1965); piano pieces (incl. *3 Intermezzi,* 1954; *Impromptu,* 1963).

Spinaccino, Francesco (Spinacino) (b. Fossombrone, near Pesaro, second half of the 15th cent.; d. Venice, after 1507). Lutenist and composer. His works were published by Petrucci in two volumes of *Intabulatura de lauto,* 1507–8, and include ricercars (the earliest pieces so called), *bassadanze,* and intabulations of sacred and secular vocal works.

Spinet [F. *épinett;* G. *Spinett;* It. *spinetta;* Sp. *espineta*]. (1) A type of small harpsichord. Originally the Italian and French terms referred to any jack-action keyboard instrument [see Harpsichord], but later they were limited to any small, single-choired, jack-action instrument in which the strings ran more or less transversely. During the 18th century the term was applied in England to small instruments having a single transverse choir of strings and a short bent side to the right. In modern English, the spinet is distinguished from the oblong virginals. Generally speaking, any single-choired, harpsichordlike instrument that is neither oblong nor of the characteristic harpsichord wing-shape may properly be called a spinet.

(2) A *piano with strings perpendicular to the keyboard (as in an upright piano) but frequently with an indirect action.

Spirito, spiritoso [It.]. Spirit, spirited.

Spiritual. A traditional sacred song of the North American Negroes. The texts of such songs draw on themes from the Bible and from conservative American Protestantism. The music, although it includes tonal and rhythmic elements likely to derive from African antecedents, is strongly influenced by the traditions of Protestant hymn-singing in

America and relies on the system of Western tonality. These songs are now known in a wide variety of arrangements for vocal soloists and for choruses.

Spohr, Ludwig (Louis) (b. Brunswick, 5 Apr. 1784; d. Kassel, 22 Oct. 1859). Violinist, conductor, and composer. Member of the Brunswick court orchestra from 1799. Concertmaster of the ducal orchestra at Gotha, 1805–12. Opera conductor at Frankfurt from 1817. *Kapellmeister* at Kassel, on Weber's recommendation, 1822–57, where he championed and performed early works of Wagner. Toured widely as a violin virtuoso. Composed operas (incl. *Faust*, Prague, 1816; *Zemire und Azor*, Frankfurt, 1819; *Jessonda*, Kassel, 1823); 9 symphonies and other orch. works; 15 violin concertos and other concerted works; choral works (incl. the oratorios *Das jüngste Gericht*, 1812; *Die letzten Dinge* [in English as The Last Judgment], 1826; *Des Heilands letzte Stunden* [Eng. Calvary], 1835); chamber music (incl. a nonet for violin, viola, cello, double bass, and wind quintet; 4 double string quartets; 34 string quartets; piano trios; pieces for violin and piano or harp); piano pieces; numerous songs. Published an autobiography and a violin method.

Spontini, Gaspare (Luigi Pacifico) (b. Majolati, near Iesi, Italy, 14 Nov. 1774; d. there, 24 Jan. 1851). Conductor and composer. Studied at the Conservatorio della Pietà de' Turchini in Naples and received advice there from Piccinni. *Maestro di cappella* to the Neapolitan court in exile in Palermo, 1798–1801. Lived in Paris from 1803, becoming music director to the Empress Josephine from 1805; director of the Italian Opera, 1810–12; court composer to Louis XVIII from 1814. Court composer and general music director to Frederick William III at Berlin, 1819–41. Composed operas (incl. *Milton*, Paris, 1804; *La vestale*, Paris, 1807; *Fernand Cortez*, Paris, 1809; *Olympie*, Paris, 1819, revised for Berlin, 1821, and for Paris, 1826; *Agnes von Hohenstaufen*, Berlin, 1829); other stage works; sacred and secular choral works; instrumental pieces.

Sprechstimme, Sprechgesang [G., speech song]. A type of voice production half-way between song and speech. It is usually notated on a staff by means of crosslike symbols indicating pitches that are to be approximated only. Both the method and the notation were introduced by Humperdinck in his melodrama *Königskinder* (1897). Schoenberg used it in *Pierrot lunaire* (1912) and *Die Glückliche Hand* (1913), and Alban Berg in *Wozzeck* and *Lulu*.

Springbogen [G.]. *Sautillé, saltando;* see Bowing (d).

Springer. An *agrément* used in 17th-century English lute and viol music that is a type of *Nachschlag.

Stabat Mater [L.]. A 13th-century *sequence (*Stabat mater dolorosa*), probably written by the Franciscan Jacopone da Todi (c. 1228–1306). It was officially added to the Roman Catholic liturgy in 1727 and is still sung at the Feast of the Seven Dolors (Sept. 15). The text has frequently been set polyphonically.

Stabreim [G.]. *Alliteration.

Staccato [It.]. Detached. A manner of performance indicated by a dot or the sign ▼ placed above or below the note, calling for a reduction of the written duration of the note with a rest substituted for half or more of its value. Earlier composers, such as K. P. E. Bach, Haydn, and Beethoven, normally indicated staccato with the wedge, reserving the dot for a less rigid staccato (*portato) occurring principally in slow movements. In modern notation the wedge often implies a very short staccato (*staccatissimo*). See also Bowing (g); Legato.

Staden, Johann (b. Nuremberg, bapt. 2 July 1581; d. there, buried 15 Nov. 1634). Court organist to the Margrave of Kulmbach and Bayreuth from 1604 until 1610 or 1611. From 1616 until his death, organist in Nuremberg, first at St. Lorenz and then at St. Sebald. Composed sacred vocal works in Latin and German, some with instruments; sacred lieder for one voice with thoroughbass; secular polyphonic lieder, some in the style of the *villanella;* pieces for instrumental ensemble, incl. dances.

Staden, Sigmund Theophil (b. Kulmbach, Bavaria, 6 Nov. 1607; d. Nuremberg, buried 30 July 1655). Son of Johann Staden. Town musician in Nuremberg from 1627. Organist at St. Lorenz in Nuremberg from 1634. Composed the earliest extant German opera, *Seelewig,* libretto by G. P. Harsdörffer, Nuremberg, 1644; *Singspiele;* oratorios; four-part chorale settings with thoroughbass; instrumental pieces.

Stadler, Maximilian (bapt. Johann Carl Dominic) (b. Melk, Austria, 4 Aug. 1748; d. Vienna, 8 Nov. 1833). Organist and composer. Benedictine abbot at Lilienfeld from 1786; at Kremsmünster from 1789. Settled in Vienna in 1796. Associate of Haydn and Mozart. Composed an oratorio, *Die Befreiung von Jerusalem,* 1816; much church music; orch. works; secular choral works; chamber music; sonatas and other pieces for piano and for organ; songs.

Staff, stave [F. *portée;* G. *Liniensystem, System;* It. *rigo;* Sp. *pentagrama, pauta*]. A series of horizontal lines, today five in number, on and between which musical notes are written, their location indicating (in connection with a *clef) their pitch. Small lines used to indicate pitches above or below the staff are called *ledger lines. Since the lines and spaces of the staff represent the pitches of the *diatonic scale (i.e., the white keys of the piano), bearing the names of the first seven letters of the alphabet, *accidentals and/or *key signatures must be used to indicate chromatic pitches (i.e., sharps and flats, played on the black keys). Piano music is normally notated on two staves connected by a brace. Several staves connected together for purposes of notating ensemble music comprise a *score.

The first use of horizontal lines for the representation of pitches appears in the treatise *Musica enchiriadis* (*c.* 900), but here the syllables of the text rather than notes are written in the appropriate spaces between lines. The invention of the staff proper is ascribed to Guido d'Arezzo (*c.* 990–1050), who recommends the use of three or four lines. The four-line staff has been preserved to the present day for the notation of Gregorian chant. For notating polyphonic music, the five-line staff (one staff for each voice-part) was used as early as the 13th

century. Six-line staves were occasionally used in the 14th century, in early 15th-century compositions with *contratenors of wide range, and in numerous 16th-century scores of keyboard music. See also Tablature.

Stainer, John (b. London, 6 June 1840; d. Verona, 31 Mar. 1901). Chorister at St. Paul's Cathedral in London, 1847–56, and organist there, 1872–88. Studied at Oxford Univ. and was professor there from 1889 until his death. Composed oratorios (incl. *The Crucifixion,* 1887); cantatas; services, anthems, and other church music; organ pieces; songs. Wrote books on harmony and the organ and edited early music.

Stamitz, Johann Wenzel Anton (Jan Václav Antonín) (b. Deutsch-Brod, now Havlíčkův Brod, Bohemia, 17 or 19 June 1717; d. Mannheim, 27 Mar. 1757). Violinist and composer. Served the electoral court at Mannheim from 1741, becoming concertmaster of the orchestra and director of chamber music in 1745. Performed in Paris, 1754–55. His pupils incl. his son Karl and Cannabich. Composed about 75 symphonies; other orch. works; concertos for violin, for clarinet, for flute, for oboe, for harpsichord; church music; violin sonatas and chamber music.

Stamitz, Karl Philipp (Karel Filip) (b. Mannheim, bapt. 8 May 1745; d. Jena, 9 Nov. 1801). Violinist and composer. Pupil of his father, J. W. A. Stamitz, and of Cannabich, Holzbauer, and F. X. Richter. Violinist in the electoral orchestra at Mannheim, 1762–70. Concertmaster to the Duc de Noailles in Paris from 1770. Conductor at Jena from 1794. Concertized widely. Composed operas and other stage works; about 80 symphonies and *sinfonie concertante;* concertos for violin, for viola, for piano, for flute, for oboe, for clarinet, for bassoon; vocal works; chamber music.

Stampita, stantipes. See *Estampie.*

Ständchen [G.]. *Serenade.

Stanford, Charles Villiers (b. Dublin, 30 Sept. 1852; d. London, 29 Mar. 1924). Organist, conductor, and composer. Studied in Dublin, Cambridge, London, Berlin, and with Reinecke in Leipzig.

Organist at Trinity College, Cambridge, 1873–92. Teacher at the Royal College of Music from 1883, and at Cambridge from 1887, until his death. His pupils incl. Bliss, Holst, and Vaughan Williams. Composed operas (incl. *The Canterbury Pilgrims*, London, 1884; *Shamus O'Brien*, London, 1896; *Much Ado about Nothing*, London, 1901); incidental music; 7 symphonies, several Irish Rhapsodies, and other orch. works; concertos for piano, for violin, for clarinet; sacred and secular choral works; 8 string quartets and other chamber music; piano pieces; organ pieces; songs and arrangements of Irish folksongs.

Stanley, John (b. London, 17 Jan. 1713; d. there, 19 May 1786). Pupil of Greene. Blind from childhood. Church organist in London from 1724. Master of the King's Band of Music from 1779, succeeding Boyce. Organist at the Chapel Royal from 1782. Friend of Handel, succeeding him, with J. C. Smith, as a conductor of oratorios. Composed stage works; oratorios (incl. *Jephtha*, 1757); cantatas; odes; concertos; pieces for flute and other instruments; keyboard pieces; songs.

Star-Spangled Banner, The. The national anthem of the United States, officially adopted in a bill passed on 3 March 1931. The words were written by Francis Scott Key (1779–1843) in September 1814, while he watched the British bombardment of Fort McHenry, near Baltimore. It is sung to a tune by John Stafford Smith (*c*. 1750–1836), an Englishman who originally composed the music for a poem beginning "To Anacreon in Heaven." It is not known whether Key had this tune in mind when he wrote the poem, or whether text and music were united later (possibly by Joseph Hopper Nicholson).

Starer, Robert (b. Vienna, 8 Jan. 1924). Pianist and composer. Pupil of Tal, Partos, and F. Jacobi. Teacher at the Juilliard School from 1947; at Brooklyn College from 1963. Has composed operas (incl. *The Intruder*, New York, 1956); ballets (incl. *The Dybbuk*, 1960; *Samson Agonistes*, choreography by Martha Graham, 1961); orch. works (incl. 3 symphonies; *Mutabili*, variants for orch., 1965); 3 piano concertos, a

Concerto a 3 for clarinet, trumpet, trombone, and strings, 1954, and other concertos; choral works; chamber music; piano pieces; songs.

Starokadomsky, Mikhail Leonidovich (b. Brest-Litovsk, 13 June 1901; d. Moscow, 24 Apr. 1954). Pupil of Vassilenko and Miaskovsky at the Moscow Conservatory, where he later taught. Composed an opera and several operettas; a concerto for orch., 1937, and other orch. works; a violin concerto, 1937; choral works; chamber music; numerous songs.

Starzer, Josef (b. Vienna, 1726 or 1727; d. there, 22 Apr. 1787). Violinist at the Vienna court chapel until 1759; court composer at St. Petersburg, 1759–69, after which he returned to Vienna. Composed ballets (incl. *Gli Orazi e gli Curiazi*, 1774; *Adèle de Ponthieu*, 1775); symphonies; choral works; string quartets and other chamber music.

Steffani, Agostino (b. Castelfranco Veneto, Italy, 25 July 1654; d. Frankfurt, 12 Feb. 1728). Priest, diplomat, and composer. Studied in Munich with Kerll and in Rome. Organist at the court in Munich from 1675 and director of chamber music there from 1681. Court *Kapellmeister* at Hanover, 1688–1710, succeeded by Handel. Composed operas (incl. *Alarico*, Munich, 1687; *Enrico Leone*, Hanover, 1689); church music; cantatas; vocal and instrumental chamber music.

Steg [G.]. *Bridge of the violin, etc. See Bowing (k).

Steibelt, Daniel (Gottlieb) (b. Berlin, 22 Oct. 1765; d. St. Petersburg, 2 Oct. 1823). Pupil of Kirnberger. Went to St. Petersburg in 1809, becoming *maître de chapelle* to Alexander I in 1810. Concertized widely in Europe and Russia as a pianist. Composed operas (incl. *Roméo et Juliette*, Paris, 1793); ballets; the intermezzo *La fête de Mars*, 1806; orch. works; 8 piano concertos; chamber music; sonatas and other piano pieces; songs. Published a piano method.

Stein, Richard Heinrich (b. Halle, Germany, 28 Feb. 1882; d. Santa Brigida, Canary Islands, 11 Aug. 1942). Settled in the Canary Islands in 1933. Worked with quarter tones. Composed an opera; orch.

works; *2 Konzertstücke* for cello and piano, with quarter tones, 1906; piano pieces; songs. Published several books on music.

Steinberg, Maximilian Osseievich (b. Vilna, 4 July 1883; d. Leningrad, 6 Dec. 1946). Pupil of Liadov, Glazunov, and Rimsky-Korsakov. Teacher at the St. Petersburg (later Leningrad) Conservatory from 1908 and its director from 1934. His pupils incl. Shostakovich. Composed ballets; 5 symphonies and other orch. works; choral works; arrangements of folksongs for voice and orch.; a violin concerto; 2 string quartets; piano pieces; songs.

Stendendo [It.]. Slowing down.

Stenhammar, Karl Wilhelm Eugen (b. Stockholm, 7 Feb. 1871; d. there, 20 Nov. 1927). Pianist, conductor, and composer. Studied in Stockholm with Hallén and in Berlin. Conductor of the Stockholm Philharmonic, 1897–1900, and of various organizations in Göteborg, 1907–22. Composed operas (incl. *Tirfing*, Stockholm, 1898; *Das Fest auf Solhaug*, after Ibsen, Stuttgart, 1899, in Swedish at Stockholm, 1902); 2 symphonies and other orch. works; 2 piano concertos; choral works; string quartets and other chamber music; piano pieces; songs.

Sterbend [G.]. Dying away.

Steso [It.]. Slow.

Stesso [It.]. Same. See *Istesso tempo.*

Steuermann, Eduard (b. Sambor, near Lvov, 18 June 1892; d. New York, 11 Nov. 1964). Pianist and composer. Pupil of Busoni, Schoenberg, and Humperdinck. Settled in the U.S. in 1937. Teacher at the Philadelphia Conservatory, 1948–64; at the Juilliard School, 1952–64. Composed orch. works; choral works; the cantata *Auf der Galerie*, text by Kafka, 1964; 2 string quartets and other chamber music; piano pieces; songs.

Stevens, Halsey (b. Scott, N.Y., 3 Dec. 1908). Studied at Syracuse Univ. and with Bloch. Teacher at the Univ. of Southern California from 1946. Has composed 2 symphonies and other orch.

works; concertos for cello, for clarinet; choral works; string quartets, piano trios, and other chamber music; piano pieces; songs. Has published *The Life and Music of Béla Bartók,* 1953, and other writings.

Stil [G.]; **stile** [It.]; **stilus** [L.]. *Style.

Stile antico [L., old style]. See under Roman school.

Stile rappresentativo [It.]. The "representative" style of *recitative used in the earliest operas and semidramatic works of about 1600.

Still, William Grant (b. Woodville, Miss., 11 May 1895). Studied at Wilberforce Univ. and Oberlin Conservatory, and with Varèse and Chadwick. Has worked as an arranger and conductor. Has composed operas; orch. works (incl. *Afro-American Symphony,* 1930, and other symphonies; *Darker America,* 1924; *From the Black Belt,* 1926); the choral ballet *Sahdji,* 1930, and other ballets; choral works; works for band; chamber music; piano pieces; songs.

Stimme [G.]. (1) Voice. (2) Voice-part.

Stimmen [G.]. (1) Plural of *Stimme.* (2) To tune.

Stimmung [G.]. (1) Mood; thus, *Stimmungsbild,* title used for pieces meant to express definite moods. (2) Tuning, intonation, e.g., *reine Stimmung,* just intonation.

Stinguendo [It.]. Fading away.

Stiracchiando, stirato [It.]. Drawing out, slowing down.

Stockhausen, Karlheinz (b. Mödrath, near Cologne, 22 Aug. 1928). Pupil of Martin and Messiaen. Associate at times of Eimert and Boulez. Has worked at the *musique concrète* studio in Paris, at the Studio for Electronic Music in Cologne, and has taught at the Darmstadt summer courses. Has worked with serial, aleatory, and electronic procedures, with spatial placement of sound sources, and with graphic notation. Some works are constructed from discrete units of musical time called "groups" or "moments." Works incl. *Kreuzspiel* for orch., 1951; *Formel* for orch., 1951–52; *Punkte* for orch., 1952, rev. 1962, 1967; *Kontra-Punkte* for 10 instruments, 1952–53; *Klavierstücke I–XI*, 1952–56 (XI, 1956, a mobile form); *Zeitmasse* for oboe, flute, English horn, clarinet, bassoon, 1955–56; **Gruppen* for 3 orchs., 1955–57; *Gesang der Jünglinge,* on tape for 5 groups of loudspeakers, 1955–56; *Zyklus* for one percussionist, 1959; *Carré* for 4 orchs., 4 choruses, 1959–60, with Cardew; *Kontakte* for piano, percussion, tape, 1959–60; *Momente* for soprano, 4 choruses, 13 instrumentalists, 1962–64; *Mikrophonie I* for tamtam, 2 microphones, and electronics, 1964, and *II* for chorus, Hammond organ, and electronics, 1965; *Telemusik,* on tape, 1966; *Prozession* for piano, electric viola, tamtam, and electronics, 1967; *Stimmung* for 6 singers, 1968; *Hymnen,* based on national anthems, in versions for tape alone, 1966–67, tape with soloists, 1966–67, and tape with orch., 1969; *Für kommende Zeiten,* 17 texts for "intuitive music" for unspecified ensemble, 1968–70; *Mantra* for 2 pianos and electronics, 1970; *Trans* for orch., 1971; *Ylem* for 19 or more players/singers, 1972; *Musik im Bauch* for 6 percussionists and music boxes, 1975.

Stoessel, Albert Frederic (b. St. Louis, 11 Oct. 1894; d. New York, 12 May 1943). Violinist, conductor, and composer. Teacher at New York Univ., 1923–30; director of the opera department at the Juilliard School, 1930–43. Composed operas; orch. works; choral works; chamber music (incl. *Suite antique* for 2 violins and piano, 1922); piano pieces; songs.

Stollen [G.]. See under *Bar* form.

Stoltzer, Thomas (b. Schweidnitz, Silesia, probably between 1480 and 1485; d. Ofen, 1526, or perhaps at the battle of Mohács on 29 Aug. 1526). Chapel master at the Hungarian court at Ofen from 1522. Composed Masses, motets, and other sacred works; polyphonic lieder; instrumental pieces.

Stölzel, Gottfried Heinrich (b. Grünstädtl, Saxony, 13 Jan. 1690; d. Gotha, 27 Nov. 1749). Studied at Schneeberg and Leipzig. Music teacher in Breslau, 1710–12. Traveled to Italy and elsewhere. Court *Kapellmeister* in

Gotha from 1719. Composed operas and other stage works; oratorios; cycles of cantatas and motets for the church year; other sacred music; concertos and *concerti grossi;* chamber music.

Stop. (1) In the *organ, the mechanical device by which the player can draw on or shut off the various registers. The term is also used for the rank (ranks) of pipes controlled by this mechanism. (2) In the *harpsichord, a set of strings and/or jacks that can be coupled with one or more other sets to provide varieties of tone color, loudness, and pitch level. For the buff stop, see under Harpsichord. See also Divided stop.

Stopped notes. See under Horn.

Stopped pipe. Any pipe closed at one end. See Acoustics; Organ; Wind instruments.

Stopping. (1) In stringed instruments (violins, lutes, etc.), pressing a string against the fingerboard with the fingertips of the left hand and thus fixing the vibrating length of the string so as to produce a desired pitch. See Acoustics; Double stop. (2) On the natural horn, see Horn.

Storace, Stephen (b. London, 4 Apr. 1762; d. there, 19 Mar. 1796). Studied with his father and at the Conservatorio di Sant' Onofrio in Naples. Lived for a time in Vienna, where he became acquainted with Mozart, returning to England in 1787. Composed operas (incl. *Gli equivoci,* Vienna, 1786; *The Haunted Tower,* London, 1789; *No Song No Supper,* London, 1790); other stage works, incl. arrangements and adaptations of works by others; chamber music; songs. His sister Nancy (Anna Selina) was a well-known singer.

Stout, Alan (b. Baltimore, 26 Nov. 1932). Pupil of Cowell, Verrall, Riegger, and Holmboe. Teacher at Northwestern Univ. from 1963. Has composed 4 symphonies and other orch. works; works for solo instruments and for solo voices with orch.; a Passion and other choral works; 10 string quartets, a cello sonata, and other chamber music; works for organ, incl. chorales.

Stradella, Alessandro (b. Montefestino,

Modena, 1 Oct. 1644; d. Genoa, 25 Feb. 1682). Singer, violinist, and composer. Active in Venice, Turin, and Genoa. Little is known of his life, though it and his murder have been the subject of various legends and of operas by Flotow and others. Composed operas (incl. *Forza dell'amor paterno*, Genoa, 1678; *Il trespolo tutore*, 1679?); oratorios (incl. *San Giovanni Battista*); numerous cantatas; motets; madrigals; arias and duets; instrumental pieces.

Straff [G.]. Rigid, firm.

Strambotto. A form of 15th- and 16th-century Italian poetry, consisting of eight-line stanzas in iambic pentameter with the rhyme scheme *ab ab ab ab*, or, more frequently, *ab ab ab cc* (the latter is known as *ottava rima*). In the publisher Petrucci's **Frottole* (1504–14) *strambotti* are provided with music for the first two lines that is then repeated for the remaining pairs of lines. Later settings are through-composed, in the manner of the madrigal.

Strang, Gerald (b. Claresholm, Alberta, Canada, 13 Feb. 1908). Pupil of Schoenberg, Toch, and Koechlin. Schoenberg's teaching assistant, 1936–38, and his editorial assistant, 1936–50. Teacher at Long Beach City College, 1938–58; San Fernando Valley State College, 1958–65; California State College at Long Beach, 1965–69. Lecturer on electronic music at the Univ. of California at Los Angeles from 1969. Has composed 2 symphonies and other orch. works; a cello concerto, 1951; chamber music; *Percussion Music for 3 Players*, 1935; electronic works, some with computer.

Strascicando, strascinando [It.]. Dragging.

Strathspey. A slow Scottish dance in 4/4 meter with many dotted notes, frequently in the inverted arrangement of the Scotch snap. The name, derived from the strath (valley) of the Spey, was originally synonymous with **reel;* later, *reel* was used for somewhat faster dances in more smoothly flowing rhythm and lacking dotted notes.

Straus, Oscar (b. Vienna, 6 Mar. 1870; d. Bad Ischl, 11 Jan. 1954). Studied in Vienna and with Bruch in Berlin. Lived in Berlin, Vienna, and Paris, becoming a French citizen in 1939. Lived in New York and Hollywood, 1940–48. Composed operas; operettas (incl. *Ein Walzertraum*, Vienna, 1907; *Der tapfere Soldat*, after Shaw, Vienna, 1908, in New York as *The Chocolate Soldier*, 1909); a ballet; orch. works; choral works; chamber music; piano pieces; music for films.

Strauss, Johann (Jr.) (the "Waltz King") (b. Vienna, 25 Oct. 1825; d. there, 3 June 1899). Son of Johann Strauss, Sr. Conductor of his own ensemble in performing his waltzes from 1844. On his father's death in 1849, merged his own orchestra with that of his father. Conductor of the court balls in Vienna, 1863–70. Toured widely and visited the U.S. in 1872. Composed operettas (incl. *Die *Fledermaus; Die Zigeunerbaron* [The Gypsy Baron], Vienna, 1885); numerous waltzes (incl. *An der schönen blauen Donau* [The Blue Danube], 1867; *Geschichten aus dem Wienerwald* [Tales from the Vienna Woods]); quadrilles, polkas, marches, galops, etc.

Strauss, Johann (Sr.) (b. Vienna, 14 Mar. 1804; d. there, 25 Sept. 1849). Conductor and composer. Pupil of Seyfried. Toured Europe with an orchestra performing his own music from 1825. Conductor of the court balls in Vienna from 1845. Composed numerous waltzes as well as polkas, galops, quadrilles, marches (incl. the *Radetzky March*), and other dances. His sons Johann (Jr.), Josef, and Eduard were also musicians and composers.

Strauss, Richard (Georg) (b. Munich, 11 June 1864; d. Garmisch, 8 Sept. 1949). Son of the composer and horn player Franz Strauss (1822–1905). Associate of Ritter and collaborator with the poet Hugo von Hofmannsthal. Conductor of the Meiningen court chapel, succeeding von Bülow, 1885–86; at the Munich court opera, 1886–89; at the court at Weimar, 1889–94; of the Berlin Philharmonic, 1894–95, succeeding von Bülow; at the Munich court opera from 1894; of the Berlin opera, 1898–1918. Co-director of the Vienna State Opera, 1919–24. President of the Reichsmusikkammer under the Nazi regime, 1933–35. Toured widely as a conductor. Works: operas (incl. *Guntram*, Weimar, 1894; *Feuers-*

not, Dresden, 1901; **Salome; *Elektra; Der *Rosenkavalier; *Ariadne auf Naxos; Die *Frau ohne Schatten; Intermezzo,* Dresden, 1924; *Die ägyptische Helena,* Dresden, 1928; **Arabella; Die schweigsame Frau,* Dresden, 1935; *Friedenstag,* Munich, 1938; *Daphne,* Dresden, 1938; *Die Liebe der Danae,* 1940, prod. Salzburg, 1952; **Capriccio*); ballets (incl. *Josephslegende,* 1914); symphonic poems and other orch. works (incl. a symphony in F min., 1884; **Aus Italien; *Don Juan; Macbeth,* 1890; **Tod und Verklärung; *Till Eulenspiegels lustige Streiche; *Also sprach Zarathustra; *Don Quixote; Ein *Heldenleben; *Symphonia domestica*); a violin concerto, 1882; 2 horn concertos, 1883, 1942; an oboe concerto, 1942; choral works; songs with orch. (incl. the so-called *4 Last Songs,* 1948); chamber music (incl. a string quartet, 1880; a cello sonata, 1883, a piano quartet, 1884; a violin sonata, 1887; pieces for winds); piano pieces; numerous songs.

Stravinsky, Igor (Feodorovich) (b. Oranienbaum, near St. Petersburg, 17 June 1882; d. New York, 6 Apr. 1971). Pianist, conductor, and composer. Son of the bass Feodor Stravinsky. Studied law and was a pupil of Rimsky-Korsakov and V. P. Kalafati. Associate of Sergei Diaghilev and his Ballets Russes, 1909–29, and of the choreographer George Balanchine thereafter. Lived in Switzerland during World War I; in Paris, 1920–39; in the U.S. after 1939, principally in Hollywood, Calif., becoming a U.S. citizen in 1945. In the course of his exceptionally long creative life he employed a wide variety of styles and techniques, including rhythmic and melodic ostinatos, elements of jazz, the diatonicism of the so-called neoclassical [see Neoclassicism] works, extremes of dissonance sometimes resulting from the juxtaposition of diatonic elements [see Bitonality], and the serialism of works composed after 1952.

Works: operas (*The *Nightingale; *Mavra; *Oedipus Rex; The *Rake's Progress*); ballets (*L'*oiseau de feu* [The Firebird]; **Petrushka; Le *sacre du printemps* [The Rite of Spring]; *Le chant du rossignol* [see *Nightingale, The*]; **Pulcinella; Les *noces; *Apollon Musagète;*

Le baiser de la fée [The Fairy's Kiss], after Tchaikovsky, 1928; **Jeu de cartes; Orpheus,* choreography by Balanchine, 1947; **Agon*); other stage works (incl. *L'*histoire du soldat; Renard* for singers, dancers, and chamber orch., Paris, 1922; **Perséphone; The Flood* for actors, tenor, 2 basses, chorus, and orch., N.B.C.-TV, 1962); orch. works (incl. a symphony in E♭, 1907; *Fireworks,* 1908; *Ragtime* for 11 instruments, 1918; *Symphonies of Wind Instruments,* 1920; *Dumbarton Oaks Concerto* in E♭ for 16 winds, 1938; *Symphony in C,* 1940; *Danses concertantes* for chamber orch., 1942; *Circus Polka,* 1942; *Scherzo à la russe,* 1944; *Symphony in 3 Movements,* 1945; a concerto in D for strings, 1946; *Variations (Aldous Huxley in memoriam),* 1964); works for solo instrument with orch. (incl. a concerto for piano and winds, 1924; *Capriccio* for piano and orch., 1929; a violin concerto in D, 1931; *Ebony Concerto* for clarinet and swing band, 1946; *Movements* for piano and orch., 1959); vocal works (incl. **Symphony of Psalms* for chorus and orch., 1930; a Mass for male voices and 10 instruments, 1948; a cantata on 15th- and 16th-century English poems, 1962; *In memoriam Dylan Thomas,* texts by Thomas, for tenor, string quartet, trombone quartet, 1954; *Canticum sacrum ad honorem Sancti Marci nominis* for tenor, baritone, organ, and orch., 1955; *Threni: id est Lamentationes Jeremiae Prophetae* for soloists and orch., 1958; *Abraham and Isaac* for baritone and chamber orch., 1963; *Elegy for J. F. K.* for baritone and instruments, 1964; *Requiem Canticles* for soloists, chorus, and orch., 1966); chamber music (incl. 3 pieces for string quartet, 1914; *Octet* for flute, clarinet, 2 bassoons, 2 trumpets, 2 trombones, 1923; *Duo concertant* for violin and piano, 1932; *Septet* for clarinet, bassoon, horn, piano, violin, viola, and cello, 1953); piano pieces (incl. 2 sonatas, 1904, 1924; a serenade in A, 1925; a concerto for 2 pianos, 1935; a sonata for 2 pianos); songs. Published *An Autobiography,* 1936; *Poetics of Music,* 1947; and a series of dialogues with Robert Craft.

Straziante [It.]. Anguished.

Street organ, hand organ. A **mechanical

instrument, based on the barrel-and-pin principle, in which the pins operate reed pipes similar to those of the organ. A crank turns the barrel and also operates a bellows, which furnishes air to make the reeds vibrate. The instrument, which is associated with the Italian street musician and his monkey, is popularly but erroneously called a *hurdy-gurdy.

Streich- [G.]. Stroke (of a bow). *Streichinstrumente,* bowed (stringed) instruments. *Streichorchester,* string orchestra. *Streichquartett (-quintett),* string quartet (quintet). *Streichklavier,* pianoviolin [see Sostenente piano].

Streit zwischen Phöbus und Pan, Der [G., The Struggle between Phoebus and Pan]. Secular cantata by J. S. Bach (1732), text by Picander, based on Ovid's account of the musical contest between Phoebus Apollo and Pan.

Strepitoso [It.]. Noisy, boisterous.

Stretta [It.]. See Stretto (2).

Stretto [It.]. (1) In a fugue, the imitation of the subject in close succession, with the answer entering before the subject is completed. (2) In nonfugal compositions, stretto (stretta) is a concluding section in faster tempo, as, e.g., at the end of the last movement of Beethoven's Fifth Symphony.

Strich [G.]. Bow stroke.

Striggio, Alessandro (b. Mantua, *c.* 1535; d. there, between 1589 and 1595). Organist, lutenist, viol player, and composer. Served the Florentine court, 1560–74, and the Mantuan court thereafter. Visited Paris and London in 1567 and the court of the Emperor Maximilian in 1574. Composed *intermedi;* the earliest madrigal comedy, *Il cicalamento delle donne al bucato,* 1567; madrigals; Masses and motets. His son Alessandro, a poet and musician, was the librettist of Monteverdi's La *favola d'Orfeo.*

String quartet [F. *quatuor à cordes;* G. *Streichquartett;* It. *quartetto di corde;* Sp. *cuarteto de cuerdas*]. Chamber music for four strings, practically always first and second violin, viola, and cello. Also an ensemble consisting of these instruments. The string quartet emerged from a variety of forms belonging to the family of the *divertimento and became established as the most serious form of *chamber music during the period of Haydn and Mozart, whose mature works continue to occupy an important place in the repertory. Its essential features were four discrete parts, each played by a single player, and the absence of keyboard accompaniment. Its form was that of the classical *sonata. The early and middle-period quartets of Beethoven build upon this foundation, but his late quartets transform it considerably and remain models of the genre in their subtlety and complexity. The vogue for opera and program music in the 19th century caused the string quartet to be cultivated somewhat less intensively after Beethoven's death. There are, nevertheless, examples by Schubert, Cherubini, Schumann, Mendelssohn, Brahms, Dvořák, Franck, and Reger. Important examples from the 20th century include works by Debussy, Ravel, Schoenberg, Berg, Webern, Bartók, Piston, Sessions, Shostakovich, Lutoslawski, Babbitt, and Carter.

String quintet. Chamber music for five strings. See Quintet.

String trio. Chamber music for three strings, often for violin, viola, and cello. See Trio (3).

Stringed instruments. Broadly, instruments in which the sound-producing agent is a stretched string. The scientific name for this category is *chordophone.* The most important members of this large group are the *violin and related instruments, *harpsichord, *harp, and *piano. Ordinarily the name *stringed instruments* ("strings") is reserved for members of the violin family and the *double bass. Gut (usually sheep intestines, the term "catgut" remaining unexplained) was the most widely used material for strings of nonkeyboard instruments from antiquity until the early 20th century, though wire was invented in the Middle Ages and used early for keyboard instruments. Strings wound (or overspun) with silver or other metal came into use for the lowest strings of the violin and related instruments in the late 17th century. Metal largely displaced gut for the uppermost string of the violin only in the early 20th century. Nylon and other synthetics are sometimes used as a substitute for gut, particularly on the guitar.

Stringendo [It.]. Compressing, i.e., quickening the tempo.

Stringfield, Lamar (b. Raleigh, N.C., 10 Oct. 1897; d. Asheville, N.C., 21 Jan. 1959). Pupil of P. Goetschius. Founded the Institute of Folk Music at the Univ. of North Carolina. Conducted the North Carolina Symphony and orchestras in Charlotte, N.C., and Knoxville, Tenn. Composed the folk drama *Carolina Charcoal,* 1952; orch. works (incl. the suite *From the Southern Mountains,* 1928, containing *Cripple Creek*); choral works; chamber music.

Stringham, Edwin John (b. Kenosha, Wis., 11 July 1890; d. Chapel Hill, N.C., 1 July 1974). Studied at Northwestern Univ., the Cincinnati Conservatory, and with Respighi. Teacher at Teachers College of Columbia Univ., 1930–38; the Juilliard School, 1930–45; Queens College in New York, 1938–46. Composed orch. works (incl. *The Ancient Mariner,* 1928; a symphony, 1929); choral works; chamber music; songs.

Strings. Colloquial name for the *stringed instruments of the orchestra (string section); also the string quartet, quintet, etc.

Strisciando [It.]. *Glissando.

Stromento [It.]. Instrument. *Stromentato,* instrumented, accompanied by instruments; see Recitative. *Stromenti a corde,* stringed instruments; *s. d'arco,* bowed instruments; *s. di legno,* woodwind instruments; *s. d'ottone* or *di metallo,* brass instruments; *s. a percossa,* percussion instrumets; *s. a fiato, di vento,* wind instruments; *s. da tasto,* keyboard instruments.

Strong, George Templeton (b. New York, 26 May 1856; d. Geneva, 27 June 1948). Pupil of Jadassohn. Associate of Liszt and his followers at Weimar and of Mac-Dowell in Wiesbaden. Taught at the New England Conservatory, 1891–92, after which he settled in Switzerland. Composed 3 symphonies and other orch.

works (incl. the symphonic poem *Undine* and the suite *Die Nacht*); choral works; chamber music; piano pieces; songs.

Strophic. Designation for a song in which all strophes or stanzas of the text are sung to the same music, in contrast to a song with new music for each stanza (*through-composed).

Strophic bass. The technique, often found in early 17th-century monody, of using the same bass line for all the strophes or stanzas of a song, with varying melodies in the upper part. The strophic bass is distinguished from the *ground (*basso ostinato*) by its greater length and definite ending. Thus, *basso ostinato* and strophic bass are examples of continuous and sectional variation, respectively [see Variations].

Strube, Gustav (b. Ballenstedt, Germany, 3 Mar. 1867; d. Baltimore, 2 Feb. 1953). Studied at the Leipzig Conservatory. Violinist in the Boston Symphony, 1891–1913. Teacher at the Peabody Conservatory in Baltimore from 1913 and its director, 1916–46. Conductor of the Baltimore Symphony, 1916–30. Composed operas; 2 symphonies and other orch. works; 2 violin concertos; choral works; chamber music. Published a textbook on harmony.

Strumento d'acciaio [It., steel instrument]. Probably an instrument like the modern celesta [see Percussion instruments I, 4]. It is called for in Mozart's *Die Zauberflöte.*

Strungk, Nicolaus Adam (b. Brunswick, bapt. 15 Nov. 1640; d. Dresden, 23 Sept. 1700). Violinist, organist, and composer. Music director at Hamburg from 1679. Member of the Hanover court chapel, 1682–86, accompanying the Elector to Italy where he met Corelli. Vice *Kapellmeister* and chamber organist at Dresden from 1688 and court *Kapellmeister* there, 1693–96. Founded an opera house in Leipzig in 1693. Composed numerous operas in German (incl. *Alceste,* Leipzig, 1693); an Easter oratorio; chamber music; ricercars and other keyboard pieces. Published a manual on string playing.

Stück [G.]. Piece, composition.

Sturgeon, Nicholas (b. Devonshire, *c.* 1390; d. London, 31 May 1454). Member of the Chapel Royal from 1413, accompanying Henry V to France in 1416. A canon of Windsor and of St. Paul's Cathedral, London, from 1442. Composed Mass sections and other sacred works found in the Old Hall manuscript.

Stürmer, Bruno (b. Freiburg im Breisgau, 9 Sept. 1892; d. Bad Homburg, 19 May 1958). Studied at the Karlsruhe Conservatory, the Univ. of Heidelberg, and the Univ. of Munich. Founded a music school in Homburg in 1926. Conductor in Kassel, 1930–45. Teacher at the Landesmusikschule in Darmstadt, 1947–52. Composed numerous choral works (incl. *Die Messe des Maschinenmenschen*, 1932); stage works; orch. works; concertos for piano, for violin, for cello; chamber music; piano pieces; songs.

Stürze [G.]. Bell of the *horn. *Stürze hoch*, the bell turned upward.

Style [F. *style;* G. *Stil;* It. *stile;* Sp. *estilo*]. In the arts, mode of expression or of performance. In a musical composition, "style" comprehends the methods of treating all of the elements—*form, *melody, *rhythm, *harmony, *texture, *timbre, etc. In practice, the term may be applied to single works (e.g., the style of *Tristan* compared to that of *Die Meistersinger*); to composers (the style of Wagner compared to that of Beethoven); to types of composition (operatic style, symphonic style, motet style, church style); to media (instrumental style, vocal style, keyboard style); to methods of composition (contrapuntal style, homophonic style, monodic style); to nations (French style, German style); to periods (baroque style, romantic style); etc. Also such terms are sometimes used in combination, e.g., "Beethoven's symphonic style," "German romantic style," "instrumental style of the baroque."

Style brisé [F., broken style]. The characteristic style of 17th-century French lute music (especially that of Denis Gaultier, *c.* 1600–72), in which melody and bass notes are sounded not simultaneously but one after the other. This style greatly influenced the harpsichord music of the French clavecinists and of Froberger.

Style galant [F.]. *Gallant style.

Subdominant. The fourth degree of the scale (e.g., F in C major or C minor), so called because this tone is a fifth below the tonic, just as the dominant is a fifth above it [see Scale degrees].

Subito [It.]. Suddenly.

Subject [F. *sujet, thème;* G. *Thema;* It. *tema, soggetto;* Sp. *tema*]. A melody or melodic fragment that, by virtue of its characteristic design, prominent position, or special treatment, is basic in the structure of a composition. In *sonata form there normally are two subjects (also called themes) or, in longer examples, two groups of subjects. A *fugue usually has only one subject, except in special types such as the double or triple fugue. Works in the fully developed imitative style of the 16th century use numerous subjects, one for each *point of imitation. See also *Soggetto cavato.*

Submediant. See under Scale degrees.

Subotnick, Morton (b. Los Angeles, 14 Apr. 1933). Studied with Milhaud and Kirchner at Mills College, where he subsequently taught, 1959–66. Co-founder of the Mills Performing Group and of the San Francisco Tape Music Center. Teacher at the California Institute of the Arts from 1969. Has worked with electronic techniques and mixed media, sometimes creating interactive sound environments. Works incl. 4 works titled *Play!* for varying combinations of instruments, electronic sounds, films, 1962–67; several serenades for instruments and tape, 1959–66; *Silver Apples of the Moon*, on tape, 1967; *The Wild Bull*, on tape, 1968; *Touch*, on tape, 1969.

Subtonic. See under Scale degrees.

Succentor [L.]. Deputy to the *precentor.

Suchoň, Eugen (b. Pezinok, near Bratislava, 25 Sept. 1908). Pupil of Novák. Teacher in Bratislava at the Music Academy and other institutions, 1933–60. Has composed operas (incl. *Krútňava* [The Whirlpool], Bratislava, 1949); orch. works; works for violin and for piano with orch.; choral works; chamber music; piano pieces; songs.

Suderburg, Robert (b. Spencer, Iowa, 28 Jan. 1936). Pupil of Donovan, Porter, and Rochberg. Teacher at Bryn Mawr College, 1960–61; Univ. of Pennsylvania, 1961–63; Philadelphia Musical Academy, 1963–66; Univ. of Washington, 1966–75. President of the North Carolina School of the Arts from 1975. Has composed orch. works (incl. *Orchestra Music I*, 1969, *II*, 1971, *III*, 1973); a piano concerto, 1974; choral works (incl. a *Concert Mass*, 1960, and 2 cantatas with orch.); chamber music; piano pieces.

Suite. (1) An important instrumental form in baroque music, consisting of a number of movements, each in the character of a dance and all in the same key.

The standard scheme of the suite used by Bach is A–C–S–O–G, with A standing for *allemande, C for *courante, S for *saraband, G for *gigue, and O for what is called an optional dance or optional group, i.e., one or several dances of various types, chiefly the *minuet, *bourrée, *gavotte, *passepied, *polonaise, *anglaise, *loure, and *air. Bach's suites for the harpsichord include six *"English Suites," six *"French Suites," and six *"Partitas." (The terms "English" and "French" for these works are unauthentic and irrelevant.) Each of the English Suites and Partitas is preceded by an introductory piece (prelude). The dance movements are invariably in *binary form. Stylistically the dances of the optional group form a contrast to the others, being simpler and more clearly suggestive of dance types. This is because the allemande, courante, saraband, and gigue are much older types that originated in the 16th century and, by the time they were adopted into the suite (*c*. 1650), had become idealized types. The optional dances, on the other hand, originated in the French ballets of the late 17th century (Lully) and retained the character of actual dance music.

This type of suite became practically extinct after 1750, leaving only traces in the *divertimento and *cassation as well as in the minuet of the classical *sonata (symphony). A few 20th-century composers, e.g., Hindemith, have modeled compositions on the baroque dance suite.

The origin of the suite is usually sought in the combinations of two dances, one in duple time, the other in triple time, that occur throughout the 16th century, e.g., pavane–galliard or *passamezzo–saltarello* [see Dance music]. While the idea of the suite as a unified musical form is clearly present in the compositions of 17th-century German composers such as S. Scheidt (1587–1654) and J. H. Schein (1586–1630), it is lacking in the works of French composers such as Jean-Baptiste Bésard (*c*. 1567–*c*. 1625), Chambonnières (*c*. 1602–72), Louis Couperin (*c*. 1626–61), and D'Anglebert (*c*. 1628–91), who merely arranged the dances either according to types or, later, according to keys, but in such large numbers as to exclude the idea of a definite form. This loose aggregation persists in the harpsichord works of François Couperin (publ. 1713–30) who, perhaps deliberately, avoids the name "suite" (used as early as 1687 by Lebègue) and uses instead the term "Ordre." The important contribution of the French clavecinists was to transform the allemande, courante, gigue, and saraband from their 16th-century plainness to baroque refinement (the courante is particularly interesting in this respect) and to enlarge the repertory by those numerous dances adopted, *c*. 1700, into the optional group of the suite.

Creation of the classical suite is the work of J. J. Froberger (1616–67). About 1650, the prevailing type of suite had only three movements, A–C–S, and indeed many suites of Froberger have this scheme. The gigue was introduced somewhat later as an "optional" dance, either before or after the courante, with the saraband retaining its position as the concluding movement: A–C–G–S or A–G–C–S. The four-movement suites in Froberger's autograph manuscripts invariably close with the saraband. Not until after Froberger's death were the positions of the saraband and gigue exchanged, as appears from the earliest printed edition of his suites (published posthumously in 1693), which bears the remark, "mis en meilleur ordre" (put in better order).

Side by side with this central development were others of a somewhat freer character, chiefly in chamber and orchestral music. In Italy the suite was cultivated mainly as a form of chamber music. The usual designation for the Italian instrumental suite of the 17th century is *sonata da camera*. Originally, this term meant any kind of dance music, mostly single dances, but later it was applied to suitelike formations. Corelli's *Sonate da camera* op. 2 (1685) and op. 4 (1694) contain twelve suites each, mostly in four movements, such as *Preludio–Allemanda–Corrente* (or *Sarabanda*)–*Giga* (or *Gavotta*).

Still another type of suite, designed for orchestral performance, originated (presumably) in the performance of Lully's operas or stage ballets "in abstracto," as a succession of their most successful dance numbers preceded by the operatic overture (ballet suite). This idea was taken over by numerous German composers, who wrote orchestral suites consisting of a French overture [see Overture] followed by a series of "modern" dances, such as the rigaudon, marche, chaconne, bourrée, traquenard, and others. Such suites, briefly called "Ouverture," were written by Georg Muffat, J. K. F. Fischer, G. P. Telemann, and J. S. Bach (4 orchestral suites). Bach also transferred this type to the keyboard in his *Französische Ouvertüre* (contained in the *Clavier-Übung* II, 1734).

(2) Any work consisting of several movements of varying character drawn from a larger work such as an opera, ballet, or incidental music to a play. Such works became common in the late 19th century; well-known examples include Tchaikovsky's *Suite from the Nutcracker* (from the ballet), Grieg's *Peer Gynt Suite* (from the incidental music to Ibsen's play), Ravel's *Daphnis et Chloé* suites (from the ballet), and Stravinsky's *Suite from Petrushka* (from the ballet).

Suite Bergamasque. Piano composition by Debussy, consisting of Prélude, Menuet, *Clair de lune*, and Passepied, composed 1890–1905. Its title is probably derived from a phrase in Verlaine's poem "Clair de lune," "masques et bergamasques."

Suk, Josef (b. Křečovice, Czechoslovakia, 4 Jan. 1874; d. Benešov, near Prague,

29 May 1935). Pupil and son-in-law of Dvořák. Second violinist in the Bohemian String Quartet, 1892–1922. Teacher at the Prague Conservatory from 1922 and its rector from 1930. Composed music for the stage (incl. *Radúz and Mahulena*, a fairy tale, Prague, 1898); orch. works (incl. a serenade in E♭ for strings, 1892; the symphony *Asrael*, 1906); choral works, some based on folksongs; 2 string quartets and other chamber music; piano pieces; songs.

Sul [It.]. On, at. *Sul G,* on the G-string of the violin. *Sul ponticello,* bowing near the bridge; *sul tasto, sulla tastiera,* bowing near the fingerboard. See Bowing (k), (1).

Sullivan, Arthur Seymour (b. London, 13 May 1842; d. there, 22 Nov. 1900). Conductor and composer. Chorister at the Chapel Royal and later studied at the Royal Academy of Music in London and at the Leipzig Conservatory. Teacher at the Royal Academy of Music from 1866. Principal of the National Training School for Music (later the Royal College of Music), 1876–81. Collaborated with the librettist W. S. Gilbert from 1871. Composed operettas (incl. the following, all with libretto by Gilbert and first produced in London unless otherwise noted: *Cox and Box,* libretto by F. C. Burnand, 1867; *Trial by Jury,* 1875; *The Sorcerer,* 1877; *H.M.S. Pinafore,* 1878; *The Pirates of Penzance,* Paignton and New York, 1879; *Patience,* 1881; *Iolanthe,* 1882; *The Mikado,* 1885; *Ruddigore,* 1887; *The Yeoman of the Guard,* 1888; *The Gondoliers,* 1889); the grand opera *Ivanhoe,* London, 1891; incidental music to plays of Shakespeare and others; ballets; overtures and other orch. works; a cello concerto, 1866; choral works (incl. the oratorio *The Prodigal Son,* 1896, and the cantata *The Golden Legend,* after Longfellow, 1886); anthems, numerous hymns (incl. "Onward, Christian Soldiers"), and other church music; piano pieces; songs.

Sumer is icumen in. A composition of the 13th century written in the form of a four-voice canon supported by a two-voice *rondellus* (called a *pes* in the original). This composition, called a *rota in the original, is the oldest surviving canon.

Summation(al) tone. See Combination tone.

Sun Quartets [G. *Sonnenquartette*]. Popular name for Haydn's six string quartets op. 20, nos. 1–6, composed in 1772. An early edition had an engraving of the rising sun as part of its frontispiece.

Suor Angelica. See under *Trittico*.

Superdominant. See under Scale degrees.

Superius. In music of the 15th and 16th centuries, the highest sounding voicepart.

Supertonic. See under Scale degrees.

Suppé, Franz von (Francesco Ezechiele Ermenegildo Cavaliere Suppe-Demelli) (b. Spalato, now Split, Dalmatia, of Belgian descent, 18 Apr. 1819; d. Vienna, 21 May 1895). Studied in Padua and with Sechter and Seyfried in Vienna. Conductor in Vienna at the Theater in der Josephstadt from 1840; at the Kaitheater, 1862–65; at the Carltheater, 1865–82. Composed about 30 comic operas and operettas (incl. the following, all first produced in Vienna: *Dichter und Bauer* [Poet and Peasant], 1846; *Die schöne Galatea* [Beautiful Galatea], 1865; *Leichte Cavallerie* [Light Cavalry], 1866; *Fatinitza*, 1876; *Boccaccio*, 1879); about 180 other works for the theater; orch. works; a *Missa dalmatica* and other choral works; string quartets and other chamber music; songs.

Sur [F.]. On, over. *Sur la touche,* bowing over the fingerboard; *sur le chevalet,* bowing near the bridge. See Bowing (k), (l).

Surinach, Carlos (b. Barcelona, 4 Mar. 1915). Studied in Barcelona, Düsseldorf, Cologne, and with Trapp in Berlin. Conductor of the Barcelona Philharmonic and at the Teatro del Liceo in Barcelona from 1945. Moved to Paris in 1947. Settled in New York in 1951. Has conducted widely in Europe and the U.S. Has composed an opera; much music for dance (incl. *Ritmo jondo,* choreography by Doris Humphrey, 1953; *Embattled Garden,* choreography by Martha Graham,

1958; *Feast of Ashes,* adapted from *Ritmo jondo* and *Doppio concertino,* 1962); 3 symphonies and other orch. works (incl. *Symphonic Variations,* 1963); a piano concerto, 1974; choral works; chamber music; piano pieces; songs. Orchestrated 7 pieces from Albéniz's *Iberia*.

Surprise Symphony. Haydn's Symphony no. 94 in G major (no. 2 of the *Salomon Symphonies), composed in 1791, so called because of a loud chord in the middle of the quiet first theme of the second movement.

Susato, Tielman (b. probably in Cologne, *c.* 1500; d. probably in Antwerp, between 1561 and 1564). Municipal musician in Antwerp, 1531–49. Established a printing firm there in 1543, publishing important collections of French chansons; sacred and secular Dutch polyphony; Masses, motets, and other sacred music; instrumental dances. Some, particularly the French, Dutch, and instrumental collections, contain his own compositions.

Suspension. (1) See under Counterpoint. (2) An 18th-century *agrément* in which the written note is slightly delayed by a short rest, e.g., a half note is played as a dotted quarter note preceded by an eighth rest.

Süssmayr, Franz Xaver (b. Schwanenstadt, Austria, 1766; d. Vienna, 17 Sept. 1803). Pupil of Salieri and of Mozart, of whom he was a close associate and whose Requiem he completed. Conductor at the National Theater in Vienna from 1792 and at the Court Opera there from 1794 until his death. Composed operas and *Singspiele* (incl. *Moses,* Vienna, 1792; *L'incanto superato,* Vienna, 1793; *Der Spiegel von Arkadien,* Vienna, 1794); *secco* recitatives for Mozart's *La *clemenza di Tito;* orch. works; church music; chamber music.

Sussurando [It.]. Whispering.

Sustaining pedal. The sostenuto pedal (middle pedal) of the *piano. The term is sometimes used for the damper pedal (right pedal).

Suter, Hermann (b. Kaiserstuhl, Switzerland, 28 Apr. 1870; d. Basel, 22 June 1926). Conductor, organist, and composer. Teacher in Zürich, 1892–1902. Director of the Basel Conservatory, 1918–21. Composed a symphony; a violin concerto; choral works (incl. the oratorio *Le laudi di San Francesco d'Assisi*, 1924); chamber music; piano pieces; songs.

Sutermeister, Heinrich (Paul) (b. Feuerthalen, Switzerland, 12 Aug. 1910). Pupil of Orff. Teacher at the Hochschule für Musik in Hanover from 1963. Has composed operas (incl. *Romeo und Julia*, Dresden, 1940; *Die Zauberinsel*, after Shakespeare's *The Tempest*, Dresden, 1942; *Raskolnikoff*, after Dostoievsky, Stockholm, 1948; *Madame Bovary*, Zürich, 1967); works for radio; a ballet; orch. works; 3 piano concertos and a cello concerto; choral works; chamber music; piano pieces; songs.

Švanda Dudák [Cz., Schwanda the Bagpiper]. Folk opera in two acts by Jaromir Weinberger (libretto by M. Karesch), produced in Prague, 1927. Setting: fairy tale.

Svelto [It.]. Quick, nimble.

Svendsen, Johan (Severin) (b. Christiania, now Oslo, 30 Sept. 1840; d. Copenhagen, 14 June 1911). Violinist and composer. Pupil of Ferdinand David, Reinecke, Hauptmann, and E. F. E. Richter. Conductor, with Grieg, of the Christiania Musical Association, 1872–77 and 1880–83. Court conductor in Copenhagen, 1883–1908. Composed 2 symphonies and other orch. works (incl. *4 Norwegian Rhapsodies*, 1877–78, and *Norwegian Artists' Carnival*, 1874); concertos for violin and for cello, and a *Romance* for violin and orch., 1881; choral works; chamber music; songs.

Sviridov, Georgy Vassilievich (b. Fatezh, near Kursk, Russia, 16 Dec. 1915). Pianist and composer. Pupil of Shostakovich in Leningrad. Settled in Moscow in 1955. Has composed musical comedies; orch. works; piano concertos; cantatas and other choral works (incl. an *Oratorio pathétique*, 1958); chamber music; piano pieces; numerous songs; music for films.

Sw. Abbr. for **swell organ*.

Swan Lake. Ballet by Tchaikovsky (choreography by M. Petipa and L. Ivanov),

completed in 1876 and produced in Moscow in 1877.

Swan of Tuonela. Symphonic poem by Sibelius, op. 22 (1893), based on a legend from the **Kalevala*.

Swan Song. See *Schwanengesang*.

Swanson, Howard (b. Atlanta, 18 Aug. 1909). Pupil of Elwell and N. Boulanger. Settled in New York in 1941. Has composed a *Short Symphony*, 1948, and other orch. works (incl. Symphony no. 3, 1970); chamber music; piano pieces; songs (incl. *4 Preludes* on texts of T. S. Eliot, 1947).

Sweelinck, Jan Pieterszoon (b. Deventer, the Netherlands, May, 1562; d. Amsterdam, 16 Oct. 1621). Succeeded his father as organist of the Oude Kerk in Amsterdam *c.* 1580, holding this position until his death. His pupils incl. Scheidt and Scheidemann. Composed pieces for organ and other keyboard instruments (incl. fantasies, ricercars, toccatas, variations, chorale settings, and dances); French chansons and Italian madrigals; motets and other sacred music.

Swell. In organs, a mechanism for obtaining a gradation of sound, crescendo and diminuendo. It consists of a large room (swell box) built around one or more divisions of the pipes and provided with shutters similar to Venetian blinds, whence the name *Venetian swell*. The chief enclosed division is called the *swell organ*, a name that also applies to the manual from which it is played. The swell box is opened and closed by a swell pedal.

Swift, Richard (b. Middlepoint, Ohio, 24 Sept. 1927). Studied at the Univ. of Chicago with L. Smith. Teacher at the Univ. of California at Davis from 1956. Has worked with serial techniques. Has composed the opera *The Trial of Tender O'Shea*, Davis, Calif., 1964; orch. works (incl. *A Coronal*, 1956; *Extravaganza*, 1962; a symphony, 1970); concertos for piano, 1961, and for violin, 1968; vocal works; 4 string quartets, a series of works titled *Stravaganza*, and other chamber music; piano pieces.

Swing. A style of jazz that became current in the 1930s and was played largely by "big bands" (e.g., four or five saxophones, three trumpets, three trombones, piano, double bass, guitar, and drums) for dancing. Among the principal novelties of the period was the shift from the two-beat rhythm of earlier styles to a rhythm in which all four pulses in duple meter received comparable emphasis. The bands in question were often led by well-known soloists such as clarinettist Benny Goodman and trombonists Glenn Miller and Tommy Dorsey.

Sydeman, William (Jay) (b. New York, 8 May 1928). Studied at the Mannes College with Travis, at Hartt College, and with Sessions and Petrassi. Teacher at the Mannes College, 1959–70. Has composed orch. works (incl. *Orchestral Abstractions,* 1958; *Oecumenicus,* 1966; several *Studies for Orchestra*); a concerto for piano four-hands with chamber orch. and tape, 1967; choral works; much chamber music (incl. several *concerti da camera*); songs and other vocal works; *Projections no. 1* for amplified violin, tape, slides, 1968.

Syllabic. The setting of a text (whether for one or more voices) is syllabic if each syllable is given only one note.

Sylphide, La. Ballet with music by Jean Schneitzhoeffer (choreography by Philippe Taglioni) first produced in Paris in 1832. A Danish production of 1836 employed music by Herman Løvenskjold (choreography by Auguste Bournonville).

Sylphides, Les. Ballet with choreography by Michel Fokine employing music by Chopin, first produced in Paris in 1909.

Sylvia. Ballet by Delibes (choreography by Louis Mérante), first produced in Paris in 1876.

Sympathetic string. A string that is not played on but serves to reinforce the sound of the bowed or plucked strings by vibrating along with them [see Resonance]. Numerous instruments have such strings, e.g., the *viola d'amore, viola bastarda [see Viol (3)], baryton [see Viol (5)], *hardingfele, and *tromba marina. They sometimes are added to the highest register of pianos, where they are called *aliquot strings.

Symphonia [Gr.]. (1) Ancient Greek term for the unison, as distinguished from *antiphonia,* the octave, and *paraphonia,* the fifth. (2) In the Middle Ages (possibly also in late Greek writings), *symphonia* means consonance as opposed to *diaphonia,* dissonance. Later the term was applied to various instruments such as the drum (Isidore of Seville, d. 636), *hurdy-gurdy, also called *cinfonie* (J. de Muris, c. 1290–c. 1351), bagpipe (hence the modern name *zampogna?), and a type of clavichord (16th cent.). (3) Beginning in the 17th century the name was used for various types of orchestral music that eventually led to the modern symphony. See *Sinfonia.*

Symphonia domestica. A programmatic symphony [see Program music] by R. Strauss, op. 53, completed in 1903 and first heard in New York the following year.

Symphonic band, concert band. A term used to distinguish the strictly musical functions of a wind band from, for example, school bands playing at athletic events. Such a distinction was prompted by the growing repertory of serious wind literature since the 1920s. The symphonic band consists of woodwind, brass, and percussion instruments, typically, 2 piccolos, 6 flutes, 2 E♭ clarinets, 4 oboes, 1 English horn, 24 B♭ clarinets, 2 alto clarinets, 2 bass clarinets, 4 bassoons, 2 alto saxophones, 1 tenor saxophone, 1 baritone saxophone, 6 cornets, 4 trumpets, 8 horns, 2 baritone horns, 4 trombones, 5 tubas, and 6 percussion. Cellos and double basses are sometimes used also.

The origin of the symphonic band is inseparable from that of the military band. About 1763 the instrumentation of the Prussian regimental bands was stabilized by Frederick the Great as 2 oboes, 2 clarinets, 2 horns, and 2 bassoons; literature by Haydn, Mozart, K. P. E. Bach, and Beethoven exists for this "standard" band of the late 18th century. The reorganization of the French bands by Sax in 1854 and the German bands by Wieprecht in 1845 led to great versatility, owing not only to the adoption of valved brass instruments but also to variation in instrumentation. By the latter half of the 19th century, however, bands in Europe and the United States played mostly marches, popular arias, and transcriptions rather than serious band literature.

The revival of the symphonic band owes much to the compositions of Gustav Holst (*First Suite for Band in E♭*, 1909; *Second Suite in F, c.* 1911; and *Hammersmith: Prelude and Scherzo*, 1930) and Ralph Vaughan Williams (*English Folk Song Suite*, 1924, and *Toccata Marziale*, 1924). Other composers of specifically band music include Hindemith, Prokofiev, Krenek, Stravinsky, Milhaud, and Schoenberg, as well as the 20th-century American composers Barber, Gould, Persichetti, and Schuman.

Symphonic Etudes. See *Études symphoniques.*

Symphonic poem. A type of 19th- and 20th-century orchestral music based on an extramusical idea, either poetic or realistic. The symphonic poem, also called a tone poem, belongs to the general category of *program music. Usually the term is reserved for compositions in one movement, in distinction to the program symphony (e.g., Berlioz's *Symphonie fantastique* and Liszt's *Dante Symphony* and *Faust-Symphonie*). The German equivalent, *Symphonische Dichtung*, was first used in 1854, in connection with a performance of Liszt's *Tasso* in Weimar.

The symphonic poem proper was inaugurated by Liszt in his one-movement compositions *Ce qu'on entend sur la montagne* (1848, after a poem of Victor Hugo), *Tasso* (1849–51, after Byron), *Les *préludes* (1848–54, after Lamartine), *Die *Hunnenschlacht* (1857, after a painting by Kaulbach, showing the slaughter of the Huns), etc. Liszt's innovation was taken up by a large number of composers to whom literary and pictorial ideas presented new sources of inspiration. Particularly favored were works descriptive of national life and landscape, first represented by Smetana's six symphonic poems *Má Vlast* (My Fatherland), composed 1874–79. These works had a host of successors, such as Borodin's *In the Steppes of Central Asia* (1880), Saint-Saëns' *Africa* (1891), Sibelius' *Finlandia* (1899), Respighi's *Fontane di Roma* (1917), F. Grofé's *Grand Canyon Suite* (1931), and E. Bloch's *America* (1926). The model of Liszt was followed by Tchaikovsky (*Romeo and Juliet*, 1869; *Francesca da Rimini*, 1876, after Dante), Saint-Saëns, Franck, and others. Especially important in the history of the genre is Richard Strauss, who preferred the term *tone poem*. His works, some of which attempt highly naturalistic depictions of their subjects, include *Aus Italien* (1886), *Don Juan* (1881–89), *Tod und Verklärung* (Death and Transfiguration, 1889), *Till Eulenspiegel* (1895), *Also sprach Zarathustra* (Thus Spake Zarathustra, 1896), *Don Quixote* (1897), *Ein *Heldenleben* (A Hero's Life, 1898), *Symphonia domestica* (1903), and *Alpensinfonie* (1911–15). Other contributors to the genre in the late 19th and early 20th centuries are Dukas (*L'*apprenti sorcier*, 1897), Sibelius (several works based on the*Kalevala), Debussy (*La *mer*, 1903–5), Stravinsky (*Feu d'artifice* [Fireworks], 1908), and Respighi (*Fontane di Roma*, 1917; *Pini di Roma*, 1924; *Feste romane*, 1929). The genre has been cultivated much less since the first few decades of the century.

Symphonic Variations. See *Variations symphoniques.*

Symphonie concertante [F.]. *Sinfonia concertante.*

Symphonie fantastique. Symphony by Berlioz, composed 1828–30 and revised in 1831; an important example of *program music [see also Symphonic poem]. The five sections of the symphony (subtitled *Episode de la vie d'un artiste*) are united by a recurring theme, called an *idée fixe.*

Symphonie pathétique. See under *Pathétique.*

Symphony. A composition for symphony *orchestra in the form of a *sonata. Like other manifestations of the sonata, it was the creation of the second half of the 18th century and reached its first great heights in the mature works of Haydn and Mozart. Although as orchestral music it numbers the baroque *concerto grosso among its antecedents, it derived principally from the Italian opera *sinfonia, which by the first half of the 18th century had largely been standardized in a three-movement form in the pattern fast–slow –fast. Associated with the adoption of this form for independent orchestral works was a shift away from the polyphonic texture of much baroque music toward the more homophonic style that characterized the *classical period. Similarly, the continuous rhythmic energy of the baroque concerto gave way to a more regular and balanced articulation of phrases. Although some of Haydn's early symphonies have only three movements, the practice of including a fourth movement (the *minuet) became common around the middle of the century in the works of the first generation of symphonists: G. B. Sammartini; the *Mannheim composers J. Stamitz and I. Holzbauer; the Viennese composers M. G. Monn and G. C. Wagenseil.

Although the symphonies of Beethoven build on the models of Haydn and Mozart, elements of some of his works in this genre point to features of many symphonies of the later 19th century: the increased length and complexity of the Third Symphony (*Eroica), the inclusion of programmatic elements in the Sixth Symphony (*Pastoral Symphony), and the inclusion of vocal soloists and chorus in the Ninth Symphony (*Choral Symphony). Composers whose symphonies represent a continuation of the tradition embodied in the nonprogrammatic works of Beethoven include Schubert, Mendelssohn, Schumann, and Brahms. Basic formal plans and the size of the required orchestras changed relatively little with these composers. Related to them, though bringing to bear some of the native musical traditions of their own countries, are Dvořák and Tchaikovsky. A tradition more closely related to Beethoven's Sixth and Ninth Symphonies begins in earnest with Berlioz's *Symphonie fantastique. Here programmatic elements assume prominence, orchestral resources are substantially expanded, and, later, the transformations of musical language wrought in Wagner's operatic works become central. The principal representative of this tradition at midcentury is Liszt, who, like other composers of similar persuasion, abandoned the symphony altogether in favor of the *symphonic poem. The symphonies of Bruckner derive important elements of tonal language and orchestration from

this tradition, though his formal procedures often hark back to Schubert. The last great representative of this tradition is Mahler.

In the 20th century, the symphony has been almost entirely neglected by composers of *serial music, but important examples have been composed by Ives, Copland, Harris, Piston, Sessions, W. Schuman, Vaughan Williams, Sibelius, Prokofiev, Shostakovich, Honegger, Hindemith, and Stravinsky.

Symphony of a Thousand. Popular name for Mahler's Symphony no. 8 in E♭ major, completed in 1907, so called because of the extremely large orchestral and choral forces required.

Symphony of Psalms. A work for chorus and orchestra (without violins or violas) by Stravinsky, completed in 1930. Its three movements are based on psalms (in Latin).

Syncopation. A momentary contradiction of the prevailing *meter. This may take the form of a temporary transformation of the fundamental character of the meter, e.g., from duple to triple or from 3/4 to 3/2 [see Hemiola (2)], or it may be simply the contradiction of the regular succession of strong and weak beats within a *measure or a group of measures whose metrical context nevertheless remains clearly defined by some part of the musical texture that does not itself participate in the syncopation. The former type may have the effect of "shifting the *bar line," e.g., of causing one of the weak beats to function as a strong beat. It is frequently encountered in the music of Beethoven, among many others. The latter type is particularly common in some styles of jazz. The accompanying example includes some common types of syncopation.

Synthesizer. An electronic instrument for the synthesis of sound, permitting independent control of the various parameters of sound: frequency, duration, intensity, envelope, and waveform [see Acoustics]. Synthesizers of varying complexity are now in use, some of which are manipulated with the aid of a keyboard like that of the piano and some of which can be used in live performances. In many cases, however, the sounds produced are first stored on magnetic tape. See also Electronic music.

Syrian chant. The liturgical chant of the Christian church of Syria, one of the first countries converted to Christianity, where the entire early development of Christian hymnody took place. Beginning with the Gnostic Psalter (hymnlike versions of the Psalms, embodying the Gnostic doctrine) of Bardesanes (d. 223) and his son, Harmonios (fl. 3rd cent.), it continued with the hymns, still used today, of St. Ephraim (306–73), which mark the beginning of Orthodox hymnody. Antiphonal *psalmody also was developed in the heretical Church of Syria. Both hymns and antiphonal psalmody were brought from Syria to Milan by St. Ambrose (340?–97). Since no early manuscripts of Syrian chant have been preserved, the present practice of Syrian chant is the only material available for study.

Syrinx. Greek name for *panpipes (perhaps also for a single flute).

System. Two or more staves connected by means of braces or bar lines for the purpose of allowing notation of music not readily accommodated on a single staff, e.g., that for ensembles or keyboard instruments.

Szabó, Ferenc (b. Budapest, 27 Dec. 1902; d. there, 4 Nov. 1969). Pupil of Leó Weiner and Kodály. Lived in the U.S.S.R. after 1932. Teacher at the Budapest Academy of Music, 1945–67, and its director, 1959–67. Composed an opera; the ballet *Ludas Matyi*, 1960; orch. works; the oratorio *Föltámadott a tenger* [The Sea is Rising], 1955, and other choral works; string quartets and other chamber music; piano pieces; songs and arrangements of folksongs; music for films.

Szalonek, Witold (b. Katowice, Poland, 2 Mar. 1927). Studied with N. Boulanger and at the State Academy of Music in Katowice, where he has taught since 1956. Has composed orch. works (incl. *Les sons*, 1965; *Mutazioni*, 1966); choral

works; chamber music; piano pieces; songs.

Szamotulczyk, Waclaw. See Waclaw of Szamotuly.

Szeligowski, Tadeusz (b. Lvov, 13 Sept. 1896; d. Poznań, 10 Jan. 1963). Studied in Cracow and with N. Boulanger in Paris. Teacher at the Vilna Conservatory, 1932–41, at the State Opera School in Poznań, 1947–50, and at the Music Academies in Poznań and Warsaw from 1950 until his death. Composed operas (incl. *Bunt Zakov* [The Students' Rebellion], Wroclaw, 1951); ballets; orch. works; concertos for violin, for piano, for clarinet; sacred choral works; string quartets and other chamber music; piano pieces; songs.

Szervánszky, Endre (b. Kistétény, Hungary, 27 Dec. 1911). Studied at the Budapest Academy of Music, where he has taught since 1948. Has worked with twelve-tone techniques. Has composed orch. works (incl. the ballet suite *Oriental Tale*, 1949; a concerto for orch., 1954; *6 Pieces*, 1959; *Variations*, 1965); concertos for clarinet and for flute; choral works; string quartets and other chamber music; piano pieces; songs.

Szokolay, Sándor (b. Kunágota, Hungary, 30 Mar. 1931). Pupil of Szabó and Farkas. Teacher at the Budapest Academy of Music from 1966. Has composed operas (incl. *Vérnász* [Blood Wedding], 1964; *Hamlet*, 1968); ballets; concertos for violin, for piano, for trumpet; oratorios and other choral works; chamber music; piano pieces.

Szymanowski, Karol (Maciej) (b. Timoshovka, Ukraine, 6 Oct. 1882; d. Lausanne, 29 Mar. 1937). Pianist and composer. Pupil of Noskowski. Lived in Berlin, 1906–8. Director of the Warsaw Conservatory, 1926–29, and rector, 1930 –31. Worked with Polish folk materials. Composed operas (incl. *Hagith*, Warsaw, 1922; *Król Roger*, Warsaw, 1926); ballets (incl. *Harnasie*, [The Highland Robbers], 1935); 4 symphonies and other orch. works; 2 violin concertos, 1917, 1933, and a *Symphonie concertante* for piano and orch., 1932; a *Stabat Mater*, 1926, and other choral works; string quartets and other chamber music; mazurkas and other piano pieces; songs.

T

T. Abbr. for *tonic, *tutti, toe* (in pedal parts of organ pieces), *trill* (in 17th-century music, usually a *mordent only). In 16th-century *partbooks, abbr. for *tenor.

Ta'amim. Notation symbols in Jewish chant. See Ecphonetic notation.

Tabarro, Il. See under *Trittico*.

Tabatière de musique [F.]. Music box; see under Mechanical instruments.

Tablature [G. *Tabulatur;* It. *intavolatura;* Sp. *tablatura*]. (1) The set of rules that regulated the musical activities of the *Meistersinger.

    (2) General name for the various early (15th–17th cent.) systems of notation (for keyboard instruments, lute, guitar, viol, flute, etc.), in which the tones are indicated by letters, figures, or other symbols instead of notes on a staff (as in the contemporary *mensural notation for vocal music). The most important are the keyboard (organ) tablatures (of which an early German type does, however, make use of a staff and notes as well as letters) and lute tablatures. Notations like the latter are still in use for guitar and ukulele. The accompanying example shows a representation of the system used in the 16th century for Italian lute music and Spanish *vihuela music together with two modern transcriptions, the first

reproducing only what is actually specified in the original, the second giving an implied polyphonic rendering. Each horizontal line of the tablature represents one *course on the instrument (here tuned G c f a d' g' beginning with the top line and reading down). The numbers indicate the frets on which the courses are to be stopped ("o" representing the open course), the notes at the top give the duration of individual attacks (each symbol applying to the attack immediately below and to all following attacks until a new symbol appears), and vertical lines mark off recurring units of time (sometimes, though not always, in ways comparable to the modern bar line). Thus, the distinguishing feature of such notations is that they instruct the player primarily in where to place the fingers on the instrument in question and only secondarily in which pitches to play.

Table. (1) The belly or upper plate of the soundbox of stringed instruments such as the violin and guitar. (2) [F.]. The *soundboard of the harp. See also under *Près*.

Tabor, taborel, tabour, tabourin, tabret. See Tambourin; also Pipe (1). For ill. see under Percussion instruments.

Tabulatur [G.]. *Tablature.

Tace [It.]; **tacet** [L.]. Be (is) silent. Term used in orchestral scores for parts not needed for a movement or a long section.

Tactus [L.]. The 15th- and 16th-century term for beat, both with its temporal meaning and as in "conductor's beat."

Tafelmusik [G.]. Table music, i.e., music to be performed at a banquet, e.g., Telemann's *Musique de table*.

Taille [F.]. Old name for a middle voice, particularly the tenor. The term was also used for instruments performing such a part, e.g., *taille de basson,* tenor oboe; *taille de violon* or simply *taille,* viola.

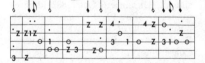

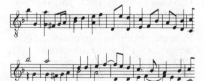

The indication *taille* in some of Bach's cantatas appears always to call for the tenor oboe, tuned, like the oboe da caccia and the modern English horn, a fifth below the oboe, but with a straight tube and an open bell. See Oboe family.

Tailleferre, (Marcelle) Germaine (b. Parc-Saint-Maur, near Paris, 19 Apr. 1892). Studied at the Paris Conservatory and with Ravel. Member of "Les *six*." Has composed operas (incl. *Il etait un petit navire*, Paris, 1951); ballets; incidental music for the theater; orch. works; a piano concerto and a concertino for harp and orch.; songs and other vocal works; chamber music; piano pieces; music for films, radio, and television.

Takahashi, Yuji (b. Tokyo, 21 Sept. 1938). Pianist and composer. Studied at the Toho School of Music, at Tanglewood, and with Xenakis. Teacher at the San Francisco Conservatory from 1970, returning to Tokyo thereafter. Has worked with stochastic processes and computers. Works incl. *Metatheses* for piano, 1968; *Orphika* for orch., 1969; *6 Stoicheia* for 4 violins, 1967; *Time*, on tape.

Takemitsu, Toru (b. Tokyo, 8 Oct. 1930). Largely self-taught. Has worked with traditional Japanese instruments, electronic techniques, and elements of serialism. Has composed orch. works (incl. *Requiem* for strings, 1957; *Music of Tree*, 1961); *November Steps* no. 1 for shakuhachi, biwa, and orch., 1967; *Asterism* for piano and orch., 1968; chamber music; piano pieces; vocal works; works on tape.

Takt [G.]. (1) *Beat* (*schwerer, leichter Takt*, i.e., strong, weak beat). (2) *Measure* (*nach 10 Takten*, after 10 measures). (3) *Meter*, time (3/4 *Takt*, 3/4 meter). *Im Takt*, in strict tempo and meter; *taktmässig*, in strict meter.

Tal, Josef (originally Gruenthal) (b. Pinne, near Poznań, Poland, 18 Sept. 1910). Pianist, conductor, and composer. Pupil of Tiessen and Trapp. Settled in Palestine in 1934. Teacher at the Jerusalem Academy of Music, 1948–53; at Hebrew Univ. from 1950. Has composed operas (incl. *Ashmedai*, Hamburg,

1973); electronic ballets; 2 symphonies and other orch. works; concertos for piano (5), for harpsichord, and for viola, some with tape; choral works; chamber music; piano pieces; songs.

Talea. See under Isorhythm.

Tales of Hoffmann, The. See *Contes d'Hoffmann, Les.*

Tallis, Thomas (b. c. 1505; d. Greenwich, 23 Nov. 1585). Organist at Canterbury Cathedral, 1540–42. Organist and Gentleman of the Chapel Royal from 1542; organist jointly with Byrd from 1572. Shared with Byrd a monopoly on printing music and music paper from 1575 until his death. Composed Masses, motets (incl. *Spem in alium* for 40 voices), Lamentations, and other Latin church music; anthems and other English church music; keyboard works; secular vocal works; *In nomine* settings.

Talma, Louise (b. Arcachon, France, 31 Oct. 1906). Studied at the Institute of Musical Art in New York and with N. Boulanger. Teacher at Hunter College from 1928. Has employed serial techniques beginning in the 1950s. Has composed the opera *The Alcestiad*, libretto by Thornton Wilder, Frankfurt, 1962; orch. works; *Dialogues* for piano and orch., 1965; *The Tolling Bell* for baritone and orch., 1969; choral works; chamber music; piano pieces; songs.

Talon [F.]. The *frog (nut) of the violin bow [see Bow].

Tambour [F.]. Drum; also, drummer. *Tambour militaire*, snare drum; *tambour de Basque*, tambourine (the modern percussion instrument).

Tambourin [F.]. (1) A small (occasionally tiny) two-headed medieval drum, cylindrical in shape, with both heads covered with skin. It was played together with the *galoubet*, a small flute [pipe and tabor; Sp. *flaviol* and *tamboril*; see Pipe (1)]. (2) In modern scores, usually the tambourine. (3) An old Provençal dance, originally accompanied by pipe and *tambourin* (or *tambour de Basque*, i.e., tambourine), in lively 2/4 meter. Rameau's operas contain many *tambourins*.

Tambourine. See Percussion instruments

II, 4. In early music, the term usually means the *tambourin.

Tambura (also *tanbura, tanpura*). Long-necked, unfretted, round-bodied drone lute of India. It has four metal strings that are plucked with one finger.

Tamburin [G.]; **tamburino** [It.]. Usually, the modern tambourine [see Percussion instruments II, 4]; rarely, the obsolete *tambourin.

Tamburo [It.]. Drum, kettledrum; *t. grande, grosso,* old name for bass drum; *t. rullante,* tenor drum; *t. militare,* snare drum [see under Percussion instruments].

Tampon [F.]. Two-headed drumstick used to produce a roll on the bass drum. It is held in the middle and moved by shaking the wrist.

Tamtam. See Percussion instruments II, 7. Not to be confused with *tom-tom.

Tanbur. See Tunbūr.

Tanbura. See Tambura.

Taneiev, Sergei Ivanovich (b. Vladimir district of Russia, 25 Nov. 1856; d. Diud-kovo, Zvenigorodsk district, 19 June 1915). Pianist and composer. Pupil of N. Rubinstein and Tchaikovsky. Teacher at the Moscow Conservatory, 1878–1906, and its director, 1885–89. His pupils incl. Glière, Rachmaninov, and Scriabin. Composed the operatic trilogy *Oresteia,* St. Petersburg, 1895; 4 symphonies and other orch. works; choral works; 6 string quartets and other chamber music; piano pieces; songs. Published a treatise on counterpoint, 1909, translated as *Convertible Counterpoint in the Strict Style,* 1962.

Tañer [Sp.]. See *Tastar.*

Tangent. See under Clavichord.

Tango [Sp.]. An urban modern dance of Argentina, performed by couples, which had adopted its characteristic features by the first decade of the 20th century in Buenos Aires. Before then it was a hybrid form, combining elements of the Andalusian tango, *habanera,* and *milonga.* It is based on syncopated patterns within a 2/4 meter.

Tannhäuser (complete title *Tannhäuser und der Sängerkrieg auf Wartburg*) [G., Tannhäuser and the Singers' Contest at Wartburg]. Opera in three acts by Wagner (to his own libretto, after a medieval legend), produced in Dresden, 1845, revised for Paris, 1861. Setting: Venusberg and in and around Wartburg, near Eisenach, early 13th century.

Tanpura. See Tambura.

Tansman, Alexandre (b. Łódź, Poland, 12 June 1897). Pianist, conductor, and composer. Studied in Warsaw. Settled in Paris in 1919. Lived in the U.S., 1941–46. Has composed operas; ballets; 8 symphonies and other orch. works; works for piano, for violin, for cello, for guitar, for oboe, and for flute with orch.; choral works; string quartets and other chamber music; piano pieces; music for the theater, radio, and films.

Tans'ur, William (originally Tanzer) (b. Dunchurch, Warwickshire, bapt. 6 Nov. 1706; d. St. Neot's, 7 Oct. 1783). Organist, lexicographer, and composer. Published numerous collections of psalm tunes, some containing his own compositions (incl. *The Royal Melody Compleat, or the New Harmony of Sion,* 1735 and numerous editions thereafter).

Tanto [It.]. So much. *Non tanto,* not so (too) much, e.g., *allegro non tanto.*

Tanz [G.]. Dance.

Tapiola. Symphonic poem by Sibelius, op. 112 (1926), named for Tapio, the forest god of Finnish legend (*Kalevala).

Tarantella. A Neapolitan dance in rapid 6/8 meter, named probably for Taranto in southern Italy, or, according to popular legend, for the tarantula spider whose poisonous bite the dance was believed to cure. In the mid-19th century it was frequently composed (Chopin, Liszt, Auber, Weber) in the style of a brilliant *perpetuum mobile.*

Tardo, tardamente [It.]. Slow, slowly. *Tardando,* slowing.

Tarogato. Hungarian instrument of ancient origin, originally a wooden *cornett having only natural tones. It was used for sounding military signals such as occur in the well-known Rákóczi march.

Later, the name was used for a wooden shawm (oboe mouthpiece) with five or more holes. The modern tarogato, built by W. J. Schunda, is a wooden saxophone, i.e., with a clarinet mouthpiece. It has a somewhat darker timbre than the normal saxophone. For ill. see under Clarinet family.

Tarp, Svend Erik (b. Thisted, Denmark, 6 Aug. 1908). Studied in Copenhagen, Munich, and Innsbruck. Teacher at the Copenhagen Conservatory, 1936–42; at the Opera School of the Royal Theater in Copenhagen, 1936–40; at Copenhagen Univ., 1939–47. Has composed operas (incl. *Prinsessen i det Fjerne,* Copenhagen, 1953); ballets; 3 symphonies and other orch. works; a *Te Deum* and other choral works; chamber music; piano pieces; music for films.

Tartini, Giuseppe (b. Pirano, Istria, 8 Apr. 1692; d. Padua, 26 Feb. 1770). Studied in Padua, Assisi, and Ancona. Solo violinist at San Antonio in Padua, 1721–23 and from 1726. Chamber musician to Count Kinsky at Prague, 1723–25. Founded a violin school in Padua, 1728. His pupils incl. Nardini. Composed about 150 violin concertos; about 100 violin sonatas (incl. *The *Devil's Trill* and *Didone abbandonata*); symphonies; sacred choral works; chamber music. Wrote several treatises on music dealing with topics such as harmony, acoustics [see Combination tone], violin playing, and ornamentation.

Tartini's tone. Same as differential tone [see Combination tone].

Taschengeige [G.]. *Kit.

Tasso. Symphonic poem by Liszt, based on a poem by Byron, composed 1849–51 and first performed as an overture to Goethe's drama, *Torquato Tasso.*

Tastar [It.]. To touch or play, as in *tastar de corde* (touching of the strings), a 16th-century term for a lute piece in the style of a free prelude. The Spanish equivalent is *tañer.*

Taste [G.]. Key (of piano, organ, etc.). *Untertaste,* white key; *Obertaste,* black key.

Tastiera [It.]. Keyboard. For the *tastiera*

per luce (*clavier à lumières*) in Scriabin's *Prometheus,* see Color organ.

Tasto [It.]. (1) The key of a keyboard. For *tasto solo* (*t.s.*), see Thoroughbass. (2) Fingerboard of the violin, etc. For *sul tasto,* see Bowing (1).

Tate, Phyllis (Margaret Duncan) (b. Gerrards Cross, Buckinghamshire, 6 Apr. 1911). Studied at the Royal Academy of Music in London. Has composed operas (incl. *The Lodger,* London, 1960); orch. works; concertos for saxophone and for cello; choral works; chamber music; songs and vocal chamber music.

Tattoo. The military signals sounded on bugles and drums for recalling soldiers to their quarters at night.

Taubert, (Karl Gottfried) Wilhelm (b. Berlin, 23 Mar. 1811; d. there, 7 Jan. 1891). Pianist, conductor, and composer. Conductor of the Berlin court orchestra from 1831 and court *Kapellmeister* in Berlin, 1845–69. Composed 6 operas; 6 symphonies and other orch. works; choral works; chamber music; piano pieces; numerous songs (incl. *Kinderlieder*).

Tauriello, Antonio (b. Buenos Aires, 20 Mar. 1931). Pianist, conductor, and composer. Pupil of Ginastera. Has worked as an opera coach in New York and Buenos Aires and has taught at the Juilliard School. Has composed an opera; orch. works; *Transparencias* for 6 instrumental groups, 1965; 2 piano concertos and works for violin and for clarinet with orch.; chamber music; piano pieces.

Tausig, Carl (b. Warsaw, 4 Nov. 1841; d. Leipzig, 17 July 1871). Virtuoso pianist and composer. Pupil of his father and of Liszt. Settled in Berlin in 1865, opening a piano school there. Composed original works for piano (incl. *2 études de concert; Ungarische Zigeunerweisen; Tägliche Studien,* a collection of exercises); transcriptions and arrangements for piano of works by others.

Taverner, John (b. probably Tattershall, Lincolnshire, *c.* 1490; d. Boston, Lincolnshire, 25 Oct. 1545). Organist and master of the choristers at Wolsey's Cardinal College (later Christ Church), Oxford, 1526–30, after which he settled in Boston, Lincolnshire. Composed Masses (incl. a *Western Wind Mass* and a *Missa Gloria tibi Trinitas* [see *In nomine*]), motets, and other Latin church music; a few secular vocal works.

Taylor, (Joseph) Deems (b. New York, 22 Dec. 1885; d. there, 3 July 1966). Music critic, radio commentator, and composer. Studied at New York Univ. President of the American Society of Composers, Authors, and Publishers, 1942–48. Composed operas (incl. *The King's Henchman*, libretto by Edna St. Vincent Millay, New York, 1926; *Peter Ibbetson*, New York, 1931); orch. works (incl. the suite *Through the Looking Glass*, 1919, rev. 1922; *Jurgen*, 1925); choral works (incl. the cantata *The Chambered Nautilus*, 1914); chamber music; piano pieces; songs. Published several books on music.

Taylor, Raynor (b. England, *c.* 1747; d. Philadelphia, 17 Aug. 1825). Chorister in the Chapel Royal. Church organist in Chelmsford from 1765. Music director at Sadler's Wells Theatre in London from 1765. Settled in the U.S. in 1792. Organist at St. Peter's in Philadelphia from 1793. Composed the ballad opera *Pizarro*, with Reinagle, 1800, and other stage works; instrumental works; piano pieces; songs.

Tchaikovsky, Piotr Ilich (b. Votkinsk, Viatka district of Russia, 7 May 1840; d. St. Petersburg, 6 Nov. 1893). Studied jurisprudence and became a clerk in the Ministry of Justice. Studied music with A. Rubinstein and others at what became the St. Petersburg Conservatory. Teacher at the Moscow Conservatory, 1866–78. Music critic for Moscow newspapers, 1868–74. For 13 years beginning in 1877 he was supported principally by commissions and then an annual allowance from the widow Nadezhda von Meck, with whom he had no direct personal contact. Traveled as a conductor, principally of his own works, in Russia and Europe and, in 1891, to the U.S. Composed operas (incl. *Eugen Onegin; The Maid of Orleans*, after Schiller, St. Petersburg, 1881; *Mazeppa*, after Pushkin, Moscow, 1884; *The *Queen of Spades*); ballets (incl. *Swan Lake; The *Sleeping Beauty; The *Nutcracker*); 6 symphonies (no. 4 in F min., 1877; no. 5

in E min., 1888; no. 6 in B min., *Pathétique*, 1893) and other orch. works (incl. *Romeo and Juliet;* the fantasy *The Tempest*, 1873; the fantasy *Francesca da Rimini*, after Dante, 1876; *Marche slave*, 1876; *Capriccio italien;* a serenade in C for strings, 1880; *Eighteen-Twelve Overture; *Manfred;* the fantasy-overture *Hamlet*, 1888; the symphonic ballad *The Voyevode*, 1891; 4 serenades, the fourth after Mozart, 1887); 3 piano concertos, 1875, 1880, 1893; a violin concerto, 1878; other works for solo instrument with orch. (incl. *Sérénade mélancolique* for violin and orch., 1875; *Variations on a Rococo Theme* for cello and orch., 1876; *Concert Fantasy* for piano and orch., 1884); choral works; 3 string quartets, a piano trio, a string sextet (*Souvenir de Florence*), and other chamber music; piano pieces; songs.

Tcherepnin, Alexander Nikolaievich (b. St. Petersburg, 21 Jan. 1899; d. Paris, 29 Sept. 1977). Son of the composer and conductor Nicolas Tcherepnin (1873–1945). Studied in St. Petersburg, Tiflis, and with Vidal in Paris. Settled in Paris in 1921. Concertized widely as a pianist in Europe, Russia, and the Orient. Teacher at De Paul Univ. in Chicago, 1949–64. Has worked with folk materials from Georgia (Russia) and the Orient. Has composed operas; ballets (incl. *Ajanta's Frescoes*, 1923); 4 symphonies and other orch. works; 6 piano concertos and other works for solo instruments with orch.; choral works; string quartets and other chamber music; piano pieces; songs. His sons Serge (b. 1941) and Ivan (b. 1943) are also composers.

Te Deum. A celebrated song of praise and rejoicing, "Te Deum laudamus" (We praise Thee, O God), also known as the hymn of thanksgiving. It was formerly attributed to St. Ambrose (hence the designation Ambrosian hymn). In the Roman Catholic liturgy it usually replaces the last responsory of Matins on feast days and Sundays and also may be sung as a hymn of thanksgiving on various occasions. The *Te Deum* has been set polyphonically by many composers, incl. Purcell, Handel, Berlioz, Bruckner, Dvořák, Britten, Kodály, and Vaughan Williams.

Tecla [Sp.]. Key or keyboard. *Música para tecla* (e.g., Cabezón's *Obras de música,* 1578) is music for keyboard instruments.

Tedesca [It.]. In the 17th century, the *allemande. About 1800, the *Ländler* and similar dances in rather quick triple meter (e.g., Beethoven, op. 79, op. 130).

Telemann, Georg Philipp (b. Magdeburg, 14 Mar. 1681; d. Hamburg, 25 June 1767). Studied law in Leipzig, where he founded a Collegium musicum. Held posts at Sorau, 1704–8; Eisenach from 1709; Frankfurt from 1712; and Hamburg, where he was town music director from 1721 until his death. Composed about 40 operas; intermezzi; 12 cycles of cantatas for the church year; 46 Passions; numerous other oratorios, cantatas, and occasional works; Masses and motets; hundreds of overtures, suites, concertos, and other orch. works; numerous sonatas, suites, and other works of chamber music; keyboard pieces.

Telephone, The. Opera in one act by Menotti, a companion piece to his *The *Medium,* produced in New York, 1947. Setting: Lucy's apartment, the present.

Tellefsen, Thomas (Dyke Ackland) (b. Trondheim, Norway, 26 Nov. 1823; d. Paris, 6 Oct. 1874). Pianist and composer. Pupil of Kalkbrenner and of Chopin, of whom he became a close associate. Employed Norwegian folk materials. Composed works for piano, incl. concertos, sonatas, nocturnes, mazurkas, waltzes; chamber music.

Telyn. The Welsh harp.

Tema [It., Sp.]. *Theme, subject.

Temperament [G. *Temperatur*]. Any system of tuning in which the intervals deviate from the acoustically "pure" intervals (i.e., those derived from the harmonic series; see Acoustics) of the *Pythagorean system and *just intonation. [See also Intervals, calculation of.] The deviations are necessary because these two systems, although perfect within a small range of tones (mainly those of the diatonic scale), become increasingly inadequate with the successive introduction of the chromatic tones. The acoustically perfect fifth, for instance, might well be used to obtain a succession of five or six fifths, c, g, d, a, e, b. However, if tones such as f♯, c♯, g♯, and d♯ are added in the same manner, the resulting tones cannot be satisfactorily used for melodies such as d e f♯ g, or d♯ f g g♯ (meaning e♭ f g a♭). Moreover, the twelfth tone of the succession of fifths, b♯, is noticeably higher than the tone c it would represent in our system of notation [see Circle of fifths]. Thus, it is necessary to devise methods that, instead of being perfect in the simple keys and intolerably wrong in the others, spread the inevitable inaccuracy over all the tones and keys. The most consistent realization of this principle is the equal temperament universally used today. Prior to its general acceptance, various other systems of tempered intervals, generally referred to as "unequal temperament," were in use, among which the mean-tone system was the only one to attain practical significance.

The *mean-tone system,* which was in use *c.* 1500, is based on a fifth that is smaller than the pure perfect fifth by one-fourth of the syntonic *comma (*c.* 22 *cents; i.e., the mean-tone fifth equals 697 instead of 702 cents), the result being that four such fifths in succession (c–g–d'–a'–e'') lead to the equivalent of a major third with the initial pitch (c–e''). In the simple keys with one or two sharps or flats, the mean-tone scale is satisfactory both melodically and harmonically. However, the continuation of the series of mean-tone fifths leads to a very noticeable discrepancy between enharmonically equivalent sharp and flat tones, indeed, a difference of almost a quarter tone (42 cents) between two such *enharmonic tones (e.g., g♯ = 772 cents above c, a♭ = 814); this difference is known as the "wolf." As a result, some 16th-century organs incorporated divided keys, the two parts of which were connected to separate pipes for pairs of pitches such as g♯ and a♭. The increased use of keys with three to six sharps and flats led in time to the system of equal temperament.

The principle of equal temperament is to divide the octave into twelve equal semitones. For a description of this system as compared with the just intonation and Pythagorean systems, see Intervals, calculation of. The system of equal temperament was first completely expounded during the 16th century, and at about the same time it began to be adopted into musical practice, at first because of the problems posed by fretted instruments such as the lute. Even the title of Bach's The *Well-Tempered Clavier (1722, 1744), however, may refer only to a close approximation of equal temperament, for the system was not universally adopted in Western Europe until the first part of the 19th century.

Temple block. A percussion instrument carved from hardwood into a round or oval shape and made hollow, with a slit spanning most of the lower half. Also called a *Chinese* or *Korean temple block* (and sometimes confused with the rectangular *Chinese block), it is usually played in a set of five of differing pitches (approximating the pentatonic scale) with soft-headed mallets or drum sticks.

Tempo [It.; pl. *tempi*]. (1) The speed of a composition or a section thereof as indicated by *tempo marks such as *largo, adagio, andante, moderato, allegro, presto, prestissimo,* or by the more accurate *metronome indications. *A tempo,* at the proper speed, e.g., following a momentary speeding up or slowing down. (2) In Italian, a *movement, e.g., of a sonata.

Tempo giusto. See *Giusto*.

Tempo marks. To indicate the *tempo of a piece, a number of Italian terms are widely used, the most important of which are, in order of slowest to quickest: *largo* (broad), *lento* (slow), *adagio* (slow; lit., at ease), *andante* (walking), *moderato* (moderate), *allegretto, allegro* (fast; lit., cheerful), *presto* (very fast), *prestissimo* (as fast as possible). In addition to these are terms calling for gradual change of speed, mainly *ritardando* (slackening) and *accelerando* (quickening); *rubato* indicates a deliberate unsteadiness of tempo. Although the Italian terms have traditionally been the most widely used, equivalent terms (many of which are found elsewhere in this book) in other languages are also used.

Prior to 1600, tempo marks were practically unknown. One of the first composers to use modern tempo marks was Adriano Banchieri (1568–1634).

Temporale. In the Roman Catholic rite, generic designation for the feasts of the Lord, as opposed to the Sanctorale, the feasts of Saints. See Gregorian chant; Proper.

Temps [F.]. *Beat; *temps fort (faible)*, strong (weak) beat.

Tempus [L.]. In 13th-century theory, the unit of musical time, comparable to the *tactus of the 16th century. Franco of Cologne describes it as "minimum in plenitudine vocis," i.e., the smallest time in which a "full sound" can be conveniently produced. In the 13th century this duration was represented by the *brevis,* whereas with the beginning of the *ars nova the semibrevis* was used instead. However, the term *tempus* continued to indicate the mensuration of the *brevis,* whether it was equal to three or to two semibreves (*tempus perfectum, imperfectum*). See Mensural notation.

Ten. Abbr. for *tenuto.

Tender Land, The. Folk drama in three acts by Copland (libretto by H. Everett), produced in New York, 1954. Setting: midwestern farm, early 1930s.

Tenebrae [L.]. In the Roman Catholic liturgy, the service of Matins and Lauds on Thursday, Friday, and Saturday of Holy Week. It is so called [lit., darkness] because of the gradual extinguishing of the candles, one after each psalm of Matins and Lauds on Thursday [*LU,* pp. 626 ff.]. At the first nocturn of Matins, the *Lamentations of Jeremiah are sung; at the beginning of Lauds, the *Miserere (Ps. 50).

Teneramente [It.]. Tenderly, gently.

Tenney, James C. (b. Silver City, N.Mex., 10 Aug. 1934). Pianist and composer. Pupil of Steuermann, Nowak, Brant, Gaburo, Hiller, Ruggles, Varèse, and Cage. Has also studied and taught engineering. Teacher at the California Institute of the Arts from 1970. Works incl. *13 Ways of Looking at a Blackbird* for tenor and 5 instruments, 1958; *Collage no. 1,* "Blue Suede Shoes," *musique concrète,* after Elvis Presley, 1961;

Erogdos 1, computer music for 2 tapes played together or separately, forward or backward, with or without certain other works; *Fabric for Ché,* computer music on tape, 1967.

Tenor. (1) In early polyphony (*c.* 1200–1500 and later), the part that carries the *cantus firmus* and is therefore the basis for the addition of other parts. It came to be called "tenor" (from L. *tenere,* to hold) in connection with the development of melismatic organum, in which the notes of the *cantus* were drawn out and sustained. (2) With the development of four-part writing (*c.* 1450), "tenor" came to mean the second-lowest part, since the *bassus* (originally *contratenor bassus*) was added below it. (3) The highest natural voice of men, of approximately the same range that the contrapuntal tenor requires [see Voices, range of]. (4) An instrument of about the same range as the vocal tenor, e.g., tenor trombone, tenor horn, tenor saxhorn, tenor violin. (5) In plainsong psalmody, the "held" (i.e., repeated) recitation tone; see Psalm tones. See also Clef.

Tenor horn. Same as tenor tuba; see under Tuba.

Tenor Mass. A polyphonic *Mass based on a cantus firmus that is used as a tenor. Most *cantus firmus* Masses of the 15th and 16th centuries are of this type.

Tenorhorn [G.]. Baritone; see Brass instruments II (c).

Tenoroon. See Oboe family II (c).

Tenso. A form of *troubadour and *trouvère poetry, in the nature of a dialogue or debate about politics or other controversial subjects. A similar form was the *jeu-parti (parture; Prov. partimen),* an actual dialogue, usually about love.

Tenth. See under Interval.

Tento [Port.]. *Tiento.*

Tenuto [It.]. Held, sustained to full value; usually equivalent to *legato. It is often indicated by a horizontal dash above or below a note or chord.

Ter Sanctus [L.]. Term used with reference to the "Sanctus, sanctus, sanctus" (Holy, holy, holy) of the *Trisagion, of the Sanctus of the *Mass, or of the *Te Deum.*

Terce. The fourth of the canonical hours. See Office.

Ternary form. See Binary and ternary form.

Terradellas, Domingo (Miguel Bernabé) (Domenico Terradeglias) (b. Barcelona, bapt. 13 Feb. 1713; d. Rome, 20 May 1751). Pupil of Durante. Traveled to England to produce his operas, 1746–47. *Maestro di cappella* at San Giacomo dei spagnuoli in Rome from 1747. Composed operas (incl. *Artaserse,* Venice, 1744; *Mitridate,* London, 1746; *Bellerofonte,* London, 1747); oratorios; church music; secular cantatas.

Tertian harmony. A harmonic system based on the third and thus the triad; hence, the common Western system of harmony as opposed to, e.g., *quartal harmony.

Terzett [G.]; **terzetto** [It.]. A vocal composition for three voices, usually with accompaniment. An instrumental piece in three parts is called a *trio.

Terzina [It.]. Triplet.

Terzo suono [It.]. Tartini's name for the *combination tones he discovered.

Tessarini, Carlo (b. Rimini, *c.* 1690; d. after 1766). Perhaps a pupil of Corelli. Violinist at San Marco in Venice from 1720; at the Urbino Cathedral, with interruptions, 1733–43 and 1750–57. Also active at various times in Rome, Brno, and Amsterdam. Composed concertos; trio sonatas and violin sonatas. Published *Grammatica di musica,* 1741.

Tessitura [It.]. In a vocal part, the particular range that is most consistently exploited, as opposed to the total range or compass of such a part. Thus, a soprano part may have a high or low tessitura.

Testo [It.]. Narrator (in oratorios, Passions, etc.).

Testudo [L., tortoise]. (1) The ancient Greek *lyra, which was frequently made of tortoise shell. (2) A 16th-century humanist name for the lute.

Tetrachord. (1) In ancient Greek music, a collection of four pitches bounded by the interval of a perfect fourth and containing one of the following three successions of intervals (proceeding downward): tone–tone–semitone (*diatonic); minor third–semitone–semitone (*chromatic); major third–quarter tone–quarter tone (*enharmonic). (2) Four pitches bounded by a perfect fourth and containing the succession of intervals (proceeding upward) tone–tone–semitone. The entire *diatonic scale can be generated from this structure. The term is sometimes applied specifically to scale degrees 5–8 of a diatonic scale (e.g., g a b c' in C major). See also Pentachord. (3) Any collection of four pitches.

Tetrardus [Gr.]. See under Church modes.

Texture. The character of a composition or passage as determined by the relationship among the elements of which it consists. Thus, the texture of a work in which emphasis is placed on the combination of several melodic lines is said to be *contrapuntal* or *polyphonic* [see Counterpoint; Polyphony]. A work consisting primarily of a succession of chords sounded as such is said to have a *chordal* or *homophonic* texture [see Chord; Homophony]. Other aspects of texture include *spacing, *tone color, and *rhythm.

Thalberg, Sigismond (Fortuné François) (b. Geneva, 8 Jan. 1812; d. Posilipo, near Naples, 27 Apr. 1871). Pupil of Hummel, Sechter, and Kalkbrenner. Concertized as a virtuoso pianist in Europe, Russia, Brazil, and the U.S. Composed 2 operas; a concerto and numerous other piano pieces, incl. sonatas, etudes, nocturnes, fantasies on operas.

Theater music. See Incidental music.

Theile, Johann (b. Naumburg, Saxony, 29 July 1646; d. there, buried 25 June 1724). Pupil of Schütz. Lived in Hamburg from 1675 and active at the opera there from 1678. *Kapellmeister* at Wolfenbüttel from 1685; at Merseburg from 1691. Composed operas (incl. the first opera to be produced at Hamburg, *Adam und Eva oder Der erschaffene, gefallene und auffgerichtete Mensch,* 1678, music

now lost); a German Passion according to St. Matthew, 1673; Masses, Magnificats, and other church music; cantatas; secular vocal music; instrumental dances.

Theme [F. *thème;* G. *Thema;* It., Sp. *tema*]. A musical idea that is the point of departure for a composition, especially a sonata (symphony, string quartet, etc., which, however, may employ several themes even within a single movement; see Sonata form), fugue, or set of variations. In sonatas and fugues it is also called the *subject.

Theorbo. See under Lute.

Theory, musical. The abstract principles embodied in music and the sounds of which it consists. In the 20th century, the study of musical theory has been concerned primarily with those aspects of music related to pitch, such as *harmony, *melody, *scales, *counterpoint, *harmonic analysis, *form, and *orchestration. These subjects are often taught in conjunction with fundamentals such as *notation and *ear training or *solfège. An important aspect of the study of musical theory is the *analysis of actual works. *Acoustics is sometimes also included in the field of musical theory. See also Musicology.

Theremin. See under Electronic instruments.

Theresienmesse [G., Theresa's Mass]. Popular name (unexplained) for Haydn's Mass in B♭, composed in 1799.

Thesis. See Arsis and thesis.

Third. See under Interval; Scale degrees.

Third-stream. A term coined by Gunther Schuller for music combining elements of jazz and Western art music.

Thirty-second note. See under Notes.

Thomas, Arthur Goring (b. Ratton Park, Sussex, 20 Nov. 1850; d. London, 20 Mar. 1892). Studied in Paris and with Sullivan, Prout, and Bruch. Composed operas (incl. *Esmeralda,* London, 1883; *Nadeshda,* London, 1885; *The Golden Web,* Liverpool, 1893); orch. works; choral works; chamber music; numerous songs.

Thomas, (Charles-Louis-) Ambroise (b. Metz, 5 Aug. 1811; d. Paris, 12 Feb. 1896). Pupil of Kalkbrenner and Lesueur. Teacher at the Paris Conservatory from 1856 and its director from 1871, succeeding Auber. Composed operas (incl. *La double échelle*, Paris, 1837; *Le caïd*, Paris, 1849; **Mignon; Hamlet*, Paris, 1868); ballets; Masses and other church music; chamber music; piano pieces; songs.

Thomas, (Georg Hugo) Kurt (b. Tönning, Schleswig-Holstein, 25 May 1904; d. Bad Oeynhausen, Westphalia, 31 Mar. 1973). Organist and composer. Studied at the Leipzig Conservatory, where he taught, 1925–34. Teacher at the Berlin Hochschule für Musik, 1934–39; in Frankfurt, 1939–45; at the Detmold Music Academy, 1947–55. Cantor at the Thomaskirche in Leipzig, 1956–61. Conductor and cantor in Frankfurt and Cologne from 1961. Composed Masses, oratorios, and other sacred and secular choral works; orch. works; chamber music; organ pieces.

Thompson, Randall (b. New York, 21 Apr. 1899). Conductor, pianist, and composer. Studied with Hill at Harvard and with Bloch. Teacher at Wellesley College, 1927–29 and 1936–37; at the Univ. of California at Berkeley, 1937–39; at the Curtis Institute, 1939–41; at the Univ. of Virginia, 1941–46; at Princeton Univ. 1946–48; at Harvard Univ., 1948–65. Has composed an opera and other music for the stage; 3 symphonies and other orch. works; numerous choral works (incl. *Americana*, 1932; *The Peaceable Kingdom*, 1936; *Alleluia*, 1940; *The Testament of Freedom*, 1943); chamber music; piano pieces; songs.

Thomson, Virgil (b. Kansas City, Mo., 25 Nov. 1896). Studied at Harvard and with Scalero and N. Boulanger. Lived in Paris, 1925–32, where he was an associate of Gertrude Stein and the followers of Satie. Music critic for the *New York Herald Tribune*, 1940–54, thereafter devoting himself to composing, writing, conducting, and lecturing. Has composed operas (incl. **Four Saints in Three Acts; The Mother of Us All*, libretto by Stein, New York, 1947; *Lord Byron*, 1970, prod. New York, 1972); ballets (incl. *Filling Station*, choreography by Lew Christensen, 1938; *The Harvest According*, choreography by Agnes de Mille, 1952); 3 symphonies (no. 3, 1976, a transcription of his String Quartet no. 2, 1932) and other orch. works; a cello concerto, 1950; choral works; 2 string quartets and other chamber music; piano pieces; organ pieces; songs; music for films (incl. *The Plough That Broke the Plains*, 1936; *The River*, 1937).

Thorne, Francis (b. Bay Shore, N.Y., 23 June 1922). Pupil of Hindemith, Donovan, Smit, and Diamond. Has worked as a jazz pianist. Teacher at the Juilliard School, 1971–73. President of the Thorne Music Fund from 1965. Executive director of the Walter W. Naumburg Foundation, 1969–72; of the Lenox Arts Center from 1972. Has worked with elements of jazz and serial techniques. Has composed 3 symphonies, a symphony in one movement, and other orch. works; a piano concerto, 1966, and other works for solo instruments and orch. (incl. *Liebesrock* for 3 electric guitars and orch., 1969); *6 Set Pieces* for 13 players, 1967, and other chamber music; vocal works; piano pieces.

Thoroughbass, figured bass [F. *basse chiffrée, continue, figurée*; G. *Generalbass, bezifferter Bass*; It. *basso continuo*; Sp. *bajo cifrado*]. Note: "thorough" (old spelling for "through") means the same as *continuo*, i.e., continuing throughout the piece.

A method of indicating an accompanying part by providing the bass notes only, together with figures designating the chief intervals and chords to be played above them. This stenographic system was universally used in the baroque period (1600–1750). The chief principles of the fully developed system (*c.* 1700) are the following [see also Ex., in which the upper staff is a realization of the figured bass of the lower staff]:

1. A figure given with a bass note calls for the corresponding interval or its octave equivalents above this note in the key indicated by the signature. In A♭ major, for example, a 6 written under (or above) a G indicates E♭, and the figures ⁶₅ indicate D♭ and E♭. Pitch classes so indicated may be played in any octave and are intended only to indicate the harmonies on which the keyboard player is to improvise a *realization* of the bass.

2. The intervals of the third, fifth, and octave often are not indicated by figures (3, 5, 8), it being understood that these were to be added where suitable. Thus, ⁶₈ implies also the inclusion of the third above the bass, as in Ex. 1.

3. Chromatic alterations are indicated by a sharp or flat placed in front of (occasionally after) the figure. A sharp or flat without a figure calls, respectively, for the major or minor third. The natural sign is used in a similar way. Sharping is frequently indicated by a diagonal stroke through the figure or by an apostrophe.

4. A horizontal dash following a figure or a vertical group of figures indicates that the pitches of the right hand are to be held, even if the bass proceeds to other pitches.

5. A small diagonal dash indicates repetition of the same figures above a changed bass note, i.e., sequential transposition of the chord.

6. The figure *O* indicates *tasto solo*, i.e., no accompaniment other than the bass note.

7. Frequently, two or more successive figures do not indicate chords proper but only voice-leading, appoggiaturas, or passing tones, e.g., 4 3, or 9 8, or 5 4 3.

The proper realization of a thorough-bass part requires at least two instruments: a keyboard instrument (most often a harpsichord) to realize the harmonies, and a melody instrument such as the cello or viola da gamba to reinforce the bass line. In the early baroque era, large and diverse groups of instruments, including lutes and other fretted instruments, were sometimes used for the purpose.

Three-Cornered Hat, The. See *Sombrero de tres picos, El.*

Threepenny Opera. See *Dreigroschenoper, Die.*

Through-composed. This term, which is widely accepted as a translation of G. *durchkomponiert,* is applied to songs in which new music is provided for each stanza. Its opposite is *strophic,* a song in which all stanzas are sung to the same melody. *Through-composed* may also refer to any composition that does not include internal repetitions.

Thuille, Ludwig (Wilhelm Andreas Maria) (b. Bozen, Tirol, 30 Nov. 1861; d. Munich, 5 Feb. 1907). Pupil of Rheinberger. Teacher at the Munich Academy of Music from 1883 until his death. Composed operas (incl. *Lobetanz,* Karlsruhe, 1898); a symphony and other orch. works; choral works; a sextet for piano and winds, 1887, and other chamber music; piano pieces; songs. Published a text on harmony, *Harmonielehre,* 1907.

Thunder machine [G. *Donnermaschine*]. A device introduced by R. Strauss in his **Alpensinfonie,* op. 64 (1911–15), to imitate thunder. It consists of a big rotating drum with hard balls inside that strike against the drumhead.

Thus Spake Zarathustra. See *Also sprach Zarathustra.*

Tibia [L.]. The Greek **aulos;* see Oboe family III.

Tie, bind. A curved line, identical in appearance to the **slur,* that connects two successive notes of the same pitch and has the function of uniting them into a single sound equal to their combined durations. The tie is used (1) to connect two notes separated by a **bar line;* (2) to produce values that cannot be indicated by a single note, e.g., the value of seven eighth notes.

Tiento [Sp.]; **tento** [Port.]. A 16th- and

17th-century Iberian counterpart of the Italian *ricercar (not, as has been stated, of the *toccata). It originated in vihuela music (Milán) as a free "study" in idiomatic style for the instrument and was later used for organ music (A. Cabezón), where it became a study in imitative counterpoint. However, the erudite formal treatment often found in the ricercar is rarely present in the *tientos*, which are also usually much shorter than the contemporary ricercars.

Tierce [F.]. (1) Third. *Tierce de Picardie*, see Picardy third. (2) An organ stop of the mutation type that sounds a note two octaves and a major third above the key played. See Organ. (3) *Tierce coulé*. See Appoggiatura, double.

Tiessen, (Richard Gustav) Heinz (b. Königsberg, East Prussia, now Kaliningrad, U.S.S.R., 10 Apr. 1887; d. Berlin, 29 Nov. 1971). Conductor, critic, and composer. Studied in Berlin and taught at the Hochschule für Musik there, 1925–55, except for 1946–49, when he directed the Municipal Conservatory. Assocate of R. Strauss. Composed the ballet *Salambo*, 1929; incidental music for plays; 2 symphonies and other orch. works; works for piano and for violin with orch.; choral works; chamber music; piano pieces; songs.

Till, Johann Christian (b. Gnadenthal, near Nazareth, Pa., 18 May 1762; d. Bethlehem, Pa., 19 Nov. 1844). Teacher, organist, piano maker, and composer. Organist of the Moravian congregation at Bethlehem, 1813–44. Composed anthems and liturgies.

Till Eulenspiegels lustige Streiche [G., Till Eulenspiegel's Merry Pranks]. Symphonic poem by R. Strauss, op. 28 (1895), based on the 16th-century German folk tale of Till Eulenspiegel.

Timbale [F.]; **timpano** or **timballo** [It.]. Kettledrum [see Percussion instruments I, 1].

Timbales [Sp.]. A pair of relatively shallow, single-headed drums, tuned to different pitches, mounted on a stand, and played with wooden sticks. They are commonly used in the popular music of Latin America.

Timbre [F.]. (1) Medieval name for *tambourin. (2) In both French and English, *tone color. (3) In French a standard melody, especially for popular tunes underlaid with new texts (as in the *opéra comique* [see Comic opera] and *vaudeville).

Time. Term used variously to indicate *meter, *tempo, *tempus, or the duration of a given note.

Time signature. The time or *meter of a work is indicated at the beginning by two numbers, one above the other; the lower indicates the chosen unit of measurement (half note, quarter note, etc.), while the upper indicates the number of such units making up a *measure. Early time signatures and their proportional modifications are explained under Mensural notation and Proportions. Two of these survive, the sign C for 4/4, and the sign ₵ for 2/2 (*alla breve).

Timpani [It.]. Kettledrums. *Timpani coperti, t. sordi,* muffled kettledrums. See under Percussion instruments.

Tinctoris, Johannes (b. probably Nivelles, near Brussels, 1436; d. there, before 12 Oct. 1511). Active at the cathedrals of Cambrai and Chartres and, *c.* 1475–87, at the court in Naples. Composed Masses, motets, and Lamentations; French chansons; an Italian secular vocal work. Wrote 12 theoretical treatises, incl. the first printed dictionary of musical terms and works on solmization, mensural notation, proportions, and counterpoint.

Tinel, (Pierre-Joseph-) Edgar (b. Sinay, Belgium, 27 Mar. 1854; d. Brussels, 28 Oct. 1912). Studied at the Brussels Conservatory, at which he taught from 1896 and was director from 1909. *Maître de chapelle* to the king from 1910. Composed 2 operas; an oratorio and other sacred choral works; orch. works; chamber music; piano pieces; organ pieces; sacred and secular songs.

Tiple [Sp.]. Soprano, upper voice. Also, a small guitar.

Tippett, Michael (Kemp) (b. London, 2 Jan. 1905). Conductor and composer. Pupil of C. Wood and R. O. Morris. Music director of Morley College, London, 1940–51. Has composed 4 operas (*The Midsummer Marriage,* London, 1955; *King Priam,* London, 1962; *The Knot Garden,* London, 1970; *Ice Break,* London, 1977); 4 symphonies and other orch. works; a piano concerto, 1955, and a *Fantasia on a Theme of Handel* for piano and orch., 1942; the oratorio *A Child of Our Time,* 1944, the cantata *The Vision of St. Augustine,* 1965, and other choral works; string quartets and other chamber music; piano pieces; organ pieces; songs.

Tirade [F.]; **tirata** [It.]. Baroque ornament consisting of a scale passage of more than three notes that serves as a transition between two principal melody notes.

Tirare [It.]. To draw. *Tira tutti* (draw all), full organ. *Tirarsi* (to be drawn), sliding mechanism of the *trombone. *Tirando,* slowing of tempo.

Tirasse [F.]. Originally, the pedals of a small organ that had no separate pipes but were mechanically connected (coupled) to the manual keys. Hence, a pedal coupler of the organ, e.g., *Tirasse du Positif* (*Tir. P.*), coupler "choir to the pedal."

Tirer, tirez, tiré [F.]. To draw, draw, drawn. Indication for downstroke of the bow [see Bowing], the drawing of organ stops, or slowing of tempo.

Tishchenko, Boris Ivanovich (b. Leningrad, 23 Mar. 1939). Pupil of Salmanov and Shostakovich. Teacher at the Leningrad Conservatory. Has composed ballets (incl. *The Twelve,* 1964; *Yaroslavna,* 1974); 3 symphonies; concertos for violin, for cello, for piano; the cantata *Lenin Lives,* 1959; chamber music; piano pieces; songs; music for films and for the theater.

Titelouze, Jean (b. Saint-Omer, France, 1563 or 1564; d. Rouen, 24 Oct. 1633). Organist at Saint-Jean in Rouen from 1585; at the Rouen Cathedral from 1588 until his death. Composed organ works, incl. settings of hymns and the Magnificat; Masses.

Toccata. (1) A keyboard (organ, harpsichord) composition in free, idiomatic keyboard style, employing full chords and running passages, with or without sections in imitative style (fugues). The earliest toccatas, by A. Gabrieli (*c.* 1515 –86) consist of full chords and interlacing scale passages only. With Claudio Merulo (1533–1604) the toccata became organized into alternating toccata (free, idiomatic keyboard style) and fugal sections, usually arranged T F T F T. The toccatas of Frescobaldi (1583–1643) are written in a series of short sections exhibiting a variety of moods in rapid succession. A special type is the short liturgical toccata (e.g., "Toccata per l'elevazione," to be played at the *Elevation of the Host). With Bernardo Pasquini (1637–1710) the Italian toccata became the arena for keyboard virtuosity and soon developed into a *perpetuum mobile* type very similar to the etudes of the early 19th century (Clementi).

The development of the toccata in Germany was twofold. The South German composers (Froberger, Kerll, Muffat) followed the Italian model of Frescobaldi. More important is the North German development, which led to an entirely novel, rhapsodic toccata that appeared first in the works of Matthias Weckmann (1621–74) and was developed by Dietrich Buxtehude (*c.* 1637–1707) and J. S. Bach (1685–1750). Most of these toccatas, particularly those of Bach, retain Merulo's five-section scheme alternating between free and contrapuntal style. The toccata style is frequently used for preludes of fugues, e.g., Bach's organ fugue in A minor. Both the North German and Italian toccatas survive in a few isolated romantic and modern works for piano.

(2) About 1600, the name *toccata* was also used for a festive brass fanfare, e.g., in the introduction of Monteverdi's *Orfeo* (1607) [see *Touche* (4); Tucket; Tusch].

Toch, Ernst (b. Vienna, 7 Dec. 1887; d. Los Angeles, 1 Oct. 1964). Studied medicine and philosophy. Largely self-taught in composition. Taught in Mannheim and Berlin. Settled in the U.S. in 1934, subsequently teaching at various institutions, incl. the Univ. of California at Los Angeles, 1940–48. Composed operas; 7 symphonies (no. 3, 1955, awarded the Pulitzer Prize) and other orch. works;

concertos for cello and for piano; choral works (incl. *Geographical Fugue* for speaking chorus, 1930); 13 string quartets and other chamber music; piano pieces; songs; music for films.

Tod und das Mädchen, Der [G., Death and the Maiden]. Schubert's String Quartet no. 14 in D minor, D. 810 (1826), whose second movement consists of variations on his song of the same name (1817).

Tod und Verklärung [G., Death and Transfiguration]. Symphonic poem by R. Strauss, op. 24, completed in 1889. The music, in four sections, depicts the fevered fantasies of a patient at the crisis of a fatal illness.

Toëschi, Carlo Giuseppe (Carl Joseph; properly Toesca della Castella-Monte) (bapt. Ludwigsburg, 11 Nov. 1731; d. Munich, 12 Apr. 1788). Pupil of J. Stamitz. Violinist in the Mannheim Court Orchestra from 1752 and its concertmaster from 1759. Music director to the court from 1780, following its removal to Munich in 1778. Composed ballets, some in collaboration with Cannabich and others; over 60 symphonies; concertos; chamber music.

Tom-tom. A drum slightly smaller than the tenor drum [see Percussion instruments] with a depth approximately equal to its diameter. It may have one or two heads, has no snares, and its pitch can be altered. It is used in dance bands and jazz groups, usually in pairs. Its sound imitates that of American Indian drums.

Tomášek, Jan Václav (Johann Wenzel) (b. Skuc, Bohemia, 17 Apr. 1774; d. Prague, 3 Apr. 1850). Pianist, organist, and composer. Much sought after as a teacher in Prague. Composed 4 operas and other stage works; symphonies and other orch. works; a piano concerto; Masses, cantatas, and other choral works; piano pieces, incl. sonatas, eclogues, rhapsodies, and 6 *Allegri capricciosi di bravura;* songs, incl. settings of Goethe.

Tomasi, Henri (Frédien) (b. Marseille, 17 Aug. 1901; d. Paris, 13 Jan. 1971). Pupil of Vidal, d'Indy, and Gaubert. Conductor of the Monte Carlo Opera, 1946–50, and of radio broadcasts and concerts

throughout Europe. Composed operas; ballets; symphonic poems and other orch. works, several on Oriental and other exotic subjects; concertos for flute, trumpet, viola, saxophone, horn, cello, clarinet, trombone, oboe, violin, guitar, harp, double bass; choral works; chamber music; piano pieces; songs.

Tomasini, (Aloisio) Luigi (b. Pesaro, 22 June 1741; d. Eisenstadt, 25 Apr. 1808). Violinist at the Esterházy residence in Eisenstadt from 1757 and concertmaster in Haydn's orchestra there from 1762. Composed violin concertos; string quartets, divertimentos for baryton, violin, and cello, and other instrumental music.

Tombeau [F., tombstone]. See under Lament (2).

Tomkins, Thomas (b. St. David's, England, 1572; d. Martin Hussingtree, near Worcester, buried 9 June 1656). Pupil of Byrd. Organist at Worcester Cathedral, *c*. 1596–1646. An organist of the Chapel Royal from 1621. Composed madrigals and ballettos; services, anthems, and other sacred music; music for virginals and for viols.

Tommasini, Vincenzo (b. Rome, 17 Sept. 1878; d. there, 23 Dec. 1950). Studied in Rome and with Bruch in Berlin. Composed 2 operas; 3 ballets (incl. *Le donne di buon umore* [The Good-humored Ladies], commissioned by Diaghilev and arranged from sonatas of D. Scarlatti, 1917); orch. works; concertos for violin, for string quartet, for piano; choral works; string quartets and other chamber music; piano pieces; songs; music for films. Published 2 books on musical aesthetics.

Ton [F.]. (1) Pitch; *donner le ton,* to give the pitch. (2) *Pitch pipe. (3) Key or mode; *ton d'ut,* key of C; *ton majeur,* major key; *ton d'église,* church mode. (4) Whole tone, as distinct from *demiton,* semitone. (5) Crook [see under Wind instruments]; *ton du cor, ton de rechange,* crook of the horn. (6) [G.] *Tone, chiefly in the meanings (1) and (3).

Tonabstand [G.]. *Interval.

Tonadilla [Sp.]. A short, Spanish, popular comic opera, with one to four characters, consisting of solo song and, occasionally, choruses. Its origins were short scenic interludes performed between the acts of a play or serious opera, but (like the Italian *opera buffa*) it later became an independent piece. It flourished from about the middle of the 18th to the early 19th century. One of the first *tonadillas* is a comic musical dialogue between a woman innkeeper and an itinerant Bohemian, written in 1757 by Luis Misón (d. 1766). Besides Misón, the chief composers of *tonadillas* were Pablo Esteve (b. *c*. 1730) and Blas de Laserna (1751–1816).

Tonal. The adjective applied to music that embodies the principles of tonic-dominant *tonality, as distinct from *modality and other systems of organizing pitch. See also Atonality.

Tonal and real. In a fugue, an answer is *real* if it is either an exact or a diatonic transposition of the subject; it is *tonal* if certain steps are modified. A subject is often so modified if it contains the interval of the fifth (d–a), this being answered not by the transposed fifth (a–e′) but by the fourth (a–d′), as illustrated in the accompanying example from Bach's *The Art of Fugue*.

Tonality. A system of organizing pitch in which a single pitch (or tone, called the *tonic* [see Scale degrees]) is made central. The term is most often applied to the particular system of tonality that prevailed in Western art music from the late 17th century until the early 20th century, sometimes called *major-minor* or *tonic-dominant tonality*. This system continues to be the basis of most Western popular music. A composition organized in this way is said to be in the *key of whatever pitch serves as the tonic, the key being either *major or minor depending on the arrangement of tones and semitones in the *scale constructed on the tonic, the scale which provides the principal pitches employed in the composition as a whole. (The term *tonality* is sometimes also used synonymously with *key* in this sense.) The tonic, or tonal center, serves as a point of repose toward which the structural tension

created by the manipulation of other pitches is resolved by means of *cadences at or near the conclusion of a composition and elsewhere. It is in its potential for the creation and release of tonal tension and for the full exploitation of the resources of the equally tempered scale that the power of tonic-dominant tonality lies. The principles of organizing pitch in this way are normally studied under the headings of tonal *harmony and *counterpoint. See also Atonality; Modality; Modulation; Tonicization.

Tonart [G.]. *Key (2).

Tonary [L. *tonarium, tonarius, tonale*]. A medieval book in which chants are listed (with their beginnings) according to mode, and often with subdivisions within each mode. Tonaries contain the chants that are (or were) connected with a psalm verse sung to one of the various recitation tones [see Tone (4); Psalm tones; Psalmody], e.g., antiphons, responsories, Introits, Communions. The purpose of the tonaries was to show the mode of a chant, a matter of great practical importance, since the selection of the proper tone depended on the mode of the antiphon, Introit, etc.

Tondichtung [G.]. Tone poem; also, any composition of a poetic character. See Symphonic poem.

Tone [F. *ton;* G. *Ton;* It., Sp. *tono*]. (1) A sound of definite pitch. (2) The *interval of a major second, i.e., a whole tone, as distinct from a semitone (minor second). This is the usual British meaning of the term, the word *note* being used for (1). (3) The quality or character of a sound. (4) In Gregorian chant, tone [L. *tonus*] is the generic name for all recitation formulas for lessons, prayers, and the like, as well as for the *psalm tones.

Tone cluster. A strongly dissonant group of tones lying close together and produced, usually on the piano, by depressing a segment of the keyboard with the fist, forearm, or a board of specified length. The term was invented by Henry Cowell.

Tone color [F. *timbre;* G. *Klangfarbe*]. The quality ("color") of a pitch as produced on a specific instrument, as distinct from the different quality of the same pitch if played on some other instrument. See Acoustics.

Tone poem. *Symphonic poem.

Tone row. See under Serial music.

Tonguing. In playing wind instruments, the use of the tongue for articulation. It consists of momentary interruptions of the windstream by an action of the tongue as if pronouncing the letter *t* or *k*. Three types of tonguing are distinguished: single tonguing (*t–t* . . .), double tonguing (*t–k t–k* . . .), and triple tonguing (*t–t–k t–t–k* . . .). The first is employed in slower passages, the last two in rapid passages for groups of two or three notes. *Flutter tonguing* (G. *Flatterzunge;* It. *frullato*) results when the tongue makes a rolling movement, as if producing *d–r–r–r*.

Tonic. The first, and main, note of a key; hence, the keynote. See Scale degrees; Tonality.

Tonic accent. An *accent caused by a pitch higher than its surroundings, rather than by an increase in loudness or by a larger note value. The last two kinds of accent are called *dynamic* and *agogic* respectively.

Tonic sol-fa. An English method of *solmization designed primarily to facilitate sight singing. It was developed from earlier methods (Lancashire system) by Sarah A. Glover and perfected *c.* 1840 by John Curwen. It is widely used for teaching in England and has also become known in some other countries, e.g., in Germany (as *Tonika-do*).

Tonic sol-fa is a system of "movable do," i.e., the tone syllables *do, re, mi, fa, sol, la, ti* are used with reference to the first through seventh *scale degrees, respectively, of the prevailing major key at any point in a composition. The initial consonants, d r m f s l t, are also used for notation. Octave repetitions are indicated for the higher octave thus: d̄ r̄ m̄ or d' r' m'; for the lower octave thus: d̲ r̲ m̲ or d, r, m,. For the minor scale the third degree becomes *do*, owing to the changed intervals of this scale: l t d r m f s l. Sharped tones are usually indicated by changing the vowel to e (*de, re, fe, se, le*), flatted tones by changing it to a (*ra, ma, la, ta*). For the sixth degree of the

ascending melodic minor scale a separate syllable *ba* is introduced, since the use of *fe* would suggest a half-step to the next note, whereas actually a whole-step follows (to *se*). Therefore the melodic minor scale is designated (up and down): l t d r m ba se l; l s f m r d t l. The tones and their relation to each other are shown in a chart called the *Modulator*.

If the piece modulates into another key, the new key is indicated (in various ways), and the tone syllables are now reckoned in the new key. For the indication of meter and rhythm, additional signs (horizontal strokes, single dots, colons, commas, etc.) are used.

Tonicization. The momentary treatment of a pitch other than the *tonic as if it were tonic, without, however, effecting a complete *modulation to the key of the pitch in question. This is most often done by the introduction of the semitone below the pitch (to suggest its leading-tone) or the introduction of the perfect fourth above.

Tonkunst [G.]. Music. *Tonkünstler*, composer.

Tonleiter [G.]. *Scale.

Tono [It.]. *Tone; whole tone; key (2); mode. *Primo (secondo*, etc.) *tono*, first (second, etc.) *church mode.

Tonsatz, Tonstück [G.]. Composition. *Tonsetzer*, composer.

Tonus [L.]. (1) Whole tone. (2) Generic name for the plainsong recitation formulas, such as *tonus lectionum, toni psalmorum, tonus peregrinus, toni v. Gloria Patri ad introitum* [see Tone (4)]. (3) *Church mode, e.g., *primus tonus, tonus authenticus, tonus plagalis.*

Torculus. See table accompanying Neumes.

Tordion. See under *Basse danse.*

Torelli, Giuseppe (Gioseffo) (b. Verona, 22 Apr. 1658; d. Bologna, 8 Feb. 1709). Violinist at San Petronio in Bologna, 1686–96, and from 1701. *Kapellmeister* to the Margrave of Brandenburg at Ansbach, 1697–99. Active in Vienna in 1699. Composed *concerti grossi*, of which he established the standard form (incl. the so-called *Christmas-Eve Concerto*, op.

8, no. 6), orchestral concertos, concertos for trumpet and other instruments, and solo violin concertos, of which he was an early exponent if not the originator; sinfonias; oratorios; trio sonatas.

Tornada. See under *Envoi*.

Tosar Errecart, Hector Alberto (b. Montevideo, Uruguay, 18 July 1923). Pianist, conductor, and composer. Studied in Montevideo and with Copland, Honegger, Milhaud, and Rivier. Teacher in Montevideo, 1951–60 and from 1966. Dean of the conservatory in San Juan, Puerto Rico, 1961–65. Has composed 3 symphonies and other orch. works (incl. a *Toccata*, 1940); a *Te Deum*, 1959, and other choral works; chamber music (incl. *Stray Birds* for baritone and 11 instruments, 1963); piano pieces; songs.

Tosca. Opera in three acts by Puccini (libretto by G. Giacosa and L. Illica, based on V. Sardou's drama of the same title), produced in Rome, 1900. Setting: Rome, June, 1800.

Tost Quartets. Twelve quartets by Haydn, written 1789–90 and dedicated to Johann Tost, Viennese merchant and violinist. They comprise op. 54, nos. 1–3; op. 55, nos. 1–3; and op. 64, nos. 1–6.

Tosti, Francesco Paolo (b. Ortona, Abruzzi, 9 Apr. 1846; d. Rome, 2 Dec. 1916). Pupil of Mercadante. Visited London first in 1875 and was singing master to the royal family from 1880. Teacher at the Royal Academy of Music from 1894. Returned to Italy in 1912. Composed songs (incl. "Forever," "Goodbye," "Mattinata," "Vorrei morire").

Tosto [It.]. Quickly, at once. *Più tosto*, either "more quickly" or the same as *piuttosto*, "rather."

Touch. In piano playing, the means by which the keys are depressed so as to produce the desired qualities of sound. Also the particular characteristics of any keyboard *action according to which greater or lesser force is required in order to depress the keys.

Touche [F.]. (1) Key of the piano. (2) Fingerboard of the violin [see Bowing (1)]. (3) A 16th-century term for fret (of a lute, guitar). (4) A 17th-century term

(also used in English sources) for the "orchestral" *toccata.

Tournemire, Charles (Arnaud) (b. Bordeaux, 22 Jan. 1870; d. Arcachon, 3 Nov. 1939). Pupil of Franck, d'Indy, and Widor. Organist at Sainte-Clothilde in Paris from 1898. Teacher at the Paris Conservatory from 1919. Toured Europe as an organ virtuoso. Composed operas; 8 symphonies and other orch. works; sacred and secular choral works (incl. the cantata *Le sang de la sirène*, 1904); chamber music; works for organ (incl. *L'orgue mystique*, containing 51 Offices for the liturgical year); piano pieces; songs. Wrote a treatise on organ playing.

Tourte bow. A violin bow made by F. Tourte (1747–1835). See Bow.

Tovey, Donald Francis (b. Eton, 17 July 1875; d. Edinburgh, 10 July 1940). Critic, pianist, conductor, and composer. Studied with W. Parratt and Parry, and at Oxford Univ. Traveled to the Continent and the U.S. as a concert pianist. Professor at Edinburgh Univ. from 1914. Composed an opera, 1907–18; a symphony, 1913; a piano concerto, 1903, and a cello concerto, 1935; choral works; string quartets and other chamber music; piano pieces; songs. Published 6 vols. of *Essays in Musical Analysis* and other books and essays.

Toy Symphony. A composition often ascribed to Haydn and scored, aside from the first and second violins and double bass, for toy instruments such as cuckoo, quail, nightingale, trumpet, drum, rattle, and triangle. It is now thought to be the work of Mozart's father, Leopold, or of Michael Haydn.

Toye. A short light composition for virginal.

Tpt. Abbr. for *trumpet*.

Tr. Abbr. for *trill, treble, transpose*.

Trabaci, Giovanni Maria (b. Montepeloso, near Potenza, Italy, c. 1575; d. Naples, 31 Dec. 1647). Organist at the Cappella reale in Naples from 1601 and *maestro di cappella* there from 1614, succeeding his teacher Macque. Composed Masses, motets, a Passion, and other sacred works; madrigals, *villa-*

nelle, and other secular vocal works; ricercars, canzonas, capriccios, toccatas,
dances, and other pieces for keyboard.

Tracker action. The purely mechanical
system of key action used in most organs
constructed before 1900. It derives its
name from the tracker, a wooden trace
rod connecting the key to the pipe valve
in the windchest. See Organ.

Tract [L., *tractus*]. In Gregorian chant,
an item of the Proper of the *Mass, used
instead of the Alleluia for various feasts
during Lent, for Ember days, and for the
Requiem Mass. It consists of two to
fourteen psalm verses, without the addition of an antiphon or response, and thus
is one of the few remaining examples of
direct *psalmody.

**Traetta, Tommaso (Michele Francesco
Saverio)** (b. Bitonto, Bari, 30 Mar. 1727;
d. Venice, 6 Apr. 1779). Pupil of Durante
and Leo. *Maestro di cappella* to the
Duke of Parma, 1758–65. Director of the
Conservatorio dell' ospedaletto in Venice, 1765–68. Court composer to Catherine the Great in St. Petersburg, 1768–
75. Composed about 50 operas, some
drawing on French as well as Italian
models (incl. *Didone abbandonata,* Venice, 1757; *Armida,* Vienna, 1761; *Sofo-
nisba,* Mannheim, 1762; *Antigona,* St. Petersburg, 1772); an oratorio; Masses,
motets, a *Stabat Mater,* and other sacred
works; secular vocal works.

Tragic Symphony. Subtitle provided by
Schubert for his Symphony no. 4 in C
minor, D. 417, composed in 1816.

Tragische Ouvertüre [G., *Tragic Overture*]. Orchestral composition by
Brahms, op. 81, composed in 1880 as a
companion piece to the *Akademische
Festouvertüre.

Transcendental Etudes. See *Études
d'exécution transcendante.*

Transcribe, transcription. See Arrangement.

Transfigured Night. See *Verklärte
Nacht.*

Transformation of themes. The modification of a musical subject with a view to
changing its character. This is a 19th-
century device that differs markedly

from earlier, more "technical" methods
of modification, such as the augmentation and diminution of a fugal subject or
the ornamentation of a theme. A characteristic example is the variety of appear-
ances of the *idée fixe* in Berlioz's *Symphonie fantastique.* Liszt exploited the
principle of "transformation des
thèmes" in his symphonic poems, and
Wagner applied it to the *leitmotiv of his
operas [see Ex. 1a, 1b, both from *Götterdämmerung*].

Transition. (1) Passing *modulation. (2)
A lasting change of key effected abruptly
rather than through regular modulation.
(3) A passage (bridge) that leads from
one main section to another, e.g., from
the first to the second theme of a movement.

Transposing instruments. Instruments
for which music is written in a key or octave other than that of their actual
sound. This method is widely used for
wind instruments, such as the clarinet in
B♭, whose natural tones are the harmonics of B♭. Since for the player of this
instrument B♭ is the simplest key, it has
become customary to present this key to
the player in the simplest notation, i.e.,
C major. The transposition to be made
from the written part to the actual sound
is indicated by the interval from C to the
pitch of the instrument, e.g., to B♭ in the
case of the B♭ clarinet, A in that of the A
clarinet [see Ex., Bruckner, Symphony
no. 7]. With certain instruments the
transposition includes a change to the
lower octave, e.g., for the horn in E♭.

The use of transposing instruments or,
more accurately, transposing notation,
dates from the time when only natural
tones were available on some instru-

Clarinet in A: *1.* As written. *2.* As it sounds.

ments. With the introduction of valves and keys in the early 19th century, every instrument could play in every key. Nevertheless, in cases where the *tone color of a particularly pitched instrument is desired, transposed notation is much more convenient for the player, since the fingering for any particular written note remains the same on, e.g., the trumpet in B♭ and the trumpet in C.

Nearly all the wind instruments not pitched in C are transposing instruments, except for the trombones, which, although pitched in E♭, B♭, etc., are written as they sound. The term is also used for instruments such as the piccolo flute, which is notated an octave lower than it sounds in order to avoid ledger lines. Orchestral scores have traditionally given the parts of transposing instruments in the transposed keys as given in the instrumental parts. Many recent compositions are published in *concert-pitch scores, however.

Transposition. The rewriting or *ex tempore* performance of a composition in a key other than the original one. This practice is particularly common with songs, as a means of accommodating different voice ranges.

Transverse flute [F. *flûte traversière;* G. *Querflöte;* It. *flauto traverso;* Sp. *flauta traversa*]. The modern flute, as opposed to the recorder. See Flute.

Trapp, (Hermann Emil Alfred) Max (b. Berlin, 1 Nov. 1887; d. there, 31 May 1971). Pupil of Dohnányi and Juon. Teacher at the Berlin Hochschule für Musik, 1920–34; at the Prussian Academy, 1934–45; at the Berlin Municipal Conservatory, 1950–53. Composed 7 symphonies, 3 concertos for orch., and other orch. works; concertos for piano, for violin, for cello; a cantata; string quartets and other chamber music; piano pieces; songs.

Traps. (1) In dance or theater orchestras, devices used for special effects (e.g., whistles, whip crack, ratchet, cowbell), usually notated for the percussion section, although many of the devices are not, strictly speaking, percussion instruments. (2) In jazz and popular music, both the devices in (1) and the complete "set of drums," which then includes

such devices along with actual percussion instruments, the latter usually including a bass drum operated by a pedal, a snare drum, one or more tom-toms, and a variety of cymbals, all arranged so as to be readily playable by a single, seated player.

Trascinando [It.]. Dragging, slowing.

Trattenuto [It.]. Delayed, slowed down.

Trauer-Ode [G., Funeral Ode]. Choral work by Bach, written in 1727 on the death of the Electress Christiane of Saxony. Based on an ode by Gottsched, it is in the form of a cantata.

Trauer-Symphonie [G., Mourning Symphony]. Popular name for Haydn's Symphony no. 44 (*c.* 1771), in E minor.

Trauermusik [G.]. Funeral music. *Trauermarsch,* funeral march.

Träumerisch [G.]. Dreamy.

Trautonium. See under Electronic instruments.

Travers, John (b. *c.* 1703; d. London, June, 1758). Chorister at St. George's Chapel, Windsor. Pupil of Pepusch and Greene. Organist of the Chapel Royal from 1737. Composed services, anthems, and other church music; *The Whole Book of Psalms* for 1–5 voices with thoroughbass, 1750; canzonets, catches, and canons; songs; voluntaries for organ or harpsichord.

Traverso [It.]; **traversière** [F.]; **Traversflöte** [G.]. See under Flute.

Traviata, La [It., The Erring One]. Opera in three acts by Verdi (libretto by F. M. Piave after Dumas' *La dame aux camélias*), produced in Venice, 1853. Setting: Paris and environs, about 1850.

Travis, Roy (Elihu) (b. New York, 24 June 1922). Pupil of B. Wagenaar, Luening, and Milhaud. Teacher at Columbia Univ., 1952–53; the Mannes College in New York, 1952–57; Univ. of California at Los Angeles from 1957. Has worked with electronic techniques and elements of African music. Has composed an opera, *The Passion of Oedipus,* 1965; orch. works (incl. *Symphonic Allegro,* 1951; *Collage,* 1968); a piano concerto, 1969; *Switched-on Ashanti* for flute,

African instruments, synthesizer, 1973; chamber music; *African Sonata*, 1966, and other piano pieces; songs.

Tre [It.]. Three. *A tre voci*, in three parts. *Tre corde*, see *Una corda*.

Treble. The highest part of a choral composition, hence synonym of *soprano*. However, treble clef is not the same as soprano clef [see Clef]. For treble viol, recorder, see under Descant; Viol; Recorder.

Treibend [G.]. Hurrying.

Treibenreif, Peter. See Tritonius, Petrus.

Tremblay, Gilles (b. Arvida, Quebec, 6 Sept. 1932). Pupil of Champagne and Messiaen, and has worked on electronic techniques with the Groupe de recherches musicales at the French Radio in Paris. Teacher at the Montreal Conservatory from 1962. Works incl. *Phases et réseaux* for piano, 1958; *Cantique de durées* for orch., 1960; *Kékoba* for Ondes Martenot, percussion, singers, 1965; *Sonorisation* on 24 tape channels, 1967; *Champs II—Souffle* for winds, double bass, piano, and percussion, 1968.

Tremblement. The most important of the French *agréments* of the 17th and 18th centuries, more commonly known as a *trill.

Tremolando [It.]. With *tremolo.

Tremolo [It.]. Usually, the quick and continuous reiteration of a single pitch. On stringed instruments it is produced by a rapid up-and-down movement of the bow, indicated as in Ex. 1. The term is also used, however, for a succession of repeated notes slightly articulated without a change in direction of the bow, as in Ex. 2, this being called a "slurred tremolo," and for a rapid alternation between two pitches of a chord, as in Ex. 3, this being called a "fingered tremolo" because it is produced by rapid movement of a finger on the fingerboard rather than by rapid movement of the bow. Some 18th-century names for the string tremolo are *bombo* [It.] and *Schwärmer* [G.].

In violin music of the 18th century (J. Stamitz, Gluck, Haydn) a special tremolo, known as an "undulating tremolo"

[0 4 0 4]

[It. *ondeggiando;* F. *ondulé*], is much used. It is produced by an undulating motion of the bow arm, resulting in alternate bowing on two strings (or more when the technique is applied to the playing of *arpeggios). This bowing can be used to produce either a reiteration of a single pitch alternately on a stopped string and an open string (in which case it is called *bariolage;* Ex. 4) or an alternation between two (or more) pitches. It was indicated by a wavy line, as in Ex. 5, a sign that is sometimes misinterpreted as indicating a vibrato. The addition of a slur indicates that several notes are to be taken in a single bow stroke, i.e., without a change in direction of the bow.

In piano music, the genuine tremolo (i.e., the rapid repetition of a single pitch) is a device used mainly in highly virtuosic compositions, such as Liszt's *La campanella,* where it also occurs in the form of quickly repeated octaves. In some cases the tremolo of the strings is imitated by the rapid alternation of a pitch and its octave, or of the several pitches of a chord. In organ music, the term is applied to the effect produced by the *tremulant stop. This effect, however, more nearly approximates the string player's *vibrato.

In singing, *tremolo* commonly means the excessive vibrato that leads to deviation of pitch. The true vocal tremolo, i.e., the quick reiteration of a single pitch, is an effect that is practically never used today. In the early 17th century the true vocal tremolo was widely used; called a *trillo,* it was usually written out in quick notes. During this period, the term *tremolo* meant a trill [see Ornamentation]. In the 18th century the true vocal tremolo fell into disuse and was henceforth known by such derogatory names as *chevrotement* [F.] and *Bockstriller* [G.], which liken it to the bleating of a goat.

Tremulant. An organ stop producing alternating increases and decreases of wind pressure, thus causing a rapid fluctuation of pitch, an expressive effect similar to the violinist's *vibrato. Although considerably abused on the theater organ, to the point where it became anathema to purists, it existed in French and German organs of the baroque period and, when properly regulated and judiciously used, it has a legitimate musical function in baroque, romantic, and contemporary organ literature.

Trent, Council of. See Council of Trent.

Trent Codices. Seven manuscript volumes of 15th-century polyphonic music discovered in the library of the Cathedral of Trent (in northern Italy). The first six volumes (Cod. 87–92) contain 1,585 compositions, mostly from the mid-15th century; a seventh volume, discovered later, contains mostly duplicates. This collection, by far the most extensive source of 15th-century music, contains compositions by about 75 French, English, Italian, and German composers, e.g., Dunstable, Power, Ciconia, Dufay, Binchois, Ockeghem, Busnois, and Isaac.

Trepak. A Cossack dance in quick duple time.

Triad. A chord of three pitches consisting of a pitch called the root and the pitches a third and fifth above it [see Interval]. There are four kinds of triad, depending on the exact sizes of the intervals comprised [see Ex.]: *major* (in which the interval between the lower two pitches is a major third and that between the upper two a minor third, the interval between the highest and lowest thus being a perfect fifth); *minor* (the lower interval a minor third, the upper a major third, and the outer a perfect fifth); *diminished* (two minor thirds, the outer interval thus being a diminished fifth); and *augmented* (two major thirds, the outer interval thus becoming an augmented fifth). The first two are consonant and the last two dissonant chords.

Triads: a. major. b. minor. c. diminished. d. augmented.

Each triad (e.g., c–e–g) has two *inversions: the *sixth (or six-three) chord (e–g–c'), so called because the intervals formed above the lowest sounding pitch are a sixth and a third, and the *six-four chord (g–c'–e'), so called because the intervals formed above the lowest sounding pitch are a sixth and a fourth. In a *major key, the tonic triad (i.e., the triad formed with the tonic as root; see Scale degrees) is major. In a minor key, the tonic triad is minor. The *primary* triads (or chords) in any major or minor key are those formed on scale degrees I, IV, and V, these triads together containing all of the pitches of the major or minor scale in question. The triad is fundamental to the harmonic practice of the 17th to 19th centuries, though triads also occur in earlier music. See Harmony; Harmonic analysis; Consonance, dissonance.

Trial of Lucullus, The. One-act opera by Sessions (libretto by B. Brecht), produced in Berkeley, California, 1947.

Triangle. See Percussion instruments II, 5.

Trichord. Any collection of three pitches (or pitch classes), particularly with reference to segments of twelve-tone rows [see Serial music].

Tricinium [L.]. A 16th-century name for a vocal composition in three voice-parts.

Trill [E., formerly *shake;* F. *cadence, tremblement;* G. *Triller;* It. *trillo;* Sp. *trino*]. A musical ornament consisting of the rapid alternation of a given pitch with the diatonic second above it.

The trill originated in the 16th century as an ornamental resolution of a suspension dissonance [see Counterpoint] at a cadence. Ex. 1 shows various forms of the 16th-century trill, 1a and 1b representing typical vocal cadences, the other variants occurring frequently in instru-

mental transciptions of vocal works and in independent keyboard compositions. It is probable, however, that even in vocal performances the singers of this period customarily embellished the simple written cadence in the more elaborate manner.

As the French name implies, the ornament was at first (early 17th cent.) invariably associated with cadences. Later it was freely introduced at other positions in the musical phrase. Until the end of the 18th century, however, it retained its primary function as the ornamental resolution of a dissonance.

In music of the 17th and 18th centuries the trill, instead of being written out in notes or left to the improvisation of the performer (as had hitherto been the case), was often indicated in the score by one of the following signs, which are synonymous:

$$tr \quad t \quad \text{\small tw} \quad \text{\small ww} \quad \text{\small w} \quad +$$

Since the sign is always placed over the consonant harmony note, the accent must fall on the upper auxiliary, which, as the dissonance, requires the greater emphasis. That is, barring specific indications to the contrary, the trill should begin on the auxiliary rather than the main note. Apart from this factor, which is constant throughout the period, the execution of the trill was varied considerably in individual cases by adding prefixes or terminations and by varying the number and rhythm of the notes making up the ornament. In the time of Bach and Handel, three ways of ending the trill were almost equally popular [Ex. 2]. The use of a simple sign (*t, tr*) for the trill left the performer free to choose interpretation a, b, or c. If the composer desired a particular execution, as at 2a or 2c, he used one of the notations shown.

The number and rhythmic distribution of the notes comprising the trill were generally left entirely to the performer's discretion. Ex. 3 shows several realizations of a cadence formula that is particularly common in the works of J. S. Bach and his contemporaries. All of these interpretations are equally correct according to the traditions of Bach's time; the choice among them should depend on the tempo and character of the passage in which the trill occurs. Sometimes the composer expressly calls for dwelling on the introductory note of the trill, known in French as *tremblement appuyé* and in German as *vorbereiteter Triller* [Ex. 4], by one of these indications: (a) inserting the sign for an *appoggiatura, (b) prefixing a vertical stroke to the sign for the trill, or (c) writing the introductory appoggiatura as an ordinary note. The excerpts in Ex. 4 show J. S. Bach's use of all three.

The beginning of a trill is often varied by the addition of a prefix, which may be indicated by one or more small notes or by a modification of the ordinary sign for the trill. The number of small notes used in the notation of the prefix does not affect the interpretation. A hook extending down from the beginning of the trill sign indicates a prefix starting below the main note [Ex. 5a]; a hook extending up represents an introductory turn beginning with the upper auxiliary [Ex. 5b]. The prefix from below is especially common; indeed, throughout the 18th century, it was customary to start a long trill with such a prefix, even when not indicated, whenever the main note was approached conjunctly from below.

The modern trill, which begins with the main note, was first introduced early in the 19th century by the Viennese pianists Hummel, Czerny, and Moscheles. It is usually played with a two-note termination [G. *Nachschlag*], shown in Ex. 6 [Liszt, *Hungarian Rhapsody* no. 14]. The "main note" trill did not entirely supplant the traditional form, which often appears in the works of Chopin, Schumann, and Liszt. It is customary, however, in the romantic and modern periods, for the composer to indicate the first note of the trill by means of a small grace note. In the absence of such an indication the trill should begin on the main note.

Triller [G.]. *Trill. Trillerkette,* chain or series of trills.

Trillo [It.]. *Trill. In the 17th century, the true vocal *tremolo.

Trimble, Lester (Albert) (b. Bangor, Wis., 29 Aug. 1923). Pupil of Lopatnikoff, Milhaud, Honegger, and N. Boulanger. Music critic for the *New York Herald Tribune,* 1951–59; *The Nation,* 1956–61. Teacher at the Univ. of Maryland, 1963–67; at the Juilliard School from 1971. Has composed an opera; 3 symphonies and other orch. works (incl. *5 Episodes,* 1962); a violin concerto, 1955, and a *Duo concertante* for 2 violins and orch., 1963; choral works; string quartets and other chamber music; songs (incl. *4 Fragments from the Canterbury Tales* for soprano, flute, clarinet, and harpsichord, 1958).

Trinklied [G.]. Drinking song.

Trio [It.]. (1) Originally, a contrapuntal composition in three parts [see Trio sonata]. (2) In the scherzo or minuet movement of the *sonata, the middle section played between the scherzo (minuet) and its repetition [see Scherzo]. For its use in the march, see March. The term *trio* comes from the 17th-century custom of writing minuets and other dances in three parts, frequently for two oboes and bassoon (Lully), a treatment that was used particularly for the second of two dances played alternately, resulting in the arrangement *Menuet, Menuet en trio, Menuet.* A good example is Bach's Brandenburg Concerto no. 1, in which the minuet is fully orchestrated whereas the trio is written for two oboes and bassoon. As late as Haydn, Mozart, and Beethoven (e.g., Symphony no. 7), the trio usually retained the lighter texture and woodwind character of Lully's trio. Schubert and others used the term for the middle section of compositions in ternary form.

(3) Music for three players. The most important type is the *piano trio* for piano, violin, and cello. In most of Haydn's 31 trios, the violin and cello are chiefly reinforcements for the piano part. Mozart's 7 piano trios (K. 254, K. 496, K. 498, K. 502, K. 542, K. 548, K. 564) show greater individuality of the parts, preparing the way for such great works as Beethoven's op. 70 and op. 97, and Schubert's op. 99 and op. 100. The standard trio repertory also includes works of Schumann (3), Mendelssohn (2), Brahms (3), Dvořák (3), Franck (4), Fauré (1), Ravel (1), and others. The *string trio,* usually for violin, viola, and cello, has attracted far fewer composers.

Trio sonata. The most important type of baroque chamber music, written in three parts, two upper parts of similar range and design and a supporting thoroughbass part. The trio sonata is usually performed on four instruments, two violins (or, in the earlier period, viols, cornetti) for the two upper parts, a cello (viola da gamba, violone) for the bass part, and a harpsichord (organ, theorbo) for the bass part together with the realization of the thoroughbass accompaniment. Other instrumentation was occasionally employed, e.g., in Biagio Marini's Sonatas for violin and organ, op. 8 (1626), in which the organ has two written parts; in Bach's six organ trios, written for organ alone in three parts without thoroughbass figures; and in G. B. Bononcini's op. 4 (1686), for which there are five partbooks, first and second violin, cello, theorbo, and organ. Toward the end of the 17th century two types of trio sonata developed, the *sonata da chiesa* (church sonata) and the *sonata da camera* (chamber sonata). The trio style became popular particularly in France, where it was known as *sonate en trio*. The form persisted into the classical period, the last examples being by Gluck (1746), the *Mannheim school, and Haydn (*Six Sonates à deux violons et basse, op. 8, c. 1766). Thereafter it changed into the classical trio for three instruments, with a fully written out part for piano [see Trio (3)].

The literature of the trio sonata includes most of the illustrious names of the late baroque, among them Corelli (48, op. 1–4), Purcell (12), Buxtehude, Handel (28, 6 of which are for two oboes and bass), F. Couperin (14), and Vivaldi (12). Bach wrote only a few trio sonatas of the standard type (i.e., for two melody instruments and thoroughbass accompaniment), including one in his *Musikalisches Opfer*.

Triole [G.]; **triolet** [F.]. *Triplet.

Tripla. (1) For *proportio tripla* see Proportions. (2) *Proportz. (3) Plural of *triplum* [see *Duplum*].

Triple concerto. A concerto for three solo instruments with orchestra, such as Bach's two concertos for three harpsichords and Beethoven's concerto for violin, cello, and piano, op. 56.

Triple counterpoint. See Invertible counterpoint.

Triple-croche [F.]. Thirty-second note. See under Notes.

Triple meter, time. See under Meter.

Triplet [F. *triolet; G. Triole; It. terzina; Sp. tresillo*]. A group of three notes to be performed in place of two of the same kind, indicated by a 3 and, usually, a slur:

For the indication of triplet rhythm by dotted notes, see under Dotted notes.

Triplum. See under *Duplum*.

Tris(h)agion [Gr.]. The Sanctus in its original Greek version. In the Roman rite it is used during the Adoration of the Cross on Good Friday, as a part of the *Improperia [*LU*, p. 737].

Tristan und Isolde. Opera in three acts by Wagner (to his own libretto, based on G. von Strassburg), produced in Munich, 1865. Setting: aboard a ship, Cornwall, Brittany, in legendary times.

Tritone. The interval of the augmented fourth (e.g., c–f♯) or diminished fifth (e.g., c–g♭), so called because it spans three whole tones. In some periods of music history it has been considered an interval to be avoided or treated with great caution [see *Diabolus in musica*].

Tritonius, Petrus (Peter Treibenreif) (b. Bozen, Tirol, c. 1465; d. probably Hall, Tirol, 1525). Pupil of the humanist Scholar Konrad Keltes. Director of the Hall Latin School, 1512–19. Composed and published four-part homorhythmic settings of odes of Horace and other Latin poems, preserving their quantitative character, 1507.

Trittico [It., Triptych]. A cycle of three independent one-act operas by Puccini, first produced together in New York, 1918: *Suor Angelica* (Sister Angelica; libretto by G. Forzano; setting, a convent near Siena, 17th century); *Gianni Schicchi* (libretto by G. Forzano, based on Dante; setting, bedroom of a house in Florence, 1299); *Il tabarro* (The Cloak; libretto by G. Adami, after D. Gold's play *La Houppelande;* setting, a barge on the Seine, 19th century).

Tritus [L.]. See under Church modes.

Triumphes of Oriana, The. A collection of English madrigals, published by Morley in imitation of an Italian collection of madrigals, *Il trionfo di Dori* (1592), and dedicated to Queen Elizabeth I. The book was scheduled to appear in 1601, but was not published until 1603, after the Queen's death. It contains 29 madrigals for five or six voices, by Morley, Weelkes, and others.

Trochee, trochaic. See under Poetic meter; Modes, rhythmic.

Trojans, The. See *Troyens, Les.*

Tromba [It.]. *Trumpet, bugle. *T. a macchina* (*ventile*), valve trumpet. *T. bassa,* bass trumpet. *T. da tirarsi, t. spezzata,* slide trumpet.

Tromba marina [It.]. A late medieval bowed instrument, still in use in the 18th century, that consisted of a tapering three-sided body, 5 to 6 feet long, over which a single string was stretched. The string was not stopped, as in violin playing, but was lightly touched with one finger to produce *harmonics, the bow playing above the "stopping" point (between it and the nut). Inside the long soundbox were a large number (up to 20 or more) of sympathetic strings tuned in unison with the playing string [see ill. accompanying Violin family]. The most peculiar feature was the bridge, in the shape of a wide inverted U whose left foot, shorter than the right, was free to vibrate against the soundboard, resulting in a drumming noise (hence G. *Trumscheit,* drum log). While its trumpetlike sound probably accounts for the *tromba* part of the name, no explanation for *marina* has been found. The instrument was frequently used by nuns and hence another German name, *Nonnengeige* (nun's fiddle).

Tromboncino, Bartolomeo (b. Verona, *c.* 1470; d. Venice?, after 1535). Musician at the court in Mantua, 1487–95 and 1501–12, after which he went to Ferrara. In Vicenza and Casale in 1499. Composed *frottole,* of which he was one of the principal exponents; sacred music.

Trombone [G. *Posaune;* Sp. *trombón*]. The modern orchestral trombone is a *brass instrument with a cylindrical bore for all but the lower third of its length, which gradually expands into the bell, and a cup-shaped mouthpiece. It incorporates a U-shaped cylindrical pipe, called a *slide,* that slides over two straight cylindrical pipes, thus varying the total effective length of pipe in the instrument. [See ill. under Brass instruments.] Including the first position, in which the slide is held closest to the player and the total effective length of the pipe is at its shortest, there are seven positions of the slide, each successive position lowering the fundamental pitch by a semitone. The combined pitches of the harmonic series [see under Acoustics; see also Wind instruments] for each of the seven fundamentals make available the complete chromatic scale over a range of almost three octaves. The fundamental for each position is called a pedal tone and is difficult to play in the three lowest positions. The practical range for each position extends upward approximately two octaves from the second harmonic (an octave above the fundamental). Although the sliding mechanism makes the execution of a true *legato difficult, a *glissando can be executed with ease. Trombones have been made in many sizes, ranging from soprano to contrabass, and in many keys. The four types used in the modern orchestra are:

(a) Tenor trombone, pitched in B♭, a complete chromatic compass as shown in Ex. 1, in addition to which four pedal tones, shown in Ex. 2, are available. It is notated at its sounding pitch (not *transposing as is, e.g., the horn).

(b) Bass trombone, pitched in F, although instruments pitched in G or E♭ are sometimes used in England. Its compass is a fourth below that of the tenor trombone. The great length of the pipe makes the slides difficult to handle, and today the instrument is generally replaced by the tenor-bass trombone.

(c) Tenor-bass trombone. It has the size (and pitch) of the tenor trombone but the bore of the bass trombone, which facilitates playing pedal tones and makes the sound similar to the bass trombone's. It has a single valve that lowers the pitch a fourth (B♭ to F), i.e., to that of the bass trombone. The tenor-bass trombone has virtually supplanted the bass trombone in the modern orchestra.

(d) Contrabass trombone (double-bass trombone), pitched an octave below the tenor trombone (British instruments are sometimes pitched in C). The difficulty caused by the great length of its pipe was overcome in 1816 (by Gottfried Weber) with the invention of the double slide, the pipe being bent into four parallel tubes. Wagner used it in his *Ring des Nibelungen,* and other composers have followed his example (e.g., d'Indy in *Jour d'été à la montagne*).

Valve trombones, employing three valves similar to those of the trumpet, have also been made [see under Trumpet].

The trombone was the first of the modern orchestral instruments to appear in its present shape. It developed in the 15th century from a large trumpet (hence the name *trombone,* i.e., large *tromba*) through the addition of a slide, and the earliest representations, in paintings of the late 15th century, show all the essentials of the present instrument. The German name *posaune* points to another line of descent, the large and straight **buysine,* the name going back to L. **buccina.* The medieval name for the trombone was *sackbut* (derived from the old Spanish *sacabuche,* "draw tube," or from old French *sacqueboute,* "pullpush"). Throughout the 16th century, trombones were commonly used in the ceremonial bands of princes and large cities as well as in churches. Their sliding mechanism made them suitable for performing art music at a time when horns and trumpets were still limited to the performance of military signals. In operas of the 17th and 18th centuries, they were frequently associated with the supernatural. Bach and Handel used the instrument occasionally, but mostly in unison with voices for the sake of greater sonority. Gluck was perhaps the first to make effective use of the trombone for accompanying chords, e.g., in the aria "Divinité du Styx" from *Alceste,* and Mozart gave the trombones a prominent place in his *Zauberflöte* and *Don Giovanni.* Beethoven introduced the trombones into symphonic music in the final movement of his Fifth Symphony, but it was not until after 1850 and the works of Berlioz and Wagner that the trombone became firmly established as a member of the orchestra. In the 20th century the trombone has been used as a solo instrument with orchestra and in chamber music combinations by Hovhaness,

Cowell, Stravinsky, Poulenc, and Hindemith.

Trommel [G.]. Drum [see Percussion instruments, II, 1–3]. *Trommelschlegel,* drumstick.

Trompete [G.]; **trompette** [F.]. **Trumpet. Trompette à coulisse,* slide trumpet.

Trope [L. *tropus*]. (1) In certain medieval treatises, designation for **church mode.

(2) Term used by J. M. Hauer in a kind of twelve-tone system devised by him that differs from that of Schoenberg [see Serial music] and has not been generally accepted. In his *Zwölftontechnik* (1926), Hauer divides each series of twelve notes into two hexachords and groups all of the series having the same notes in each of the hexachords into a class called a *trope.* Thus, one such trope (no. 44) contains all series beginning with the tones c d e f♯ g♯ a♯ (in any order). There are 44 such tropes.

(3) Loosely, any interpolation of text, music, or both into a liturgical chant. The principal types are (a) the addition of a new text to a preexistent *melisma, whether newly composed or part of a traditional *Gregorian chant; (b) the composition of a new melody and text, which is then sung together with a traditional chant in various ways, e.g., before and/or after it, or by alternation of the phrases of the trope with those of the original chant; (c) the composition of a melody without text, which is then added to an item of the standard repertory. The term is sometimes further extended to include polyphonic elaborations of liturgical chants. The only historically correct use of the term, namely that of medieval manuscripts, restricts it to (b) above, which characteristically takes the form of introductions to the lines of antiphonal chants [see Psalmody], particularly the Introit, and additions to the Gloria, Sanctus, and Agnus Dei of the *Ordinary. The origins of *liturgical drama are usually thought to lie in such Introit tropes. The principal examples of type (c) are the *sequentiae,* extended melismas sung following the Alleluia verse. Additions of type (a) occur in conjunction with responsorial chants and Kyries and bear the term *prosula* or, in the case of the longer texts added to *sequentiae, prosa.* The latter results in

what is now most often called a *sequence. In the case of the Kyries, however, there is some doubt as to whether the melodies actually antedate the "interpolated" texts. All of these phenomena flourished from the 10th through the 12th centuries. With few exceptions [see Sequence] they were suppressed in the 16th century by the *Council of Trent, though Kyrie melodies continue to be identified by the texts formerly associated with them (e.g., *Kyrie Cunctipotens genitor*).

Troper [L. *troparium*]. A liturgical book containing *tropes.

Troppo [It.]. Too (much). *Allegro non troppo,* not too fast.

Troubadour. Any of a large number of 12th- and 13th-century poet-musicians of southern France (Provence). Their Provençal name was *trobador.* The movement was begun by Guilhem IX, seventh Count of Poitiers (fl. 1087–1127), and included members of the French nobility as well as commoners, all devoted to poetry and music in the service of chivalrous love. In the mid-12th century it spread to northern France (*trouvères) and Germany (*minnesingers). Scholars do not agree about the origins of this movement. Arab-Spanish models as well as Carolingian love lyrics and liturgical hymns in honor of the Virgin Mary have all been cited as sources. The relationship of the troubadours to the *jongleurs* [see under Minstrel] is also not fully understood. Among the troubadours whose melodies survive are Guilhem IX, Marcabru, a commoner (d. *c.* 1150), Bernart de Ventadorn (*c.* 1127–95), Peire Vidal, a commoner (d. 1215), Rambault de Vaqueiras (d. 1207), Folquet de Marseille (*c.* 1155–1231), Raimon de Miraval (d. *c.* 1220), Aimeric de Peguillan (1205–75), and Guiraut Riquier (d. 1294), the "last of the troubadours."

About 300 troubadour poems (*c.* 30 with devotional texts; most are love lyrics) are preserved with melodies. Special types are the *alba, pastorela* (pastoral), *planc* [see Lament (2)], *partimen* [see *Tenso*], and *sirventes.* Practically all of them are strophic poems, normally with five or six stanzas and a concluding half-stanza (*tornada;* see Envoi). Most often the stanza is through-composed, but the form with initial repeat, A A B, also occurs [see *Canzo*]. For the notation and rhythmic interpretation of the troubadour songs, see under Trouvère.

Trout Quintet. Popular name for Schubert's Quintet in A, op. 114, D. 667 (1819), for violin, viola, cello, double bass, and piano, in five movements, the fourth being a set of variations on his song "The Trout" [G. *Die Forelle*].

Trouvère. Any of the 12th- and 13th-century poet-musicians active in northern France who imitated the movement initiated by the Provençal *troubadours. The development began in the late 12th century with Blondel de Nesles (b. *c.* 1155), Gace Brulé (d. 1220), the Châtelain de Coucy (d. 1203), and Conon de Béthune (*c.* 1160–1219); continued with Gautier d'Epinal (fl. 1220–40), Thibaut IV (Count of Champagne and later King of Navarre, 1201–53), Colin Muset, Moniot d'Arras, Perrin d'Angicourt, and others; and closed with Jehan Bretel (d. 1272), Adam de la Hale (*c.* 1240–87), and Gillebert de Berneville (d. *c.* 1300).

Of more than 4,000 trouvère poems, about 1,400 are preserved with their melodies. A large majority of the songs are love lyrics in the form of strophic poems; special literary types are the *aube* [see *Alba*], *chanson de toile, jeu-parti* [see *Tenso*], and *pastourelle* (pastoral). Through-composed stanzas, which occur in the majority of troubadour songs, are relatively rare. The form with initial repeat, A A B, is the most important form of trouvère music. This form is similar to the 14th-century *ballade. Occasionally, other repeat structures are encountered, such as A A B B, A A B B C, A B B, etc. In addition to strophic songs, the trouvère repertory includes a considerable number of *lais. The *rondeau* and *virelai,* however, cannot be considered forms of trouvère music.

The melodies of the trouvères (and troubadours) are practically all notated without clear indication of rhythm, and their rhythmic interpretation has been widely studied and disputed.

Trovatore, Il. [It., The Troubadour, or The Minstrel]. Opera in four acts by Verdi (libretto by S. Cammarano, based on a play by A. Gutiérrez), produced in Rome, 1853. Setting: Spain, 15th century.

Troyens, Les [F., The Trojans]. Opera in five acts by Berlioz (to his own libretto, after Virgil), in two parts, *La prise de Troie* (The Taking of Troy) and *Les Troyens à Carthage* (The Trojans at Carthage), composed 1856–58. Only the second part was produced during Berlioz's lifetime (Paris, 1863); the whole work was first produced (in German) in Karlsruhe, 1890. Setting: Troy and Carthage, 1200 B.C.

Trumpet [F. *trompette;* G. *Trompete;* It. *tromba;* Sp. *trompeta*]. The modern orchestral trumpet is a *brass instrument with a cup-shaped mouthpiece and a narrow tube that is cylindrical for about three-fourths of its length, then widening into a moderate-sized bell. These characteristics distinguish it from the horn, which has a prevailingly conical bore and funnel-shaped mouthpiece. [For ill. see Brass instruments.] The trumpet has three *valves (rotary or piston), which, singly or in combination, lower the natural pitch of the instrument by one to six semitones; hence, the name *valve trumpet* [F. *trompette-à-pistons* or *chromatique;* G. *Ventiltrompete;* It. *tromba ventile, t. a macchina, t. a pistoni*] to distinguish it from the earlier *natural trumpet.* How tones are produced on the trumpet is explained under Wind instruments.

The modern orchestral trumpet is pitched in B♭ and has the written chromatic compass shown in the accompanying example. Instruments pitched in D are also relatively common. At the end of the 19th century, a larger trumpet, pitched in F (or, for military bands, E♭), was popular. Bass trumpets, pitched in low E, D, or C, were demanded by Wagner for his *Ring des Nibelungen* but have proved impracticable. The instruments known by this name and used as substitutes are actually *valve trombones,* pitched in C.

The oldest ancestors of the modern trumpet are discussed under Brass instruments; Buccina; Buysine; Cornett; Lituus; Lur. Prior to *c.* 1700 the trumpet existed mainly in the form known as a *natural trumpet, a plain brass cylindrical bore without any such devices as side-holes, crooks, slides, or valves to bridge the gaps of the harmonics. From the 14th century on, it became associated with military and ceremonial functions. After 1600 the trumpet began to be used in art music, the *clarino* and *trombe sordine* of Monteverdi's *Orfeo* (1607) being an early though isolated instance. Toward the end of the 17th century, trumpets were quite frequently used in operas, cantatas, etc., for military scenes or for expressing joyful triumph (Purcell, Buxtehude). At this time the art of playing the highest register of the trumpet, where the harmonics form a full scale, was developed; formerly only the low and middle registers, in which only fanfarelike motifs are possible, had been used [see Clarino (2)].

During the 18th century, various attempts were made to overcome the limitation in the natural trumpet's compass. As early as Bach's time crooks—additional lengths of tubing—were inserted between the mouthpiece and the instrument. Toward the end of the 18th century, both side-holes covered with keys and a sliding mechanism were introduced. *Key trumpets* were invented in 1801 by the court trumpeter Anton Weidinger of Vienna, but they were soon abandoned because side-holes, though fairly satisfactory on conical instruments such as cornets and bugles (*key bugle*), produce a muffled sound on instruments with a cylindrical bore. More successful was the application of the sliding mechanism, which had always been used for trombones. In an earlier construction, documented as early as the 15th century, the slide was part of the elongated mouthpiece, which could be pulled out so that all the gaps in the natural scale could be filled. It is probably this instrument [F. *trompette à coulisse;* G. *Zugtrompete*] that Bach meant when he indicated *tromba da tirarsi* (Cantatas no. 5, 20, 77). The terms *tromba o corno da tirarsi* (Cantata no. 46) and *corno da tirarsi* (Cantatas 67, 162) probably mean the same instrument. [See ill. under Brass instruments.] At the beginning of the 19th century another construction was made by John Hyde (1804; or by Richard Woodham, c. 1810?) in which the U of the upper coil was transformed into a movable slide, similar to that of the trombone, and provided with springs to bring it back to its normal position. This instrument was in constant use in England throughout the 19th century. Although it had the fine sound of the natural trumpet, it lacked the agility demanded in modern scores and was therefore finally abandoned in favor of the valve trumpet.

The invention of *valves (c. 1815) opened the way for the permanent establishment of the trumpet in the orchestra. One of the first parts for the valve trumpet is that in Halévy's *La juive* (1835), in which two valve trumpets are used along with two natural trumpets with crooks. The modern development of a brilliant trumpet technique has enabled composers to use the trumpets as melody instruments equal and occasionally superior in importance to the woodwinds. The scores of Stravinsky, Shostakovich, and others contain many interesting trumpet passages. The repertory for trumpet includes concertos by Haydn and Hummel, a sonata by Hindemith, and works by Purcell, Bach, Vivaldi, and Enesco.

Trumpet marine. *Tromba marina.

Trythall, Richard (b. Knoxville, Tenn., 25 July 1939). Pianist and composer. Pupil of Van Vactor, Sessions, and Kim. Has lived principally in Italy from 1968. Works incl. *Composition for Piano and Orchestra*, 1965; *Penelope's Monologue* for soprano and orch., 1966; *Costruzione per orchestra*, 1967; *Coincidences* for piano, 1969; *Variations on a Theme of Haydn* for woodwind quintet and tape, 1975.

T.s. Abbr. for *tasto solo* [see under Thoroughbass].

Tuba. (1) [L.] Ancient Roman straight trumpet.

(2) In modern usage, generic name loosely used for any bass-pitched brass instrument other than the trombones. This group comprises instruments of many sizes and shapes, depending on when and where and by whom they were made, a fact partly explained by their extensive use in military and other bands. The most important of these band instruments, such as the euphonium, helicon, sousaphone, and baritone, are briefly described under Brass instruments II.

The tubas of the modern orchestra are bass instruments with an oblong shape, a conical bore, a bell pointing upward, a cupped mouthpiece, and three to five valves [see ill. under Brass instruments]. There are three sizes: (a) tenor tuba [G. *Baryton*] in B♭; (b) bass tuba, pitched either in E♭ (E♭ or EE♭ bass tuba) or in F (F bass tuba); (c) double-bass or contrabass tuba (usually called BB♭ [double B-flat] bass tuba or BB♭ bass), pitched an octave below the tenor tuba.

Wagner tuba and *Bayreuth tuba* are names given to instruments designed for Wagner's *Ring*. They have a somewhat narrow bore (similar to that of the *cornet) and a funnel-shaped mouthpiece like that of the horn. Wagner used two tenor and two bass instruments of this type, together with a normal double-bass tuba for the lowest part. The Wagner tubas combine the agility of the cornet with the mellow timbre of the true tubas. They have also been used by Bruckner and R. Strauss (*Elektra*). See ill. under Brass instruments.

(3) For *tuba* in Gregorian chant, see under Psalm tones.

Tucket, tuck. Elizabethan name for a trumpet flourish. The word appears to be an anglicization of *toccata* [see Toccata (2)].

Tudor, David (Eugene) (b. Philadelphia, 20 Jan. 1926). Pianist, bandoneon player, and composer. Pupil of Wolpe. Close associate of Cage and Feldman. Associate of the Merce Cunningham Dance Company from 1953. Has been a particularly prominent performer and realizer of music of the avant garde, incl. works of Cage, Bussotti, Boulez, and Stockhausen. Has employed aleatory procedures and a wide variety of electronic techniques as well as lasers and other visual elements. Works incl. *Bandoneon!* [Bandoneon Factorial] with projections by Lowell Cross, 1966; *Rainforest* for Merce Cunningham, 1968; *Video/Laser II* with Cross and Carson Jeffries, 1970.

Ṭunbūr. A long-necked lute with a pear-shaped body that is found throughout the Balkans and Near East. It has a variable number of metal strings. See Lute.

Tunder, Franz (b. Burg auf Fehmarn, near Lübeck, 1614; d. Lübeck, 5 Nov. 1667). Organist at the court in Gottorp, 1632–41; at the Marienkirche in Lübeck, 1641 until his death; succeeded by his son-in-law Buxtehude. Composed cantatas; pieces for organ, incl. preludes, fugues, and chorale settings.

Tune. *Melody.

Tune book. Generic term for the many volumes of three- and four-part vocal music published in the American colonies and United States as well as in England in the 18th and 19th centuries, which contain psalm tunes, hymn tunes, fuging tunes, anthems, odes, "motettos," and occasionally even a cantata.

Tuning. Adjustment of an instrument to its proper pitch. In stringed instruments (including the piano, the harp, and the harpsichord as well as the violin and related instruments) this is done by adjusting the tension of the strings; in wind instruments by adjusting the effective length of the pipe through the use of *tuning slides (in brass instruments and the organ) or through changing the position of the mouthpiece (in the clarinet family) or reed (in the oboe family). For various systems of tuning see Temperament.

Tuning fork [F. *diapason;* G. *Stimmgabel;* It. *corista;* Sp. *diapasón*]. A two-pronged steel fork used as a standard of *pitch. Its tone, which is largely free of *harmonics other than the fundamental, is produced by the vibration of the two prongs created when one of them is struck. The sound produced is considerably amplified if the tip of the stem is held against a table or similar solid object. Invented in the early 18th century, the device can be made in any size required to produced any desired pitch. The most common tuning forks now in use produce the pitch a' at the international standard of 440 cycles per second.

Tuning slide. In organ building, a movable metal clip or tube attached to the upper end of an open flue pipe. By lowering or raising it, the length of the pipe, and hence its pitch, can be adjusted. Also the U-shaped slides on modern *brass instruments by means of which the pitch of an instrument can be adjusted slightly.

Tuning wire. In organ building, a wire by means of which the length of the vibrating tongue of reed pipes is changed.

Turandot. Unfinished opera in three acts by Puccini, completed by F. Alfano (libretto by G. Adami and R. Simoni, based on C. Gozzi's play), produced in Milan, 1926. Setting: China, legendary times.

Turba [L., crowd]. In oratorios, Passions, etc., a choral movement representing the Jews or heathens.

Turca, alla [It.]. In the Turkish style, i.e., in imitation of Turkish military music (*Janizary music), which became popular in Europe in the late 18th century.

Turina, Joaquín (b. Seville, 9 Dec. 1882; d. Madrid, 14 Jan. 1949). Pianist, conductor, critic, and composer. Studied in Seville and Madrid and with d'Indy and Moszkowski in Paris. Teacher at the Madrid Conservatory from 1931. Worked with native Spanish materials. Composed operas (*Margot,* Madrid, 1914; *Jardín de oriente,* Madrid, 1923); incidental music; orch. works (incl. *La procesión del rocío,* 1912; *Danzas fantásticas,* 1920; *Sinfonía sevillana,* 1920); church music; a string quartet, 2 piano trios, and other chamber music (incl. *Escena andaluza* for viola, string quartet, and piano, 1912; *La oración del torero* for string quartet, 1925); numerous piano pieces; organ pieces; guitar pieces; songs.

Türk, Daniel Gottlob (b. Clausnitz, Saxony, 10 Aug. 1750; d. Halle, 26 Aug. 1813). Violinist, organist, and composer. Pupil of Homilius and J. A. Hiller. Cantor at the Ulrichskirche in Halle, 1776–87. Music director at Halle University, 1779–87. Organist at the Liebfrauenkirche in Halle from 1787. Composed an opera; symphonies; oratorios and cantatas; church music; piano pieces; songs. Published a piano method and several books on music theory.

Turkish crescent [also *Turkish* or *Chinese pavilion* or *hat, jingling Johnny;* F. *chapeau chinois;* G. *Schellenbaum;* Turk. *chaghāna*]. A percussion instrument consisting of a wooden stick surmounted by crescent-shaped crossbars and an ornament shaped like a pavilion or Chinese hat, all hung with numerous small bells and jingles. [For ill. see under Percussion instruments.] The instrument was used in Turkish *Janizary music, whence it was introduced into the military bands of many European nations.

Turn [F. *double cadence, doublé, brisé;* G. *Doppelschlag;* It. *fioritura;* Sp. *grupito*]. An ornament consisting of a group of four or five notes that turn around the principal note. The most common form of turn in the music of the 17th and 18th centuries is indicated by a curved line; it contains four notes and begins on the beat with the note above the written note [Ex. 1].

The sign for the turn was originally used only for the first trill of the compound ornament known as a *double cadence*. The formula shown in Ex. 2 and occurring frequently in the works of J. S. Bach and his contemporaries actually constitutes a single ornament; there should be no break between the turn and the ensuing trill. So closely was the sign in question associated with this formula that it was retained for the isolated turn (as shown in Ex. 1) along with its name, *double cadence*.

In Ex. 2 the sign for the turn is placed slightly to the right of the written note instead of directly above it, showing that the main note should be sounded first. In Bach's works this occurs only when another ornament (generally a trill) is to be played immediately afterward, as in the *double cadence*. Later, however, this practice became quite common, as seen in the accompanying examples by Mozart [Ex. 3] and Beethoven [Ex. 4]. The practice of indicating the turn by small grace notes became popular during the classical period.

The romantic composers often used five- or six-note turns. Their rhythm is exceedingly flexible, the only definite rule being that they are to be performed in the time value of the preceding note [Ex. 5 and 6, Chopin].

Among the unusual forms of turn are the *geschnellter Doppelschlag*, a rapid five-note turn beginning with the main note [Ex. 7, K. P. E. Bach], known in Italy as *gruppo* (*groppo*) or *gruppetto* and in Germany as *Rolle;* the *prallender Doppelschlag*, a turn combined with an appoggiatura and short trill [Ex. 8, K. P. E. Bach]; the *inverted turn*, sometimes indicated by the ordinary sign upside down or in a vertical position but more often represented by tiny notes as in Ex. 9 (Mozart).

Turn of the Screw, The. Opera in two acts and a prologue by Britten (libretto by M. Piper, based on H. James's tale), produced in Venice, 1954.

Turner, William (b. Oxford, 1651; d. London, 13 Jan. 1740). Singer and composer. Chorister at Christ Church, Oxford, and at the Chapel Royal under Cooke. Gentleman of the Chapel Royal from 1669. Vicar choral of St. Paul's Cathedral, London, and lay vicar of Westminster Abbey. Composed services, anthems, and other church music;

occasional works; songs, some for stage works; catches.

Tusch [G.]. A fanfare played on brass instruments. See Tucket.

Tutte le corde. See under *Una corda.*

Tutti [It., all]. In orchestral works, particularly *concertos, indication for passages for the whole orchestra as distinct from those for the soloist.

Twelve-tone technique. See under Serial music.

Twilight of the Gods, The. Wagner's *Götterdämmerung.* See under *Ring des Nibelungen, Der.*

Tye, Christopher (b. *c.* 1500; d. Doddington-cum-Marche, Isle of Ely, 1573). Studied at Cambridge. Master of the choristers at Ely Cathedral, 1541–61. Rector at Doddington from 1561. Composed Masses, motets, and other Latin church music; anthems and other English church music; settings of the Acts of the Apostles; *In nomine* settings and other instrumental pieces.

Tympanon, tympanum [Gr.; L.]. A frame drum beaten with the hand. In the Middle Ages the name designated the kettledrum, although some writers applied it to the *dulcimer. In modern writings *tympani* occurs as a misspelling of *timpani.*

Tyrwhitt-Wilson, Gerald Hugh. See Berners, Lord.

U

Übung [G.]. Excercise, study.

U.c. *Una corda.*

Uccellini, Marco (b. Forlimpopoli?, Italy, *c.* 1603; d. there, 10 Sept. 1680). Violinist and composer. *Maestro di cappella* at the ducal court in Modena, 1641–62; at the cathedral in Modena, 1647–65. Musician at the court in Parma from 1665. Composed an opera; ballets; concerted sacred music; instrumental chamber music, incl. sonatas, canzonas, dances, etc., for the violin, some of which make novel technical demands on the performer, employing the 6th position.

'Ūd, oud [Arab.]. See under Lute.

Ugolini, Vincenzo (b. Perugia, *c.* 1570; d. Rome, 6 May 1638). Pupil of Nanino. *Maestro di cappella* at Santa Maria Maggiore, 1592–1603; at the Benevento Cathedral, 1609–15; at San Luigi dei Francesi in Rome, 1616–20 and 1631 until his death; of the Cappella Giulia at St. Peter's, 1620–26. His pupils incl. Benevoli. Composed Masses, motets, Vesper psalms, and other sacred music, some with thoroughbass; madrigals.

Uguale [It.]. Equal, uniform.

Uhl, Alfred (b. Vienna, 5 June 1909). Pupil of Schmidt. Teacher at the Vienna Academy of Music from 1943. Has composed an opera; ballets; orch. works; a *Konzertante Sinfonie* for clarinet and orch., 1944; an oratorio, *Gilgamesch,* 1956, rev. 1969, a cantata, and other choral works; string quartets and other chamber music; *48 Etudes* for clarinet, 1938.

Uhlig, Theodor (b. Wurzen, near Leipzig, 15 Feb. 1822; d. Dresden, 3 Jan. 1853). Pupil of F. Schneider. Violinist in the Dresden court orchestra from 1841. Associate of Wagner and Liszt. Composed *Singspiele;* symphonies; a violin concerto; choral works; chamber music; piano pieces; songs. Published writings on music theory.

Uilleann pipes. Irish *bagpipe. The name was later corrupted into "union pipes."

Ukrainian Symphony. Tchaikovsky's Symphony no. 2 in C minor, op. 17 (1872), also called *Little-Russian Symphony,* "Little Russia" being the common 19th-century name for the Ukraine.

Ukulele. A Hawaiian instrument of the guitar family, with four strings and a long fingerboard, usually fretted. It probably developed from a Portuguese guitar called a *machete*. It became popular in the United States c. 1920. See ill. under Guitar family. See also Tablature.

Umlauff, Ignaz (Umlauf) (b. Vienna, 1746; d. Meidling, near Vienna, 8 June 1796). Violinist at the Vienna court theater from 1772. Conductor of the Nationalsingspiel in Vienna from 1778. Second *Kapellmeister* to Salieri at the Viennese court from 1789. Composed *Singspiele* (incl. *Die Bergknappen*, Vienna, 1778; *Das Irrlicht*, Vienna, 1782); other music for the stage; church music; chamber music.

Umstimmen [G.]. To change the tuning, e.g., of kettledrums.

Un ballo in maschera [It.]. See *Ballo in maschera, Un*.

Un peu [F.], **un poco** [It.]. See *Peu; Poco*.

Una corda [It., one string]. In piano playing, direction (abbr. *u.c.*) to use the left pedal (soft pedal; F. *pédale douce;* G. *Verschiebung*), which, by moving the entire action, keyboard, and hammers (on grand pianos; see Piano) a little to the right, causes the hammers to strike a single string (in modern instruments usually two strings) instead of all three. The indication is canceled by *tre corde* or *tutte le corde* (*t.c.;* "three strings" or "all strings"). See Mute.

Unequal voices. Mixture of men's and women's voices.

Unfinished Symphony. Schubert's Symphony no. 8 in B minor, D. 759, so called because only the first two movements exist. They were written in 1822, six years before the composer's death. That Schubert intended to complete the work appears from the fact that he had sketched out the beginning of the Scherzo. Schubert sent the two movements to his friend Hüttenbrenner, and not until the latter's death in 1868 was the work published, though its first performance took place in 1865.

Ungarische Tänze. See *Hungarian Dances*.

Ungebunden [G.]. Unrestrained, free.

Ungerader Takt [G.]. Uneven, i.e., triple, meter.

Ungestüm [G.]. Violent, raging.

Union pipes. See Uilleann pipes.

Unis [F.]. In orchestral music, unison (after **divisi*). In organ music, it means 8' pitch (stops) only; also, without octave couplers.

Unison (1) Simultaneous performance of the same notes or melody by various instruments or by the whole orchestra, either at exactly the same pitch or in different octaves, e.g., violin and cello in unison (*all'unisono*). (2) The **interval formed by a tone and its duplication [G. *Prime*], e.g., c–c, as distinguished from the second, c–d, etc.

Unisono, all' [It.]. See Unison; *A due*.

Unmerklich [G.]. Imperceptible.

Unruhig [G.]. Restless.

Unterwerk [G.]. **Choir organ.

Upbeat. Anacrusis. One or several notes that occur before the first complete measure and thus before the first metrically accented **beat (downbeat) of a work or phrase. Sometimes also called the pickup.

Uribe Holguín, Guillermo (b. Bogotá, Colombia, 17 Mar. 1880; d. there, 26 June 1971). Pupil of d'Indy. Director of the National Conservatory in Bogotá, 1910–35. Worked with native Colombian materials. Composed an opera; 11 symphonies and other orch. works; a piano concerto and 2 violin concertos; sacred choral works; string quartets and other chamber music; piano pieces (incl. about 350 *Trozos en el sentimiento popular*); songs.

Urio, Francesco Antonio (b. Milan, *c*. 1660). *Maestro di cappella* at the Church of the 12 Apostles in Rome in 1690; at the Church of the Frari in Venice in 1697; at other times at churches in Assisi and Genoa. Composed motets, psalms, and other church music, some with instruments (incl. a *Te Deum* from which Handel borrowed material for his *Dettingen Te Deum*).

Urlar. See under Pibroch.

Urrutia Blondel, Jorge (b. La Serena,

Chile, 17 Sept. 1905). Pupil of Allende, Santa Cruz, Koechlin, Dukas, N. Boulanger, and Hindemith. Teacher at the Santiago Conservatory from 1931. Has worked with Chilean folk materials. Has composed a ballet, *La guitarra del diablo,* 1942; other stage works; orch. works; choral works; chamber music; piano pieces; songs.

Usandizaga, José María (b. San Sebastián, Spain, 31 Mar. 1887; d. there, 5 Oct. 1915). Pupil of d'Indy. Worked with native Basque and Spanish musical materials. Composed operas (incl. *Mendy-Mendiyan,* Bilbao, 1910; *Las golondrinas,* Madrid, 1914); orch. works; vocal works; 2 string quartets; numerous piano pieces; organ pieces.

Usper, Francesco (Francesco Spongia) (b. Parenzo, Istria, late 16th cent.; d. Venice, early 1641). Pupil of A. Gabrieli and Monteverdi. Organist in Venice at San Salvatore, *c.* 1614; at San Marco, 1621–23. Director of the school of San Giovanni Evangelista in Venice from 1627. Composed Masses, motets, Vesper psalms and other concerted sacred music; instrumental chamber music, incl. ensemble canzonas, trio sonatas, and violin sonatas, the latter among the first pieces to use the tremolo; madrigals.

Ussachevsky, Vladimir (b. Hailar, Manchuria, of Russian parents, 3 Nov. [21 Oct. old style] 1911). Settled in the U.S. in 1930. Pupil of Hanson, Bernard Rogers, and Luening. Teacher at Columbia Univ., 1947–72; at the Univ. of Utah from 1972. Co-director of the Columbia-Princeton Electronic Music Center from 1959. Has composed orch. works; a

piano concerto, 1951; choral works (incl. a *Jubilee Cantata* for narrator, baritone, chorus, and orch., 1938; *The Creation* for 4 choruses, orch., and tape, 1961); electronic works (incl. *Sonic Contours* for tape and instruments, 1952; *Incantation,* on tape, with Luening, 1953; *Poem of Cycles and Bels* for tape and orch., with Luening, 1954; *Piece for Tape Recorder,* 1956; *Computer Piece* no. 1, 1969).

Ustvol'skaia, Galina Ivanovna (b. Petrograd, 17 July 1919). Pupil of M. Steinberg and Shostakovich. Teacher at the Leningrad Conservatory from 1948. Has composed 2 symphonies (no. 1, 1955, for 2 boy sopranos and orch.; no. 2, 1967, for voice, winds, percussion, and piano) and other orch. works; a piano concerto, 1946; *The Dream of Stenka Razin* for bass and orch., 1948; chamber music; 3 sonatas and other piano pieces; music for films.

Ut. The first of the Guidonian syllables of solmization; see Hexachord. In French nomenclature, name for C [see Pitch names].

Ut supra [L.]. As above, as before.

Uttini, Francesco Antonio Baldassare (b. Bologna, 1723; d. Stockholm, 25 Oct. 1795). Pupil of Padre Martini. President of the Accademia dei filarmonici in Bologna from 1751. Conductor of an Italian opera company in Stockholm from 1755 and conductor of the court opera there, 1767–88. Composed operas in Italian, French, and Swedish (incl. *Thetis och Pelée,* the first opera on a Swedish text, Stockholm, 1773); sacred music; trio sonatas and other instrumental pieces.

V

V. Abbr. for (1) *vide,* see; (2) *violin* (also abbr. V°); *VV,* violins; (3) *voci,* e.g., 3 v, for three voices; (4) in liturgical books, ℣ means *verse or versicle.

Va. Abbr. for *viola.*

Vaccai, Nicola (b. Tolentino, Italy, 15

Mar. 1790; d. Pesaro, 5 Aug. 1848). Singer and composer. Pupil of Paisiello. Singing teacher at various times in Venice, Trieste, Vienna, Paris, and London. Teacher at the Milan Conservatory, 1838 –44. Composed operas (incl. *Giulietta e Romeo,* Milan, 1825, the last scene of which was sometimes used in productions of Bellini's *I Capuleti e i Montecchi*); sacred choral works; cantatas; songs; pedagogic works.

Vaet, Jacobus (b. Courtrai or Harlebeke, Flanders, 1529; d. Vienna, 8 Jan. 1567). Chorister at Notre Dame in Courtrai, 1543–46. *Kapellmeister* from 1554 until his death to Maximilian, then King of Bohemia and from 1564 Emperor Maximilian II in Vienna. Composed Masses, motets (incl. some for state occasions), Magnificats, hymns; chansons.

Vaghezza, con [It.]. With longing; with charm.

Vainberg, Moissei Samuilovich (b. Warsaw, 8 Dec. 1919). Studied at the Warsaw Conservatory. Settled in Moscow in 1943. Has composed operas; ballets; 11 symphonies and other orch. works; works for solo instruments with orch. (incl. a cello concerto; a trumpet concerto; *Moldavian Rhapsody* for violin and orch.); string quartets and other chamber music; piano pieces; songs; music for films.

Valderrábano, Enríquez de (b. Peñaranda de Duero, Spain, fl. 16th cent.). Vihuelist and composer. Court musician to the Count of Miranda. Compiled the *Libro de musica de vihuela, intitulado Silva de Sirenas*, a tablature book containing transcriptions and original compositions for vihuela.

Valen, (Olav) Fartein (b. Stavanger, Norway, 25 Aug. 1887; d. Valevåg, 14 Dec. 1952). Studied in Oslo and with Bruch in Berlin. Music librarian at Oslo Univ., 1927–38. Composed 5 symphonies and other orch. works; concertos for piano and for violin; choral works; works for soprano and orch.; string quartets and other chamber music; piano pieces; organ pieces; songs.

Valkyrie, The. Wagner's *Die Walküre*. See under *Ring des Nibelungen, Der*.

Valle, Francisco (Valls) (b. Barcelona, 1665 or *c.* 1672; d. there, 2 Feb. or July 1747). *Maestro de capilla* in Gerona, 1688–96. Assistant *maestro de capilla* at the Barcelona Cathedral from 1696 and *maestro* there from 1709. Composed Masses, motets, and other church music.

Valse [F.]; **vals** [Sp.]. *Waltz. Valse à*

deux temps, a waltz whose melody proceeds in units of two beats instead of three, in cross-rhythm with the accompaniment. The best-known example is in Gounod's *Faust*.

Valse, La. "Poème choréographique" (dance poem) for orchestra by Ravel, composed in 1920, imitating and cleverly parodying the Viennese waltz of Johann Strauss, Jr. It is often used for ballet performances.

Valse triste [F., Sad Waltz]. A popular waltz for orchestra by Sibelius, originally composed (1903) as part of the incidental music to the play *Kuolema*.

Valses nobles et sentimentales. A set of waltzes for piano by Ravel, composed in 1911 and later orchestrated by the composer to serve as music for the ballet *Adélaïde, ou Le langage des fleurs*. The title ("Noble and Sentimental Waltzes") alludes to Schubert's *Valses nobles* op. 77 and *Valses sentimentales* op. 50 for piano.

Valve [F. *piston;* G. *Ventil;* It. *pistone;* Sp. *pistón*]. A mechanism invented *c.* 1815 by Blühmel (in Silesia) and, simultaneously, by Stölzel (in Berlin) that makes available all the tones of the chromatic scale on brass instruments. The device alters an instrument's pitch by increasing or decreasing the tube length through which the wind must pass. Descending valves bring extra lengths of tube (loops) into play, lowering the pitch; ascending valves eliminate a portion of the main tubing, raising the pitch. Horns and trumpets usually have three valves, which lower the pitch a whole tone, semitone, and minor third, respectively. Using one, two, or all three valves together can lower the pitch by as many as six semitones, making possible a complete chromatic scale [see Wind instruments].

Two types of valve are in use, piston valves and rotary (or cylinder) valves. In the former a piston works up and down in a casing. The rotary valve, preferred for the French horn in the United States and on the Continent though not in England, is a four-way stopcock turning in a cylindrical case and controlled by a metal spring. See Horn; Trumpet; Tuba; Wind instruments.

Valve instruments. Brass instruments provided with a *valve mechanism. Today all brass instruments (trumpets, horns, tubas, etc.) except the trombone are built with valves. The terms *valve horn, valve trumpet,* etc., distinguish the modern instruments from the earlier *natural or keyed instruments.

Van Hagen, Peter Albrecht (b. Holland, 1750; d. Boston, 1803). Settled in the U.S. in 1774, living first in Charleston, S.C., then in New York, 1798–96, and thereafter in Boston. Composed music for the theater; a *Federal Overture,* 1797; *Funeral Dirge for George Washington,* 1800.

Van Vactor, David (b. Plymouth, Ind., 8 May 1906). Studied at Northwestern Univ. with Oldberg and Borowski, at the Vienna Academy with Schmidt, at the Paris Conservatory with Dukas. Flutist with the Chicago Symphony, 1931–47. Teacher at the Univ. of Tennessee and conductor of the Knoxville Symphony from 1947. Has composed ballets (incl. *Suite on Chilean Folk Tunes,* 1963); 2 symphonies and other orch. works (incl. *Overture to a Comedy* nos. 1 and 2, 1923 and 1941; *Variazioni solenne,* 1941; *Music for the Marines,* 1943; *Fantasia, Chaconne, and Allegro,* 1957; *Sinfonia breve,* 1964); concertos for flute, for viola, for violin, and for 3 flutes and harp; choral works (incl. *Walden,* with orch., 1969); string quartets and other chamber music; works for voice and piano.

Vanessa. Opera in four acts by Barber (libretto by G. C. Menotti), produced in New York, 1958.

Vaňhal, Jan Křtitel (Johann Baptist Wanhal) (b. Nechanice, Bohemia, 12 May 1739; d. Vienna, 20 Aug. 1813). Studied with Dittersdorf in Vienna, where he later settled, and in Italy. Composed operas; about 100 symphonies; numerous concertos; much church music; about 100 string quartets and much other chamber music; numerous piano pieces; organ pieces; songs.

Varèse, Edgard (-Victor-Achille-Charles) (b. Paris, 22 Dec. 1883; d. New York, 6 Nov. 1965). Conductor and composer. Studied in Turin and with d'Indy, Roussel, and Widor in Paris. Lived in Berlin, 1909–14; principally in New York after 1915. Founded the New Symphony Orchestra, 1919; the International Composers' Guild, with Salzedo, 1921; the Pan-American Association of Composers, with Slonimsky, Cowell, Ives, and Chávez, 1928. Began to experiment with electronic means in the 1920s. Works incl. *Amériques* for orch., 1921; *Offrandes* for soprano and orch., 1922; *Hyperprism,* for woodwinds, brass, percussion, 1923; *Octandre* for 7 winds and double bass, 1924; *Intégrales* for woodwinds, brass, percussion, 1925; *Arcana* for orch., 1927; *Ionisation* for percussion and 2 sirens, 1931; *Equatorial* for bass, brass, piano, organ, Theremins, percussion, 1934; *Density 21.5* for flute, 1936; *Déserts* for winds, brass, percussion, tape, 1949–54; *Poème électronique,* on tape, 1958; *Nocturnal* for soprano, chorus of basses, and orch, 1961, completed by Chou Wen-chung, 1968.

Variation. The modification or transformation of a musical idea in a way that retains one or more essential features of the original. Also the result of such modification or transformation. A wide range of techniques may be used in the process, including *ornamentation, *transposition, *inversion, *retrograde motion, *augmentation, *imitation, *diminution, change of tempo, and rhythmic alteration of various kinds. The elements most likely to play a fundamental role in variation are melody, harmony, and phrase structure, one or more of which usually provides the basis for identification of the original material with its varied form.

Usually the term refers to the immediate restatement, in varied form, of a musical theme (tune). Examples are the varied repeat, the *double,* and the musical form known as "theme with variations." The varied repeat is often used in the late 16th-century *pavane, each of whose three sections is repeated in a varied form. The *double* is a simple variation on a dance of a suite. The theme with variations is a musical form resulting from the consistent application of variation techniques so that a musical theme is followed by a number of modified restatements, each called a variation. Such compositions appear as independent works (Bach, Goldberg Variations, *Clavier-Übung,* part IV; Beethoven, Diabelli Variations op. 120) or as a movement of a sonata or symphony, usually the slow movement (Beethoven, Appassionata Sonata op. 57; Ninth Symphony).

The theme in this last type is usually a simple tune in binary form, from 16 to 32 measures long and frequently borrowed from another composer (e.g., Beethoven's variations on a theme by Diabelli; Brahms' variations on a theme by Handel, op. 24, for piano solo with fugue). There is, however, a special kind of variation technique in which the theme is not a complete tune but only a four- or eight-measure scheme of harmonies or a bass line of the same length. Of this kind are the examples known as *chaconne, passacaglia, *ground, and basso ostinato. These two kinds of variations might be distinguished as "sectional variations" and "continuous variations." In sectional variations the theme is a full-grown tune with a definite ending, and hence each variation has a definite end (except in cases where the composer prescribes segue subito, "follow immediately," with the next variation). In continuous variations the theme is a short succession of harmonies to be repeated over and over without interruption.

Stability of the harmonic scheme at least in its main outlines is a prerequisite for practically all variations, except the entirely free variations of modern composers (e.g., Stravinsky, Sonata for Two Pianos, 2nd movt. [1943–44]). Stability of the melody is an additional restriction that was traditionally observed in the early period of variation (16th and 17th cent.) but is the exception rather than the rule with composers such as Mozart, Beethoven, Schubert, and Brahms.

Occasionally in sectional variations the melody is retained but the harmonies are altered, as for example, in variation no. 6 of Beethoven's Eroica Variations op. 35, in which the original melody is harmonized in C minor instead of E♭ major. This technique was most important in the contrapuntal variations of the baroque, in which the melody is treated as a *cantus firmus surrounded with contrapuntal parts, sometimes imitative or even canonic in nature.

The documented history of variations as a musical form begins in the early 16th century. Judging from the surviving examples, Spain and England have about an equal claim to precedence, England in continuous variations (H. Aston's "Hornepype"; "My Lady Careys Dompe," both c. 1525; see Dump; Ostinato), and Spain in both continuous variations and sectional variations based on a fully developed theme (vihuela variations by Narváez, 1538). By 1550 the evolution of the Spanish variations, called *diferencias [see also Glosa], had culminated in the works of Antonio de Cabezón (c. 1510–66). Cabezón's variations are mostly contrapuntal, a type that continued to prevail with the later masters (Sweelinck, Scheidt, Frescobaldi). Toward the end of the 16th century the English virginalists (Byrd, Bull, J. Munday, Gibbons) established the figural variation, frequently in brilliant virtuoso style (rapid scales, broken-chord figures, figures in parallel thirds, etc.).

In Italy the traceable history of variations begins with the 16th- and 17th-century Neapolitan composers Valente, Trabaci, and A. Mayone, who, probably influenced by Cabezón, wrote *partitas to popular bass patterns such as the *romanesca, *ruggiero, zefiro, etc. [see also Folia]. Their tradition was continued in the numerous partitas of Frescobaldi (1583–1643). Froberger's (1616–67) partitas "Auff die Meyerin" are the first examples of variations in the style of dances. They represent a trend, quite common in the baroque era, toward merging the form of variations with that of the *suite. Of particular importance is the German 17th-century tradition of variations based on a chorale [see Chorale variations]. For other types, see Chaconne and passacaglia; Ground; Strophic bass; Noel.

Compared to the elaborate variation technique of the baroque, that of Mozart's piano variations is fairly simple and standardized. The first variations usually are ornamented with triplets or sixteenth notes, followed by some with special pianistic or contrapuntal devices. After these there is usually a slow variation, sometimes in a minor key, and then a final fast variation in a different meter (duple instead of triple, or vice versa). Haydn's greatest contributions to the repertory are in his symphonies and, particularly, in his late quartets, notably the Emperor Quartet (op. 76, no. 3, 2nd movt.) with its variations on "Gott erhalte Franz den Kaiser." For the more conventional methods, particularly ornamentation, Beethoven substituted a wealth of individual treatments and ideas. He was also the first to organize the succession of variations into contrasting groups, a procedure particularly evident in his "continuous" variations in C minor op. 32 (sometimes described as a chaconne). Other important examples are his Eroica Variations op. 35, Diabelli Variations op. 120 (1823), and movements from the piano sonatas op. 109 and op. 111.

Franz Schubert contributed to the genre in such works as his variations for piano four-hands in B minor op. 84, no. 1, and in Ab major op. 35. Schumann's greatest contributions are the *Études symphoniques* op. 13, the first instance of free variations, since in some of them the theme serves as no more than a springboard.

Franz Liszt made use of a brilliant, virtuosic variation technique in many of his rhapsodies as well as in his variations on a theme by Paganini (his *Paganini Etudes, no. 6), one also used by Brahms. However, Brahms' fame as a master of this form rests chiefly on his Variations on a Theme by Handel (op. 24) for piano and his orchestral Variations on a Theme by Haydn (op. 56; also for two pianos). In his variations Brahms treats the harmonies with considerable freedom while still retaining the structural outlines of the theme. Following the precedent of Beethoven's Eroica and Diabelli Variations, he climaxes the series of variations with an elaborate fugue (in the Haydn Variations, a passacaglia).

Shortly before 1900 two important examples of "free variation" appeared, Vincent d'Indy's *Istar* Variations (1896) and Richard Strauss' *Don Quixote* (1897). The former are "variations in reverse" insofar as the "theme" (properly, two thematic motifs) appears at the end, a procedure of "disrobing" that is implied by the story of Istar, the Babylonian goddess of love. Compared to these two works, Elgar's *Enigma Variations* are considerably more conven-

tional, approximately along the lines of Schumann's *Études symphoniques*. Reger's numerous variations continued this tradition. Among later composers of variations are Busoni, Krenek, Webern, and Copland.

Variations on a Theme by Diabelli (Handel, etc.). See under *Diabelli Variations, Handel Variations, etc.*

Variations symphoniques [F., Symphonic Variations]. Work for piano and orchestra by Franck (composed 1885) in which the expected theme-and-variations structure is expanded by a developmental treatment more characteristic of a symphony with two themes.

Varsovienne. A Polish dance, named for the city of Warsaw, in slow mazurka rhythm, usually with an accented dotted note on the first beat of every second and fourth measure. It was popular in ballrooms from about 1850 to 1870.

Vásquez, Juan (b. Badajoz, Spain, c. 1500; d. Seville, c. 1560). *Maestro de capilla* at the Badajoz Cathedral, 1545–51. Served various noble families in and around Seville thereafter. Composed polyphonic settings of *villancicos, canciones,* and sonnets; an Office and a Mass for the dead.

Vassilenko, Sergei Nikiforovich (b. Moscow, 30 Mar. 1872; d. there, 11 Mar. 1956). Conductor and composer. Pupil of Grechaninov, Taneiev, and Ippolitov-Ivanov. Teacher at the Moscow Conservatory, 1906–50. Composed operas (incl. *Buran,* Tashkent, 1939, employing Uzbek materials); ballets; 5 symphonies and other orch. works (incl. *Hircus nocturnus,* 1909; *Chinese Suite,* 1927; *Hindu Suite,* 1927; *Uzbek Suite,* 1942); concertos for violin, for cello, for trumpet, for balalaika; choral works; string quartets and other chamber music; piano pieces; songs and arrangements of folksongs.

Vater unser [G., Our Father]. German version of the Lord's Prayer [L. *Pater noster*]. It is sung as a hymn [G. *Choral*] to a 16th-century melody (by Luther?) that has been used as the basis for compositions by Hans Leo Hassler, Bach (organ chorales), and others.

Vaudeville [F.]. In the late 16th century, a song with a short lyrical or amorous text, composed in a simple chordal style with the melody in the highest voice. The preface to A. Le Roy and R. Ballard's *Livre d'airs de cour* (1571) states that the songs formerly called *voix de ville* (same as *vaudeville?*) were now called *airs de cour. Despite this alleged transformation, the *vaudeville* continued an independent existence as a satirical poem sung to a popular melody (usually preexistent). The same melody (*timbre*) commonly served for many different texts. The *vaudeville* was the principal type of song in the early *opéra comique* (1715–c. 1735). In the 19th century, *vaudeville* was the name given to short comedies interspersed with popular songs. More recently, in the U.S., the name has been used for miscellaneous popular entertainments, including songs, presented in cafés or variety theaters.

Vaughan Williams, Ralph (b. Down Ampney, Gloucestershire, 12 Oct. 1872; d. London, 26 Aug. 1958). Pupil of C. Wood, W. Parratt, Parry, Stanford, Bruch, and Ravel. Teacher at the Royal College of Music from 1919. Active as a collector of folksongs. Conducted and lectured in the U.S. on several occasions. Composed operas (incl. *The Shepherds of the Delectable Mountains*, after Bunyan, London, 1922; *Hugh the Drover*, London, 1924; *Sir John in Love*, after Shakespeare's *Merry Wives of Windsor*, London, 1929; *The Poisoned Kiss*, Cambridge, 1936; *Riders to the Sea*, on the play of J. M. Synge, London, 1937; *The Pilgrim's Progress*, after Bunyan, incorporating *The Shepherds of the Delectable Mountains*, London, 1951); ballets; incidental music for Aristophanes' *The Wasps*, 1909; 9 symphonies (no. 1, **Sea Symphony;* no. 2, *London Symphony*, 1913; no. 3, *Pastoral Symphony*, 1922) and other orch. works (incl. *3 Norfolk Rhapsodies*, 1906–7, nos. 2 and 3 withdrawn; *In the Fen Country*, 1904, rev. 1905, 1907, 1935; *Fantasia on a Theme by Tallis* for strings, 1910; *Job*, a masque for dancing, 1930; *5 Variants of "Dives and Lazarus,"* 1939; *Fantasia on "Greensleeves,"* arranged by Ralph Greaves from *Sir Robert in Love*, 1934); works for solo instrument with orch.

(incl. *The Lark Ascending* for violin, 1914; *Concerto accademico* for violin, 1925; a piano concerto, also arranged for 2 pianos, 1933; a suite for viola, 1934; an oboe concerto, 1944; *Romance* for harmonica, 1952; a tuba concerto, 1954); *Folksong Suite* for band; choral works (incl. *Toward the Unknown Region*, 1905, rev. 1918; *Flos campi* for viola, chorus, and orch., 1925; the oratorio *Sancta Civitas*, 1926; *5 Tudor Portraits*, 1936; the cantata *The Sons of Light*, 1951; the cantata *Hodie*, 1953); a Mass, motets, services, and other church music; 2 string quartets and other chamber music; piano pieces; organ pieces; numerous songs; music for films. Published some of his lectures, other writings, and editions of folksongs and other music.

Vcl. Abbr. for *violoncello*, i.e., cello.

Vecchi, Orazio (b. Modena, bapt. 6 Dec. 1550; d. there, 19 or 20 Feb. 1605). *Maestro di cappella* at Salò, 1581–84; at the cathedral in Modena, 1584–86; at Reggio Emilia in 1586. Canon at Correggio, 1586–95. *Maestro di cappella* at the Modena Cathedral, 1596–1604, and at the court in Modena from 1598. Composed the madrigal comedy *L'Amfiparnaso*, Modena, 1594; madrigals and *canzonette;* Masses, motets, and other church music; instrumental pieces.

Vega, Aurelio de la (b. Havana, 28 Nov. 1925). Critic and composer. Studied in Havana and with Toch and Pisk. Dean of the school of music at the Universidad de Oriente in Santiago de Cuba, 1954–59. Teacher at California State Univ. at Northridge from 1960. Has worked with serial techniques. Has composed orch. works (incl. *Overture to a Serious Farce*, 1950; *Symphony in 4 Parts*, 1960; *Intrata*, 1972); chamber music (incl. *Structures* for piano and string quartet, 1962; *Segments* for piano and violin, 1964); piano pieces; electronic works (incl. *Vectors*, on tape, 1963; *Tangents* for violin and tape, 1973).

Vejvanovský, Pavel Josef (b. Hlučín, Bohemian Silesia, or Hukvaldy, Moravia, c. 1640; d. Kroměříž, buried 24 June 1693). Trumpeter at Kroměříž from 1664 and *Kapellmeister* there from 1670.

Composed Masses, motets, Vespers, and other church music; sonatas, *balletti*, and other instrumental music.

Velato [It.]. Veiled, subdued.

Veloce [It.]. Fast.

Venetian school. A 16th-century school of Flemish and Italian composers working in Venice. Inaugurated by Adrian Willaert (*c*. 1490–1562; appointed *maestro di cappella* at St. Mark's in 1527), it included his pupils Andrea Gabrieli (*c*. 1520–86) and Cipriano de Rore (1516–65), as well as Gioseffe Guami (*c*. 1540–1611), Giovanni Gabrieli (*c*. 1555–1612), and Giovanni Croce (*c*. 1557–1609); also the organ composers Jacques Buus (d. 1565), Annibale Padovano (*c*. 1527–75), and Claudio Merulo (1533–1604); and the theorists Nicola Vicentino (1511–76) and Gioseffo Zarlino (1517–90).

Among their contributions are Willaert's chromaticism and freer use of modulation, the toccata style of A. Gabrieli and C. Merulo, and G. Gabrieli's broad masses of sound, *polychoral treatment, echo effects, and progressive use of instruments, the latter setting the Venetian school particularly apart from composers of the contemporaneous *Roman school. The style spread especially to Germany, where Jacobus Gallus (Händl, 1550–91), Hieronymus Praetorius (1560–1629), Hans Leo Hassler (1564–1612), and Michael Praetorius (1571–1621) became the most important representatives of the Venetian style. Among the German composers influenced by this school was Heinrich Schütz (1585–1672), who studied in Venice with G. Gabrieli.

Venetian swell. See under Swell.

Veni Sancte Spiritus [L.]. The *sequence for Whitsunday (Pentecost).

Venite exsultemus [L.]. See under Invitatory.

Vent [F.]. Wind. *Instruments à vent,* *wind instruments.

Ventil [G.]; **ventile** [It.]. *Valve. *Ventilhorn* [G.], valve horn.

Veracini, Francesco Maria (b. Florence, 1 Feb. 1690; d. there, 31 Oct. 1768). Solo violinist at the Italian Opera in London in 1714; at the Dresden court, 1717–23. In London, where he composed operas, 1735–45. Toured widely as a virtuoso. Composed operas; violin concertos; symphonies; oratorios and cantatas; 24 violin sonatas with thoroughbass; arias.

Veränderungen [G.]. *Variations.

Verbunkos [Hung.]. A Hungarian soldiers' dance that was used to attract recruits for enlistment in the army. The name is a corruption of G. *Werbung,* enlistment. The dance was used from *c*. 1780 until 1849, when the Austrian government imposed conscription, and it has survived as a ceremonial dance. In its fully developed form it consisted of two or more sections, some in the character of a slow introduction (*lassu*), others very rapid and wild (*friss*). Many collections of *verbunkos* were published during the 19th century. In art music, the *verbunkos* were imitated by Liszt (Hungarian Rhapsody no. 2), Bartók (rhapsodies for piano or violin with orchestra), and Kodály (Intermezzo from the opera *Háry János*).

Verdelot, Philippe (b. probably Caderousse, near Orange, France; d. Florence?, before 1552). Lived principally in Italy. *Maestro di cappella* at San Giovanni in Florence, 1523–27. Composed Masses and motets; madrigals, of which he was among the first composers; chansons.

Verdi, Giuseppe (Fortunino Francesco) (b. Le Roncole, near Busseto, Parma, 10 Oct. 1813; d. Milan, 27 Jan. 1901). Studied in Busseto and privately with Vincenzo Lavigna in Milan, where he had failed to gain admission to the Conservatory. Director of the music school and the Philharmonic Society in Busseto, 1835–38, after which he returned to Milan. Visited London in 1847 and lived nearly two years thereafter in Paris. Returned in 1849 to Italy, where he lived in relative seclusion in Busseto with his second wife, making occasional trips to oversee the production of new operas. Works: operas (*Oberto, Conte di San Bonifacio,* Milan, 1839; *Un giorno di regno, ossia Il finto Stanislao,* Milan, 1840; *Nabucco; I Lombardi alla prima *crociata*, Milan, 1843, rev. for Paris as *Jérusalem*, 1847; **Ernani; I due Foscari*, Rome, 1844; *Giovanna d'Arco*, Milan, 1845; *Alzira*, Naples, 1845; *Attila*, Venice, 1846; **Macbeth; I masnadieri*, London, 1847; *Il corsaro*, Trieste, 1848; *La battaglia di Legnano*, Rome, 1849; *Luisa Miller*, Naples, 1849; *Stiffelio*, Trieste, 1850, rev. as *Aroldo*, Rimini, 1857; **Rigoletto; Il *trovatore; La *traviata; Les vêpres siciliennes*, Paris, 1855, Italian version first called *Giovanna di Guzman* and later *I vespri siciliani*, Milan, 1856; **Simon Boccanegra; Un *ballo in maschera; La *forza del destino; *Don Carlos; *Aida; *Otello; *Falstaff*); sacred choral works (incl. the **Manzoni Requiem; Pater noster*, 1880; *4 pezzi sacri*, incl. *Ave Maria, Stabat Mater, Te Deum*, and *Laudi alla Vergine Maria*, 1898); 2 cantatas; *Ave Maria* for soprano and strings, 1880; a string quartet, 1873; songs.

Veress, Sándor (b. Kolozsvár, Hungary, 1 Feb. 1907). Pupil of Bartók, Kodály, and Lajtha. Assisted Bartók in Budapest in work on folk music, 1936–41. Teacher at the Budapest Academy of Music, 1943 –48; at the Bern Conservatory from 1950; at Bern Univ. from 1968. Has composed ballets; 2 symphonies and other orch. works; concertos for piano, for violin, and for string quartet and orch.; choral works; string quartets and other chamber music; piano pieces; songs.

Verhallend [G.]. Fading away.

Verismo [It.]. An Italian operatic school of the late 19th century that is the musical counterpart of the literary realism of Zola, Flaubert, Ibsen, and others. Instead of the idealistic librettos of earlier operas, realistic subjects from everyday life were chosen, often embellished with violent and theatrical incidents. Coloratura arias and other features of earlier Italian opera were abandoned in favor of a melodramatic recitative that was considered more naturalistic. Mascagni's *Cavalleria rusticana* of 1890 (scenes from peasant life) and Leoncavallo's *I pagliacci* of 1892 (circus life) were the first products of the new movement. They were followed, in 1900, by Charpentier's more naturalistic *Louise*, to which, however, the term "naturalism"

is usually applied instead. Puccini's *La bohème* (1896) represents a somewhat modified, more lyrical veristic opera.

Verklärte Nacht [G., Transfigured Night]. Sextet in one movement, for two violins, two violas, and two cellos, by Schoenberg (op. 4, 1899), inspired by a poem of R. Dehmel. It was later arranged for full string orchestra, and finally became the music for the ballet *Pillar of Fire*.

Verrall, John (Weedon) (b. Britt, Iowa, 17 June 1908). Pupil of R. O. Morris, Kodály, D. Ferguson, Copland, Harris, and Jacobi. Teacher at Hamline Univ., 1934–42; Mt. Holyoke College, 1942–46; Univ. of Washington, 1948–73. Has composed 3 operas; 2 symphonies and other orch. works; concertos for violin, for viola, for piano; choral works; 7 string quartets and other chamber music; piano pieces. Has published 2 books on music theory.

Vers [F., G.]. (1) See Verse (2). (2) See under *Canzo*. (3) [F.] A line of a poem. (4) [G.] A stanza of a poem.

Vers mesuré [F.]. Late 16th-century French poetry resulting from the application of the quantitative principles of classical Greek and Latin, also known as *vers mesurés à l'antique*. This type of poetry became established mainly through Jean Antoine de Baïf, founder of the Académie de poésie et musique, who in 1567 translated the psalms into *vers mesuré* and also wrote *chansonettes mesurées*. Some composers set texts of this kind in a homophonic style in which all short syllables were set with notes of a single rhythmic value, and all long syllables were set with a rhythmic value twice as long. Called *musique mesurée*, such settings consist of an irregular succession of, e.g., the equivalent of half notes and quarter notes. This style was similar to and in part merged with the **air de cour*. The foremost composers of *musique mesurée* were Claude Le Jeune (c. 1530–1600), Jacques Mauduit (1557– 1627), and François Eustache Du Caurroy (1549–1609).

Verschiebung [G.]. Soft pedal. See *Una corda;* Mute.

Verschwindend [G.]. Disappearing, fading away.

Verse [F. *vers;* G. *Vers;* It., Sp. *verso;* L. *versus*]. (1) In poetry, a line of metrical writing; also a larger unit, e.g., a stanza of a poem. [See Vers (3) (4).] (2) In Gregorian chant, the term (abbreviated ℣) denotes a verse of a psalm or canticle, or a sentence from other scriptural texts. Single verses of this kind are found chiefly in *Graduals, *Alleluias, *Introits, and *responsories [see Psalmody II, III]. They are always sung by the soloist (though usually with a short choral opening). Association of plainsong verse with solo singing survived in the verse service and verse *anthem of the Anglican Church, settings that include sections for solo voices as distinguished from the purely choral full service and full anthem. (3) For organ verse, see Verset.

Verset [F. *verset;* G. *Versett, Versetl;* It. *verso, versetto;* Sp. *versillo*]. Organ verse, i.e., a short organ piece, usually in fugal style, designed to be played in place of a plainsong *verse of a psalm, canticle, or other short item of the service such as a section of a Kyrie. From the 16th to 18th centuries it was customary to have alternate verses of a psalm or canticle replaced by organ versets, in alternation with plainsong performance for the others [see Magnificat].

Versetto [It.]. *Verset.

Versetzung [G.]. *Transposition. *Versetzungszeichen,* *accidental.

Versicle. In the Roman Catholic and Anglican rites, a short text from the Scriptures or another source sung by the officiant, to which the choir (or the congregation) responds in like fashion, e.g., "℣. Dominus vobiscum. ℟. Et cum spiritu tuo" (℣. The Lord be with you. ℟. And with thy spirit). Also, a line from a sequence [see Sequence (2)].

Versillo [Sp.]. *Verset.

Verso [It.]. *Verse; *verset.

Verstärken [G.]. To reinforce (the sound).

Verstovsky, Alexei Nikolaievich (b. district of Tambov, Russia, 1 Mar. 1799; d.

Moscow, 17 Nov. 1862). Studied in St. Petersburg with Field and others. Inspector of the imperial opera in Moscow from 1825. Composed operas (incl. *Askold's Tomb,* Moscow, 1835; *Thunder,* Moscow, 1857), operettas, and vaudevilles; sacred and secular choral works; songs.

Versus [L.]. (1) Psalm verse. *Versus alleluiaticus,* the verse added to the *Alleluia. (2) A type of rhymed, strophic Latin poetry set to music in the *St. Martial repertory.

Vespers. The seventh of the canonical hours. See Office.

Via [It.]. Away. *Via sordini,* remove the mutes.

Viadana, Lodovico Grossi da (b. Viadana, near Mantua, *c.* 1560; d. Gualtieri, 2 May, probably 1627). *Maestro di cappella* at the Mantua Cathedral at least from 1593 until 1597 and at other Italian churches thereafter. Composed Masses, motets, psalms, and other sacred music (incl. the collection *Cento concerti ecclesiastici a 1, a 2, a 3, e a 4 con il basso continuo per sonar nell' organo,* 1602, containing early examples of the sacred concerto style and of the thoroughbass, though without figures).

Viana da Mota, José (b. the island of São Tomé, Portuguese West Africa, 22 Apr. 1868; d. Lisbon, 1 June 1948). Pianist and composer. Pupil of the brothers Scharwenka, and of Liszt and H. von Bülow. Associate of Busoni. Director of the Geneva Conservatory, 1915–17; of the Lisbon Conservatory, 1919–38. Concertized widely in Europe and the Americas. Composed orch. works (incl. the symphony *A patria*); *Invocação dos Lusíadas* for chorus and orch.; chamber music; numerous piano pieces (incl. *5 Portuguese Rhapsodies*); songs. Published numerous writings on music and edited the piano works of Liszt.

Vibraphone, vibraharp. A percussion instrument originating in the United States. It is similar to the *marimba but has metal bars, foot-operated dampers, and electrically driven rotating propellers in the resonators under each bar, causing a *vibrato effect.

Vibrations. See under Acoustics.

Vibrato. (1) In stringed instruments, a slight, rapid fluctuation of pitch produced on sustained notes by an oscillating motion of the left hand. Through the 18th century, it was generally regarded as an ornament to be added only in certain circumstances. Although known in the 18th century, the continuous vibrato now almost universally practiced (except where the specific instruction *senza vibrato,* "without vibrato," is given) became the norm only in the 19th century. Lute players of the 17th century distinguished between vibrato produced by a motion of the finger [E. *close shake;* F. *langeur;* It. *ondeggiamento*] and one performed with the aid of a second finger that lightly taps the string as close as possible to the stopping finger [E. *sting;* F. **battement*]. For vibrato on the clavichord see *Bebung.*

(2) In singing, some authorities use the term *vibrato* for the quick reiteration of a single pitch produced by an intermittent stream of breath with fixed vocal cords. This effect corresponds to what string players call **tremolo.* Most singers, however, use the term *vibrato* for a fluctuation in pitch corresponding to the violinist's moderate vibrato. (3) In wind instruments, a slight, rapid fluctuation of pitch produced by variations in wind pressure created by the diaphragm, by movement of the jaw and/or lips on the mouthpiece or reed, or, sometimes in the case of the trumpet, by an oscillating motion of the right hand causing variations in the pressure of the mouthpiece against the lips. See also Tremulant.

Vicentino, Nicola (b. Vicenza, 1511; d. probably Milan, 1576). Pupil of Willaert. Served Cardinal Ippolito d'Este in Ferrara and Rome for most of his career. *Maestro di cappella* at the Vicenza Cathedral, 1563–65. Composed motets; madrigals, some highly chromatic. His treatise *L'antica musica ridotta alla moderna prattica,* 1555, sought to revive the three genera of classical antiquity; it includes music employing microtones and describes his **arcicembalo.*

Victimae paschali laudes [L.]. The sequence for Easter Sunday. See Sequence (2).

Victoria, Tomás Luís de (b. Ávila, Spain, *c.* 1548; d. Madrid, 27 Aug. 1611). Went to Rome in 1565 and was perhaps a pupil there of Palestrina, whom he succeeded as *maestro di cappella* at the Roman Seminary in 1571. *Maestro di cappella* at the Collegium germanicum in Rome from 1573. Returned to Spain in 1585, though he later visited Italy, and was organist and choirmaster to the Empress María (sister of Philip II) at the Convent of the Descalzas reales in Madrid from at least 1587 until his death. Composed Masses, motets, Magnificats, and other sacred works.

Vidal, Paul (-Antoine) (b. Toulouse, 16 Apr. 1863; d. Paris, 9 Apr. 1931). Studied at the Paris Conservatory, where he later taught from 1884. Choral director at the Paris Opéra from 1889 and conductor there in 1906. Composed the opera *Guernica,* Paris, 1895, and other stage works (incl. the ballet *La maladetta,* 1893); orch. works; choral works; chamber music; piano pieces; songs. Published several textbooks.

Vide. (1) [F.] Empty. *Corde à vide,* open string. (2) [L.] See. The term is used, with its syllables *Vi-* and *-de* placed at separate places of the score, to indicate an optional omission, the player being permitted to proceed from the place marked *Vi-* immediately to the place marked *-de.*

Vielle [F.]. The most important bowed stringed instrument of the 13th to 15th centuries, mentioned by numerous writers and described in detail, though not quite clearly, in the 13th century by Hieronymus de Moravia, according to whom it had a drone string and four fingered strings. Later (in the 15th cent.) the name was applied to the **hurdy-gurdy,* properly called *vielle à roue* (wheel viol). See under Violin; ill. under Violin family.

Viennese classical school. Collective name for the masters of **classical music,* Haydn, Mozart, and Beethoven, who worked in Vienna.

Vierne, Louis-Victor-Jules (b. Poitiers, 8 Oct. 1870; d. Paris, 2 June 1937). Blind from birth. Pupil of Franck and Widor. Assistant organist to Widor at Saint-Sulpice in Paris from 1892. Organist at Notre Dame from 1900 until his death. Teacher at the Paris Conservatory from 1894; at the Schola cantorum from 1912. Composed orch. works; choral works; chamber music; songs; organ works (incl. 6 symphonies).

Viertel [G.]. Quarter. *Viertelnote,* quarter note; *Viertelton,* quarter tone.

Vieru, Anatol (b. Iaşi, Rumania, 8 June 1926). Studied in Bucharest and with Khachaturian. Conductor of the National Theater Orchestra in Bucharest, 1947–49. Teacher at the Bucharest Conservatory from 1958. Has composed orch. works (incl. a concerto, 1954, and *Sanduhr,* 1969); concertos for cello and for violin, and *Jeux* for piano and orch., 1963; the oratorio *Miorita,* 1957, and other choral works; string quartets and other chamber music; piano pieces; electronic works.

Vieuxtemps, Henri (Joseph François) (b. Verviers, Belgium, 17 Feb. 1820; d. Mustapha, Algiers, 6 June 1881). Violinist and composer. Studied in Brussels and with Sechter in Vienna and Reicha in Paris. Teacher at the St. Petersburg Conservatory from 1846 until about 1851; at the Brussels Conservatory, 1871–73. Concertized widely in Europe, Russia, and the U.S. Composed 7 violin concertos and other works for violin with orch.; 2 cello concertos; works for violin and piano and other chamber music.

Vif [F.]. Lively.

Vihuela [Sp.]. (1) *Vihuela de arco,* a viol. (2) *Vihuela de Flandres* (from Flanders), the lute. (3) *Vihuela de mano,* or simply *vihuela,* a six-course *guitar of the 16th century. The tuning and stringing were similar to those of the lute and the notation like Italian lute *tablature.

Villa-Lobos, Heitor (b. Rio de Janeiro, 5 Mar. 1887; d. there, 17 Nov. 1959). Largely self-taught. Played the cello as a youth. Lived in Europe, principally Paris, 1923–30. Held various official posts in music education in Brazil from 1930. Worked extensively with elements of Brazilian folk music. Traveled widely in Europe and the Americas, often conducting his own works. His more than

3,000 works incl. 4 operas; 12 symphonies; 9 *Bachianas brasileiras;* 14 *Chôros* for various instruments; choral works; 16 string quartets and other chamber music; piano pieces (incl. 2 suites titled *Prole do bebé; As tres Marias,* 1939); etudes and other pieces for guitar; songs.

Villancico [Sp.]. In the 15th and 16th centuries, a type of Spanish poetry, idyllic or amorous in subject matter and consisting of several stanzas (*copla*) linked by a refrain (*estribillo*). The *copla* consists of two sections, *mundanza* and *vuelta,* which correspond exactly to the *piedi* and *volta* of the Italian *ballata,* while the *estribillo* corresponds to the Italian *ripresa.* The number of lines in each section varies. In the following diagram for an example with a two-line refrain, the refrain is indicated by italics in the textual structure and by capital letters in the musical structure:

	estribillo	copla		estr.	copla	
		mudanza	vuelta		mud.	vuelta
music	A	b b	a	A	b b	a
text	a a	b b	b a	a a	b b	b a etc.

The late 13th-century *Cantigas de Santa Maria* include numerous songs showing the metrical and musical form of the *villancico,* though the term does not come into use until the 15th century. [See also *Virelai.*]

Many *villancicos* composed for three or four voices are preserved in the Spanish *cancioneros* beginning in about 1500. Juan del Encina (1468–1529) is probably the most important of the early composers of such pieces. After 1500 the *villancico* was also composed as a solo song with *vihuela accompaniment. In the 17th century the *villancico* reappeared as a religious composition comparable to the church cantata or anthem, and during the 17th and 18th centuries a considerable number of such *villancicos* were produced both in Spain and in Latin America. Many of these works were intended for church use at Christmas. Today the term is loosely used for any Christmas carol.

Villanella. A 16th-century type of vocal music that originated in Naples (*v. alla napoletana*) and that, in both text and music, represents a sharp contrast to the refinements of the contemporary madrigal. A parodistic device of the *villanella* is its frequent use of "forbidden" parallel fifths. The earliest collections of *villanelle* are by G. D. da Nola (1541, the earlier term *villanesca* being used, however), T. Cimello (1545), A. Willaert (1545), and B. Donati (1550). The *villanella* style spread, particularly to Germany, where it was used for drinking songs, jesting songs, etc.

Subspecies of the *villanella* are the *greghesca, giustiniana, mascherata,* and *moresca.* The *greghesca* is in three voice-parts, the text a mixture of Venetian and Greek. The *giustiniana* is a type of *villanella,* always in three voice-parts, whose text ridicules the ineffectual stuttering Venetian patrician. The poems have no relationship whatever to lyrics, called *giustiniani,* of the early 15th-century poet Leonardo Giustiniani. The *mascherata* is a type to be sung during a masked ball or procession. The *moresca* is a type in which the singers represent Moorish girls. It has no relationship to the dance called the **moresca.*

More recent composers, among them Berlioz, Chabrier, Granados, and Loeffler, have used the terms *villanella* and *villanesca* for instrumental pieces in the style of a rustic dance, usually in quick 6/8 meter.

Villanesca. An earlier name for what was later called **villanella.*

Villota. A type of 16th-century Italian song of irregular structure, often including a popular or street song in its texture. Some *villote* close with a more rapid section, called *nio.*

Viṇa. A melody instrument of India belonging to the **zither family. See ill. under Zither.

Vincent, John (b. Birmingham, Ala., 17 May 1902; d. Los Angeles, 21 Jan. 1977). Conductor, critic, and composer. Pupil of Chadwick, Piston, N. Boulanger, and Harris. Teacher at the Univ. of California at Los Angeles, 1946–69. Composed an opera, *Primeval Void,* 1969; a ballet; 2 symphonies and other orch. works (incl. *Symphonic Poem after Descartes,* 1958; *Benjamin Franklin Suite* with glass harmonica, 1962; *Rondo Rhapsody,* 1965; *The Phoenix,* 1965); choral works; 2 string quartets and other chamber music; songs.

Vinci, Leonardo (b. probably Strongoli, Calabria, or Naples, between 1690 and 1696; d. Naples, 27 or 29 May 1730). Vice *maestro* of the Cappella reale in Naples from 1725. *Maestro di cappella* at the Conservatorio dei poveri di Gesù Cristo in Naples from 1728. Composed about 40 operas (incl., for Naples, *Silla dittatore,* 1723; *Astianatte,* 1725; *La caduta dei Decemviri,* 1727; *Artaserse,* 1730); oratorios and cantatas; Masses and motets; arias.

Vingt-quatre violons du roi. A string orchestra of 24 players, in the service of the French kings Louis XIII, Louis XIV, and Louis XV (*c.* 1650–1761), that became particularly famous under Lully.

Viol. Any of a family of bowed stringed instruments in use mainly during the 16th and 17th centuries, replacing the various types of medieval fiddle (*rabāb, *vielle) and in turn superseded by the *violin family. The viols differ from the violins in the following ways: (a) the shoulders slope from the neck instead of being set at right angles to it; (b) the back is usually flat instead of bulging; (c) the ribs are deeper; (d) the normal number of strings is six instead of four; (e) the fingerboard generally has frets; (f) the sound holes are usually in the shape of a C instead of an f [see Sound hole]; (g) the bridge is wider and less arched, facilitating the playing of full chords; (h) the strings are thinner and less tense; (i) it is played with an older type of bow whose stick curves outward from the hair [see Bow], and the hand is held palm up; (j) the instrument is held upright, resting on the player's lap or between the legs. See ill. accompanying Violin family.

In the 17th century, the classical period of the viols, they were built in three sizes, treble viol [F. *dessus de viole*], tenor viol [*taille de viole*], and bass viol [*basse de viole*], the last also known as the *viola da gamba. According to T. Mace (*Musick's Monument,* 1676), a good set of viols (a so-called "chest of viols") consisted of "2 basses, 2 tenors, and 2 trebles: all truly, and proportionably suited." The tuning of these instruments was in fourths around a central third: bass viol, D G c e a d'; tenor viol, A d g b e' a'; treble viol, d g c' e' a' d''. Toward the end of the 17th century, French musicians added a small viol tuned a fourth above the treble viol, called the *pardessus de viole*. The corresponding English term is *descant viol,* a name also used for the treble viol. The French bass viol often had a seventh string, usually tuned A_1.

In addition to the standard types, the viol family included several other instruments.

1. Double-bass viol [F. *contre-basse de viole;* It. *violone;* Sp. *contrabajo*]. A six-stringed instrument tuned an octave below the bass viol. It is the ancestor of the modern *double bass, which has retained some features of the viols together with the alternate name "bass viol." The *violone* frequently called for in Bach's cantatas probably was an intermediate instrument between the old six-stringed type and the modern double bass.

2. Division viol. A slightly smaller bass viol, which was preferred for playing *divisions upon a ground and similar solo performance.

3. Lyra viol. An instrument still smaller than the division viol. Since its size was between the bass viol and tenor viols, it was also called a *viola bastarda.* [See ill. accompanying Violin family.] The lyra viol was tuned principally in fifths and fourths, e.g., C G c e a d' or A_1 E A e a d', unlike the other viols but like the older *lira da gamba;* hence the name *lyra-way* for this manner of tuning, which greatly facilitated playing chords. It was also known as "harp-way tuning" (T. Mace). The music for this instrument was not written in ordinary notation but in *tablature.

4. Viola d'amore. See separate entry.

5. Baryton. An 18th-century instrument that might be regarded as a viola da gamba provided with sympathetic strings, or as a larger *viola d'amore. The broad neck was usually carved out under the fingerboard (leaving only an oblong frame) so that the sympathetic strings could be plucked from underneath with the thumb of the left hand [see ill. accompanying Violin family]. A number of late 18th-century compositions for the baryton survive. Many of

them were written for Prince Nikolaus Esterházy, who was very fond of the instrument. They include 175 compositions by Haydn.

Viola. (1) In modern usage, the second member of the violin family [F. *alto;* G. *Bratsche*]. It is tuned a fifth lower than the violin, c g d' a'. Nonetheless, it is only one-seventh larger than the violin (body length 15 to 17 1/4 in.), a disproportion that makes its timbre more nasal and veiled than those of the violin and cello. For modern constructions in various sizes, see Violin family (c), (d). In contrast to the violin, the viola has been used almost exclusively as an ensemble instrument, in the orchestra or in chamber music [see String quartet].

About 1600 the viola was called a *violino (violino ordinario)*, the smaller violin being called a *violino piccolo*. In the 17th and 18th centuries it was frequently called a *violetta,* the name "viola" being used for the viola da gamba.

(2) In the Renaissance and baroque periods, *viola* was the generic Italian name for all bowed stringed instruments. There were two main classes: *viole da gamba* (leg viols) and *viole da braccio* (arm viols). The former, which were held on or between the legs, are the *viols; the latter, which were held against the shoulder (at least the smaller sizes), are the immediate forerunners of the violins. Later, each of these collective terms became identified with a particular member of the group, the viola da gamba [G. *Gambe*] with the bass viol and the viola da braccio [viola; G. *Bratsche*] with the alto violin.

Viola, Alfonso della (b. Ferrara, *c*. 1508; d. probably Ferrara, *c*. 1570). Viol player and composer. *Maestro di cappella* to Duke Ercole II d'Este at Ferrara. Composed music for plays (incl. *Il sacrifizio,* 1554); madrigals.

Viola alta. See Violin family (c).

Viola bastarda [It.]. Lyra *viol.

Viola da gamba [It.]. Originally, any of the *viols, because they were held on or between the legs; see Viola (2). Specifically, the bass size of this family, also called a bass viol [see also Double bass, however]. It has six strings, normally tuned D G c e a d'. The instrument was often used as a solo instrument.

Viola da spalla [It.]. An 18th-century variety of cello that was held across the player's chest suspended by a strap over the shoulder [*spalla,* shoulder].

Viola d'amore [It.; F. *viole d'amour;* G. *Liebesgeige*]. An instrument the size of a treble viol but having *sympathetic strings, made of thin wire, stretched behind the bowed strings. Unlike the viols proper, it had no frets and was held like a violin. Along with this type there existed viole d'amore without sympathetic strings, and with metal strings replacing the gut strings of the ordinary viols. See ill. accompanying Violin family.

Viola di bordone [It.]; **viola paradon** [Eng.]. Baryton [see Viol, 5].

Viola pomposa. An 18th-century instrument of the violin (not viol) family, whose invention is erroneously ascribed to J. S. Bach. The only works for the instrument are two compositions by Telemann, a concerto by J. G. Graun, and a *Sonata per la Pomposa col Basso* by Cristiano G. Lidarti from *c.* 1760. From these pieces it has been deduced that the viola pomposa was a larger viola held on the arm (not under the chin) and with five strings, tuned c g d' a' e''. The *violino pomposo* mentioned in some sources was the same instrument.

Viole [F.]. *Viol. Viole d'amour,* *viola d'amore.

Viole-ténor [F.]. See Violin family (g).

Violet. A name sometimes given to the *viola d'amore.

Violetta. (1) A 16th-century three-stringed instrument of the violin type [see under Violin]. (2) A 17th- and 18th-century name for the viola, used by J. Rosenmüller, Bach, and other German composers; *violetta marina,* for viola d'amore; *violetta piccola,* according to M. Praetorius (*Syntagma musicum,* 1614 –20), a small viol, but it may also have meant a violin.

Violin [F. *violon;* G. *Violine, Geige;* It. *violino;* Sp. *violín*]. The most important of the stringed instruments, in the or-

chestra as well as in chamber and solo music. Its main parts are: (a) the body, consisting of the table (soundboard or belly), back, and ribs (bouts, side walls); (b) the unfretted fingerboard, ending in a pegbox and scroll; (c) the string holder (tail piece); (d) the bridge. [See the illustrations accompanying Violin family.] Inside the body is the *bass-bar, which is glued to the table, reinforcing blocks glued to the corners of the bouts and to the back, and the *sound post, fixed between the table and the back. Its overall length is about 23 1/2 in.; its body length about 14 in. The violin has four strings tuned in fifths g d' a' e''. For the material of the strings, see Stringed instruments.

Whereas all other modern instruments (except the organ) were not perfected until the late 19th century, the great period of violin building followed soon after the instrument emerged as a definite type. From 1600 to 1750 Cremona was the center for masters of violin making, notably Niccolò Amati (1596–1684), Antonio Stradivari (1644–1737), and Giuseppe B. Guarneri (Giuseppe del Gesù, 1698–1744). Although the instruments of these masters continue to be regarded as the finest ever produced, virtually all surviving examples were altered during the course of the 19th century to conform with new designs intended primarily to produce the more powerful sound required for large concert halls. The changes included a higher, more arched bridge, a slightly longer neck set back at an angle to the belly rather than more nearly parallel to it, and a heavier bass-bar, all of which produced or permitted greater tension on the strings. The chin rest, which aids in holding the instrument on the shoulder, came into use around 1800. [See also Bow; Bowing.]

The violin has a relatively short history. There is no evidence of the use of a bow prior to the 9th century, when it is mentioned in Persian and Chinese sources. There is some evidence that the fiddle originated in Central Asia, whence it spread to the Far East as well as to Europe. A Chinese fiddle called *huchyn* (*hu ch'in*) has a small cylindrical soundbox made of bamboo, wood, or coconut, with the lower end open and the upper end covered with snakeskin. A long neck, in the form of a stick, pierces the body, and over it two strings are stretched. The bow cannot be removed since it passes between the strings. A similar instrument is the Persian *kemânǧe* or *kamānja*. In India a folk instrument called a *sārangī* comes in a variety of shapes. The Arab *rabāb* was imported into Europe, where it was usually called a *rebec* [see Rabāb].

The earliest European fiddles were shaped like a slender bottle or pear and were known by various names, among them *rebec*, **gigue*, and **lyra*. The slightly pear-shaped form was retained in the Italian **lira da braccio* and *lira da gamba*. The slender fiddle (rebec) persisted in the *klein geigen* [see below] and **kit*. The most important medieval fiddle was the **vielle* of the 13th century. The development during the next two centuries is obscure, but sometime between *c*. 1550 and 1600 the violin developed from several earlier types, each of which contributed some essential features. In view of the differences between the violin and the earlier **viols*, a number of the violin's forerunners can be singled out. The practice of leaning the instrument against the shoulder and bowing palm-downward was used with the vielle. Tuning in consecutive fifths is documented as early as 1533 and was consistently used with the three-stringed *klein geigen* (descendants of the slender rebec) throughout the 16th century. The right angle between the fingerboard and upper end of the body is present in a **lira* designed by Rafael (*c*. 1510) as well as in **violettas* mentioned in 1543. The latter instruments, with no frets and with three strings tuned in fifths, were very similar to the classical violin. A picture by Gaudenzio Ferrari from *c*. 1535 shows *violettas* with shallow ribs, pointed corners, round shoulders, a depression running around the edge, f-holes, and a scroll. Only the addition of a fourth string was needed to create what might be called the first violin.

The emergence of the name *violin* did not coincide with the emergence of the instrument. Throughout the 16th century, names such as *violini* and *violons* were used for viols and similar instruments. About 1600, *violino* meant **viola* rather than violin, as, e.g., in G. Gabrieli's *Symphoniae sacrae* (1597). In Monteverdi's *Orfeo* (1607), *violino ordinario* means viola and *violino piccolo* probably means violin [see Violin family (a)].

The first known makers of true violins were Gasparo (Bertolotti), called after his birthplace "da Salò" (1540–1609), G. Paolo Maggini (1580–*c*. 1630), both working in Brescia, and the brothers Amati (Antonio, 1550–1638; Girolamo, 1556–1630), who made Cremona famous as the center of violin making. Girolamo's son Niccolò was the first of the great three violin makers, the other two being A. Stradivari and G. Guarneri.

Violin family. The chief members of this family are the **violin*, **viola*, **cello*, and, for all practical purposes, the **double bass* (though this instrument, strictly speaking, belongs to the **viol family*). These four instruments form the string section of the orchestra, the first three also being used extensively in chamber music (**string quartet*, etc.) and the last in **jazz*. For more details, see the separate entries.

A great number of in-between sizes have been constructed, none of which has achieved permanent importance. Among them are (in order of size):

(a) Violino piccolo [G. *Quartgeige*]. Tuned a fourth above the violin. Bach scored for this instrument in his Cantata no. 140 and his first Brandenburg Concerto. The *violini piccoli* of Monteverdi's *Orfeo* (1607) have been interpreted variously as true violins, as Bach's *violino piccolo*, as the *pochette* or **kit*, and as a 3/4-size violin tuned a major third above the violin.

(b) Contra-violin, introduced (1917) by H. Newbould. Slightly bigger than the normal violin and designed to take the place of the second violin in chamber music.

(c) Viola alta, introduced by H. Ritter and used during the Bayreuth festivals of 1872–75. This was a slightly oversized viola (body length 19 in. instead of 15 to 17 1/4 in.) and was later provided with a fifth string tuned e″.

(d) Contralto, an oversized viola with

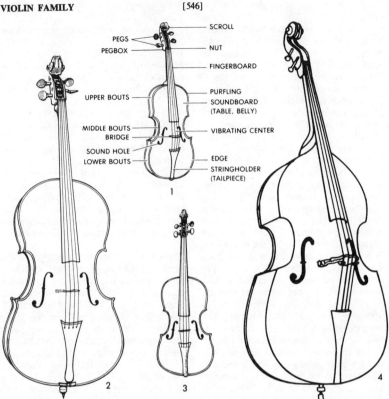

Violin family and related instruments: 1. Violin. 2. Cello. 3. Viola. 4. Double bass (reduced in this illustration in comparison to other instruments shown).

a fuller tone, constructed by J.-B. Vuillaume, 1855.

(e) Violotta, constructed by A. Stelzner in 1891, a tenor violin with a body length of 16 1/8 in. and an overall length of 28 in., tuned G d a e'.

(f) Tenor violin. Name for various instruments between the viola and cello in size (overall length 27 1/2 to 29 1/2 in.). They were used from the mid-16th century but became obsolete in the 18th century. The most common baroque tuning appears to have been F c g d'. Later attempts to build similar instruments include those of Vuillaume (1855), H. Ritter, and A. Stelzner [see (c), (d), (e) above].

(g) Viole-ténor [F.], constructed by R. Farramon in 1930; it is held like a cello. Also called *alto-moderne*.

(h) Violoncello piccolo. An instrument 36 to 38 in. long that Bach frequently preferred to the cello because its smaller size facilitated the execution of solo passages. It was tuned like the cello. The *violoncello à cinque cordes,* which Bach scored for in the sixth of his suites for cello solo, was probably only slightly smaller than the usual cello.

(i) Cellone, constructed by Stelzner [see (e) above]. A large cello (length 46 in.), tuned G_1 D A e (a fourth lower than the cello) and intended chiefly as a contrabass for chamber music.

(j) Octobasse, constructed by J.-B. Vuillaume in 1849. A giant double bass, about 13 feet high, with three strings tuned C_2 G_2 C_1. They were stopped by a mechanical system of levers and pedals. An American model made by John Geyer in 1889 measures almost 15 feet.

See also Quinton.

5. Vielle (fidel). 6. Hardanger fiddle. 7. Hurdy-gurdy. 8. Lira da braccio. 9. Viola da gamba. 10. Viola d'amore. 11. Lyra viol.

[548]

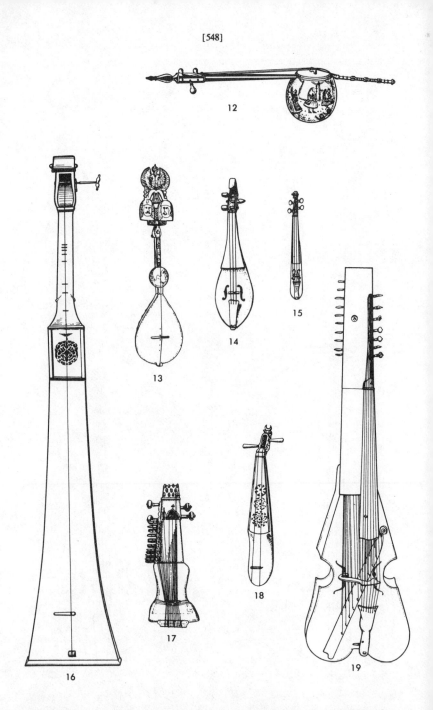

12. Kamãnja. 13. Gusle. 14. Rebec. 15. Kit. 16. Tromba marina. 17. Sãrangĩ.
18. Rabãb. 19. Baryton.

Violino piccolo. See Violin family (a).

Violon [F.]. Violin. *Violón* [Sp.]; viol, bass viol, double bass.

Violoncello. See Cello.

Violoncello piccolo. See Violin family (h).

Violoncino. Old name for violoncello (*cello).

Violone [It.]. The largest size of the *viols.

Violotta. See Violin family (e).

Viotti, Giovanni Battista (b. Fontanetto da Po, Italy, 12 May 1755; d. London, 3 Mar. 1824). Violinist and composer. Pupil of Pugnani. Associate of Cherubini. Court musician to Marie Antoinette in Paris, 1784–86. Lived in London, 1792–98, as an opera conductor and violinist and returned there in 1801. Director of the Italian Opera in Paris, 1819–22. Concertized widely in Europe and Russia. Composed 29 violin concertos, 10 piano concertos, and 2 *symphonies concertantes;* 21 string quartets and other chamber music; piano sonatas; songs.

Virelai [F.]. An important form of medieval French poetry and music (also called *chanson balladée*), consisting of a refrain (R) that usually alternates with three stanzas (S): R S₁ R S₂ R S₃ R. The stanzas begin with two rhyming versicles and close with a versicle paralleling the refrain (*versicle* here means a section of the text; it may consist of one, two, three, or more lines of the poem). The musical structure corresponds exactly to that of the poem, the two parallel versicles being sung to the same music and the closing versicle to that of the refrain. In the following diagram, for R S₁ R and a two-line refrain, the refrain is indicated by italics in the textual structure and by capital letters in the musical structure:

	R	S₁	R	
Text	*a b*	c c a b	*a b*	etc.
Music	A	b b a	A	

It was Machaut who established the *virelai* as one of the *formes fixes* of French poetry and music. It continued to be composed in the late 14th century, and sparingly throughout the 15th by Dufay,

Ockeghem, and Busnois, the last of whom preferred the shorter *bergerette,* as did others after him.

The *virelai* is not a form of *trouvère music, as was formerly assumed. More likely its origins are Spanish, and perhaps ultimately Hispano-Arabic [see *Zejel*]. The Spanish *cantigas of the second half of the 13th century (some possibly even earlier) include, among *c.* 400 songs, more than 100 in strict *virelai* form and many more showing essentially the same form with some modifications. The Italian *laude* of the same period also have a general *virelai* structure but with some variants of the musical form. The strict form appears in 14th-century Italian music as the *ballata,* and in Spanish music of the 15th and 16th centuries as the *villancico.* Unlike the French type, the Italian and Spanish forms do not always restate the refrain after each stanza, nor do they always have the strict conformity of poetic structure to musical form that is characteristic of the French *virelai.* This is especially evident in their rhyme structure, which in many cases is asymmetrical, e.g., *ab cccb,* instead of symmetrical, *ab ccab.* Practically all the Italian *ballate* (e.g., those by Landini) are asymmetrical.

Virga [L.]. See table accompanying Neumes.

Virginal. In England, a type of *harpsichord with one choir of transverse strings, described as early as 1511, in S. Virdung's *Musica getutscht.* The earliest virginals were in the shape of a small oblong box, to be placed on a table or even held in the player's lap. Toward the end of the 16th century the term was indiscriminately applied to all types of harpsichord, whether rectangular, wing-shaped, or trapezoidal [see Spinet]. Thus it cannot be assumed that the virginalist composers wrote for the oblong virginals. The common term was *pair of virginals,* an idiom whose origin is not known, nor is the origin of the term *virginal* itself known, despite various hypotheses. The most important composers of virginal music were William Byrd (1543–1623), Thomas Morley (1557–1602), Peter Philips (1561–1628), Giles Farnaby (*c.* 1565–1640), John Bull (*c.* 1562–1628), Thomas Weelkes (*c.* 1575–

1623), Thomas Tompkins (1572–1656), Orlando Gibbons (1583–1625). The repertory of the virginalist composers comprises dances (mainly pavanes and galliards), variations, preludes, fantasias, liturgical pieces (organ hymns; see also *In nomine*), and transcriptions of madrigals. The largest manuscript collection of these works is the *Fitzwilliam Virginal Book.

Virtuoso. A performer who excels in technical ability; sometimes, one who excels in this only.

Visée, Robert de (b. *c.* 1660; d. Paris, after *c.* 1725). Guitarist, lutenist, theorbist, singer, and composer. Musician to the French court, *c.* 1686–1721. Composed pieces for guitar, for lute, and for theorbo.

Visigothic chant. See Mozarabic chant.

Visitation, The. Opera by Gunther Schuller (libretto by the composer, based on Kafka), produced in Hamburg, 1966.

Vitali, Filippo (b. Florence, *c.* 1590; d. there, 1653). Singer in the pontifical choir in Rome from 1631. *Maestro* of the ducal chapel in Florence and of the Cathedral of San Lorenzo there from 1642. *Maestro di cappella* at Santa Maria Maggiore in Bergamo, 1648–49. Composed the opera *L'Aretusa*, Rome, 1620; *intermedi;* madrigals; vocal chamber music; motets, Vesper psalms, and other sacred music.

Vitali, Giovanni Battista (b. Bologna, 18 Feb. 1632; d. Modena, 12 Oct. 1692). Violinist and composer. Pupil of Cazzati. *Viola da braccio* player at San Petronio in Bologna from *c.* 1667. Vice *maestro di cappella* at the court in Modena from 1674 and *maestro* from 1684. Composed trio sonatas; sonatas, dances, and other pieces for ensembles; concerted sacred music; oratorios and cantatas; operas.

Vitali, Tommaso Antonio (b. Bologna, 7 Mar. 1663; d. Modena, 9 May 1745). Violinist and composer. Son of Giovanni Battista Vitali. Musician to the Duke of Modena, 1675–1742. Composed trio sonatas and violin sonatas with thoroughbass. A well-known chaconne for violin with thoroughbass, of uncertain authorship, is also sometimes attributed to him.

Vite, vitement [F.]. Fast, quickly.

Vitry, Philippe de (b. Vitry, Champagne, or Paris, 31 Oct. 1291; d. Meaux or Paris, 9 June 1361). Poet, theorist, diplomat, and composer. Held several ecclesiastical posts and served Jean II both before and after his accession to the French throne in 1350. Bishop of Meaux from 1351 until his death. Composed motets. His treatise *Ars nova* (1322 or 1323) gave its name to the 14th century as a period in French musical history and systematized the use of both duple and triple meter in mensural notation.

Vivace [It.]. Quick, lively. *Vivacissimo,* very quick.

Vivaldi, Antonio (Lucio) (the "Red Priest") (b. Venice, 4 Mar. 1678; d. Vienna, 28 July 1741). Violinist and composer. Teacher at the Seminario musicale dell' Ospedale della pietà at Venice, 1703–40, with interruptions. *Maestro di cappella* to Prince Philip, Landgrave of Hesse-Darmstadt, at Mantua, from 1718 or 1719 until 1723. Settled in Vienna in 1741. Composed over 40 operas; 3 oratorios (incl. *Juditha triumphans,* 1716); 38 secular cantatas; Vespers and other church music; numerous *concerti grossi* for various combinations of instruments (incl. *The *Seasons*) and solo concertos; sonatas and other chamber music; arias.

Vivement [F.]. Lively.

Vives, Amadeo (Roig) (b. Collbató, near Barcelona, 18 Nov. 1871; d. Madrid, 1 Dec. 1932). Pupil of Pedrell. Co-founder of the choral society Orfeó català in 1891. Composed operas (incl. *Maruxa,* Madrid, 1914); numerous *zarzuelas* (incl. *Doña Francisquita,* Madrid, 1923); piano pieces; songs.

Vl. Abbr. for *violin. Vla.,* viola. *Vlc.,* violoncello. *Vll.,* violins.

Vlad, Roman (b. Cernauti, Rumania, 29 Dec. 1919). Critic, pianist, and composer. Studied in Cernauti and with Casella after settling in Italy in 1938. Artistic director of the Accademia filarmonica in Rome, 1955–58; of the Teatro comunale in Florence from 1968. Has worked with twelve-tone techniques. Has composed operas; ballets; incidental music for plays; music for films; orch. works; choral works; chamber music; piano pieces; songs. Has published books on Stravinsky, on twelve-tone techniques, and on other topics.

Vladigerov, Pantcho (b. Zürich, of Bulgarian parents, 13 Mar. 1899). Pupil of Juon. Theater pianist, conductor, and composer in Berlin, 1921–32. Teacher at the Sofia Conservatory from 1932. Has composed the opera *Tsar Kaloyan*, Sofia, 1936; a ballet; 5 symphonies and other orch. works; concertos for piano and for violin; chamber music; piano pieces; songs.

Vlasov, Vladimir Alexandrovich (b. Moscow, 7 Jan. 1903 [old style 25 Dec. 1902]). Conductor, ethnomusicologist, and composer. Studied at the Moscow Conservatory. Artistic director of the National Opera at the Kirgiz capital, Frunze, 1936–43. Has composed several operas based on Kirgiz folk materials; ballets; orch. works; 2 cello concertos; oratorios and cantatas; chamber music; songs.

Vlijman, Jan van (b. Rotterdam, 11 Oct. 1935). Pianist and composer. Pupil of van Baaren. Director of the Amersfoort School of Music, 1961–65. Teacher at the Utrecht Conservatory, 1965–67. Assistant director of the Royal Conservatory at The Hague from 1967. Has worked with twelve-tone techniques. Works incl. the opera *Reconstructie*, with L. Andriessen, Schat, and others, 1969; *Interpolations* for orch. and tape, 1968; *Sonata* for piano and orch. in 3 groups, 1966; *Gruppi* for 20 instruments and percussion, 1962; a wind quintet, 1959; songs.

Vocalization [F. *vocalise;* G. *Vokalise;* It. *vocalizzo;* Sp. *vocalización*]. A long melody sung on a vowel, i.e., without text. The term is used chiefly for vocal exercises (*solfège).

Voce [It.; pl. *voci*]. Voice. *A due (tre) voci,* for two (three) voices. *Colla voce,* see *Colla. Voci pari* or *eguali,* *equal voices.

Voces [L.]. See *Vox.*

Vogel, Wladimir (b. Moscow, of a German father and Russian mother, 29 Feb. 1896). Pupil of Tiessen and Busoni. Settled in Switzerland in 1935. Has worked with twelve-tone techniques and the adaptation of rhythmic procedures to these. Has composed choral works with orch., *Sprechstimmen,* and speaking chorus (incl. *Thyl Claes,* 1945; *Die Flucht,* 1964); orch. works; concertos for violin and for cello; chamber music (incl. *12 variétudes* for violin, flute, clarinet, cello, 1940); piano pieces; songs.

Vogler, Georg Joseph ("Abbé Vogler") (b. Würzburg, 15 June 1749; d. Darmstadt, 6 May 1814). Pupil of Padre Martini. Took holy orders in 1773. Second *Kapellmeister* at the court in Mannheim from 1775 and founded a school there in 1776. Followed the court to Munich in 1780 and became first *Kapellmeister* in 1784. Court *Kapellmeister* in Stockholm, 1786–88; in Darmstadt from 1807. Traveled widely as a pianist and organist. His pupils incl. Weber and Meyerbeer. Composed operas, ballets, and other stage works; symphonies and other orch. works; sacred and secular choral works; chamber music; piano pieces; organ pieces. Published numerous works on music theory.

Voice. (1) The human mechanism for producing sound, consisting of the larynx containing the vocal cords; the lungs and diaphragm, which supply the wind; and the various parts of the mouth and head that articulate and give resonance to the sound. See also Voices, range of. (2) Any single part or line in polyphonic music [see Polyphony], whether or not intended for vocal performance and regardless of the number of performers performing it. Thus, e.g., four-voice fugue (perhaps intended for keyboard performance), five-voice motet (to be sung with several singers on each "voice"). The terms *part* and *voice-part* are also used in this way.

Voice exchange [G. *Stimmtausch*]. The restatement of a contrapuntal passage with the voice-parts exchanged, so that, e.g., the soprano part sings the alto part and vice versa (without the octave transposition found in *invertible counterpoint). The device is an important feature of some 13th-century polyphony, particularly that of England.

Voice-leading. See under Counterpoint.

Voice-part. See Voice (2).

Voices, range of. Human voices are usually divided into six ranges: three female voices—soprano, mezzo-soprano, and contralto—and three male voices—tenor, baritone, and bass. For the male alto or countertenor, see Alto (2). In choral singing the middle voices of each group may be omitted. The normal range of these voices is roughly an octave (or a seventh) below and above the notes d, f, a, and e′, g′, b′ in order from bass to soprano [see Ex.]. The indication of range

Bass Baritone Tenor Contralto Mezzo Soprano

differs markedly in different countries. Trained soloists frequently exceed these ranges. Opera singers are further classified, mainly with regard to the character and timbre of the voice: *Dramatic soprano,* with powerful voice and marked declamatory and histrionic ability; *lyric soprano,* with lighter quality and pleasant cantabile style; *coloratura soprano,* with great agility and a high range. *Dramatic contralto,* with slightly lower range than the dramatic soprano (one or two tones) but capable of producing a powerful sound as well as great dramatic expression.

Tenore robusto (robust tenor), with full voice and vigor; *lyric tenor,* corresponding to the lyric soprano; *Heldentenor* (heroic tenor), combining agility, brilliant timbre, and expressive power. *Basso profondo* [F. *basse profonde*], with low range, powerful voice, and solemn character; *basso cantante* [*basse chantante*], with qualities similar to the lyric soprano; *basso buffo,* comical, agile bass.

Voicing. In organ building, adjustment of the timbre and pitch of the pipes. In piano (or harpsichord) building, the adjustment of the hammer felts (or jacks) to produce the desired timbre.

Voilé [F.]. Veiled, subdued.

Voix [F.]. Voice. *Voix céleste,* an organ stop of the string family. *Voix humaine,* an organ stop of the reed family.

Voix de ville [F.]. See under *Vaudeville.*

Vokal [G.]. Vowel. *Vokalisieren,* to vocalize; *Vokalise,* *vocalization.

Volante [It.]. Rushing.

Volkmann, (Friedrich) Robert (b. Lommatzsch, Saxony, 6 Apr. 1815; d. Budapest, 29 Oct. 1883). Studied with his father and in Leipzig, where he became acquainted with Schumann. Teacher in Prague, 1839–42, settling in Prague thereafter. Teacher at the National Academy of Music in Budapest from 1875. Composed 2 symphonies and other orch. works; a cello concerto and a *Konzertstück* for piano and orch.; sacred and secular choral works; 6 string quartets and other chamber music; piano pieces; songs.

Volkonsky, Andrei (Mikhailovich) (b. Geneva, of Russian parents, 14 Feb. 1933). Studied in Geneva, with N. Boulanger in Paris, and with Shaporin in Moscow, where he lived for some years before returning to Geneva in 1973. Has composed a concerto for orch., 1953; 2 cantatas and other choral works; *Wanderer Concerto* for soprano, violin, percussion, and orch., 1968; a piano quintet, 1954, a string quartet, 1955, and other chamber music; piano pieces; music for films.

Volkslied [G.]. Folksong.

Volles Werk [G.]. Full organ.

Volta, volte [It.]. (1) A dance of the period *c.* 1600, usually in dotted 6/8 meter. English writers (e.g., Shakespeare) and musicians often called it *Lavolta* or *Levalto.* (2) See under *Ballata.* (3) In modern scores, *prima and seconda volta* indicate the first and second ending of a section that is repeated. See also *Ouvert, clos.*

Volteggiando [It.]. Crossing the hands (in piano playing).

Volti [It.]. Turn over (the page); *volti subito* (abbr. *v.s.*), turn quickly.

Voluntary. An organ piece, often in a free, improvisatory style, played before, during, or after an Anglican church service. The first such pieces date from the middle of the 16th century.

Voormolen, Alexander (Nicolaas) (b. Rotterdam, 3 Mar. 1895). Music critic and composer. Pupil of J. Wagenaar, Ravel, and Roussel. Librarian at the Royal Conservatory at The Hague, 1938–55. Has composed ballets; orch. works (incl. *The Three Horsemen*, variations on a Dutch folksong, 1927; *Arethusa*, 1947; *Chaconne en Fuga*, 1958); concertos for oboe, for 2 oboes, for cello, for 2 harpsichords; string quartets and other chamber music; piano pieces; songs.

Vorbereiten [G.]. To prepare in advance (e.g., organ stops).

Voříšek, Jan Hugo (Woržischek) (b. Wamberg, Bohemia, 11 May 1791; d. Vienna, 19 Nov. 1825). Pianist, conductor, and composer. Pupil of Tomášek. Associate of Beethoven, Hummel, Meyerbeer, and Moscheles. Court organist in Vienna from 1823. Composed orch. works; a piano concerto; choral works, incl. church music; chamber music; piano pieces (incl. rhapsodies, 1818, and impromptus, 1822); songs.

Vorschlag [G.]. See Appoggiatura (2). *Kurzer, langer Vorschlag*, short, long appoggiatura.

Vorspiel [G.]. Prelude, overture. Also, performance (*vorspielen*, to perform before an audience).

Vorwärts [G.]. Go ahead, continue.

Vox [L.; pl. *voces*]. (1) Voice, sound, tone color. (2) In polyphonic music, voice-part. (3) Note, pitch; i.e., any of the seven pitches of the scale. Also any of the six pitches of the *hexachord, called *sex voces* or *voces musicales*.

Vox humana. An organ stop of the reed family.

V.s. Abbr. for *volti subito*.

Vulpius, Melchior (real name Fuchs) (b. Wasungen, near Meiningen, *c.* 1570; d. Weimar, buried 7 Aug. 1615). Cantor at Schleusingen, Thuringia, 1589–96; at Weimar from 1596 until his death. Composed a St. Matthew Passion; chorale settings and other German and Latin sacred works.

Vuoto [It.]. Empty, toneless. *Corda vuota*, open string.

Vv. Abbr. for *violins*.

Vycpálek, Ladislav (b. Prague, 23 Feb. 1882; d. there, 9 Jan. 1969). Pupil of Novák. Head of the music department at the National and University Library in Prague, 1922–42. Employed folksongs and folk poetry. Composed numerous choral works (incl. a *Czech Requiem*, 1940); chamber music; piano pieces; songs and arrangements of folksongs.

Vyshnegradsky, Ivan (b. St. Petersburg, 16 May 1893). Studied at the St. Petersburg Conservatory. Settled in Paris in 1919. Has worked principally with microtones, especially quarter tones, for which he designed a piano that was constructed by the firm of Pleyel. Has composed microtonal orch. works; choral works; string quartets and other chamber music; piano pieces, principally for 2 pianos tuned a microtone apart.

W

Wachsend [G.]. Growing, increasing.

Waclaw of Szamotuly (Szamotulczyk) (b. Szamotuly, near Poznań, between 1524 and 1526; d. probably Pińczow, *c.* 1560). Composer to the King of Poland, 1547–54. Court musician to the Calvinist Prince Mikolaj Radziwill at Vilna from 1555. Composed motets and other Latin church music; sacred choral works with Polish texts.

Waelrant, Hubert (b. perhaps Tongerloo, North Brabant, *c.* 1517; d. Antwerp, 19 Nov. 1595). Singer at Notre Dame in Antwerp, 1544–45. Teacher in Antwerp, 1553–57, and publisher there, with Jean Laet, 1554–58. Composed motets, madrigals, *canzoni alla napolitana,* and chansons. A seven-syllable system of solmization called bocedization is attributed to him.

Wagenaar, Bernard (b. Arnhem, the Netherlands, 18 July 1894; d. York, Maine, 19 May 1971). Pupil of his father, J. Wagenaar, at the Utrecht Music School. Settled in the U.S. in 1920. Violinist in the New York Philharmonic, 1921–23. Teacher at the Juilliard School, 1927–68. Composed the opera *Pieces of Eight,* New York, 1944; 4 symphonies and other orch. works; a violin concerto, a triple concerto for flute, cello, and harp, and 5 *Tableaux* for cello and orch.; choral works; 4 string quartets and other chamber music; piano pieces; songs.

Wagenaar, Johan (b. Utrecht, 1 Nov. 1862; d. The Hague, 17 June 1941). Organist, conductor, and composer. Studied in Utrecht and with Herzogenberg in Berlin. Organist at the Utrecht Cathedral from 1888. Teacher at the Utrecht Music School from 1887 and its director from 1904. Director of the Royal Conservatory at The Hague, 1919–37. Composed operas (incl. *De Doge van Venetie,* Utrecht, 1904; *De Cid,* Utrecht, 1916); symphonic poems and other orch. works; choral works; organ pieces; songs.

Wagenseil, Georg Christoph (b. Vienna, 29 Jan. 1715; d. there, 1 Mar. 1777). Pupil of Fux. Served the Vienna court as composer from 1739 until his death; as organist to the Dowager Empress Elizabeth Christine, 1741–50; and as music master to the Empress Maria Theresa and the princesses. Composed operas; about 30 symphonies; concertos for harpsichord (almost 30), for violin, for flute, for cello; oratorios and cantatas; church music; divertimenti and other chamber music; organ pieces; harpsichord pieces; arias.

Wagner, Joseph Frederick (b. Springfield, Mass., 9 Jan. 1900; d. Los Angeles, 12 Oct. 1974). Pupil of Converse, Casella, and N. Boulanger. Assistant director of music in the Boston public schools, 1923–44. Teacher at Boston Univ., 1929–40; Brooklyn College, 1945–47; Los Angeles Conservatory, 1960–63; Pepperdine Univ., 1963–72. Founder and conductor of the Boston Civic Symphony, 1925–44. Conductor of the National Orchestra of Costa Rica, 1950–54. Composed an opera; ballets; 4 symphonies and other orch. works; works for violin, for trumpet, for harp, and for piano with orch.; band works; choral works; chamber music; piano pieces; organ pieces; songs.

Wagner, (Wilhelm) Richard (b. Leipzig, 22 May 1813; d. Venice, 13 Feb. 1883). Pupil of Theodor Weinlig, cantor of the Thomasschule in Leipzig. Chorusmaster at the Würzburg Theater in 1833. Conductor of the Magdeburg Theater from 1834; of the Königsberg Theater from 1836; of the opera and of orchestral concerts in Riga, 1837–39. Lived in Paris, 1839–42. Music director of the Saxon court at Dresden, 1843–49, from which he fled for political reasons to Switzerland by way of Weimar, where he was received by Liszt. The following years saw travels to Paris, London, Moscow, St. Petersburg, Venice, Vienna, and Stuttgart, the latter in flight from his creditors, as well as a period of residence in 1857–58 on the Wesendonck estate in Zürich. Ludwig II of Bavaria summoned him to Munich with promises of support in 1864, but he was obliged to leave at the end of 1865, settling in Switzerland on Lake Lucerne, where he was joined by Cosima von Bülow, wife of the conductor Hans von Bülow and daughter of Liszt. She became Wagner's second wife in 1870, following her own divorce. In 1863 he met Nietzsche. Wagner settled in Bayreuth in 1872 and oversaw there the construction of the Festspielhaus according to his own design for a theater for his works. Works: operas (*Die Hochzeit,* unfinished, 1832; *Die Feen,* 1833–34, prod. Munich, 1888; *Das Liebesverbot,* Magdeburg, 1836; **Rienzi; Der *fliegende Holländer; *Tannhäuser; *Lohengrin; Der *Ring des Nibelungen,* consisting of *Das Rheingold, Die Walküre, Siegfried,* and *Götterdämmerung; *Tristan und Isolde; Die *Meistersinger von Nürnberg; *Parsifal*); a symphony in C, 1832, several overtures (incl. *Eine Faust Ouvertüre,* 1840), and other orch. works (incl. *Huldingungsmarsch,* 1864; **Siegfried Idyll*); choral works; some chamber music (incl. a lost string quartet and perhaps the adagio for clarinet and strings often attributed to him); a few piano pieces; songs (incl. settings of 5 poems by Mathilde Wesendonck, 1857–58). His literary works incl. the "poems" or librettos of his operas and numerous prose works in which he set forth his theories of music and opera (incl. *Die Kunst und die Revolution* [Art and Revolution], 1849; *Das Kunstwerk der Zukunft* [The Artwork of the Future], 1850; *Oper und Drama* [Opera and Drama], 1851; *Eine Mittheilung an meine Freunde* [A Communication to My Friends], 1851). See Opera.

Wagner-Régeny, Rudolf (b. Régen, Transylvania, 28 Aug. 1903; d. East Berlin, 18 Sept. 1969). Studied at the Leipzig Conservatory and with Schreker and others at the Berlin Hochschule. After work in the theaters and for films in Berlin, became director of the Hochschule in Rostock, 1947–50; at the Music Academy in East Berlin, 1950–68. Associate of Brecht. Composed operas (incl. *Der Günstling,* Dresden, 1935; *Die Bürger von Calais,* Berlin, 1939; *Das Bergwerk zu Falun,* text by Hofmannsthal, Salzburg, 1961); ballets; orch. works; choral works; chamber music; piano pieces; songs.

Wait. Originally, an English town watchman who sounded the hours of the night. In the 15th and 16th centuries the waits developed into bands of musicians, paid by the town and supplied with uniforms, who played on ceremonial occasions. At Christmas they performed before the houses of notables; it is this meaning that has survived, a wait today being a street performer of Christmas music. The term *wait* (wayte) was also used for the waits' characteristic instrument, a shawm, as well as for the tunes played by the various local guilds.

Waldhorn [G.]. The French *horn, either natural or with valves.

Waldstein Sonata. Beethoven's Piano Sonata in C, op. 53 (1803–4), dedicated to Count Ferdinand von Waldstein.

Waldteufel, Emil (Charles-Émile Lévy) (b. Strasbourg, 9 Dec. 1837; d. Paris, 16 Feb. 1915). Studied at the Strasbourg Conservatory with his father and at the Paris Conservatory. Chamber musician to the Empress Eugénie in Paris from 1865 and director of the court balls there from 1866. Toured throughout Europe conducting his own music. Composed waltzes and other dances for orch.

Walker, Ernest (b. Bombay, 15 July 1870; d. Oxford, 21 Feb. 1949). Studied at Balliol College, Oxford, where he remained and taught most of his life. Composed some orch. works; sacred and secular choral works (incl. *Ode to a Nightingale* for baritone, chorus, and orch., 1908); chamber music; piano pieces; organ pieces; songs. Published a *History of Music in England,* 1907, and other writings.

Walker, George (b. Washington, D.C., 27 June 1922). Pianist and composer. Studied at the Oberlin Conservatory, at the Eastman School, and with Scalero, N. Boulanger, R. Casadesus, and Menotti. Teacher at Smith College, 1961–68; at Rutgers Univ. at Newark from 1969 and at the Peabody Conservatory as well from 1972. Has composed orch. works (incl. a symphony; *Variations; Passacaglia*); a trombone concerto; choral works; 2 string quartets and other chamber music; piano pieces (incl. 2 sonatas; *Spatials; Spektra*).

Walküre, Die. See *Ring des Nibelungen, Der.*

Wallace, William (b. Greenock, Scotland, 3 July 1860; d. Malmesbury, Wiltshire, 16 Dec. 1940). Ophthalmologist and composer. Largely self-taught in music, he studied briefly at the Royal Academy of Music in London and taught there from 1927. Composed orch. works (incl. the symphonic poems *The Passing of Beatrice,* 1892; *François Villon,* 1909); choral works; chamber music; songs (incl. *Freebooter Songs,* with orch., 1899). Published books on Wagner, Liszt, and other subjects.

Wallace, William Vincent (b. Waterford, Ireland, 11 Mar. 1812; d. Château de Bagen, Haute-Garonne, France, 12 Oct. 1865). Toured extensively as a violinist in Europe, the Americas, and Australia. Composed operas (incl. *Maritana,* London, 1845; *Lurline,* London, 1860); piano pieces; songs.

Walmisley, Thomas Attwood (b. London, 21 Jan. 1814; d. Hastings, 17 Jan. 1856). Pupil of his father, Thomas Forbes Walmisley, and of his godfather, Thomas Attwood. Associate of Mendelssohn. Organist at Trinity and St. John's Colleges, Cambridge, from 1833, and professor of music at Cambridge from 1836 until his death. Composed services, anthems, and other church music; choral odes; chamber music; organ pieces; songs.

Walter, Johann (Johannes Walther) (b. probably Kahla, Thuringia, 1496; d. Torgau, 25 Mar. 1570). Singer in the chapel of the Elector of Saxony, 1517–26. Assisted Martin Luther in Wittenberg in the composition of the German Mass. Cantor at Torgau, 1526–48. *Kapellmeister* at the court chapel in Dresden, 1548–54. Composed polyphonic settings of German sacred melodies, some with texts by Luther (incl. the collection *Geystlich Gesangk Buchleyn*, 1524, the first Protestant hymn book); German Passion music; Latin motets; Magnificats; instrumental pieces.

Walther, Johann Gottfried (b. Erfurt, 18 Sept. 1684; d. Weimar, 23 Mar. 1748). Organist at the Thomaskirche in Erfurt from 1702. Town organist and court music teacher at Weimar from 1707 and court musician there from 1720. Composed organ pieces, incl. concertos, chorale variations, preludes, fugues, toccatas. Published the *Musikalisches Lexikon oder Musikalische Bibliothek*, 1732, an influential dictionary and the first to include biographies as well as terms; a treatise on composition.

Walther, Johann Jakob (b. Witterda, near Erfurt, *c.* 1650; d. Mainz, 2 Nov. 1717). Violinist and composer. Concertmaster at the court in Dresden from 1674. Secretary to the Elector of Mainz from 1688. Composed pieces for violin with thoroughbass, some making advanced technical demands.

Walton, William (Turner) (b. Oldham, Lancashire, 29 Mar. 1902). Pupil of his father and at the Christ Church Cathedral Choir School at Oxford, after which he was largely self-taught in music. Became an undergraduate at Christ Church, Oxford, at age 16 and later received some advice from Busoni and

Ernst Ansermet. Has composed the operas *Troilus and Cressida*, London, 1954, and *The Bear*, Aldeburgh Festival, 1967; the ballet *The Quest*, 1943, and the ballet suite, arranged from works of Bach, *The Wise Virgins*, 1940; 2 symphonies, 1935 and 1960, and other orch. works (incl. *Portsmouth Point Overture*, 1926; 2 suites from *Façade*, 1926 and 1938; *Partita*, 1958; *Variations on a Theme by Hindemith*, 1963); concertos for viola, 1929, rev. 1962, for violin, 1939, for cello, 1957; the oratorio *Belshazzar's Feast*, 1931, and other choral works; *Façade* for reciter and 6 instruments, text by Edith Sitwell, 1923; chamber music; piano pieces; songs; music for films (incl. *Henry V*, 1944; *Hamlet*, 1947; *Richard III*, 1955).

Waltz [G. *Walzer;* F. *valse*]. A dance in moderate triple time that originated in the late 18th century as an outgrowth of the **Ländler*. The waltzes of Beethoven still resemble the earlier *Ländler* or *deutsche Tanz*, as do, to some extent, Schubert's numerous waltzes. Weber's **Aufforderung zum Tanz* (Invitation to the Dance, 1819) is the first example of the characteristic rhythm and accompaniment associated with the waltz. Later notable composers of waltzes include Chopin, Johann Strauss (father and son), Brahms (*Liebeslieder*), Richard Strauss (in *Der Rosenkavalier*), and Ravel (*Valses nobles et sentimentales; also La valse*, for orchestra).

Walze [G.]. (1) **Swell pedal of the organ. (2) An 18th-century term for stereotyped undulating figures, such as an **Alberti bass.

Wanderer-Fantasie [G., Wanderer Fantasy]. Schubert's Fantasy (actually a sonata) in C for piano, op. 15, D. 760 (1822), so called because the second movement is a series of variations on a theme from his song "Der Wanderer" (1816). The initial pattern of this theme is also used at the beginning of the other three movements.

Wanhal, Johann Baptist. See Vaňhal, Jan Křtitel.

War of the Buffoons [F. *querelle* (*guerre*) *des bouffons*]. A famous quarrel that developed in 1752 between two parties of

Parisian musicians and opera enthusiasts —those favoring the national French serious opera (exemplified by the works of Lully, Rameau, and Destouches) and those preferring the Italian *opera buffa* (e.g., that of Pergolesi). Pergolesi's comic opera *La *sèrva padrona*, composed in 1733 as an *intermezzo, had been first given in Paris in 1746 without arousing more than moderate interest. The second performance, however, given in 1752 by a troupe of Italian comedians (*buffi*), led to a quarrel that split Paris in two. The national party consisted largely of the aristocracy (including Louis XV and Madame de Pompadour) and plutocracy, while the Italian side was taken by intellectuals and connoisseurs of music (including the Queen, Rousseau, D'Alembert, and Diderot). The latter considered Italian opera superior because it had more melody, expression, and naturalness and because it had shaken off completely the "useless fetters of counterpoint." The efforts of French musicians to compete with the popular *opera buffa* resulted in a new kind of French comic opera known as *comédie mêlée d'ariettes* [see Comic opera].

Ward, John (b. Canterbury, bapt. 8 Sept. 1571; d. before 31 Aug. 1638). Served Sir Henry Fanshawe. Composed madrigals, published in 1613; services and anthems; pieces for viols and for virginals.

Ward, Robert (Eugene) (b. Cleveland, 13 Sept. 1917). Conductor and composer. Pupil of Bernard Rogers, Hanson, Jacobi, B. Wagenaar, and Copland. Teacher at Columbia Univ., 1946–48; the Juilliard School, 1946–56. Executive vice president and managing editor of Galaxy Music Corp. and Highgate Press, 1956–67. President of the North Carolina School of the Arts, 1967–75, and subsequently professor of composition there. Has composed operas (incl. *The Crucible*, after Arthur Miller, New York, 1961, awarded the Pulitzer Prize; *The Lady from Colorado*, Central City, Colorado, 1964); 4 symphonies and other orch. works; a piano concerto, 1968; choral works; chamber music; piano pieces; songs.

Ward-Steinman, David (b. Alexandria,

La., 6 Nov. 1936). Pupil of B. Phillips, N. Boulanger, Riegger, Milhaud, and Babbitt. Teacher at San Diego State College, 1961–70; at California State Univ. at San Diego from 1972. Has composed an opera; ballets; incidental music for the theater; orch. works (incl. a symphony, 1959; *Prelude and Toccata*, 1962; *Arcturus*, with tape or synthesizer, 1972); a cello concerto, 1966; band works; the oratorio *The Song of Moses*, 1964, and other choral works; chamber music, some with voice; piano pieces; electronic works, some with instruments; works for mixed media.

Warlock, Peter. See Heseltine, Philip Arnold.

Wärme, mit [G.]. With warmth.

Warner, Harry Waldo (b. Northampton, 4 Jan. 1874; d. London, 1 June 1945). Violist and composer. Member of the London String Quartet, 1907–28. Composed an opera; orch. works (incl. *Hampton Wick*, 1932); choral works; 3 piano trios, works for string quartet, and other chamber music; piano pieces; songs.

Water Music. Orchestral suite by Handel, *c*. 1717, perhaps for a royal event on the Thames.

Webbe, Samuel (b. London, 1740; d. there, 25 May 1816). Organist and choirmaster at the chapel of the Portuguese Embassy in London from 1776 and later at the Sardinian Embassy as well. Composed numerous catches and glees; other sacred and secular vocal works; instrumental pieces. His son, Samuel, Jr. (1770–1843), was a pianist, organist, composer, and pupil of Clementi who also composed catches, glees, and other works.

Weber, Ben (b. St. Louis, 23 July 1916). Studied at De Paul Univ. in Chicago but is largely self-taught. Received encouragement from Schnabel and Schoenberg. Has worked with twelve-tone techniques. Has composed a ballet; orch. works (incl. *Prelude and Passacaglia*, 1955; *Dolmen, an Elegy*, 1964); concertos for violin, 1954, for piano, 1961, and *Concert Poem* for violin and orch., 1970; choral works; *Symphony on Poems of William Blake* for baritone and

12 instruments, 1951; chamber music; piano pieces; songs.

Weber, Carl Maria (Friedrich Ernst) von (b. Eutin, near Lübeck, 18 or 19 [bapt. 20] Nov. 1786; d. London, 5 June 1826). Pupil of M. Haydn and Abbé Vogler. Conductor of the Breslau City Theater, 1804–6. Secretary to Duke Ludwig at Stuttgart and music master to his children, 1807–10. Conductor of the German opera in Prague, 1813–16. *Kapellmeister* of the German opera at the court in Dresden from 1816 until his death. Toured as a pianist and conductor. Composed operas (incl. *Peter Schmoll und seine Nachbarn*, Augsburg, 1803; *Silvana*, Frankfurt, 1810; *Abu Hassan*, Munich, 1811; *Preciosa*, after Cervantes, Berlin, 1821; *Der *Freischütz; Die drei Pintos*, 1821, finished by Mahler, Leipzig, 1888; *Euryanthe*, Vienna, 1823; *Oberon*, London, 1826); incidental music; 2 symphonies, 1807, and other orch. works; works for solo instrument with orch. (incl. 2 piano concertos, 1810 and 1812, and a *Konzertstück* for piano and orch., 1821; 2 clarinet concertos and a clarinet concertino, all 1811; a horn concertino, 1806, rev. 1815; a bassoon concerto, 1811, and an andante and rondo for bassoon, 1813); 2 Masses and other sacred choral works; cantatas; a clarinet quintet, 1815, and other chamber music; piano pieces (incl. 4 sonatas; *Aufforderung zum Tanz* [Invitation to the Dance]); songs.

Weber, (Jacob) Gottfried (b. Freinsheim, near Mannheim, 1 Mar. 1779; d. Kreuznach, 21 Sept. 1839). Conductor, pianist, theorist, jurist, and composer. Founded the Mannheim Conservatory in 1806. Founded the magazine *Caecilia* in 1824 and edited it until his death. Composed Masses and other sacred and secular choral works; chamber music; songs. Published several theoretical works (incl. *Versuch einer geordneten Theorie der Tonsetzkunst*, 3 vols., 1817–21 and later editions, published in English in Boston, 1846, and London, 1851).

Webern, Anton (Friedrich Wilhelm von) (b. Vienna, 3 Dec. 1883; d. Mittersill, near Salzburg, 15 Sept. 1945). Studied at the Univ. of Vienna, from which he received a doctorate under Guido Adler with a dissertation on Isaac's *Choralis constantinus*. Pupil of Schoenberg, and his associate in Vienna in the Society for Private Musical Performances. Conductor at theaters in Vienna, Danzig, Prague, and elsewhere from 1908. Conductor of the Vienna Workers' Symphony Concerts, 1922–34, and of the Vienna Workers' Chorus. Guest conductor at the British Broadcasting Corp. in London on several occasions. Taught privately in Vienna and was associated with the publishing firm of Universal Edition there. His use of twelve-tone techniques and *Klangfarbenmelodie* has been particularly influential. Composed orch. works (incl. *Passacaglia*, op. 1, 1908; *6 Pieces*, op. 6, 1910; *5 Pieces*, op. 10, 1913; *Symphony* for small orch., op. 21, 1928; *Variations*, op. 30, 1940); *Das Augenlicht*, op. 26, 1935, 2 cantatas, op. 29 and op. 31, 1940 and 1943, and other choral works; chamber music (incl. *5 Movements* for string quartet, op. 5, 1909; *6 Bagatelles* for string quartet, op. 9, 1913; a string trio, op. 20, 1927; a quartet for violin, clarinet, saxophone, and piano, op. 22, 1930; a concerto for 9 instruments, op. 24, 1934; a string quartet, op. 28, 1938; *4 Pieces* for violin and piano, 1910; *3 Little Pieces* for cello and piano, 1914); piano pieces (incl. *Variations*, op. 27, 1936); songs, some with instruments; arrangements (incl. one of the *Ricercar a 6 voci* no. 2 from Bach's *Musical Offering*).

Weckerlin, Jean-Baptiste Théodore (b. Gebweiler, Alsace, 9 Nov. 1821; d. Buhl, near Gebweiler, 20 May 1910). Scholar and composer. Pupil of Halévy. Assistant librarian at the Paris Conservatory from 1869 and head librarian there, 1876–1909, succeeding Félicien David. Composed operas (incl. *L'organiste dans l'embarras*, Paris, 1853); orch. works; numerous choral works; numerous songs. Published several collections of early French songs and folksongs.

Weckmann, Matthias (b. Niederdorla, near Mühlhausen, Thuringia, 1621; d. Hamburg, 24 Feb. 1674). Pupil of Schütz, Reinken, and Scheidemann. Court organist in Copenhagen, 1643–47. Court *Kapellmeister* in Dresden, 1647–55. Organist at the Jakobkirche in Hamburg (where he was one of the founders of the Collegium musicum) from 1655. Composed sacred choral works with instruments; solo cantatas; instrumental pieces; organ pieces, incl. preludes, fugues, chorale settings.

Wedge Fugue. Popular name for Bach's great organ fugue in E minor, so called because of the increasingly wider intervals in the subject.

Weelkes, Thomas (b. *c*. 1575; d. London, 30 Nov. 1623). Organist at Winchester College in 1600; at Winchester Cathedral from about 1602. Composed services and anthems; several collections of madrigals as well as balletts and polyphonic airs; pieces for viols.

Weerbecke, Gaspar van (b. probably Oudenaarde, Flanders, *c*. 1440; d. after 1518). Possibly a pupil of Ockeghem. Member of the ducal court chapel in Milan, 1472–81. Singer in the papal choir, 1481–89 and from 1499 until at least 1514, having served in the intervening years at Milan and in the chapel of Philip the Handsome. Composed Masses, motets, and Lamentations; chansons.

Wegelius, Martin (b. Helsinki, 10 Nov. 1846; d. there, 22 Mar. 1906). Studied in Vienna and with E. F. E. Richter, Rheinberger, Reinecke, and Jadassohn. Conductor of the Finnish Opera in Helsinki, 1878–79. Founded and directed the Helsinki Conservatory from 1882 until his death. His pupils incl. Sibelius. Composed orch. works; cantatas and other vocal works; chamber music; piano pieces; songs. Published several books on music history and theory.

Wehmütig [G.]. Sad, melancholy.

Weigel, Eugene (b. Cleveland, 11 Oct. 1910). Pupil of Shepherd and Hindemith. Violist of the Walden String Quartet at the Univ. of Illinois from 1947 and teacher there, 1950–56. Teacher at Montana State Univ. from 1956. Has composed operas; orch. works (incl. *Prairie Symphony*, 1953); a Requiem, 1956; chamber music; piano pieces; songs.

Weigl, Joseph (b. Eisenstadt, Austria, 28 Mar. 1766; d. Vienna, 3 Feb. 1846). Godson of Haydn. Pupil of Salieri and Albrechtsberger. Assistant conductor to Salieri at the Vienna court theater from 1790 and composer and *Kapellmeister* there, 1792–1823. Vice *Kapellmeister* of the court from 1827. Composed over 30 operas (incl. *La Principessa d'Amalfi*, Vienna, 1794; *Die Schweizerfamilie*, a *Singspiel*, Vienna, 1809); ballets; oratorios and cantatas; Masses and other church music; instrumental pieces; songs.

Weigl, Karl (b. Vienna, 6 Feb. 1881; d. New York, 11 Aug. 1949). Studied in Vienna with R. Fuchs and Zemlinsky and earned a doctorate in musicology there under Guido Adler. Coach at the Vienna opera under Mahler, 1904–6. Teacher at the New Vienna Conservatory from 1918 and at the Univ. of Vienna from 1930. Settled in the U.S. in 1938 and taught at Brooklyn College, the Boston Conservatory, and the Philadelphia Music Academy. Composed 6 symphonies and other orch. works; concertos for violin, for cello, for piano; choral works; 8 string quartets and other chamber music; piano pieces; songs.

Weihe des Hauses, Die [G., The Consecration of the House]. Overture by Beethoven (op. 124) composed in 1822 for the opening of the Josephstadt Theater in Vienna.

Weihnachts-Oratorium [G.]. See *Christmas Oratorio*.

Weill, Kurt (b. Dessau, 2 Mar. 1900; d. New York, 3 Apr. 1950). Pupil of Humperdinck and Busoni. Associate of Bertolt Brecht. Settled in the U.S. in 1935. Employed elements of jazz in some works. Composed operas (incl. *Der Protagonist*, Dresden, 1926; *Aufstieg und Fall der Stadt Mahagonny*, a *Singspiel* with text by Brecht, Baden-Baden, 1927, rev. as an opera, Leipzig, 1930; *Der Zar lässt sich photographieren*, Leipzig, 1928; *Die *Dreigroschenoper; Der Jasager*, Berlin, 1930; *Die Bürgschaft*, Berlin, 1932; *Der Silbersee*, Berlin, 1933; *Down in the Valley*); musical comedies (incl. *Knickerbocker Holiday*, libretto by Maxwell Anderson, Hartford, Conn., 1938; *Street Scene*, libretto by Elmer Rice, New York, 1947); music for films; incidental music; 2 cantatas and other vocal works; orch. works; chamber music; piano pieces; songs.

Weinberg, Henry (b. Philadelphia, 7 June 1931). Pupil of Rochberg, Babbitt, Sessions, and Dallapiccola. Teacher at the Univ. of Pennsylvania, 1962–65; at Queens College in New York from 1965. Works incl. a *Sinfonia* for chamber orch., 1957; 2 string quartets and other chamber music (incl. *Cantus commemorabilis I*, 1966); songs and other vocal works.

Weinberger, Jaromir (b. Prague, 8 Jan. 1896; d. St. Petersburg, Fla., 8 Aug. 1967). Pupil of Křička, Karel, Novák, and Reger. Settled in St. Petersburg, Fla., in 1939. Composed operas (incl. **Švanda Dudák*); orch. works; choral works; band works; chamber music; piano pieces; organ pieces; songs.

Weiner, Lazar (b. Cherkassy, near Kiev, 27 Oct. 1897). Studied at the Kiev Conservatory and in 1914 settled in the U.S., where he studied with Jacobi, Robert Russell Bennett, and Schillinger. Conductor in New York of the Workmen's Circle Chorus, 1929–64; of the choir of Central Synagogue from 1930. Teacher at Hebrew Union College School of Sacred Music from 1953. Has composed an opera; ballets on Jewish subjects; Jewish sabbath services; cantatas; orch. works; chamber music; piano pieces; songs, some on Yiddish texts.

Weiner, Leó (b. Budapest, 16 Apr. 1885; d. there, 13 Sept. 1960). Studied in Budapest with Koessler and in Germany and France. Teacher at the Budapest Academy of Music, 1908–60. Made some use of Hungarian folk materials. Composed orch. works (incl. a serenade, 1906, and 5 divertimenti); a concertino for piano and orch.; 3 string quartets and other chamber music; piano pieces. Transcribed for orch. works of Bach, Beethoven, and others, and published textbooks on form and harmony.

Weingartner, (Paul) Felix (von) (b. Zara, Dalmatia, 2 June 1863; d. Winterthur, Switzerland, 7 May 1942). Pupil of Reinecke and Jadassohn. Received encouragement from Brahms and Liszt. Traveled widely as a conductor and held conducting posts at the Berlin Opera, 1891–98; the Vienna State Opera, 1908–11, succeeding Mahler, and 1935–36; the Hamburg Municipal Opera, 1912–14; the Vienna Volksoper, 1919–24. Director of the Basel Conservatory, 1927–35. Also active as a pianist. Composed operas (incl. *Sakuntala*, Weimar, 1884; *Genesius*, Berlin, 1892; the trilogy *Orestes*, Leipzig, 1902); 7 symphonies and other orch. works; concertos for violin and for cello; choral works; 5 string quartets and other chamber music; songs. Orchestrated Weber's **Aufforderung zum Tanz* and works of other composers and published books on conducting and other subjects.

Weinzweig, John (Jacob) (b. Toronto, 11 Mar. 1913). Pupil of Willan and Bernard Rogers. Teacher at the Toronto Conservatory from 1939 and at the Univ. of Toronto from 1952. Has worked with serial techniques and elements of jazz and folklore. Has composed a ballet; orch. works (incl. a symphony, 1940; *Symphonic Ode*, 1958; *Dummiyah*, 1969); concertos for violin, for piano, for harp; choral works; string quartets, divertimenti, and other chamber music; piano pieces; songs; music for radio and films.

Weis, Karel (Weiss) (b. Prague, 13 Feb. 1862; d. there, 4 Apr. 1944). Conductor, organist, and composer. Pupil of Fibich. Active as a collector of Bohemian folksongs. Composed operas (incl. *Der polnische Jude,* Prague, 1901); a symphony and a symphonic poem; chamber music; piano pieces; songs and arrangements of folksongs.

Weisgall, Hugo (b. Ivančice, Czechoslovakia, 13 Oct. 1912). Conductor and composer. Settled in the U.S. in 1920, where he studied at the Peabody Conservatory, at Johns Hopkins Univ., and with Sessions and Scalero. Teacher at the Jewish Theological Seminary in New York from 1952; the Juilliard School from 1957; Queens College in New York from 1961; the Peabody Conservatory, 1974–75. Has composed operas (incl. *The Tenor,* Baltimore, 1952; *The Stronger,* after Strindberg, Westport, Conn., 1952; *Six Characters in Search of an Author,* after Pirandello, 1956; *Purgatory,* after Yeats, Washington, D.C., 1961; *Athaliah,* after Racine, New York, 1964; *Nine Rivers from Jordan,* New York, 1968); ballets; vocal works; chamber music; songs.

Weismann, Julius (b. Freiburg im Breisgau, 26 Dec. 1879; d. Singen, near Lake Constance, 22 Dec. 1950). Pupil of Rheinberger, Thuille, and Herzogenberg. Composed operas (incl. *Leonce und Lena,* after Büchner, Freiburg im Breisgau, 1925; *Die pfiffige Magd,* Leipzig, 1939); ballets; 3 symphonies and other orch. works; concertos for piano and for violin; choral works; much chamber music; piano pieces; songs.

Weiss, Adolph (b. Baltimore, 12 Sept. 1891; d. Van Nuys, Calif., 21 Feb. 1971). Pupil of Schoenberg. Bassoonist with various orchestras, incl. the New York Philharmonic under Mahler, the Chicago Symphony, and the Rochester Philharmonic. Also active as a conductor. Worked with twelve-tone techniques. Composed orch. works (incl. *American Life,* 1928); works for dance; 3 string quartets and other chamber music; piano pieces; songs.

Weiss, Silvius Leopold (b. Breslau, 12 Oct. 1686; d. Dresden, 16 Oct. 1750). Lutenist to the Prince of Poland in Rome, 1708–14; at the Dresden court from 1717 until his death. Composed suites and other pieces for lute; chamber music with lute. Published a treatise on the lute.

Well-Tempered Clavier, The [G. *Das wohltemperierte Clavier*]. Bach's collection of 48 preludes and fugues, grouped in two parts (1722, 1744), each of which contains 24 preludes and fugues, one for each major and minor key. The name refers to the then novel system of equal *temperament, which made it possible to play equally well in all the keys and of which Bach's collection was the first complete realization. The pieces in the two collections date from various periods of Bach's life and employ a variety of styles. Whether harpsichord or clavichord is the "proper" instrument for these pieces has long been disputed.

Wellesz, Egon (Joseph) (b. Vienna, 21 Oct. 1885; d. Oxford, 9 Nov. 1974). Musicologist and composer. Pupil of the musicologist Guido Adler and of Schoenberg. Teacher at the Univ. of Vienna, 1913–38; at Oxford Univ. from 1939. Composed operas (incl. *Alkestis,* libretto by H. von Hofmannsthal, Mannheim,

1924; *Die Bakchantinnen,* Vienna, 1931); ballets; 9 symphonies and other orch. works; concertos for piano and for violin; sacred and secular choral works; 9 string quartets and other chamber music; piano pieces; songs. Published numerous books and articles, particularly on Byzantine chant and on Schoenberg.

Wellingtons Sieg [G., Wellington's Victory]. A "battle" symphony [see *Battaglia*] by Beethoven (full title *Wellingtons Sieg oder die Schlacht bei Vittoria,* op. 91, 1813), written in celebration of Wellington's victory over Napoleon. It consists of English and French fanfares, settings of "Rule Britannia" and "Marlborough s'en va-t-en guerre," the Battle (punctuated by English and French guns), a Charge, and, in the second part, a Victory Symphony containing a quotation from "God Save the King." It was originally written for a mechanical instrument invented by Maelzel but was orchestrated by the composer.

Werk principle. In organs, a rule often followed in the 16th, 17th, and 18th centuries, according to which the pipework controlled by any one keyboard of the organ is set forth in its own separate tone cabinet, separated both aurally and visually from the pipework controlled by the other keyboards.

Werner, Gregor Joseph (bapt. Ybbs on the Danube, 29 Jan. 1693; d. Eisenstadt, 3 Mar. 1766). *Kapellmeister* to Prince Esterházy at Eisenstadt from 1728 until his death, when he was succeeded by Haydn, who had been his assistant from 1761. Composed Masses, motets, and other church music; oratorios; instrumental pieces, incl. fugues for string quartet arranged by Haydn.

Wernick, Richard (b. Boston, 16 Jan. 1934). Pupil of Fine, ⌐hapero, Berger, Kirchner, Toch, Blacher, and Copland. Music director and composer for the Royal Winnipeg Ballet, 1957–58. Composed for films, television, and theater in New York, 1958–64. Teacher at the Univ. of Chicago, 1965–68; the Univ. of Pennsylvania from 1968. Works incl. *Aevia* for orch., 1965; *Haiku of Bashō* for soprano and instruments, 1967; *Moonsongs from the Japanese* for 1 or 3 sopranos with tape, 1969; *Visions of Ter-*

ror and Wonder for soprano and orch., awarded the Pulitzer Prize in 1977; *Requiem-Kaddish; A Prayer for Jerusalem,* 1971; 2 string quartets and other chamber music.

Wert, Giaches de (b. Wert, Flanders, 1535; d. Mantua, 6 May 1596). *Maestro di cappella* to the Duke of Mantua from 1565 until his death, with occasional absences to Ferrara. Composed numerous madrigals, some for the celebrated "three ladies" who were singers at Ferrara; canzonets and *villanelle;* music for Mantuan theatrical performances; motets.

Werther. Opera in four acts by Massenet (libretto by E. Blau, P. Milliet, and G. Hartmann, based on Goethe's *Die Leiden des jungen Werthers*), produced (in German) in Vienna, 1892. Setting: Germany, 1772.

Wesley, Samuel (b. Bristol, 24 Feb. 1766; d. London, 11 Oct. 1837). Organ virtuoso and composer. Pupil of his brother Charles Wesley. Nephew of John Wesley. Composed works for organ, incl. 11 concertos with orch.; 4 symphonies and other orch. works; church music, incl. Masses, motets, services, and anthems; chamber music; piano pieces; glees; songs.

Wesley, Samuel Sebastian (b. London, 14 Aug. 1810; d. Gloucester, 19 Apr. 1876). Natural son of Samuel Wesley. Chorister at the Chapel Royal. Organist at various churches, incl. the cathedrals at Hereford, Exeter, Winchester, and Gloucester. Teacher at the Royal Academy of Music from 1850. Composed services, anthems (incl. "The Wilderness") and other sacred music; piano pieces; organ pieces; glees; songs.

Westergaard, Peter (b. Champaign, Ill., 28 May 1931). Pupil of Piston, Sessions, Babbitt, Milhaud, and Fortner. Teacher at Columbia Univ., 1958–66; Amherst College, 1967–68; Princeton Univ., 1966 –67 and from 1968. Has composed 2 chamber operas, *Charivari,* 1953, and *Mr. and Mrs. Discobbolos,* 1965; orch. works (incl. *5 Movements for Small Orchestra,* 1958); 3 cantatas (incl. *Leda and the Swan* for mezzo-soprano, clarinet, viola, vibraphone, marimba, 1961); chamber music.

Wetz, Richard (b. Gleiwitz, Upper Silesia, 26 Feb. 1875; d. Erfurt, 16 Jan. 1935). Pupil of Thuille, though largely self-taught. Conductor and teacher in Erfurt from 1906 until his death, teaching also in Weimar from 1916. Composed 2 operas; 3 symphonies and a *Kleist-Ouvertüre;* a violin concerto; a Christmas Oratorio and other choral works; chamber music; piano pieces; numerous songs.

Wetzler, Hermann Hans (b. Frankfurt, 8 Sept. 1870; d. New York, 29 May 1943). Pupil of I. Knorr, Clara Schumann, and Humperdinck. Settled in New York in 1892, establishing the Wetzler Symphony Concerts there in 1903. Held a series of conducting posts in European cities such as Hamburg, Riga, Halle, Lübeck, and Cologne, 1905–40, after which he returned to the U.S. Composed an opera; orch. works (incl. *Assisi,* 1925); choral works; chamber music; songs.

Weyse, Christoph Ernst Friedrich (b. Altona, near Hamburg, 5 Mar. 1774; d. Copenhagen, 8 Oct. 1842). Pupil of J. A. P. Schulz. Church organist in Copenhagen from 1794; court composer there from 1819. Composed operas (incl. *Sovedrikken* [The Sleeping-Potion], Copenhagen, 1809); 7 symphonies and other orch. works; sacred choral works; cantatas; organ pieces; piano pieces; songs and arrangements of Danish folksongs.

Whistle. A small, simple, end-blown pipe, made of wood, cane, metal, or plastic.

Whistle flute. In the classification of instruments, generic designation for flutes blown by means of a flue. A synonymous term is *fipple flute.* The upper end of the pipe is stopped by a plug or fipple [G. *Block,* hence *Blockflöte* for recorder], with a narrow slit (flue) remaining. The breath is led through the flue towards the sharp edge of a small opening below the fipple. The same principle is used in organ flue pipes. The whistle flutes include the *recorders and flageolets. Flageolets differ from recorders mainly in that they have fewer finger holes, four in front and two thumb holes in the rear. In the 19th century the flageolet acquired keys. For ill. see under Flute.

White, Clarence Cameron (b. Clarksville, Tenn., 10 Aug. 1880; d. New York, 30 June 1960). Violinist and composer. Studied at Howard Univ., at Oberlin College, and with Coleridge-Taylor and Laparra. Teacher at West Virginia State College, 1924–31; at Hampton Institute, 1931–35. Composed the opera *Ouanga*, on a Haitian subject, 1932; a symphony, 1928, an *Elegy*, 1954, and other orch. works; choral works; violin pieces; piano pieces; songs. Published *American Negro Folk Songs*, 1928.

White, Robert. See Whyte, Robert.

Whithorne, Emerson (b. Cleveland, 6 Sept. 1884; d. Lyme, Conn. 25 Mar. 1958). Pianist, critic, and composer. Studied in Cleveland and with Leschetizky, R. Fuchs, and Schnabel. Composed a ballet; orch. works (incl. 2 symphonies; *New York Days and Nights*, 1926, originally for piano; *Moon Trail*, 1933); incidental music to O'Neill's *Marco Millions*, 1928, employing Chinese materials; a piano quintet and other chamber music; piano pieces (incl. *The Aeroplane*, 1920, orch. version, 1926); songs.

Whiting, Arthur Battelle (b. Cambridge, Mass., 20 June 1861; d. Beverly, Mass., 20 July 1936). Pianist, harpsichordist, and composer. Nephew of George E. Whiting. Pupil of Chadwick and Rheinberger. Gave educational concerts at Harvard, Yale, Columbia, and Princeton Universities from 1907. Composed orch. works; a piano concerto, 1888, and a *Fantasie* for piano and orch., 1897; anthems; chamber music; piano pieces, some pedagogic; songs.

Whiting, George Elbridge (b. Holliston, Mass., 14 Sept. 1840; d. Cambridge, Mass., 14 Oct. 1923). Studied in New York, Liverpool, and Berlin. Organist at King's Chapel in Boston. Taught organ at the New England Conservatory, 1876–79 and 1883–97, and in the interim at the Cincinnati College of Music. Composed an opera; a symphony and other orch. works; Masses and other sacred music; secular cantatas; piano pieces; organ pieces; songs.

Whittenberg, Charles (b. St. Louis, 6 July 1927). Pupil of B. Phillips and Bernard Rogers. Teacher at the Univ. of Connecticut at Storrs from 1967. Has worked with electronic and serial techniques. Works incl. a *Fantasy*, 1962, and *Games of Five*, 1968, for wind quintet; *Tryptich* for brass quintet, 1962; *Variations for 9 Players*, 1965; a string quartet in one movement, 1965; *Polyphony for Solo Trumpet*, 1965; *The Run Off*, an electronic collage.

Whole note. See under Notes.

Whole tone. The interval of the major second. See Interval.

Whole tone scale. A scale consisting of whole tones only, there being six to the octave. Only two such scales exist: c d e f♯ g♯ b♭ c′ and c♯ d♯ f g a b c♯′.

Whole-tube instruments. See under Wind instruments.

Whyte, Robert (White) (b. *c.* 1535; d. London, buried 11 Nov. 1574). Master of the choristers at Ely Cathedral from about 1561 until 1566, perhaps at Chester thereafter, and at Westminster Abbey from 1570. Composed Latin and English church music; *In nomine* settings; organ pieces; lute pieces.

Whythorne, Thomas (b. 1528; d. Aug. 1595). Teacher at Trinity College, Cambridge, and in London. Traveled on the Continent. Published a collection of "songes" in 3 to 5 voices, 1571, and a collection of duos for singing or playing, 1590. He also wrote an autobiography.

Widmann, Erasmus (bapt. Hall, Württemberg, 15 Sept. 1572; d. Rothenburg on the Tauber, 31 Oct. 1634). Organist in Graz, 1596–98; cantor in Hall, 1599–1602; *Kapellmeister* in Weickersheim, 1602–13; cantor in Rothenburg, 1613–34. Composed church music; instrumental dances; songs.

Widor, Charles-Marie (-Jean-Albert) (b. Lyon, 21 Feb. 1844; d. Paris, 12 Mar. 1937). Pupil of Lemmens and Fétis. Organist at Saint-Sulpice in Paris, 1869–1934. Teacher at the Paris Conservatory from 1890. Composed operas (incl. *Les pêcheurs de Saint-Jean*, Paris, 1905); 4 symphonies and other orch. works; concertos for piano (2), for cello; church music and other choral works; chamber music; piano pieces; organ works (especially the 8 symphonies, the *Symphonie* *gothique,* and the *Symphonie romaine*); songs. Published an edition of Bach's organ works, in collaboration with his student Albert Schweitzer; an edition, with supplement, of Berlioz's treatise on instrumentation; music criticism and other writings.

Wie aus der Ferne. See *Ferne.*

Wieniawski, Henryk (Henri) (b. Lublin, Poland, 10 July 1835; d. Moscow, 31 Mar. 1880). Violin virtuoso and composer. Studied at the Paris Conservatory, graduating at the age of 11. Toured widely in Russia, Europe, and the U.S., at times with his brother Joseph (1837–1912), a pianist and composer, and at times with Anton Rubinstein. Violinist to the Czar from 1859. Teacher at the St. Petersburg Conservatory, 1862–67; at the Brussels Conservatory, 1874–77. Composed 2 violin concertos, *Légende,* and other works for violin and orch.; pieces for violin with piano.

Wigglesworth, Frank (b. Boston, 3 Mar. 1918). Pupil of Luening, Cowell, and Varèse. Teacher at Columbia Univ., 1946–51; at the New School for Social Research, in New York, from 1954. Has composed 2 symphonies and other orch. works; stage works; choral works; chamber music.

Wihtol, Joseph (Jazeps Vitols) (b. Volmar, Latvia, 26 July 1863; d. Lübeck, 24 Apr. 1948). Pupil of Rimsky-Korsakov. Teacher at the St. Petersburg Conservatory, 1886–1918, succeeding Rimsky-Korsakov and teaching Prokofiev. Founder in 1919 of the National Conservatory in Riga and teacher there until 1944, when he settled in Germany. Employed Latvian folksongs. Composed orch. works (incl. a symphony, 1887, and the Latvian fairy tale *Spriditis,* 1908); choral works; chamber music; piano pieces; songs and arrangements of folksongs.

Wilbye, John (b. Diss, Norfolk, England, bapt. 7 Mar. 1574; d. Colchester, Sept. 1638). Household musician to the younger Sir Thomas Kytson and his wife at Hengrave Hall, near Bury St. Edmunds, and at their London townhouse, from about 1595 until 1628, when he retired to Colchester. Composed madrigals for 3, 4, 5, and 6 voices; a few sacred pieces with English and Latin texts.

Wildberger, Jacques (b. Basel, 3 Jan. 1922). Pupil of Vogel. Teacher at the Karlsruhe Hochschule für Musik, 1959–66; at the Basel Music Academy from 1966. Has worked with serial techniques. Has composed orch. works (incl. *Mouvements,* 1964); an oboe concerto, 1963; cantatas and other choral works (incl. *Épitaphe pour Évariste Galois* with soloists, speaking chorus, orch., and tape, 1964); chamber music; *La notte* for mezzo-soprano, 5 instruments, and tape, 1967.

Wilder, Alec (b. Rochester, N.Y., 16 Feb. 1907). Studied at the Eastman School of Music. Active as a composer for theater and films. Has composed short operas (incl. *The Lowland Sea,* 1951); a ballet; orch. works; chamber music, much of it for winds; piano pieces; songs. Published a book on American popular song, 1972.

Willaert, Adrian (b. probably Bruges, *c.* 1490; d. Venice, 7 Dec. 1562). Pupil of Mouton. *Maestro di cappella* at San Marco in Venice from 1527 until his death. His pupils incl. Zarlino, Rore, Vicentino, and A. Gabrieli. Composed Masses, motets, and other sacred music, incl. some psalms that are among the earliest polychoral works; madrigals, *canzoni villanesche,* and chansons with French and with Dutch texts; ricercars and fantasies for instrumental ensembles.

Willan, Healey (b. Balham, Surrey, England, 12 Oct. 1880; d. Toronto, 16 Feb. 1968). Teacher at the Royal Conservatory in Toronto from 1913 and vice principal there, 1920–36; at the Univ. of Toronto, 1936–50, and organist there from 1932. Organist and director of music at the Church of St. Mary Magdalene, 1921–68. Composed 3 operas for radio (incl. *Deirdre,* 1946); 2 symphonies and other orch. works; much Anglican church music; other choral works; chamber music; piano pieces; organ pieces; songs.

William Tell. See *Guillaume Tell.*

Williams, Alberto (b. Buenos Aires, 23 Nov. 1862; d. there, 17 June 1952). Pupil of Guiraud, Godard, and Franck. Founded a conservatory in Buenos Aires in 1893, with branches in other cities, and a publishing house. Employed native

Argentine musical materials as well as the whole-tone scale and related devices. Composed 9 programmatic symphonies and other orch. works, incl. suites of Argentine dances; choral works; chamber music; numerous piano pieces; songs. Published books of poetry and numerous didactic works.

Williamson, Malcolm (Benjamin Graham Christopher) (b. Sydney, 21 Nov. 1931). Pianist, organist, and composer. Pupil of Goossens and Lutyens. Has lived in England since 1953. Master of the Queen's Music from 1975, succeeding Bliss. Has composed operas (incl. *Our Man in Havana*, after Graham Greene, London, 1963; *The Happy Prince*, for children, after Oscar Wilde, Farnham, 1965; *Julius Caesar Jones*, for children and adults, London, 1966; *The Violins of St. Jacques*, London, 1966); ballets; 2 symphonies and other orch. works; concertos for piano (3), for organ, for violin; choral works; chamber music; piano pieces; organ pieces; songs (incl. the cycle *From a Child's Garden*, texts by Robert Louis Stevenson, 1968).

Wilson, George Balch (b. Grand Island, Nebr., 28 Jan. 1927). Pupil of Finney, Absil, Sessions, and N. Boulanger. Teacher at the Univ. of Michigan from 1961 and director of the Electronic Music Studio there from 1964. Works incl. *6 Pieces* for orch., 1960; a string quartet, 1950, *Concatenations* for 12 instruments, 1969, and other chamber music; *Exigencies*, on tape, 1968; *Polarity* for percussion and tape, 1971.

Wilson, John (b. probably Faversham, Kent, 5 Apr. 1595; d. London, 22 Feb. 1674). Lutenist, singer, and composer. One of the King's musicians from 1635. Professor of Music at Oxford Univ., 1656–61. Gentleman of the Chapel Royal from 1662, succeeding Lawes. Composed over 200 songs with unfigured bass, and in some cases lute accompaniment, to English texts of Shakespeare and others and to Latin texts, incl. odes of Horace; music for plays; about 30 fantasies for lute.

Wilson, Olly (b. St. Louis, 7 Sept. 1937). Studied at Washington Univ. in St. Louis, at the Univ. of Illinois, and with Bezanson at the Univ. of Iowa. Teacher

at the Oberlin Conservatory from 1964; at the Univ. of California at Berkeley from 1972. Has composed orch. works (incl. *Akwan* for piano, electric piano, amplified strings, and orch., 1973); choral works (incl. *In memoriam—Martin Luther King, Jr.*, with tape, 1968); piano pieces with tape; works for voice with instruments.

Wilson, Richard (b. Cleveland, 15 May 1941). Pupil of Moevs and R. Thompson. Teacher at Vassar College from 1966. Has composed orch. works (incl. *Initiation*, 1970); choral works; chamber music (incl. *Music for Violin and Cello*, 1964; *Music for Solo Flute*, 1972; *Concert Piece* for violin and piano, 1967; a string quartet, 1968).

Wind chest. In organs, an airtight box that receives the wind from the bellows and controls its passage to the pipes. See Organ.

Wind instruments. Generic name for all instruments in which the sound-generating medium is an enclosed column of air. They are also known as *aerophones*. The main wind instruments are the *brass instruments (*trumpets, *horns, *trombones, *tubas, etc.), and *woodwinds (*flutes, *clarinets, and *oboes). See also Reed.

In each wind instrument an enclosed column of air, cylindrical or conical (depending on the bore of the instrument), is set into vibration [see Acoustics]. Neither the material (whether brass or wood) nor the shape (whether straight or bent) is important. The pitch of the sound produced depends on the length of the pipe and whether the pipe is an open or closed resonator; its timbre depends on the mouthpiece (single reed in the clarinets, double reed in the oboes, mouth-hole in the flutes, cupped mouthpiece in the trumpets, funnel mouthpiece in the horns, etc.), shape of the bore, widening of the bell, etc.

A pipe of given length gives one tone only. However, by proper control of the breath and lips, called *overblowing*, a pipe can easily be made to sound not only its normal tone, the fundamental, but also the higher *harmonics. These tones constitute the *natural tones* of a wind instrument. Another name for the fundamental tone is *pedal tone*. In a

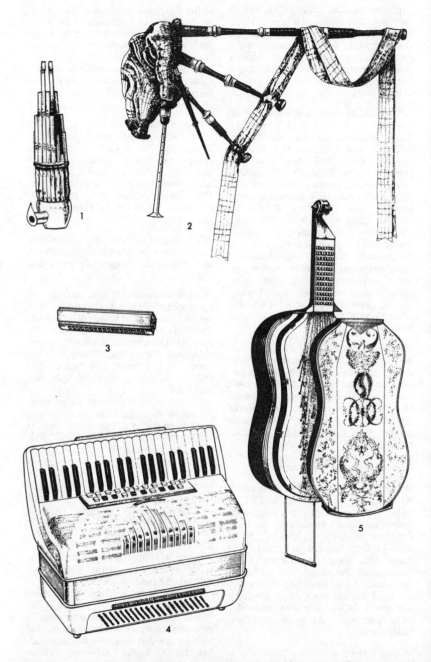

Miscellaneous wind instruments: 1. Sheng. 2. Bagpipe. 3. Harmonica (shown twice its actual size in relation to the others). 4. Accordion. 5. Mélophone.

number of instruments the pedal tone is practically unobtainable, and a distinction is made between *whole-tube instruments,* in which the air column can be made to vibrate as a whole, thus producing the pedal tone, and *half-tube instruments,* in which even the slightest air pressure is likely to set up vibrations of the half length, thus producing the harmonic just above the fundamental. To the former category belong all the woodwinds and the brass instruments of wide bore (tubas); to the latter, nominally, the brass instruments of narrow bore (trumpets, horns, trombones, higher saxhorns). Today, however, skilled players can obtain the pedal notes on trumpets and saxhorns, so that the French horn and the trombone in the lower positions of the slide remain, for all practical purposes, the only half-tube instruments.

The description above applies to the so-called *open pipes,* i.e., pipes that are open at their lower end. If a pipe of the same length is closed at the lower end (*stopped pipe*), its fundamental is an octave lower than in the open pipe, and, moreover, only the odd-numbered harmonics above this fundamental are obtainable. Stopped pipes are frequently used in organ building to obtain lower tones from relatively short pipes. Wind instruments with a cylindrical bore usually act as stopped pipes although they are not actually stopped at the lower end. The most important instrument of this type is the clarinet, which is said to "overblow at the fifth" (actually, at the twelfth), whereas the instruments with a conical bore (oboes, horns, etc.) overblow at the octave.

In a wind instrument that consists simply of a pipe, only the natural tones are available (e.g., the natural horn or trumpet). In order to obtain the numerous tones between the gaps of the natural series, there must be a means of temporarily shortening or lengthening the pipe. Four main kinds of device are so used: (a) slides; (b) crooks; (c) valves; (d) side holes.

(a) Slide. An instrument so equipped consists of two separate portions of tubing, one sliding inside the other so that it can be drawn out. Thus the tube can actually be lengthened, and in each position a series of natural tones becomes available. Since the largest gap in the series of overtones is the fifth (which contains seven semitones), a complete chromatic scale can be obtained by the combined tones of seven series of overtones whose fundamentals are separated by seven adjacent semitones. This principle is used with a *trombone.

(b) Crook or shank. An additional piece of tubing is inserted by the player when needed. Since adding a crook or shank takes time, it does not really serve to fill in the gaps of the natural scale but only gives the instrument a different (lower) tuning for different pieces or different sections of a piece. This method was used with trumpets in the 18th century [see Trumpet; also Horn].

(c) Valves. The name is misleading, since what is really meant are crooks attached permanently to the instrument, to be opened and closed momentarily by means of valves. Normally the instrument is provided with three valves (I, II, III) that lower the pitch, respectively, by 2, 1, or 3 semitones, while their combined use yields a lowering of 5 (I + III), 4 (II + III), and 6 (I + II + III) semitones. Thus seven series of overtones become available, resulting in a complete chromatic scale, as explained under (a). Also see Valve.

(d) Side holes. These are holes bored in the side wall of the instrument (today, in woodwinds only; formerly, also in trumpets and cornets, e.g., key trumpet, key bugle) that can be opened and closed by the fingers, usually with the help of a key mechanism [see Key (1)]. If all the holes are closed, the pipe sounds its fundamental. If some of the holes are opened, the acoustical length of the air column is shortened and higher tones are produced.

In the horns, pitch can also be altered by stopping [see Horn].

Wind machine [F. *Éoliphone;* G. *Windmaschine*]. A device designed to imitate the sound of the wind, occasionally used for descriptive purposes (R. Strauss, *Don Quixote, Eine Alpensinfonie*). It consists of a barrel framework covered with cloth, which is rotated so that the cloth rubs against cardboard or wood.

Winter, Peter (von) (b. Mannheim, bapt. 28 Aug. 1754; d. Munich, 17 Oct. 1825).

Pupil of Abbé Vogler. Music director at the court theater in Mannheim, 1776–78, following the Electoral Court to Munich thereafter and becoming its vice *Kapellmeister* in 1787, serving as its *Kapellmeister* from 1798 until his death. Composed German and Italian operas (incl. *Das unterbrochene Opferfest*, Vienna, 1796); ballets; 9 symphonies and other orch. works; concertos for clarinet, bassoon, and other instruments; 26 Masses and much other church music; oratorios and cantatas; string quartets and other chamber music.

Winterreise, Die [G., Winter Journey]. Cycle of 24 songs by Schubert, D. 911, in two parts, composed in 1827 to poems by Wilhelm Müller.

Wirbel [G.]. (1) Peg of a violin; *Wirbelkasten*, pegbox. (2) A drum roll.

Wirén, Dag Ivar (b. Nora, Sweden, 15 Oct. 1905). Studied in Stockholm and Paris. Music critic for *Svenska Morgonbladet,* 1938–46. Member of the Swedish Musical Academy from 1946. Has composed radio operas; incidental music; ballets; 5 symphonies, a *Serenade* for strings, 1937, and other orch. works; concertos for violin, for cello, for piano; string quartets and other chamber music; piano pieces; songs; music for films.

Wise, Michael (b. Wiltshire, England, *c.* 1648; d. Salisbury, 24 Aug. 1687). Pupil of Cooke. Organist at Salisbury Cathedral from 1668. Gentleman of the Chapel Royal from 1676. Master of the choristers at St. Paul's Cathedral, London, in 1687. Composed anthems and services; catches.

Witt, Friedrich (b. Hallenbergstetten, now Niederstetten, Württemberg, 8 Nov. 1770; d. Würzburg, 3 Jan. 1836). *Kapellmeister* in Würzburg from 1802, first to the Prince-Bishop and then to the Grand Duke; at the Würzburg Theater after 1814. Composed operas; symphonies, incl. perhaps the "Jena Symphony" at one time attributed to Beethoven; concertos; Masses and other church music; oratorios and cantatas; chamber music.

Wohltemperierte Clavier, Das [G.]. See *Well-Tempered Clavier, The.*

Wolf [G.]. Any disagreeable effect resulting from imperfect tuning in instruments. Specifically: (1) The slight difference in pitch between G ♯ and A♭ in the mean-tone system, and similar discordance in other systems of unequal *temperament. (2) In violins and cellos, *Wolfnote* is a term used for certain tones that differ markedly in both intensity and quality from those in adjoining parts of the compass.

Wolf, Hugo (Philipp Jakob) (b. WindischGräz, Austria [since 1919 Slovenjgradec, Yugoslavia], 13 Mar. 1860; d. Vienna, 22 Feb. 1903). Studied at the Vienna Conservatory with R. Fuchs. Music critic for a weekly newspaper in Vienna (*Wiener Salonblatt*), 1883–87. After an attempted suicide in 1898, he entered an insane asylum, where he remained until his death. Composed the opera *Der Corregidor,* after Alarcón, Mannheim, 1896, and part of another; a few orch. works (incl. the symphonic poem *Penthesilea,* 1885); choral works; some chamber music (incl. a string quartet in D min., 1878–84, and a serenade in G maj. for string quartet, 1887, transcribed for orch. in 1892 as *Italienische Serenade*); piano pieces; about 300 songs with piano accompaniment (incl. collections on poems by Mörike, 1888, Eichendorff, 1886–88, and Goethe, 1888–89; the *Spanisches Liederbuch;* the *Italienisches Liederbuch,* after Paul Heyse, 1890–96, publ. in 2 parts, 1892 and 1896), some 20 of which he later orchestrated.

Wolf-Ferrari, Ermanno (b. Venice, of a German father and an Italian mother, 12 Jan. 1876; d. there, 21 Jan. 1948). Pupil of Rheinberger. Director of the Liceo B. Marcello in Venice, 1902–7. Teacher at the Salzburg Mozarteum from 1939. Lived mostly near Munich. Composed operas (incl. the following works all first produced in Munich in German translations: *Le donne curiose,* 1903; *I quattro rusteghi,* 1906; *Il segreto di Susanna,* 1909; *I gioielli della Madonna,* 1911, in English as *The Jewels of the Madonna,* New York, 1913); orch. works; choral works; chamber music; piano pieces; songs.

Wolff, Christian (b. Nice, France, 8 Mar. 1934). Largely self-taught in music.

Earned a Ph.D. in classics at Harvard Univ. and taught classics there, 1962–70. Teacher of music and classics at Dartmouth College from 1971. Associate of Cage, Tudor, and Feldman. Has worked with aleatory procedures and novel kinds of notation. Works incl. dance scores for Merce Cunningham; *For Prepared Piano*, 1951; several pieces for one or more pianists; *Summer* for string quartet, 1961; *For 1, 2, or 3 People* on any instruments, 1964; *Burdocks* for one or more orchestras, any instruments or sound sources, 1971.

Wölfl, Joseph (Woelfl, Wölffl) (b. Salzburg, 24 Dec. 1773; d. London, 21 May 1812). Pupil of L. Mozart and M. Haydn. Successful pianist in Vienna from 1795, Paris from 1801, and London from 1805. Composed operas; ballets; 2 symphonies and other orch. works; piano concertos; string quartets, piano trios, violin sonatas, and other chamber music; piano pieces, incl. 58 sonatas and 24 sets of variations; songs. Wrote a piano method with numerous etudes.

Wolkenstein, Oswald von (b. probably Schloss Schöneck, Pustertal, Tirol, *c.* 1377; d. Merano, Italy, 2 Aug. 1445). Sometimes regarded as the last of the minnesingers. Traveled to Russia, the Holy Land, Persia, Africa, Greece, Spain, France, Italy, and elsewhere. Served King (later Emperor) Sigismund from 1415. Composed music and poetry for sacred and secular monophonic songs and some polyphony.

Wolle, Peter (b. New Herrnhut, St. Thomas, West Indies, 5 Jan. 1792; d. Bethlehem, Pa., 14 Nov. 1871). Moravian minister, bishop, and composer. Studied in Nazareth, Pa., and served in Lancaster, Philadelphia, and Lititz. Composed anthems and music for winds; edited the *Moravian Tune Book,* 1836.

Wolpe, Stefan (b. Berlin, 25 Aug. 1902; d. New York, 4 Apr. 1972). Pupil of Juon, Schreker, Busoni, and Webern. Lived in Palestine, 1934–38. Settled in the U.S. in 1938. Teacher at the Settlement Music School in Philadelphia, 1939–42; Philadelphia Academy of Music, 1949–52; Black Mountain College, 1952–56; C. W. Post College of Long Island Univ., 1957–68; the Mannes College of

Music, from 1968. Employed at various times elements of jazz, Semitic music, and twelve-tone techniques. Composed 2 operas; the ballet *The Man from Midian,* 1942; other stage works; 5 symphonies and other orch. works; cantatas; chamber music (incl. *Chamber Piece* no. 1 and no. 2 for 14 players, 1964, 1966); piano pieces (incl. *Enactments* for 3 pianos, 1953); songs.

WoO. In the catalog of Beethoven's works by G. Kinsky and H. Halm, abbr. for *Werk ohne Opuszahl,* work without opus number.

Wood block. See Chinese block.

Wood, Charles (b. Armagh, Ireland, 15 June 1866; d. Cambridge, 12 July 1926). Organist and composer. Pupil of Stanford and Bridge. Teacher at the Royal College of Music in London from 1888; at Cambridge Univ. from 1897 and professor there from 1924, succeeding Stanford. Composed church music and other choral works; orch. works; incidental music; 8 string quartets; organ pieces; songs and arrangements of Irish folksongs.

Woodbury, Isaac Baker (originally Woodberry) (b. Beverly, Mass., 23 Oct. 1819; d. Charleston, S.C., 26 Oct. 1858). Studied in Paris and London, taught in Boston, and published a music magazine in New York from 1850. Composed sacred and secular songs and published the collection of sacred songs *The Dulcimer,* collections of church music, and a manual on composition and thoroughbass.

Woodwinds. See under Orchestra; Wind instruments.

Woollen, Russell (b. Hartford, Conn., 7 Jan. 1923). Pianist and composer. Studied at the Pius X School of Liturgical Music in New York, at the Benedictine Abbey of Solesmes in France, and with Nabokov, N. Boulanger, and Piston. Teacher at the Catholic Univ. and at Howard Univ. in Washington, D.C. Has composed Masses and other sacred and secular choral works; orch. works; chamber music; piano pieces; songs.

Worcester, school of. A repertory of English compositions of *c.* 1300, many of which seem to have originated at the Cathedral of Worcester. They are preserved only in fragments, the original sources having been cut up to serve as fly-leaves. A characteristic trait of the Worcester style is the frequent use of *voice exchange. Some pieces are remarkable for their extensive employment of *sixth-chord style.

Word painting. The illustration through music of the ideas presented or suggested by the words of a song or other vocal piece. The term usually refers to the portrayal of single words or phrases that lend themselves to specific treatment, rather than the rendition of the general mood of the text. In the late Renaissance and in the baroque period it played a prominent role. The devices used rely principally on the relationship between qualities of the thing illustrated and certain characteristics of music. In the simplest cases, natural sounds, such as those of birds, thunder, sobbing, and the like, are imitated. Otherwise, music that is high, low, ascending, descending, loud, soft, fast, or slow may be associated, respectively, with these same concepts in the abstract or with concepts that share these qualities. Thus, for example, in baroque music, "heaven" is almost certain to be associated with music that is high or ascending in pitch. Such devices are sometimes important in *program music. See also Eye music.

Wordsworth, William (Brocklesby) (b. London, 17 Dec. 1908). Pupil of Tovey. Has composed 5 symphonies and other orch. works; concertos for piano, for cello, for violin; choral works; 6 string quartets and other chamber music; piano pieces; organ pieces; songs; music for radio.

Wozzeck. Opera in three acts by Alban Berg (to his own libretto, based on G. Büchner's drama of 1836), produced in Berlin, 1925. Setting: Germany in the 1830s.

Wranitzky, Anton (Antonín Vranický) (b. Neureisch, Moravia, 13 June 1761; d. Vienna, 6 Aug. 1820). Violinist and composer. Pupil of his brother Paul Wranitzky and of Albrechtsberger, Haydn, and Mozart. *Kapellmeister* to Prince Lobkowitz in Raudnitz, Prague, and Vienna from at least 1790. Composed 16

symphonies and other orch. works; concertos, incl. 15 for violin; church music; marches for winds; chamber music; piano pieces.

Wranitzky, Paul (Pavel Vranický) (b. Neureisch, Moravia, 30 Dec. 1756; d. Vienna, 28 Sept. 1808). Violinist and composer. Brother of Anton Wranitzky. Pupil of Joseph Martin Kraus in Vienna. Member of Prince Esterházy's orchestra at Eisenstadt from 1780. Concertmaster of the Vienna Opera from 1785 until his death. Composed *Singspiele* (incl. *Oberon, König der Elfen,* Vienna, 1789), ballets, and other stage works; over 20 symphonies; concertos for violin, for flute, for cello, etc.; sacred and secular vocal works; about 50 string quartets and other chamber music; piano pieces.

Wuchtig [G.]. Weighty, heavy.

Wüllner, Franz (b. Münster, 28 Jan. 1832; d. Braunfels-on-the-Lahn, 7 Sept. 1902). Pianist, conductor, and composer. Studied with Beethoven's biographer Anton Schindler and others. Teacher at the Munich Conservatory, 1856–58. Municipal music director at Aachen, 1858–64. Director of the Munich court chapel from 1864. Conductor of the Munich court theater from 1869, succeeding von Bülow, and *Kapellmeister* there from 1870. Conductor at the court in Dresden from 1877. Director of the Cologne Conservatory from 1884 until his death. Composed sacred and secular choral works, with and without orch., incl. Masses and other church music; chamber music; piano pieces; songs.

Wuorinen, Charles (b. New York, 9 June 1938). Pianist, conductor, and composer. Pupil of Luening, Beeson, and Ussachevsky. Co-founder, with Sollberger, of the Group for Contemporary Music, 1962. Teacher at Columbia Univ., 1964–71; at the Mannes College of Music from 1971. Has worked with serial and electronic techniques. Has composed 3 symphonies and other orch. works (incl. *Orchestral and Electronic Exchanges,* with tape, 1965); 2 piano concertos; choral works; chamber music (incl. chamber concertos for cello, 1963, for flute, 1964, and for oboe, 1965, all with 10 players; a string quartet, 1971; *Tashi* for violin, cello, piano, and clarinet, also with orch., 1975); works for percussion; piano pieces (incl. a sonata, 1969, and *Making Ends Meet* for piano four-hands, 1966); pieces for organ and for harpsichord; works for voice with instruments; *Time's Encomium,* on tape, 1969, awarded a Pulitzer Prize.

Würdig [G.]. Stately, with dignity.

Wyner, Yehudi (b. Calgary, Canada, of naturalized U.S. parents, 1 June 1929). Pianist, conductor, and composer. Son of Lazar Weiner. Pupil of Donovan, Hindemith, and Piston. Teacher at Yale, 1964–77. Has composed Jewish liturgical works; *Da camera* for piano and orch., part 1, 1967; chamber music (incl. *Serenade* for 7 instruments, 1958; *Passover Offering* for flute, clarinet, trombone, and cello, 1959; *Cadenza* for clarinet and harpsichord or piano, 1970); piano pieces; songs.

Wyschnegradsky, Iwan. See Vyshnegradsky, Ivan.

X

Xácara [Sp.]. *Jácara.

Xenakis, Yannis (Iannis) (b. Braila, Rumania, of Greek parents, 29 May 1922). Architect and composer. Lived with his family in Greece from 1932. After work in the resistance, escaped to Paris in 1947 and studied with Honegger, Milhaud, and Messiaen. Worked with the architect Le Corbusier, 1948–59. Founded the School of Mathematical and Automated Music in Paris in 1966 and has taught there and at Indiana Univ., where he founded a similar center. Has worked with computers and various mathematical techniques, incl. game theory and stochastic processes, producing primarily fully notated works for conventional instruments. Works incl. *Metastaseis* for orch., 1954; *Pithoprakta* for orch., 1956; *Stratégie,* game for 2 orchs., 1962; *Akrata* for 16 winds, 1965; *Terretektorh,* 1966, and other works for orch. scattered among the audience (incl. *Polytope,* 1967; *Nomos Gamma,* 1968); *Eonta* for piano and brass, 1964; *ST/4* for string quartet, 1966. Has published *Musique formelles,* 1963, and other writings.

Xylophone. A percussion instrument consisting of graduated bars of hardwood that are struck with a stick. For the modern orchestral instrument, see Percussion instruments I, 3; also Marimba. Xylophones are commonly used in non-Western cultures.

Y

Yamada, Kosaku (Kôsçak) (b. Tokyo, 9 June 1886; d. there, 29 Dec. 1965). Studied in Tokyo and with Bruch in Berlin. Organized the Tokyo Philharmonic Orchestra in 1914. Toured Russia, Europe, and the U.S. as a conductor. Composed operas (incl. *Kurofune* [Black Ships], Tokyo, 1940); 5 symphonies and other orch. works; numerous choral works; chamber music; piano pieces; numerous songs.

Yannay, Yehuda (b. Timisoara, Rumania, 26 May 1937). Studied in Israel with Boskovich and Seter and in the U.S. with Berger, Shapero, Krenek, Schuller, Martirano, and Brün. Dean of the Israeli Conservatory of Music in Tel

Aviv, 1966–68. Teacher at the Univ. of Wisconsin from 1968. Has worked with aleatory procedures, graphic notation, elements of theater, and electronics. Has composed *Wraphap* for actress, amplified aluminum sheet, and Yannachord, 1969; *Houdini's 9th* for double bass, escape artist, and others, 1969; orch. works; choral works; chamber music; *Coheleth,* an electronic environment with mobile chorus, 1970; works on tape.

Yardumian, Richard (b. Philadelphia, 5 Apr. 1917). Largely self-taught in composition. Has taught piano privately and worked as a church musician. Has composed 2 symphonies and other orch. works; concertos for violin and for piano; choral works; chamber music; piano pieces.

Yevgeny Onyegin. See *Eugen Onegin.*

Yodel [G. *Jodel*]. A special type of singing practiced by the mountain peoples of Switzerland and Austria (Tirol) and characterized by frequent and rapid passing from a low chest voice to a high falsetto. A *Jodler* is a vocalization appended to a song, with low vowels (a, o) used for the low tones and high vowels (e, i) for the high ones.

Yon, Pietro Alessandro (b. Settimo Vittone, Italy, 8 Aug. 1886; d. Huntington, N.Y., 22 Nov. 1943). Studied at the conservatories in Milan and Turin and at Santa Cecilia in Rome. Organist at St. Peter's in Rome, 1905–7; at St. Francis-Xavier's in New York, 1907–19 and 1921–26; at St. Patrick's in New York, 1926–43. Composed Masses, motets, and other church music; an oratorio; numerous organ works (incl. a *Concerto gregoriano* with orch.; *Gesù Bambino,* 1917); chamber music; piano pieces; songs.

Young, La Monte (b. Bern, Idaho, 14 Oct. 1935). Studied at the Univ. of California at Los Angeles and at Berkeley; with Maxfield and Stockhausen; Indian vocal music in New York and New Delhi. Has collaborated with his wife, Marian Zazeela, in producing sound-light environments and theater pieces, incl. some works in which relatively few sounds are sustained with slight variations over very long periods. Works incl.

word scores, e.g., "Draw a straight line and follow it"; *The Tortoise, His Dreams and Journeys* for "continuous performance" over several days, with strings, voices, and projections, realized in various parts and under various titles beginning in 1964.

Young, William (Joung, Jough) (d. London, before 21 Dec. 1671). Court musician at Innsbruck in 1653. Flutist and later violinist in the orchestra of Charles II of England from 1660. A collection of chamber sonatas and dances for 2, 3, and 4 violins with thoroughbass, published at Innsbruck in 1653, is usually attributed to him, though not with absolute certainty. Other works perhaps by the same composer incl. ayres and dances for viols; madrigals.

Youth's Magic Horn, The. See *Knaben Wunderhorn, Des.*

Yradier, Sebastián (Iradier) (b. Sauciego, Álava, Spain, 20 Jan. 1809; d. Vitoria, 6 Dec. 1865). Singing master to the Empress Eugénie in Paris after 1851. At other times lived in Cuba and taught singing at the Madrid Conservatory. Composed songs (incl. "El arreglito," also titled "Chanson havanaise," and used, with modifications, by Bizet for the "Habanera" in *Carmen;* "La paloma"; "Ay chiquita").

Ysaÿe, Eugène (b. Liège, 16 July 1858; d. Brussels, 12 May 1931). Violin virtuoso, conductor, and composer. Pupil of H. Wieniawski and Vieuxtemps. Teacher at the Brussels Conservatory, 1886–98. Conductor of the Cincinnati Symphony Orchestra, 1918–22. Composed 2 Walloon operas, the second unfinished; 8 concertos and other works for violin with orch.; 6 sonatas for violin solo. His brother Théophile Ysaÿe (1865–1918) was a pianist and composer.

Yuehchyn (yüeh ch'in). A Chinese guitar. See under Guitar family.

Yun, Isang (b. Tongyoung, South Korea, 17 Sept. 1917). Studied in Korea and Japan. Teacher at the universities in Pusan and Seoul, 1952–56. Subsequently studied with T. Aubin in Paris and with Blacher in Berlin, living in Germany from 1960. Teacher at the Berlin Hochschule für Musik from 1970. Has worked with serial techniques and elements of Oriental music. Has composed operas (incl. *Der Traum des Liu-Tung*, Berlin,

1965); orch. works; choral works; chamber music (incl. *Music for 7 Instruments*, 1959; *Loyang* for 8 instruments and percussion, 1962); piano pieces.

Z

Zachow, Friedrich Wilhelm (Zachau) (b. Leipzig, 19 Nov. 1663; d. Halle, 14 Aug. 1712). Organist at the Liebfrauenkirche in Halle from 1684 until his death. His pupils incl. Handel. Composed cantatas and other church music; chamber music; organ pieces.

Zádor, Eugen(e) (b. Bátaszék, Hungary, 5 Nov. 1894; d. Los Angeles, 3 Apr. 1977). Studied at the Vienna Conservatory and with Reger. Teacher at the New Vienna Conservatory, 1922–38. Settled in the U.S. in 1939, working as an orchestrator of film scores in Hollywood. Composed operas; a ballet, *The Machine-Man*, 1934; symphonies, symphonic poems, and other orch. works (incl. *Contrasts*, 1965); a trombone concerto, 1966, and a rhapsody for cimbalom and orch., 1968; choral works; chamber music; piano pieces; songs; music for films.

Zählzeit [G.]. Beat.

Zajal. *Zejel.

Zampogna [It.]. A mouth-blown *bagpipe.

Zandonai, Riccardo (b. Sacco, Trento, Italy, 28 May 1883; d. Pesaro, 5 June 1944). Pupil of Mascagni. Composed operas (incl. *Conchita*, Milan, 1911; *Francesca da Rimini*, Turin, 1914); orch. works; concertos for violin, for cello; a Requiem and other choral works; chamber music; songs; music for films.

Zanfoña [Sp.]. *Hurdy-gurdy.

Zapateado [Sp.]. A Spanish solo dance in triple time, the rhythm being marked by stamping of the heels, frequently in syncopation.

Zarabanda [Sp.]. *Saraband.

Zarlino, Gioseffo (b. Chioggia, Italy, probably before 22 Apr. 1517; d. Venice, 14 Feb. 1590). Pupil of Willaert. *Maestro di cappella* at San Marco in Venice, succeeding Rore, from 1565 until his death. Composed motets and other sacred music; madrigals. Published several very influential treatises (incl. *Istitutioni harmoniche*, 1558 and later editions; *Dimostrationi harmoniche*, 1571; *Sopplimenti musicali*, 1588).

Zart [G.]. Tender, soft.

Zarzuela [Sp.]. The most important type of Spanish opera, distinguished from ordinary opera in that the music is intermingled with spoken dialogue, as in *comic opera. Its subjects, however, are not restricted to comedy. Its name comes from the Palace of La Zarzuela (a royal country seat near Madrid) where festive representations called *Fiestas de Zarzuela* were given. The earliest on record is Lope de Vega's *eclogue *La selva sin amor* (The Forest Without Love) of 1629. The earliest known composer of zarzuelas is Juan Hidalgo, whose *Los celos hacen estrellas* (text by Vélez de Guevara; produced 1644?) uses recitative as well as choruses in the style of the madrigal. He also composed the music for Calderón de la Barca's *Ni amor se libra de Amor* (c. 1640) and *Celos aun del aire matan* (1662). In the latter part of the 17th century the *zarzuela* resembled the French *ballet de cour*, with its emphasis on elaborate stage production and the addition of ballets and popular dances accompanied by guitar and castanets (José Clavijo y Fajardo, 1730–1806). This type of "aristocratic opera," based largely on mythological subjects, reached its zenith with Sebastián Durón (1660–1716) and Antonio Literes Carrión

(c. 1675–1747). At the same time there arose a "popular" reaction against the *zarzuela* in the *tonadilla*. The increasing influence of Italian opera—clearly present in the works of José de Nebra (1702–1768)—also contributed to the decline of the *zarzuela*.

An attempt at revival in a more popular form, made c. 1770 by the dramatist Ramón de la Cruz in collaboration with the composer Antonio Rodríguez de Hita (1724–87), was only briefly successful. It was not until the middle of the 19th century that a forceful national movement led to a new era for the *zarzuela*. This revival began chiefly with Francisco A. Barbieri (1823–94; *Jugar con fuego*, 1851) and Pascual Arrieta y Corera (1823–94; *Marina*, 1871). In 1865 the *Teatro de la Zarzuela* was founded, and the movement found numerous participants, e.g., Ruperto Chapí y Lorente (1851–1909), M. Fernández Caballero (1835–1906), Tomás Bretón y Hernández (1850–1923), Joaquín Valverde (1846–1910), Federico Chueca (1846–1908), and Amadeo Vives (1871–1932). The modern *zarzuelas* are classified as *zarzuela grande*, in three acts, and *género chico* or *zarzuelita*, in one act. The former tend to deal with serious, dramatic subjects; the latter are essentially comic. Bretón y Hernández' *La Dolores* (1895) and *La verbena de la paloma* (1897) are outstanding examples of each type. Later, important composers of the *zarzuela grande* are Francisco Alonso (b. 1887) and Federico Moreno Torroba (b. 1891); of the *género chico* (with features derived from Viennese operetta and even American jazz), Jacinto Guerrero (1895–1951) and others.

Zauberflöte, Die [G., The Magic Flute]. Opera in two acts by Mozart (libretto by E. Schikaneder), produced in Vienna, 1791. Setting: magical world.

Zeitmass [G.]. Tempo.

Zejel [also *zajal*]. A type of medieval Hispano-Arabic poetry that has been cited as the model for the *virelai* or, more properly, its Spanish counterpart as found in many of the 13th-century *cantigas*.

Zelenka, Jan Dismas (b. Louňovice, Bohemia, bapt. 16 Oct. 1679; d. Dresden,

22 or 23 Dec. 1745). Pupil of Fux and Lotti. Vice *Kapellmeister* at the court in Dresden from 1719, succeeding Heinichen as *Kapellmeister* in 1729 and becoming court composer in 1735. Composed a melodrama; much church music, incl. Masses, Requiems, and motets; Italian oratorios and cantatas; instrumental pieces, incl. sontatas for woodwinds with thoroughbass and the suite *Hypocondria*.

Zelter, Carl Friedrich (b. Berlin, 11 Dec. 1758; d. there, 15 May 1832). Pupil of K. F. C. Fasch and Kirnberger. Associate of Goethe. Teacher at the Berlin Academy of Fine Arts from 1809. Founded the Royal Institute for Church Music in Berlin in 1822 and directed it until his death. His pupils incl. Mendelssohn and Meyerbeer. Composed numerous songs, particularly settings of Goethe (incl. "König von Thule" and "Es ist ein Schuss gefallen"); choral works; church music; symphonies; concertos; piano pieces.

Zemlinsky, Alexander von (b. Vienna, 14 Oct. 1871; d. Larchmont, N.Y., 15 Mar. 1942). Studied at the Vienna Conservatory. Conductor of the German Opera in Prague, 1911–27; of the Krolloper in Berlin, 1927–30. Settled in the U.S. in 1934. His pupils incl. Schoenberg. Composed operas (incl. *Es war einmal*, Vienna, 1900); a ballet; 3 symphonies and other orch. works; choral works; string quartets and other chamber music; piano pieces; songs.

Zhizn za Tsarya. See *Life for the Czar, A*.

Ziani, Marco Antonio (b. Venice, c. 1653; d. Vienna, 22 Jan. 1715). Nephew of Pietro Andrea Ziani. Vice *Kapellmeister* at the court in Vienna from 1700 and *Kapellmeister* there from 1712. Composed operas; oratorios; church music.

Ziani, Pietro Andrea (b. Venice, c. 1620; d. Naples, 12 Feb. 1684). Organist at San Marco in Venice from 1669. Teacher at the Conservatorio di Sant' Onofrio in Naples, 1678–80. *Maestro di cappella* of the Cappella reale in Naples, 1680–84, where he was succeeded by A. Scarlatti. Composed operas; oratorios and cantatas; church music; instrumental pieces; madrigals; arias and duets.

Zibaldone [It.]. *Quodlibet.

Ziehharmonika [G.]. *Accordion.

Zielenski, Mikolaj (Nikolaus) (b. c. 1550; d. c. 1615). Organist and composer. In the service of the Primate of Poland, Archbishop Baranowski, 1608–15. Composed Offertories, Communions, and a Magnificat for 1 to 12 voices, with and without the organ and other instruments, some in polychoral style, published in Venice in 1611.

Ziemlich [G.]. Rather. *Ziemlich schnell,* rather fast.

Zigeunermusik [G.]. Gypsy music.

Zilcher, Hermann (**Karl Josef**) (b. Frankfurt, 18 Aug. 1881; d. Würzburg, 1 Jan. 1948). Pianist, conductor, and composer. Pupil of I. Knorr. Teacher at the Akademie der Tonkunst in Munich, 1908–20. Director of the Würzburg Conservatory, 1920–44. Composed a comic opera; incidental music for plays; 5 symphonies and other orch. works; choral works; chamber music; piano pieces; numerous songs.

Zimbalon. *Cimbalom.

Zimmermann, Bernd Alois (b. Bliesheim, near Cologne, 20 Mar. 1918; d. Königsdorf, 10 Aug. 1970). Pupil of Jarnach, Fortner, and Leibowitz. Teacher at the Univ. of Cologne, 1950–52; at the Hochschule für Musik in Cologne from 1957. Worked at various times with serial, electronic, and collage techniques and with mixed media and graphic notation. Composed the opera *Die Soldaten,* for mixed media, Cologne, 1965; ballets; 4 symphonies and other orch. works; concertos for violin, for oboe, for cello, for trumpet; choral works; chamber music; piano pieces; songs; music for the theater and for films.

Zingarelli, Nicola Antonio (b. Naples, 4 Apr. 1752; d. Torre del Greco, near Naples, 5 May 1837). Studied at the Conservatorio Santa Maria di Loreto in Naples. *Maestro di cappella* at the Milan Cathedral, 1792–94; at Loreto, 1794–1804; at the Sistine Chapel, 1804–11; at the Naples Cathedral from 1816, succeeding Paisiello. His pupils incl. Bellini and Mercadante. Composed 37 operas (incl. *Giulietta e Romeo,* Milan, 1796);

oratorios; much church music; secular cantatas; chamber music; organ pieces; arias and solfeggi.

Zingarese, alla [It.]. In the style of gypsy music.

Zink(en) [G.]. *Cornett.

Zipoli, Domenico (b. Prato, Tuscany, 16 Oct. 1688; d. Córdoba, Argentina, 2 Jan. 1726). Pupil of Pasquini. Organist at the Jesuit church in Rome from 1715. Joined the Jesuit Order in 1716 and was a church organist in Córdoba from 1718 until his death. Composed oratorios and other sacred vocal works; sonatas and other pieces for harpsichord and for organ.

Zither (1) A folk instrument used chiefly in Bavaria and Austria, consisting of a flat wooden soundbox over which 4 or 5 melody strings and as many as 37 accompaniment strings are stretched. The melody strings, nearest to the player, are stopped on a fretted fingerboard with the fingers of the left hand and are plucked by a plectrum worn on the right thumb. The accompaniment strings are plucked by the fingers on the right hand. (2) A large class of stringed instruments, also called *psalteries. See accompanying ill. For the instruments illustrated under Zither, see the separate entry for each. (3) Old German spelling for *cittern.* See Guitar family.

Znamenny chant. The chant of the Russian Church, as used from the 11th through 17th centuries. The name is derived from *znamia,* sign or neume. The oldest extant musical sources date from the 11th century and are notated in signs very similar to those of early Byzantine notation. Later sources (11th to 17th cent.) are written in the so-called *kriuki* (or *znamenny*) notation, a system including more than 90 different signs for single notes as well as for stereotyped melodic formulas. They have not yet been deciphered.

Zöllner, Heinrich (b. Leipzig, 4 July 1854; d. Freiburg im Breisgau, 4 May 1941). Pupil of Reinecke, Jadassohn, and E. F. E. Richter. Teacher and choral conductor at the Cologne Conservatory from 1885. Conductor of the Deutscher Liederkranz in New York from 1890.

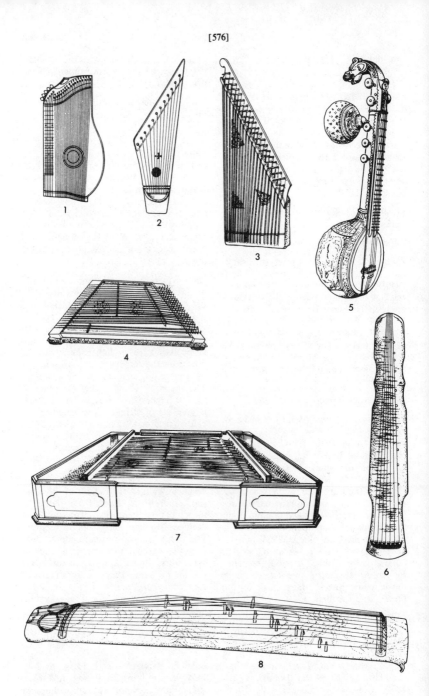

Zithers: 1. Zither. 2. Kantele. 3. Kanun. 4. Psaltery. 5. Vīṇa. 6. Chyn. 7. Cimbalom (Hungarian). 8. Koto.

Music director at Leipzig Univ. from 1898. Teacher and choral conductor at the Leipzig Conservatory, 1902–6. Conductor at the Flemish Opera in Antwerp, 1907–14. Composed operas (incl. *Die versunkene Glocke*, Berlin, 1899); choral works; 5 symphonies and other orch. works; chamber music; piano pieces; songs.

Zoppa, alla [It.]. Inverted dotted rhythm [see Dotted notes]. The term *zoppa* also was used for 17th-century dance movements in syncopated rhythm, e.g., by Vitali.

Zug [G.]. Slide. *Zugposaune,* slide trombone, the ordinary trombone. *Zugtrompete,* slide trumpet.

Zumsteeg, Johann Rudolf (b. Sachsenflur, Baden, Germany, 10 Jan. 1760; d. Stuttgart, 27 Jan. 1802). Associate of Schiller. Director of the Stuttgart court theater from 1792. Composed operas (incl. *Die Geisterinsel,* after Shakespeare's *The Tempest,* Stuttgart, 1798); other music for the stage; church cantatas and other choral works; ballades

for voice and piano (incl. Schiller's "Maria Stuart"; Bürger's "Lenore"; Goethe's "Colma"; also "Des Pfarrers Tochter von Taubenhayn"; "Die Entführung").

Zunge [G.]. Reed. *Zungenpfeife,* reed pipe.

Zurückhalten [G.]. To hold back, *rallentando*.

Zusammen [G.]. Together, e.g., after a passage in which an instrumental group has been divided [G. *geteilt;* see *Divisi*].

Zwischenspiel [G.]. Interlude, particularly the instrumental interludes between the stanzas of a song (*ritornello*) or the *tutti* sections in a concerto. Also, name for fugal episodes [see *Durchführung*], or the episodes in rondo form.

Zymbel [G.]. *Cymbal.

Zymbelstern [G.]. A percussion stop found in many organs of the baroque period that produces a random tinkling sound of fairly high pitch.